WOMEN
IMAGES AND REALITIES

WOMEN
IMAGES AND REALITIES

A Multicultural Anthology

Third Edition

Amy Kesselman
State University of New York, New Paltz

Lily D. McNair
The University of Georgia

Nancy Schniedewind
State University of New York, New Paltz

Boston   Burr Ridge, IL   Dubuque, IA   Madison, WI   New York
San Francisco   St. Louis   Bangkok   Bogotá   Caracas   Kuala Lumpur
Lisbon   London   Madrid   Mexico City   Milan   Montreal   New Delhi
Santiago   Seoul   Singapore   Sydney   Taipei   Toronto

McGraw-Hill Higher Education

*A Division of The **McGraw-Hill** Companies*

WOMEN: IMAGES AND REALITIES: A MULTICULTURAL ANTHOLOGY
Published by McGraw-Hill, a business unit of The McGraw-Hill Companies, Inc., 1221 Avenue of the Americas, New York, NY, 10020. Copyright © 2003, 1999, 1995, by The McGraw-Hill Companies, Inc. All rights reserved. No part of this publication may be reproduced or distributed in any form or by any means, or stored in a database or retrieval system, without the prior written consent of The McGraw-Hill Companies, Inc., including, but not limited to, in any network or other electronic storage or transmission, or broadcast for distance learning. Some ancillaries, including electronic and print components, may not be available to customers outside the United States.

This book is printed on acid-free paper.

5 6 7 8 9 0 FGR/FGR 0 9 8 7 6

ISBN-13: 978-0-7674-2089-1
ISBN-10: 0-7674-2089-6

Publisher: *Kenneth King*
Sponsoring editor: *Katherine Bates*
Marketing manager: *Katherine Bates*
Project manager: *Ruth Smith*
Production supervisor: *Susanne Riedell*
Coordinator of freelance design: *Mary E. Kazak*
Cover design: *Ryan Brown*
Cover image: *"From Head to Hand" by Lisa L. Kriner*
Typeface: *10/13 Plantin*
Compositor: *G&S Typesetters*
Printer: *Quebecor World Fairfield Inc.*

Library of Congress Cataloging-in-Publication Data

    Women : images and realities : a multicultural anthology / [edited by] Amy Kesselman, Lily D. McNair, Nancy Schniedewind.—3rd ed.
      p. cm.
    ISBN 0-7674-2089-6 (softcover : alk. paper)
      1. Feminism—United States.   2. Women—United States—Social conditions.   3. Women's studies—United States.   I. Kesselman, Amy Vita, 1944– II. McNair, Lily D., 1957–
    III. Schniedewind, Nancy, 1947–
    HQ1421.W653 2003
    305.42′0973—dc21

                                     2002070991

www.mhhe.com

Dedicated to our students,

our sisters: Laura Kesselman Devlin (1938–1981)
 Naomi McNair Vliet
 Carol Schniedewind

our mothers: Ethel Pickelny Kesselman (1908–1996)
 Kazuko Takijima McNair
 Grace Douglass Schniedewind (1912–1995)

and to: Virginia Blaisdell
 George, Randall, and Marguerite Roberts
 Dave Porter and Jesse and Daniel Schniedewind

 Preface

This third edition of *Women: Images and Realities* has emerged from a process of reflective teaching and research. It builds upon our experience in writing the first and second editions, which grew out of our practice as teachers of introductory women's studies and psychology of women courses. Dissatisfied with the available texts, we spent many years foraging among journals and anthologies to bring our students a view of feminism that reflected their diverse experience and spoke in a language that was accessible and compelling. While we wanted to include some of the fruits of feminist research, we felt it most important that students' first encounters with women's studies be ones that engaged them and evoked the flash of recognition and connection that has drawn women to feminism. To this end, *Women: Images and Realities* included a great many first person and fictional accounts of women's experiences. In order to address issues that emerge from discussions of the lives of women with diverse backgrounds, we not only included pieces about a variety of female experiences, but also, in Part VI, directly addressed some of the systems of domination that interact with gender in women's lives.

The introductory women's studies course at the State University of New York at New Paltz, called Women: Images and Realities, provided both the inspiration and structure for this anthology. Since it was first offered in 1974, the course has developed to reflect the responses of thousands of students who have taken it. Instructors found that students were more adept at analyzing social structures after they had discussed ideas about gender and its effect on individual women's lives. We have therefore structured the book to move from the more visible manifestations of sexism in our culture to the forms of discrimination that are embedded in social institutions.

This third edition reflects the experiences of students and faculty who have used this book in the past seven years. In our classrooms we have engaged students with the material and each other, reflected on what we have learned, and reconceived the book anew. We have benefited from the feedback of others who have shared their learning from this process as well.

We are all academics: a historian, a clinical psychologist, and an educator. Amy has written about women workers during World War II and is currently researching the history of women's liberation. Lily's research focuses on women's issues in addictive behaviors, especially African-American women's experiences in psychotherapy. Nancy's work is in the areas of multicultural/social justice education, feminist pedagogy, and cooperative learning.

Our interest in women's studies and feminism, however, is not merely academic; we are all deeply committed to feminist social change. We have tried, in *Women: Images and Realities,* to stimulate an intellectual interest in women's studies by presenting a wide variety of women's studies topics. In addition, by demonstrating the ways that women have been able to make significant changes in our society and culture, we hope to encourage a political commitment to creating a just and generous world.

ACKNOWLEDGMENTS

The third edition of this book, like the first and second, has truly been a collaborative effort. Our cooperative working arrangements and consensual decision making process, characteristic of feminist process, have been both stimulating and arduous. We appreciate each other's patience and commitment.

Many people have made invaluable contributions to this third edition. Lanette Fisher-Hertz's excellent research, writing, and editing skills were indispensable. Lucia Ferrante, Monique Harris, Amanda Kim, Vernique Jefferson, Carissa Bergmann, and Anne Byrer have been resourceful, able, and dedicated research assistants. We continue to be grateful for the ongoing contributions of Virginia Blaisdell, David Porter, and George Roberts.

Pat Clarke, the Program Assistant at the Women's Studies Program at S.U.N.Y. New Paltz, has helped in innumerable and invaluable ways over the years. We also appreciate the clerical assistance of Erin Fisher, Cathy Ragsdale, Kristin Aycock, Lorraine Fazio, Teresa Maphis, and Devon McDermott.

The work of many who contributed to the first and second editions was also essential to the completion of this collection. Candace Watson, Lisa DeBoer, Lori Gross, Lena Hatchett, Stephanie Brown, Shalom Palacio, Kellie-Ann Ffrench, and Sarah Ellis were able and dedicated research assistants. We appreciate the ideas and perspectives that Johnella Butler and Elisa Dávila contributed to the early stages of this project. Stacey Yap offered many valuable resources on Asian-American women. Rayna Green and Paula Gunn Allen provided helpful suggestions regarding a number of pieces included here. Alison Nash, Eudora Chikwendu, Lee Bell, and Rickie Solinger also gave useful feedback. Virginia Blaisdell's thoughtful editorial assistance improved several parts of this manuscript.

Serena Beauparlant, sponsoring editor at Mayfield Publishing Company, was encouraging in initiating the third edition of this book. We are grateful to Katherine

Bates for easing the transition from Mayfield to McGraw-Hill and for her cheerful support in the revising process. We appreciate the thoughtful feedback of reviewers who read earlier drafts of the manuscript, some of which has been incorporated into the text. Finally, we especially thank all the contributors to this volume, some of whom rewrote earlier pieces for this book.

Contents

PART III
GENDER AND
WOMEN'S BODIES   117

PART IV
INSTITUTIONS THAT
SHAPE WOMEN'S LIVES 179

Women and Work 187

WOMEN
IMAGES AND REALITIES

Introduction

Inspired by the very positive responses to the first and second editions of *Women: Images and Realities: A Multicultural Anthology,* we are pleased to bring even more diverse women's voices, more voices of young women, additional feminist issues, and updated information and resources to this third edition. We have tried to gather into this book, once again, readings that will be meaningful to you and challenge your thinking.

In *Women: Images and Realities: A Multicultural Anthology* you will enter the lives of many different women. By exploring their experiences and ideas, you will learn more about yourself and what it means to be female in the United States today. You will hear the voices of women of different racial, cultural and socio-economic backgrounds who have made various choices in their lives. Because the selections reflect a wide variety of female experience, some parts of this book will resonate with your experience while others will not. We hope the book will enable you to understand what women have in common as well as the different ways that the experience of being female is shaped by race, class, and culture.

The structure of this book is inspired by the consciousness-raising process that has been a central part of contemporary feminism. The goal of consciousness raising is to use insights from personal experience to enhance a political critique of the position of women in society. Echoing this process, the book moves back and forth between personal experience and social realities, illuminating the way sexism in society affects women's lives. We hope the selections in this book will stimulate your thinking about your own life.

ORGANIZATION AND USE OF THIS BOOK

This third edition of *Women: Images and Realities* is organized somewhat differently from the previous editions. We have reorganized it so as to make issues facing women emerge in a more clear and focused way.

Women: Images and Realities is divided into eight parts. We begin by introducing the subject of women's studies, an approach to knowledge that emerged as part of the contemporary feminist movement. Because a feminist perspective provides the groundwork for women's studies, Part I explores the meaning of feminism and women's studies for different groups of women and, to a lesser extent, for men.

It examines the impact of women's studies and feminist scholarship on other academic disciplines.

Part II presents prevailing ideas about what it means to be female in our society and describes the way we learn and internalize these ideas. Part III explores the effects of these ideas on women's attitudes toward our bodies and our sexuality. Because this anthology is designed to enable you to make connections between your personal life and social realities, it moves from a focus on individual experience in Parts II and III to an examination of the social institutions that shape women's lives in Part IV. Articles in this part demonstrate the ways that the subordination of women is deeply embedded in social institutions such as the legal system, the workplace, the family, and religion. Part V examines the sexism in the medical care system and women's efforts to take control of their health. This includes women's ongoing struggle for reproductive rights, including access to birth control and abortion and protection from sterilization abuse.

While all parts in *Women: Images and Realities* include accounts by women from diverse social groups, Part VI directly addresses the ways that socially defined differences among women have been used to divide women from each other. It examines the ways that inequities in our society based on race, class, sexual orientation, and age have often separated women. It analyzes the interplay between institutional discrimination and the relationships among different groups of women. Part VII explores violence against women in various forms, particularly battering, rape, and incestuous sexual abuse. Part VIII reviews ways that women have worked together to make social and political change. By reminding us of the rich tradition of female resistance both within and outside an organized feminist movement, the selections in Part VIII provide inspiration and hope for changing our lives and the world around us. The resurgence of political activism on college campuses in the 1990s reinforces, as well, a renewed sense of the possibility for change.

We have tried to create a rich brew—a mixture of short stories, poems, autobiographical accounts, and journal excerpts as well as analytical and descriptive essays from a variety of disciplines. We hope this mixture will engage you intellectually and emotionally. Introductions to sections provide a framework that places the selections in the broader context of the part. While most of the material is current, some articles provide a historical perspective. Those written in the earlier years of the contemporary feminist movement are important because they laid the conceptual groundwork for further research and analysis.

While there are theoretical insights in *Women: Images and Realities,* this book does not provide a theoretical introduction to women's studies in all the various disciplines. Theory is discussed in those women's studies courses that explore feminist issues and particular disciplines in depth. Here, you will hear the words of a wide variety of writers, some prominent feminist writers, and some students like yourself. Because the emotions provoked by this material can sometimes be unsettling, you may find it useful to discuss your responses outside of class as well as in the classroom. These discussions might take place with friends, family members, or a counselor, depending on the intensity of the personal connection with the issue.

This book may raise specific questions for African-American, Asian-American, Latina, Arab-American, American Indian, and Jewish women. Women of color are struggling against the sexism in minority communities and the particular ways that sexism and racism interact in their lives. The different priorities and emphases that emerge from various cultural and racial contexts enrich and deepen a feminist perspective. The focus of *Women: Images and Realities* is on the struggle for freedom of women in the U.S. The feminist movement in the U.S., however, is part of a global women's movement that has raised significant questions for women in the U.S. While the connections between U.S. women's efforts and issues raised by the global feminist movement are touched on in this book, they are explored more fully in other women's studies courses.

Men who have taken women's studies courses have often found it intellectually and emotionally challenging to be in a course focused on women, taught by women, and usually including a majority of female students. By listening to women's experiences and sharing the experience of being a male in a sexist society, men can both benefit from and contribute to a women's studies course.

Many students will use this book in the introductory women's studies course, an interdisciplinary course that familiarizes students with the field of women's studies and the feminist perspective that shapes women's studies scholarship. In such a course, you may also read *Our Bodies, Our Selves for the New Century* written by the Boston Women's Health Book Collective (Simon and Schuster, 1998). Even if the book is not assigned in your course, it is an excellent complement to *Women: Images and Realities,* and we recommend it.

HOW WE SEE FEMINISM

Because *Women: Images and Realities* is informed by a feminist perspective, we want to describe what feminism means to us. We see sexism as a central fact of all women's lives, even though it wears many different faces. The life of a single mother struggling to support her family on the wages she earns doing domestic work is very different from the life of a woman struggling to succeed in a scientific establishment dominated by men. But both survive in a world where women are paid less than men on all levels, both live in a society in which one woman is raped every three minutes, and both face the possibility of losing their jobs if they resist their employer's sexual advances. Feminism is a social movement whose goal is to eliminate the oppression of women in all its forms. This means making major social, economic, and political and cultural changes in our society—changes so fundamental and numerous that the task sometimes seems overwhelming. Yet feminists have succeeded in making changes that would have appeared unthinkable 50 years ago—and such accomplishments give us hope and courage.

One of the most important ideas that contemporary feminism has generated is that "the personal is political"—what happens in our private lives reflects the power relations in our society. This book examines the inequities both in women's personal lives and in the world. The belief in our right to determine our lives empowers us to expand our choices: to develop relationships based on equality and mutual respect, to choose when and if to have children, to work toward career goals that are meaningful to us.

Because of the connection between personal and political life, our ability to control our own lives is limited by the environment in which we live. We cannot, for example, choose when and if we have children unless safe, effective, and legal birth control and abortion are available and accessible. Feminism is more than an individual lifestyle. It involves a commitment to social change, which can take a variety of forms. It might mean working to make your campus safer for women; forming a support group for women in your school, department, or office to discuss the conditions of your lives and ways to improve them; organizing a forum about sexual harassment at your workplace or on your campus; or establishing a cooperative child-care center in your community. Feminism means making changes wherever you are.

THE AUTHORS: THREE FEMINIST JOURNEYS

Because this book affirms the differences among us, we want to tell you who we are and what feminism means to each of us.

Amy   Growing up Jewish in New York City in the 1950s, I always felt different from the boys and girls whose images I confronted in grade school textbooks. The blond children and white picket fences represented normalcy to me, while my apartment building and multi-ethnic neighborhood seemed deviant. I went to a large city college in which men dominated the intellectual and cultural life, and I struggled to be taken seriously in and out of the classroom. The movements of the 1960s for civil rights and peace in Vietnam gave direction and meaning to my life, but I found that even as we worked toward a fairer world, women were treated in demeaning ways. In the late 1960s, when feminism was a foreign word to most people, I began talking with other women about my experiences and participated in the birth of the women's liberation movement.

Feminism saved my life. It replaced the self-hatred of being female in a woman-hating culture with the power of anger at injustice. It replaced isolation with a sense of connection and identification with other women. It replaced despair with a vision of a world in which everyone is able to develop fully in loving connection with each other. But feminism did not liberate me. I am still subject to rape, sexual harassment, discrimination, and unremitting degradation by the media and other woman-hating institutions. Ultimately, I see feminism as a political movement. Its power to change the world depends on its ability to mobilize women to challenge the power relations of the institutions in our society.

Lily   I grew up in a rural community on the outskirts of a major military installation in New Jersey. My childhood memories are filled with images of other children who, like me, were of mixed racial backgrounds. Most had mothers who were Asian (Japanese, Korean, or Filipino) and fathers who were African American. This setting made it impossible for me to ignore the effects of race and class on the lives of people around me. I began to realize that the world was unfair and that this unfairness shaped the lives of most of the people I knew.

My parents taught me, very early, that I was a black child in a racist society. There were times when I didn't quite understand why they attached so much significance to this fact, but I gradually learned about the world from their history. My mother talked about her experiences as a Japanese girl-child during World War II, and as a "war bride" in the Deep South of the 1950s. Bitter toward a society that treated him as less than a person because of his black skin, my father promised me that one day I would understand what he meant.

When I went away to an Ivy League college, I saw inequity both in the structure of the institution (such as hiring and tenure practices) and within the student body. Blacks and women were still viewed as unwanted and unqualified newcomers to this formerly all-white, all-male bastion. Fortunately, the African-American community provided me with peers and a black, female mentor who helped to strengthen my commitment to fighting racial, sexual, and class oppression.

For me, feminism is a natural extension of my experiences as an African-American-Asian woman. Feminism provides me with a framework for looking at and understanding power relationships in our society. I recognize that I must be aware of the realities of oppression because this knowledge forces me to challenge racism and sexism. A feminist perspective is consistent with my view of a more just society—one in which differences among people can be appreciated and celebrated, not merely tolerated or dismissed. Feminism is a positive force in my personal life as well. My feminist beliefs have strongly influenced my parenting practices, as I am committed to teaching my children to challenge the social inequities they see in the world around them. It enables me to develop relationships that are based on equality, cooperation, and an affirmation of the strengths of women and men.

Nancy   Growing up as a white female in a semi-rural New England community, I was not aware of the price I was paying for being female. I did not wonder why I hated science. No one called my attention to how few females appeared in my textbooks or discussed the ways that the absence of role models inhibits learning and stunts expectations. I never wondered why no one encouraged me to become a scientist despite my aptitude for science. Though I knew I loved sports, I never connected my failure to take myself seriously as an athlete with the fact that the high school athletic budget and programs for boys' sports were extensive, while those for girls were nonexistent.

I was also unaware of the privileges I received by being white. I didn't realize that because we were white, my family was able to move to our town and to find housing and thereby benefit from better public schools. I didn't wonder why there were only two African-American families in our town. I never thought about the comfort of being in the racial majority in my school and how my sense of being "normal" enhanced my ability to learn. I didn't ask why I had the privilege to go home to play when my African-American classmates went home to help their mothers do the laundry they took in to support their families.

I saw my life as my own. Even throughout my masters degree program, I failed to see patterns of discrimination and privilege. I thought the sexual harassment I experienced was my own problem, not part of a pattern experienced by millions of women. There were no women's studies courses in the late 1960s, and it was only through long talks with friends and co-workers that I opened my eyes to sexism. Subsequently, I read much of what the burgeoning women's movement was producing. Looking back at my life, I saw how I had been affected by gender, race, and class, and look to the future with a renewed commitment to work for change.

Feminism offers me the support, values, and ideas for living an authentic life. It provides me a way to understand women's experience and a vision of a more just and humane future. Feminism contributes to my role as an educator by helping me understand how sexism limits men's and women's educational potential. Its values underlie my feminist approach to teaching which is more equitable, cooperative, and empowering than traditional approaches. As a family member, feminism gives me the consciousness and strength to encourage more equitable family relations. Finally, feminism sustains my faith in women's collective power to transform our individual lives and social institutions.

As our own stories demonstrate, the experience of integrating feminism into one's life can be challenging and exhilarating. We hope this book makes you feel stronger and better able to both make choices in your own life and participate in the process of creating a more just and generous world.

PART I

What Is Women's Studies?

Before the late 1960s there were no women's studies courses. Most college courses focused on male experience and women were shadowy, marginal figures. The resurgence of feminism in the late 1960s led students and faculty to ask "where are the women?" and work to establish courses that focused on women's experience. Today there are women's studies programs throughout the world, close to 1,000 of them in the United States.

What *is* women's studies? You will probably hear this question often when you tell people that you are taking women's studies classes. Despite the spectacular growth in women's studies programs and courses in the past three decades, some faculty members and students still view women's studies as marginal to the main business of the university. Yet to countless others, women's studies is an important and exciting experience that introduces new ways of seeing both the world and oneself. Women's studies courses investigate women's experience, perspectives, and contributions and place women at the center of inquiry.

As Barrie Thorne has pointed out, women's studies has been a two-pronged project: it has created courses within disciplines, such as women and literature or sociology of women, which seek to incorporate the experience of women into the subject matter of the disciplines. But the boundaries that separate the disciplines begin to blur and appear arbitrary when we seek to answer questions about women's lives. The second prong of the women's studies project, therefore, is to create interdisciplinary courses and lines of inquiry. The Introduction to Women's Studies course in most colleges is an example of an interdisciplinary course that draws on theory and approaches from a variety of disciplines to render women's lives visible.[1] Women's studies scholars working both within and across disciplines have generated new concepts and approaches to understanding the world. A basic premise of women's studies is that we cannot understand the world without understanding women's experiences, perspectives, and contributions.

A women's studies approach to education emphasizes an interactive learning process which challenges students intellectually and emotionally. Women's studies emerged from the questions women asked about their own experiences as well as about the subjects they were studying, and this process remains a central part of a women's studies education. Women's studies instructors usually encourage students to ask questions of the material, and to bring their own experiences to bear on the material they are studying. Women's studies instructors see themselves as resources and guides in this process, not as authorities who are handing down knowledge to passive recipients. The values of feminism, including a critique of all forms of domination, an emphasis on cooperation, and a belief in the integration of theory and practice, have shaped an approach to teaching termed feminist pedagogy, which makes the women's studies classroom an interactive learning environment.

---

[1] Barrie Thorne, "A Telling Time for Women's Studies," *Signs: A Journal of Women in Culture and Society* 25, #4 (2000), p. 1183.

The realities of schooling in America contradict these approaches to learning. Education has often been a bittersweet experience for women. We expect that knowledge of our world can be empowering, enabling us to change our lives and our communities. For many women, particularly those of us who have experienced racial or ethnic discrimination, educational achievement assures greater access to resources and opportunities. But the educational institutions of our society have too often been limiting, rather than empowering, for women. The practices of educational institutions frequently encourage girls and women to pursue occupations in traditionally "female" areas rather than in traditionally "male" domains, such as math and the sciences. Schools and teachers tend to reinforce girls' compliance and passivity rather than their assertiveness and inquisitiveness. Men have historically exercised authority in institutions of higher learning, determining "valid" areas of inquiry and "legitimate" methods of analysis and research. In sum, the dominant message is that human experience equals male experience. Sometimes this message is overt, and sometimes so subtle and deeply imbedded in the educational experience that we are not aware of it. There has been some progress in the past three decades, but for the most part the massive outpouring of research by women's studies scholars has not been integrated into mainstream education.

Women's studies was born out of the conviction that women are worth learning about, and that understanding women's experiences helps us to change the condition of women. Emerging from the feminist movement of the late 1960s and 70s, women's studies courses and programs were deeply political. The Buffalo women's studies program asserted, for example, "This education will not be an academic exercise; it will be an ongoing process to change the ways in which women think and behave. It must be part of the struggle to build a new and more complete society." [2] From their beginnings in the 1960s, women's studies courses spread rapidly across the country. By 1989, over 500 colleges in the United States had women's studies programs. In the past 30 years, thousands of books and articles about women have been published, challenging old assumptions and charting new territory. Today, women's studies has become part of the academy and offers majors, minors, master's degrees and, at a few universities, doctorates in women's studies. Women's studies flourishes in conferences, workshops, journals, and research institutes, and in countless Internet sites and discussion lists.

As feminist scholars began to chart female experience, they sometimes found the available vocabulary inadequate and confusing. As a result, feminist scholarship has generated several new words or has endowed familiar words with new meaning. The word "gender," for example, used to pertain only to grammar, but has come to mean the socially constructed behaviors and characteristics that are associated with each sex. While gender is a social category, the word "sex" describes the physiological

---

[2] Quoted in Florence Howe and Carol Ahlum, "Women's Studies and Social Change" in *Academic Women on the Move,* ed. Alice Rossi and Ann Calderwood (New York: Russell Sage, 1973), p. 420.

identities of women and men. The distinction between sex and gender enables us to see that the particular expectations for women and men in our culture are neither immutable nor universal. Recently, however, feminist scholars have argued that sex itself is not a purely biological category but has been powerfully shaped by gender. For many years, for example, doctors have insisted that sexually ambiguous genitalia be surgically altered so that they fit into the prevailing divisions between male and female, thereby showing the power of gender to constitute sex.[3] In addition, scholars have pointed out that the social construction of gender is a complex process in which individuals and groups sometimes challenge gender norms. Tina Chanter suggests that we think of "sex and gender" as always in dynamic relation and the distinctions between the two realms as not fixed or rigid but malleable and flexible.[4]

The word "sexism" appeared because the available phrase, "sex discrimination," did not adequately describe the pervasive bias against women in our culture. Sexism therefore has come to mean behaviors, attitudes, and institutions based on the assumption of male superiority. Patriarchy refers to "power of the fathers" and is used by feminists in two ways: 1) to describe a society in which older men are in positions of power, and 2) a male-dominated society. This new vocabulary has been instrumental in shaping the ways in which we now think about the experiences of women and girls in our society.

Over the past three decades women's studies has developed and changed as it seeks to understand more effectively the experiences of all women. Initially, women scholars endeavored to address the absence of women in the literature of varied academic areas by uncovering women's achievements. For example, psychology has benefited from the work of scholars who focused on the important contributions of women such as Mamie Phipps Clark, Carolyn Sherif, and Margaret Harlow to psychological research. It quickly became apparent, however, that the central concepts of many academic disciplines excluded women or assumed women's inferiority to men. Even the language used to describe these concepts and ideas is often laden with assumptions about female inferiority. As Emily Martin points out, "scientific" descriptions of the egg and sperm rely on stereotyped notions of male and female roles, and reinforce widely held myths about female passivity and male power.[5] A women's studies perspective allows us to critique these interpretations, thereby challenging some of the basic tenets that structure academic knowledge. In this way, women's experiences can be at center stage rather than an anomalous footnote.

In the field of history, for example, subject matter was traditionally limited to the

---

[3] Ann Fausto-Sterling, *Sexing the Body.* (New York: Basic Books, 2000).
[4] Tina Chanter, "Gender Aporias," *Signs: Journal of Culture and Society* 25, (2000). p. 1241. See also Judith Butler, *Gender Trouble: Feminism and the Subversion of Identity* (Routledge, 1990) and Ann Fausto-Sterling, *Sexing the Body* (Ibid.).
[5] Emily Martin, "The Egg and the Sperm: How Science Has Constructed a Romance Based on Stereotypical Male-Female Roles," *Signs* 16 (1991), pp. 485–501.

public arena such as political parties, wars, and the economy. The domestic world, where many women spent a great deal of their time, was considered trivial or irrelevant; and the relationship between the domestic and public worlds was ignored. In literature, the very definition of great literature, or "the canon," was based on standards that white male authors generated. By emphasizing the contributions of women, critically challenging the conceptual frameworks underlying traditional scholarship, and presenting theory and research focusing on women's experiences, women's studies research is transforming the terrain of human knowledge. When women are placed at the center of inquiry, everything dramatically changes, as if a kaleidoscope has been turned.

As Michael Kimmel points out, "Women's studies has made gender visible."[6] Thus, examining gender is more than examining women's lives; it also includes acknowledging the enormous influence of gender on *all* of our lives. Boys' and men's experience is powerfully affected by ideas about masculinity and femininity. Women's studies has, as a result, generated the broader field of gender studies. Gender studies examines the ways that ideas about the social relations of women and men structure our politics and culture and the way we all experience our world. By reaffirming the significance of gender in our lives, gender studies is very much related to women's studies in its content. Elizabeth Minnich aptly describes this complementary relationship: "Gender Studies requires Women's Studies, just as Women's Studies requires the study of gender. One does not substitute for the other; they are mutually enriching."[7]

The ideas of feminism have inspired the development of women's studies theory and courses. "Feminism" refers to the belief that women have been historically subordinate to men, as well as to the commitment to working for freedom for women in all aspects of social life. While feminist beliefs, values, and practices are continually evolving, reflecting new ideas, movements, and historical research, it is clear that similar values have informed the lives and work of many different groups of women, even when they may not have identified their beliefs as "feminist." Paula Gunn Allen, a Native American writer, pointed out that roots of contemporary feminism can be found in many Native American cultures.[8] Some of these societies were gynarchies (governed by women), which were egalitarian, pacifist, and spiritually based. These values and practices are comparable to those of present-day feminism, such as cooperation and respect for human freedom. As we understand the varied ways that women have worked toward self-determination in different contexts and cultures

---

[6]Michael Kimmel, "Men and Women's Studies: Premises, Perils, and Promise in Talking Gender." *Public Images, Personal Journeys and Political Critiques.* Nancy Hewitt, Jean O'Barr, and Nancy Rosebaugh, eds. Chapel Hill, NC: University of North Carolina Press, 1996.
[7]Elizabeth Minnich, *Transforming Knowledge.* Philadelphia: Temple University Press, 1990, p. 139.
[8]Paula Gunn Allen, *The Sacred Hoop: Recovering the Feminine in American Indian Traditions.* Boston: Beacon Press, 1986.

throughout history, our definition of feminism becomes broader and richer. We also acknowledge and incorporate the struggles of women who have worked for equality and freedom for women, though they may not have called themselves "feminists."

The word "feminism" originated in France and was introduced into this country in the early 1900s after efforts to expand women's political rights had been flourishing throughout the world for many decades.[9] The women who first identified themselves as feminist in the early twentieth century believed that the "emancipation of women" required changes in the relations between women and men and between women and the family, as well as between women and the state.

For many women, the goal of freedom for women was inextricably linked with the end of all forms of domination. Women of color in particular saw the connections between sexual and racial oppression. African-American activists like Anna Cooper argued for a women's movement that challenged all forms of domination and made alliances with all oppressed peoples.

U.S. historians often refer to the movement that began in the nineteenth century and culminated with the Nineteenth Amendment, granting women the right to vote, as the first wave of feminism. The legal, educational, and political achievements of the movement were considerable, despite the fact that it faced enormous opposition to every demand. Yet the organizations that led the movement did not speak for all women, and often refused to seriously consider the concerns of African-American and immigrant women. The history of the suffrage movement demonstrates how race and class divisions can prevent a movement from working effectively to achieve freedom for all women.

In the decades after women won the right to vote in 1920, the organized women's rights movement in the United States dissipated, and the word "feminism" fell into disuse and ill repute. In the 1960s, a new generation revived the fight for what they now called "women's liberation" and a vision of a world free of domination and subordination. This movement struck a responsive chord for countless women. The feminist movement grew rapidly throughout the 1970s, permeating every aspect of social, political, and cultural life. The new feminist movement has argued that reproductive rights are essential for women's freedom. It has criticized the disadvantaged position of women in the workplace and the subordination of women in the family, pointing out the connection between the place of women in the labor force and the family. By declaring that "the personal is political," contemporary feminists have brought into the open subjects that had only previously been discussed in whispers, such as sexuality, rape, incestuous sexual abuse, and violence against women. For feminists, all of these struggles are inextricably connected, and changes in all of them are necessary to attain freedom for women.

Feminism is continually developing a more multicultural and inclusive perspective, reflecting the lives of women of all races, ethnic groups, and classes. Feminists

[9]Nancy Cott, *The Grounding of Modern Feminism.* New Haven, CT: Yale University Press, 1987.

of varied races and ethnicities are generating theory and practice that address their particular experiences and consciousness, broadening and deepening the scope of feminist analysis. It is important to recognize that while gender affects all of us, these effects are powerfully shaped by other aspects of our experience.

Black feminist thought, for example, reflects the unique position of African-American women in American society. As eloquently expressed by Alice Walker, black feminism, or "womanism," draws on the historical strength of black women in their families and communities and the rich African-American tradition of resistance, persistence, and survival. By describing a "womanist" with a broad brush that celebrates the everyday lives of black girls and women, as well as the political implications of their activism, Walker's definition resonates with the experiences of many black women. African-American feminists have also emphasized the concept of "multiple consciousness" or "intersectionality": the idea that distinct systems of racism, sexism, and class oppression interact simultaneously in the lives of women of color in the U.S. They have also suggested an African-centered rather than a Euro-centric perspective on the history of women, allowing for an appreciation of the powerful roles that women have played in some African societies.

Jewish feminists have also reclaimed their tradition of Jewish female resistance and have reexamined insulting stereotypes like "pushy Jewish mother" and "Jewish American Princess" to express the legitimacy of female assertiveness. They have revived Rabbi Hillel's question, "If I am not for myself, who will be? If I am only for myself, what am I?" to explore both the meaning of anti-Semitism for Jewish women and the importance of the connections between different groups of suppressed people. Reflecting on this project, Melanie Kaye/Kantrowitz has pointed out that "what is best in people is a sturdy connection between respect for the self and respect for the other: reaching in and out at the same time." [10]

Asian and Latina feminists have pointed out the tensions between immigrant and U.S. cultures, and the concurrent need to affirm their cultural heritage and reject its sexism. Traditional Japanese culture, for instance, expects women to be docile and to put family honor ahead of their own needs. One's self is inextricably tied to one's family; to break away is often viewed as an act of betrayal. Asian-American feminists have also confronted the myths about Asian women's sexuality, myths that have emerged from an interplay between Western stereotypes and the expectations of women in Asian cultures. Latina feminists have demonstrated the need to negotiate a path between the sometimes conflicting demands of the Latino community's expectations and female self-determination. Feminism for Latina women, and women of other oppressed groups, means simultaneously working with Latino men against their common oppression and challenging sexist or "macho" attitudes and behavior.

---

[10]Melanie Kaye/Kantrowitz, "To Be a Radical Jew in the Late Twentieth Century." *Sinister Wisdom* 29–30 (1986), p. 280.

Contemporary American Indian feminists carry many of the traditional values and practices of women-centered Native American cultures into the present. In addition, Native American women's history and their vision of connectedness to the earth and spiritual world, along with a legacy of responsibility toward the environment, are emerging as important concerns for many feminists. For example, eco-feminism addresses the connection between women's oppression and the exploitation of the earth's natural resources, and emphasizes women's role in confronting these environmental issues.

One of the most exciting developments of the past decade has been the emergence of a powerful global feminist movement that has worked throughout the world to challenge violence against women, defend women's rights as human rights, expand the education of girls, champion women's sexual and reproductive freedom, and support women's access to economic independence. The activities and ideas of women throughout the world have enriched and broadened feminist theory and practice.

The ideas and concerns of different groups of women are expanding the boundaries of feminism, contributing to multicultural feminist theory and practice aimed at liberating all people. To emphasize the diversity within feminism, some scholars have begun to refer to "feminisms."

Speaking up for ourselves is an essential first step for women taking an active role in their education. In the first selection, bell hooks writes from the context of the Southern black community in which she grew up, where "talking back" as a girl was an act of daring. It often takes courage for women to speak up for themselves in educational settings where male-oriented norms, curricula, and classroom processes often silence women's voices. Mai Kao Thao echoes this message in her essay, "Sins of Silence," as she describes the pain she and other "good Hmong women" have endured when they have kept silent about the realities of their lives.

Adrienne Rich, feminist author and poet, wrote the next selection as an address to a primarily white, female graduating class in 1977. Its message, about the importance of women "claiming an education" that is meaningful to them, continues to be relevant today in any educational setting. Rich provides a personal context for understanding the role of women's studies courses in shaping such an education.

Just as feminism has become more inclusive of women from diverse backgrounds, so too has the content of women's studies expanded over the years, embodying the experiences of women from varying racial, ethnic, and class groups. In their classic essay, Gloria Hull and Barbara Smith place the development of black women's studies in a political and historical context. By highlighting the legacy of black women's struggles to obtain an education during and after slavery, Hull and Smith show us the connection between black women's studies and the politics of oppression.

The next essay focuses on men and women's studies. Originally delivered as a lecture by Michael Kimmel at an anniversary of the women's studies program at a major university, the essay begins by stating that "many readers are wondering . . . what I'm doing in such a volume of essays."[11] A sociologist who studies men's relation to feminism, Kimmel gives us another important example of the relevance of women's studies for all students.

In the next six selections, women's studies students and one instructor speak of the value of a women's studies education to their intellectual, political, and personal lives. Because the authors of these pieces come from varied backgrounds, women's studies took on different meanings for each of them.

We end this section with an essay examining the influence of women's studies across a variety of disciplines within American colleges and universities. By documenting the changes that have been prompted by the evolution of women's studies, Carol Christ highlights the far-reaching impact of a feminist perspective in research and teaching, and considers the future contributions of women's studies to academia.

 1

Talking Back

BELL HOOKS

In the world of the southern black community I grew up in, "back talk" and "talking back" meant speaking as an equal to an authority figure. It meant daring to disagree and sometimes it just meant having an opinion. In the "old school," children were meant to be seen and not heard. My great-grandparents, grandparents, and parents were all from the old school. To make yourself heard if you were a child was to invite punishment, the back-hand lick, the slap across the face that would catch you unaware, or the feel of switches stinging your arms and legs.

To speak then when one was not spoken to was a courageous act—an act of risk and daring. And yet it was hard not to speak in warm rooms where heated discussions began at the crack of dawn, women's voices filling the air, giving orders, making threats, fussing. Black men may have excelled in the art of poetic preaching in the male-dominated church, but in the church of the home, where the everyday rules

of how to live and how to act were established, it was black women who preached. There, black women spoke in a language so rich, so poetic, that it felt to me like being shut off from life, smothered to death if one were not allowed to participate.

It was in that world of woman talk (the men were often silent, often absent) that was born in me the craving to speak, to have a voice, and not just any voice but one that could be identified as belonging to me. To make my voice, I had to speak, to hear myself talk—and talk I did—darting in and out of grown folks' conversations and dialogues, answering questions that were not directed at me, endlessly asking questions, making speeches. Needless to say, the punishments for these acts of speech seemed endless. They were intended to silence me—the child—and more particularly the girl child. Had I been a boy, they might have encouraged me to speak believing that I might someday be called to preach. There was no "calling" for talking girls, no legitimized rewarded speech. The punishments I received for "talking back" were intended to suppress all possibility that I would create my own speech. That speech was to be suppressed so that the "right speech of womanhood" would emerge.

[11] Michael Kimmel, "Men and Women's Studies." *Talking Gender, Public Images: Personal Journeys and Political Critiques,* eds. Nancy Hewitt, Jean O'Barr and Nancy Rosebaugh. Chapel Hill, N.C.: University of North Carolina Press, 1996.

Within feminist circles, silence is often seen as the sexist "right speech of womanhood"—the sign of woman's submission to patriarchal authority. This emphasis on woman's silence may be an accurate remembering of what has taken place in the households of women from WASP backgrounds in the United States, but in black communities (and diverse ethnic communities), women have not been silent. Their voices can be heard. Certainly for black women, our struggle has not been to emerge from silence into speech but to change the nature and direction of our speech, to make a speech that compels listeners, one that is heard.

Our speech, "the right speech of womanhood," was often the soliloquy, the talking into thin air, the talking to ears that do not hear you—the talk that is simply not listened to. Unlike the black male preacher whose speech was to be heard, who was to be listened to, whose words were to be remembered, the voices of black women—giving orders, making threats, fussing—could be tuned out, could become a kind of background music, audible but not acknowledged as significant speech. Dialogue—the sharing of speech and recognition—took place not between mother and child or mother and male authority figure but among black women. I can remember watching fascinated as our mother talked with her mother, sisters, and women friends. The intimacy and intensity of their speech—the satisfaction they received from talking to one another, the pleasure, the joy. It was in this world of woman speech, loud talk, angry words, women with tongues quick and sharp, tender sweet tongues, touching our world with their words, that I made speech my birthright—and the right to voice, to authorship, a privilege I would not be denied. It was in that world and because of it that I came to dream of writing, to write.

Writing was a way to capture speech, to hold onto it, keep it close. And so I wrote down bits and pieces of conversations, confessing in cheap diaries that soon fell apart from too much handling, expressing the intensity of my sorrow, the anguish of speech—for I was always saying the wrong thing, asking the wrong questions. I could not confine my speech to the necessary corners and concerns of life. I hid these writings under my bed, in pillow stuffings, among faded underwear. When my sisters found and read them, they ridiculed and mocked me —poking fun. I felt violated, ashamed, as if the secret parts of my self had been exposed, brought into the open, and hung like newly clean laundry, out in the air for everyone to see. The fear of exposure, the fear that one's deepest emotions and innermost thoughts will be dismissed as mere nonsense, felt by so many young girls keeping diaries, holding and hiding speech, seems to me now one of the barriers that women have always needed and still need to destroy so that we are no longer pushed into secrecy or silence.

Despite my feelings of violation, of exposure, I continued to speak and write, choosing my hiding places well, learning to destroy work when no safe place could be found. I was never taught absolute silence, I was taught that it was important to speak but to talk a talk that was in itself a silence. Taught to speak and yet beware of the betrayal of too much heard speech, I experienced intense confusion and deep anxiety in my efforts to speak and write. Reciting poems at Sunday afternoon church service might be rewarded. Writing a poem (when one's time could be "better" spent sweeping, ironing, learning to cook) was luxurious activity, indulged in at the expense of others. Questioning authority, raising issues that were not deemed appropriate subjects brought pain, punishments—like telling mama I wanted to die before her because I could not live without her—that was crazy talk, crazy speech, the kind that would lead you to end up in a mental institution. "Little girl," I would be told, "if you don't stop all this crazy talk and crazy acting you are going to end up right out there at Western State."

Madness, not just physical abuse, was the punishment for too much talk if you were female. Yet even as this fear of madness haunted me, hanging over my writing like a monstrous shadow, I could not stop the words, making thought, writing speech. For this terrible madness which I feared, which I was sure was the destiny of daring women born to intense speech (after all, the authorities emphasized this point daily), was not as threatening as imposed silence, as suppressed speech.

Safety and sanity were to be sacrificed if I was to experience defiant speech. Though I risked them both, deep-seated fears and anxieties characterized my childhood days. I would speak but I would not ride a bike, play hardball, or hold the gray kitten. Writing about the ways we are traumatized in our growing-up years, psychoanalyst Alice Miller makes the point in *For Your Own Good* that it is not clear why childhood wounds become for some folk an opportunity to grow, to move forward rather than backward in the process of self-realization. Certainly, when I reflect on the trials of my growing-up years, the many punishments, I can see now that in resistance I learned to be vigilant in the nourishment of my spirit, to be tough, to courageously protect that spirit from forces that would break it.

While punishing me, my parents often spoke about the necessity of breaking my spirit. Now when I ponder the silences, the voices that are not heard, the voices of those wounded and/or oppressed individuals who do not speak or write, I contemplate the acts of persecution, torture—the terrorism that breaks spirits, that makes creativity impossible. I write these words to bear witness to the primacy of resistance struggle in any situation of domination (even within family life); to the strength and power that emerges from sustained resistance and the profound conviction that these forces can be healing, can protect us from dehumanization and despair.

These early trials, wherein I learned to stand my ground, to keep my spirit intact, came vividly to mind after I published *Ain't I A Woman* and the book was sharply and harshly criticized. While I had expected a climate of critical dialogue, I was not expecting a critical avalanche that had the power in its intensity to crush the spirit, to push one into silence. Since that time, I have heard stories about black women, about women of color, who write and publish (even when the work is quite successful) having nervous breakdowns, being made mad because they cannot bear the harsh responses of family, friends, and unknown critics, or becoming silent, unproductive. Surely, the absence of a humane critical re-

sponse has tremendous impact on the writer from any oppressed, colonized group who endeavors to speak. For us, true speaking is not solely an expression of creative power; it is an act of resistance, a political gesture that challenges politics of domination that would render us nameless and voiceless. As such, it is a courageous act—as such, it represents a threat. To those who wield oppressive power, that which is threatening must necessarily be wiped out, annihilated, silenced.

Recently, efforts by black women writers to call attention to our work serve to highlight both our presence and absence. Whenever I peruse women's bookstores, I am struck not by the rapidly growing body of feminist writing by black women, but by the paucity of available published material. Those of us who write and are published remain few in number. The context of silence is varied and multidimensional. Most obvious are the ways racism, sexism, and class exploitation act to suppress and silence. Less obvious are the inner struggles, the efforts made to gain the necessary confidence to write, to re-write, to fully develop craft and skill—and the extent to which such efforts fail.

Although I have wanted writing to be my lifework since childhood, it has been difficult for me to claim "writer" as part of that which identifies and shapes my everyday reality. Even after publishing books, I would often speak of wanting to be a writer as though these works did not exist. And though I would be told, "you are a writer," I was not yet ready to fully affirm this truth. Part of myself was still held captive by domineering forces of history, of familial life that had charted a map of silence, of right speech. I had not completely let go of the fear of saying the wrong thing, of being punished. Somewhere in the deep recesses of my mind, I believed I could avoid both responsibility and punishment if I did not declare myself a writer.

One of the many reasons I chose to write using the pseudonym bell hooks, a family name (mother to Sarah Oldham, grandmother to Rosa Bell Oldham, great-grandmother to me), was to construct a writer-identity that would challenge and subdue all impulses leading me away from speech into silence. I was a young girl buying bubble gum at the corner store when I first really heard the full name bell hooks. I had just "talked back" to a grown person. Even now I can recall the surprised look, the mocking tones that informed me I must be kin to bell hooks—a sharp-tongued woman, a woman who spoke her mind, a woman who was not afraid to talk back. I claimed this legacy of defiance, of will, of courage, affirming my link to female ancestors who were bold and daring in their speech. Unlike my bold and daring mother and grandmother, who were not supportive of talking back, even though they were assertive and powerful in their speech, bell hooks as I discovered, claimed, and invented her was my ally, my support.

That initial act of talking back outside the home was empowering. It was the first of many acts of defiant speech that would make it possible for me to emerge as an independent thinker and writer. In retrospect, "talking back" became for me a rite of initiation, testing my courage, strengthening my commitment, preparing me for the days ahead—the days when writing, rejection notices, periods of silence, publication, ongoing development seem impossible but necessary.

Moving from silence into speech is for the oppressed, the colonized, the exploited, and those who stand and struggle side by side a gesture of defiance that heals, that makes new life and new growth possible. It is that act of speech, of "talking back," that is no mere gesture of empty words, that is the expression of our movement from object to subject—the liberated voice.   [1989]

 2

Sins of Silence

MAI KAO THAO

My mother used to tell me that I should always be a good, obedient woman, and smile silently as I swallow the bitterness that others give me. "Nod your head and say yes even if you don't agree. It's much easier. No trouble," she would say. Through these words, I heard, "Silence is power! It is a woman's strength." I remember hearing my father criticize my mother, even about the smallest things. "The rice doesn't taste good enough! Now the meat is too hard! You are a bad woman, a stupid woman! No good." And all the while, my mother would go about fixing what she did "wrong" without uttering a word, just wearing her usual, invisible mask of sadness. Oh well. At least there was no trouble.

I was trained to avoid conflict. When my brother lectured me, I'd reply "uh" and shake my head in agreement. I was punished with harsh reprimands and scorching displeasure if I talked back or offered an opinion, so I was silent. I was declared insolent if I spoke a little louder than I should have, so I learned to whisper. My voice was soft, sweet, and so delicious to the ear of authority. Yes. I was a good girl. Wordless. Humble. Obedient. A perfect Hmong woman.

Sexism laid comfortably on top of my silent submission. I smiled politely when older men gave me kisses on my cheek, more like wet, slow licks that made my innocent skin crawl. Hands grappled my body. Was that a bad touch or a good touch? Must have been a good touch. Relieved. No one will say that I was wrong in thinking that it was a bad touch, because it wasn't, and no one will call me stupid girl. There will be no trouble. Yes, it must be a good touch! Racism grinned at my passivity, while I, the "damned chink," gave it my pride, tears, and forgiveness. But no matter! I was stone. Silent. Hard. Emotionless. Nothing was going to hurt me!

In reality, I wasn't stone. I was flesh and blood. I was a cup, continuously filled, half with anger, dissatisfaction, and anxiety, and the other half with emptiness. My silence had killed my Self, the essence which holds and molds an individual together in order to form one complete organism. Without it, I was but an empty shell; a bird without the courage to fly. I suppressed my ideas of independence and ignored my innate disposition to feel and need. I had not learned to listen to the voice within, and so I did not know how to express these feelings or needs to others. Sadly, not only did I alone deprive my Self of its necessary nutrients, but I also allowed others to do it. And I wondered why no one understood me or gave me the respect I hungered for.

With love, my mother gave me her legacy, a shield of silence to protect me from pain and to prevent me from troubles. It gave me a source of inner strength, but it also barred inner peace from reaching the premises of my soul. Although my mother's words are wise, they are in some cases unsuitable to deal with problems which I faced in the context of my experiences in this new country. Back in Laos, my mother's life consisted of devotion to others, her parents, her husband, her children, because she was never expected to go beyond the role of the traditional Hmong woman. Here in America, opportunities are more plentiful. Education delivers knowledge. Employment offers financial independence. Women's support groups give an identity not solely in relation to men, but within the boundaries of our own person. And I can possess all of this!

In addition, I realized that I could not avoid every dragon or retreat from every problem. I was tired of running, of being voiceless, of being afraid, and I no longer wanted to be stepped on, suppressed, or taken for granted. I couldn't continue pretending that I was less than others. I craved to belong in the world, not as a silent observer, but as a human being; shaping, creating, questioning, reforming, or advocating. I wanted to exist!

Silence is power? In my silence, I was the sacrificial lamb. I was the martyr, like my mother. We suffered pain in the name of obedience just so no one will accuse us of being insolent or naughty, and in the struggle for harmony, loving the people around us. These can be good causes, but when we are silent even in the face of injustice, then I cannot in all fairness pronounce them good ones. As a Hmong woman, I am expected to perfect the art of hiding the painful reality of sexual, physical, or mental abuse. These conflicts cannot be resolved with silence, only deepened and catalyzed through it. If to be a good Hmong woman means to ignore my identity, to swallow my pride so others can abuse me, or to shut my eyes in the face of injustice by turning

the other cheek, I do not want to be a good Hmong woman. [1996]

 3

Claiming an Education

ADRIENNE RICH

For this convocation, I planned to separate my remarks into two parts: some thoughts about you, the women students here, and some thoughts about us who teach in a women's college. But ultimately, those two parts are indivisible. If university education means anything beyond the processing of human beings into expected roles, through credit hours, tests, and grades (and I believe that in a women's college especially it *might* mean much more), it implies an ethical and intellectual contract between teacher and students. This contract must remain intuitive, dynamic, unwritten; but we must turn to it again and again if learning is to be reclaimed from the depersonalizing and cheapening pressures of the present-day academic scene.

The first thing I want to say to you who are students is that you cannot afford to think of yourselves as being here to *receive* an education; you will do much better to think of yourselves as being here to *claim* one. One of the dictionary definitions of the verb "to claim" is: to take as the rightful owner; to assert in the face of possible contradiction. "To receive" is to come into possession of; to act as receptacle or container for; to accept as authoritative or true. The difference is that between acting and being acted-upon, and for women it can literally mean the difference between life and death.

One of the devastating weaknesses of university learning, of the store of knowledge and opinion that has been handed down through academic training, has been its almost total erasure of women's experience and thought from the curriculum, and its exclusion of women as members of the academic community. Today, with increasing numbers of women students in nearly every branch of higher learning, we still see very few women students in nearly every branch of higher learning, we still see very few women in the upper levels of faculty and administration in most institutions. Douglass College itself is a women's college in a university administered overwhelmingly by men, who in turn are answerable to the state legislature, again composed predominantly of men. But the most significant fact for you is that what you learn here (and I mean not only at Douglass but any college in any university) is how *men* have perceived and organized their experience, their history, their ideas of social relationships, good and evil, sickness and health, etc. When you read or hear about "great issues," "major texts," "the mainstream of Western thought," you are hearing about what men, above all white men, in their male subjectivity, have decided is important.

Black and other minority peoples have for some time recognized that their racial and ethnic experience was not accounted for in the studies broadly labeled human; and that even the sciences can be racist. For many reasons, it has been more difficult for women to comprehend our exclusion, and to realize that even the sciences can be sexist. For one thing, it is only within the last hundred years that higher education has grudgingly been opened up to women at all, even to white, middle-class women. And many of us have found ourselves poring eagerly over books with titles like: *The Descent of Man; Man and His Symbols; Irrational Man; The Phenomenon of Man; The Future of Man; Man and the Machine; From Man to Man; May Man Prevail?; Man, Science and Society; One-Dimensional Man*—books to describe a "human" reality that does not include over one-half the human species.

Less than a decade ago, with the rebirth of a feminist movement in this country, women students and teachers in a number of universities, began to demand and set up women's studies courses—to *claim* a woman-directed education. And, despite the inevitable accusations of "unscholarly," "group therapy," "faddism," etc., despite backlash and budget cuts, women's studies are still growing, offering to more and more women a new intellectual grasp on their lives, new understanding of our history, a fresh vision of the human experience, and also a critical

basis for evaluating what they hear and read in other courses, and in the society at large.

But my talk is not really about women's studies, much as I believe in their scholarly, scientific, and human necessity. While I think that any Douglass student has everything to gain by investigating and enrolling in women's studies courses, I want to suggest that there is a more essential experience that you owe yourselves, one which courses in women's studies can greatly enrich, but which finally depends on you, in all your interactions with yourself and your world. This is the experience of *taking responsibility toward yourselves*. Our upbringing as women has so often told us that this should come second to our relationships and responsibilities to other people. We have been offered ethical models of the self-denying wife and mother; intellectual models of the brilliant but slapdash dilettante who never commits herself to anything the whole way, or the intelligent woman who denies her intelligence in order to seem more "feminine," or who sits in passive silence even when she disagrees inwardly with everything that is being said around her.

Responsibility to yourself means refusing to let others do your thinking, talking, and naming for you; it means learning to respect and use your own brains and instincts, hence, grappling with hard work. It means that you do not treat your body as a commodity with which to purchase superficial intimacy or economic security; for our bodies and minds are inseparable in this life, and when we allow our bodies to be treated as objects, our minds are in mortal danger. It means insisting that those to whom you give your friendship and love are able to respect your mind. It means being able to say, with Charlotte Bronte's Jane Eyre: "I have an inward treasure born with me, which can keep me alive if all the extraneous delights should be withheld or offered only at a price I cannot afford to give."

Responsibility to yourself means that you don't fall for shallow and easy solutions—predigested books and ideas, weekend encounters guaranteed to change your life, taking "gut" courses instead of ones you know will challenge you, bluffing at school and life instead of doing solid work, marrying early as an escape from real decisions, getting pregnant as an evasion of already existing problems. It means that you refuse to sell your talents and aspirations short, simply to avoid conflict and confrontation. And this, in turn, means resisting the forces in society which say that women should be nice, play safe, have low professional expectations, drown in love and forget about work, live through others, and stay in the places assigned to us. It means that we insist on a life of meaningful work, insist that work be as meaningful as love and friendship in our lives. It means, therefore, the courage to be "different"; not to be continuously available to others when we need time for ourselves and our work; to be able to demand of others—parents, friends, roommates, teachers, lovers, husbands, children—that they respect our sense of purpose and our integrity as persons. Women everywhere are finding the courage to do this, more and more, and we are finding that courage both in our study of women in the past who possessed it, and in each other as we look to other women for comradeship, community, and challenge. The difference between a life lived actively, and a life of passive drifting and dispersal of energies, is an immense difference. Once we begin to feel committed to our lives, responsible to ourselves, we can never again be satisfied with the old, passive way.

I have said that the contract on the student's part involves that you demand to be taken seriously so that you can also go on taking yourself seriously. This means seeking out criticism, recognizing that the most affirming thing anyone can do for you is demand that you push yourself further, show you the range of what you *can* do. It means rejecting attitudes of "take-it-easy," "why-be-so-serious," "why-worry-you'll-probably-get-married-anyway." It means assuming your share of responsibility for what happens in the classroom, because that affects the quality of your daily life here. It means that the student sees herself engaged with her teachers in an active, ongoing struggle for a real education. But for her to do this, her teachers must be committed to the belief that women's minds and experience are intrinsically valuable and indispensable to any civilization worthy of the name; that there is no more exhilarating and intellectually fertile place in the academic world today than a women's college—*if*

both students and teachers in large enough numbers are trying to fulfill this contract. The contract is really a pledge of mutual seriousness about women, about language, ideas, methods, and values. It is our shared commitment toward a world in which the inborn potentialities of so many women's minds will no longer be wasted, raveled-away, paralyzed, or denied.   [1977]

 4

The Politics of Black Women's Studies

AKASHA (GLORIA T.) HULL
and BARBARA SMITH

Merely to use the term "Black women's studies" is an act charged with political significance. At the very least, the combining of these words to name a discipline means taking the stance that Black women exist—and exist positively—a stance that is in direct opposition to most of what passes for culture and thought on the North American continent. To use the term and to act on it in a white-male world is an act of political courage.

Like any politically disenfranchised group, Black women could not exist consciously until we began to name ourselves. The growth of Black women's studies is an essential aspect of that process of naming. The very fact that Black women's studies describes something that is really happening, a burgeoning field of study, indicates that there are political changes afoot which have made possible that growth. To examine the politics of Black women's studies means to consider not only what it is, but why it is and what it can be. Politics is used here in its widest sense to mean any situation/relationship of differential power between groups or individuals.

Four issues seem important for a consideration of the politics of Black women's studies: (1) the general political situation of Afro-American women and the bearing this has had upon the implementation of

Black women's studies; (2) the relationship of Black women's studies to Black feminist politics and the Black feminist movement; (3) the necessity for Black women's studies to be feminist, radical, and analytical; and (4) the need for teachers of Black women's studies to be aware of our problematic political positions in the academy and of the potentially antagonistic conditions under which we must work.

The political position of Black women in America has been, in a single word, embattled. The extremity of our oppression has been determined by our very biological identity. The horrors we have faced historically and continue to face as Black women in a white-male-dominated society have implications for every aspect of our lives, including what white men have termed "the life of the mind." That our oppression as Black women can take forms specifically aimed at discrediting our intellectual power is best illustrated through the words of a "classic" American writer.

In 1932 William Faulkner saw fit to include this sentence in a description of a painted sign in his novel *Light in August*. He wrote:

> But now and then a negro nursemaid with her white charges would loiter there and spell them [the letters on the sign] aloud with *that vacuous idiocy of her idle and illiterate kind*.[1] [Italics ours]

Faulkner's white-male assessment of Black female intellect and character, stated as a mere aside, has fundamental and painful implications for a consideration of the whole question of Black women's studies and the politics that shape its existence. Not only does his remark typify the extremely negative ways in which Afro-American women have been portrayed in literature, scholarship, and the popular media, but it also points to the destructive white-male habit of categorizing all who are not like themselves as their intellectual and moral inferiors. The fact that the works in which such oppressive images appear are nevertheless considered American "masterpieces" indicates the cultural-political value system in which Afro-American women have been forced to operate and which, when possible, they have actively opposed.

The politics of Black women's studies are totally connected to the politics of Black women's lives in this country. The opportunities for Black women to carry out autonomously defined investigations of self in a society which through racial, sexual, and class oppression systematically denies our existence have been by definition limited.

As a major result of the historical realities which brought us enslaved to this continent, we have been kept separated in every way possible from recognized intellectual work. Our legacy as chattel, as sexual slaves as well as forced laborers, would adequately explain why most Black women are, to this day, far away from the centers of academic power and why Black women's studies has just begun to surface in the latter part of the 1970s. What our multilayered oppression does not explain are the ways in which we have created and maintained our own intellectual traditions as Black women, without either the recognition or the support of white-male society.

The entry entitled "A Slave Woman Runs a Midnight School" in Gerda Lerner's *Black Women in White America: A Documentary History* embodies this creative, intellectual spirit, coupled with a practical ability to make something out of nothing.

> [In Natchez, Louisiana, there were] two schools taught by colored teachers. One of these was a slave woman who had taught a midnight school for a year. It was opened at eleven or twelve o'clock at night, and closed at two o'clock a.m. . . . Milla Granson, the teacher, learned to read and write from the children of her indulgent master in her old Kentucky home. Her number of scholars was twelve at a time and when she had taught these to read and write she dismissed them, and again took her apostolic number and brought them up to the extent of her ability, until she had graduated hundreds. A number of them wrote their own passes and started for Canada. . . .
>
> At length her night-school project leaked out, and was a for a time suspended; but it was not known that seven of the twelve years subsequent to leaving Kentucky had been spent in this work. Much excitement over her night-school was produced. The subject was discussed in their legis-

lature, and a bill was passed, that it should not be held illegal for a slave to teach a slave. . . . She not only [re]opened her night-school, but a Sabbath-school. . . . Milla Granson used as good language as any of the white people.[2]

This document illuminates much about Black women educators and thinkers in America. Milla Granson learned to read and write through the exceptional indulgence of her white masters. She used her skills not to advance her own status, but to help her fellow slaves, and this under the most difficult circumstances. The act of a Black person teaching and sharing knowledge was viewed as naturally threatening to the power structure. The knowledge she conveyed had a politically and materially transforming function, that is, it empowered people to gain freedom.

Milla Granson and her pupils, like Black people throughout our history here, made the greatest sacrifices for the sake of learning. As opposed to "lowering" educational standards, we have had to create our own. In a totally antagonistic setting we have tried to keep our own visions clear and have passed on the most essential kind of knowledge, that which enabled us to survive. As Alice Walker writes of our artist-thinker foremothers:

> They dreamed dreams that no one knew—not even themselves, in any coherent fashion—and saw visions no one could understand. . . . They waited for a day when the unknown thing that was in them would be made known; but guessed, somehow in their darkness, that on the day of their revelation they would be long dead.[3]

The birth of Black women's studies is perhaps the day of revelation these women wished for. Again, this beginning is not unconnected to political events in the world outside university walls.

The inception of Black women's studies can be directly traced to three significant political movements of the twentieth century. These are the struggles for Black liberation and women's liberation, which themselves fostered the growth of Black and women's studies, and the more recent Black feminist movement, which is just beginning to show its strength.

Black feminism has made a space for Black women's studies to exist and, through its commitment to all Black women, will provide the basis for its survival.

The history of all these movements is unique, yet interconnected. The Black movements of the 1950s, '60s, and '70s brought about unprecedented social and political change, not only in the lives of Black people, but for all Americans. The early women's movement gained inspiration from the Black movement as well as an impetus to organize autonomously both as a result of the demands for all-Black organizations and in response to sexual hierarchies in Black- and white-male political groupings. Black women were a part of that early women's movement, as were working-class women of all races. However, for many reasons—including the increasing involvement of single, middle-class white women (who often had the most time to devote to political work), the divisive campaigns of the white-male media, and the movement's serious inability to deal with racism—the women's movement became largely and apparently white.

The effect that this had upon the nascent field of women's studies was predictably disastrous. Women's studies courses, usually taught in universities, which could be considered elite institutions just by virtue of the populations they served, focused almost exclusively upon the lives of white women. Black studies, which was much too often male-dominated, also ignored Black women. Here is what a Black woman wrote about her independent efforts to study Black women writers in the early 1970s:

> . . . At this point I am doing a lot of reading on my own of Black women writers ever since I discovered Zora Neale Hurston. *I've had two Black Lit courses and in neither were any women writers discussed.* So now I'm doing a lot of independent research since the Schomburg Collection is so close.[4] [Italics ours.]

Because of white women's racism and Black men's sexism, there was no room in either area for a serious consideration of the lives of Black women. And even when they have considered Black women, white women usually have not had the capacity to analyze racial politics and Black culture, and Black men have remained blind or resistant to the implications of sexual politics in Black women's lives.

Only a Black *and* feminist analysis can sufficiently comprehend the materials of Black women's studies; and only a creative Black feminist perspective will enable the field to expand. A viable Black feminist movement will also lend its political strength to the development of Black women's studies courses, programs, and research, and to the funding they require. Black feminism's total commitment to the liberation of Black women and its recognition of Black women as valuable and complex human beings will provide the analysis and spirit for the incisive work on Black women. Only a feminist, pro-woman perspective that acknowledges the reality of sexual oppression in the lives of Black women, as well as the oppression of race and class, will make Black women's studies the transformer of consciousness it needs to be.

Women's studies began as a radical response to feminists' realization that knowledge of ourselves has been deliberately kept from us by institutions of patriarchal "learning." Unfortunately, as women's studies has become both more institutionalized and at the same time more precarious within traditional academic structures, the radical life-changing vision of what women's studies can accomplish has constantly been diminished in exchange for acceptance, respectability, and the career advancement of individuals. This trend in women's studies is a trap that Black women's studies cannot afford to fall into. Because we are so oppressed as Black women, every aspect of our fight for freedom, including teaching and writing about ourselves, must in some way further our liberation. Because of the particular history of Black feminism in relation to Black women's studies, especially the fact that the two movements are still new and have evolved nearly simultaneously, much of the current teaching, research, and writing about Black women is not feminist, is not radical, and unfortunately is not always even analytical. Naming and describing our experience are important initial steps, but not alone sufficient to get us where we need to go. A descriptive approach to the lives of Black women, a "great Black women" in history or literature approach, or any traditional male-identified approach will not result in intellectually groundbreaking or politically transforming work. We cannot change our lives by teaching solely about "exceptions" to the ravages of white-male oppression. Only through exploring the experience of supposedly "ordinary" Black women whose "unexceptional" actions enabled us and the race to survive, will we be able to begin to develop an overview and an analytical framework for understanding the lives of Afro-American women.   [1982]

NOTES

1. William Faulkner, *Light in August* (New York: Modern Library 1932), p. 53.
2. Laura S. Haviland, *A Woman's Life-Work, Labors and Experience* (Chicago: Publishing Association of Friends, 1889; copyright 1881), pp. 300–301; reprinted in Gerda Lerner, ed., *Black Women in White America: A Documentary History* (New York: Vintage, 1973), pp. 32–33.
3. Alice Walker, "In Search of Our Mother's Gardens," *Ms.* (Magazine 1974): 64–70. 105.
4. Bernette Golden, Personal letter, April 1, 1974.

 5

Men and Women's Studies: Premises, Perils, and Promise

MICHAEL KIMMEL

What does women's studies have to do with men? For one thing, it clears an intellectual space for talking about gender. I am not suggesting that among all the other things women's studies has to do, it must now also drop everything and take care of men in some vaguely academic version of the second shift. (I have heard arguments from men suggesting that women's studies must provide us with "a room of our own" within the curriculum, to appropriate the words of Virginia Woolf—and make sure that room has a rather commanding view of the traditional campus!)

When I say women's studies is about men, I mean that *women's studies has made men visible.* Before women's studies, men were invisible—especially to themselves. By making women visible, women's studies also made men visible both to women and to men themselves. If men are now taking up the issue of gender, it is probably less accurate to say, "Thank goodness they've arrived," the way one might when the cavalry appears in a western film, than to say, "It's about time."

Of course, making men visible has not been the primary task of women's studies. But it has been one of its signal successes. The major achievement of women's studies, acting independently and as a force within traditional disciplines, has been making *women* visible through the rediscovery of long-neglected, undervalued, and understudied women who were accomplished leaders, artists, composers, and writers and placing them in the pantheons of significance where they rightly belong. In addition, women's studies has rediscovered the voices of ordinary women—the laundresses and the salesgirls, the union maids and the union organizers, the workers and the wives—who have struggled to scratch out lives of meaning and dignity. For this—whether they know it or not, whether they acknowledge it or not—women all over the world owe a debt.

But in making women visible, women's studies has been at the epicenter of a seismic shift in the university as we know it. Women's studies has made *gender* visible. Women's studies has demonstrated that gender is one of the axes around which social life is organized, one of the most crucial building blocks of our identities. Before women's studies, we didn't know that gender mattered. Twenty-five years ago, there were no women's studies courses in colleges or universities, no women's studies lists at university presses across the country. In my field of sociology, there were no gender courses, no specialty area called the Sociology of Gender. We had, instead, a field called Marriage and the Family—to my mind the Ladies' Auxiliary of Sociology. By making women visible, women's studies decentered men as the unexamined, disembodied authorial voice of the academic canon and showed that men, as well as women, are utterly embodied, their identities are as socially constructed as those of women. When the voice of the canon speaks, we can no longer *assume* that voice is going to sound masculine or that the speaker is going to look like a man.

The problem is that many men do not yet know this. Though ubiquitous in positions of power, many men remain invisible to themselves as gendered beings. Courses on gender in the universities are populated largely by women, as if the term applied only to them. "Woman alone seems to have 'gender' since the category itself is defined as that aspect of social relations based on difference between the sexes in which the standard has always been man," writes historian Thomas Lacquer.[1] Or, as the Chinese proverb has it, the fish are the last to discover the ocean.

I know this from my own experience: women's studies made gender visible to me. In the early 1980s I participated in a graduate-level women's studies seminar in which I was the only man among about a dozen participants. During one meeting, a white woman and a black woman were discussing whether all women were, by definition, "sisters" because they all had essentially the same experiences and because all women faced a common oppression by all men. The white women asserted that the fact that they were both women bonded them, in spite of racial differences. The black woman disagreed.

"When you wake up in the morning and look in the mirror, what do you see?" she asked.

"I see a woman," replied the white woman.

"That's precisely the problem," responded the black woman. "I see a *black* woman. To me, race is visible every day, because race is how I am *not* privileged in our culture. Race is invisible to you, because it's how you are privileged. It's why there will always be differences in our experience."

As I witnessed this exchange, I was startled, and groaned—more audibly, perhaps, than I had intended. Someone asked what my response meant. "Well," I said, "when I look in the mirror, I see a human being. I'm universally generalizable. As a middle-class white man, I have no class, no race, no gender. I'm the generic person!"

Sometimes, I like to think it was on that day that I *became* a middle-class white man. Sure, I had been all those before, but they had not meant much to me. Since then, I have begun to understand that race, class, and gender do not refer only to other people, who are marginalized by race, class, or gender privilege. Those terms also describe me. I enjoy the privilege of invisibility. The very processes that confer privilege to one group and not another group are often invisible to those upon whom that privilege is conferred. American men have come to think of ourselves as genderless, in part because gender privilege affords us the luxury of ignoring the centrality of gender. But women's studies offers the possibility of making gender visible to men as well and, in so doing, creating the possibilities of alliances between women and men to collaboratively investigate what gender means, how it works, and what its consequences are.

In *Fire with Fire*, Naomi Wolf returns often to her book's epigraph, that famous line of Audre Lorde, "the Master's tools cannot dismantle the Master's house." Wolf believes that her book is a refutation of that position, and when one considers the impact of women's studies on the university and the culture at large, it seems that on this score at least, Wolf is quite right—that passionate, disciplined scholarship, inspired and dedicated teaching, and committed, engaged inquiry can contribute to the reorientation of the university as an institution. All over the country, schools are integrating "gender awareness" into their first-year curricula, even orienting the entire curriculum around gender awareness. Within the professional organization of my discipline, sociology, the Sex and Gender section is now the largest section of the entire profession. Gender has moved from the margins—Marriage and the Family—to the center and is the largest single constituency within the field.

Most commentators laud the accomplishments of women's studies programs in transforming women's lives, but it is obvious that women's studies programs have also been transformative for men. The Duke case is a particularly successful one: the popular house course "Men and Gender Issues" has been offered under the umbrella of Women's Studies for five years. Men Acting for Change (MAC), the campus group for pro-feminist men that has become a model for similar groups on campuses around the country, found a supportive harbor in the Women's Studies Program. The first time I came to lecture at Duke three years ago, my lecture was jointly sponsored by the Women's Studies Program and the Inter-Fraternity Council—the first time, I'm told, that those two organizations had cooperated on anything. Women's studies can—and does—forge creative alliances!

Essentially, however, the program at Duke and women's studies in general has centered around the same two projects as any other discipline: teaching and research. And to speak personally, the perspectives of women's studies have transformed both my research and my teaching. Women's studies made it *possible* for me to do the work I do. And for that I am grateful. Inspired by the way women's studies made gender visible, I offered a course called "Sociology of the Male Experience" in 1983 at Rutgers University, where I was then a young assistant professor. This was the first such course on men and masculinity in the state of New Jersey, and I received enormous support both from my own department and from the Women's Studies Program at Rutgers, then chaired by Catharine Stimpson. Today, I teach that course as well as a course entitled "Sex and Society" at Stony Brook to over 350 students each semester. Now, as then, the course is cross-listed with women's studies. But I also teach our department's classical sociological theory course, the course on the historical development of social and political theory. In that course, students traditionally read works by Hobbes, Locke, Rousseau, Smith, Marx, Durkheim, Tocqueville, Weber, and Freud. This is probably the most intractably canonical "Dead White European Men" course we offer in the social sciences. But it has become impossible for me to teach the works of those "great men" without reference to gender—without noting, for example, the gendered creation myths that characterize the move from the state of nature to civil society in the thought of Locke or Hobbes, or the chronic anxiety and loss of control attendant upon modern society documented by Tocqueville, Marx, Weber, or Freud. Moreover, I find that I cannot teach about the rise of nineteenth-century liberal individualism without including Frederick Douglass or Mary Wollstonecraft; nor can I teach about the late nineteenth-century critiques of individualism without references to W. E. B. Du Bois or to Charlotte Perkins Gilman.

If women's studies has made gender, and hence *men,* visible, then it has also raised a question about men: where are they? where have they been in women's struggles for equality? Taking my cues from women's history, I began to research men's responses to feminism. *Against the Tide* tries to provide part of the answer, a missing chapter from women's history: the chapter about the men who supported women's equality.[2] When I began *Against the Tide,* I mentioned to Catharine Stimpson, then dean of the Graduate School at Rutgers, what I intended to do. "A book about men who supported feminism?" she asked. "Now that will surely be the world's shortest book!" she joked. Of course, she knew better, but I did not really know what I would find. It turns out that in every arena in which women have struggled for equal rights—education (the right to go to college or professional school, the right to go to college with men), economic life (the right to work, join unions, receive equal wages), social life (the right to own property, have access to birth control, get a divorce), or political life (the right to vote, to hold elective office, to serve on juries)—there have been American men, some prominent, many unheralded, who have supported them: men such as Thomas Paine, who sat before the Declaration of Independence in 1776 and recognized that women would not be included under its provisions, although women had, as he put it, an "equal right to virtue." Men such as famed abolitionists William Lloyd Garrison and Frederick Douglass, who campaigned tirelessly for women's rights from Seneca Falls onward. Men such as Matthew Vassar, William Alan Neilson,

and Henry Durant, founders of Vassar, Smith, and Wellesley colleges. It was Durant, founder of Wellesley, who in 1877 called the higher education of women a "revolt": "We revolt against the slavery in which women are held by the customs of society— the broken health, the aimless lives, the subordinate position, the helpless dependence, the dishonesties and shams of so-called education. The Higher Education of Women is one of the great world battle cries for freedom; for right against might. It is the cry of the oppressed slave. It is the assertion of absolute equality."[3]

Pro-feminist men have included educators such as John Dewey, who urged that women be admitted to the University of Chicago and was one of the founders of the Men's League for Woman Suffrage, the nation's first pro-feminist men's organization. The group of pro-feminist men included W. E. B. Du Bois, Ralph Waldo Emerson, and Eugene Debs among the most vigorous supporters of woman suffrage. And there have been academic men such as Lester Ward and George Herbert Mead, to name but two, who pointed toward the scholarly study of women and opposed gender inequality. In one of his major treatises, *Applied Sociology,* Ward provided an epigraph for the advent of women's studies, arguing that "the universal prevalence of the androcentric worldview acts as a wet blanket on all the genial fire of the female sex."[4] Pro-feminist men are also policymakers such as Robert Reich, secretary of labor in the Clinton administration, who wrote a furious letter (reprinted in *Ms.* magazine) to a college president when his wife was denied tenure, and Representative Don Edwards of California, who has introduced the ERA in every session of Congress since 1974, as well as former Supreme Court justice Harry Blackmun, that vigilant defender of women's right to control their own bodies.

Supporters of women's equality have also included the less-celebrated men who simply lived out their principles of equality without fanfare. Men such as James Mott (married to Lucretia), Theodore Weld (married to Angelina Grimké), and Wendell Phillips, ardent abolitionist and suffrage supporter. In 1856, Lucy Stone called her husband, Henry Brown Blackwell, "the best husband in the world. In the midst of all the extra care, hurry and perplexity of business, you stop and look after all my little affairs," she wrote, "doing everything you can to save me trouble."[5] More than a half a century later, Margaret Sanger quotes her husband, William, as telling her to "go ahead and finish your writing, and I'll get dinner and wash the dishes."[6] (She also comments that she drew the curtains in the kitchen of their first-floor Greenwich Village apartment, lest passersby see her husband wearing an apron.) It appears that long before Ted Kramer and Mr. Mom, real men did housework!

Men *have* been there supporting women's equality every step of the way. And if men have been there, it means that men *can* be there and that they *will* be there. This legacy of men who supported women's equality allows contemporary men to join what I like to think of as the Gentlemen's Auxiliary of the Women's Movement. Neither passive bystanders nor the front-line forces—and especially not the leaders of those troops—men still have a pivotal role to play. Men can join this epochal struggle and provide support both individually and collectively. This strikes me as an utterly honorable relationship to feminism, quite different from an impulse I've encountered among newly enlightened men that goes something like, "Thanks for bringing all this to my attention, ladies. We'll take it from here." It also serves as an important corrective to many men's fears, which often boil down to "How can I support feminism without feeling like—or being seen as—a wimp?" To be a member of the Auxiliary is to know that the cental actors in the struggle for gender equality will be, as they always have been, women.

But women's studies has done more than make the study of gender possible; it has made it *necessary.* The issues raised by women in the university and outside it have not "gone away" or subsided now that women have been offered a few resources and an academic room of their own. Women's studies has not been content with one room while the rest of the university goes about its androcentric business, any more than the women's movement has been convinced of its political victory because 100 percent of the U.S. senators from California in 1993 are women. Think about the shockwaves that rippled outward from Clarence Thomas's confirmation hearings over two years ago. Remember how the media responded to that event; recall the shameful way Anita Hill was treated by the Senate Judiciary Committee. The phrase the media used, as if with one voice, was that Thomas's confirmation would have a "chilling effect" on American women —that women would be less likely to come forward to describe their experiences of sexual harassment in the workplace, that women would be less likely to speak of the inequities and humiliations that permeated their working lives. Have the media ever been more wrong? Not only was there no "chilling effect," there was a national thaw. Women have been coming forward in unprecedented numbers to talk about their working lives. And they have not gone away. On campuses and off all across the country, women's studies students and faculty have joined in this virtual national seminar about men, masculinity, and power.

Gender as a power relation is the "it" that men "just don't get" in the current discussion. Women's studies scholars have demonstrated that masculinity and femininity are identities that are socially constructed in a field of power. Gender, like race and class, is not simply a mode of classification by which biological creatures are sorted into their respective and appropriate niches. Gender is about power. Just because both masculinity and femininity are socially constructed does not mean that they are equivalent, that there are no dynamics of power and privilege in operation. The problem with bringing men into this discussion about gender and power is that these issues are invisible to men.   [1996]

NOTES

1. Thomas Lacquer, *Making Sex: Body and Gender from the Greeks to Freud* (Cambridge: Harvard University Press, 1990), 22.
2. Michael S. Kimmel and Thomas Mosmiller, eds., *Against*

the Tide: *Pro-Feminist Men in the United States, 1776–1990. A Documentary History* (Boston: Beacon Press, 1992).
3. Thomas Paine, "An Occasional Letter on the Female Sex," 1775, and Henry Fowle Durant, "The Spirit of the College," 1877, in *Against the Tide,* ed. Kimmel and Mosmiller, 63–66, 132.
4. Lester Frank Ward, *Applied Sociology: A Treatise on the Conscious Improvement of Society by Society* (Boston: Ginn and Company, 1906), 232.

 6

Have You Ever Heard of Asian-American Feminists?

STACEY G. H. YAP

I can say that I stumbled into women's studies accidentally. I had no intention in my younger days to choose this area. It's true that there were few to no courses offered in women's studies in the early 1970s when I first arrived at college on the East Coast, and it's also true that I stereotyped women's liberation as a group of white women gone mad! I didn't see myself identifying with "them" even if I had seen courses offered in the women's studies area then. It was only when I went to graduate school and unintentionally selected a course about "men and women in corporations" that I was first introduced to the research in women's studies without ever knowing it. And from then on, my life was transformed.

Today I am a faculty member and chair of the women's studies (minor) program in my college, and teaching a course in women's studies, I cannot help thinking how much my life has changed from an undergraduate business major to a women's studies/sociology college teacher. My students must wonder about the irony of any Asian (American) teacher teaching them about women's studies and the American women's movement. The unexpected role that I play in influencing my students' lives will probably help them remember how much common ground we share even though we are ethnically different. What will transform my life and my students' lives is the complete element of surprise that women's studies can offer. It is the story of our lives, our mothers' and our grandmothers' lives, and the conditions and experiences we women have gone through and are going through now. Feminist scholars have researched experiences in great detail and told stories of our lives that have never been told before in colorful and powerful language.

What is more surprising are the uncharted territories women's studies offers, and what is not documented. Particularly, since I look and speak differently from my students, women's studies presents an opportunity for my women students to ask me more questions about me: How do I feel about American white men? What do I think about American black women? Do I think that the socialization process they learn is different in the Asian context? What is different about mother-daughter relationships among whites and those that are written by Chinese Americans like Amy Tan and Maxine Hong Kingston? The fact that Asian-American women are not represented in the mainstream of women's studies literature made my students and myself more intense in our search to wonder about their absence. As a feminist, I acknowledge their absence but do not feel upset nor angry by their lack of recognition. This neglected treatment by white American women who dominated this field in producing women's anthologies for women's studies courses is understandable. I try to remedy this by teaching my students and my friends about Asian-American women and their experiences. I center my research in the "unearthing" of Asian women's experiences. Whether they are Asian-born women or American-born Asian women, I recognize that their experiences have helped shape the history, politics, and literature of this country.

Women's studies has taught me that women must be studied on their own terms and not judged by male-defined standards. Similarly, Asian women must be allowed to speak for themselves because, while we share a great deal with other women, our experiences are unique, and women of other backgrounds can't speak for us. Asian women come to feminism in a variety of ways. Some of us stumbled into politics through fighting against unfair wage practices, and others protested against the Vietnam war. Including Asian women's experiences in women's studies courses is important, for we, like most women around the world, do not passively or silently accept the oppression we share with all women.

[1992]

 7

Voices of Women's Studies Students

Women's Studies as a Growth Process

DANISTA HUNTE

I remember trying to fit Introduction to Women's Studies into my schedule for five semesters and feeling frustrated each time that chemistry or some other requirement took precedence. Finally, first semester senior year, I was able to fit it into my schedule. After three years at Vassar College, I thought my feminist development was far beyond the introductory level and there would not be much for me to learn from the class. I was wrong. My politics were challenged daily. It seemed that everything that was changing and developing could be linked to a reading or discussion in women's studies. I learned life lessons that take some people all of their lives to learn. The most important lesson was that the many parts of myself—black, female, feminist, Caribbean, pro-choice, working class, etc.—could coexist as one healthy individual. I gained a better understanding of how our society consistently seeks to "divide and conquer" or to squash any possible coalition

among oppressed individuals. I confronted a lot of the anger I felt toward white society. I do not know whether I will ever resolve that anger, but identifying its source and understanding the way in which it can stifle my own growth and development are valuable lessons. I gained a better understanding of the environment and the culture in which my mother was raised and in turn how she raised me. I realized how difficult it is to be someone's mother, and I appreciate my mother even more. Although I left some class sessions feeling confused and schizophrenic, by the end of first semester I felt empowered and confident that I could handle anything.

On the first day of class, I counted the number of women of color in the class. There were two of us. I had a reputation of being a vocal student, and nothing less was expected of me in this class. I also knew that I would be the official spokeswoman of color and the voice of all black women on campus. Initially I resented having to occupy the "speaker" role, and I was even angry at the other sister in class who never spoke in concert with me. As a matter of fact she never spoke at all, which may tell another tale altogether. There was no support or comfort upon which to depend.

These feelings were not new. For the three years prior to women's studies, my being was fueled by anger and the thrill of battle. I craved the opportunities for combat with the administration of the college. I enjoyed sitting on committees with faculty and feeling confident about what I had to contribute or debating with a white man who presumed to know "who I was and what my life was about" based upon his proficiency in two Africana studies courses! These encounters excited me and made me feel powerful; however, by the time I had reached senior year, I was *tired* and did not want to fight anymore. After reading Audre Lorde's "The Uses of Anger: Women Responding to Racism" in *Sister Outsider,* those feelings of anger and resentment began to subside. Through Lorde's writings I identified some of the reasons for the anger I was feeling about the class, my experiences at Vassar College, and toward myself. Lorde warns black women not to let our justified anger eat away at our compassion to love ourselves and others. She advocates that black women must find ways in which to channel their anger into *healthy* and *productive* actions that will hopefully transform our situations. Anger should not be denied, but explored and used to produce something positive that will move the individual forward.

Introduction to Women's Studies was painful, but I learned a lot. There is *much* work to be done on the part of all women, and especially by women of color. The class offered very little feminist theory by African-American women, Hispanic women, Asian women, or Native American women, which angered me. From my own personal readings I had found a wealth of writings by women of color on issues of motherhood and parenting, male domination, and the portrayal of women in film, etc. There are time constraints when developing a syllabus. However, when the theoretical and critical analyses that comprise the syllabus are written by white feminists, this conveys only one perspective. This imbalance facilitates the myth that black women do not theorize or are not capable of critically analyzing their own situations or of offering criticism of their society. We as black women need to pursue fields in which we can create and command our own destinies and have an impact upon our lives and the lives of our sisters.

Lorde says that, "for survival, Black children in america must be raised to be warriors."[1] Unfortunately, that often means we grow up justifiably paranoid and untrusting of anyone who is not like us. Women's studies rejuvenated my spirit and reassured me that people can grow and things can change. As a result of the class, I try not to build walls around myself and I want to be more inclusive in my politics. Each new experience, whether categorized as "good" or "bad," facilitates growth. I look upon my experience in Introduction to Women's

Studies as a growth process—and, for the record, it was "good." [1991]

Finding My Latina Identity Through Women's Studies

LUANA FERREIRA

Taking a women's studies course entitled Women: Images and Realities helped me to become the person that I am today. It enabled me to share both my experience as a woman and my experience of Latino culture with other women and understand more fully the position of women in society.

When I lived in the Dominican Republic, I'd see the same scene over and over, especially around the holidays: women were in the kitchen cooking and setting the table while the men were in the living room discussing sports or politics. My grandmother always told me that once a woman learned how to do house chores, she was ready for marriage, and that a woman should always depend on a man because a woman will always need the *strength* of a man. At this point in my life I was beginning to feel frustrated and anxious. I asked myself why at the age of 17 I still was not engaged, or in a relationship, and what would happen if I never got married.

Once I arrived in the United States and enrolled in college, I began to see male-female relationships differently. I saw that women were indeed more career-oriented and independent. However, as a college student, I thought that the women's movement, womanism, and feminism were a little too radical for me. The word "feminist" to me meant "man hater."

The course taught me a great deal about women in the United States and around the world. I could not believe how much I had been missing out! I must admit that I was biased in choosing the teacher. Looking in the catalogue, I saw three different names, but one stood out: Delgado. Since I am Latina, the idea of having a teacher I can relate to pleased me. Professor Linda Delgado, a proud Puerto Rican woman, taught me how to detach myself from traditional ideas about women without los-

---

[1] Audre Lorde, "Man Child: A Black Lesbian Feminist's Response," *Sister Outsider* (Freedom, CA: The Crossing Press, 1984), p. 75.

ing my cultural values and awareness. At the same time, having a Latina teacher for this course has helped me to become more involved in my community. I learned about sexism in religion and in the labor force, and I became more aware of issues such as rape, abortion, and sexual harassment.

In my traditional family, my parents always taught me "where a woman's place in society is." According to them, rape victims deserve to get raped because of the way they were dressed, pregnancy is a punishment for the irresponsibility of a woman, virginity is a proof of purity and decency and is the best wedding gift to a man, a spouse can be found through one's cooking, and so forth. I can go on forever with these myths and taboos.

The course made me realize that clothing should not determine the reputation of a woman, that women have the right to make their own decisions about sex, and that both men and women should be concerned about pregnancy. I also learned that one should learn to do chores for survival, not to please someone else. I have become more secure about myself. I am able to make my own decisions because I am using my own judgment, *not* doing what my parents expect or what society dictates. I am also more firm in my decisions. Before, if I were involved in a discussion with a male, I always worried that if I opened my mouth he would lose interest in me. I cannot believe that I used to think this way! I operated on the assumption that if I were too articulate or too much of an activist, I would lose the relationship of my dreams. I thank my teacher and the course for making me understand that standing up for your rights and for what you believe in will raise your self-confidence and self-esteem. Now I find myself having interesting discussions with many colleagues, males and females, and I am more open with my female friends.

Today I am happy to say that I am a woman striving for a career. I am very involved in my community, and I am not afraid to state my beliefs and ideas. Now I know that being a feminist, far from being a man hater, is rather fighting for equal rights, struggling against discrimination, and educating one's self and others about women's issues.   [1992]

What Women's Studies Has Meant to Me

LUCITA WOODIS

I had no understanding of what women's studies meant when I first looked through the spring catalogue at the University of New Mexico, but it sounded intriguing. So I went to the Women's Studies Center on campus and asked lots of questions: What is women's studies? What can I gain from a course like this? Can I use the information from women's studies courses outside the university? Can I use this for a certain area of my life?

Well, my questions were answered in such a positive way that the very same day, I stepped into the Women's Center and signed up as a women's studies minor.

Now that I've been introduced to the curriculum, I believe that women's studies means empowerment for women. We as women want equality in our lives—in areas such as the workplace, where we want to have acknowledged that people should be paid on the basis of their experience, not their sex; that regardless of sex, we are human. As women, we need respect for making our choices and decisions. We need power and control—not power over others, but shared power with other human beings who work together cooperatively. This is especially meaningful to me as a woman of color, a Native American artist who grew up on the Navajo Reservation.

I have never experienced a more close, supportive, nurturing, and expressive multicultural group of women as I did in the Women in Contemporary Society class at the University of New Mexico. Our bond as women enabled us to break through the barriers of race, creed, and color to interact as human beings and discover a common ground. In our class discussions, we were able to express our intolerance at being victims of pornography and sexual abuse, knowing that with every issue there has been some change for the better. We saw how we as women have bonded together through self-help groups, have opened up shelters for battered women, and in a sense have been saying that we do have power —power to overcome these intolerable abuses and survive as powerful women into the 1990s.

The knowledge I gained through the course came from the classroom, my classmates, and my professor, Deborah Klein. Ms. Klein was very avid in our discussions and presentations, as we bonded together through our openness. She helped the class evolve to an intimate level. With no remorse or self-consciousness, we created an atmosphere of acceptance, shared a great deal of ourselves, and enhanced each other's lives. As a sister to women of color, I experienced support, nurturing, and the embrace of other women as we expressed our experiences openly and individually.

I used part of my class experience to take the group on a journey about the meaning of sexual abuse in a woman's life, particularly in mine. I chose to present my journey as a narrative. I told my story with the visual images of my artwork, as well as with my words. My goal was to convey to others that confronting one's self can be a positive path toward strength, confidence, and the ability to be true to one's self.

Exploring women's issues has truly been a journey for me, a spiritual journey filled with healing and cleansing and enlightenment. My explorations have led me toward harmony and balance and enable me to feel peaceful, calm, and serene.

As a Native American (Navajo), I can only stress that women are powerful. We are a maternal society, the bearers of children. We are patient yet very strong in our decision making. I can say I have benefited from the women's studies program and won't be silent long. I will be verbally expressive as well as visually expressive, because that is who I am—an artist. I share a very intimate part of myself through my art. I will always be a Native first, as I am from a traditional family, and I'm proud to know my clan through my ancestors. Yet I can also say that I'm from the Navajo Nation *and* part of the larger women's experience in our society.

Today, I understand that I am not alone. I am important. I am not a second-class citizen, I am a capable, strong, and independent Native American Navajo woman. I will always carry my culture and traditions in my heart whether on the Reservation or in the outside world. Through my spirit, I will carry a message visually and verbally that to survive and heal from abuse is to come full-circle to contentment, that we are all part of a larger whole.

Nishțı́nı́gíí shit beehozin   (Navajo)
I know who I am   (English)   [1992]

Why Women's Studies?

DEBORAH HALSTEAD LENNON

Whenever I tell people I am majoring in women's studies, the response is usually along the lines of, "Whatever are you going to *do* with *that?*" I know they are expecting me to respond by specifying some kind of practical job application for the degree. I could say, "I'm going to be a personnel consultant, increasing morale and productivity through understanding and meeting the needs of the work force." But that's not why I enrolled in the program.

I returned to school as a women's studies major at the age of 31. My intended purpose was to validate the perspective I had developed from my life experiences. I have found that—and so much more. Women's studies shows us women's lives and their art of living, how women's contributions to society are so intricately woven into the fabric of their daily lives that they go unrecognized because they are so familiar. It has ended my isolation by showing me that other women have had similar experiences. Through nurturing my growth and self-esteem, I have regained my voice and learned how to use it. Women's studies has united me with women and oppressed peoples from all over the world.

Women's studies has enabled me to discuss issues such as birth control, abortion, rape, and domestic violence with my children. Addressing these and other issues as part of my coursework greatly decreased the apprehension parents and children often experience when approaching these topics. My daughter is now a year younger than I was when these became issues in my life. I am now able to look forward to her teenage years with confidence that when these things touch her life, as they almost surely will in some form, she will not feel the confusion and devastation that I endured. The reason for this confidence is twofold: She has an awareness and understanding that precede her experience, enabling her to avoid some situations that ignorance may have otherwise drawn her into; and she knows how to network and form a supportive community with other women.

Women's studies has been, for me, a metamorphosis; it teaches a way of being, a different mode of perception that pervades our very essence. Now when I hear of a woman in an abusive situation, I can see the factors that keep her trapped: housing, earning potential, child care, fear. I also see how our society perpetuates women's fears through promoting the idea that women are defenseless without a male companion. Women's studies teaches us to crack the shell of fear so that we may spread our wings and fly. What do I *do* with *that?* I help other women (and men) be strong and secure in who they are, in following their dreams. Some of us will do this as lawyers, as teachers, as wives and mothers . . . the possibilities are endless.

Welcome to the beginning of *your* journey. You will find your beauty in your strength, and your wings will take you wherever you want to go.

[1992]

Women's Studies: A Man's Perspective

EVAN WEISSMAN

Bob Marley once sang, "Don't forget, no way, who you are and where you stand in your struggles." Because I was interested in examining my role in society as a young man and exploring what I could do for women's struggles for freedom and equality, I registered for the course "Women: Images and Realities." I have always been aware of the feminist fight for equality; I grew up surrounded by feminists, but I never had the opportunity to take a class focused on women and was eager to learn more about the struggle today.

Although most of the reactions of my friends and family were positive and encouraging, some men ridiculed me for taking a women's studies class. I remember one individual who constantly challenged my "manliness" by saying things like "My, Evan, you look very feminine today; is that class rubbing off on you?" I often felt hopeless in the face of such ridicule, but I realized the mockery came from ignorance. Rather than becoming defensive, I would ask him whether he was insecure about his manhood, since anyone secure in themselves could easily take a women's studies class. Men are often unfamiliar with the facts of women's subordination, the extent to which it is practiced, and the role we can play in changing it. From my experience, it is often easier for people to joke about things they are scared to face or know nothing about. It is much easier for a man to criticize women's studies than to take a critical look at one's self and the advantages given to men in a society based on gender hierarchy.

Because the media portray feminists as "dykes who hate men," I brought into my first women's studies class a fear that my female classmates would hate me because I was a man, I was the oppressor. I learned in the course the difference between acting against men and acting against the actions of men. My classmates judged me by my beliefs and actions, not by what I have between my legs. Feminism, I learned, does not call for men's subordination but for the fair and equal treatment of women.

I learned in "Women: Images and Realities" that sexism is far deeper than I had previously thought. I also came to realize that I have many privileges as a white man. I learned that my skin color and gender give me an unfair advantage in American society, a realization that was extremely difficult to deal with. These privileges make life easier for me than for those who do not benefit from their skin color or sex. Without these privileges, my life goals and dreams would be more distant and difficult to achieve. Once I acknowledged this fact, I had to figure out what I could do with this information. It is not possible for me to divest myself individually of these privileges simply because I now recognize them. But I can work to change the system while being conscious of what these privileges have done for me.

Through "Women: Images and Realities," I became more aware of the prevalence of sexism in everyday life and the many small, seemingly insignificant ways in which men keep women in subordinate roles. I decided to stand up for my beliefs at all times, even when they were not popular. I wanted to contribute to women's struggles by dissenting from sexism in groups of men, but I soon learned that men don't always welcome such intervention.

A few months after the class ended, I was at a party and got into an argument with an acquaintance, who I'll call Bill, who was talking about how "pussy" needed to be "fucked." None of the other guys around had anything to say, so I asked him to clarify himself. When he repeated his statement, I asked him whether his mom had a "pussy" that needed a good "fuck." He replied, "Yeah, for someone else." I was disgusted and tried to explain to him how disrespectful his comment was. I argued that he could never make that comment to a woman's face. After a while I walked off, realizing that I could not make him take his comment back, especially with all of his friends around. I went up to my cousin and told her about what Bill had said. She immediately went over to him and said "I don't have a pussy that needs to be fucked." In a few minutes Bill approached me ready for a fistfight. "Why did you do that?" he asked. "I was making the point that you couldn't make your comment to a woman's face because it is disrespectful," I responded and walked off.

To this day Bill holds a grudge against me, but I don't regret my action. It was important to me to let Bill know that I would not tolerate sexist behavior. I have to be true to myself and stand for what I believe in. I must fight against injustice whenever possible, even when it is difficult. My male friends seldom say insulting things about women in my presence, and I feel good about this even though they probably continue to say these things when I'm not around. At least I've made them think. I now see myself as a feminist, making the struggle for women's equality my own, and I will not forget who I am and where I stand in this struggle.   [1998]

 8

The American University and Women's Studies

CAROL T. CHRIST

The institutionalization of women's studies has been so rapid and so powerful that it prompts us to ask why. The most important cause of the development of women's studies is the feminist movement. Indeed, in the early years of women's studies, it was hard to separate the two. Early discussions of the field forthrightly asserted that one of the principal goals of women's studies courses was consciousness raising. Women's studies conferences in the early 1970s often focused on the relationship of women's studies to a feminist political agenda. Women's studies took its inspiration, its energy, and many of its issues from the women's movement. The women's movement in turn found a model and an analogue in the civil rights movement, and found energy and license from the various rebellions of the '60s. Black studies, ethnic studies, and women's studies developed together and evolved conceptual frameworks that borrowed from one another.

Although the women's movement clearly stimulated the development of women's studies, I don't think it offers a sufficient explanation for its academic institutionalization. Essential to the emergence of women's studies as an academic field has been the increasing representation of women on the faculty of colleges and universities. When I joined the Berkeley faculty in 1970, I became the fourth woman faculty member in an English Department of about eighty tenure-track faculty. In 1970, 3% of the entire Berkeley faculty were women. Now, 23%

of the faculty are women. Of this 23%, the largest proportion is in the social sciences and humanities. In the English Department, for example, twenty-eight out of sixty faculty are now women.

If you think for a moment of what the historical experience of the cohort of women currently on the faculty of colleges and universities is likely to be, you will realize that many, like me, will have matured as scholars and teachers during the women's movement and will have experienced the growth in their numbers on the faculties on which they teach. In many fields this increase in the proportion of women on the faculty seems a simple equity issue. In English, for example, women for decades earned a substantial portion of the Ph.D.s yet held few faculty positions in major universities. For many women academics, the increased hiring of women faculty was immediate evidence of the changes the women's movement had brought. The increased hiring of women faculty facilitated the growth of women's studies because it created a cohort of women in colleges and universities throughout the country who had reason to feel that the women's movement had changed their professional world.

Thus far I have identified political factors that facilitated the growth of women's studies—the women's movement, the civil rights movement, the increased presence of women on college and university faculties. There are intellectual factors as well that facilitated the growth of women's studies. A number of disciplines in which women's studies took strongest root experienced paradigm shifts in the '70s that were particularly hospitable to work on gender. Indeed, one of the most interesting issues in the history of women's studies has been the way in which it has developed and located itself in different disciplines. As I was writing this talk, I sent an e-mail to a number of colleagues of mine in different departments asking them the following question: have there been paradigm shifts in your discipline in the past twenty-five years that have facilitated the development of women's studies? I got back a fascinating set of stories that showed how differently women's studies had developed from discipline to discipline. I will spend the next portion of my talk

describing how dominant and emerging paradigms in different disciplines have affected the positions of women's studies.

I will begin with my own discipline, English. English is a field in which women's studies emerged as an early and powerful force. In *Female Studies II,* thirty of its sixty-six syllabi were courses in literature. Kate Millett's *Sexual Politics* was developed from a doctoral dissertation in English. Germaine Greer earned her doctorate as a Shakespeare scholar. A number of factors contributed to the early emergence of women's studies in the field of English. First, English is a large field and has always attracted a large number of women graduate students. Women's studies moved quickly into the curriculum in the field of English in part because English departments had a substantial number of women faculty. Secondly, literature is necessarily gendered. Authors, obviously, are male or female; furthermore, any story or drama is likely to represent relationships between men and women. It therefore will make assumptions about gender or display conceptions of it. Finally, English literature contains many extraordinary women writers.

Because literature so obviously concerns gender, work in women's studies did not necessarily need to challenge critical paradigms. Scholars focusing on gender issues could and did use traditional critical methods. Although interpretations of individual literary works could be radically revisionary, they often used standard critical procedures. Take, for example, the feminist reinterpretation of *Jane Eyre,* which gives Sandra Gilbert and Susan Gubar's seminal book, *The Madwoman in the Attic,* its name. Although the arguments that a number of women critics made, that *Jane Eyre* concerns women's anger at the restrictions of their lives, entailed a radical re-seeing of the novel, the critical methodologies they used were often traditional—analysis of character, analysis of theme, placement of a work in its historical context. Likewise, the work on women writers that emerged in the '70s and '80s, was not necessarily revisionary in its methodology. The fact that women's studies in literature did not associate itself with a single methodology and did not for the most part attack traditional critical procedures helped its early and rapid institutionalization.

If one turns to other fields, one can see how the development of women's studies has been shaped and situated by the paradigms of those fields. In history, for example, another field in which women's studies has established an early and powerful presence, the development of women's studies has gone hand in hand with the increased attention to social history. In the first chapter of her book, *Disorderly Conduct: Visions of Gender in Victorian America,* the historian Carroll Smith-Rosenberg reflects on both her own development as a historian and on the development of women's history within the field of history. She locates the motivation for women's history in the feminist movement. "Aroused by feminist charges of economic and political discrimination, angered at the sexualization of women by contemporary society and at the psychological ramifications of that sexualization, we turned to our history to trace the origins of women's second-class status." But, Smith-Rosenberg goes on to argue:

> while a sense of personal oppression and of revolt against marginality and invisibility shaped the questions women's historians first addressed, those questions in turn pushed the methodological approaches and conceptual framework of traditional history to new frontiers. They revolutionized historians' understanding of the family, of the processes of economic change, and of the distribution of power within both traditional and industrial societies.[1]

The work of women's historians both built upon the new social history and transformed its conceptual framework. It did this in part by making women visible, not just in the words of men but in the words of women, in diaries and letters in which women gave voice to their experience.

The location of women's studies in the different fields of the social sciences shows some fascinating contrasts. Women's studies established itself fastest and most easily in psychology and in anthropology. In both fields, a focus on gender is central to the discipline, but in both fields women's studies motivated important shifts in how gender was understood.

Professor Christina Maslach, of Berkeley's Psychology Department, answered my e-mail inquiry about the institutionalization of women's studies in a particularly interesting way. She begins by recognizing that psychology was no stranger to issues of sex and gender before the 1960s. Freud's conception of sex roles, the focus of developmental psychologists on sex differences in children's behavior, research on the biological side of the field on the role of sex hormones on sexual behavior, and the use by personality psychologists of masculinity/femininity as a core set of traits all depended upon a bipolar model of masculinity and femininity as opposites that are linked to biological sex. In the late 1960s and early 1970s many scholars questioned the biological determinism of this model and placed increasing emphasis on the social context of behavior and development. Masculinity and femininity were conceptualized as two independent dimensions rather than opposite poles of one dimension, and they were unlinked from sex. Thus a crucial distinction was made between biological sex and social/psychological gender. At the same time, the emergence of new paradigms in cognitive psychology entailed a greater focus on processes of thinking, reasoning, perceiving, and judging. Work on social cognition in particular underscored the notion that gender is a constructed category rather than the expression of innate qualities.

In the 1970s, when feminist work in psychology first emerged, it focused upon the psychology of women, and this focus helped contribute to the legitimacy of women's studies. More recently, emphasis has shifted to include the psychology of men. Across the entire range of psychological research, gender is now understood as a fundamental category. As in the field of history, an interest in women that was at first motivated by the women's movement has broadened and deepened research in the field.

Anthropology, like psychology, seemed to have a natural fit with the concerns of women's studies. As Judy Stacey and Barrie Thorne observe in their article on "The Missing Feminist Revolution in Sociology," the traditional subject matter of anthropology—preliterate tribal cultures in which kinship is central to social life—has always encouraged anthropologists, even those concerned with law, religion, politics, and the economy, to attend to the sexual division of labor and structural and symbolic dimensions of gender relationships. As in literature and psychology, women were a visible subject of study in the discipline. However, placing women at the center of inquiry, as Stacey and Thorne observe, created dramatic conceptual shifts in anthropologists' understanding of the relationship of nature and culture, of the connection between gender and power, and of the connection between public and private life.[2] Furthermore, the fact that social and cultural anthropology were very much involved in the theoretical ferment in the humanities facilitated work on gender. The challenge to the idea of an objective anthropology, in which the anthropologist can describe a society without considering the perspective created by his or her own culture; the argument that all discourse must be understood as text, with a text's instabilities; the absorption of social anthropology into cultural studies— all reinforced the legitimacy of women's studies in anthropology.

Sociology and political science offer interesting contrasts to psychology and anthropology. In neither field has the influence of women's studies been as powerful as it has been in the fields I have described. The reasons reflect the methodologies and the sociology of the disciplines. In an e-mail in response to my question, Professor David Leonard of Berkeley's Political Science Department observed that in political science women's studies was picked up by the most humanistic part of the discipline —political theory—at the same time that political scientists from other subfields were questioning the explanatory force of theory. Women's studies helped political theory maintain some credibility, at the same time that the alliance of women's studies with political theory marginalized it within the rest of the discipline. The position of women's studies within the discipline distanced it from orientations that were more quantitative and scientific. This was not a necessary result. Women's studies could influence the study of social movements or political behavior, particularly the behavior of voters. (Remember the

soccer Moms.) However, women's studies within political science took on a position that was critical of power, and this position put it at odds with the center of the discipline.

Women's studies, of course, is only one of a number of different kinds of studies that have become current in the last two decades. All of the subfields of ethnic studies, international and area studies, urban studies, American studies are interdisciplinary concentrations that, like women's studies, bring together the subjects of inquiry and methodologies of a number of disciplines in the humanities and social sciences in order to understand a specific population. In considering the allocation of faculty positions across departments, university administrators are now used to thinking not only about the ideal composition of a political science department or a history department but about the range of scholars on a campus studying Latin America, for example, or East Asia. In general, universities have become more alert to the fact that traditional departments do not represent the only organization of knowledge, that there is a horizontal axis in the social sciences and the humanities that represents populations as well as a vertical axis that represents traditional disciplines. Women's studies has been an important participant in this interdisciplinary reorganization of knowledge.

I would like now to turn to the question of what have been the fundamental contributions of women's studies. The most important has been the renewed recognition that social position necessarily shapes experience and perspective. Scholars now understand gender, race, and class as socially constructed categories that shape experience not only for women and for ethnic minorities but for everyone in society. This change has been important both in the humanities and in the social sciences. No critic can provide a fully adequate account of a text without taking gender into account; similarly, social science research must consider how gender shapes its data.

Secondly, women's studies has contributed a new sensitivity to the metaphoric and figurative use of gendered terms. For example, we cannot any longer read work that uses gendered metaphors without

This segment of a longer piece by Emily Martin (Signs, 16, 1991) provides an example from the discipline of biology of how gender bias can subtly be reinforced in academic disciplines, Martin examined major scientific textbooks and research articles that discuss reproduction and found significant evidence of gender stereotyping in the scientific language.

The Egg and the Sperm: How Science Has Constructed a Romance Based on Stereotypical Male-Female Roles

EMILY MARTIN

How is it that positive images are denied to the bodies of women? A look at language—in this case, scientific language—provides the first clue. Take the egg and the sperm. It is remarkable how "femininely" the egg behaves and how "masculinely" the sperm. The egg is seen as large and passive. It does not *move* or journey, but passively "is transported," "is swept," or even "drifts" along the fallopian tube. In utter contrast, sperm are small, "streamlined," and invariably active. They "deliver" their genes to the egg, "activate the developmental program of the egg," and have a "velocity" that is often remarked upon. Their tails are "strong" and efficiently powered. Together with the forces of ejaculation, they can "propel the semen into the deepest recesses of the vagina." For this they need "energy," "fuel," so that with a "whiplashlike motion and strong lurches" they can "burrow through the egg coat" and "penetrate" it.

At its extreme, the age-old relationship of the egg and the sperm takes on a royal or religious patina. The egg coat, its protective barrier, is sometimes called its "vestments," a term usually reserved for sacred, religious dress. The egg is said to have a "corona," a crown, and to be accompanied by "attendant cells." It is holy, set apart and above, the queen to the sperm's king. The egg is also passive, which means it must depend on the sperm for rescue. Gerald Schatten and Helen Schatten liken the egg's role to that of Sleeping Beauty: "a dormant bride awaiting her mate's magic kiss, which instills the spirit that brings her to life." Sperm, by contrast, have a "mission," which is to "move through the female genital tract in quest of the ovum." One popular account has it that the sperm carry out a "perilous journey" into the "warm darkness," where some fall away "exhausted." "Survivors" "assault" the egg, the successful candidates "surrounding the prize." Part of the urgency of this journey, in more scientific terms, is that "once released from the supportive environment of the ovary, an egg will die within hours unless rescued by a sperm." The wording stresses the fragility and dependency of the egg, even though the same text acknowledges elsewhere that sperm also live for only a few hours.

being alert to their implications. In *Thinking About Women,* Ellman makes this point by quoting the following paragraph by Balzac, describing the art of writing:

> To pass from conception to execution, to produce, to bring the idea to birth, to raise the child laboriously from infancy, to put it nightly to sleep surfeited, to kiss it in the mornings with the hungry heart of a mother, to clean it, to clothe it fifty times over in new garments which it tears and casts away, and yet not revolt against the trials of this agitated life—this unwearying maternal love, this habit of creation—this is execution and its toils.[3]

Similarly, women's studies has created a self-consciousness of the gendered terms in everyday language. We now say chair and not chairman, police officer and not policeman, and we do not use "he" as a generic pronoun. This change sometimes has its awkwardnesses—waitperson for waiter, or, as a colleague of mine insists, person-person for mailman. Nonetheless, there is a stratum of assumptions about gender in language to which we are sensitive.

Finally, women's studies has contributed the discovery of an extraordinary body of women's writing and of women's history. Women's studies has brought a new attention to women's lives, experiences, and achievements. Critics have discovered the work of many women writers and have shown rich new dimensions in the work of those already well known. The canon has changed. And the way in which critics construct literary history has changed as well, as we understand increasingly more about the role of women writers in the production of literature.

What is in the future for women's studies? In the early days of women's studies, its first proponents imagined it as always on the margin of the academy, as always in opposition, using its place on the edge to critique the center. Although one can still find this view of women's studies, I do not think it is accurate nor do I think it is very fruitful. As I have shown today, women's studies has profoundly affected work in a range of core disciplines to such an extent that questions about gender are at the center of those fields. In the early days of women's studies, women often debated the question of whether women's studies should be located in the various departments that it could hope to transform. That form of the question no longer makes sense. Whether or not a college or university chooses to have a women's studies program, women's studies is represented across the disciplines of the humanities and social sciences. I believe that women's studies will become an increasingly prominent part of our intellectual landscape. Indeed, the use of gender as a focus for analysis has become so pervasive throughout the humanities and social sciences that I occasionally wonder whether the idea of a discipline that bounds the study of women is adequate to the wealth and variety of work being done.   [1997]

NOTES

1. Carroll Smith-Rosenberg, *Disorderly Conduct: Visions of Gender in Victorian America* (New York: Oxford University Press, 1985), pp. 12, 11.
2. Judy Stacey and Barrie Thorne, "The Missing Feminist Revolution in Sociology," *Social Problems,* 32, No. 4 (1985), 305.
3. Honoré de Balzac, quoted in Ellman, *Thinking About Women* (New York: Harcourt Brace Jovanovich, 1968), p. 17.

PART II

Becoming a Woman in Our Society

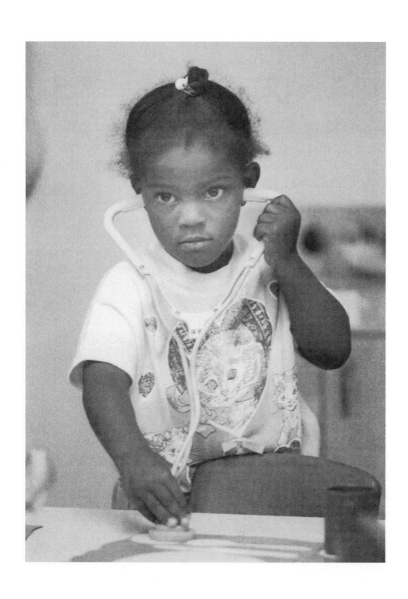

Images of women convey powerful beliefs about what is considered appropriate behavior for girls and women. Regardless of the context of these images, they tend to illustrate prevailing norms. From the adorable and delicate baby girl to the seductively attractive young woman, such images are part and parcel of our culture's portrayal of females. What *does* it mean to be a woman? Ideas about what it means to be a woman permeate all cultures, powerfully shaping the way that women are perceived and treated. These ideas vary from culture to culture, yet they are presented as if they were ordained by either God or nature. In this chapter we explore the notion of "femininity" as a social construct: a prevailing set of ideas, myths, stereotypes, norms, and standards that affect the lives of all women in a variety of ways. Disentangling "nature" from "culture" has been a central task of women throughout history as they struggle to free themselves from constricting myths, stereotypes, and standards.

Western concepts of femininity include a combination of ideas about female good and evil that feminists have identified as the madonna/whore dichotomy. Female virtue has traditionally been presented as pure, selfless, and maternal while female evil has been presented as deceitful, dangerous, and sinful. In a society which is racist as well as sexist, it is frequently the white woman who appears as pure and selfless while women of racial and ethnic minorities are seen as deviant. In the United States, ideas about femininity have been inextricably linked with ideas about race and class. In the nineteenth century, for example, urban, white middle-class women were told it was "woman's nature" to be frail and demure while slave women worked alongside men in the fields. For these reasons, women's studies scholars often describe gender norms as racialized. Thus, we often hear of the African-American woman's domineering nature; the exotic, mysterious sensuality of the Asian-American woman; the Chicana woman's stereotype as evil, sexually uncontrollable, and betrayer of her race; and the status-conscious Jewish American woman.

Although specific to different racial and ethnic groups, these images of women reflect the negative half of the madonna/whore and good girl/bad girl stereotypes that have historically defined standards of behavior for all women. One learns very early—from peers, family, educational institutions, and the media—what are acceptable behaviors, attitudes, and values. From infancy on, young girls are bombarded with messages about what "good" girls do and, even more insistently, what they don't do.

Consider the many ways in which American society communicates expectations of females and males from the moment of birth. Gender markers in the form of color of clothing immediately differentiate female infants from male infants: pink gowns with frills and bows convey a feminine gentleness, purity, and fragility, while blue sleepers decorated with animals, trains, and sports scenes evoke strength and vigor. From the family outward to the community, children are continuously exposed to direct and indirect messages regarding appropriate sex-role behavior. For example, different household chores are typically assigned to boys and girls at home:

dishwashing and housecleaning for girls, and washing cars and yard work for boys. Such divisions in responsibility reinforce the notion that the domestic world is girls' domain, while the world outside the home is reserved for boys.

Prevailing norms of behavior also influence the ways women's behavior is judged. Women have traditionally been defined in relation to male standards and needs. Man is seen as strong, woman weak, and the resulting dichotomy perpetuates the superiority of males. Women have historically been viewed as men's subordinate, someone different from and inferior to him. "Masculine" traits are socially desirable and valued, while "feminine" ones are not. In one of the most frequently cited studies of sexism in psychotherapy, Broverman and her colleagues asked mental health professionals to rate the behavior of a psychologically healthy woman, man, and adult. The results indicated that the standard for mental health reflected attributes considered characteristic of men (e.g., independent, intelligent, aggressive). The findings of this study forcefully demonstrate the pervasive use of male behavior as the norm for everyone, with "femininity" carrying negative connotations for perceptions of women.[1]

As we explore the experience of being female, we call attention to the ways in which society has limited and trapped women through myths and stereotypes. In American culture, ideas of success are associated with male traits. Women's self-perceptions are often distorted, reflecting cultural values about women rather than realistic appraisals of women's worth. All too often, these self-images take the form of diminished notions of ability and strength, and exaggerated ideas of inferiority and weakness. Ultimately, many girls and women begin to question themselves and feel powerless, whether they are in the classroom, at work, or in relationships with others. To value oneself beyond these limiting expectations can be an arduous task when the majority of society's messages are undermining one's self-respect.

Stereotypes about girls and women make it easier for individuals to think they can predict behavior, allowing a quick evaluation and categorization of behavior. For example, adhering to stereotypes leads people to (erroneously) evaluate attractive women as unintelligent, particularly if they are blonde. Stereotypes of women's mental capability give rise to snap judgments that women are not as qualified as men for certain positions requiring what are presumed to be masculine attributes (e.g., intelligence, decisiveness, logical reasoning skills). In general, stereotypes are tightly woven into the social fabric of this culture, and reinforce dichotomous notions of "femininity" and "masculinity."

In her classic work in psychology, Naomi Weisstein detailed the ways in which psychologists have lent a mantle of scientific "authority" to these ideas by promoting the concept of a "female essence" and ignoring the powerful influence of social

---

[1] Inge K. Broverman, D. M. Broverman, F. E. Clarkson, P. S. Rosenkrantz, & S. R. Vogel. "Sex Role Stereotypes and Clinical Judgments of Mental Health." *Journal of Consulting and Clinical Psychology 34* (1970), 1–7.

context and environment on behavior.[2] Weisstein exposed the ways that scientists, rather than pursuing evidence, have created theories based on ideas of femininity they inherited from the culture. A more effective way of understanding the behavior of both women and men, she argued, would be to study the power of social expectations to influence behavior.

There are few cultural institutions and practices that do not promote and reinforce the stereotyping of women. In language, for example, maleness is the standard; consider the terms mankind, chairman, policeman, postman, and so on. From subtle uses of language to more overt messages transmitted through the media, advertisements, and classroom settings, girls are bombarded with sexist views of the world and of themselves. The dynamics of the classroom often reinforce existing power relationships between males and females. These patterns are so pervasive that we don't usually notice them. However, studies of classrooms reveal that teachers call on female students less frequently than on male students and discourage females' classroom participation, thus eroding their self-confidence. Ultimately, we see females and males literally tracked into "feminine" and "masculine" fields of study and careers.

In the second section of this part, selections focus on family and cultural norms, educational experiences, nonverbal communication, and the media, which have all had powerful effects on the way women and girls see themselves and their world. The lyrics of many mainstream contemporary songs, as well as the images in the music videos accompanying them, promote sexist notions of women, emphasizing women's sexuality and subordination to men. The power of these images is so strong that girls as young as five and six, who are exposed to constant messages of women's sexual objectification, often desire the revealing and sexually suggestive "Britney Spears" look in fashion. When girls and women are constantly exposed to messages of male superiority, they will inevitably feel powerless and insignificant. However, there is a growing number of contemporary young women musicians who are defying these stereotypes by portraying women as strong and assertive, active and rebellious. By challenging restrictive norms and practices, these women provide more realistic and positive models of "what it means to be a woman."

----

[2]Naomi Weisstein. *Psychology Constructs the Female*, Cambridge, MA: New England Free Press, 1969.

Dominant Ideas About Women

Images of femininity, while powerful in our culture, vary according to class, ethnic group, and race, and have been manipulated to serve the needs of those in power. Precisely because these portrayals of women interact with specific stereotypes, it is critical to examine the ways they affect the experiences of different groups of women. Betty Friedan exposed the myths and realities of the "happy middle-class housewife" of the 1960s in her book *The Feminine Mystique.* This book represented a pivotal point in the consciousness of many white middle-class women, who identified with Friedan's characterization of many women's discontent and frustration with the decorative supportive roles glorified in the popular culture of the 1950s and 1960s. Marge Piercy echoes this theme in her poem "A Work of Artifice," as she equates the fragile beauty of the bonsai tree with traditional expectations of femininity. Piercy suggests that women pay a price for complying with these social norms, as does the bonsai tree, which is artificially stunted for ornamental purposes.

Often when girls enter puberty they encounter our culture's ideas of femininity. Girls are suddenly treated differently and face restrictions they don't understand. In "Purification," gracepoore describes a rite of passage from southern India that acknowledges a girl's first menstruation. This ritual traditionally signals a girl's readiness for the "wife-mother" role and includes a cleansing ceremony that is meant to "purify" her of her blood. While the ritual functions as a way of bringing family and community together, it can also render girls invisible as individuals.

Danzy Senna shares her experiences as an adolescent "growing up mixed in the racial battlefield of Boston," where she struggles to become clear about her identity and what kind of woman she wanted to be. Torn between her observation of the real-life power dynamics between men and women and her desire to conform to the racialized gender norms of popular culture, Senna shows us that young women with multiple racial and ethnic backgrounds negotiate a complex path as they consider conflicting messages of what they "should" be.

Susan Schnur confronts myths and stereotypes about Jewish women, highlighting the anti-Semitism and sexism inherent in the term "JAP." Another widely held misconception is that women with physical disabilities do not have sexual lives. Debra Kent challenges the assumption that women have to be attractive and perfect in order to be sexual. In doing so, she shows us that the struggle of women with disabilities to claim their sexual live reflects "everyone's battle against the binding rules of conformity."

Like the ceremony in "Purification," the ritual surrounding weddings preserves traditional notions of femininity, even while increasing numbers of women see themselves as independent individuals who are not becoming their husbands' property.

This section concludes with two pieces that challenge the ever-present image of the sweet innocent girl who grows up and becomes the passive helpless woman. Elisa Dávila describes how she learned to be a "good girl" in a patriarchal and sexist society. Developing an understanding of the different standards imposed for men's and women's behavior, Dávila challenged them, creating a life in the United States that resonates with her own needs for self-fulfillment. However, she reminds us that regardless of where she is or what she does, she is still subject to being judged by artificial ideals of womanhood. In "Not a Pretty Girl," Ani DiFranco squarely defies the idea of women as decorative, fragile, and in need of rescuing.

 9

The Problem That Has No Name

BETTY FRIEDAN

Gradually I came to realize that the problem that has no name was shared by countless women in America. As a magazine writer I often interviewed women about problems with their children, or their marriages, or their houses, or their communities. But after a while I began to recognize the telltale signs of this other problem. I saw the same signs in suburban ranchhouses and split-levels on Long Island and in New Jersey and Westchester County; in colonial houses in a small Massachusetts town; on patios in Memphis; in suburban and city apartments; in living rooms in the Midwest. Sometimes I sensed the problem, not as a reporter, but as a suburban housewife, for during this time I was also bringing up my own three children in Rockland County, New York. I heard echoes of the problem in college dormitories and semi-private maternity wards, at PTA meetings and luncheons of the League of Women Voters, at suburban cocktail parties, in station wagons waiting for trains, and in snatches of conversation overheard at Schrafft's. The groping words I heard from other women, on quiet afternoons when children were at school or on quiet evenings when husbands worked late, I think I understood first as a woman long before I understood their larger social and psychological implications.

Just what was this problem that has no name? What were the words women used when they tried to express it? Sometimes a woman would say "I feel empty somehow . . . incomplete." Or she would say, "I feel as if I don't exist." Sometimes she blotted out the feeling with a tranquilizer. Sometimes she thought the problem was with her husband, or her children, or that what she really needed was to redecorate her house, or move to a better neighborhood, or have an affair, or another baby. Sometimes, she went to a doctor with symptoms she could hardly describe: "A tired feeling. . . . I get so angry with the children it scares me. . . . I feel like crying without any reason." (A Cleveland doctor called it "the housewife's syndrome.") A number of women told me about great bleeding blisters that break out on their hands and arms. "I call it the housewife's blight," said a family doctor in Pennsylvania. "I see it so often lately in these young women with four, five and six children who bury themselves in their dishpans. But it isn't caused by detergent and it isn't cured by cortisone."

Sometimes a woman would tell me that the feeling gets so strong she runs out of the house and walks through the streets. Or she stays inside her house and cries. Or her children tell her a joke, and she doesn't laugh because she doesn't hear it. I talked to women who had spent years on the analyst's couch, working out their "adjustment to the feminine role," their blocks to "fulfillment as a wife and mother." But the desperate tone in these women's voices, and the look in their eyes, was the same as the tone and the look of other women, who were sure they had no problem, even though they did have a strange feeling of desperation.

A mother of four who left college at nineteen to get married told me:

> I've tried everything women are supposed to do—hobbies, gardening, pickling, canning, being very social with my neighbors, joining committees, running PTA teas. I can do it all, and I like it, but it doesn't leave you anything to think about—any feeling of who you are. I never had any career ambitions. All I wanted was to get married and have four children. I love the kids and Bob and my home. There's no problem you can even put a name to. But I'm desperate. I begin to feel I have no personality. I'm a server of food and putter-on of pants and a bedmaker, somebody who can be called on when you want something. But who am I?

A twenty-three-year-old mother in blue jeans said:

> I ask myself why I'm so dissatisfied. I've got my health, fine children, a lovely new home, enough money. My husband has a real future as an electronics engineer. He doesn't have any of these feelings. He says maybe I need a vacation, let's go to New York for a weekend. But that isn't it. I always had this idea we should do everything together. I can't sit down and read a book alone. If the children are napping and I have one hour to myself I just walk through the house waiting for them to wake up. I don't make a move until I know where the rest of the crowd is going. It's as if ever since you were a little girl, there's always been somebody or something that will take care of your life: your parents, or college, or falling in love, or having a child, or moving to a new house. Then you wake up one morning and there's nothing to look forward to.

A young wife in a Long Island development said:

> I seem to sleep so much. I don't know why I should be so tired. This house isn't nearly so hard to clean as the cold-water flat we had when I was working. The children are at school all day. It's not the work. I just don't feel alive.

In 1960, the problem that has no name burst like a boil through the image of the happy American housewife. In the television commercials the pretty housewives still beamed over their foaming dishpans and *Time*'s cover story on "The Suburban Wife, an American Phenomenon" protested: "Having too good a time . . . to believe that they should be unhappy." But the actual unhappiness of the American housewife was suddenly being reported—from the *New York Times* and *Newsweek* to *Good Housekeeping* and CBS Television ("The Trapped Housewife"), although almost everybody who talked about it found some superficial reason to dismiss it. It was attributed to incompetent appliance repairmen (*New York Times*), or the distances children must be chauffeured in the suburbs (*Time*), or too much PTA (*Redbook*). Some said it was the old problem—education: more and more women had education, which naturally made them unhappy in their role as housewives. "The road from Freud to Frigidaire, from Sophocles to Spock, has turned out to be a bumpy one," reported the *New York Times* (June 28, 1960). "Many young women—certainly not all—whose education plunged them into a world of ideas feel stifled in their homes. They find their routine lives out of joint with their training. Like shut-ins, they feel left out. In the last year, the problem of the educated housewife has provided the meat of dozens of speeches made by troubled presidents of women's colleges who maintain, in the face of complaints, that sixteen years of academic training is realistic preparation for wifehood and motherhood."

There was much sympathy for the educated housewife. ("Like a two-headed schizophrenic . . . once she wrote a paper on the Graveyard poets; now she writes notes to the milkman. Once she determined the boiling point of sulfuric acid; now she determines her boiling point with the overdue repairman. . . . The housewife often is reduced to screams and tears. . . . No one, it seems, is appreciative, least of all herself, of the kind of person she becomes in the process of turning from poetess into shrew.")

Home economists suggested more realistic preparation for housewives, such as high-school workshops in home appliances. College educators suggested more discussion groups on home management and the family, to prepare women for the adjustment to domestic life. A spate of articles appeared in the mass magazines offering "Fifty-eight Ways to Make Your Marriage More Exciting." No month went by without a new book by a psychiatrist or sexologist offering technical advice on finding greater fulfillment through sex.

A male humorist joked in *Harper's Bazaar* (July, 1960) that the problem could be solved by taking away women's right to vote. ("In the pre-19th Amendment era, the American woman was placid, sheltered and sure of her role in American society. She left all the political decisions to her husband and he, in turn, left all the family decisions to her. Today a woman has to make both the family *and* the political decisions, and it's too much for her.")

A number of educators suggested seriously that women no longer be admitted to the four-year colleges and universities: in the growing college crisis, the education which girls could not use as housewives was more urgently needed than ever by boys to do the work of the atomic age.

The problem was also dismissed with drastic solutions no one could take seriously. (A woman writer proposed in *Harper's* that women be drafted for compulsory service as nurses' aides and baby-sitters.) And it was smoothed over with the age-old panaceas: "love is their answer," "the only answer is inner help," "the secret of completeness—children," "a private means of intellectual fulfillment," "to cure this toothache of the spirit—the simple formula of handing one's self and one's will over to God."

The problem was dismissed by telling the housewife she doesn't realize how lucky she is—her own boss, no time clock, no junior executive gunning for her job. What if she isn't happy—does she think men are happy in this world? Does she really, secretly, still want to be a man? Doesn't she know yet how lucky she is to be a woman?

The problem was also, and finally, dismissed by shrugging that there are no solutions: this is what being a woman means, and what is wrong with American women that they can't accept their role gracefully? As *Newsweek* put it (March 7, 1960):

She is dissatisfied with a lot that women of other lands can only dream of. Her discontent is deep, pervasive, and impervious to the superficial remedies which are offered at every hand. . . . An army of professional explorers have already charted the major sources of trouble. . . . From the beginning of time, the female cycle has defined and confined woman's role. As Freud was credited with saying: "Anatomy is destiny." Though no group of women has ever pushed these natural restrictions as far as the American wife, it seems that she still cannot accept them with good grace. . . . A young mother with a beautiful family, charm, talent and brains is apt to dismiss her role apologetically. "What do I do?" you hear her say. "Why nothing. I'm just a housewife." A good education, it seems, has given this paragon among women an understanding of the value of everything except her own worth. . . .

And so she must accept the fact that "American women's unhappiness is merely the most recently won of women's rights," and adjust and say with the happy housewife found by *Newsweek*: "We ought to salute the wonderful freedom we all have and be proud of our lives today. I have had college and I've worked, but being a housewife is the most rewarding and satisfying role. . . . My mother was never included in my father's business affairs . . . she couldn't get out of the house and away from us children. But I am an equal to my husband; I can go along with him on business trips and to social business affairs."

The alternative offered was a choice that few women would contemplate. In the sympathetic words of the *New York Times:* "All admit to being deeply frustrated at times by the lack of privacy, the physical burden, the routine of family life, the confinement of it. However, none would give up her home and family if she had the choice to make again." *Redbook* commented: "Few women would want to thumb their noses at husbands, children and community and go off on their own. Those who do may be talented individuals, but they rarely are successful women."

The year American women's discontent boiled over, it was also reported (*Look*) that the more than 21,000,000 American women who are single, widowed, or divorced do not cease even after fifty their frenzied, desperate search for a man. And the search begins early—for seventy per cent of all American women now marry before they are twenty-four. A pretty twenty-five-year-old secretary took thirty-five different jobs in six months in the futile hope of finding a husband. Women are moving from one political club to another, taking evening courses in accounting or sailing, learning to play golf or ski, joining a number of churches in succession, going to bars alone, in their ceaseless search for a man.

Of the growing thousands of women currently getting private psychiatric help in the United States, the married ones were reported dissatisfied with their marriages, the unmarried ones suffering from anxiety and, finally, depression. Strangely, a number of psychiatrists stated that, in their experience, unmarried women patients were happier than married ones. So the door of all those pretty suburban houses opened a crack to permit a glimpse of uncounted thousands of American housewives who suffered alone from a problem that suddenly everyone was talking about, and beginning to take for granted, as one of those unreal problems in American life that can never be solved—like the hydrogen bomb. By 1962 the plight of the trapped American housewife had become a national parlor game. Whole issues of magazines, newspaper columns, books learned and frivolous, educational conferences and television panels were devoted to the problem.

Even so, most men, and some women, still did not know that this problem was real. But those who had faced it honestly knew that all the superficial remedies, the sympathetic advice, the scolding words and the cheering words were somehow drowning the problem in unreality. A bitter laugh was beginning to be heard from American women. They were admired, envied, pitied, theorized over until they were sick of it, offered drastic solutions or silly choices that no one could take seriously. They got all kinds of advice from the growing armies of marriage and child-guidance counselors, psychotherapists, and armchair psychologists, on how to adjust to their role as housewives. No other road to fulfillment was offered to American women in the middle of the twentieth century. Most adjusted to their role and suffered or ignored the problem that has no name. It can be less painful, for a woman, not to hear the strange, dissatisfied voice stirring within her.

[1964]

🌿 10

A Work of Artifice

MARGE PIERCY

The bonsai tree
in the attractive pot
could have grown eighty feet tall
on the side of a mountain
till split by lightning.
But a gardener
carefully pruned it.
It is nine inches high.
Every day as he
whittles back the branches
the gardener croons,
It is.your nature
to be small and cozy,
domestic and weak;
how lucky, little tree,
to have a pot to grow in.
With living creatures
one must begin very early
to dwarf their growth:
the bound feet,

the crippled brain,
the hair in curlers,
the hands you
love to touch.   [1973]

🦎 11

Purification

GRACEPOORE

It was there one afternoon—a stain on my panties, the colour of dried plantain juice. "Amma, I have a brown patch on my pants," I said at the lunch table.

Mother dropped the ball of curried rice she was about to pop in her mouth, and stared at me. "What patch? Where?" she rapped.

"I dunno. It just came. On my knickers." I noticed a strange look on her face. In silence, she kept her eyes on me, then tossed the ball of rice into her mouth and chewed.

I bit into a piece of chicken. Of all the chicken curries I had tasted at other people's homes at Deepavali,[1] Mother's was the best. She made it so her chicken was tender without falling apart in shreds inside the gravy. Her spices blended just right so the hotness didn't stick in your throat. I picked another chicken off my plate, curry collecting in the creases of my palms and soaking my finger tips. Long after I had eaten, the scent would remain as it always did with the curries that my mother made.

"Ma, can I ride Peter's bike after I finish my homework?" Jeevan's voice crashed through the silence. He was my nine-year old brother. Dad did not like him riding bicycles since the time he fell and grazed his knee so badly, he had a purple scab for two months.

Mother ignored Jeevan. She went on shaping another ball of rice in her plate while he sat licking his fingers. Jeevan tried again, "Ma, can I. . . ."

"How many times have I told you not to lick your fingers? If you've finished eating, go and wash your hands," Mother scolded even before he could complete his sentence.

"But I haven't finished eating," Jeevan complained.

"Then hurry up and finish," Mother snapped and poured a glass of water.

Jeevan was not ready to give up on the bicycle and went on pestering her. "So can I ride Peter's. . . ."

"Take your food and go into the hall, Jeevan," Mother jerked her head sideways and turned to him. I looked at her.

"But you're the one who told us not to eat in the hall," Jeevan argued.

"Take your food and eat it in the hall. I want to talk to Geeta."

"But why?" Jeevan whined.

"Will you stop asking bloody questions and just do what I tell you? Take your plate and get out there!" Mother yelled, her hands furiously mixing curry and rice.

Jeevan knew he was in for trouble if he stayed one minute longer. He picked up his plate and walked out of the kitchen. Mother thrust back her chair, went to the sink, washed her hands and disappeared into the bedroom. I followed her, my lunch and hers half-eaten on the table.

Behind closed doors, she thrust a soft white object at me and said in a cold voice, "Put this between your legs." I stared at what she held out, a large slice of bread with a loop on each end. "Put it into your panties," she ordered.

I took the bread from her. One side felt smooth like one of Mother's saris, the other side a little rough, with a fine-net like surface and a blue line running up and down the middle.

"Go on. What are you waiting for? Adjust that between your thighs," Mother broke into my thoughts.

I had no idea what to do. "How, Amma?" I asked.

"Can't you do a simple thing?" she bristled and snatched the pad from me. Then she picked up her sari, lifted it halfway up, and held the pad between her thighs. I had never seen anything above my mother's knees, so the sight of her thighs made me forget the pad. There she stood, exposed, green lines snaking under her light brown skin. Instantly, Mother noticed and pulled her sari down. In her eyes I saw what I felt in my heart, and I wished I had never seen my mother's thighs. Then it was my turn.

I kept trying to hold my skirt down while fumbling with the pad inside my panties, unable to see what I was doing, yet unwilling to expose myself like she had. Then, I heard her say, "This evening, when Dad comes home, he'll get a belt for the pad." I wondered where the belt would go. Mother went on. "You put the loops into the belt hooks so the pad won't move."

"How long do I wear this?"

"Till your period is over. Every time it gets dirty, you change it. There's newspaper under the sink. Wrap the pads in that and throw them in the front dustbin, not the one in the kitchen. Take it to the front, understand?" I pulled the panties up over the pad. "Tomorrow, you stay home. I'll write a note to your teacher."

But I had a netball game. I had to go. "Ma, Mrs. Koh told us not to be absent. I'm playing netball."

"I'll write a note," she silenced me.

"But Mrs. Koh said not to be absent."

"I'm telling you, you can't go."

"But I'm not sick, why can't I go?"

"When did you get such a big mouth? You aren't going and that's final."

"But Mrs. Koh. . . ."

"Who the hell is Mrs. Koh? Is she feeding you or am I? If Dad hears you talking like this, you'll get a bloody lashing." I felt the pad lodged between my thighs, I remembered Dad's terrible temper, I thought about the brown stain, and held my breath.

Mother opened the door and walked out. I sat on the bed and cried quietly. How would I explain to my teammates? What would Mrs. Koh think? Through the open door, I watched Mother clearing away the lunch dishes and felt tears roll down the bridge of my nose.

The next five days were a mystery. Mother gave rules she had never given before. "Don't take the dog out, don't let Jeevan sit on your bed, don't dare wash your hair today, you'll get black circles under your eyes. Wait another three days."

Then she screamed, "How many times have I got to tell you, throw the pads in the front dustbin!"

When I yelled back, "I forgot, Ma," she got angry and screamed even louder, "I've told you before, that's girl's stuff and you have to be careful not to let Jeevan see it."

Jeevan never knew why I stayed home from school. Dad told him to mind his own business when he asked about me. I never said a word because Mother said not to. So Jeevan told the neighborhood boys that I had chicken pox.

Twice a day, Mother made me eat a stiff sweet paste of green peas mixed with brown sugar. In the mornings, she forced me to swallow raw egg yolks and drink gingelly oil to strengthen my womb. Meanwhile, a tight pink elastic belt girdled my waist and cut into my flesh. My brown stain became a sticky red liquid which Mother called "menses." My stomach ached below my belly button and all through my lower back.

For a week I missed school. I thought about the netball games and wondered if I would ever play again. Once or twice, I asked Dad if I could go to school. At first he said no. The second time, he threatened to smack me so I stopped asking. Most of the week I stayed in bed and read Enid Blyton's mystery books. This part was fun, the only part that was fun.

Soon the pain in my stomach stopped and the blood started to go away. Mother told me I could soak my clothes with the other's again, and I did not have to hang my panties at the far end of the clothes line where spiders built cobwebs to catch beetles.

Just when my sickness was nearly gone, Mother gave me something I had only seen in Tamil movies, a costume that women wore when they danced before a king or some rich man who turned out to be a villain. She gave me a satin, yellow midriff blouse and a sweeping, yellow sequinned skirt made from one of her new georgette saris. The skirt came down to the ankles and the blouse had press studs down the front and little eared sleeves.

"Tomorrow you wear this," she said. "Unless and aunts are coming here and pastor is doing a prayer service for you."

"Why are they praying?" I asked.

"It's our custom. Every girl must go through it," she answered, ending the conversation.

All day that day, Mother stood over the kerosene stove, cooking Indian sweets. She grumbled about the price of cardamom and worried about not having enough food to feed the guests. When I asked her again why people were coming to our house, she said it was a celebration. When I asked what we were celebrating, she scolded me for wasting her time and told me to leave the kitchen.

At three o'clock the next afternoon, relatives poured into our small terrace house, invading every room except mine. Mother said I had to stay in the room until she called. I lay in bed, listening to the laughter and chatter around me. Two aunts came in to ask how I felt. My cousins peeked through open window louvres. Uncles stood at the door, glancing at me occasionally, but never venturing close.

After awhile they all left me alone. I tried to read *The Mystery Of The Missing Red Coat* but my mind kept wandering outside. Soon, only my eyes were in the book. My ears pulled my head outside, to the stories floating around behind the closed door. Uncle Arthur was having a cataract operation. Aunt Esther was going to marry an engineer. Mrs. Dorai's daughter failed Oxford. Cousin Joshua's son was coming back with a Jaffna bride.

From the kitchen, smells of mother's cooking wafted through the house. I had watched her pile our special rose-colored plates with gulab jamuns glistening with thick sugar syrup. She had unwrapped fish-shaped steel trays from tissue paper and arranged golden ladhus next to creamy white burfi. This morning, she filled Pyrex bowls with chicken curry and yellow rice spiked with cloves and cinnamon sticks. I lay on the bed and tasted her food on the back of my tongue, wondering when we would eat.

As the sun turned a bright orange outside, Mother came into my room. "Grandcousin Ivy is going to bathe you now," she said and left. I sat on the edge of my bed, terrified. I didn't know grandcousin Ivy.

"Geeta, come. Your bath is waiting," I heard Mother call. I waited by the door. Someone knocked and said, "Geeta, your Amma is calling," but I did not move. Maybe if I stayed in the room, Mother would come in again and I'd ask her about grand-

cousin Ivy. But Mother did not come in. Instead, Dad tapped on the louvres. "Oi! Geeta, Amma is calling you. Are you deaf?"

I turned the door knob and stepped out. The uncles stopped talking. The aunts smiled. I suddenly felt trapped and ashamed. Why were they looking at me? What had I done?

The hallway leading to the bathroom seemed to go on forever. I kept walking, my eyes on the floor. Something gripped the middle of my stomach and I felt my legs grow weak.

When I reached the bathroom, grandcousin Ivy was waiting. I had never seen her before. I looked down at her feet and saw a covered pot. I entered the bathroom.

"Come, take off your clothes." she said. I had never undressed before another human being. Not since I was seven and knew the meaning of shame, knew that Jeevan was no longer my brother but a boy, that uncles were no longer uncles but men, and girls were girls who must hide their bodies.

I looked shyly at grandcousin Ivy and tried to catch her eye, but she fussed with the towels and pretended not to see me. I shifted from one foot to the other, all the time looking at her face.

Suddenly she snapped, "Tcheh! Come on, come on. Hurry up. I haven't got all day." I tried to unfasten the buttons on my dress but my fingers were frozen.

"I say, what's this nonsense? Don't stand there like a statue child. I've seen dozens of crotches before." I winced at her vulgarity. Who was this woman with a hard, proud face? Why did Mother invite her?

Grandcousin bent down and took the cover off the pot. A powerful smell of warm milk rose up and filled the air. Then she straightened up and looked at me, hands on her hips, waiting.

My hands shook as they passed over each button. Finally, the last one was undone. I stood naked against the cool tiles of the bathroom wall. Grandcousin signalled for me to come forward. I moved towards her and squatted on the floor. Mumbling a prayer in Tamil, she picked up the pot and tipped it over my head. Warm milk streamed lazily down my eyes, soaked into my hair and clung to my eyelashes.

"Okay, everything is done!" she announced. I saw the whiteness of the milk against my skin and remembered the time when we had moved into this house. Dad had boiled milk on a charcoal stove in the middle of the living room floor so that our house would be protected from evil spirits. Mother said the milk would purify the air.

I remembered that time six years ago, and suddenly I understood everything. The milk was purifying me. It was taking away the pollution of my blood.

Grandcousin left the bathroom. I stayed to wash up, to scrub away the sickening liquid, drying quickly on my body. I soaped and scratched at the milk, hating it, hating her, hating them . . . most of all, hating my blood.

When the bath was over, I dressed in the sequinned skirt and shiny blouse. Mother led me out in front of the relatives and made me sit next to her. The Reverend Thangaraj read a prayer and offered a blessing. A hymn was sung, the benediction received. Then, all eyes fell on me. They studied my face, my hair, the color of my skin. They looked carefully to see if I would make a suitable daughter-in-law someday. Finally, done with their scrutiny, they came over and shook my hand.

At the other end of the room, Dad stood up and invited the guests to begin eating. Soon, one by one, they swarmed over the feast Mother had laid out for them and forgot my presence. I sat in my chair and watched them. Amidst the smells of ladhus and gulab jamuns, chicken curry and spiced rice, I became invisible.

EPILOGUE:

The Tamil custom of observing a girl's first menstruation through ritual and ceremony is an acknowledgement of her rite of passage to womanhood. While this custom can serve as a positive affirmation of her femaleness, in practice it evolved as a means for the girl's family to publicize their daughter's availability for marriage. Hence, the ceremony is more for the family than for the girl herself.

In time, as more and more middle-class urban Tamil families like mine encouraged marriage later, women put off marriage until their mid or late twen-

ties, even thirties. With this development, it seemed as if the custom of celebrating a girl's period would become an actual honoring of her rite of passage rather than a mechanism for placing her on the marriage market. Yet it hasn't. For while a Tamil girl may no longer need to marry when she is an adolescent or young teenager, her puberty marks the point at which she is ready to produce children via the institution of marriage. Hence, everything from her dietary changes during her period to her ceremonial clothes inform her and others around her that she has inherited the role and responsibility of being a potential wife-mother.

In my family, the menstruation ritual took on an added dimension due to their belief that menstrual blood is impure. Not only was a girl to be "celebrated" for coming of age but she was also to be "cleansed."

The use of milk to purify is a Tamil and Hindu customn. However, as with many in the South Asian diaspora, cultural practices persist in co-opted forms irrespective of religious affiliation or belief systems. Hence, cleansing with milk became simply a Tamil no longer a Hindu custom, while serving a Tamil Christian function. Likewise, the idea that plants will die if touched by a menstruating girl/woman is Hindu and, most likely, agrarian. This too has been adopted by a Tamil Christian family like mine living in an industrialized city.

Further, since my family migrated to Malaysia which has large populations of Chinese and Malays, some of the menstrual taboos observed in these ethnic communities also became part of Tamil custom. For instance, the belief that black circles under the eyes will form if one washes one's hair during the first three days of menstruation is a Southern Chinese custom. Hence, the source of many menstrual customs appears to matter less than the actual imposing and observing of "period rules" during menstruation.

Exposing one's culture to a foreign audience is like sharing a family secret that discredits family honor. Yet there are practices in all cultures that need to be revised, re-interpreted, and/or eventually discarded because they disempower individuals. There was great hesitation in writing this story, an even greater hesitation in submitting it for publication, but it was a necessary act—to give voice to anger and to transform experience into narrative.

"Purification" is written for several reasons: to expose a custom that is meant to celebrate but in fact humiliates girls and women; to defy the silence that all cultures impose on those who question and challenge repressive customs; to protest forced participation of children in rituals that have no meaning to them, that frighten and strip them of their dignity as people; and to confront adults who practice the very customs that disempowered them as children, who perpetuate these customs in exchange for social stuatus, and pass on these traditions to the generations after them in the name of preserving cultural heritage. I write this story for my nieces so they will not have to go through what Geeta went through for growing up female in a christianized Tamil family.

For a menstruation ritual to be truly celebratory, the very premise on which this ritual is currently based must be changed, and silence around women's sexuality must be lifted. Only then can She who becomes the center of attention in a menstruation ritual be free of the stigma and shame she inherits for getting her period. Only then will she not be punished for being female.

NOTES

1. Deepavali is a Hindu Festival of Lights, celebrated in October or November.

 12

To Be Real

DANZY SENNA

Growing up mixed in the racial battlefield of Boston, I yearned for something just out of my reach— an "authentic" identity to make me real. Everyone but me, it seemed at the time, fit into a neat cultural box, had a label to call their own. Being the daughter of both feminist and integrationist movements, a white socialist mother and a black intellectual fa-

ther, it seemed that everyone and everything had come together for my conception, only to break apart in time for my birth. I was left with only questions. To Be or Not to Be: black, Negro, African-American, feminist, femme, mulatto, quadroon, lesbian, straight, bisexual, lipstick, butch bottom, femme top, vegetarian, carnivore? These potential identities led me into the maze of American identity politics, and hopefully out the other side.

When I was eleven years old, an awkward child with knobby knees and a perpetually flat chest, I was preoccupied with questions of womanhood and what kind of woman I would become. Even then, I was aware of two kinds of power I could access as a female. There was the kind of power women got from being sexually desired, and the kind women got from being sexually invisible—that is, the power in attracting men and the power in being free of men. I also noticed that women fought one another for the first kind and came together for the second. Even as a child, I knew people craved power. I just wasn't sure which kind I wanted.

I liked the power of looking pretty, but wasn't certain men were worth attracting. I didn't like the effect they had on the women around me. Like most of my friends, I lived in a female-headed household. My mother raised us with the help of other women, a series of sidekick moms who moved in and out of our lives. In the evenings, we all converged in the kitchen, an orange-painted room on the second floor of our house. In the kitchen, laughter, food, and talk formed a safe space of women and children. On those occasions when men did enter the picture —for dinner parties or coffee—the fun of wild, unabashed laughter and fluid gossip seemed to float out the window. In walked huge, serious, booming creatures who quickly became the focus of attention. The energy of the room shifted from the finely choreographed dance of womentalk, where everyone participated in but no one dominated the conversation, to a room made up of margins and centers. The relative kindness of men didn't change the dynamic of their presence. From my perspective, it appeared that they immediately became the center of the kitchen, while the women were transformed into fluttering, doting frames around them.

The women who had a moment before seemed strong, impenetrable heroines, became, in the presence of men, soft and powerless girls.

My confusion about which kind of power I wanted to have—which kind of woman I wanted to be—is reflected in a diary entry from that year. In round, flowery script I wrote vows. "Always wear lipstick. Never get married." The prospect of being able to turn heads, to be asked out on dates—to be desired—was an aspect of my impending adolescence which looked thrilling. Lipstick became the symbol of this power in my mind. At the same time, I noticed that once Lipstick Women had attracted men, often they became old and beaten, pathetic, desperate creatures, while the men remained virile and energized. At ten, I hoped there was a space in between the two extremes— a place where I could have both kinds of power—a place where I could wear lipstick and still be free.

My mother and her friends seemed to have settled for only one of these forms of power—the power of feminism—and their brazen rejection of the "lipstick world" insulted and embarrassed my burgeoning adolescent consciousness. I remember one dusky evening in particular, when a group of women from the local food cooperative came banging on our door. They wanted my mother's support in a march protesting violence against women. She liked these tough, working-class women and what they stood for, so while other mothers called their kids into dinner, ours dragged us into the streets. My sister, brother, and I were mortified as we ran alongside the march, giggling and pointing at the marching women chanting "Women Unite—Take Back the Night!" The throngs were letting it all hang out: their breasts hung low, their leg hair grew wild, their thighs were wide in their faded blue jeans. Some of them donned Earth shoes and T-shirts with slogans like "A Woman Needs a Man Like a Fish Needs a Bicycle." They weren't in the least bit ashamed. But I was. I remember thinking, "I will never let myself look like that."

Shortly after the march, I began to tease my mother. "Why can't you be a *real* mother?" I asked. It became a running joke between us. She'd say, "Look, a real mother!" pointing at prim women in matching clothes and frosted lipstick at the shopping mall. We'd laugh together, but there was a serious side to it all. I wanted my sixties mother to grow up, to stop protesting and acting out—to be "normal." I loved her, but at the same time craved conformity. In my mind, real mothers wore crisp floral dresses and diamond engagement rings; my mother wore blue jeans and a Russian wedding ring given to her from a high-school boyfriend. (She had lost the ring my father gave to her.) Real mothers got married in white frills before a church; my mother wed my father in a silver lamé mini-dress which she later donated to us kids for Barbie doll clothes. Real mothers painted their nails and colored their hair; my mother used henna. And while real mothers polished the house with lemon-scented Pledge, our house had dog hair stuck to everything.

My mother scolded me, saying I wanted her to be more "bourgeois." Bourgeois or not, to me, *real* equaled what I saw on television and in the movies, whether it was the sensible blond Carol Brady or the Stephen Spielberg suburban landscape—a world so utterly normal that the surreal could occur within it. At night, visions of white picket fences and mothers in housedresses danced in my head. I dreamed of station wagons, golden retrievers, and brief-case-toting fathers who came home at five o'clock to the smell of meat loaf wafting from the kitchen. But *real* was something I could never achieve with my white socialist mother, my black intellectual father who visited on Sundays, and our spotted mongrel from the dog pound, because most of all, real was a white girl—and that was something I could never, ever be.

I was fourteen when I first sat perched on a kitchen stool and allowed a friend to put an iron to my head —a curling iron, that is. She wasn't pressing my hair straight. Just the opposite. She was trying to give my straight, chestnut-brown hair some curl, and I wasn't taking no for an answer. So far, I had been mistaken for almost everything—Italian, Greek, Jewish, Pakistani—but never for black. My features and hair brought me forever short of Negritude. In a 1980s twist on the classic tragic mulatta, I was determined to pass as black. And if that wasn't possible, at least with my hair-sprayed "crunchy curls"

I could pass as Puerto Rican. I remember lying in bed at night and smelling Spanish cooking from the apartment downstairs; I would close my eyes and fantasize that I was actually Puerto Rican, that everything else had been just a bad dream, that my name was Yolanda Rivera, and that I lived in the barrio.

I had dropped my quest for a "real mother" and yearned for something within my reach: a real ethnicity, something other than the half-caste purgatory to which I had been condemned. Now I yearned for Blackness, which, like femininity, was defined by the visible signifiers of the times. In my father's era, these had been a daishiki, an Afro, a fisted pik. No longer. This was still Boston in the 1980s and to be authentically black meant something quite different. Now you had to wear processed hair and Puma sneakers. I remember gazing at my best friend's straightened black hair, at the sheen of the chemicals and the way it never moved, and thinking it was the most beautiful hair I had ever seen. I believed the answer to that ubiquitous question "How can I be down?" lay in cultural artifacts: a Louis Vuitton purse, a Kangol, a stolen Ralph Lauren parka.

On my first day of high school, I went decked out in two-toned jeans, Adidas sneakers, and a red bomber with a fur-lined collar. My hair was frozen in hard curls all over my head and I wore frosty pink lipstick. I snapped my bubblegum and trailed after my sister. She is a year older than me and like most firstborn children, had inherited what I saw as the riches: kinky hair and visible blackness. We sauntered into the cafeteria where everyone hung out before class began. Doug E. Fresh beats boomed from someone's radio. Old friends greeted my sister with hugs; she introduced me and, to my relief, everyone smiled and commented on how much we looked alike. A dark-skinned boy with a shaved-bald head asked my sister where she had been hiding me, and I blushed and glanced away from his steady brown-eyed stare. There, across the cafeteria, my gaze fell on a girl, and we stared at each other with that intensity that could only mean love or hate.

She looked a little like me, but right away I knew she was more authentic than I would ever be. With an olive complexion, loose dark curls, and sad brown eyes, she sat in a cluster of pretty brown-skinned girls. She was smoking and squinting at me from across the hazy cafeteria.

I whispered to my sister: "Who's that girl?"

"That's Sophia."

Sophia whispered something just then to the girls at her table and they giggled. My cheeks began to burn.

I nudged my sister. "Why's she staring at me?"

"Cause David, her boyfriend, has been eyeing you ever since you came in here."

The bald-headed boy—David—winked at me when our eyes met and I heard my sister's voice beside me warn: "Just keep your distance and it'll be okay."

It wasn't. As the year progressed, the tension between me and Sophia escalated. It was as if we took one look at each other and said, "There ain't room in this school for both of us." From her point of view, I threatened her position not only with David, who had a fetish for light-almost-white girls, but also her position in the school. She, like me, had gotten used to her role as "the only one." Her "whiteness" had brought her status within the black world, and she didn't want that threatened by anyone, and certainly not by me with my crunchy-curls.

In a strange way I idolized Sophia, though I would have never admitted it at the time. To me, she was a role model, something to aspire to. She represented what I had spent my whole life searching for: she was the genuine article. While I lived with my white mother in a rambling brown-shingled house, Sophia lived with her black mother in an inner-city townhouse. While my curls were painstakingly acquired, Sophia's were natural. While I was soft, Sophia was hard-core. And of course, while I was the tragedy trying to walk-the-walk and talk-the-talk, Sophia didn't need to try.

David became our battleground. I told my friends and family that I was in love with him and that I despised Sophia. The truth is that Sophia was the real object of my desire. I wanted to be her. But it was just dawning on me that certain things could not be manufactured. By curling my hair, wearing heavy gold hoop earrings, and a bomber jacket, I could not recreate her experience. My imitation of her life could only go skin deep. So my desire for her was transformed into an obsessive envy. If I couldn't be her, I would beat her.

One day I discovered obscenities about me splattered on the girls' room wall—just the regular catty slander, nothing too creative, saying I was a bitch and a ho. But there was a particular violence to the way it had been written, in thick red marker around the bathroom mirrors. In tears, I went to find my big sister. Always my protector, she dragged me to the girls' room after lunch period to set things straight with Sophia once and for all. We found her in there with her girls, skipping class and preening in front of a mirror.

Sister: "Did you write this about my sister?"

Sophia: "She been trying to get with my man all year. That bitch had it comin' to her."

Sister: "I asked you a question. Did you write this about my sister?"

Sophia: "Yeah, I did. And what are you gonna do about it?"

Soon, in the bright spring sunshine, my sister and Sophia came to blows while I stood on the sidelines with the rest of the black population of our school. I had been warned by Sophia's rather hefty cousin that if I jumped in the fight, she would whip my ass. I didn't jump in. And after all was said and done, my sister ended up with a broken nose, Sophia with two black eyes and a scratched up face. The war was over and I got out without a scar. My sister had protected me, and I knew I was a coward, a fake. And as I sat holding my sister's hand in the hospital waiting room, I knew it wasn't blackness I had failed in. It was sisterhood. [1995]

🌿 13

Blazes of Truth

SUSAN SCHNUR

When I was 12 years old, my parents sent me off to Camp Ramah in the Poconos. That June, I was a dull kid in an undershirt from Trenton, New Jersey, outfitted in lime-green, mix-and-match irregulars from E. J. Korvette's. By the end of August, though—exposed as I was, for two months, to suburban Philadelphia's finest pre-adolescent fashion cognoscenti—I had contracted that dread disease: "*JAP*itis."

Symptoms included not only the perfection of an elaborate, all-day triple-sink procedure for dyeing white-wool bobby socks to the requisite shade of dirty white (we called it oyster), but also my sudden, ignominious realization that the discount "Beatlemania" record my mother had bought for me the previous spring was not, after all, sung by the real group.

I'm not even sure that the term *JAP* existed yet back then (I don't think it did), but, in any case, by October I was—more or less—cured. I put the general themes of entitlement, of materialism, of canonized motifs (in those days, Lord and Taylor was the label of choice rather than Bloomingdale's) at the back of my mental medicine chest for the next two decades.

It wasn't until six months ago, actually—while teaching a course at Colgate University called "Contemporary Issues of Jewish Existence"—that I again gave the subject of *JAP*s a moment's pause.

A unit on *JAP*s was decidedly *not* on my course syllabus (I taught the standards: Holocaust—Faith—Immigration—Assimilation—Varieties of Religious Experience—Humor—Israel—Women). But my students, as it turned out, were obsessed with *JAP*s.

Week after week, in personal journals that they were keeping for me, they talked *JAP*s: the stereotypes, dating them, hating them, not *being* them, *JAP* graffiti, *JAP* competitiveness, *JAP*s who gave them the willies back home in Scarsdale over spring break.

I had been raised on moron jokes; *they* had been raised on *JAP* jokes. ("What does a *JAP* do with her asshole in the morning? Dresses him up and sends him to work.")

Little by little, I came to realize that the *JAP* theme was by no means a one-note samba. It was kaleidoscopic and self-revealing; the students plugged it into a whole range of Jewish issues. I began to encourage them to look at their throwaway *JAP* comments with a measure of scrutiny.

The first, and most striking, ostinato in the students' journals was the dissociative one. As one Jewish student framed it, "There are so many *JAP*s in this class, it makes me sick." (An astonishing number of students were desperate to let me know this.)

Since over one-third of the class was not Jewish (the enrollment was 30), and since there was no one in the class that I would have identified sartorially as a *JAP*, this was an interesting fillip.

"That's funny," I started commenting back in these students' journals. "The other students think *you're* a *JAP*."

Eventually, one Jewish student wrote, "Maybe when I talk about *JAP*s and that whole negative thing, it's a way for me to get 'permission' to assimilate."

Another wondered why he feels "like every *JAP* on campus somehow implicates me. That's a very 'minority culture' reflex, isn't it? Why am I so hung up on how everyone else perceives Jews?"

Some students perceived the *JAP* phenomenon, interestingly, as a developmental phase in American Judaism—a phase in which one parades both one's success and one's entitlement. "When my best girlfriend from childhood was bat mitzvahed," wrote one student after reading *A Bintel Brief* and *World of Our Fathers,* "her grandmother gave her a '*JAP*-in-training' diamond-chip necklace. It's like the grandmother was saying, 'When I was your age, I had to sew plackets in a Lower East Side sweatshop. So you girls be *JAP*s. Take whatever you can and be proud of it.'"

A Black student mentioned—during a talk about the socialization of Jewish women—that Jewish women, like their Black counterparts, are encouraged to be extremely competent, but then are double-bound with the message that their competence must *only* be used for frivolous purposes. (Like Goldie Hawn, in *Private Benjamin,* scolding her upholsterer with impressive assertiveness: "I specifically said—the ottoman in mushroom!", or informing her superior officer that she refused to go to Guam because "my hair will frizz.") "Minority women are warned not to be a real threat to anyone," the student explained, "That's how *JAP*s evolve."

Another theme of the students touched on their perception that Jews are sometimes discriminated against not because they are *less* endowed than others, but because they are more endowed (smarter, richer, more "connected"). *JAP*s, then, become, in the words of an Irish Catholic student who was doing readings on theology and the theme of chosenness, "the 'chosen of the chosen.' Unlike Irish Catholics who have been discriminated against because we seem 'un-chosen'," she mused, "people hate *JAP*s because they seem to have everything: money, confidence, style."

Of course, it's probably unnecessary for me to point out that the most prolific *JAP* references had to do with that venerable old feud—the Jewish War-Between-The-Sexes.

One pre-law Jewish male in the class (who was under a lot of pressure and had developed colitis during that semester) stated point-blank that he did not date Jewish women. I was shocked by the number of 20-year-old, seemingly fully-assimilated Jewish males who were right up there with Alexander Portnoy on this subject.

Several students responded to his comment in their journals. "He's angry at *JAP*s," one woman wrote, "because they get to be needy and dependent, whereas the expectations on him are really high."

Another student related the experience of two friends of hers at SUNY Binghamton: "Someone spray-painted the word *JAP* on their dormitory door," she recounted. "But now I wonder—which one of the girls was being called a *JAP*? The one with the dozen Benetton sweaters, or the one who'd gotten 750 on her L-SATs?" The question being, of course, which is ultimately more threatening: the demanding woman or the self-sufficient one?

An Hispanic woman in the class talked about what she called "the dialectic of prejudice"—that is, the contradictory nature of racist or sexist slurs as being, in itself, a diagnostic of irrational bias. "A *JAP* is portrayed as both frigid and nymphomaniacal," she wrote. "She's put down both because of her haughty strut that says, 'I'm indepen-

JAP: The New Antisemitic Code Word

FRANCINE KLAGSBRUN

Isn't it odd that the term *JAP,* referring to a spoiled, self-indulgent woman, should be so widely used at a time when women are working outside their homes in unprecedented numbers, struggling to balance their home lives and their work lives to give as much of themselves as they can to everybody—their husbands, their kids, their bosses?

Jewish women, like women throughout society, are trying to find their own paths, their own voices. And, along with other changes that have taken place, they have been finding themselves Jewishly. And yet we hear the term *JAP* being used, perhaps almost more now than ever before. Why?

The new-found, or rather newly-accepted, drive of women for achievement in many arenas threatens many men. What better put-down of the strong woman than to label her a "Princess"? She is not being attacked as a competitor—that would be too close to home. No—she's called a princess, and that label diminishes her, negating her ambition and her success.

One may note, and rightly so, that there *are* materialistic Jewish women—and men too. But are Jews the only people guilty of excesses in spending? Why should the word "Jewish" be used pejoratively to describe behavior we don't approve of?

I think the answer is that there is an underlying antisemitic message in that label. Loudness is somehow "Jewish." Vulgarity is somehow "Jewish." All the old stereotypes of Jews come into play in the use of the term *JAP.* In this day, polite Christian society would not *openly* make anti-Jewish slurs. But *JAP* is O.K. *JAP* is a kind of code word. It's a way of symbolically winking, poking with an elbow, and saying, "well you know how Jews are—so materialistic and pushy."

What is interesting is that this code word can be used in connection with *women*—the Jewish American *Princess*—and nobody protests its intrinsic antisemitism.   [1980]

---

dent,' and because of her *kvetching* that says, 'I'm dependent.'"

A twist on this theme was provided by a Jewish woman who commented, "Whatever Jewish men call us—cold, hot, leech, bitch—it's all the same thing: They're afraid they can't live up to our standards."

A psych major in the class took a different tack. "It's not that the Jewish male really believes Jewish women are terrible, rather that he simply wants majority culture males to believe it. It's like when territorial animals urinate on a tree," she explained. "It's a minority male's possessive instinct. Like a sign that says, 'Robert Redfords—stay away!'"

Finally, several Jewish students framed their rela-

tions with one another in the context of Jewish family systems. "Lashing out at Jewish women— calling them all *JAP*s or refusing to marry them— is a way to get back at the entire high-expectation, high-pressure Jewish family," stated one student in response to a film I showed in class called "Parenting and Ethnicity." "You can lash out by becoming an academic failure," he went on, "or you can become a doctor—which is less self-destructive—and then simply refuse to marry a Jewish woman."

Towards the end of the term, a feminist friend pointed out to me something I had not considered: that the characterizations of *JAP*s and Yuppies are often identical—the difference being, of course, that a Yuppie designation is still generally taken as neutral or even positive, whereas there is hardly one of us left—I don't think—who would compete for the label of *JAP.*

All in all, I trust that the larger lessons in all of these *JAP* ruminations have not been lost on my students. For example: Why has it become socially sanctioned to use a *Jewish* designation (*JAP*) for a description that fits as many Christians as Jews? Or why—along the same lines—is it okay to use a *female* designation (again, *JAP*) for a description that fits as many men as women? Or, sensing what we now sense, shouldn't we refuse any truck altogether with the term *JAP?*   [1987]

❧ 14

In Search of Liberation

DEBRA KENT

When I joined a women's consciousness-raising group a few years ago, I'm not quite sure what I expected—to discover some bond of understanding with other women, perhaps, to feel myself part of the growing sisterhood of the liberation movement. But through session after session, I listened in amazement and awe as the others delivered outraged accounts of their exploitation at the hands of bosses, boyfriends, and passersby. They were tired of being regarded as sex objects by male chauvinist pigs. All their lives, they lamented, they had been programmed for the confining roles of wife and mother, roles in which their own needs were submerged by those of the men they served.

I had to admit that their indignation was justified. But it was impossible for me to confess my own reaction to their tales of horror, which was a very real sense of envy. Society had provided a place for them as women, however restricting that place might be, and they knew it.

Totally blind since birth, I was seldom encouraged to say, "When I grow up I'll get married and have babies." Instead, my intellectual growth was

nurtured. I very definitely received the unspoken message that I would need the independence of a profession, as I could not count on having the support of a husband.

For myself and for other disabled women, sex discrimination is a secondary issue—in life and in the job market. To the prospective employer, a visible handicap may immediately connote incompetence, and whether the applicant is male or female may never come under consideration at all. In fact, the connotations that disability holds for the public seem, in many ways, to negate sexuality altogether. In a culture where men are expected to demonstrate strength and dominance, the disabled man is regarded as weak and ineffectual. But in social situations he may have an advantage over the disabled woman.

Our culture allows the man to be the aggressor. If he can bolster himself against the fear of rejection, he can make overtures toward starting a relationship. At least he doesn't have to sit home waiting for the telephone to ring.

According to the stereotype, women are helpless creatures to be cuddled and protected. The disabled woman, however, is often merely seen as helpless. A man may fear that she will be so oppressively dependent upon him that a relationship with her may strike him as a terrifying prospect. To prove him wrong she may strive for self-sufficiency, only to have him say that she's too aggressive and unfeminine.

People may pity the disabled woman for her handicap, or admire her for her strength in overcoming it, but she is too unlike other females to be whistled at on the street. Somehow she is perceived as a nonsexual being. If men don't make passes at girls who wear glasses, what chance does a blind girl have, or one in a wheelchair, or a woman with spastic hands?

American culture still pictures the ideal woman: slender, blonde, blue-eyed, and physically perfect. Of course, there is plenty of leeway, and not every man is worried about these cultural stereotypes when choosing a mate. But as long as a woman remains a status symbol to the man who "possesses" her, the living proof of his prowess, the woman with a disability will be at a severe disadvantage. The man who is not completely secure will be afraid to show her off with pride because she is too different.

The worst period for most disabled men and women is probably adolescence, when conformity to the group's norms is all-important. Then, even overweight or a bad case of acne is enough to brand one as a pariah. Things may become easier later on, as emphasis on outward appearances gradually yields to concern with qualities as well. But it is hard to shake off the sense of being an outcast.

Even when she establishes a healthy relationship with a man, the disabled woman may sometimes find herself wondering, "Why does he want me unless there is something wrong with him? If someone else comes along, won't he leave me for her?"

But why, I ask myself, should it ever make a difference to society whether people with disabilities are ever accepted intact—as human beings with minds, feelings, and sexuality? Though we have become more vocal in recent years, we still constitute a very small minority.

Yet the Beautiful People—the slender, fair, and perfect ones—form a minority that may be even smaller. Between these two groups are the average, ordinary citizens: Men who are too short, women who are too tall, people who are too fat or too thin, people with big noses, protruding ears, receding hairlines, and bad complexions. Millions of people go through life feeling self-conscious or downright inadequate, fearing that others will reject them for these physical flaws. Perhaps the struggle of disabled people is really everyone's battle against the binding rules of conformity, the struggle for the right to be an individual.

As I sat in that consciousness-raising group, I realized that disabled women have a long and arduous fight ahead. Somehow we must learn to perceive ourselves as attractive and desirable. Our struggle is not unlike the striving for self-acceptance of the millions of nonhandicapped who also fall short of the Beautiful People image.

Our liberation will be a victory for everyone.

[1987]

🌿 15

Brideland

NAOMI WOLF

Brideland exists primarily in the bridal magazines, which conjure up a fantastic, anachronistic world that really exists nowhere beyond itself. It is a nineteenth-century world, in which major late-twentieth-century events, like the sexual revolution and the rise of the financially self-supporting woman, seem to have transpired only glancingly, to be swept away by a dimity flounce like so much unsightly grit. It is a theme park of upward mobility; in Brideland, in the events surrounding The Event, everyone is temporarily upper middle class: everyone routinely throws catered events and hires musicians and sends engraved invitations and keeps carriages or vintage cars awaiting. At the ceremony itself, things become downright feudal: the bride is treated like a very queen with her court of "maids." She has, perhaps, a child to lift her train, a child to bear her ring, and a sparkling tiara upon her hair. Cinderella is revealed in her true aristocratic radiance at last, and, in the magazines, she is perpetually arriving at the ball.

Brideland has very little to do with the relationship or even the marriage: it is, like any theme park, eternally transient: you enter, you are transformed completely, and then, presumably, you depart. It is a world of lush feminine fantasy, eerily devoid of men, who appear, if at all, as shadow figures retrieving luggage or kneeling before the bride in a state of speechless awe. Brideland has an awful lot to say about what women want that they are not getting, and it taught me a thing or two about myself.

My own initiation was abrupt. Shortly after we made our announcement, I picked up one of those magazines, mostly to find out what the rules were that I was bound to be breaking. As I turned page after page, I started to change. Long-buried yearnings surfaced, a reminder, which little else gives me, that until I was six, I inhabited a world unchanged by the 1970s' women's movement. Somehow, I had picked up atavistic feelings about The Bride that I would never have recognized in my conscious, feminist, and more skeptical mind.

By page 16 my capacity for irony was totally paralyzed. I tried hard to activate it but, as in a dream, I was powerless; it wouldn't budge. By page 32 I was hypnotized; by the time I reached the end, the honeymoon section—for the magazines are structured chronologically, as if they want to be sure you know what comes first—I had acquired new needs; blind, overwhelming, undeniable needs. The fantasies I had put away in 1966 with Bridal Barbie resurfaced with a vengeance. I needed . . . garters! And engraved stationery—engraved, not printed! And fetching little lace mitts; and a bouquet that trailed sprays of stephanotis! And heavens, maybe a veil or mantilla of some kind—down my back, of course, not over my face—would not be as unthinkable as I had thought.

You must understand: this is coming from a woman who had viewed all traditional wedding appurtenances as if they represented death by cuteness. While I am the product of an egalitarian marriage, and fervently believe in the possible goodness of life partnership, I have had such a strong resistance to all things matrimonial that when I pass Tiffany's I break out in a cold sweat. I could imagine eloping; or a civil ceremony; or even an alternative ceremony, so creatively subversive that it would be virtually unrecognizable for what it is. But not—never—a wedding.

Part of my aversion comes from my ambivalence, not about the man—about whom I have no doubts —but about the institution. How can I justify sealing such a private, precious relationship with a legal bond that lets a man rape his wife in fourteen states? How can I endorse an institution that, in the not-too-distant past, essentially conveyed the woman over to her husband as property, denying her even the right to her own property? How can I support a system that allows me to flaunt my heterosexual relationship brazenly, but forbids deeply committed gay and lesbian friends of mine to declare their bonds in the same way? How can I ask my love to be sanctioned by a legal order that leaves divorcing women to struggle in a desperately unevenly matched battle in sexist courts for money and custody of children? And, less profoundly, but no less urgently, if I were to do it, what on earth would I wear?

Brideland lulls the reader into a haze of romantic acquisitiveness that leaves most such political considerations firmly outside the threshold. The magazines' articles about the origins of different rituals leave no doubt as to the naked patriarchalism of the ceremony's origins. Bridesmaids were originally dressed similarly to the bride so as to confuse marauders who would wish to abduct the woman. Groomsmen were warriors whose role was to help the bridegroom fight off the would-be kidnapers. The cedar chest and mother-of-the-bride embroidered handkerchiefs—even the beading and faux-pearling and glitter down the bodices of many dresses—are all vestigial reminders that brides and their trousseaus were essentially chattel to be bartered, bearing a specific value. Even the word *honeymoon* derives from the Old English custom of sending the couple off for a month to drink honeyed ale, as a way to relax sexual inhibitions and, presumably, ease the anxieties of virginal teenage brides who most likely had had little contact with their mates, and whose attraction to them was generally considered an irrelevance. But in the glossy pages, these fairly unnerving details fade into quaintness.

The centerpiece of Brideland is, of course, the dress, and it is this that has elicited my deepest buried fantasies. For a reason that for a long time was mysterious, I felt that I had to, but absolutely had to, create a wedding dress that had an eighteenth-century bodice, three-quarter-length sleeves, and an ankle-length skirt with voluminous panniers. I have since homed in on the trace-memory, and realize that the transcendentally important look of my dress on the critical day was predetermined by a drawing of a milkmaid in the A. A. Milne (creator of Pooh) children's book, *Now We Are Six*.   [1995]

16

On Being a "Good Girl": Implications for Latinas in the United States

ELISA DÁVILA

I am an immigrant Latina. My gender, my ethnicity, and my status as an "émigré," shape and define my life and the work I do. I was born in Colombia, a beautiful but violent country. The early years of my life were marked by the horrors of civil war.[1] I grew up witnessing not only the desolation left by civil war but also experiencing the inner devastation forced upon women by the socially constructed demands of *good-girlism*.[2] As a woman, I have had a major struggle to overcome the senseless impositions of a patriarchal and sexist society, which has established different standards of behavior for men and women. This is particularly relevant for Latina women living in a *machista* society and having to conform to the dictates of *marianismo*.

The origins and ideology of *marianismo* and how it affects women were first discussed by Evelyn Stevens in 1973. In the essay "Marianismo: The Other Face of Machismo in Latin America," she writes:

> Latin American mestizo cultures—from the Rio Grande to the Tierra del Fuego—exhibit a well-defined pattern of beliefs and behavior centered on popular acceptance of a stereotype of the ideal woman. This stereotype, like its *macho* counterpart, is ubiquitous in every social class. There is near universal agreement on what a "real woman" is like and how she should act. Among the characteristics of this ideal are semidivinity, moral superiority, and spiritual strength. This spiritual strength engenders abnegation, that is, an infinite capacity for humility and sacrifice. No self-denial is too great for the Latin American woman, no limit can be divined to her vast store of patience with the men of her world. Although she may be sharp with her daughters—and even cruel to her daughter-in-law—she

is and must be complaisant toward her own mother and her mother-in-law for they, too, are reincarnations of the great mother. She is also submissive to the demands of the men: husbands, sons, fathers, brothers.[3]

Stevens's definitions of *machismo* and *marianismo* have been criticized and, at times, dismissed by some Latin American feminists who consider them as an exaggerated portrayal of gender relations in Latin America.[4] But the basic premises of *marianismo* have been accepted by therapists, counselors, and other health practitioners working with Hispanic/Latina women in the United States. In a recent book, Rosa María Gil and Carmen Inoa Vazquez explain:

> But there is another side to the coin of *machismo*, which is equally rigidly enforced and deeply woven into the fabric of Latino/a life. It is called *marianismo;* it is the mortar holding antiquated cultural structures firmly in place, and it forms the core of the Maria Paradox. While discussed in academic literature—first in a ground-breaking essay by Evelyn P. Stevens in 1973, and subsequently by such eminent academicians as Sally E. Romero, Julia M. Ramos McKay, Lillian Comas-Diaz, and Luis Romero—as far as we know, it has never before been presented to the general reader.[5]

As a young woman, I realized that I did not like being what was considered a *good girl* in my culture. I was aware of the different treatment given to the males in the family (brothers, cousins, friends). While men were allowed the freedom to go alone into town, to stay up late, to party all night long, and particularly to wait around to be served by the women around them, my sisters and I were held to different standards. The *Manual de urbanidad y buenas maneras (The Manual of Urbanity and Good Manners)* by Manuel Antonio Carreño was constantly enforced on my sisters and me.[6]

Carreño's book was (still is) the catechism of the do's and don'ts for children, but particularly for young women. It covered everything including how to be a good Catholic and a good patriot; how to pray, how to dress, to socialize, to sit at the table and how to eat; how to respond to adults, how to look or not to look at people, particularly at boys; and so on. The topics discussed had to do with the conduct and behavior women should exhibit in order to gain social acceptance. Many of the prescriptions would help females keep appearances, thereby reinforcing the oppressive notions of Catholic morality, race, and class. Compulsory heterosexuality was emphasized, but sexual education was taboo, except for the absolute commandment of no premarital sex and virginity for unmarried women. If one learned to behave according to these rules, one would be praised as a good and adorable girl who would be able to get married and have a family.

Being a *good girl* meant denying big chunks of myself such as the freedom to choose a career over a husband, to work and live away from home, or the basic right to know my feelings and to experience my own body. In a patriarchal society like Colombia's, a woman is expected to conform to a set of rules that dictate the manner by which she can act, dress, talk, have sex, even think. A woman is supposed to accept domesticity and motherhood as the two guiding forces of her life.

> Home. Family. Honor. These are the guiding principles of female-male relations that have remained constant from 1492 to the present. The typical Latin American family is portrayed as patriarchal in structure with an authoritarian male head, bilateral kinship, and a submissive mother and wife concerned with the domestic sphere.[7]

To survive under *goodgirlism,* a woman undergoes a major displacement or disconnection inside her own self. Caught between the expectations of family and community and her individual needs and desires, a Latina is at war with herself. The rewards given to her by society for conforming—protection, security, relationships, alliances, and all the other status-related goods and benefits of a good woman —do not serve to end the war. For in the long process of adjustment to the imperatives of *machismo and marianismo,* a woman suffers from emotional alienation from her own feelings, physical and aesthetic estrangement from her body, social isolation, betrayal of her own gender, and silencing of her own voice.

As an adolescent, I also realized that in order to be other than the ideal subservient, suffering, and chaste woman, destined for motherhood and domesticity, I had to be different from the women in my family, from the women in the large household where I grew up, and from the women around me at school, at church, in the neighborhood. It was a painful realization, for I had to reconcile the expectations of my family and community that were at odds with my own inner imperatives.

It is in the process of reconciling these contradictory messages that a Latina may find the roots of her inner strength and the driving impetus for change. I did not come to these realizations alone or in a vacuum, nor did I arrive at the place where I am now without the example and encouragement of other women, many of them ignored by the recorders of history. Since the early days of European colonization, women's presence in the larger social structure and their universe have been ignored. Historians have traditionally excluded such experience from their writings, except for some notable examples (mostly notorious ones), such as queens, courtesans, mistresses, and nuns. The norm has been to ignore women (women as absence) or to portray them as obstacle, as the other, as atavism, or as foible.

In my own life, I have been inspired by teachers, union organizers, women fighting for human rights in Argentina, Chile, Guatemala, El Salvador, and immigrant women working in sweat shops and maquiladoras in New York City and the Mexican-American border to understand their strength and to emulate their courage to change. These women have some character traits in common: they all have aspired to be *other than* the externally imposed cultural model of the *good woman,* and they do it with unabashed dignity and great courage.

To become *other than,* which means, unlike many of the women in my household, or in my neighborhood, or in my school, I had to cross many borders: educational, sexual, national, linguistic, cultural. With each crossing, I was breaking familiar, many times, psychological bonds that tethered me to the extended family structure and the community.

As I wandered into new inner and outer spaces and geographies, I entered new worlds where there were no female roles to emulate. In the pursuit of my own individuality and my own voice, I went abroad to college, and later I went to teach away from home. In doing so my life became a difficult experiment in overcoming loneliness and fear. Not having received as a child and as a young woman the skills to be anything else but a *good girl,* I did not know how to survive away from *marianismo* and from a class system that determined my place in the social organization. It seemed that my identity was directly linked to being a "señora [casada] de," a married woman, which in Spanish literally means *the woman of* so-and-so.[8] The future depended not so much on my intelligence but on having a home of my own, with a husband, children, and all the other status-related goods, relationships, alliances, and cultural identifiers of an upper-middle-class woman.[9]

After crossing national and linguistic borders and immigrating to the United States, I began living away from the expectations and demands of the family core and the extended family of friends and acquaintances. I entered the realm of being the *alien/ other.* A major displacement took place. In a *machista* society, like Colombia where I was born and raised, a woman is the *other* in terms of intergender and class relations. As the *other* she is the object of sexual and sexist oppression and dominance on the part of the males of the society, condoned, of course, by the *marianista* female culture. But, as a Latina immigrant in the United States, one becomes the *other* in terms of ethnic and linguistic categorizations. Also, within the prejudicial male chauvinism of Anglo culture, a Latina becomes either a desirable *other,* objectified and used as a sensuous and passionate being, or an undesirable "illegal" with no rights.[10]

Married to an Anglo man who brought into my life a new set of expectations and ideas of the concept of a "good American wife" and striving to acculturate and function in the new environment, I began to feel at the margins of society, and on the edge of disintegration. With my hyphenated name that caused a severe rift with my mother-in-law, I became no more than a hyphen to the new family.[11] This *otherness* made me long for what I had left behind. In this new environment, lacking recognition from the family I had married into and not quite understanding its cultural norms and social trans-

actions, I began to idealize my past and my background (family, traditions, friends, etc.). I needed my "cultural security blanket." In *The Maria Paradox,* Rosa María Gil and Carmen Inoa Vazquez explain this syndrome:

> In our new life in the United States, there is so much that is unfamiliar and frightening, even to the best-adjusted among us. When we are adjusting to the new culture, or acculturating, some Latinas might feel extremely vulnerable and especially terrified of losing the affection and esteem of loved ones, whose presence helps to anchor our sense of self. Too often, out of that fear, they regress rather than move on.[12]

Patriarchy offers some rewards to the women who conform. Among others, there is social recognition, stability, financial security, and "machista gallantry." There is some attraction to the discourse of family unity and support, motherhood and domestic security. Being a *good girl* seemed attractive to the lonely, newly married woman walking the empty streets of a suburban American neighborhood. Homesickness and silence fueled the desire to return, to give up, to find refuge under the normative system of male oppression and Catholic patriarchy I had left. After all, cultural and familiar oppression and gallant machismo seemed better than the cultural exile I was experiencing in the new country.

To survive, I plunged into working and learning English, as well as the language of acculturation. Alongside my new skills came a divorce, different jobs, other lovers, and a new identity. One family rejected me, the other wanted me to go back to Colombia and be protected by the extended family. I refused to go back with the excuse of finishing my Ph.D., which I could not have done in Colombia. But guilt and solitude made me doubt my decision to stay in the United States. Was I becoming a *bad girl?* The dualistic and manichean worldview that Western culture imposes on us did not give me anything but a set of oppositions to characterize my new reality: good/bad, male/female, decent/prostitute, mother/spinster. New labels and new categories were superimposed on the old ones: divorced, immigrant, Hispanic, alien, "mojada" (wet back).

They did not replace the identity of the young woman who came; they just covered the rupture of separation, of not belonging to either one of the two cultures. As time passed, I abandoned the idea of going back home, and the security of a tenured academic job sealed the impossibility of return.

In the eyes of the society where I grew up, I am successful and, perhaps, secretly admired. But I am also the object of pity and compassion for being a failure as a woman, for not having procreated, and particularly for not having a male at my side. When I travel home or to other Latin American countries, invariably men and women ask me not about my work, or the articles and poems I write, but about husband and children. My responses usually elicit some pitiful comments by women that go more or less like the following:

- "Y no te sientes solita, mi hijita?" (And, don't you feel very alone, my child?)
- "Y dónde está tu familia?" (And where is your family?)
- "Pero, de verdad, no piensas volver donde tu familia?" (But, tell me the truth, don't you want to go back to your family?)
- "Si, mi hija, está bien estudiar, pero también hay que hacer la casa." (Yes, my dearest, it is good to study, but it is also important to make a home.)
- "Y, eso del Ph.D., te va a cuidar cuando estés viejita?" (And that thing called the Ph.D., is it going to take care of you when you are old?)

Men's responses can be very aggressive because they interpret my divorced status either as an invitation to sexual advances or they feel some unstated discomfort about my sexuality that does not include them.

No matter how far I have traveled, the powerful ideological force of sexism that determines the behavior of men and women, and the ways in which girls are raised, or the manner in which women are expected to act, dress, talk, have sex, continues to haunt me. The basic and culturally constructed definers of the female condition are still the parameters by which I am judged and accepted.   [1998]

NOTES

1. Colombia's history, like that of so many Latin American countries, can be described as a relentless unsuccessful attempt to define and practice democracy. For almost two decades, beginning in the mid-1940s, the traditional conservative forces, supported by the Catholic church and the military, unleashed a bloody period of civil strife in Colombia. Liberal forces made up primarily of intellectuals, union workers, students, poor farm laborers, and the disenfranchised masses of urban centers fought against the military and the police. As in the case of the Mexican Revolution of 1910, the Bolivian and Guatemalan Revolutions of the 1950s, and many other revolutionary movements in Latin America, a popular uprising with political overtones and civil rights goals resulted in indiscriminate killing and devastation. A military coup and dictatorship ended the civil war, but not the abuse of the poor by the rich or the poverty and illiteracy of the masses. The dream of equality and freedom was crushed.

2. In 1995, for about eight months, a group of college professors at SUNY–New Paltz (Drs. Sue Books, Ann V. Dean, and Elaine Kolitch), a pastoral counselor (Rev. Kathy Brady), and I worked on trying to understand what it meant to be a *good girl* in different cultures. We presented a panel discussion on this topic at the April 1996 American Educational Research Association (AERA) Conference in New York, "A Cross-Cultural Autobiographical Excavation of *Good-Girlism.*" The following was the group's definition of *good-girlism.*

   > *Good-girlism*
   > ". . . is a powerful ideology, often invisible to us in our everyday practices and relations, that can be used to monitor female identity in private and public spheres.
   > . . . is a historical, cross-cultural phenomenon, constantly reified by institutions (family, school, church, state, etc.) that benefit from having oppressed members.
   > . . . thrives in discursive practices that mediate moral selfhood.
   > . . . is bred and nurtured in the moral/emotional tyranny that threatens to render us illegitimate should we opt out of the unspoken agreement: protect me and I will legitimate/love/protect you."

3. Evelyn P. Stevens. "Marianismo: The Other Face of Machismo in Latin America," in Ann Pescatello (ed.), *Female and Male in Latin America* (Pittsburgh, PA: University of Pittsburgh Press, 1973), pp. 94–95.

4. See, for example, Josefina Zoraida Vásquez, "Women's Liberation in Latin America: Toward a History of the Present," in Gertrude M. Yeager (ed.), *Confronting Change, Challenging Tradition. Women in Latin American History* (Wilmington, DE: Scholarly Resources Books, 1994), pp. 18–25.

5. Rosa Maria Gil and Carmen Inoa Vazquez, *The Maria Paradox* (New York: Putnam's, 1996), p. 6.

6. Manual Antonio Carreño, *Compendio manual de urbanidad y buenas maneras,* Unica edición completa (Colombia, 1994). *Urbanidad* is a Spanish noun that means how to behave in an urban manner, exhibiting the characteristics of a person living in a city. Carreño, like many other Spanish and Latin American male educators, believes that education consists of a set of norms and rules of behavior that will teach children how to act in a decent, patriotic, and moral manner inspired by European tradition. The oppo-

sitions—civilization versus barbarism, urban versus rural, Christian versus non-Christian—emphasized a hierarchical order based on gender and class differences. The education of girls, and of members of the "weaker sex" in Latin America, was traditionally influenced by the dictates of the Catholic church and the state. See Zoraida Vásquez's, op. cit., pp. 18–25. Carreño's book has influenced generations of Latin American men and women all over the continent.

7. Yeager, "Introduction," op. cit. p. xi.

8. "In Spanish the verb 'to marry,' *casarse*, literally means 'to put oneself into a house.' A married woman is referred as *casada* (housed in) not only because of a perceived biological tie to children or because she may not be physically or mentally suited for other labor but also because, under the patriarchal system, family honor resides with her." Yeager, op. cit., p. xi.

9. Hispanic culture limits us "by defining us first and foremost as mothers [and wives], and because it refuses to accept families headed by lesbian or gay couples." Ana María Isasi-Díaz, *En la lucha. In the Struggle: Elaborating a mujerista Theology* (Minneapolis: Fortress Press, 1993), p. 20.

10. I recommend the film *Carmen Miranda: Bananas Is My Business* by Helena Solberg (New York: Noon Pictures, 1994) to understand some of the issues of exploitation, discrimination, and stereotyping of Latin American women in the United States.

11. My former mother-in-law could never understand why I did not want to be just Mrs. Smith and preferred to be called Mrs. Dávila-Smith.

12. Gil and Inoa Vazquez, op. cit., p. 24.

 17

not a pretty girl

ANI DI FRANCO

i am not a pretty girl
that is not what i do
i ain't no damsel in distress
and i don't need to be rescued
so put me down punk

wouldn't you prefer a maiden fair
isn't there a kitten
stuck up a tree somewhere

i am not an angry girl
but it seems like
i've got everyone fooled
every time I say something
they find hard to hear
they chalk it up to my anger
and never to their own fear
imagine you're a girl
just trying to finally come clean
knowing full well they'd prefer
you were dirty
and smiling
and i'm sorry
but I am not a maiden fair
and I am not a kitten
stuck up a tree somewhere
generally my generation
wouldn't be caught dead
working for the man
and generally I agree with them
trouble is you got to have yourself
an alternate plan
i have earned my disillusionment
i have been working all of my life
i am a patriot
i have been fighting the good fight
and what if there are
no damsels in distress
what if i knew that
and I called your bluff
don't you think every kitten
figures out how to get down
whether or not you ever show up

i am not a pretty girl
i don't really want to be a pretty girl
i want to be more than a pretty girl   [1995]

Learning Gender

We learn about gender—ideas about what it means to be female and male—in a variety of overt and subtle ways. Images of women are communicated through the language we use, media depictions of women, direct messages from family, friends, and teachers, and many other sources. In this section, we begin exploring this process through three women's descriptions of how family expectations, peer norms, and cultural traditions affected them and their ideas of what it meant to be a girl.

Murielle Minard's poem, "The Gift," describes a doll given to a girl on her seventh birthday. Beautiful and perfect, the fragile doll symbolizes the essence of femininity. The doll is to be admired for her beauty, never played with lest she be damaged. In "Allegra Maud Goldman" by Edith Konecky, a young girl becomes aware of her family's expectations that she be graceful in dance class and nurturing and protective of her older brother. Allegra astutely realizes that her brother enjoys privileges that she does not.

Susan Jane Gilman considers the powerful influence that Barbie has on young girls' emerging sense of femininity. She recalls that many women have a nostalgic reaction to Barbie, but that she and her friends realized that "if you didn't look like Barbie, you didn't fit in." The voices of these ethnically diverse women show us that they have experienced similar messages about girls' value and worth in our society.

School experiences are another powerful socializing force. In a variety of ways, female students learn more than academic material in the classroom. Here, they also learn about the norms for appropriate behavior in our culture and begin to consider how well they will measure up to those standards. Myra Sadker, David Sadker, and colleagues describe a series of classroom practices and dynamics prevalent in today's schools that perpetuate a bias against girls' educational achievement. Lee Anne Bell describes dilemmas that interfere with girls' success in school, and highlights strategies girls use to deal with the individualistic, competitive atmosphere of the classroom.

Accepted patterns of interpersonal and nonverbal communication reinforce unequal power relationships between men and women. The ways in which women and men address one another, disclose personal information, and even look at each other during conversations communicate messages about differences in status and power. Nancy Henley and Jo Freeman's article, written in 1979, was instrumental in calling attention to subtle yet powerful patterns of sexism in male-female communication.

One of the most influential purveyors of social norms is the media. From television to print and electronic media, norms projected through these avenues shape our views of what it means to female. Anastasia Higginbotham addresses the impact of fashion and beauty magazines on teenage girls. Through both advertising and editorial materials, these magazines encourage their readers to pursue strategies for "getting a guy, and dropping 20 pounds." Similarly, much attention has been directed at the negative portrayal of women in music. The lyrics of many contemporary songs depict women in demeaning ways, often reducing them to sex objects and caricatures of passivity and dependence. Venise Berry and Naomi Weisstein approach this issue from two vantage points. Berry traces the shift from degrading images of women in rap music dominated by male singers, to the current efforts of African-American women rap artists who challenge these images by rapping about women taking control in their lives. Recalling an earlier time when she was a member of a women's band that "challenged all the demeaning imperatives for women in music," Weisstein celebrates the emerging voices of women whom she dubs "mutineers." These women depart from the tradition of singing "endless litanies of Suffering Abject Devotion to men." Instead, they represent a new breed of women who are angry about women's position in society. Berry and Weisstein show us that despite the pervasive sexist images of women in our culture, young women are finding new and exciting avenues for creatively expressing themselves in a positive and empowering way. This is illustrated in the song "Video," as India.Arie forcefully asserts, "I'm not the average girl in your video, my worth is not determined by the price of my clothes . . ." Indi.Arie is part of a movement of young black women musicians defying traditional expectations of femininity. Along with artists such as Erykah Badu, Macy Gray, and Jill Scott, she is forging a powerful new direction in contemporary music.

   This part closes with a fictional exploration of what might happen if society abandoned all traditional gender expectations of girls and boys. In "X: A Fabulous Child's Story," Lois Gould tells the story of Baby X, a child whose gender is unspecified as part of a social experiment. This engaging account highlights the many seemingly insignificant ways children and adults learn sexism, giving us a glimpse of what might occur if we risked changing our ideas about traditional sex roles.

 18

The Gift

MURIELLE MINARD

On my seventh birthday
A beloved uncle
Gave me a doll.
She was a beautiful creature
With blue eyes
That opened and shut,

Golden curls
And a blue velvet dress.

Once a week,
On Sunday afternoon,
My mother would sit me
In a chair
And place the doll in my arms.
I was not to disturb its perfection
In any way,
I would sit there
Transfixed
By its loveliness

And mindful
Of my mother's wishes.

After a time
She would take the doll from me,
Rewrap it carefully
In tissue,
Put it back into its own
Long, gray box
And place it
High on the closet shelf,
Safe from harm.

To this doll
Nothing must happen.   [1984]

 19

klaus barbie, and other dolls i'd like to see

SUSAN JANE GILMAN

For decades, Barbie has remained torpedo-titted, open-mouthed, tippy-toed and vagina-less in her cellophane coffin—and, ever since I was little, she has threatened me.

Most women I know are nostalgic for Barbie. "Oh," they coo wistfully; "I used to *loooove* my Barbies. My girlfriends would come over, and we'd play for hours . . ."

Not me. As a child, I disliked the doll on impulse; as an adult, my feelings have actually fermented into a heady, full-blown hatred.

My friends and I never owned Barbies. When I was young, little girls in my New York City neighborhood collected "Dawns." Only seven inches high, Dawns were, in retrospect, the underdog of fashion dolls. There were four in the collection: Dawn, dirty blond and appropriately smug; Angie, whose name and black hair allowed her to pass for Italian or Hispanic; Gloria, a redhead with bangs and green eyes (Irish, perhaps, or a Russian Jew?); and Dale, a black doll with a real afro.

Oh, they had their share of glitzy frocks—the tiny wedding dress, the gold lamé ball gown that shredded at the hem. And they had holes punctured in the bottoms of their feet so you could impale them on the model's stand of the "Dawn Fashion Stage" (sold separately), press a button and watch them revolve jerkily around the catwalk. But they also had "mod" clothes like white go-go boots and a multi-colored dashiki outfit called "Sock It to Me" with rose-colored sunglasses. Their hair came in different lengths and—although probably only a six-year-old doll fanatic could discern this—their facial expressions and features were indeed different. They were as diverse as fashion dolls could be in 1972, and in this way, I realize now, they were slightly subversive.

Of course, at that age, my friends and I couldn't spell subversive, let alone wrap our minds around the concept. But we sensed intuitively that Dawns were more democratic than Barbies. With their different colors and equal sizes, they were closer to what we looked like. We did not find this consoling—for we hadn't yet learned that our looks were something that required consolation. Rather, our love of Dawns was an offshoot of our own healthy egocentrism. We were still at that stage in our childhood when little girls want to be everything special, glamorous and wonderful—and believe they can be.

As a six-year-old, I remember gushing, "I want to be a ballerina, and a bride, and a movie star, and a model, and a queen . . ." To be sure, I was a disgustingly girly girl. I twirled. I skipped. I actually wore a tutu to school. (I am not kidding.) For a year, I refused to wear blue. Whenever the opportunity presented itself, I dressed up in my grandmother's pink chiffon nightgowns and rhinestone necklaces and paraded around the apartment like the princess of the universe. I dressed like my Dawn dolls—and dressed my Dawn dolls like me. It was a silly, fabulous narcissism—but one that sprang from a crucial self-love. These dolls were part of my fantasy life and an extension of my ambitions. Tellingly, my favorite doll was Angie, who had dark brown hair, like mine.

But at some point, most of us prima ballerinas experienced a terrible turning point. I know I did. I have an achingly clear memory of myself, standing before a mirror in all my finery and jewels, feeling suddenly ridiculous and miserable. *Look at yourself,* I remember thinking acidly. *Nobody will ever like you.* I could not have been older than eight. And then later, another memory: my friend Allison confiding in me, "The kids at my school, they all hate my red hair." Somewhere, somehow, a message seeped into our consciousness telling us that we weren't good enough to be a bride or a model or a queen or anything because we weren't pretty enough. And this translated into not smart enough or likable enough, either.

Looks, girls learn early, collapse into a metaphor for everything else. They quickly become the defining criteria for our status and our worth. And somewhere along the line, we stop believing in our own beauty and its dominion. Subsequently, we also stop believing in the power of our minds and our bodies.

Barbie takes over.

Barbie dolls had been around long before I was born, but it was precisely around the time my friends and I began being evaluated on our "looks" that we became aware of the role Barbie played in our culture.

Initially, my friends and I regarded Barbies with a sort of vague disdain. With their white-blond hair, burnt orange "Malibu" skin, unblinking turquoise eyes and hot-pink convertibles, Barbie dolls represented a world utterly alien to us. They struck us as clumsy, stupid, overly obvious. They were clearly somebody else's idea of a doll—and a doll meant for vapid girls in the suburbs. Dawns, my friend Julie and I once agreed during a sleepover, were far more hip.

But eventually, the message of Barbie sunk in. Literally and metaphorically, Barbies were bigger than Dawns. They were a foot high. They merited more plastic! More height! More visibility! And unlike Dawns, which were pulled off the market in the mid-'70s, Barbies were ubiquitous and perpetual bestsellers.

We urban, Jewish, Black, Asian and Latina girls began to realize slowly and painfully that if you didn't look like Barbie, you didn't fit in. Your status was diminished. You were less beautiful, less valuable, less worthy. *If you didn't look like Barbie, companies would discontinue you.* You simply couldn't compete.

I'd like to think that, two decades later, my anger about this would have cooled off—not heated up. (I mean, it's a *doll* for chrissake. Get over it.) The problem, however, is that despite all the flag-waving about multiculturalism and girls' self-esteem these days, I see a new generation of little girls receiving the same message I did twenty-five years ago, courtesy of Mattel. I'm currently a "big sister" to a little girl who recently moved here from Mexico. When I first began spending time with her, she drew pictures of herself as she is: a beautiful seven-year-old with café au lait skin and short black hair. Then she began playing with Barbies. Now she draws pictures of both herself and her mother with long, blond hair. "I want long hair," she sighs, looking woefully at her drawing.

A coincidence? Maybe, but Barbie is the only toy in the Western world that human beings actively try to mimic. Barbie is not just a children's doll; it's an adult cult and an aesthetic obsession. We've all seen the evidence. During Barbie's thirty-fifth anniversary, a fashion magazine ran a "tribute to Barbie," using live models posing as dolls. A New York museum held a "Barbie retrospective," enshrining Barbie as a pop artifact—at a time when most human female pop artists continue to work in obscurity. Then there's Pamela Lee. The Barbie Halls of Fame. The websites, the newsletters, the collectors' clubs. The woman whose goal is to transform herself, via plastic surgery, into a real Barbie. Is it any wonder then that little girls have been longing for generations to "look like Barbie"—and that the irony of this goes unchallenged?

For this reason, I've started calling Barbie dolls "Klaus Barbie dolls" after the infamous Gestapo commander. For I now clearly recognize what I only sensed as a child. This "pop artifact" in an icon of Aryanism. Introduced after the second world war, in the conservatism of the Eisenhower era (and rumored to be modeled after a German prostitute by a man who designed nuclear warheads), Barbies, in their "innocent," "apolitical" cutesiness, propagate the ideals of the Third Reich. They ultimately succeed where Hitler failed: They instill in legions of little girls a preference for whiteness, for blond hair, blue eyes and delicate features, for an impossible *über*figure, perched eternally and submissively in high heels. In the Cult of the Blond, Barbies are a cornerstone. They reach the young, and they reach them quickly. *Barbie, Barbie!* The Aqua song throbs. *I'm a Barbie girl!*

It's true that, in the past few years, Mattel has made an effort to create a few slightly more p.c. versions of its best-selling blond. Walk down the aisle at Toys-R-Us (and they wonder why kids today can't spell), and you can see a few boxes of American Indian Barbie, Jamaican Barbie, Cowgirl Barbie. Their skin tone is darker and their outfits ethnicized, but they have the same Aryan features and the same "tell-me-anything-and-I'll-believe-it" expressions on their plastic faces. Ultimately, their packaging reinforces their status as "Other." These are "special" and "limited" edition Barbies, the labels announce: clearly *not* the standard.

And, Barbie's head still pops off with ease. Granted, this makes life a little sweeter for the sadists on the playground (there's always one girl who gets more pleasure out of destroying Barbie than dressing her), but the real purpose is to make it easier to swap your Barbies' Lilliputian ball gowns. Look at the literal message of this: Hey, girls, a head is simply a neck plug, easily disposed of in the name of fashion. Lest anyone think I'm nit-picking here, a few years ago, a "new, improved" Talking Barbie hit the shelves and created a brouhaha because one of the phrases it parroted was *Math is hard.* Once again, the cerebrum took a backseat to "style." Similarly, the latest "new, improved" Barbie simply trades in one impossible aesthetic for another: The bombshell has now become the waif. Why? According to a Mattel spokesperson, a Kate Moss figure is better suited for today's fashions. Ah, such an improvement.

Now, I am not, as a rule, anti-doll. Remember, I once wore a tutu and collected the entire Dawn family myself. I know better than to claim that dolls are nothing but sexist gender propaganda. Dolls can be a lightning rod for the imagination, for compan-

ionship, for learning. And they're *fun*—something that must never be undervalued.

But dolls often give children their first lessons in what a society considers valuable—and beautiful. And so I'd like to see dolls that teach little girls something more than fashion-consciousness and self-consciousness. I'd like to see dolls that expand girls' ideas about what is beautiful instead of constricting them. And how about a few role models instead of runway models as playmates? If you can make a Talking Barbie, surely you can make a Working Barbie. If you can have a Barbie Townhouse, surely you can have a Barbie business. And if you can construct an entire Barbie world out of pink and purple plastic, surely you can construct some "regular" Barbies that are more than white and blond. And remember, Barbie's only a doll! So give it a little more inspired goofiness, some real *pizzazz!*

Along with Barbies of all shapes and colors, here are some Barbies I'd personally like to see:

Dinner Roll Barbie. A Barbie with multiple love handles, double chin, a real, curvy belly, generous tits and ass and voluminous thighs to show girls that voluptuousness is also beautiful. Comes with miniature basket of dinner rolls, bucket o' fried chicken, tiny Entenmann's walnut ring, a brick of Sealtest ice cream, three packs of potato chips, a T-shirt reading "Only the Weak Don't Eat" and, of course, an appetite.

Birkenstock Barbie. Finally, a doll made with horizontal feet and comfortable sandals. Made from recycled materials.

Bisexual Barbie. Comes in a package with Skipper and Ken.

Butch Barbie. Comes with short hair, leather jacket, "Silence = Death" T-shirt, pink triangle buttons, Doc Martens, pool cue and dental dams. Packaged in cardboard closet with doors flung wide open. Barbie Carpentry Business sold separately.

Our Barbies, Ourselves. Anatomically correct Barbie, both inside and out, comes with spreadable legs, her own speculum, magnifying glass and detailed diagrams of female anatomy so that little girls can learn about their bodies in a friendly, nonthreatening way. Also included: tiny Kotex, booklets on sexual responsibility. Accessories such as contraceptives, sex toys, expanding uterus with fetus at various stages of development and breast pump are all optional, underscoring that each young women has the right to choose what she does with her own Barbie.

Harley Barbie. Equipped with motorcyle, helmet, shades. Tattoos are non-toxic and can be removed with baby oil.

Body Piercings Barbie. Why should Earring Ken have all the fun? Body Piercings Barbie comes with changeable multiple earrings, nose ring, nipple rings, lip ring, navel ring and tiny piercing gun. Enables girls to rebel, express alienation and gross out elders without actually having to puncture themselves.

Blue Collar Barbie. Comes with overalls, protective goggles, lunch pail, UAW membership, pamphlet on union organizing and pay scales for women as compared to men. Waitressing outfits and cashier's register may be purchased separately for Barbies who are holding down second jobs to make ends meet.

Rebbe Barbie. So why not? Women rabbis are on the cutting edge in Judaism. Rebbe Barbie comes with tiny satin *yarmulke,* prayer shawl, *tefillin,* silver *kaddish* cup, Torah scrolls. Optional: tiny *mezuzah* for doorway of Barbie Dreamhouse.

B-Girl Barbie. Truly fly Barbie in midriff-baring shirt and baggy jeans. Comes with skateboard, hip hop accessories and plenty of attitude. Pull her cord, and she says things like, "I don't *think* so," "Dang, get outta my face" and "You go, girl." Teaches girls not to take shit from men and condescending white people.

The Barbie Dream Team. Featuring Quadratic Equation Barbie (a Nobel Prize–winning mathematician with her own tiny books and calculator), Microbiologist Barbie (comes with petri dishes, computer and Barbie Laboratory) and Bite-the-Bullet Barbie, an anthropologist with pith helmet, camera, detachable limbs, fake blood and kit for performing surgery on herself in the outback.

Transgender Barbie. Formerly known as G.I. Joe. [2000]

 # 20

Allegra Maud Goldman

EDITH KONECKY

"What are you going to be when you grow up?"

My favorite question. Everyone over a certain height asked it. You'd think the whole world turned on what Allegra Maud Goldman was going to *be* when she grew up. I never gave the same answer twice.

"A gentleman farmer," I said to Mrs. Oxfelder, who was helping me into a blue butterfly dress with big gauze wings. She was about to give me my first dancing lesson.

"Ha, ha," said Mrs. Oxfelder, not unkindly. "You can't be a gentleman farmer, Allegra. You're a girl."

"I'm going to change," I said. A girl was something else I was beginning to learn I might be stuck with, and it was not the best thing to be. I had an older brother, David, and he was something it was better to be. He was a boy. He had a bicycle.

"Wouldn't you like to be a dancer?" Mrs. Oxfelder said. "A lovely, graceful vision, music for the eye, making all the people sigh and dream and weep and cry *bravo?*"

"No."

"Using your body to say all the magical, miracle things music says? And love says?"

"No."

"Perhaps you'll change your mind," she said, leading me by the hand into a large room where I stood shivering among a lot of other butterflies, some of them fat.

"This is Allegra, girls, our newest *danseuse.*" She sat down at the piano and played a few arpeggios. "Now, girls, I am going to play some airy spring music and I want you to listen to it. Then I want you to think of yourselves as lovely butterflies, free and joyous in the beautiful sunlit sky. And remember, the delicious flowers are blooming everywhere."

She played and the girls started to flit about, flapping their arms and sucking on imaginary flowers. I couldn't believe my eyes. I clamped them shut and threw myself onto the floor, where I lay spread-eagled. The music abruptly ceased.

"Allegra! What kind of butterfly is that?"

"A dead one in a glass case in the Museum of Natural History," I muttered.

"This is the *dance*," Mrs. Oxfelder said, her voice shrill. "It is not science. Get up off the floor."

It was a long hour, and when my mother came to get me at the end of it, she was wearing her brave face. Where I was concerned, she was usually filled with forebodings.

"Twinkletoes she's not," Mrs. Oxfelder said, handing me over.

"That's why she's here," my mother said.

On the way home in the car I sulked. "I'm not ever going back there again," I said.

"Yes you are."

"David doesn't have to."

"David is a boy."

"I'll kill myself," I said. "I don't see why I have to be some crummy bug."

"You're learning to dance."

"The main thing I'm not going to be when I grow up," I said, "is a dancer."

"You have to learn to be graceful and feminine. You walk like a lumberjack."

The rest of that day I made it a point to flit and leap, waving my hands above my head and giving off whirring sounds. Grandma, my mother's mother, was living with us. She was a widow. She had run away from an arranged marriage and also from something called pogroms (I thought Pogroms was the name of a place) in Russia when she was sixteen, a long time ago, but her English still left something to be desired. Though she spoke Russian, German, Hebrew and Yiddish, and knew a little Polish and Rumanian, her English had obviously been grudgingly acquired out of necessity rather than inclination. She had gone to night school for a term to learn

the English alphabet so we could identify her preserves, thereafter labeled phonetically in Grandma's voice: "Blegber," "Agelber" and "Crebebl."

"St. Vita's dance she's got?" Grandma said to my mother after watching me for a while.

"Ignore her," my mother said.

"Your underwear itches?" she said to me.

"Whirr, whirr," I said.

"Meshugenah," she said, shrugging and returning to her labors. It was the cook's night out and Grandma's night in. She was making kreplach. If it hadn't been for Grandma, we'd have had no ethnic tone at all. For a while, I hovered about, flapping my wings and watching her. These were not your ordinary kreplach. In fact, I've never had any like them since. I've had the meat kind, boiled in soup. I've had ravioli. I've had empanadas and Chinese wontons. But these were dainty, thin-skinned pockets filled with cottage cheese, or pot cheese, or maybe both, sautéed like blintzes in sweet butter until they were slightly crisp, golden, and delicious. I wish I could find them again.

I drifted upstairs to see what David was doing, though I had a pretty good idea what it would be. I was right. He was making one of his transatlantic liners, an elaborate construction using a number of cardboard boxes of different sizes, paper cut into various shapes and colored with crayons, and a lot of paste. David was chiefly concerned with the interiors of his ships. Our father, a dress manufacturer, went to Paris once every year and sometimes twice, and occasionally we would go with our mother to see him off. He always went first-class on a deluxe ship like the *Ile de France* and had a party in his stateroom with champagne and caviar, and while the grown-ups were dealing with these, David and I would trot around exploring the ship. We never really got to see the outside of it, as it was huddled against a pier and we made our entrance through a kind of canopied and carpeted gangplank, so that we could hardly tell where shore ended and ship began. But the inside, we thought, was gorgeous, and we never really believed that all of that endless luxury would actually float. It was like a fairy tale.

So what David was intent on fabricating, in painstaking detail, was the ship's innards, and only the first-class parts. We'd never seen the parts of the ship that made it work. He'd make three or four levels, but the top one was open until the very end, cross-sectioned and fitted with cubicles representing the staterooms, the dining salons, the bar, nightclub, gym, swimming pool and movie theater. He even had little bathrooms with carefully cut out toilets. I had to admire the detail. It was an achievement that took him hours, and sometimes the project spanned a whole weekend. When it was finished, he'd put a top on it with smokestacks, fill the bathtub with water, and sink the ship.

Much later I realized that what he was doing was killing our father, though I don't recall that he ever put any people in the ship. I didn't know about Oedipus then, though I was beginning to learn about other complexes. At the time I thought that David was simply doing one of those dopey destructive things boys did. Sometimes he didn't even wait to watch the ship go down. He'd leave it floating in the tub and some time later he'd come back and fish out the soggy, disintegrated mess and throw it away.

This particular day, he was working on the swimming pool when I fluttered up to watch. He had a mirror from one of our mother's handbags and was carefully fitting it into a square of cardboard.

"How was the dancing lesson?"

"I'd rather not talk about it."

"What'd they make you do?"

I flopped onto the floor and scrutinized his handiwork. He had outdone himself with the movie theater. There was even a screen with a cowboy riding a horse on it, a picture cut out of *The Saturday Evening Post*. Black and white. That was before Technicolor.

"You walked in your sleep again last night," I said. "You peed on the bathroom chair instead of in the toilet."

He looked up, interested, a pale, thin boy with a lot of curly brown hair and greenish eyes, not quite a year and a half older than me. Though we fought a lot, we were close. He didn't have any friends because he was shy and also because he didn't like to do any of the things the kids on the block did, punch-

ball and stickball and territory. The other boys called him a sissy and shunned him. He was taking piano lessons and he was already up to "The Turkish March."

"What I'd like to know," I said, "is why you have to come wake me up and tell me you have to go to the bathroom. I can understand it when you come to tell me the house is on fire or there's a robber looking in the window. But why when you have to go to the bathroom? You know where it is."

"I really peed on the chair?"

"Why do you?"

"Pee on the chair?"

"Wake me up."

"How should I know? I'm asleep, aren't I?"

One of the things I was learning about who I was was that I was sometimes expected to be an older sister to my older brother. With none of the privileges. Because, as my mother explained from time to time, "David is so sensitive. He's not like other boys. He has a lot of fears and an inferiority complex."

"What's an inferiority complex?"

"He doesn't know his own worth."

This was a new idea, and one that surprised me, for David was always lording it over me and telling me how stupid I was.

"We have to help him gain self-confidence."

"What's that?"

"Knowing his own worth."

I thought about this for a while.

"How much *is* David worth?" I said.

It was one of my jobs when he sleepwalked into my room to unburden himself of whatever was on his mind, to fix it somehow and then see him back to his bed. If the house was on fire, I'd say, "I'll go look." Then I'd go look and tell him, "It's okay, the house isn't on fire." Or, "There's nobody at the window. If there was, he's gone away." The night before I'd led him to the toilet and gone out into the hall to wait for him. Then, when I went back in, he was standing at the chair fixing his pajama pants. The chair was at the other end of the bathroom, a white chair with a cane bottom, and there was a puddle underneath it. He must have done it on purpose, even in his sleep. But I didn't say anything; I couldn't see much point in making unnecessary conversation with a sleepwalker. I took his arm and led him back to his bed and waited for him to get into it and said, "Go to sleep," which he was anyhow the whole time, and "Good night." In the morning I got blamed.

"You'd think *I* did it," I protested.

"You shouldn't have let him," my mother said and then added, irrelevantly, "Thank God you'll be starting school soon."   [1987]

❧ 21

Gender Equity in the Classroom: The Unfinished Agenda

MYRA SADKER, DAVID SADKER, LYNN FOX, and MELINDA SALATA

"In my science class the teacher never calls on me, and I feel like I don't exist. The other night I had a dream that I vanished." [1]

Our interviews with female students have taught us that it is not just in science class that girls report the "disappearing syndrome" referred to above. Female voices are also less likely to be heard in history and math classes, girls' names are less likely to be seen on lists of national merit finalists, and women's contributions infrequently appear in school textbooks. Twenty years after the passage of Title IX, the law prohibiting gender discrimination in U.S. schools, it is clear that most girls continue to receive a second-class education.

The very notion that women should be educated at all is a relatively recent development in U.S. history. It was not until late in the last century that the concept of educating girls beyond elementary school took hold. Even as women were gradually allowed to enter high school and college, the guiding principle in education was separate and unequal. Well into the twentieth century, boys and girls were assigned to sex-segregated classes and prepared for very different roles in life.

In 1833 Oberlin became the first college in the United States to admit women; but these early female college students were offered less rigorous courses and required to wait on male students and wash their clothes. Over the next several decades, only a few colleges followed suit in opening their doors to women. During the nineteenth century, a number of forward-thinking philanthropists and educators founded postsecondary schools for women—Mount Holyoke, Vassar, and the other seven-sister colleges. It was only in the aftermath of the Civil War that coeducation became more prevalent on campuses across the country, but even here economics and not equity was the driving force. Since the casualties of war meant the loss of male students and their tuition dollars, many universities turned to women to fill classrooms and replace lost revenues. In 1870 two-thirds of all universities still barred women. By 1900 more than two-thirds admitted them. But the spread of coeducation did not occur without a struggle. Consider that as late as the 1970s the all-male Ivy League colleges did not admit women, and even now state-supported Virginia Military Institute fights to maintain both its all-male status and its state funding.

CYCLE OF LOSS

Today, most female and male students attend the same schools, sit in the same classrooms, and read the same books; but the legacy of inequity continues beneath the veneer of equal access. Although the school door is finally open and girls are inside the building, they remain second-class citizens.

In the early elementary school years, girls are ahead of boys academically, achieving higher standardized test scores in every area but science. By middle school, however, the test scores of female students begin a downward spiral that continues through high school, college, and even graduate school. Women consistently score lower than men on the Graduate Record Exams as well as on entrance tests for law, business, and medical schools. As a group, women are the only students who actually lose ground the longer they stay in school.

Ironically, falling female performance on tests is not mirrored by lower grades. Some have argued that women's grade-point averages are inflated because they tend not to take the allegedly more rigorous courses, such as advanced mathematics and physics. Another hypothesis suggests that female students get better grades in secondary school and college as a reward for effort and better behavior rather than a mastery of the material. Another possibility is that the standardized tests do not adequately measure what female students know and what they are really able to do. Whatever the reason, course grades and test grades paint very different academic pictures.

Lower test scores handicap girls in the competition for places at elite colleges. On average, girls score 50 to 60 points less than boys on the Scholastic Aptitude Test (SAT), recently renamed the Scholastic Assessment Test, which is required for admission to most colleges. Test scores also unlock scholarship money at 85 percent of private colleges and 90 percent of the public ones. For example, in 1991, boys scored so much higher on the Preliminary SAT/National Merit Scholarship Qualifying Test (PSAT/NMSQT) that they were nominated for two-thirds of the Merit Scholarships—18 thousand boys compared to 8 thousand girls in 1991.[2]

The drop in test scores begins around the same time that another deeply troubling loss occurs in the lives of girls: self-esteem. There is a precipitous decline from elementary school to high school. Entering middle school, girls begin what is often the most turbulent period in their young lives. According to a national survey sponsored by the American Association of University Women, 60 percent of elementary school girls agreed with the statement "I'm happy the way I am," while only 37 percent still agreed in middle school. By high school, the level had dropped an astonishing 31 points to 29 percent, with fewer than three out of every 10 girls feeling good about themselves. According to the survey, the decline is far less dramatic for boys: 67 percent report being happy with themselves in elementary school, and this drops to 46 percent in high school.[3]

Recent research points to the relationship between academic achievement and self-esteem. Students who do well in school feel better about themselves; and in turn, they then feel more capable. For most female students, this connection has a negative twist and a cycle of loss is put into motion. As girls feel less good about themselves, their academic performance declines, and this poor performance further erodes their confidence. This pattern is particularly powerful in math and science classes, with only 18 percent of middle school girls describing themselves as good in these subjects, down from 31 percent in elementary school. It is not surprising that the testing gap between boys and girls is particularly wide in math and science.[3]

INEQUITY IN INSTRUCTION

During the past decade, Myra and David Sadker have investigated verbal interaction patterns in elementary, secondary, and college classrooms in a variety of settings and subject areas. In addition, they have interviewed students and teachers across the country. In their new book, *Failing at Fairness: How America's Schools Cheat Girls*, they expose the microinequities that occur daily in classrooms across the United States—and they show how this imbalance in attention results in the lowering of girls' achievement and self-esteem.[1] Consider the following:

• From grade school to graduate school, girls receive less teacher attention and less useful teacher feedback.

• Girls talk significantly less than boys do in class. In elementary and secondary school, they are eight times less likely to call out comments. When they do, they are often reminded to raise their hands while similar behavior by boys is accepted.

• Girls rarely see mention of the contributions of women in the curricula; most textbooks continue to report male worlds.

• Too frequently female students become targets of unwanted sexual attention from male peers and sometimes even from administrators and teachers.

From omission in textbooks to inappropriate sexual comments to bias in teacher behavior, girls experience a powerful and often disabling education climate. A high school student from an affluent

Gender Bias in the SAT Math Exams

Several studies of large student groups and individual institutions such as MIT, Rutgers, and Princeton demonstrate that although young women typically earn the same or higher grades as their male counterparts in math and other college courses, their SAT scores were 30 to 50 points lower. Researchers Kathy Kessel and Marcia Lynn of the University of California suggest that the disparity is caused by the SAT exam's emphasis on speed and multiple-choice questions. Tests require students to solve 25 to 35 short problems in 30 minutes. Studies show that males do better on speeded tests because they are more self-confident and therefore spend less time checking their answers and reflecting on problems. In countries such as the Netherlands, England, and Australia where exams require solutions to several long problems, there is less disparity between the scores of male and female students. College courses in the United States are increasingly emphasizing the solution of the complex problems. The ability to engage in the sustained reasoning required to solve such problems is not adequately measured by the college entrance examinations.

As a result of these factors, young women receive lower SAT math scores and lose out on college admissions, scholarships, placement into advanced courses, and various career opportunities. Yet given a chance, they are likely to outperform their male counterparts. Kessel and Linn endorse new forms of assessments that use portfolios and projects and applaud those schools where test scores are optional in the admission process.

Adapted from "Fair Test Examiner," National Center for Fair and Open Testing, Winter 1996–97.

Race, Ethnicity, and Self-Confidence

Research by the American Association of University Women and Peggy Orenstein, author of *Schoolgirls*, indicates that race and ethnicity as well as gender affect girls' experience of self-confidence. While all girls' self-esteem declines during adolescence, African-American girls retain a stronger sense of self, feel more entitled to speak out, and are more satisfied with their appearance than other groups of girls. They are, however, less confident about school than other girls and often feel undermined and stigmatized by the low expectations and racism of their teachers. Latinas experience the most radical decline in both personal and academic self-confidence during adolescence. According to the American Association of University Women, the number of Latina girls who are "happy with the way I am" plunges by 38 percentage points, compared with a 33 percent drop for white girls and a 7 percent drop for black girls.

AAUW Report, Executive Summary, Washington, D.C., 1991, p. 27.

Northeastern high school describes her own painful experience:

> My English teacher asks the class, "What is the purpose of the visit to Johannesburg?" . . . I know the answer, but I contemplate whether I should answer the question. The boys in the back are going to tease me like they harass all the other girls in our class . . . I want to tell them to shut up. But I stand alone. All of the other girls don't even let themselves be bold. Perhaps they are all content to be molded into society's image of what a girl should be like—submissive, sweet, feminine . . . In my ninth period class, I am actually afraid—of what [the boys] might say . . . As my frustration builds, I promise myself that I will yell back at them. I say that everyday . . . and I never do it.[4]

Teachers not only call on male students more frequently than on females; they also allow boys to call out more often. This imbalance in instructional attention is greatest at the college level. Our research shows that approximately one-half of the students in college classrooms are silent, having no interaction whatsoever with the professor. Two-thirds of these silent students are women. This verbal domination is further heightened by the gender segregation of many of today's classes. Sometimes teachers seat girls and boys in different sections of the room, but more often students segregate themselves. Approximately one-half of the elementary and high school classrooms and one-third of the coeducational college classrooms that the Sadkers visited are sex-segregated. As male students talk and call out more, teachers are drawn to the noisier male sections of the class, a development that further silences girls.

Not only do male students interact more with the teacher but at all levels of schooling they receive a higher quality of interaction. Using four categories of teacher responses to student participation—praise, acceptance, remediation, and criticism—the Sadkers' studies found that more than 50 percent of all teacher responses are mere acceptances, such as "O.K." and "uh huh." These nonspecific reactions offer little instructional feedback. Teachers use remediation more than 30 percent of the time, helping students correct or improve answers by asking prob-

ing questions or by phrases such as "Try again." Only 10 percent of the time do teachers actually praise students, and they criticize them even less. Although praise, remediation, and criticism provide more useful information to students than the neutral acknowledgment of an "O.K." these clearer, more precise teacher comments are more often directed to boys.

Who gets taught—and how—has profound consequences. Student participation in the classroom enhances learning and self-esteem. Thus, boys gain an educational advantage over girls by claiming a greater share of the teacher's time and attention. This is particularly noteworthy in science classes, where, according to the AAUW report, *How Schools Shortchange Girls,* boys perform 79 percent of all student-assisted demonstrations. When girls talk less and do less, it is little wonder that they learn less.[5] Even when directing their attention to girls, teachers sometimes short-circuit the learning process. For example, teachers frequently explain how to focus a microscope to boys but simply adjust the microscope for the girls. Boys learn the skill; girls learn to ask for assistance.

When female students do speak in class, they often preface their statements with self-deprecating remarks such as, "I'm not sure this is right," or "This probably isn't what you're looking for." Even when offering excellent responses, female students may begin with this self-criticism. Such tentative forms of speech project a sense of academic uncertainty and self-doubt—almost a tacit admission of lesser status in the classroom.

Women are not only quiet in classrooms; they are also missing from the pages of textbooks. For example, history textbooks currently in use at middle and high schools offer little more than 2 percent of their space to women. Studies of music textbooks have found that 70 percent of the figures shown are male. A recent content analysis of five secondary school science textbooks revealed that more than two-thirds of all drawings were of male figures and that not a single female scientist was depicted. Furthermore, all five books used the male body as the model for the human body, a practice that contin-

*Sexism and racism are so embedded in curriculum material that it requires a conscious effort to cre-
ate a classroom climate that is truly inclusive. The questions below have been helpful to instructors
in examining their texts and lectures. How have teachers' choices of materials and patterns of classroom interaction affected you?*

Checklist for Inclusive Teaching

MERCILEE JENKINS

TEXTS, LECTURES, AND COURSE CONTENT

1. Are you and your texts' language sex-neutral, using words with relation to both sexes
   whenever this is the author's intent? If your texts use the masculine generic, do you
   point this out in the classroom?
2. Is content addressed equitably to men, to women, people of color?
3. Do you and your texts portray equitably the activities, achievements, concerns, and
   experiences of women and people of color? If your texts do not, do you provide
   supplemental materials? Do you bring omissions to the attention of your students?
4. Do you and your texts present the careers, roles, interests, and abilities of women and
   people of color without stereotyping? If there are stereotypes in your texts, do you
   point this out?
5. Do you and your texts' examples and illustrations (both verbal and graphic) represent an equitable balance in terms of gender and race? If your texts do not, do you
   point this out?
6. Do your texts and lectures reflect values that are free of sex and race bias, and if not,
   do you discuss your/their biases and values with your students?
7. Do your texts incorporate new research and theory generated by feminist and ethnic
   scholarship? If not, do you point out areas in which feminist and ethnic studies are
   modifying perceived ideas? Do you provide additional bibliographic references for

ues even in medical school texts.[6] At the college
level, too, women rarely see themselves reflected in
what they study. For example, the two-volume *Norton Anthology of English Literature* devotes less than
15 percent of its pages to the works of women. Interestingly, there was greater representation of women
in the first edition of the anthology in 1962 than in
the fifth edition published in 1986.[7]

PRESENCE AND POWER

Not only are women hidden in the curriculum and
quiet in the classroom, they are also less visible in
other school locations. Even as early as the elementary grades, considered by some to be a distinctly
feminine environment, boys tend to take over the
territory. At recess time on playgrounds across the
country, boys grab bats and balls as they fan out
over the school yard for their games. Girls are likely
to be left on the sideline—watching. In secondary
school, male students become an even more powerful presence. In *Failing at Fairness*, high school
teachers and students tell these stories:

> A rural school district in Wisconsin still has the
> practice of having the cheerleaders (all girls, of
> course) clean the mats for the wrestling team before
> each meet. They are called the "Mat Maidens."

students who want to pursue these issues? When you order books for the library, do they reflect these issues?

8. Do your exams and assignments for papers, projects, etc. allow and encourage students to explore the nature, roles, status, contributions and experience of women and people of color?

9. Do your texts and materials make it clear that not everyone is heterosexual?

CLASSROOM INTERACTIONS

1. Are you conscious of sex- or race-related expectations you may hold about student performance?

2. How do you react to uses of language (accent, dialect, etc.) that depart from standard English or that are different from your own? Do you discount the speaker's intelligence and information?

3. What is the number of males versus females or of various cultural and racial groups called on to answer questions? Which students do you call by name? Why?

4. Which of these categories of students participate in class more frequently through answering questions or making comments? Is the number disproportional enough that you should encourage some students to participate more frequently?

5. Do interruptions occur when an individual is talking? If so, who does the interrupting? If one group of students is dominating classroom interaction, what do you do about it?

6. Is your verbal response to students positive? Aversive? Encouraging? Is it the same for all students? If not, what is the reason? (Valid reasons occur from time to time for reacting or responding to a particular student in a highly specific manner.)

7. Do you tend to face or address one section of the classroom more than others? Do you establish eye contact with certain students more than others? What are the gestures, postures, facial expressions, etc. used and are they different for men, women, people of color?

In our local high school, boys' sports teams received much more support from the school system and the community. The boys' team got shoes, jackets, and played on the best-maintained grounds. The girls' softball team received no clothes and nobody took care of our fields. Cheerleaders did not cheer for us. When we played, the bleachers were mostly empty.

Sports are not the only fields where women lose ground. In many secondary schools, mathematics, science, and computer technology remain male domains. In the past, girls were actively discouraged or even prohibited from taking the advanced courses in these fields. One woman, now a college professor, recalls her high school physics class:

> I was the only girl in the class. The teacher often told off-color jokes and when he did he would tell me to the leave the room. My great regret today is that I actually did it.

Today, we hope such explicitly offensive behavior is rare, yet counselors and teachers continue to harbor lower expectations for girls and are less likely to encourage them to take advanced classes in math and science. It is only later in life that women realize the price they paid for avoiding these courses as they are screened out of lucrative careers in science and technology.

By the time they reach college, male students' control of the environment is visible. Male students are more likely to hold positions of student leadership on campus and to play in heavily funded sports programs. College presidents and deans are usually men, as are most tenured professors. In a sense, a "glass wall" divides today's college campus. On one side of the glass wall are men, comprising 70 percent of all students majoring in chemistry, physics, and computer science. The percentage is even higher in engineering. While the "hard sciences" flourish on the men's side of the campus, the women's side of the glass wall is where education, psychology, and foreign languages are taught. These gender walls not only separate programs, they also indicate social standing. Departments with higher male enrollment carry greater campus prestige and their faculty are often paid higher salaries.

These gender differences can be seen outside academic programs, in peer relationships both at college and in high school. In 1993 a national survey sponsored by the AAUW and reported in *Hostile Hallways* found that 76 percent of male students and 85 percent of female students in the typical high school had experienced sexual harassment.[8] What differed dramatically for girls and boys was not the occurrence of unwanted touching or profane remarks but their reaction to them. Only 28 percent of the boys, compared to 70 percent of the girls, said they were upset by these experiences. For 33 percent of the girls, the encounters were so troubling that they did not want to talk in class or even go to school. On college campuses problems range from sexist comments and sexual propositions to physical assault. Consider the following incidents:

• A UCLA fraternity manual found its way into a campus magazine. Along with the history and bylaws were songs the pledges were supposed to memorize. The lyrics described sexual scenes that were bizarre, graphic, and sadistic.[9]
• One fraternity on a New England campus hosted "pig parties" where the man bringing the female date voted the ugliest wins.[1]

• A toga party on the campus of another elite liberal arts college used for decoration the torso of a female mannequin hung from the balcony and splattered with paint to look like blood. A sign below suggested the female body was available for sex.[10]

When one gender is consistently treated as less important and less valuable, the seeds of contempt take root and violence can be the result.

STRATEGIES FOR CHANGE

One of the ironies of gender bias in schools is that so much of its goes unnoticed by educators. While personally committed to fairness, many are unable to see the microinequities that surround them. The research on student-teacher interactions led the Sadkers to develop training programs to enable teachers and administrators to detect this bias and create equitable teaching methods. Program evaluations indicate that biased teaching patterns can be changed, and teachers can achieve equity in verbal interactions with their students. Research shows that for elementary and secondary school teachers, as well as college professors, this training leads not only to more equitable teaching but to more effective teaching as well.

During the 1970s, content analysis research showed women missing from schoolbooks. Publishers issued guidelines for equity and vowed to reform. But recent studies show that not all publishing companies have lived up to the promise of their guidelines. The curriculum continues to present a predominately male model of the world. Once again publishers and authors must be urged to incorporate women into school texts. Teachers and students need to become aware of the vast amount of excellent children's literature, including biographies that feature resourceful girls and strong women. *Failing at Fairness*[1] includes an extensive list of these resources for both elementary and secondary schools.

In postsecondary education, faculty members typically select instructional materials on the basis of individual preference. Many instructors would benefit from programs that alert them to well-written, gender-fair books in their academic fields. And individual professors can enhance their own lectures and discussions by including works by and about women.

Education institutions at every level have a responsibility for students in and beyond the classroom. Harassing and intimidating behaviors that formerly might have been excused with the comment "boys will be boys" are now often seen as less excusable and less acceptable. Many schools offer workshops for students and faculty to help eliminate sexual harassment. While controversy surrounds the exact definition of sexual harassment, the education community must take this issue seriously and devise strategies to keep the learning environment open to all.

After centuries of struggle, women have finally made their way into our colleges and graduate schools, only to discover that access does not guarantee equity. Walls of subtle bias continue to create different education environments, channeling women and men toward separate and unequal futures. To complete the agenda for equity, we must transform our education institutions and empower female students for full participation in society.

[1994]

REFERENCES

1. M. Sadker and D. Sadker, *Failing at Fairness: How America's Schools Cheat Girls* (New York: Charles Scribner's Sons, 1994). The research for this article as well as the anecdotes are drawn from this book.
2. Test data were obtained from Educational Testing Service.
3. The Analysis Group, Greenberg-Lake. *Shortchanging Girls, Shortchanging America* (Washington, D.C.: American Association of University Women, 1990).
4. L. Kim, "Boys Will Be Boys . . . Right?" *The Lance*, Livingston High School (June 1993), 32:5.
5. The Wellesley College Center for Research on Women. *How Schools Shortchange Girls: The AAUW Report* (Washington, D.C.: American Association of University Women Educational Foundation, 1992).
6. J. Bazler and D. Simonis, "Are Women Out of the Picture?" *Science Teacher 57* (December 1990):9.
7. W. Sullivan, "*The Norton Anthology* and the Canon of English Literature." Paper presented at the Annual Meeting of the College English Association, San Antonio, Texas, 1991.
8. Louis Harris and Associates. *Hostile Hallways: The AAUW Survey on Sexual Harassment in America's Schools* (Washington, D.C.: American Association of University Women, 1993).
9. J. O'Gorman and B. Sandler, *Peer Harassment: Hassles for Women on Campus* (Washington, D.C.: Project on the Status and Education of Women. Association of American Colleges, 1988).
10. B. A. Crier, "Frat Row," *Los Angeles Times* (February 9, 1990).

 22

Something's Wrong Here and It's Not Me: Challenging the Dilemmas That Block Girls' Success

LEE ANNE BELL

"I bet all you do is study. You probably never have fun."
"I was just lucky. I'm sure yours was just as good."

These quotes are taken from a discussion with a group of third and fourth grade girls in Project REACH, a project designed to explore internal barriers to girls' achievement.[1] Two students were comparing their achievement on a project for which one of them has received an award. In the initial role play of this incident, the girl who did not win was envious and responded by teasing the other girl. The other girl, in an attempt to minimize the differences between them, downplayed her achievement. This taunt and the response to it encapsulate a core dilemma girls experience in school, the perceived disjunction between achievement and affiliation.

Something *is* wrong here. Each girl ends up feeling bad about herself. The "winner" at best feels uncomfortable and at worst undeserving. The "loser" feels inadequate, jealous and guilty for her reaction. Yet, this discomfort with competitive achievement situations is not uncommon among girls (Dweck, et al., 1978; Homer, 1972; Nicholls, 1975; Stein & Bailey, 1973). Suggested interventions often seek to raise female aspirations and self-esteem but whether intentional or not, present the problem as something *in* girls that needs to be fixed (Kerr, 1983; Wilson, 1982).

Girls who exhibit outstanding academic ability,

intense commitment to their chosen interests, leadership and critical judgment are at risk in public schools today (Callahan, 1980; Rodenstein, Pfleger & Colangelo, 1977). By fourth grade, they begin to lose self-confidence, become extremely self-critical, and often lower their effort and aspirations in order to conform to gender stereotyped social expectations (Entwisle & Baker, 1983; Robinson-Awana, Kehle & Jenson, 1986). Underachievement among girls with high potential begins to emerge by fourth or fifth grade and becomes widespread by junior high school (Fitzpatrick, 1978; Olshen & Matthews, 1987; Callahan, 1980). As girls pull back from achieving to their fullest they drastically reduce their options for the future.

Project REACH sought to understand the core dilemmas girls experience in school from the perspective of the girls themselves. We identified a pool of high potential girls in one urban elementary school. From this pool, we randomly selected a group of 26 girls within racial/ethnic and economic categories which matched the diversity of the district as a whole (15% Hispanic, 28% Black, 57% White, 39% eligible for free or reduced lunch). Thirteen were in third and fourth grade and thirteen in fifth and sixth grade.[2] We met weekly for one hour with each group for fourteen weeks to explore achievement-related issues identified in educational and psychological literature as problematic for females. The dilemmas posed in this paper came from discussions with this diverse group of eight to eleven year old girls.

DILEMMA #1: SMART VS. SOCIAL

The segment of dialogue quoted at the beginning of this article illustrates one core dilemma girls experience, the perception that achievement and affiliation are mutually exclusive. We asked the girls to examine the science contest situation more closely and think of alternatives that would enable both girls to feel good about themselves *and* get what they want; to feel good about achieving *and* get the friendship and support they value. The girls eagerly engaged in a discussion which yielded the following options: "tear the trophy in half," "give it to the teacher," "leave it in school," "give half to the other girls,"

"give the trophy away, it's just a piece of metal." All of the suggested options sacrificed achievement in order to preserve the relationship.

We reiterated our challenge to the group to find a solution that would affirm both girls. They struggled and seemed stuck until Hadley, a fourth grader, offered:

> When they [the judges] pick, probably a lot of people *could* have gotten first place, but they can only pick one. She wasn't there [to hear the judging process], she could have won too.

The sense of breakthrough was palpable. Immediately several new solutions emerged. All aimed at restructuring the situation to allow many people to do creative, high quality projects by working together cooperatively. The problem was externalized onto the system of judging rather than internalized as defects in individual girls. By expanding the problem to the larger context, in this case the competitive structure of the situation, the girls broke through the either/or dilemma and generated new options for confronting competitive situations. This process was used to examine additional dilemmas presented below.

DILEMMA #2: SILENCE VS. BRAGGING

Success is a loaded experience for females that incorporates a myriad of conflicting feelings, values and cultural messages about femininity. Girls receive contradictory messages about success from a competitively-oriented society that on the one hand claims females can be and do anything, but on the other promotes the belief that females should be "feminine" (e.g., passive and protected from risk) (Chodorow, 1974). The literature on achievement often claims that females avoid success because it conflicts with the feminine role (Horner, 1972), but discussions with Project REACH girls revealed just how complicated this issue is. The girls expressed pride in success but did not want to achieve it at the expense of others. Their responses support Sassen's (1980) assertion that females don't fear success itself so much as the social isolation with which they associate success.

This theme of hiding success for fear of seeming

to put oneself above others was prevalent among all the girls in our sample regardless of grade. The student who won the science prize grappled with the dilemma in the following way:[3]

Jane: (after receiving a compliment on her prize): Well, I don't feel that great when you say that to me because I feel like everybody's equal and everybody should have gotten a prize no matter what they did. I think Chris should've gotten it.

Myra: OK, Jane, tell the group why you didn't say "I feel good about winning this prize."

Jane: Well, because I feel like um, like everybody's looking at me and um saying "Oh, she shouldn't have won that prize, I should have won," and everybody's gonna be mad at me because, um, I won and they didn't.

Myra: Is there any situation that you could think of where you won an honor that you were deserving of and feel good about it?

Jane: If other people won also.

While Jane feels uncomfortable about acknowledging her success publicly, she does feel good about her accomplishment.

Myra: When you said you didn't want to accept a compliment and thought other people should win, did you also really think you deserved it deep down? Just within yourself, not worrying about other people?

Jane: Yeah, I thought I deserved it but I didn't want to say it because then other people might think I was bragging.

Betsy: Jane, when you got the part of [a lead in the school play] and people said like congratulations and stuff, what did you do?

Jane: Well, I tried not to talk about it too much. I talked about it sometimes but you know, like with Tommy. You know I always eat with Melissa, Linda and Tommy. Well, um, he really wanted that part so I tried not to talk about it cuz I didn't want to make anyone feel bad.

The literature on achievement motivation indicates that girls are more likely to attribute success to external causes such as luck, timing or the help of others while boys are more likely to take credit for success by attributing it to ability or effort (Dweck, et al., 1978; Maehr & Nicholls, 1980). Our research found that girls learn to muffle acknowledgement of their successes in order to avoid the appearance of "bragging."

The term "bragging" was brought up so repeatedly by girls in both groups that we began to see it as symbolizing a core issue. This issue has at least two aspects. First, girls do not like to place themselves above others, partly because they fear ostracism but also because they value social solidarity. Second, girls may see more clearly the actual conditions that govern success in a competitive system.

Black and Hispanic children evidence similar conflicts with success (Lindstrom & Van Sant, 1986). Marginality provides insight into the unspoken norms governing social situations, norms that are often invisible to those who benefit from and thus have no reason to question the status quo (Miller, 1986). As members of subordinate groups, perhaps girls and minority boys experience a value conflict that the dominant group does not. Part of the difficulty they have in taking credit for success may be the result of perceptive insight into a competitive system that mystifies the conditions for success. That is, although the system purports that individual effort alone is necessary, in fact, social class, race, status and opportunity have a great deal to do with actual achievement.

To the extent that girls do not become conscious of the conflicting values embedded in their reaction to success, they internalize the problem. Their ambivalence about success can lead to failure to own their achievements, an unwillingness to take risks in order to achieve, and ultimately an avoidance of success situations. When girls learn to publicly affirm their achievements and at the same time take seriously their aversion to competitive structures, they can then consider more than an either/or option to this dilemma.

DILEMMA #3: FAILURE VS. PERFECTION

Girls also receive conflicting messages about failure. The literature suggests that girls are more likely to internalize failure while boys are more likely to externalize it (Frieze, 1980). Boys' ability to more easily accept and learn from failure is attributed to their wider experience with competitive, team sports and the greater amount of critical, academic feedback they receive from teachers (Sadker & Sadker, 1982). The failure dilemma for girls is further confounded by race since many teachers give less attention and hold lower expectations for Black students (Rubovitz & Maehr, 1973); reward nonacademic, custodial behaviors in Black girls (Scott-Jones & Clark, 1986; Grant, 1984); and give Black girls fewer opportunities to respond in the classroom than they do boys and White girls (Irvine, 1986).

We asked each of our girls to tell about a time when she did poorly or failed. Many described athletic or academic situations. One fourth grader gave this representative example:

Alexis: I was at baseball and we were losing the game. I was the last person to bat and I had to not get out. And I got out and they all said, "You're no good."

Evy: How did that make you feel?

Alexis: Like a basket case!

The result of doing poorly or failing was embarrassment and humiliation. We asked, "When you make a mistake or fail like everyone does, what do you do to make yourself feel better?" Their responses were to withdraw from the situation and to express or avoid feelings. None focused on ways to improve their performance or challenge the dynamics of the situation itself.

Anika: I lie to myself and say I don't care.

Judith: I turn my head away from everyone till everyone stops laughing. When they try to act nice, I'll be cheered up by them.

Rosa: I call my friend up and talk for two or three hours.

Celeste: I write something on notes then I hide them away in my treasure box.

We asked them to consider how they might respond differently. They struggled to move beyond the all or nothing dilemma of performing with perfection or withdrawing, but no other alternatives emerged until we suggested the possibility of asserting their feelings and ideas for change within the situation itself.

We described a formula used in assertiveness training for learning to make an assertive statement:

"I feel ——— when you ——— because ———."

The girls rehearsed this statement in response to the failure situations they had recounted previously.

Kamillah: I feel angry when you say that I can't act because I study a lot and I learn my lines.

Amy: I feel insulted when you say I should give up on math because it's not fair. I could just work harder and I could try to do it.

DILEMMA #4: MEDIA "BEAUTY" VS. MARGINALITY

The girls were extremely self-conscious about how they looked on the videotapes. This led us to explore the role physical appearance plays in girls' attitudes toward success. We asked them to list the media messages females receive about how we should look in order to be successful. The following list (a composite of both groups) was generated:

tall
thin
beautiful
pretty
long, wavy hair
dainty personality
matching clothes
look neat and in place, even with babies
blonde
rich
skinny
popular
fur coats
nice figure
accessories (extra stuff)
blue-eyed
long hair
good looking
famous
wear makeup
nice smile
clothes and dress for every occasion

We then displayed a collection of pictures we had assembled on three walls of the room. These pictures included girls and women of all sizes, shapes, races, ages, and social classes doing a variety of interesting things. We asked the girls to examine the pictures and make a list of all the ways in which they contradicted the media messages. Their new list said: "You can be successful and look . . .

fat
old
poor
dressy
handicapped
wrinkly
many different ways
lots of different shades and colors
skinny
black
rich
Spanish
not rich
beautiful or not beautiful
doing different things
young
white
sloppy
in the middle
tough
boyish or feminine
old, young, and in-between

The girls discussed the differences between the two lists and then worked together on a definition of beauty that would include all the females in the pictures:

> Beauty is . . . doing your own thing
> having lots of interests
> believing in yourself
> looking how you want to . . .

Through this activity the girls challenged the "Success = Beauty" dilemma and created new options for themselves. This proved to be a powerful session having a lasting impact as evidenced by their continual references to it. At the beginning of this session one third grade Black girl whispered to me, "I really want to be white. I told my parents and that's what I want." At the end of the session we asked each

girl to write an essay entitled: "Ways in which I am beautiful." This girl then wrote, "I am beautiful because I am proud of my race, I'm smart and I have pretty brown eyes." Another girl who had initially stated that she wanted to look like Vanna White, a stereotypic blonde, blue-eyed television game show hostess, later wrote, "I am beautiful because I'm good in school, I'm Puerto Rican and Dominican, and I'm good at sports."

DILEMMA #5: PASSIVE VS. AGGRESSIVE

Research indicates that boys, especially White boys, demand and receive more attention from teachers than girls (Grant, 1984; Irvine, 1986). Our girls expressed annoyance with the greater attention boys receive and with their method of getting this attention.

Judith: Sometimes, when the boys are uh with us they always misbehave and make the teachers scream and I hate it. I hate to hear people scream.

In addition to giving boys more attention, teachers often reward passivity and punish assertiveness in girls as well (Sadker & Sadker, 1982).

For our girls the alternatives to competing with boys for teacher attention were either to withdraw and be passive ("I just won't raise my hand anymore") or fight back ("I'll punch him out"). In this dilemma, clear racial differences emerged, with White and Hispanic girls more likely to withdraw and Black girls more likely to fight back. Either way, boys' behavior defines the situation and the girls are left to react.

The consequences are often negative for girls. Those girls who withdraw in response to boys' behavior lose opportunities to respond in class, to verbally explore their ideas, to actively shape the classroom, and to meet their own needs and desires. Those girls who fight back also receive more teacher disapproval and punishment for their assertiveness. This dilemma is especially damaging for Black girls whose resistance becomes a source of teacher hostility and disciplinary action.

We explored this dilemma by asking the girls to describe various situations in school that bothered them and develop alternative responses. Those girls who tended to withdraw or avoid expressing their needs were encouraged to respond actively. Those girls who tended to fight back in self-defeating or in-effective ways practiced asserting themselves more effectively, assertively rather than aggressively.

An interesting outcome of one discussion was observed in one fourth grade classroom following this session. The teacher was working with a small reading group and, as we had noticed repeatedly in our classroom observations, boys dominated the group by raising their hands more, calling out for the teacher's attention and misbehaving. One of our girls, small for her age and usually quiet, turned to a boy next to her who was pounding the table to get the teacher's attention and said, "When you do that it annoys me. Please control yourself. I want a chance to answer the question."

Group support for such endeavors is crucial. Students, especially girls, who respond assertively to authority figures run a high risk of punishment. Group support may increase the likelihood of being taken seriously.

Until adults change, however, girls are caught in the bind of conforming or being punished. Educators and counselors concerned about girls' achievement must work to challenge and change adult attitudes, behaviors and classroom structures that block girls' potential. Without such changes girls' resistance will continue to be met with individual and structural, conscious and unconscious barriers that undermine their attempts to participate fully and successfully in all areas of school.

CONCLUSION

Discussing dilemmas about achievement in a supportive environment with others can be a powerful form of consciousness raising for girls. The group context counteracts isolation by showing us that the problems we experience as "mine alone" are in fact shared by many others.

Group discussion and support also provide a way to analyze the social messages and behaviors that reinforce feelings of inadequacy and fears about achievement. Girls can help each other understand and critique the situations that create achievement related conflicts and explore alternatives that would allow for achievement and connection to others. By defining the problem collectively, girls can then brainstorm ways to change the situation. Finally, females of all ages can organize to implement changes in the oppressive structures and situations that devalue female capacities and choices. Like consciousness raising for adults, these groups help their participants to stop asking "What's wrong with me?" and instead learn to say "What's wrong out there and what can we do collectively to change it for the better?"[4]   [1992]

NOTES

1. The research for Project REACH was conducted during the 1987–88 school year. Methods included ethnographic observations in classrooms, interviews with teachers and fourteen one hour sessions with third/fourth and fifth/sixth grade groups. This article draws upon only one portion of the data collected, the transcripts of the videotapes of the sessions with the girls.

2. The pool from which the sample girls were drawn was established in cooperation with already established procedures of the gifted/talented program in the district. These procedures focused on academic ability and included IQ scores and parent and teacher nomination. Additional methods to identify athletic, artistic, creative and social ability were added to the criteria used by the district in developing the pool from which our sample was drawn.

3. Fictitious names were used for all the girls quoted in this article.

4. The Coopersmith Self-Esteem Inventory was administered as a pre/post test but these data have not yet been analyzed. Anecdotal comments from the principal, teachers and parents suggest that the program had a positive effect in raising the confidence of the girls in the sample group. We have also received letters from parents requesting that their daughters be allowed to continue with the program.

REFERENCES

Callahan, C. (1980). The gifted girl: An anomaly? *Roeper Review*. Vol. 2, No. 3, Feb–Mar.

Chodorow, N. (1974). Family structure and feminine personality. In M. Rosaldo and L. Lamphere (Eds.). *Women, Culture and Society*. Stanford, CA: Stanford University Press.

Dweck, C., Davidson, W., Nelson, S., and Enna, B. (1978). Sex differences in learned helplessness: II. The contingencies of evaluative feedback in the classroom and III. An experimental analysis. *Developmental Psychology*. Vol. 14, No. 3, 268–276.

Entwisle, D., and Baker, D. (1983). Gender and young children's expectations for performance in arithmetic. *Developmental Psychology, 19*, 200–209.

Fitzpatrick, J. (1978). Academic achievement, other-directedness and attitudes toward women's roles in bright adolescent females. *Journal of Educational Psychology*. Vol. 70, No. 4, 650–654.

Frieze, I. (1980). Beliefs about success and failure in the classroom. In J. H. McMillen (Ed.), *The Social Psychology of School Learning.* New York: Academic Press.

Grant, L. (1984). Black females' "place" in desegregated classrooms. *Sociology of Education.* Vol. 57 (April): 98–111.

Horner, M. (1972). Toward an understanding of achievement-related conflicts in women. *Journal of Social Issues.* Vol. 28, 157–175.

Irvine, J. (1986). Teacher-student interactions: Effects of student race, sex and grade level. *Journal of Educational Psychology.* Vol. 78, No. 1, 14–21.

Kerr, B. (1983). Raising the career aspirations of gifted girls. *Vocational Guidance Quarterly.* Vol. 32, 37–43.

Lindstrom, R., and Van Sant, S. (1986). Special issues in working with gifted minority adolescents. *Journal of Counseling and Development.* Vol. 64, May, 583–586.

Maehr, M. and Nicholls, J. (1980). Culture and achievement motivation: A second look. In N. Warren (Ed.), *Studies in Cross-Cultural Psychology.* Vol. 2. New York: Academic Press.

Miller, J. B. (1986). *Toward a New Psychology of Women.* Boston: Beacon Press.

Nicholls, J. (1975). Causal attributions and other achievement-related cognitions: Effects of task outcomes, attainment value and sex. *Journal of Personality and Social Psychology.* Vol. 31, 379–389.

Olshen, S., and Matthews, D. (1987). The disappearance of giftedness in girls: An intervention strategy. *Roeper Review.* Vol. 9, No. 4, 251–254.

Robinson-Awana, P., Kehle, T., and Jenson, W. (1986). But what about smart girls? Adolescent self-esteem and sex role perceptions as a function of academic achievement. *Journal of Educational Psychology.* Vol. 78, No. 3, 179–183.

Rodenstein, J., Pfleger, L., and Colangelo, N. (1977). Career development of gifted women. *The Gifted Child Quarterly, 21,* 340–347.

Rubovitz, P. and Maehr, M. (1973). Pygmalion, black and white. *Journal of Personality and Social Psychology.* Vol. 25, 210–218.

Sadker, M., and Sadker, D. (1982). *Sex Equity Handbook for Schools.* New York: Longman.

Sassen, G. (1980). Success anxiety in women: A constructivist interpretation of its sources and significance. *Harvard Educational Review, 50,* 13–25.

Scott-Jones, D., and Clark, M. (March, 1986). The school experience of black girls: The interaction of gender, race and socioeconomic status. *Phi Delta Kappan,* 520–526.

Stein, A., and Bailey, N. (1973). The socialization of achievement orientation in females. *Psychological Bulletin, 80,* 345–366.

Wilson, S. (1982). A new decade: The gifted and career choice. *Vocational Guidance Quarterly, 31,* 53–59.

 23

The Sexual Politics of Interpersonal Behavior

NANCY HENLEY and JO FREEMAN

Social interaction is the battlefield where the daily war between the sexes is fought. It is here that women are constantly reminded where their "place" is and that they are put back in their place, should they venture out. Thus, social interaction serves as the most common means of social control employed against women. By being continually reminded of their inferior status in their interactions with others, and continually compelled to acknowledge that status in their own patterns of behavior, women learn to internalize society's definition of them as inferior so thoroughly that they are often unaware of what their status is. Inferiority becomes habitual, and the inferior place assumes the familiarity—and even desirability—of home.

Different sorts of cues in social interaction aid this enforcement of one's social definition, particularly the verbal message, the nonverbal message transmitted within a social relationship, and the nonverbal message transmitted by the environment. Our educational system emphasizes the verbal messages and teaches us next to nothing about how we interpret and react to the nonverbal ones. Just how important nonverbal messages are, however, is shown by the finding of Argyle et al. that nonverbal cues have over four times the impact of verbal ones when both verbal and nonverbal cues are used.[1] Even more important for women, Argyle found that female subjects were more responsive to nonverbal cues (compared with verbal ones) than male subjects. If women are to understand how the subtle forces of social control work in their lives, they must learn as much as possible about how nonverbal cues affect people, and particularly about how they perpetuate the power and superior status enjoyed by men.

Even if a woman encounters no one else directly in her day, visual status reminders are a ubiquitous part of her environment. As she moves through the day, she absorbs many variations of the same status theme, whether or not she is aware of it: male bosses dictate while female secretaries bend over their steno pads; male doctors operate while female nurses assist; restaurants are populated with waitresses serving men; magazine and billboard ads remind the woman that home maintenance and child care are her foremost responsibilities and that being a sex object for male voyeurs is her greatest asset. If she is married, her mail reminds her that she is a mere "Mrs." appended to her husband's name. When she is introduced to others or fills out a form, the first thing she must do is divulge her marital status acknowledging the social rule that the most important information anyone can know about her is her legal relationship to a man.

These environmental cues set the stage on which the power relationships of the sexes are acted out, and the assigned status of each sex is reinforced. Though studies have been made of the several means by which status inequalities are communicated in interpersonal behavior, they do not usually deal with power relationships between men and women. Goffman has pointed to many characteristics associated with status:

> Between status equals we may expect to find interaction guided by symmetrical familiarity. Between superordinate and subordinate we may expect to find asymmetrical relations, the superordinate having the right to exercise certain familiarities which the subordinate is not allowed to reciprocate. Thus, in the research hospital, doctors tended to call nurses by their first names, while nurses responded with "polite" or "formal" address. Similarly, in American business organizations the boss may thoughtfully ask the elevator man how his children are, but this entrance into another's life may be blocked to the elevator man, who can appreciate the concern but not return it. Perhaps the clearest form of this is found in the psychiatrist-patient relation, where the psychiatrist has a right to touch on aspects of the patient's life that the patient might not even allow himself to touch upon, while of course this privilege is not reciprocated.
>
> Rules of demeanor, like rules of deference, can be symmetrical or asymmetrical. Between so-

cial equals, symmetrical rules of demeanor seem often to be prescribed. Between unequals many variations can be found. For example, at staff meetings on the psychiatric units of the hospital, medical doctors had the privilege of swearing, changing the topic of conversation, and sitting in undignified positions; attendants, on the other hand, had the right to attend staff meetings and to ask questions during them . . . but were implicitly expected to conduct themselves with greater circumspection than was required of doctors. . . . Similarly, doctors had the right to saunter into the nurses' station, lounge on the station's dispensing counter, and engage in joking with the nurses; other ranks participated in this informal interaction with doctors, but only after doctors had initiated it.[2]

A status variable widely studied by Brown and others is the use of terms of address.[3] In languages that have both familiar and polite forms of the second person singular ("you"), asymmetrical use of the two forms invariably indicates a status difference, and it always follows the same pattern. The person using the familiar form is always the superior to the person using the polite form. In English, the only major European language not to have dual forms of address, status differences are similarly indicated by the right of first-naming; the status superior can first-name the inferior in situations where the inferior must use the superior's title and last name. An inferior who breaks this rule by inappropriately using a superior's first name is considered insolent.[4]

According to Brown, the pattern evident in the use of forms of address applies to a very wide range of interpersonal behavior and invariably has two other components: (1) whatever form is used by a superior in situations of status inequality can be used reciprocally by intimates, and whatever form is used by an inferior is the socially prescribed usage for nonintimates; (2) initiation or increase of intimacy is the right of the superior. To use the example of naming again to illustrate the first component, friends use first names with each other, while strangers use titles and last names (though "instant" intimacy is considered proper in some cultures, such as our own, among status equals in informal settings). As an example of the second component, status superiors, such as professors, specifically tell status inferiors, such as students, when they can use the first name, and often rebuff them if they assume such a right unilaterally.

Although Brown did not apply these patterns to status differences between the sexes, their relevance is readily seen. The social rules say that all moves to greater intimacy are a male prerogative: It is boys who are supposed to call girls for dates, men who are supposed to propose marriage to women, and males who are supposed to initiate sexual activity with females. Females who make "advances" are considered improper, forward, aggressive, brassy, or otherwise "unladylike." By initiating intimacy they have stepped out of their place and usurped a status prerogative. The value of such a prerogative is that it is a form of power. Between the sexes, as in other human interaction, the one who has the right to initiate greater intimacy has more control over the relationship. Superior status brings with it not only greater prestige and greater privileges, but greater power.

These advantages are exemplified in many of the various means of communicating status. Like the doctors in Goffman's research hospital, men are allowed such privileges as swearing and sitting in undignified positions, but women are denied them. Though the male privilege of swearing is curtailed in mixed company, the body movement permitted to women is circumscribed even in all-women groups. It is considered unladylike for a woman to use her body too forcefully, to sprawl, to stand with her legs widely spread, to sit with her feet up, or to cross the ankle of one leg over the knee of the other. Many of these positions are ones of strength or dominance. The more "feminine" a woman's clothes are, the more circumscribed the use of her body. Depending on her clothes, she may be expected to sit with her knees together, not to sit cross-legged, or not even to bend over. Though these taboos seem to have lessened in recent years, how much so is unknown, and there are recurring social pressures for a "return to femininity," while etiquette arbiters assert that women must retain feminine posture no matter what their clothing.

Prior to the 1920s women's clothes were designed to be confining and cumbersome. The dress reform movement, which disposed of corsets and long skirts, was considered by many to have more significance for female emancipation than women's suffrage.[5] Today women's clothes are designed to be revealing, but women are expected to restrict their body movements to avoid revealing too much. Furthermore, because women's clothes are contrived to reveal women's physical features, rather than being loose like men's, women must resort to purses instead of pockets to carry their belongings. These "conveniences" have become, in a time of blurred sex distinctions, one of the surest signs of sex, and thus have developed the character of stigma, a sign of woman's shame, as when they are used by comics to ridicule both women and transvestites.

Women in our society are expected to reveal not only more of their bodies than men but also more of themselves. Female socialization encourages greater expression of emotion than does that of the male. Whereas men are expected to be stolid and impassive, and not to disclose their feelings beyond certain limits, women are expected to express their *selves*. Such self-expression can disclose a lot of oneself, and, as Jourard and Lasakow found, females are more self-disclosing to others than males are.[6] This puts them at an immediate disadvantage.

The inverse relationship between disclosure and power has been reported by other studies in addition to Goffman's earlier cited investigation into a research hospital. Slobin, Miller, and Porter stated that individuals in a business organization are "more self-disclosing to their immediate superior than to their immediate subordinates."[7] Self-disclosure is a means of enhancing another's power. When one has greater access to information about another person, one has a resource the other person does not have. Thus not only does power give status, but status gives power. And those possessing neither must contribute to the power and status of others continuously.

Another factor adding to women's vulnerability is that they are socialized to *care* more than men —especially about personal relationships. This puts them at a disadvantage, as Ross articulated in what he called the "Law of Personal Exploitation": "In any sentimental relation the one who cares less can exploit the one who cares more."[8] The same idea was put more broadly by Waller and Hill as the "Principle of Least Interest": "That person is able to dictate the conditions of association whose interest in the continuation of the affair is least."[9] In other words, women's caring, like their openness, gives them less power in a relationship.

One way of indicating acceptance of one's place and deference to those of superior status is by following the rules of "personal space." Sommer has observed that dominant animals and human beings have a larger envelope of inviolability surrounding them—i.e., are approached less closely—than those of a lower status.[10] Willis made a study of the initial speaking distance set by an approaching person as a function of the speaker's relationship.[11] His finding that women were approached more closely than men—i.e., their personal space was smaller or more likely to be breached—is consistent with their lower status.

Touching is one of the closer invasions of one's personal space, and in our low-contact culture it implies privileged access to another person. People who accidently touch other people generally take great pains to apologize; people forced into close proximity, as in a crowded elevator, often go to extreme lengths to avoid touching. Even the figurative meanings of the word convey a notion of access to privileged areas—e.g., to one's emotions (one is "touched" by a sad story), or to one's purse (one is "touched" for ten dollars). In addition, the act of touching can be a subtle physical threat.

Remembering the patterns that Brown found in terms of address, consider the interactions between pairs of persons of different status, and picture who would be more likely to touch the other (put an arm around the shoulder or a hand on the back, tap the chest, hold the arm, or the like: teacher and student; master and servant; policeman and accused; doctor and patient; minister and parishioner; adviser and advisee; foreman and worker; businessman and secretary. As with first-naming, it is considered presumptuous for a person of low status to initiate touch with a person of higher status.

There has been little investigation of touching by social scientists, but the few studies made so far indicate that females are touched more than males are.

Goldberg and Lewis[12] and Lewis[13] report that from six months on, girl babies are touched more than boy babies. The data reported in Jourard[14] and Jourard and Rubin[15] show that sons and fathers tend to refrain from touching each other and that "when it comes to physical contact within the family, it is the daughters who are the favored ones."[16] An examination of the number of different regions in which subjects were touched showed that mothers and fathers touch their daughters in more regions than they do their sons; that daughters touch their fathers in more regions than sons do; that males touch their opposite-sex friends in more regions than females do. Overall, women's mean total "being-touched" score was higher than men's.

Jourard and Rubin take the view that "touching is equated with sexual interest, either consciously, or at a less-conscious level,"[17] but it would seem that there is a sex difference in the interpretation of touch. Lewis reflects this when he writes, "In general, for men in our culture, proximity (touching) is restricted to the opposite sex and its function is primarily sexual in nature."[18] Waitresses, secretaries, and women students are quite used to being touched by their male superordinates, but they are expected not to "misinterpret" such gestures. However, women who touch men are often interpreted as conveying sexual intent, as they have often found out when their intentions were quite otherwise. Such different interpretations are consistent with the status patterns found earlier. If touching indicates either power or intimacy, and women are deemed by men to be status inferiors, touching by women will be perceived as a gesture of intimacy, since it would be inconceivable for them to be exercising power.

A study by Henley puts forward this hypothesis.[19] Observations of incidents of touch in public urban places were made by a white male research assistant, naive to the uses of his data. Age, sex, and approximate socioeconomic status were recorded, and the results indicated that higher-status persons do touch lower-status persons significantly more. In particular, men touched women more, even when all other variables were held constant. When the settings of the observations were differentially examined, the pattern showed up primarily in the outdoor setting, with indoor interaction being more evenly spread over sex combinations. Henley has also reported observations of greater touching by higher status persons (including males) in the popular culture media; and a questionnaire study in which both females and males indicated greater expectancies of being touched by higher status persons, and of touching lower status and female ones, than vice versa.[20]

The other nonverbal cues by which status is indicated have likewise not been adequately researched —for humans. But O'Connor argues that many of the gestures of dominance and submission that have been noted in primates are equally present in humans.[21] They are used to maintain and reinforce the status hierarchy by reassuring those of higher status that those of lower status accept their place in the human pecking order.

The most studied nonverbal communication among humans is probably eye contact, and here too one finds a sex difference. It has repeatedly been found that women look more at another in a dyad than men do.[22] Exline, Gray, and Schuette suggest that "willingness to engage in mutual visual interaction is more characteristic of those who are oriented towards inclusive and affectionate interpersonal relations,"[23] but Rubin concludes that while "gazing may serve as a vehicle of emotional expression for women, [it] in addition may allow women to obtain cues from their male partners concerning the appropriateness of their behavior."[24] This interpretation is supported by Efran and Broughton's data showing that even male subjects "maintain more eye contact with individuals toward whom they have developed higher expectancies for social approval."[25]

Another possible reason why women gaze more at men is that men talk more,[26] and there is a tendency for the listener to look more at the speaker than vice versa.[27]

It is especially illuminating to look at the power relationships established and maintained by the manipulation of eye contact. The mutual glance can be seen as a sign of union, but when intensified into a stare it may become a way of doing battle.[28] Research reported by Ellsworth, Carlsmith, and Henson supports the notion that the stare can be inter-preted as an aggressive gesture. These authors write, "Staring at humans can elicit the same sort of responses that are common in primates; that is, staring can act like a primate threat display."[29]

Though women engage in mutual visual interaction in its intimate form to a high degree, they may back down when looking becomes a gesture of dominance. O'Connor points out, "The direct stare or glare is a common human gesture of dominance. Women use the gesture as well as men, but often in modified form. While looking directly at a man, a woman usually has her head slightly tilted, implying the beginning of a presenting gesture or enough submission to render the stare ambivalent if not actually submissive."[*][30]

The idea that the averted glance is a gesture of submission is supported by the research of Hutt and Ounsted into the characteristic gaze aversion of autistic children. They remark that "these children were never attacked [by peers] despite the fact that to a naive observer they appeared to be easy targets; this indicated that their gaze aversion had some signalling function similar to 'facing away' in the kittiwake or 'head-flagging' in the herring gull— behavior patterns which Tinbergen has termed 'appeasement postures.' In other words, gaze aversion inhibited any aggressive or threat behavior on the part of other conspecifics."[31]

Gestures of dominance and submission can be verbal as well as nonverbal. In fact, the sheer use of verbalization is a form of dominance because it can quite literally render someone speechless by preventing one from "getting a word in edgewise." As noted earlier, contrary to popular myth, men do talk more than women, both in single-sex and in mixed-sex groups. Within a group a major means of asserting dominance is to interrupt. Those who want to dominate others interrupt more; those speaking will not permit themselves to be interrupted by their inferiors, but they will give way to those they consider their superiors. Zimmerman and West found in a

---

*"Presenting" is the term for the submissive gesture seen in primates, of presenting the rump to a dominant animal; O'Connor also points out that it is a human female submissive gesture as well, seen, for example, in the can-can.

sample of 11 natural conversations between women and men that 46 of the 48 interruptions were by males.[32]

Other characteristics of persons in inferior status positions are the tendencies to hesitate and apologize, often offered as submissive gestures in the face of threats or potential threats. If staring directly, pointing, and touching can be subtle nonverbal threats, the corresponding gestures of submission seem to be lowering the eyes from another's gaze, falling silent (or not speaking at all) when interrupted or pointed at, and cuddling to the touch. Many of these nonverbal gestures of submission are familiar. They are the traits our society assigns as desirable secondary characteristics of the female role. Girls who have properly learned to be "feminine" have learned to lower their eyes, remain silent, back down, and cuddle at the appropriate times. There is even a word for this syndrome that is applied only to females: coy.

In verbal communication one finds a similar pattern of differences between the sexes. As mentioned earlier, men have the privilege of swearing, and hence access to a vocabulary not customarily available to women. On the surface this seems like an innocuous limitation, until one realizes the psychological function of swearing: it is one of the most harmless and effective ways of expressing anger. The alternatives are to express one's feelings with physical violence or to suppress them and by so doing turn one's anger in on oneself. The former is prohibited to both sexes (to different degrees) but the latter is decisively encouraged in women. The result is that women are "intropunitive"; they punish themselves for their own anger rather than somehow dissipating it. Since anger turned inward is commonly viewed as the basis for depression, we should not be surprised that depression is considerably more common in women than in men, and in fact is the most prevalent form of "mental illness" among women. Obviously, the causes of female depression are complex.[33]

Swearing is only the most obvious sex difference in language. Key has noted that sex differences are to be found in phonological, semantic, and grammatical aspects of language as well as in word use.[34]

In one example, Austin has commented that "in our culture little boys tend to be nasal . . . and little girls, oral," but that in the "final stages" of courtship the voices of both men and women are low and nasal.[35] The pattern cited by Brown,[36] in which the form appropriately used by status superiors is used between status equals in intimate situations, is again visible: in the intimate situation the female adopts the vocal style of the male.

In situations where intimacy is not a possible interpretation, it is not power but abnormality that is the usual interpretation. Female voices are expected to be soft and quiet—even when men are using loud voices. Yet it is only the "lady" whose speech is refined. Women who do not fit this stereotype are often called loud—a word commonly applied derogatorily to other minority groups or out-groups.[37] One of the most popular derogatory terms for women is "shrill," which, after all, simply means loud (out of place) and high-pitched (female).

In language, as in touch and most other aspects of interpersonal behavior, status differences between the sexes mean that the same traits are differently interpreted when displayed by each sex. A man's behavior toward a woman might be interpreted as an expression of either power or intimacy, depending on the situation. When the same behavior is engaged in by a woman and directed toward a man, it is interpreted only as a gesture of intimacy—and intimacy between the sexes is always seen as sexual in nature. Because our society's values say that women should not have power over men, women's nonverbal communication is rarely interpreted as an expression of power. If the situation precludes a sexual interpretation, women's assumption of the male prerogative is dismissed as deviant (castrating, domineering, unfeminine, or the like).*

Of course, if women do not wish to be classified either as deviant or as perpetually sexy, then they

---

*We are not suggesting that just because certain gestures associated with males are responded to as powerful, women should automatically adopt them. Rather than accepting male values without question, individual women will want to consider what they wish to express and how, and will determine whether to adopt particular gestures or to insist that their own be responded to appropriately meanwhile.

must persist in playing the proper role by following the interpersonal behavior pattern prescribed for them. Followed repeatedly, these patterns function as a means of control. What is merely habitual is often seen as desirable. The more men and women interact in the way they have been trained to from birth without considering the meaning of what they do, the more they become dulled to the significance of their actions. Just as outsiders observing a new society are more aware of the status differences of that society than its members are, so those who play the sexual politics of interpersonal behavior are usually not conscious of what they do. Instead they continue to wonder that feminists make such a mountain out of such a "trivial" molehill.   [1979]

NOTES

1. M. Argyle, V. Salter, H. Nicholson, M. Williams, and P. Burgess, "The Communication of Inferior and Superior Attitudes by Verbal and Non-verbal Signals," *British Journal of Social and Clinical Psychology,* 9 (1970), 222–31.
2. Goffman, "The Nature of Deference and Demeanor," *American Anthropologist,* 58 (1956), 473–502.
3. R. Brown, *Social Psychology* (Glencoe, Ill.: Free Press, 1965). See also R. Brown and M. Ford, "Address in American English," *Journal of Abnormal and Social Psychology,* 62 (1961), 375–85; R. Brown and A. Gilman, "The Pronouns of Power and Solidarity," in T. A. Sebeak, ed., *Style in Language* (Cambridge, Mass.: M.I.T. Press, 1960).
4. Brown, *Social Psychology,* pp. 92–97.
5. W. L. O'Neill, *Everyone Was Brave: The Rise and Fall of Feminism* (Chicago: Quadrangle, 1969), p. 270.
6. S. M. Jourard and P. Lasakow, "Some Factors in Self-Disclosure," *Journal of Abnormal and Social Psychology,* 56 (1958), 91–98.
7. D. I. Slobin, S. H. Miller, and L. W. Porter, "Forms of Address and Social Relations in a Business Organization," *Journal of Personality and Social Psychology,* 8 (1968), 289–93.
8. E. A. Ross, *Principles of Sociology* (New York: Century, 1921), p. 136.
9. W. W. Waller and R. Hill, *The Family: A Dynamic Interpretation* (New York: Dryden, 1951), p. 191.
10. R. Sommer, *Personal Space* (Englewood Cliffs, N.J.: Prentice-Hall, 1969), Chap. 2.
11. F. N. Willis, Jr., "Initial Speaking Distance as a Function of the Speakers' Relationship," *Psychonomic Science,* 5 (1966), 221–22.
12. S. Goldberg and M. Lewis, "Play Behavior in the Year-old Infant: Early Sex Differences," *Child Development,* 40 (1969), 21–31.
13. M. Lewis, "Parents and Children: Sex-role Development," *School Review,* 80 (1972), 229–40.
14. S. M. Jourard, "An Exploratory Study of Body Accessi-bility," *British Journal of Social and Clinical Psychology,* 5 (1966), 221–31.
15. S. M. Jourard and J. E. Rubin, "Self-Disclosure and Touching: A Study of Two Modes of Interpersonal Encounter and Their Interrelation," *Journal of Humanistic Psychology,* 8 (1968), 39–48.
16. Jourard, "Exploratory Study," p. 224.
17. Jourard and Rubin, "Self-Disclosure and Touching," p. 47.
18. Lewis, "Parents and Children," p. 237.
19. N. Henley, "The Politics of Touch," American Psychological Association, 1970. In P. Brown ed., *Radical Psychology* (New York: Harper & Row, 1973).
20. N. Henley, *Body Politics: Sex, Power and Nonverbal Communication* (Englewood Cliffs, N.J.: Prentice-Hall, 1977).
21. L. O'Connor, "Male Dominance: The Nitty Gritty of Oppression," *It Ain't Me Babe,* 1 (1970), 9.
22. R. Exline, "Explorations in the Process of Person Perception: Visual Interaction in Relation to Competition, Sex, and Need for Affiliation," *Journal of Personality,* 31 (1963), 1–20; R. Exline, D. Gray, and D. Schutte, "Visual Behavior in a Dyad as Affected by Interview Control and Sex of Respondent," *Journal of Personality and Social Psychology,* 1, (1965), 201–09; and Z. Rubin, "Measurement of Romantic Love," *Journal of Personality and Social Psychology,* 16 (1970), 265–73.
23. Exline, Gray, and Schuette, "Visual Behavior in a Dyad," p. 207.
24. Rubin, "Measurement of Romantic Love," p. 272.
25. J. S. Efran and A. Broughton, "Effect of Expectancies for Social Approval on Visual Behavior," *Journal of Personality and Social Psychology,* 4 (1966), p. 103.
26. M. Argyle, M. Lalljee, and M. Cook, "The Effects of Visibility on Interaction in a Dyad," *Human Relations,* 21 (1968), 3–17.
27. Exline, Gray, and Schuette, "Visual Behavior in a Dyad."
28. Exline, "Explorations in the Process of Person Perception."
29. P. C. Ellsworth, J. M. Carlsmith, and A. Henson, "The Stare as a Stimulus to Flight in Human Subjects: A Series of Field Experiments," *Journal of Personality and Social Psychology,* 21 (1972), p. 310.
30. O'Connor, "Male Dominance."
31. C. Hutt and C. Ounsted, "The Biological Significance of Gaze Aversion with Particular Reference to the Syndrome of Infantile Autism," *Behavioral Science,* 11 (1966), p. 154.
32. D. Zimmerman and C. West, "Sex Roles, Interruptions and Silences in Conversation," in B. Thorne and N. Henley, *Language and Sex* (Rowley, Mass.: Newbury House, 1975).
33. For more on this see P. B. Bart, "Depression in Middle-aged Women," in V. Gornick and B. K. Moran, *Woman in Sexist Society* (New York: Basic Books, 1971); and P. Chesler, *Women and Madness* (New York: Doubleday, 1972).
34. See also M. R. Key, *Male/Female Language* (Metuchen, N.J.: Scarecrow, 1975); R. Lakoff, *Language and Woman's Place* (New York: Harper & Row, 1975); C. Miller and K. Swift, *Words and Women* (New York: Doubleday, 1976); B. Thorne and N. Henley, *Language and Sex: Dif-*

ference and Dominance (Rowley, Mass.: Newbury House, 1975).

35. W. M. Austin, "Some Social Aspects of Paralanguage," *Canadian Journal of Linguistics,* 11 (1965), pp. 34, 37.
36. Brown, *Social Psychology.*
37. Austin, "Some Social Aspects of Paralanguage," p. 38.

🌿 24

Teen Mags: How to Get a Guy, Drop 20 Pounds, and Lose Your Self-Esteem

ANASTASIA HIGGINBOTHAM

I used to be the teen magazine market's ideal consumer: vain, terribly insecure, white, and middle class. I craved affection and approval from boys (often at the expense of meaningful relationships with girls), spent far too much time staring at myself in the mirror, and trusted the magazines' advice on all sorts of really, really important issues, like lip gloss and *luv.*

I plastered my family's refrigerator with pictures of models I'd torn out of *YM, Seventeen, Sassy,* and *'Teen,* and also *Vogue, Cosmopolitan,* and *Mademoiselle*—a strategy I used to remind me not to eat. I hoped they would inspire me to do great things, like be in a David Lee Roth video. I wish I were kidding.

Though this characterization might lead you to believe I was kind of a doorknob, I assure you I was merely acting like most girls my age at whom these magazines are directed, aspiring to an ideal that I knew would bring me much success in the social world. In my first 14 years, I learned that the pretty girl who knows how to play the game wins the prize. The "prize" being older, cooler, all-star boyfriends, multiple mentions and pictures throughout the school yearbook, and seasonal dubbings as makeshift teen royalty (Homecoming Queen, May Queen, blow-job queen, and so on). And so I absorbed the rules of the game, with teen magazines serving as a reliable source of that information.

Ten years later, I pore over these magazines to see what they're telling girls today. As I flip through the pages of *YM, Seventeen, Sassy,* and *'Teen,* my blood begins to boil and my eyes cloud with anger; teen magazines make millions off of girls by assuming that girls need improving, and then telling girls how to make themselves prettier, cooler, and better. Has anything changed?

As horrified as I am by these magazines, I cannot deny their raging success. *Seventeen* and *YM* (which used to stand for *Young Miss* and now stands for *Young and Modern*) rake in nearly two million subscriptions each from their teen-to-early-twenties market. *'Teen* and *Sassy,* with readerships of 1.3 million and 800,000 respectively, cater to the younger end of the spectrum.

In each of the magazines, cover lines offer the girls "Model hair: how to get it," "Boy-magnet beauty," "Your looks: what they say about you," and "Mega makeovers: go from so-so to supersexy." Their image of the ideal girl is evidenced by the cover models: white, usually blond, and invariably skinny.

When I asked why this is, Caroline Miller, editor in chief of *Seventeen,* explained, "There's a traditional expectation that African Americans don't sell magazines." *Seventeen* has recently tested this proposition (which, by the way, fails to address the invisibility of Asian and Native American models) by featuring pop star Brandy on its April cover and another African American model on October's cover (both months' are normally hot sellers). October sold just as well as the typical white-model cover, while the Brandy cover was possibly *Seventeen*'s best-selling April issue ever. Despite *Seventeen*'s success, rather than jeopardize newsstand sales and advertising dollars, well-intentioned editors at other magazines like *'Teen* and *Sassy* compromise by featuring some white-looking black model in a month that typically has the worst sales. Meanwhile, *YM* would probably be satisfied with a different shot of Drew Barrymore each month.

In the wake of *Sassy*'s transmogrification from bold, feminist teen mag into dumbed-down, superficial teen rag (*Sassy* was sold to Peterson Publishing, the same company that owns *'Teen,* in December 1994 after years of controversy with advertisers and parents over its content), *Seventeen,* under Miller, has taken up the *Sassy* mantle with smart stories about interracial dating, student activists, and African American girls' body image. *YM,* on the other hand, offers nothing more than bullshit and bad advice, and *'Teen* is not much better. The new *Sassy* lacks much of the brains, courage, and wit of the old *Sassy;* something that its editors, tragically, see as a good thing.

Just what are the messages in the teen magazines? A series of catch-22s—ugliness is next to nothingness and a girl with insufficient interest in boys is referred to as a "deserted island," yet one who is too sexy is also in trouble. For instance, April 1995 *Sassy* warns girls to watch who they flirt with because men cannot distinguish between harmless flirting and a full-on pass. According to *Sassy,* while a girl is flirting, "there's always a chance [men are] wondering what you look like without your clothes on." This mentality is used to justify the behavior of grown men who "get a little carried away sometimes" and harass, insult, and assault young women. A girl bears the responsibility of attracting every "hottie" (hot guy) on the beach, but if one of them jumps her, well then, it sucks to be her. Using *Sassy's* logic, that girl should have known she was dealing with a potential psychopath.

YM echoes this sentiment in the July 1995 episode of "Love Crisis," a column in which Editor in Chief Sally Lee solves "agonizing love problems." A girl reveals that she was invited by her boyfriend to a party that turned out to be just him and his two male friends. They got her really drunk and she "ended up . . . having sex with all of them!" She writes, "I feel so dirty. . . . How could I have been so stupid?" The letter is signed "Mortified." *YM* apparently wonders the same thing: a caption on the page with her letter reads "Wake up and face the facts: you made a pretty big mistake." Lee then chastises the girl for underage drinking and not asserting herself.

Even if the girl has not actually been gang-raped, Lee's complete disregard for a girl who was tricked and humiliated by her boyfriend and his friends is unforgivable. *YM* shamelessly promotes boy-catching tactics with articles like "the ultimate get-a-guy guide," then acts surprised, even judg-

mental, when the tricks actually work. Girls are bombarded with messages about the thrill of catching boys, so why is it shocking when a girl's pursuit includes a little creative compromise, like forgiving her boyfriend for lying about the party, drinking when he tells her to drink, and being too drunk to care (or too drunk to resist) when he and his friends fuck her? *YM* shows girls 100 asinine ways to be supersexy and then provides them with no follow-up skills, self-defense, or self-esteem—as if ignorance will keep them from going all the way. If *YM* ever changes its name again, I suggest *Dicktease.*

Likewise, when it comes to body image, teen magazines send a convoluted message. Girls are encouraged to love their bodies, no matter what they look like, by magazines with fashion spreads featuring only stick-thin, flawless-faced white models in expensive outfits. Granted, there is that one light-skinned black girl in every fashion layout. But she's just as thin as the white girl standing next to her, and that white girl is *always* there—like a chaperone. Like it's the white girl's responsibility to keep the black girl in line, make sure she doesn't mingle with other black folks, start a riot or something. The black model doesn't have any black girlfriends; she's lucky if she gets a similarly nonthreatening black boyfriend for the prom. Maybe they think if they surround her with enough white people no one will even notice she's black.

The thin factor is equally dismaying. While the old *Sassy* strictly enforced a no-diet policy, forbidding publication of any and all diet advice (including the kind masquerading as a fitness article), the new *Sassy* eats it up. Catherine Ettlinger, until recently the editorial director of the new *Sassy,* rejects the connection between articles offering diet tips and girls' obsession with thinness: "We present them with options. 'If you want to eat more low-fat stuff, here's some information; if you don't, fine.'"

If it were that simple, girls would not be getting sick. In a culture that all but demands that a women weigh no more than 120 pounds, girls do not want for diet advice. Girls do not need more low-fat options, nor do they need to learn how to shed or hide "excess fat." Similarly, when *'Teen, YM,* and *Seven-*

teen take a turn on the self-love/body-pride trip, they tend to fall flat on their faces. Photos that accompany the stories typically depict a model—who isn't the least bit fat. Readers are supposed to empathize with girls who weigh 125 pounds but who are afraid to put on a bathing suit, exposing what they perceive to be huge thighs and bulging stomachs. Girls are reminded that because of their "low self-esteem" (certainly not because of patriarchy), they imagine their bodies to be much larger than they actually are. So, if they can get over that self-esteem thing and realize that they're not fat, they have nothing to worry about.

While body hatred of this type is epidemic, presenting body image as being about thin girls who think they're fat does nothing to undermine the essential prejudice against fatness, especially fat women. Is a fat girl beautiful? Should she worry? If she relies on these magazines for affirmation of her self-worth, yes, she should. And so should we.

Teen magazines' glorification of boy-focused, looks-based, prom-obsessed idiocy reinforces every negative stereotype that has ever been used to justify —and ensure—women's second-class status. But as a woman with very clear memories of high school, I understand the trauma associated with fitting in and finding love. I was not prepared for a feminist revolution at 16; I could barely deal with what the humidity did to my hair.

I wanted to find out what girls think about teen magazines nowadays, so I staged an informal survey with a group of teenagers and showed them issues of *'Teen, Sassy, Seventeen,* and *YM.* Some girls criticized the magazines for being too white, too into skinny, and too superficial, but readily admitted to delighting in them anyway.

Kate Stroup from Philadelphia subscribes to *Seventeen,* as well as to various "adult" fashion magazines. "I like the ads," she says. Stroup and her friends can spend hours looking at the pictures, talking about the articles, "even talking about how bad it is." She explains, "It gives us something to bond over."

Girls looking for something easy and entertaining are sure to find it within the pages of teen magazines. Just as I lapped up celebrity gossip while researching this story, the girls I spoke with see no harm in learning a stupid hair trick.

Some girls read them for tips on navigating the social scene and dealing with relationships. "Sometimes I like to read about what guys say, not saying that I would actually follow their advice," says Kenya Hooks of Memphis.

But Roshanda Betts from Dallas no longer reads teen magazines. "I can't relate to them and I don't really think that they're made for me," she says, referring to the unrealistic size requirements for girls, racist definitions of beauty, and what she sees as the magazines' self-contradictions. "They have articles talking about, 'You should love yourself for who you are,' and then they have the seven-day diet."

The girls all like *Seventeen*'s "School Zone," which each month features six pages of photos and quotes from a different high school and which, according to Betts, "shows the spectrum of what's really happening." It's the only place in any of the magazines where kids from various racial and ethnic backgrounds, with "imperfect" shapes and "flawed" complexions, are portrayed in all their splendor. "School Zone" puts the rest of the images in the magazine to shame merely by providing a glimpse of truth.

In the articles, reality often comes in the form of "real-life stories" injected into each magazine, it seems, to scare the hell out of the girl reading it. We can choose from "one girl's battle with depression," another's physically abusive relationship, the story of a woman who sank to 55 pounds, a girl who was "raped, shot, and left for dead," and many more. Without some analysis or a context in which to place these stories (Why did she starve herself? How can we avert these tragedies?), they are nothing more than tales of tabloid horror.

Several months' worth of *'Teen, Seventeen, YM* and *Sassy* left me with a blur of contradictory messages about how to navigate life as an adolescent girl. The sum of it is this: be pretty, but not so pretty that you intimidate boys, threaten other girls, or attract inappropriate suitors, such as teachers, bosses, fathers, and rapists; be smart, but not so smart that you intimidate boys or that, god forbid, you miss the prom to study for finals; be athletic, but not so athletic that you intimidate boys or lead people to believe that you are aggressive, asexual, or (gasp!) a lesbian or bisexual; be happy with yourself, but not if you're fat, ugly, poor, gay, disabled, antisocial, or can't at least pass as white.

The creators of teen magazines claim to reflect the reality of girls' lives; they say that they're giving girls what the girls say they want and, I'm sure that sometimes what girls want is, in fact, a new hairstyle and a prom date. But filling girls full of fluff and garbage—under the pretense that this is their reality—is patronizing, cowardly, and just plain lazy. Magazines that pride themselves on teaching girls beauty tips to "hide what they hate" ought to stop reflecting a reality marred by heterosexist double standards and racist ignorance and start changing it.

I understand the tremendous pressures that editors deal with from parents and advertisers who hold pristine ideas about teendom and girlhood and impose those ideas backed by the mighty dollar. But it's very clear where these editors and advertisers draw their lines. If they really wanted girls to love their bodies, they'd give them a few more shapes and colors to choose from, they'd provide articles exploring some of the real reasons why a girl might plow through a box of Oreos one moment, yak her guts out the next, and then zone in front of the television for sixteen hours a day. If they can be so brazen about teaching a girl how to kiss the boy of her dreams, they can teach her how to kiss a girl. They just won't.   [1996]

✣ 25

Media Images, Feminist Issues

DEBORAH L. RHODE

For those committed to feminism, a central concern has always been how the media reflect and recast feminist issues. For those committed to feminist

research, media studies offer a particularly useful perspective on the social construction of a political movement. Indeed, even formulating this topic as a research question yields unexpected insights. In the *Readers' Guide to Periodical Literature,* "feminism" traditionally has not been significant enough to warrant a separate entry. In the listings for the 1950s, the feminist heading has only a cross-reference to "Women, social and moral questions." This entry lists a handful of articles and a "see also" reference to alcoholism, divorce, harem, and prostitution. Over the next two decades, these cross-references expand and eventually come to include "Women, equal rights." But it is not until the early eighties that feminism becomes a topic heading in its own right.

The following discussion chronicles this evolution and certain persistent limitations in media texts and subtexts. The basic story is one of partial progress. Over the last quarter century, much has improved in press portraits of feminism, feminists, and gender-related issues. Yet much still needs improvement. This article suggests what and why. At issue is what the media choose to present (or not to present) as news about women and how they characterize (or caricature) the women's movement. This issue deserves greater attention from those interested in social movements in general and the women's movement in particular. The press is increasingly responsible for supplying the information and images through which we understand our lives (Hall 1977, 340–42). For any social movement, the media play a crucial role in shaping public consciousness and public policy. Journalists' standard framing devices of selection, exclusion, emphasis, and tone can profoundly affect cultural perceptions (Gitlin 1980, 3–7; Goffman 1974, 10–11).

For the contemporary women's movement, mass communications networks have done much both to frustrate and to advance feminist objectives. As subsequent discussion suggests, the mainstream press appeared largely uninterested or unsympathetic during the movement's early years. And female journalists often lacked the critical mass and professional leverage to ensure systematic, evenhanded treatment of gender-related issues. That has changed dramatically in recent years, in part because of women's increasing involvement in the media and in part because of broader cultural changes in gender roles. As media theorists remind us, audiences always exert some control over the message they receive, and the public's growing concern about women's issues has reshaped popular discourse (Rapping 1993; 1994, 10–12, 284). The press is increasingly an ally in making those issues into political priorities.

However, despite substantial improvements, we still remain stuck in some familiar places. The discussion that follows identifies persistent feminist concerns. Analysis focuses on the absence of women: their underrepresentation in positions of influence; and the not-so-benign neglect of women's issues. By gaining a better understanding of how media images construct and constrain feminist objectives, we may come closer to realizing them.

NEGLECT

Underrepresentation of Women

The frequent absence of women in, on, and behind the news has been chronicled at length elsewhere and does not require extended treatment here. A few illustrative statistics reveal the gaps in women's representation and in the coverage of women's issues, as well as the relationship between the two. In the late 1940s, only one female journalist appeared on any television news. By 1960, the number had increased to one per network. These female reporters handled "women's" stories, such as those involving political wives, and sometimes filled in as weather girls (Marzolf 1993, 33, 36–44). In the print media, the small group of female journalists generally had a separate, and anything but equal, status. Most were relegated to work as researchers rather than writers or to positions on the women's page, traditionally limited to food, fashion, furnishings, and society "dots and doings" (Ross 1974; Davis 1991, 110–11; Robertson 1992; Beasley and Gibbons, 1993; 16; Mills 1993; Quindlen 1993a, 2). The absence of women on news staffs typified broader patterns from prime-time drama to children's cartoons (Tuchman 1978, 8–10; Robertson 1992, 7, 181).

During the 1960s, the situation began to improve, in response both to the feminist movement and to the broader socioeconomic changes that the movement reflected and reinforced. Between the mid-1960s and the early 1990s, women's representation among television network news reporters rose from under 5 percent to over 15 percent, and among print journalists it increased from under 20 percent to almost 40 percent (Marzolf 1993, 43). Female representation also grew to some 68 percent of journalism school graduates (Marzolf 1993, 43). Yet women in the media continue to be grossly underrepresented in positions of the greatest status and power and dramatically overrepresented in the lowest. Women account for less than 10 percent of editors-in-chief, news publishers, and deans or directors of journalism programs (Mills 1993, 19, 25; Otto 1993, 157–58). A recent survey of newspapers and network news programs found that men wrote about two-thirds of the front-page stories and provided 85 percent of the television reporting (Bridge 1993). Women of color are even less visible. They account for only about 7 percent of the newspaper workforce and 3 percent of its executives and managers. In the broadcast media, representative studies from the early 1990s found that women of color filed only 2 percent of the total surveyed stories and that no nonwhite women figured in an annual survey of the fifty most prominent reporters (Beasley and Gibbons 1993, 307, 317).

Once again, these gender imbalances in journalism are symptomatic of broader media patterns. Men hold 90 percent of upper-level Hollywood executive positions, play two-thirds of the leads in prime-time television, supply 90 percent of the narrator's voices in television commercials, and monopolize 90 percent of televised sporting events (Lovdal 1989, 716; Dutka 1990, 8; Carmody 1993, B12; Messner, Duncan, and Jensen 1993). Rarely do women of color exceed what is commonly described as a "sprinkling of minorities" (Edwards 1993, 215–18; Minnesota Advisory committee 1993, 5–7; Women, Men and the Media 1993).

Inattention to Women and "Women's Issues"

The inadequate representation of women in media decision making is mirrored in the media's inadequate representation of women's perspectives and concerns. In recent surveys, men provided 85 percent of newspaper quotes or references, accounted for 75 percent of the television interviewees, and constituted 90 percent of the most frequently cited pundits (Bridge 1993; O'Reilly 1993, 127, 129). This proportionality, or lack thereof, held up across subject matter areas, even on issues that centrally involved women, such as breast implants (Douglas 1992; Bridge 1993; O'Reilly 1993, 125, 127). During the much-fabled "Year of the Woman" in politics, not one representative of a major women's policy organization appeared on any leading TV talk show (Wolf 1993, 80). Despite increased efforts at token representation, all-male talk shows persist even on topics like single motherhood (Pollitt 1994). When women commentators do appear, it is often on explicitly "women's issues." How often, asks Katha Pollitt, do women show up on *Nightline* or *Crossfire* when the subject is not "Hillary Clinton: Does Whitewater Stigmatize All Women?" or "Is the Wonderbra Sexist?" (quoted in Pollitt 1994, 409). Female commentators who write on general topics often remain in the Rolodex under "F"; "as St. Augustine put it, men need women only for the things they can't get from a man" (Pollitt 1993, 409). The result is much as Kirk Anderson portrays it in his cartoon of a talk show anchor stating that, "in the next half-hour, my wealthy white conservative male friends and I will discuss the annoyingly persistent black underclass, and why women get so emotional about abortion" (Ward, 1993, 192).

Women's issues are also underrepresented in the mainstream media (Kahn and Goldenberg 1991, 105–7). To be sure, the situation has improved dramatically since the 1960s and early 1970s, when leading papers rarely discussed matters such as child care and domestic violence or did so only in the "style" section (Quindlen 1993a, 3). Coverage has steadily increased, and dramatic events like the Hill-Thomas hearings or the Tailhook scandal can create a sudden cottage industry of commentary on issues that for centuries had gone unchalleged and unchanged. But on a day-to-day basis, gender biases remain. Subjects that are of greater interest to male than female readers have greater priority among

largely male editors. Topics with the most appeal to men but the least to women, such as local sports, obtain substantially greater newspaper resources than topics for which the relative interest levels are reversed, such as fashion or lifestyle issues (Miller 1993, 167–68).

Issues of particular concern to women of color are often ignored, as are the women themselves. For example, despite the prominent role that black female politicians played during the 1992 Democratic National Convention, few appeared in media coverage (Women, Men, and the Media 1993). "How Can 29 Million People Be Invisible to Democrats?" asked a recent *Los Angeles Times* headline, referring to the Latino population. The same question could have been asked about the author's own profession, which rarely focuses on that constituency (Rogovin 1992, 51, 55–58; Minnesota Advisory Committee 1993, 5–7; Women, Men and the Media 1993).

What coverage does occur often presents biased images. The mainstream media prefer to center stories on deviance rather than on achievements or victimization among people of color and to explain such deviance in terms of race rather than other, more complicated factors (Minnesota Advisory Committee 1993, 5–7). For example, rapes of white women by black men receive a grossly disproportionate amount of media attention, although they account for only a small minority of reported rapes. Sexual assaults against black women are largely overlooked, even though this is the group likeliest to be victims of such brutality (Benedict 1992, 9). During the week of the highly publicized rape of a white investment banker in Central Park by a non-white gang, twenty-eight other women in New York also reported rapes. Nearly all of these were women of color, and their assaults, including at least one of comparable brutality, went largely unreported by the press (Benedict 1992, 219; Terry 1993, 160).

Moreover, despite the enormous volume of commentary attempting to account for the Central Park rape, the most obvious gender-related explanations were notable for their absence. Almost all the coverage focused on race and poverty; almost none surveyed the research on gang rape, which reveals that such crimes are frequently committed by white middle-class athletes and fraternity members. As sociologist Jane Hood put it, "Like the proverbial fish who cannot describe water, Americans see everything but gender at work in the [New York] assault. Given more than 30 years of research on rape, that myopia is hard to explain" (quoted in Benedict 1992, 210).

Any adequate explanation would have to include the media's own selective vision. In Helen Benedict's recent survey, only one of some thirty reporters who routinely covered sex crimes had ever read a book on rape and few had made any effort to consult experts (Benedict, in press, 7). Indeed, many defended their inattention. According to one *Newsday* editor, attempts to analyze sexual brutality are "thumb-sucking journalism. . . . Once you write a piece about rape experts talking about why people do a gang rape, there's no follow-up" (quoted in Benedict, in press, 3). In explaining the *New York Times*'s selective coverage of the Central Park rape, the metropolitan editor acknowledged, "I can't imagine the range of reaction to the sexual aspect of the crime would be very strong. I may be wrong but I can't think right off what questions one ought to ask about that" (quoted in Benedict, in press, 3).

Efforts to increase the coverage of women's perspectives are often met with confession and avoidance. The standard response, reflected in one recent interview with a *New Republic* editor, is that "it's really hard to get women; regrettably, writers of opinion pieces tend to be men" (quoted in Wolf 1993, 84). If so, the media are in part responsible. Female journalists frequently bump up against what Anna Quindlen describes as the "quota of one" (Quindlen 1993a, 12). In explaining their unwillingness to carry a column by a woman who writes about women, editors will note that they "already have one" (O'Reilly 1993, 125; Quindlen 1993a, 12). This somehow turns out not to be a problem for columns by and about white men. It is the notion of women pontificating, and not just about women, that seems to be the problem (O'Reilly 1993, 125–26).

The marginalization of women occurs not only through failure to represent their perspectives but also through failure to recognize them as independent agents, apart from their relation to men. This symbolic erasure was apparent in television descriptions of ethnic cleansing in Bosnia, in which the subjects of gang rape figured as wives and daughters (Ward 1993, 190). Like early English common law, which treated rape as a crime against men's property interest, some contemporary media accounts carry similar subtexts: "Five [males] broke into the home of a . . . school teacher, beat him, raped his wife, and looted everything they could find" (Beasley and Gibbons 1993, 34). Similarly, a recent newspaper headline—"Widow, 70, Dies after Beating by Intruder"—reflects the significance of women's marital status even after death (Ward 1993, 191). Other information, such as the victim's work as a crime prevention volunteer, is of less apparent importance. Such persistent value hierarchies are aptly captured in a recent Cath Jackson cartoon. It features a male editor lecturing a female staffer on the obvious problems with an article titled "Wheelchair Woman Climbs Mt. Everest": "You've missed the main points: WHO is her husband? WHAT does he do? WHERE would she be without him and WHY isn't she at home looking after the kids?" (Jackson 1993, 4).   [1995]

REFERENCES

Beasley, Maurine H., and Shiela J. Gibbons. 1993. *Taking Their Place: A Documentary History of Women and Journalism.* Washington, D.C.: American University Press.

Benedict, Helen. 1992. *Virgin or Vamp: How the Press Covers Sex Crimes.* New York: Oxford University Press.

———. In press. "Covering Rape without Feminism." In *Women and Law in the Media,* ed. Martha Fineman. New York: Routledge.

Bridge, M. Junior. 1993. "The News: Looking Like America? Not Yet. . . ." In *Women, Men and Media.* Los Angeles: Center for Women, Men, and the Media.

Carmody, John. 1993. "Minorities Still Shut Out Survey Reports." *Washington Post,* June 16, B12.

Davis, Flora. 1991. *Moving the Mountain: The Women's Movement in America since 1960.* New York: Simon & Schuster.

Douglas, Susan J. 1992. "Missing Voices: Women and the U.S. News Media." *Fairness and Accuracy in Reporting Extra* (Special Issue), 4.

Dutka, Elaine. 1990. "Women and Hollywood: It's Still a Lousy Relationship." *Los Angeles Times,* November 11, Calendar, 8.

Edwards, Audrey. 1993. "From Aunt Jemima to Anita Hill: Media's Split Image of Black Women." *Media Studies Journal,* vol. 7.

Gitlin, Todd. 1980. *The Whole World Is Watching*. Berkeley and Los Angeles: University of California Press.

Goffman, Irving. 1974. *Frame Analysis: An Essay on the Organization of Experience*. New York: Harper & Row.

Hall, Stuart. 1977. "Culture, Media, and the Ideological Effect." In *Mass Communication and Society*, ed. James Curran, Michael Gurevitch, and Janet Woollacott. London: Edward Arnold.

Jackson, Cath. 1993. "Trouble and Strife" (cartoon). In Caryl Rivers, "Bandwagons, Women and Cultural Mythology." *Media Studies Journal*, vol. 7.

Kahn, Kim Fridkin, and Edie N. Goldenberg. 1991. "The Media, Obstacle or Ally of Feminists." *Annals of the American Academy of Political and Social Science*, vol. 515.

Lovdal, Lynn T. 1989. "Sex-Role Messages in Televison Commercials: An Update." *Sex Roles* 21 (11–12): 715.

Marzolf, Marion Tuttle. 1993. "Deciding What's Women's News." *Media Studies Journal*, vol. 7.

Messner, Michael A., Margaret Carlisle Duncan, and Kerry Jensen. 1993. "Separating the Men from the Girls: The Gendered Language of Televised Sports." *Gender and Society*, vol. 7.

Miller, Susan. 1993. "Opportunity Squandered—Newspapers and Women's News." *Media Studies Journal*, vol. 7.

Mills, Kay. 1993. "The Media and the Year of the Woman." *Media Studies Journal*, vol. 7.

Minnesota Advisory Committee to the U.S. Commission on Civil Rights. 1993. *Stereotyping of Minorities by the News Media in Minnesota*. Washington, D.C.: Government Printing Office.

O'Reilly, Jane. 1993. "The Pale Males of Punditry." *Media Studies Journal*, vol. 7.

Otto, Jean. 1993. "A Matter of Opinion." *Media Studies Journal*, vol. 7.

People. 1994. "Hillary Pillary." *People*, June 20, 42.

Pollitt, Katha. 1993. "Not Just Bad Sex." *New Yorker*, October 4, 220.

———. 1994. "Subject to Debate." *The Nation*, October 17, 409.

Quindlen, Anna. (1992) 1993. "The Two Faces of Eve." In her *Thinking Out Loud*, 197. New York: Random House.

Quinn, Sally. 1992. "Feminists Have Killed Feminism." *Los Angeles Times*. January 23, B7.

Rapping, Elayne. 1993. "Gender and Media Theory: A Critique of the 'Backlash Model.'" Unpublished manuscript, Adelphi University, Garden City, N.Y.

———. 1994. *Media-tions: Forays into the Culture and Gender Wars*. Boston: South End.

Robertson, Nan. 1992. *The Girls in the Balcony*. New York: Fawcett Columbine.

Rogovin, Wendy M. 1992. "The Regulation of Television in the Public Interest: On Creating a Parallel Universe in Which Minorities Speak and Are Heard." *Catholic Law Review*, vol. 92.

Ross, Ishbel. 1974. *The Ladies of the Press*. New York: Arno.

Terry, Don. 1993. "In the Week of an Infamous Rape, 28 Other Victims Suffer." In *Gender and Public Policy*, ed. Kenneth Winston and Mary Jo Bane. Boulder, Colo.: Westview.

Tuchman, Gaye. 1978. "Introduction: The Symbolic Annihilation of Women by the Mass Media." In *Hearth and Home: Images of Women in the Mass Media*, ed. Arlene Kaplan Daniels and Jane Benet. New York: Oxford University Press.

Ward, Jean. 1993. "Talking (Fairly) about the World: A Reprieve on Journalistic Language." *Media Studies Journal*, vol. 7.

Wolf, Naomi. 1993. *Fire with Fire*. New York: Random House.

Women, Men and the Media. 1993. "The News, As If All People Mattered." New York: Women, Men and the Media, New York University.

 26

Female Images and Roles in Music

VENISE T. BERRY

Music is a business. It is the business of marketing a product for profit, and research has shown that sex can sell.[1] A study by Larry Lance and Christina Berry found a significant increase between 1968 and 1977 in the number of popular songs with implications of sexual intercourse and in the number of females initiating those sexual encounters.[2]

Negative sexual images of females in the male-dominated music industry is a prominent topic of criticism. Men dominate the pop music arena, defining sex role standards from a patriarchal perspective.[3] Research indicates that in country music a woman's role and status is usually related to her ability to get and hold a man.[4] Colleen Hyden and N. Jane McCandless have found that women are typically portrayed as youthful, passive, and childlike in contemporary popular music.[5] Susan Butruille and Anita Taylor have identified three prominent female images in popular music: the ideal woman or saint; the evil/fickle witch, sinner, or whore, and the victim (usually dead). In the same study women were most often shown as sex objects, possessions, or providers in black music culture.[6]

Rock music and music videos have come under intense scrutiny. Barry Sherman and Joseph Dominick examined 366 rock music videos and found a significant amount of violence, sex, and other aggressive acts directed at women.[7] Women were also portrayed in a condescending manner in an overwhelming number of music videos examined by Richard Vincent, Dennis Davis, and Lilly Boruszkowski.[8] Christine Hansen and Ronald Hansen found in their studies that images in rock music videos suggest women are considered more non-threatening, submissive, sexual, and sympathetic when they return the man's advances.[9] Finally, Jane Brown and Kenneth Campbell report that females, both black and white, are rarely portrayed on MTV or Video Soul as professionals; however, black women in their study were least likely to be found in roles projecting antisocial behavior or victimization.[10]

Research on the acceptance and perpetuation of stereotypical images of women in American culture is prominent and has shown that the application of gender labels and other stereotypical attributes are learned as early as the age of three.[11] Sex role stereotypes are linked to specific gender-related activities and domains, such as girls playing inside with dolls and boys outside playing with guns.[12] Many studies have illustrated the importance of gender relations and appropriate activity selection in the United States, suggesting that children are taught these roles through peer interaction, socialization, and cultural experience.[13]

Many critics have acknowledged that other music, such as the blues, reflects the sexual exploitation of women. Themes that emerged in a 1988 book about the blues by Daphne Harrison included infidelity, sexual exploitation, and mistreatment. Harrison argued that women in blues usually do not joke about lost love but instead sing of grief, while men brag about their conquests and exploits with women.[14] Mary Ellison, in her book *Lyrical Protests: Black Music's Struggle against Discrimination*, agreed. She discussed such female blues singers as Ma Rainey, Bessie Smith, and Victoria Spivey, who often sang about inadequate men, but she also found the music of female blues reflects black women's strong determination to lead their own lives.[15] Hazel Carby's analysis of the sexual politics of women's blues explained how important "classic blues" were

for women: "What has been called 'Classic Blues,' is the women's blues of the twenties and early thirties. It is a discourse that articulates a cultural and political struggle over sexual relations; a struggle that is directed against the objectification of female sexuality within a patriarchal order, but which also tries to reclaim women's bodies as the sexual and sensual subjects of women's songs."[16]

The struggle for independence, equality, and freedom among black women, Ellison also pointed out, has been a part of black music styles from slavery to the present: "There is an explosive dynamism coursing through the songs that black women write specifically about themselves—a tension that springs from the determination to free themselves from male domination and misuse, conflicting with a strong resolution to stand with black men in the fight for the liberation of all black people."[17]

This spirit of rebellion and independence was a major part of music in the 1960s. Ellison observed that Aretha Franklin's popular hit "Respect," insisting that respect be given to black women and men, became a banner for the civil rights movement.[18] She also discussed other contemporary black women, like Millie Jackson and Grace Jones, who sang of independence and individuality through female role reversals.[19]

EVOLVING RAP MUSIC STYLE

The negative images and messages concerning women in rap music have spawned tremendous publicity. As Reebee Garofalo explained, it is the frankness of rap that creates many of its problems. While making no excuses for rap stars, he suggests that the sexism in rap is a product of all genres of popular music and life in the United States.[20] Music has long been a powerful form of expression in black culture, with rap music stretching and redefining previous boundaries. Born in the New York streets of Harlem and the South Bronx, rap evolved as part of the privileged black male urban street culture, popularizing black dialect, street fashion, style, attitude, and mannerisms.

David Toop in *The Rap Attack* related the evolution of rap music to the griot in West Africa, who was a great singing storyteller and served as a living history book. He went on to link this oral genre to other powerful black traditions, like oral preaching, rhyming stories called toasts, and verbal rhyming word games, such as the "dozens" and "signifying," all popular in urban black neighborhoods and resembling the rhythmic talking style of rap. These cultural legacies were specifically black male traditions. They were a prominent part of the black male experience carried out wherever black men gathered —on street corners or in bars, the armed forces, and prisons.[21]

Male-privileged space is a primary issue for Lisa Lewis in her evaluation of female images on MTV. She explains that the street is traditionally a place for males to explore freedom, rebellious practice, male bonding, and female pursuit. For women, however, the streets are dangerous, feared, and inappropriate. Women on the street are considered prostitutes, or whores, objects of male desire and dominance.[22]

Rap music, a product of black male tradition and experience, has defined the images of women from that limited perspective. Many male rap groups tend to view women with a common lack of respect, but controversial groups like the 2 Live Crew, The Ghetto Boys, Easy E, and Too Short perpetuate extreme negatives. In many male rap videos, the female body is presented as a product of male sexual pleasure; candid shots of breasts, crotches, and buttocks are the norm. Women in these raps are called "skeezers," "hoes," "sluts," "whores," and "bitches." They are described as objects to be sexually used, physically and verbally abused.

The most controversial example is 2 Live Crew, a group whose music has killed love and romance and has taken sex into the realm of perversion, violence, and pain. Many of their song titles can serve as examples of their sexist ideology: "We Want Some Pussy," "Me So Horny," "Head, Booty, and Cock," "Bad Ass Bitch," "Face Down, Ass Up," and "Dick Almighty." The cover of their album "As Nasty as They Wanna Be" flaunts the well-endowed buttocks of four black women in G-strings standing on a table with their backs turned and legs spread. Members of the 2 Live Crew position themselves in front of the women, each centered between a pair of legs, facing the camera. Luther Campbell, leader of the group,

argues that his music is no worse than the work of Eddie Murphy or Andrew Dice Clay. In his defense he explains that "bitch" is an endearing term: "We're talking about a hell of a woman who ain't gonna take shit—one of those Dynasty, Alexis type motherfuckers. That's what I like in a woman. I want me a real Bitch, not some pushover."[23]

The hearings of Parents Music Resource Center (PMRC) have led to questions of censorship; however, it must again be noted that music is a business and that sex sells. Major record companies are currently dealing with the controversy of labeling sexually explicit and violent albums as they see fit. Geffen, for example, chose to drop The Ghetto Boys because of their obscenity, while Atlantic Records, in the midst of the media controversy, purchased an interest in the 2 Live Crew's Luke Records.[24]

In the profit-oriented music industry the success of sexually explicit acts is fantastic, considering the lack of radio and television airplay. The 2 Live Crew's album *Nasty as They Wanna Be,* with no video or other major advertising, made the *Rolling Stone* top fifty album chart. Because of the controversy created in their obscenity trials, the album leaped from number forty-four to sixteen in a two-week period.[25] It also outsold the clean version, *As Clean as They Wanna Be,* by nine to one.[26]

In all fairness it should be noted there is a significant number of male rap groups that do not advocate misogyny or violence toward women. Rappers like KRS One, A Tribe Called Quest, Jungle Brothers, and De La Soul are attempting to unify rappers and rap fans through positive information and education. Positive rap efforts are bringing male and female rap stars together to speak against gang violence and black-on-black crime, while empowering the black rap community as a whole.

While it is crucial to confront the perpetuation of sexism in rap music, Lewis suggests moving away from an emphasis on male attitude and behavior and instead focusing on the powerful messages and images of today's popular female stars.[27] Women as contrasting voices, "others," have created a new dialogue in rap music, challenging those negative, male-oriented perspectives. Their music reflects the same macho style and aggressive delivery, but it includes black feminist ideology that tests the line between socially accepted male and female roles.

According to Toop, male rappers were willing to accept female rappers but considered them lacking in the competitiveness necessary to survive and succeed in rap.[28] To compete in the male-dominated music industry, women are serious and hard-hitting in their lyrics and delivery style. The stereotypical portrayals of women as weak, stupid, and sexually out of control conflict with the new identity projected by female rappers. Their lyrical story line and performance style demonstrate an unyielding intelligence and strength.

The popularity of black female rappers comes as no surprise in light of the cultural experience of black women in the United States. The foundation of black music as a spoken song has always included women. Toop describes African women who also developed cultural legacies, such as lampoons and galla abusive poems. These expressions of hostility or hate were usually sung. In this tradition the hostile words of Yoruba women became lyrical poetry. Toop also mentions other prominent black women singers who serve as evolutionary examples of the black feminine voice in African American music: Dorothy Norwood, a prominent gospel storyteller; the sermonette singer Edna Gallman Cooke; the pioneer soul rappers Laura Lee and Irma Thomas; and finally, Millie Jackson, who was dubbed the mistress of musical raps. These women have all played a crucial role in the development of the rap music genre.[29]   [1994]

NOTES

1. See, for example, Lance and Berry, "Has There Been a Sexual Revolution?"; Zillman and Mundorf, "Image Effects"; and Abramson and Mechanic, "Sex and the Media."
2. Lance and Berry, "Has There Been a Sexual Revolution?" 162.
3. Endres, "Sex Role Standards."
4. Saucier, "Healers and Heartbreakers."
5. Hyden and McCandless, "Lyrics of Contemporary Music."
6. Butruille and Taylor, "Women in American Popular Song."
7. Sherman and Dominick, "Violence and Sex in Music Videos."
8. Vincent, Davis, and Boruszkowski, "Sexism on MTV."
9. Hansen and Hansen, "Influence of Sex and Violence."
10. Brown and Campbell, "Race and Gender in Music Videos."
11. See, for example, Thompson, "Gender Labels"; Weinraub, Clemens, and Sockloff, "Development of Sex Role Stereotypes"; and Masters and Wilkerson, "Consensual and Discrimination Stereotypy."
12. See, for example, Blakemore, Larve, and Olejnik, "Sex Appropriate Toy Preference"; Eisenberg, Murray, and Hite, "Children's Reasoning"; and Ruble, Balaban, and Cooper, "Gender Constancy."
13. See, for example, Masters and Furman, "Friendship Selection"; Lamb and Roopnarine, "Peer Influences on Sex Role Development"; and Langlois and Downs, "Mothers, Fathers, and Peers as Socialization Agents."
14. Harrison, *Black Pearls*, 63–113.
15. Ellison, *Lyrical Protest*, 111.
16. Carby, "'It Jus Be's Dat Way Sometime,'" 241.
17. Ellison, *Lyrical Protest*. 107.
18. Ibid., 115.
19. Ibid., 113.
20. Garofalo, "Crossing Over," 115.
21. Toop, *Rap Attack*, 47, 94.
22. Lewis, "Female Address in Music Video," 75.
23. Quoted in Ressner, "On the Road," 20, 24.
24. See, for example, Dimartino and Rosen, "Labeling Albums," 6; and Newman, Lichtman, and Haring, "Atlantic Invests in Crew Label."
25. "Top Fifty Albums," 74.
26. Roberts-Thomas, "Say It Loud," 30.
27. Lewis, "Form and Female Authorship," 356.
28. Toop, *Rap Attack*, 94.
29. Ibid., 47–48.

 27

Mutineers in Mainstream Music: Heralds of a New Feminist Wave?

NAOMI WEISSTEIN

"He punched out my dog/ he totalled my van/ he beat me up/ I love my man," roared The Chicago Women's Liberation Rock Band 25 years ago, parodying the masochistic lyrics expected of girl vocalists in rock. We challenged all the demeaning imperatives for women in music. We performed at the hurricane-high of the radical second wave of feminism, and audiences danced, shouted, and sang along with our insurrection, mobbing the stage afterward, hugging us and our instruments—even our amplifiers.

In 1973 the band dissolved, and, for a long time afterward (with the splendid but marginalized exception of folkie "women's music"), female vocalists sang endless litanies of Suffering Abject Devotion to men. I despaired of the music and mourned for the politically energized audience that had resonated with our mutinous performance.

And then I could not listen at all. A catastrophic neurological illness attacked me, and for years I have lain supine in a bed without sound or light, the detritus of mass misogynist culture humming in my head.

Recently, a new anti-seizure medication has enabled me to listen again, in tiny bytes over many months—not recommended for music lovers, but it gives you plenty of time to ponder the material. What I hear astonishes me! By turns joyful, angry, moving, original, and hilarious, a cadre of folkateers, funkateers, punkateers, pop stars, rockers, and rappers have left gender church and are rebelling against the frenzied worship of men that defined female popular song for so long.

Many of the new lyrics are marvelously angry. "Did you forget about me, Mr. Duplicity?" asks Alanis Morissette in a tone-perfect shriek, ". . . I'm not gonna fade." "You thought I was a little mouse, . . . but now I'm here, burning down your house," growls Shirley Manson of Garbage. "I'm packing a rod and it's all for you," grunts mock-tough L7. ". . . fucking Napoleon," sneers Ani DiFranco. "Keep him on a leash cuz he's a D-O-G," snarl the usually amiable Salt 'n Pepa.

In these new lyrics, if men are allowed to stick around, it's on *terms:* "I need my car waxed and my floor shellac/I need my back rubbed and da bubbles in the tub," instructs hip-hopper M. C. Lyte. Lil Kim puts in her order: "No dick tonight, eat my pussy right." Even the bubblegum-feminist Spice Girls warn, "If you can't dance, . . . you can't do nothing for me."

While few musical mutineers—as I'll call them —would out themselves as "feminist" (a currently tainted word), protest against women's subjugation

pervades the songs. Anti-rape: "Did she ask you for it? Did she ask you nice?" laments Courtney Love of Hole. Anti-harassment: "Who you calling bitch?" demands Queen Latifah. "Who you calling ho?" Anti-beauty traps: "You made me crazy," Kathleen Hanna of Bikini Kill shouts at her mirror. "Ugly girl . . . do you hate her?" rails Jewel.

The new lyrics do more than burn down the man's mission: they build mansions above the ruins. Defying the women-must-love-men injunction, mutineers celebrate lesbian love. "If you must dance, dance for me," funkateer Me'shell Ndegeocello begs Mary Magdalene. "I am your passion, your promise, your end," hard-rocking Melissa Etheridge resoundingly reassures her female partner.

In a stunning departure from anything that has ever gone before, female songwriters also empathically illuminate the lives of other women—clearly not themselves. Joan Osborne elegizes a homeless mother in "St. Theresa." "Lolita, go on home," Suzanne Vega advises a love-hungry teenager. In "Ordinary Morning," Sheryl Crow, the virtuoso of such empathic character sketches, imagines herself a runaway housewife-turned-hooker who is becoming psychotic: "Just an ordinary day . . . Just an ordinary woman . . . slipping away."

The phenomenon-manipulators have not ignored these feminist developments in pop music. All year long they've been hype-ranting about "girl power," a mindless cheer that rises up equally for sales of battery-powered brassieres, lawsuits against high school dress codes, and adoration of *Titanic*'s Leonardo DiCaprio.

But what really *is* happening? Have the six megacorporations that virtually own entertainment only *now* realized that transgression is the cash crop of rock and rap and that, to reverse the current disastrous sag in music sales, they should start encouraging women to be *bad?* (Followed, of course, in five minutes, by a campaign to dress women musicians in little see-through slave uniforms and encourage them to be *good?*) Or is there such widespread resistance to the old minification that the industry is helpless to contain it?

Blind and bedridden and unable to answer this

question myself, I enlisted a few pop-culture junkie friends and some old band members to help me figure this out. Their report was that *it's both.* Some mutineer women are being heavily promoted. But a new energy is also present—an explosion of youthful anti-sexist consciousness. This market empowers female rebels to kick out.

Indeed, the story of the interaction between women's musical mutiny and the passionate audience that is supporting it is almost a feminist fantasy of how political change can work.

Here is a brief history. It has always been difficult to break into rock and rap, but for women it approached impossibility. Performance tours did not include women and (except for the more-timid-than mutinous but nevertheless wildly successful Lilith Fair, they still do not); labels would not sign them; and the radio would air only one woman per playlist.

Recalls Rana Ross, the bassist for Phantom Blue and Vixen (easily the decade's two tightest hard-rock girl bands), "A few years ago, a rock superstar was auditioning players. I sent in my bio and tape, but no picture. I got an excited call, but when they found out I was female, they wouldn't even let me audition. My tape was good enough, but my gender wasn't."

American history professor Rachel Devlin recounts that about ten years ago a tornado of militant feminist musicians blew away anti-woman business-as-usual. Riot Grrrls, Foxcore groups, and others organized showstring production companies and friends-of-friends distribution networks, spreading their openly confrontational music from city to city.

These independents, with their zines and punk bars, might just have ended up as another exercise in the marginality of "women's music," but—mirabile dictu!—the acts got hot. To give an example of how hot, Ani DiFranco, the most successful Indie yet, male or female, played to a sold-out crowd at Jones Beach with—zowie!—*Bob Dylan!* "[She is] One of the decade's defining voices," raved *Rolling Stone* magazine.

Mainstream mutineers followed on the heels of the Indies. "The Indies . . . influenced and set the stage for Alanis, Sheryl, and Melissa," says Devlin. Minimally, Indies influenced *some* labels to record *some* women, if only as weirdo novelty acts to revive dying revenues. Maximally, they struck forked terror into the hearts of Megalopolated Entertainment.

Ultimately, insurrection marched into mainstream music because the fans devoured it. Receipts soared. Alanis Morissette's debut album sold *15 million* units. (Platinum is a million.) Jewel's debut sold 5 million units. Erykah Badu's goodbye rap to the boyfriend ("Tyrone") got so popular with women that some black radio stations started calling it "the female national anthem." The *New York Times*, I'm told, reports that the slump in record sales was over last summer due primarily to mutineer albums.

People who have been there tell me that audiences for mutineers act more like they are at a political rally than at a mere concert. Overwhelmingly female (the ratio of girls to boys at Lilith Fair was 3 : 1), they are wildly participatory and proprietary. Fans admonish Ani DeFranco when her *attitude* decompresses.

Indeed, these audiences *are* at a political rally. Female rebels are singing to the anger, confusion, and aspirations of a generation of young women now coming of age. Despite the relentless attempt by the rest of the media to ridicule feminist ideas and raise victim blaming to religion, these young women suspect, or know already, that they live in a violent, often woman-hating world. They cannot count on lovers to love them or husbands to honor them. Romance lies bleeding in a battered women's shelter. They seek feminist truths and female heroes, and they are finding them on the soundstages (and on the women's pro-basketball courts and at countless other female venues) across America.

My observers' reports of the intensity of the crowds reminds me—happily—of the ecstatic performance of my rock band a quarter century ago. People might call it "girl power" this time—or some other cute phrase that simultaneously trivializes, commodifies and distances it from feminism, but I believe that we are poised for a renewed surge of women's militance in the world. From what I hear, some restless folks are gathering at the gates.

Rap

Queen Latifa: *Black Reign.*	Moving, politically savvy, dramatic
M C. Lyte: *bad as i wanna b.*	Sexually graphic, hilarious
Salt 'n Pepa: *Very Necessary.*	Amiable, sexy, playful, comic theater
Missy Eliot: *Supadupa Fly.*	Breathtakingly rhythmic mumbling that defies the gotta-be-sexy conventions

Rock

Sheryl Crow: *Sheryl Crow.*	Sophisticated, novelistic, sixties-legatee
Joan Osborne: *Relish.*	Bluesy, gritty-voiced, complex poetry
Alanis Morissette: *Jagged Little Pill.*	Rousingly angry, breakneck tempoed, tone-perfect shrieking

Funk/Jazz/R&B

Me'shell Ndegeocello: *Peace Beyond Passion.*	Many-layered personal/political
Erykah Badu: *Baduizm.*	Smooth Jazz from a most imperious presence

Funk

L7: *Smell the Magic.*	Tough, hip, observant, girls-only band

Indies

Bikini Kill: *Reject American*	Swiftian satire from the original riot grrrls
Ani DiFranco: *Living in Clip.*	The angriest, most vulnerable, toughest, softest, outest feminist

[1998]

ACKNOWLEDGEMENTS

Grateful thanks to rock critics Robert Christgau and Ben Kim; to Rana Ross, John Ross, Rachel Devlin, Anne Snitow, Virginia Blaisdell, and Amy Kesselman; and to Carmen Balkaran, Aleatha Carter, and Maureen Josephs.

🌿 28

Video

INDIA.ARIE

Sometimes I shave my legs and sometimes I don't
Sometimes I comb my hair and sometimes I won't
Depend on how the wind blows I might even paint
my toes
It really just depends on whatever feels good in my
soul

I'm not the average girl from your video
And I ain't built like a supermodel
But I learned to love myself unconditionally,
Because I am a queen

When I look in the mirror and the only one there
is me
Every freckle on my face is where it's supposed
to be
And I know my creator didn't make no mistakes
on me
My feet, my thighs, my lips, my eyes, I'm loving
what I see

Am I less of a lady if I don't wear pantyhose?
My momma said a lady ain't what she wears but
what she knows
But I've drawn the conclusion, it's all an illusion
Confusion's the name of the game
A misconception, a vast deception,
Something's got to change

Now don't be offended this is all my opinion
Ain't nothing that I'm saying law
This is a true confession
Of a life-learned lesson
I was sent here to share with y'all
So get in when you fit in
Go on and shine

Clear your mind
Now's the time
Put your salt on the shelf
Go on and love yourself
'Cause everything's gonna be alright

Keep your fancy drink, and your expensive minks
I don't need that to have a good time
Keep your expensive cars and your caviar
All's I need is my guitar

Keep your Cristal and your pistol
I'd rather have a pretty piece of crystal
Don't need no silicone, I prefer my own
What God gave me is just fine.

I'm not the average girl from your video
And I ain't built like a supermodel
But I learned to love myself unconditionally,
Because I am a queen.   [2001]

🌿 29

X: A Fabulous Child's Story

LOIS GOULD

Once upon a time, a baby named X was born. This baby was named X so that nobody could tell whether it was a boy or a girl. Its parents could tell, of course, but they couldn't tell anybody else. They couldn't even tell Baby X, at first.

You see, it was all part of a very important Secret Scientific Xperiment, known officially as Project Baby X. The smartest scientists had set up this Xperiment at a cost of Xactly 23 billion dollars and 72 cents, which might seem like a lot for just one baby, even a very important Xperimental baby. But when you remember the prices of things like strained carrots and stuffed bunnies, and popcorn for the movies and booster shots for camp, let alone 28 shiny quarters from the tooth fairy, you begin to see how it adds up.

Also, long before Baby X was born, all those sci-

entists had to be paid to work out the details of the Xperiment, and to write the *Official Instruction Manual* for Baby X's parents and, most important of all, to find the right set of parents to bring up Baby X. These parents had to be selected very carefully. Thousands of volunteers had to take thousands of tests and answer thousands of tricky questions. Almost everybody failed because, it turned out, almost everybody really wanted either a baby boy or a baby girl, and not Baby X at all. Also, almost everybody was afraid that a Baby X would be a lot more trouble than a boy or a girl. (They were probably right, the scientists admitted, but Baby X needed parents who wouldn't *mind* the Xtra trouble.)

There were families with grandparents named Milton and Agatha, who didn't see why the baby couldn't be named Milton or Agatha instead of X, even if it *was* an X. There were families with aunts who insisted on knitting tiny dresses and uncles who insisted on sending tiny baseball mitts. Worst of all, there were families that already had other children who couldn't be trusted to keep the secret. Certainly not if they knew the secret was worth 23 billion dollars and 72 cents—and all you had to do was take one little peek at Baby X in the bathtub to know if it was a boy or a girl.

But, finally, the scientists found the Joneses, who really wanted to raise an X more than any other kind of baby—no matter how much trouble it would be. Ms. and Mr. Jones had to promise they would take equal turns caring for X, and feeding it, and singing it lullabies. And they had to promise never to hire any baby-sitters. The government scientists knew perfectly well that a baby-sitter would probably peek at X in the bathtub, too.

The day the Joneses brought their baby home, lots of friends and relatives came over to see it. None of them knew about the secret Xperiment, though. So the first thing they asked was what kind of a baby X was. When the Joneses smiled and said, "It's an X!" nobody knew what to say. They couldn't say, "Look at her cute little dimples!" And they couldn't say, "Look at his husky little biceps!" And they couldn't even say just plain "kitchy-coo." In fact, they all thought the Joneses were playing some kind of rude joke.

But, of course, the Joneses were not joking. "It's an X" was absolutely all they would say. And that made the friends and relatives very angry. The relatives all felt embarrassed about having an X in the family. "People will think there's something wrong with it!" some of them whispered. "There *is* something wrong with it!" others whispered back.

"Nonsense!" the Joneses told them all cheerfully. "What could possibly be wrong with this perfectly adorable X?"

Nobody could answer that, except Baby X, who had just finished its bottle. Baby X's answer was a loud, satisfied burp.

Clearly, nothing at all was wrong. Nevertheless, none of the relatives felt comfortable about buying a present for a Baby X. The cousins who sent the baby a tiny football helmet would not come and visit any more. And the neighbors who sent a pink-flowered romper suit pulled their shades down when the Joneses passed their house.

The *Official Instruction Manual* had warned the new parents that this would happen, so they didn't fret about it. Besides, they were too busy with Baby X and the hundreds of different Xercises for treating it properly.

Ms. and Mr. Jones had to be Xtra careful about how they played with little X. They knew that if they kept bouncing it up in the air and saying how *strong* and *active* it was, they'd be treating it more like a boy than an X. But if all they did was cuddle it and kiss it and tell it how *sweet* and *dainty* it was, they'd be treating it more like a girl than an X.

On page 1,654 of the *Official Instruction Manual,* the scientists prescribed: "plenty of bouncing and plenty of cuddling, *both.* X ought to be strong and sweet and active. Forget about *dainty* altogether."

Meanwhile, the Joneses were worrying about other problems. Toys, for instance. And clothes. On his first shopping trip, Mr. Jones told the store clerk, "I need some clothes and toys for my new baby." The clerk smiled and said, "Well, now, is it a boy or a girl?" "It's an X," Mr. Jones said, smiling back. But the clerk got all red in the face and said huf-

fily, "In *that* case, I'm afraid I can't help you, sir." So Mr. Jones wandered helplessly up and down the aisles trying to find what X needed. But everything in the store was piled up in sections marked "Boys" or "Girls." There were "Boys' Pajamas" and "Girls' Underwear" and "Boys' Fire Engines" and "Girls' Housekeeping Sets." Mr. Jones went home without buying anything for X. That night he and Ms. Jones consulted page 2,326 of the *Official Instruction Manual.* "Buy plenty of everything!" it said firmly.

So they bought plenty of sturdy blue pajamas in the Boys' Department and cheerful flowered underwear in the Girls' Department. And they bought all kinds of toys. A boy doll that made pee-pee and cried, "Pa-pa." And a girl doll that talked in three languages and said, "I am the Pres-i-dent of Gen-er-al Mo-tors." They also bought a storybook about a brave princess who rescued a handsome prince from his ivory tower, and another one about a sister and brother who grew up to be a baseball star and a ballet star, and you had to guess which was which.

The head scientists of Project Baby X checked all their purchases and told them to keep up the good work. They also reminded the Joneses to see page 4,629 of the *Manual,* where it said, "Never make Baby X feel *embarrassed* or *ashamed* about what it wants to play with. And if X gets dirty climbing rocks, never say 'Nice little Xes don't get dirty climbing rocks.'"

Likewise, it said, "If X falls down and cries, never say 'Brave little Xes don't cry.' Because, of course, nice little Xes *do* get dirty, and brave little Xes *do* cry. No matter how dirty X gets, or how hard it cries, don't worry. It's all part of the Xperiment."

Whenever the Joneses pushed Baby X's stroller in the park, smiling strangers would come over and coo: "Is that a boy or a girl?" The Joneses would smile back and say, "It's an X." The strangers would stop smiling then, and often snarl something nasty —as if the Joneses had snarled at *them.*

By the time X grew big enough to play with other children, the Joneses' troubles had grown bigger, too. Once a little girl grabbed X's shovel in the sandbox, and zonked X on the head with it. "Now, now,

Tracy," the little girl's mother began to scold, "little girls mustn't hit little—" and she turned to ask X, "Are you a little boy or a little girl, dear?"

Mr. Jones, who was sitting near the sandbox, held his breath and crossed his fingers.

X smiled politely at the lady, even though X's head had never been zonked so hard in its life. "I'm a little X," X replied.

"*You're a what?*" the lady exclaimed angrily. "You're a little b-r-a-t, you mean!"

"But little girls mustn't hit little Xes, either!" said X, retrieving the shovel with another polite smile. "What good does hitting do, anyway?"

X's father, who was still holding his breath, finally let it out, uncrossed his fingers, and grinned back at X.

And at their next secret Project Baby X meeting, the scientists grinned, too. Baby X was doing fine.

But then it was time for X to start school. The Joneses were really worried about this, because school was even more full of rules for boys and girls, and there were no rules for Xes. The teacher would tell boys to form one line, and girls to form another line. There would be boys' games and girls' games, and boys' secrets and girls' secrets. The school library would have a list of recommended books for girls, and a different list of recommended books for boys. There would even be a bathroom marked BOYS and another one marked GIRLS. Pretty soon boys and girls would hardly talk to each other. What would happen to poor little X?

The Joneses spent weeks consulting their *Instruction Manual* (there were 249½ pages of advice under "First Day of School"), and attending urgent special conferences with the smart scientists of Project Baby X.

The scientists had to make sure that X's mother had taught X how to throw and catch a ball properly, and that X's father had been sure to teach X what to serve at a doll's tea party. X had to know how to shoot marbles and how to jump rope and, most of all, what to say when the Other Children asked whether X was a Boy or a Girl.

Finally, X was ready. The Joneses helped X button on a nice new pair of red-and-white checked overalls, and sharpened six pencils for X's nice new pencilbox, and marked X's name clearly on all the books in its nice new bookbag. X brushed its teeth and combed its hair, which just about covered its ears, and remembered to put a napkin in its lunchbox.

The Joneses had asked X's teacher if the class could line up alphabetically, instead of forming separate lines for boys and girls. And they had asked if X could use the principal's bathroom, because it wasn't marked anything except BATHROOM. X's teacher promised to take care of all those problems. But nobody could help X with the biggest problem of all— Other Children.

Nobody in X's class had ever known an X before. What would they think? How would X make friends?

You couldn't tell what X was by studying its clothes—overalls don't even button right-to-left, like girls' clothes, or left-to-right, like boys' clothes. And you couldn't guess whether X had a girl's short haircut or a boy's long haircut. And it was very hard to tell by the games X liked to play. Either X played ball very well for a girl or played house very well for a boy.

Some of the children tried to find out by asking X tricky questions, like "Who's your favorite sports star?" That was easy. X had two favorite sports stars: a girl jockey named Robyn Smith and a boy archery champion named Robin Hood. Then they asked, "What's your favorite TV program?" And that was even easier. X's favorite TV program was "Lassie," which stars a girl dog played by a boy dog.

When X said that its favorite toy was a doll, everyone decided that X must be a girl. But then X said that the doll was really a robot, and that X had computerized it, and that it was programmed to bake fudge brownies and then clean up the kitchen. After X told them that, the other children gave up guessing what X was. All they knew was they'd sure like to see X's doll.

After school, X wanted to play with the other children. "How about shooting some baskets in the gym?" X asked the girls. But all they did was make faces and giggle behind X's back.

"How about weaving some baskets in the arts and

crafts room?" X asked the boys. But they all made faces and giggled behind X's back, too.

That night, Ms. and Mr. Jones asked X how things had gone at school. X told them sadly that the lessons were okay, but otherwise school was a horrible place for an X. It seemed as if the Other Children would never want an X for a friend.

Once more, the Joneses reached for the *Instruction Manual.* Under "Other Children," they found the following message: "What did you Xpect? *Other Children* have to obey all the silly boy-girl rules, because their parents taught them to. Lucky X—you don't have to stick to the rules at all! All you have to do is be yourself. P.S. We're not saying it'll be easy."

X liked being itself. But X cried a lot that night, partly because it felt afraid. So X's father held X tight, and cuddled it, and couldn't help crying a little, too. And X's mother cheered them both up by reading an Xciting story about an enchanted prince called Sleeping Handsome, who woke up when Princess Charming kissed him.

The next morning, they all felt much better, and little X went back to school with a brave smile and a clean pair of red-and-white checked overalls.

There was a seven-letter-word spelling bee in class that day. And a seven-lap boys' relay race in the gym. And a seven-layer-cake baking contest in the girls' kitchen corner. X won the spelling bee. X also won the relay race. And X almost won the baking contest, except it forgot to light the oven. Which only proves that nobody's perfect.

One of the Other Children noticed something else, too. He said: "Winning or losing doesn't seem to count to X. X seems to have fun being good at boys' skills *and* girls' skills."

"Come to think of it," said another one of the Other Children, "maybe X is having twice as much fun as we are!"

So after school that day, the girl who beat X at the baking contest gave X a big slice of her prize-winning cake. And the boy X beat in the relay race asked X to race him home.

From then on, some really funny things began to happen. Susie, who sat next to X in class, suddenly refused to wear pink dresses to school any more. She insisted on wearing red-and-white checked overalls —just like X's. Overalls, she told her parents, were much better for climbing monkey bars.

Then Jim, the class football nut, started wheeling his little sister's doll carriage around the football field. He'd put on his entire football uniform, except for the helmet. Then he'd put the helmet *in* the carriage, lovingly tucked under an old set of shoulder pads. Then he'd start jogging around the field, pushing the carriage and singing "Rockabye Baby" to his football helmet. He told his family that X did the same thing, so it must be okay. After all, X was now the team's star quarterback.

Susie's parents were horrified by her behavior, and Jim's parents were worried sick about him. But the worst came when the twins, Joe and Peggy, decided to share everything with each other. Peggy used Joe's hockey skates, and his microscope, and took half his newspaper route. Joe used Peggy's needlepoint kit, and her cookbooks, and took two of her three baby-sitting jobs. Peggy started running the lawn mower, and Joe started running the vacuum cleaner.

Their parents weren't one bit pleased with Peggy's wonderful biology experiments, or with Joe's terrific needlepoint pillows. They didn't care that Peggy mowed the lawn better, and that Joe vacuumed the carpet better. In fact, they were furious. It's all that little X's fault, they agreed. Just because X doesn't know what it is, or what it's supposed to be, it wants to get everybody *else* mixed up, too!

Peggy and Joe were forbidden to play with X any more. So was Susie, and then Jim, and then *all* the Other Children. But it was too late; the Other Children stayed mixed up and happy and free, and refused to go back to the way they'd been before X.

Finally, Joe and Peggy's parents decided to call an emergency meeting of the school's Parents' Association, to discuss "The X Problem." They sent a report to the principal stating that X was a "disruptive influence." They demanded immediate action. The Joneses, they said, should be *forced* to tell whether X was a boy or a girl. And then X should be *forced* to behave like whichever it was. If the Joneses refused to tell, the Parents' Association said, then X must take an Xamination. The school psychiatrist must Xamine it physically and mentally, and issue a full report. If X's test showed it was a boy, it would have to obey all the boys' rules. If it proved to be a girl, X would have to obey all the girls' rules.

And if X turned out to be some kind of mixed-up misfit, then X should be Xpelled from the school. Immediately!

The principal was very upset. Disruptive influence? Mixed-up misfit? But X was an Xcellent student. All the teachers said it was a delight to have X in their classes. X was president of the student council. X had won first prize in the talent show, and second prize in the art show, and honorable mention in the science fair, and six athletic events on field day, including the potato race.

Nevertheless, insisted the Parents' Association, X is a Problem Child. X is the Biggest Problem Child we have ever seen!

So the principal reluctantly notified X's parents that numerous complaints about X's behavior had come to the school's attention. And that after the psychiatrist's Xamination, the school would decide what to do about X.

The Joneses reported this at once to the scientists, who referred them to page 85,759 of the *Instruction Manual.* "Sooner or later," it said, "X will have to be Xamined by a psychiatrist. This may be the only way any of us will know for sure whether X is mixed up—or whether everyone else is."

The night before X was to be Xamined, the Joneses tried not to let X see how worried they were. "What if—?" Mr. Jones would say. And Ms. Jones would reply, "No use worrying." Then a few minutes later, Ms. Jones would say, "What if—?" and Mr. Jones would reply, "No use worrying."

X just smiled at them both, and hugged them hard and didn't say much of anything. X was thinking, What if—? And then X thought: No use worrying.

At Xactly 9 o'clock the next day, X reported to the school psychiatrist's office. The principal, along with a committee from the Parents' Association, X's teacher, X's classmates, and Ms. and Mr. Jones, waited in the hall outside. Nobody knew the details of the tests X was to be given, but everybody knew

they'd be *very* hard, and that they'd reveal Xactly what everyone wanted to know about X, but were afraid to ask.

It was terribly quiet in the hall. Almost spooky. Once in a while, they would hear a strange noise inside the room. There were buzzes. And a beep or two. And several bells. An occasional light would flash under the door. The Joneses thought it was a white light, but the principal thought it was blue. Two or three children swore it was either yellow or green. And the Parents' Committee missed it completely.

Through it all, you could hear the psychiatrist's low voice, asking hundreds of questions, and X's higher voice, answering hundreds of answers.

The whole thing took so long that everyone knew it must be the most complete Xamination anyone had ever had to take. Poor X, the Joneses thought. Serves X right, the Parents' Committee thought. I wouldn't like to be in X's overalls right now, the children thought.

At last, the door opened. Everyone crowded around to hear the results. X didn't look any different; in fact, X was smiling. But the psychiatrist looked terrible. He looked as if he was crying! "What happened?" everyone began shouting. Had X done something disgraceful? "I wouldn't be a bit surprised!" muttered Peggy and Joe's parents. "Did X flunk the *whole* test?" cried Susie's parents. "Or just the most important part?" yelled Jim's parents. "Oh, dear," sighed Mr. Jones.

"Oh, dear," sighed Ms. Jones.

"*Sssh,*" ssshed the principal. "The psychiatrist is trying to speak."

Wiping his eyes and clearing his throat, the psychiatrist began, in a hoarse whisper. "In my opinion," he whispered—you could tell he must be very upset—"in my opinion, young X here—"

"Yes? Yes?" shouted a parent impatiently.

"*Sssh!*" ssshed the principal.

"Young *Sssh* here, I mean young X," said the doctor, frowning, "is just about—"

"Just about *what?* Let's have it!" shouted another parent. ". . . just about the *least* mixed-up child I've ever Xamined!" said the psychiatrist.

"Yay for X!" yelled one of the children. And then the others began yelling, too. Clapping and cheering and jumping up and down.

"*SSSH!*" SSShed the principal, but nobody did.

The Parents' Committee was angry and bewildered. How *could* X have passed the whole Xamination? Didn't X have an *identity* problem? Wasn't X mixed up at *all?* Wasn't X *any* kind of a misfit? How could it *not* be, when it didn't even *know* what it was? And why was the psychiatrist crying?

Actually, he had stopped crying and was smiling politely through his tears. "Don't you see?" he said. "I'm crying because it's wonderful! X has absolutely no identity problem! X isn't one bit mixed-up! As for being a misfit—ridiculous! X knows perfectly well what it is! Don't you, X?" The doctor winked. X winked back.

"But what *is* X?" shrieked Peggy and Joe's parents. "*We* still want to know what it is!"

"Ah, yes," said the doctor, winking again. "Well, don't worry. You'll all know one of these days. And you won't need me to tell you."

"What? What does he mean?" some of the parents grumbled suspiciously.

Susie and Peggy and Joe all answered at once. "He means that by the time X's sex matters, it won't be a secret any more!"

With that, the doctor began to push through the crowd toward X's parents. "How do you do," he said, somewhat stiffly. And then he reached out to hug them both. "If I ever have an X of my own," he whispered, "I sure hope you'll lend me your instruction manual."

Needless to say, the Joneses were very happy. The Project Baby X scientists were rather pleased, too. So were Susie, Jim, Peggy, Joe, and all the Other Children. The Parents' Association wasn't, but they had promised to accept the psychiatrist's report, and not make any more trouble. They even invited Ms. and Mr. Jones to become honorary members, which they did.

Later that day, all X's friends put on their red-and-white checked overalls and went over to see X. They found X in the back yard, playing with a very tiny baby that none of them had ever seen before. The baby was wearing very tiny red-and-white checked overalls.

"How do you like our new baby?" X asked the Other Children proudly.

"It's got cute dimples," said Jim.

"It's got husky biceps, too," said Susie.

"What kind of baby is it?" asked Joe and Peggy.

X frowned at them. "Can't you tell?" Then X broke into a big, mischievous grin. "*It's a Y!*"

[1972]

PART III

Gender and Women's Bodies

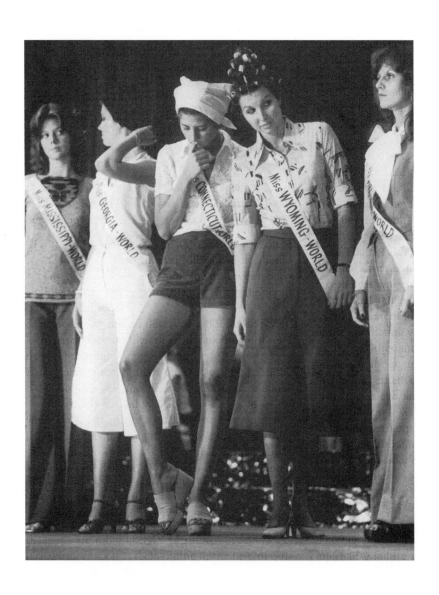

In many ways, women's value in our culture has been defined by their bodies. Girls quickly learn that their worth is evaluated by physical appearance; more attention is directed to girls' beauty, clothes, and hair than to their intelligence, skills, and talents. As Rhoda Unger and Mary Crawford state, "Learning to care about looks is a life-long process."[1]

Just as the psychological experience of being female affects girls' and women's self-perceptions, it also shapes perceptions of their bodies and sexuality. Although women's attitudes about bodies are changing, reflecting a greater appreciation of athleticism, strength, and health, most women still find fault with their bodies and physical appearance. For all too many adolescent girls and women, negative body image is related to lowered self-esteem. Bombarded with messages of ideal beauty and body size, many adolescent girls who are physically maturing struggle with meeting these unrealistic standards. The greater incidence of eating disorders among females than males reflects the extreme pressures placed on girls and women to achieve impossible weight standards. For these women, concerns about weight and appearance become the guiding focus of their lives. Their bodies become focal points for achieving control, social acceptance, and self-worth. The experiences of women dealing with eating disorders remind us that messages about body weight and attractiveness can have devastating psychological and physical consequences.

All girls and women in our culture are exposed to a constant barrage of messages and expectations regarding physical attractiveness. Whether presented as images of tall, thin supermodels on magazine covers, or closely fitting clothing sold on department store racks, girls and women see the obvious markings of the prevalent standards for female beauty: thinner is better, fat is bad, dieting is good. Even more striking is the reality that such expectations are being held by girls as young as seven and eight.

The advertising world generates standards of beauty that exclude most women, particularly women of color and women who depart from the "ideal" of the white, Anglo-Saxon, thin model. When women strive to fit these standards, they often fail to appreciate their own uniqueness. Along the way, women often compare themselves harshly and critically to "classic beauties," subjecting themselves to beauty aids, unnecessary (and sometimes dangerous) cosmetic surgeries, unhealthy diets and dangerous appetite-suppressing drugs to achieve the "right look." More frequently than not these attempts do not succeed, and women end up feeling dissatisfied and defeated, often blaming themselves for their perceived imperfections.

For women of color, white definitions of female beauty are less powerful now than they were 30 years ago. For example, the shift to celebrating African roots of African-American culture has expanded the ideals for African-American women's beauty, providing many possibilities for self-expression through fashion and hair-

---

[1]Rhoda Unger and Mary Crawford, *Women and Gender: A Feminist Psychology,* 2nd ed. (New York: Mc-Graw-Hill, 1996), p. 317.

style. Similarly, a resurgence in ethnic and urban pop culture show alternatives to traditional norms for beauty to young people, particularly in urban areas. However, despite these changes, unbearably thin, waif-like white women remain the dominant image of female beauty promoted in the media.

Expressions of sexuality are also closely related to how women view themselves and their bodies. Male-defined attitudes about women's sexuality have created powerful myths and stereotypes that have damaged women by restricting their ideas about what it means to be accepted in this culture. These myths and stereotypes have historically defined women's sexuality, prescribing certain behaviors and expressions of sexuality as appropriate for women.

Attitudes about female sexuality in Western culture have changed radically over the years, reflecting shifts in social and cultural norms about sexuality and the role of women in society. In Europe from the 1400s to the 1700s, women were seen as sexually insatiable. Female sexuality was viewed as dangerous, evil, and in need of control. The embodiment of this uncontrollable sexuality was the "witch," who was thought to consort with the devil to satisfy her lustful desires. During the 1800s, these attitudes changed dramatically, reflecting the Victorian values of 19th century Europe. White women were regarded as pure, genteel, and passionless, while darker-skinned women were cast as sexual potentates. During the years of slavery in the United States, this double standard for white and black women was played out in the continued sexual exploitation and rape of slave women by the very same white slaveowners who viewed their own wives as sexually pure and innocent.

Prevailing stereotypes about women's sexuality reflect the interaction of racism and sexism in our culture. Viewed as "other" relative to white women, Latinas are cast as "hot-blooded," and Asian women as exotic and geisha-like. Their sexuality takes on the added dimension of being unfeminine: to be hot-blooded, seductive, and erotic is at odds with being pure and genteel.

The sexual revolution of the 1960s signalled for many a loosening of restrictions on sexual behavior for men and women. However, the double standard for male and female sexuality has persisted. The cultural climate of the United States is now more conducive to accepting women's sexuality, and we see greater acceptance among college students of people's exploration of their sexual identities. However, we continue to see men's sexuality described in positive terms, while the descriptors for women's sexuality are decidedly negative, frequently stigmatizing women's personal attributes. According to this double standard, a sexually active man who has several partners is "virile," but a woman who has several partners is described as "easy," "promiscuous," and thus "not a good woman." Prevailing social notions of the "appropriate" expression of women's sexuality continue to affect women's sexual behavior, and to cloud expectations of appropriate behavior for women in general.

Sexual scripts are messages about expected behavior in sexual interactions that derive from stereotypes about men's and women's sexuality. In our culture, these scripts refer to heterosexual behavior, totally excluding the sexual expressions of lesbian and bisexual women. In fact, when these women's sexuality is considered, it is often in the context of being compared to the heterosexual "norm." For example, the definition of "sex" that is often used to survey couples' sexual behavior typically assumes heterosexual behavior, that is, penile-vaginal intercourse. For lesbian couples, this definition is meaningless, and fails to capture the range of emotional and physical aspects of "sex" between two women. As Marilyn Frye asserts, "The suspicion arises that what 85% of heterosexual couples are doing more than once a month and what 47% of what lesbian couples are doing less than once a month is not the same thing."[2]

A common sexual script for heterosexuals in our culture contains the following do's and don'ts: The man initiates sex, therefore the woman should not appear too interested at first; good sex is spontaneous and "just happens"; women should not appear to enjoy sex "too much"; and women should not desire sex "too much." Sexual scripts often place women in the position of being the "gatekeeper": the partner who is responsible for saying "no" to sexual advances, thereby exerting passive and indirect control. College students tend to describe men and women as having opposing goals in sexual interactions: men attempt to have sex, while women's goal is to avoid sex.[3] This portrayal of women's sexuality reaffirms the dichotomous images of the pure, sexually reticent woman and sexually uncontrollable man.

Taboos about women's sexuality, shaped by cultural ideology and mythology, directly affect a woman's experience of her own sexuality. It is not unusual to hear women discuss ambivalent feelings about their sexual desires and relationships, or to question whether or not "something is wrong" because they do not experience sex the way they think they "should." Again, we see the influence of sexual scripting on women's perceptions of their own behavior. As we explore these different issues in this section, we introduce the feminist perspective, which asserts that for women living in a sexist culture, sexuality encompasses both pleasure and danger. Previously, women's right to sexual pleasure was denied or restricted. In some cultures they still are, especially regarding behaviors such as masturbation and sex outside of marriage. A feminist approach to sexuality affirms women's right to sexual pleasure and desire. Feminists believe that women should make their own sexual choices, and reject the double standard that governs attitudes toward male and female sexuality. On the other hand, because of the ongoing danger of AIDS and other sexually transmitted infections, along with the possibility of unwanted pregnancy, women's right to sexual pleasure must be balanced with the responsibility of taking care of themselves. Thus, it is important for women to take control of their sexual behavior, making decisions that reduce their risk for HIV/AIDS, STDs, and unwanted pregnancy. In

---

[2]Marilyn Frye, "Lesbian Sex." *Sinister Wisdom* 35 (1988), reprinted in Amy Kesselman, Lily McNair, and Nancy Schniedewind, *Woman: Images and Realities* (Mountain View, CA: Mayfield Press, (1995), p. 122.
[3]M. N. LaPlante, N. McCormick, & G. G. Brannigan, "Living the Sexual Script: College Students' Views of Influence in Sexual Encounters." *Journal of Sex Research* 16 (1980), pp. 338–55.

doing so, women can more fully experience and enjoy those aspects of sexual intimacy that are pleasurable and fulfilling with the knowledge that they are active partners taking responsibility for their actions.

Women's attitudes about beauty, their bodies, and sexuality begin developing early in life. The unrealistic expectations created by a society that sexually objectifies women restrict women's choices, and limit their growth. As the selections that follow reveal, understanding how gender socialization and sexism create damaging stereotypes and expectations can help us develop our own standards of personal beauty and ideas about sexuality.

Female Beauty

"The beauty myth," as Naomi Wolf calls it in her book by that name, is omnipotent and far-reaching. It consists of the belief that women must possess an immutable quality, "beauty," in order to be successful and attractive to men. In essence, femininity is equated with beauty and beauty is seen as the central measure of women's worth. In fact, standards of beauty vary greatly from culture to culture and have changed radically over time. In our culture, prevailing notions of beauty emphasize being young, thin, white, and Anglo-Saxon. Naomi Wolf questions the foundation of this myth, and states that "the beauty myth is not about women at all. It is about men's institutions and institutional power."

Images of beauty vary across ethnic groups, demonstrating how racism and sexism interact to shape expectations of women. Nellie Wong, Inés Hernandez-Avila, Aishe Berger, and Lucille Clifton describe the effects of stereotyped notions of beauty on Asian-American, Latina, Jewish, and African-American women. As these selections demonstrate, such standards create anguish and confusion for most women, and particularly women of color, who are outside the prevailing "norms" of beauty.

In addition to affecting a woman's sense of self-worth, ideals of physical beauty often have destructive effects on a woman's physical health. The increasing rates of eating disorders in the United States are just one example of the unhealthy consequences of rigid standards of beauty. In "One Spring," Leslea Newman recounts the events that propelled her into a journey toward "disappearing" so that she would not attract attention to her emerging physical maturity. Although many other factors contribute to the development of eating disorders, her account reveals the cultural pressures that make it difficult for many girls to be comfortable with their sexual and physical selves. Abra Fortune Chernik captures the intensity of a woman's experience with anorexia, drawing the connection between dramatically losing weight and "starving away my power and vision, my energy and inclinations." While Linda Delgado points out that Latino/Latina culture prizes women of fuller proportions, Graciela Rodriguez's account shows that Latinas are not immune to eating disorders. In fact, Graciela states that "the media's and society's images of women . . . promised acceptance and happiness if I could only look like them." The pervasive pressure to be thin goes hand in hand with a fat-hating attitude in our culture. Viewed as "the other," many big women face hostility from a culture that considers them, as July Siebecker writes, "too loud and too laughing, too big for our britches." In "The Fat Girl Rules the World," Siebecker addresses the unrelenting negative attitudes toward fat girls and women and our society, and praises their resilience and strength.

When women begin to defy social scripts for physical beauty, they can begin to see the beauty within themselves and define beauty in a more meaningful way. This section concludes with two pieces reflecting contemporary women's new ideas about beauty. Written by African-American women, both of these selections convey important messages for women of all racial and ethnic backgrounds who are freeing themselves from restrictive standards of personal beauty.

🌿 30

The Beauty Myth

NAOMI WOLF

At last, after a long silence, women took to the streets. In the two decades of radical action that followed the rebirth of feminism in the early 1970s, Western women gained legal and reproductive rights, pursued higher education, entered the trades and the professions, and overturned ancient and revered beliefs about their social role. A generation on, do women feel free?

The affluent, educated, liberated women of the First World, who can enjoy freedoms unavailable to any women ever before, do not feel as free as they want to. And they can no longer restrict to the subconscious their sense that this lack of freedom has something to do with—with apparently frivolous issues, things that really should not matter. Many are ashamed to admit that such trivial concerns—to do with physical appearance, bodies, faces, hair, clothes—matter so much. But in spite of shame, guilt, and denial, more and more women are wondering if it isn't that they are entirely neurotic and alone but rather that something important is indeed at stake that has to do with the relationship between female liberation and female beauty.

The more legal and material hindrances women have broken through, the more strictly and heavily and cruelly images of female beauty have come to weigh upon us. Many women sense that women's collective progress has stalled; compared with the heady momentum of earlier days, there is a dispiriting climate of confusion, division, cynicism, and above all, exhaustion. After years of much struggle and little recognition, many older women feel burned out; after years of taking its light for granted, many younger women show little interest in touching new fire to the torch.

During the past decade, women breached the power structure; meanwhile, eating disorders rose exponentially and cosmetic surgery became the fastest-growing medical specialty. During the past five years, consumer spending doubled, pornography became the main media category, ahead of legitimate films and records combined, and thirty-three thousand American women told researchers that they would rather lose ten to fifteen pounds than achieve any other goal. More women have more money and power and scope and legal recognition than we have ever had before; but in terms of how we feel about ourselves *physically,* we may actually be worse off than our unliberated grandmothers. Recent research consistently shows that inside the majority of the West's controlled, attractive, successful working women, there is a secret "underlife" poisoning our freedom; infused with notions of beauty, it is a dark vein of self-hatred, physical obsessions, terror of aging, and dread of lost control.

It is no accident that so many potentially powerful women feel this way. We are in the midst of a violent backlash against feminism that uses images of female beauty as a political weapon against women's advancement: the beauty myth. It is the modem version of a social reflex that has been in force since the Industrial Revolution. As women released themselves from the feminine mystique of domesticity, the beauty myth took over its lost ground, expanding as it waned to carry on its work of social control.

The contemporary backlash is so violent because the ideology of beauty is the last one remaining of the old feminine ideologies that still has the power to control those women whom second wave feminism would have otherwise made relatively uncontrollable: It has grown stronger to take over the work of social coercion that myths about motherhood, domesticity, chastity, and passivity, no longer can manage. It is seeking right now to undo psychologically and covertly all the good things that feminism did for women materially and overtly.

This counterforce is operating to checkmate the inheritance of feminism on every level in the lives of Western women. Feminism gave us laws against job discrimination based on gender; immediately case law evolved in Britain and the United States that institutionalized job discrimination based on women's appearances. Patriarchal religion declined; new religious dogma, using some of the mind-altering techniques of older cults and sects, arose around age and weight to functionally supplant traditional ritual. Feminists, inspired by Friedan, broke the stranglehold on the women's popular press of advertisers for household products, who were promoting the feminine mystique; at once, the diet and skin care industries became the new cultural censors of women's intellectual space, and because of their pressure, the gaunt, youthful model supplanted the happy housewife as the arbiter of successful womanhood. The sexual revolution promoted the discovery of female sexuality; "beauty pornography"—which for the first time in women's history artificially links a commodified "beauty" directly and explicitly to sexuality—invaded the mainstream to undermine women's new and vulnerable sense of sexual self-worth. Reproductive rights gave Western women control over our own bodies; the weight of fashion models plummeted to 23 percent below that of ordinary women, eating disorders rose exponentially, and a mass neurosis was promoted that used food and weight to strip women of that sense of control. Women insisted on politicizing health; new technologies of invasive, potentially deadly "cosmetic" surgeries developed apace to re-exert old forms of medical control of women.

Every generation since about 1830 has had to fight its version of the beauty myth. "It is very little to me," said the suffragist Lucy Stone in 1855, "to have the right to vote, to own property, etcetera, if I may not keep my body, and its uses, in my absolute right." Eighty years later, after women had won the vote, and the first wave of the organized women's movement had subsided, Virginia Woolf wrote that it would still be decades before women could tell the truth about their bodies. In 1962, Betty Friedan quoted a young woman trapped in the Feminine Mystique: "Lately, I look in the mirror, and I'm so afraid I'm going to look like my mother." Eight years after that, heralding the cataclysmic second wave of feminism, Germaine Greer described "the Stereotype": "To her belongs all that is beautiful, even the very word beauty itself . . . she is a doll . . . I'm sick of the masquerade." In spite of the great revolution of the second wave, we are not exempt. Now we can look out over ruined barricades: A revolution has come upon us and changed everything in its path, enough time has passed since then for babies to have grown into women, but there still remains a final right not fully claimed.

The beauty myth tells a story: The quality called "beauty" objectively and universally exists. Women must want to embody it and men must want to possess women who embody it. This embodiment is an imperative for women and not for men, which situation is necessary and natural because it is biological, sexual, and evolutionary: Strong men battle for beautiful women, and beautiful women are more reproductively successful. Women's beauty must correlate to their fertility, and since this system is based on sexual selection, it is inevitable and changeless.

None of this is true. "Beauty" is a currency system like the gold standard. Like any economy, it is determined by politics, and in the modern age in the West it is the last, best belief system that keeps male dominance intact. In assigning value to women in a vertical hierarchy according to a culturally imposed physical standard, it is an expression of power relations in which women must unnaturally compete for resources that men have appropriated for themselves.

"Beauty" is not universal or changeless, though the West pretends that all ideals of female beauty stem from one Platonic Ideal Woman; the Maori admire a fat vulva, and the Padung, droopy breasts. Nor is "beauty" a function of evolution. Its ideals change at a pace far more rapid than that of the evolution of species, and Charles Darwin was himself unconvinced by his own explanation that "beauty" resulted from a "sexual selection" that deviated from the rule of natural selection; for women to compete with women through "beauty" is a reversal of the way in which natural selection affects all other mammals. Anthropology has overturned the notion that females must be "beautiful" to be selected to mate: Evelyn Reed, Elaine Morgan, and others have dismissed sociobiological assertions of innate male polygamy and female monogamy. Female higher primates are the sexual initiators; not only do they seek out and enjoy sex with many partners, but "every nonpregnant female takes her turn at being the most desirable of all her troop. And that cycle keeps turning as long as she lives." The inflamed pink sexual organs of primates are often cited by male sociobiologists as analogous to human arrangements relating to female "beauty," when in fact that is a universal, nonhierarchical female primate characteristic.

Nor has the beauty myth always been this way. Though the pairing of the older rich men with young, "beautiful" women is taken to be somehow inevitable, in the matriarchal Goddess religions that dominated the Mediterranean from about 25,000 B.C.E. to about 700 B.C.E., the situation was reversed: "In every culture, the Goddess has many lovers. . . . The clear pattern is of an older woman with a beautiful but expendable youth—Ishtar and Tammuz, Venus and Adonis, Cybele and Attis, Isis and Osiris . . . their only function the service of the divine 'womb.'" Nor is it something only women do and only men watch: Among the Nigerian Wodaabes, the women hold economic power and the tribe is obsessed with male beauty; Wodaabe men spend hours together in elaborate makeup sessions, and compete—provocatively painted and dressed, with swaying hips and seductive expressions—in beauty contests judged by women. There is no legitimate historical or biological justification for the beauty myth; what it is doing to women today is a result of nothing more exalted than the need of today's power structure, economy, and culture to mount a counteroffensive against women.

If the beauty myth is not based on evolution, sex, gender, aesthetics, or God, on what is it based? It claims to be about intimacy and sex and life, a celebration of women. It is actually composed of emotional distance, politics, finance, and sexual repression. The beauty myth is not about women at all. It is about men's institutions and institutional power.

The qualities that a given period calls beautiful in women are merely symbols of the female behavior that that period considers desirable: *The beauty myth is always actually prescribing behavior and not appearance.* Competition between women has been made part of the myth so that women will be divided from one another. Youth and (until recently) virginity have been "beautiful" in women since they stand for experiential and sexual ignorance. Aging in women is "unbeautiful" since women grow more powerful with time, and since the links between generations of women must always be newly broken: Older women fear young ones, young women fear old, and the beauty myth truncates for all the female life span. Most urgently, women's identity must be premised upon our "beauty" so that we will remain vulnerable to outside approval, carrying the vital sensitive organ of self-esteem exposed to the air.

Though there has, of course, been a beauty myth in some form for as long as there has been patriarchy, the beauty myth in its modern form is a fairly recent invention. The myth flourishes when material constraints on women are dangerously loosened. Before the Industrial Revolution, the average woman could not have had the same feelings about "beauty" that modern women do who experience the myth as continual comparison to a mass-disseminated physical ideal. Before the development of technologies of mass production—daguerrotypes, photographs, etc.—an ordinary woman was exposed to few such images outside the Church. Since the family was a productive unit and women's work complemented men's, the value of women who were not aristocrats or prostitutes lay in their work skills, economic shrewdness, physical strength, and fertility. Physical attraction, obviously, played its part; but "beauty" as we understand it was not, for ordinary women, a serious issue in the marriage marketplace. The beauty myth in its modern form gained ground after the upheavals of industrialization, as the work unit of the family was destroyed, and urbanization and the emerging factory system demanded what social engineers of the time termed the "separate sphere" of domesticity, which supported the new labor category of the "breadwinner" who left home for the workplace during the day. The middle class expanded, the standards of living and of literacy rose, the size of families shrank; a new class of literate, idle women developed, on whose submission to enforced domesticity the evolving system of industrial capitalism depended. Most of our assumptions about the way women have always thought about "beauty" date from no earlier than the 1830s, when the cult of domesticity was first consolidated and the beauty index invented.

For the first time new technologies could reproduce—in fashion plates, daguerreotypes, tintypes, and rotogravures—images of how women should look. In the 1840s the first nude photographs of prostitutes were taken; advertisements using images of "beautiful" women first appeared in mid-century. Copies of classical artworks, postcards of society beauties and royal mistresses, Currier and Ives prints, and porcelain figurines flooded the separate sphere to which middle-class women were confined.

Since the Industrial Revolution, middle-class Western women have been controlled by ideals and stereotypes as much as by material constraints. This situation, unique to this group, means that analyses that trace "cultural conspiracies" are uniquely plausible in relation to them. The rise of the beauty myth was just one of several emerging social fictions that masqueraded as natural components of the feminine sphere, the better to enclose those women inside it. Other such fictions arose contemporaneously: a version of childhood that required continual maternal supervision; a concept of female biology that required middle-class women to act out the roles

of hysterics and hypochondriacs; a conviction that respectable women were sexually anesthetic; and a definition of women's work that occupied them with repetitive, time-consuming, and painstaking tasks such as needlepoint and lacemaking. All such Victorian inventions as these served a double function —that is, though they were encouraged as a means to expend female energy and intelligence in harmless ways, women often used them to express genuine creativity and passion.

But in spite of middle-class women's creativity with fashion and embroidery and child rearing, and, a century later, with the role of the suburban housewife that devolved from these social fictions, the fictions' main purpose was served: During a century and a half of unprecedented feminist agitation, they effectively counteracted middle-class women's dangerous new leisure, literacy, and relative freedom from material constraints.

Though these time- and mind-consuming fictions about women's natural role adapted themselves to resurface in the post-war Feminine Mystique, when the second wave of the women's movement took apart what women's magazines had portrayed as the "romance," "science," and "adventure" of homemaking and suburban family life, they temporarily failed. The cloying domestic fiction of "togetherness" lost its meaning and middle-class women walked out of their front doors in masses.

So the fictions simply transformed themselves once more: Since the women's movement had successfully taken apart most other necessary fictions of femininity, all the work of social control once spread out over the whole network of these fictions had to be reassigned to the only strand left intact, which action consequently strengthened it a hundredfold. This reimposed onto liberated women's faces and bodies all the limitations, taboos, and punishments of the repressive laws, religious injunctions and reproductive enslavement that no longer carried sufficient force. Inexhaustible but ephemeral beauty work took over from inexhaustible but ephemeral housework. As the economy, law, religion, sexual mores, education, and culture were forcibly opened up to include women more fairly, a private reality colonized female consciousness. By using ideas about "beauty," it reconstructed an alternative female world with its own laws, economy, religion, sexuality, education, and culture, each element as repressive as any that had gone before.

Since middle-class Western women can best be weakened psychologically now that we are stronger materially, the beauty myth, as it has resurfaced in the last generation, has had to draw on more technological sophistication and reactionary fervor than ever before. The modern arsenal of the myth is a dissemination of millions of images of the current ideal; although this barrage is generally seen as a collective sexual fantasy, there is in fact little that is sexual about it. It is summoned out of political fear on the part of male-dominated institutions threatened by women's freedom, and it exploits female guilt and apprehension about our own liberation— latent fears that we might be going too far. This frantic aggregation of imagery is a collective reactionary hallucination willed into being by both men and women stunned and disoriented by the rapidity with which gender relations have been transformed: a bulwark of reassurance against the flood of change. The mass depiction of the modern woman as a "beauty" is a contradiction: Where modern women are growing, moving, and expressing their individuality, as the myth has it, "beauty" is by definition inert, timeless, and generic. That this hallucination is necessary and deliberate is evident in the way "beauty" so directly contradicts women's real situation.

And the unconscious hallucination grows ever more influential and pervasive because of what is now conscious market manipulation; powerful industries—the $33-billion-a-year diet industry, the $20-billion cosmetics industry, the $300-million cosmetic surgery industry, and the $7-billion pornography industry—have arisen from the capital made out of unconscious anxieties, and are in turn able, through their influence on mass culture, to use, stimulate, and reinforce the hallucination in a rising economic spiral.

This is not a conspiracy theory; it doesn't have to be. Societies tell themselves necessary fictions in the same way that individuals and families do. Henrik Ibsen called them "vital lies," and psychologist

Daniel Goleman describes them working the same way on the social level that they do within families: "The collusion is maintained by directing attention away from the fearsome fact, or by repackaging its meaning in an acceptable format." The costs of these social blind spots, he writes, are destructive communal illusions. Possibilities for women have become so open-ended that they threaten to destabilize the institutions on which a male-dominated culture has depended, and a collective panic reaction on the part of both sexes has forced a demand for counterimages.

The resulting hallucination materializes, for women, as something all too real. No longer just an idea, it becomes three-dimensional, incorporating within itself how women live and how they do not live: It becomes the Iron Maiden. The original Iron Maiden was a medieval German instrument of torture, a bodyshaped casket painted with the limbs and features of a lovely, smiling young woman. The unlucky victim was slowly enclosed inside her; the lid fell shut to immobilize the victim, who died either of starvation or, less cruelly, of the metal spikes embedded in her interior. The modern hallucination in which women are trapped or trap themselves is similarly rigid, cruel, and euphemistically painted. Contemporary culture directs attention to imagery of the Iron Maiden, while censoring real women's faces and bodies.

Why does the social order feel the need to defend itself by evading the fact of real women, our faces and voices and bodies, and reducing the meaning of women to these formulaic and endlessly reproduced "beautiful" images? Though unconscious personal anxieties can be a powerful force in the creation of a vital lie, economic necessity practically guarantees it. An economy that depends on slavery needs to promote images of slaves that "justify" the institution of slavery. Western economies are absolutely dependent now on the continued underpayment of women. An ideology that makes women feel "worth less" was urgently needed to counteract the way feminism had begun to make us feel worth more. This does not require a conspiracy; merely an atmosphere. The contemporary economy depends right now on the representation of women within the beauty myth. Economist John Kenneth Galbraith offers an economic explanation for "the persistence of the view of homemaking as a 'higher calling'": the concept of women as naturally trapped within the Feminine Mystique, he feels, "has been forced on us by popular sociology, by magazines, and by fiction to disguise the fact that woman in her role of consumer has been essential to the development of our industrial society. . . . Behavior that is essential for economic reasons is transformed into a social virtue." As soon as a woman's primary social value could no longer be defined as the attainment of virtuous domesticity, the beauty myth redefined it as attainment of virtuous beauty. It did so to substitute both a new consumer imperative and a new justification for economic unfairness in the workplace where the old ones had lost their hold over newly liberated women.

Another hallucination arose to accompany that of the Iron Maiden: The caricature of the Ugly Feminist was resurrected to dog the steps of the women's movement. The caricature is unoriginal; it was coined to ridicule the feminists of the nineteenth century. Lucy Stone herself, whom supporters saw as "a prototype of womanly grace . . . fresh and fair as the morning," was derided by detractors with "the usual report" about Victorian feminists: "a big masculine woman, wearing boots, smoking a cigar, swearing like a trooper." As Betty Friedan put it presciently in 1960, even before the savage revamping of that old caricature: "The unpleasant image of feminists today resembles less the feminists themselves than the image fostered by the interests who so bitterly opposed the vote for women in state after state." Thirty years on, her conclusion is more true than ever: That resurrected caricature, which sought to punish women for their public acts by going after their private sense of self, became the paradigm for new limits placed on aspiring women everywhere. After the success of the women's movement's second wave, the beauty myth was perfected to checkmate power at every level in individual women's lives. The modern neuroses of life in the female body spread to woman after woman at epidemic rates. The myth is undermining—slowly, imperceptibly, without our being aware of the real forces of erosion—the ground women have gained through long, hard, honorable struggle.

The beauty myth of the present is more insidious than any mystique of femininity yet. A century ago, Nora slammed the door of the doll's house; a generation ago, women turned their backs on the consumer heaven of the isolated multiapplianced home; but where women are trapped today, there is no door to slam. The contemporary ravages of the beauty backlash are destroying women physically and depleting us psychologically. If we are to free ourselves from the dead weight that has once again been made out of femaleness, it is not ballots or lobbyists or placards that women will need first; it is a new way to see.   [1991]

✿ 31

When I Was Growing Up

NELLIE WONG

I know now that once I longed to be white.
How? you ask.
Let me tell you the ways.

    when I was growing up, people told me
    I was dark and I believed my own darkness
    in the mirror, in my soul, my own narrow vision

        when I was growing up, my sisters
        with fair skin got praised
        for their beauty, and in the dark
        I fell further, crushed between high walls

    when I was growing up, I read magazines
    and saw movies, blonde movie stars, white skin,
    sensuous lips and to be elevated, to become
    a woman, a desirable woman, I began to wear
    imaginary pale skin

        when I was growing up, I was proud
        of my English, my grammar, my spelling
        fitting into the group of smart children

smart Chinese children, fitting in,
belonging, getting in line

when I was growing up and went to high
   school,
I discovered the rich white girls, a few yellow
   girls,
their imported cotton dresses, their cashmere
   sweaters,
their curly hair and I thought that I too should
   have
what these lucky girls had

    when I was growing up, I hungered
    for American food, American styles,
    coded: white and even to me, a child
    born of Chinese parents, being Chinese
    was feeling foreign, was limiting,
    was unAmerican

when I was growing up and a white man
   wanted
to take me out, I thought I was special,
an exotic gardenia, anxious to fit
the stereotype of an oriental chick

    when I was growing up, I felt ashamed
    of some yellow men, their small bones,
    their frail bodies, their spitting
    on the streets, their coughing,
    their lying in sunless rooms,
    shooting themselves in the arms

when I was growing up, people would ask
if I were Filipino, Polynesian, Portuguese.
They named all colors except white, the shell
of my soul, but not my dark, rough skin

    when I was growing up, I felt
    dirty. I thought that god
    made white people clean
    and no matter how much I bathed,
    I could not change, I could not shed
    my skin in the gray water

when I was growing up, I swore
I would run away to purple mountains,
houses by the sea with nothing over
my head, with space to breathe,

uncongested with yellow people in an area
called Chinatown, in an area I later learned
was a ghetto, one of many hearts
of Asian America

I know now that once I longed to be white.
How many more ways? you ask.
Haven't I told you enough?   [1981]

🌿 32

To Other Women Who Were Ugly Once

INÉS HERNANDEZ-AVILA

Do you remember how we used to panic
when Cosmo, Vogue and Mademoiselle
   ladies
      would Glamour-us
      out of existence
         so ultra bright
         would be their smile
         so lovely their
         complexion
their confianza[a] based on
someone else's fashion
and their mascara'd mascaras[b]
      hiding the cascaras[c]
      that hide their ser?[d]

I would always become cold inside
          mata*onda*[e] to compete
      to need
      to dress right
      speak right
      laugh in just the
      right places
      dance in just
      the right way

---

[a]Confidence. [b]Masks. [c]Shells. [d]Being. [e]Dampener: *onda* is a "trip" in the positive sense—to *matar onda* is to kill, to frustrate the "trip"—to dishearten.

My resistance to this type of
   existence
   grows stronger every day
Y al cabo ahora se
   que se vale
   preferir natural luz[f]
           to neon.   [1980]

 33

Nose Is a Country . . . I Am the Second Generation

AISHE BERGER

for Emma Eckstein

Emma Eckstein was a socialist and a writer before she became a patient of Freud's. He diagnosed her as an hysteric because she was prone to emotional outbursts and masturbated frequently. Freud turned Emma over to his colleague Dr. Fleiss, who believed operating on the nose would inhibit sexual desire. Fleiss broke Emma's nose and left a large wad of gauze inside her nasal passage. This "error" wasn't discovered until years later, long after Emma's physical and emotional health was ruined and she was left an invalid.

"Such a nice girl, you have the map of Israel all over your face."

        —Woman in fruitstore when I was thirteen

I. Rhinoplasty

Nose that hangs on my face like a locket
with a history inside   you kiss
on our once a week date like lovers
in their mid forties
or maybe just my mother who is a lover
in her mid forties who had a nose job
in her mid twenties
the bump
the bumpy roads that troubled my father

the trouble with my father
who liked *zoftig*[1] women
all sides moldable
no bumps on the nose
map of Israel   on the face
map of Israel   on the map
a place on the edge of a deep blue
romantic sea on the map
a place that keeps shuffling its feet
backward   shrinking
like her nose under gauze
under wraps
under hemorrhage that accidentally
happened when the doctor left
the operating room and didn't
return till the anesthesia was already
loosening to sound
like an avalanche
in preparation
her nose bleeding under that
temporary wrap
a change in the landscape
my mother passes me down
this nation
this unruly semitic landmass on my face

My teeth were always
complimented for their four years
of braces
the rumblings of my jaw as my face
continentally drifted and my nose
grew
not like my mother's which is
like a border with its bone gates
levelled neutral
a passive face my mother's
bumpless smile

II. Hemorrhage

I think of Emma Eckstein
whose cartilage
was hammered out of her   the ancient
steppes on her face   the long view

---

[f]And now anyway I know that it is worthy to prefer natural light.

---

[1]Plump.

of the world flooded
with large quantities of blood

Emma Eckstein who took her hands lovingly
inside her
who perhaps merely rubbed her legs together
in her seat and orgasmed
told she is hysterical
she wants too much in the final analysis
in the final analysis
the nose is inextricably linked
to the clitoris and the need to take hands
to yourself lovingly
is abnormal
Which was then a fresh new word
abnormal
the desire to treat oneself with kindness

Take your hands and put them on your lap

Take your nose and put it on inside out

On the ancient steps
up Emma Eckstein's nose
a man named Fleiss committed

strange unnatural acts in the name of
Psycho therapy
which was then a fresh new word

Emma
Levelled
Neutral
a passive face
a bumpless smile
her hands
jerk
at the thought
of herself
the hammer
reinforced
the hammer

III. Assimilation into the modern world

and the gauze
under my own eyes
black and blue staying

in my house for a week
like sitting *shiva*[2]
fourteen years old
the most important days of my life

My mother promises me
a profile
like Greta Garbo

She used to tell me
my best friend Hilary
was prettier than me

The little Yeshiva boys yelled
that I took all their air up
when I walked down the hall
Then the boys at camp said
they'd kiss me if they could
ever find my lips

My dermatologist pierces
my ears
when I'm ten and advises me
to wear big earrings
it will distract people away
from my face

At eight I learn the word *rhinoplasty*
and it becomes a goal in my future
like becoming the first woman president
or flying to the moon

I am the second generation

Nose is a country where little wooden puppets
tell lies
where paintings of Shylock
are in every hotel lobby
Nose is a country where women have to
walk with their heads down
Where I await my new
modern look
assimilated
deconstructed

---

[2]Practice of mourning the death of a relative by sitting in the house for a week.

IV. Bridges

The body doesn't let go
of bridges

they expose me to the world after seven days
I expect to be noseless erased
but I am there   long and sloped
like a mountain after a fierce rain

I am there
the body knows

Mine stopped breathing at the crucial moment
the moment where they smash
bridges
the moment where the enemy
takes over

This time they couldn't finish
what they started
a part of me revolted
against the gas   they had to
revive me before the last
bone was broken

The suspension of my long
winding bridge where my Jewish soul
still wanders over
the slightly altered terrain

the body knows

My desert nose my sweet ripe nose
    my kosher nose
my zoftig nose my mountain nose
    my gentle nose
my moon of nose my sea of nose
    my heart pumping
lungs stretching fire of nose
    my full bodied
wine of nose   my acres of *sheyne
    sheyne meydele*[3]
nose

that you kiss at night

Nose that I put my loving hands on.   [1986]

_____
[3]Pretty, pretty girl.

 34

Homage to My Hair

LUCILLE CLIFTON

when i feel her jump up and dance
i hear the music! my God
i'm talking about my nappy hair!
she is a challenge to your hand
black man,
she is as tasty on your tongue as good greens
black man,
she can touch your mind
with her electric fingers and
the grayer she do get, good God,
the blacker she do be!   [1976]

 35

One Spring

LESLÉA NEWMAN

The air was thick with the promise
of lilacs and rain that evening
and the clouds hovered about my shoulders
like the mink stole in my mother's closet
I tried on from time to time.
I was sixteen and I knew it.
I tossed my head like a proud pony
my hair rippling down my back in one black wave
as I walked down the sultry street
my bare feet barely touching the ground
past the sounds of a television
a dog barking
a mother calling her child,
my body slicing through the heavy air
like a sailboat gliding on lazy water.

When the blue car slowed alongside me
I took no notice

until two faces leaned out the open window.
"Nice tits you got there, honey."
"Hey sweetheart, shine those headlights over
   here."
"Wanna go for a ride?"
I stopped,
dazed as a fish thrust out of water
into sunlight so bright it burns my eyes.
I turn and walk away fast
head down, arms folded,
feet slapping the ground.
I hear, "Nice ass, too,"
then laughter
the screech of tires
silence.

All at once I am ashamed of my new breasts
round as May apples,
I want to slice them off with a knife
sharp as a guillotine.

All at once I am mortified by my widening hips,
I want to pare them down with a vegetable peeler
until they are slim and boyish.
All at once I want to yank out my hair by the roots
like persistent weeds that must not grow wild.
But I am a sensible girl.
I do none of these things.

Instead I go home, watch TV with my parents,
brush my teeth and braid my hair for the night.
And the next day I skip breakfast,
eat only an apple for lunch
and buy a calorie counter,
vowing to get thinner and thinner
until I am so slim I can slip
through the cracks in the sidewalk
and disappear. And I do.   [1993]

36

The Body Politic

ABRA FORTUNE CHERNIK

My body possesses solidness and curve, like the ocean. My weight mingles with Earth's pull, drawing me onto the sand. I have not always sent waves into the world. I flew off once, for five years, and swirled madly like a cracking brown leaf in the salty autumn wind. I wafted, dried out, apathetic.

I had no weight in the world during my years of anorexia. Curled up inside my thinness, a refugee in a cocoon of hunger, I lost the capacity to care about myself or others. I starved my body and twitched in place as those around me danced in the energy of shared existence and progressed in their lives. When I graduated from college crowned with academic honors, professors praised my potential. I wanted only to vanish.

It took three months of hospitalization and two years of outpatient psychotherapy for me to learn to nourish myself and to live in a body that expresses strength and honesty in its shape. I accepted my right and my obligation to take up room with my figure, voice and spirit. I remembered how to tumble forward and touch the world that holds me. I chose the ocean as my guide.

Who disputes the ocean's fullness?

Growing up in New York City, I did not care about the feminist movement. Although I attended an all-girls high school, we read mostly male authors and studied the history of men. Embracing mainstream culture without question, I learned about womanhood from fashion magazines, Madison Avenue and Hollywood. I dismissed feminist alternatives as foreign and offensive, swathed as they were in stereotypes that threatened my adolescent need for conformity.

Puberty hit late; I did not complain. I enjoyed living in the lanky body of a tall child and insisted on the title of "girl." If anyone referred to me as a "young woman," I would cry out, horrified, "Do not call me the *W* word!" But at sixteen years old, I could no longer deny my fate. My stomach and breasts rounded. Curly black hair sprouted in the most embarrassing places. Hips swelled from a once-flat plane. Interpreting maturation as an unacceptable lapse into fleshiness, I resolved to eradicate the physical symptoms of my impending womanhood.

Magazine articles, television commercials, lunchroom conversation, gymnastics coaches and write-ups on models had saturated me with diet savvy. Once I decided to lose weight, I quickly turned expert. I dropped hot chocolate from my regular breakfast order at the Skyline Diner. I replaced lunches of peanut butter and Marshmallow Fluff sandwiches with small platters of cottage cheese and cantaloupe. I eliminated dinner altogether and blunted my appetite with Tab, Camel Lights, and Carefree bubble gum. When furious craving overwhelmed my resolve and I swallowed an extra something, I would flee to the nearest bathroom to purge my mistake.

Within three months, I had returned my body to its preadolescent proportions and had manipulated my monthly period into drying up. Over the next five years, I devoted my life to losing my weight. I came to resent the body in which I lived, the body that threatened to develop, the body whose hunger I despised but could not extinguish. If I neglected a workout or added a pound or ate a bite too many, I would stare in the mirror and drown myself in a tidal wave of criticism. Hatred of my body generalized to hatred of myself as a person, and self-referential labels such as "pig," "failure" and "glutton" allowed me to believe that I deserved punishment. My self-hatred became fuel for the self-mutilating behaviors of the eating disorder.

As my body shrank, so did my world. I starved away my power and vision, my energy and inclinations. Obsessed with dieting, I allowed relationships, passions and identity to wither. I pulled back from the world, off of the beach, out of the sand. The waves of my existence ceased to roll beyond the inside of my skin.

And society applauded my shrinking. Pound after pound the applause continued, like the pounding ocean outside the door of my beach house.

The word "anorexia" literally means "loss of appetite." But as an anorexic, I felt hunger thrashing inside my body. I denied my appetite, ignored it, but never lost it. Sometimes the pangs twisted so sharply, I feared they would consume the meat of my heart. On desperate nights I rose in a flannel nightgown and allowed myself to eat an unplanned something.

No matter how much I ate, I could not soothe the pangs. Standing in the kitchen at midnight, spotlighted by the blue-white light of the open refrigerator, I would frantically feed my neglected appetite: the Chinese food I had not touched at dinner; ice cream and whipped cream; microwaved bread; cereal and chocolate milk; doughnuts and bananas. Then, solid sadness inside my gut, swelling agitation, a too-big meal I would not digest. In the bathroom I would rip off my shirt, tie up my hair, and prepare to execute the desperate ritual, again. I would ram the back of my throat with a toothbrush handle, crying, impatient, until the food rushed up. I would vomit until the toilet filled and I emptied, until I forgave myself, until I felt ready to try my life again. Standing up from my position over the toilet, wiping my mouth, I would believe that I was safe. Looking in the mirror through puffy eyes in a tumescent face, I would promise to take care of myself. Kept awake by the fast, confused beating of my heart and the ache in my chest, I would swear I did not miss the world outside. Lost within myself, I almost died.

By the time I entered the hospital, a mess of protruding bones defined my body, and the bones of my emaciated life rattled me crazy. I carried a pillow around because it hurt to sit down, and I shivered with cold in sultry July. Clumps of brittle hair clogged the drain when I showered, and blackened eyes appeared to sink into my head. My vision of reality wrinkled and my disposition turned mercurial as I slipped into starvation psychosis, a condition associated with severe malnutrition. People told me that I resembled a concentration camp prisoner, a chemotherapy patient, a famine victim or a fashion model.

In the hospital, I examined my eating disorder under the lenses of various therapies. I dissected my childhood, my family structure, my intimate relationships, my belief systems. I participated in experiential therapies of movement, art and psychodrama. I learned to use words instead of eating patterns to communicate my feelings. And still I refused to gain more than a minimal amount of weight.

I felt powerful as an anorexic. Controlling my body yielded an illusion of control over my life; I received incessant praise for my figure despite my sickly mien, and my frailty manipulated family and friends into protecting me from conflict. I had reduced my world to a plate of steamed carrots, and over this tiny kingdom I proudly crowned myself queen.

I sat cross-legged on my hospital bed for nearly two months before I earned an afternoon pass to go to the mall with my mother. The privilege came just in time; I felt unbearably large and desperately wanted a new outfit under which to hide gained weight. At the mall, I searched for two hours before finally discovering, in the maternity section at Macy's, a shirt large enough to cover what I perceived as my enormous body.

With an hour left on my pass, I spotted a sign on a shop window: "Body Fat Testing, $3.00." I suggested to my mother that we split up for ten minutes; she headed to Barnes & Noble, and I snuck into the fitness store.

I sat down in front of a machine hooked up to a computer, and a burly young body builder fired questions at me:

"Age?"

"Twenty-one."

"Height?"

"Five nine."

"Weight?"

"Ninety-nine."

The young man punched my statistics into his keyboard and pinched my arm with clippers wired to the testing machine. In a moment, the computer spit out my results. "Only ten percent body fat! Unbelievably healthy. The average for a woman your age is twenty-five percent. Fantastic! You're this week's blue ribbon winner."

I stared at him in disbelief. *Winner? Healthy? Fantastic?* I glanced around at the other customers in the store, some of whom had congregated to watch my testing, and I felt embarrassed by his praise. And then I felt furious. Furious at this man and at the society that programmed him for their ignorant approbation of my illness and my suffering.

"I am dying of anorexia," I whispered. "Don't congratulate me."

I spent my remaining month in the hospital supplementing psychotherapy with an independent examination of eating disorders from a social and political point of view. I needed to understand why society would reward my starvation and encourage my vanishing. In the bathroom, a mirror on the open door behind me reflected my backside in a mirror over the sink. Vertebrae poked at my skin, ribs hung like wings over chiseled hip bones, the two sides of my buttocks did not touch. I had not seen this view of myself before.

In writing, I recorded instances in which my eating disorder had tangled the progress of my life and thwarted my relationships. I filled three and a half Mead marble notebooks. Five years' worth of: *I wouldn't sit with Daddy when he was alone in the hospital because I needed to go jogging; I told Derek not to visit me because I couldn't throw up when he was there; I almost failed my comprehensive exams because I was so hungry; I spent my year at Oxford with my head in the toilet bowl; I wouldn't eat the dinner my friends cooked me for my nineteenth birthday because I knew they had used oil in the recipe; I told my family not to come to my college graduation because I didn't want to miss a day at the gym or have to eat a restaurant meal.* And on and on for hundreds of pages.

This honest account of my life dissolved the illusion of anorexic power. I saw myself naked in the truth of my pain, my loneliness, my obsessions, my craziness, my selfishness, my defeat. I also recognized the social and political implications of consuming myself with the trivialities of calories and weight. At college, I had watched as classmates involved themselves in extracurricular clubs, volunteer work, politics and applications for jobs and graduate schools. Obsessed with exercising and exhausted by starvation, I did not even consider joining in such pursuits. Despite my love of writing and painting and literature, despite ranking at the top of my class, I wanted only to teach aerobics. Despite my adolescent days as a loud-mouthed, rambunctious class leader, I had grown into a silent, hungry young woman.

And society preferred me this way: hungry, fragile, crazy. *Winner! Healthy! Fantastic!* I began reading feminist literature to further understand the disempowerment of women in our culture. I digested the connection between a nation of starving, self-obsessed women and the continued success of the patriarchy. I also cultivated an awareness of alternative models of womanhood. In the stillness of the hospital library, new voices in my life rose from printed pages to echo my rage and provide the conception of my feminist consciousness.

I had been willing to accept self-sabotage, but now I refused to sacrifice myself to a society that profited from my pain. I finally understood that my eating disorder symbolized more than "personal psychodynamic trauma." Gazing in the mirror at my emaciated body, I observed a woman held up by her culture as the physical ideal because she was starving, self-obsessed and powerless, a woman called beautiful because she threatened no one except herself. Despite my intelligence, my education, and my supposed Manhattan sophistication, I had believed all of the lies; I had almost given my life in order to achieve the sickly impotence that this culture aggressively links with female happiness, love and success. And everything I had to offer to the world, every tumbling wave, every thought and every passion, nearly died inside me.

As long as society resists female power, fashion will call healthy women physically flawed. As long as society accepts the physical, sexual and economic abuse of women, popular culture will prefer women who resemble little girls. Sitting in the hospital the summer after my college graduation, I grasped the absurdity of a nation of adult women dying to grow small.

Armed with this insight, I loosened the grip of the starvation disease on my body. I determined to re-create myself based on an image of a woman warrior. I remembered my ocean, and I took my first bite.

Gaining weight and getting my head out of the toilet bowl was the most political act I have ever committed.

I left the hospital and returned home to Fire Island. Living at the shore in those wintry days of my new life, I wrapped myself in feminism as I hunted sea shells and role models. I wanted to feel proud of my womanhood. I longed to accept and honor my body's fullness.

During the process of my healing, I had hoped that I would be able to skip the memory of anorexia like a cold pebble into the dark winter sea. I had dreamed that in relinquishing my obsessive chase after a smaller body, I would be able to come home to rejoin those whom I had left in order to starve, rejoin them to live together as healthy, powerful women. But as my body has grown full, I have sensed a hollowness in the lives of women all around me that I had not noticed when I myself stood hollow. I have made it home only to find myself alone.

Out in the world again, I hear the furious thumping dance of body hatred echoing every place I go. Friends who once appeared wonderfully carefree in ordering late-night french fries turn out not to eat breakfast or lunch. Smart, talented, creative women talk about dieting and overeating and hating the beach because they look terrible in bathing suits. Famous women give interviews insulting their bodies and bragging about bicycling twenty-four miles the day they gave birth.

I had looked forward to rejoining society after my years of anorexic exile. Ironically, in order to preserve my health, my recovery has included the development of a consciousness that actively challenges the images and ideas that define this culture. Walking down Madison Avenue and passing emaciated women, I say to myself, *those women are sick.* When smacked with a diet commercial, I remind myself, *I don't do that anymore.* I decline invitations to movies that feature anorexic actors, I will not participate in discussions about dieting, and I refuse to shop in stores that cater to women with eating-disordered figures.

Though I am critical of diet culture, I find it nearly impossible to escape. Eating disorders have woven their way into the fabric of my society. On television, in print, on food packaging, in casual conversation and in windows of clothing stores populated by ridiculously gaunt mannequins, messages to lose my weight and control my appetite challenge my recovered fullness. Finally at home in my body, I recognize myself as an island in a sea of eating disorder, a sea populated predominantly by young women.

A perversion of nature by society has resulted in a phenomenon whereby women feel safer when starving than when eating. Losing our weight boosts self-esteem, while nourishing our bodies evokes feelings of self-doubt and self-loathing.

When our bodies take up more space than a size eight (as most of our bodies do), we say, *too big*. When our appetites demand more than a Lean Cuisine, we say, *too much*. When we want a piece of a friend's birthday cake, we say, *too bad*. Don't eat too much, don't talk too loudly, don't take up too much space, don't take from the world. Be pleasant or crazy, but don't seem hungry. Remember, a new study shows that men prefer women who eat salad for dinner over women who eat burgers and fries.

So we keep on shrinking, starving away our wildness, our power, our truth.

Hiding our curves under long T-shirts at the beach, sitting silently and fidgeting while others eat dessert, sneaking back into the kitchen late at night to binge and hating ourselves the next day, skipping breakfast, existing on diet soda and cigarettes, adding up calories and subtracting everything else. We accept what is horribly wrong in our lives and fight what is beautiful and right.

Over the past three years, feminism has taught me to honor the fullness of my womanhood and the solidness of the body that hosts my life. In feminist circles I have found mentors, strong women who live with power, passion and purpose. And yet, even in groups of feminists, my love and acceptance of my body remains unusual.

Eating disorders affect us all on both a personal and a political level. The majority of my peers —including my feminist peers—still measure their beauty against anorexic ideals. Even among feminists, body hatred and chronic dieting continue to consume lives. Friends of anorexics beg them to

please start eating; then these friends go home and continue their own diets. Who can deny that the millions of young women caught in the net of disordered eating will frustrate the potential of the next wave of feminism?

Sometimes my empathy dissolves into frustration and rage at our situation. For the first time in history, young women have the opportunity to create a world in our image. But many of us concentrate instead on recreating the shape of our thighs.

As young feminists, we must place unconditional acceptance of our bodies at the top of our political agenda. We must claim our bodies as our own to love and honor in their infinite shapes and sizes. Fat, thin, soft, hard, puckered, smooth, our bodies are our homes. By nourishing our bodies, we care for and love ourselves on the most basic level. When we deny ourselves physical food, we go hungry emotionally, psychologically, spiritually and politically. We must challenge ourselves to eat and digest, and allow society to call us too big. We will understand their message to mean too powerful.

Time goes by quickly. One day we will blink and open our eyes as old women. If we spend all our energy keeping our bodies small, what will we have to show for our lives when we reach the end? I hope we have more than a group of fashionably skinny figures.   [1995]

 37

Breaking the Model

GRACIELA (CHELY) RODRIGUEZ

"Are you a model?"

I had been walking through the metal detector at the Los Angeles airport last month when one of the attendants addressed me.

"Would a model be eating these?" I replied, pulling a huge bag of Doritos out of my purse.

I know the question was meant as a compliment, but it brought back a lot of painful memories. You see, I spent the best part of my teenage years "train-

[ing] to be a model . . . or just look like one." I didn't end up on the catwalk, but rather, in the hospital, recovering from anorexia and bulimia.

That's right, me—an eighteen-year-old Latina who's supposed to be immune to such things. Or so I'm told. Everyone from magazine publishers to television producers has suggested that Latina and African-American girls aren't likely to develop eating disorders, that we're less influenced by the skinny-girl images than our white peers.

But how do they explain me? I come from a traditional, hardworking Mexican family. We celebrate all the Mexican holidays, practice the Catholic religion, and, by nature, our appearance resembles that of our ancestors—prominent facial features, thick bodies and brown skin. I learned Spanish at an early age, as my parents had emigrated to California from Mazatlán, Sinaloa, when they were nineteen.

I've lived in the small town of Carpinteria, California, for my whole life. It's one of the few towns I know to be truly multicultural. My schools have always been filled with kids from all backgrounds—different ethnicities, races, religions. My own Latina identity has been just one among many—and it's never held me back. I've worked hard to fit in and be accepted.

As a young teen, I shared the dream of many girls: I wanted to be a model and an actress. Like most girls, I wanted to be popular, and more than anything that meant I had to be attractive. When I was thirteen, I was scanning a fashion magazine and saw an ad for a model search contest that was coming to Beverly Hills. I jumped at the chance and begged my parents to take me.

At first, my father was against the idea. But with a lot of pleading, I convinced my parents to make the two-hour drive one Saturday afternoon. I entered the contest with more than two thousand little girls, boys, teens and adults. There was no cost to enter, and it seemed like the chance of a lifetime. And it was easy. I just had to parade down a runway and introduce myself to a panel of judges by stating my name, my age and my interests.

Three weeks later, I got a phone call from one of the representatives, saying that I was a finalist. I wasn't one of the top *five* finalists, who were awarded money and free modeling classes. I was, however, a runner-up, which made me eligible for a partial scholarship to help cover modeling and acting lessons. My parents would only have to pay two thousand dollars, the rep told me. To this day, I'm not sure why they did it, but my parents withdrew the money from their savings. Every Saturday, we made the two-hour drive to Beverly Hills, and they waited for eight hours while I learned how to strut, pose and walk with a supermodel sashay.

On my first day, an agent named Pat took my measurements. He frowned and clucked his tongue as he scribbled my dimensions onto a clipboard—five-foot-three, 130 pounds, size seven. Then, he told me that the average model wore a size three and recommended that I drop down to that as quickly as possible.

For motivation, Pat handed me a stack of fashion magazines. He suggested I study the models in *Teen* and *Seventeen* and watch *Beverly Hills 90210* to "get an idea of what real models look like." It didn't matter that I was only thirteen years old and not even fully developed. I was expected either to lose the weight or to get lost.

I left depressed, thinking I would never look like a model because I came from a line of full-figured Mexican women. Even if I lost the weight, I would still never look like most of the girls in the magazines. I remember wishing I'd been born with blond hair, blue eyes and a small waist. I also started to think that if I got a nose job to create that perfect "button" nose, then maybe this career I really wanted could happen. Though I still had doubts whether my genetically given body could be shaped into model material, I believed that if I worked hard enough, I could succeed. As I entered junior high, my goal was not just to *look* like the characters on *90210,* but to *live* like them. I wanted to be popular, like the typical girl on TV. I wanted to be thin—to fit in.

I've been told that sometimes the desire for thinness is learned or reinforced at home. For me, that was true to a degree. My mother is a full-figured woman who's always been concerned about her weight. When I was younger, she used to exercise and limit her portions at mealtime. In fact, she even did some small-scale runway modeling for friends who had boutiques or clothing lines.

But my mother's example didn't spark my desire to model, even though she supported my decision. I feel the media's and society's images of women were more responsible. Like they do for so many girls, these images promised acceptance and happiness if I could only look like them.

However, my mother's habits and shaky self-image did make it easier when I began to diet and exercise obsessively at age thirteen. Early on, I discovered her diet pills and began taking them secretly. When she caught on that some were missing, she confronted me and I denied it. She didn't believe me, though, and even had the principal search my school locker. I remember thinking, "God, now people are going to know why I'm losing weight." I wanted everyone to think it was natural, and I felt like my secret had been revealed. In reality, no one else knew except for a friend (also Latina), who'd given me the idea in the first place. Soon after, I started to buy my own appetite suppressants, which I hid in my change purse.

I was eager to lose weight, and the modeling agency was happy to help. They gave me a list of "forbidden" foods, which was basically anything that didn't taste like sawdust or water. Every day, I had a salad with lemon juice or a plain baked potato, and that was it. I ate only once a day, limiting my intake to a 250-calorie maximum. After a year, my body submitted to this starvation regimen, and my appetite nearly disappeared. Although my stomach would rumble loudly in class, I learned to drink lots of water to fill it for long enough to spare me the embarrassment.

My parents noticed the dramatic change in my appearance, but they mistakenly trusted that the agency had put me on a healthy diet. Since they both worked long hours, and I was busy with extracurricular activities, they didn't have time to monitor my eating habits anyway. On the rare occasions that the family ate together, I would eat enough to escape their scrutiny, and then secretly throw it up later.

Bingeing and purging became a ritual. The same friend who introduced me to diet pills taught me that I could eat whatever I wanted and then force it back up so I wouldn't gain any weight. After a while, I didn't even have to stick my finger down my throat; I could throw up just by eating a chip. I also exercised for at least two hours a day at a local gym and at the park near my house. I was so obsessed with losing weight that I would wake up as early as 3 o'clock in the morning to run, and then jog again in the afternoon. I also enrolled in aerobics classes, and in eighth grade, I became captain of the cheerleading squad and president of the student body.

People ask me how I found the energy to do all this, especially with no food in my stomach. I can only answer that I was so driven to achieve "perfection" that it wiped out any concern I might have had for my body or my health. I would come home from school exhausted some days and flop down on my bed. But I was surrounded by pictures of teen models that I'd ripped from magazines and taped to my walls. My response was instant—one look at the wall and I'd be lacing up my Nikes and heading for the track.

But by eight o'clock, I was exhausted. Some nights, I was too tired to finish my homework, and I usually declined invitations from friends so I could stay home and work out. I wasn't the only one, though. Many of my friends—who were mostly Latina and African-American—were going through the same thing. Although there were few models who looked like us in *Teen* and *Seventeen,* we read those magazines anyway and bought into their messages. At the very least, all the girls at my junior high cared about their weight. Most of us worked out, and a lot of our conversations centered around how little we'd eaten that day. There was an unspoken competition, or at least a comparison, to see who had the most "willpower." Somehow, the quest for that power made us overlook the throbbing headaches and the gnawing hunger pangs that came with the territory of thinness.

At the modeling agency, most of the girls were also on strict diets and concerned about their bodies. In the end, going to extremes never paid off. None of us ever got any real modeling jobs. I did a couple of department store fashion shows, but that was it. It never amounted to the money my parents shelled out for my lessons.

But I did lose weight. After three years of hard work, the scales put me at one hundred pounds. In fact, I outdid myself—I dropped down to a size one. Finally, I felt okay wearing a bathing suit in public. I wore cropped tank tops and shorts all the time. There was no lack of attention or praise. People commented on how great and "healthy" I looked, and my self-esteem soared. I might not have been as "beautiful" as some models—after all, none of the models I saw on TV were Latina—but at least I was as skinny as they were.

Still, like most girls with eating disorders, I was never satisfied. In fact, I was unaware that I even had an eating disorder. All I knew was that I didn't feel "perfect" yet. My quest for the perfect body ended when a family member caught me throwing up in a restaurant bathroom. She told my parents, who took me to the hospital immediately, where I was diagnosed with anorexia and bulimia.

My family was as surprised as I was. Fortunately, I began counseling immediately. My counselor helped me to recover from my insecurity and to rebuild my self-esteem. I began to recognize that my worth was not based solely on my looks. It took me about a year to recover. I started to eat more and more and turned to healthier sources to stay in shape. I still exercised, but not nearly as much.

To this day, weight is a big issue in my life and may always be. Last night, I was watching an interview with Janet Jackson, and the thought of looking like her crept into my mind. I started to think, *God, I wish I had abs and a firm butt like hers.* I caught myself falling into an old trap. But I was able to stop myself by refocusing my thoughts on all of my good qualities and reminding myself that this was only an image.

One of the most influential things my counselor said to me was, "Chely, you are beautiful inside and out." It seems basic, yet somewhere in my quest for the perfect body, I had forgotten this. I decided never to change for anyone or try so hard to fit in. If

I had had real role models—girls with round stomachs and pimples—I would probably have felt more acceptable. After all, that's what most teenage girls look like. Of course, that kind of beauty doesn't sell the way the fantasy kind does. There's a reason we're given an image that's so hard to achieve. As long as we're chasing an impossible weight, we'll always have a reason to buy more diet products, to watch *90210* and to read *Seventeen*.

I now weigh 130 pounds again, and I'm proud of my body. But I need a lot of support to maintain that. Whenever I feel bad, I remind myself, "If people don't accept me the way I am, it's their problem." I also continue to heal myself by helping others. I'm actively involved as a peer advocate, countering unrealistic images in magazines, TV shows, websites and other media that can damage girls' body image. I promote healthy eating habits and exercise and encourage girls to get involved in sports. I'm now a high school senior, and I'm still involved in cheerleading and soccer (I often find myself "counseling" younger teammates about body acceptance). I'm also active in a number of girls clubs that help me maintain my self-esteem in the face of negative body image messages.

After recovering from my eating disorder, I participated in an organization called Girls Incorporated, which helps nurture young girls to become strong, self-confident women. Girls Inc. recently awarded me ten thousand dollars toward my college tuition. I've never been prouder. It felt incredible to receive a scholarship that was based on my achievements, rather than on the way I looked.

When I talk to girls, I tell them what I've learned—that it can be okay to want to look attractive and to be concerned about body weight, but we have to understand how far to take it. Finding that balance is tricky. The influence of the media is extremely powerful. I tell my story at conferences where big-time media executives are in attendance. I challenge them to provide young people with better role models and to stop portraying girls as victims and sex objects.

Eating disorders affect girls of color, too. I'm a perfect example of a Latina who developed an eating disorder because I so badly wanted to look and be like the thin, popular girls I saw in the media. I saw very few Latina role models on TV, and if I did see any, they were in gangs, wearing bikinis or cleaning houses. I have rarely seen a Latina get acknowledged for her accomplishments rather than her large breasts. If I'd had positive Latina role models, I might never have felt ashamed to come from a full-figured line of women. I would have felt proud.

In the meantime, I've decided to become my own role model by reminding myself who I am every day. I am an eighteen-year-old Latina, a full-figured former model. I have survived an eating disorder. And I'm learning to love my body.   [2000]

🦎 38

Arroz Con Pollo vs. Slim-Fast

LINDA DELGADO

To many white American women, thinness and tallness are essential parts of beauty. Yet in Spanish, the words *delgada* and *flaca* have a different connotation. Both words mean thin. *Delgada* connotes thin and weak, while *flaca* connotes thin as in skinny. Neither is very flattering. In fact, the question that usually follows after someone notices you are looking rather *delgada* is whether you have been ill.

Weight problems, aside from their health implications, are not seen as important in Latino culture as they are in mainstream American culture. There is a ceremonial importance to food and many rituals assigned to the sharing of food with others. Recently during a warm-up exercise in a new class, students were asked to introduce themselves by identifying with a particular food. A young Dominican woman said she was like *arroz con pollo* (rice with chicken). Her reason for picking this dish was that rice with chicken symbolized warmth, love, and acceptance. It is a dish made for new neighbors, new in-laws, and new friends to celebrate important events. It means welcome and good luck.

The breaking of bread with family, friends, and strangers is part of Latino hospitality. "*Mi casa, su casa*" is an unaltered tradition. When you visit my aunt's house, for example, go there hungry! The variety and amounts of food are quite extraordinary. I get full just looking at the table! Not only must you partake of everything there, you must also keep in mind that there are at least three or four desserts to follow. On special occasions, such as Easter, Christmas, and Mother's Day, everyone has a signature dish, and part of the celebration is sharing these delicacies. Failure to eat the right amount will cause personal distress to the hostess. What did she do wrong? At my aunt's house, usually my grandmother will ask if you have been sick or if your children have been giving you a hard time. There must be some explanation why you have not eaten your share of food. By "your share of food" they mean enough to feed a small army! The word "diet" or "calories" is never mentioned. For the current generations, these messages can be confusing.

Putting weight on your bones, as my grandmother explains it, is necessary for many reasons. First of all, how else can you carry the burdens of being a woman? You have to eat in order to have the strength to deal with a husband and/or children (regardless of the fact that, at present, you may be 11 years old). You have to eat to have the strength to deal with *lo que Dios te mande*, whatever God sends you because *uno nunca sabe lo de mañana, so uno tiene que aprobechar lo de hoy*, we never know what tomorrow may bring, so we have to enjoy what we have today. Living in New York, you also have to eat in order to deal with the cold, wintry weather. There is always a good reason for a second or third helping of food. In the film *Acting Our Age*, an African-American woman about the age of 65 expresses her concern for the next generation of young women. She says, "Now that black women are being used as models and thought of as beautiful, they will pick up the same false notions about beauty as white women." I think this is also true for Latinas in the United States.

The Body of Evidence: Dangerous Intersections between Development and Culture in the Lives of Adolescent Girls

MARY K. BENTLEY

As I was walking through a major department store in our local mall I was stopped dead in my tracks by a mannequin in front of me. I'm sure many of you have had the experience of being "snuck up on" by a mannequin, but the reason for my fear was not its placement, its wild hair, or strange dress, it was the mannequin itself. It (it was a she) looked sick, emaciated, as if it could hardly stand under the burden of its own weight. . . . As I peered around the display, I saw two girls about twelve or thirteen years old strolling toward the cosmetic department, clutching plastic bags and drinking Diet (in large letters) Cokes. Neither one of them was overweight. They looked like healthy middle school girls. This scene bothered me so much that I decided to go back to the store with a measuring tape and actually take the measurements of this form. When I attempted this, I was stopped by a sales clerk who wished to direct me to the rack where I could find the dress on display. I tried to explain the situation to her, but she got very uncomfortable and called the manager. . . . After some additional explanation, I was given the phone number of a man who is in charge of dressing displays. A brief phone conversation with him led to a visit.

He was a wealth of information and gave me a fascinating account of the historical evolution of the mannequin. He explained that mannequins have gone through many incarnations over the past thirty years. He was very animated in his descriptions of mannequins that had exaggerated body parts, like cinched waists and large hips and breasts in the 1950s, mannequins that were actual body casts of models complete with genitalia in the 1970s, and the advent of the girlish flat-busted form of the 1980s. The mannequins he currently uses for displays are generally very thin. He explained: "The waif-like heroin addict is the look that dominates most of the young women's displays." He further added that in some of the displays they now "add a substantial breast to the form, the Pamela Anderson kind of thing, for more provocative displays."

He was in the process of dressing two mannequins and agreed to measure them for me. The first was 5'8" tall. Her measurements were 30" bust (she had no pads on, a la Pamela Anderson), 23" waist, and 32" hips. The second was 6 ft. tall with a 32" bust, 23" waist, and 31" hips. They both had 18" thighs and upper arms of less than ten inches. When I asked how the proportions of the mannequins were determined, he replied: "They were made so the clothes fit right and the way they are supposed to."

A mannequin is by definition a life-sized model of the human body, used to fit or display clothes. If the forms he measured were real bodies, there would be very little life in them. The average woman in the United States is a size 14. According to international sizing charts, this means she has a 38–39" bust, 29–31" waist, and 39–40" hips, more than 6 inches larger than this mannequin (32–23–31).

One of my childhood memories was an episode involving my grandmother when I was in the fifth grade. She picked me up at school and told my mother we were going shopping. Well, we did, but first she had someplace to take me. For as long as I could remember, I was a tall and very skinny child. That day, my grandmother and I took a bus ride into Manhattan to a nutrition clinic. She swore I was undernourished and that something was wrong. The doctor said I was healthy and of a good weight. My grandmother was quite surprised and, in fact, didn't believe him.

Having a "good set of hips" means not only that you can carry a child well but also that you can manage whatever your husband has in store for you. "You have to eat in order to have strength." So, from the time you are an infant, chubbiness is applauded as healthy. As you grow older, mental and physical well-being are assessed by your outer appearance. Thin is not sexy. It is unhealthy, unappealing, and sad. My grandmother told me that I didn't look strong enough to carry my bookbag and asked how was I going to carry whatever God sent my way. I learned early in life to expect to bear something! That was part of the gender-role experience.

Interestingly, flabbiness is not acceptable, either. Flabbiness is a sign of laziness and overindulgence. Formal exercise is not part of the Latino culture for women, while men often play softball, handball, or paddle ball. It is generally accepted that women who are flabby and out of shape must not be taking care of their homes, themselves, or their children. They must be watching *novelas*. Women's exercise happens in the course of cleaning, cooking, and caring for children.

In the dating game, life gets really confusing for young Latinas. If women look too much like the models, they will be considered the kind of women men play with but don't necessarily marry. A man brings a woman who is a size 10 or 12 home to mother and a family dinner, but a woman who is size 5 or 6, you have to keep away from your brother! A 16-year-old Puerto Rican student recently told me that her boyfriend wanted her to put on some weight before the summer. She said that he was not pleased at the fact that other men were watching her on the beach last summer. The other side of the problem was that her mother had taught her that if she gained weight, she would not have any boyfriends. When I heard this story, it reminded me of the African-American woman in the film and her description of "false notions about beauty."

Some of my fondest memories are wrapped in the warmth of mealtimes. Special foods are part of special holidays. Watching generations of women cook and exchange recipes, taking in all the wonderful aromas and feeling their sense of pride and accomplishment as they fulfilled their understood role, was positive for me. Although their place of power was in the kitchen, I learned how that power worked. Being in the kitchen did not mean being passive or subservient. It meant doing your share of the business of parenting and partnering, since the kitchen is the center of family activity. It is a place of importance in the Latino household. Feeding those whom you care about is nurturing the entire unit, and eating all of your *arroz con pollo* means you are loved for your efforts in return.

There are many mixed messages to negotiate in a cross-cultural environment. Immigrants, like everyone else, want to belong. They find themselves trapped somewhere between the cultural values of their home and their host country. Although some can negotiate the conflict better than others, it nevertheless distorts views of the self. Reconciliation of different cultural repertoires is quite a challenge, especially for young Latinas who are trying to "fit in."

[1992]

 39

JULY SIEBECKER

The Fat Girl Rules the World

From the plush velvet throne
in her subterranean lair

The fat girl rules the world.
We hate her, oh we hate her
Her voracious will
Her demanding spread
Her unrepentant appetite
Too loud and too laughing
Too big for our britches
She gives us these urges
She makes us all crazy
Ribs us to excess
and though we try to deny her
we secretly know that
we each are just barely
a licentious whisper
and a dangerous curve
from joy-running naked
and shrieking with laughter
through night-blackened woods.
She cannot be handled.
She cannot be trusted.
she makes us
very
nervous.
And so we shame her to silence,
And stuff her underground
And imagine that she is controlled.
But you can't kill the fat girl
she's laughing way down there
You drive her below
and she rules the roots
Leaving you wanting
and making you flustered
never quite sure if your
feet can be trusted
to walk you to work without
suddenly dancing.
She's down there right now
saying
I won't be denied
Saying
Deal with me
Saying
YES!   [2002]

 40

Homage to My Hips

LUCILLE CLIFTON

these hips are big hips
they need space to
move around in.
they don't fit into little
petty places. these hips
are free hips.
they don't like to be held back.
these hips have never been enslaved,
they go where they want to go
they do what they want to do.
these hips are mighty hips.
these hips are magic hips.
i have known them
to put a spell on a man and
spin him like a top!   [1976]

 41

Beauty: When the Other Dancer Is the Self

ALICE WALKER

It is a bright summer day in 1947. My father, a fat, funny man with beautiful eyes and a subversive wit, is trying to decide which of his eight children he will take with him to the county fair. My mother, of course, will not go. She is knocked out from getting most of us ready: I hold my neck stiff against the pressure of her knuckles as she hastily completes the braiding and then beribboning of my hair.

My father is the driver for the rich old white lady up the road. Her name is Miss Mey. She owns all the land for miles around, as well as the house in which we live. All I remember about her is that she once offered to pay my mother thirty-five cents for cleaning her house, raking up piles of her magnolia leaves, and washing her family's clothes, and that my mother—she of no money, eight children, and a chronic earache—refused it. But I do not think of this in 1947. I am two and a half years old. I want to go everywhere my daddy goes. I am excited at the prospect of riding in a car. Someone has told me fairs are fun. That there is room in the car for only three of us doesn't faze me at all. Whirling happily in my starchy frock, showing off my biscuit-polished patent-leather shoes and lavender socks, tossing my head in a way that makes my ribbons bounce, I stand, hands on hips, before my father. "Take me, Daddy," I say with assurance; "I'm the prettiest!"

Later, it does not surprise me to find myself in Miss Mey's shiny black car, sharing the back seat with the other lucky ones. Does not surprise me that I thoroughly enjoy the fair. At home that night I tell the unlucky ones all I can remember about the merry-go-round, the man who eats live chickens, and the teddy bears, until they say: that's enough, baby Alice. Shut up now, and go to sleep.

It is Easter Sunday, 1950. I am dressed in a green, flocked, scalloped-hem dress (handmade by my adoring sister, Ruth) that has its own smooth satin petticoat and tiny hot-pink roses tucked into each scallop. My shoes, new T-strap patent leather, again highly biscuit-polished. I am six years old and have learned one of the longest Easter speeches to be heard that day, totally unlike the speech I said when I was two: "Easter lilies / pure and white / blossom in / the morning light." When I rise to give my speech I do so on a great wave of love and pride and expectation. People in the church stop rustling their new crinolines. They seem to hold their breath. I can tell they admire my dress, but it is my spirit, bordering on sassiness (womanishness), they secretly applaud.

"That girl's a little *mess*," they whisper to each other, pleased.

Naturally I say my speech without stammer or pause, unlike those who stutter, stammer, or, worst of all, forget. This is before the word "beautiful" exists in people's vocabulary, but "Oh, isn't she the *cutest* thing!" frequently floats my way. "And got so much sense!" they gratefully add . . . for which thoughtful addition I thank them to this day.

It was great fun being cute. But then, one day, it ended.

I am eight years old and a tomboy. I have a cowboy hat, cowboy boots, checkered shirt and pants, all red. My playmates are my brothers, two and four years older than I. Their colors are black and green, the only difference in the way we are dressed. On Saturday nights we all go to the picture show, even my mother; Westerns are her favorite kind of movie. Back home, "on the ranch," we pretend we are Tom Mix, Hopalong Cassidy, Lash LaRue (we've even named one of our dogs Lash LaRue); we chase each other for hours rustling cattle, being outlaws, delivering damsels from distress. Then my parents decide to buy my brothers guns. These are not "real" guns. They shoot "BBs," copper pellets my brothers say will kill birds. Because I am a girl, I do not get a gun. Instantly I am relegated to the position of Indian. Now there appears a great distance between us. They shoot and shoot at everything with their new guns. I try to keep up with my bow and arrows.

One day while I am standing on top of our makeshift "garage"—pieces of tin nailed across some poles—holding my bow and arrow and looking out toward the fields, I feel an incredible blow in my right eye. I look down just in time to see my brother lower his gun.

Both brothers rush to my side. My eye stings, and I cover it with my hand. "If you tell," they say, "we will get a whipping. You don't want that to happen, do you?" I do not. "Here is a piece of wire," says the older brother, picking it up from the roof; "say you stepped on one end of it and the other flew up and hit you." The pain is beginning to start. "Yes," I say. "Yes, I will say that is what happened." If I do not say this is what happened, I know my brothers will find ways to make me wish I had. But now I will say anything that gets me to my mother.

Confronted by our parents we stick to the lie agreed upon. They place me on a bench on the porch and I close my left eye while they examine the right. There is a tree growing from underneath the porch that climbs past the railing to the roof. It is the last thing my right eye sees. I watch as its trunk, its branches, and then its leaves are blotted out by the rising blood.

I am in shock. First there is intense fever, which my father tries to break using lily leaves bound around my head. Then there are chills: my mother tries to get me to eat soup. Eventually, I do not know how, my parents learn what has happened. A week after the "accident" they take me to see a doctor. "Why did you wait so long to come?" he asks, looking into my eye and shaking his head. "Eyes are sympathetic," he says. "If one is blind, the other will likely become blind too."

This comment of the doctor's terrifies me. But it is really how I look that bothers me most. Where the BB pellet struck there is a glob of whitish scar tissue, a hideous cataract, on my eye. Now when I stare at people—a favorite pastime, up to now—they will stare back. Not at the "cute" little girl, but at her scar. For six years I do not stare at anyone, because I do not raise my head.

Years later, in the throes of a mid-life crisis, I ask my mother and sister whether I changed after the "accident." "No," they say, puzzled. "What do you mean?"

What do I mean?

I am eight, and, for the first time, doing poorly in school, where I have been something of a whiz since I was four. We have just moved to the place where the "accident" occurred. We do not know any of the people around us because this is a different county. The only time I see the friends I knew is when we go back to our old church. The new school is the former state penitentiary. It is a large stone building, cold and drafty, crammed to overflowing with boisterous, ill-disciplined children. On the third floor there is a huge circular imprint of some partition that has been torn out.

"What used to be here?" I ask a sullen girl next to me on our way past it to lunch.

"The electric chair," says she.

At night I have nightmares about the electric chair, and about all the people reputedly "fried" in it. I am afraid of the school, where all the students seem to be budding criminals.

"What's the matter with your eye?" they ask, critically.

When I don't answer (I cannot decide whether it was an "accident" or not), they shove me, insist on a fight.

My brother, the one who created the story about the wire, comes to my rescue. But then brags so much about "protecting" me, I become sick.

After months of torture at the school, my parents decide to send me back to our old community, to my old school. I live with my grandparents and the teacher they board. But there is no room for Phoebe, my cat. By the time my grandparents decide there *is* room, and I ask for my cat, she cannot be found. Miss Yarborough, the boarding teacher, takes me under her wing, and begins to teach me to play the piano. But soon she marries an African—a "prince," she says—and is whisked away to his continent.

At my old school there is at least one teacher who loves me. She is the teacher who "knew me before I was born" and bought my first baby clothes. It is she who makes life bearable. It is her presence that finally helps me turn on the one child at the school who continually calls me "one-eyed bitch." One day I simply grab him by his coat and beat him until I am satisfied. It is my teacher who tells me my mother is ill.

My mother is lying in bed in the middle of the day, something I have never seen. She is in too much pain to speak. She has an abscess in her ear. I stand looking down on her, knowing that if she dies, I cannot live. She is being treated with warm oils and hot bricks held against her cheek. Finally a doctor comes. But I must go back to my grandparents' house. The weeks pass but I am hardly aware of it. All I know is that my mother might die, my father is not so jolly, my brothers still have their guns, and I am the one sent away from home.

"You did not change," they say.

Did I imagine the anguish of never looking up?

I am twelve. When relatives come to visit I hide in my room. My cousin Brenda, just my age, whose father works in the post office and whose mother is a nurse, comes to find me. "Hello," she says. And then she asks, looking at my recent school picture, which I did not want taken, and on which the "glob," as I think of it, is clearly visible, "You still can't see out of that eye?"

"No," I say, and flop back on the bed over my book.

That night, as I do almost every night, I abuse my eye. I rant and rave at it, in front of the mirror. I plead with it to clear up before morning. I tell it I hate and despise it. I do not pray for sight. I pray for beauty.

"You did not change," they say.

I am fourteen and baby-sitting for my brother Bill, who lives in Boston. He is my favorite brother and there is a strong bond between us. Understanding my feelings of shame and ugliness, he and his wife take me to a local hospital, where the "glob" is removed by a doctor named O. Henry. There is still a small bluish crater where the scar tissue was, but the ugly white stuff is gone. Almost immediately I became a different person from the girl who does not raise her head. Or so I think. Now that I've raised my head I win the boyfriend of my dreams. Now that I've raised my head I have plenty of friends. Now that I've raised my head classwork comes from my lips as faultlessly as Easter speeches did, and I leave high school as valedictorian, most popular student, and *queen,* hardly believing my luck. Ironically, the girl who was voted most beautiful in our class (and was) was later shot twice through the chest by a male companion, using a "real" gun, while she was pregnant. But that's another story in itself. Or is it?

"You did not change," they say.

It is now thirty years since the "accident." A beautiful journalist comes to visit and to interview me. She is going to write a cover story for her magazine that focuses on my latest book. "Decide how you want to look on the cover," she says. "Glamorous, or whatever."

Never mind "glamorous," it is the "whatever" that I hear. Suddenly all I can think of is whether I will get enough sleep the night before the photography session: if I don't, my eye will be tired and wander, as blind eyes will.

At night in bed with my lover I think up reasons why I should not appear on the cover of a magazine. "My meanest critics will say I've sold out," I say. "My family will now realize I write scandalous books."

"But what's the real reason you don't want to do this?" he asks.

"Because in all probability," I say in a rush, "my eye won't be straight."

"It will be straight enough," he says. Then, "Besides, I thought you'd made your peace with that."

And I suddenly remember that I have.

I remember:

I am talking to my brother Jimmy, asking if he remembers anything unusual about the day I was shot. He does not know I consider that day the last time my father, with his sweet home remedy of cool lily leaves, chose me, and that I suffered and raged inside because of this. "Well," he says, "all I remember is standing by the side of the highway with Daddy, trying to flag down a car. A white man stopped, but when Daddy said he needed somebody to take his little girl to the doctor, he drove off."

I remember:

I am in the desert for the first time. I fall totally in love with it. I am so overwhelmed by its beauty, I confront for the first time, consciously, the meaning of the doctor's words years ago: "Eyes are sympathetic. If one is blind, the other will likely become blind too." I realize I have dashed about the world madly, looking at this, looking at that, storing up images against the fading of the light. *But I might have missed seeing the desert!* The shock of that possibility—and gratitude for over twenty-five years of sight—sends me literally to my knees. Poem after poem comes—which is perhaps how poets pray.

On Sight

I am so thankful I have seen
The Desert

And the creatures in the desert
And the desert itself.

The desert has its own moon
Which I have seen
With my own eye.
There is no flag on it.

Trees of the desert have arms
All of which are always up
That is because the moon is up
The sun is up
Also the sky
The stars
Clouds
None with flags.

If there *were* flags, I doubt
the trees would point.
Would you?

But mostly, I remember this:

I am twenty-seven, and my baby daughter is almost three. Since her birth I have worried about her discovery that her mother's eyes are different from other people's. Will she be embarrassed? I think. What will she say? Every day she watches a television program called "Big Blue Marble." It begins with a picture of the earth as it appears from the moon. It is bluish, a little battered-looking, but full of light, with whitish clouds swirling around it. Every time I see it I weep with love, as if it is a picture of Grandma's house. One day when I am putting Rebecca down for her nap, she suddenly focuses on my eye. Something inside me cringes, gets ready to try to protect myself. All children are cruel about physical differences, I know from experience, and that they don't always mean to be is another matter. I assume Rebecca will be the same.

But no-o-o-o. She studies my face intently as we stand, her inside and me outside her crib. She even holds my face maternally between her dimpled little hands. Then, looking every bit as serious and lawyerlike as her father, she says, as if it may just possibly have slipped my attention: "Mommy, there's a *world* in your eye." (As in, "Don't be alarmed, or do anything crazy.") And then, gently but with great interest: "Mommy, where did you *get* that world in your eye?"

For the most part, the pain left then. (So what, if my brothers grew up to buy even more powerful pellet guns for their sons and to carry real guns themselves. So what, if a young "Morehouse man" once nearly fell off the steps of Trevor Arnett Library because he thought my eyes were blue.) Crying and laughing I ran to the bathroom, while Rebecca mumbled and sang herself off to sleep. Yes indeed, I realized, looking into the mirror. There *was* a world in my eye. And I saw that it was possible to love it: that in fact, for all it had taught me of shame and anger and inner vision, I *did* love it. Even to see it drifting out of orbit in boredom, or rolling up out of fatigue, not to mention floating back at attention in excitement (bearing witness, a friend has called it), deeply suitable to my personality, and even characteristic of me.

That night I dream I am dancing to Stevie Wonder's song "Always" (the name of the song is really "As," but I hear it as "Always"). As I dance, whirling and joyous, happier than I've ever been in my life, another bright-faced dancer joins me. We dance and kiss each other and hold each other through the night. The other dancer has obviously come through all right, as I have done. She is beautiful, whole and free. And she is also me.   [1983]

Sexuality and Relationships

Our sexual experiences, on both emotional and physical levels, are closely tied to what we learn about the meaning of sexuality and its relationship to other dimensions of our lives. As Rebecca Walker points out, experiencing our sexuality allows us to explore what it means to be a woman, discover our erotic power, and learn about love and intimacy, among other things. For many young women, however, emerging sexuality is shrouded in shame and fear—the shame associated with being a "bad girl" and fear of pregnancy, sexually transmitted diseases, and AIDS. Walker proclaims the importance of young women knowing that "my body is not my enemy and pleasure is my friend and my right." Through acquiring this knowledge, women can become empowered to experience more fully the many dimensions of their lives. However, as Yen Espiritu and Caridad Sousa describe, in some communities it is not acceptable for a young woman to be openly sexual, and girls are expected to conform to explicitly stated roles regarding sexual behavior.

No discussion of contemporary sexuality, especially among young adults, would be complete without attending to the effects of AIDS on sexual attitudes and behaviors. Adolescents and young adults, who often consider themselves invulnerable to disease and mortality, continue to be at high risk for contracting HIV. In "Safer Sex Is Real Sex," Zoe Leonard explores some of the ways that having an HIV-positive partner has affected not only her sexual behavior but her emotional relationship with her partner as well. As she deals with the necessity of practicing safer sex, she presents strategies she has adopted that allow her to explore and enjoy her sexuality, as well as protect her health. Her essay reminds us how pleasure and safety can and must be compatible as we develop new ways of relating sexually in the age of AIDS. What happens when women are able to move beyond the limited stereotypes of "acceptable" sexuality? The next two selections relate the experiences of two lesbians, one of whom is disabled. The portrayal of these women as sexually active and sensual challenges the confining norms that our society prescribes for women's sexual behavior and offers a vision of the many possibilities that exist for women's sexual expression.

This section concludes with two essays that integrate many of the issues related to sexuality and relationships that we have addressed. In "The Turn On," Marge Piercy contemplates the meaning of sex and sensuality in her relationships, going beyond prevailing conceptions of sexual arousal to appreciate relationship qualities and experiences that are exciting and intimate. Robin Ochs shares her exploration of the relation between her feminist ideals and beliefs, her sexual experiences with women and men, and what she has learned about herself in the process. Ochs's essay conveys the subtle ways in which heterosexuals take their privilege for granted as they move through the world of male-female couples. Both of these selections help us see that women can grow beyond the stereotyped images of female sexuality to claim sexual relationships that are truly gratifying.

 42

Lusting for Freedom

REBECCA WALKER

I had sex young and, after the initial awkwardness, loved it. For days and nights, I rolled around in a big bed with my first boyfriend, trying out every possible way to feel good body to body. I was able to carry that pleasure and confidence into my every-day life working at the hair salon, raising my hand in English class, hanging out with my best girlfriend, and flirting with boys. I never felt any great loss of innocence, only great rushes of the kind of power that comes with self-knowledge and shared intimacy.

But experiences like mine are all too rare. There are forces that subvert girls' access to freeing and empowering sex—forces like AIDS, limited access to health care, and parental notification laws that force thousands of young women to seek out illegal and sometimes fatal abortions. The way we experience, speak about and envision sex and sexuality can either kill us or help us to know and protect ourselves better. The responsibility is enormous. Unfortunately, moral codes and legal demarcations complicate rather than regulate desire. And judgments like "right" and "wrong" only build barriers between people and encourage shame within individuals. I personally have learned much more from examining my own life for signs of what was empowering for me and what was not, and from listening to and asking questions of my friends: What did you feel then, what did you learn from that?

When I look back at having sex during my teenage years, I find myself asking: What was it in my own life that created the impulse and the safety; the wanting that led me and the knowing that kept me from harm?

If you are a girl, sex marks you, and I was marked young. I am ashamed to tell people how young I was, but I am too proud to lie. Eleven. I was eleven, and my mother was away working. One autumn night Kevin, a boy I had met in the neighborhood, called and said he had a sore throat. I told him I would make him some tea if he wanted to come over. He said he was on his way. I had told him that I was sixteen, so I ran around for a few minutes, panicking about what to wear. I settled on a satin leopard-print camisole from my mother's bureau and hid it beneath a big red terry-cloth robe.

I have a few vivid memories of that night: I remember being cold and my teeth chattering. I remember his black Nike high tops and red-and-gray football jersey, and the smell of him, male and musky, as he passed me coming through the front door. I remember sitting on our green sofa and telling him rather indignantly that I was not a virgin. I remember faking a fear that I might get pregnant (I didn't have my period yet). I remember his dry penis, both of us looking elsewhere as he pushed it inside of me. I remember that I wanted him to stay with me through the night, but that instead he had to rush home to make a curfew imposed upon him by his football coach.

Shocking, right? Not really. Sex begins much earlier than most people think, and it is far more extensive. It is more than the act of intercourse, much more than penis and vagina. Sex can look like love if you don't know what love looks like. It gives you someone to hold on to when you can't feel yourself. It is heat on your body when the coldness is inside of you. It is trying out trusting and being trusted. Sex can also be power because knowledge is power, and because yeah, as a girl, you can make it do different things. I can give it to you, and I can take it away. This sex is me, you can say. It is mine, take it. Take me. Please keep me.

By the time I was eighteen I was fluent in the language of sex and found myself in restaurants with men twice my age, drinking red wine and artfully playing Woman. By then I had learned about the limitations of male tenderness, men's expectations about black female desire, the taboo of loving other women, the violence of rape. And, like women all over the world, I had mastered the art of transforming myself into what I thought each man would fall in love with. Not at all in control of each affair, but very much in control of the mask I put on for each man, I tried on a dozen personas, played out a dozen roles, decided not to be a dozen people. When Bryan said I was too black, I straightened my hair. When Ray said I was too young, I added four years. For Miles I was a young virgin, nervous and giggly. For Jacob I was a self-assured student of modern art. For Robbie I was a club girl. I was Kevin's steady.

When I think of what determined my chameleon-like identity then, I think of the movie *Grease,* with the dolled-up Olivia Newton-John getting the guy and popularity too after she put on pumps and a push-up bra and became "sexy." I also think about my best girlfriend in the fourth grade who stopped speaking to me and "stole" my boyfriend over Christmas break. It was a tricky world of alliances in those younger years. You could never be sure of who was going to like you and why, so I tried my best to control what parts I could. That explains my attempts to be cool and sexy, my pretending to know everything, my smoking cigarettes, and of course, my doing it with boys. I did what I thought had to be done.

But there were also other elements, other factors. Like curiosity, desire and my body. These are the urges that account for the wet, tonguey ten-minute kiss outside the laundry room that I remembered with a quivering belly for weeks afterwards. Ditto for my desire to bury my face in my boyfriend's armpits in order to learn his smell well enough to recognize it anywhere. This very same desire to know also made me reach down and feel a penis for the first time, checking almost methodically for shape, sensitivity and any strange aberrations on the skin. My quest was not simply a search for popularity, but a definite assertion of my own nascent erotic power. This strange force, not always pleasurable but always mine, nudged me toward physical exploration and self-definition, risk taking and intimacy building, twisting each element into an inextricable whole.

Because my mother was often away, leaving me with a safe and private space to bring my boyfriends, and because my common sense and experience of nonabusive love led me to decent men, my relationships consisted of relatively safe explorations of sex that were, at the time, fulfilling physically and emotionally. I also began to play with different kinds of strength. While I learned about my partners' bodies, I learned that I had the power to make them need me. While I learned how much of myself to reveal, I learned how to draw them out. While I learned that they were not "right" for me, I learned that I was more than what they saw.

Did I know then that I was learning to negotiate the world around me and answering important questions about the woman I would become? Probably not, but looking back, it seems obvious: I peeled back endless layers of contorted faces, checking out fully the possibilities of the roles I took on. I left them again and again when I felt I could not bring all of myself to the script. I couldn't just be the football player's cheerleader girlfriend, or the club girl friend of a bartender. I wasn't happy faking orgasm (self-deceit for male ego) or worrying about getting pregnant (unprotected ignorance) or having urinary tract infections (victim of pleasure) or sneaking around (living in fear). Instinctively I knew I wanted more pleasure and more freedom, and I intuitively knew I deserved and could get both.

When I think back, it is that impulse I am most proud of. The impulse that told me that I deserve to live free of shame, that my body is not my enemy and that pleasure is my friend and my right. Without this core, not even fully jelled in my teenage mind but powerful nonetheless, how else would I have learned to follow and cultivate my own desire? How else would I have learned to listen to and develop the language of my own body? How else would I have learned to initiate, sustain and develop healthy intimacy, that most valuable of human essences? I am proud that I did not stay in relationships when I couldn't grow. I moved on when the rest of me would emerge physically or intellectually and say, Enough! There isn't enough room in this outfit for all of us.

It is important to consider what happens when this kind of self-exploration is blocked by cultural taboo, government control or religious mandate. What happens when we are not allowed to know our own bodies, when we cannot safely respond to and explore our own desire? As evinced by the world-wide rape epidemic, the incredible number of teen-age pregnancies, and the ever-increasing number of sexually transmitted diseases, sex can be an instrument of torture, the usher of unwanted responsibility or the carrier of fatal illness.

It is obvious that the suppression of sexual agency and exploration, from within or from without, is often used as a method of social control and domination. Witness widespread genital mutilation and the homophobia that dictatorially mandates heterosexuality; imagine the stolen power of the millions affected by just these two global murderers of self-authorization and determination. Without being able to respond to and honor the desires of our bodies and our selves, we become cut off from our instincts for pleasure, dissatisfied living under rules and thoughts that are not our own. When we deny ourselves safe and shameless exploration and access to reliable information, we damage our ability to even know what sexual pleasure feels or looks like.

Sex in silence and filled with shame is sex where our agency is denied. This is sex where we, young women, are powerless and at the mercy of our own desires. For giving our bodies what they want and crave, for exploring ourselves and others, we are punished like Eve reaching for more knowledge. We are called sluts and whores. We are considered impure or psychotic. Information about birth control is kept from us. Laws denying our right to control our bodies are enacted. We learn much of what we know from television, which debases sex and humiliates women.

We must decide that this is no longer acceptable, for sex is one of the places where we do our learning solo. Pried away from our parents and other authority figures, we look for answers about ourselves and how the world relates to us. We search for proper boundaries and create our very own slippery moral codes. We can begin to take control of this process and show responsibility only if we are encouraged to own our right to have a safe and self-created sexuality. The question is not whether young women are going to have sex, for this is far beyond any parental or societal control. The question is rather, what do young women need to make sex a dynamic, affirming, safe and pleasurable part of our lives? How do we build the bridge between sex and sexuality, between the isolated act and the powerful element that, when honed, can be an important tool for self-actualization?

Fortunately, there is no magic recipe for a healthy sexuality; each person comes into her or his own sexual power through a different route and at her or his own pace. There are, however, some basic requirements for sexual awareness and safe sexual practice. To begin with, young women need a safe space in which to explore our own bodies. A woman needs to be able to feel the soft smoothness of her belly, the exquisite softness of her inner thigh, the full roundness of her breasts. We need to learn that bodily pleasure belongs to us; it is our birthright.

Sex could also stand to be liberated from pussy and dick and fucking, as well as from marriage and procreation. It can be more: more sensual, more spiritual, more about communication and healing. Women and men both must learn to explore sexuality by making love in ways that are different from what we see on television and in the movies. If sex is about communicating, let us think about what we want to say and how will we say it. We need more words, images, ideas.

Finally, young women are more than inexperienced minors, more than property of the state or legal guardians. We are growing, thinking, inquisitive, self-possessed beings who need information about sex and access to birth control and abortion. We deserve to have our self-esteem nurtured and our personal agency encouraged. We need "protection" only from poverty and violence.

And even beyond all of the many things that will have to change in the outside world to help people in general and young women in particular grow more in touch with their sexual power, we also need to have the courage to look closely and lovingly at our sexual history and practice. Where is the meaning? What dynamics have we created or participated in? Why did we do that? How did we feel? How much of the way we think about ourselves is based on someone else's perception or label of our sexual experiences?

It has meant a lot to me to affirm and acknowledge my experiences and to integrate them into an empowering understanding of where I have been and where I am going. Hiding in shame or running fast to keep from looking is a waste of what is most precious about life: its infinite ability to expand and give us more knowledge, more insight and more complexity.   [1995]

🌿 43

"We Don't Sleep Around Like White Girls Do": Family, Culture, and Gender in Filipina-American Lives

YEN LE ESPIRITU

Sexuality, as a core aspect of social identity, is fundamental to the structuring of gender inequality (Millett 1970). Sexuality is also a salient marker of otherness and has figured prominently in racist and imperialist ideologies (Gilman 1985; Stoler 1991). Historically, the sexuality of subordinate groups—particularly that of racialized women—has been systematically stereotyped by the dominant groups.[1]

---

[1] Writing on the objectification of black women, Patricia Hill Collins (1991) argues that popular representations of black females—mammy, welfare queen, and Jezebel—all pivot around their sexuality, either desexualizing or hypersexualizing them. Along the same line, Native American women have been portrayed as sexually excessive (Green 1975), Chicana women as "exotic and erotic" (Mirande 1980), and Puerto Rican and Cuban women as "tropical bombshells, . . . sexy, sexed and interested" (Tafolla 1985, 39).

At stake in these stereotypes is the construction of women of color as morally lacking in the areas of sexual restraint and traditional morality. Asian women—both in Asia and in the United States—have been racialized as sexually immoral, and the "Orient"—and its women—has long served as a site of European male-power fantasies, replete with lurid images of sexual license, gynecological aberrations, and general perversion (Gilman 1985). In colonial Asia in the nineteenth and early twentieth centuries, for example, female sexuality was a site for colonial rulers to assert their moral superiority and thus their supposed natural and legitimate right to rule. The colonial rhetoric of moral superiority was based on the construction of colonized Asian women as subjects of sexual desire and fulfillment and European colonial women as the paragons of virtue and the bearers of a redefined colonial morality (Stoler 1991). The discourse of morality has also been used to mark the "unassimilability" of Asians in the United States. At the turn of the twentieth century, the public perception of Chinese women as disease-ridden, drug-addicted prostitutes served to underline the depravity of "Orientals" and played a decisive role in the eventual passage of exclusion laws against all Asians (Mazumdar 1989, 3–4). The stereotypical view that all Asian women were prostitutes, first formed in the 1850s, persisted. Contemporary American popular culture continues to endow Asian women with an excess of "womanhood," sexualizing them but also impugning their sexuality (Espiritu 1997, 93).

Filipinas—both in the Philippines and in the United States—have been marked as desirable but dangerous "prostitutes" and/or submissive "mail-order brides" (Halualani 1995; Egan 1996). These stereotypes emerged out of the colonial process, especially the extensive U.S. military presence in the Philippines. Until the early 1990s, the Philippines, at times unwillingly, housed some of the United States's largest overseas airforce and naval bases (Espiritu 1995, 14). Many Filipino nationalists have charged that "the prostitution problem" in the Philippines stemmed from U.S. and Philippine government policies that promoted a sex industry—brothels, bars, and massage parlors—for servicemen stationed or on leave in the Philippines. During the Vietnam War, the Philippines was known as the "rest and recreation" center of Asia, hosting approximately ten thousand U.S. servicemen daily (Coronel and Rosca 1993; Warren 1993). In this context, *all* Filipinas were racialized as sexual commodities, usable and expendable. A U.S.-born Filipina recounted the sexual harassment she faced while visiting Subic Bay Naval Station in Olongapo City:

> One day, I went to the base dispensary. . . . I was dressed nicely, and as I walked by the fire station, I heard catcalls and snide remarks being made by some of the firemen. . . . I was fuming inside. The next thing I heard was, "How much do you charge?" I kept on walking. "Hey, are you deaf or something? How much do you charge? You have a good body." That was an incident that I will never forget. (Quoted in Espiritu 1995, 77)

The sexualized racialization of Filipina women is also captured in Marianne Vilanueva's short story "Opportunity" (1991). As the protagonist, a "mail-order bride" from the Philippines, enters a hotel lobby to meet her American fiancé, the bellboys snicker and whisper *puta* (whore): a reminder that U.S. economic and cultural colonization in the Philippines always forms a backdrop to any relations between Filipinos and Americans (Wong 1993, 53).

Cognizant of the pervasive hypersexualization of Filipina women, my respondents, especially women who grew up near military bases, were quick to denounce prostitution, to condemn sex laborers, and to declare (unasked) that they themselves did not frequent "that part of town." As one Filipina immigrant said,

> Growing up [in the Philippines], I could never date an American because my dad's concept of a friendship with an American is with a G.I. The only reason why my dad wouldn't let us date an American is that people will think that the only way you met was because of the base. I have never seen the inside of any of the bases because we were just forbidden to go there.

Many of my respondents also distanced themselves culturally from the Filipinas who serviced U.S. sol-

diers by branding them "more Americanized" and "more Westernized." In other words, these women were sexually promiscuous because they had assumed the sexual mores of white women. This characterization allows my respondents to symbolically disown the Filipina "bad girl" and, in so doing, to uphold the narrative of Filipina sexual virtuosity and white female sexual promiscuity. In the following narrative, a mother who came to the United States in her thirties contrasted the controlled sexuality of women in the Philippines with the perceived promiscuity of white women in the United States:

> In the Philippines, we always have chaperones when we go out. When we go to dances, we have our uncle, our grandfather, and auntie all behind us to make sure that we behave in the dance hall. Nobody goes necking outside. You don't even let a man put his hand on your shoulders. When you were brought up in a conservative country, it is hard to come here and see that it is all freedom of speech and freedom of action. Sex was never mentioned in our generation. I was thirty already when I learned about sex. But to the young generation in America, sex is nothing.

Similarly, another immigrant woman criticized the way young American women are raised: "Americans are so liberated. They allow their children, their girls, to go out even when they are still so young." In contrast, she stated that, in "the Filipino way, it is very important, the value of the woman, that she is a virgin when she gets married."

The ideal "Filipina," then, is partially constructed on the community's conceptualization of white women. She is everything that they are not: she is sexually modest and dedicated to her family; they are sexually promiscuous and uncaring. Within the context of the dominant culture's pervasive hypersexualization of Filipinas, the construction of the "ideal" Filipina—as family-oriented and chaste—can be read as an effort to reclaim the morality of the community. This effort erases the Filipina "bad girl," ignores competing sexual practices in the Filipino communities, and uncritically embraces the myth of "Oriental femininity." Cast as the embodiment of perfect womanhood and exotic femininity,

Filipinas (and other Asian women) in recent years have been idealized in U.S. popular culture as more truly "feminine" (i.e., devoted, dependent, domestic) and therefore more desirable than their more modern, emancipated sisters (Espiritu 1997, 113). Capitalizing on this image of the "superfemme," mail-order bride agencies market Filipina women as " 'exotic, subservient wife imports' for sale and as alternatives for men sick of independent 'liberal' Western women" (Halualani 1995, 49; see also Ordonez 1997, 122).

Embodying the moral integrity of the idealized ethnic community, immigrant women, particularly young daughters, are expected to comply with male-defined criteria of what constitute "ideal" feminine virtues. While the sexual behavior of adult women is confined to a monogamous, heterosexual context, that of young women is denied completely (see Dasgupta and DasGupta 1996, 229–31). In the next section, I detail the ways Filipino immigrant parents, under the rubric of "cultural preservation," police their daughters' behaviors in order to safeguard their sexual innocence and virginity. These attempts at policing generate hierarchies and tensions within immigrant families—between parents and children and between brothers and sisters.

THE CONSTRUCTION(S) OF THE "IDEAL" FILIPINA: "BOYS ARE BOYS AND GIRLS ARE DIFFERENT"

As the designated "keepers of the culture" (Billson 1995), immigrant women and their behavior come under intensive scrutiny both from men and women of their own groups and from U.S.-born Americans (Gabbacia 1994, xi). In a study of the Italian Harlem community from 1880 to 1950, Orsi reports that "all the community's fears for the reputation and integrity of the domus came to focus on the behavior of young women" (1985, 135). Because women's moral and sexual loyalties were deemed central to the maintenance of group status, changes in female behavior, especially that of growing daughters, were interpreted as signs of moral decay and ethnic suicide and were carefully monitored and sanctioned (Gabbacia 1994, 113).

Although details vary, young women of various groups and across space and time—for example, second-generation Chinese women in San Francisco in the 1920s (Yung 1995), U.S.-born Italian women in East Harlem in the 1930s (Orsi 1985), young Mexican women in the Southwest during the interwar years (Ruiz 1992), and daughters of Caribbean and Asian Indian immigrants on the East Coast in the 1990s (Dasgupta and DasGupta 1996; Waters 1996)—have identified strict parental control on their activities and movements as the primary source of intergenerational conflict. Recent studies of immigrant families also identify gender as a significant determinant of parent-child conflict, with daughters more likely than sons to be involved in such conflicts and instances of parental derogation (Rumbaut and Ima 1988; Woldemikael 1989; Matute-Bianchi 1991; Gibson 1995).

Although immigrant families have always been preoccupied with passing on their native culture, language, and traditions to both male and female children, it is daughters who have the primary burden of protecting and preserving the family. Because sons do not have to conform to the image of an "ideal" ethnic subject as daughters do, they often receive special day-to-day privileges denied to daughters (Haddad and Smith 1996, 22–24; Waters 1996, 75–76). This is not to say that immigrant parents do not place undue expectations on their sons; rather, these expectations do not pivot around the sons' sexuality or dating choices.[2] In contrast, parental control over the movement and action of daughters begins the moment they are perceived as young adults and sexually vulnerable. It regularly consists of monitoring their whereabouts and forbidding dat-

---

[2] The relationship between immigrant parents and their sons deserves an article of its own. According to Gabbacia, "Immigrant parents fought with sons, too, but over different issues: parents' complaints about rebellious sons focused more on criminal activity than on male sexuality or independent courtship" (1994, 70). Moreover, because of their mobility, young men have more means to escape—at least temporarily—the pressures of the family than young women. In his study of Italian American families, Orsi reports that young men rebelled by sleeping in cars or joining the army, but young women did not have such opportunities (1985, 143).

ing (Wolf 1997). For example, the immigrant parents I interviewed seldom allowed their daughters to date, to stay out late, to spend the night at a friend's house, or to take an out-of-town trip.

Many of the second-generation women I spoke to complained bitterly about these parental restrictions. They particularly resented what they saw as gender inequity in their families: the fact that their parents placed far more restrictions on their activities and movements than on their brothers'. Some decried the fact that even their younger brothers had more freedom than they did. "It was really hard growing up because my parents would let my younger brothers do what they wanted but I didn't get to do what I wanted even though I was the oldest. I had a curfew and my brothers didn't. I had to ask if I could go places and they didn't. My parents never even asked my brothers when they were coming home." As indicated in the following excerpt, many Filipino males are cognizant of this double standard in their families:

My sister would always say to me, "It's not fair, just because you are a guy, you can go wherever you want." I think my parents do treat me and my sister differently. Like in high school, maybe 10:30 at night, which is pretty late on a school night, and I say I have to go pick up some notes at my friend's house, my parents wouldn't say anything. But if my sister were to do that, there would be no way. Even now when my sister is in college already, if she wants to leave at midnight to go to a friend's house, they would tell her that she shouldn't do it.

When questioned about this double standard, parents generally responded by explaining that "girls are different":

I have that Filipino mentality that boys are boys and girls are different. Girls are supposed to be protected, to be clean. In the early years, my daughters have to have chaperones and curfews. And they know that they have to be virgins until they get married. The girls always say that is not fair. What is the difference between their brothers and them? And my answer always is, "In the Philippines, you know, we don't do that. The girls stay home. The boys go out." It was the way that I was raised. I still want to

have part of that culture instilled in my children. And I want them to have that to pass on to their children.

Even among self-described Western-educated and "tolerant" parents, many continue to ascribe to "the Filipino way" when it comes to raising daughters. As one college-educated father explains,

Because of my Western education, I don't raise my children the way my parents raised me. I tended to be a little more tolerant. But at times, especially in certain issues like dating, I find myself more towards the Filipino way in the sense that I have only one daughter so I tended to be a little bit stricter. So the double standard kind of operates: it's alright for the boys to explore the field but I tended to be overly protective of my daughter. My wife feels the same way because the boys will not lose anything, but the daughter will lose something, her virginity, and it can be also a question of losing face, that kind of thing.

Although many parents discourage or forbid dating for daughters, they still fully expect these young women to fulfill their traditional roles as women: to marry and have children. A young Filipina recounted the mixed messages she received from her parents:

This is the way it is supposed to work: Okay, you go to school. You go to college. You graduate. You find a job. *Then* you find your husband, and you have children. That's the whole time line. *But* my question is, if you are not allowed to date, how are you supposed to find your husband? They say "no" to the whole dating scene because that is secondary to your education, secondary to your family. They do push marriage, but at a later date. So basically my parents are telling me that I should get married and I should have children but that I should not date.

In a study of second-generation Filipino Americans in northern California, Diane Wolf (1997) reports the same pattern of parental pressures: Parents expect daughters to remain virgins until marriage, to have a career, *and* to combine their work lives with marriage and children.

The restrictions on girls' movement sometimes spill over to the realm of academics. Dasgupta and DasGupta (1996, 230) recount that in the Indian

American community, while young men were expected to attend faraway competitive colleges, many of their female peers were encouraged by their parents to go to the local colleges so that they could live at or close to home. Similarly, Wolf (1997, 467) reports that some Filipino parents pursued contradictory tactics with their children, particularly their daughters, by pushing them to achieve academic excellence in high school but then "pulling the emergency brake" when they contemplated college by expecting them to stay at home, even if it meant going to a less competitive college, or not going at all. In the following account, a young Filipina relates that her parents' desire to "protect" her surpassed their concerns for her academic preparation:

> My brother [was] given a lot more opportunity educationally. He was given the opportunity to go to Miller High School that has a renowned college preparatory program but [for] which you have to be bussed out of our area.[3] I've come from a college prep program in junior high and I was asked to apply for the program at Miller. But my parents said "No, absolutely not." This was even during the time, too, when Southside [the neighborhood high school] had one of the lowest test scores in the state of California. So it was like, "You know, mom, I'll get a better chance at Miller." "No, no, you're going to Southside. There is no ifs, ands, or buts. Miller is too far. What if something happens to you?" But two years later, when my brother got ready to go on to high school, he was allowed to go to Miller. My sister and I were like, "Obviously, whose education do you value more? If you're telling us that education is important, why do we see a double standard?"

The above narratives suggest that the process of parenting is gendered in that immigrant parents tend to restrict the autonomy, mobility, and personal decision making of their daughters more than that of their sons. I argue that these parental restrictions are attempts to construct a model of Filipina womanhood that is chaste, modest, nurturing, and family-oriented. Women are seen as responsible for holding the cultural line, maintaining racial boundaries, and marking cultural difference. This is not to say that parent-daughter conflicts exist in all Filipino immigrant families. Certainly, Filipino parents do not respond in a uniform way to the challenges of being racial-ethnic minorities, and I met parents who have had to change some of their ideas and practices in response to their inability to control their children's movements and choices:

> I have three girls and one boy. I used to think that I wouldn't allow my daughters to go dating and things like that, but there is no way I could do that. I can't stop it. It's the way of life here in America. Sometimes you kind of question yourself, if you are doing what is right. It is hard to accept but you got to accept it. That's the way they are here. (Professional Filipino immigrant father)

> My children are born and raised here, so they do pretty much what they want. They think they know everything. I can only do so much as a parent. . . . When I try to teach my kids things, they tell me that I sound like an old record. They even talk back to me sometimes. . . . The first time my daughter brought her boyfriend to the house, she was eighteen years old. I almost passed away, knocked out. Lord, tell me what to do? (Working-class Filipino immigrant mother)

These narratives call attention to the shifts in the generational power caused by the migration process and to the possible gap between what parents say they want for their children and their ability to control the young. However, the interview data do suggest that intergenerational conflicts are socially recognized occurrences in Filipino communities. Even when respondents themselves had not experienced intergenerational tensions, they could always recall a cousin, a girlfriend, or a friend's daughter who had.

SANCTIONS AND REACTIONS: "THAT IS NOT WHAT A DECENT FILIPINO GIRL SHOULD DO"

I do not wish to suggest that immigrant communities are the only ones in which parents regulate their daughters' mobility and sexuality. Feminist schol-

---

[3]The names of the two high schools in this excerpt are fictitious.

ars have long documented the construction, containment, and exploitation of women's sexuality in various societies (Maglin and Perry 1996). We also know that the cultural anxiety over unbounded female sexuality is most apparent with regard to adolescent girls (Tolman and Higgins 1996, 206). The difference is in the ways immigrant and nonimmigrant families sanction girls' sexuality. To control sexually assertive girls nonimmigrant parents rely on the gender-based good girl/bad girl dichotomy in which "good girls" are passive, threatened sexual objects while "bad girls" are active, desiring sexual agents (Tolman and Higgins 1996). As Dasgupta and DasGupta write, "the two most pervasive images of women across cultures are the goddess and whore, the good and bad women" (1996, 236). This good girl/bad girl cultural story conflates femininity with sexuality, increases women's vulnerability to sexual coercion, and justifies women's containment in the domestic sphere.

Immigrant families, though, have an additional strategy: they can discipline their daughters as racial/national subjects as well as gendered ones. That is, as self-appointed guardians of "authentic" cultural memory, immigrant parents can attempt to regulate their daughters' independent choices by linking them to cultural ignorance or betrayal. As both parents and children recounted, young women who disobeyed parental strictures were often branded "nonethnic," "untraditional," "radical," "selfish," and "not caring about the family." Female sexual choices were also linked to moral degeneracy, defined in relation to a narrative of a hegemonic white norm. Parents were quick to warn their daughters about "bad" Filipinas who had become pregnant outside marriage.[4] As in the case of "bar girls" in the Philippines, Filipina Americans who veered from acceptable behaviors were deemed "Americanized"—as women who have adopted the sexual mores and practices of white women. As one Filipino immigrant father de-

scribed "Americanized" Filipinas: "They are spoiled because they have seen the American way. They go out at night. Late at night. They go out on dates. Smoking. They have sex without marrying."

From the perspective of the second-generation daughters, these charges are stinging. The young women I interviewed were visibly pained—with many breaking down and crying—when they recounted their parents' charges. This deep pain, stemming in part from their desire to be validated as Filipina, existed even among the more "rebellious" daughters. One twenty-four-year-old daughter explained:

> My mom is very traditional. She wants to follow the Filipino customs, just really adhere to them, like what is proper for a girl, what she can and can't do, and what other people are going to think of her if she doesn't follow that way. When I pushed these restrictions, when I rebelled and stayed out later than allowed, my mom would always say, "That is not what a decent Filipino girl should do. You should come home at a decent hour. What are people going to think of you?" And that would get me really upset, you know, because I think that my character is very much the way it should be for a Filipina. I wear my hair long, I wear decent makeup. I dress properly, conservative. I am family oriented. It hurts me that she doesn't see that I am decent, that I am proper and that I am not going to bring shame to the family or anything like that.

This narrative suggests that even when parents are unable to control the behaviors of their children, their (dis)approval remains powerful in shaping the emotional lives of their daughters (see Wolf 1997). Although better-off parents can and do exert greater controls over their children's behaviors than do poorer parents (Wolf 1992; Kibria 1993), I would argue that all immigrant parents—regardless of class background—possess this emotional hold on their children. Therein lies the source of their power: As immigrant parents, they have the authority to determine if their daughters are "authentic" members of their racial-ethnic community. Largely unacquainted with the "home" country, U.S.-born children depend on their parents' tutelage to craft and affirm their ethnic selves and thus are particu-

---

[4] According to a 1992 health assessment report of Filipinos in San Francisco, Filipino teens have the highest pregnancy rates among all Asian groups and, in 1991, the highest rate of increase in the number of births as compared with all other racial or ethnic groups (Tiongson 1997, 257).

larly vulnerable to charges of cultural ignorance and/ or betrayal (Espiritu 1994).

Despite these emotional pains, many young Filipinas I interviewed contest and negotiate parental restrictions in their daily lives. Faced with parental restrictions on their mobility, young Filipinas struggle to gain some control over their own social lives, particularly over dating. In many cases, daughters simply misinform their parents of their whereabouts or date without their parents' knowledge. They also rebel by vowing to create more egalitarian relationships with their own husbands and children. A thirty-year-old Filipina who is married to a white American explained why she chose to marry outside her culture:

> In high school, I dated mostly Mexican and Filipino. It never occurred to me to date a white or black guy. I was not attracted to them. But as I kept growing up and my father and I were having all these conflicts, I knew that if I married a Mexican or a Filipino, [he] would be exactly like my father. And so I tried to date anyone that would not remind me of my dad. A lot of my Filipina friends that I grew up with had similar experiences. So I knew that it wasn't only me. I was determined to marry a white person because he would treat me as an individual.[5]

Another Filipina who was labeled "radical" by her parents indicated that she would be more open-minded in raising her own children: "I see myself as very traditional in upbringing but I don't see myself as constricting on my children one day and I wouldn't put the gender roles on them. I wouldn't lock them into any particular way of behaving." It is important to note that even as these Filipinas desired new gender norms and practices for their own families, the majority hoped that their children would remain connected to Filipino culture.

My respondents also reported more serious reactions to parental restrictions, recalling incidents of someone they knew who had run away, joined a

gang, or attempted suicide. A Filipina high-school counselor relates that most of the Filipinas she worked with "are really scared because a lot of them know friends that are pregnant and they all pretty much know girls who have attempted suicide." A 1995 random survey of San Diego public high schools conducted by the Federal Centers for Disease Control and Prevention (CDC) found that, in comparison with other ethnic groups, female Filipino students had the highest rates of seriously considering suicide (45.6 percent) as well as the highest rates of actually attempting suicide (23 percent) in the year preceding the survey. In comparison, 33.4 percent of Latinas, 26.2 percent of white women, and 25.3 percent of black women surveyed said they had suicidal thoughts (Lau 1995).

CONCLUSION

Because the policing of women's bodies is one of the main means of asserting moral superiority, young women face numerous restrictions on their autonomy, mobility, and personal decision making. This practice of cultural (re)construction reveals how deeply the conduct of private life can be tied to larger social structures.

The construction of white Americans as the "other" and American culture as deviant serves a dual purpose: It allows immigrant communities both to reinforce patriarchy through the sanctioning of women's (mis)behavior and to present an unblemished, if not morally superior, public face to the dominant society. Strong in family values, heterosexual morality, and a hierarchical family structure, this public face erases the Filipina "bad girl" and ignores competing (im)moral practices in the Filipino communities. Through the oppression of Filipina women and the denunciation of white women's morality, the immigrant community attempts to exert its moral superiority over the dominant Western culture and to reaffirm to itself its self-worth in the face of economic, social, political, and legal subordination. In other words, the immigrant community uses restrictions on women's lives as one form of resistance to racism. This form of cultural resistance, however, severely restricts the lives of women, particularly those of the second generation, and it casts

---

[5]The few available studies on Filipino American intermarriage indicate a high rate relative to other Asian groups. In 1980, Filipino men in California recorded the highest intermarriage rate among all Asian groups, and Filipina women had the second-highest rate, after Japanese American women (Agbayani-Siewert and Revilla 1995, 156).

the family as a potential site of intense conflict and oppressive demands in immigrant lives.   [2001]

REFERENCES

Agbayani-Siewert, Pauline, and Linda Revilla. "Filipino Americans." In *Asian Americans: Contemporary Trends and Issues,* ed. Pyong Gap Min. Thousand Oaks, Calif.: Sage, 1995.

Billson, Janet Mancini. *Keepers of the Culture: The Power of Tradition in Women's Lives.* New York: Lexington, 1995.

Coronel, Sheila, and Ninotchka Rosca. "For the Boys: Filipinas Expose Years of Sexual Slavery by the U.S. and Japan." *Ms.,* November/December 1993, pp. 10–15.

Dasgupta, Shamita Das, and Sayantani DasGupta. "Public Face, Private Space: Asian Indian Women and Sexuality." In *"Bad Girls/Good Girls": Women, Sex, and Power in the Nineties,* ed. Nan Bauer Maglin and Donna Perry. New Brunswick, N.J.: Rutgers University Press, 1996.

di Leonardo, Micaela. *The Varieties of Ethnic Experience: Kinship, Class, and Gender among California Italian-Americans.* Ithaca, N.Y.: Cornell University Press, 1984.

Egan, Timothy. "Mail-Order Marriage, Immigrant Dreams and Death." *New York Times,* May 26, 1996, p. 12.

Espiritu, Yen Le. "The Intersection of Race, Ethnicity, and Class: The Multiple Identities of Second Generation Filipinos." *Identities* 1(2–3) (1994) pp. 249–73.

———. 1995. *Filipino American Lives.* Philadelphia: Temple University Press.

———. 1997. *Asian American Women and Men: Labor, Laws, and Love.* Thousand Oaks, Calif.: Sage.

Espiritu, Yen Le, and Diane L. Wolf. Forthcoming. "The Paradox of Assimilation: Children of Filipino Immigrants in San Diego." In *Ethnicities: Children of Immigrants in America,* ed. Ruben Rumbaut and Alejandro Portes. Berkeley: University of California Press; New York: Russell Sage Foundation.

Frankenberg, Ruth. *White Women, Race Matters: The Social Construction of Whiteness.* Minneapolis: University of Minnesota Press, 1993.

Gabbacia, Donna. *From the Other Side: Women, Gender, and Immigrant Life in the U.S., 1820–1990.* Bloomington: Indiana University Press, 1994.

Gibson, Margaret A. "Additive Acculturation as a Strategy for School Improvement." In *California's Immigrant Children: Theory, Research, and Implications for Educational Policy,* ed. Ruben Rumbaut and Wayne A. Cornelius. 77–105. La Jolla: Center for U.S.-Mexican Studies, University of California, San Diego, 1995.

Gilman, Sander L. *Difference and Pathology: Stereotypes of Sexuality, Race, and Madness.* Ithaca, N.Y.: Cornell University Press, 1985.

Green, Rayna. "The Pocahontas Perplex: The Image of Indian Women in American Culture." *Massachusetts Review* 16(4) (1975) pp. 698–714.

Haddad, Yvonne Y., and Jane I. Smith. "Islamic Values among American Muslims." In *Family and Gender among American Muslims: Issues Facing Middle Eastern Immigrants and Their Descendants,* ed. Barbara C. Aswad and Barbara Bilge. Philadelphia: Temple University Press, 1996.

Halualani, Rona Tamiko. "The Intersecting Hegemonic Discourses of an Asian Mail-Order Bride Catalog: Pilipina 'Oriental Butterfly' Dolls for Sale." *Women's Studies in Communication* 18(1) (1995): pp. 45–64.

Kibria, Nazli. 1993. *Family Tightrope: The Changing Lives of Vietnamese Immigrant Community.* Princeton, N.J.: Princeton University Press.

Lau, Angela. 1995. "Filipino Girls Think Suicide at Number One Rate." *San Diego Union-Tribune,* February 11, A-1.

Maglin, Nan Bauer, and Donna Perry. "Introduction." In *"Bad Girls/Good Girls": Women, Sex, and Power in the Nineties,* ed. Nan Bauer Maglin and Donna Perry. New Brunswick, N.J.: Rutgers University Press, 1996.

Matute-Bianchi, Maria Eugenia. "Situational Ethnicity and Patterns of School Performance among Immigrant and Nonimmigrant Mexican-Descent Students." In *Minority Status and Schooling: A Comparative Study of Immigrant and Involuntary Minorities,* ed. Margaret A. Gibson and John U. Ogbu. New York: Garland, 1991.

Mazumdar, Suchetta. "General Introduction: A Woman-Centered Perspective on Asian American History." In *Making Waves: An Anthology by and about Asian American Women,* ed. Asian Women United of California. Boston: Beacon, 1989.

Millett, Kate. *Sexual Politics.* Garden City, N.Y.: Doubleday, 1970.

Ordonez, Raquel Z. "Mail-Order Brides: An Emerging Community." In *Filipino Americans: Transformation and Identity,* ed. Maria P. Root. Thousand Oaks, Calif.: Sage, 1997.

Orsi, Robert Anthony. *The Madonna of 115th Street: Faith and Community in Italian Harlem, 1880–1950.* New Haven, Conn.: Yale University Press, 1985.

Ruiz, Vicki L. "The Flapper and the Chaperone: Historical Memory among Mexican-American Women." In *Seeking Common Ground: Multidisciplinary Studies,* ed. Donna Gabbacia. Westport, Conn.: Greenwood, 1992.

Rumbaut, Ruben, and Kenji Ima. *The Adaptation of Southeast Asian Refugee Youth: A Comparative Study.* Washington, D.C.: U.S. Office of Refugee Resettlement, 1988.

Stoler, Ann Laura. "Carnal Knowledge and Imperial Power: Gender, Race, and Morality in Colonial Asia." In *Gender at the Crossroads of Knowledge: Feminist Anthropology in the Postmodern Era,* ed. Micaela di Leonardo. Berkeley: University of California Press, 1991.

Tiongson, Antonio T., Jr. "Throwing the Baby out with the Bath Water." In *Filipino Americans: Transformation and Identity,* ed. Maria P. Root. Thousand Oaks, Calif.: Sage, 1997.

Tolman, Deborah L., and Tracy E. Higgins. "How Being a Good Girl Can Be Bad for Girls." In *"Bad Girls/Good Girls": Women, Sex, and Power in the Nineties,* ed. Nan Bauer Maglin and Donna Perry. New Brunswick, N.J.: Rutgers University Press, 1996.

Villanueva, M. *Ginseng and Other Tales from Manila.* Corvallis, Ore.: Calyx, 1991.

Warren, Jenifer. "Suit Asks Navy to Aid Children Left in Philippines," *Los Angeles Times,* March 5, 1993, p. A3.

Waters, Mary C. 1996. "The Intersection of Gender, Race, and Ethnicity in Identity Development of Caribbean American Teens." In *Urban Girls: Resisting Stereotypes,*

Creating Identities, ed. Bonnie J. Ross Leadbeater and Niobe Way, 65–81. New York: New York University Press.

Woldemikael, T. M. *Becoming Black American: Haitians and American Institutions in Evanston, Illinois.* New York; AMS Press, 1989.

Wolf, Diane L. *Factory Daughters: Gender, Household Dynamics, and Rural Industrialization in Java.* Berkeley: University of California Press, 1992.

———. 1997. "Family Secrets: Transnational Struggles among Children of Filipino Immigrants." *Sociological Perspectives* 40(3):457–82.

Wong, Sau-ling. *Reading Asian American Literature: From Necessity to Extravaganza.* Princeton, N.J.: Princeton University Press, 1993.

Yung, Judy. *Unbound Feet: A Social History of Chinese Women in San Francisco.* Berkeley: University of California Press, 1995.

 44

Esta Risa No Es De Loca[1]

CARIDAD SOUZA

Esta risa no es de loco. Se están riendo de mí. Me dicen que yo estoy loco pero se están cayendo de un coco. Porque de mí no pueden reír . . .[2]
—Hector La Voe, *Vamos a Reír Un Poco,* 1978

ESTA LOCURA TIENE RAÍCES.[3]

I'm not exactly sure when it was that I began to feel crazy, but I think it has something to do with being Puerto Rican, and working class, from a woman-headed family, and a girl-child who has come of age in the late twentieth century. It's really quite a feat to be a Puerto Rican woman in the late twentieth century. You barely exist outside your own imagination except in the form of vicious stereotypes. The only way to bring your own self out of oblivion is to remind folks about that peculiarly colonial/postcolonial relationship the U. S. has with a small island in the Caribbean and its people in diaspora. The huge wall of silence that always stops a conversation among people in the United States whenever you bring up those "controversial" issues they'd rather forget speaks to the way Puerto Rican women continually get erased. It always makes me feel so crazy.

My first lessons in erasure happened during my early childhood within my extended family. I was born in the South Bronx at the tail end of the baby boom, my Puerto Ricanness was questioned by my mother's family. Although on the surface I seemed to fit all the appropriate Puerto Rican identity markers, there were wrinkles in this fabric. My father was the child of dual migrations. His mother, an orphan from Ponce, Puerto Rico, migrated to the United States as a domestic servant during the first significant wave of Puerto Rican migration in the early part of the century. My paternal grandfather migrated to the U.S. from the Cape Verde Islands. I was four years old when he died, so I had little contact with his relatives. My father, although New York born and bred, brought that culture alive for me through religious beliefs and practices that connected me to my African heritage through a particular cosmological worldview. My mother, on the other hand, was part of the "great migration" of Puerto Ricans to the U. S. that began at midcentury. She passed down to her children some historically and regionally specific cultural values and practices that connect me to my *puertorriqueñidad.* But her Puerto Rico was the one of her childhood in the fifties, a Puerto Rico partly constructed through the imaginings of a migrating female, colonial subject. She fed us the nostalgic narrative of an island paradise interspersed with stories of poverty and hardship that made sense only after we moved to the island when I was eight years old. That's how I got to be a child of multiple diasporas. But the glaring contradictions in my family's narrative were what started me off feeling crazy.

When my father moved us back to the United States we ended up in the small seaside community of Far Rockaway, Queens. It was in Far Rockaway that I spent the rest of my formative years, and it had an important impact on my sense of *puertorriqueñidad,* and my craziness. Shortly after my family moved to Far Rockaway, my parents permanently separated. The change in our household composition, and our subsequent fall from the working class into the ranks of the poor, meant we were subjected to severe material deprivation. In the multiethnic context of my childhood I had to constantly negotiate different sociocultural politics as a Puerto Rican girl. This meant that whenever I visited friends, I was subjected to a certain scrutiny by wary mothers who wanted to assure themselves I wasn't *that* kind of Puerto Rican. No matter the ethnic background of any of my friends, whether Colombian, Jewish, Dominican, or Italian-American, once their mothers found out I was Puerto Rican, I could expect an interrogation at my first visit. My parents raised me to respect my elders and inculcated in me an ethic of respect that won me the approval, sometimes even the affection, of my friend's parents. But the fact that I was Puerto Rican and poor was enough to render me suspicious. Despite passing the entry exams, I was still subject to undue questioning whenever anything was lost or missing and whenever my friends got into mischief. I worked hard to please the adults, going out of my way to comport myself appropriately and to abide by any household rules. But my racial, ethnic, and class position marked me no matter how well I behaved, no matter how respectful I was, no matter how much I followed the rules. My name was always the first to come up whenever something went wrong. I learned to anticipate this scrutiny and develop elaborate arguments in my own defense. It annoyed the hell out of the adults and didn't endear me to them, but it saved me the pain of their scrutiny.

THAT PUTA *THING THAT JUST DOESN'T GO AWAY*

Specific gender and sexual ideologies governed my behavior as a young girl and adolescent in this community. The label of *puta* (whore) was used within this Latino community for girls and young women to uphold the rigid lines of sexual propriety. Any woman who didn't conform to the prevailing gender and sexual norms was a *puta*. The word tethered us like a huge ball and chain. So great was the power of this label that none of us escaped constructing our sexual identities without, at some level, addressing the *puta* thing. For someone like me who was poor, from a woman-headed family on welfare, and Puerto Rican, the label *puta* had a particular resonance. My explicit sexualization meant that I didn't merit the respect "ladies" get by virtue of living in households with a male head. For better or for worse, I did not get the kind of patriarchal protection most Latinas do. The lack of male presence at home left me open to whatever assaults and attacks men deemed appropriate for someone of my station. It didn't matter that I wasn't even interested in sex with men, that I didn't have a boyfriend, and that I was not actively pursuing a man. Junior whores-in-training like me, guilty by association, bore the brunt of the psychological and sociopolitical impact of the *puta* label. More than anything, it was this label that taught me the most important lessons about patriarchal domination and masculine violence.

Sexual stigma was status- and color-oriented among Puerto Ricans in this community, but it was more intensely racialized outside of the Puerto Rican enclave among Latinos and other ethnic groups. I lived with the stigma of the word *puta*, carrying it around like a marker of my worth, an index of how I should be treated. Even before I had a chance to define my own sexuality, my own identity, the label preceded me like a calling card. Once a friend's older brother, who was on a home visit from the military, decided I had grown up enough to bestow his masculine virility on me. He cornered me in his sister's bedroom and tried to kiss me. I pushed him away with such force that he slammed against the wall. He seemed surprised by this and he said, in all earnestness, "What? You want to go to a hotel?" Perhaps my friend's constant refrain—that the only thing Puerto Rican women were good for was to cook, dance, and fuck—should have tipped me off. Until that moment, I really didn't know that I was open season even to the boys I grew up with once they became men. It was another one of those revelatory moments.

These types of incidents taught me to anticipate whether or not knowledge about my woman-headed-household-on-public-assistance background might matter to people. I carefully selected my friends based on the position they took. This *puta* thing also meant men assumed that I was sexually available to them, especially after they learned that I was Puerto Rican. Somehow *puertorriqueña* became synonymous with *puta*. And since I was undoubtedly a *puta*, the logic went, then I must also be interested in casual sex with any man who approached me. Whenever I wasn't grateful enough to oblige a man's sexual interest in me, I was treated abusively, sometimes even violently. Since for me the sexual attention of men was always dangerous, usually painful, and always unsolicited, I avoided contact with them. I steered clear from sexual encounters with men and worked hard never to find myself in a position where I was alone with a man for fear of his expectations and their consequences. I constantly fended off unwanted sexual attentions and sexual attacks, becoming an expert in dodging and evasiveness to avoid such encounters. I learned to watch for the ways people might misperceive me sexually, to read between the lines, to intuit whether double entendres meant a dangerous situation was brewing. Consequently, I was never all-consumed with finding a man to settle down with in a relationship, unlike many of the women I knew. Since my gender and sexual identity were not defined relationally by attachment to a man, I concentrated on developing relationships with women. Yet, despite my lack of engagement with men, the stigma of being a *puta* even when I wasn't, made me feel more than a little crazy.

NO GREAT EXPECTATIONS

No one expected much out of me. There are no great expectations for little Puerto Rican girls from women-headed families on welfare. I achieved in spite of this, exceeding all their expectations for someone from my background, and sometimes even my own. In many respects I've become the quintessential American achievement story. From an outsider's view, I've defied the odds. My achievements are celebrated by the very people who expected nothing from me. After struggling to get out from under the weight of my sociopolitical inheritance, after struggling against the stereotypes about me within and outside of the Latino community I lived in, after struggling to get beyond the structural constraints on my life and after grappling with my low self-esteem, I've become successful by their standards. More importantly I've become successful by my own standards. But the damage is still there. Now I wage a new struggle to remind people that

none of my achievements are guaranteed. And that it's all been at a cost. And while, yes, I'm better off materially, and perhaps even more in control of my life, while academia and intellectual work offer me a certain refuge, and while a lot of hard work on my part has paid off, much of it is a result of institutional support. The end result is that all of this has enhanced my ability to see contradictions and to grapple with them in ways that can benefit me.

For a long time my ability to read the cultural, social, and political contradictions in my life made me feel really crazy. They tore me apart. But the basis for my sense of craziness is really a world that compartmentalized me *a priori* into social categories that I did not fit. I was born into these categories without much say, and the expectations and stereotypes about my potential really only measure the biases upon which they were based and not my social worth as a person. No matter my own values, I realized I would be judged by societal assumptions about who I ought to be, not who I actually was. These assumptions used superficial understandings of me that certainly never considered my views. My fate was sealed before I could have a say. In the world I was born into, I used to feel like I was crazy. These days I've learned that what is crazy is a world that is so structured by inequality and injustice that it doesn't nurture poor Puerto Rican girls simply because they are poor, Puerto Rican girls.

Only recently I have been able to appreciate my ability to "see" beyond the surface; how these experiences have taught me to be aware of my surroundings; and what it means to be marked by race, class, gender, and ethnicity. It's given me an edge. I've learned, for example, that political allies come in a variety of shapes and forms, and I've learned to choose them on the basis of ideological and poetical persuasion. I've also learned about partially situated perspectives, about the transparency of claims to objectivity, and about the importance of cross-referencing. The life situations I've narrated have taught me much about how people come to view things, about how our biases mediate our perspectives. From my family I've learned a healthy distrust for authority and for the "official story." From the way that race, class, gender, and ethnicity have come together in my life, I've learned that people will question facts before they question their convictions, especially if those convictions support stereotypes about others that benefit them in some way. I have witnessed how the adults around me were wrong about their perceptions, how authority figures made mistakes. Much later I learned that racist ethnocentrism was actually a very logical, rational system of oppression.

One of the most important ways my life experiences have prepared me for academia has been to develop my own internal standards, and to look to those standards for validation. Otherwise I would have to accept the assessment of a world that despises me. The world I live in does not validate little Puerto Rican girls. So I've developed my own measures of success, of progress, of achievement. Learning to redefine categories, to question received ones, and to create new definitions and concepts means I participate in creating alternative perspectives. Why accept definitions of others when they were not only possibly wrong, but potentially harmful and inaccurate anyway? I've learned to question everything. People have their own sense of meaning, and they also make meaning as they move along the trajectories of their lives. I learned that I don't have to accept their meanings, especially if those meanings were constructed to devalue me. My own meanings, perspectives, and interpretations are just as valid, just as useful.

Laughter has always been a part of my survival mechanism, one that I learned in my family. Although I'm usually serious, I find myself almost ready to explode with giggles at the most inappropriate times. Or a word sounds strange and I laugh to myself. Sometimes I will remember a silly moment and will chuckle out loud to myself while sitting on the train or bus. That kind of laughter has always marked me as crazy. Laughter helps to heal the crazies. Lately, my laughter sounds less like the screech of a crazy woman than of someone who delights in the world I see, disorderly, contradictory, and complex as it may be. Recently, I was taking one of my students to an awards banquet. Her mother, who was in the car with us, turned to me and said, "Cari, *tú no te crees nadie.*"[4] An immigrant

from Latin America, I understood her words to mean that I am not pretentious. I laughed heartily at this. It's hard to be pretentious in a world that devalues you at every turn. *Pero esta risa no es de loca.*[5] I'm having the last laugh. Only this time it's the laughter of a woman grounded in who she is regardless of how she's been marked.

So I guess the last laugh is on me.   [2002]

NOTES

1. Jus' Cuz I'm Laughin' Don't Mean I'm Crazy
2. This laughter doesn't mean I'm crazy. They're laughing at me. They say I'm crazy but *'se están cayendo de un coco'* (untranslatable word play, possibly for the purpose of rhyming *loco*[crazy] with *coco*[coconut]). But they can't laugh at me . . .
3. This Madness Has Roots.
4. "Cari, you don't believe yourself to be better than other people."
5. "But jus' cuz I'm laughin' doesn't mean I'm crazy."

 45

Safer Sex Is Real Sex

ZOE LEONARD

I have a lover who is HIV positive.

I am HIV negative.

I want to talk about my experience with safer sex and loving someone who is HIV positive.

Safer sex is often spoken about as a major drag . . . necessary, but fundamentally unerotic. People never seem to say, "Yeah, I do this with my lover and it's really hot."

Well, I do it with my lover and it's really hot.

I knew he was HIV positive before I slept with him. I had felt surprised when I found out; he just looked so damned healthy. I didn't envision having a sexual relationship with him, mainly because I've been an out and happy lesbian for years. So, when we realized we had crushes on each other, it was a big shock and really scary. I was doing AIDS activism and supposedly I knew all about safer sex, but suddenly I couldn't remember what I knew. All the grey areas of "low-risk" and "safer" sex seemed unclear and menacing; was kissing really OK? Secret fears snuck in. What if everyone is wrong about safer sex, about saliva? I felt I couldn't ask about these scary thoughts, like I should know the answers and had no right to feel so threatened. I didn't want to reinforce the stigma that he fights: feeling infectious, reading about himself as an "AIDS carrier." It had been relatively easy to be supportive and accepting of my friends with AIDS, to be sex positive, to talk about safer sex, but now it was in my bedroom, and I'm wondering: can he put his finger inside me without a glove, can he go down on me, can I touch his penis? Safer sex is different when you know your partner is infected. I don't want to appear frightened. I don't want to make him feel bad by talking about it, but I really, really don't want to get infected. (I tested negative for HIV about two years ago, and swore that I would never again place myself at any risk whatsoever.) And, here I was, a dyke at that, kissing this man goodnight after our first date.

In the beginning I was overwhelmed, terrified after that first kiss. So, we didn't dive right into bed and "do the nasty." We took our time and messed around for months, figuring out what we were comfortable with. It was great, all that sex building up. I always came, but we never did anything outside the strictest confines of "no risk" sex without talking about it first. We talked a lot about limits and seeing each other's points of view: my understanding that he doesn't want to feel like a pariah, or like he represents disease, his understanding that I had a right to be frightened, cautious, curious. It is important that I never do anything out of pressure, out of a need to prove that I'm not prejudiced. I realize that, as much as he cares about my health, I have to decide for myself what is safer, and stick to it. I knew I would resent him if we did something I wasn't sure about, and I would fly into a panic the next day.

I also realize that he is at risk for any infection that I might be carrying, and that safer sex is to protect him, too. A mild infection that might be harmless to me could be devastating to him.

I'm afraid of making him sick. I had hepatitis this summer, and we were worried that I might give it to him. Hepatitis can be very dangerous to anyone with an impaired immune system. I felt frightened and guilty. Later on I got angry that my *being* sick was

somewhat overlooked in the panic surrounding the possibility of his *getting* sick. I found myself anxious and worried about his health at a time when I needed comfort and care. Sometimes I don't feel legitimate in feeling sorry for myself or being concerned about my own health.

A great thing about safer sex is that we . . . don't have intercourse all the time. We get off a lot of different ways, so our sex is varied and we don't just fall into one pattern.

The main thing is not to form a hierarchy of what "real sex" is, or equate "real sex" with high-risk practices. We can't think that humping is fake and intercourse is real.

Condoms are great. They are really sexy to me now, like lingerie or the perfume of a lover. Maybe I'm just immature, or particularly responsive to Pavlovian training, but the mere sight of condoms, lube, or dental dams sends a sexy feeling through me. The tools of safer sex become as significant and fetishized as other toys for pleasure. I'm always hearing about how condoms and other latex barriers take away all the spontaneity, as if sex before AIDS was always spontaneous and perfect. There are many barriers to good sex, like being too anxious, too busy, or too tired, or the *phone ringing,* or not finding someone you want to have sex with in the first place.

You can use safer sex to tease each other, waiting until you want something really badly before you screw up the courage to ask for it (or beg for it). Then you stop, and hang in this state of anticipation, feeling like a teenager, waiting while he (for instance) gets the first condom out, squirts the lube in it, and gets it on. Then he gets the second condom out and on. It's tense and full of anticipation, and I rarely feel either of us cooling off. It can be exciting to admit what you want, to articulate it, and to know what your partner wants, and to use the confines of safer sex to create tension and escalate desire.

Also, it can be a gift, like the time we went away for the weekend and he showed up with a shopping bag full of every form of latex known to humankind. It's a way of showing that you care about someone's health, and that you want him or her to be considerate and romantic at the same time.

We've had to negotiate so many aspects of our relationship that otherwise might have remained mute, but this has given us the context to discuss other things: what feels good, what we want, what freaks us out. The need to figure all those things out has built trust between us; it's made us honest.

But divisions do occur between the sick and the well. My lover is asymptomatic, so HIV often seems like an abstract issue to me. When I'm talking about something in the future, he blurts out, "I don't know if I'll be alive in five years." Can I understand the depression? I feel guilty sometimes and cut off other times.

It's one thing to learn to [have safer sex] and quite another to feel committed to someone that you are afraid might get really sick or die. I think: can I do it? Will I have the patience, will I be adequate? What if he really does get sick, what then? . . . can I handle feeling this responsible? Do I want to take care of him? And what if he really does die? What about that?

I've had friends die of AIDS. I have visceral memories of Dan in the hospital just before he died, massaging his feet, feeling the thick lumps of KS lesions through his sweat socks. I remember him semi-conscious, making noises, responding to the pressure of my hands, his lover saying yes, he likes that.

I was once very much in love with a woman who got cancer. For a year my whole world telescoped into just her room, her health. My life was filled with nightmares and worrying, cooking, obsessing. My days were spent in the hospital, knowing the staff, being a regular. I knew every detail of her treatment, read all the articles, took notes. Running into friends, everyone would ask, "How's Simone?" People stopped asking, "How are you?" There was a certain relief in turning myself over to this greater cause, where everything was always about her—humidifiers, macrobiotic food, appointments. Even now, we are friends, and still there is a subtext: will she get sick again, will she die?

I wonder, do I just thrive on drama? Do I have a martyr complex, or a death wish? Did I fall for him because of his status? Do I want to get infected; is this my most recent and subtle form of self-destruction? Friends and family are anxious, ask me about *it*. They tell me I'm crazy, and speak of illness and health in hushed tones.

And I have to admit, after all these months, sometimes I'm still scared. I see an article and I think,

---

Demanding a Condom

KAT DOUD

Before I understood AIDS, who got it, and how it could be prevented, I was scared, really scared. I felt at risk but for the wrong reasons. I was afraid of casual contact with people instead of being afraid of having unsafe sex with a man I was seeing at the time. Max (not his real name) was putting a lot of pressure on me to get birth control pills for protection, [but] the only protection pills would offer would be for pregnancy—not AIDS. During this time, my fear of AIDS was growing. I was getting really paranoid, so I called the hotline. They talked a lot about condoms and safer sex. I went immediately to Max to tell him how I was feeling and that I wouldn't have sex with him without condoms. His reaction was horrible. He got very angry and full of contempt and accused me of having AIDS, and angry that I insinuated that he did. I began to try to explain, then realized he wasn't worth my time. Why would I want to sleep with this creature who didn't care about my life? I never saw him again after that night.   [1990]

could I be the first case of saliva transmission? Why am I still scared? I forget for weeks, and then when I get sick, feverish, peaked, HIV is there like a threat. I worry secretly, and when I tell him, he's angry, defensive.

All around us, his friends, my friends, into the hospital, out of the hospital, dying. When will it start with him? He gets a cold, the flu. He's tired, glands swollen.

I hate this virus.

This started out to be about the joys of safer sex, but I guess it's complicated.

I am HIV negative, as of my last test. I've learned a lot and had some really hot sex and lots of flirty, sexy stuff, and there's been a lot of love and happiness in this relationship. There's a difference between rational fears and irrational ones. I try to act on the rational ones. I try to protect myself and my lover from real threats, and try to overcome the irrational fears.

You *can* make decisions about your life and love based on what you want, and not let illness, or fear of illness, make all the decisions for you.   [1990]

46

Pleasures

DIANE HUGS

We both sat there, two disabled lesbians in our wheelchairs, each on opposite sides of the bed. Sudden feelings of fear and timidity came over us. But once we finished the transferring, lifting of legs, undressing and arranging of blankets, we finally touched. Softly and slowly we began to explore each other, our minds and bodies. Neither could make assumptions about the sensations or pleasures of the other. It was wonderful to sense that this woman felt that my body was worth the time it took to explore, that she was as interested in discovering my pleasure as I was in discovering hers.

From the first touch it was a stream of sensations; to listen to every breath, each sigh, and to feel

every movement of our love intermingling. It was so intense, so mutual that I must say this beginning was one of the deepest and most fulfilling that I have ever experienced.

When I was an able-bodied lesbian, my approach to relating sexually had been to find out what moves turned someone on and go from there. Never before have I taken the time or had the opportunity to begin a relationship with such a beautiful feeling of pleasure, not only from the pot of gold at the end of the rainbow, but also from the exploration itself.

[1985]

47

Loving Another Woman

ANNE KOEDT

The following is from a taped interview with a woman who talked about her love relationship with another woman. Both of these women, who requested anonymity, had previously had only heterosexual relationships; both are feminists. The interview was conducted by Anne Koedt.

Question: You said you had been friends for a while before you realized you were attracted to each other. How did you become aware of it?

Answer: I wasn't conscious of it until one evening when we were together and it all just sort of exploded. But, looking back, there are always signs, only one represses seeing them.

For example, I remember one evening—we are in the same feminist group together—and we were all talking very abstractly about love. All of a sudden, even though the group was carrying on the conversation in a theoretical way, we were having a personal conversation. We were starting to tell each other that we liked each other. Of course one of the things we discussed was: What is the thin line between friendship and love?

Or, there were times when we were very aware of having "accidentally" touched each other. And Jennie told me later that when we first met she remembered thinking, "abstractly" again, that if she were ever to get involved with a woman, she'd like to get involved with someone like me.

The mind-blowing thing is that you aren't at all conscious of what you are feeling; rather, you subconsciously, and systematically, refuse to deal with the implications of what's coming out. You just let it hang there because you're too scared to let it continue and see what it means.

Q: What did you do when you became aware of your mutual attraction?

A: We'd been seeing a lot of each other, and I was at her house for dinner. During the evening—we were having a nice time, but I remember also feeling uncomfortable—I became very aware of her as we were sitting together looking at something. There was an unusual kind of tension throughout the whole evening.

It was quite late by the time we broke up, so she asked me whether I wanted to stay over and sleep on her couch. And I remember really being very uptight—something I certainly wouldn't have felt in any other situation with a friend. Yet, even when I was uptight and felt that in some way by staying I would get myself into something, I wasn't quite sure what—something new and dangerous—I decided to stay anyway.

It wasn't really until I tried to fall asleep, and couldn't, that all of a sudden I became very, very aware. I was flooded with a tremendous attraction for her. And I wanted to tell her, I wanted to sleep with her, I wanted to let her know what I was feeling. At the same time I was totally bewildered, because here I was—not only did I want to tell her, but I was having a hard time just facing up to what was coming out in myself. My mind was working overtime trying to deal with this new thing.

She was awake too, and so we sat and talked. It took me about two hours to build up the courage to even bring up the subject. I think it is probably one of the most difficult things I ever had to do. To say—to in any way whatsoever open up the subject—to say anything was just so hard.

When I did bring it up in an oblique way and told her that I was attracted to her, she replied somewhat generally that she felt the same way. You see, she was as scared as I was, but I didn't know it. I thought she seemed very cool, so I wasn't even sure if she was interested. Although I think subconsciously I knew, because otherwise I wouldn't have asked her—I think I would have been too scared of rejection.

But when I finally did bring it up, and she said she felt the same way, well, at that point there was really no space left for anything in your mind. So we agreed to just drop it and let things happen as they would at a later time. My main, immediate worry was that maybe I had blown a good friendship which I really valued. Also, even if she did feel the same way, would we know what to do with it?

Q: When you first realized that you were possibly getting involved with a woman, were you afraid or upset?

A: No. The strange thing is that the next morning, after I left, I felt a fantastic high. I was bouncing down the street and the sun was shining and I felt tremendously good. My mind was on a super high.

When I got home I couldn't do any kind of work. My mind kept operating on this emergency speed, trying to deal with my new feelings for her. So I sat down and wrote a letter to myself. Just wrote it free association—didn't try to work it out in any kind of theory—and as I was writing I was learning from myself what I was feeling. Unexpectedly I wasn't feeling guilty or worried. I felt great.

Q: When did you start sleeping with each other?

A: The next time we were together. Again, we really wanted each other, but to finally make the move, the same move that with a man would have been automatic, was tremendously difficult . . . and exhilarating. Although we did sleep together, it wasn't sexual; just affectionate and very sensual. After that evening we started sleeping together sexually as well.

I guess it was also a surprise to find that you weren't struck down by God in a final shaft of lightning. That once you fight through that initial wall of undefined fears (built to protect those taboos), they wither rapidly, and leave you to operate freely in a new self-defined circle of what's natural. You have a new sense of boldness, of daring, about yourself.

Q: Was it different from what you had thought a relationship with a woman would be like?

A: Generally, no. Most of the things that I had thought intellectually in fact turned out to be true in my experience. One thing, however, was different. Like, I'd really felt that very possibly a relationship with a woman might not be terribly physical. That it would be for the most part warm and affectionate. I think I probably thought this because with men sex is so frequently confused with conquest. Men have applied a symbolic value to sex, where the penis equals dominance and the vagina equals submission. Since sensuality has no specific sex and is rather a general expression of mutual affection, its symbolic value, power-wise, is nil. So sex with a man is usually genitally oriented.

Perhaps I wasn't quite sure what would happen to sexuality once it was removed from its conventional context. But one of the things I discovered was that when you really like somebody, there's a perfectly natural connection between affection and love and sensuality and sexuality. That sexuality is a natural part of sensuality.

Q: How is sex different with a woman?

A: One of the really mind-blowing things about all this has been that it added a whole new dimension to my own sexuality. You can have good sex, technically, with a woman or a man. But at this point in time I think women have a much broader sense of sensuality. Since she and I both brought our experiences as women to sexuality, it was quite something.

Another aspect of sexuality is your feelings. Again, this is of course an area that has been delegated to women; we are supposed to provide the love and affection. It is one of our duties in a male-female relationship. Though it has been very oppressive in the context that we've been allowed it, the *ability* to show affection and love for someone else is, I think, a fine thing—which men should develop more in themselves, as a matter of fact. Love and affection are a necessary aspect of full sexuality. And one of the things I really enjoy with Jennie is this uninhibited ability to show our feelings.

Q: Is the physical aspect of loving women really as satisfying as sex with a man?

A: Yes.

Q: You've been together a while now. What's your relationship like?

A: Once we got over the initial week or so of just getting used to this entirely new thing, it very quickly became natural—natural is really the word I'd use for it. It was like adding another dimension to what we'd already been feeling for each other. It is quite a combination to fall in love with your friend.

We don't have any plans, any desire, to live together, although we do see a great deal of each other. We both like our own apartments, our own space.

I think one of the good things we did in the beginning was to say: Let's just see where it will go. We didn't say that we loved each other, just that we liked each other. We didn't immediately proclaim it a "relationship," as one is accustomed to do with a man—you know, making mental plans for the next ten years. So each new feeling was often surprising, and very intensely experienced.

Q: What would you say is the difference between this relationship and those you have had with men?

A: Well, one of the biggest differences is that for the first time I haven't felt those knots-in-the-stomach undercurrents of trying to figure out what's *really* happening under what you *think* is happening.

I think it all boils down to an absence of role-playing; I haven't felt with Jen that we've fallen into that. Both of us are equally strong persons. I mean, you can ask yourself the question, if there were going to be roles, who'd play what? Well, I certainly won't play "the female," and I won't play "the male," and it's just as absurd to imagine her in either one of them. So in fact what we have is much more like what one gets in a friendship, which is more equalized. It's a more aboveboard feeling.

I don't find the traditional contradictions. If I do something strong and self-assertive, she doesn't find that a conflict with her having a relationship with me. I don't get reminded that I might be making myself "less womanly." And along with that there's less *self*-censorship, too. There's a mutual, unqualified, support for daring to try new things that I have never quite known before.

As a result, my old sense of limits is changing. For example, for the first time in my life I'm beginning to feel that I don't have a weak body, that my body isn't some kind of passive baggage. The other day I gritted my teeth and slid down a fireman's pole at a park playground. It may sound ordinary, but it was something I had never dared before, and I felt a very private victory.

Q: Given the social disapproval and legal restrictions against lesbianism, what are some of the external problems you have faced?

A: One thing is that I hesitate to show my affection for her in public. If you're walking down the street and you want to put your arm around someone or give them a kiss—the kind of thing you do without thinking if it is a man—well, that's hardly considered romantic by most people if it's done with someone of your own sex. I know that if I were to express my feelings in public with Jennie, there would be a lot of social intrusion that I would have to deal with. Somehow, people would assume a license to intrude upon your privacy in public; their hostile comments, hostile attitudes, would ruin the whole experience. So you're sort of caught in a bind. But we have in fact begun to do it more and more, because it bothers me that I can't express my feeling as I see fit, without hostile interference.

Q: What made you fall in love with a woman?

A: Well, that's a hard question. I think maybe it's even a bit misleading the way you phrased it. Because I didn't fall in love with "a woman," I fell in love with Jen—which is not exactly the same thing. A better way to ask the question is: How were you able to *overcome* the fact that it was a woman? In other words, how was I able to overcome my heterosexual training and allow my feelings for her to come out?

Certainly in my case it would never have happened without the existence of the women's movement. My own awareness of "maleness" and "femaleness" had become acute, and I was really probing what it meant. You see, I think in a sense I never wanted to be either male *or* female. Even when I was quite little and in many ways seemed feminine and "passive"—deep down, I never felt at home with the kinds of things women were supposed to be. On the other hand, I didn't particularly want to be a man either, so I didn't develop a male identity. Before I even got involved with the women's movement, I was already wanting something new. But the movement brought it out into the open for me.

Another thing the movement helped me with was shedding the notion that, however independent my life was, I must have a man; that somehow, no matter what I did myself, there was something that needed that magical element of male approval. Without confronting this I could never have allowed myself to fall in love with Jennie. In a way, I am like an addict who has kicked the habit.

But most important of all, I like her. In fact I think she's the healthiest person I have ever been involved with. See, I think we were lucky, because it happened spontaneously and unexpectedly from both sides. We didn't do it because we felt compelled to put our ideological beliefs into reality.

Many feminists are now beginning to at least theoretically consider the fact that there's no reason why one shouldn't love a woman. But I think that a certain kind of experimentation going on now with lesbianism can be really bad. Because even if you do ideologically think that it is perfectly fine—well, that's a *political* position; but being able to love somebody is a very personal and private thing as well, and even if you remove political barriers, well, then you are left with finding an individual who particularly fits *you*.

So I guess I'm saying that I don't think women who are beginning to think about lesbianism should get involved with anyone until they are really attracted to somebody. And that includes refusing to be seduced by lesbians who play the male seduction game and tell you, "you don't love women," and "you are oppressing us" if you don't jump into bed with them. It's terrible to try to seduce someone on ideological grounds.

Q: Do you now look at women in a more sexual way?
A: You mean, do I now eye all women as potential bed partners? No. Nor did I ever see men that way. As a matter of fact, I've never found myself being attracted to a man just because, for example, he had a good physique. I had a sexual relationship with whatever boyfriend I had, but I related to most other men pretty asexually. It's no different with women. My female friends—well, I still see them as friends, because that's what they are. I don't sit around and have secret fantasies of being in bed with them.

But there's a real question here: What is the source, the impetus, for one's sexuality? Is it affection and love, or is it essentially conquest in bed? If it's sex as conquest in bed, then the question you just asked is relevant, for adding the category of women to those you sleep with would mean that every woman—who's attractive enough to be a prize worth conquering, of course—could arouse your sexuality. But if the sexual source lies in affection and love, then the question becomes absurd. For one obviously does not immediately fall in love with every woman one meets simply because one is *able* to sleep with women.

Also, one thing that really turns me off about this whole business of viewing women as potential bedmates is the implied possessiveness of it. It has taken me this long just to figure out how

men are treating women sexually; now when I see some lesbians doing precisely the same kinds of things, I'm supposed to have instant amnesia in the name of sisterhood. I have heard some lesbians say things like, "I see all men as my rivals," or have heard them proudly discuss how they intimidated a heterosexual couple publicly to "teach the woman a political lesson." This brings out in me the same kind of intense rage that I get when, for example, I hear white men discussing how black men are "taking their women" (or vice versa). Who the hell says we belong to anyone?

Q: Do you think that you would have difficulty relating to a man again if this relationship broke up? That is, can you "go back" to men after having had a relationship with a woman?
A: It's an interesting thing that when people ask that question, most often what they're really asking is, are you "lost" to the world of what's "natural"? Sometimes I find myself not wanting to answer the question at all just because they're starting out by assuming that something's wrong with having a relationship with a woman. That's usually what's meant by "go back to men"—like you've been off someplace wild and crazy and, most of all, unsafe, and can you find your way home to papa, or something. So first of all it wouldn't be "going back."

And since I didn't become involved with a woman in order to make a political statement, by the same token I wouldn't make the converse statement. So, sure I could have a relationship with a man if he were the right kind of person and if he had rejected playing "the man" with me —that leaves out a lot of men here, I must add. But if a man had the right combination of qualities, I see no reason why I shouldn't be able to love him as much as I now love her.

At a certain point, I think, you realize that the final qualification is not being male or female, but whether they've joined the middle. That is —whether they have started from the male or the female side—they've gone toward the center where they are working toward combining the healthy aspects of so-called male and female characteristics. That's where I want to go and that's what I'm beginning to realize I respond to in other people.

Q: Now that you've gotten involved with a woman, what is your attitude toward gay and lesbian groups?

A: I have really mixed feelings about them. To some extent, for example, there has been a healthy interplay between the gay movement and the feminist movement. Feminists have had a very good influence on the gay movement because women's liberation challenges the very nature of the sex role system, not just whether one may be allowed to make transfers within it. On the other hand, the gay movement has helped open up the question of women loving other women. Though some of this was beginning to happen by itself, lesbians made a point of pressing the issue and therefore speeded up the process.

But there is a problem to me with focusing on sexual choice, as the gay movement does. Sleeping with another woman is not *necessarily* a healthy thing by itself. It does not mean—or prove, for that matter—that you therefore love women. It doesn't mean that you have avoided bad "male" or "female" behavior. It doesn't guarantee you anything. If you think about it, it can be the same game with new partners: On the one hand, male roles are learned, not genetic; women can ape them too. On the other, the feminine role can be comfortably carried into lesbianism, except now instead of a woman being passive with a man, she's passive with another woman. Which is all very familiar and is all going nowhere.

The confusing of sexual *partners* with sexual *roles* has also led to a really bizarre situation where some lesbians insist that you aren't really a radical feminist if you are not in bed with a woman. Which is wrong politically and outrageous personally.

Q: Did the fact that lesbians pushed the issue in the women's movement have a major effect upon your own decision to have a relationship with a woman?

A: It's hard to know. I think that the lesbian movement has escalated the thinking in the women's movement, and to that extent it probably escalated mine.

But at the same time I know I was slowly getting there myself anyway. I'd been thinking about it for a long time. Because it is a natural question; if you want to remove sexual roles, and if you say that men and women are equal human beings, well, the next question is: Why should you only love men? I remember asking myself that question, and I remember it being discussed in many workshops I was in—what is it that makes us assume that you can only receive and give love to a man?   [1973]

 48

The Turn On

MARGE PIERCY

Fantasies are sex in the head. I have often observed that what turns me on in thinking about sex is not at all what turns me on in real time. My erotic fantasies and my sexual reality are quite distinct. My fantasies run to the exotic: a great many of them occur in other times and even in other worlds.

When I was younger, this distinction was not so sharp to me as it is now. In my blue and spiky youth, I was under the spell of various literary incubi; what attracted me was what had been programmed into me as attractive, for purposes far from my own. I was taught to choose men who tried to reduce my autonomy and who attempted to control me in ways that would have prevented me from doing any useful work of my own. Very negative human qualities had been programmed into me by literary and popular culture as triggers to sexual response: male self-pity, sullenness, posing, narcissism, self-dramatization, being or pretending to be violent. I responded to several sorts of men, none of them suitable—but I am not at all persuaded there existed then the sort of men I find attractive now.

Besides the Heathcliff mood-monsters, I was sometimes attracted to men who told me they were geniuses, generally scientists, since that was one field in which I could in no way contest their assertions. I was moved by these contorted, bright types who seemed to yearn for the land of the emotions as for some lush jungle that they could not penetrate. I would of course be their guide.

I imagined that some store of warmth was hidden in these oysters, a pearl of great price and a love that would be worth the incredible work of trying to open a shell not by force but by persuasion and passion. I believe this tendency could probably be better satisfied by that fad of a few years ago, the Pet Rock.

What turns me on not in the head, not in theory, not on paper, but in daily life? Truthfully, my most passionate moments have never been brief encounters. I have given a lot of rope to my sexual curiosity over the years and it has led me into many adventures and strange encounters; but none of them offered the pure sexual pleasure of being in my own bed with someone I trust and love. In my adventures, my omnivorous curiosity was always far better satisfied than my sexuality.

I do not find orgasm easy with a new sexual partner. A woman never quite knows what she is going to find when someone takes off his clothes. Often the polite social mask falls with the pants and she may find a passionate animal, or a four-year-old who wants to make mud pies and scream at mommy, or a machine freak who wants to program her the way he programs his personal computer.

A woman is never quite sure what she has got herself into, and she is generally committed to it, no matter how rough the ride, at least for the duration of the evening or night. Sex with someone new is exciting in the head, but to me tense with anxiety in reality. Even if the new partner's manner is wholly benign, there is anxiety over whether your own body will please. Unless you are plastic perfect, your body reflects the life you have lived. It has its scars, its stretch marks, its wounds of pleasure or pain, its signs of hard use or soft living. You are offering up your skin, your flesh, and there is always that element of suffering oneself to be judged.

There is also the awkwardness of finding out what each other likes and dislikes once the relationship has been established. Our sexual preference may be quite different with different partners. Some men are never any good at oral sex so it is pointless to try to tell them how you like to be eaten. They approach the vagina with such fear and loathing you might as well give up. Hardly any man nowadays goes about saying how sex disgusts him, so you only find out that cold naysaying hatred after you've already climbed into bed. Some men with the best will in the world are simply incompetent. I have never been able to decide if this is real or feigned incompetence. It reminds me of the old trick of volunteering to do the dishes and being sure to do them so badly that you will not be asked to do them again.

Unless you are overprogrammed in your pleasures, clearly what you enjoy most with one partner may be different from what you enjoy most with another. All those small adjustments and explanations and verbal or nonverbal requests occur over a period of time. In a good sexual relationship you don't ever quite stop making them, but they occur after a while in a context of permission and ease.

Once that ease is created, often I find situations of working together on a common household project or job erotic. I don't necessarily mean something intellectual. That doesn't seem to work nearly as well as something physical. It could be planting beans or building a grape arbor or laying flagstones. The context of working together for a common good that is tangible acts directly on my sexual center.

I do not respond to the skinny icons of our culture. They speak to me of control, anxiety, mistrust of the flesh and of our animal natures. I like a fair amount of flesh and I also appreciate muscles: the kind that ordinary women and men develop when they do physical work. I do not like bodies that appear carved out of plastic resin. I like some belly and some bounce to snuggle against. My partner working outside with me looks good to me, in filthy jeans and an old shirt, as we carry around bags of bone meal and manure. In warmer weather, working in the garden tends to turn us both on, but in truth there is little fine sensual pleasure in attempting to copulate among the rows of cabbages while trying not to crush any, and the bugs do bite bare flesh. It is nicer to take the turned-on feeling inside. I am a great one for enjoying the out-of-doors and then going in for good food, good wine, and a comfortable bed.

Shared laughter is erotic too. Sometimes we are passionate and grunty in our sex, but sometimes we are silly, and silliness can be just as delightful. The permission to play in bed is something that perhaps only people who are fully at ease with each other can signal. It is permission to take on roles, to make noises, to try out spontaneous gestures and notions.

My sexuality is close to my sensuality. I find the common link in our culture between sex and violence peculiar, as if others around me were whipped into a frenzy of desire by the sight of a traffic light or the smell of wet wool. The difference between pleasure and pain is a sharply marked boundary to me. Whatever pleases me tends to express itself in sex eventually.

Sex is one of the few times, at its best, when the conscious mind ceases to be aware of its own machinations. We become our feelings, our sensations, our appetite, without all the quibbling and second-guessing and motive-scouring that normally goes on. While I value, perhaps even overvalue, my own intellect and honed consciousness, I seek those moments of respite from the constant chatter of evaluation. My cats soothe me by their animal presence; my garden soothes me as it requires my hard work and my attention. Sex is the ultimate cave, short of sleep and the sinking of the mind into the body. Sleep and sex are connected as animal functions: when I have trouble with one, I may well have trouble with the other. Insomnia and difficulty in orgasm are both warning signs of something wrong at the core, a problem that has to be dealt with.

When I have good sex with someone, I put up with more and am infinitely more motivated to work out problems. When someone withdraws sexually —a great way to manipulate a partner who likes sex—then already part of the motivation for getting through the muck is diminished. It's all part of the same whole. If you feel closer, the sex tends to be better; if you feel more distant, then the sex tends to be weaker.

I am not someone who is turned on by jealousy. That kind of competition and insecurity makes me ill at ease with my own sexuality. One of my prerequisites for sexual response is that I have a sense that the other person also finds me attractive—though our relationship doesn't have to be sexually exclusive.

That may seem contradictory, but it isn't. I require being able to trust my sexual partner, to feel sure that my partner is willing to offer real intimacy and love. Without that trust, I can never approach full sexual response. Women have such a range of pleasure, anyhow, from little bitty orgasms that are like buzzes and blips to orgasms that pick you up and carry you off and drop you after what feels like miles and years of intensity. I like sex pretty often and have never required that ecstasy be presented to me. I figure it's a mutual responsibility. But there are prerequisites to letting go that have to be there.

To be afraid of a partner, unable to speak my mind or lose my temper or express my will, would dampen my sexuality. Under the gross inequality that has existed between almost all men and women, I think few women can flourish sexually. To be defined as a sexual receptacle for someone else means to be negated as the one who desires.

For some in our culture, sex is possessing. For some, sex is conquering. For some, sex is doing something to someone before they can do it to you. For me, it is primarily knowing, both the other and oneself. In sex I know my body in an immediate way, from deep within it.

In good sex, my partner opens to me his full vulnerability, his capacity for pleasure, tenderness, and passion. We are communicating directly skin on skin. We are communicating through pressure and smell and taste and little sounds, far more than in the occasional words that may be spoken.

If I say that talk is erotic to me, I don't mean spatting and I don't mean those where-were-you-last-night? ordeals. I have had lovers who seemed turned on by fighting, and relationships in which a kind of tearing and gouging and screaming seemed essential, and might end up with fairly heated sex; but those relationships were with basically inarticulate men who needed a fair amount of shouting and banging around to feel in touch. I find I often do want to make love after a fight, but not because I am aroused. It is simply to affirm that the relationship continues.

No, the talking that is most erotic to me is simply conversation at its own pace, a combination of the intense and the casual, the free association of two people who know each other well but who always have something new to report, to question, to discuss. When we are talking that way, I feel caressed.

Since my partner and I both write at home computers and raise much of our food organically, we are always sharing new skills—whether about the construction of a pitched roof or the recovery of some inadvertently erased data. Bringing to each other new glittering bits of knowledge in our hot beaks is surely part of our mating dance. We like to admire each other, as I think most people in egalitarian couples do.

On such occasions, we often feel especially close. I think it is feeling intimate that produces the best sex—not a great surprise, finally. The more trips we take together, whether by car or by computer or by walking in the dunes, the more opportunities we give each other to explore the rich variables of each other's mind and body. The best sex for me arises out of such an intimacy, constantly stimulated and renewed.   [1984]

🌿 49

Bisexuality, Feminism, Men and Me

ROBYN OCHS

Where does feminist consciousness come from? Why do some women begin to question what has been presented to us as given and, as a result of that questioning, come to understand the ways in which women have been systemically limited? Each of us takes a different road to feminism. Many of our journeys begin with a pivotal event or transition that forces us to question our assumed reality.

My own route to feminism was long, convoluted and closely connected with my developing bisexual consciousness. In my early twenties I realized that my emotional and sexual attractions toward women as well as men were not going to go away, and I began to address those feelings. Forced off-balance by the turbulence of these emotions and their implications for my future, I began for the first time to consciously question the assumptions I had made about my life. I began to understand that many of my choices had not been freely made, but rather had been made within the context of a system that Adrienne Rich calls "compulsory heterosexuality," a system that posits heterosexuality as the only way to be.[1] In this essay I describe my own journey: what I learned and what I unlearned, and how these changes in my thinking have fundamentally changed my relationships with men.

I grew up believing that women deserved equal pay for equal work and that we had the right not to be raped or battered and the right to control our own reproduction. These beliefs were firmly held by my mother and grandmothers. In the kitchen of the house I grew up in, a cartoon showing two toddlers looking into their diapers was tacked to the bulletin board next to the telephone. One of the toddlers was saying to the other, "So *that* explains the difference in our salaries." Had I been asked as a young person whether I was a feminist I would have answered in the affirmative. To me, these issues were the essence of feminism.

But despite adopting the feminist label for external causes, I did not escape female socialization. I learned some "basic truths": that as a woman my value was in my body, and that mine was not "good enough": that sooner or later every woman needs a man; and that I would have to behave in certain ways in order to get myself one. These truths, which very much shaped my behavior for many years, I'll describe in greater detail below.

MY BODY AND ME

Like many women, I grew up hating my body. I remember wearing shorts over my bathing suit as a preteen to hide my "ugly" fat thighs. As a teenager, I spent a lot of time worrying whether I was attractive enough. Of course, I was never quite up to standard. I wanted very much to have the kind of exterior that would cause scouting agents from pinup magazines or from modeling agencies to approach me on the street to recruit me. Needless to say, this never happened, reinforcing my belief that physically I was a total failure as a woman. I fantasized about being a dancer but knew I did not have the requisite "dancer's body." I thought my size 7½ feet were enormous. For the record, I have always been more or less average in weight. But average was not good enough. As long as I didn't look like one of those women in *Playboy*, I wasn't pretty enough.

Too big too short too stocky too busty too round too many zits blackheads disgusting pinch an inch fail the pencil test cellulite don't go out without makeup don't let them see what you really *look like they'll run away in terror but if you are really lucky and have a few beers and do it in the dark he might not notice so make sure to turn off the light before . . .*

I never questioned my standards of measurement, never realized that these standards are determined by a male-dominated culture and reinforced by a multibillion-dollar "femininity" industry that sells women cosmetics, diet aids, plastic surgery, fashion magazines, liposuction, creams and girdles. I took my inability to live up to these standards as personal failure and never drew any connections between my experience and that of other women.

MEN AND ME

Men, you can't live without 'em. Sooner or later I would end up with one. My grandfather used to tell me that it was good that I was short, as that way I would have the option of marrying either a tall man or a short one. There aren't enough men to go around and it gets harder and harder to find one as you get older. Men aren't comfortable with women who are more educated/smarter/earn more than they. My fifty-year-old aunt never married. She waited *too long*, and by then it was *too late* because she was *too old, poor dear.* It's just as easy to fall in love with a rich man as a poor man. Men lead.

I always had a boyfriend. From age thirteen until after college, I don't remember going for more than

a month without being in a relationship or at least having a crush. Having a boyfriend was a measure of my worth. I would select the boy and flirt with him until he asked me out. Most times, like the Mounties, I got my man. In dance, this is called backleading, directing the action from the follower's position. It allows the man to look like he is in control.

I learned that there's a man shortage. There are more women than men. And "good men" are extremely rare. Therefore, if you manage to get hold of a good one, you'd better hang on to him. This message got louder as I moved into my twenties. I saw older women in their thirties and beyond searching frantically for a suitable partner with whom to reproduce the human species and make their lives meaningful. I learned that you'd better pay attention to your "biological clock."

THE UNLEARNING

These messages had a powerful grip on me. How did I begin to unlearn them? The women's studies class I took in college helped a bit. However, I continued to consider feminism only in terms of situations outside of myself. I looked at my environment and catalogued the injustices, but did not look inside.

It wasn't until I was considering a relationship with a woman that I began to see the relevance of the feminist theory I had read as a first-year college student to my own life. My perspective changed dramatically. For example, in my first relationship with a woman, it became quickly apparent that in many ways I fit quite neatly into the passive "femme" role of the butch/femme stereotype. I was behaving as I had always behaved in relationships, but for the first time, now that my lover was a woman, my "normal" behavior appeared to me (and probably to her as well) strange and unbalanced. Why were my lover and I behaving so differently? Suddenly our roles appeared constructed rather than natural. I won't pretend that I woke up one day and found myself suddenly freed of my conditioning. Rather, I spent several years unfolding and unraveling the layers of misinformation I had internalized, learning more with each subsequent relationship or incident.

My body image began to change. Through the firsthand experience of my own attractions, I learned that women, and their bodies, are beautiful, though I did not immediately apply this knowledge to my opinion of my own body. There was one woman friend on whom I had a crush for more than two years. I thought she was beautiful, with her solid, powerful angles and healthy fullness. One day, with a sense of shock, I realized that her body was not so very different from mine and that I had been holding myself to a different, unattainable standard than I had been holding her and other women to. It was this experience of seeing my image reflected in another woman that finally allowed me to begin developing a positive relationship with my own body.

I learned from firsthand experience about the privilege differential that results when the gender of your partner changes. Before I had experienced some of society's disapproval and disregard, I had no sense of the privileges I had experienced in heterosexual relationships. In subsequent years, each time I changed partners I was painfully aware of this absurd double standard and began to strategize ways to live in such a way that I could challenge rather than collaborate with these injustices. I have made a personal commitment to be "out" as bisexual at every possible opportunity and to avoid taking privileges with a male lover that I would not have with my female lover. For these reasons, I have chosen not to marry, though I hope someday to establish a "domestic partnership" and have a "commitment ceremony." If I feel someone would be unwilling to hear me talk about a same-sex lover, I disclose nothing about *any* of my relationships, even if my current partner is of the opposite sex. This is not very easy, and occasionally I backslide, but I am rewarded with the knowledge that I am not contributing to the oppression of lesbian, gay, and bisexual people when I am in an opposite-sex relationship.

It was empowering to realize that men as romantic partners were optional, not required. I no longer felt pressured to lower my relationship standards in light of the shortage of good men. Yes, I might get involved with and spend the rest of my life with one, but then again I might choose to spend my life with a woman. Or perhaps simply with myself. This was to be my choice.

I realized how I had been performing my designated gender role. It's amazing how being in a same-sex relationship can make you realize just how much of most heterosexual relationships is scripted from the first date to the bedroom to the dishes. In relationships with women, I learned how to lead and learned that I like to lead sometimes. As sometimes I like to follow. And as sometimes I prefer to negotiate every step with my partner, or to dance alone.

Finally, I made a personal commitment to hold men and women to the same standards in relationships. I realized that in our society women are grateful when a man behaves in a sensitive manner, but expect sensitivity of a woman as a matter of course. I decided that I would not settle for less from men, realizing that it means that I may be categorically eliminating most men as potential partners. So be it.

My experience with being in relationships with women has been in a way like a trip abroad. I learned that many of the things I had accepted as natural truths were socially constructed, and the first time I returned to a heterosexual relationship things felt different. I hadn't yet learned how to construct a relationship on my own terms, but I was aware that things were not quite right. As time passed, my self-awareness and self-confidence increased. I gathered more experience in lesbian relationships and began to apply my knowledge to subsequent heterosexual relationships.

It is not possible to know who or where I would be today had I remained heterosexual in my attractions and in my self-identity. Perhaps other events in my life would have triggered a feminist consciousness. At any rate, it is entirely clear to me that it was loving a woman that made me realize I had fallen outside my "script," which in turn forced me to realize there *was* a script. From there, I moved toward a critical self-awareness and the realization that I could shape and write my own life.

[1992]

NOTES

Thanks to Marti Hohmann, Rebecca Kaplan and Annie Senghas for their feedback and support while I was writing this essay.

1. Rich, Adrienne. "Compulsory Heterosexuality and Lesbian Existence," *Signs: Journal of Women in Culture and Society* 5, no. 4, (1980), pp. 631–60.

PART IV

Institutions That Shape Women's Lives

We have examined the ways that sexist attitudes about women's potential, abilities, and social roles have limited their sense of self, impeded their growth, and damaged their self-confidence. Sexism, however, is more than a set of attitudes; it is firmly entrenched in the structure of society. Part IV examines the position of women in four of the major institutions that shape women's lives: the legal system, the economy, the family, and religion. Together they have reinforced women's subordination in all areas of social life. Although we are accustomed to thinking of relationships such as family and motherhood as emotional and biological, they serve social and political purposes.

Feminist analysis has revealed that institutions tend to allocate power and resources in complex and subtle ways that systematically support patriarchy and other systems of domination. While overt personal prejudice is apparent to most people, institutionalized sexism is so deeply embedded in our social life that it appears to be the natural order. Much of it remained unnoticed until the feminist movement called attention to it, revealing layer upon layer of discriminatory patterns. The deeper we look, the more patterns emerge. For example, women's analysis of the work force first exposed a great deal of outright discrimination. Employers paid women less and excluded them from jobs because they were women. But when the Equal Pay Act of 1963 and Title Seven of the Civil Rights Act of 1964 made such discrimination illegal, women remained in a disadvantaged position in the work force. This was caused not only by discrimination that eluded the law but by occupational segregation, the clustering of women into female-dominated occupations that pay less and offer fewer opportunities for advancement than male-dominated occupations.

Our society has been organized around the notion that the public arenas of work, politics, and education are the province of men, and the private world of home and family is female terrain. While this division of activities and resources is powerful as ideology, it has never been an accurate description of the lives of all women. As Patricia Hill Collins argues, for example, most black women have occupied both public and private worlds, bearing both economic and nurturing responsibility for families.[1] Today a large proportion of women of all races and ethnic groups work outside the home. Despite these facts, the belief that women's natural role is in the family and men's in the public world shapes the primary institutions of social life. The contradiction between the realities of many women's lives and the social institutions structured by the belief in this division of labor is one of the major sources of tension in contemporary American life.

In fact, women have always played crucial economic roles both inside and outside the family. The work that women do in the home is absolutely essential to economic life. Because it is unpaid, however, it is invisible and difficult to measure. Women have also been working outside the home for centuries. Female slaves worked

---

[1] Patricia Hill Collins, *Black Feminist Thought* (New York: Routledge, 1990).

in the fields and young women factory workers were the first employees of the American textile industry. Until the middle of the twentieth century, most white women left their jobs when they married, but African-American women continued to work outside the home while caring for their own homes and children. In the past several decades women of all racial and ethnic groups have entered the work force in increasing numbers. Women constitute 46% of the total work force. Nevertheless, the belief that women's primary role is in the home continues to shape women's workplace experience, restricting opportunities, creating pay inequity, and preserving women's responsibility for childcare and housework even while they hold full-time jobs.

Affirmative action policies have increased the hiring, promotion, job stability, and wages of women. A Department of Labor study estimated that 5 million people of color and 6 million women are in higher occupational classifications today than they would have been without affirmative action policies. Affirmative action has spurred companies and other organizations to create innovative programs to open up new oppotunities for women. For example, an employee development program established by a Pennsylvania chemical company encourages students of color and white female students to pursue careers in chemistry and engineering and extensively recruits promising, qualified female candidates and candidates of color for entry-level positions.[2]

Although sex discrimination is against the law, significant wage gaps based on sex and race persist. Overall, women who work full-time, year-round earn on average 73% percent of what men earn who also work full-time, year-round. White women in 2000 earned 72% of the salary of white men, while black women, Latinas, and Asian-American women were paid 64%, 52%, and 80% respectively.[3] On an annual basis the average woman earns $13,087 less than the average man.[4]

While there has been progress in the labor market position of women, the reduction in the wage gap in the past twenty years is more a result of stagnant earnings for men than significant increases for women. Women continue to encounter sexual harassment, sexual double standards, and what has been described as the glass ceiling, an invisible barrier of discrimination that has prevented women from advancing beyond a certain level.

Recognizing that the clustering of women in low-paid, low-status jobs has been a major source of the wage inequities between women and men, some women have begun to enter occupations that have been historically male-dominated. Another approach to this problem is the demand for comparable worth or pay equity—the

---

[2]"Affirmative Action Helps Boost Women's Pay and Promotes Economic Security for Women and Their Families," National Partnership for Women and Families. http://www.national partnership.org/workand family/workplace/affirmact/aa_newwage.htm. 1/27/02.
[3]"Little Progress in Closing Wage Gap in 2000," National Committee on Pay Equity/U.S. Census Bureau, March 2001, http://www.feminist.com/fairpay/f_wagegap.htm. 1//27/02.
[4]"The Wage Gap Over Time," National Committee on Pay Equity, http://www.feminist.com/fairpay/f-change.htm.

reevaluation of male- and female-dominated jobs on the basis of the required skill, effort, responsibility, and working conditions.

Women's responsibility for child care remains one of the biggest obstacles to economic equality for women. The United States lags behind other countries in providing child care facilities, parental leave, and other features that make the work-place compatible with parenting. It is one of the few industrialized countries without a national maternity leave policy, and one of the few industrialized countries that does not provide universal health care or income support to families with children. Without a fundamental restructuring of the work place to accommodate workers with family responsibilities—both male and female—women will continue to be in a disadvantaged position.

In recent years some employers have provided more "family-friendly" policies, policies that enable women to better balance work and family life. Benefits often include on-site childcare, flexible work schedules, summer programs, and sick-child care, among others. Since over three-quarters of women who have school-age children are in the work force, employers have found that such policies boost recruitment and lower absenteeism. Unfortunately these options are more often available to professionals and managers than to women with low-wage jobs.

The Family and Medical Leave Act of 1993 requires employers to give workers up to 12 weeks of unpaid leave during a 12 month period for birth or adoption; to care for a seriously ill parent, spouse, or child; or to undergo medical treatment for their own serious illness. While helpful to some women workers, the law covers only employers with 50 or more employees. It is estimated that the Act affects 5% of U.S. employers and 62% of all employees. Since the leave is unpaid, it is difficult for women in low-paying jobs to take advantage of the leave.

Women face many barriers in the workplace, among them sexual harassment. For centuries women and girls have endured various forms of harassment, from ogling on the street to demands for sex in return for rewards with threat of reprisal. Such retribution in the workplace can cause job loss, denial of promotion, and an intimidating atmosphere, making working conditions very stressful.

Women, however, have a long history of organizing for better working conditions for themselves and others. Recently associations of working women such as 9to5, organizations for union women such as the Congress of Labor Union Women, and renewed commitments by the AFL/CIO to organize low-wage women workers have resulted in both economic gains for women and solidarity among women workers who often felt isolated.

The legal system and social policies enforce the subordination of women generally, as well as in the workplace. As recently as 1961, the Supreme Court upheld a law exempting women from jury service because "woman is still regarded as the center of home and family life"[5] and therefore not subject to the same public

---

[5] *Hoyt v. Florida,* 1961.

obligations as men. Laws have changed in the last 35 years, and the courts now recognize women's right to equal protection, but the legal system remains male-dominated and biased against women in many ways. At the same time, women have used the judicial system to challenge sexism and to fight for reproductive freedom, child support, domestic safety, and workplace justice, among others.

Social policy, typically drafted and passed into law by white, affluent, male legislators, can particularly burden poor, single women with children who are consigned to poverty by the absence of affordable child care and the low pay of most women's jobs. Prior to 1996 these poor women were assured some cash assistance through Aid to Families with Dependent Children (AFDC). The Personal Responsibility and Work Opportunity Act (1996) eliminated AFDC and replaced it with the Temporary Assistance for Needy Families (TANF), a block grant program which removes any guarantee of assistance. It mandates states to force poor mothers into the low-wage labor market by adding a work requirement and imposing time limits.

Despite claims of the success of welfare-to-work policies by politicians, very serious problems exist. Sufficient funding has not been provided to create jobs, increase child care, or provide job training and health coverage to low-wage workers. Randy Albelda writes, "The welfare-to-work solution is a match made in hell. It joins together poor mothers with few resources whose family responsibilities require employment flexibility with jobs in the low-wage labor market that often are most inflexible, have the least family-necessary benefits and provide levels of pay that often are insufficient to support a single person, let alone a family." Since the jobs most poor mothers get don't provide much dignity or sufficient wages to support a family, the experience is not only demoralizing, but economically crippling. "For many, welfare-to work policies are a cruel hoax that makes legislators feel better about themselves, but leaves poor families in the lurch."[6] Social policy changes that promote education, training and access to jobs that pay a living wage would be true reforms. 9to5 urges changing the purpose of the bill itself—to end child and family poverty.

In exchange for welfare, TANF violates women's rights to vocational freedom and sexual privacy, while it seeks to restore the patriarchal family. "Mothers who are married do not have to work outside the home, for labor market work by only one parent in a two-parent family satisfies TANF's work requirement. . . . Far from 'ending dependency,' the TANF regime actually fosters poor mothers' dependence on individual men."[7] If women's caregiving work was valued and supported, welfare could be rethought of as income owed to women, married or not, whose work is now unpaid.

The position of women in the workforce is inextricably connected with the position of women in the family. The division of power and resources in the patriarchal family has often subordinated the needs of married women to those of their spouses.

---

[6]Randy Albelda, "Fallacies of Welfare-to-Work Policies." *Annals, AAPSS,* 577 (September 2001), pp. 68, 74.

[7]Gwendolyn Mink, "Violating Women: Rights Abuses in the Welfare Police State," *Annals,* op.cit. p. 81.

The sentimental rhetoric that often surrounds the family not only obscures the unequal power relations but also conveys the impression that only the patriarchal family is legitimate. In fact, the family, a group of people who are committed to each other and share resources, can take a variety of forms. The African-American family, often sustained by mothers, aunts, and grandmothers, has proved remarkably durable in the face of almost insurmountable odds.

Feminist theorists have found it useful to view motherhood as an institution as well as a relationship between mother and child. As an institution, motherhood was for a long time assumed to be women's primary function, one that made women unfit for full participation in other realms. The sentimentalization of motherhood obscures the realities of mothers' experience in a number of ways. While most mothers love and enjoy their children, motherhood can be lonely and sometimes painful in a society in which there are few social supports. The image of perfect mother leads people to blame mothers when they don't live up to that idealized image. When motherhood takes place outside the patriarchal family, the mantle of sentimentality disappears. Lesbian mothers have lost custody of their children, and single mothers face social censure. Sentimentalized motherhood also obscures the fact that not all women enjoy motherhood, and that mothers who have no other sources of identity and satisfaction can become disoriented when children grow up. Some essays in this section tell the stories of real women whose lives belie the myths. They demonstrate the need to see motherhood as a more varied experience and to envision social supports that enable women to be mothers while participating fully in other aspects of human life.

Our society glorifies the nuclear family and disparages people, particularly women, who live outside it. Feminists believe that women should be able to choose how and with whom they live. Since one can choose freely only if a variety of lifestyles are considered legitimate, feminists seek to expand women's options, recognizing that different women will choose different ways to live and love.

Feminists insist that the nuclear family is not the only viable form in which to build lasting relationships and raise children. For feminists, a broadened definition of family includes any living arrangement in which people share time and space, contribute to the physical and psychological tasks of making a household function, share common history and ritual, and make a commitment to stay together over time. Members are not necessarily tied by biology or by the sanction of the state or church, or by living in the same house all the time. Feminists work toward building families in which all members both give and receive support and love and have space to grow as autonomous individuals.

By supporting their families and maintaining nurturing homes, single mothers are defying the notion that children do not stand a chance in life because their father isn't present; lesbian parents affirm the validity of their families. Some women have created cooperative living arrangements in which they share household and parenting responsibilities.

The struggle for public recognition of one alternative family form, lesbian and gay marriage, has caused considerable controversy and backlash in recent years. The Defense of Marriage Act, passed by large majorities in Congress and signed into law by President Clinton in 1996, affirms that states are not required to recognize marriages that were performed in other states. For the first time ever in our country's history it creates a federal definition of "marriage" as a legal union between one man and one woman as husband and wife.

Nevertheless feminists still struggle to defend a variety of democratic, cooperative living arrangements in which responsibility and power are shared, and where women can find both freedom and love. Our personal experiences in equitable communities and relationships will help us envision and create similar communities of care in our society at large.

The final institution that this part considers is institutionalized religion, in which women have been the members, men the decision makers. "It has been said that women are the 'backbone' of the church," writes Jacquelyn Grant, who studies black women and the church. "On the surface, this may appear to be a compliment, considering the function of the backbone in the human anatomy. . . . The telling part of the word 'backbone' is 'back'. It has become apparent to me that most of the ministers who use this term are referring to location rather than function. What they really mean is that women are in the 'background' and should be kept there; they are merely support workers."[8]

Patriarchal religion has had a powerful effect on women's lives not only by systematically excluding them from many leadership positions in most organized religions, but by justifying subordination and enveloping it in divine sanction. Religious symbolism can reinforce both sexism and racism, as in the case of Christianity. Jacquelyn Grant writes, "Though we insist that God is a spirit and Jesus died for us all, we persist in deifying the maleness of both God and Jesus, certainly giving men a social, political and theological advantage over women. . . . We have consistently and historically represented God and Jesus as White."[9] Women who have spoken and acted on behalf of women's freedom have often found themselves colliding with church dogma.

Since the 1990s religious fundamentalism has become more influential in the U.S. and world-wide. In all of fundamentalism's forms—whether Christian, Muslim, Hindu, Jewish, or Buddhist—women are confined to a traditional, secondary status in the family and in society. Charlotte Bunch writes, ". . . fundamentalisms insist that women identify with the particular narrow identity of their group and disavow 'the other.' Most demand that women be carriers of the cultural purity of their

---

[8]Jacquelyn Grant, "Black Women and the Church," in *Some of Us Are Brave*, Gloria Hull, Patricia Bell Collins, and Beverly Smith, eds. (New York: Feminist Press, 1982).
[9]Jacquelyn Grant, "Womanist Jesus and the Mutual Struggle for Liberation," in *The Recovery of Black Presence, An Interdisciplinary Exploration*, Randall Bailey and Jacquelyn Grant, eds. (Nashville, TN: Abington Press, 1995), p. 134.

group. When women are identified with culture—as reproducers and bearers of tradition. . . . they are used as the front line against feminism."[10] In their efforts to influence governmental policy, fundamentalists have spearheaded efforts to challenge women's reproductive rights and right to sexual freedom, both in the U.S. and in international forums such as the Women's Conference in Beijing in 1995.

Recently women's struggle for equality in institutional religion has contributed to the decision of some religious groups to ordain women ministers and rabbis. This presence of women clergy may help change many people's vision of God as masculine. Women are doing some of the most challenging and innovative work in theology and ministry by infusing religious traditions with an emphasis on female experience. Other women have taken their quest for spirituality beyond organized religion, and are developing their own forms of feminist spirituality that often have links both to historic female-centered religious practices and to the natural world.

All these institutions are intimately connected to each other. Women's experience in one reinforces their position in another, indicating that change in the position of women in our society needs to take place on many fronts. The selections in this part show that within our social institutions, gender, class, and race work together to shape female experience. While our culture teaches us to believe that hard work and talent will be rewarded, institutions place white men in advantageous social positions. Understanding institutional barriers enables us to see that all people do not have equal opportunity in our society, and that to create it, we must make fundamental changes in our social institutions. Unless we recognize the historic advantages of white men, it is impossible to move toward a more equitable society. Affirmative action programs, which commit organizations to give preference to women and members of other historically disadvantaged groups, recognize that in many ways a "white male affirmative action program" has been in place for centuries.

Finally, the selections in Part IV testify to the durability of patriarchy. While women have made significant advances in the past 35 years, sexism is proving to be a stubborn adversary. As women occupy new territory in our society, new problems emerge or come into view. We are just beginning to understand, for example, the extent to which sexual harassment has crippled women in the workplace, particularly in nontraditional occupations. When barriers to women's equality are toppled, they often reappear in different forms, requiring us to develop new strategies for change.

---

[10]Charlotte Bunch, "Women's Human Rights: The Challenge of Global Feminism and Diversity," in *Feminist Locations: Global and Local, Theory and Practice,* Marianne DeKoven, ed. (New Brunswick, NJ, Rutgers University Press, 2001), pp. 133–134.

Women and Work

The selections in this section consider the ways sexism shapes women's work both in and outside the home, and suggest approaches to change.

While the media gives the impression that women have unlimited opportunities and have made unprecedented career advances, the reality of the workplace is much more discouraging. While women have made significant progress in a few areas, the majority of women face a sex-segregated labor market that devalues the work that most women do. Ellen Bravo and Gloria Santa Anna, Co-Directors of 9to5 National Association of Working Women, detail the problems women face at work, and suggest policy changes needed to bring gender equity to the workplace. Data about the wage gap between men and women and a plan for eliminating sex and race discrimination in wages through a system of pay equity follow. Since most women and people of color are still segregated into a small number of jobs that are underpaid, a system of pay equity would ensure that the criteria employers use to set wages would be sex and race neutral.

Another barrier to equity in the workplace is sexual harassment. Women who are sexually harassed come from all walks of life, reflecting their shared vulnerability to unwanted sexual attention. Julia Whealin provides an overview of recent research on sexual harassment in the United States. She shows the extent of this problem, describing some of the effects of sexual harassment on women.

Since their studies are the bulk of college students' work, we include in this section a guide for women students who have experienced sexual harassment in their college or university. Because sexual harassment is about power and control, many women victims feel unable to confront their harassers. This article provides clear, concise information about strategies for dealing with harassment so that women can reclaim their dignity and stand up for their rights.

The work that women do in the home—housework, child care, and nurturing —is extremely demanding in time, energy, and skill. Women still do most work in the home despite their increasing participation in the labor force. "The Politics of Housework" is a classic piece from the early days of the women's liberation movement that points to the struggle involved in getting men to take responsibility for housework. Because it is associated with women, housework is seen as demeaning and lacking in value. Like many of the writings from this period, this article demonstrates that an activity that has been treated as private is indeed political; that is, it involves the allocation of power and resources.

Women pay a significant economic price for becoming mothers, as Ann Crittendon describes in "The Price of Motherhood." When mothers do the necessary work of raising children and sustaining families, their reward is often professional marginalization, a loss of status, and long-term losses in income and benefits due to lost time in the workplace. While some corporations boast "family-friendly policies," low-wage workers are least likely to get the benefits of those policies, as the article by Betty Holcomb points out.

Collective efforts by women make a significant difference in gaining equity in the workplace. Union membership under a collective bargaining agreement is associated with higher wages and longer job tenure, as well as a smaller pay gap between women and men. The selection about 9to5 describes the history of an association for working women that for over 25 years has organized low-wage women to fight for equity at work. In the process of doing so, it has helped women see that their struggles are not personal, but based on the need to redistribute power in the workplace.

Alice Walker ends the section with a poem that pays tribute to the strength and resourcefulness of her mother and the many black women whose labors of love and creativity made possible a future for their daughters.

🦎 50

An Overview of Women and Work

ELLEN BRAVO and
GLORIA SANTA ANNA

Any commentator reviewing progress in the United States during the twentieth century will list prominently the gains of working women. Swept away were laws and customs that prevailed for the centuries—allowing lower pay for women doing the same work as men, permitting women to be fired for being pregnant, considering women fair game for harassment on the job. From doctor to drill sergeant, carpenter to CEO, women changed the face of the nation's workforce. The notion that women had been absent from certain jobs because they weren't capable was dealt a significant blow.

And yet, women in this country still earn less than men for equivalent jobs. Many women today lose their jobs when they give birth. Sexual harassment remains a persistent problem in the workplace. While women appear in almost every occupational category, they are woefully underrepresented in higher-paying positions.

In fact, the picture for working women is decidedly mixed. Gains have been real and important, but many women have not been significantly affected by them. A close look at three areas—pay, work/family balance, and welfare—helps illustrate the problems and their impact on women and their families. If women as a whole are to benefit, concern for equality must be joined with fundamental change in the way this society does business.

WHO'S WORKING

A quick look at the numbers shows how greatly the workforce has changed. By 1998 women accounted for 46.3% of the total U.S. labor force, compared with 37.7% in 1960. Nearly six out of every ten women—59.8%—age 16 and over were working or looking for work. Women are expected to make up 48% of the workforce by 2005.

While marriage and childbirth had never spelled the end of employment for certain groups of women, especially African Americans and immigrants, the majority of women in the past left the workforce to care for their families. That reality has changed drastically, as a result of shrinking real wages and growing expectations. Debate about whether women should work has become moot. Most women—including most married mothers—are in the labor force. More than 62% of mothers of children under 3 work outside the home, compared to 39.4% in 1978. Employment, however, has brought women neither equality nor an end to poverty.

PAY

Despite dramatic increases in pay for some, earnings for women as a group remain not just lower than men's but often very low indeed:

- Of women working full-time in 2000, 13.3% earned less than $15,000 for the year. For Latinas, the figure is 26.9%; for African-Americans, 17.3%.
- 27% of employed mothers are in a household with income less than $25,000/year.

Why do women make so little money? Because their employers pay them so little. And why is that? Aside from the continuation of blatant discrimination, the reasons include the following factors:

1) Although there have been huge changes in jobs formerly closed to women, most women do the same jobs they've always done, and those jobs pay less than comparable jobs done by men.

- Nearly 60% of women workers are employed in service, sales and clerical jobs.
- Even within certain occupations, women are clustered in the lower-paying jobs. In retail trades, for instance, women in 2000 constituted 78% of employees in gift and novelty shops but only 20% of those employed in higher-paying car dealerships.
- More women are in professional and managerial positions, but they've made little headway in skilled construction trades and other traditionally male, blue-collar occupations or at the top of the corporate ladder. Women account for only 2% of firefighters and electricians, 11.5% of police and 5% of senior managers.
- Women of color are concentrated in the lowest-paying jobs, including domestic workers, nurses' aides and child-care workers.[1]

Many people talk about the need to increase the number of women in science and math. While those efforts are needed, they ignore the underlying question: why does society value accountants more than social workers? Embedded in the market value of jobs is the legacy of past discrimination, based on gender and on race.

2) Women disproportionately are employed in part-time and temporary jobs. No law says these jobs have to pay the same as full-time and permanent positions, or give any, much less equivalent benefits.

Tracy was a temp for more than 6 years because she could not find permanent employment. She had to leave her house—and her school-aged son—at 5 a.m. to ride a bus that took her to a van which transported her (for a fee) to jobs in the outlying areas. Her annual income was less than $13,000 and she had no benefits. Tracy could not afford a car and sometimes was without a home. "Even though I was always working," said Tracy, "I was living in poverty."

When Linda's marriage fell apart, she tried to find full-time employment but had to make do with three part-time jobs. None of her jobs provided health insurance, including one at a nursing home. At age 38, Linda had a serious heart attack. She eventually found a doctor and hospital willing to do the surgery and was able to have hospital bills waived. Still, she owed $20,000 to 16 different health care professionals. After she recovered, Linda found a full-time job and a second, part-time position to pay something every month on those bills. She suffered another heart attack and died on that job the day before her 42nd birthday.

3) Moonlighting—working more than one job—has been one area where women have made great gains in recent years. Between 1978 and 1998, women constituted 72% of the additional 3.4 million people in this category, accounting for nearly half (47.8%) of all multiple jobholders. Three out of ten of these women work two part-time jobs.[2]

Part-time or temporary positions can be beneficial for women, as long as they are voluntary and equitable. Increasingly, these positions are neither. Regular part-time female workers are paid 20% less than regular full-time workers with similar characteristics. In 1997, median weekly earnings of temp workers were $329 a week, as compared to $510 a week for workers in traditional jobs.[3] Being paid less than full-time or permanent workers often means poverty wages. According to a report by the Economic Policy Institute 28.1% of women employed by temporary help agencies earn less than $5.95 an hour. So do 36.7% of female part-timers. Fewer than one of ten women temps and two in ten part-timers receive health insurance from their employers.[4]

4) Women are still largely responsible for family. The penalty for that is significant—and most women never make it up. One study of professional women who took an average of 8.8 months leave showed them earning 17% less than women who hadn't taken leave.[5] For lower-wage women, taking a leave may also mean losing a job and having to start over—often having to go on welfare. In a 1980 speech, Clarence Thomas spoke with disdain of his sister who had gone on welfare. He neglected to mention that she'd done so in order to care for an aunt who had a stroke.

5) The globalization of the economy has affected women's pay in several ways. Large numbers of women from Asia, Central America and elsewhere find themselves in the United States, their native economies turned upside-down by transnational corporations. Here they fill jobs U.S.-born workers try to avoid, sewing garments and assembling products in old-fashioned sweatshops, picking crops, not uncommonly with their children by their side. The most basic employment protections often elude them. Globalization has costs for U.S. workers as well, as the same transnationals move jobs overseas in the quest for ever cheaper labor. Decent-paying manufacturing jobs disappear, replaced by lower-paying industries or low-wage service jobs.

6) Women are disproportionately represented among minimum-wage earners, accounting for more than 3/5 of all those in this category. Of these women in 2000, 15% were married, 10% were women maintaining families.

7) Unionized women earn 31% more than non-union women. Despite talk of "supply and de-mand," wage levels depend above all on bargaining power. Being able to bargain collectively for pay and benefits helps diminish the undervaluation of women's work and to create more opportunities for women to move into higher-paying jobs. A contract also ensures greater protection against arbitrary firing and a greater likelihood of paid maternity leave —with the longer job tenure ensuring higher pay. However, only 11.4% of all women are unionized. Although women have increased their percentage of all union members, up to 40% in 1998 from 35% a decade earlier, that gain also reflects the loss of union jobs for men—only 16.2% are in unions, down from 20.4% in 1988.

Clearly, the solution to women's low pay must be much more far-reaching than elevating greater numbers of women into jobs traditionally performed by men. To end poverty among women and their families will require fundamental restructuring of the economy.

WORK/FAMILY ISSUES

Today 55% of working women provide half or more of their families' income. Only ⅕ of families with children fit the stereotype of Dad as breadwinner, Mom full-time at home. Yet the workplace has not kept pace with these changes in the workforce. Passage of the Family and Medical Leave Act in 1993 was an important step forward. This law allows women and men to take up to 12 weeks unpaid leave to care for a new child, a seriously ill child, spouse or parent, or for a personal illness. But the impact of the bill remains unacceptably narrow. Consider these findings from an updated study originally done for the bipartisan Commission on Leave:[6]

• Only 62% of U.S. workers both work for covered employers (those with 50 or more employees) and meet the eligibility requirements (at least 12 months on the job, working for at least 1,250 hours).

• Only 11% of private sector work sites are covered.

• Two-fifths of non-covered firms with 25-49 employees do not provide leave for all FMLA reasons.

• 62% of employees at covered establishments do not know if the FMLA applies to them. 16% of those employers do not know if they are covered or mistakenly report that they are not when, in fact, they are.

• Women, younger workers, workers with low family incomes, and those not protected by collective bargaining are most likely to be ineligible or unable to afford leave. Of all ethnic groups, Latino workers are least likely to be protected.

• Of those who needed leave but didn't take it, 78% said they couldn't afford to lose their wages. Nearly one out of ten leave-takers used public assistance to deal with lost income during leave.

Not all workers in the U.S. have access to paid sick leave or even vacation. According to a study reported in *Pediatrics* magazine, 60% of the working poor do not have sick leave they can use to care for sick family members.[7] Nearly three out of four of the working poor did not consistently have paid sick leave between 1994 and 1998.[8] Adding to the problem has been the view in U.S. culture that care of family members is a private problem to be solved by individual employees.

WELFARE

In 1996 we saw the passage of national welfare reform legislation—the stunning reversal of U.S. policy that for decades had guaranteed assistance to poor women and children. Unfortunately, the new policy is based on faulty assumptions and an unrealistic view of where women will work.

Many architects of welfare reform start with the premise that the majority of women are on welfare because they won't work. Their strategy is to force them to work—any job will do. They design extensive punishments for those who don't comply. Since women can't work without some assistance, they provide some help with insurance and child care. The measure of success is reduction in the welfare rolls.

In fact, 70% of women on welfare during a two-year period were working or looking for work.[9] They're cyclers (on and off welfare) or combiners (combine work and welfare). According to a study of six midwest states by Northern Illinois University, only 6.3% of Aid to Families with Dependent Children (AFDC) recipients never worked; only 3.4% of adults were under 18.[10]

The most serious problem with the program implemented in 1996 is that it's missing the key component: jobs. There aren't enough jobs, the ones that are available don't pay enough, and there's a mismatch between the job seekers and where good jobs are located and the skills they require.

We need to understand that most women are on welfare because of problems with work or with some other system in their lives, such as marriage or education. The strategy must be to find solutions for those problems—job training, creation of living wage jobs with affordable leave, adequate quality child care, health insurance, along with efforts to eliminate domestic violence, reach equity and quality in all schools, and so forth. Since the problems affect more people than those on welfare, the solutions need to be universal. The measure of success must be reduction in poverty, not in caseloads, and rise in self-sufficiency for families.

CONCLUSION

Often policy makers and advocates for women's rights speak of "women" as if one size fits all. But women exist in splendid diversity. Only a thorough understanding of specific conditions of various groups, an understanding that looks through the lens of class, race and ethnicity, and sexual orientation, can lead us to the range of solutions that women need. Progress for women cannot be measured only by what happens to women in professional and managerial jobs. In order for women as a whole to benefit, the fight for gender equality must go hand in hand with the struggle against all forms of oppression.   [2002]

ENDNOTES

1. See Karen Rosenblum, "The Wage Gap: Myths and Facts," for occupational concentrations by race, ethnicity and gender. In Kesselman et al. *Women: Images and Realities, a Multicultural Anthology.* (California: Mayfield Publishing Company, 1999).
2. Cynthia Costello, and Anne J. Stone, eds., *The American Woman 2001–2002.* (New York: Norton, 2001).

Gender Segregation and Pay Differentials in Occupations

DATA FROM BUREAU OF LABOR STATISTICS, 2001

occupation	median weekly wage	% male	% female
automobile mechanic	$541	99%	1%
electrician	$714	98%	2%
truck driver	$593	95%	5%
industrial engineer	$1053	82%	18%
architect	$981	76%	24%
therapist	$788	29%	71%
elementary school teacher	$740	19%	81%
registered nurse	$829	10%	90%
dental assistant	$435	3%	97%
prekindergarten and kindergarten teacher	$480	2%	98%
secretary	$475	2%	98%
private child care worker	$246	2%	98%

3. National Alliance For Fair Employment, *Contingent Workers Fight for Fairness.* (Boston: National Alliance for Fair Employment, 2000).

4. Anne Kalleberg, et al., *Nonstandard Work, Substandard Jobs.* (Washington, D.C.: Economic Policy Institute, 1997.)

5. This 1994 study by business professors Joy Schneer and Frieda Reiton compared 128 women MBAs who had never taken a break with 63 who had taken some leave and gone back full time by 1987.

6. *Balancing the Needs of Families and Employers: Family and Medical Leave Surveys 2000 Update,* conducted by Westat for the U.S. Department of Labor. (Washington, D.C.: U.S. Department of Labor, 2000).

7. Jody Heymann, "Parental Availability for the Care of Sick Children," *Pediatrics* magazine, 98, No. 2 (August 1996).

8. Jody Heymann, et al., *Work-Family Issues and Low-Income Families.* (New York: Ford Foundation, 2002).

9. Roberta Spalter-Roth, et al., *Welfare That Works: The Working Lives of AFDC Recipients.* (Washington, D.C.: Institute for Women's Policy Research, 1995.)

10. Paul Kleppner and Nikolas Theodore, *Work After Welfare: Is the Midwest's Booming Economy Creating Enough Jobs?* (Chicago: Northern Illinois University: 1997.)

 51

Questions and Answers on Pay Equity

NATIONAL COMMITTEE FOR PAY EQUITY

WHAT IS PAY EQUITY?

Pay Equity is a means of eliminating sex and race discrimination in the wage-setting system. Many women and people of color are still segregated into a small number of jobs such as clerical, service workers, nurses and teachers. These jobs have historically been undervalued and continue to be underpaid to a large extent because of the gender and race of the people who hold them. Pay equity means that the criteria employers use to set wages must be sex- and race-neutral.

WHAT IS THE LEGAL STATUS OF PAY EQUITY?

Two laws protect workers against wage discrimination. The Equal Pay Act of 1963 prohibits unequal pay for equal or "substantially equal" work performed by men and women. Title VII of the Civil Rights Act of 1964 prohibits wage discrimination on the basis of race, color, sex, religion or national origin. In 1981, the Supreme Court made it clear that Title VII is broader than the Equal Pay Act, and prohibits wage discrimination even when the jobs are not identical. However, wage discrimination laws are poorly enforced and cases are extremely difficult to prove and win. Stronger legislation is needed to ease the burden of filing claims and clarify the right to pay equity.

HOW LARGE IS THE WAGE GAP?

2000 Median Annual Earnings of Year-Round, Full-Time Workers

All Men $37,339(100%)		All Women $27,355(73%)	
Men		Women	
White	$38,869	White	$28,080
Black	$30,409	Black	$25,117
Asian & Pacific Islander	$40,946*	Asian & Pacific Islander	$31,156*
Hispanic	$24,638	Hispanic	$20,527

*Due to the small size of the survey sample, these data may not be representative.
Source: U.S. Census Bureau, Current Population Reports, Series P-60

WHY IS THERE A WAGE GAP?

The wage gap exists, in part, because many women and people of color are still segregated into a few low-paying occupations. More than half of all women workers hold sales, clerical and service jobs. Studies show that the more an occupation is dominated by women or people of color, the less it pays. Part of the wage gap results from differences in education, experience or time in the workforce. But a significant portion cannot be explained by any of those factors; it is attributable to discrimination. In other words, certain jobs pay less because they are held by women and people of color.

HASN'T THE WAGE GAP CLOSED CONSIDERABLY IN RECENT YEARS?

The wage gap has narrowed by about ten percentage points during the last seventeen years, ranging from 62 percent in 1982 to 73 percent in 2000. Since 1973, however, approximately 60 percent of the change in the wage gap is due to the fall in men's real earnings. About 40 percent of the change in the wage gap is due to the increase in women's wages. The wage gap has fluctuated often, ranging from a low of 57 percent in the early 1970s, and peaking at 74 percent in 1997.

IS IT POSSIBLE TO COMPARE DIFFERENT JOBS?

Yes, employers have used job evaluations for nearly a century to set pay and rank for different occupations within a company or organization. Today, two out of three workers are employed by firms that use some form of job evaluation. The federal government, the nation's largest employer, has a 70-year old job evaluation system that covers nearly two million employees.

WHO REALLY NEEDS PAY EQUITY?

Women, people of color, and white men who work in jobs that have been undervalued due to race or sex bias need pay equity. Many of these workers are the sole support for their families. In addition, it is estimated that 70 percent of women with children under 18 work outside the home. (Up from 44.9 percent twenty years ago.) Discriminatory pay has consequences as people age and across generations. Everyone in society is harmed by wage discrimination. Therefore, everyone needs pay equity.

IS PAY EQUITY AN EFFECTIVE ANTI-POVERTY STRATEGY?

Yes, pay equity helps workers become self-sufficient and reduces their reliance on government assistance programs. A recent study found that nearly 40 percent of poor working women could leave welfare programs if they were to receive pay equity wage increases. Pay equity can bring great savings to tax payers at a minimal cost to business. Adjustments would cost no more than 3.7 percent of hourly wage expenses.

WILL WHITE MEN'S WAGES BE REDUCED IF PAY EQUITY IS IMPLEMENTED?

No, Federal law prohibits reducing pay for any employee to remedy discrimination. Furthermore, male workers in female-dominated jobs benefit when sex discrimination is eliminated, as do white workers in minority-dominated jobs. Pay equity means equal treatment for all workers.

WILL ACHIEVING PAY EQUITY REQUIRE A NATIONAL WAGE-SETTING SYSTEM?

No, pay equity does not mandate across-the-board salaries for any occupation, nor does it tamper with supply and demand. It merely means that wages must be based on job requirements like skill, effort, responsibility and working conditions without consideration of race, sex, or ethnicity.

DOESN'T PAY EQUITY COST EMPLOYERS TOO MUCH?

In Minnesota, where pay equity legislation meant raises for 30,000 state employees, the cost was only 3.7 percent of the state's payroll budget over a four-year period—less than one percent of the budget each year. In Washington State, pay equity was achieved at a cost of 2.6 percent of the state's personnel costs and was implemented over an eight-year period. Voluntary implementation of pay equity is cost effective, while court-ordered pay equity adjustments can lead to greater costs. Discrimination is costly and illegal.

ARE WAGE INEQUALITIES THE RESULT OF WOMEN'S CHOICES?

Again, part of the wage gap is attributed to differences in education, experiences and time in the workforce. However, the overwhelming evidence that wage discrimination persists in America can be found in numerous court cases and legal settle- ments, Department of Labor investigations, surveys of men and women on the job, and salary surveys that control for age, experience and time in the work-force. While women sometimes take time out of the workforce to raise children, it should be noted that when couples are deciding who should stay home with children, the fact that the wife is earning a lower salary impacts that decision. In addition, some of the other explainable factors can sometimes be attributed to discrimination. For example, if women and men have different jobs in a company, women may not be choosing the lower paying jobs. They may have trouble advancing in a company due to bias about women's abilities or levels of commitment.

WILL IMPLEMENTING PAY EQUITY DISRUPT THE ECONOMY?

No. The Equal Pay Act, minimum wage, and child labor laws all provoked the same concerns and all were implemented without major disruption. What disrupts the economy and penalizes families is the systematic underpayment of some people because of their sex or race. When wages for women and people of color are raised, their purchasing power will increase, strengthening the economy. One survey found that a growing number of businesses support the elimination of wage discrimination between different jobs as "good business" and that pay equity is consistent with remaining competitive.

WHAT IS THE STATUS OF EFFORTS TO ACHIEVE PAY EQUITY?

Pay equity is a growing national movement building on the progress made in the 1980s, when twenty states made some adjustments of payrolls to correct for sex or race bias. (Seven of these states successfully completed full implementation of a pay equity plan. Twenty-four states including Washington, D.C. conducted studies to determine if sex was a wage determinant. Four states examined their compensation systems to correct race bias, as well.)

In the last 2–3 years, bills have been introduced in over 25 legislatures. On the federal level, the Fair Pay Act has been introduced in the U.S. House of Representatives by Delegate Eleanor Holmes-Norton,

Office Double Standards

A businessman is aggressive, a businesswoman is pushy.
He's careful about details, she's picky.
He follows through, she doesn't know when to quit.
He's firm, she's stubborn.
He makes judgments, she reveals her prejudices.
He's a man of the world, she's "been around."
He exercises authority, she's bossy.
He's discreet, she's secretive.
He says what he thinks, she's opinionated.

(original sources, unfortunately, unknown)

and in the U.S. Senate by Senator Tom Harkin. The Fair Pay Act would expand the Equal Pay Act's protections against wage discrimination to workers in equivalent jobs with similar skills and responsibilities, even if the jobs are not identical. In addition, the Paycheck Fairness Act has been introduced in the U.S. Senate by Senator Tom Daschle and in the U.S. House by Representative Rosa DeLauro. The Paycheck Fairness Act would amend the Equal Pay Act and the Civil Rights Act of 1964 to provide more effective remedies to workers who are not being paid equal wages for doing equal work.   [2002]

 52

The Politics of Housework

PAT MAINARDI OF REDSTOCKINGS

Though women do not complain of the power of husbands, each complains of her own husband, or of the husbands of her friends. It is the same in all other cases of servitude; at least in the commencement of the emancipatory movement. The serfs did not at first complain of the power of the lords, but only of their tyranny.

—John Stuart Mill
On the Subjection of Women

Liberated women—very different from Women's Liberation! The first signals all kinds of goodies, to warm the hearts (not to mention other parts) of the most radical men. The other signals—HOUSEWORK. The first brings sex without marriage, sex before marriage, cozy housekeeping arrangements ("I'm living with this chick") and the self-content of knowing that you're not the kind of man who wants a doormat instead of a woman. That will come later. After all, who wants that old commodity anymore, the Standard American Housewife, all husband, home and kids? The New Commodity, the Liberated Woman, has sex a lot and has a Career, preferably something that can be fitted in with the household chores—like dancing, pottery, or painting.

On the other hand is Women's Liberation—and housework. What? You say this is all trivial? Wonderful! That's what I thought. It seemed perfectly reasonable. We both had careers, both had to work a couple of days a week to earn enough to live on, so why shouldn't we share the housework? So I suggested it to my mate and he agreed—most men are too hip to turn you down flat. You're right, he said. It's only fair.

Then an interesting thing happened. I can only explain it by stating that we women have been brainwashed more than even we can imagine. Probably too many years of seeing television women in ecstasy over their shiny waxed floors or breaking down over their dirty shirt collars. Men have no such conditioning. They recognize the essential fact of housework right from the very beginning. Which is that it stinks.

Here's my list of dirty chores: buying groceries, carting them home and putting them away; cooking meals and washing dishes and pots; doing the laundry, digging out the place when things get out of control; washing floors. The list could go on but the sheer necessities are bad enough. All of us have to do these things, or get someone else to do them for us. The longer my husband contemplated these chores, the more repulsed he became, and so proceeded the change from the normally sweet, considerate Dr. Jekyll into the crafty Mr. Hyde who would stop at nothing to avoid the horrors of—housework. As he felt himself backed into a corner laden with dirty dishes, brooms, mops and reeking garbage, his front teeth grew longer and pointier, his fingernails haggled and his eyes grew wild. Housework trivial? Not on your life! Just try to share the burden.

So ensued a dialogue that's been going on for several years. Here are some of the high points:

• "I don't mind sharing the housework, but I don't do it very well. We should each do the things we're best at." MEANING: Unfortunately I'm no good at things like washing dishes or cooking. What I do best is a little light carpentry, changing light bulbs, moving furniture (how often do *you* move furniture?). ALSO MEANING: Historically the lower classes (black men and us) have had hundreds of years experience doing menial jobs. It would be a waste of manpower to train someone else to do them now. ALSO MEANING: I don't like the dull, stupid, boring jobs, so you should do them.

• "I don't mind sharing the work, but you'll have to show me how to do it." MEANING: I ask a lot of questions and you'll have to show me everything every time I do it because I don't remember so good. Also don't try to sit down and read while I'M doing my jobs because I'm going to annoy hell out of you until it's easier to do them yourself.

• "We used to be so happy!" (Said whenever it was his turn to do something.) MEANING: I used to be so happy. MEANING: Life without housework is bliss. No quarrel here. Perfect Agreement.

• "We have different standards, and why should I have to work to your standards? That's unfair." MEANING: If I begin to get bugged by the dirt and crap I will say, "This place sure is a sty" or "How can anyone live like this?" and wait for your reaction. I know that all women have a sore called "Guilt over a messy house" or "Household work is ultimately my responsibility." I know that men have caused that sore—if anyone visits and the place *is* a sty, they're not going to leave and say, "He sure is a lousy housekeeper." You'll take the rap in any case. I can outwait you. ALSO MEANING: I can provoke innumerable scenes over the housework issue. Eventually doing all the housework yourself will be less painful to you than trying to get me to do half. Or I'll suggest we get a maid. She will do my share of the work. You will do yours. It's women's work.

• "I've got nothing against sharing the housework, but you can't make me do it on your schedule." MEANING: Passive resistance. I'll do it when I damned well please, if at all. If my job is doing dishes, it's easier to do them once a week. If taking out laundry, once a month. If washing the floors, once a year. If you don't like it, do it yourself oftener, and then I won't do it at all.

• "I hate it more than you. You don't mind it so much." MEANING: Housework is garbage work. It's the worst crap I've ever done. It's degrading and humiliating for someone of *my* intelligence to do it. But for someone of *your* intelligence. . . .

• "Housework is too trivial to even talk about." MEANING: It's even more trivial to do. Housework is beneath my status. My purpose in life is to deal with matters of significance. Yours is to deal with matters of insignificance. You should do the housework.

• "This problem of housework is not a man-woman problem. In any relationship between two people one is going to have a stronger personality and dominate." MEANING: That stronger personality had better be *me*.

• "In animal societies, wolves, for example, the top animal is usually a male even where he is not chosen for brute strength but on the basis of cunning and intelligence. Isn't that interesting? MEANING: I have historical, psychological, anthropological and biological justification for keeping you down. How can you ask the top wolf to be equal?

• "Women's liberation isn't really a political movement." MEANING: The revolution is coming too close to home. ALSO MEANING: I am only interested in how I am oppressed, not how I oppress others. Therefore the war, the draft and the university are political. Women's liberation is not.

• "Man's accomplishments have always depended on getting help from other people, mostly women. What great man would have accomplished what he did if he had to do his own housework?" MEANING: Oppression is built into the system and I, as the white American male, receive the benefits of this system. I don't want to give them up.

Participatory democracy begins at home. If you are planning to implement your politics, there are certain things to remember.

1. He *is* feeling it more than you. He's losing some leisure and you're gaining it. The measure of your oppression is his resistance.

2. A great many American men are not accustomed to doing monotonous, repetitive work which never issues in any lasting, let alone important, achievement. This is why they would rather repair a cabinet than wash dishes. If human endeavors are like a pyramid with man's highest achievements at the top, then keeping oneself alive is at the bottom. Men have always had servants (us) to take care of this bottom stratum of life while they have confined their efforts to the rarefied upper regions. It is thus ironic when they ask of women—Where are your great painters, statesmen, etc.? Mme. Matisse ran a military shop so he could paint. Mrs. Martin Luther King kept his house and raised his babies.

3. It is a traumatizing experience for someone who has always thought of himself as being against any oppression or exploitation of one human being by another to realize that in his daily life he has been accepting and implementing (and benefiting from) this exploitation; that his rationalization is little different from that of the racist who says, "Black people don't feel pain" (women don't mind doing the shitwork); and that the oldest form of oppression in history has been the oppression of 50 percent of the population by the other 50 percent.

4. Arm yourself with some knowledge of the psychology of oppressed peoples everywhere, and a few facts about the animal kingdom. I admit playing top wolf or who runs the gorillas is silly but as a last resort men bring it up all the time. Talk about bees. If you feel really hostile bring up the sex life of spiders. They have sex. She bites off his head.

The psychology of oppressed peoples is not silly. Jews, immigrants, black men and all women have employed the same psychological mechanisms to survive: admiring the oppressor, glorifying the oppressor, wanting to be like the oppressor, wanting the oppressor to like them, mostly because the oppressor held all the power.

5. In a sense, all men everywhere are slightly schizoid—divorced from the reality of maintaining life. This makes it easier for them to play games with it. It is almost a cliché that women feel greater grief at sending a son off to a war or losing him to that war because they bore him, suckled him, and raised him. The men who foment those wars did none of those things and have a more superficial estimate of the worth of human life. One hour a day is a low estimate of the amount of time one has to spend "keeping" oneself. By foisting this off on others, man has seven hours a week—one working day more to play with his mind and not his human needs. Over the course of generations it is easy to see whence evolved the horrifying abstractions of modern life.

6. With the death of each form of oppression, life changes and new forms evolve. English aristocrats at the turn of the century were horrified at the idea of enfranchising working men—were sure that it signaled the death of civilization and a return to barbarism. Some working men were even deceived by this line. Similarly with the minimum wage, abolition of slavery, and female suffrage. Life changes but it goes on. Don't fall for any line about the death of everything if men take a turn at the dishes. They will imply that

you are holding back the revolution (their revolution). But you are advancing it (your revolution).

7. Keep checking up. Periodically consider who's actually *doing* the jobs. These things have a way of backsliding so that a year later once again the woman is doing everything. After a year make a list of jobs the man has rarely if ever done. You will find cleaning pots, toilets, refrigerators and ovens high on the list. Use time sheets if necessary. He will accuse you of being petty. He is above that sort of thing (housework). Bear in mind what the worst jobs are, namely the ones that have to be done every day or several times a day. Also the ones that are dirty—it's more pleasant to pick up books, newspapers, etc., than to wash dishes. Alternate the bad jobs. It's the daily grind that gets you down. Also make sure that you don't have the responsibility for the housework with occasional help from him. "I'll cook dinner for you tonight" implies it's really your job and isn't he a nice guy to do some of it for you.

8. Most men had a rich and rewarding bachelor life during which they did not starve or become encrusted with crud or buried under the litter. There is a taboo that says women mustn't strain themselves in the presence of men—we haul around 50 pounds of groceries if we have to but aren't allowed to open a jar if there is someone around to do it for us. The reverse side of the coin is that men aren't supposed to be able to take care of themselves without a woman. Both are excuses for making women do the housework.

9. Beware of the double whammy. He won't do the little things he always did because you're now a "Liberated Woman," right? Of course he won't do anything else either. . . .

I was just finishing this when my husband came in and asked what I was doing. Writing a paper on housework. Housework? he said. *Housework?* Oh my god how trivial can you get? A paper on housework.   [1970]

 53

The Price of Motherhood: Why the Most Important Job in the World Is Still the Least Valued

ANN CRITTENDEN

In the United States, motherhood is as American as apple pie. No institution is more sacrosanct; no figure is praised more fulsomely . . .

When I was on a radio talk show in 1998, several listeners called in to say that child-rearing is the most important job in the world. A few weeks later, at a party, Lawrence H. Summers, a distinguished economist who subsequently became the secretary of the treasury, used exactly the same phrase. "Raising children," Summers told me in all seriousness, "is the most important job in the world." As Summers well knows, in the modern economy, two-thirds of all wealth is created by human skills, creativity, and enterprise—what is known as "human capital." And that means parents who are conscientiously and effectively rearing children are literally, in the words of economist Shirley Burggraf, "the major wealth producers in our economy." [1]

But this very material contribution is still considered immaterial. All of the lip service to motherhood still floats in the air, as insubstantial as clouds of angel dust. On the ground, where mothers live, the lack of respect and tangible recognition is still part of every mother's experience. Most people, like infants in a crib, take female caregiving utterly for granted.

The job of making a home for a child and developing his or her capabilities is often equated with "doing nothing." Thus the disdainful question frequently asked about mothers at home: "What do they *do* all day?" I'll never forget a dinner at the end of a day in which I had gotten my son dressed and fed and off to nursery school, dealt with a plumber about a leaky shower, paid the bills, finished an op-ed piece, picked up and escorted my son to a reading group at the library, run several miscellaneous errands, and put in an hour on a future book project. Over drinks that evening, a childless female friend commented that "of all the couples we know, you're the only wife who doesn't work." . . .

In my childless youth I shared these attitudes. In the early 1970s I wrote an article for the very first issue of *Ms.* magazine on the economic value of a housewife. I added up all the domestic chores, attached dollar values to each, and concluded that the job was seriously underpaid and ought to be included in the Gross National Product. I thought I was being sympathetic, but I realize now that my deeper attitude was one of compassionate contempt, or perhaps contemptuous compassion. Deep down, I had no doubt that I was superior, in my midtown office overlooking Madison Avenue, to those unpaid housewives pushing brooms. "Why aren't they making something of themselves?" I wondered. "What's wrong with them? They're letting our side down."

I imagined that domestic drudgery was going to be swept into the dustbin of history as men and women linked arms and marched off to run the world in a new egalitarian alliance. It never occurred to me that women might be at home because there were children there; that housewives might become extinct, but mothers and fathers never would. . . .

The devaluation of mothers' work permeates virtually every major institution. Not only is caregiving not rewarded, it is penalized. These stories illustrate the point:

• Joanna Upton, a single mother working as a store manager in Massachusetts, sued the company for wrongful dismissal after it fired her for refusing to work overtime—until nine or ten at night and all day Saturday. Upton had been hired to work 8:15 A.M. until 5:30 P.M.; she could not adequately care for or barely even see her son if she had to work overtime. Yet she lost her suit. The Massachusetts Supreme Judicial Court ruled that under state contract law, an at-will employee may be fired "for any reason or for no reason at all" unless the firing violates a "clearly established" public policy. Massachusetts had no public policy dealing with a parent's responsibility to care for his or her child.[2]

• A woman in Texas gave up a fifteen-year career in banking to raise two children. Her husband worked extremely long hours and spent much of his time on the road. She realized that only if she left her own demanding job would the children have the parental time and attention they needed. For almost two decades she worked part-time as a consultant from her home, and for several years she had little or no income. Recently the Social Security Administration sent her an estimate of her retirement income—a statement that was full of zeroes for the years spent caregiving. Social Security confirmed that her decision to be the responsible, primary parent had reduced the government pension by hundreds of dollars a month in retirement income.

• A mother in Maryland had a son who had been a problem child ever since kindergarten. At junior high, the boy was suspended several times; he was finally caught with a gun in his backpack and expelled. The boy's father sued for custody, and the mother countered with a request for more child support, to help pay the $10,000 tuition for a special private school. She also quit her full-time job to have more time for her family. At his new school, the boy showed dramatic improvement both in his academic work and in his behavior. When the case came to court, the father was denied custody, but the judge refused to require him to pay half the costs of the boy's rehabilitation, including therapy and tutoring, despite evidence that the father could afford to do so. A mother who did not work full-time was, in the judge's view, a luxury that "our world does not permit." So the mother was in effect penalized for having tried to be a more attentive mother, and the boy was forced to leave the only school in which he had enjoyed any success. . . .[3]

As these examples reveal the United States is a society at war with itself. The policies of American business, government, and the law do not reflect Americans' stated values. Across the board, individuals who assume the role of nurturer are punished and discouraged from performing the very tasks that everyone agrees are essential. We talk endlessly about the importance of family, yet the work it takes to make a family is utterly disregarded. This contradiction can be found in every corner of our society.

First, inflexible workplaces guarantee that many women will have to cut back on, if not quit, their employment once they have children. The result is a loss of income that produces a bigger wage gap between mothers and childless women than the wage gap between young men and women. This forgone income, the equivalent of a huge "mommy tax," is typically more than $1 million for a college-educated American woman.

Second, marriage is still not an equal financial partnership. Mothers in forty-seven of the fifty states—California, Louisiana, and New Mexico are the exceptions—do not have an unequivocal legal right to half of the family's assets. Nor does a mother's unpaid work entitle her to any ownership of the primary breadwinner's income—either during marriage or after a divorce. Family income belongs solely to "he who earns it," in the phrase coined by legal scholar Joan Williams. A married mother is a "dependent," and a divorced mother is "given" what a judge decides she and the children "need" of the father's future income. As a result, the spouse who principally cares for the children—and the children—are almost invariably worse off financially after divorce than the spouse who devotes all his energies to a career.

Third, government social policies don't even define unpaid care of family dependents as work. A family's primary caregiver is not considered a full productive citizen, eligible in her own right for the major social insurance programs. Legal nannies earn Social Security credits; mothers at home do not. Unless she is otherwise "employed," the primary parent is not entitled to unemployment insurance or workman's compensation. The only safety net for a caregiver who loses her source of support is welfare, and even that is no longer assured.

For all these reasons, motherhood is the single biggest risk factor for poverty in old age. American mothers have smaller pensions than either men or childless women, and American women over sixty-five are more than twice as likely to be poor as men of the same age.

The devaluation of a mother's work extends to those who do similar work for pay. Even college-educated teachers of infants are often characterized as "baby-sitters," and wages for child care are so low that the field is hemorrhaging its best-trained people. Increasingly, day care is being provided by an inexperienced workforce—what one expert calls "Kentucky Fried Day Care"—while highly trained Mary Poppins–style nannies are officially classified as "unskilled labor," and as such largely barred from entry into the United States.

The cumulative effect of these policies is a heavy financial penalty on anyone who chooses to spend any serious amount of time with children. This is the hard truth that lies beneath all of the flowery tributes to Mom. American mothers may have their day, but for the rest of the year their values, their preferences, and their devotion to their children are short-changed. As the twenty-first century begins, women may be approaching equality, but mothers are still far behind. Changing the status of mothers, by gaining real recognition for their work, is the great unfinished business of the women's movement. . . .

Unpaid female caregiving is not only the life blood of families, it is the very heart of the economy. A spate of new studies reveals that the amount of work involved in unpaid child care is far greater than economists ever imagined. Indeed, it rivals in size the largest industries of the visible economy. By some estimates, even in the most industrialized countries the total hours spent on unpaid household work—much of it associated with child-rearing—amount to at least half of the hours of paid work in the market.[4] Up to 80 percent of this unpaid labor is contributed by women.

This huge gift of unreimbursed time and labor explains, in a nutshell, why adult women are so much poorer than men—even though they work longer hours than men in almost every country in the world.[5] One popular economics textbook devotes four pages to problems of poverty without once mentioning the fact that the majority of poor people are women and children. The author never considers that this poverty might be related to the fact that half the human race isn't paid for most of the work it does.

In economics, a "free rider" is someone who benefits from a good without contributing to its provision: in other words, someone who gets something for nothing. By that definition, both the family and the global economy are classic examples of free riding. Both are dependent on female caregivers who offer their labor in return for little or no compensation.

It may well be that mothers and others who care for children and sick and elderly family members will go on giving, whatever the costs or consequences for themselves. Maternal love, after all, is one of the world's renewable resources. But even if this is so, there is still a powerful argument for putting an end to free riding on women's labor. It's called *fairness*.

An analogy to soldiers might be helpful here. Soldiers, like mothers, render an indispensable national service to their country. The ultimate rationale for offering honors and material rewards to military veterans is to avoid free riding on their services. The public feels it owes its warriors some quid pro quo. The G.I. Bill, for example, was not originally a recruitment tool, as military benefits later became, but repayment of a debt that a grateful nation owed to its fighting men. No one, after World War II, dreamed of being a free rider on the sacrifices of Normandy Beach and Guadalcanal.

By the same token, it isn't fair to demand that the nurturing of human capabilities, the national service primarily rendered by women, be valued any less. It isn't fair that mothers' life-sustaining work forces women to be society's involuntary philanthropists. It isn't fair to expect mothers to make sacrifices that no one else is asked to make, or have virtues that no one else possesses, such as a dignified subordination of their personal agenda and a reliance on altruism for life's meaning. Virtues and sacrifices, when expected of one group of people and not of everyone, become the mark of an underclass.[6]

Establishing a fair deal for mothers would go beyond "wages for housewives," an idea that surfaced in the 1970s; or even mothers' benefits similar to veterans' benefits. What is needed is across-the-board recognition—in the workplace, in the family, in the law, and in social policy—that someone has to do the necessary work of raising children and sustaining families, and that the reward for such vital work should not be professional marginalization, a loss of status, and an increased risk of poverty.

Such recognition would end the glaring contradiction between what we tell young women—go out, get an education, become independent—and what happens to those aspirations once they have a child. It would demolish the anachronism that bedevils most mothers' lives: that although they work as hard as or harder than anyone else in the economy, they are still economic *dependents*, like children or incapacitated adults.

The standard rationale for the status quo is that women choose to have children, and in so doing, choose to accept the trade-offs that have always ensued. As an African safari guide once said of a troop of monkeys, "The mothers with the little babies have a hard time keeping up." But human beings, unlike apes, have the ability to ensure that those who carry the babies—and therefore our future—aren't forever trailing behind.   [2001]

NOTES

1. In no known human culture have males ever had the primary task of rearing small children. According to two preeminent scholars of children's history, one of the few things that can be said with certainty, amid the "extraordinary variety" in the historical treatment of children, is that "the vast majority of human infants have been and continue to be cared for primarily by females." N. Roy Hiner and Joseph M. Hawes, *Children in Historical and Comparative Perspective* (New York: Greenwood Press, 1991), p. 6. If this ever changed, writes Marion J. Levy, a sociologist at Princeton University, the implications would be more radical than the discovery of fire, the invention of agriculture, or the switch from animate to inanimate sources of power. Marion J. Levy, Jr., *Maternal Influence* (New Brunswick, N.J.: Transaction Publishers, 1992), pp. xix, 20–23.
2. Unpublished data from the March 1999 Current Population Survey, provided by Steve Hipple.
3. Female university graduates' labor force participation rates were provided by Agneta Stark, an economist at the University of Stockholm, during an interview in August 1997 in Stockholm.
4. More than 2 million American women work in a home-based business. They average twenty-three hours of work (in the business) a week.
5. Deborah Fallows made this comment during a panel discussion at the Harvard/Radcliffe twenty-fifth reunion in 1996, attended by the author.
   Council of Economic Advisers, *Families and the Labor Market, 1969–1999: Analyzing the "Time Crunch,"* (Washington, D.C., 1999) p. 4.

6. Louis Uchitelle, "As Labor Supply Shrinks, a New Supply Is Tapped," *New York Times*, December 20, 1999.

 54

Friendly for Whose Family?

BETTY HOLCOMB

One might assume that Lynnell Minkins, a single mother of three, would be thrilled to work for Marriott International. Last year, Marriott made *Working Mother* magazine's list of the 100 best companies for working mothers, largely because it offers flexible work schedules, hot lines to help employees deal with child-care emergencies, and three on-site child-care centers. Minkins, a food server at the San Francisco Marriott, could use that sort of help. But it's not available to her. Instead, she never knows from week to week what her hours will be, making it hard to find and hold on to decent child care, let alone make plans. "How can I get doctor appointments if I don't know when I'll be working?" she asks. "A month ahead, the clinic says there are only these days. I take them, and then I have to work."

When her kids were younger, she relied on a neighbor, paying a flat rate to send them over whenever she had to work. But now that they're in school, she has to figure out how to get them there on days she has to be at work early. A simple schedule change could solve everything, but she hasn't asked for one. "I don't dare bring it up. I'm afraid I'll get written up." A write-up means getting disciplined, and too many write-ups can lead to losing her job.

The irony is that, at least officially, Marriott offers flextime to its approximately 135,000 U.S. employees. Yet the one time Minkins tried it, her supervisors constantly pressed her to fix the "problem," and in her annual performance review that year she was described as being "challenged" by time management. "I should have called them on it, but I let it go," she says. "People who work in these jobs, they need the money. So you don't tell anybody what's going on." Senior managers, says Minkins, don't seem to suffer the same scrutiny. "It doesn't look like their job is being challenged. The lower people, the people in the back of the house, they're having the problems."

So it goes for hundreds of thousands of lower-level workers at companies widely recognized for their "family-friendly" policies. In fact, the research conducted by the Families and Work Institute exclusively for this article shows that the workers who most need benefits such as child care and flexible hours are the least likely to get them.

Consider these facts from the study. Workers in low-wage jobs are:

- half as likely as managers and professionals to have flextime;
- less likely to have on-site child care;
- more likely to lose a day's pay when they must stay home to care for a sick child;
- three times less likely to get company-sponsored tax breaks to help pay for child care.

In addition, other studies show that workers in entry-level, low-paying, or low-status jobs are much less likely to be offered a paid maternity leave than managers are, and in the case of unpaid leave, they are less likely to get as much time off after having a baby.

"It's clear that more advantaged workers have more access to certain benefits," says Ellen Galinsky, president of the Families and Work Institute. Put another way, some families seem to count more than others. "You ask yourself if people really care about the family benefits of people who clean the toilets, who clean the office buildings after everyone else leaves," says Netsy Firestein, director of the Labor Project for Working Families in Berkeley, California. "Who's taking care of their kids? Often it's older children putting younger ones to bed, while the parents struggle to make wages and get health insurance paid."

"For the first time, research shows that the gap between the haves and have-nots is becoming wider," says Ellen Galinsky of the Families and Work Institute, which ran the numbers below for *Ms.* "Some of the statistics are startling," she adds. "Only two in

The Job/Family Challenge

Almost half the workforce has responsibilities for young or elderly relatives. Passage of the FMLA has helped, but leave is still difficult because:

- Most workers can't afford to take much unpaid leave.
- The corporate culture discourages most men from sharing family responsibilities.
- Smaller firms are not covered by the FMLA.

Parents' problems with child care are taking a toll on family life and on business.

Working families need flexible schedules—and most don't have them.

---

five low-wage workers are allowed time off—without pay—to care for a sick child." Equally startling is how few family-related benefits are available to anyone: less than a quarter of workers get help finding child care. Trying to right the imbalance for low-income workers, in 1996 the Institute helped found the Employer Group, which is searching for new solutions. "The picture is bleak, but there is light ahead," says Galinksy. "The problem has been that nobody has paid attention to this."

The less you have, the less you get
Family-friendly benefits by job title and income:

	Earn $45,000 or more	Earn $29,000 or less
Have daily flextime	42.4%	16.6%
Allowed time off without pay for a sick child	63.3%	39.1%
Employer offers service to help find child care	26.9%	16.7%
Employer offers pre-tax account for child care	42.8%	21.2%
Employer offers service to help find elder care	32.6%	19.7%

9to5: Organizing Low-Wage Women

ELLEN BRAVO and GLORIA SANTA ANNA

When 9to5 was founded in Boston in 1973, the terms "sexual harassment," "pay equity" and "family leave" did not yet exist. But experiences with sexual degradation on the job, undervaluation of women's work and lack of consideration for family responsibilities were common. So were the consequences, both financially and emotionally, for women workers.

The women who started 9to5 worked as secretaries in Boston's prestigious colleges. Karen Nussbaum and Ellen Cassedy were angry over the daily reminders from those with power that support staff had none. They attended a weekend workshop for office workers at the YWCA where women listed the problems: low pay, limited advancement opportunity, little say over working conditions. A teller said she didn't make enough to get a loan from the bank she worked for. A clerk in a hospital couldn't afford to get sick; a university secretary couldn't afford to send her children to college. For the most part, workshop participants were proud of their skills and their work. Their goal was not so much to get out of office work as to upgrade it—to change the way they were treated and paid.

Ten women got together after the workshop and printed a short newsletter. In the mornings on the way to work they passed out the newsletters in front of subway stops and large office complexes. The response was overwhelming. The group called a meeting and 300 women showed up, bursting with grievances. In November 1973, they formed an association of working women and called it "9to5" after the usual hours of the business day.

The organization's early focus was on clericals, who represented the sphere of traditionally female jobs. The founders learned that one-third of all working women were employed in administrative support positions, the largest and fastest-growing sector of the workforce. Many of the women in these jobs lived near or in poverty—yet they were not being reached by anti-poverty groups, nor were they the focus of feminist organizations. At the time, most unions ignored them.

The movement began to grow. Women in other cities, motivated by experiences in the social movements of the 1960s as well as the huge influx of women into the workforce, formed similar groups. In the mid–1970s, they joined together to make 9to5 a national association. Staff and volunteers answered questions about job problems and held workshops on how to ask for a raise, plan for retirement and organize to win better treatment. And many began to celebrate actual victories. Women reported asking for raises for the first time in their lives—and getting them. Groups of clericals met with managers to demand policy changes, including accurate job descriptions and job postings. Women in the publishing, insurance and banking industries filed discrimination charges and won millions of dollars in back pay as well as new promotion and training programs. A few corporations, pressured by 9to5 activists, set aside money to help pay for child care.

Inspired by the group, Jane Fonda decided to make a movie about the concerns of office workers and called it "Nine to Five," greatly increasing the group's visibility. (The original plot involved murdering the boss. "That's not really on our agenda,"

9to5 activists persuaded Fonda, who changed the story to include a kidnapping and fantasies of murder—all based on interviews with 9to5 members.)

Some actions brought quick results. When a bank in Milwaukee told its employees they would have to take over payments for dependent health coverage —the equivalent of a week's take home pay—9to5 organized a demonstration outside the bank, with flyers that read "Should banks care about kids?" Within days the bank gave the women a raise equivalent to the health premium. Other campaigns dragged on for years, such as the successful efforts by the Delta 9to5 Network to gain recognition for their class action lawsuit against the employer. Workers for the airline had numerous complaints of discrimination against employees with physical disabilities, including the practice of identifying and firing employees with HIV.

From the early days, 9to5 leaders were interested in the intersection between the women's movement and the labor movement. Would unionization work for clerical workers? After some local efforts in Boston, 9to5 began exploring a relationship with an international union. In 1981, District 925 was born as an affiliate of Service Employees International Union. Today that group, which functions as a separate organization from 9to5, has organized women office workers across the country to bargain collectively. Union women overall make higher wages than non-union employees and often have greater benefits. In addition, a union contract can give protection from arbitrary firing and recognition for seniority. 9to5 found that working as a non-profit association had advantages as well, particularly in involving women for whom unionization wasn't an immediate option and in attracting media visibility.

In addition to empowering women individually and in groups, 9to5 helped change the policy environment. Issues that were trivialized when the group started became part of the public agenda. Using interviews with the media, actions, testimony and educational programs, 9to5 members also influenced the laws. They watched years of hard work result in passage of the 1978 Pregnancy Discrimination Act, the 1991 Civil Rights Act and the 1993 Family and

Medical Leave Act on the federal level, as well as numerous state pay equity and family leave laws, and some state statutes establishing protections for computer users.

The group's victories didn't escape the notice of management. In one midwestern city, the start of a 9to5 chapter was greeted with a seminar called "9to5: Not Just a Movie—How to Keep 9to5 Out of Your Office." The planners made one miscalculation: they'd forgotten who opens the mail. Several secretaries mailed the notice to the fledgling chapter, who sent someone to the seminar—and called a press conference immediately afterwards to denounce the tactics of trying to prevent employees from organizing.

In the late 1980s, 9to5's agenda expanded to address the needs of those who work at the margins of the economy—part-time and temporary workers, women who cycle on and off welfare. 9to5 activists with direct experience of welfare drew attention to the connections between women's problems in the workforce and their need to rely on public assistance. What happens to women who lose their job because of discrimination or lack of family leave, they asked? If you really want to reform welfare, they told policymakers, start by looking at the need to reform work. In the 1990s, 9to5 became involved in struggles for a living wage and state self-sufficiency standards. The group has also been prominent in struggles around removal of the social safety net. While working for short-term improvements, 9to5 points to the root causes of poverty and discrimination and the need for lasting solutions, as well as the need for alliances with other women's groups, labor, faith-based groups and community organizations.

Technological developments added another issue: electronic surveillance. In 1989, 9to5 started a hotline to track computer users who were being monitored on the job, often without their awareness. Workers resented being spied on. Spying, one woman said, is what you do to the enemy.

Electronic surveillance wasn't the only reason people dialed the hotline. They called with every type of job problem, eager to find out if they had any rights. After the Clarence Thomas hearings in 1991, the line was deluged with calls about sexual harassment. Many had experienced the harassment years earlier. As one woman put it, "I've never told anyone before. I thought that's just what you had to put up with."

9to5 has worked hard to make visible the problems working women face and to identify solutions. The vehicle at times is humorous, such as the contest for many years to "Rate Your Job: The Good, the Bad and the Downright Unbelievable." Winners included the manager who sent his secretary to bars on Saturday nights with a beeper to save him the trouble of scoping out women he might like; the doctor who demanded his nurse return to the office after she found her children's babysitter had died in her home; and a chain store in California that cut a 15-year employee's hours, ending all her benefits and sick days. The most recent version of the contest calls on women to rate their employer on a scorecard and nominate co-workers who've helped "Raise the Score" at work.

Over the years 9to5 helped raise the expectations of low-wage women. Most women were already aware of problems on the job. As a popular 9to5 button put it, "My consciousness is fine—it's my pay that needs raising." Thanks to 9to5, women workers have gained greater awareness that they deserve better treatment. Yet most still lack the belief that change is possible—or the concept that they themselves are the real agents of change. 9to5 tries to address this gap by helping members recognize and expand their leadership skills, and above all by showing the difference collective action can make. The organization popularizes success stories to demystify the change process, revealing the many small steps that lead to a victory.

Nearly thirty years after its founding, 9to5 is still transforming itself. The group has always been multiracial and multicultural, with an emphasis on fighting all forms of discrimination. But for many years the highest level staff were all or predominantly white. In the mid-1990s, with leadership from many parts of the organization, 9to5 set about examining how to become a genuinely anti-oppression organization. The process included structural

Going Public

ELLEN BRAVO

For many years in April, in honor of National Secretaries Day, 9to5 sponsored a national contest called "Nominate Your Boss: The Good, the Bad and the Downright Unbelievable." We used Public Service Announcements to attract entries to the contest. Subsequent publicity about the "winners" helped draw attention to problems faced by working women, kept the spotlight on offenders, called attention to positive steps taken by employers, and honored the courageous women who are turning their private pain into public action. Among the Unbelievable winners:

OUTRAGEOUS REQUESTS BY A MANAGER OF HIS ASSISTANT

Repair a hole in his trousers—while he's wearing them.
Clip his nose hairs.
Wax the hair off his back.
Take his urine sample (or stool sample) to the lab.
Cup her hands for his cigarette ashes.
Dress up in spandex and lure workers off a competitor's construction site.

OUTRAGEOUS COMMENTS / ACTIONS

A stockbroker asked his secretary to take home his trading jacket to wash by hand because "you don't have a college degree."
A manager fired his support staff person because her son was due for a liver transplant —he claimed she wouldn't be able to keep her mind on her performance.
When a suspicious-looking package arrived in the mail, the manager said: "This might be a letter bomb. You open it."
A stockbroker held a contest among the office help to see who was most proficient at forging clients' signatures on stocks and bonds.
Managers at a newspaper that was merging and laying off hundreds of employees urged them to "demonstrate your ability to take a punch."
The manager of a canteen vending company told his administrative assistant, the only African American in the front office, "Some of the people are racist. They did not want me to hire you. Maybe you should quit."   [2002]

changes such as adding caucuses to create safe space for women of color, lesbian/bisexual women and women in poverty to come together. Board and staff reviewed everything from mission to program to methods of resolving conflict in order to make sure that the group consistently "walked its talk." A management team developed a more collaborative structure for itself and welcomed flattening of the organization overall.

Above all, 9to5 strives to be a vehicle where working women can see that the particular pain they've experienced isn't personal—it's not about one bad manager or one set of policies or one election, but about power. Rather than striving simply to put more women into power, 9to5 aims to put more power in the hands of all women and all other groups who've been denied it. [2002]

56

Sexual Harassment: An Overview of Its Impact on Women

JULIA WHEALIN

A growing awareness of exploitation and oppression has developed in the wake of the civil rights and women's movements. With this, our conception of violence and exploitation has expanded from that of "the criminal on the street" to encompass interpersonal behavior among acquaintances, such as sexual harassment. The awareness of such exploitation has encouraged people to stand up legally for their rights both to strangers and to those with whom they may have a close relationship, such as an employer, teacher, physician, or peer.

In 1980, the Equal Employment Opportunities Commission used the following definition to describe sexual harassment:

> Unwelcome sexual advances, requests for sexual favors, and other verbal or physical conduct of a sexual nature constitute sexual harassment when 1) submission to such conduct is made either explicitly or implicitly a term or condition of an indi-

---

Unions Benefit Working Women

ADAPTED FROM AFL-CIO WEBSITE

PAY FOR WOMEN IN UNIONS IS HIGHER THAN FOR THEIR NONUNION COUNTERPARTS

In 1997, women union members earned 40 percent more than nonunion women, according to union wage data based upon the median weekly earnings of full-time wage and salary workers. Union women earned 84 percent of what union men earned in 1997, while nonunion women earned only 76 percent of what nonunion men earned.

African-American women who belonged to unions earned 44 percent more than their nonunion counterparts. Latina union members earned 42 percent more than nonunion Latina workers. Unions work to increase equality in wages between women and men.[1]

In 2001 union women earned 30% more than their nonunion counterparts.[2]

UNION WORKERS ARE MORE LIKELY THAN NONUNION WORKERS TO HAVE HEALTH AND PENSION BENEFITS

85 percent of full-time union workers in medium-sized and large private establishments had health benefits in 1995, compared with 74 percent of full-time nonunion workers.

87 percent of full-time union workers in medium-sized and large private establishments had retirement benefits, compared with 78 percent of full-time nonunion workers.[3]

[1] All the above statistics are from Bureau of Labor Statistics, Employment and Earnings, January 1998.
[2] Bureau of Labor Statistics, *Employment and Earnings,* January 2002.
[3] The above statistics are from U.S. Department of Labor Employee Benefits Survey, "Full-Time Workers in Medium and Large Private Establishments, stats.bls.gov/ebs2/ebb10013.pdf.

vidual's employment, 2) submission to or rejection of such conduct by an individual is used as a basis for employment decisions affecting such individual, or 3) such conduct has the purpose or effect of unreasonably interfering with an individual's work performance or creating an intimidating, hostile, or offensive working environment.

Sexual harassment therefore differs from flirtation, flattery, or requests for a date to the extent that it lacks mutuality. Two types of sexual harassment are currently recognized by the law. The first, "*quid pro quo,*" occurs when sexual favors are requested in exchange for an employment or academic opportunity. The second type of sexual harassment has come to be known as the "hostile environment." It occurs when unwelcome, severe, and pervasive sexual conduct interferes with the target individual's performance or otherwise creates an intimidating or hostile environment (Lewis, Hastings, & Morgan, 1992).

EXTENT OF THE PROBLEM

The extent of sexual harassment among adults has been documented in the past two decades. The first study to investigate the prevalence of sexual harassment was a readers' poll conducted by *Redbook* magazine (Safran, 1976). Ninety percent of the 9,000 women who responded to this survey reported that they had been sexually harassed at some point in their lives. Although this prevalence is probably biased by the fact that a random sampling research design was not used, the response rate made it apparent that sexual harassment was a widespread problem for women.

In 1981, a carefully designed, random-sample survey of 24,000 U.S. government workers revealed that 42% of women and 15% of men experienced sexual harassment on the job in the prior two years (U.S. Merit Systems Protection Board, 1981). The consequences of the harassment were often extensive. For instance, of those who had experienced harassment, 52% reported that they had quit because of it or were fired. Furthermore, the survey showed that most of those who were harassed did not take formal action against the harasser: only 5% filed

complaints. This widely publicized study was replicated in 1988 with similar results. Comparable rates of sexual harassment are also reported in smaller studies of specific professions, such as airline personnel, social workers, and female lawyers. Moreover, similar rates of sexual harassment have been reported by white-collar as well as blue-collar workers (Kissman, 1990). However, workers in settings composed predominantly of the opposite sex tend to report higher rates of harassment than workers in occupations traditional for their sex (Mansfield, Koch, Henderson, & Vicary, 1991; U.S. Merit Systems Protection Board, 1988).

Surveys in college settings reveal that sexual harassment is also a problem there, although less than that reported by studies of other settings (Charney & Russell, 1994). For instance, about one-fourth of female students surveyed at three large Northeastern universities said that they had been harassed by a professor. In another study, 16% of female university counseling center clients reported experiencing sexual harassment while at the university. Rates are reportedly higher for graduate students and medical students than for undergraduates. In addition to educational and occupational settings, individuals are sexually harassed by various other perpetrators, from physicians to strangers on the street.

HARASSERS AND HARASSEES

One commonality among various settings is that women are often the victims of sexual harassment. Furthermore, those who experience sexual harassment in occupational settings are more likely in lower-level positions in the organization, nonwhite, and young (U.S. Merit Systems Protection Board, 1988). Those who report harassment often hold lower-income occupations and are the sole supporters of families (Crull, 1979). Conversely, perpetrators of sexual harassment are more likely to be men. For example, in a sample of medical residents, 96% of female victims and 55% of male victims reported sexually harassing behaviors by a male (Komaromy, Bindman, Haber, & Sande, 1993).

Understanding the reported characteristics of harassers, based on reports of those harassed, helps to explain some of the dynamics of the behavior. The U.S. Merit Systems Protection Board study (1981) found, for example, that most harassers were married. Furthermore, most harassers of women were older than their victims, whereas most harassers of men were younger than the victims. Harassers of both women and men tended to act alone rather than with another person. Moreover, both women and men reported that their harasser had bothered others at work. Perpetrators of harassment were more likely to be co-workers, while supervisors were harassers in 40% of the cases. Women in this study, however, were more likely than men to be harassed by a supervisor. This result is consistent with that of another study (Crull, 1979) in which 70% of women reported that their harassers had "the power to fire or promote" them. Thus, much of the time, harassers target women who in some way are less powerful than they.

To obtain information about men who harass, Pryor (1987) developed the Likelihood to Sexually Harass Scale. This scale is a self-report inventory in which men are asked to imagine themselves in ten situations in which they control an important reward or punishment for an attractive woman. They are then asked to rate the likelihood of using this power to sexually exploit the woman (and thus engage in quid pro quo sexual harassment). Several attitudes were evidenced among men who admitted to harassing behaviors. Specifically, men who were high on the Likelihood to Sexually Harass Scale (1) held adversarial sexual beliefs, (2) found it difficult to assume another's perspective, (3) endorsed traditional male sex role stereotypes, (4) were high in authoritarianism, and (5) reported a higher likelihood to rape a woman, assuming that they would not be held responsible for their actions. In another study using the scale, men who scored high on the scale showed significantly more thoughts associating themes of sexuality with social power (Pryor & Stoller, 1992, cited in Pryor, Lavite, & Stoller, 1993).

RESPONSE TO SEXUAL HARASSMENT

The victim's response to sexual harassment varies from ignoring the behavior to filing a grievance complaint. In the U.S. Merit Systems Protection Board (1981, 1988) studies, about 11% of victims responded by reporting the harassment to a higher authority. As few as 2.5% of those harassed initiated an official grievance procedure. Of those who responded actively by filing a formal complaint, 47% reported that the action "made things better," regardless of whether the complaint was successful. Thirty-three percent, however, felt that their filing a complaint "made things worse" because of retaliation by the harasser or social stigmatization.

In another investigation, which surveyed 304 women and 205 men by telephone, 17% of those reporting harassment in a work situation reported that they had quit their jobs or asked for a transfer as a result of the harassment. Additionally, about one-third of victims in this study chose to ignore the harassment, while almost 40% said something themselves to the harasser. Only 8% said something to their boss regarding the harassment, and 3% of those harassed actually reported the behavior (Loy & Stewart, 1984). Respondents in this study were also asked about the organization's response to their experiences of harassment. Many of those harassed reported negative outcomes at their place of employment. Social stigmatization among co-workers was the most common negative outcome, reported by one-third of the victims. Other negative responses reported included being ignored by the harasser, being given lower performance evaluations, or being denied a promotion. Moreover, a negative response was reported more often when those harassed responded by saying something to the harasser. Fewer negative responses were reported, however, when those harassed ignored the behavior or went to their supervisors with complaints.

Organizational effects linked with sexual harassment can be quite profound. For example, harassment in an occupational setting can result in the deterioration of interpersonal work relationships and can strain working alliances with the opposite sex. Often, those harassed leave their jobs as a result of sexual harassment (Loy & Stewart, 1984; U.S. Merit Systems Protection Board, 1988). The effects of harassment in universities have also been substantial, as they has led students to drop courses, change majors, as well as give up career intentions (Fitzgerald et al., 1990). In summary, the research performed to date suggests that sexual harassment can have a serious, detrimental effect on one's interpersonal relationships with co-workers, on the career path one feels able to choose, and on one's evaluation and promotion in that career.

EFFECTS OF SEXUAL HARASSMENT ON WOMEN

In addition to direct work- or school-related consequences, sexual harassment can lead to negative personal ramifications. For example, difficulties with work relationships decrease access to work-related information and support from others (DiTomasio, 1989) that is needed for women to advance in their careers. Lowered self-esteem and self-confidence may follow the realization that rewards were due to one's sexual attraction rather than one's work ability. Furthermore, work performance has been purported to decline owing to a loss of motivation, feelings of anxiety, and the distracting nature of the harassment (Woody & Perry, 1993).

Physical and psychological symptoms are another personal ramification of sexual harassment. For instance, physical ailments such as headaches, decreased appetite, weight loss, sleep problems, and an increase in respiratory or urinary tract infections are reported by victims of harassment. Psychological difficulties associated with harassment include anger, fear, sadness, anxiety, irritability, loss of self-esteem, feelings of humiliation and alienation, and a sense of helplessness and vulnerability (Jenson & Gutek, 1992).

Gender-based abuse, such as sexual harassment, may be related to the increased depression rates seen in women (Hamilton, Alagna, King, & Lloyd, 1987). Indeed, substantial depressive symptoms reportedly resulted from sexual harassment in one sample of women in a community (Loy & Stewart, 1984). Furthermore, 84 professional women experienced feelings of depression and self-blame after simply listening to an audio simulation of sexual harassment in

which they were asked to imagine themselves as the victim (Samoluk & Pretty, 1994).

In some cases, the stress induced by the victimization may result in a posttraumatic stress reaction (Hamilton et al., 1987). Flashbacks, shock, emotional numbing, sleep disturbance, anxiety, and constriction of affect have accompanied the symptoms of depression seen in those who have been harassed. Sexual harassment can reinforce the internalization of social stereotypes and prejudice that define women as a devalued group. When such a stereotype is internalized, reactions such as isolation, extreme irrationality, and the tendency to minimize or deny harassment may result.

GENDER DIFFERENCES AND SEXUAL HARASSMENT

Research has demonstrated that men and women tend to perceive sexual harassment differently. For instance, women generally perceive a greater number of behaviors to be harassing than men (Baker, Terpstra, & Cutler, 1990; Gutek, Morasch, & Cohen, 1983). In particular, women are more likely than men to perceive harassing incidents as actual harassment when they include touching, when they are accompanied by a negative comment about their work, and when they are initiated by a man or a higher-status person (Gutek et al., 1983). Findings additionally show that women are less likely than men to blame women for being sexually harassed (Jensen & Gutek, 1982).

Studies of the effects of sexual harassment show that similar behaviors may have a different impact on women than on men. Women view behavior such as sexual propositions as inappropriate and likely to cause discomfort, while men more often do not see them as inappropriate or as causing as much discomfort (Garlick, 1994; Roscoe, Strouse, & Goodwin, 1994). In one study, approximately half of working men said they would respond positively to unsolicited sexual attention (Berdahl, Magley, & Waldo, 1996). Written descriptions of the men's view of the situations included comments that the sexual harassment "doesn't bother me" or that it "makes the job more fun." A second viewpoint that emerged was that the men felt as though they had control over the situation. Men's responses indicated that, when they did not like the behavior, they would confront the perpetrator or report that person to a supervisor. This reaction is in contrast to women's responses, which more often included perceived threat and lack of control, as well as passive responding (Fitzgerald et al., 1990).

In general, the same behaviors women may experience as sexually harassing may be more often experienced by men as nonthreatening social-sexual behavior. However, the term *harassment* implies that the behavior must be stressful to the victim (Fitzgerald, Swan, & Fischer, 1995). Although males may like or dislike the unsolicited sexual attention, the behaviors do not tend to have the strong impact on men that they do on women. Thus, research suggests that the sexual advances of women toward men often do not result in a perceived hostile or offensive environment that may interfere with one's ability to perform.

SUMMARY OF SEXUAL HARASSMENT

To review the current findings regarding sexual harassment of adults, the most extensive and carefully designed studies to date suggest that approximately 42% of women and 15% of men report that they have been sexually harassed in their workplaces in the preceding two years. About one-fourth of female students experience harassment while at college. Perpetrators of sexual harassment are most often men, and victims are more often women. Sexual harassment frequently has negative ramifications for the victim. Victims report negative workplace responses, such as poor performance evaluations. In colleges, women have changed majors and dropped courses because of harassment. Additionally, the stress resulting from harassment can have significant physical and psychological consequences on the victim.

Despite the negative impact of harassment, research performed to date suggests that much can be done to address its perpetration. As sexual harassers often bother several victims, a woman can realize that she is not singled out by the harasser. Other women have likely come before her, and if nothing is done, more women will be harassed in the future. Most women report that going to supervisors with complaints helps end the harassment. While few women report filing formal grievances, those who do usually find that it helps end the harassment. Unfortunately, women who address harassment can suffer personal and occupational stresses as a result. It therefore may be important to gain aid from others. Peers likely will assist and support their friends. When peers are not able to provide the help that is needed, supervisors, friends, women's organizations, and therapists are available to lend needed advice.

Finally, while investigations have helped to identify the victims and perpetrators of sexual harassment, research is necessary that explores ways to prevent the behavior. Interventions are much needed at the organizational level to teach employers and educators about the legal and personal ramifications of harassment. Women are demanding the right they deserve to have harassment-free work and school environments, and institutions must respond by making sexual harassment a serious offense.

REFERENCES

Baker, D. D., Terpstra, D. E., & Cutler, B. D. (1990). Perceptions of sexual harassment: A re-examination of gender differences. *Journal of Psychology, 124,* 409–416.

Berdahl, J. L., Magley, V. J., & Waldo, C. R. (1996). The sexual harassment of men? Exploring the concept with theory and data. *Psychology of Women Quarterly, 20,* 527–547.

Charney, D. A., & Russell, R. C. (1994). An overview of sexual harassment. *American Journal of Psychiatry, 151,* 10–17.

Crull, P. (1979). The impact of sexual harassment on the job: A profile of the experiences of 92 women. *Working Women's Institute Research Series Report, 3,* 1–7.

DiTomasio, N. (1989). Sexuality in the workplace: Discrimination and harassment. In J. Hearn, D. L. Sheppard, P. Tancred-Sherriff, & G. Burrell (Eds.), *The sexuality of the organization* (pp. 71–90). Newbury Park, CA: Sage.

Fitzgerald, L. F., Swan, S., & Fischer, K. (1995). Why didn't she just report him? The psychological and legal implications of women's responses to sexual harassment. *Journal of Social Issues, 51,* 117–138.

Fitzgerald, L. F., Shullman, S. L., Bailey, N., Richards, M.,

Swecker, J., Gold, Y., Ormerod, A. J., & Weitzman, L. M. (1990). The incidence and dimensions of sexual harassment in academia and the workplace. *Journal of Vocational Behavior, 32,* 152–175.

Garlick, R. (1994). Male and female responses to ambiguous instructor behaviors. *Sex Roles, 30,* 124–158.

Gutek, B. A., Morasch, B., & Cohen, A. G. (1983). Interpreting social-sexual behavior in a work setting. *Journal of Vocational Behavior, 22,* 30–48.

Hamilton, J. A., Alagna, S. W., King, L. S., & Lloyd, C. (1987). The emotional consequences of gender-based abuse in the workplace: New counseling programs for sexual discrimination. *Women and Therapy, 14,* 155–182.

Jensen, I. W., & Gutek, B. A. (1982). Attributions and assignment of responsibility in sexual harassment. *Journal of Social Issues, 38,* 121–138.

Kissman, K. (1990). Women in blue-collar occupations: An exploration of constraints and facilitators. *Journal of Sociology and Social Welfare, 17,* 139–149.

Komaromy, M., Bindman, A. B., Haber, R. J., & Sande, M. A. (1993). Sexual harassment in medical training. *New England Journal of Medicine, 328,* 322–326.

Lewis, J. F., Hastings, S. C., & Morgan, A. C. (1992). *Sexual harassment in education.* Topeka, KS: National Organization on Legal Problems in Education.

Loy, P. H., & Stewart, L. P. (1984). The extent and effects of sexual harassment of working women. *Sociological Focus, 17,* 31–43.

Mansfield, P. K., Koch, P. B., Henderson, J., Vicary, J. R., Cohen, M., & Young, E. W. (1991). The job climate for women in traditionally male blue-collar occupations. *Sex Roles, 25,* 63–75.

Pryor, J. B. (1987). Sexual harassment proclivities in men. *Sex Roles, 17,* 269–290.

Pryor, J. B., Lavite, C. M., & Stoller, L. M. (1993). A social psychological analysis of sexual harassment: The person/situation interaction. *Journal of Vocational Behavior, 42,* 68–83.

Roscoe, B., Strouse, J. S., & Goodwin, M. P. (1994). Sexual harassment: Early adolescents' self-reports of experiences and acceptance. *Adolescence, 29,* 515–523.

Safran, C. (1976). Sexual harassment: A view from the top. *Redbook, 156,* 1–7.

Samoluk, S. B., & Pretty, G. M. H. (1994). The impact of sexual harassment simulations on women's thoughts and feelings. *Sex Roles, 30,* 679–697.

U.S. Merit Systems Protection Board Office of Merit Systems Review. (1981). *Sexual Harassment in the Federal Government: Is it a problem?* Washington, D.C.: U.S. Government Printing Office.

U.S. Merit Systems Protection Board. (1988). *Sexual harassment in the Federal government: An update.* Washington, D.C.: U.S. Government Printing Office.

Woody, R. H., & Perry, N. W. (1993). Sexual harassment victims: Psycholegal and family therapy considerations. *American Journal of Family Therapy, 21,* 136–144.

 57

In Case of Sexual Harassment: A Guide for Women Students

BERNICE SANDLER

MYTHS ABOUT SEXUAL HARASSMENT

Myth: Sexual harassment only happens to women who are provocatively dressed.

Fact: Sexual harassment can happen to anyone, no matter how she dresses.

Myth: If the women had only said "NO" to the harasser, he would have stopped immediately.

Fact: Many harassers are told "NO" repeatedly and it does no good. NO is too often heard as YES.

Myth: If a woman ignores sexual harassment, it will go away.

Fact: No, it won't. Generally, the harasser is a repeat offender who will not stop on his own. Ignoring it may be seen as assent or encouragement.

Myth: All men are harassers.

Fact: No, only a few men harass. Usually there is a pattern of harassment: one man harasses a number of women either sequentially or simultaneously, or both.

Myth: Sexual harassment is harmless. Women who object have no sense of humor.

Fact: Harassment is humiliating and degrading. It undermines school careers and often threatens economic livelihood. No one should have to endure humiliation with a smile.

Myth: Sexual harassment affects only a few people.

Fact: Surveys on campus show that up to 30 percent of all female college students experience some form of sexual harassment. Some surveys of women in the working world have shown that as many as 70 percent have been sexually harassed in some way.

WHAT YOU CAN DO ABOUT SEXUAL HARASSMENT

Ignoring sexual harassment does not make it go away. Indeed, it may make it worse because the harasser may misinterpret no response as approval of his behavior. However, there are things you can do, from informal strategies to formal ones. Here are some of your options.

• Know your rights. Sexual harassment is illegal in many instances. Your college or university may also have specific policies prohibiting faculty and staff from sexually harassing students and employees. Familiarize yourself with these policies. (For example, you can ask the Dean of Students if there is a policy.)

• Speak up at the time. Be sure to say "NO" clearly, firmly and without smiling. This is not a time to be polite or vague. (For example, you can say, "I don't like what you are doing," or "Please stop— you are making me very uncomfortable.") There is a chance—albeit small—that the harasser did not realize that his behavior was offensive to you. Additionally, if you decide to file charges at a later date, it is sometimes helpful, but not essential, to have objected to the behavior.

• Keep records, such as a journal and any letters or notes received. Note the dates, places, times, witnesses and the nature of the harassment—what he said and did and how you responded.

• Tell someone, such as fellow students or co-workers. Find out if others have been harassed by the same person and if they will support you should you decide to take action. Sharing your concern helps to avoid isolation and the tendency to blame yourself. Sexual harassment incidents are usually not isolated; most sexual harassers have typically harassed several or many people.

• Identify an advocate, perhaps a counselor, who can give you emotional support as well as help and information about both informal and formal institutional procedures.

• Write a letter. Many people have successfully stopped sexual harassment by writing a special kind of letter to the harasser. This letter should be polite, low-key and detailed, and consists of three parts:

• Part I is a factual account of what has happened, without any evaluation, as seen by the writer. It should be as detailed as possible with dates, places and a description of the incident(s). (For example, "Last week at the department party you asked me to go to bed with you." Or "On Oct. 21, when I came to you for advice on my test, you patted my knee and tried to touch my breast.")

• Part II describes how the writer feels about the events described in Part I, such as misery, dismay, distrust, and revulsion. (For example, "My stomach turns to knots when I come to class," or "I'm disgusted when I look at you.")

• Part III consists of what the writer wants to happen next. This part may be very short, since most writers usually just want the behavior to stop. (For example, "I don't ever want you to touch me again or to make remarks about my sexuality," or "Please withdraw my last evaluation until we can work out a fair one.")

The letter should be delivered either in person or be registered or certified mail. Copies are not sent to campus officers or the press. The writer should keep at least one copy of the letter. (In the unlikely event that it fails to achieve its purpose, the letter can later be used to document retaliation or in support of a formal complaint or lawsuit.)

In most cases, the harasser is often astonished that his behavior is viewed in the way the writer sees it. He may also be fearful of a formal charge, and worry about who else has seen the letter. The letter also seems to be far more powerful than a verbal request—even those who may have ignored verbal requests to stop, often respond differently when the request is put into writing. The recipient of the letter rarely writes back; usually he just stops the sexual harassment immediately, and typically does not harass anyone else either.

Occasionally the harasser may want to apologize or discuss the situation. You don't need to discuss it if you don't want to—you can simply reiterate that you want the behavior to stop and it's not necessary to discuss it.

There are many advantages to writing a letter:

- It helps the victim regain a sense of being in control of the situation;
- it often avoids formal charges and a public confrontation;
- it keeps the incident(s) confidential;
- it provides the harasser with a new perspective on his behavior;
- it may minimize or prevent retaliation against the writer;
- it is not necessary to address questions such as legality, confidentiality, evidence and due process; and
- it usually works.   [1992]

🌿 58

Women

ALICE WALKER

They were women then
My mama's generation
Husky of voice—Stout of
Step
With fists as well as
Hands
How they battered down
Doors
And ironed
Starched white
Shirts
How they led
Armies
Headragged Generals
Across mined
Fields
Booby-trapped
Kitchens
To discover books

Desks
A place for us
How they knew what we
Must know
Without knowing a page
Of it
Themselves   [1974]

Women, the Law, and Social Policy

Laws and social policies shape women's experience of all institutions in our society. Although more women have entered the legal profession, legislatures, and government agencies in recent years, sexism continues to permeate the policies and practices of these institutions.

In the first article, attorney Kristin Miccio paints both a historical and contemporary picture of women's secondary status under the law. She describes the ways that the legal system has constrained women and the ways feminists have used the law to fight for civil rights in the areas of work, reproductive rights, and violence against women. Despite feminists' efforts, reforms have been slow to take effect because of the sexist attitudes that still shape police and attorney practices, judicial rulings, and jury verdicts. Miccio concludes that systemic change will "require the infusion of feminist politics at every level of the justice system from the police to the courts."

Similarly, sexism pervades social policies that shape women's lives. Compared to European countries, for example, the United States has few governmental supports, such as child and maternal benefits, that protect mothers and children from poverty. In "How to Bring Children Up Without Putting Women Down," Ann Crittenden describes the ways that employers could redesign work around parents' needs, and governmental policies that would replace the welfare state with a caring state supportive of women.

The dual role women workers are expected to take on without support combined with inequities in the workplace trap many women in poverty. When women had children and couldn't find work that paid enough to support their families and pay for childcare, they often had to turn to welfare. A former welfare recipient, Rita Henley Jensen, describes the realities of being a woman on welfare. She shows how in the early 1970s Aid to Families with Dependent Children (AFDC) provided her a way out, and how and why it does not now. In "Farewell to Welfare, But Not to Poverty," Randy Albelda and Chris Tilly describe the welfare "reform" legislation of 1996, pointing out the ways TANF (Temporary Aid to Needy Families) worsens the lives of women in poverty, and suggesting reforms that would work. Finally Linda Burnham describes the ways in which, in the years since the 1995 World Conference on Women, the U.S. government has contradicted the Beijing platform for action, going back on its pledges to uphold women's human rights, by driving more U.S. women into poverty through "welfare reform." She shows how women of color on welfare rolls are especially vulnerable to the negative effects of these policies.

59

Women and the Law

KRISTIAN MICCIO

America prides itself on the notion that we are a society of laws. The legal system provides a framework upon which we as a society define ourselves. It is a statement of our collective values and traditions. Within the American context, law has an additional function. It is a compact between equals: A self-governance contract between the governed and the governors. Yet women have been conspicuously missing from the fabric of our legal traditions. In fact, women were at one time specifically excluded from the body politic.[1]

The framers of the Constitution believed that the public sphere and the exercise of citizenship were the domain of men. As Jefferson wrote, "Were the state a pure democracy there would still be excluded from our deliberation women, who, to prevent deprivation of morals and ambiguity of issues should not mix promiscuously in gatherings of men."[2] Clearly, Jefferson believed that the presence of women would pollute and corrupt not only the morals of men but the system itself. Jefferson's position echoed the prevailing view that women's social and political identity should be restricted and that her sexuality should be controlled.

The legal concept that women and men are equal before the law was not the original understanding of the Constitution's framers. Indeed, women's exclusion from the body politic was a direct consequence of our sex. Our body of law and our legal traditions restricted and confined women to that of the private sphere, and, in setting up this gilded cage, women's legal identity was shaped by and dependent on the men within the home.

In the eyes of the law, women were neither separate nor distinct legal beings. Simply put, because a woman derived her legal identity from men, she had no claim to rights commonly associated with citizenship. She could not vote, and her acquisition and control of private property was severely restricted.[3] Consequently, women's social status was defined by her ability to reproduce, and her legal status was shaped by her relationship to men within the family —as one's wife or as one's daughter. Women's legal identity, then, was subsumed into that of the husband or father. She had no separate legal character.

The British common-law tradition of "covered woman," which defined married women's legal status, was incorporated into American jurisprudence. William Blackstone, an eighteenth-century British legal theorist, summarized the doctrine of "femme couverte" in his Commentaries on the Law of England:

> By marriage, the husband and wife are one person in the law: that is, the very being or legal existence of the woman is suspended during the marriage, or at least is incorporated and consolidated into that of the husband; under whose wing, protection, and cover, she performs everything. . . . Upon this principle, of a union of person in husband and wife depend almost all the legal rights, duties and disabilities, that either of them acquire by the marriage. . . . a man can not grant anything to his wife, or enter into covenant with her: for the grant would be to suppose her separate existence; and to covenant with her would be only to covenant with himself

---

[1]The Fourteenth Amendment to the Constitution, which enfranchised black men, specifically referred to males over the age of 21 as citizens with the right to vote. This excluded all women, regardless of race, class, or creed.

[2]Quoted in Kay, Herma Hill, *Sex Discrimination and the Law* (West Publications, 1988, p. 1).

[3]In *Minor v. Happersett*, 88 U.S. 162, 22 L.Ed. 627 (1874), Virginia Minor attempted to vote in the elections of 1872. The U.S. Supreme Court ruled that the right to vote was not among the "privileges and immunities" of United States or federal citizenship. Therefore, the States were not prohibited by the Constitution from inhibiting this right and restricting it, "[the] important trust to men alone." The Court did state, however, that women, like children, were "persons" and may be citizens within the meaning of the Fourteenth Amendment. Women received the right to vote with passage of the Nineteenth Amendment in 1920. This followed a century of struggle by the first wave of feminists (suffragists).

and therefore it is also generally true that all compacts made between husband and wife, when single, are voided by the intermarriage. A woman indeed may be attorney for her husband, for that implies no separation from, but is rather a representation of her lord.[4]

This tradition guided our law until the mid-nineteenth century. With the passage of the Married Women's Property Act of 1848, many of the civil disabilities consistent with the acquisition of private property were lifted. Women as the sexual property of men and restrictions on their participation in public life remained intact until the late twentieth century.[5]

Upon marriage, a woman experienced a legal death. The first step in this process was the surrender of her name. This loss was more than a symbolic act; it was the initial step toward utter suspension of her legal existence.

Since married women were invisible in the eyes of the law, they could not take part in civil life. And the effects of such a civil death were profound. Women could not sue; they could not keep wages; they could not own property; they could not seek employment without spousal consent; they could not exercise any control over their children; and, finally, they had no control over their reproductive and sexual lives.

The doctrine of covered women transformed married women into the sexual property of their husbands. And because they were property, women could not exercise free will. Husbands, then, had complete control over their wives' bodies. Rape within marriage was not only a legal fiction, it was socially sanctioned and legally condoned. For women, the concept of a right to (bodily) privacy was alien.

A further consequence of "civil death" was economic dependency. Women could not work without the consent of their husbands. And if a woman was permitted to work outside the home, she was not entitled to keep her wages. This forced dependency kept women economically subservient and tied to hearth and home.

WOMEN AND WORK

In 1873, Myra Bradwell's application for a license to practice law was denied by the Illinois Supreme Court. This denial was due solely to her sex—she was born female. Bradwell's case was heard by the U.S. Supreme Court, and it upheld the lower state court's decision to deny her access to the legal profession. Justice Bradley, in a concurring opinion, written for himself and his brethren Justices Swayne and Field, stated:

> The civil law, as well as nature herself, has always recognized a wide difference in the respective spheres and destinies of man and woman. Man is or should be woman's protector and defender. The natural and proper timidity and delicacy which belongs to the female sex evidently unfits it [*sic*] for many of the occupations of civil life. The constitution of the family organization, which is founded in divine ordinance, as well as in the nature of things, indicates the domestic sphere as that which properly belongs to the domain and function of womanhood. The harmony, not to say identity, of interests and views which belong, or should belong, to the family institution is repugnant to the idea of a woman adopting a distinct and independent career from that of her husband.[6]

Critical to Bradley's concurrence in *Bradwell* is his reliance on "divine ordinance" in upholding an arbitrary denial of admission to the Illinois bar. Once invoked, it is difficult to rebut the notion of the "divine ordinance," and in so doing, Justice Bradley couched a misogynist assumption in rather lofty and untouchable rhetoric.[7]

---

[4] *Blackstone's Commentaries* [1966 ed.], t. 430, as quoted in Kay, Herma Hill, *Sex Discrimination and the Law* (West Publications, 1988, p. 913).

[5] Marital rape exemptions fell in many states in the late 1980s; however, a limited number of jurisdictions still cling to this vestige of women as chattel.

---

[6] 83 U.S. (16 Wall) 130, 141–142, 21 L.Ed. 442 (1873).

[7] Notwithstanding reference to a "divine ordinance," the doctrine of separation of church and state was not violated. The Court's decision and Bradley's concurrence did not establish a state religion. Rather, it put into perspective the val-

Such reliance on "divinity" formed the basis for Constitutional interpretations that denied women access to occupations and restricted the scope of their labor. By invoking "divine ordinance," the Court placed its imprimatur on a set of social values that defined women as reproductive instruments of the state.

In *Muller v. Oregon*, a decision that followed *Bradwell*, the Court clearly outlined its view of women in relationship to the state. Oregon had prohibited women from working in any mechanical establishment, factory, or laundry for more than 10 hours per day. Not less than three years before *Muller*, the Supreme Court in *Lochner* had declared restricting the hours of bakers as unconstitutional since such regulations violated the workers' liberty interest—the right to contract. The Court resolved this obvious conflict by focusing on the unique function of women's reproductive ability and its value to the state.

The *Muller* Court held that

As healthy mothers are essential to vigorous off-spring, the physical well-being of woman becomes an object of public interest in order to preserve the strength and vigor of the race. . . . The limitations which this statute places upon her contractual powers, upon her right to agree with her employer as to the time she shall labor are not imposed solely for her benefit, but also largely for the benefit of all. Many words cannot make this plainer. The two sexes differ in structure of body, in the functions to be performed by each, in the amount of physical strength . . . the influence of vigorous health upon the future well-being of the race, the self-reliance which enables one to assert full rights, and in the capacity to maintain the struggle for subsistence. This difference justifies a difference in legislation and upholds that which is designed to compensate for some of the burdens which rest upon her.[8]

By viewing women's reproductive ability as a tool for the state, the Court was comfortable in restricting women's ability to contract freely. Yet in the nineteenth century, the right to contract was considered a fundamental right. Restrictions on this right were rare and only in those instances where the Court believed that the state had a strong or compelling interest. Limiting women's right to contract was premised solely on the state's interest in protecting the reproductive functions of women. Clearly, fundamental rights were premised on gender, and women did not hold this right in the same manner as men. And such "protection" carried with it a profound price—the eradication of a fundamental right.

Although much has changed concerning women's participation in the "public sphere," equality for women remains an ongoing struggle. It is important to recognize that the modern improvements women experience in the workplace were won through women's tireless campaign to ensure equality and to improve the quality of life for workers.

In 1963, women won a critical battle with the passage of the Equal Pay Act. Prior to its passage, employers were permitted to discriminate in pay, based on sex, notwithstanding similar work. With the EPA, employers were barred from paying women less as long as the work performed was of essentially the same nature as that performed by their male counterparts.

When issues of comparable worth are raised, EPA analysis is of little benefit. The EPA does not require that men and women be paid the same. Rather, it requires that workers who perform the same job must be paid the same wage. Therefore, a woman firefighter could not be paid less than her male counterparts as long as she performed the same tasks. Sex alone was not sufficient to warrant a difference in pay. Where a wage differential is predicated on a "factor other than sex," e.g., market factors, this difference is permissible. Compa-

---

ues and mores of society at the time the decision was written. It is important to note, however, that the Court has explicitly relied on Judeo-Christian doctrine to deny protections afforded by the Fourteenth Amendment to such groups as gay men and lesbians (*Hardwick v. Bowers*).

[8]It is important to note that the control of women's procreative ability served two functions: Women of "Yankee stock"

---

should reproduce to propagate the (white) race, while immigrant and black women's reproductive ability was useful only in so much as their reproductive capabilities delivered future workers. *Muller v. Oregon;* 208 U.S. 412, 28 S. Ct. 324, 52 L.Ed 551 (1908).

rable worth cases have failed because litigants have been unable to demonstrate that pay differences are based on sex and the devaluation of women's work, rather than as a consequence of "market factors."

In the mid-1960s, the advent of the civil rights and women's movements brought substantial changes in employment opportunities for male members of the ethnic minority communities and for women. In 1964, the Civil Rights Acts were passed, and at the eleventh hour, at the behest of Rep. Martha Griffin, "sex" was added to Title VII of the Civil Rights Act. Title VII, in combination with various executive orders signed by President Johnson, paved the way for a sustained attack on gender asymmetry in the workplace.

Following passage of Title VII, it was unlawful to discriminate "against any individual with respect to . . . compensation, terms, conditions or privileges of employment because of that individual's race, color, religion, sex or national origin."[9] Additionally, with Johnson's executive orders in 1967, federal contractors were mandated to establish goals and timetables to eradicate past and/or continuing discrimination. The latter orders, commonly referred to as affirmative action programs, placed an affirmative burden on all recipients of federal moneys not only to hire qualified women and minorities but to construct a plan to compensate for past discrimination.

It was the affirmative action laws of the 1960s that opened up "nontraditional" job classifications for women and minorities. Women were finding both job training and employment in such industries as the building trades, uniform occupations (police, fire, and sanitation), and "white-collar" professions. These laws, in conjunction with Title IX of the Educational Amendments which prohibited sexism in educational programs, did much to open doors previously closed to women.

With the election of Ronald Reagan in 1980 and his subsequent appointments to the Supreme Court and the federal bench, the gains made by women in employment were systematically eroded. Various Supreme Court decisions weakened the affirmative action laws of the 1960s, and the promise of the Civil Rights Act was broken. In the next century, women will have to recapture lost ground, while helping construct a legal theory that attacks the root cause of gender asymmetry in the workplace. This is a difficult task because it raises issues concerning biologic difference and challenges long-held notions concerning equal protection. . . .

REPRODUCTIVE RIGHTS

The state's position concerning birth control and abortion has been nothing short of schizophrenic. According to the common law, abortions in the U.S. were permitted before "quickening," the period at which the fetus became ensouled. Prior to this point, the fetus was viewed as part of the mother's body, and abortions were not proscribed. In the mid-nineteenth century, this common-law distinction was eradicated as state after state passed new laws criminalizing abortion. By the end of the nineteenth century, abortion was illegal at any stage of pregnancy throughout the U.S.

During the mid-1960s and early 1970s, challenges to the states' restrictive birth control and abortion laws were undertaken. Where legislative reform seemed hopeless, feminists turned to the courts to identify and protect women's right to reproductive freedom.[10]

Central to a feminist politic was the belief that women's control over their bodies was a fundamental right. To deny women the right to decide when and if to procreate was a denial of a basic civil liberty. Overturning restrictive abortion and birth control laws became a primary political goal of the feminist civil rights struggles of this era.

Birth Control

In 1965, the Supreme Court struck down a Connecticut law that criminalized counseling for and using

---

[9]Title VII, Civil Rights Act, 1964.

[10]In 1970, New York state reformed its abortion laws. New York's new law was one of the most liberal abortion statutes, and it foreshadowed the *Roe* decision handed down by the U.S. Supreme Court in 1973.

contraceptives. The director of Planned Parenthood was convicted of providing a married couple with birth control information. She faced a possible fine and imprisonment of not less than 60 days and a maximum of one year. The case was appealed, and, after exhausting the state appellate process, the Supreme Court was petitioned to review the matter. In the now famous case of *Griswold v. Connecticut,* the Supreme Court ruled that the Connecticut statute was unconstitutional.

Writing for the majority, Justice William O. Douglas recognized that specific guarantees in the Bill of Rights "have penumbras, formed by emanations from those guarantees that help give them [the first ten amendments to the Constitution] life and substance . . . various guarantees create zones of privacy."[11] Douglas found that these zones of privacy included a marital right of privacy that was protected from intrusion by the state.

Central to the Court's analysis in *Griswold* was the belief that the decision to procreate is at the heart of a cluster of constitutionally protected choices. No doubt the Court was repulsed by the idea that the state could intrude into a married couple's bedroom to regulate sexual practices and behavior,[12] but it was the nature of the decision (procreation) that the Court found worthy of privacy protection.

Following *Griswold,* the Court expanded the right of privacy to unmarried individuals. In *Eisen-* *stadt v. Baird,* the Court struck down as unconstitutional a law that prohibited the distribution of contraceptives to unmarried persons. In *Eisenstadt,* the Court held that the liberty interest found in the Fourteenth Amendment involved a right of privacy, and "if the right of privacy [meant] anything, it [was] the right of the individual, married or single, to be free of unwarranted governmental intrusion into matters so fundamentally affecting a person as the decision whether to bear or beget a child."[13]

To the Court, marital status was irrelevant. What was critical and worthy of Constitutional protection was the decision to procreate. Such decisions, then, fell under the scope of Fourteenth Amendment protection.

Five years later, in *Carey v. Population Services,* the Supreme Court invalidated a New York law that regulated the availability of nonprescription contraceptives to minors.[14] Carey was a critical decision because it reaffirmed that women have a fundamental right not only to decide whether or not to procreate, but also to exercise that choice. Relying on *Roe v. Wade,* the abortion decision decided only four years earlier, the Court recognized that the right to decide or choose is meaningless without the right to access. In *Carey,* the Court strengthened the principle that women's reproductive freedom was more than a theoretical right. Rather, the exercise of this right was an inherent part of the "right to choose." In the context of human existence, anything less would make it meaningless.

Abortion Decisions

In 1973, the Supreme Court expanded fundamental rights protection to the right to decide to terminate a pregnancy. In *Roe v. Wade,* the majority held that the Fourteenth Amendment liberty interest involved a right of privacy concerning a woman's decision to terminate a pregnancy. The state could only intrude on that decision if there existed a compelling state interest, and the means chosen (regulatory plan) was narrowly drawn and closely tailored

---

[11] Since the Constitution does not specifically enumerate a right of privacy, the Court located this right in existing amendments and provisions. In doing this, the Court recognized that the Constitution is a living, breathing document, and that the already existing provisions, if understood historically and contextually, could accommodate a privacy right analysis. The Court did not create a "new right"; rather, it interpreted existing law as incorporating this right. See, by way of contrast, articles on original intent and strict constructionist theory.

[12] This repulsion was dissipated when the Court was faced with the question of whether a right of privacy extends to homosexuality. In *Hardwick v. Bowers,* the Court upheld a Georgia statute that criminalized sodomy (a sex act anything other than intercourse) even if the acts were between consenting adults. The majority was quite clear that the right of privacy did not extend to the homosexual bedroom. Lurking behind the *Hardwick* decision was the majority's reliance on Judeo-Christian dogma. See *Hardwick v. Bowers,* specifically the Burger concurring opinion and Blackmun's dissent.

[13] *Eisenstadt v. Baird, supra,* 405 U.S. at 453.
[14] *Carey v. Population Services,* 431 U.S. 678 (1977).

to the governmental objective. The burden, then, was on the state to justify its position and its methodology if they restricted access to abortion.

In *Roe*, and its companion case *Doe v. Bolton*, the Court did not vest women with an absolute right to terminate a pregnancy. Rather, it recognized that the state has a compelling interest to regulate abortion in order to protect the right of the fetus and maternal health.[15] The Court, then, did not view the issue through the prism of a woman's right to exercise control over her body; rather, the Court recognized competing rights and interests of the state and that of the fetus. In doing so, it set the stage for the erosion of the original premise that the fundamental right to decide when and if to procreate was at the center of a "cluster" of constitutionally protected choices located in the Fourteenth Amendment.

Finally, by recognizing fetal rights at the point of viability, the Court not only compromised women's bodily integrity, it subordinated her right to that of the fetus and the state. Under the scheme articulated by the Court, the state could proscribe abortions at the point of fetal viability. At this time in the pregnancy, set at the third trimester, the state can prohibit all abortions unless this procedure is necessary to save the life of the mother. The woman's fundamental right to decide (which included accessibility), then, is now lessened in relation to that of the fetus's right to life and the state's interest in protecting fetal life. At the point of viability, the rights and interests of the woman, the fetus, and the state all converge, and it is the woman's right that is subordinated.

From 1976 to 1992, there was a series of abortion decisions that chipped away at the fundamental right articulated in *Roe*. These decisions were the consequence of two important factors. First, with the election of Ronald Reagan in 1980 and of George Bush in 1988, an anti-women's rights political attitude was reflected in the federal appointments made by both presidents. Five Supreme Court Justices were appointed during this 8-year period.[16] The Supreme Court was being filled with jurists who were hostile to women's reproductive freedom.

Second, following *Roe*, the Right-to-Life (RTL) Movement went on the political offensive. Through a combination of direct political action (such as the Operation Rescue blockade of abortion clinics), election politics, and community-based politics, the abortion issue was cast from the perspective of the anti-women's rights activists.

During this period, Medicaid funds for abortion were cut off (*McRae v. Harris*), minors' rights were subordinated to parents' rights (*Webster* and *Casey*), mandatory waiting periods were imposed (*Webster* and *Casey*), and the state's interest in promoting childbirth was recognized and elevated to a compelling interest.

The combined effects of these decisions resulted in weakening women's fundamental right. Access was no longer an inherent part of the right to decide. Unlike the birth control decisions, the right to decide was construed in its literal form—the mental process of reaching a decision in a social vacuum. The Court then permitted a cutoff of Medicaid funds to poor women who wished to exercise their right to terminate a pregnancy. The Court believed that the state's cutoff did not place an affirmative burden on the decision-making process since the state did not create poverty.

The Court decision in *Harris* was sinister for two reasons. First, it removed access from contempla-

---

[15] The Court set up an intricate system to accommodate what it viewed as conflicting rights and interests. During the first trimester, a woman's right to terminate a pregnancy was paramount; therefore, the state could not proscribe abortion. During the second trimester, the state's interest in protecting maternal health was compelling; therefore, the state could regulate the procedure as long as accessibility to abortion was not restricted. In the third trimester (viability), the combined interest of the state in protecting fetal life and the fetus's right to life were sufficiently compelling as to permit proscription of abortion unless maternal life was at issue.

[16] Justices O'Connor, Kennedy, Scalia, Souter, and Thomas. Following the newest decision, *Casey*, it is clear that Thomas and Scalia are aligned with Chief Justice Rehnquist in his opposition to the right of privacy and the protections that this right affords women in deciding to terminate a pregnancy. O'Connor, Kennedy, and Souter are on the record in support of the right but would permit more extensive compromise of that right.

tion of what constitutes a right, thereby creating an abstract right. Second, it placed the state's interest in promoting childbirth on a par with a woman's right to reproductive freedom.[17] *Harris*, then, severely weakened *Roe* and women's right to choose.

In July of 1992, in *Planned Parenthood v. Casey*, the Court changed the compelling interest test to one of undue burden. This shifted the burden to women to prove that the state's actions were "unduly burdensome" before strict scrutiny could be triggered. This was a severe deviation from *Roe*, which had placed the onus on the state, thereby invoking strict scrutiny at the outset.

Although reaffirming *Roe*, *Casey* weakened the fundamental character of woman's right to terminate her pregnancy. Indeed, it is questionable at best if what remains of *Roe* is mere form over substance, since a woman's right to choose is no longer treated as a fundamental right.[18]

Conclusion

The Court's decisions in the abortion and birth control cases are dissimilar in one striking aspect. The birth control cases did not exorcise access from fundamental rights analysis. The fundamental character of an *individual's* right to decide to use contraceptives remains undisturbed. In contrast, in the abortion cases, a woman's fundamental right of privacy has been severely compromised. This is due in large part to who holds the right (women) with the convergence of "rights" now vested in the fetus and the state. Abortion, unlike birth control, implicates the fundamental right only of the woman. In birth control, the Court protected the right of women and men to decide (and act). It is no coincidence, then, that the right to terminate a pregnancy has been circumscribed according to the sex of the person who is vested with it.

VIOLENCE AGAINST WOMEN

The problem of violence against women is at once simple and quite complex. It is simple because it is so obvious—indeed, such violence is everywhere. Women are beaten, abused, raped, and tortured on the streets, in the boardroom, and in the bedroom. Statistics tell us that violence against women is the leading cause of injury to women—more than car accidents, more than office-related accidents, and more than drug-related incidents.[19] Women are beaten, shot, and stabbed to death, not at the hands of strangers but by the men closest to them. In New York City in 1988, over 20,000 petitions for orders of protection were filed in New York County Family Court. Nationwide, 40% of all homicide victims are female; of that number, over 90% were killed by their husbands or boyfriends. Women are killed by intimates at a rate six times higher than men.[20]

The question is: Why are women killed and beaten at epidemic proportions?[21] Simply put, violence against women has been legally sanctioned and socially condoned. Wife-beating was legal, and marital rape is still sanctioned in some jurisdictions. This privilege extended to males was a direct outgrowth of the legal doctrine of "femme couverte," or "covered woman." Under this doctrine, women's legal existence was suspended or subsumed in that of the males. In the eyes of the law, women were invisible and, within the home, subject to the tyranny of the

---

[17]At issue in *Harris* was the Hyde Amendment, which restricted Medicaid funds for pregnant poor women. Under Hyde, the federal government would reimburse states only for prenatal care and birthing. If a poor woman wanted to exercise her right to terminate her pregnancy, no federal funds could be used. In effect, due to the cost of hospitalization, poor women would have no other choice but to carry to term or revert to back-alley abortions. The framers of Hyde justified this total ban on poor women's right to abort in the state's right to promote and favor childbirth. The Court recognized this interest. Moreover, it held that since the state did not create poverty, it was under no affirmative duty to ensure that poor women could actualize their decision to abort. The dissent in *Harris* understood the effects of the majority decision. Characterizing the majority decision as callous, the dissenters recognized that *Harris* obliterated the access component of a right—but only for poor women.

[18]It is important to note that the Court is *one* vote away from overturning *Roe*. As Justice Blackmun, the architect of *Roe*, commented: "I am 83 years old. I shall not be on this Court much longer."

[19]FBI Statistics, 1989.
[20]Department of Justice Statistics, 1990.
[21]Indeed, the U.S. Surgeon General has stated that domestic violence is the chief health risk faced by women.

husband. Husbands could offer "subtle chastisement" or beat their wives as they beat their children.[22]

This cultural position vis-à-vis women's relationship to men in the family influenced American jurisprudence. The states codified this misogyny. Indeed, the decriminalization of assaults in the family and the marital rape exemption were a direct result of such misogyny in the law.

Prior to 1962 in New York state, assaults in the family that were low-level felonies if committed by strangers were routinely handled in family court. If a case managed to find its way into criminal court, it was automatically transferred because the criminal courts lacked "subject matter" jurisdiction.[23] Following hearings in the State Capitol, hearings that detailed the horrific violence experienced by women, New York modified its laws, and cases previously barred from prosecution were, theoretically, prosecutable under existing penal law statutes.

During the 1960s and 1970s, feminists were challenging the gender asymmetry of the laws involving "domestic violence." One such challenge called into question police-arrest avoidance in domestic violence cases. In *Bruno v. Codd,* the New York City Police Department (NYPD) was sued because line officers were refusing to arrest boyfriends and husbands accused of beating their girlfriends and wives. The plaintiffs in *Bruno* proved that the police were mediating cases even where the woman was beaten with a weapon. Clearly, the doctrine of "subtle chastisement" affected police performance.

A settlement agreement flowed from *Bruno,* and the NYPD assured battered women and their advocates that they would, at the very least, exercise discretion. Therefore, when responding to domestic violence incidents, the police would assess whether an arrest was warranted rather than engage in a *de facto* refusal to arrest in cases where the victim and assailant were known to each other.

In *Sorichetti v. NYPD,* all discretion was removed from police where violations of a court order of protection were at issue. In *Sorichetti,* the police refused to enforce an order of protection which mandated that the noncustodial father return the minor child at 5:00 p.m. following visitation and that he refrain from harassing and assaultive conduct.

The father in this case has been adjudicated an abuser in the New York Family Court, and he was known to the police as a "wife beater." When Ms. Sorichetti appealed to the police to look for her daughter and her ex-husband, she was rebuffed. Yet her fear was well grounded. After Ms. Sorichetti had dropped her daughter off for a visit with the father, he had made a death threat. In addition, he had failed to return the child at the time prescribed by the Court. The death threat and the failure to adhere to the time schedule constituted two separate violations of the order. Yet, notwithstanding a valid court order, two violations of the order, and a state law which said that the police should arrest where there has been a violation of an order of protection, the police refused to act.

Following repeated requests for assistance to enforce the order, the police searched for and found young Dina Sorichetti. Her father had carried through on his threat by attempting to dismember the child. In this case, the Court awarded Ms. Sorichetti and her daughter $2.3 million for the police's failure to enforce the order, which resulted in a failure to protect her and her daughter. As a result of this damage award, the NYPD changed its police procedures, mandating a must-arrest policy where there is probable cause to believe that an order of protection has been violated.

Such New York cases illustrate that the gender asymmetry in law has resulted in unequal protection for female citizens.[24]

Rape

Marital Rape Exemption   The marital rape exemption was a vestige of the common-law system that viewed women as inferior to men and as sub-

---

[22] See *Blackstone's Commentaries, supra.*
[23] See NYS Family Court Act Section 813 and Besharov's Commentaries.

[24] See also *Thurman v. Torrington.* Here, the police did nothing while Tracy Thurman's husband stomped on her face, threw her to the ground, and choked her. The police claimed that their refusal to arrest was premised on the fact that this was a domestic dispute.

jects of their husbands. At the core of this system was the view that a woman is the property of either her husband or her father. The purpose of rape law generally was to preserve the "value" of the sexual object.[25] Under Mosaic law, the rapist of a virgin was penalized by forcing him to pay the bride price to the father to marry the woman.[26] Under ancient Babylonian law, criminal rape was the "theft of virginity, an embezzlement of the woman's fair price on the market."[27] These ancient laws found themselves in Western jurisprudence. According to common law, the female victim could save her attacker from death by marriage.[28]

Within the family and against a third party, the husband had a property interest in the body and a right to the "personal enjoyment of his wife."[29] Moreover, since the person of the married woman merged into that of the husband, it was a legal impossibility to hold the husband accountable for rape because it would be as if he were charged with raping himself.

Finally, based on the marital contract, because a woman was incapable of withholding consent, rape of one's wife was a legal nullity. As Lord Matthew Hale stated in the seventeenth century:

> But the husband cannot be guilty of rape committed by himself upon his lawful wife, for by their mutual matrimonial consent and contract, the wife hath given up *herself in this kind unto her husband which she cannot retract* [emphasis added].[30]

Jurisdictions accepted Hale's notion without any question and codified this exemption into their statutes.[31] States then willingly constructed a system of unequal justice based on marital status and gender. Indeed, the laws were allowed to stand in the face of the Fourteenth Amendment and various state constitutions, which incorporated equal protection standards from the federal constitution into their own. Woman as sexual property of the husband superseded the right of female citizens to be secure in their persons.

The marital rape exemptions of most jurisdictions did not fall until the 1980s. With the re-emergence of the battered women's and anti-rape movements, the states were confronted with legal challenges to these exemptions. Based on federal and state equal protection laws, the highest courts in the various states struck these provisions as constitutionally offensive.[32]

Rape: A Category of Crime Unto Itself   Cultural misogyny found its way into the rules of evidence as well as into the states' penal laws. Rape, therefore, was treated unlike any other crime. Up until recently, women's testimony was considered incredible as a matter of law. States, therefore, enacted strict corroboration requirements in sexual assault (rape) and sodomy cases.[33]

Under the independent corroboration rule, the testimony of the victim was insufficient to sustain an indictment for rape. The state needed evidence of a "different character" to make out every element of the crime. Therefore, to prove that the sex act had occurred, one would need either physical trauma to the vaginal or anal area, or evidence of semen. To prove the identity of the defendant, if unknown to the victim, one would need a witness. To meet the sufficiency burden concerning consent, evidence of bodily injury was critical. Rape is the only crime that required its victim to be victimized again—via assault (physical injury).

In addition, because most states required that force be viewed through the eyes of the defendant,

[25] See S. Brownmiller, *Against Our Will: Men, Women, and Rape* (New York: Simon & Schuster, 1975, p. 9).
[26] Deuteronomy 22:13–29.
[27] Brownmiller, p. 9.
[28] Rape and Battery Between Husband and Wife, 6 Stan. L.Rev. 719 724 & n. 269 1954.
[29] *Oppenheim v. Krindel*, 140 N.E. 227, 228 (1923).
[30] I. Hale, *History of Pleas of the Crown;* pp. 6–9, as quoted in Kay, Herma Hill, *Sex Discrimination and the Law* (West Publications, 1992, p. 911).
[31] See *People v. Meli*, 19 NYS 365 (1922).

[32] See *People v. Liberta*, 64 NY 2d 152 [1984].
[33] Usually, such corroboration requirements exist when the victim (complainant) is either a minor or mentally incompetent. Under these circumstances, minors and mental incompetents could not normally testify under oath. Therefore, to sustain a conviction, the state needed independent corroboration to support the uncorroborated testimony of the victim. Such complainants were viewed, due to age and mental status, as legally incompetent.

where he interposed a reasonable belief that the victim consented, this operated as a complete defense. The level of fear, actual or perceived by the victim, was irrelevant in these jurisdictions.

Finally, women's character was under attack at trials involving rape charges. The prevailing defense theory was that if the complainant consented to sex once, this operated as a blanket consent and was relevant to the issue of "force" in current prosecution. It was not uncommon for a victim's past sexual history to be paraded before the Court.

Feminists systematically challenged the independent corroboration rules and the evidentiary "fishing expeditions" into the victim's prior sexual history. As a result, states passed rape shield laws and repealed the independent corroboration rule.

Nevertheless, because misogynist attitudes die hard, rape convictions are difficult to achieve where the victim has had a sexual life or has had a dating relationship with the defendant. The underlying premise is that a woman is not empowered to refuse sexual advances, especially when she has either socialized or had an intimate relationship with the defendant. Hence, marital rape, date rape, and acquaintance rape cases are still very difficult to prosecute. Juries are loathe to convict under these circumstances: They will do everything in their power to discredit the victim while crediting the defendant.

Although the law has been reformed to, theoretically, treat women as full human beings, these reforms are slow to take effect. This is because the justice system is still influenced by attitudes that view women as sexual property, reproductive instruments of the state, and unworthy of belief. Such attitudes shape police practices, prosecutorial discretion, judicial rulings, and jury verdicts.[34]

Creating systemic change will require the infu-sion of feminist politics at every level of the justice system, from the police to the courts. We will also need to evaluate the feminist theory and practice that has developed during the past decade to make sure that they adequately represent women's lives and defend women's rights. For example, the idea of the battered woman's syndrome was first developed by Lenore Walker to explain to juries why women who killed their assailants felt they had no choice even though there was a break in the violence. Further research and analysis has shown, however, that such situations often are, in fact, life-threatening to the woman. It does a disservice to the woman to refer to a psychological state rather than to see her as someone who has reasonably appraised her choices. Perhaps the real challenge of the twenty-first century will be to transform a legal system crafted to protect male power into one that brings women to the center of human discourse. *We* can then create a new legal tradition in which women's experience is no longer marginal.   [1992]

60

How to Bring Children Up Without Putting Women Down

ANN CRITTENDON

The feminist task is neither to glorify nor discount the differences between men and women, but to challenge the adverse consequences of whatever differences there may be.
—Christine Littleton

In the early spring of 1995, I attended an international conference in the fashionably faded Villa Schifanoia, a Renaissance estate in the elegant Florentine suburb of Fiesole. The topic was "The Cost of Being a Mother; the Cost of Being a Father."

The meetings were conducted in an ornate, high-ceilinged former theater hung with tapestries. Some fifty assembled scholars from Europe, the United States, and the United Kingdom listened through

---

[34]See New York State Task Force Report on Women in the Courts (1985), in which a judicial commission documented the misogyny in the justice system. It found that women litigants, rape victims, domestic violence victims, as well as female attorneys, were all treated with disrespect and in many cases with outright contempt. In New York, as in most states, women still await the full benefits of legal personage before the law.

headsets to simultaneous translations as they sat beneath murals of cherubs playing lyres. Between sessions, the participants strolled through the grounds along avenues of stately cypress trees.

I had gone to this unlikely setting to get beyond the often sterile American debate over family values and the work-family conflict, by learning more about other advanced countries' policies toward caregivers. Were the Europeans really as successful as they are said to be in protecting mothers and children from poverty? Had they been able to promote caring for others without hindering women's progress in all the other arenas of work and life?

What I learned at this gathering, sponsored by the European University Institute, was heartening. First, despite severe budget cuts in virtually every European country, not one government was cutting its generous maternal and child benefits, with the important exception of reduced subsidies for child care in the former East Germany. In recent elections in both France and Norway, politicians had even competed over how to increase governmental support for families.

The American assumption that Europe can no longer afford its investment in good care for those who need it is clearly not shared by most Europeans. The public strongly supports policies that have kept poverty among children and their mothers substantially lower than in the United States. . . .

Moreover, the European debate seems to be more candid about the fact that family support issues are very much women's issues. The conference itself was organized around the idea that the costs of caring have to be better understood and more fairly shared between men and women and by society as a whole. Several commentators noted that unless this cost sharing occurs, women will never escape a precarious, semidependent economic status.

The implicit assumption in all of the papers presented was that caring needs to be conceptualized as work if it is ever to be properly valued socially, legally, or economically. By the same token, those who provide care, unpaid as well as paid, must be seen as productive citizens who deserve the same social rights as all other workers and citizens. . . .

The United States is not Europe, and Americans may never accept the kind of compassionate capitalism or caring state that western Europeans demand. But it doesn't strike me as beyond our reach to revise a new social contract as well. I can easily imagine adding care to our pantheon of national values, along with liberty, justice, and the pursuit of happiness through the pursuit of money.

But this will never happen unless women demand it. Women have to insist that caretaking and early education can no longer depend on their cheap or unpaid labor. And before that can happen, women have to understand that the true costs of care include their exclusion from full participation in the economy and in society.[1]

The only way women can achieve equal citizenship is for the entire society to contribute to the provision of a public good that everyone desires: well-raised children who will mature into productive, law-abiding citizens. And that means that all free riders—from employers to governments to husbands to communities—have to pitch in and help make the most important job in the world a top national priority—and a very good job. . . .

EMPLOYERS: REDESIGN WORK AROUND PARENTAL NORMS

Give Every Parent the Right to a Year's Paid Leave

In 1997, American pediatricians officially recommended that new mothers breast-feed for a full year. This was a sick joke in a country that entitles new mothers to no paid leave at all. American mothers are guaranteed only three months' maternity leave without pay—forcing most working mothers to return to their jobs within a few weeks after giving birth, because they can't afford to take three months off without a paycheck.[2] As a consequence, poor mothers are far less likely to breast-feed than their better-off sisters, and infants as young as six weeks are going into day care, with some spending as many as ten hours a day in group settings. No other women or children in the industrialized world are forced to live under these conditions, which child development experts agree are deplorable, if not downright harmful.

Those concerned about family values or parental neglect of children could find no better place to attack the problem than by demanding a paid leave, which could be shared by both parents, of at least one year. This would do more to improve infant care, increase family income, enhance fathers' emotional ties to their offspring, and promote economic equality between husbands and wives than almost any other single measure.

More generous leaves allowing parents to stay home with a sick child are also essential. Fewer than half of working parents stay home when their children are sick, even though research shows that sick children recover more quickly when a parent is there.[3] According to a recent survey by the AFL-CIO, 54 percent of working women are not entitled to any paid leave for taking care of a sick child or other family member.

Corporate lobbyists have vehemently opposed the most minimal paid parental or family leaves, claiming that the cost would bankrupt American business. This is blatantly untrue. Generous paid parental leaves are a basic right in every other economically advanced nation, and in none of them does business have to foot the entire bill. In some countries the leaves are paid for by contributions of employers and employees to the national old-age insurance system; in others they come out of general tax revenues or some combination of taxes, Social Security, and employer or employee insurance funds.

The costs to the economy can be offset by reduced turnover and the creation of a wider labor pool of women who will remain in the paid workforce if they don't have to quit to take care of an infant or a sick child.

Shorten the Workweek

Experts estimate that roughly 5 to 7 million American children are left unattended at home every day. Why? Because parents of young children don't have the right to work a day that coincides with the school day.

In Sweden, parents can opt to work a six-hour day until their children are eight years old. In the Netherlands the official workweek is thirty-six hours, and workers have a right to a four-day week. The legal workweek in France was reduced from thirty-nine to thirty-five hours in 2000, and pressure is rising for the rest of Europe to follow suit.[4]

American parents have complained for years that they need a shorter workweek, but for many the workday is getting steadily longer instead. The average workweek has crept up to almost forty-eight hours for professionals and managers, and even so-called part-time work is now edging toward forty hours a week. . . .

Despite their adamant opposition, American companies might discover gains in a shorter workweek. Overwork-related stress disorders, absenteeism, and turnover would surely be reduced, and productivity in some cases improved, as a number of French companies have already discovered.

Provide Equal Pay and Benefits for Equal Part-time Work

A shorter workweek would have to be accompanied by a federal law requiring companies to pay part-time workers at the same hourly rates as full-timers doing the same job, as well as prorated fringe benefits, including vacations, sick leave, and inclusion in company pension plans. Currently, only about 22 percent of part-time workers have any health insurance, compared with 78 percent of full-time workers, and only 26 percent have any private pensions, compared with 60 percent of full-timers. These inequities give employers a huge incentive to hire nonstandard workers—most of them mothers—on cheap, exploitative terms.

A model for ending the exploitation and marginalization of part-time work has been established in the Netherlands, where one-third of all jobs are now part-time. Dutch part-timers enjoy all of the benefits that accrue to full-time workers, on a prorated basis. The Canadian province of Saskatchewan has also set a precedent by becoming the first jurisdiction in North America to rewrite its labor laws to extend benefits to part-time workers.

Eliminate Discrimination Against Parents in the Workplace

Only eight states currently have laws prohibiting parental discrimination. Although such bias is hard to quantify, parents believe that it is widespread. One obvious example would be people who are penalized for declining to work overtime because of family responsibilities.

In the 1997 Massachusetts case of *Upton v. JWP Businessland,* a single mother working as a store manager brought suit for wrongful dismissal after she was fired for refusing to work much longer hours than she had originally been hired to do, including all day Saturday. The woman argued that the compulsory overtime would prevent her from being an adequate mother to her son—indeed she would scarcely be able to see him. Yet the Massachusetts Supreme Judicial Court ruled against her. The court decided that state contract law permitted at-will employees to be fired "for any reason or for no reason at all" unless the firing violates a "clearly established" public policy. It found that Massachusetts had no public policy dealing with the responsibility of a parent to care for his or her child.[5] Perhaps it is time for governments to establish such policies.

GOVERNMENT: REPLACE THE WELFARE STATE WITH A CARING STATE

Equalize Social Security for Spouses

Under this reform, both spouses would automatically earn equal Social Security credits during their marriage. They would combine these credits with whatever credits they might have earned before or after marriage, for their own individual retirement benefits. This so-called earnings sharing would increase benefits for working and stay-at-home mothers alike, and for divorced women, who are among the poorest old people in the country.

Currently, the Social Security system penalizes anyone who spends time working as an unpaid caregiver, and anyone who earns significantly less than their spouse—that is, the great majority of married mothers. In 1992 Congress issued a report on the inequities surrounding women and retirement, with the intention of launching a national debate on the

issue. But the expected debate never occurred. As soon as the new 1994 Republican Congress came into power, it abolished the Select Committee on Aging that had issued the report.

The avatars of free enterprise had a very different debate in mind. Soon we began to hear about privatization of Social Security: allowing individuals to keep and invest for themselves money that would have gone into the Social Security Trust Fund.

One of the versions of privatization favored by Republicans would allow a sizable portion of a person's Social Security contributions to be put into a so-called PSA: a personal savings account to be invested as he or she saw fit. At retirement everyone would receive a flat minimum stipend from Social Security plus whatever had accumulated in their PSA.

This scheme would mean that the spouse who makes the home, wipes the runny noses, kisses away the bruises, cuts the corners off her own career, and earns less money would not necessarily have a stake in the accumulated savings of her family. There would be no "family" savings, only "personal" savings. The millions of women who are primary caregivers would have smaller PSAs than their husbands, to match their lower lifetime earnings. If they wanted anything more than a below-subsistence retirement income, they would either have to go out and earn their own money to invest for themselves or have to "depend on what he felt like giving her," according to attorney Edith Fierst. It would be hard to dream up a more anticaregiver retirement plan.

If any version of privatization ever does occur, it should mandate an FSA—a family savings account—for all married couples with children, jointly owned by both spouses, rather than individual PSAs that would allow the big breadwinner to salt away most of the family savings and future retirement income as his own. An alternative would be simply to give Social Security credits to family caregivers. Both France and Germany give women pension credits for time spent out of the labor market caring for family members, young or old. During the 2000 election campaign such a "caregiver's credit" was proposed by Vice President Albert Gore. He would credit any stay-at-home parent with $16,500 annual income for up to five years. This would lift the bene-fits of as many as 8 million people, almost all of them mothers, by an average of $600 a year.

Offer Work-Related Social Insurance Programs to All Workers

The artificial distinction between "members of the labor force," who work for wages, and those who provide unpaid care should be abolished. A "worker" would be defined as anyone who either is employed in the provision of goods and services or is engaged in the unpaid provision of care and services to dependent adults and children. Primary caregivers would be considered to be "in the labor force," and eligible for temporary unemployment compensation and job training in the event of divorce, and workmen's compensation for job-related injuries.

Provide Universal Preschool for All Three- and Four-Year-Olds

A caring state would also guarantee that all children have access to developmental education in their critical early years. In the nineteenth century the United States led the world in establishing free public education for all children starting at age six. The early twentieth century saw the expansion of public education through high school. Yet the country has become a laggard in providing young children with the early education that can prepare them for success in school and in life. This failure to invest in human capital is surely one major reason why one out of every six adult Americans is functionally illiterate.

The remedy is universal preschool for all American three- and four-year-olds. We have seen that quality early education is beyond the means of most parents, just as most parents cannot afford the full costs of primary or secondary education. Even middle-class families are routinely priced out of licensed nursery schools and child-care centers. According to the Census Bureau, child care is the single biggest expense of young families, after housing and food.

Among low-income families, government-subsidized early education and child care is so scarce that only about one-twelfth of the poor families who are eligible for subsidies receive them, according to a 1999 study by the Department of Health and Human Services.[6]

No state offers universal early education to three-year-olds, and only one state, Georgia, offers subsidized preschool to every four-year-old (although in 2000 Oklahoma and New York were also starting to take steps in that direction).

The practical effect of this neglect is to deny an early education to poor children, who are the very ones who need it the most. Nationally, only 36 percent of three- to five-year-olds from families earning less than $15,000 a year attend any kind of pre-kindergarten, compared with 79 percent from families earning more than $75,000.

In France, by contrast, 99 percent of three- to five-year-olds attend preschools at no or minimum charge. The French government also finances a licensed network of subsidized crèches, where 20 percent of younger children are cared for in a family setting. . . .

Stop Taxing Mothers More Than Anyone Else

We know that children as well as women benefit when mothers have significant control over family income and some financial independence. . . . One of the fairest, most effective ways of accomplishing this would be to lower taxes on mothers' incomes, as opposed to family tax cuts per se. . . .

The current tax regime, like the Social Security system, was set up between the 1930s and 1950s with a traditional male breadwinner, dependent female spouse in mind. To some degree intentionally, the tax laws discourage two-earner families at all income levels by taxing the lower-earning spouse at much higher rates than the primary earner.

The government could actually raise more revenue, without lowering families' income by a penny, by taxing married men more and married women less. Economists have discovered that in response to high tax rates, married women do shift from work outside the home to unpaid work in the home, while lower taxes, and more take-home pay, draw them back into the paid labor force. When taxes go up for married men, by contrast, either their work patterns are not affected by the change, or, if anything, the men work harder to make up for the loss of income. . . .

One simple way to remedy this tax bias against married working mothers is to restore separate filing of federal income tax returns, as was done in the United States before 1948. Separate filing, the most common method of taxing married persons in other advanced democracies would currently put the first $10,000 earned by the secondary earner, usually the mother, in a zero tax bracket, rather than having every dollar of her income taxed at the family's highest marginal rate. Separate filing would also eliminate the anachronistic designation of one spouse as "head of household" and the other as "spouse." I may earn less money than my husband, but that doesn't make him the "head of the household" and me the "spouse." Let us file and be taxed (or not taxed) separately, as financial equals in the family.

A mother's taxes could also be reduced considerably by allowing her to deduct child-care expenditures. If business executives can deduct half the cost of meals and entertainment as a legitimate cost of doing business, then surely the family's primary caregiver should be allowed to deduct the cost of substitute child care as a business expense, which it certainly is.

A Child Allowance; or Social Security for Children

The big problem with tax deductions and tax credits for children and for child care is that tax breaks do nothing for the roughly 30 percent of parents whose income is so low they pay no federal taxes. Far better than tinkering with the tax code would be a *child allowance* paid to *all* primary caregivers of young children, whether they work outside the home or not. Such a "salary" for every mother is paid in a number of countries, including Britain and France, and is truly neutral regarding parents' decisions on how to raise their children, for the money can be used either to help pay for child care or to help pay the bills in households where one parent stays home.

A child allowance, with the check made out to the person who is the family's primary caregiver, would target children far more effectively than a "family tax cut." Tax cuts, including the child tax credit, increase the income of the major breadwinner—and not even that in families who earn too little to pay income taxes. Child-care deductions, for their part, don't help families where the mother provides the care. An allowance, or "family wage" paid directly to caregivers, would help all families with kids. It could be paid out of a Children's Trust Fund, similar to the Social Security Trust Fund, supported by a dedicated income stream, possibly including contributions from employers and employees, as in the case of Social Security. One version of the family wage idea calls it Social Security for Children.

Provide Free Health Coverage for All Children and Their Primary Caregivers

Another minimal element in a caring state is adequate health insurance for *all* dependents, including children as well as the elderly and disabled. An American journalist whose wife recently had a baby in Paris discovered how nice it is to live in a place that values maternal and child health more highly. "[I] have become French enough to feel, stubbornly," he wrote, "that in a prosperous society all pregnant women should have three sonograms and four nights in a hospital if they want to. . . . It doesn't seem aristocratically spoiled to think that a woman should keep her job and have some paid leave afterward. . . . All human desires short of simple survival are luxurious, and a mother's desire to have a slightly queenly experience of childbirth . . . seems as well worth paying for as a tobacco subsidy or another tank."[7]

Even in Britain, where the Darwinian struggle was invented, all new mothers receive several home visits from a nurse to ensure that everything is going well. Among other things, the nurses make sure that new mothers have a grasp of the techniques of successful breast-feeding. In the United States, by contrast, new mothers are routinely sent home from hospitals after one day, often knowing less about babies than they do about their cat. Recently, a young American mother was indicted for manslaughter because she didn't know enough about breast-feeding to realize that her baby was slowly starving to death."[8]

Add Unpaid Household Labor to the GDP

A final, and relatively cheap, step the government could take toward valuing unpaid child care would be to include it in the GDP. In the early 1990s, the United Nations Statistical Commission recommended that member countries prepare so-called satellite GDP accounts estimating the value of unremunerated work. Countries all over the globe are complying.   [2001]

NOTES

1. For an elaboration of this point, see Mona Harrington, *Care and Equality* (New York: Knopf, 1999).
2. Jacob Alex Kierman and Arleen Leibowitz, "The Work-Employment Distinction Among New Mothers," *Journal of Human Resources* 29, no. 2 (spring 1994): 296. Unfortunately, another female boss who separated a new mother from her job was Washington senator Patty Murray, who had campaigned as "a Mom in tennis shoes" with the promise that as a woman she could understand other women's problems. But apparently not enough; her legislative aide Pam Norick was forced to resign after becoming pregnant with her second baby. The story is summarized by Clara Bingham in *Women on the Hill* (New York: Times Books, 1997), pp. 114–15, 253.
3. Alvin Powell, "Parents' Presence Helps Heal Children," *Harvard University Gazette*, November 4, 1999.
4. Suzanne Daley, "A French Paradox at Work," *New York Times*, November 11, 1999. In France not even managers are supposed to work more than thirty-nine hours a week.
5. See Mona Harrington, *Care and Equality*, pp. 51–52, 153.
6. Raymond Hernandez, "Millions in State Child Care Funds Going Unspent in New York," *New York Times*, October 25, 1999.
7. Adam Gopnik, "Like a King," *New Yorker*, January 31, 2000.
    The mother was subsequently committed on a lesser charge and released on probation. Among the conditions of her release was a requirement that she attend parenting classes.
8. The mother, a poor, twenty-one-year-old living in the Bronx, was subsequently convicted of criminally negligent homicide, despite the fact that she had twice taken the baby to her HMO for checkups and been turned away because the baby's Medicaid card hadn't yet arrived in the mail. She was sentenced to five years' probation, including a condition that if she had another child during the probation period, she take parenting classes. See Katha Pollitt, "A Bronx Tale," *The Nation*, June 14, 1999; Nina Bernstein, "Mother Convicted in Infant's Starvation Death Gets 5 Years' Probation," *New York Times*, September 9, 1999.

🌿 61

Exploding the Stereotypes: Welfare

RITA HENLEY JENSEN

I am a woman. A white woman, once poor but no longer. I am not lazy, never was. I am a middle-aged woman, with two grown daughters. I was a welfare mother, one of those women society considers less than nothing.

I should have applied for Aid to Families with Dependent Children when I was 18 years old, pregnant with my first child, and living with a boyfriend who slapped me around. But I didn't.

I remember talking it over at the time with a friend. I lived in the neighborhood that surrounds the vast Columbus campus of Ohio State University. Students, faculty, hangers-on, hippies, runaways, and recent émigrés from Kentucky lived side by side in the area's relatively inexpensive housing. I was a runaway.

On a particularly warm midsummer's day, I stood on High Street, directly across from the campus' main entrance, with an older, more sophisticated friend, wondering what to do with my life. With my swollen belly, all hope of my being able to cross the street and enroll in the university had evaporated. Now, I was seeking advice about how merely to survive, to escape the assaults and still be able to care for my child.

My friend knew of no place I could go, nowhere I could turn, no one else I could ask. I remember saying in a tone of resignation, "I can't apply for welfare." Instead of disagreeing with me, she nodded, acknowledging our mutual belief that taking beatings was better than taking handouts. Being "on the dole" meant you deserved only contempt.

In August 1965, I married my attacker.

Six years later, I left him and applied for assistance. My children were 18 months and five and a half years old. I had waited much too long. Within a year, I crossed High Street to go to Ohio State. I graduated in four years and moved to New York City to attend Columbia University's Graduate School of Journalism. I have worked as a journalist for 18 years now. My life on welfare was very hard—there were times when I didn't have enough food for the three of us. But I was able to get an education while on welfare. It is hardly likely that a woman on AFDC today would be allowed to do what I did, to go to school and develop the kind of skills that enabled me to make a better life for myself and my children.

This past summer, I attended a conference in Chicago on feminist legal theory. During the presentation of a paper related to gender and property rights, the speaker mentioned as an aside that when one says "welfare mother" the listener hears "black welfare mother." A discussion ensued about the underlying racism until someone declared that the solution was easy: all that had to be done was have the women in the room bring to the attention of the media the fact that white women make up the largest percentage of welfare recipients. At this point, I stood, took a deep breath, stepped out of my professional guise, and informed the crowd that I was a former welfare mother. Looking at my white hair, blue eyes, and freckled Irish skin, some laughed; others gasped—despite having just acknowledged that someone like me was, in fact, a "typical" welfare mother.

Occasionally I do this. Speak up. Identify myself as one of "them." I do so reluctantly because welfare mothers are a lightning rod for race hatred, class prejudice, and misogyny. Yet I am aware that as long as welfare is viewed as an *African American* woman's issue, instead of a *woman's* issue—whether that woman be white, African American, Asian, Latina, or Native American—those in power can continue to exploit our country's racism to weaken and even eliminate public support for the programs that help low-income mothers and their children.

I didn't have the guts to stand up during a 1974 reception for Ohio state legislators. The party's hostess was a leader of the Columbus chapter of the National Organization for Women and she had opened up her suburban home so that representatives of many of the state's progressive organizations could lobby in an informal setting for an increase in the state's welfare allotment for families. I was invited as a representative of the campus area's single mothers' support group. In the living room, I came across a state senator in a just-slightly-too-warm-and-friendly state induced by the potent combination of free booze and a crowd of women. He quickly decided I looked like a good person to amuse with one of his favorite jokes. "You want to know how a welfare mother can prevent getting pregnant?" he asked, giggling. "She can just take two aspirin—and put them between her knees," he roared, as he bent down to place his Scotch glass between his own, by way of demonstration. I drifted away.

I finally did gather up my courage to speak out. It was in a classroom during my junior year. I was enrolled in a course on the economics of public policy because I wanted to understand why the state of Ohio thought it desirable to provide me and my two kids with only $204 per month—59 percent of what even the state itself said a family of three needed to live.

For my required oral presentation, I chose "Aid to Families with Dependent Children." I cited the fact that approximately two thirds of all the poor families in the country were white; I noted that most welfare families consisted of one parent and two children. As an audiovisual aid, I brought my own two kids along. My voice quavered a bit as I delivered my intro: I stood with my arms around my children and said, "We are a typical AFDC family."

My classmates had not one question when I finished. I don't believe anyone even bothered to ask the kids' names or ages.

If I were giving this talk today, I would hold up a picture of us back then and say we still represent typical welfare recipients. The statistics I would cite to back up that statement have been refined since the 1970s and now include "Hispanic" as a category. In 1992, 38.9 percent of all welfare mothers were white, 37.2 percent were black, 17.8 percent were "Hispanic," 2.8 percent were Asian, and 1.4 percent were Native American.

My report, however, would focus on the dramatic and unrelenting reduction in resources available to low-income mothers in the last two decades.

Fact: In 1970, the average monthly benefit for a

family of three was $178. Not much, but consider that as a result of inflation, that $178 would be approximately $680 today. And then consider that the average monthly payment today is only about $414. That's the way it's been for more than two decades: the cost of living goes up (by the states' own accounting, the cost of rent, food, and utilities for a family of three has doubled), but the real value of welfare payments keeps going down.

Fact: The 1968 Work Incentive Program (the government called it WIN; we called it WIP) required that all unemployed adult recipients sign up for job training or employment once their children turned six. The age has now been lowered to three, and states may go as low as age one. What that means is you won't be able to attend and finish college while on welfare. (In most states a college education isn't considered job training, even though experts claim most of us will need college degrees to compete in the workplace of the twenty-first century.)

Fact: Forty-two percent of welfare recipients will be on welfare less than two years during their entire lifetime, and an additional 33 percent will spend between two and eight years on welfare. The statistics haven't changed much over the years: women still use welfare to support their families when their children are small.

In 1974, I ended my talk with this joke: A welfare mother went into the drugstore and bought a can of deodorant. I explained that it was funny because everyone knew that welfare mothers could not afford "extras" like personal hygiene products. My joke today would be: A welfare mother believed that if elected public officials understood these facts, they would not campaign to cut her family's benefits.

The idea that government representatives care about welfare mothers is as ridiculous to me now as the idea back then that I would waste my limited funds on deodorant. It is much clearer to me today what the basic functions of welfare public policy are at this moment in U.S. history.

By making war on welfare recipients, political leaders can turn the public's attention away from the government's redistribution of wealth to the wealthy. Recent studies show that the United States has become the most economically stratified of industrial nations. In fact, Federal Reserve figures reveal that the richest 1 percent of American households—each with a minimum net worth of $2.3 million—control nearly 40 percent of the wealth, while in Britain, the richest 1 percent of the population controls about 18 percent of the wealth. In the mid-1970s, both countries were on a par: the richest 1 percent controlled 20 percent of the wealth. President Reagan was the master of this verbal shell game. He told stories of welfare queens and then presided over the looting of the nation's savings and loans by wealthy white men.

Without a doubt, the current urgency for tax cuts and spending reductions can be explained by the fact that President Clinton tried to shift the balance slightly in 1992 and the wealthy ended up paying 16 percent more in taxes the following year, by one estimate.

The purpose of this antiwelfare oratory and the campaigns against sex education, abortion rights, and aid to teenage mothers is to ensure a constant supply of young women as desperate and ashamed as I was. Young women willing to take a job at any wage rate, willing to tolerate the most abusive relationships with men, and unable to enter the gates leading to higher education.

To accomplish their goals, political leaders continually call for reforms that include demands that welfare recipients work, that teenagers don't have sex, and that welfare mothers stop giving birth (but don't have abortions). Each "reform" addresses the nation's racial and sexual stereotypes: taking care of one's own children is not work; welfare mothers are unemployed, promiscuous, and poorly motivated; and unless the government holds their feet to the fire, these women will live on welfare for years, as will their children and their children's children.

This type of demagoguery has been common throughout our history. What sets the present era apart is the nearly across-the-board cooperation of the media. The national news magazines, the most prestigious daily newspapers, the highly regarded broadcast news outlets, as well as the supermarket tabloids and talk-radio hosts, have generally abandoned the notion that one of their missions is to sometimes comfort the afflicted and afflict the comfortable. Instead, they too often reprint politicians' statements unchallenged, provide charts comparing one party's recommendations to another's without really questioning those recommendations, and illustrate story after story, newscast after newscast, with a visual of an African American woman (because we all know they're the only ones on welfare) living in an urban housing project (because that's where all welfare recipients live) who has been on welfare for years.

When *U.S. News & World Report* did a major story on welfare reform this year, it featured large photographs of eight welfare recipients, seven of whom were women of color: six African Americans and one Latina or Native American (the text does not state her ethnicity). Describing the inability of welfare mothers to hold jobs (they are "hobbled not only by their lack of experience but also by their casual attitudes toward punctuality, dress, and co-workers"), the article offers the "excuse" given by one mother for not taking a 3 P.M. to 11 P.M. shift: "'I wouldn't get to see my kids,'" she told the reporter. You can't win for losing—should she take that 3-to-11 job and her unsupervised kids get in trouble, you can be sure some conservative would happily leap on her as an example of one of those poor women who are bad mothers and whose kids should be in orphanages.

Why don't the media ever find a white woman from Ohio or Iowa or Wisconsin, a victim of domestic violence, leaving the father of her two children to make a new start? Or a Latina mother like the one living in my current neighborhood, who has one child and does not make enough as a home health care attendant to pay for her family's health insurance? Or a Native American woman living on a reservation, creating crafts for pennies that will be sold by others for dollars?

Besides reinforcing stereotypes about the personal failings of welfare recipients, when my colleagues write in-depth pieces about life on welfare they invariably concentrate on describing welfare mothers' difficulties with the world at large: addictions, lack of transportation, dangerous neighbors, and, most recently, shiftless boyfriends who begin beating them when they do get jobs—as if this

phenomenon were limited to relationships between couples with low incomes.

I wonder why no journalist I have stumbled across, no matter how well meaning, has communicated what I believe is the central reality of most women's lives on welfare: they believe all the stereotypes too and they are ashamed of being on welfare. They eat, breathe, sleep, and clothe themselves with shame.

Most reporting on welfare never penetrates the surface, and the nature of the relationship between the welfare system and the woman receiving help is never explored. Like me, many women fleeing physical abuse must make the welfare department their first stop after seeking an order of protection. Studies are scarce, but some recent ones of women in welfare-to-work programs across the U.S. estimate that anywhere from half to three fourths of participants are, or have been, in abusive relationships. And surveys of some homeless shelters indicate that half of the women living in them are on the run from a violent mate.

But if welfare is the means of escape, it is also the institutionalization of the dynamic of battering. My husband was the source of my and my children's daily bread and of daily physical and psychological attacks. On welfare, I was free of the beatings, but the assaults on my self-esteem were still frequent and powerful, mimicking the behavior of a typical batterer.

As he pounds away, threatening to kill the woman and children he claims to love, the abuser often accuses his victims of lying, laziness, and infidelity. Many times, he threatens to snatch the children away from their mother in order to protect them from her supposed incompetence, her laziness, dishonesty, and sexual escapades.

On welfare, just as with my husband, I had to prove every statement was not a lie. Everything had to be documented: how many children I had, how much I paid for rent, fuel, transportation, electricity, child care, and so forth. It went so far as to require that at every "redetermination of need" interview (every six months), I had to produce the originals of my children's birth certificates, which were duly photocopied over and over again. Since birth certificates do not change, the procedure was a subtle and constant reminder that nothing I said was accepted as truth. Ever.

But this is a petty example. The more significant one was the suspicion that my attendance at Ohio State University was probably a crime. Throughout my college years, I regularly reported that I was attending OSU. Since the WIN limit at that time was age six and my youngest daughter was two when I started, I was allowed to finish my undergraduate years without having to report to some job-training program that would have prepared me for a minimum-wage job. However, my caseworker and I shared an intuitive belief that something just had to be wrong about this. How could I be living on welfare and going to college? Outrageous! Each day I awoke feeling as if I were in a race, that I had to complete my degree before I was charged with a felony.

As a matter of fact, I remember hearing, a short time after I graduated, that a group of welfare mothers attending college in Ohio were charged with food stamp fraud, apparently for not reporting their scholarships as additional income.

Batterers frequently lie to their victims—it's a power thing. Caseworkers do too. For example, when I moved to New York to attend graduate school and applied for assistance, I asked my intake worker whether I could apply for emergency food stamps. She told me there was no emergency food program. The kids and I scraped by, but that statement was false. I was unaware of it until welfare rights advocates successfully sued the agency for denying applicants emergency food assistance. In another case, when someone gave me a ten-year-old Opel so I could keep my first (very low paying) reporting job, my caseworker informed me in writing that mere possession of a car made me ineligible for welfare. (I appealed and won. The caseworker was apparently confused by the fact that although I was not allowed to have any assets, I did need the car to get to work. She also assumed a used car had to have some value. Not this one.)

Then there's the issue of sexual possessiveness: states rarely grant assistance to families with fathers still in the home. And as for feeling threatened about losing custody, throughout the time I was on welfare, I knew that if I stumbled at all, my children could be taken away from me. It is widely understood that any neighbor can call the authorities about a welfare mother, making a charge of neglect, and that mother, since she is less than nothing, might not be able to prove her competency. I had a close call once. I had been hospitalized for ten days and a friend took care of my children. After my return home, however, I was still weak. I would doze off on the sofa while the kids were awake—one time it happened when they were outside playing on the sidewalk. A neighbor, seeing them there unattended, immediately called the child welfare agency, which sent someone out to question me and to look inside my refrigerator to see if I had any food. Luckily, that day I did.

Ultimately, leaving an abusive relationship and applying for welfare is a little like leaving solitary confinement to become part of a prison's general population. It's better, but you are still incarcerated.

None of this is ever discussed in the context of welfare reform. The idiot state legislator, the prosecutor in Ohio who brought the charges against welfare mothers years ago, Bill Clinton, and Newt Gingrich all continue to play the race and sex card by hollering for welfare reform. They continue to exploit and feed the public's ignorance about and antipathy toward welfare mothers to propel their own careers. Sadly, journalists permit them to do so, perhaps for the same reason.

Lost in all this are the lives of thousands of women impoverished by virtue of their willingness to assume the responsibility of raising their children. An ex-boyfriend used to say that observing my struggle was a little like watching someone standing in a room, with arms upraised to prevent the ceiling from pressing in on her. He wondered just how long I could prevent the collapse.

Today, welfare mothers have even less opportunity than I did. Their talent, brains, luck, and resourcefulness are ignored. Each new rule, regulation, and reform make it even more unlikely that they can use the time they are on welfare to do as I did: cross the High Streets in their cities and towns, and realize their ambitions. Each new rule makes it more likely that they will only be able to train for

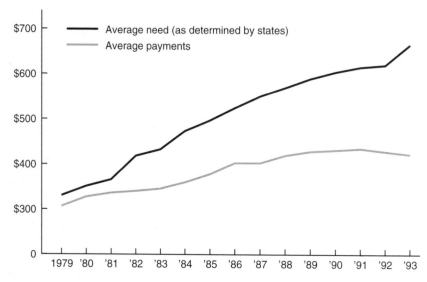

Monthly AFDC Payments vs. Cost of Living for a Family of Three
Source: U.S. Department of Health and Human Services

a minimum-wage job that will never allow them to support their families.

So no, I don't think all we have to do is get the facts to the media. I think we have to raise hell any way we can.

Our goal is simple: never again should there be a young woman, standing in front of the gates that lead to a better future, afraid to enter because she believes she must instead choose poverty and battery.

[1995]

 62

Farewell to Welfare but Not to Poverty

RANDY ALBELDA and CHRIS TILLY

Welfare as we knew it is gone.

What is in its place? A federal mandate to states to force poor mothers into the low-wage labor mar-

ket any way they see fit. What is not in place, however, is sufficient funding, guarantees or even incentives to create the jobs or work supports that might make this poverty-fighting strategy possible. There are no federal requirements to increase the supply or funding of child care, little is being done to create jobs for women that pay living wages, there are no plans to expand health care to low wage workers, and there is no talk of boosting the educational and training opportunities for single mothers.

Welfare as we knew it—AFDC (Aid to Families with Dependent Children)—was no one's dream program, but it did guarantee cash assistance to very poor families, mainly single women and their children. Welfare as we have it—TANF (Temporary Assistance to Needy Families)—does more than remove the guarantee that needy families will receive assistance. It provides incentives for the states to spend less than they did under AFDC, includes a 60-month lifetime limit for assistance, and requires states to put a substantial percentage of all adult recipients into paid or unpaid jobs almost immediately.

Besides further eroding the safety net and fracturing an already ill-funded program, TANF provisions make it more difficult for states to help low-income mothers support their families through their own earnings. TANF's financial incentives are to place recipients directly into jobs—any jobs—making states less likely to provide education or meaningful job training. And while the new legislation will reduce welfare rolls, unless there are creative state initiatives and some federal changes to the law, poverty as we know it will increase.

EVERY MOTHER A WORKING MOTHER

Jobs have always been promoted as this country's best solution to poverty, but this has never worked well for women, since women's wages alone are too low to support families. Yet work has never before been so explicitly forced on mothers, especially those with young children. The 1988 Family Support Act required states to turn AFDC into a jobs and training program for single parents. But more than half of them fulfilled the requirement by going to school. The 1980s emphasis on making recipients work-ready has turned into a 1990s mandate that mothers work. What happened?

Close to 70% of mothers are in the paid labor force. Public sentiment appears to say that if other mothers must work, why not single mothers? This rationale has been used to push poor women into an unrelenting labor market, but it won't work—and not just for poor single mothers. Our economy depends on women for free care of children and for doing low-wage jobs, yet there is an increasing expectation that every adult earn wages sufficient to support a family. For mothers, this is virtually impossible—you can't both provide free care and work enough hours to earn a family wage.

While many families fare poorly under society's new work expectations for women, single-mother families fare the worst for three simple reasons. First, like all women, single-mothers earn less, on average, than men do when they work. Second, raising children is time-consuming work, and children increase the cost of family life (they need food, clothing, shelter and care). Finally, in single-mother families, there is only one adult to both earn income and take care of children.

The difficulties single mothers face are borne out in the poverty statistics. In 1994, half of single-mother families were poor, compared to one out of every 20 married couples with no children. While only 8% of all people in the United States live in single mother families, they make up 28% of all poor persons.

ENDING WELFARE

In August 1996, President Clinton signed the Personal Responsibility and Work Opportunity Act. Along with 22% cuts to Food Stamps and Supplemental Security Income (SSI) over the next six years, the bill eliminates AFDC. In its place is the Temporary Assistance for Needy Families (TANF) block grant.

The Republican Congress takes credit for this bill, but it is a scaled-down version of previous efforts to reform welfare. They also hoped to eliminate the Medicaid entitlement and severely reduce Food Stamps for all, but were repeatedly stymied because the political stakes were too high. State medical establishments receive too much Medicaid money to let it be discarded. Agribusiness made it clear they didn't intend to lose their best customer—the federal government—by cutting Food Stamps.

AFDC, on the other hand, didn't have strong enough "interest groups" protecting it. Two-thirds of the 13 million people receiving AFDC in 1996 were children. The Catholic church and women's groups—the two most active groups lobbying against passage of this bill—clearly did not hold much sway among these Republican legislators. Once the Republicans were able to isolate AFDC from Medicaid and drastic Food Stamps cuts, the President (running as an un-Democrat for reelection) couldn't resist signing a bill that assured him of much coveted suburban votes.

THE TERMS OF TANF

There are four main components to TANF:

• ending the guarantee of cash assistance to poor families.

• establishing a new fiscal relationship, under which the federal government will provide fixed block grants to states, while no longer providing them with a financial incentive to spend additional money on low-income families.

• establishing a lifetime time limit of 60 months (not necessarily consecutive) on receiving assistance from federal TANF funds.

• penalizing states which do not force a substantial percentage of their adult recipients into narrowly defined work programs.

While the first change has received the most attention, all four drastically change the nature of poverty programs. Relying on the rhetoric that states know best and dependency is bad, the Republican Congress eliminated the federal promise of cash assistance to needy families. The hard-earned struggles of the welfare rights movements of the 1960's and 1970's to assure that those eligible to receive AFDC (particularly African Americans) know their rights and receive their assistance were erased with a stroke of the pen.

With federal eligibility requirements eliminated, states may now define "needy" any way they want. They don't even have to use the same definition of needy across their state: needy in the city can be defined differently than needy in the suburbs.

States no longer have to provide cash assistance if they don't want to and can completely privatize their welfare system. The lack of uniform eligibility provisions opens the door to the systematic disentitlement of groups of people that was prevalent before the welfare rights movement. Anyone convicted of a drug-related felony cannot receive TANF funds, and immigrants who come to the United States are denied benefits until they have been here for five years (unless a state changes its own law).

FIXED FEDERAL FUNDING

TANF also profoundly alters the fiscal relationship between states and the feds. The new law requires the Federal government to provide each state with the highest of their 1995, 1994 or average of 1992–1994 federal allocation of AFDC during every year from 1997 to 2002. There are no automatic adjustments for inflation or for need. This represents a dramatic change from AFDC, which was a matching grant: for every dollar a state spent on the pro-

gram, it received a dollar (or more than a dollar for poor states). Although many states did not take full advantage of the match, this funding mechanism intentionally provided a strong incentive to increase spending.

Under the new block grant structure, states can spend as much as they please, but will not receive an extra penny from the feds. And once the money is gone, there is no more. With a recession and an increase in poor families, states will not necessarily have more resources to help out than they did in the past. There are several pools of money that states may tap into in case of deep recession, or if they reduce their TANF rolls, or if they reduce the number of out-of-wedlock births. But these are small bundles of cash and are set at fixed amounts to be split by all qualifying states.

Further, TANF actually permits states to spend less money. As long as states meet federal work participation requirements, they can cut up to a quarter of their 1994 spending levels without penalty (although to qualify for additional assistance in a recession, states must maintain full funding). One aspect of the bill that helped assure its passage was that most states will actually see a windfall for the first year or so of TANF, provided there is no recession. Because national AFDC rolls have fallen since 1994, federal and state spending levels were higher than in 1996. But, as inflation erodes the grant and as the business cycle turns, states will find themselves with less money from the feds and permission to spend less of their own money.

A particularly cruel aspect of the new law is the time limit. States are not allowed to allocate TANF money to any adult who has received TANF money for 60 months—regardless of how much assistance was received in any month or how long it took to accrue 60 months of aid. When AFDC was in place, the average amount of time any recipient receives aid over her lifetime was seven years. Sixty months is an arbitrary number and it will not serve the needs of many poor families. If fully enforced, this provision will throw many families into the street.

The time limit also works against the most positive reform already implemented by many states: allowing employed AFDC recipients to keep more of their cash assistance, even though it may be a small amount. Given the difficulties that single mothers face juggling jobs and kids, and given their relatively low average wages, most will need some form of support until their children are old enough to take care of themselves. That usually is more than 60 months.

The 60-month time limit pushes states concerned about families hitting the limit to avoid giving aid in small monthly amounts, even though this is precisely what some families need in order to make holding a job possible. While states can use their own funds to extend the limit or boost other programs that supplement work, the current political climate makes that unlikely. The only good thing about the time limit provision is that the federal government did not set up or fund a national registry for TANF recipients, so implementing time limits will be difficult.

WORK, WORK, WORK

The final major piece of TANF is the federal requirement that states put recipients to work. The new law requires recipients whose youngest child is more than one year old to do some form of paid or unpaid work after 24 months of receiving benefits. Most schooling and job training will not count as "work." Further, unless states specifically opt out, adult recipients with children older than one must perform community service (meaning workfare) after only two months of obtaining benefits.

Although previous federal provisions also had work requirements, the 1988 law exempted women with a disabled child or whose youngest child was less than three, and most education qualified as being part of a work program. Plus, it provided day care and transportation costs for mothers, neither of which is required under the new law.

In addition to the work requirements, states must meet work participation rates or risk losing some of their federal grant. Every year a certain percentage of all adult recipients (whose youngest child is older than one) must be in a work program for a certain number of hours a week. In 1997, 20% of single mother families had to be at "work" for at least 20 hours a week, gradually increasing to 50% working for at least 30 hours during the year 2002.

The work requirements are structured in such a way to discourage states from providing education and training that would allow at least some women to move into decent paying jobs. States can provide education and training if they want, but most of the programs cannot count toward the work participation requirement. For states to hit their "quotas" they will want to place women into the labor market immediately.

The bottom line? The new law is designed to encourage states to reduce funding and welfare rolls by pushing women into an unrelenting low-wage labor market without the vital supports that make employment possible.

WHY MANY SINGLE MOTHERS CAN'T WORK THEIR WAY OUT OF POVERTY

The clear message of TANF is "work your way out of poverty." And states are saddled with the responsibility of making mothers work. But they will find that for women, especially those with low educational attainment and little job experience, this is not possible without the supports necessary for mothers to work.

It's not for want of trying that single mothers have not been able to make ends meet. They work for pay about as many hours per year, on average, as other mothers, about 1,000 hours a year (a year-round, full-time job logs 2,000 hours). But less than full-time work for most women in this country just doesn't pay enough to feed mouths, make rent payments, and provide care for children while at work.

Not all single mothers are poor—but half of them are (compared to a 5% poverty rate for married couples). For poor single mothers, the labor market usually doesn't provide a ticket off of welfare or out of poverty. That's why AFDC (Aid to Families with Dependent Children, the program known as welfare) worked like a revolving door for so many of them.

Heidi Hartmann and Roberta Spalter-Roth of the Institute for Women's Policy Research (IWPR) report that half of single mothers who spend any time on welfare during a two-year period also work for pay. But that work only generates about one-third of their families' incomes. In short, work is not enough; like other members, they "package" their income from three sources: work in the labor market, support from men or other family members, and government aid. "Mothers typically need at least two of those sources to survive," says Spalter-Roth.

THE TRIPLE WHAMMY

While all women, especially mothers, face barriers to employment with good wages and benefits, single mothers face a "triple whammy" that sharply limits what they can earn. Three factors—job discrimination against women, the time and money it takes to care for children, and the presence of only one adult—combine to make it nearly impossible for women to move off welfare through work alone, without sufficient and stable supplemental income supports.

First, the average woman earns about two-thirds as much per hour as her male counterpart. Women who need to rely on welfare earn even less, since they often have lower skills, less work experience and more physical disabilities than other women. Between 1984 and 1988, IWPR researchers found, welfare mothers who worked for pay averaged a disastrous $4.18 per hour. Welfare mothers with jobs received employer-provided health benefits only one quarter of the time. Mothers on welfare are three times as likely as other women to work as maids, cashiers, nursing aides, child care workers, and waitresses—the lowest of the low-paid women's jobs.

Second, these families include kids. Like all mothers, single mothers have to deal with both greater demands on their time and larger financial demands—more "mouths to feed." A 1987 time-budget study found that the average time spent in household work for employed women with two or more children was 51 hours a week. Child care demands limit the time women can cut into their jobs, and interrupt them with periodic crises, ranging from a sick child to a school's summer break. This takes its toll on both the amount and the quality of work many mothers can obtain. "There's a sad match between women's needs for a little flexibility and time, and the growth in contingent jobs, part-time jobs, jobs that don't last all year," comments Spalter-Roth. "That's the kind of jobs they're getting."

Finally, and unlike other mothers, single mothers have only one adult in the family to juggle child care and a job. Fewer adults means fewer opportunities for paid work. And while a single mother may receive child care from an absent father, she certainly cannot count on the consistent assistance—be it financial support or help with the childcare—that a resident father can provide.

What kind of prospects will welfare recipients face when they have been pushed into the workforce by TANF regulations? Two-thirds of welfare recipients hold no more than a high school diploma. The best way to tell how work requirements will work is to look at the women who already have the jobs that welfare recipients will be compelled to seek.

The news is not good. An unforgiving labor market, in recession and recovery alike, has hammered young, less-educated women, according to economists Jared Bernstein and Lawrence Mishel of the Economic Policy Institute, a Washington, D.C. think tank. Between 1979 and 1989, hourly wages plummeted for these women, falling most rapidly for African American women who didn't finish high school. This group's hourly wages, adjusted for inflation, fell 20% in that ten year period. Most young high school-or-less women continued to lose during 1989–93. At the end of this losing streak, average hourly wages ranged from $5 an hour for younger high school dropouts to $8 an hour for older women with high school diplomas.

Unemployment rates in 1993 for most of these young women are stunning: 42% for black female high school dropouts aged 16–25, and 26% for their Latina counterparts.

But young women don't have a monopoly on labor market distress: workforce-wide hourly wages fell 14% between 1973 and 1993, after controlling for inflation. Given the collapse of wage rates, work simply is not enough to lift many families out of poverty. Two-thirds of all people living in poor families with children—15 million Americans—live in families *with a worker* in 1991, report Isaac Shapiro and Robert Greenstein of the Center on Budget and Policy Priorities. And 5.5 million of these people in poverty had a family member who worked *year-round, full-time.*

REFORMS THAT WOULD WORK

The problems of insufficient pay and time to raise children that face single-mother families—and indeed many families—go far beyond the welfare system. So the solution must be much more comprehensive than simply reforming that system. What we need is a set of thorough changes in the relations among work, family, and income.

• *Provide supports for low-wage workers.* The two most important supports are universal health coverage—going down in flames in Congress at the time of this writing—and a universal child care plan. Two-thirds of welfare recipients leave the rolls within two years, but lack of health insurance and child care drive many of them back: over half of the women who left welfare to work went back to AFDC. A society that expects all able-bodied adults to work—regardless of the age of their children—should also be a society that socializes the costs of going to work, by offering programs to care for children of all ages.

• *Create jobs.* This item seems to have dropped off the national policy agenda. Deficit-probing has hogtied any attempt at fiscal stimulus, and the Federal Reserve seems bent on stamping out growth in the name of preventing inflation. Government spending could be used to boost job growth, and even invest in creating public service jobs.

• *Make work pay by changing taxes and government assistance.* Make it not only for women working their way off welfare, but for everybody at the low end of the labor market. Clinton's preferred tool for this has been the Earned Income Tax Credit (EITC)—which gives tax credits to low-wage workers with children (this tax provision now outspends AFDC). Although they get the EITC, women on welfare who work suffer a penalty that takes away nearly a dollar of the AFDC grant for every dollar earned. Making work pay would mean reducing or eliminating this penalty.

• *Make work pay by shoring up wages and benefits.* To ensure that the private sector does its part, raise the minimum wage. A full-time, year-round minimum wage job pays less than the poverty income threshold for a family of one. Conservatives and the small business lobby will trot out the bogeyman of job destruction, but studies on the last minimum wage increase showed a zero or even positive effect on employment. Hiking the minimum wage does eliminate lousy jobs, but the greater purchasing power created by a higher wage floor generates roughly the same number of *better* jobs. In addition, mandate benefit parity for part-time, temporary, and subcontracted workers. This would close a loophole that a growing number of employers use to dodge fringe benefits.

• *Make a serious commitment to life-long education and training.* Education and training do help welfare recipients and other disadvantaged workers. But significant impacts depend on longer-term, intensive—and expensive—programs. We also need to expand training to a broader constituency, since training targeted only to the worst-off workers helps neither these workers, who get stigmatized in the eyes of employers, nor the remainder of the workforce, who get excluded. In Sweden, half the workforce takes some time off work for education in any given year.

• *Build flexibility into work.* "Increasingly," says Spalter-Roth, "all men and all women are workers *and* nurturers." Some unions have begun to bargain for the ability to move between full-time and part-time work, but in most work places changing hours means quitting a job and finding a new one. And though employees now have the right to unpaid family or medical leave, many can't afford to take time off. *Paid* leave would, of course, solve this problem. Failing that, temporary disability insurance (TDI) that is extended beyond disability situations to those facing a wide range of family needs could help. Five states (California, New York, New Jersey, Rhode Island, and Hawaii) currently run TDI systems funded by payroll taxes.

• *Mend the safety net, for times when earnings aren't enough.* Unemployment insurance has important gaps: low-wage earners receive even lower unemployment benefits, the long-term unemployed get cut off, new labor market entrants and reentrants have no access to benefits, and in many states people seeking part-time work cannot collect. Closing these gaps would help welfare "packagers," as well as others at the low end of the labor market, to make ends meet. But even with all of these policies in place, there will be times when single mothers will either choose or be compelled to set aside paid work, sometimes for extended periods, to care for their families.

So welcome to reality. Most single mothers *cannot* work their way out of poverty—definitely not without supplemental support. There are many possible policy steps that could be taken to help them and other low-wage workers get the most out of an inhospitable labor market. But ultimately, old-fashioned welfare must remain part of the formula.

Resources: Heidi Hartmann and Robert Spalter-Roth, "The real employment opportunities of women participating in AFDC: What the market can provide" (1993) and "Welfare that works: An assessment of the administration's welfare reform proposal" (1994), Institute for Women's Policy Research; Jared Bernstein and Lawrence Mishel, "Trends in the low-wage labor market and welfare reform: The constraints on making work pay," Economic Policy Institute (1994); Isaac Shapiro and Robert Greenstein, *Making Work Pay: The Unfinished Agenda,* Center on Budget and Policy Priorities (1993); Randy Albelda and Chris Tilly, *Glass Ceilings and Bottomless Pits: Women, Income, and Poverty in Massachusetts,* Women's Statewide Legislative Network (Massachusetts) (1994).

[1994 and 1996]

✣ 63

Welfare Reform, Family Hardship, and Women of Color

LINDA BURNHAM

Six years ago, tens of thousands of women's and human rights activists gathered at the United Nations Fourth World Conference on Women, held in Beijing, China, to focus their attention on improving the condition and status of women worldwide. Working through cultural, religious, political, economic, and regional differences, women from the nations of the world produced a comprehensive document, the Beijing Platform for Action, that detailed actions to be taken by governments, nongovernmental organizations, and multilateral financial and developmental institutions to improve women's conditions. The platform for action called on governments to take action to relieve "the persistent and increasing burden of poverty on women" and address gender "inequality in economic structures and policies, in all forms of productive activities and in access to resources" (United Nations 1995).

Yet, in the six years since Beijing, in a time of unparalleled national prosperity, policies contradictory to the spirit and intent of the platform for action were promulgated in the United States, targeting the most vulnerable citizens and, rather than assisting women onto the path of economic security, driving many deeper into poverty. While U.S. officials pledged in international forums to uphold women's human rights, those rights were substantially undermined by the 1996 passage of the Personal Responsibility and Work Opportunities Reconciliation Act (PRWORA).

INCREASING FAMILY HARDSHIP

Several studies document how much worse off many women are in the wake of welfare reform (Sherman et al. 1998; USGAO 1999a). Those who remain on welfare, those in transition from welfare to work, and those who have been pushed off welfare into the low-wage economy often face worse conditions, with less support than the woefully inadequate previous system provided. A few indicators of the increasing hardships will be highlighted here, before turning to the particular problems facing women of color and immigrant women, and then placing the impact of welfare reform in the context of international human rights.

The stated intent of welfare reform was at least twofold: to reduce the welfare rolls and to move women toward economic self-sufficiency. The first objective has been achieved; welfare rolls have declined dramatically since 1996. Welfare reform has stripped single mothers of any sense that they are entitled to government support during the years when they are raising their children.

Despite the "success" of welfare reform, research has repeatedly found that many women who move from welfare to work do not achieve economic independence (USGAO, 1999; Rangarajan and Wood, 1999, Loprest, 1999). Instead, most find only low-paid, insecure jobs that do not lift their families above the poverty line. They end up worse off economically than they were on welfare: they work hard and remain poor. Others are pushed off welfare and find no employment. They have no reported source of income.

Women in transition from welfare to work—or to no work—face particular difficulties and crises related to housing insecurity and homelessness and food insecurity and hunger.

Low-income people in the United States faced a housing crisis long before the passage of the PRWORA. In most states, the median fair-market cost of housing for a family of three is considerably higher than total income from a Temporary Aid to Needy Families (TANF) grant (Dolbeare 1999). Further, as a consequence of two decades of declining federal support for public and subsidized housing, the great majority of both current and former TANF recipients are at the mercy of an unforgiving private housing market.

The withdrawal of the federal government's commitment to need-based income support adds a powerful destabilizing element to already tenuous conditions. The evidence that welfare reform is contributing to rising levels of housing insecurity and homelessness is piling up. The author of one recent study of over 17,000 children noted, "Young children are without homes in the largest numbers since the Great Depression. Welfare reform has made things much worse. Shelters are overflowing and gridlocked" (Griffin 1999, 4A).

Utility payment problems are another important indicator of housing insecurity because they reveal that many families, while they may have a roof over them, spend at least some time without heat and light. And utility problems are often a prelude to inability to pay the rent. A 1998 survey of social service clients who had left welfare within the previous six months found that 25 percent had had their heat cut off (Sherman et al. 1998, 13). A recent Illinois study found that 61 percent of TANF recipients who were not working could not pay their utility

bills. But former recipients who were working were also struggling with their budgets, and 48 percent were unable to meet their utility payments (Work, Welfare and Families 2000, 25).

Confronting the absurd and agonizing decision of whether to feed their children or house them, most mothers will use the rent money to buy food and then struggle to deal with the consequences. In one national study of three hundred and four families 23 percent of former welfare recipients moved because they could not pay the rent (Sherman et al. 1998, 13). A New Jersey survey found that 15.8 percent of respondents who had had their benefits reduced or terminated in the previous 12 months had lost their housing (Work, Poverty and Welfare Evaluation Project 1999, 53). Furthermore, in Illinois, 12 percent of former recipients who were not working and 5 percent of former recipients who were working experienced an eviction (Work, Welfare and Families 2000, 25).

Welfare reform has also put severe pressures on an already strained shelter system. The U.S. Conference of Mayors reported that requests for emergency shelter increased by 12 percent between 1998 and 1999 in the 26 cities surveyed and were at their highest levels since 1994 (U.S. Conference of Mayors 1999, 94). "When I started here three years ago, we had plenty of family space. Since welfare reform, I don't have a bed," said a social service worker in a Salvation Army Shelter in New Orleans (Cobb 1999, 1).

According to a survey conducted by social service agencies in six states, 8 percent of the single parents who had stopped getting welfare in the previous six months had to turn to homeless shelters to house their families (Sherman et al. 1998, 16). In an Illinois study, 7 percent of former recipients who were not working became homeless. Prospects were not much better for former recipients who were working, of whom 5 percent became homeless (Work, Welfare and Families 2000, 25).

Although the PRWORA was trumpeted as a step toward strengthening families, increased housing insecurity and homelessness have led to families being split apart. Most family shelters do not take men, so the fathers of two-parent families that become homeless must either go to a single men's shelter or make other housing arrangements. Many shelters also do not accommodate adolescent boys or older male teens. Family breakup may be required for a shelter stay.

The housing instability of poor women and their children has profound consequences, both for them and for society as a whole. Homelessness compromises the emotional and physical health of women and children, disrupts schooling, and creates a substantial barrier to employment. It widens the chasm between those who are prospering in a strong economy and those who fall ever further behind. In the six years since the United States made its Beijing commitments to improving women's lives, welfare policy, rather than widening poor women's access to safe and affordable housing, has created higher levels of housing instability and homelessness.

Like homelessness, the problems of food insecurity predate welfare reform. Low-income workers and welfare recipients alike have struggled for years to provide adequate food for themselves and their families. The robust economy of the late 1990s did not fundamentally alter this reality. Of families headed by single women, 1 in 3 experience food insecurity and 1 in 10 experience hunger (Work, Welfare and Families 2000, 25).

Welfare reform has made women's struggles to obtain food for themselves and their families more difficult. Several studies document that former recipients cannot pay for sufficient food and that their families skip meals, go hungry, and/or use food pantries or other emergency food assistance.

The figures are astoundingly high. In New Jersey, 50.3 percent of former recipients who were not working reported an inability to sufficiently feed themselves or their children. Former recipients who were working were no better off: 49.7 percent reported the very same problem (Work, Poverty and Welfare Evaluation Project 1999, 58). The situation conveyed by an Illinois study is even more disturbing. Here, the population reporting the most difficulty with food insecurity was former recipients who were participating in the labor force. Sixty-three percent of them said that there was a time when they could not buy the food they needed, a significantly

higher proportion than either former recipients who were not working or current recipients. (Work, Welfare and Families 2000, 25). In other words, the higher costs associated with participating in the labor force, combined with reduction or elimination of the food stamp allotment, meant women's access to adequate food became more precarious rather than less so as they moved from welfare to work. Entering the workforce came at a very high price.

The Food Stamp Program is intended to ensure that no family goes hungry, but many families do not receive the food stamps to which they are entitled. Even before welfare reform, the rate of participation in the Food Stamp Program was declining more rapidly than the poverty rate. The number of people receiving food stamps dropped even more steeply later, from 25.5 million average monthly recipients in 1996 to 18.5 million in the first half of 1999 (U.S. General Accounting Office 1999, 46). The rate of participation is the lowest it has been in two decades, with a growing gap between the need for food assistance and families' use of food stamps.

Welfare reform has itself contributed to the underutilization of food stamps. Many families that leave the welfare system do not know that as long as their income remains below a certain level, they are still eligible for food stamps. Believing that termination of TANF benefits disqualifies them for food stamps as well, they fail to apply or to reconfirm eligibility. Confusion and misinformation on the part of eligibility workers, or their withholding of information, are also factors in the low participation of former recipients. Additional contributing factors include the lack of bilingual staff and burdensome application and recertification processes (Venner, Sullivan, and Seavey 2000, 17). Among families who had left welfare, only 42 percent of those who were eligible for food stamps were receiving them (Zedlewski and Brauner 1999, 1–6).

Not surprisingly, demands for food from other sources are increasing. As the welfare rolls shrink, requests for food from charities rise. Catholic Charities reported a 38 percent rise in demand for emergency food assistance in 1998. "For many low-income people, the 'emergency' need for food assistance has become 'chronic'—a basic component of their efforts to survive" (U.S. Conference of Mayors 1999, 20). The U.S. Conference of Mayors's study showed that 85 percent of the cities surveyed experienced increased demand for emergency food and that requests for emergency food assistance increased by an average of 18 percent between 1998 and 1999 (U.S. Conference of Mayors 1999, 94). In many cases, the demand for food goes unmet. As one report states, "The bottom line is that . . . for millions of households, work force participation has been accompanied by hunger" (Venner, Sullivan, and Seavey 2000, 16).

WOMEN OF COLOR AND IMMIGRANT WOMEN

Welfare reform is a nominally race-neutral policy suffused with racial bias, both in the politics surrounding its promulgation and in its impact. It may not have been the intent to racially target women of color for particular punishment, yet women of color and immigrant women have nonetheless been particularly hard hit in ways that were highly predictable.

Feminist theory has for some time recognized that the social and economic circumstances women of color must negotiate are shaped by the intersection of distinct axes of power—in this case primarily race, class, and gender. The relationships of subordination and privilege that define these axes generate multiple social dynamics that influence, shape, and transform each other, creating, for women of color, multiple vulnerabilities and intensified experiences of discrimination.

Welfare reform might legitimately be regarded as a class-based policy intended to radically transform the social contract with the poor. Poverty in the United States, however, is powerfully structured by racial and gender inequities. It is not possible, therefore, to institute poverty policy of any depth that does not also reconfigure other relations, either augmenting or diminishing race and gender inequalities. By weakening the social safety net for the poor, PRWORA necessarily has its greatest effect on those communities that are disproportionately represented among the poor. Communities of color and immigrant communities, already charac-

terized by significantly higher levels of minimum wage work, homelessness, hunger, and poor health, are further jeopardized by the discriminatory impact of welfare reform.

As a consequence of the historical legacy and current practices of, among other things, educational inequity and labor market disadvantage, patterns of income and wealth in the United States are strongly skewed along racial lines; for example, the disproportionate burden of poverty is carried by people of color. While the white, non-Hispanic population constituted 72.3 percent of the total population in 1998, they made up only 45.8 percent of the population living below the poverty line. In stark contrast, blacks made up just over 12 percent of the general population, but 26.4 percent of the U.S. population in poverty. People of Hispanic origin, of all races, comprise 23.4 percent of the people below the poverty line, while making up 11.2 percent of the total population. While 8.2 percent of the white, non-Hispanic population lives in poverty, 12.5 percent of Asian and Pacific Islanders do (U.S. Census Bureau 1999, 2000).[1]

Economic vulnerabilities due to race and ethnicity may be further compounded by disadvantages based on gender and immigration/citizenship status. Thus, for households headed by single women, the poverty rates are also stark. Over 21 percent of such white, non-Hispanic households were below the poverty line in 1998, as compared to over 46 percent of black and 48 percent of Hispanic female-headed households (U.S. Census Bureau 1999). Immigrants, too, are disproportionately poor, with 18 percent below the poverty line as compared to 12 percent of the native born (U.S. Census Bureau 1999). Given the disproportionate share of poverty experienced by people of color, and the significant poverty of single-mother households, it is no surprise that the welfare rolls are racially unbalanced, with women of color substantially overrepresented (see table).

This racial imbalance has been cynically used for decades in the ideological campaign to undermine support for welfare—a crude but ultimately effective interweaving of race, class, gender, and anti-immigrant biases that prepared the consensus

TANF Recipients by Race, 1998 (in percentages)

White	32.7
Black	39.0
Hispanic	22.2
Native	1.5
Asian	3.4
Other	0.6
Unknown	0.7

Source: U.S. Department of Health and Human Services 1999.

to "end welfare as we know it." Having been maligned as lazy welfare cheats and something-for-nothing immigrants, Latinas, African-American women, and Asian women of particular nationality groups are now absorbing a punishing share of welfare reform's negative impacts.

Much of the data on welfare reform are not disaggregated by race. We will not know the full impact of welfare reform on women of color until we have countywide, statewide, and national studies of women transitioning from welfare to work that consistently include race as a variable. However, to the extent that communities of color experience some of the most devastating effects of poverty at exceptionally high rates, and to the extent that welfare reform has rendered these communities more rather than less vulnerable, we may expect that the policy will deepen already entrenched inequalities.

For example, African-American women are massively overrepresented in the urban homeless population. Their particular vulnerability to homelessness has been shaped by, among many factors, high rates of reliance on welfare in a period in which the value of the welfare grant plummeted and housing costs climbed steeply; low marriage rates and, therefore, lack of access to a male wage; overconcentration on the bottom rungs of the wage ladder; and high unemployment rates, especially for young women with less than a high school education.

Beyond intensified impact due to disproportionate representation in the affected population, additional factors compound the disadvantages of women of color and immigrant women. One Virginia study found noteworthy differences in how caseworkers interact with black and white welfare recipients. A substantial 41 percent of white recipients were encouraged to go to school to earn their high school diplomas, while no black recipients were. A much higher proportion of whites than blacks found their caseworkers to be helpful in providing information about potential jobs (Gooden 1997). Other studies showed that blacks were removed from welfare for noncompliance with program rules at considerably higher rates than white recipients, while a higher proportion of the cases of white recipients were closed because their earnings rose too much to qualify for welfare (Savner 2000).

Further, while welfare use is declining among all races, white recipients are leaving the welfare rolls at a much more rapid rate than blacks or Latinos. In New York City, for example, the number of whites on welfare declined by 57 percent between 1995 and 1998, while the rate of decline for blacks was 30 percent and that of Latinos, 7 percent. White recipients have also been leaving the rolls at faster rates than minorities in states such as Illinois, Pennsylvania, Michigan, and Ohio. And nationally, the decline has been 25 percent for whites but only 17 percent for African Americans and 9 percent for Latinos (DeParle 1998, A1).

The causes of this phenomenon have been insufficiently studied, but some of the factors may include higher average educational levels among white recipients, greater concentrations of recipients of color in job-poor inner cities, racial discrimination in employment and housing, and discriminatory referral policies on the part of welfare-to-work caseworkers. Whatever the combination of contributing factors, it appears that white recipients are making a more rapid transition into the labor force.

Some of the most punitive provisions of PRWORA are directed at immigrants. The 1996 legislation banned certain categories of legal immigrants from a wide array of federal assistance programs, including TANF, food stamps, Supplementary Security Income, and Medicaid. In the year following passage, 940,000 legal immigrants lost their food stamp eligibility. Strong advocacy restored some of the cuts and removed some restrictions, but legal immigrants arriving in the United States after the 22 August 1996 legislation passed are ineligible for benefits for five years. States have the discretion of barring pre-enactment legal immigrants from TANF and nonemergency Medicaid as well (National Immigration Law Center 1999).

These restrictions have had profound effects on immigrant communities. First of all, many immigrant women who are on welfare face significant barriers to meeting TANF work requirements. Perhaps the most formidable obstacles are limited English proficiency and low educational levels. A study of one hundred and fifty immigrant recipients in California found that 87 percent of the Vietnamese women had limited or no proficiency in English, as did 48 percent of the Mexican-American women. Many of these women were also not literate in their native languages, with the Mexican Americans averaging 6.5 years in school and the Vietnamese 8.7 years (Equal Rights Advocates 1999, 7). A study of one hundred and thirty seven Hmong women found 90 percent with little or no English proficiency, 70 percent with no literacy in the Hmong language, and 62 percent with no formal education whatsoever (Moore and Selkowe 1999).

Limited English, lack of education, and limited job skills severely restrict immigrant women's options in the job market, making it very difficult for them to comply with welfare-to-work requirements. Language problems also impede their ability to negotiate the welfare bureaucracy, which provides very limited or no translation services. These women lack information about programs to which they are entitled, and they worry about notices that come to them in English. When immigrant women recipients are able to find work, it is most often in minimum wage or low-wage jobs without stability or benefits (Center for Urban Research and Learning 1999, 5; Equal Rights Advocates 1999, 31).

It should come as no surprise that immigrant women report high levels of hardship. In a study of Santa Clara County, California, 50 percent of the Mexican-American recipients had experienced food shortages, as had 26 percent of the Vietnamese women (Equal Rights Advocates 1999, 32). One out

of three Hmong women recipients in Wisconsin reported running out of food in the six months prior to the survey, and 51.8 percent said they had less food on the state's W-2 program than they had had on AFDC (Moore and Selkowe 1999, 4). Of 630 Latino and Asian households surveyed in California, Texas, and Illinois, 79 percent faced food insecurity, and 8.5 percent reported experiencing severe hunger. A study of Los Angeles and San Francisco immigrant households whose food stamps had been cut found that 33 percent of the children in the San Francisco households were experiencing moderate to severe hunger (Venner, Sullivan, and Seavey 2000, 21).

Immigrant women recipients are also likely to experience severe overcrowding and to devote a huge portion of their income to housing. They share housing with relatives or with unrelated adults; live in garages or other makeshift, substandard dwellings; and worry constantly about paying the rent.

A more hidden, but still pernicious, impact of welfare reform has been the decline in applications for aid from immigrants who would be eligible to receive it. One report documents PRWORA's "chilling effect on immigrants" who mistakenly believe they are no longer eligible for any benefits. Reporting on the numbers of TANF applications approved each month, this study showed a huge drop —71 percent—in the number of legal immigrant applicants approved for TANF and MediCal between January 1996 and January 1998. That number fell from 1545 applicants in January 1996 to only 450 in January 1998 (Zimmerman and Fix 1998, 5). The intensive anti-immigrant propaganda that accompanied the passage of PRWORA and statewide anti-immigrant initiatives appear to have discouraged those who need and are entitled to aid from applying for it, surely undermining the health and welfare of immigrant women and their families.

WELFARE REFORM IS INCOMPATIBLE WITH WOMEN'S HUMAN RIGHTS

One of the chief accomplishments of the Beijing conference and the Platform for Action was to position women's issues squarely within the context of human rights. Building on the foundational work of activists worldwide, Beijing became the first U.N. women's conference in which "women's rights are human rights" was articulated not as a platitude but as a strategic assertion. Indeed, the phrase was taken up by former First Lady Hillary Rodham Clinton who, in her 5 September 1995 speech to the conference, asserted that "women will never gain full dignity until their human rights are respected and protected."

PRWORA is wholly incompatible with the strategic objectives of the Beijing Platform for Action and profoundly compromises the exercise of women's human rights. Rather than improving the status of poor women, the legislation has deepened the misery of tens of thousands of women and their children. By undermining women's access to a stable livelihood, welfare reform constructs barriers to their exercise of political, civil, cultural, and social rights.

Undoing the damage of welfare reform—and bringing U.S. policy in line with its stated commitments to the world community—will require the promulgation and implementation of policies that restore and strengthen the social safety net for women and children while funding programs that support women along the path to economic self-sufficiency. In the absence of the political will for such a comprehensive reworking of U.S. social welfare policy, advocates for poor women and families face an extended, defensive battle to ameliorate the cruelest and most discriminatory effects of this radically regressive policy.

NOTE

1. In citing Census Bureau statistics, I use their terminology. Elsewhere, I use the term "Latino" to refer to immigrants from Mexico, Central and South America, and the Spanish-speaking Caribbean and their descendants in the United States.

REFERENCES

Center for Urban Research and Learning. 1999. *Cracks in the System: Conversations with People Surviving Welfare Reform.* Chicago: Center for Urban Research and Learning, Loyola University, Howard Area Community Center, Organization of the NorthEast.

Clinton, Hillary. Remarks by First Lady Hillary Rodham Clinton for the United Nations Fourth World Conference on Women, September 5, 1995.

Cobb, Kim. "Homeless Kids Problem Worst in Louisiana; Welfare Reform, Housing Crunch Are Among Reasons." *Houston Chronicle,* August 15, 1999.

DeParle, Jason. "Shrinking Welfare Rolls Leave Record High Share of Minorities." *New York Times,* July 24, 1998.

Dolbeare, Cushing. *Out of Reach: The Gap Between Housing Costs and Income of Poor People in the United States.* Washington, DC: National Low-Income Housing Coalition, 1999.

Equal Rights Advocates. *From War on Poverty to War on Welfare: The Impact of Welfare Reform on the Lives of Immigrant Women.* San Francisco: Equal Rights Advocates, 1999.

Gooden, Susan. Examining Racial Differences in Employment Status Among Welfare Recipients. In *Race and Welfare Report.* Oakland, CA: Grass Roots Innovative Policy Program, 1997.

Griffin, Laura. "Welfare Cuts Leaving More Families Homeless, Study Finds." *Dallas Morning News,* July 1, 1999.

Loprest, Pamela. *How Families That Left Welfare Are Doing: A National Picture.* Washington, DC: Urban Institute, 1999.

Moore, Thomas and Vicky Selkowe. *The Impact of Welfare Reform on Wisconsin's Hmong Aid Recipients.* Milwaukee: Institute for Wisconsin's Future, 1999.

National Immigration Law Center. *Immigration Eligibility for Public Benefits.* Washington, DC: National Immigration Law Center, 1999.

Rangarajan, Anu and Robert G. Wood. *How WFNJ Clients Are Faring Under Welfare Reform: An Early Look.* Princeton, NJ: Mathematical Policy Research, Inc., 1999.

Savner, Steve. Welfare Reform and Racial/Ethnic Minorities: The Questions to Ask. *Poverty & Race* 9(4):3–5, 2000.

Sherman, Arloc, Cheryl Amey, Barbara Duffield, Nancy Ebb, and Deborah Weinstein. *Welfare to What: Early Findings on Family Hardship and Well-Being.* Washington, DC: Children's Defense Fund and National Coalition for the Homeless, 1998.

United Nations. *Fourth World Conference on Women Platform for Action.* Geneva, Switzerland: United Nations, 1995.

U.S. Census Bureau. *Poverty Thresholds in 1998 by Size of Family and Number of Related Children Under 18 Years.* Washington, DC: U.S. Census Bureau, 1999.

———. *Resident Population Estimates of the United States by Sex, Race, and Hispanic Origin.* Washington, DC: U.S. Census Bureau, 2000.

U.S. Conference of Mayors. *A Status Report on Hunger and Homelessness in America's Cities.* Washington, DC: U.S. Conference of Mayors, 1999.

U.S. Department of Health and Human Services. *Characteristics and Financial Circumstances of TANF Recipients.* Washington, DC: U.S. Department of Health and Human Services, Administration for Children and Families, 1999.

U.S. General Accounting Office. *Food Stamp Program: Various Factors Have Led to Declining Participation.* Washington, DC: U.S. General Accounting Office, 1999.

Venner, Sandra H., Ashley F. Sullivan, and Dorie Seavey. *Paradox of Our Times: Hunger in a Strong Economy.* Medford, MA: Tufts University, Center on Hunger and Poverty, 2000.

Work, Poverty and Welfare Evaluation Project. Assessing Work First: What Happens After Welfare? Report for the Study Group on Work, Poverty and Welfare. Legal Services of New Jersey, New Jersey Poverty Research Institute, Edison, NJ, 1999.

Work, Welfare and Families. *Living with Welfare Reform: A Survey of Low Income Families in Illinois*. Chicago: Chicago Urban League and UIC Center for Urban Economic Development, 2000.

Zedlewski, Sheila R. and Sarah Brauner. *Are the Steep Declines in Food Stamp Participation Linked to Falling Welfare Caseloads?* Washington, DC: Urban Institute, 1999.

Zimmerman, Wendy and Michael Fix. *Declining Immigrant Applications for MediCal and Welfare Benefits in Los Angeles County*. Washington, DC: Urban Institute, 1998.

Women and the Family

The family and motherhood are often thought of as "natural" entities rather than institutions that, in traditional forms, reinforce sexism and maintain women's subordinated status. The selections in this section first explore women's situation in the family and then some of their varied experiences with motherhood. The fictional pieces serve to highlight the emotional realities of some women's lives in the family, realities that are often obscured by rosy images of family life.

While families can be a source of support for some women, sexism in families can hurt us in various ways. Women no longer lose their legal identity and right to contract as they did in earlier centuries, yet, as Susan Lehrer points out, "the nuclear family is a different place for women and men." The family offers women the hope of love, but also the potential of entrapment, as Rosie learns in Hisaye Yamamoto's short story.

As discussed in the introduction to this Part, feminists distinguish the experience of mothering from the institution of motherhood. "A Long Story" depicts the pain experienced by mothers when the state's prerogatives, rather than women's emotional ties to their children, define motherhood. Even the experience of mothering can be agonizing, especially for immigrant women for whom language barriers can isolate them from others, including their children, as Pat Mora suggests in "Elena."

At the same time that women are limited by the institutions of the family and motherhood, they are sometimes blamed for its problems. June Jordan points to the way that black single mothers in particular are blamed for black poverty. Rather than eliminating the racism and sexism that undermine black families and praising black women for their success in keeping families together, the media "experts" and government officials "talk about our mamas." Writing in 1987, she compares the "crisis of the black family" to what she saw as the truly significant crises of the day that the U.S. government was perpetuating through its international policy. Jordan suggests governmental, institutional, and social changes necessary to support all women and families.

The ability to make conscious choices about personal relationships is central to women's freedom. Because choice is integral to feminism, this section also presents alternatives to the traditional family. Women who are single or celibate are often stigmatized in our society. Yet some women have found the experience of living with oneself to be satisfying and liberating. Mary Helen Washington speaks of the strength she finds in living on her own.

Including children in a male-female relationship brings challenges as well as rewards. Alix Kates Shulman describes the agreement that she and her husband made in their attempt to bring equity to parenting. While it may appear mechanical and extreme, it reflects the resolve and intentionality many parents find necessary to change gendered patterns in the family.

🌿 64

Family and Women's Lives

SUSAN LEHRER

We tend to think about the family as a natural, biological unit. After all, everyone knows it takes two to make a baby. What is meant by family is more than biological relations, of course. In current debates, one specific form of family is referred to as "traditional": the nuclear family—mother, father, and their children, living together, with the father the main breadwinner and the mother responsible for the home. It is maintained and reinforced by law and the state, and forms the basis for social policy toward women and children. Yet only about 25% of American households are married couples and their children.

Work is now the norm. In 2000, both parents were employed in 64.2% of married-couple families with children under 18, while the father, but not the mother, was employed in only 29.2% (little changed since 1994). The proportion of "traditional" families, that is, families in which the father, but not the mother, is employed, is larger among couples with preschool children (under 6 years of age) than among families whose youngest child was 6 to 17 years old (BLS Current Pop Survey info on Families: Employment Characteristics of Families Summary, USDL 01-103, Internet address: http://stats.bls.gov/newsrels.htm).

Overwhelmingly, women's family life includes responsibility for children and the home (called "women's work"). But women also work outside the home in the paid labor force—including over half of women with children under one year of age. Using the outdated, inaccurate picture of "family," however, prevents the needs of women and real-life families from being recognized. This essay explores some of the broad historical changes that have changed the family, and the way in which family structure defines the opportunities, economic situation, and social position of women.

HISTORICAL OVERVIEW

Before industrialization, the family was a working, productive unit, with women producing goods for family consumption, as well as maintaining the family's health and material well-being. For example, in *Little House on the Prairie*, Laura Ingalls Wilder describes her childhood frontier family in which Ma's contribution was clear and valued, and Pa's work took place within the family setting as well. This continued into the late nineteenth and early twentieth centuries in rural areas.

With the beginnings of industrialization, a major shift occurred, as "work" became something done outside the home, for pay, by men. "Women's work" within the home (called housework) was not paid labor and hence not seen as "real work." Thus, the roles of breadwinner and homemaker that are often taken for granted as "natural" are the result of specific historical changes like industrialization, and are, as Jesse Bernard (1981) put it, specific to a very short period in human history. The household itself changed from a unit of production to one primarily of consumption.

Although men were the main workers (for pay), right from the beginning of industrialization, women also worked outside their homes. For example, in making cloth (which was one of the first industries affected by the Industrial Revolution), young women were the main source for factory workers, because men's labor was needed in agricultural production and therefore scarce. Women received wages that were one-quarter to one-half those of men. From the beginning of wage labor and capitalist production for profit, the wage structure itself has been different (and lower) for female workers than for male workers. Although male workers were not well paid, their wages were expected to support a family; women were not expected to be self-supporting, let alone able to support anyone else. This meant women were dependent upon men for support, even when they did work outside the home.

The "power of the purse" reinforced the husband's control over his family. Under English common law, which our legal system is based on, when a woman married, she lost her own legal identity and her legal right to contract. For instance, her husband had control over all the money and property of the family, including her wages. Marriage represented a legal contract in which a woman's status was subordinate to her husband's. Women's current subordination in marriage is rooted in legal tradition as well as in economic arrangements.

As commercial and industrial development expanded and a national economy emerged in the late 1800s, women's world was still supposed to be centered within the household—she was the "angel of the hearth," available to provide material and emotional comfort for the man, who braved the world of commercial competition. This idealized version of family was never quite accurate even in the nineteenth century. For middle-class women, it meant complete economic dependence on the goodwill of their husbands and fathers. Less well-off women worked in factories and sweatshops as young women or whenever they were not supported by a man's income. Women also added to the household income by taking in boarders or doing washing—usually ignored by official counts of family income and employment (Bose, 1987:113).

Enslaved African-American women were expected to perform tasks similar to men, and in the United States, unlike other countries, even slave marriage was not recognized by white law. African-American women worked in the fields as well as in the slave master's household. Nonetheless, studies indicate that many enslaved families sought to maintain strong ties (which amounted to an act of subversion under slavery), and after emancipation, large-scale relocations of African Americans were often an attempt to reunite families broken apart by slavery (Gutman, 1983). After slavery, whites still expected African-American wives to work for them; they were considered lazy if they presumed to stay home and act like ladies (Jones, 1985:59). Thus we see that the "traditional" family was only expected to apply to certain groups and not others—white, middle-class families primarily.

From this brief historical survey, it is clear that the family is not a natural, unchanging entity, but it changes along with social and economic shifts in the larger social world. We are again in a time when these larger social forces are visibly changing the way families function. Although the number of women working outside the home has been slowly increasing since the early 1900s, the increase in the past two decades has been astounding. The vast majority of women now combine outside work and family life, and in addition, the proportion of women who are heads of households, never married, and working has increased dramatically.

THE NUCLEAR FAMILY: IT'S A DIFFERENT PLACE FOR WOMEN THAN MEN

The idealized image of family relationships is that they are warm, loving, and occasionally quarrelsome but, in the long run, supportive. As the saying goes, family is where, when you go there, they have to take you in. The image of the nuclear family—with the father the main money-maker and responsible for making the important decisions in the family—continues to be a very strong influence on family lifestyles. Choices made within the family setting that appear to be simply logical or natural are, in fact, the consequence of the nuclear family structure. For instance, since the man's job is considered the mainstay of the family, his occupational shifts take first place over other family concerns. Because his earnings are likely to be greater than his wife's if she works, her job is considered the logically expendable one. If they have children, the wife is the one who is going to quit work and "stay home with the baby." If his career plans favor relocating to a different city, hers are likely to suffer. This, in turn, reinforces the disparity in their earnings, making it seem natural that his job is the one that is really important, while hers is secondary. Many women's reluctance to plan a career (as distinguished from a job to earn money) reflects the reality that they are expected to fit it in around everything else in the family. Many men agree that their wife's education, job, and career plans are worthwhile, as long as dinner is still on the table, the house in order, and the kids taken care of when he walks in the door. Some men still talk about taking responsibility for their own child as "baby-sitting."

The reality is that different family members experience the same family very differently. Where money is short, it is women who "bridge the gap between what a household's resources really are and what a family's position is supposed to be" (Rapp, 1982:175). They stretch the available food, clothing, and resources to make ends meet. Where a family consistently comes up short at the end of the paycheck, it is the woman who eats less and does without, so that the kids and husband can have enough. To talk about a family's standard of living as if all family members shared the same level of well-being or poverty is misleading. Yet social scientists typically use the husband's occupation in defining social class and just assume that the rest of the family is included. And defining a family's class by the husband's occupation does not provide a basis for understanding the very different life chances that men and women face within the same family, given the realities of divorce and single parenthood.

FAMILIES: A MULTITUDE OF POSSIBILITIES

Probably the most talked-about change in American families in recent years has been the increase in family households headed by women. More than a quarter of America's children now live with one parent; 26% of all families are headed by mothers (5% by fathers), in 2000, which is up from 12% and 1% in 1970. The number of single mothers increased between 1970 and 2000, from 3 million to 10 million; over the same time frame, the number of single fathers increased also, from 393,000 to 2 million. (Single mothers and fathers include all those who are not currently living with a spouse.) (U.S. Census Brief 97-1, "Children With Single Parents–How They Fare," September 1997.)

Women heading families face a series of obstacles that reflect the unwillingness of policy makers to recognize and address their condition. In order to work and support their families, women must have child care; then they must earn enough to provide for their families. Women's earnings have risen from 62% of men's in 1970, to 76.5% by 2000. The good news is that this is a greater proportion than it has been in the recent past; the bad news is that this is mostly because of the relative decline in men's earnings rather than an increase in women's overall income. There are important race and ethnic differences that change this picture somewhat: white women's earnings are about 75% of white men's, while black women's are 85% of black men's and Hispanic women's are almost 87% of Hispanic men's. What this shows is that the wage gap is affected by both gender and race. The relatively lower pay of black and Hispanic men compared with white men means the gender gap is correspondingly less, but of course this translates to lower overall family incomes for these families (*Highlights of Women's Earnings in 2000*, U.S. Department of Labor Bureau of Labor Statistics, August 2001, Report 952). Women heading households are more likely to be poor, not only because there is only one earner in the family but because that earner is a woman. Nearly 6 of ten children living with only their mother were near or below the poverty line. (U.S. Census Brief 97-1, *Children With Single Parents—How They Fare*, September 1997.) It also means that the lack of affordable child care hits women who are heads of family especially hard. Yet American social policy has not recognized that child care is just as much a social necessity as educating children. The United States is far behind most European countries, which train child-care specialists and provide care for children from the youngest ages.

For many women, the descent to poverty occurs as a result of divorce. This is more likely to happen for white women than for black women, partly because of the overall lower earnings of black men relative to white men. Despite all the jokes about men paying their life fortune in alimony to ex-wives, the reality is that men's standard of living goes up following divorce, while women's drops precipitously. The Working Women's Defense Fund calculated that mothers' standard of living declined an average of 26%, while fathers' improved by 34% (Masnerus, 1995).

The transition from Mrs. to ex-Mrs. is especially difficult for older, long-married women, who often do not have marketable skills with which to support themselves. The tragic irony is that it is precisely those women who acceded to cultural expectations to stay at home and be good wives and mothers who suffer the most, both economically and emotionally. Women whose whole sense of identity centers around being a wife and mother must cope with profound loss of meaning as well as the economic shock of divorce. These older women are the ones more likely to get alimony (as distinguished from child support). Younger women from shorter-term marriages are unlikely to be awarded alimony and often are unable to even collect child support. Despite all the movies depicting the hilarious, heart-warming adventures of men raising children, custodial parents are most likely women: Mothers are still 85% of custodial parents, and almost half of them (47%) are likely to be working full time. Custodial mothers were three times as likely to be poor as custodial fathers were. This is not surprising, given the wage gap between men and women. Only 42% of custodial parents received the full amount of child support they were supposed to get from the other parent (that includes women paying the custodial father as well) (Grall, Timothy, Current Population Reports, P60-212, "Custodial Support for Mothers and Fathers," October 2000 using 1997 data). Chasing down so-called deadbeat dads has become standard rhetoric; and the emphasis on child support has resulted in more fathers who actually pay up. It does not, however, necessarily mean more money in the mother's household for families receiving public assistance, because the father's contribution is usually deducted from their welfare grant.

The reasons for the increase in families headed by women are complex and cannot be reduced to a simple explanation. Young women are more likely

to have worked. Young women are postponing marriage (or not marrying at all). In the 30 years from 1970 to 2000, the median age for women to get married increased from 20 years to 25 years of age. This increases the likelihood of having children though not married. (*Current Population Reports*, "America's Families and Living Arrangements, 2000," issued June 2001, by Jason Fields and Lynne Casper.) Shotgun weddings are less common now than in the past (judging by the fact that many fewer pregnant women marry before their first child is born). The options of abortion, and refusing to marry someone you don't like, are more acceptable now. Other explanations look at economic factors affecting couples' financial prospects as they consider marriage. Coontz and Folbre state that "nonmarriage is often a result of poverty and economic insecurity rather than the other way around," and low income families can also be two parent as well. In fact, more than a third of young children in poverty do in fact live with both parents (Coontz and Folbre, 2002). The reality is, over 25% of families with children were headed by women in 1995, compared with less than 12% in 1970. Single-parent families are 31% of families with children under 18; less than 16% of them are headed by the father. Many African-American families are headed by women—58%, compared with 21% for white families and 31% for Hispanic-American families. And remember, not all families involve children—they also include elders or other relatives in the household (U.S. Bureau of the Census, Statistical Abstracts, 1996, p. 62).

Married couples with children still depend upon the wife to do the "second shift"—the housework. Even when both husband and wife work full-time, throughout the 1980s, two-thirds of working wives reported that they did most or all of the housework. The time women spent on housework remained about the same whether they worked or not. This may be beginning to change—partly because women have simply stopped doing so much of it, but also because couples believe in sharing household work (Schor, 1991:103). Despite the variety of social arrangements in which people live their lives, social policy and law persist in penalizing those who do not live in nuclear family settings. One of the ways this has harmed non-traditional families is by excluding non-legally married family members from health insurance plans—without which Americans cannot afford to be sick. The high cost of medical coverage has now reached crisis proportions nationally. (The United States is the only major industrial nation that does not assure national health coverage for everybody.) However, there are signs of changes in employment coverage for non-traditional family units. Some employers (both private and public) are now including "domestic partners" in health coverage, life insurance and other employment-related benefits. One or two states also are formalizing "gay marriages" as domestic partners. Bear in mind that "marriage" is a legal status, with entitlements and responsibilities, as well as a traditionally approved social arrangement. So, to consider broadening the conventional scope of "marriage" indicates a real shift in public attitudes, and recognition of the diversity of possible living arrangements for people.

Currently, however, government emphasizes marriage as the "solution" for a host of social ills, especially for low income and poor people. Encouraging "Responsible Fatherhood" seems to take the form of government sponsored marital counseling, sometimes with religious auspices. Instead of policies aimed at, for example, improving child care options, education, and job training for single mothers, this approach promotes marriage as the "cure", and suggests "abstinence only" for sex education. However, it is a measure of the progress of the women's movement that even these conservative approaches aimed at "strengthening marriage" recognize that domestic violence is a real problem for many women (and children) for whom marriage is not the answer.

The Institute for Women's Policy Research, among others, disputes this emphasis on marriage as the "cure" for poverty and "dependency" on welfare. They state: "despite its virtues, marriage does not address the root causes of women's poverty . . . factors that do influence [women's] marital decisions include increased male unemployment and decreased men's real wages, the potential for increased domestic violence, increased housework, and other economic and emotional considerations, [are] most

associated with single-parenthood for many low-income women." (December 2000, IWPR's Statement on Marriage Promotion and TANF Reauthorization, citing Francine Blau et al. 2000 and Kathryn Edin 2000.)

MOM AND APPLE PIE?

The conservatives who attack the women's movement for being anti-family have a specific form of the family in mind—one that certainly does not correspond to what real families are like. These fundamentalist doctrines of the political far right rigidly interpret the Bible to justify the patriarchal family, attack women's rights, and use the power of the laws to support their views. It is interesting that in times of social change—like the mid-1800s in the throes of industrialization, and our own time—ideologies advocating a return to an earlier, "golden age" surface.

Now, even the basic, biological fact that it takes two to make a baby seems to be blurring at the edges with the advances of reproductive technologies. A woman may be pregnant and give birth to a child to whom she is not genetically related, from an ovum that was fertilized in vitro (outside the woman's body). The child then may potentially have two completely different sets of parents. What is the legal status of the woman who was pregnant with the child? What "right," if any, has she to be considered the "mother"? Is a "contract" to give up the child after birth enforceable if she changes her mind? These are unresolved questions. Typically, the couple wishing to become parents is wealthy enough to pay large medical and legal fees, while the woman having the child has much lower income and less to spend on lawyers. Our thinking about women, pregnancy, parenting, and family will need to take these issues into account.

Another possibility is that a woman who wants to become pregnant but is having difficulties can opt for series of fertility treatments or implanting of fertilized eggs—procedures that are experimental and extremely expensive, uncomfortable, and uncertain. Others want to be parents but not within a male-female household, either gay/lesbian couples or single persons. All of these can also become families with parents who raise children, wipe sniffly noses, and clap at school plays. The challenge is to creatively respond to changed conditions, and to help shape that change in ways that will enhance rather than stifle peoples lives.   [2002]

REFERENCES

Bernard, Jessie. "The Good Provider Role: Its Rise and Fall," *American Psychologist* 36, no. 1 (January 1981) pp. 1–12.

Bose, Christine, "Devaluing Women's Work: The Undercount of Women's Employment in 1900 and 1980," in *Hidden Aspects of Women's Work*, Christine Bose, Roslyn Feldberg, and Natalie Sokoloff, New York: Praeger, 1987, pp. 95–115.

Coontz, Stephanie and Nancy Folbre, "Marriage, Poverty and Public Policy" (2002), Council on Contemporary Families", paper for Annual Conference 4/02.

Grall, Timothy. U.S. BLS Current Population Reports, Custodial Support for Mothers and Fathers, Oct. 2000 using 1997 data, pp. 60–212.

Gutman, Herbert, "Persistent Myths About the Afro-American Family" in *The American Family in Social-Historical Perspective*, Michael Gordon, ed. 3rd ed. New York: St. Martin's Press, 1983, pp. 459–481.

Institute for Women's Policy Research, "Statement on Marriage Promotion and TANF Reauthorization," December 2001 (www. IWPR.org) (citing Blau, Francine et al., 2000).

Edin, Kathryn. "Understanding Young Women's Marriage Decisions: The Role of Labor and Marriage Market Conditions," *Industrial Labor Relations Review* 53 no. 4: 624–48; 2000.

"Few Good Men: Why Low-Income Single Mothers Don't Get Married," *American Prospect* no.11 pp. 4, 26–31.

Jones, Jacqueline. *Labor of Love, Labor of Sorrow: Black Women. Work and the Family from Slavery to the Present.* New York: Vintage, 1985.

Masnerus, Laura. "The Divorce Backlash: For Professional Women, the Price of Getting Out of a Marriage—and Keeping the Children—Is Getting Higher." *Working Woman* 20 no. 2 (Feb. 1995), p. 40.

Rapp, Rayna. "Family and Class in Contemporary America: Notes Toward an Understanding of Ideology," in *Rethinking the Family: Some Feminist Questions,* Barrie Thorne and Marilyn Yalom, eds. New York: Longman, 1982.

Thompson, Karen, and Andrzejewski, Julie. *Why Can't Sharon Kowalski Come Home?* San Francisco: Spinster/ Aunt Lute Book Company, 1988.

U.S. Bureau of Labor Statistics, Highlights of Women's Earnings in 2000, August 2001, Report 952.

U.S. Bureau of Labor Statistics, Current Pop Survey "Employment Characteristics of Families Summary", USDL 01-103; Internet: http://stats.bls.gov/newsrels.htm.

U.S. Bureau of the Census, U.S. Department of Commerce, "Household and Family Characteristics: March 1990 and 1989," Current Population Reports, Population Characteristics, Series P-20, No. 447, 1991.

U.S. Bureau of the Census, U.S. Department of Commerce, Statistical Abstracts of the U.S. Washington D.C.: U.S. Government Printing Office, 1996.

U.S. Census Brief 97-1, "Children With Single Parents—How They Fare" Sept 1997. Fields, Jason and Lynne Casper, "America's Families and Living Arrangements, 2000" U.S. BLS, Current Population Reports issued June 2001.

 65

Seventeen Syllables

HISAYE YAMAMOTO

The first Rosie knew that her mother had taken to writing poems was one evening when she finished one and read it aloud for her daughter's approval. It was about cats, and Rosie pretended to understand it thoroughly and appreciate it no end, partly because she hesitated to disillusion her mother about the quantity and quality of Japanese she had learned in all the years now that she had been going to Japanese school every Saturday (and Wednesday, too, in the summer). Even so, her mother must have been skeptical about the depth of Rosie's understanding, because she explained afterwards about the kind of poem she was trying to write.

See, Rosie, she said, it was a *haiku,* a poem in which she must pack all her meaning into seventeen syllables only, which were divided into three lines of five, seven, and five syllables. In the one she had just read, she had tried to capture the charm of a kitten, as well as comment on the superstition that owning a cat of three colors meant good luck.

"Yes, yes, I understand. How utterly lovely," Rosie said, and her mother, either satisfied or seeing through the deception and resigned, went back to composing.

The truth was that Rosie was lazy; English lay ready on the tongue but Japanese had to be searched for and examined, and even then put forth tentatively (probably to meet with laughter). It was so much easier to say yes, yes, even when one meant no, no. Besides, this was what was in her mind to say: I was looking through one of your magazines from

Japan last night, Mother, and towards the back I found some *haiku* in English that delighted me. There was one that made me giggle off and on until I fell asleep—

It is morning, and lo!
I lie awake, *comme il faut*,
sighing for some dough.

Now, how to reach her mother, how to communicate the melancholy song? Rosie knew formal Japanese by fits and starts, her mother had even less English, no French. It was much more possible to say yes, yes.

It developed that her mother was writing the *haiku* for a daily newspaper, the *Mainichi Shimbun*, that was published in San Francisco. Los Angeles, to be sure, was closer to the farming community in which the Hayashi family lived and several Japanese vernaculars were printed there, but Rosie's parents said they preferred the tone of the northern paper. Once a week, the *Mainichi* would have a section devoted to *haiku*, and her mother became an extravagant contributor, taking for herself the blossoming pen name, Ume Hanazono.

So Rosie and her father lived for awhile with two women, her mother and Ume Hanazono. Her mother (Tome Hayashi by name) kept house, cooked, washed, and, along with her husband and the Carrascos, the Mexican family hired for the harvest, did her ample share of picking tomatoes out in the sweltering fields and boxing them in tidy strata in the cool packing shed. Ume Hanazono, who came to life after the dinner dishes were done, was an earnest, muttering stranger who often neglected speaking when spoken to and stayed busy at the parlor table as late as midnight scribbling with pencil on scratch paper or carefully copying characters on good paper with her fat, pale green Parker.

The new interest had some repercussions on the household routine. Before, Rosie had been accustomed to her parents and herself taking their hot baths early and going to bed almost immediately afterwards, unless her parents challenged each other to a game of flower cards or unless company dropped in. Now if her father wanted to play cards, he had to resort to solitaire (at which he always cheated fearlessly), and if a group of friends came over, it was bound to contain someone who was also writing *haiku,* and the small assemblage would be split in two, her father entertaining the non-literary members and her mother comparing ecstatic notes with the visiting poet.

If they went out, it was more of the same thing. But Ume Hanazono's life span, even for a poet's, was very brief—perhaps three months at most.

One night they went over to see the Hayano family in the neighboring town to the west, an adventure both painful and attractive to Rosie. It was attractive because there were four Hayano girls, all lovely and each one named after a season of the year (Haru, Natsu, Aki, Fuyu), painful because something had been wrong with Mrs. Hayano ever since the birth of her first child. Rosie would sometimes watch Mrs. Hayano, reputed to have been the belle of her native village, making her way about a room, stooped, slowly shuffling, violently trembling (*always* trembling), and she would be reminded that this woman, in this same condition, had carried and given issue to three babies. She would look wonderingly at Mr. Hayano, handsome, tall, and strong, and she would look at her four pretty friends. But it was not a matter she could come to any decision about.

On this visit, however, Mrs. Hayano sat all evening in the rocker, as motionless and unobtrusive as it was possible for her to be, and Rosie found the greater part of the evening practically anaesthetic. Too, Rosie spent most of it in the girls' room, because Haru, the garrulous one, said almost as soon as the bows and other greetings were over, "Oh, you must see my new coat!"

It was a pale plaid of grey, sand, and blue, with an enormous collar, and Rosie, seeing nothing special in it, said, "Gee, how nice."

"Nice?" said Haru, indignantly. "Is that all you can say about it? It's gorgeous! And so cheap, too. Only seventeen-ninety-eight, because it was a sale. The saleslady said it was twenty-five dollars regular."

"Gee," said Rosie. Natsu, who never said much and when she said anything said it shyly, fingered the coat covetously and Haru pulled it away.

"Mine," she said, putting it on. She minced in the aisle between the two large beds and smiled happily. "Let's see how your mother likes it."

She broke into the front room and the adult conversation and went to stand in front of Rosie's mother, while the rest watched from the door. Rosie's mother was properly envious. "May I inherit it when you're through with it?"

Haru, pleased, giggled and said yes, she could, but Natsu reminded gravely from the door, "You promised me, Haru."

Everyone laughed but Natsu, who shamefacedly retreated into the bedroom. Haru came in laughing, taking off the coat. "We were only kidding, Natsu," she said. "Here, you try it on now."

After Natsu buttoned herself into the coat, inspected herself solemnly in the bureau mirror, and reluctantly shed it, Rosie, Aki, and Fuyu got their turns, and Fuyu, who was eight, drowned in it while her sisters and Rosie doubled up in amusement. They all went into the front room later, because Haru's mother quaveringly called to her to fix the tea and rice cakes and open a can of sliced peaches for everybody. Rosie noticed that her mother and Mr. Hayano were talking together at the little table —they were discussing a *haiku* that Mr. Hayano was planning to send to the *Mainichi,* while her father was sitting at one end of the sofa looking through a copy of *Life,* the new picture magazine. Occasionally, her father would comment on a photograph, holding it toward Mrs. Hayano and speaking to her as he always did—loudly, as though he thought someone such as she must surely be at least a trifle deaf also.

The five girls had their refreshments at the kitchen table, and it was while Rosie was showing the sisters her trick of swallowing peach slices without chewing (she chased each slippery crescent down with a swig of tea) that her father brought his empty teacup and untouched saucer to the sink and said, "Come on, Rosie, we're going home now."

"Already?" asked Rosie.

"Work tomorrow," he said.

He sounded irritated, and Rosie, puzzled, gulped one last yellow slice and stood up to go, while the sisters began protesting, as was their wont.

"We have to get up at five-thirty," he told them, going into the front room quickly, so that they did not have their usual chance to hang onto his hands and plead for an extension of time.

Rosie, following, saw that her mother and Mr. Hayano were sipping tea and still talking together, while Mrs. Hayano concentrated, quivering, on raising the handleless Japanese cup to her lips with both her hands and lowering it back to her lap. Her father, saying nothing, went out the door, onto the bright porch, and down the steps. Her mother looked up and asked, "Where is he going?"

"Where is he going?" Rosie said. "He said we were going home now."

"Going home?" Her mother looked with embarrassment at Mr. Hayano and his absorbed wife and then forced a smile. "He must be tired," she said.

Haru was not giving up yet. "May Rosie stay overnight?" she asked, and Natsu, Aki, and Fuyu came to reinforce their sister's plea by helping her make a circle around Rosie's mother. Rosie, for once having no desire to stay, was relieved when her mother, apologizing to the perturbed Mr. and Mrs. Hayano for her father's abruptness at the same time, managed to shake her head no at the quartet, kindly but adamant, so that they broke their circle and let her go.

Rosie's father looked ahead into the windshield as the two joined him. "I'm sorry," her mother said. "You must be tired." Her father, stepping on the starter, said nothing. "You know how I get when it's *haiku,*" she continued, "I forget what time it is." He only grunted.

As they rode homeward silently, Rosie, sitting between, felt a rush of hate for both—for her mother for begging, for her father for denying her mother. I wish this old Ford would crash, right now, she thought, then immediately, no, no, I wish my father would laugh, but it was too late: already the vision had passed through her mind of the green pick-up crumpled in the dark against one of the mighty eucalyptus trees they were just riding past, of the three contorted, bleeding bodies, one of them hers.

Rosie ran between two patches of tomatoes, her heart working more rambunctiously than she had ever known it to. How lucky it was that Aunt Taka and Uncle Gimpachi had come tonight, though, how very lucky. Otherwise she might not have really kept her half-promise to meet Jesus Carrasco. Jesus was going to be a senior in September at the same school she went to, and his parents were the ones helping with the tomatoes this year. She and Jesus, who hardly remembered seeing each other at Cleveland High where there were so many other people and two whole grades between them, had become great friends this summer—he always had a joke for her when he periodically drove the loaded pick-up up from the fields to the shed where she was usually sorting while her mother and father did the packing, and they laughed a great deal together over infinitesimal repartee during the afternoon break for chilled watermelon or ice cream in the shade of the shed.

What she enjoyed most was racing him to see which could finish picking a double row first. He, who could work faster, would tease her by slowing down until she thought she would surely pass him this time, then speeding up furiously to leave her several sprawling vines behind. Once he had made her screech hideously by crossing over, while her back was turned, to place atop the tomatoes in her green-stained bucket a truly monstrous, pale green worm (it had looked more like an infant snake). And it was when they had finished a contest this morning, after she had pantingly pointed a green finger at the immature tomatoes evident in the lugs at the end of his row and he had returned the accusation (with justice), that he had startlingly brought up the matter of their possibly meeting outside the range of both their parents' dubious eyes.

"What for?" she had asked.

"I've got a secret I want to tell you," he said.

"Tell me now," she demanded.

"It won't be ready till tonight," he said.

She laughed. "Tell me tomorrow then."

"It'll be gone tomorrow," he threatened.

"Well, for seven hakes, what is it?" she asked, more than twice, and when he had suggested that the packing shed would be an appropriate place to find out, she had cautiously answered maybe. She had not been certain she was going to keep the appointment until the arrival of her mother's sister and her husband. Their coming seemed a sort of signal of permission, of grace, and she had definitely made up her mind to lie and leave as she was bowing them welcome.

So as soon as everyone appeared settled back for the evening, she announced loudly that she was going to the privy outside, "I'm going to the *benjo!*" and slipped out the door. And now that she was actually on her way, her heart pumped in such an undisciplined way that she could hear it with her ears. It's because I'm running, she told herself, slowing to a walk. The shed was up ahead, one more patch away, in the middle of the fields. Its bulk, looming in the dimness, took on a sinisterness that was funny when Rosie reminded herself that it was only a wooden frame with a canvas roof and three canvas walls that made a slapping noise on breezy days.

Jesus was sitting on the narrow plank that was the sorting platform and she went around to the other side and jumped backwards to seat herself on the rim of a packing stand. "Well, tell me," she said without greeting, thinking her voice sounded reassuringly familiar.

"I saw you coming out the door," Jesus said. "I heard you running part of the way, too."

"Uh-huh," Rosie said. "Now tell me the secret."

"I was afraid you wouldn't come," he said.

Rosie delved around on the chicken-wire bottom of the stall for number two tomatoes, ripe, which she was sitting beside, and came up with a left-over that felt edible. She bit into it and began sucking out the pulp and seeds. "I'm here," she pointed out.

"Rosie, are you sorry you came?"

"Sorry? What for?" she said. "You said you were going to tell me something."

"I will, I will," Jesus said, but his voice contained

disappointment, and Rosie fleetingly felt the older of the two, realizing a brand-new power which vanished without category under her recognition.

"I have to go back in a minute," she said. "My aunt and uncle are here from Wintersburg. I told them I was going to the privy."

Jesus laughed. "You funny thing," he said. "You slay me!"

"Just because you have a bathroom *inside*," Rosie said. "Come on, tell me."

Chuckling, Jesus came around to lean on the stand facing her. They still could not see each other very clearly, but Rosie noticed that Jesus became very sober again as he took the hollow tomato from her hand and dropped it back into the stall. When he took hold of her empty hand, she could find no words to protest; her vocabulary had become distressingly constricted and she thought desperately that all that remained intact now was yes and no and oh, and even these few sounds would not easily come out. Thus, kissed by Jesus, Rosie fell for the first time entirely victim to a helplessness delectable beyond speech. But the terrible, beautiful sensation lasted no more than a second, and the reality of Jesus' lips and tongue and teeth and hands made her pull away with such strength that she nearly tumbled.

Rosie stopped running as she approached the lights from the windows of home. How long since she had left? She could not guess, but gasping yet, she went to the privy in back and locked herself in. Her own breathing deafened her in the dark, close space, and she sat and waited until she could hear at last the nightly calling of the frogs and crickets. Even then, all she could think to say was oh, my, and the pressure of Jesus' face against her face would not leave.

No one had missed her in the parlor, however, and Rosie walked in and through quickly, announcing that she was next going to take a bath. "Your father's in the bathhouse," her mother said, and Rosie, in her room, recalled that she had not seen him when she entered. There had been only Aunt Taka and Uncle Gimpachi with her mother at the table, drinking tea.

She got her robe and straw sandals and crossed the parlor again to go outside. Her mother was telling them about the *haiku* competition in the *Mainichi* and the poem she had entered.

Rosie met her father coming out of the bathhouse. "Are you through, Father?" she asked. "I was going to ask you to scrub my back."

"Scrub your own back," he said shortly, going toward the main house.

"What have I done now?" she yelled after him. She suddenly felt like doing a lot of yelling. But he did not answer, and she went into the bathhouse. Turning on the dangling light, she removed her denims and T-shirt and threw them in the big carton for dirty clothes standing next to the washing machine. Her other things she took with her into the bath compartment to wash after her bath. After she had scooped a basin of hot water from the square wooden tub, she sat on the grey cement of the floor and soaped herself at exaggerated leisure, singing "Red Sails in the Sunset" at the top of her voice and using da-da-da where she suspected her words. Then, standing up, still singing, for she was possessed by the notion that any attempt now to analyze would result in spoilage and she believed that the larger her volume the less she would be able to hear herself think, she obtained more hot water and poured it on until she was free of lather. Only then did she allow herself to step into the steaming vat, one leg first, then the remainder of her body inch by inch until the water no longer stung and she could move around at will.

She took a long time soaking, afterwards remembering to go around outside to stoke the embers of the tin-lined fireplace beneath the tub and to throw on a few more sticks so that the water might keep its heat for her mother, and when she finally returned to the parlor, she found her mother still talking *haiku* with her aunt and uncle, the three of them on another round of tea. Her father was nowhere in sight.

At Japanese school the next day (Wednesday, it was), Rosie was grave and giddy by turns. Preoccupied at her desk in the row for students on Book Eight, she made up for it at recess by performing wild mimicry for the benefit of her friend Chizuko. She held her nose and whined a witticism or two in what she considered was the manner of Fred Allen; she assumed intoxication and a British accent to go over the climax of the Rudy Vallee recording of the pub conversation about William Ewart Gladstone; she was the child Shirley Temple piping, "On the Good Ship Lollipop"; she was the gentleman soprano of the Four Inkspots trilling, "If I Didn't Care." And she felt reasonably satisfied when Chizuko wept and gasped, "Oh, Rosie, you ought to be in the movies!"

Her father came after her at noon, bringing her sandwiches of minced ham and two nectarines to eat while she rode, so that she could pitch right into the sorting when they got home. The lugs were piling up, he said, and the ripe tomatoes in them would probably have to be taken to the cannery tomorrow if they were not ready for the produce haulers tonight. "This heat's not doing them any good. And we've got no time for a break today."

It *was* hot, probably the hottest day of the year, and Rosie's blouse stuck damply to her back even under the protection of the canvas. But she worked as efficiently as a flawless machine and kept the stalls heaped, with one part of her mind listening in to the parental murmuring about the heat and the tomatoes and with another part planning the exact words she would say to Jesus when he drove up with the first load of the afternoon. But when at last she saw that the pick-up was coming, her hands went berserk and the tomatoes started falling in the wrong stalls, and her father said, "Hey, hey! Rosie, watch what you're doing!"

"Well, I have to go to the *benjo*," she said, hiding panic.

"Go in the weeds over there," he said, only half-joking.

"Oh, Father!" she protested.

"Oh, go on home," her mother said. "We'll make out for awhile."

In the privy Rosie peered through a knothole toward the fields, watching as much as she could of Jesus. Happily she thought she saw him look in the direction of the house from time to time before he finished unloading and went back toward the patch where his mother and father worked. As she was heading for the shed, a very presentable black car purred up the dirt driveway to the house and its driver motioned to her. Was this the Hayashi home, he wanted to know. She nodded. Was she a Hayashi? Yes, she said, thinking that he was a good-looking man. He got out of the car with a huge, flat package and she saw that he warmly wore a business suit. "I have something here for your mother then," he said, in a more elegant Japanese than she was used to.

She told him where her mother was and he came along with her, patting his face with an immaculate white handkerchief and saying something about the coolness of San Francisco. To her surprised mother and father, he bowed and introduced himself as, among other things, the *haiku* editor of the *Mainichi Shimbun*, saying that since he had been coming as far as Los Angeles anyway, he had decided to bring her the first prize she had won in the recent contest.

"First prize?" her mother echoed, believing and not believing, pleased and overwhelmed. Handed the package with a bow, she bobbed her head up and down numerous times to express her utter gratitude.

"It is nothing much," he added, "but I hope it will serve as a token of our great appreciation for your contributions and our great admiration of your considerable talent."

"I am not worthy," she said, falling easily into his style. "It is I who should make some sign of my humble thanks for being permitted to contribute."

"No, no, to the contrary," he said, bowing again.

But Rosie's mother insisted, and then saying that she knew she was being unorthodox, she asked if she might open the package because her curiosity was so great. Certainly she might. In fact, he would like her reaction to it, for personally, it was one of his favorite Hiroshiges.

Rosie thought it was a pleasant picture, which looked to have been sketched with delicate quickness. There were pink clouds, containing some graceful calligraphy, and a sea that was a pale blue except at the edges, containing four sampans with indications of people in them. Pines edged the water and on the far-off beach there was a cluster of thatched huts towered over by pine-dotted mountains of grey and blue. The frame was scalloped' and gilt.

After Rosie's mother pronounced it without peer and somewhat prodded her father into nodding agreement, she said Mr. Kuroda must at least have a cup of tea after coming all this way, and although Mr. Kuroda did not want to impose, he soon agreed that a cup of tea would be refreshing and went along with her to the house, carrying the picture for her.

"Ha, your mother's crazy!" Rosie's father said, and Rosie laughed uneasily as she resumed judgment on the tomatoes. She had emptied six lugs when he broke into an imaginary conversation with Jesus to tell her to go and remind her mother of the tomatoes, and she went slowly.

Mr. Kuroda was in his shirtsleeves expounding some *haiku* theory as he munched a rice cake, and her mother was rapt. Abashed in the great man's presence, Rosie stood next to her mother's chair until her mother looked up inquiringly, and then she started to whisper the message, but her mother pushed her gently away and reproached, "You are not being very polite to our guest."

"Father says the tomatoes. . . ." Rosie said aloud, smiling foolishly.

"Tell him I shall only be a minute," her mother said, speaking the language of Mr. Kuroda.

When Rosie carried the reply to her father, he did not seem to hear and she said again, "Mother says she'll be back in a minute."

"All right, all right," he nodded, and they worked again in silence. But suddenly, her father uttered an incredible noise, exactly like the cork of a bottle popping, and the next Rosie knew, he was stalking angrily toward the house, almost running in fact, and she chased after him crying, "Father! Father! What are you going to do?"

He stopped long enough to order her back to the shed. "Never mind!" he shouted. "Get on with the sorting!"

And from the place in the fields where she stood, frightened and vacillating, Rosie saw her father enter the house. Soon Mr. Kuroda came out alone, putting on his coat. Mr. Kuroda got into his car and backed out down the driveway onto the highway. Next her father emerged, also alone, something in his arms (it was the picture, she realized), and, going over to the bathhouse woodpile, he threw the picture on the ground and picked up the axe. Smashing the picture, glass and all (she heard the explosion faintly), he reached over for the kerosene that was used to encourage the bath fire and poured it over the wreckage. I am dreaming, Rosie said to herself, I am dreaming, but her father, having made sure that his act of cremation was irrevocable, was even then returning to the fields.

Rosie ran past him and toward the house. What had become of her mother? She burst into the parlor and found her mother at the back window watching the dying fire. They watched together until there remained only a feeble smoke under the blazing sun. Her mother was very calm.

"Do you know why I married your father?" she said without turning.

"No," said Rosie. It was the most frightening question she had ever been called upon to answer. Don't tell me now, she wanted to say, tell me tomorrow, tell me next week, don't tell me today. But she knew she would be told now, that the telling would combine with the other violence of the hot afternoon to level her life, her world to the very ground.

It was like a story out of the magazines illustrated in sepia, which she had consumed so greedily for a period until the information had somehow reached her that those wretchedly unhappy autobiographies, offered to her as the testimonials of living men and women, were largely inventions: Her mother, at nineteen, had come to America and married her father as an alternative to suicide.

At eighteen she had been in love with the first son of one of the well-to-do families in her village. The two had met whenever and wherever they could, secretly, because it would not have done for his family to see him favor her—her father had no money; he was a drunkard and a gambler besides. She had learned she was with child; an excellent match had already been arranged for her lover. Despised by her family, she had given premature birth to a stillborn son, who would be seventeen now. Her family did not turn her out, but she could no longer project herself in any direction without refreshing in them the memory of her indiscretion. She wrote to Aunt Taka, her favorite sister in America, threatening to kill herself if Aunt Taka would not send for her. Aunt Taka hastily arranged a marriage with a young man of whom she knew, but lately arrived from Japan, a young man of simple mind, it was said, but of kindly heart. The young man was never told why his unseen betrothed was so eager to hasten the day of meeting.

The story was told perfectly, with neither groping for words nor untoward passion. It was as though her mother had memorized it by heart, reciting it to herself so many times over that its nagging vileness had long since gone.

"I had a brother then?" Rosie asked, for this was what seemed to matter now; she would think about the other later, she assured herself, pushing back the illumination which threatened all that darkness that had hitherto been merely mysterious or even glamorous. "A half-brother?"

"Yes."

"I would have liked a brother," she said.

Suddenly, her mother knelt on the floor and took her by the wrists. "Rosie," she said urgently, "Promise me you will never marry!" Shocked more by the request than the revelation, Rosie stared at her mother's face. Jesus, Jesus, she called silently, not certain whether she was invoking the help of the son of the Carrascos or of God, until there returned sweetly the memory of Jesus' hand, how it had touched her and where. Still her mother waited for an answer, holding her wrists so tightly that her hands were going numb. She tried to pull free. Promise, her mother whispered fiercely, promise. Yes, yes, I promise, Rosie said. But for an instant she turned away, and her mother, hearing the familiar glib agreement, released her. Oh, you, you, you, her eyes and twisted mouth said, you fool. Rosie, covering her face, began at last to cry, and the embrace and consoling hand came much later than she expected.   [1988]

 66

A Long Story

BETH BRANT

*Dedicated to my Great-Grandmothers
Eliza Powless and Catherine Brant*

"About 40 Indian children took the train at this depot for the Philadelphia Indian School last Friday. They were accompanied by the government agent, and seemed a bright looking lot."

—*The Northern Observer*
(Massena, New York, July 20, 1892)

"I am only beginning to understand what it means for a mother to lose a child."

—Anna Demeter, *Legal Kidnapping*
(Beacon Press, Boston, 1977)

1890

It has been two days since they came and took the children away. My body is greatly chilled. All our blankets have been used to bring me warmth. The women keep the fire blazing. The men sit. They talk among themselves. We are frightened by this sudden child-stealing. We signed papers, the agent said. This gave them rights to take our babies. It is good for them, the agent said. It will make them civilized, the agent said. I do not know *civilized*.

I hold myself tight in fear of flying apart in the air. The others try to feed me. Can they feed a dead woman? I have stopped talking. When my mouth opens, only air escapes. I have used up my sound screaming their names—She Sees Deer! He Catches The Leaves! My eyes stare at the room, the walls of scrubbed wood, the floor of dirt. I know there are people here, but I cannot see them. I see a darkness, like the lake at New Moon. Black, unmoving. In the center, a picture of my son and daughter being lifted onto the train. My daughter wearing the dark blue, heavy dress. All of the girls dressed alike. Never have I seen such eyes! They burn into my head even now. My son. His hair cut. Dressed as the white men, his arms and legs covered by cloth that made him sweat. His face, streaked with tears. So many children crying, screaming. The sun on our bodies, our heads. The train screeching like a crow, sounding like laughter. Smoke and dirt pumping out the insides of the train. So many people. So many children. The women, standing as if in prayer, our hands lifted, reaching. The dust sifting down on our palms. Our palms making motions at the sky. Our fingers closing like the claws of the bear.

I see this now. The hair of my son held in my hands. I rub the strands, the heavy braids coming alive as the fire flares and casts a bright light on the black hair. They slip from my fingers and lie coiled on the ground. I see this. My husband picks up the braids, wraps them in cloth; he takes the pieces of our son away. He walks outside, the eyes of the people on him. I see this. He will find a bottle and drink with the men. Some of the women will join him. They will end the night by singing or crying. It is all the same. I see this. No sounds of children playing games and laughing. Even the dogs have ceased their noise. They lay outside each doorway, waiting. I hear this. The voices of children. They cry. They pray. They call me. *Nisten ha.* I hear this. *Nisten ha.**

1978

I am wakened by the dream. In the dream my daughter is dead. Her father is returning her body to me in pieces. He keeps her heart. I thought I screamed . . . *Patricia!* I sit up in bed, swallowing air as if for nourishment. The dream remains in the air. I rise to go to her room. Ellen tries to lead me back to bed, but I have to see once again. I open her door. She is gone. The room empty, lonely. They said it was in her best interests. How can that be? She is only six, a baby who needs her mothers. She loves us. This has not happened. I will not believe this. Oh god, I think I have died.

Night after night, Ellen holds me as I shake. Our sobs stifling the air in our room. We lie in our bed

---

and try to give comfort. My mind can't think beyond last week when she left. I would have killed him if I'd had the chance! He took her hand and pulled her to the car. The look in his eyes of triumph. It was a contest to him, Patricia the prize. He will teach her to hate us. He will! I see her dear face. That face looking out the back window of his car. Her mouth forming the words *Mommy, Mama.* Her dark braids tied with red yarn. Her front teeth missing. Her overalls with the yellow flower on the pocket, embroidered by Ellen's hands. So lovingly she sewed the yellow wool. Patricia waiting quietly until she was finished. Ellen promising to teach her designs—chain stitch, french knot, split stitch. How Patricia told everyone that Ellen made the flower just for her. So proud of her overalls.

I open the closet door. Almost everything is gone. A few things hang there limp, abandoned. I pull a blue dress from the hanger and take it back to my room. Ellen tries to take it from me, but I hold on, the soft blue cotton smelling of my daughter. How is it possible to feel such pain and live? "Ellen?!" She croons my name. "Mary, Mary, I love you." She sings me to sleep.

1890

The agent was here to deliver a letter. I screamed at him and sent curses his way. I threw dirt in his face as he mounted his horse. He thinks I'm a crazy woman and warns me, "You better settle down Annie." What can they do to me? I am a crazy woman. This letter hurts my hand. It is written in their hateful language. It is evil, but there is a message for me.

I start the walk up the road to my brother. He works for the whites and understands their meanings. I think about my brother as I pull the shawl closer to my body. It is cold now. Soon there will be snow. The corn has been dried and hangs from our cabin, waiting to be used. The corn never changes. My brother is changed. He says that *I* have changed and bring shame to our clan. He says I should accept the fate. But I do not believe in the fate of child-stealing. There is evil here. There is much wrong in our village. My brother says I am a crazy woman because I howl at the sky every evening. He is a fool. I am calling the children. He says the people are becoming afraid of me because I talk to the air and laugh like the raven overhead. But I am talking to the children. They need to hear the sound of me. I laugh to cheer them. They cry for us.

This letter burns my hands. I hurry to my brother. He has taken the sign of the wolf from over the doorway. He pretends to be like those who hate us. He gets more and more like the child-stealers. His eyes move away from mine. He takes the letter from me and begins the reading of it. I am confused. This letter is from two strangers with the names Martha and Daniel. They say they are learning civilized ways. Daniel works in the fields, growing food for the school. Martha cooks and is being taught to sew aprons. She will be going to live with the schoolmaster's wife. She will be a live-in girl. What is a *live-in girl?* I shake my head. The words sound the same to me. I am afraid of Martha and Daniel, these strangers who know my name. My hands and arms are becoming numb.

I tear the letter from my brother's fingers. He stares at me, his eyes traitors in his face. He calls after me, "Annie! Annie!" That is not my name! I run to the road. That is not my name! There is no Martha! There is no Daniel! This is witch work. The paper burns and burns. At my cabin, I quickly dig a hole in the field. The earth is hard and cold, but I dig with my nails. I dig, my hands feeling weaker. I tear the paper and bury the scraps. As the earth drifts and settles, the names Martha and Daniel are covered. I look to the sky and find nothing but endless blue. My eyes are blinded by the color. I begin the howling.

1978

When I get home from work, there is a letter from Patricia. I make coffee and wait for Ellen, pacing the rooms of our apartment. My back is sore from the line, bending over and over, screwing the handles on the doors of the flashy cars moving by. My work protects me from questions, the guys making jokes at my expense. But some of them touch my shoul-

der lightly and briefly as a sign of understanding. The few women, eyes averted or smiling in sympathy. No one talks. There is no time to talk. No room to talk, the noise taking up all space and breath.

I carry the letter with me as I move from room to room. Finally I sit at the kitchen table, turning the paper around in my hands. Patricia's printing is large and uneven. The stamp has been glued on halfheartedly and is coming loose. Each time a letter arrives, I dread it, even as I long to hear from my child. I hear Ellen's key in the door. She walks into the kitchen, bringing the smell of the hospital with her. She comes toward me, her face set in new lines, her uniform crumpled and stained, her brown hair pulled back in an imitation of a french twist. She knows there is a letter. I kiss her and bring mugs of coffee to the table. We look at each other. She reaches for my hand, bringing it to her lips. Her hazel eyes are steady in her round face.

I open the letter. *Dear Mommy. I am fine. Daddy got me a new bike. My big teeth are coming in. We are going to see Grandma for my birthday. Daddy got me new shoes. Love, Patricia.* She doesn't ask about Ellen. I imagine her father standing over her, coaxing her, coaching her. The letter becomes ugly. I tear it in bits and scatter them out the window. The wind scoops the pieces into a tight fist before strewing them in the street. A car drives over the paper, shredding it to garbage and mud.

Ellen makes a garbled sound. "I'll leave. If it will make it better, I'll leave." I quickly hold her as the dusk moves into the room and covers us. "Don't leave. Don't leave." I feel her sturdy back shiver against my hands. She kisses my throat, and her arms tighten as we move closer. "Ah Mary, I love you so much." As the tears threaten our eyes, the taste of salt is on our lips and tongues. We stare into ourselves, touching the place of pain, reaching past the fear, the guilt, the anger, the loneliness.

We go to our room. It is beautiful again. I am seeing it new. The sun is barely there. The colors of cream, brown, green mixing with the wood floor. The rug with its design of wild birds. The black ash basket glowing on the dresser, holding a bouquet of dried flowers bought at a vendor's stand. I remember the old woman, laughing and speaking rapidly in Polish as she wrapped the blossoms in newspaper. Ellen undresses me as I cry. My desire for her breaking through the heartbreak we share. She pulls the covers back, smoothing the white sheets, her hands repeating the gestures done at work. She guides me onto the cool material. I watch her remove the uniform of work. An aide to nurses. A healer of spirit.

She comes to me in full flesh. My hands are taken with the curves and soft roundness of her. She covers me with the beating of her heart. The rhythm steadies me. Her heat is centering me. I am grounded by the peace between us. I smile at her face above me, round like a moon, her long hair loose and touching my breasts. I take her breast in my hand, bring it to my mouth, suck her as a woman—in desire, in faith. Our bodies join. Our hair braids together on the pillow. Brown, black, silver, catching the last light of the sun. We kiss, touch, move to our place of power. Her mouth, moving over my body, stopping at curves and swells of skin, kissing, removing pain. Closer, close, together, woven, my legs are heat, the center of my soul is speaking to her, I am sliding into her, her mouth is medicine, her heart is the earth, we are dancing with flying arms, I shout, I sing, I weep salty liquid, sweet and warm it coats her throat. This is my life. I love you Ellen, I love you Mary, I love, we love.

1891

The moon is full. The air is cold. This cold strikes at my flesh as I remove my clothes and set them on fire in the withered corn field. I cut my hair, the knife sawing through the heavy mass. I bring the sharp blade to my arms, legs, and breasts. The blood trickles like small red rivers down my body. I feel nothing. I throw the tangled webs of my hair into the flames. The smell, like a burning animal, fills my nostrils. As the fire stretches to touch the stars, the people come out to watch me—the crazy woman. The ice in the air touches me.

They caught me as I tried to board the train and search for my babies. The white men tell my husband to watch me. I am dangerous. I laugh and laugh. My husband is good only for tipping bottles and swallowing anger. He looks at me, opening his mouth and making no sound. His eyes are dead. He wanders from the cabin and looks out on the corn. He whispers our names. He calls after the children. He is a dead man.

Where have they taken the children? I ask the question of each one who travels the road past our door. The women come and we talk. We ask and ask. They say there is nothing we can do. The white man is like a ghost. He slips in and out where we cannot see. Even in our dreams he comes to take away our questions. He works magic that resists our medicine. This magic has made us weak. What is the secret about them? Why do they want our children? They sent the Blackrobes many years ago to teach us new magic. It was evil! They lied and tricked us. They spoke of gods who would forgive us if we believed as they do. They brought the rum with the cross. This god is ugly! He killed our masks. He killed our men. He sends the women screaming at the moon in terror. They want our power. They take our children to remove the inside of them. Our power. They steal our food, our sacred rattle, the stories, our names. What is left?

I am a crazy woman. I look to the fire that consumes my hair and see their faces. My daughter. My son. They still cry for me, though the sound grows fainter. The wind picks up their keening and brings it to me. The sound has bored into my brain. I begin howling. At night I dare not sleep. I fear the dreams. It is too terrible, the things that happen there. In my dream there is wind and blood moving as a stream. Red, dark blood in my dream. Rushing for our village. The blood moves faster. There are screams of wounded people. Animals are dead, thrown in the blood stream. There is nothing left. Only the air echoing nothing. Only the earth soaking up blood, spreading it in the four directions, becoming a thing there is no name for. I stand in the field watching the fire, The People watching me. We are waiting, but the answer is not clear yet. A crazy woman. That is what they call me.

1979

After taking a morning off work to see my lawyer, I come home, not caring if I call in. Not caring, for once, at the loss in pay. Not caring. My lawyer says there is nothing more we can do. I must wait. As if there has been something other than waiting. He has custody and calls the shots. We must wait and see how long it takes for him to get tired of being a mommy and a daddy. So, I wait.

I open the door to Patricia's room. Ellen and I keep it dusted and cleaned in case my baby will be allowed to visit us. The yellow and blue walls feel like a mockery. I walk to the windows, begin to systematically tear down the curtains. I slowly start to rip the cloth apart. I enjoy hearing the sounds of destruction. Faster, I tear the material into strips. What won't come apart with my hands, I pull at with my teeth. Looking for more to destroy, I gather the sheets and bedspread in my arms and wildly shred them to pieces. Grunting and sweating, I am pushed by rage and the searing wound in my soul. Like a wolf, caught in a trap, gnawing at her own leg to set herself free, I begin to beat my breasts to deaden the pain inside. A noise gathers in my throat and finds the way out. I begin a scream that turns to howling, then becomes hoarse choking. I want to take my fists, my strong fists, my brown fists, and smash the world until it bleeds. Bleeds! And all the judges in their flapping robes, and the fathers who look for revenge, are ground, ground into dust and disappear with the wind.

The word *lesbian*. Lesbian. The word that makes them panic, makes them afraid, makes them destroy children. The word that dares them. Lesbian. *I am one.* Even for Patricia, even for her, *I will not cease to be!* As I kneel amidst the colorful scraps, Raggedy Anns smiling up at me, my chest gives a sigh. My heart slows to its normal speech. I feel the blood pumping outward to my veins, carrying nourishment and life. I strip the room naked. I close the door.   [1985]

 67

Elena

BY PAT MORA

My Spanish isn't enough.
I remember how I'd smile
listening to my little ones,
understanding every word they'd say,
their jokes, their songs, their plots.
> *Vamos a pedirle dulces a mamá. Vamos.*
But that was in Mexico.
Now my children go to American high schools.
They speak English. At night they sit around
the kitchen table, laugh with one another.
I stand by the stove and feel dumb, alone.
I bought a book to learn English.
My husband frowned, drank more beer.
My oldest said, "*Mamá*, he doesn't want you
to be smarter than he is." I'm forty,
embarrassed at mispronouncing words,
embarrassed at the laughter of my children,
the grocer, the mailman. Sometimes I take
my English book and lock myself in the bathroom,
say the thick words softly,
for if I stop trying, I will be deaf
when my children need help.   [1994]

68

"Don't You Talk About My Mama!"

JUNE JORDAN

I got up that morning, with malice toward no one. Drank my coffee and scanned the front page of *The New York Times*. And there it was. I remember, even now, the effrontery of that headline four years ago: "Breakup of Black Family Imperils Gains of Decades." I could hardly believe it. Here were these clowns dumping on us yet again. That was 1983, three years into the shameless Real Deal of Ronald Reagan. He'd taken or he'd shaken everything we Black folks needed just to hang in here, breathing in and out. And yet the headline absolutely failed to give credit where it was due. Instead, "politicians and scholars—black and white" dared to identify the *victims*—the Black single mothers raising 55 percent of all of our Black children *with no help from anybody anywhere*—as the cause of Black poverty! These expense-account professionals presumed to identify "the family crisis" of Black folks as "a threat to the future of Black people without equal." And this was not somebody's weird idea about how to say "thank you." (I could relate to that: somebody finally saying thank you to Black women!) No: This was just another dumb, bold insult to my mother.

Now when I was growing up, the one sure trigger to a down-and-out fight was to say something—anything—about somebody's mother. As a matter of fact, we refined things eventually to the point where you didn't have to get specific. All you had to do was push into the face of another girl or boy, close as you could, almost nose to nose, and just spit out the two words: "Your mother!" This item of our code of honor was not negotiable, and clearly we took it pretty seriously: Even daring to refer to someone's mother put you off-limits. From the time you learned how to talk, everybody's mama remained the holiest of holies. And we did not ever forget it, this fact, that the first, the last and the most, that the number-one persevering, resourceful, resilient and devoted person in our lives was, and would always be, your mother and my mother.

But sometimes, as you know, we grow up without growing wise. Sometimes we become so sophisticated we have to read *The New York Times* in order to figure out whether it's a hot or a rainy day. We read the fine print in order to find out the names of our so-called leaders. But what truly surprises me is Black folks listening to a whole lot of white blasphemy against Black feats of survival, Black folks paying attention to people who never even notice us except to describe us as "female-headed" or some-thing equally weird. (I would like to know, for a fact, has anybody ever seen a female-headed anything at all? What did it look like? What did it do?)

Now I am not opposed to sophistication per se, but when you lose touch with your mama, when you take the word of an absolute, hostile stranger over and above the unarguable truth of your own miraculous, hard-won history, and when you don't remember to ask, again and again, "Compared to what?" I think you don't need to worry about enemies anymore. You'd better just worry about yourself.

Back in 1965, Daniel P. Moynihan (now a U.S. senator from New York) issued a broadside insult to the national Black community. With the full support of a Democratic administration that was tired of Negroes carrying on about citizenship rights and integration and white racist violence, Moynihan came through with the theory that we, Black folks, and we, Black women in particular, constituted "the problem." And now there are Black voices joining the choruses of the absurd. There are national Black organizations and purported Black theoreticians who have become indistinguishable from the verified enemies of Black folks in this country. These sophisticated Black voices jump to the forefront of delighted mass-media exposure because they are willing to lament and to defame the incredible triumph of Black women, the victory of Black mothers that is the victory of our continuation as a people in America.

Archly delivering jargon phrases about "the collapse of Black family structure" and "the destructive culture of poverty in the ghetto" and, of course, "the crisis of female-headedness," with an additional screaming reference to "the shame of teenage pregnancy," these Black voices come to us as the disembodied blatherings of peculiar offspring: Black men and women who wish to deny the Black mother of their origins and who wish to adopt white Daniel P. Moynihan as their father. I happen to lack the imagination necessary to forgive, or understand, this phenomenon. But the possible consequences of this oddball public outcry demand our calm examination.

According to these new Black voices fathered by

Mr. Moynihan, it would seem that the Black family subsists in a terrible, deteriorating state. That's the problem. The source of the problem is The Black Family (that is, it is not white; it suffers from "female-headedness"). The solution to The Black Family Problem is—you guessed it—The Black Family. It must become more white—more patriarchal, less "female-headed," more employed more steadily at better and better-paying jobs.

Now I would agree that the Black family is not white. I do not agree that the problem is "female-headedness." I would rather suggest that the problem is that women in general and that Black women in particular cannot raise our children and secure adequately paying jobs because this is a society that hates women and that believes we are replaceable, that we are dispensable, ridiculous, irksome facts of life. American social and economic hatred of women means that any work primarily identified as women's work will be poorly paid, if at all. Any work open to women will be poorly paid, at best, in comparison to work open to men. Any work done by women will receive a maximum of 64 cents on the dollar compared with wages for the same work done by men. Prenatal, well-baby care, day care for children, children's allowances, housing allowances for parents, paid maternity leave—all of the elemental provisions for the equally entitled citizenship of women and children are ordinary attributes of industrialized nations, except for one: the United States.

The problem, clearly, does not originate with women in general or Black women specifically, who, whether it's hard or whether it's virtually impossible, nevertheless keep things together. Our hardships follow from the uncivilized political and economic status enjoined upon women and children in our country, which has the highest infant mortality rate among its industrial peers. And, evidently, feels fine, thank you, about that. (Not incidentally, Black infant-mortality rates hold at levels twice that for whites.)

The Black Family persists *despite* the terrible deteriorating state of affairs prevailing in the United States. This is a nation unwilling and progressively unable to provide for the well-being of most of its citizens: Our economic system increasingly concentrates our national wealth in the hands of fewer and fewer interest groups. Our economic system increasingly augments the wealth of the richest sector of the citizenry, while it diminishes the real wages and the available livelihood of the poor. Our economic system refuses responsibility for the equitable sharing of national services and monies among its various peoples. Our economic system remains insensitive to the political demands of a democracy, and therefore it does not yield to the requirements of equal entitlement of all women and all children and Black, Hispanic and Native American men, the elderly and the disabled. If you total the American people you have an obvious majority of Americans squeezed outside the putative benefits of "free enterprise."

Our economic system continues its trillion-dollar commitment *not* to the betterment of the lives of its citizens but, rather, to the development and lunatic replication of a military-industrial complex. In this context, then, the Black family persists, yes, in a terrible deteriorating state. But we did not create this state. Nor do we control it. And we are not suffering "collapse." Change does not signify collapse. The nuclear, patriarchal family structure of white America was never our own; it was not *African*. And when we arrived to slavery here, why or how should we have emulated the overseer and the master? We who were counted in the Constitution as three-fifths of a human being? We who could by law neither marry nor retain our children against the predations of the slave economy? Nonetheless, from under the whip through underpaid underemployment and worse, Black folks have formulated our own family, our own home base for nurture and for pride. We have done this through extended kinship methods. And even Black teenage parents are trying, in their own way, to perpetuate the Black family.

The bizarre analysis of the Black family that blames the Black family for being not white and not patriarchal, not endowed with steadily employed Black husbands and fathers who enjoy access to middle-income occupations is just that: a bizarre analysis, a heartless joke. If Black men and Black women *wanted* Black men to become patriarchs of their families, if Black men wanted to function as head of the house—shouldn't they probably have some kind of a job? Can anyone truly dare to suggest that the catastrophic 46-percent unemployment rate now crippling working-age Black men is something that either Black men or Black women view as positive or desirable? Forty-six percent! What is the meaning of a man in the house if he cannot hold out his hand to help his family make it through the month, and if he cannot hold up his head with the pride and authority that regular, satisfying work for good pay provides? How or whom shall he marry and on what basis? Is it honestly puzzling to anyone that the 46-percent, Depression-era rate of unemployment that imprisons Black men almost exactly mirrors the 50 percent of Black households now maintained by Black women? Our Black families persist despite a racist arrangement of rewards such as the fact that the median Black family has only about 56 cents to spend for every dollar that white families have to spend. And a Black college graduate still cannot realistically expect to earn more than a white high-school graduate.

We, children and parents of Black families, neither created nor do we control the terrible, deteriorating state of our unjust and meanly discriminating national affairs. In its structure, the traditional Black family has always reflected our particular jeopardy within these unwelcome circumstances. We have never been "standard" or predictable or stabilized in any normative sense, even as our Black lives have never been standard or predictable or stabilized in a benign national environment. We have been flexible, ingenious and innovative or we have perished. And we have not perished. We remain and we remain different, and we have become necessarily deft at distinguishing between the negative differences —those imposed upon us—and the positive differences—those that joyously attest to our distinctive, survivalist attributes as a people.

Today we must distinguish between responsibility and consequence. We are not responsible for the systematic underemployment and unemployment of Black men or women. We are not responsible for racist hatred of us, and we are not responsible for the American contempt for women per se. We are not responsible for a dominant value system that quibbles over welfare benefits for children and squanders deficit billions of dollars on American pie in the sky. But we must outlive the consequences of this inhumane, disposable-life ideology. We have no choice. And because this ideology underpins our economic system and the political system that supports our economy, we no longer constitute a minority inside America. We are joined in our precarious quandary here by all women and by children, Hispanic Americans and Native Americans and the quickly expanding population of the aged, as well as the temporarily or permanently disabled.

At issue now is the "universal entitlement" of American citizens (as author Ruth Sidel terms it in her important book *Women and Children Last: The Plight of Poor Women in Affluent America* [Viking Press, 1986]): What should American citizenship confer? What are the duties of the state in relation to the citizens it presumes to tax and to govern?

It is not the Black family in crisis but American democracy in crisis when the majority of our people oppose U.S. intervention in Central America and, nevertheless, the President proceeds to intervene. It is not the Black family in crisis but American democracy at stake when the majority of our people abhor South African apartheid and, nonetheless, the President proceeds to collaborate with the leadership of that evil. It is not the Black family in crisis but American democracy at risk when a majority of American citizens may no longer assume that social programs beneficial to them will be preserved and/ or developed.

But if we, Black children and parents, have been joined by so many others in our precarious quandary here, may we not also now actively join with these other jeopardized Americans to redefine and to finally secure universal entitlement of citizenship that will at last conclude the shameful American history of our oppression? And what should these universal entitlements—our new American Bill of Rights— include?

1. Guaranteed jobs and/or guaranteed income to ensure each and every American in each and every one of the 50 states an existence *above* the poverty line.
2. Higher domestic minimum wages and, for the sake of both our narrowest and broadest self-interests, a coordinated, international minimum wage so that exhausted economic exploitation in Detroit can no longer be replaced by economic exploitation in Taiwan or Soweto or Manila.
3. Government guarantees of an adequate minimum allowance for every child regardless of the marital status of the parents.
4. Equal pay for equal work.
5. Affirmative action to ensure broadly democratic access to higher-paying occupations.
6. Compensation for "women's work" equal to compensation for "men's work."
7. Housing allowances and/or state commitments to build and/or to subsidize acceptable, safe and affordable housing for every citizen.
8. Comprehensive, national health insurance from prenatal through geriatric care.
9. Availability of state education and perpetual reeducation through graduate levels of study on the basis of student interest and aptitude rather than financial capacity.
10. A national budget that will invariably commit the main portion of our collective monies to our collective domestic needs for a good life.
11. Comprehensive provision for the well-being of all our children commensurate with the kind of future we are hoping to help construct. These provisions must include paid maternity and paternity leave and universal, state-controlled, public child-care programs for working parents.
12. Nationalization of vital industries to protect citizen consumers and citizen workers alike from the greed-driven vagaries of a "free market."
13. Aggressive nuclear-disarmament policies and, concurrently, aggressive state protection of what's left of the life-supportive elements of our global environment.

I do not believe that a just, a civilized nation can properly regard any one of these 13 entitlements as optional. And yet not one of them is legally in place in the United States. And why not? I think that, as a people, we have yet to learn how to say thank you in real ways to those who have loved us enough to keep us alive despite inhumane and unforgivable opposition to our well-being. For myself, I do not need any super-sophisticated charts and magical graphs to tell me my own mama done better than she could, and my mama's mama, *she* done better than I could. And *everybody's mama* done better than anybody had any right to expect she would. And that's the truth!

And I hope you've been able to follow my meaning. And a word to the wise, they say, should be sufficient. So, I'm telling you real nice: Don't you talk about my mama!   [1987]

 69

Working at Single Bliss

MARY HELEN WASHINGTON

I

Apart from the forest
have you seen
that a tree alone
will often take inventive form . . .
                              —Paulette Childress White
                              "A Tree Alone"

She who has chosen her Self, who defines her Self, by choice, neither in relation to children nor men; who is Self-identified, is a Spinster, a whirling dervish spinning in a new time/space.

                              —Mary Daly
                              Gyn/Ecology (Beacon Press)

Last year I was asked to be on the "Tom Cottle Show," a syndicated television program that originates here in Boston. The psychiatrist-host wanted to interview six single women about their singleness. I hesitated only a moment before refusing. Six single women discussing the significance of their lives? No, I instinctively knew that the interview would end up being an interrogation of six unmarrieds (a pejorative, like coloreds)—women trying to rationalize lives of loss. Losers at the marriage game. *Les femmes manqués.*

I watched the program they put together without me, and sure enough, Cottle asked a few perfunctory questions about singleness and freedom, and then moved on rapidly to the real killer questions. I found it painful to watch these very fine women trapped in the net he'd laid. "Don't you ever come home from these glamorous lives of freedom [read selfishness] and sit down to dinner alone and just cry?" "What about sex?" "What about children?" The women struggled to answer these insulting questions with dignity and humor, but clearly the game was rigged against them. Imagine the interviewer lining up six couples and asking them the same kinds of questions: "Well, what about your sex lives?" "Why don't you have any children?" (or "Why do you have so many?") "Don't you ever come home at night, sit down to dinner, and wonder why you ever married the person on the other side of the table?" Of course, this interview would never take place—the normal restraint and politeness that are reserved for people whose positions are socially acceptable assure married folks some measure of protection and, at least, common decency.

"You're so lucky, footloose and fancy-free, with no responsibilities," a friend with two children once said to me. Ostensibly that's a compliment, or at least, it's supposed to be. But underneath it is really a critique of single people, implying that their lives do not have the moral stature of a life with "responsibilities." It's a comment that used to leave me feeling a little like a kid, a failed adult; for what's an adult with no responsibilities? A kid. I have had to learn to recognize and reject the veiled contempt in this statement because, of course, single people do have responsibilities.

At age 40, I have been a single adult for 20 years. No, I am neither widowed nor divorced. I am single in the pristine sense of that word—which unleashes that basic fear in all of us, "What will I do if I'm left by myself?" As I have more or less successfully dealt with that fear over the years, I am somewhat indignant at being cast as an irresponsible gadfly, unencumbered by the problems of Big People. I have earned a living and "kept myself," and I have done that without being either male or white in a world dominated by men and corroded by racism. I've sat up nights with students' papers and even later with their problems. Without any of the social props married people have, I have given many memorable parties. Like my aunts before me, I've celebrated the births, birthdays, first communions, graduations, football games, and track meets of my 10 nephews. And not a hair on my mother's head changes color without my noticing it.

As Zora Hurston's Janie says, "Two things everybody's got tuh do fuh theyselves. They got tuh go tuh God, and they got tuh find out about livin' fuh theyselves." If anything, a single person may be more aware of the responsibility to discover and create meaning in her life, to find community, to honor her creativity, to live out her values, than the person whose life is circumferenced by an immediate and intimate family life.

II

To be single and busy—nothing bad in that. Such people do much good.

—Elizabeth Hardwick
Sleepless Nights (Random House)

To some extent my adolescent imagination was bewitched by the myth that marriage is *the* vertical choice in a woman's life—one that raises her status, completes her life, fulfills her dreams, and makes her a valid person in society. In the 1950s, all the movies, all the songs directed us to this one choice: to find our worldly prince and go two by two into the ark. Nothing else was supposed to matter quite as much and it was a surprise to discover that something else matters just as much, sometimes more.

But in spite of the romance-marriage-motherhood bombardment, I grew up in a kind of war-free zone where I heard the bombs and artillery all around me but was spared from a direct attack. I was raised in two very separate but mutually supportive communities—one black, one Catholic, both of which taught me that a woman could be her own person in the world.

In the all-women's Catholic high school and college in Cleveland, Ohio, where I put in eight formative years, we were required to think of ourselves as women with destinies, women whose achievements mattered—whether we chose marriage or religious life or, as it was called then, a life of "single blessedness." In fact, marriage and the single life seemed to my convent-honed ninth-grade mind to have a clearly equal status: they were both inferior to the intrinsically superior religious life.

The program of spiritual, intellectual, social, and physical development the nuns demanded of us allowed an involvement with myself I craved even in the ninth grade. *Some* dating was encouraged at Notre Dame Academy (ninth through twelfth grades)—not as a consuming emotional involvement but as part of a "normal social development." Boys had their place—on the periphery of one's life. (A girl who came to school with her boyfriend's taped class ring on her finger was subject to expulsion.) You were expected to be the central, dominant figure in the fabric of your own life.

The nuns themselves were vivid illustrations of that principle. For me they were the most powerful images of women imaginable—not ladies-in-waiting, not submissive homebodies, not domestic drudges, not deviants. They ran these women-dominated universes with aplomb and authority. Even if "Father" appeared on Monday morning for our weekly religious lesson, his appearance was tolerated as a kind of necessary token of the male hierarchy, and, when he left, the waters ran back together, leaving no noticeable trace of his presence.

Nuns were the busiest people I knew then. No matter how graceful and dignified the pace, they always seemed to be hurrying up and down the corridors of Notre Dame planning something important and exciting. Sister Wilbur directed dramatics and went to New York occasionally to see the latest Off-Broadway productions. Sister Kathryn Ann wrote poetry and went to teach in Africa. Another sister coached debate and took our winning teams to state championships in Columbus. Though technically

nuns are not single, they do not have that affiliation with a male figure to establish their status. (After Mary Daly it should not be necessary to point out that God is not a man.) They also have to ward off the same stigma of being different from the norm as single people do. So it's only a little ironic that I got some of my sense of how a woman could be complete and autonomous and comfortable in the world —*sans* marriage—from the Sisters of Notre Dame.

The message I got from the black community about single life was equally forceful. So many black girls heard these words, they might have been programmed tapes: "Girl, get yourself an education, you can't count on a man to take care of you." "An education is something no one can take from you." "Any fool can get married, but not everyone can go to school."

I didn't know it then, but this was my feminist primer. Aim high, they said, because that is the only way a black girl can claim a place in this world. Marriage was a chancy thing, not dependable like diplomas: my mother and aunts and uncles said that even if you married a Somebody—a doctor or a lawyer —there was no assurance that he'd have a good heart or treat you right. They thought that the worst thing a woman could do was to get into financial dependency with a man—and it was not that they hated or distrusted men so much as they distrusted any situation that made an already vulnerable woman more powerless.

There was such reverence in my mother's voice for women of achievement that I never connected their social status with anything as mundane as marriage. The first black woman with a Ph.D., the first black woman school principal, the first woman doctor—I knew their names by heart and wanted to be one of them and do important things.

My third-grade teacher, the first black teacher at Parkwood Elementary in Cleveland, Ohio, was a single woman in her thirties. At age nine, I saw her as a tall, majestic creature who wore earrings, drove her own car, and made school pure joy. To my family and the neighborhood, Miss Hilliard was like a totem of our tribe's good fortune: an independent, self-sufficient, educated woman bringing her treasures back to their children. She was a part of that tradition of 19th-century black women whose desire for "race uplift" sent them to teach in the South and to schools like Dunbar High in Washington, D.C., and the School for Colored Youth in Philadelphia. Though many of these women were married, the majority of them were widowed for a great many years and those were often the years of achievement for them.

One of these 19th-century stellar examples, Anna Julia Cooper, dismissed the question of marriage as a false issue. The question should not be "How shall I so cramp, stunt, simplify, and nullify myself as to make me eligible for the horror of being swallowed up into some little man," but how shall a generation of women demand of themselves and of men "the noblest, the grandest and the best" in their capacities.

III

In the places of their childhoods, the
troubles they had getting grown,
the tales of men they told among
themselves as we sat unnoted
at their feet, we saw some image
of a past and future self.
The world had loved them even
less than their men but this did
not keep them from scheming
on its favor.

—Sherley Anne Williams
Some One Sweet Angel Chile (William Morrow)

I learned early about being single from my five aunts. By the time I was old enough to notice, four were widowed and one divorced, so from my 12-year-old perspective, they were single women for a good part of their lives. They ran their own households, cooked, entertained, searched for spirituality, helped my mother to raise eight children, traveled some, went to work, cared for the sick, planned picnics. In short, they made up their lives by themselves, inventing the forms that satisfied them. And in the course of their "scheming" they passed on to me something about the rituals and liturgy of single life.

The eldest of these aunts, Aunt Bessie, lived as a single woman for 26 years. Her husband of 40 years died when she was 60 and she began to live alone for the first time since she was 18. She bought a huge old house, painted, decorated, and furnished every room with Oriental rugs and secondhand furniture purchased at estate sales. (Black people discovered this bonanza in the 1940s long before it became a middle-class fad.) She put in a new lawn, grew African violets, and started a whole new life for herself on Ashbury Avenue.

Aunt Bessie was secretly proud of how well she was doing on her own, and she used to tell me slyly how many of these changes she could not have made as a married woman: "Uncle wouldn't have bought this house, baby; he wouldn't have wanted this much space. He wouldn't have changed neighborhoods." She was finally doing exactly what pleased her, and the shape of her life as she had designed it in her singularity was much more varied, dynamic, and daring. What I learned from her is symbolized by that multilevel house on Ashbury Avenue. She had three bedrooms—she needed them for guests; on the third floor she made hats, which she sold for a living; the huge old basement was for her tools and lawn work. All this room was essential to the amount of living she planned to do.

Since she willed all of her furniture to me, my own flat resembles that house in many ways, and her spirit came with the furnishings: I have the sense of inhabiting every corner of my life just as she lived in all 10 rooms of her house. Even my overstocked refrigerator is a reflection of something I learned from her about taking care of your life. Another aunt, Hazel, died only a few years after she was widowed, and I remember Aunt Bessie's explanation of her untimely death as a warning about the perils of not taking your life seriously. "Hazel stopped cooking for herself after her husband died, just ate snacks and junk food instead of making a proper dinner for herself. And she got that cancer and died." The message was clear to me—even at age 12—that single life could be difficult at times and that living it well required some effort, but you were not supposed to let it kill you.

IV

[Friendship] is a profound experience which calls forth our humanness and shapes our being. . . . This is true for all persons, but it has a special significance for single persons. For it is in the context of friendship that most single persons experience the intimacy and immediacy of others.
 —Francine Cardman
 "On Being Single"

Girded up with all of this psychological armament from my past, I still entered adult life without the powerful and sustaining myths and rituals that could provide respect and support for single life. Terms like "old maid" and "spinster," not yet redefined by a feminist consciousness, could still be used to belittle and oppress single women. By the time I was 35, I had participated in scores of marriage ceremonies, and even had begun sending anniversary cards to my married friends. But never once did I think of celebrating the anniversary of a friendship—even one that was by then 25 years old. (Aren't you entitled to gifts of silver at that milestone?)

Once, about 10 years ago, five of us single women from Cleveland took a trip to Mexico together. (Actually only four of the group were single; the fifth, Ernestine, was married and three months pregnant.) I remember that trip as seven days and eight nights of adventure, laughter, discovery, and closeness.

We were such typical tourists—taking snapshots of ancient ruins, posing in front of cathedrals, paying exorbitant sums to see the cliff divers (whose entire act took about 20 seconds), floating down debris-filled waterways to see some totally unnoteworthy sights, learning the hard way that in the hot Acapulco sun even us "killer browns" could get a sunburn. We stayed up at night talking about our lives, our dreams, our careers, our men, and laughing so hard in these late-night sessions that we hardly had the energy for the next morning's tour.

It was the laughter and the good talk (remember Toni Cade Bambara's short story "The Johnson Girls") that made the trip seem so complete. It was so perfect that even in the midst of the experience I knew it was to be a precious memory. Years later I asked my friend, Ponchita, why she thought the five

of us never planned another trip like that, why we let such good times drift out of our lives without an attempt to recapture them. "Because," she said, "it wasn't enough. It was fun, stimulating, warm, exciting, but it wasn't 'The Thing That Made Life Complete,' and it wasn't leading us in that direction; I guess it was a little like 'recess.'" We wanted nests, not excitement. We wanted domestic bliss, not lives lived at random, no matter how thrilling, how wonderful. So there was the potential—those "dependable and immediate supports" existed. But without the dependable myths to accompany them, we couldn't seriously invest ourselves in those experiences.

When my friend Meg suggested we celebrate Mother's Day this year with a brunch for all our single, childless women friends, and bring pictures of the nieces and nephews we dote on, I recognized immediately the psychic value in honoring our own form of caretaking. We were establishing rituals by which we could ceremonially acknowledge our particular social identities.

My oldest friend Ponchita and I did exchange gifts last year on the twenty-fifth anniversary of our friendship, and never again will the form "anniversary" mean only a rite (right) of the married. My journey through the single life was beginning to have its own milestones and to be guided by its own cartography.

V

A life of pure decision, of thoughtful calculations, every inclination honored. They go about on their own, nicely accompanied in their singularity by the companion of possibility.

 —Elizabeth Hardwick
 Sleepless Nights

Our Mexico trip was in 1971. In the next 10 years, I earned a Ph.D., became director of black studies at the University of Detroit, edited two anthologies, threw out my makeshift bricks-and-board furniture, began to think about buying a house and adopting a child, and in the process, decided that my life was no longer "on hold." These deliberate choices made me begin to regard my single status as an honorable estate. But you know, when I look back at that checklist of accomplishments and serious life plans, I feel resentful that I had to work so hard for the honor that naturally accompanies the married state. Overcompensation, however, sometimes has its rewards: I had established a reputation in my profession that brought the prospect of a fellowship year at Radcliffe and a new job in Boston.

When I was leaving Detroit, I was acutely aware of my single status. What kind of life was it, I wondered, if you could start all over again in a new city with nothing to show for your past except your furniture and your diplomas? I didn't even have a cat. Where were the signs and symbols of a coherent, meaningful life that others could recognize? What was I doing living at *random* like this? I had made this "pure" decision and was honoring my inclination to live in another city, to take a job that offered excitement and challenge. As I packed boxes alone, signed contracts with moving companies, and said good-bye at numerous dinners and going-away parties to all the friends I had made over 10 years, I felt not so very different from a friend who was moving after separating from his wife: "like a rhinoceros being cut loose from the herd."

I think it was the wide-open, netless freedom of it all that scared me, because I was truly *not* alone. I moved into a triple-decker in Cambridge where I live in a kind of semi-cooperative with two other families. Here, I feel secure, but independent and private. The journalist on the second floor and I read each other's work, and I exchange ideas about teaching methods with the three other professors in the house. We all share meals occasionally; we've met one another's extended families; and we celebrate one another's assorted triumphs. I have put together another network of friends whose lives I feel intimately involved in, and who, like me, are interested in making single life work—not disappear.

But I do not yet have the solid sense of belonging to a community that I had in Cleveland and Detroit, and sometimes I am unsettled by the variousness and unpredictableness of my single life. This simply means that I still have some choices to make—about

deepening friendships, about having children (possibly adopting them), about establishing closer ties with the black community in Boston. If and when I do adopt a child, she or he will have a selection of godparents and aunts and uncles as large and varied as I had. That is one of the surest signs of the richness of my single life.

VI

You're wondering if I'm lonely:
OK then, yes, I'm lonely
as a plane rides lonely and level
on its radio beam, aiming
across the Rockies
for the blue-strung aisles
of an airfield on the ocean

—Adrienne Rich
"Song" from *Diving into the Wreck* (Norton)

Last year Elizabeth Stone wrote an article in the *Village Voice* called "A Married Woman" in which she discussed how much her life had changed since she married at the age of 33. Somewhat boastfully, she remarked at the end that she had hardly made any reference in the whole article to her husband. But if a single woman describes her life without reference to romance—no matter how rich and satisfying her life may be, no matter what she says about wonderful friends, exciting work, cultural and intellectual accomplishments—in fact, the *more* she says about these things—the more skeptical people's reactions will be. That one fact—her romantic involvement—if it is not acceptable can cancel out all the rest. This is how society keeps the single woman feeling perilous about her sense of personal success.

Still, everybody wants and needs some kind of special alliance(s) in her life. Some people have alliances called marriage. (I like that word alliance: it keeps marriage in its proper—horizontal—place.) I'd like an alliance with a man who could be a comrade and kindred spirit, and I've had such alliances in the past. Even with the hassles, they were enriching and enjoyable experiences for me, but I have never wanted to forsake my singularity for this kind of emotional involvement. Whatever psychic forces drive me have always steered me toward autonomy and independence, out toward the ocean's expanse and away from the shore.

I don't want to sound so smooth and glib and clear-eyed about it all, because it has taken me more than a decade to get this sense of balance and control. A lot of rosaries and perpetual candles and expensive long-distance calls have gotten me through the hard times when I would have chosen the holy cloister over another day of "single blessedness." The truth is that those hard times were not caused by being single. They were part of every woman's struggle to find commitment and contentment for herself. Singleness does not define me, is not an essential characteristic of me. I simply wish to have it acknowledged as a legitimate way to be in the world. After all, we started using Ms. instead of Mrs. or Miss because *none* of us wanted to be defined by the presence or absence of a man.

VII

Apart from the forest
a single tree will sometimes grow awry
in brave and extraordinary search
for its own shape

—Paulette Childress White
"A Tree Alone"

When I first started running in 1972, I ran regularly with a man. As long as I had this male companion, the other men passing by either ignored me or gave me slight nods to show their approval of my supervised state. Eventually I got up the nerve to run alone around Detroit's Palmer Park, and then the men came out of the trees to make comments— usually to tell me what I was doing wrong ("Lift your legs higher" or "Stop waving your arms"), or to flirt ("Can I run with you, baby?" was by far the most common remark, though others were nastier).

Once a carload of black teenagers who were parked in the lot at the end of my run started making comments about my physical anatomy, which I started to dismiss as just a dumb teenage ritual. But on this particular day, something made me stop my run, walk over to the car, and say, "You know, when you see a sister out trying to get some exercise, as hard as that is for us, you ought to be trying to support her, because she needs all the help she can get." I didn't know how they would respond, so I was surprised when they apologized, and somewhat shamefaced, one of them said: "Go on, sister; we're with you."

Now, that incident occurred because I was alone, and the image has become part of my self-definition: I am a woman in the world—single and powerful and astonished at my ability to create my own security, "in brave and extraordinary search for my own shape." [1982]

 70

A Marriage Agreement

ALIX KATES SHULMAN

When my husband and I were first married, a decade ago, keeping house was less a burden than a game. We both worked full-time in New York City, so our small apartment stayed empty most of the day and taking care of it was very little trouble. Twice a month we'd spend Saturday cleaning and doing our laundry at the laundromat. We shopped for food together after work, and though I usually did the cooking, my husband was happy to help. Since our meals were simple and casual, there were few dishes to wash. We occasionally had dinner out and usually ate breakfast at a diner near our offices. We spent most of our free time doing things we enjoyed together, such as taking long walks in the evenings and spending weekends in Central Park. Our domestic life was beautifully uncomplicated.

When our son was born, our domestic life suddenly became *quite* complicated; and two years later, when our daughter was born, it became impossible. We automatically accepted the traditional sex roles that society assigns. My husband worked all day in an office; I left my job and stayed at home, taking on almost all the burdens of housekeeping and child raising.

When I was working I had grown used to seeing people during the day, to having a life outside the home. But now I was restricted to the company of two demanding preschoolers and to the four walls of an apartment. It seemed unfair that while my husband's life had changed little when the children were born, domestic life had become the only life I had.

I tried to cope with the demands of my new situation, assuming that other women were able to handle even larger families with ease and still find time for themselves. I couldn't seem to do that.

We had to move to another apartment to accommodate our larger family, and because of the children, keeping it reasonably neat took several hours a day. I prepared half a dozen meals every day for from one to four people at a time—and everyone ate different food. Shopping for this brood—or even just running out for a quart of milk—meant putting on snowsuits, boots and mittens; getting strollers or carriages up and down the stairs; and scheduling the trip so it would not interfere with one of the children's feeding or nap or illness or some other domestic job. Laundry was now a daily chore. I seemed to be working every minute of the day—and still there were dishes in the sink; still there wasn't time enough to do everything.

Even more burdensome than the physical work of housekeeping was the relentless responsibility I had for my children. I loved them, but they seemed to be taking over my life. There was nothing I could do, or even contemplate, without first considering how they would be affected. As they grew older, just answering their constant questions ruled out even a private mental life. I had once enjoyed reading, but now if there was a moment free, instead of reading for myself, I read to them. I wanted to work on my own writing, but there simply weren't enough hours in the day. I had no time for myself; the children were always *there*.

As my husband's job began keeping him at work later and later—and sometimes taking him out of town—I missed his help and companionship. I wished he would come home at six o'clock and spend time with the children so they could know him better. I continued to buy food with him in mind and dutifully set his place at the table. Yet sometimes whole weeks would go by without his having dinner with us. When he did get home the children often were asleep, and we both were too tired ourselves to do anything but sleep.

We accepted the demands of his work as unavoidable. Like most couples, we assumed that the wife must accommodate to the husband's schedule, since it is his work that brings in the money.

As the children grew older I began free-lance editing at home. I felt I had to squeeze it into my "free" time and not allow it to interfere with my domestic duties or the time I owed my husband—just as he felt he had to squeeze in time for the children during weekends. We were both chronically dissatisfied, but we knew no solutions.

After I had been home with the children for six years I began to attend meetings of the newly formed Women's Liberation Movement in New York City. At these meetings I began to see that my situation was not uncommon; other women too felt drained and frustrated as housewives and mothers. When we started to talk about how we would have chosen to arrange our lives, most of us agreed that even though we might have preferred something different, we had never felt we had a choice in the matter. We realized that we had slipped into full domestic responsibility simply as a matter of course, and it seemed unfair.

When I added them up, the chores I was responsible for amounted to a hectic 6 A.M.–9 P.M. (often later) job, without salary, breaks or vacation. No employer would be able to demand these hours legally, but most mothers take them for granted—as I did until I became a feminist.

For years mothers like me have acquiesced to the strain of the preschool years and endless household maintenance without any real choice. Why, I asked myself, should a couple's decision to have a family mean that the woman must immerse years of her life in their children? And why should men like my husband miss caring for and knowing their children?

Eventually, after an arduous examination of our situation, my husband and I decided that we no longer had to accept the sex roles that had turned us into a lame family. Out of equal parts love for each other and desperation at our situation, we decided to re-examine the patterns we had been living by, and starting again from scratch, to define our roles for ourselves.

We began by agreeing to share completely all responsibility for raising our children (by then aged five and seven) and caring for our household. If this new arrangement meant that my husband would have to change his job or that I would have to do more free-lance work or that we would have to live on a different scale, then we would. It would be worth it if it could make us once again equal, independent and loving as we had been when we were first married.

Simply agreeing verbally to share domestic duties didn't work, despite our best intentions. And when we tried to divide them "spontaneously," we ended up following the traditional patterns. Our old habits were too deep-rooted. So we sat down and drew up a formal agreement, acceptable to both of us, that clearly defined the responsibilities we each had.

It may sound a bit formal, but it has worked for us. Here it is:

MARRIAGE AGREEMENT

I. Principles

We reject the notion that the work which brings in more money is more valuable. The ability to earn more money is a privilege which must not be compounded by enabling the larger earner to buy out of his/her duties and put the burden either on the partner who earns less or on another person hired from outside.

We believe that each partner has an equal right to his/her own time, work, value, choices. As long as all duties are performed, each of us may use his/her extra time any way he/she chooses. If he/she wants to use it making money, fine. If he/she wants to spend it with spouse, fine. If not, fine.

As parents we believe we must share all responsibility for taking care of our children and home— not only the work but also the responsibility. At least during the first year of this agreement, *sharing responsibility* shall mean dividing the *jobs* and dividing the *time*.

In principle, jobs should be shared equally, 50-50, but deals may be made by mutual agreement. If jobs and schedule are divided on any other than a 50-50 basis, then at any time either party may call for a re-examination and redistribution of jobs or a revision of the schedule. Any deviation from 50-50 must be for the convenience of both parties. If one party works overtime in any domestic job, he/she must be compensated by equal extra work by the other. The schedule may be flexible, but changes must be formally agreed upon. The terms of this agreement are rights and duties, not privileges and favors.

II. Job Breakdown and Schedule

(A) Children

1. Mornings: Waking children; getting their clothes out; making their lunches; seeing that they have notes, homework, money, bus passes, books; brushing their hair; giving them breakfast (making coffee for us). Every other week each parent does all.

2. Transportation: Getting children to and from lessons, doctors, dentists (including making appointments), friends' houses, park, parties, movies, libraries. Parts occurring between 3 and 6 P.M. fall to wife. She must be compensated by extra work from husband (see 10 below). Husband does all weekend transportation and pickups after 6.

3. Help: Helping with homework, personal problems, projects like cooking, making gifts, experiments, planting; answering questions; explaining things. Parts occurring between 3 and 6 P.M. fall to wife. After 6 P.M. husband does Tuesday, Thursday and Sunday; wife does Monday, Wednesday and Saturday. Friday is free for whoever has done extra work during the week.

4. Nighttime (after 6 P.M.): Getting children to take baths, brush their teeth, put away their toys and clothes, go to bed; reading with them; tucking them in and having nighttime talks; handling if they wake or call in the night. Husband does Tuesday, Thursday and Sunday. Wife does

Monday, Wednesday and Saturday. Friday is split according to who has done extra work during the week.

5. Baby sitters: Getting baby sitters (which sometimes takes an hour of phoning). Baby sitters must be called by the parent the sitter is to replace. If no sitter turns up, that parent must stay home.

6. Sick care: Calling doctors; checking symptoms; getting prescriptions filled; remembering to give medicine; taking days off to stay home with sick child; providing special activities. This must still be worked out equally, since now wife seems to do it all. (The same goes for the now frequently declared school closings for so-called political protests, whereby the mayor gets credit at the expense of the mothers of young children. The mayor closes only the schools, not the places of business or the government offices.) In any case, wife must be compensated (see 10 below).

7. Weekends: All usual child care, plus special activities (beach, park, zoo). Split equally. Husband is free all Saturday, wife is free all Sunday.

(B) Housework

8. Cooking: Breakfast; dinner (children, parents, guests). Breakfasts during the week are divided equally; husband does all weekend breakfasts (including shopping for them and dishes). Wife does all dinners except Sunday nights. Husband does Sunday dinner and any other dinners on his nights of responsibility if wife isn't home. Whoever invites guests does shopping, cooking and dishes; if both invite them, split work.

9. Shopping: Food for all meals, housewares, clothing and supplies for children. Divide by convenience. Generally, wife does local daily food shopping; husband does special shopping for supplies and children's things.

10. Cleaning: Dishes daily; apartment weekly, biweekly or monthly. Husband does dishes Tuesday, Thursday and Sunday. Wife does Monday, Wednesday and Saturday. Friday is split according to who has done extra work during week. Husband does all the house cleaning in exchange for wife's extra child care (3 to 6 daily) and sick care.

11. Laundry: Home laundry, making beds, dry cleaning (take and pick up). Wife does home laundry. Husband does dry-cleaning delivery and pickup. Wife strips beds, husband remakes them.

Our agreement changed our lives. Surprisingly, once we had written it down, we had to refer to it only two or three times. But we still had to work to keep the old habits from intruding. If it was my husband's night to take care of the children, I had to be careful not to check up on how he was managing. And if the baby sitter didn't show up for him, I would have to remember it was *his* problem.

Eventually the agreement entered our heads, and now, after two successful years of following it, we find that our new roles come to us as readily as the old ones had. I willingly help my husband clean the apartment (knowing it is his responsibility) and he often helps me with the laundry or the meals. We work together and trade off duties with ease now that the responsibilities are truly shared. We each have less work, more hours together and less resentment.

Before we made our agreement I had never been able to find the time to finish even one book. Over the past two years I've written three children's books, a biography and a novel and edited a collection of writings (all will have been published by spring of 1972). Without our agreement I would never have been able to do this.

At present my husband works a regular 40-hour week, and I write at home during the six hours the children are in school. He earns more money now than I do, so his salary covers more of our expenses than the money I make with my free-lance work. But if either of us should change jobs, working hours or income, we would probably adjust our agreement.

Perhaps the best testimonial of all to our marriage agreement is the change that has taken place in our family life. One day after it had been in effect for only four months our daughter said to my husband, "You know, Daddy, I used to love Mommy more than you, but now I love you both the same."

[1971]

Women and Religion

Institutionalized religion has a powerful impact on women's views of themselves and the values and policies that affect their life choices. Many women appreciate the spiritual aspects of their religious traditions but find the discriminatory practices and policies of religious institutions confining and unjust.

Mary Ann Sorrentino, a Roman Catholic, writes about her experience of being publicly excommunicated for helping other women obtain abortions. She describes the pain imposed on her family when the Church refused to confirm her daughter unless she repudiated what her mother stood for.

While throughout most of Jewish history the synagogue has primarily been the domain of men, recently women have been ordained as rabbis. Laura Geller discusses some of the implications of women having this position of power in Judaism. Since the social distance between the congregant and the clergy diminishes when the rabbi is a woman, she foresees a breakdown of religious hierarchy, leading Jews to see their rabbi not as a "priest" but as a teacher and enabling congregants to become more active participants in the life of the synagogue.

Fundamentalism in many religious traditions, whether Christian, Jewish, Muslim, Hindu, or Buddhist, reinforces patriarchy. In "Christian Fundamentalism: Patriarchy, Sexuality, and Human Rights" Susan Rose focuses on the ways in which Christian fundamentalism, in particular, privileges men's rights over women's rights, reinforces the difference between men and women, and controls women's expression of sexuality.

Quotes from religious writings, like the Bible, are often used to justify women's oppression. In "Revelations" an African-American journalist, Linda Villarosa, describes how her own Biblical research illuminated ways that those in the Religious Right take the Bible literally only when it suits them, ignoring anything that does not easily support their beliefs. She describes the process of bolstering herself intellectually and emotionally to more confidently confront homophobia based in literal interpretations of the Bible.

"In Her Own Image" describes the work of Christian women of various faiths who have written about theology or entered the clergy. In addition to their feminist theological ideas, their very presence in churches challenges tradition. For example Episcopal priest Carter Heyward, a lesbian, argues that it is important for gay and lesbian priests to be as "visible as we can be just to show that we are already here. It is not like the Church has a choice. We are in it already." These women's voices make visible and legitimate female experiences in churches and synagogues today.

❧ 71

My Church Threw Me Out

MARY ANN SORRENTINO

I have never had an abortion myself, nor have I ever performed one. But my Church has told me that because I believe that women should be able to have abortions if they so desire, I have automatically excommunicated myself. I still believe that I am a Catholic; I will always be a Catholic—whether or not I can take communion or be buried with the Church's rites. I intend to keep my faith and to fight to change my Church.

I had no idea that I was excommunicated until last May, two days before my daughter's confirmation. Her religion teacher called me that Friday morning and asked me to bring Luisa, who was then 15, to an afternoon meeting with Father Egan, our pastor. Although the teacher was not allowed to tell me why, she said that Luisa's confirmation hung in the balance. I was stunned. Luisa had passed all her tests, and another parish priest had already interviewed her once. I was expecting 20 guests on Sunday to celebrate. I called Father Egan immediately. He told me that Luisa could not be confirmed until he had interrogated her about her views on abortion.

His message was clear: I was the problem. For the last nine years I have been executive director of Planned Parenthood of Rhode Island. As far as the Catholic Church was concerned, my only child could not be confirmed until she had repudiated what her mother stood for.

No one had told Luisa why she was being dismissed from school early, so when I picked her up, she was in tears. She said, "I thought Daddy or Grandma died and that's why you came to get me." When I told her the reason, she began to sob.

I was so outraged at the idea of this ordeal Luisa had to go through that I decided to tape the meeting, in case we needed a record later. My husband, Al, who is a lawyer, accompanied Luisa and me, even though Father Egan had not invited him. When the priest arrived, Al told him he didn't understand why his daughter had to be singled out for ques-

tioning from a class of 75. "Because she lives in a particular atmosphere," Father Egan said. "Her mother is an advocate of abortion. I have to ascertain whether Luisa believes in abortion. That's all." Then Father Egan said to me, "You're the one who ties my hands. I *want* your daughter to be confirmed. But if she believes in a doctrine that conflicts with that confirmation, then one thing contradicts another."

I said, "Father, I want to go on record that I don't advocate abortion. What I advocate is that every woman who is pregnant should be allowed to exercise her own conscience and her own choice."

"Well," Luisa spoke up, "I don't have any opinion of abortion. What my mother does for a living is her business."

"If you feel abortion is right, then we can't administer the sacrament," Father Egan replied.

Finally Luisa stated that she herself wouldn't have an abortion.

"But do you believe in abortion?" Father Egan persisted.

"I don't know," Luisa replied.

I felt I had to intervene. I asked Luisa, "But you wouldn't have one, right?"

"No," Luisa answered.

"Then you don't believe in it," Father Egan told her. He added to Al and me, "All I want her to say is that she doesn't advocate abortion." Luisa, by now very upset, left the room, tears running down her cheeks.

Then Father Egan said that he could not give me communion at the confirmation "because you're excommunicated. You should know that already."

I was stunned. Every now and again a "Right-to-Lifer" would accuse me of being excommunicated, but to hear this from a member of the Catholic clergy shocked me.

"I haven't been formally notified," I answered. "And I've taken communion as recently as Christmas." If I, a lifelong Catholic, were indeed excommunicated, I could no longer receive the sacraments of my faith, including communion and the last rites. Excommunication is a formal, official procedure: canon law requires that the local bishop, not a parish priest, inform a church member of excommunication. I knew that no American has been publicly excommunicated for more than 20 years. And I now know that church policy states that those who perform abortions and those who undergo them can be excommunicated. But I didn't know this last spring, and I don't fit either category.

"Your excommunication is automatic because abortion is a sin," said Father Egan. "When you publicly advocate abortion, you become what is known as a public sinner, and you cannot receive the sacraments."

"I don't believe this," I said. I was deeply hurt. But I was also very angry. The Church was trying to blackmail me through my child. The only reason we had allowed Luisa to be interrogated was that she had worked so hard to prepare for confirmation. The Church had us over a barrel.

For six months I did not discuss publicly what had happened to me because Al and I wanted to protect Luisa. On January 21, the eve of the anniversary of *Roe* v. *Wade*, the Supreme Court decision legalizing abortion, a "Right-to-Life" priest in my hometown of Providence, Rhode Island, placed a newspaper ad for a cable TV program he had produced. The ad asked whether Rhode Island's leading abortion advocate was really a Catholic.

The next day I watched with horrified fascination as he went on the air and called me the state's "public enemy number one of babies in the womb." Then he gave his own answer to the question he had posed in his ad: He said that I wasn't really a Catholic because I had been excommunicated.

Many times during the past nine years, I've been quoted in newspapers and have appeared on radio and television shows in my state—the most Catholic in the union—where Catholics comprise 65 percent of the state's population. I can't count the number of times I've called, not for abortion, but for a pregnant woman's right to exercise her own conscience. Until Luisa's interrogation, no Church authority had ever contacted me or challenged my views. And to this day, the bishop of Providence has never addressed a word to me directly.

For second-generation Italian-Americans like me, excommunication seems like something that could just never happen. Catholicism is part of who

I am. For me and for many Italians, Church dogma is closely interwoven with our ethnic and cultural fabric. We want our children to be initiated with God, so we make a big deal out of baptism. We're romantic—we love marriages, so the wedding ceremony has particular meaning for us. We mourn very deeply, so the last rites, the funeral and burial in holy ground are very much a part of our lives. But we tend to be flexible about Church rules. When I was growing up, I remember hearing my uncle say, "It doesn't matter what the Church says about birth control; no one is going to tell me what to do in my own bedroom."

I was raised to be a traditional Italian wife and mother; still, I've always had a history of fighting back. My father, who died when I was nine, was very proud that he could send me to an exclusive Catholic school, the Convent of the Sacred Heart, in Providence. But I felt the nuns there treated us Italians as second-class citizens, compared with the Irish girls. Once, when one of my Italian girlfriends didn't know an answer during an oral exam, the nuns pressed her so hard that she wet her pants. I got into a lot of trouble because I told them to stop picking on her.

Al and I got married right after my graduation. He still had a year of college to go, so I became a social worker. I soon found that I would have to take on the state government. My clients were welfare mothers who asked me for birth-control information. I gave it to them. My superior called me in and told me that the taxpayers of Rhode Island weren't paying my salary to have me discuss something they didn't believe in. So I complained to the head of the state welfare department and got other social workers to back me up. The policy eventually changed.

After his graduation, Al announced his plans to attend law school in Boston. This meant I had to keep on working and that we had to move. I was sad to leave my mother—I was extremely close to her—and all the rest of my family.

I cried a lot in those years—I wasn't very independent. I was still a typical Italian wife. Every night I made a three- or four-course gourmet meal. All Al did was study and work, not because he was lazy, but because I would't let him do anything else. Even though I kept getting promoted at work, I continued to take care of everything at home. I discovered my talent for administration and became a unit manager at a local hospital.

I always knew I wanted to have children, but we couldn't afford a baby then. I was taking the Pill, and that's how I first got into trouble with the Church.

During confession, when the priest heard I was practicing birth control, he refused to give me absolution. "I want you to go to Catholic Social Services to learn about the rhythm method," he said. "Father," I replied, "I'm a social worker. Do you know how many rhythm babies are born every year?" Friends told me I should confess to other priests who didn't think the Pill was a sin. I said no. It didn't make any sense to me to have to shop around for absolution. I stopped going to Mass regularly—but I never abandoned the Church.

I was pregnant at Al's law school graduation, which was exactly what I had wanted. When Luisa was born, she became the job of our lives, and she still is. Yet I have often wondered what I would do if I found myself pregnant today, at 42. I think the only honest answer is that I don't know. A fertilized egg that grows into a fetus is the beginning of human life, but I don't think of a fertilized egg as a person.

I do know that for the last nine years, the proudest work I've done has been holding the hands of women who needed someone with them during an abortion. And by helping these women, I have never considered myself any different from the hundreds of Catholic administrators of hospitals across this country where birth-control techniques are distributed, where sterilizations and abortions are performed. That's our work. I've never thought of myself as being any different from a Catholic lawyer who handles divorces. That's your work and you help people who come to you.

What I resent is the way I've been singled out and punished, considering what else is going on today in the diocese of Providence. Two priests are awaiting trial for the alleged sexual abuse of children. Another priest has been charged with perjury in the Von Bulow case. And the headmaster of a Catholic prep school here was recently arrested for transporting a male minor for immoral purposes. These men are passing out communion on one side of the altar rail while trying to keep me away on the other. I want my Church to explain.

Luisa's confirmation took place on a beautiful sunny Sunday, but as far as I was concerned, it was a funeral. I felt a terrible sense of helplessness because our child would be hurt no matter what I did. If I talked openly about the interrogation, she would be denied the sacrament. If I said nothing, we seemed to be accepting the Church's judgment. I felt as if my hands were tied. The guests all came to the party afterward, but Al, Luisa and I were just going through the motions.

I still cry when I think I might not be buried with my parents. I've told my husband that if I go first and the Church will not allow me to be buried alongside them at our Catholic cemetery, he should have my body cremated and scatter my ashes over their graves. That way I can be with them.

Part of my faith is a strong belief that nothing happens without a reason. I'm not a mystic, but I think there is some reason God singled me out for this trial. If the Catholic Church thinks it has embarrassed me or that I will go quietly and give up, the Church is mistaken. As God, Al and Luisa know, I am and will die a Catholic.　　　　　[1986]

 72

Reactions to a Woman Rabbi

LAURA GELLER

At the conclusion of High Holiday services during my first year as an ordained rabbi, two congregants rushed up to talk to me. The first, a middle-aged woman, blurted out, "Rabbi, I can't tell you how different I felt about services because you are a woman. I found myself feeling that if you can be a rabbi, then maybe I could be a rabbi too. For the first time in my life I felt as though I could learn those prayers, I could study Torah, I could lead this service, I could do anything you could do. Knowing that made me feel much more involved in the service—much more involved with Judaism! Also, the service made me think about God in a different way. I'm not sure why." The second congregant had something very similar to tell me, but with a slightly different emphasis. He was a man, in his late twenties. "Rabbi, I realized that if you could be a rabbi, then certainly I could be a rabbi. Knowing that made the service somehow more accessible for me. I didn't need you to 'do it' for me. I could 'do it,' be involved with Jewish tradition, without depending on you."

It has taken me five years to begin to understand the significance of what these people told me.

Throughout most of Jewish history the synagogue has primarily been the domain of men. It has also been a very important communal institution. Was the synagogue so important because it was the domain of men, or was it the domain of men because it was so important? Perhaps the question becomes more relevant if we ask it in another way. If women become leaders in the synagogue, will the synagogue become less important? This concern was clearly expressed in 1955 by Sanders Tofield of the Conservative Movement's Rabbinical Assembly, when he acknowledged that one reason women are encouraged to remain within the private sphere of religious life is the fear that if women were to be completely integrated into all aspects of Jewish ritual, then men might relegate religious life to women and cease being active in the synagogue.[1] The fear connected with the "feminization" of Judaism is, largely, that once women achieve positions of power within the synagogue, men will feel that the synagogue is no longer sufficiently important to occupy their attention. The other side of the question is also being asked. Is the fact that women are becoming leaders in synagogues a sign that the synagogue is no longer an important institution?

The fact that these questions are posed increasingly suggests to me that the synagogue is not very healthy. Are synagogues so marginal in the life of American Jews that men really would limit their involvement because women are active participants?

The participation of women as leaders and especially as rabbis raises another concern for synagogues. Those two congregants on Rosh Hashanah expressed a feeling that has been echoed many times since then. When women function as clergy, the traditional American division between clergy and lay people begins to break down. Let me give an example from another religious tradition. A woman who is an Episcopal priest told me that when she offers the Eucharist people take it from her differently from the way they would take it from a male priest, even though she follows the identical ritual. People experience her as less foreign, and so the experience is more natural, less mysterious.

People don't attribute to women the power and prestige that they often attribute to men. Therefore, when women become rabbis or priests, there is often less social distance between the congregant and the clergy. The lessening of social distance and the reduction of the attribution of power and status leads to the breakdown of hierarchy within a religious institution. "If you can be a rabbi, then certainly I can be a rabbi!"

Clearly some would argue that the breakdown of traditional religious hierarchy is bad. However, in my view this change could bring about a profound and welcome change in American Judaism. It could lead to synagogues that see their rabbi not as "priest" but as teacher, and that see the congregations not as passive consumers of the rabbi's wisdom but as active participants in their own Jewish lives.

The ordination of women will lead to change in another important area of Judaism: the way Jews think about God. On a basic, perhaps subconscious, level, many Jews project the image of their rabbi onto their image of God. As Dr. Mortimer Ostow has pointed out, "While it is true that no officiant in the service actually represents God, to the average congregant God is psychologically represented by the rabbi, since he is the leader and the teacher and preacher of God's word."[2]

Most adult Jews know that it is inappropriate to envisage God as a male. But given the constant references in Jewish prayer to God as "Father" and "King," and given our childhood memories of imaging God as an old man with a long white beard, it is no surprise that to the extent Jews do conceptualize God in human terms, they often think of God as male or masculine.

Jewish tradition recognizes that God is not male. To limit God in this or any way is idolatrous; God is understood by tradition to encompass both masculinity and femininity and to transcend masculinity and femininity. Unfortunately, many Jews have never incorporated this complex image of God into their theology.

As long as the rabbi is a man, a Jew can project the image of the rabbi onto God. But when Jews encounter a rabbi who is a woman, it forces them to think about God as more than male or female. It provokes them to raise questions that most Jews don't like to confront: What or who is God? What do I believe about God? That primary religious question leads to others. How can we speak about God? What are the appropriate words, images and symbols to describe our relationship to God? Does the English rendering of Hebrew prayers convey the complexity of God? How can we change language, images, and symbols so they can convey this complexity?

All of these questions could lead to a more authentic relationship to Jewish tradition and to God. Once Jews begin to explore their image of God, they will also reevaluate their image of themselves. Because all of us are created in God's image, how we think about God shapes how we think about ourselves. That thinking leads to a reevaluation of men's and women's roles within our tradition and our world.

The ordination of women has brought Judaism to the edge of an important religious revolution. I pray we have the faith to push it over the edge.

[1983]

NOTES

1. Sanders Tofield, Proceedings of the Rabbinical Assembly 19 (1955), p. 190 as cited in Ellen M. Umansky, "Women and Rabbinical Ordination: A Viable Option? *Ohio Journal of Religious Studies*, vol. 4, Number 1 (March 1976), p. 63.

2. Dr. Mortimer Ostow, "Women and Change in Jewish Law," *Conservative Judaism* (Fall 1974), p. 7.

🌿 73

Christian Fundamentalism: Patriarchy, Sexuality, and Human Rights

SUSAN D. ROSE

I. INTRODUCTION

The Universal Declaration of Human Rights (Universal Declaration) adopted by the United Nations (UN) proclaims that "[a]ll human beings are born free and equal in dignity and rights,"[1] yet women's freedom, dignity, and equality are persistently compromised by law, custom, and religious tradition in ways that men's are not. This chapter will focus on Christian fundamentalism and patriarchy, and how they interactively help shape and rationalize both cultural views and social policy related to gender, sexuality, health, reproductive choice, and violence against women and girls.

The reinforcement of patriarchy is the trait that Christian fundamentalism most clearly shares with the other forms of religious belief that have also been called "fundamentalist." This characteristic is most evident across the Abrahamic tradition of the three major monotheistic religions—among fundamentalist Israeli Jews, within both Sunni and Shi'ite Muslim communities in various countries, and within the current revival of evangelical Protestantism emanating from the United States—but is also evident in fundamentalist Hindu and Buddhist movements.[2] All seek to control women and the expression of sexuality. Fundamentalists argue that men and women are by divine design "essentially" different, and they aim to preserve the separation between public and private, male and female, spheres of action and influence.[3] As Charlotte Bunch notes:

The distinction between private and public is a dichotomy largely used to justify female subordination and to exclude human rights abuses in the home from public scrutiny. . . . When women are denied democracy and human rights in private, their human rights in the public sphere also suffer, since what occurs in "private" shapes their ability to participate fully in the public arena.[4]

The most common rationale given for denial of human rights to women is the preservation of family and culture. While article 16 of the Convention on the Elimination of All Forms of Discrimination Against Women (CEAFDAW) requires state parties to take "all appropriate measures" to ensure the equality of women and men in marriage and in parental rights and responsibilities,[5] fundamentalists across these traditions maintain that women are the keepers of the heart and hearth, whereas men are the keepers of the mind and marketplace.

The struggle for women's and children's rights as human rights poses a fundamental threat to "traditional" cultural orders and social structures, and especially to "secondary-level male elites."[6] When "secondary-level male elites" are struggling to maintain male dominance in the middling areas of society where jobs are increasingly contested by women, they find that they can reassert themselves in the family, school, and church, which are the social institutions most accessible to them.[7] In contrast, the first-level male elite, who control the major financial institutions and/or manage the corporate structures, are not so concerned with this kind of patriarchal restoration.[8]

II. MAKING MEN, SUBDUING WOMEN IN LATE-TWENTIETH-CENTURY AMERICA

In the early twentieth century, the original, U.S. Christian fundamentalist movement explicitly stated that reining in women was essential to maintaining social cohesion.[9] Fundamentalists were also aware that although religion remained important to women, its appeal was declining among men.[10] In addition, the shift from an agrarian to an industrial society made it more difficult for men to live out "traditional" notions of masculinity.[11] As a result, concerns about the feminization of men and of

Christianity developed into a kind of militant, virile masculinity that became the hallmark of the Christian warrior, and the movement's literature became "rife with strident anti-feminist pronouncements, some of them bordering on outright misogyny."[12]

This is no less true today. As Martin Riesebrodt argues, fundamentalism is primarily a "radical patriarchalism" that represents a protest movement against the increasing egalitarianism between the sexes.[13] Within the vast majority of fundamentalist, Pentecostal, neo-Pentecostal, and charismatic Protestant churches (which I refer to under the umbrella terms "evangelical" or "fundamentalist")[14] spreading both within and beyond the United States, the downward lines of authority of the nuclear, patriarchal family are still being firmly reinforced: children are to be obedient to their parents, wives to their husbands, and husbands to their God.[15]

One of the most prominent evangelical groups today to promote a modernized form of patriarchy is the "Promise Keepers." Founded in 1990 by Bill McCartney, head coach of the University of Colorado football team, the Promise Keepers (and their female counterpart, the Promise Reapers) has embraced the goal of motivating men toward Christ-like masculinity. For example, Pastor Tony Evans, in *Seven Promises of a Promise Keeper,* argues that the primary cause of (our) national crisis—the decline of family structure—is "[t]he Feminization of Men," and he urges men to take back their male leadership role: "Unfortunately, however, there can be no compromise here. . . . Treat the lady gently and lovingly. But *lead!*"[16]

The Promise Keepers are promoting good old-fashioned patriarchy with a new twist. They are encouraging men to become more involved in family life, and more responsible to and for their children, but their approach would not meet the obligations of equality under article 16 of CEAFDAW—which they would be bound to oppose in any event. Rather than working toward greater equality for both men and women, leaders reassure men that they will *gain* rather than lose power and authority within the family. Within the fundamentalist framework, family life continues to be gendered along patriarchal lines, and while men are called back to the private sphere, gender apartheid is still maintained. This has significant consequences for social policy that affect the lives and choices of all citizens, particularly in the arenas of reproductive choice and health.

III. LEGISLATING THE CHRISTIAN PATRIARCHAL AGENDA

The pro-family political platform of the contemporary Christian Right in the United States unabashedly supports patriarchy, and privileges men's rights over women's rights, and parents' rights over children's and states' rights. This approach is particularly pernicious given that studies of domestic violence indicate that wife and child abuse is more common among families that adhere to traditional, patriarchal sex role norms.[17]

Over the past several years, conservative groups such as the Christian Coalition, Focus on the Family, the Eagle Forum, and Of the People have campaigned for "parental-rights" legislation at the federal level and in more than 25 states. These various attempts have included the "Pupil Protection Act," also known as the Hatch Amendment of 1978, which requires parental consent when a federally funded program in a school calls for a student to submit to a survey or evaluation that may reveal information concerning, among other things: political affiliations; mental and psychological problems potentially embarrassing to the student or his family; sex behavior and attitudes; and illegal, anti-social, self-incriminating, and demeaning behavior.[18] The Christian Religious Right used the Hatch Amendment to attack the curricula of public education and to prohibit curricula dealing with: health issues of suicide, drug and alcohol abuse, and sex education; globalism and world issues such as information on the Holocaust and news reporting from worldwide magazines (*Time* and *Newsweek*); diversity issues, including exposing children to books by African-American and homosexual authors; and general programs concerning political participation, including mock elections.[19] The breadth and depth of the attack on the integrity of a free public education was so great that even Senator Orrin Hatch, the sponsor of the bill, called for "the rule of commonsense [to] prevail."[20]

The patriarchal approach of the Christian Right is also apparent in the recently proposed "Parental Rights and Responsibilities Act of 1995," which prohibits any government from interfering with or usurping the right of the parent in the upbringing of the child in such areas as education, health, discipline (including corporal punishment), and religious teachings.[21] Such a bill would, among other things, have an obvious "chilling" effect on intervention in child-abuse cases.[22]

The Christian Right's support for parents' rights over children's rights and its attacks on public education demonstrate the clear conflict of interest between, on the one hand, the rights of children to an informed education (including their health) and the duty of all states to provide informed education and, on the other hand, the extent of the parental right to socialize and educate their children within the parameters of their religious faith. It is also important to note that the strongest impact will be on girls because the Christian Right educational agenda includes the promotion of patriarchy and thus unequal roles for men and women. It is hard to imagine how girls can take away from such education the Universal Declaration's proclamation that "[a]ll human beings are born free and equal in dignity and rights."[23]

The most recent victory for the conservative crusaders in their influence on public school education was their successful lobbying of Congress, in 1996, to pass welfare reform that included a provision to promote teen sexual abstinence programs in public schools. The federal government had previously funded similar programs and had been sued for providing public funding to those programs that promoted specific religious teachings.[24] Although the settlement in the case included a requirement that funded programs be medically accurate and free of religious teachings,[25] it is unclear that this standard is being met under the newly funded programs.

IV. THE SEXUAL POLITICS OF ABSTINENCE

Contemporary evangelicals have concerns about sex and sexuality that focus on issues regarding social order and control—especially over women's bodies and desires. Within the evangelical framework, lack of control over sex and the desires of the body are thought to threaten the integrity of the soul.

Exposure to information about sex, many evangelical leaders argue, leads to sex. Therefore, the political platform of the Religious Right aims to curtail sex education in the schools, and severely limit contraceptive research and dissemination at large. With the United States holding the record for the highest rate of teenage (ages 15 to 19) pregnancies and abortions in the industrialized world,[26] these issues have become all the more critical. Rightfully concerned about the high rates of teenage pregnancy, abortion, sexually transmitted diseases, and AIDS, evangelicals are active in trying to influence public policy. Although the US. teenage pregnancy rate has actually fallen to its lowest level in 20 years,[27] teenage pregnancy *is* still a problem—but when, where, how, and why it became constructed as a social problem is important to examine. For example, cross-national data indicate that the countries that have low teen pregnancy rates tend to have more open attitudes toward sexuality and sex education, access to contraceptives and a national health care system, and greater socioeconomic equality.[28] But rather than dealing with the complex problems associated with high rates of teenage pregnancy, including the fact that the United States has one of the highest rates of child poverty, child death, and infant mortality in the industrialized world, and that young teens often become pregnant as a result of rape or incest,[29] abstinence-only advocates simply advise young people to "just say no." Abstinence-only advocates have "just said no" to substantial and well-documented empirical data that show that the degree to which an effect of comprehensive sexuality education has been identifiable in studies, it has *postponed* initiation of sexual intercourse.[30]

A. *"Just Say No"*

Sex education has always been a point of conflict between public educators and conservative religious groups. Since the 1960s, Religious Right political groups have opposed the teaching of comprehensive sexuality education in public schools. By the 1980s, however, it was clear that the Religious Right was having little success in removing sex education from the schools because the general American public favors comprehensive sex education.[31] As a result, Religious Right groups, including the Eagle Forum, Concerned Women for America, Focus on the Family, and Citizens for Excellence in Education have all devoted major resources to promoting "abstinence-only" curricula in the public schools as a substitute for comprehensive sex education programs. As noted, in 1996, bowing to the Religious Right, Congress allocated fifty million dollars annually for abstinence-only education programs.[32] The provision funds programs to teach children that "sexual activity outside of the context of marriage is likely to have harmful psychological and physical effects."[33]

Religious Right groups use sophisticated, fear-based tactics in their abstinence-only programs: "Just say no or die."[34] For example, the video, *No Second Chance*, juxtaposes images of men dying from AIDS with an evangelical sex educator interacting with a classroom of teenagers. She compares having sex outside of marriage with playing Russian roulette: "every time you have sex, it's like pulling the trigger." When one teenage boy asks, "[w]hat if I do have sex before I get married?" She responds, "I guess you'll just have to be prepared to die."[35]

Leslie Kantor, the former director of the Sexuality, Information, and Education Council of the United States (SIECUS) Community Advocacy Project, conducted an extensive content analysis of abstinence-only sex education programs produced and promoted by Christian Right groups and that are used in public schools. She concluded that these programs omit the most fundamental information on contraception and disease prevention, perpetuate medical misinformation, and rely on religious doctrine and images of fear and shame in discouraging sexual activity.[36]

B. *Holding Girls Responsible*

When reading through these Christian abstinence materials, one becomes aware of an old, traditional message: the cautionary story of sex as one of male predators and female prey. On the one hand, from an evangelical perspective, humans are not animals (which is at the crux of the evolution-creation debate), rather they stand only a little lower than angels. Yet, beyond a certain point, humans—especially men—are regarded as not being able to control their sexual urges. In fact, according to the sexual arousal time line in *Sexual Common Sense: Affirming Adolescent Abstinence,* "the prolonged kiss" is pinpointed as the "beginning of danger."[37]

After this point of "danger," there is no turning back from sexual arousal. The sexual arousal time line also indicates that while females too have sexual instincts, they take longer to become aroused. Therefore, they hold greater responsibility in exercising constraint. Women are considered to be less controlled by their sexuality and more responsible not only for their own sexual behavior but for the sexual behavior of men. Evangelist James Robison, whose book *Sex is Not Love* sold over half a million copies, warns that "[s]ex before marriage . . . develops sensual drives that can never be satisfied and may cause a man to behave like an animal."[38] He states that "[s]ome girls become that way, too . . . but most of them don't. When they do, it's the most awful thing that can happen to humanity."[39]

However, it would appear that there are more awful things that can happen: the use of tax dollars to support abstinence-only programs that provide medical misinformation and promote fear and ignorance, and the failure to provide support to implement effective social policy that could effectively curb teenage pregnancy and provide better economic, educational, and health opportunities for all young people.

V. WHOSE RIGHTS?

Central to the sex education debate is the Religious Right's attempt to preserve men's rights over women's rights, and parental rights over children's rights. The Family Research Council in 1995 critiqued the Fourth World Conference on Women, stating that the conference reflected "a radical feminist agenda" that "denigrate[d] motherhood and the traditional family" by noting that there were "unequal power relations" in the family.[40] Radical? Yes, writes evangelical psychologist James Dobson, who heads up the largest Christian Right Organization in the United States, Focus on the Family. He warns that

the UN Conference on Women represents "the most radical, atheistic, anti-family crusade in the history of the world"[41] and that "[t]he Agency for International Development will channel hundreds of millions of dollars to support women's reproductive and sexual rights and family planning services. The only hope for derailing this train is the Christian church."[42]

As we enter the new millennium, family planning, reproductive and sexual health, and economic well-being are vital concerns for individuals, communities, and nations. Rates of pregnancy, and AIDS and other sexually transmitted diseases, remain alarmingly high among America's youth, yet opponents of sexuality education are trying to censor vital, life-saving information that has proven effective in dealing with these problems. Instead, the Religious Right continues to blame the "fallen girl/woman" and the feminization of men for the ills of our society rather than economic and structural forces that perpetuate inequality between men and women, and between the very wealthy and the middle and impoverished classes. In the battle over sexuality and choice and education, it's girls' and women's bodies, lives, and livelihoods that are all too often sacrificed.

With respect to girls' rights in education, it is important to remember that the International Covenant on Civil and Political Rights (ICCPR)—to which the United States is a party—prohibits discrimination against women or girls.[43] The Human Rights Committee, the monitoring body of the ICCPR, has interpreted ICCPR provisions as allowing parents to ensure that their children receive a religious and moral education but that public schools are limited to teaching the general history of religion in a nondiscriminatory manner and only if it is given "in a neutral and objective manner" because the "instruction in a particular religion or belief is inconsistent" with the ICCPR.[44] Does the Christian Right educational agenda meet this standard?

While evangelicals represent only 25 percent of the U.S. population, their influence on social policy regarding sexuality education, sexual orientation, teen pregnancy, reproduction, family planning, and economic equity has been significant, though less in establishing their agenda than in putting the brakes on research, education, and funding that could reduce the rates of teen pregnancy, abortion, and violence against women and children; increase the equality between women and men; and better protect and prepare children for healthy, active, responsible lives in the twenty-first century. Their impact is also felt beyond the borders of the United States. Today North American evangelicals are the largest group of missionaries moving across the globe on mission quests.[45] They are effective in establishing churches, schools, and health clinics in various places around the world. What kind of messages will they be disseminating? What kinds of influence may evangelical "sex experts" have as they fund programs and advise people and political leaders, not only in the United States, but around the world about gender, family planning, sex, contraception, violence—about life and death?   [1999]

NOTES

1. *See* Universal Declaration of Human Rights, *adopted* Dec. 10, 1948, G.A. Res. 217A (III), U.N. GAOR, 3d Sess., pt. 1,183d plen. mtg., at 71, art. 1, U.N. Doc. A/810 (1948) [hereinafter Universal Declaration].

2. *See* Steve Brouwer, Paul Gifford, & Susan Rose, Exporting the American Gospel: Global Christian Fundamentalism 218–26 (New York/London: Routledge, 1996) [hereinafter Brouwer, Exporting]; Helen Hardacre, *The Impact of Fundamentalism on Women, the Family, and Impersonal Relations, in* 2 The Fundamentalism Project, Fundamentalisms and Society 129, 131–47 (Martin E. Marty & R. Scott Appleby, eds.) (Chicago /London: The University of Chicago Press, 1993) [hereinafter Fundamentalism and Society]; John S. Hawley, *Hinduism: Sati and Its Defenders, in* Fundamentalism and Gender 79, 93–103 (John Stratton Hawley, ed.) (New York/Oxford: Oxford University Press, 1994); *see also* Jan Goodwin, Price of Honor: Muslim Women Lift the Veil of Silence on the Islamic World (New York/Boston/Toronto/London: Little, Brown, and Company, 1994). For a further discussion of "fundamentalism" across religions, see John Stratton Hawley, Fundamentalism, in this volume.

3. *See* Courtney W. Howland, *The Challenge of Religious Fundamentalism to the Liberty and Equality Rights of Women: An Analysis under the United Nations Charter,* 35 Colum. J. Transnat'l L. 271, 283–85 (1997).

4. Charlotte Bunch, *Transforming Human Rights from a Feminist Perspective, in* Women's Rights, Human Rights: International Feminist Perspectives 11, 14 (Julie Peters & Andrea Wolper, eds.) (New York/London: Routledge, 1995).

5. *See* Convention on the Elimination of All Forms of Discrimination Against Women, *adopted* Dec. 18, 1979, G.A. Res. 34/180, U.N. GAOR, 34th Sess., Supp. No. 46, at 193, 196, art. 16 (1). U.N. Doc. A/34/46 (1979), 1249 U.N.T.S. 13, 20.

6. Bruce B. Lawrence, Defenders of God: The Fundamentalist Revolt Against the Modern Age 100 (Columbia, SC: University of South Carolina Press, 1989).

7. *See* Susan D. Rose, Keeping Them out of the Hands of Satan: Evangelical Schooling in America 1–10 (New York/London: Routledge, 1988).

8. *See* Brouwer, Exporting, *supra* note 2, at 219 & n.19.

9. See Brouwer, Exporting, *supra* note 2, at 219–20.

10. *See* Margaret Lamberts Bendroth, Fundamentalism and Gender, 1875 to the Present 13, 17 (New Haven/London: Yale University Press, 1993).

11. *Id.* at 17; Brouwer, Exporting, *supra* note 2, at 219–20.

12. *See* Bendroth, *supra* note 10, at 31.

13. Martin Riesebrodt, Pious Passion: The Emergence of Modern Fundamentalism in Iran and the United States 176–208 (Berkeley/Los Angeles/London: University of California Press, 1993).

14. For a more detailed discussion of these different groups and terminology, including the use of the umbrella term "evangelical," see Brouwer, Exporting, *supra* note 2, at 263–71; Nancy T. Ammerman, *North American Protestant Fundamentalism, in* 1 The Fundamentalism Project: Fundamentalisms Observed 1, 2–5 (Chicago/London: the University of Chicago Press, 1991); Laurence R. Innaccone, *Heirs to the Protestant Ethic? The Economies of American Fundamentalists, in* 3 The Fundamentalism Project: Fundamentalisms and the State 342, 343–44 (Chicago/London: The University of Chicago Press, 1993).

15. *See, e.g.,* Dr. Edward Hindson, former Director of Counseling at Jerry Falwell's Thomas Road Baptist Ministries, *quoted in* Rose, *supra* note 7, at xvii ("The Bible clearly states that the wife is to submit to her husband's leadership.").

16. Tony Evans, *Spiritual Purity; in* Seven Promises of a Promise Keeper 73, 80 (Al Janssen & Larry K.Weeden, eds.) (Colorado Springs, CO: Focus on the Family Publishing, 1994).

17. *See* Gender Violence: Interdisciplinary Perspectives (Laura L. O'Toole & Jessica R. Schiffman, eds.) (New York/London: New York University Press, 1997); James Alsdurf & Phyllis Alsdurf, Battered Into Submission: The Tragedy of Wife Abuse in the Christian Home 10, 16–18 (Downers Grove, IL; InterVarsity Press, 1989).

18. Protection of pupil rights, 20 U.S.C. §1232h (1994). The Hatch Amendment itself was amended in 1994, but the key provisions remain intact. The current regulations are those that were written before the 1994 amendments. *See* Student Rights in Research, Experimental Programs, and Testing, 34 C.F.R. §98 (1996); *see generally* Anne C. Lewis, Little-Used Amendment Becomes Divisive, Disruptive Issue, Phi Delta Kappan, June 1985, at 667.

19. *See* Susan Rose, *Christian Fundamentalism and Education in the United States, in* Fundamentalisms and Society, *supra* note 2, at 452, 467–473.

20. Pupil Protection Rights Regulations, 131 Cong. Rec. 2449, 2451 (1985).

21. *See* H.R. 1946, 104th Cong. (1995); S. 984, 104th Cong. (1995).

22. The Alan Guttmacher Institute, *Supremacy of Parental Authority New Battlecry For Conservative Activists,* Washington Memo, Dec. 21, 1995, at 4.

23. For a discussion of how international human rights law can protect the girl child's right to education, see Deirdre Fottrell & Geraldine Van Bueren, *The Potential of International Law to Combat Discrimination Against Girls in Education,* in this volume.

24. *See* Brown v. Kendrick, 487 U.S. 589 (1988) (remanded for trial).

25. *See* Leslie M. Kantor, *Attacks on Public School Sexuality Education Programs: 1993–94 School Year,* 22 SIECUS Report, Aug./Sept. 1994, at 11, 11.

26. *See* Andrew L. Shapiro, We're Number One! Where America Stands—And Falls—in the New World Order 11–16 (New York: Vintage Books, 1992); Sex and America's Teenagers 40–43 (New York/Washington, D.C.: The Alan Guttmacher Institute, 1994); Elise F. Jones et al., Teenage Pregnancy in Industrialized Nations 1 (New Haven/London: Yale University Press, 1986).

27. *See* Patricia Donovan, *Falling Teen Pregnancy, Birthrates: What's Behind the Decline?,* The Guttmacher Report: On Public Policy, Oct. 1998, at 6, 6.

28. Jones et al., *supra* note 26, at 216–27.

29. *See* Debra Boyer & David Fine, *Sexual Abuse as a Factor in Adolescent Pregnancy and Child Maltreatment,* 24 Fam. Plan. Persp. 4 (1992); Patrick A. Langan, Ph.D. & Caroline Wolf Harlow, Ph.D., Child Rape Victims, 1992 (Washington, D.C.: U.S. Department of Justice, 1994).

30. *See* People for the American Way, Teaching Fear: The Religious Right's Campaign Against Sexuality Education 22–26 (Washington, DC: People for the American Way, 1994) [hereinafter Teaching Fear].

31. *See* The Best Intentions: Unintended Pregnancy and the Well-Being of Children and Families 132 (Sarah Brown & Leon Eisenberg, eds.) (Washington, D.C.: National Academy Press, 1995).

32. Maternal and Child Health Services Block Grant, Pub. L. 104–193, 110 Stat. 2353 (1996), 42 U.S.C.A. §710 (Supp. 1.998).

33. The Alan Guttmacher Institute, *Snapshot Welfare Reform Law,* Washington Memo, Oct. 8, 1996, at 5.

34. *See* Teaching Fear, *supra* note 30, at 6; Kantor, *supra* note 25, at 11–12; *see, e.g., Sex, Lies, and the Truth,* video distributed by James Dobson's organization, Focus on the Family.

35. *See* Teaching Fear, *supra* note 30, at 8 (quoting *No Second Chance,* film used for Sex Respect programs developed by the Committee on the Status of Women, an anti-choice organization founded by Phyllis Schafly).

36. Leslie M. Kantor, *Scared Chaste? Fear-Based Educational Curricula,* 21 SIECUS Report, Dec. 1992/Jan. 1993, at 1, 1–15; *see also Sexuality Education Around the World,* 24 SIECUS Report, Feb./Mar. 1996, at 1.

37. Coleen Kelly Mast, Sex Respect: The Option of True Sexual Feeling-Student Handbook 7, 90 (Bradley, IL: Respect Incorporated, rev. ed., 1997) *reprinting chart from* Patricia B. Driscoll & Mary Rose Osborn, Sexual Common Sense: Affirming Adolescent Abstinence (Walnut Creek, CA: Womanity Publications, 1982).

38. William Martin, *God's Angry Man,* Texas Monthly, April 1981, at 153, 223.

39. *Id.* (quoting James Robison).

40. Family Research Council, *UN: Bound for Beijing,* 6 Washington Watch: Special Report, Aug. 24, 1995, at 1.

41. James Dobson, *The Family Under Fire By the United Nations,* Focus On the Family Newsletter, August 1995, at 1.

42. Letter from James Dobson, President, Focus on the Family, mass mailing to members, 6 (Oct. 1995) (footnote omitted).

43. *See* International Covenant on Civil and Political Rights, *adopted* Dec. 16, 1966, G.A. Res. 2200 (XXI), U.N. GAOR, 21st Sess., Supp. No. 16, at 52, arts. 2(1), 3, 23(4), 24(1), 26 U.N. Doc. A/6316, 999 U.N.TS. 171, 6 I.L.M. 368 (1967) [hereinafter ICCPR].

44. Human Rights Committee, General Comments Adopted under Article 40, Paragraph 4, of the ICCPR: General Comment No. 22 (48) (art. 18), UN. Doc. A/48/40 (Pt. I) 208, para. 6, at 209 (1993).

45. *See generally* Brouwer, Exporting, *supra* note 2, at 182–86.

 74

Revelations

LINDA VILLAROSA

In the May 1991 issue of *Essence* magazine, my mother and I each wrote about my coming out as a lesbian. That article received a tremendous reception—most of it positive—and it remains the most responded-to article in the history of the magazine. Due to the avalanche of mail, my mother and I followed up with "Readers Respond to Coming Out," which ran later that year in the October issue. This article was much more political, allowing me to speak out directly against homophobia in Black communities. Almost overnight, I was unexpectedly catapulted into the public arena, which began a wave of national speaking engagements that left me to cope with both adulation and condemnation.

Before I came out in print, I never had someone tell me I was going to go to hell. Now people say it to me regularly. When my mother and I addressed a conference of Black social workers about how families may confront their homophobia and accept lesbian and gay children, a sad-eyed man, round-shouldered in a baggy suit, approached me. "I enjoyed hearing what you had to say," he offered, his hand extended. My hand in his, he continued, barely missing a beat, "But you're a sinner. You're going to hell." He said this casually, through a half-smile, as though ready to add, "Have a nice day."

Some people put their condemnation in writing, spitting angry religion-like curse words. These are two of the several letters I received at *Essence*:

From Smyrna, Georgia: [Your] behavior is a sin against God that can be forgiven by sincere repentance and turning away from the sin of homosexuality. In fact, the word of God is very clear on the immorality of homosexuality. Read 1 Corinthians 6:9. Homosexuals and the homosexual lifestyle will never be accepted. I believe that sharing the Word with those individuals afflicted with the sin of homosexuality and imparting love and patience, they can receive the loving salvation of Jesus Christ. This is the only way you, and other homosexuals, can become normal, saved persons.

From Westchester, New York: [Essence] should be ashamed of itself for having a woman like Linda Villarosa on your staff. Lesbian [sic] is not a sickness, it's a sin, and if that woman does not repent, she is going to perish. She should read Mathew [sic] chapter 19 verses 4 and 5. Read it and see what it says. Linda, no one wants to know who you are!

The worst verbal attack came at Oregon State University, where I was to address a large group of students about being Black, lesbian, and out. The trouble started before I arrived. I had requested that the organizers contact African-American student groups about coming to my lecture, because I believe that it's extremely important for Blacks—gay and straight—to know that Black lesbians exist and can be happy and out and secure in their identities. A member of the school's Black Women's Alliance (BWA), who was also friendly with the gay group

on campus, agreed to make an announcement at BWA's next meeting to garner support and ensure a strong Black presence at the lecture. At the end of the meeting she told the other sisters that an editor from *Essence* would be speaking the following evening. Several women clapped and nodded. "She'll be talking about what it's like to be a Black lesbian," the young woman continued. At that point, the room fell silent. Finally, one woman stood up and said, "Lesbianism is nastiness and they should get a vaccine to make them normal." Spurred on, another declared, "Gays are against God, and because of my religion, I can't hear this woman speak." In the end, another exasperated sister said, " Can we please stop talking about this, I'm getting physically ill."

Thankfully, I didn't know about this backlash or I would've been too freaked to do the lecture. Expressions of homophobia hurt deeply, but coming from other Black women the pain is particularly acute. Knowing that I would be facing such resistance in what was already a largely white audience on a conservative college campus may well have paralyzed me.

The lecture went fine. The question-and-answer period was particularly long with interested students —gay, straight, and of many races and ethnicities— hungry for answers and information. After a while I became tired and announced that I'd answer one final question. A clean-cut white guy wearing a baseball cap waved his hand frantically from the balcony. And there it was: "You and all gays are going to hell. I'm telling you this because God taught me to love you." Then he cited a Bible passage: "Read Leviticus 20:13."

Bedlam broke out in the room. After several minutes, I got things quieted down and looked out into the expectant faces of the audience. The challenge had been made, and I felt that all of the young, gay people there expected me to defend us all with authority. My voice shook with anger and a little bit of fear that I wouldn't be able to meet this challenge. "Listen, you don't love me, you don't know me, you don't understand me," I said, barely able to remain composed and keep from crying. "You're using religion to cloak your horrible message in the language of love. People like you have used religion to suppress everything you find offensive. In the past the Bible was used to justify slavery and now you're using it to justify your fear and hatred of those of us who are living our lives as gays and lesbians."

The tension broke and the crowd began to applaud, but I felt empty. Even the reporters covering the event saw through my strong front and brave smile. The next day's edition of the *Corvallis (Ore.) Gazette-Times* reported that as I stepped from the podium, I had seemed stunned. It was true: I was stunned. And sad. My words had sounded hollow to me, as though I had been reading from a textbook. I hadn't felt them. My reaction had been a knee-jerk response to being attacked in public; but deep within me, I knew I wasn't so sure about myself. Where do I really stand spiritually? That heckler knew exactly how he felt and where he stands, why didn't I?

Nothing in my own religious upbringing prepared me for these attacks. My family attended an integrated, "progressive" Episcopal church. There were a handful of families of color like us and lots of groovy white people, interracial couples, and aging hippies with their adopted children of color in tow. Our choir didn't sing gospel music, but folky spiritual ballads accompanied by the organ, guitar, and African and Native American drumming.

I don't remember learning many specific religious lessons from our minister. With his long hair flowing over his Roman collar, Father Hammond preached through sleepy eyes, as though he'd been out late drinking the night before. His words were inspirational and easy to understand, filled with references to pop culture. A quote from *Playboy* magazine could seamlessly segue into biblical verse. My mother taught my fourth-grade Sunday school class, stressing discipline and openmindedness. One Saturday morning the group of us gathered for a field trip to a nearby synagogue. We looked like a bunch of "We Are the World" poster children. "It's important to learn about the way other people worship," my mother explained, looking over our group to make sure our two lines were straight and orderly and no noses were running.

To further my religious studies, I attended weeks and weeks of confirmation classes every Thursday night. On confirmation day, I walked down the church aisle, clutching a white prayer book in white-gloved hands. I was wearing a white dress, white lace socks, white patent-leather shoes, and had a white handkerchief pinned to my head. I looked like a brown-skinned vestal virgin awaiting sacrifice. I don't remember one spiritual lesson from that time, but I do remember how hard it was to try to stay clean in all those bleached-white clothes.

We also visited St. John's, my grandmother's Baptist church, on trips back to Chicago, where I was born. Getting dressed for service was a major production. My grandmother had to decide which of her many wigs and hats to wear and whether or not to put on her fur, a decision that had little to do with the temperature outside. After the frenzied preparations, we'd all pile into my grandfather's Electra 225 and float to church in the boat-sized car.

Once inside, I'd always scrunch into my grandmother's side and maneuver a way to sit by her. I knew she was important in this community from the way heads would turn as she led the family— straight-backed—down the aisle to our pew, and I wanted a little of that limelight.

The service really wasn't as fun as the preparation, mainly because of its three-hour length. Until someone got the Spirit. I'd hold my breath as the organ pounded out the same repetitive note and the singing rang louder, rising to more and more tremorous shouts. Inevitably, some well-dressed woman would take to the aisle, chanting and skipping. Then two strong, well-practiced sisters, dressed in white gloves and nurse's uniforms, would walk briskly over and efficiently bring the saved soul back to this world and dispatch her into the care of family members. I would tug at Grandmother's sleeve asking questions about the moment of high drama, but she would slap my Vaselined knees together and hiss into my ear, "Stop-staring-close-your-lips-don't-bite-your-cuticles-put-your-gloves-back-on." The only thing I knew for certain was that no one in our family would ever get the spirit, because my grandmother would die of embarrassment.

From my parents' church I learned about respect for difference and community across seemingly unbridgeable differences, and through my grandmother's church I connected with my Southern Baptist roots. But nothing from my religious past had prepared me to deal with the continued abuse I was receiving from so-called religious people. It was time for me to begin studying the Bible, but, more importantly, it was time to discover my own spiritual core.

First, I dug out the dusty copy of the Revised Standard Version of the Bible left over from my days in confirmation classes, and I looked up the passages that had been thrown in my face. I started with 1 Corinthians 6:9 and 10, which read: "Do not be deceived; neither the immoral, nor idolaters, nor adulterers, nor homosexuals, nor thieves, nor the greedy, nor drunkards, nor revilers, nor robbers will inherit the kingdom of God."

I felt skeptical: had the authors of the Bible really used the word "homosexual" two thousand years ago? No, they had not. The New Testament had been written in Greek and then translated into Hebrew. In 1382 the Bible was first translated into English, and in 1611 came the King James (or authorized) Version. The Bible I was reading had been revised 335 years later. I purchased a paperback copy of the King James Version and looked up 1 Corinthians 6:9 and 10. This earlier version never used the word "homosexual" but listed the "effeminate" and "abusers of themselves with mankind" in its inventory of the "unrighteous," and that had been translated to mean "homosexual" in the revised version. Something had been lost—or gained—in translation.

I decided not to spend much more time trying to sort out what the authors meant and what lessons they were trying to teach about homosexuality—if that's even what they were talking about—in the context of social systems from twenty centuries past. In fact, even after reading Genesis 19 many times, I still didn't see how the story of Sodom had anything to do with gay sex. In that story, Lot, a holy man and resident of the evil city of Sodom, is visited by two angels. Genesis 19:4-8 reads:

. . . the men of the city, the men of Sodom, both young and old, all the people to the last man, surrounded the house; and they called to Lot, "Where are the men who came to you tonight [i.e., the angels]? Bring them out to us, that we may know them." Lot went out of the door to the men, shut the door after him, and said, "I beg you, my brothers, do not act so wickedly. Behold, I have two daughters who have not known man; let me bring them out to you, and do to them as you please; only do nothing to these men. . . ."

Eventually, the angels strike the men blind, and God rains fire and brimstone on the city and burns it down. From this story comes the word "sodomy" —a pejorative term for gay sex. And now, when a city like New York is described as a modern-day Sodom, the underlying assumption is that it's full of sin and sex and gays. Even assuming that the word "know" refers to sex, it seems a stretch to use it to condemn gays and lesbians. Why isn't anyone questioning Lot for offering to turn over his virginal daughters to the mob of men, which is the most obvious aberrance relayed there?

Moving on, I looked up Matthew 19:4 and 5, which says: "He answered, 'Have you not read that he who made them from the beginning made them male and female,' and said, 'For this reason a man shall leave his father and mother and be joined to his wife, and the two shall become one flesh.'"

Upon further reading, it was easy to see that the letter writer from Westchester, New York, had taken these verses completely out of context. The passage had nothing to do with lesbians and gay men but was clearly a condemnation of divorce. In fact, the verses she cited were an answer to the question "Is it lawful to divorce one's wife for any cause?" (Matthew 19:3). Verse 9 says that "whoever divorces his wife, except for unchastity, and marries another, commits adultery." In case there's any question about the seriousness of adultery, Leviticus 20:10 spells it out clearly: "If a man commits adultery with the wife of his neighbor, both the adulterer and the adulteress shall be put to death." What does this have to do with queerness?

Next I looked up Leviticus 20:13: "If a man

lies with a male as with a woman, both of then have committed an abomination; they shall be put to death, their blood is upon them." I guess they could be murdered along with the divorced remarried couple from earlier Leviticus verses. At this point, I started getting angry.

It doesn't take a biblical scholar to figure out that people use the Bible selectively. The people who write me letters are not sending hate mail to people who are divorced or to those who have cheated on their spouses. The man who lashed out at me in Oregon is not condemning people who eat pork ("And the swine, because it parts the hoof and is cloven-footed but does not chew the cud, is unclean to you. Of their flesh you shall not eat, and their carcasses you shall not touch; they are unclean to you": Leviticus 11:7-8) or shellfish (". . . anything in the seas or the rivers that has not fins and scales, of the swarming creatures in the waters and of the living creatures that are in the waters, is an abomination to you": Leviticus 11:10).

Neither is he cursing or carrying on about cattle. breeders, farmers who grow two different crops, or anyone who wears a poly-cotton blend of clothing despite Leviticus 19:19: "You shall not let your cattle breed with a different kind; you shall not sow your field with two different kinds of seed; nor shall there come upon you a garment of cloth made of two kinds of stuff."

These people are also overlooking beautiful, lyrical passages in the Bible that celebrate same-sex love. In Ruth 1:16-17 of the Old Testament, Ruth says to Naomi: "Entreat me not to leave you or to return from following you; for where you go I will go, and where you lodge I will lodge; your people shall be my people, and your God my God; where you die I will die, and there will I be buried."

David and Jonathan of the Old Testatment seem to be deeply in love: ". . . the soul of Jonathan was knit to the soul of David, and Jonathan loved him as his own soul" (1 Samuel 18:1). When Jonathan dies in the war, David writes: ". . . your love to me was wonderful, passing the love of women" (2 Samuel 1:26).

Many so-called righteous people are taking the Bible literally when it suits them, ignoring anything that doesn't easily support their narrow condemnations or calls into question their own life styles. And many Black people are using the Bible against their lesbian and gay sisters and brothers just as whites used the scriptures against our ancestors when they interpreted passages such as Ephesians 6:5-6—"Slaves, be obedient to those who are your earthly masters, with fear and trembling, in singleness of heart, as to Christ; not in the way of eyeservice, as men-pleasers, but as servants of Christ"—to mean that our people should remain enslaved.

It is, in fact, a sad irony that the overwhelmingly white Christian Right movement is capitalizing on homophobia in Black communities. Groups like the Moral Majority and the Christian Coalition have never marched side by side with or fought for issues affecting people of color. In fact, the Christian Right has actively lobbied against issues such as voting rights and affirmative action. But now they're recruiting our people, taking advantage of the deep spiritual commitment of the African-American community and distorting Christianity to pass anti-gay and lesbian legal initiatives and turn straight Blacks against gays—similar to the way their ancestors distorted Christianity to justify slavery.

My Bible studies behind me, I felt fortified intellectually but still on shaky ground spiritually. But I knew exactly what I needed to do. I had heard about Unity Fellowship Church and its lively congregation of hundreds of mostly Black lesbians and gay men that worshipped on Sundays at New York City's Lesbian and Gay Community Services Center. Although I had always found excuses to avoid going, now it was time.

When I arrived that first Sunday, the room at the Center was packed with people; in fact, close to one hundred latecomers had to be turned away. The service began with testimonials. Person after person stood up and testified to what had happened over the week: breakups, gay bashing, rejections by parents, eviction from apartments, illness, sadness, loneliness, addiction, sorrow, seemed to silence the news of triumphs and causes for celebration. Pain filled the room, Black pain, gay pain. But when the pastor, Elder Zachary Jones, marched into the room to the tune of "We've come this far by faith . . . ," the mood in the room changed to one of joy.

"It doesn't have nothing to do with who you sleep with, but what's in your heart," Rev. Zach shouted over the low hum of the choir. "Who says God doesn't love gay people? There's love in this room." And there was. A measure of healing had begun. His simple words struck a chord in me, and I felt relieved and then cleansed. As I looked around at the hundreds of other Black lesbian and gay people in the room—who like me had been searching for a spiritual home—I knew I had found a place where I could be comfortable and explore my own spirituality.

Fortified in mind and spirit, from my connection with this community, I felt ready to face the world. And an opportunity presented itself while I was giving a talk at a Black cultural center on the West Coast. After going through my usual song and dance about how it felt to be Black and a lesbian, I began fielding questions. I noticed a woman raising her hand tentatively. She was a sister in her mid-thirties, turned out in an expensive, corporate-looking suit and bright gold jewelry, with her hair freshly done in braided extensions. "You seem like a really nice woman and I enjoyed hearing your story," she began slowly. "But as a Christian woman I need to share this with you. I went through a period in my life when I thought I was attracted to women. But then I discovered Jesus Christ. By reading the Bible, I realized that homosexuality was unnatural and that I was a sinner. If I continued in the life, I would be condemned."

"Where does the Bible say that?" I asked.

Opening her purse, she pulled out a small, worn copy of the New Testament and began to read from a marked passage. "For this reason God gave them up to dishonorable passions. Their women exchanged natural relations for unnatural, and the men likewise gave up natural relations with women and were consumed with passion for one another, men committing shameless acts with men and receiving in their own persons the due penalty for their error.' Romans 1, verses 26 and 27."

I listened politely as she read. When she had finished, I reached into my backpack and pulled out my own copy of the Bible. "'In like manner that the women adorn themselves in modest apparel with propriety and moderation, not with braided hair or gold or pearls or costly clothing,' 1 Timothy, chapter 2, verse 9," I read. "And 1 Timothy 2:11 and 12 say, 'Let a woman learn in silence with all submissiveness. I permit no woman to teach or to have authority over men; she is to keep silent.' I'm sure in your work you have had to supervise men. I know I have. And even by standing up and speaking out today, I guess we're both sinning."

"Wait, that's not fair," she said, her face looking at once confused and angry. "It's not right to take the Bible out of context like that."

"Why?" I countered. "That's what you're doing."

Even as I hit her close to home, I felt sorry for this woman. She was obviously confused and probably a closet case, and I knew I was preying on that, attacking her with scriptures almost as I had been attacked. I was aiming at a place she had only recently uncovered—where she was still vulnerable.

"Listen," I said softly: "I don't want to do this. All of us need to stop taking the Bible literally, and begin to read it critically and intelligently. You know, there are some important messages that we can understand and agree on." I opened my Bible to Leviticus 19:17 and read in a clear voice, "You shall not hate your brother in your heart, but you shall reason with your neighbor, lest you bear sin because of him. You shall not take vengeance or bear any grudge against the sons of your own people, but you shall love your neighbor as yourself." And this time my words sounded strong and confident, and were definitely my own.   [1995]

 75

In Her Own Image

ROSE SOLARI

For as long as she can remember, Vienna Cobb Anderson wanted to be a priest. "I played priest when

I was a child," she recalls. "I dressed up in my choir robes and performed marriage ceremonies. I held funerals for the neighborhood pets." Anderson, now rector of St. Margaret's Episcopal Church in Washington, D.C., gave up a career as an actress to enter the seminary in 1964, 12 years before the Episcopal Church approved the ordination of women. As far as she was concerned, her calling took precedence over the Church politics of the time.

"The men in seminary kept telling me not to rock the boat," she says of her early questions about sexism in the Church, "but I couldn't keep quiet. Once in class, the professor—who was, of course, also a priest—became so angry with me that he said, 'You must realize that there is a difference between a priest and other Christians.'" when Anderson pushed him to clarify his point, he blurted out, "I can celebrate the Eucharist, and you can't!"

Three decades later, Anderson celebrates the Eucharist every Sunday, proving her former teacher wrong.

She is not alone. Over the last 35 years, scores of Christian women of all denominations have brought feminism into their churches, re-examining everything from scripture to sexuality. Today, some of the most challenging and innovative work in both theology and ministry is being done by women professors and preachers who combine their religious traditions with a powerful emphasis on female identity and experience. This work is not limited to Christianity alone, nor to the United States: Feminists have formulated critiques and prescriptions for change in Jewish, Buddhist, and Islamic traditions, and feminist theologians have emerged in Asia, Africa, and Latin America. But even if one limits one's gaze to this country and to Christianity, it is clear that—whether their primary identification is as ethicists, womanists, or ecofeminists, whether they lead congregations or classes—women are breaking open the traditional definitions of what it means to be a disciple of Christ.

Their work is not without negative consequences. As the organizers of 1993's ecumenical Re-Imagining Conference discovered, many churches are willing to go only so far to accommodate the demands of these increasingly vocal and well-educated women. According to its planners, the aim of the conference was to provide a forum in which women from a variety of denominations could come together to explore feminist issues in the Church, as well as to celebrate their faith. However, the backlash experienced by the participants extended from ridicule in the press to punishment by their church hierarchies.

Yet they are undaunted. "I am just going on with my work," says Delores S. Williams, a pioneer in the African American, or "womanist," branch of feminist theology, who was singled out for some of the strongest criticism in the Christian press following the Re-Imagining Conference. "We all got backlash in one way or another. I'm not paying a bit of attention to it."

Williams has company in her fearlessness. Books and articles exploring a feminist approach to Christianity continue to proliferate, with more and more conferences, newsletters, and organizations springing up every year. Before 1960, one could find little literature on the role of women in the Church; with the emergence of feminism, however, women across the country began to turn a critical eye on all of the systems that might be contributing to their oppression. One of those systems was religion.

"I am a student of theology; I am also a woman." With these words, Valerie Saiving began her essay "The Human Situation: A Feminine View," which appeared in the April 1960 issue of the *Journal of Religion* and ushered in the opening decade of feminist theology. Saiving, then a doctoral student, discussed the ways in which her experiences as a woman seemed disconnected from the theology she was studying. She wrote, "I am no longer as certain as I once was that, when theologians speak of 'man,' they are using the word in its generic sense."

For the next three decades, women would echo Saiving's statement, both in conversation and in print. Beginning in academic journals and presses, then moving into the mainstream on a growing tide of feminist literature, women were discovering that, both on paper and in practice, Christian denominations had as a part of their foundation certain sexist assumptions that were damaging not only to the psyches of individual Christian women but also to the structure of the Church as a whole. Women writers and thinkers began to note such problematic elements of Christianity as the emphasis on Eve as the bringer of sin, the concept of God as father and son, and the theological writing of such thinkers as Thomas Aquinas, whose statements on the inferior nature of women were taught in theological seminaries all over the world.

Since the 1960s, feminist theologians have not simply been looking to make space for the feminine in a male hierarchy. Noting that the history of Christianity was shaped by a male bias that precluded women from participation in the formation of theology, teaching, and preaching, they have been demanding something much more radical. For most of them, the goal has been not to renovate the existing structure but to tear the whole building down and start over, creating something that they believe to be much closer to the roots of Christ's actual teachings and intentions.

FOUNDING MOTHERS

Although the list of writers and thinkers in this field continues to grow—and new approaches are being developed every day—many women cite three early, key figures who helped make their work possible: Mary Daly, now a professor of philosophy at Yale University, whose first book, *The Church and the Second Sex,* was an impassioned critique of sexism in Christianity and who has now abandoned that tradition; Rosemary Radford Ruether, a professor at Garrett-Evangelical Theological Seminary in Illinois and the author or editor of over 25 books, including groundbreaking work on the cultural and historical roots of sexism in Christianity; and Beverly Wildung Harrison, a professor of Christian ethics at Union Theological Seminary in New York City, who works on some of the most controversial and difficult ethical subjects facing Christians today —such as the ethics of abortion rights and the obligation that Christians have to the poor—while encouraging and mentoring countless students in the field.

Unlike those whom they have inspired and guided, these women began their research and writing with relatively few sources and no guideposts.

What they had was their own well-schooled intellects, which combined with the political climate of the 1960s to create a new way of looking at religion.

Mary Daly, who grew up a Roman Catholic and obtained doctorates in both philosophy and theology in Europe in the 1960s, was the first to bring the battle cry for feminist theology to a mainstream audience. Combining a thorough academic background with fiery prose, Daly, in her 1968 book, *The Church and the Second Sex,* blasted Christianity for providing women with images of themselves as inherently sinful and inferior. In a subsequent volume, *Beyond God the Father,* published in 1975, her critique gained momentum, and by her third book, *Gyn/Ecology,* published in 1978, she had left Christianity behind, positing that it was beyond hope of feminist reform. Unlike feminist theologians who work to separate what they see as Christianity's original, egalitarian message from subsequent patriarchal interpretations, Daly felt that such a task was impossible and unnecessary; to be a truly radical feminist, she asserted, one must part with Christianity altogether.

While Daly was working on her first two books, Rosemary Radford Ruether, then a young member of the Theology Department at Garrett-Evangelical Theological Seminary, began publishing articles that pushed the critique of Christianity in a different direction. Scholarly and reserved where Daly was impassioned and personal, Ruether theorized that the oppression of women stemmed from the dualistic thinking—placing, for example, the soul in opposition to the body, and spirit in opposition to nature—that has come to be a central aspect of Christian thought. This dualism, she maintained, resulted in a hierarchical structure wherein men are placed above nature and believe that it is their right to dominate it.

But while Ruether emphasizes the intellectual nature of her enterprise, a rare personal revelation can be found in her essay "The Question of Feminism," published in the early '70s. Having devoted herself early on to the pursuit of an academic career, Ruether was astonished when, just after her marriage, the monsignor of her husband's parish informed the young couple that if Rosemary was not pregnant within a year, he would know that they were "living in sin." Noting that she was fortunate in choosing a husband who did not share these expectations, Ruether says that it nonetheless seemed to her that her culture and religion were "bent on destroying the entire identity and future that I had constructed for myself."

If her own struggle seemed hard, she soon had an example of what might happen to a non-white, uneducated woman of the same religion. Ruether writes that in 1963, having just given birth to her third child, she met in the maternity ward a Mexican American woman named Assumptione, who had just delivered her ninth child and who tearfully described to Ruether and the attending physician the circumstances of her life. "The house was without central heating," Ruether writes. "She had to turn on the stove to keep the place warm and was always in danger of being asphyxiated by the fumes. There was little food. Her husband beat her." When the doctor suggested that the woman should avail herself of some form of birth control, "she could only reply that her priest did not allow her." This incident catalyzed Ruether's critique of sexism in the Church, ". . . not just for my own sake, but for those millions of Assumptiones weeping in maternity beds around the world."

FROM FEMINIST TO WOMANIST

Among the rewards reaped by Ruether and Daly—both of them white and traditionally educated—is seeing their work inspire and instruct other groups of women across the country. One such group is African American women, who have developed their own approach to the role of feminism in Christianity, an approach that takes into account their experiences of oppression in a predominantly white culture.

For Delores S. Williams, an ordained Presbyterian minister who studied theology at Union Theological Seminary and is now on the faculty there, being in graduate school during the early days of feminist theology provided her with inspiration but also with some questions.

"Many of us [African Americans] were favorably disposed to the kinds of claims that theologians like Rosemary Ruether and Beverly Harrison were making," Williams says, "but we did understand that the women's experiences described in these texts did not fit the facts of our lives. So we were looking for a kind of anthropological understanding of womanhood that took seriously what our cultural context had been about. Then Alice Walker came out with this definition of 'womanist,' and right away we recognized that this was it."

Writer Alice Walker coined and defined "womanist" in a kind of preface to her 1974 collection of essays, *In Search of Our Mothers' Gardens*. The definition is composed of four parts that have since been claimed and explored by various womanist writers and theologians. The passage begins with such definitions as "a black feminist or feminist of color. . . . Responsible. In charge. *Serious*," and moves on to "A woman who loves other women, sexually and/or nonsexually," and concludes with "womanist is to feminist as purple is to lavender."

Walker, like Daly, opened a door that other women could step through. Whereas feminist theologians at that time were working to uncover and analyze the ways in which male bias had precluded them from participation in their religious traditions, the women who would come to call themselves womanists noted that their oppression had been perpetuated by all of white society. A womanist analyzing sexism in religion takes into account not only race but also such interrelated factors as class, economic background, and culture. Over the next 20 years, Williams and many other African American women—notably Katie Geneva Cannon, Renita Weems, Toinette Eugene, Cheryl Townsend Gilkes, and Emilie M. Townes—would bring womanist perspectives to the study of theology, ethics, sociology, and literature, as well as the ministry.

Another distinctive element of womanist thought is an emphasis on taking its dialogue out into the public arena, or building bridges between the academy and people's everyday lives. A large number of womanist professors are also ordained ministers, who speak to their congregations about such issues as feeding and maintaining the self-image of black women, or of the importance of encouraging a younger generation to stay in school. Both from the pulpit and in print, womanists pay particular attention to issues of oppression and violence. Gilkes, for instance, is currently at work on a book about how African American slaves interpreted the English Bible to help them survive their exploitation and envision the possibility of future empowerment; Townes recently edited the collection *A Troubling in My Soul: Womanist Perspectives on Evil & Suffering,* in which a variety of voices speak to such subjects as the psychological violence that racist standards of beauty inflict on black women and the history of black Christian theological definitions of sin.

Williams has done some of her most controversial work on the link between biblical images of atonement, such as the crucifixion, and violence in contemporary society, and she is currently concerned with bringing womanist voices into political issues, such as the welfare debate. "We need to be in there as Christians," she says, "describing what kind of reform ought to take place, a reform without stereotyping, that helps people to discover dignity in work, and that provides supplements that will help families stay together and establish themselves." Williams believes that by bringing discussion of such issues into church congregations as well as academia, womanists can help reshape public policy along more humane lines.

ORDINATION AND CELEBRATION

One area where women theologians have had to fight a number of disparate battles is in the area of ordination. The subject of how women worship, and the question of who, if anyone, should be designated to lead, is one of the most imaginative and diverse areas of contemporary feminist thought. Currently, of the major denominations in the United States, the Roman Catholic Church is alone in not allowing the ordination of women at all. Many Catholic women have switched their focus from the battle for ordination to the pursuit of new, nonhierarchical models of worship. Meanwhile, in some Protestant denominations, there are arguments over a variety of issues that women have brought to the ministry, including the ordination of openly gay and lesbian priests.

The history of women's ordination in Protestant churches in the U.S. is not easy to track, in part because so many denominations are split into individual conferences or bodies with their own autonomous powers. In the Methodist Church, for example, Anna Howard Shaw—suffragist and protégée of Susan B. Anthony—seems to have been the first woman minister in the U.S., ordained by the Methodist Episcopal Church, North, in 1880; however, other Methodist churches did not grant women the right to ordination until 1968. Mary Kay Sauter, cofounder of the Re-Imagining Community and a candidate for ordination by the United Church of Christ, says that her denomination ordained its first woman minister in 1850; it would take the two mainstream Presbyterian bodies in this country—divided between the northern and southern United States and called, respectively, "the Presbyterian Church in the U.S.A." and "the Presbyterian Church in the U.S."—another century to make the same move, with the northern body approving ordination in 1955 and the southern in 1964.

Overall, change seems to come earlier to local chapters than to national associations, partly because in some denominations, church leaders who approve women's ordination resist the idea that women should be able to move into positions of higher authority, such as that of bishop. Additionally, as Episcopal priest Carter Heyward points out, "Any real, deep social change is not going to occur because a majority votes in favor of it. It takes some kind of prophetic voice or prophetic action, and then the people come along, sometimes many years later, and say, 'Oh, yes, that's right.'"

Heyward should know: Now a professor of theology at Episcopal Divinity School in Boston and the author of a number of books on feminist theology, including *Speaking of Christ: A Lesbian Feminist Voice* and *Staying Power,* she is one of 11 women ordained by the Episcopal Church in 1974—two years before that church officially sanctioned women's ordination.

"The Church had voted down ordination twice," she remembers, "so 11 of us, 4 bishops, and several thousand people said, 'Well, the time has come to really push the question.'" On July 29 of that year, Heyward and 10 other women were ordained in a ceremony in Philadelphia. For the next two years, issues raised by these "irregular" ordinations—from how to deal with the bishops involved to ways to respond to the new women priests—dominated Episcopal Church dialogue. Finally, in 1976, the Church retroactively recognized the ordination of those first women priests; the following year would see the first "regular" women's ordination in that tradition.

Now, according to Heyward, a different question rocks her denomination—whether or not to endorse the ordination of openly gay and lesbian priests. Although members of both groups have already been ordained, there is a movement in the Episcopal Church to bring charges against the bishops who ordained them.

Heyward, who came out as a lesbian in 1979, says that it is important for gay and lesbian priests to be "as visible as we can be just to show that we are already here. It is not like the Church has a choice. We are in it already." Heyward, who has written often on the subject of sexuality and spirituality, sees the linking of those two areas—for so long kept apart by institutionalized Christianity—as a particular gift that gay and lesbian theologians can bring to the Church. "Everybody, regardless of sexual identity, needs to look at issues of what it means to be responsible adults sexually and spiritually. Gays and lesbians are bringing an enormous gift to the Church, simply by raising these questions."

It is a gift that many churches find hard to accept. In 1993, the Presbyterian Church's General Assembly passed a resolution "to be engaged in the discipline of open, diligent, prayerful study and dialogue on the issues of human sexual behavior and orientation as they relate to membership, ministry, and ordination." The Assembly also agreed that the results of this study and dialogue would be discussed at their annual meeting in 1996. But Lisa Larges, a candidate for the ministry and an out lesbian, worries that this three-year period of reflection and study could become "a stalling tactic." So she founded her own organization, the Witness for Reconciliation Project, to help Presbyterian churches in the San Francisco Bay Area, where she lives, further their examination of the subject of gay and lesbian

ordination. The organization has sponsored discussion groups and even a play based on the topic.

For Roman Catholic women, however, the ordination question has turned into an entirely new approach to worship. As early as the 1950s, Catholic nuns and laywomen were re-examining liturgy and their role in it. For example, at Grailville, a community of Catholic women based in rural Ohio, members were celebrating Mass with gender-inclusive language in the 1950s. Such events, followed by the changes established by the Second Vatican Council in the 1960s—including allowing priests to celebrate the Mass in the language of the congregation rather than in Latin and to face the congregation during the Eucharistic prayer rather than away from it—and by the 1975 formation of the Women's Ordination Conference, seemed to indicate that the ordination of women might come to Catholicism within the century. But while such optimism was extinguished with the selection in 1978 of the current pope, the conservative John Paul II, Catholic women have pursued a new approach to worship, one that does not require a priest at all.

Based on the work of New Testament scholar Elisabeth Schüssler Fiorenza, whose research maintains that early Christianity was a countercultural movement that smashed hierarchical patterns altogether, many Catholic feminists are now active in a movement called "Women-Church," an approach to church as a community in which all Christians are engaged in equal ministry to one another. While Women-Church communities are springing up all over the country, it is hard to say just how many women are currently involved. Mary Hunt, one of the leading proponents of Women-Church, says that there are over a hundred such communities in the Washington, D.C., area alone and that national conferences on the subject attract an audience of several thousand.

WHY THEY STAY

The diversity of approaches and the liveliness of the dialogue that are hallmarks of feminist theology will no doubt continue to flourish in the 21st century. But while the women involved have made progress in changing the face of Christianity—both in academia and in the ministry—feminist theologians in the United States are also aware that an increasingly conservative political climate here may make their work harder. Yet few of the women interviewed for this article seem interested in following Mary Daly's path out of the Church. Rather, many are invigorated by the fight itself, while others find more pragmatic or personal reasons for continuing to rework Christian ground.

For many women, their inspiration to continue the fight for a church free of sexism derives from something closer to home—the influence, perhaps, of a loving mother or a kind aunt who embodied the particular gifts that women can bring to the ministry. Vienna Cobb Anderson, the first woman rector called to a major urban Episcopal parish, grew up in an old and powerful Episcopal family. Their family Bible dated back to 1607, and her grandfather was the senior warden of the parish where she grew up.

Nonetheless, it was her grandmother who had the greatest effect on her future calling.

"Her concern for the whole community, and her desire to offer them something real, had a powerful effect on me," the rector says. "In many ways, she is my role model in the priesthood."

As feminist theologians in this country continue to work on issues ranging from ordination to birth control, from liturgy to world hunger, the image of Anderson's grandmother seems a telling one. In their emphasis on bringing the truth of women's experiences to their churches, what these scholars and ministers are offering may be, in a sense, the real bread of daily life, offered with a commitment to the principles of love and justice that are for them the basis of Christianity. Whether or not their church hierarchies ultimately accept this gesture seems to these women beside the point. What concerns them is the wholeness of their vision and the persistence of their calling to equality.   [1995]

PART V
Health and Reproductive Freedom

Women's health and reproductive lives are profoundly influenced by prevailing attitudes toward women's bodies and sexuality, their subordinate position in the social structure, and the political context of health and reproductive policy. Although women are the majority of health care consumers and provide a great deal of the direct care services, most doctors, researchers, and managers of clinics and hospitals are men. As a result, women's health needs have not been adequately or accurately addressed. All too often the criteria used to diagnose particular disorders are based on studies of men, and as a result women's symptoms are easily ignored or misinterpreted. Even when exercise is examined, male behavior is the norm. For example, many measures of physical activity focus on activities that are more common in men's lives, and do not include everyday activities that some women regularly engage in, such as those related to household tasks and child care. The male norm of behavior shapes conceptualizations of health as well as illness.

One particularly grievous example of this failure has been the slowness of the medical community to focus on the experiences of women with AIDS. During the first 20 years of the AIDS epidemic, men were the majority of people with AIDS. Consequently, the medical criteria for diagnosis reflected men's health needs. In fact, during the first 13 years of the epidemic, the Centers for Disease Control and Prevention (CDC) did not include one female-specific condition related to HIV in its diagnostic criteria for AIDS.[1] As the incidence of HIV/AIDS in women increased, however, it was clear that women with AIDS experienced a high rate of reproductive tract diseases, which is not the case for men with AIDS. Thus, because AIDS is manifested differently in women, women who were HIV positive and actually had AIDS often did not meet the diagnostic criteria. In 1993, following pressure from feminist health activists, the CDC altered its definition of AIDS to include cervical cancer. More attention is currently being paid to the symptoms that HIV-positive women typically experience, with recognition of the high rates of reproductive system disorders among women. However, women are still underrepresented in the AIDS Clinical Trial Group, which is an experimental drug trial study. Rates of HIV/AIDS infection are increasing faster among women than men, especially for African-American women and Latinas, who represent over 75% of all women with AIDS.[2] Therefore, it is imperative that the medical community conduct more systematic research on AIDS in women.[3]

A woman's health status reflects the interaction between her biology and the social/physical environment in which she lives and works. However, the biomedical assumptions of the medical community focus on the biological mechanisms of dis-

---

[1] Nancy Goldstein and Jennifer L. Manlowe. *The Gender Politics of HIV/AIDS in Women* (New York: New York University Press, 1997).
[2] Ibid.
[3] Nancy Krieger and Elizabeth Fee, "Man-Made Medicine and Women's Health: The Biopolitics of Sex/Gender and Race/Ethnicity," *International Journal of Health Sciences,* 24 (1994), pp. 265–283.

ease transmission, without addressing the sociocultural influences on health. These assumptions lead to emphasizing individual, rather than social factors in health.[4] For example, an individual risk factor for hypertension is high sodium intake. A social risk factor is unrelenting stress related to being a woman of color living in poverty—which ultimately influences diet and nutrition. The implications for understanding the health status of women are startling, particularly when examining women of color. Socioeconomic status is closely related to indices of health. In particular, racial disparities in the health status of women are associated with differences due to socioeconomic status.[5] For example, while heart disease is the number one cause of death for all women, women of color, those with lower socioeconomic status, and older women are at higher risk.

Differences in breast cancer rates and survival also illustrate the role of race and social class in health outcomes. Although African-American women have a lower incidence of breast cancer than white women, their death rates are higher. The incidence rate for breast cancer is increasing most rapidly among Latinas, and they are least likely to survive five years after being diagnosed. On the other hand, Native American women have low rates of breast cancer yet experience the lowest survival rate when compared with all other groups of women in the United States. These differences in breast cancer incidence and survival are related to factors such as poor access to health care and diagnosis at a later stage of cancer, both of which are associated with poverty, lack of health insurance, discrimination, and language barriers.[6] Thus, it continues to be important to address the social and political context of women's health issues in the United States.

For the past several decades women in the United States have been systematically excluded from the majority of research to develop new drugs, medical treatments, and surgical techniques. A major study of the activities of the National Institutes of Health in 1990 found that women were underrepresented in studies of diseases affecting both men and women. At that time, some of the largest and most important medical studies of recent years had failed to enroll a single woman. In 1993 the National Institutes of Health strengthened its guidelines for including women and minorities in clinical studies. However, since these are guidelines—and not regulations—they are not enforced and do not mandate national change in the conduct of health-related research.

Studies show that for many women, sexism permeates the doctor-patient relationship. Professor Ann Turkel reports, "Women are patronized and treated like

---

[4] Ibid.

[5] Lily D. McNair and George W. Roberts, "African American women's health," in *Behavioral Medicine and Women: A Comprehensive Handbook,* Elaine A. Blechman and Kelly D. Brownell, eds. (New York: Guilford, 1998), pp. 821–825.

[6] Susan J. Ferguson and Anne Kasper, "Living with breast cancer," in *Breast Cancer: Society Shapes an Epidemic* (New York: St. Martins, 2000), pp. 1–22.

little girls. They're even referred to as girls. Male physicians will call female patients by their first names but they themselves are always called 'Doctor.' They don't do that with men."[7] Often women's symptoms are not taken seriously because physicians erroneously believe that they have no physical basis and are just "in their heads." Unfortunately, this frequently results in overreliance on psychiatric medications, such as anti-anxiety drugs, to "calm women's nerves" when they have somatic complaints that are not understood by their physicians.

The women's health movement has been a vital part of the rebirth of feminism. Through books such as *Our Bodies, Ourselves for the New Century* (Simon & Schuster, 1998) and organizations such as the National Black Women's Health Project and the National Asian Women's Health Organization, women have reclaimed their bodies, challenged the priorities of the medical establishment, and made women's experiences and needs visible. A striking example of this movement has been breast cancer grassroots activism, which experienced a resurgence in the 1990s.[8] Angry about the limited range of treatments provided to women with breast cancer, as well as the low levels of funding for breast cancer research, women across the country mobilized to mount a multifaceted campaign. In 1991, the National Breast Cancer Coalition united over 180 advocacy groups to push for more money for research into the causes of breast cancer. By putting political pressure on Congress, attracting media attention, and raising awareness of this crisis in women's health—which has a disproportionately high mortality rate among African Americans—organized women across the nation have had a dramatic effect on increasing research funding for breast cancer.

As Margaret Sanger said in 1914, "enforced motherhood is the most complete denial of a woman's right to life and liberty."[9] Women have tried to control their reproductive lives throughout history, sharing contraceptive and abortion information among themselves. In the early twentieth century Margaret Sanger led the crusade to legalize birth control and improve the contraceptive technology available to women. Undeterred by arrests and harassment, she and other crusaders succeeded in establishing birth control clinics throughout the country and legalizing the distribution of birth control information and devices.

Unfortunately, while the birth control movement began with a firm commitment to all women's right to determine their own reproductive lives, it later made alliances with eugenicists, who saw the goal of family planning as the control of population, particularly of elements they saw as less desirable. Dorothy Roberts, in *Killing the Black Body,* comments that Sanger "promoted two of the most perverse tenets of

---

[7]Leslie Laurence and Beth Weinhouse, "Outrageous Practices: The Alarming Truth about How Medicine Mistreats Women," in *Clashing Views on Abnormal Psychology,* Susan Nolen-Hoeksema (Guildford, CT: Dushkin/McGraw Hill, 1998) p. 226.

[8]Maureen Hogan Casamayou, *The Politics of Breast Cancer* (Washington, DC: Georgetown University Press, 2001).

[9]*The Woman Rebel,* June 1914, p.25.

eugenic thinking: that social problems are caused by reproduction of the socially disadvantaged and that their childbearing should therefore be deterred."[10] This kind of thinking contributed to the sterilization of thousands of women of color throughout the 1960s and 70s. Believing that women's procreation was the cause of their poverty, doctors in poor communities sterilized women, mostly women of color, without their informed consent, often supported by federal funds. In the 1970s Latina, African-American, and Native American women successfully pressured government agencies to enact and enforce guidelines ensuring that women were fully informed about their choices before being sterilized.

While birth control was widely used by the 1960s, some states still restricted its use until the Supreme Court declared such restrictions unconstitutional in 1965 (*Griswold v. Connecticut*). As we have shown in the discussion of women and the law, the Supreme Court, in *Roe v. Wade*, in 1973 drew on the "right to privacy" ideas articulated in the Griswold decision to declare unconstitutional state laws that criminalized abortion. Since 1973 women's reproductive rights have been under fierce attack and the Supreme Court has retreated from its support of all women's right to decide whether to bear a child.

The activities of the anti-abortion movement have brought reproductive rights to the center of the political stage in the last two decades. Opponents of abortion have harassed abortion clinics and doctors who perform abortion and pressured legislatures to limit abortions. Between 1993 and 1998 seven staff members of abortion clinics were murdered and there have been over 1,000 incidents of arson and bombings at abortion clinics.[11]

The advocates of women's reproductive rights have called themselves the "pro–choice" movement emphasizing a woman's right to choose when she has a child. The anti–abortion forces have called themselves "the right to life" movement, contending that human life exists from the moment of conception. Beneath this argument lie conflicting views of sexuality, women's role in society, and individual liberty. As Kristin Luker has shown in *Abortion and the Politics of Motherhood,* most activists in the "right to life movement" adhere to traditional views about women's role, believe that sexuality should be confined to the family, and that women's most important role is motherhood. Advocates of women's reproductive rights believe that these decisions should be made by individual women and that all women have a right to choose how they live, with whom they have sex, and when and if they have children.[12] The debate about abortion is inextricably entangled with the broader debate about women's position in society.

Although the majority of the American people favor legal abortion, the "right

---

[10] Dorothy Roberts, *Killing the Black Body: Race, Reproduction and the Meaning of Liberty* (New York: Vintage, 1997), p. 81.

[11] National Abortion Federation Website. Http//www.prochoice.org/violence.

[12] Kristin Luker, *Abortion and the Politics of Motherhood* (Berkeley: University of California Press, 1984).

to life" movement has succeeded in severely curtailing women's access to abortion on both federal and state levels. Since the "Hyde Amendment" was passed in 1976, women on welfare have been denied federal funding for abortion, and most states prohibit the use of state funds for abortion as well. As a result of congressional action, women in the U.S. armed services can no longer obtain abortions in overseas military hospitals, women who work for the federal government can no longer choose a health plan that covers abortion, and funding for international family planning clinics has been radically reduced. Between 1995 and 2001 state legislatures passed 301 measures restricting abortions including parental consent requirements for minors, waiting periods, and restrictions of late-term abortions.[13] Abortion services are becoming harder to obtain, since the threat of violence has resulted in fewer doctors who will perform abortions. Rural women have less access to abortion since providers are concentrated in metropolitan areas. According to Marlene Fried, "Ninety-four percent of non-metropolitan counties have no services."[14]

Without access to abortion services, the legal right is meaningless. For this reason Billye Avery, the founder of the National Black Woman's Health Project, has urged feminists to speak out on reproductive health, which includes both the right to make decisions about one's reproductive life and access to the services required to make that right a reality. Rickie Solinger has pointed out in *Beggars and Choosers* that *choice* has come to mean the possession of resources, and suggests instead that we work for reproductive *rights*—which require no resources. "After a generation of practicing 'choice,'" she argues, "it is clear that all women—regardless of race and class—can achieve the status of full citizen in the United States (and around the world) only when reproductive autonomy is a full blooded right, not merely a consumer's choice."[15] Working for reproductive rights means fighting to maintain the access of young, poor, and rural women to safe, legal abortions, access that has been increasingly restricted in the past ten years, as well as working for the right of all women to have babies if they so choose.

As the selections in this section make clear, returning to the days of illegal abortion would not eliminate abortion; women would continue to try to control their reproductive lives and would find illegal and sometimes unsafe ways to do it. Since they would have even less access to safe abortions than they do today, it is poor women who would suffer. Studies suggest that in many areas, the majority of the women who died as a result of unsafe, illegal abortions before *Roe v. Wade* were women of color.[16] The anti–abortion forces in the United States, in asserting the right of the state to control the behavior of pregnant women, are not only elevating

---

[13] Who Decides? A State-by-state Review of Abortion and Reproductive Rights. 2002, NARAL Foundation.
[14] Marlene Fried, "Legal and Inaccessible," in *Abortion Wars: A Half Century of Struggle, 1950–2000,* edited by Rickie Solinger (Berkeley: University of California Press, 1998), p. 214.
[15] Rickie Solinger, *Beggars and Choosers: How the Politics of Choice Shapes Adoption, Abortion and Welfare in the United States.* (New York: Hill and Wang, 2001), p. 224.
[16] Loretta J. Ross, "African-American Women and Abortion," in Solinger, *Abortion Wars,* p. 161.

the fetus to the status of human life, but also relegating the woman to the status of carrier, or as the writer Katha Pollitt has put it, "potting soil."[17] As Ruth Hubbard points out, however, the concern for fetal life which allegedly motivates the regulation of pregnant women's behavior appears hypocritical when little is being done to improve the social and economic conditions of poverty that endanger so many babies.

Defending reproductive freedom must be a multifaceted campaign which defends the reproductive rights of all women and addresses the social and economic conditions that affect women's ability to determine their reproductive lives.

---

[17]Katha Pollitt, "The New Assault on Feminism," *The Nation,* March 26, 1990, p. 418.

The Health Care System

Historically, women have been healers and have supported each other with skill and understanding when experiencing physical pain. The legacy of midwives in this country is one example. Yet beginning in the late eighteenth century, male physicians in the United States led a successful campaign to eliminate midwives. In the mid-nineteenth century, they also mounted an assault against the many women medical practitioners who were trained outside of the male-dominated medical establishment.

Some of you may be reading *Our Bodies, Ourselves for the New Century* (Simon and Schuster, 1998) along with *Women: Images and Realities. Our Bodies, Ourselves* was written by a group of women who, impelled by the lack of available information about women's bodies, began meeting in 1969 to share information and experiences and publish what became the first of many editions of *Our Bodies, Ourselves*. Women of varied racial and class backgrounds from different parts of the country organized similarly to spawn the now extensive women's health movement.

Despite the strength of this movement, sexism in the medical system is wide-ranging. Women's health activists report many types of abuse. Personnel in medical settings have not listened to women or believed what they said. They have withheld knowledge or lied; treated women without their consent; failed to warn them of risks; experimented on them; discriminated against them because of race, sexual preference, age, or disability; offered tranquilizers or moral advice instead of medical care or useful referrals to community resources; administered treatments that were unnecessarily mutilating; performed unnecessary operations; or sexually abused them. Carol Stevens's piece, "How Women Get Bad Medicine," describes some of these types of abuse in more detail. Diane Hugs's description of her sexually abusive doctor reminds us of how institutional practices reinforce the continued maltreatment and abuse of women. Her story suggests steps to take if it does occur.

Women of color are particularly vulnerable in the health care system. Suffering from AIDS, Elizabeth Ramos describes how doctors initially misdiagnosed and mistreated her, and how this led to her educational work with Latino teenagers. Evelynn Hammonds's article depicts the stereotypical way the media portray African-American women with AIDS, and contrasts this with the reality of their lives.

Breast cancer has become a very serious health threat for women. The *Ms.* article, "Breast Cancer: Is It the Environment?" points to the need for increased research in two areas: environmental risks such as exposure to toxic chemicals, and prevention strategies. Through greater understanding of the environmental links to breast cancer, prevention efforts can be developed to reduce women's exposure to toxins. Such research could prove pivotal in preventing breast cancer in thousands of women each year.

76

How Women Get
Bad Medicine

CAROL STEVENS*

By the time Sara and Bernie Blumenthal pulled up to the Washington Hospital Center, the emergency-room staff was waiting. They had been told to expect someone having a heart attack. When the Blumenthals arrived, they rushed toward Bernie. But Sara was the one having the heart attack.

It was a continuation of what Sara had been through for two days, ever since waking up in the middle of the night with a stabbing pain between her shoulder blades. She had gone to the hospital, only to be diagnosed with back spasms. But the pain didn't go away, and after repeated injections of muscle relaxants, her doctor gave her an electrocardiogram.

His face turned pale as he watched the needle jump. Sara Blumenthal had been having a heart attack—one that had destroyed one fifth of her heart muscle. The doctor sent Sara and her husband rushing to the hospital.

The failure to detect Sara's heart attack was understandable, considering that she was only 41, not overweight, and a nonsmoker for the past year. Also, as a woman, she was less likely than a man to have a heart attack. Still, her experience reflected a troubling side of modern medicine: that for all its progress, all its sophistication, it does not treat women and men the same.

It is true of patient care, with no less a source than the National Institutes of Health's director, Dr. Bernadine Healy, contending that "women's medical complaints aren't taken seriously" and that women with "men's diseases"—such as coronary heart disease—aren't treated as aggressively as male patients. And it's true of medical research, in which studies traditionally have been done with only male subjects. Even when medical technology has been geared to women, the results have been rife with problems.

When that happens, as it has most recently with breast implants, the calls come pouring into places like the National Women's Health Network here. The "what" questions—What health problems can be blamed on implants?—are easy to answer. The "whys" are harder. Why weren't women told about the serious health risks before getting implants? Why did federal agencies allow implants to be marketed in spite of safety questions? Why was this allowed to happen to women?

"You can hear it in their voices," says Toni Young of the Women's Health Network. "They're feeling helpless."

In the nineteen years since the Boston Women's Health Collective published the first edition of *Our Bodies, Ourselves,* one health crisis after another has seemed to justify the book's distrust of and dissatisfaction with the medical system. First it was the Dalkon Shield, an intrauterine contraceptive device (IUD) that was linked with high rates of pelvic infection, miscarriages, hysterectomies, and seventeen deaths before it was pulled from the market in 1974. Eight years later toxic shock syndrome, a life-threatening illness, was tied to the use of high-absorbency tampons. Tampon manufacturers were required to place warning labels on packages in 1982, but it wasn't until 1989 that the Food and Drug Administration, under court order, required manufacturers to standardize tampon absorbency levels.

Other studies discovered problems with estrogen. At the high levels found in some birth-control pills, researchers discovered a link with strokes, blood clots, and heart attacks. When prescribed in supplements for post-menopausal women, estrogen appeared to increase the risk of breast cancer.

All of these examples had one thing in common: women who had been healthy were put at risk by their exposure to medical technology.

Would these health-care crises have occurred if it were men's bodies being subjected to the same drugs and devices? "It's kind of like wondering how men would handle pregnancy," says Cindy Pearson, program director for the National Women's Health Network. "We'll never know, because men have never been put in that position."

The fact is that women have more contact with

---

*Leslie Milk contributed to this article.

physicians than men. According to government estimates, 81 percent of women visit the doctor at least once a year, compared to 67 percent of men. "Women receive more examinations, lab tests, blood-pressure checks, drug prescriptions, and return appointments than men," says the American Medical Association.

Thanks to the reproductive process alone, millions of healthy women visit doctors' offices, clinics, and hospitals each year. "Women interact with the health-care system for contraceptives to avoid getting pregnant. They get involved again each time they get pregnant. And when they go back again during menopause," Pearson says.

This close contact with the medical field has its benefits. Regular gynecological checkups have allowed more and more women to detect cervical and breast cancer at an early stage, resulting in rising survival rates. But there are those who feel that too much medicine also has its costs, that because of their biology women are more likely to be exposed to the risk of infections, unnecessary procedures, and medical errors.

The truth is that in a society that rewards doctors for treating diseases, many physicians find it hard to leave well-enough women alone. "[The] inexhaustible capacity to cut and medicate women in this country comes, in part, from a cultural view that women's natural biological processes are treatable illnesses," writes Dr. Sidney Wolfe, director of the Public Citizen Health Research Group, in *Women's Health Alert.* "Menstruation, pregnancy, childbirth, and lactation are all normal female reproductive functions. But a series of paths, paved initially with good and legitimate intentions, have led to the commercialization of treatment for each of these normal female functions."

The inequality between health care for men and women exists on another level, too: Women who are sick don't often get the same quality of treatment. An AMA study confirms that women are less likely than men to receive kidney transplants, undergo coronary bypass surgery, or have their lung cancer diagnosed.

NIH's Bernadine Healy goes even further, contending that a "Yentl syndrome" exists, in which heart disease is too often considered a "man's disease in disguise" when, in fact, it is the leading cause of death among American women.

"Women who have chest pains are not treated the same as men unless tests show they are having a heart attack," Healy says. "This suggests that women are being treated by different standards and, at a broader level, that women have to act like men to be taken seriously."

Women's dissatisfaction with the medical system is based on the widely held belief that their doctors don't always take their complaints seriously. "If you scratch the surface of any woman's experience, you're likely to hear at least one example of how she believes she was treated inappropriately," says National Women's Health Network's Cindy Pearson.

Such as the Oakton teacher whose HMO blamed a bad drug reaction on "postpartum blues." Or the DC writer whose doctor wouldn't take her high fever seriously until her irate husband got on the phone. Or the 22-year-old Arlington woman whose doctor recommended surgery to treat her menstrual cramps.

Says a 28-year-old Annandale woman, "I kept asking my doctor whether the pains in my elbows were somehow related to my breast implants. But he told me I was being silly. When I finally changed doctors, my new physician found pools of silicone in the joints of my arms and legs. I'll always resent the first doctor for belittling me."

For years, women have treated these anecdotes as veterans do their war stories: harrowing tales to tell in private. But research has begun to confirm that these stories are not isolated incidents but part of a pattern. A 1979 study in the *Journal of the American Medical Association* found that doctors treat men and women complaining of the same symptoms differently. Researcher Karen Armitage found that doctors were more likely to refer male patients for diagnostic tests and to attribute women's complaints to stress or hypochondria.

In its own analysis of gender disparities, the AMA discovered that female heart patients were twice as likely as males to have the abnormal results of an exercise test blamed on "psychiatric or other noncardiac causes."

"There is evidence that physicians are more likely to perceive women's maladies than men's as the result of emotionality," the AMA concluded.

Another example: As recently as six years ago, the nation's leading urology textbook was rewritten after it was discovered that interstitial cystitis, an illness that afflicts 450,000 people nationwide—90 percent of them women—was not a psychosomatic condition that manifests itself in urinary problems—as doctors had been taught for nearly 100 years. Better diagnostic equipment showed that the bladder disorder, which does not respond to antibiotics, is the result of ulcers and bladder adhesions.

"When doctors couldn't see anything wrong with the women who came to them crying in pain, they'd conclude they were crazy," says Judith Heller, director of Affiliate Affairs for the Interstitial Cystitis Association. "They'd advise them to get married, to have a baby, or to get psychiatric help."

It would be simplistic to suggest that all doctors are sexist. But it would be fair to say that medical tradition has been often sexist. As part of their training, all doctors are taught to rely on generalizations and stereotypes to make diagnoses. "As physicians we are overwhelmed with information," says Dr. Jean Hamilton, an associate professor of psychiatry at the University of Texas's Southwestern Medical School. "Doctors use stereotypes to help them process some of this information."

Conventional medical wisdom, for instance, holds that heart disease is primarily a male disease. Yet for the last two years more American women have died of heart disease than men. The medical community also considers lung cancer a man's health problem. Yet the death rate for lung cancer has increased more than 100 percent in the last twenty years—virtually all due to the growing number of women who smoke.

Even doctors who try hard to provide equal health care are hampered by the fact that they often don't know if what works for men will work for women. Should, for instance, women join men in taking an aspirin a day to prevent heart attacks? It's hard to say. The frequently cited study touting the benefits of aspirin involved 22,071 men and no women. Will the same oat-bran recipes recommended for men with high cholesterol also cut a woman's risk of heart attack? Not necessarily. Early studies excluding women showed that low-fat diets helped men ward off heart attacks by lowering their levels of LDL, or bad cholesterol. Yet subsequent studies of women have shown that they are at greater risk when their HDL, or good cholesterol, is too low. A diet that cuts a woman's good cholesterol along with her bad could be dangerous.

It's not surprising that most research into heart and lung disease has focused on men. Men die of heart disease at a younger age than women. And until women started smoking in numbers equal to men, they weren't at the same risk of developing lung cancer. It's not as easy to explain the medical-research community's fixation on men when it comes to studying diseases of primary concern to women.

Clinical depression is a case in point. Women are twice as likely as men to suffer from it. Yet initial research on antidepressants was conducted exclusively on men.

"I plan on having a second child, and I worry about how the antidepressants I'm on will affect my pregnancy," says a 35-year-old Maryland lawyer. "My doctor gives me an educated guess, but no one can tell me for sure because the research has never been done."

Diseases of the aging are another example. Women live an average of seven years longer than men, and often are plagued with arthritis and osteoporosis as they age. Yet women were excluded from a National Institute on Aging long-term study for its first twenty years.

The exclusion of women from medical research was a deliberate policy. Women were excluded for two reasons: Their bodies are more complicated. And they can have babies.

Women's changing hormone levels during their menstrual cycles were thought to skew test results. Researchers also feared that experimental treatments and drugs might harm women's reproductive systems or damage the fetuses of women who didn't know they were pregnant.

These are legitimate concerns. Unfortunately, once drugs and medical treatments are approved, they end up being prescribed for women despite women's fluctuating hormone levels and ability to reproduce and despite the fact that they have never been proven safe or effective for women.

"First the medical system excludes women from research, then it wants to turn around and extrapolate its findings to women. But you can't have it both ways," says Joanne Howes, a partner with Bass and Howes, a DC consulting firm specializing in women's health.

That proved true in the case of the antidepressants tested only on men. Only after they were prescribed for women was it discovered that changing female hormone levels limited their effectiveness. Subsequent studies showed that when women received the same doses as men, they were inappropriately medicated for parts of each month.

The pattern holds true in analyzing early warning signs for diseases. The assumption has been that symptoms of illnesses for women are the same as for men. But there is growing evidence that life-threatening illnesses manifest themselves differently in men and women.

The same treadmill tests that can identify men at risk for heart disease are not as accurate when used on women. Chest pains and angina also are more likely to be early warning signals of heart disease in men than in women. The result is that women are less likely to survive bypass surgery and heart attacks because their heart problems are more advanced by the time they are diagnosed.

Medicine's reliance on the male model also is causing problems for women with AIDS. Opportunistic infections and diseases such as Kaposi's sarcoma are common among gay men with the virus, but not among infected women. Instead, HIV-positive women are more likely to suffer from gynecological problems. But because the Centers for Disease Control's official definition of AIDS focuses on the symptoms that manifest themselves most frequently in men, infected women are excluded from taking part in clinical trials, receiving experimental drugs and, to some extent, qualifying for Social Security disability payments. At a hearing of the House human resources subcommittee last year, it was estimated that because of the CDC's limited definition, the number of women with AIDS is undercounted by at least one third.

Who's to blame for medical science that treats men better than women?

Some critics say the National Institutes of Health, the government's primary source of medical research, is the prime offender. Five years after the Public Health Service first concluded that the nation's research policies put women at a disadvantage, the General Accounting Office released a 1990 report criticizing NIH for failing to do anything about it. "The GAO report showed that when it came to women's health, no one was home at NIH," says Howes. The publicity that followed turned up other gender bias at NIH. For instance, only 3 of NIH's 2,000 researchers specialized in obstetrics and gynecology. Also, not one of the divisions within NIH is dedicated exclusively to obstetrics and gynecology. Plus, the research center was spending less than 14 percent of its annual budget on women's-health research.

The revelations were enough to prompt women scientists and researchers to form groups such as the Institute for Research in Women's Health, and the Society for the Advancement of Women's Health Research. One of their first stops was Capitol Hill, where their cause was adopted by the Congressional Caucus for Women's Issues. The women researchers formed their own political-action committee and began awarding research grants.

The pressure was effective. In 1990 Healy was named NIH's first woman director, and last October she unveiled the first step in her plan for correcting the medical system's gender bias: a $500-million Women's Health Initiative to track diseases including cancer, heart disease, and osteoporosis in some 140,000 women over the next decade. In the meantime, a newly created NIH Office of Research on Women's Health will identify other gaps in medical knowledge about women. The office is headed by Dr. Vivian W. Pinn, the former chairman of pathology at Howard University's College of Medicine.

"All of a sudden the issue has taken off . . . there is all this interest in increasing the budget for women's health," says Dr. Florence Hazeltine, director of NIH's Center for Population Research and the president of the board of directors of the Society for Advancement of Women's Health Research. "Part of it is that the issue is so clear-cut. It is obvious to everyone that women weren't being treated fairly."

Earlier this year, the Bush administration's budget request included $89 million for its women's- and minority-health initiatives. This included a 40 percent increase in its funding for breast- and cervical-cancer research. In 1991, twenty grants were awarded by the Office of Research on Women's Health. Some $2.5 million has been earmarked for the study of interstitial cystitis, including funding for a data bank to track women with the disease.

As part of NIH's new focus, the University of Texas's Jean Hamilton and Sheryle Gallant, an associate professor at the Bethesda-based Uniformed Services University of the Health Sciences, have received a grant for nearly $600,000 to study the same subject Hamilton was told to stay away from as an NIH researcher more than a decade ago: the differences in the way men and women respond to drugs. "Now the idea that men and women will react differently to drugs seems so obvious it is embarrassing," Hamilton says. "But at the time, I was told there couldn't possibly be differences. The subject was very low priority."

One sign of the success of the women's medical movement is the eagerness of some men's health groups to imitate it. Chicago resident Edward Kaps co-founded an international support group for survivors of prostate cancer named Us Too after hearing a talk from Sharon Green, the executive director of Y-Me?, a support group for breast-cancer survivors.

"The men's movement is gradually growing, but it's still far behind where women are with diseases like breast cancer," says Dr. Mark Soloway, chairman of the urology department at the University of Miami. "Men are rapidly learning that it can be very productive to talk about their health problems."

That's especially true if the men are powerful politicians such as Republican Senators Bob Dole and Ted Stevens, and Democrat Alan Cranston, all of whom were treated for prostate cancer last year. "Now with senators who have had the disease, there's no doubt more money will be available for research," Soloway says.

Such predictions make leaders of the women's-health movement uneasy. Men have the same odds of developing prostate cancer as women face for breast cancer, about one in nine. If medical research becomes dependent on first-person testimonials, men have many more potential advocates in positions of power.

That's one more reason the promotion of women scientists and doctors to higher positions in the medical establishment has become a key issue. "Now that we have women in medical studies we need to have women doing medical studies. That's next," says Florence Haseltine.

The AMA says the number of women physicians has quadrupled in the last twenty years, with women now accounting for 34 percent of medical school graduates and nearly 17 percent of all practicing physicians. This year, for the first time, women made up more than 54 percent of the doctors in the first year of residency for obstetrics and gynecology.

Yet women are not well represented in the upper echelons of the medical establishment. Only 14 percent of NIH's top positions are held by women. The AMA's latest count shows no women serving as deans at U.S. medical schools and less than 10 percent female medical-school faculty. Women also are underrepresented outside of the primary-care specialties. Women doctors now account for almost 19 percent of all pediatricians, 15 percent of all internists, but less than 3 percent of all surgeons.

Medical research can be a particularly lonely field for women. "At NIH, women scientists are not valued. The prevailing attitude is, 'You're a girl. You should be taking care of patients because that's what girl doctors do,'" says Jean Hamilton, who filed a 1980s administrative complaint against the institutes, charging that they provided a hostile workplace for women scientists. Under the terms of her settlement, she cannot talk about its resolution.

There's also ongoing debate about the merits of women's-health research, with critics pointing out that it will result in an expensive and time-consuming replication of studies that have already been conducted on men.

"Sure, a lot of it is catch-up work. But there's nothing the matter with catch-up work if there is something that can be learned from it," says Haseltine.

More troubling to women scientists is the political climate surrounding research into the female reproductive process. They see a growing need for investigating such problems as the nation's high infant-mortality rate, the 22-year increase in the incidence of ectopic pregnancies, and the epidemic of sexually transmitted disease. But that raises issues of sexuality and birth control and, for some politicians, questions of morality. And that can become a stumbling block for research funding.

In recent years, the federal government has discouraged scientists from pursuing several areas of reproductive health. Responding to pressures from anti-abortion groups, the FDA in 1989 placed an import ban on RU-486, the so-called French abortion pill. As a result, scientists have had trouble obtaining the drug for study, even though it has shown promise as a treatment for infertility, fibroid tumors, breast cancer, and Cushing's syndrome, a disease caused by excessive cortisone. Similarly, a ban on federal funding of placental-tissue research has jeopardized research into its uses to help diabetics and patients suffering from Parkinson's, Alzheimer's and Huntington's diseases.

Some scientists have decided to stay away from reproductive health until the political climate changes. Instead they are focusing their research proposals on other areas of women's health.

Also, a push is on to make the health-care system more responsive to women. The Society for the Advancement of Women's Health Research has spent the last year talking to women at a series of roundtable meetings around the country.

What the group is hearing is that women are frustrated that no one specialty exists to handle all their medical needs, that they are still more likely than men to be shuffled from one specialist to another. Women would like to see the development of a "women's health" specialty, one that is broader than ob/gyn in that it would also address the effects of

drugs and diseases on women. The researchers also are hearing that doctors still place a low priority on preventive medicine and are not very well trained in dealing with matters that aren't strictly medical, such as the issue of battered women.

Such complaints come at a time when the nation's health-care system has become a major campaign issue and is ripe for an overhaul. More than any time before, women are in a position to have a say in how the country approaches health care— from the kind of research it does to the priorities of doctor-patient relationships.

Leaders of the women's-health movement are optimistic. They say it's only a matter of time before the traditional male model of medical care is replaced by a system more user-friendly to women.

"There's been an awakening to the fact that women are treated unfairly in medical research and patient care," says Bernadine Healy. "Now we have to make sure people stay awake and make women a part of mainstream medicine. We can't let people go back to sleep."　　　　　　　　　　[1992]

 77

Mandatory Doctor's Visit

DIANE HUGS

Being a disabled woman with a progressive disability requires that I document some of that disability through Social Security. Knowing that my primary physician documented what she saw on my visits, it surprised me a little when Social Security sent me a letter stating that I must see their doctor or I might no longer be considered disabled. This was funny because the small progression of my disability was not even the reason I was on Social Security and could no longer work. But they set up an appointment for me with a doctor I had never heard of and assigned the day and time of this appointment, and they stipulated that I had to go to that appointment.

As usual I took along a friend to the doctor's office; I've found it useful to have someone with me as a patient advocate and to help me remember what I wanted to ask. The doctor's office was in an old building with many rooms in his suite. When we got there it was unusually quiet for an office. We checked around and could not find anyone there. So we picked out what we thought might be the waiting room and waited for the doctor to show up.

The exam was routine and did not require that I remove my clothing. During the exam the doctor started by stroking my thigh as he looked over my chart sent by Social Security. He then asked me about my level of sensation since I am a paraplegic and cannot feel below the point of my paralysis. I held out my hands in front of me indicating that my sensation ended about the same level as my breasts. The doctor stroked my breast and asked me if I could feel that. Since he was below where I can feel I told him no, biting my lip so I wouldn't scream at him. Then he moved up to my level of sensation and touched my breast again with a stroking motion. I said, "Yes I can feel that. But is this necessary?" The reason I wondered was because he was checking neurological data and he was not a neurologist. He answered. "Actually it isn't, I was just curious."

During the exam he rubbed my shoulders and even kissed me; in fact he tried to kiss me on the lips but I turned away. There was no safe way I could think of to stop him; after all, his report would affect my Social Security status, and that is all the income I have in the world. Even though he could not deny I was disabled, he could have messed with my case to stop my checks at least temporarily. This was a psychological weapon which I felt was held over me the entire time I was there. So I kept my mouth shut and held myself back from hitting him during the exam.

As soon as I made it out of the office I burst into tears. My friend felt terrible for not having stood up for me but she was afraid of making more trouble for me. I was numb as I waited for the accessible van to pick me up and drive me home. Once inside the van I broke into tears again and told the driver what had happened. She was furious and told me to call the Center for Independent Living to get some advice. That was very helpful because at that time I could barely think at all.

Upon returning home I called the Center and the first person I talked to told me to call the rape crisis line. At first I was surprised at this suggestion; I had not been raped, just molested. But then I remembered that the local rape crisis center did more than counsel women who had been raped. They also gave information about what you can do or who you can contact in situations like this. So I called the crisis line and talked to one of their counselors. She told me to file a complaint with the police, that this was a crime and I should prosecute. It took me by surprise to have my feelings validated so strongly. Keeping the momentum up I called the police immediately after speaking with the counselor. During the hour and a half that it took before the officer arrived I went through a tornado of feelings. Was I taking this all too seriously? Would the officer think I was paranoid to be making such a charge? Were my perceptions accurate or was I blowing this out of proportion?

While the officer was not the most understanding or sensitive person, he did take what I was saying seriously. He wrote out the complaint and told me they would be back in touch with me for more information and that the medical ethics board would be notified. A few days later my friend was asked to meet with the police and an investigator from the Board of Medical Quality Assurance. She told me the investigator was a really nice guy who seemed seriously interested in seeing this case prosecuted. The next day the investigator came by to take my statement. He was disgusted by the story and hoped they would be able to do something to stop this doctor. It made me feel stronger to be taken so seriously and the investigator thanked me for filing the charges. He had two similar cases with physicians he was working on but it had taken the women years to come forward, making it a lot more difficult to prosecute. Because I had reported the event so quickly, there was a better chance of the investigator being able to prosecute. He first contacted Social Security to obtain a list of others who had been sent to this particular doctor. He needed to know if there were other women who had been similarly mistreated but who had not had the courage to report it. Although he went through every channel including the police, Social Security would not release any information. They claimed it would violate rights to privacy of Social Security recipients. He even asked if they would have their own people contact other patients they had sent to this doctor to see if anyone else had been abused, but they simply refused his requests. I was so angry—it was a lame excuse for Social Security to say it was a violation of our rights to privacy when they were the ones that made me (and how many other women) go to see this doctor.

Finally the investigator came up with a plan that Social Security would go along with. An undercover policewoman was to be sent in to see the doctor as if she were a disabled woman being sent in by Social Security. She sat in a wheelchair and had all the same forms as I had from Social Security. The exam went the same, the doctor did almost exactly the same things to her. When I learned of this, I realized this must be routine for him to mistreat and abuse Social Security or disabled patients during the exam. And although the undercover policewoman felt horrible and powerless when he kissed her and fondled her breasts, she wrote in her report that she wasn't sure if his actions were criminal. What I think she and the system did not understand was that he had power over my life through what he could do to my Social Security payments. I know it wasn't a weapon he could hold over the undercover policewoman, but I wished she had understood that he had no way of stopping her income. She could have fought back without risking her livelihood.

The district attorney did not see grounds to prosecute. This same D.A. was known for not prosecuting sex-related crimes; in fact later that year he was required by the City Council to prosecute over seventy rape cases he had passed by. Knowing that he did not take sex crimes very seriously, I checked to see if there was any other way to get this into court. But the sad fact is that the D.A. has the final call on whether or not to prosecute a case, and nothing I could do or say could change that fact. My next hope was the Board of Medical Quality Assurance. They brought him up before the discipline board and asked him to explain himself. The doctor admitted to everything that had happened; he just didn't think there was anything wrong with it. The Board warned

him to keep his hands to himself and left it at that. Even though I wrote the Board an impassioned plea to reconsider on the grounds that his position of working for Social Security was a weapon against disabled women, they would not hear me.

This was more than I could take. On one hand I was told that I was right, that he had no right to fondle and kiss me, that in fact it was criminal; on the other hand no one would do anything to stop him from doing it to every woman he came into contact with. It really bothered me that he was not only going to get away with what he had done, but there was also no way for my testimony to keep other women safe. I told Social Security that his report on me was invalid since I was a victim, not a client; they told me they didn't want to hear about my personal problems. No way could I make them stop sending people to this doctor. It was driving me crazy to feel so helpless.

Having exhausted all means of legal prosecution, I decided to take him into civil court. There was a lawyer, Leslie Levy, with an outstanding reputation, so I decided to call her. She took the case even though I didn't have a dime and went right to work on it. The malpractice insurance company jumped into defending him even though they said they were in no way liable, because there is an exclusion for the insurance companies for any act that may be deemed criminal rather than a malpractice claim. So we had to battle these high-priced lawyers even though their company assumed no responsibility. There were two years of foot dragging and legal manipulation which my lawyer had to fight while the doctor continued to practice. He said he would settle for five hundred dollars. I rejected this because I could see no indication that he had the slightest clue that he had done something wrong.

Two years after filing this case and having every legal trick in the book thrown at us, we finally got around to doing court depositions. I was unable to sit upright at the time so not only was I unable to go to his deposition, I had to give mine from my bed. Instead of having all these strangers in my bedroom I used the bed in the living room. That was a very good thing because the doctor decided to show up and listen to my statement. A deposition requires the presence of lawyers from both sides along with a court reporter, and that felt like a huge invasion in itself. The deposition lasted about three hours and I was very lucky to have such a brilliant lawyer on my side. She did not let them get away with asking anything that was not relevant. She jumped up and down a lot, screaming at the other lawyer to back off. Since Leslie was familiar with abusive lawyers and litigants, she protected me from unnecessary harassment and abuse, for which I am eternally grateful to her.

That deposition did the job. The doctor seemed to realize I had been hurt. For the first time he understood that he had done damage, though he was not willing to pay for it. So onwards towards court we went. It was finished four months later and while I cannot divulge the outcome, I can say that the judge was understanding and resolved the case so I didn't have to go before a whole courtroom with it. The terms of the settlement prohibit me from saying anything.

I am still left with feelings of rage and sadness about what he did to me and how the system let him get away with it. If it had not been for the interest of Leslie Levy I would have been left out in the cold. There are not enough lawyers like her.

The legal system is still predominately male and does not take women seriously. It is not a lucrative business for lawyers to take on such cases since there's not that much money in these cases even if you get the court system to see the damage done. For me that was the hardest part, being asked, "Describe how this hurt you" in front of strangers who were not sensitive to my feelings. How to explain what having this uncaring authority figure run his hands all over me did to me, how he made me feel like a whore.

I used to trust doctors, but not anymore. I lost trust not only in the system which ignored my pain, but also I lost trust in people in general. It took over four years for me to let a stranger touch me at all. I had to explain to the doctor's lawyer that this lack of trust, not wanting to be touched, was damage in itself. He tried to downplay it by asking me if I would ever let anyone touch me again. I told him I had every intention of healing from this and hoped to be

able to regain my trust. I fought hard. I fought long. It was worth the effort. The doctor knows he was wrong now. I just wish I had been able to stop him from continuing to practice. But I did everything I could and I can live with that.

What I would like to say to other women, disabled or not, is that a doctor does not have the right to touch you in any inappropriate way. We all have the right to fight back. More women need to fight the doctors who don't know the limits of conduct. If you are not sure whether your doctor went too far, but you do not feel good about what happened, follow it through. Contact the Board of Medical Quality Assurance, rape crisis centers and please, if you think there is even a possibility of a criminal case, call the police. The more women who call doctors on misconduct, the fewer doctors will continue to do harm to their women patients. If you cannot do this for yourself, please consider doing it for the next woman. Even though your doctor may not have taken you seriously, having to answer to all the different authorities will make him think twice before he treats another patient the same way again.

[1992]

 78

Elizabeth Ramos

BEBE NIXON

Elizabeth was the mother of two hyperactive young sons, Christopher and Matthew. After her husband left her, she raised them alone while working full-time at the John Hancock Insurance Company. In April 1985 she started to have trouble breathing. Her doctor treated her for bronchitis, but she didn't get better. The doctor didn't test or treat her for anything else. Oddly, in May, she received notification from the Red Cross that blood she had routinely donated in February had tested positive for HIV infection. She didn't even know what that meant. When she asked the doctor if it could have anything to do with what was wrong with her, he said no. As her illness worsened, the doctor treated her again for bronchitis, then for stress, and finally, for hysteria.

In late September she developed pneumonia; frantic, she went on her own to the emergency room at Boston City Hospital. There, on October 1, she was diagnosed with PCP, the signature pneumonia of AIDS. She was in intensive care for nearly five weeks, being kept alive on a respirator. Her lungs were severely damaged.

When she got out of the hospital, she did two uncharacteristic and drastic things. First, she went public with her illness. She decided to devote all her time to speaking out against AIDS ignorance, to reaching the Hispanic community, especially teenagers, to making them know what AIDS was and how to avoid it. Second, she and two lawyers drew up a malpractice suit against the doctor who had so badly misdiagnosed and mistreated her illness. She wanted people to know what had happened to her, to highlight the price she had paid, and, if she won, to provide money for her sons after she was gone.

FALL 1987

Because of my condition, I can't have many goals in life. I could go to school again, but I never could use it in any professional way. Talking about AIDS, reaching out to people in the community, this is my joy right now. I have to use all my time to spread my message. I believe there's a mission for me to accomplish. If people see me and hear me, and even touch me, they'll know this is for real. It can happen to women, it can happen to men. Then maybe they'll start doing something about it.

I got AIDS from my boyfriend, José. I never used drugs. I wasn't promiscuous. But he had the virus, and I got it from him. He was an IV drug user. For the longest time, he denied that I got it from him. He said some bad things about me, about how *he* thought I got it. Then he got sick. He said it was this, he said it was that, he said it was skin cancer. Finally I asked him straight out. "Do you think I got it from you?" And he said yes. And yes, he had been sharing needles with different people around here, around the apartment complex. Clean needles are very hard to find here: once somebody has one, everybody uses it. I asked him, "I wonder if their wives know?" I talked to them. They don't know anything. And they don't believe me when I tell them what's happening, and what happened to me. The neighborhood is so congested, so close, everyone ends up living with everyone else. And I'm worried that if these men are infected, they will infect these women, and the women will infect other men, and they will infect their unborn babies. I want to do something to stop it. AIDS is one of the facts of life now, like the birds and the bees. We just have to add it on to everything else.

I'm an ordinary person. I got AIDS. It can happen to anyone. Anyone at all. If people know that, if they see me and really know that, then I will have made a difference. That's my goal. I know about people and places that a lot of the organized outreach can't reach out to. I know about drug users. I know about teenage girls in the projects. I know how they tell you anything they think you want to hear, and then go do exactly as they please. It takes a special kind of knowing, a having been there, to talk to them so they *listen.*

The teenagers I talk to, they're mostly girls. And usually by the time they come to hear me, they've already had some sexual experience. That's why they come. They're scared. And I tell them, "You make sure that guy puts a condom *on* before he puts that thing *in.* You just make him. It won't be easy, because a lot of them are goin' to say, 'Bye, baby,' if you make them. But it boils down to this: are you willing to *die* for this dude? Because if he has the virus, and he won't wear a condom, that's just what you'll do. Is it worth it?" They listen.

My kids are afraid that when they come home from school, they'll find me gone. Gone to the hospital, gone to heaven, just gone. It's hard to prepare them for my death. They hate this illness. Christopher once told me he wanted to be back inside my stomach. I asked him, "Why?" He said, "So I could fight the virus from inside you." They know, even my Chris, and he's only eight years old, they know there's no cure. They are very scared.

When I die, I want everyone to know why I died. And I want people to know that I tried very hard to get them to understand.

In January 1988 a jury awarded Elizabeth $750,000 in her lawsuit against the doctor who had misdiagnosed her illness. Her greatest satisfaction was in knowing that her children could be taken care of after her death, that they would not be a financial burden to anyone.

She also had two dreams that could now come true. One was to buy a real house for her and the boys to live in. After much searching, she found one that she thought was just right for her, and she bought it, even though the price was way too high. She was ready to move in, but there was something she wanted to do first: Her other dream was to take the boys to Disney World. The trip was a prize she'd been given by the top fundraiser in the

AAC's annual Walk for Life in June. With much fan-fare and a great public send-off, Elizabeth, Matthew, and Christopher all went to Florida in mid-October. They did everything at Disney World; the boys went on every ride. But Elizabeth was exhausted by it, and she was getting sick again. After five days in Florida, she came home.

By this time, she had been hospitalized more than a dozen times. The disease was wearing her down. The day after she came back to Boston, she went into the hospital again. Within three days she had slipped into a coma. Less than ten days later, on November 4, 1988, Elizabeth Ramos died. She never spent a single night in her new house.

The boys now live in New York with their Aunt Lucy. The dream house is on the market. [1991]

79

Missing Persons: African American Women, AIDS, and the History of Disease

EVELYNN HAMMONDS

Nobody is ever in to see me or hear my complaints. They are never there when I try to make an appointment to get anything done. Nobody cares. I continue to get sick over and over again, and nobody listens to what I have to say. I don't think that's fair, because I feel I deserve better, because not only am I a woman, I am also a human being; and it's hard enough for me to deal with the issue of having AIDS, dying a day at a time and to have to live under the circumstances that I am under.[1]

WHY DO AFRICAN AMERICAN WOMEN DISPROPORTIONATELY GET AIDS?

In spite of the fact that the majority of women with AIDS are African American, the devastating toll that AIDS is taking on the lives of these women has yet to be perceived as a national crisis. Neither scientific, epidemiological, nor historical or cultural studies about AIDS have addressed the question of why African American women are at such greater risk for HIV infection and why their survival rates are so abysmally low. Now that the percentages for women

with AIDS have more than doubled in the last two years (in some cities women make up twenty-five percent of the AIDS cases), research on women is in process. One might wonder, however, whether the government's recent focus on women is not mainly directed at their reproductive lives; that is, women become the risk factor for HIV in children. In this essay I want to look at a number of factors that have supported the invisibility of African American women with AIDS. First, I look at examples of the representation of these women in the media, in particular focusing on how media reports shape and re-flect the social context of the epidemic with regard to African American women with AIDS. Secondly, I discuss how AIDS is affecting the lives of poor, Af-rican American women. In sum, I argue that African American women are disproportionately vulnerable to the ravages of AIDS in part because of the long-term and persistent failure of public health practices to control sexually transmitted diseases in the Afri-can American community.

It goes without saying that gender has not been at the center of discussions or research about AIDS. The way in which AIDS was first conceptualized as a disease of gay men, then a disease of various "risk groups," e.g., intravenous drug users, foreclosed the recognition of women as potentially a significant proportion of the AIDS caseload.[2] This is even more apparent when examining gender within racial cate-gories. In the broadest sense, little attention has been paid to the plight of African American women with AIDS because they are women. Overall, the medi-cal establishment and most activist groups have fo-cused on men, who make up the larger numbers of people with AIDS.[3] And as feminists and other activists have documented, women have historically received unequal treatment in the United States health care system. African American women, as evidenced by their higher rates of many diseases, have long been among the least served by the health care system. AIDS appears in African American communities at the end of a long trail of neglect in the Reagan-Bush years—including the cut-off of federal funds for abortion, jobs, housing, and the failure to control *sexually transmitted diseases*. The conditions that African American women live under in their communities, their roles as mothers, wives, workers, and lovers, all shape their responses to AIDS.

MEDIA IMAGES: "MOST ARE POOR, MANY ARE RECKLESS"

The impact of HIV infection on African American women and other women of color has received an odd sort of coverage in the media. On the one hand when the threat of AIDS to women is discussed, no mention is made of African American women. When African American women are discussed, they are relegated to the drug abuser category or partners of drug abusers or bad mother category for passing AIDS on to their children. A good example of this appeared in August 1987 in an article by Jane Gross, which appeared on the front page of the *New York Times*. The headline read: "Bleak Lives: Women Carrying AIDS," followed by "Women Who Carry the AIDS Virus: Most Are Poor, Many are Reckless."[4] I refer to this article in part to underline how little has changed since it appeared in 1987 and because it so clearly lays out the assumptions about women who become infected with HIV.

First, the article stated the grim statistics; in New York City in August 1987 there were 50,000 women infected with HIV; eighty percent were black and Hispanic. The first paragraph of the article announced:

> They are the primary carriers of the disease from the world of drug abuse to the larger community, making their education an increasingly urgent task.

The identification of women as "carriers" was stated without supporting scientific data. Perhaps the writer was unaware of the scientific data but, by 1987, studies showed that women were at greater risk of infection from infected men than the other way around. Or, in the rhetoric of the medical literature, female to male transmission of HIV is "less efficient."[5] The women in this article are portrayed as passive victims in abusive relationships with men who are most often drug abusers. Their lives are described as "unruly," "chaotic," "despairing." The most demeaning attack is made on African American women who, though HIV positive, become pregnant and choose to continue their pregnancies rather than have an abortion. Gross reported that

> . . . Women explain that they want to have another child to leave something behind in the face of dearth, that they view a fifty-fifty chance of having a healthy baby acceptable odds. But counselors say these explanations usually do not surface until a pregnancy has proceeded past the point when abortion is possible. They wind up having babies more by default than intent.[6]

The behaviors highlighted by these experts' comments suggest that these African American women are not responsible to themselves or to the children they bear. The prevalence of such attitudes is attested to by reports from women of color who are HIV positive, who are, in many cities, being subjected to hostility from hospital staff and counselors because they want to have their babies. Gross, like other writers, portrays African American women largely from the perspective of neonatal infection, which implies that the women themselves are not patients but only vectors of disease, or put another way, the risk factor for their children.

The article goes on to quote a social worker who commented that from her experience running a counseling group, only the middle-class women in her group expressed concern about their health. "Among the poorest women, who are often indifferent or ignorant about health care, there is no demonstrated concern about their physical well-being. . . ." The sense of powerlessness that African American women who are HIV positive experience is used to emphasize their irresponsibility. Such comments leave unexamined the personal and economic difficulties that these women face in their attempts to get access to good health care and counseling. Gross does not present a portrait of women who are fighting a disease, and the reader is not drawn to be sympathetic toward them. Instead, it is a portrait of the by now classic stereotype of black women who are unstable and irresponsible, even more so because they now carry a deadly disease. They are blamed for not having control over their lives.

The article does not report that these women are being diagnosed at later stages in the disease. We are not told about the different opportunistic infections in women that could possibly mask early diagnosis. We are not told how many of these women have lost their homes and custody of children when their HIV status is made known, nor that their opportunities for anonymous testing, good counseling, or access to drug treatment programs are severely limited. There have now been recommendations to implement testing of all pregnant women. African American women are likely to become the first non-incarcerated, civilian United States citizens to confront mass screening for HIV. And I would suggest, in the wake of this recommendation, there is also the possibility that some might call for mandatory abortions or, given that Medicaid monies are not allowed to cover abortion in most states, preemptive sterilization for these same HIV-infected pregnant women.

QUICK: NAME ONE BLACK WOMAN WITH AIDS

Gross's article is not atypical. I have read few stories in the mainstream media detailing the emotional trauma that HIV infection causes for African American women; nothing about survival strategies; no stories of daily life—how living with AIDS affects jobs, family relationships, or friendships. On Sunday, June 17, 1990, the *New York Times* ran a full page of profiles of black and white gay people living with AIDS. One woman was interviewed though no picture of her was printed. She said, "You want so much for someone to hold you, and no one wants to touch you." Her response only hints at the emotional trauma such women are facing. So many questions remain unasked in such accounts—how are these women dealing with the stigma associated with a disease that is perceived to be associated largely with white gay males? How are they dealing with the loss of their children or how are they preparing their children for their own impending deaths? What is happening to women who don't have children or extended families? Perhaps the problem is that, to date, no "famous" black woman has died of

AIDS for the media to create a symbol that would garner support for African American women with the disease.

The tactics used by the media to make the American public aware of the various dimensions of the AIDS epidemic have been troubling. One tactic has been to take one person's story and transform it into a symbol for some particular aspect of the epidemic that needs to be addressed. For example, Ryan White epitomized the "innocent" child, made a victim of the bigoted attitudes of parents who barred him from his local school and town. White's story became the vehicle to educate the public about the small risk of AIDS being transmitted casually and the plight of "innocent" children who are stigmatized because of their infection. Similarly, the story of Kimberly Bergalis, alleged to have been infected by her dentist, has been the centerpiece of the debate over whether there should be restrictions on dentists, physicians, and health care workers who are HIV positive. White gay male artists, entertainers, and writers suffering and dying from AIDS are featured in articles that eloquently reveal to the larger heterosexual world the emotional toll that AIDS has taken in gay communities while breaking down stereotypes about gay life. These articles serve to reveal the junctures and disjunctures in our beliefs about sexuality and sexual practices as well as the anxieties in American life about sex and morality.

In each of these cases, in some way the media has used such symbols to subtly urge the public to embrace people with AIDS. African American women with AIDS are constantly represented with respect to drug use—either their own or their partner's. They are largely poor or working class. They are single mothers. Media portrayals of these people with AIDS allude to the spectre of drug abuse and uncontrolled sexuality coupled with welfare "dependency" and irresponsibility. Such allusions undermine any representations of African American women with AIDS that would allow them to be embraced by the larger public.

Public health educators have been challenged to deal with the issue of cultural sensitivity in AIDS prevention and education material, and thus have created advertising campaigns displaying African American women in a positive light. This advertising often presents nameless figures who may look more like the average black woman, and thus encourage other African American women to identify with the ads' message on AIDS prevention; but these ads may not be able to elevate the threat AIDS poses to African American women, or the plight of those already infected, to the levels of recognition that could dethrone the more prevalent negative imagery.

THE FACE OF AIDS FOR AFRICAN AMERICAN WOMEN

The average age of African American women with AIDS at the time of diagnosis is thirty-six years. A significant number of the women were diagnosed when they were in their twenties and thus would have been infected as adolescents.[7] Most of these young women live in urban areas in the Northeast. The fact that many of the African American women with AIDS are so young is a startling statistic. It suggests that they were infected at an age when they had the least control over their sexual lives. They were at an age when they were vulnerable to the demands not just of partners of their own age, but older men as well. In contrast to a picture of women in their twenties aware of the consequences of their actions, instead some number of African American women contracted AIDS at an age when their ideas about sex were just being formed. Many of these young women also live in urban communities where few support systems exist to protect them and allow them to grow unmolested to adulthood. Additionally, it is reported that few HIV-infected individuals in communities of color with high rates of infection, such as in sections of New York City, know their infection status.[8] Many African American women and men simply do not know that they are in danger. Far too many are only found to have AIDS upon autopsy.

Though fifty-one percent of women with AIDS were infected through intravenous (IV) drug use, twenty-nine percent were infected through hetero-sexual contact.[9] As Ernest Drucker notes, in New York City, ". . . even those women who did have histories of IV drug use were, almost universally, *also* the sexual partners of men (sometimes many men) who were IV drug users. . . . Thus, it becomes extremely difficult to attribute these women's infection to one exposure or the other, since they were dually exposed for sustained periods of time to both risks of infection."[10] It is obvious then that African American women in such contexts are both dually exposed and dually victimized in a social setting now being ravaged by an incurable disease.

Every aspect of family life is touched by the presence of AIDS. "As AIDS cuts a swath through family after family, some have four or five members already sick with the disease and more infected."[11] Few people are aware of what these families face. Suki Ports, of the Minority Task Force on AIDS, reported the following story:

> Frances worked. She had difficulty after the birth of her six-year-old and needed many transfusions. She had a second child, who is fourteen months old. This baby was diagnosed with AIDS, so Frances quit work to take care of her . . . She then had to make a choice. She could move into an SRO, with two children, one sick, no cooking facilities except a hot plate, and get full benefits, or move in with her mother and receive no benefits, because her mother works . . . Her choice was made. It is difficult, and it's straining the mother's resources and good nature. Family benefits to assist the whole family are not available without creating a new precedent for payments in an already strained financial outlook.[12]

Many women are also hiding the fact that members of their family have AIDS. Long-practiced and familiar cultural beliefs are breaking down in the face of AIDS in African American communities. There is little evidence that fear or stigma is decreasing. Anecdotal reports suggest that some families who have relatives die of AIDS are refusing to have public funerals or indicate the cause of death in obituary notices. I found Frances's story as the debate was being waged in Congress on the bill that would mandate that businesses protect the jobs of workers who had to take leave to care for family members who are ill. I heard no one speak to the need for this bill because of the spread of the AIDS epidemic.

CONCLUSION

I believe that the invisibility and objectification of African American women in the AIDS epidemic is tied to the historical treatment of African American women with respect to sexually transmitted disease. The Tuskegee syphilis experiment is just one example of the legacy of danger and death that sexually transmitted diseases represent for African American communities. For a black woman to expose that she had a sexually transmitted disease was, for much of this century, to render herself multiply stigmatized, bringing up older images of immorality and uncontrolled sexuality that neither class nor educational privilege could protect her from. It possibly meant that pregnancy carried more risks; it often precipitated long-term health problems and even early death. That physicians and public health experts have long accepted higher rates of sexually transmitted diseases among African American women is a sign that somehow this had quietly become a norm. That overt racial comments from white health care providers on the cause of this higher incidence of sexually transmitted disease and the attendant problems for fetal and maternal health are less evident today than in the 1920s is not necessarily a sign that attitudes have changed or that the stigma associated with these diseases has diminished.

Current public health efforts must address the long-term stigma that African American women continue to experience with respect to sexually transmitted diseases. As the uninterrupted disparity in the incidence of these diseases within this community over the last fifty years indicates, those efforts have largely failed. Bringing to the fore the historical treatment and experience of African American women, their children, and their partners with respect to sexually transmitted diseases in the past is a necessary step.

In addition, most of all, what is needed is a viable black feminist movement. African American feminists need to intervene in the public and scientific debates about AIDS, making plain the impact that medical and public health policy will have on African American women. An analysis of gender is desperately needed to frame the discussion of sexual relations in the black community. Sexism lies behind the disempowerment and lack of control that African American women experience in the face of AIDS. African American women are multiply stigmatized in the AIDS epidemic—only a multifaceted African American feminist analysis attentive to issues of race, sex, gender, and power can adequately expose the impact of AIDS on our communities and formulate just policies to save women's lives.   [1995]

NOTES

1. Testimony of Margaret Rivera, Report of the Public Hearing, "AIDS: Its Impact on Women, Children and Families." (New York State Division for Women, 12 June 1987), 21.
2. IV drug users were constructed as male in the mass media before the spectacle of "crack babies." Moreover, drug treatment models and facilities continue to favor male clients while the despair of women's addiction to crack disappears quickly behind our image of them as monsters for "delivering drugs" to their babies.
3. By using the term "attention," it is not my intent in this essay to disparage or belittle the heroic efforts of the many health care workers, activists, and others who *have* labored to bring the plight of African American women and other women with AIDS to light. By using the term "attention," I only mean to address the fact that the deaths of African American women with AIDS have not garnered the kind of front-page headlines or other prominent popular media attention given to other people with AIDS, as will be discussed more fully later in the essay.
4. Jane Gross, "Bleak Lives, Women Carrying AIDS," *New York Times*, 27 August 1987.
5. N. S. Padian, "Heterosexual Transmission of Acquired Immunodeficiency Syndrome: International Perspectives and National Projections," *Review of Infectious Diseases* 9 (1987): 947–960.
6. Gross, "Bleak Lives."
7. Ellerbrock, "Epidemiology," 2973.
8. Ernest Drucker, "Epidemic in the War Zone: AIDS and Community Survival in New York City," *International Journal of Health Services* 20, no. 4 (1990): 605. Drucker notes that fewer than ten percent of the estimated 150 to 250 thousand people infected with HIV in New York City know their HIV status.
9. Ellerbrock, "Epidemiology," 2974.
10. Drucker, "Epidemic," 609.
11. Drucker, "Epidemic," 613.
12. "AIDS: Its Impact on Women, Children and Families," 51.

✣ 80

Breast Cancer: Is It the Environment?

MS.

"For too long now breast cancer research has been dominated by the elusive search for the cure," says Andrea Martin, founder and executive director of the Breast Cancer Fund, a San Francisco–based group that has launched a major campaign to draw attention to the links between the environment and breast cancer. Citing the fact that only 5 to 10 percent of breast cancer cases are genetically caused and that the number of women with breast cancer nearly doubled between 1970 and 1990, the fund has teamed up with the Susan G. Komen Breast Cancer Foundation to urge the public to agitate for more research into environmental causes of the disease. In 1999 the two groups rallied 70 individuals and organizations (including local breast cancer groups, the Coalition of Labor Union Women, and the YWCA) to call for increased funding for research examining environmental links; monitoring by the Centers for Disease Control (CDC) of what chemicals are in our bodies and in what amounts; full funding for the Environmental Protection Agency's (EPA) program to screen for environmental toxins; and a cross-agency committee to oversee government funding for environmental health research.

The following is excerpted from the Breast Cancer Fund's publication *Examining the Environmental Links to Breast Cancer.*

Since 1971, the year President Richard Nixon declared a "war on cancer," more than $35 billion has been committed to research. Yet we still cannot pinpoint with certainty the causes behind the vast majority of breast cancer cases, nor have treatment options changed or improved much over the years. Women still must choose from surgery, radiation, and/or chemotherapy.

In addition, some in the medical establishment have misleadingly focused on mammography as a prevention measure, with the assumption that early detection can prevent serious illness. Mammography, however, is *not* prevention. It can only detect cancer that already exists and may have been present for eight to ten years. It fails to detect breast cancer 20 percent of the time in women over 50, and as much as 40 percent of the time in younger women.

WHAT WE KNOW

Hundreds of scientific studies of laboratory animals and wildlife have drawn links between exposure to toxic chemicals and cancer. Emerging science suggests that synthetic chemicals in the environment pose a risk to the human reproductive system, the endocrine system, and to human growth and development both *in utero* and after birth.

A rapidly evolving field of research involves the study of "endocrine disrupters" or "hormone mimickers"—synthetic chemicals found in pesticides like DDT, some fuels, plastics, detergents, and pharmaceutical drugs. We know that estrogen binds with receptors in mammary glands, signaling cells to grow. In 1993, scientists at Cornell University cautioned that growing evidence seemed to indicate that exposure to estrogen-mimicking chemicals, called xenoestrogens, can cause cells to rapidly grow out of control and form tumors. It has been postulated that xenoestrogens may be responsible for increasing a woman's chances of getting breast cancer. Researchers at Tufts University Medical School have demonstrated that xenoestrogens make human breast cancer cells grow in the laboratory, just as natural estrogen does.

There are also studies that show drastic changes in development, particularly in the reproductive system, when laboratory mice are exposed to estrogen mimickers during critical windows of vulnerability *in utero.* When cells are rapidly developing and proliferating, there can be a key period of vulnerability during which damaging or altering cell development can lead to cancer. Other windows of vulnerability include puberty and a woman's first pregnancy.

Studies tracking patterns of breast cancer development in humans also strongly suggest the influence of environmental factors. In Asia, women are four to seven times less likely to develop breast cancer than women in the U.S. Yet when Asian women migrate to the U.S., their risk of breast cancer rises over a two-generation span. Women who live in the U.S. for a decade or more have an 80 percent higher risk of developing breast cancer than more recent immigrants, and those whose grandparents were born in the U.S. have a 60 percent greater risk than women whose grandparents were born overseas.

Estrogen mimickers may be either beneficial or detrimental. Estrogen-mimicking compounds found in foods such as broccoli, soy products, and cauliflower may act as "good" estrogens, providing some protection against the effects of estradiol, the chief "bad" estrogen, made naturally by our bodies. Critics of the "xenoestrogen theory" argue that these beneficial compounds found in foods can balance possible hazards posed by human-made chemicals. Other scientists point out that the human body has been fine-tuned to handle plant estrogens through thousands of years of evolution, while human-made estrogen mimickers have been in the environment only since the 1940s. Since we do not yet understand how women's natural estrogen affects breast cancer, it is difficult to predict how estrogen mimickers might behave, even at low doses.

Studies have identified the presence of more than 200 foreign chemicals in women's breast milk, including significant levels of dioxin, a carcinogen that has been shown to disrupt children's hormone systems. Within six months of being breast-fed, a baby in the U.S. or Europe receives the maximum recommended lifetime dose of dioxin.

MORE RESEARCH NEEDED

Chemicals that are persistent in the environment accumulate in body fat and are carried by women in their breast tissue. Thus far, human data about the link between these chemicals and breast cancer are inconclusive. For example, some studies have shown that women with breast cancer have the same or lower levels of pesticide residue in their system than women without the disease.

However, other studies, by U.S. and Canadian scientists, have found that women with higher levels of organochlorines in their blood have four to ten times the risk of breast cancer than those with lower levels. [Organochlorines are hydrocarbon-based chemicals containing chlorines like DDT. Many of these compounds break down very slowly in the environment and can be stored in the fat of animals, fish, and humans.] These seemingly inconsistent results point to the need for long-term prospective studies on this issue.

There are only two recognized causes of breast cancer: exposure to ionizing radiation and inherited genetic defects in breast cells. Other factors, though they have not been shown to *cause* the disease, are associated with higher risk: beginning menstruation before age 12, onset of menopause after 55, bearing children late in life or not at all, not breast-feeding, and prolonged use of estrogen after menopause.

More research is needed to examine why the established risk factors increase a woman's vulnerability. However, additional and different research is needed to determine which of the thousands of chemicals in the environment cause the disease, and how. Most important, we must conduct long-term prospective studies that measure exposures to chemicals during critical windows of breast development.

RESEARCH PRIORITIES

For many years the focus of the National Cancer Institute (NCI), the largest single government funding source for cancer investigations, has been on earlier detection with mammography, improved radiation and chemotherapy, and improved surgical techniques designed to help women survive the disease and live longer. Much research continues to be focused on the role of inherited gene defects. Currently, there is no breast cancer prevention research strategy at the NCI except for chemo-prevention through the use of raloxifene and tamoxifen in high-risk, healthy women.

The federal government has funded one multi-million-dollar, multiyear environment research study, the Long Island Breast Cancer Study Project, to determine whether environmental contaminants increase breast cancer risk. But overall, funding for environmental research represents only a tiny fraction of the government's budget for disease research. Of the National Institutes of Health's $15.7 billion budget last year, just $382 million, or 2.4 percent, went to the National Institute of Environmental Health Sciences, the primary agency conducting research on environmental health. Similarly, the CDC's National Center for Environmental Health received just $172 million for 1999.

A CALL FOR ACTION

Over the years, a growing movement has emerged calling for prevention-based research.

Breast cancer advocates and researchers have identified three important types of research currently underfunded by the federal government: testing and screening of industrial chemicals and pesticides for their toxicity and hormone-mimicking effects; measuring the levels of these chemicals in our bodies—a process known as "bio-monitoring"; and learning how girls and women are exposed to these chemicals, so we can study health effects and ultimately reduce health risks.

In 1996, an advisory committee of scientists and experts established by the EPA recommended the creation of a program to test the toxicity and hormonal effects of 9,000 chemicals, as required under the Food Quality Protection Act. However, this program has been grossly underfunded. Further, as currently devised, the tests do not screen for toxicity during the prenatal and early development period when chemicals have been known to have different and often more harmful effects.

To fully understand the impact of environmental contaminants on humans, the EPA's data on the toxicity of these chemicals must be completed and complemented by an ongoing systematic program of bio-monitoring data to identify what chemicals exist in our bodies and at what levels.

Unfortunately, the CDC's National Environmental Health Laboratory, the agency that spearheads bio-monitoring research, is also severely underfunded. The Breast Cancer Fund is calling for more broad-based testing as well as testing on breast milk, a fluid that absorbs chemicals differently, and, in some cases, at higher and potentially more dangerous levels. Not only do women have the right to know what chemicals are in their breasts and breast milk, but investing in this kind of research is also a critical step to developing public policies and prevention strategies that will effectively address the breast cancer epidemic and other serious illnesses.

Yet research into the environmental causes of breast cancer remains a low priority among leading cancer organizations and government agencies. Advocates have attributed this lack of commitment, in part, to pressure from industry. Pharmaceutical companies, in particular, have a vested interest in keeping breast cancer research focused on drug therapies and away from environmental pollution. Breast Cancer Awareness Month was initiated by the pharmaceutical giant Zeneca, the maker of tamoxifen. [Activists often note Zeneca's link to Imperial Chemical Industries (ICI), the maker of pesticides, plastics, pharmaceutical, and paper. Zeneca was a spin-off company of ICI, which was sued in 1990 by state and federal agencies for dumping DDT and PCBs in California harbors.] In 1999, Zeneca merged with the Swedish pharmaceutical company Astra to become the world's third-largest drug concern. AstraZeneca continues to be the primary sponsor of Breast Cancer Awareness Month.

A MATTER OF LIFE AND DEATH

If exposure to chemicals in the environment was shown to be associated with only 10 to 20 percent of breast cancer cases, and the U.S. acted to reduce or eliminate these hazardous chemicals, we would be able to prevent between 9,000 and 36,000 women from contracting the disease each year.   [2000]

Reproductive Freedom

The *Roe v. Wade* decision of 1973 legalized abortion in the United States, guaranteeing for the first time a woman's right to choose between pregnancy and abortion. Since this landmark decision, however, women's right to safe and legal abortions has been steadily eroded, as documented in the introduction to this part.

We begin this section with Ellen Willis's examination of the implications of anti-abortion arguments. Contending that the "nitty gritty of the abortion debate is not life, but sex," Willis argues that the control of one's reproductive life is central to women's right to be sexually active and autonomous. Arguments against abortion, she maintains, falsely separate the fetus from the woman whose body it inhabits.

Anti-abortion legislation, particularly parental consent and notification laws that require teenage women to obtain a parent's approval for abortion, have diminished a woman's right to legal abortion. Mike Males compares the assumptions about the lives of adolescent females, upon which some of these laws are based, with the reality of their lives. The devastating effects of such legislation on young women are explored in "Abortion Denied." William Bell provides a personal narrative of the tragic consequences of Indiana's parental consent laws. His daughter, Becky, was 18 years old when she died from an infection resulting from an illegal abortion. Rather than risk her parents' disappointment by telling them about her pregnancy, Becky had chosen to obtain an abortion on her own.

Because of the violence that has been directed at abortion clinics, some activists on both sides of the debate have sought to understand each other more fully. The group of women who met in Boston after the murder of two abortion workers tried to avert violence and create a dialogue between the two sides of the abortion debate.

The struggle for reproductive freedom has taken different forms for different groups of women. In the excerpt from her book *Killing the Black Body: Race, Reproduction and the Meaning of Liberty,* Dorothy Roberts demonstrates that African-American women have had to struggle for the right to procreate and continue to battle against attempts to control their fertility. Ruth Hubbard shows that pregnant women's rights are often subordinated to those of the fetus, and argues for meeting the economic, social, and educational needs of women and their children. We conclude with an agenda for the future that conceives of reproductive freedom broadly, including its connection to economic and sexual self-determination.

🌿 81

Abortion:
Is a Woman a Person?

ELLEN WILLIS

If propaganda is as central to politics as I think, the opponents of legal abortion have been winning a psychological victory as important as their tangible gains. Two years ago, abortion was almost always discussed in feminist terms—as a political issue affecting the condition of women. Since then, the grounds of the debate have shifted drastically; more and more, the right-to-life movement has succeeded in getting the public and the media to see abortion as an abstract moral issue having solely to do with the rights of fetuses. Though every poll shows that most Americans favor legal abortion, it is evident that many are confused and disarmed, if not convinced, by the antiabortionists' absolutist fervor. No one likes to be accused of advocating murder. Yet the "pro-life" position is based on a crucial fallacy—that the question of fetal rights can be isolated from the question of women's rights.

Recently, Garry Wills wrote a piece suggesting that liberals who defended the snail-darter's right to life and opposed the killing in Vietnam should condemn abortion as murder. I found this notion breathtaking in its illogic. Environmentalists were protesting not the "murder" of individual snail-darters but the practice of wiping out entire species of organisms to gain a short-term economic benefit; most people who opposed our involvement in Vietnam did so because they believed the United States was waging an aggressive, unjust and/or futile war. There was no inconsistency in holding such positions and defending abortion on the grounds that women's welfare should take precedence over fetal life. To claim that three very different issues, each with its own complicated social and political context, all came down to a simple matter of preserving life was to say that all killing was alike and equally indefensible regardless of circumstance. (Why, I wondered, had Wills left out the destruction of hap-

less bacteria by penicillin?) But aside from the general mushiness of the argument, I was struck by one peculiar fact: Wills had written an entire article about abortion without mentioning women, feminism, sex, or pregnancy.

Since the feminist argument for abortion rights still carries a good deal of moral and political weight, part of the antiabortionists' strategy has been to make an end run around it. Although the mainstream of the right-to-life movement is openly opposed to women's liberation, it has chosen to make its stand on the abstract "pro-life" argument. That emphasis has been reinforced by the movement's tiny left wing, which opposes abortion on pacifist grounds and includes women who call themselves "feminists for life." A minority among pacifists as well as right-to-lifers, this group nevertheless serves the crucial function of making opposition to abortion respectable among liberals, leftists, and moderates disinclined to sympathize with a right-wing crusade. Unlike most right-to-lifers, who are vulnerable to charges that their reverence for life does not apply to convicted criminals or Vietnamese peasants, anti-abortion leftists are in a position to appeal to social conscience—to make analogies, however facile, between abortion and napalm. They disclaim any opposition to women's rights, insisting rather that the end cannot justify the means—murder is murder.

Well, isn't there a genuine moral issue here? If abortion *is* murder, how can a woman have the right to it? Feminists are often accused of evading this question, but in fact an evasion is built into the question itself. Most people understand "Is abortion murder?" to mean "Is the fetus a person?" But fetal personhood is ultimately as inarguable as the existence of God; either you believe in it or you don't. Putting the debate on this plane inevitably leads to the nonconclusion that it is a matter of one person's conscience against another's. From there, the discussion generally moves on to broader issues: whether laws defining the fetus as a person violate the separation of church and state; or conversely, whether people who believe an act is murder have not only the right but the obligation to prevent it. Unfortunately, amid all this lofty philosophizing, the concrete, human reality of the pregnant woman's dilemma gets lost, and with it an essential ingredient of the moral question.

Murder, as commonly defined, is killing that is unjustified, willful, and malicious. Most people would agree, for example, that killing in defense of one's life or safety is not murder. And most would accept a concept of self-defense that includes the right to fight a defensive war or revolution in behalf of one's independence or freedom from oppression. Even pacifists make moral distinctions between defensive violence, however deplorable, and murder; no thoughtful pacifist would equate Hitler's murder of the Jews with the Warsaw Ghetto rebels' killing of Nazi troops. The point is that it's impossible to judge whether an act is murder simply by looking at the act, without considering its context. Which is to say that it makes no sense to discuss whether abortion is murder without considering why women have abortions and what it means to force women to bear children they don't want.

We live in a society that defines child rearing as the mother's job; a society in which most women are denied access to work that pays enough to support a family, child-care facilities they can afford, or any relief from the constant, daily burdens of motherhood; a society that forces mothers into dependence on marriage or welfare and often into permanent poverty; a society that is actively hostile to women's ambitions for a better life. Under these conditions the unwillingly pregnant woman faces a terrifying loss of control over her fate. Even if she chooses to give up the baby, unwanted pregnancy is in itself a serious trauma. There is no way a pregnant woman can passively let the fetus live; she must create and nurture it with her own body, in a symbiosis that is often difficult, sometimes dangerous, always uniquely intimate. However gratifying pregnancy may be to a woman who desires it, for the unwilling it is literally an invasion—the closest analogy is to the difference between lovemaking and rape. Nor is there such a thing as foolproof contraception. Clearly, abortion is by normal standards an act of self-defense.

Whenever I make this case to a right-to-lifer, the exchange that follows is always substantially the same:

RTL: If a woman chooses to have sex, she should be willing to take the consequences. We must all be responsible for our actions.

EW: Men have sex, without having to "take the consequences."

RTL: You can't help that—it's biology.

EW: You don't think a woman has as much right as a man to enjoy sex? Without living in fear that one slip will transform her life?

RTL: She has no right to selfish pleasure at the expense of the unborn.

It would seem, then, that the nitty-gritty issue in the abortion debate is not life but sex. If the fetus is sacrosanct, it follows that women must be continually vulnerable to the invasion of their bodies and loss of their freedom and independence—unless they are willing to resort to the only perfectly reliable contraceptive, abstinence. This is precisely the "solution" right-to-lifers suggest, usually with a touch of glee; as Representative Elwood Rudd once put it, "If a woman has a right to control her own body, let her exercise control before she gets pregnant." A common ploy is to compare fucking to overeating or overdrinking, the idea being that pregnancy is a just punishment, like obesity or cirrhosis.

In 1979 it is depressing to have to insist that sex is not an unnecessary, morally dubious self-indulgence but a basic human need, no less for women than for men. Of course, for heterosexual women giving up sex also means doing without the love and companionship of a mate. (Presumably, married women who have had all the children they want are supposed to divorce their husbands or convince them that celibacy is the only moral alternative.) "Freedom" bought at such a cost is hardly freedom at all and certainly not equality—no one tells men that if they aspire to some measure of control over their lives, they are welcome to neuter themselves and become social isolates. The don't-have-sex argument is really another version of the familiar anti-feminist dictum that autonomy and femaleness—that is, female sexuality—are incompatible; if you choose the first, you lose the second. But to pose this choice is not only inhumane; it is as deeply disingenuous as "Let them eat cake." No one, least of all the anti-abortion movement, expects or wants significant numbers of women to give up sex and marriage. Nor are most right-to-lifers willing to allow abortion for rape victims. When all the cant about "responsibility" is stripped away, what the right-to-life position comes down to is, if the effect of prohibiting abortion is to keep women slaves to their biology, so be it.

In their zeal to preserve fetal life at all costs, antiabortionists are ready to grant fetuses more legal protection than people. If a man attacks me and I kill him, I can plead self-defense without having to prove that I was in danger of being killed rather than injured, raped, or kidnapped. But in the annual congressional battle over what if any exceptions to make to the Medicaid abortion ban, the House of Representatives has bitterly opposed the funding of abortions for any reason but to save the pregnant woman's life. Some right-to-lifers argue that even the danger of death does not justify abortion; others have suggested "safeguards" like requiring two or more doctors to certify that the woman's life is at least 50 percent threatened. Antiabortionists are forever worrying that any exception to a total ban on abortion will be used as a "loophole": better that any number of women should ruin their health or even die than that one woman should get away with not having a child "merely" because she doesn't want one. Clearly this mentality does not reflect equal concern for all life. Rather, antiabortionists value the lives of fetuses above the lives and welfare of women, because at bottom they do not concede women the right to an active human existence that transcends their reproductive function. Years ago, in an interview with Paul Krassner in *The Realist,* Ken Kesey declared himself against abortion. When Krassner asked if his objection applied to victims of rape, Kesey replied—I may not be remembering the exact words, but I will never forget the substance—"Just because another man planted the seed, that's no reason to destroy the crop." * To this day I have not heard a more eloquent or chilling metaphor for the

essential premise of the right-to-life movement: that a woman's excuse for being is her womb. It is an outrageous irony that antiabortionists are managing to pass off this profoundly immoral idea as a noble moral cause.

The conservatives who dominate the right-to-life movement have no real problem with the antifeminism inherent in their stand; their evasion of the issue is a matter of public relations. But the politics of antiabortion leftists are a study in self-contradiction: in attacking what they see as the violence of abortion, they condone and encourage violence against women. Forced childbearing does violence to a woman's body and spirit, and it contributes to other kinds of violence: deaths from illegal abortion; the systematic oppression of mothers and women in general; the poverty, neglect, and battering of unwanted children; sterilization abuse.

Radicals supposedly believe in attacking a problem at its roots. Yet surely it is obvious that restrictive laws do not keep women from seeking abortions; they just create an illicit, dangerous industry. The only way to drastically reduce the number of abortions is to invent safer, more reliable contraceptives, ensure universal access to all birth control methods, eliminate sexual ignorance and guilt, and change the social and economic conditions that make motherhood a trap. Anyone who is truly committed to fostering life should be fighting for women's liberation instead of harassing and disrupting abortion clinics (hardly a nonviolent tactic, since it threatens the safety of patients). The "feminists for life" do talk a lot about ending the oppression that drives so many women to abortion; in practice, however, they are devoting all their energy to increasing it.

Despite its numerical insignificance, the antiabortion left epitomizes the hypocrisy of the right-to-life crusade. Its need to wrap misogyny in the rhetoric of social conscience and even feminism is actually a perverse tribute to the women's movement; it is no longer acceptable to declare openly that women deserve to suffer for the sin of Eve. I suppose that's progress—not that it does the victims of the Hyde Amendment much good.   [1981]

---

*A reader later sent me a copy of the Kesey interview. The correct quotation is "You don't plow under the corn because the seed was planted with a neighbor's shovel."

82

Lost Woman Song

ANI DIFRANCO

I opened a bank account
When I was nine years old
I closed it when I was eighteen
I gave them every penny
That I'd saved
And they gave my blood and urine a number
Now I'm sitting in this waiting room
Playing with the toys
I am here to exercise my freedom of choice
I passed their hand held signs
I went thru their picket lines
They gathered when they saw me coming
They shouted when they saw me cross
I said why don't you go home
Just leave me alone
I'm just another woman lost
You are like fish in the water who don't know that
     they are wet as far as I can tell
The world isn't perfect yet
His bored eyes were obscene
On his denimed thighs a magazine
I wish he'd never come here with me
In fact I wish he'd never come near me
I wish his shoulder wasn't touching mine
I am growing older waiting in this line
But some of life's best lessons are learned at the
     worst times
Under the fierce fluorescent she offered her hand
     for me to hold
She offered stability and calm
And I was crushing her palm
Through the pinch pull wincing
My smile unconvincing
On that sterile battlefield that sees
Only casualties
Never heroes
My heart hit absolute zero
Lucille, your voice
Still sounds in me
Mine was a relatively easy tragedy

The profile of our country looks a little less hard-
     nosed
But that picket line persisted and that clinic has
     since been closed
They keep pounding their fists on reality
Hoping it will break
But I don't think there's one of them that leads a
     life free
Of mistakes
You can't make me sacrifice my freedom of choice

[1990]

83

Talking with the Enemy

ANNE FOWLER, NICKI NICHOLS
GAMBLE, FRANCES X. HOGAN,
MELISSA KOGUT,
MADELINE MCCOMISH,
and BARBARA THORP

For nearly six years, leaders on both sides of the abortion debate have met in secret in an attempt to better understand each other. Now they are ready to share what they have learned.

On the morning of Dec. 30, 1994, John Salvi walked into the Planned Parenthood clinic in Brookline and opened fire with a rifle. He seriously wounded three people and killed the receptionist, Shannon Lowney, as she spoke on the phone. He then ran to his car and drove two miles down Beacon Street to Preterm Health Services, where he began shooting again, injuring two and killing receptionist Lee Ann Nichols.

Salvi's 20-minute rampage shocked the nation. Prochoice advocates were grief-stricken, angry, and terrified. Prolife proponents were appalled as well as concerned that their cause would be connected with this horrifying act. Governor William F. Weld and Cardinal Bernard Law, among others, called for talks between prochoice and prolife leaders.

We are six leaders, three prochoice and three prolife, who answered this call. For nearly 5½ years, we have met together privately for more than 150 hours —an experience that has astonished and enriched us. Now, six years after the shootings in Brookline, and on the 28th anniversary of the US Supreme Court's landmark Roe v. Wade decision, we publicly disclose our meetings for the first time.

How did the six of us, activists from two embattled camps, ever find our way to the same table?

In the months following the shootings, the Public Conversations Project, a Boston-based national group that designs and conducts dialogues about divisive public issues, consulted many community leaders about the value of top-level talks about abortion.

Encouraged by these conversations, the project in July 1995 invited the six of us to meet together four times. The meetings would be confidential and we would attend as individuals, not as representatives of our organizations.

Our talks would not aim for common ground or compromise. Instead, the goals of our conversations would be to communicate openly with our opponents, away from the polarizing spotlight of media coverage; to build relationships of mutual respect and understanding; to help deescalate the rhetoric of the abortion controversy; and, of course, to reduce the risk of future shootings.

Still shaken by the murderous attacks in Brookline, we each agreed to participate.

As we approached the first meeting, we all were apprehensive.

Before the meeting, the prolife participants prayed together in a booth at a nearby Friendly's. Frances X. Hogan, a lawyer and president of Women Affirming Life and executive vice president of Massachusetts Citizens for Life, worried that a dialogue with prochoice leaders might generate "a scandal if people thought I was treating abortion merely as a matter of opinion on which reasonable people could differ."

Madeline McComish, a chemist and president of Massachusetts Citizens for Life, had a "gut fear of sitting with people who were directly involved with taking life."

Barbara Thorp was "deeply anguished over the murders at the clinics." She feared that "if lines of direct communication between prolife and prochoice leaders were not opened, polarization would only deepen." Despite misgivings, Thorp, a social worker

and director of the ProLife Office of the Archdiocese of Boston, was "anxious to meet the other side."

The prochoice participants were also skeptical and concerned. As president and CEO of the Planned Parenthood League of Massachusetts, Nicki Nichols Gamble was directly affected by the shootings. Although she felt that dialogue might help, she "wondered if the talks would divert my energies from coordinating my organization's response to the shootings and from assisting in the healing of my employees and their families."

Melissa Kogut, newly appointed executive director of Mass NARAL, the state affiliate of the National Abortion Rights Action League, wondered how she would "justify to my board and colleagues spending time on something that arguably could be futile."

The Rev. Anne Fowler, rector of St. John's Episcopal Church in Jamaica Plain, believed that her perspective as a Christian leader who is prochoice would be essential, but worried that her viewpoint might not be respected by either side. "However, as a priest, peacemaker, and activist, I had to accept this invitation."

The two facilitators who would moderate all the meetings were also anxious. Laura Chasin, director of the Public Conversations Project, "was afraid that talks might do more harm than good." Susan Podziba, an independent public policy mediator from Brookline, recalls, "The threat of violence was palpable. What if the wrong person found out about the dialogue?"

The first meeting took place at the project's office in Watertown on Sept. 5, 1995, a sweltering Tuesday evening. "I had wanted to wear my clerical collar, but it was too hot," recalls Fowler.

That first discussion was grueling. We could not agree on what to call each other. All but one of us were willing to use each side's preferred designation, in virtual or actual quotation marks: "prolife" and "prochoice."

Our first of many clashes over language, this disagreement remains unresolved. To this day, Gamble still cannot call the other side prolife because "I believe my cause is also prolife," she says. This stand frustrates Thorp and her colleagues. "I have tolerated Nicki's refusal to call us prolife but, frankly, it angers me. I wasn't eager to call Nicki's side prochoice, but I did it because it seemed to be necessary for showing respect and for moving the conversation forward," Thorp says.

Kogut questioned her own willingness to agree to these terms, "but I came to two conclusions," Kogut says. "To proceed with a civil dialogue, we needed to call each other what we each wanted to be called. Second, over time, I began to see 'prolife' as descriptive of the others' beliefs—that life itself, more important than the quality of life, was their preeminent value."

We also struggled over how to refer to what grows and develops in a pregnant woman's womb. The prochoice women found "unborn baby" unacceptable and the prolife women would not agree to "fetus." For the sake of proceeding, we all assented, uneasily, to the term "human fetus."

These opening exchanges brought us to the heart of our differences. Nerves frayed. The chasm between us seemed huge.

To help us listen and speak across this divide, ground rules were critical. We would seek to use terms acceptable (or at least tolerable) to all participants. We would not interrupt, grandstand, or make personal attacks. We would speak for ourselves, not as representatives of organizations. Most important, the meetings would be completely confidential unless all of us could agree upon a way to go public.

We also made a commitment that some of us still find agonizingly difficult: to shift our focus away from arguing for our cause. This agreement was designed to prevent rancorous debates.

And indeed, we believe this ground rule has been essential to the long life of our dialogue. Knowing that our ideas would be challenged, but not attacked, we have been able to listen openly and speak candidly.

But it has not been easy.

"From the beginning, I have felt an enormous tension," Hogan says, "between honoring the agreement to not argue for our position and my deep hope —which I still feel—that these women for whom I have such great respect will change their minds about abortion."

Our ground rules also required us to refrain from polarizing rhetoric. In one early session, we generated a list of "hot buttons"—words and phrases that make it almost impossible for some of us to think clearly, listen carefully, or respond constructively.

Prochoice members are inflamed when called "murderers" or when abortions are likened to the Holocaust or to "genocide." Prolife participants are incensed by dehumanizing phrases such as "products of conception" and "termination of pregnancy" that obscure their belief that abortion is killing.

We also discussed stereotypes we thought were applied to us by people "on the other side."

Prolife participants feel maligned when characterized as religious fanatics taking orders from men, or as uneducated, prudish individuals, indifferent to women in crisis and to children after they are born. Prochoice members are offended by labels such as anti-child, anti-men, anti-family, elitist, frivolous, self-centered, and immoral.

Despite the strains of these early meetings, we grew closer to each other. At one session, each of us told the group why she had devoted so much of her time, energy, and talents to the abortion issue. These accounts—all deeply personal—enlightened and moved us.

After the fourth meeting, we agreed to extend our sessions through the one-year anniversary of the shootings—an occasion, we feared, when tensions over abortion might ignite in Boston.

On the evening of Dec. 30, 1995, about 700 people gathered at Temple Ohabei Shalom in Brookline to honor the memory of Lowney and Nichols. All our prochoice participants attended the service. Fowler and Gamble officiated. In the solemn crowd were Podziba, one of our facilitators, and two of our prolife members, Hogan and Thorp, accompanied by David Thorp, her husband.

"Seeing the other members of the group walk in was one of the most meaningful moments of the service for me." Fowler recalls.

In her remarks, Gamble expressed gratitude "for the prayers of those who agree with us and the prayers of those who disagree."

Fowler, in her sermon, reminded us of the "God who calls out to all who love peace." She drew from the words of the Hebrew prophet Isaiah, saying "and new things have sprung forth in the year since Lee Ann's and Shannon's deaths. Much has been transformed, and much will be."

Indeed, to those of us involved in the confidential dialogues, much had been transformed. By the time of this sad anniversary, each one of us had come to think differently about those "on the other side."

While we struggled over profound issues, we also kept track of personal events in one another's lives, celebrating good times and sharing sorrows. As our mutual understanding increased, our respect and affection for one another grew.

This increased understanding affected how we spoke as leaders of our respective movements. The news media, unaware that we were meeting, began noting differences in our public statements.

In an article after the first-year anniversary of the shootings, Globe reporter Don Aucoin wrote, "Has the past year brought the lowering of voices . . . called for by Cardinal Law, Governor William Weld and others? The answer seems to be a qualified yes, at least among some activists."

The article quoted Gamble as saying, "There are numbers of people on both sides of this question who have tried to be thoughtful about the rhetoric they use." Gamble added that she was hearing fewer uses of such labels as "baby-killer, murderer, Nazi."

In the same article, Hogan is quoted as saying she uses "prochoice because that is what they want to be called. I have a basic respect for the person, even though I don't agree with or respect the position."

Thorp, too, was quoted. "This call for a lowering of voices sent a signal that we really needed to listen to each other with care and respect. I'm more mindful now than I've ever been of speaking in love, speaking in peace, and speaking in respect to anyone no matter how wide the differences are."

In a National Public Radio interview about the anniversary, Hogan explained that while she believed that abortion is killing, she did not call it murder. Hogan also said, "Toning down the rhetoric is critical. It's not just better manners, but it turns out it's also better politics. . . . We reach people we may never otherwise have reached with the message."

Kogut felt and acted differently when she appeared with prolife spokespeople on news shows and at speaking engagements. Kogut recalls, "I was struck by the media's desire for conflict. One host of a radio talk show actually encouraged me to attack my opponent personally."

In early 1996, we continued to meet, anticipating that the upcoming Salvi trial would present new challenges to protect activists and the public from danger.

At one point, prolife advocates acted to keep proponents of violence away from Massachusetts. In February 1996, the Rev. Donald Spitz, head of Pro-Life Virginia, made it known that he was planning to come to Boston to show support for what he had called, according to the Globe, Salvi's "righteous deed."

McComish wrote a letter to Spitz, signed also by Hogan and Thorp. "Your public statements on the acceptability of violence . . . are counter to everything that the prolife movement represents," McComish wrote. "At this very difficult time, you are not welcome in Massachusetts."

Spitz and several of his allies objected to McComish's charge. They suggested that she was betraying the cause. But he did not come.

A growing trust opened a "hot line" channel of reliable communication between us. The prolife leaders alerted Gamble when there was a possibility of imminent physical danger. "It lowered my anxiety —and moved me deeply—to know that there were people on the other side who were concerned about my safety," Gamble says.

Throughout these 5½ years, though external events claimed much of our attention, we managed to explore many aspects of the abortion controversy, such as when life begins, the rights of women, the rights of the unborn, why women get abortions, and the aftermath of abortion.

We spent especially tense hours discussing the issue that prochoice members describe as "bans on certain abortion procedures" and that prolife participants call "partial-birth abortions." We also probed a host of other complex and challenging subjects: feminism, sex education, euthanasia, suicide, the death penalty, the role of law in society, and individual responsibility.

Prochoice

The prochoice members of the group describe their views this way:

We recognize no single, universal truth that determines our moral decisions. On the contrary, we must consider a broad range of values whenever we seek to make wise, ethical, and compassionate choices. We respect a woman's moral capacity to make decisions regarding her health and welfare, including reproductive decisions.

A woman's choices reflect how she weighs her various life circumstances: her important relationships, her economic, social, and emotional resources and obligations, her health, her religious or philosophical beliefs, and the well-being of others for whom she has responsibility.

We live out our destinies in a world of vast and profound complexity, where claims upon our compassion and our judgment compete and often conflict. A woman respects the preciousness of human life by acknowledging and honoring the intricate tapestry of her relationships and commitments; indeed, we believe that the complexity of human life can be a source of moral wisdom and courage.

Prolife

The prolife members of the group describe their views this way:

We believe in one universal truth. We three, as Catholics, believe that each human life has its origin in the heart of God. This divine genesis of the human person calls us to protect and respect every human life from the moment of conception to natural death.

The truth regarding the intrinsic dignity of the human person can also be understood through reason and scientific principles of human reproduction and genetics. Indeed, faith and reason resonate, both affirming the inviolable truth that every human life is inherently sacred.

Abortion kills the most vulnerable member of the human family: the unborn child. The right to be born is the most basic of human rights. If it is not protected then all other rights are threatened.

We understand, all too well, the often desperate and overwhelming circumstances that some pregnant women face. We remain committed to creating an environment in which no pregnant woman feels that she must choose between her own well-being and the life of her child. It is an utter failure of love and community for a pregnant woman to feel that abortion is her only choice.

When addressing divisive topics, we expected to disagree. But at times, conflicts caught us by surprise—flaring when one side unwittingly used certain words in a way that struck the other as presumptuous or offensive.

One provocative word has been "violence." While the prochoice leaders use it to refer to shootings and other attacks on clinics, doctors, and staff, the prolife activists believe that abortion also is a violent act.

In writing this article, we came to an impasse when one side mentioned the Declaration of Independence. The prolife participants wished to cite the Declaration as a presentation of their core belief

has no law. "The law has, more than anything, disrupted and harmed families" and "can provoke violence," U.S. District Judge Donald Alsop wrote in a compelling opinion ignored by the Supreme Court.

In briefs filed in Judge Alsop's court reviewing parental consent and notification laws, Minnesota and Massachusetts judges recounted harassed, terrified, angry girls forced to reveal intimate details of their lives in intimidating court proceedings. "They find it a very nerve-racking experience," wrote one judge; another described "incredible amounts of stress" shown in "tone of voice, tenor of voice, shaking, wringing of hands," even physical illness. Judges, some personally opposed to abortion, unanimously agreed parental consent laws are useless and punitive.

While the Supreme Court upheld parental and judicial "rights" to decide that a minor girl must have a baby, there is no mandate that parents or the court pay her pregnancy expenses and the 18-year, $200,000 cost of raising a child she did not want to have—one an adult woman would have been allowed to abort. Bizarrely, a judge who finds a girl too immature for an abortion may force her to be a mother.

ADULT-TEEN SEX

There is, further, no requirement that the male partner in "teenage" abortions face similar sanctions. The reason: It is *adult men,* not teenage boys, who cause or collaborate in the vast majority of all "teenage" pregnancies and abortions, including the 5 percent of all "teen" pregnancies that result from rape. Vital and health statistics records indicate 90 percent of all pregnancies among girls under age 18 are caused by adult men over age 18, and more than half by men over age 20. The "adult-teen" pregnancy and abortion reality is one lawmakers and justices refuse to face.

Thus the only ones left to punish are young girls. And yet, minor girls are hardly the cause of the prevalence of abortion that anti-abortion forces find so offensive. Only one out of 10 abortions is performed on a girl under age 18; less than 2 percent of all abortions in the country involve a pregnancy caused by a couple in which *both* partners are under age 18. The young, like the poor, are targeted for oppressive restrictions because they can't fight back.

Punishment appears, in the end, both the motive and result of parental consent laws. In a . . . *Dateline* NBC report, the legislative sponsor of Ohio's parental notification law equated a pregnant teenage girl with a criminal who commits theft or vandalism. The laws' chief effects are delay, fear, stress, expense, hazard, forced motherhood and—now that the Supreme Court has invited states to experiment with harsher restrictions against teenagers and other vulnerable women—a return to dangerous illicit and self-induced measures.   [2002]

 85

Testimony of William Bell (on Raised Bill #5447)

CONNECTICUT STATE LEGISLATURE

My name is Bill Bell and I reside in Indianapolis, Indiana, with my wife Karen and my 20 year old son Bill.

I submit this testimony with mixed emotions: dreading to relive the death of my daughter but also realizing a responsibility to others, that the punitive and restrictive laws that are being heard before this committee are understood by all. In writing and in theory these laws appear reasonable and safe. But in practice they are punishing.

My daughter Becky made a mistake and became pregnant. Parental consent laws, very similar to those you are considering today, dictated that in order to terminate her pregnancy she must obtain approval of her parents, petition the courts, or travel to another state that would allow her a safe clinical abortion, *or* seek back-alley assistance. She died [from] an illegal abortion.

In confiding with her best friend she said, "I don't want to disappoint my mother and dad, I love them so much."

Knowing my daughter, I believe that the judicial option would have been too intimidating, given her desperate emotional state. She would also have been faced with the prospect of appearing before a pro-life judge. Hardly a reasonable option considering the fact that she had decided to terminate her pregnancy. She chose the last option available to her, an illegal abortion.

Unfortunately, we have been unable to piece together all the circumstances and today we struggle with the question, why did our daughter have to endure such mental torture in making what turned out to be her final decision?

She was intelligent enough to pursue her options, yet we live with the pain of knowing our daughter was desperate and alone, and because of these punishing and restrictive laws, she further compounded her initial mistake with another, and paid for it with her life.

My daughter was a quality child. She was raised in a functional family environment and was encouraged to develop her own thinking and reasoning skills. Yet, in her time of crisis, others had dictated how she must react, thus denying her a legitimate option that all women should enjoy, the right of self-determination.

Had our daughter come to us, her mother and I would have counseled her, made her aware of all her options, the circumstances and the consequences, to the best of our ability. But I can state emphatically that the final decision would have been hers.

As it stands today, legislators, judges, self-appointed moralists, and parents are making the decisions for these young women, allowing little or no input from them. Decisions that are clearly along the lines of their own political, moral or religious beliefs. How can we legislate or dictate that families communicate? How can we dictate to people how they must act or react in a time of crisis?

I realize a great number of young women are going to their parents for counsel and for this I am grateful. Since the death of our daughter, my wife and I have counseled several young women and have been fortunate to get the parents involved. But what about the young woman who doesn't want to disappoint her family?

If I understand correctly, the legislation before you offers no accommodation for a real life situation like that of a Becky Bell. Nor does it consider the young lady from a dysfunctional home who may fear for her physical well-being. These laws speak to theories and hypotheticals, they do not address the real life issues taking place today. I submit to you, these punitive and restrictive laws being considered, if enacted, will serve to further isolate the young women of this state. They will serve as a punishment to those who have made a mistake. In the interest of political gain and in the name of God, my daughter was punished.

Others took it upon themselves to decide my daughter's fate, thus denying her a safe option, the best care. Their theories and political stance were placed ahead of and valued more than the life of my daughter.

These laws clearly denied her a safe and reasonable option. And because she had decided to terminate her pregnancy, forced her into making a fatal mistake. My beautiful Becky Bell died on September 16th, 1988.

My daughter's death *will* count for something. She was somebody, somebody beautiful. I will not sit idly by and not speak out to others that could face the same torment that the Bell family now lives with. Not as long as there are those who will go to any length to take away basic human rights.

I am not promoting abortion, far from it. But I am speaking out against those who want to punish, who suggest that we can reduce teenage pregnancy through legislation. I am speaking out against those who will simply not address the needs of birth control and sex education.

Sex among teenagers will not be regulated by legislation, nor will it be eliminated.

I am a man with a broken heart, and it is my desire that speaking out will in some way prevent others from living this same nightmare.

I urge you to consider real life situations and not punish the young women of this state and uphold the rights of all the people of Connecticut, not just the parents.

Rebecca Suzanne Bell was not a theory, she was a beautiful human being. She was my daughter, taken away because others *thought* they had all of the answers. The bill before you doesn't have all of the answers either and I urge you to defeat this legislation.

[1990]

✣ 86

Using Pregnancy to Control Women

RUTH HUBBARD

Strange things have been happening to this culture's ideas about pregnancy. More and more, physicians, judges, legislators, and the media are presenting pregnancy as a contest in which pregnant women and the embryos and fetuses we nourish in our bodies are represented as lined up on opposing sides. But construing the "interests" of embryos and fetuses as opposed to those of the women whose bodies sustain them makes no sense biologically or socially. A pregnant woman's body is an organic unit, of which the fetus is a part. She shares with her fetus one blood supply as well as other essential functions. Any foods or digestive products, hormones or drugs, or anything else that involves either can have an impact on the other.

This does not mean that pregnant women should scan all their feelings, thoughts, and actions for possible ill effects on the fetus within them. It is probably true that stresses they experience will be transmitted to the fetus, but that includes the stresses and anxieties that would arise from trying to live a life free of stress and anxiety. What it does mean, however, is that it is counterproductive to heap needless stress on pregnant women by worrying them about possible sources of harm to their fetus and by subjecting them to often still-experimental tests and procedures to detect fetal disabilities for which they or the fetus are not specifically predicted to be at risk. Some of today's stresses of pregnancy are evoked by exaggerated concerns and watchfulness intended to avert relatively unlikely risks.

Precisely because anything that is done to a pregnant woman or to her fetus has an impact on both, pregnant women must be the ones to decide whether to carry their pregnancy to term. Only they can know whether they are prepared to sustain the pregnancy as well as the future relationship to their child.

As part of this trend of looking upon embryos and fetuses as though their "interests" could be separated from those of the women whose bodies sustain them, we have been witnessing: (1) prosecutions of pregnant women or of women who have recently given birth for so-called fetal abuse; (2) court-mandated Caesarean sections; and (3) so-called fetal protection practices in which employers bar women of child-bearing age (defined in one instance as 16 to 54 years) from certain kinds of jobs that are said to put a potential fetus at risk, in case these women become pregnant.

I want to look at these three situations and then speculate about why this is happening now and why only in the United States.

"DISTRIBUTING DRUGS TO A MINOR"

Across the nation in the last few years women have been charged with the crime of "distributing drugs to a minor via the umbilical cord" or similarly Orwellian accusations. Since the legal status of the fetus is uncertain, most of these have not stood up in court. Presumably for this reason, in Florida, Jennifer Johnson, a woman who had just birthed her baby, so that it was now legally a born child, was charged with delivering an illicit drug to a minor via the umbilical cord while it was still attached to the cord. Despite the absurdity of this construct, she was convicted.

It seems reasonable to assume that drug use during pregnancy can harm the fetus, though it is not at all clear how dangerous it is. The designation "crack baby" usually is not the result of health-care workers noting behavioral abnormalities in a newborn. It came on the scene because a test was devised that can detect metabolic products resulting from women's drug use close to the time of birth. As a result, babies of mothers who fall into certain "suspect" categories—young, unmarried, poor, of color—are tested more or less routinely and especially in public hospitals. (In one recent instance where the test result was challenged by the young woman and her mother—though not until after the young woman and her baby had been forcibly separated—it turned out that the drugs the test detected were medically administered to the woman during labor.)

A recent article in the medical journal *The Lancet* explains that there are no accurate assessments of the dangers to the fetus of drug use by pregnant women. Its authors show that Canada's Society of Pediatric Research between 1980 and 1989 much more frequently accepted papers for presentation at its annual meeting that documented adverse effects of drug use during pregnancy than papers of the same, or superior, scientific quality that failed to detect any harm. As the authors point out, this kind of bias in publication of research reports makes it impossible to know how great the risk actually is. But even if we go with the common wisdom that drugs taken by pregnant women are likely to harm the fetus, the problem is that very few drug-treatment programs accept women, fewer yet pregnant women, and even fewer, women on Medicaid. In fact, Jennifer Johnson's sentence in Florida included as a condition of her fifteen-year probation that she enter a drug-treatment program, something she had tried, but been unable, to do while pregnant. Another was that she be gainfully employed, something she had also tried, but been unable, to achieve. In other words, she was first victimized by an unresponsive system and then blamed for not availing herself of the remedies she had tried, but been unable, to obtain. She ended up convicted for the government's negligence and neglect.

It is important to realize that just about all the women who have been prosecuted for prenatal injuries to their babies have been poor and of color. Most of them have had little or no prenatal care and have given birth in public or teaching hospitals. None has been a white, suburban drug user, in the care of a private obstetrician. The so-called war on drugs requires public hospitals to report instances of suspected drug use, while private physicians can avoid doing so. Obviously, this policy is counterproductive, since it will make women who could benefit from medical and social services avoid them for fear of being declared unfit to care for their children.

COURT-MANDATED CAESAREANS

In most cases, a woman submits to a Caesarean section when a physician warns that giving birth vaginally would endanger her baby. This is true in this country, as elsewhere, despite the fact that the incidence of Caesarean sections in the United States is higher (about one in four) than in any other industrialized country (it is one in ten in the Netherlands, which has one of the lowest infant mortality rates in the world). But occasionally, a woman refuses on religious grounds, out of fear of surgery, or for other reasons. Whereas physicians and attorneys argued in print as late as 1979 that physicians have it in their power to cajole or threaten, but that cutting someone open against her will constitutes battery, since 1980 obstetricians have been granted court orders for performing Caesarean sections against the explicit will of the pregnant woman. In a number of instances pregnant women have escaped the operation by going underground or by giving birth vaginally before the court order could be implemented. In all of them the babies have been born unharmed, despite the obstetrician's direst predictions. In one case, the physician had testified that without a Caesarean there was a 99 percent risk that the baby would die and a 50 percent risk of death to the woman if she gave birth vaginally. She did, and both she and the baby were fine, which just shows that birth outcomes are notoriously unpredictable, except to say that most births end well. These situations, too, have involved mostly poor women—many of them of color, and whose primary language is not English—presumably because of the range of power imbalances between obstetricians and pregnant women. The prevalent differences in class, race, sex, and education that interfere with communication even in the best of circumstances are exacerbated when the women have unusual religious convictions or are young or unmarried or don't speak the same language as the doctor.

There is hope that a recent decision handed down by the District of Columbia Court of Appeals may make courts more reluctant to order Caesareans against the wishes of pregnant women. On April 26, 1990, this court ruled on the case of Angela Carder, a woman who was pregnant and dying of cancer. After 26 weeks of gestation, when it became clear that she would not survive until the end of her pregnancy, Georgetown Hospital in Washington, D.C., got a court order to perform a Caesarean section against her wishes as well as those of her parents, her husband, and her attending physicians. Both she and the baby died within 24 hours of surgery. The American Public Health Association, the American Medical Association, the American College of Obstetricians and Gynecologists, and other health and civil liberties organizations joined, as friends of the court, in a suit brought against the hospital. The majority of the D.C. Court of Appeals held that "in virtually all cases, the question of what is to be done is to be decided by the patient—the pregnant woman —on behalf of herself and the fetus." Though this decision governs only in the District of Columbia, we can hope that it will lend weight to refusals of surgery by pregnant women in other jurisdictions.

FETAL ENDANGERMENT IN THE WORKPLACE

Reproductive hazards in the workplace were cited in 1977 as grounds for requiring five women at the American Cyanamid plant in Willow Island, West Virginia, to be sterilized, if they wanted to retain jobs paying $225 per week plus substantial overtime instead of being transferred to janitorial jobs at $175 per week with no extras. None of these women was pregnant or planning a pregnancy, yet without the operation, they were considered "potentially pregnant." A number of such situations have arisen since, and currently the U.S. Supreme Court has agreed to hear an appeal against a lower court decision supporting Johnson Controls' "fetal protection" policy. . . .*

---

*Editor's note: In March, 1991 in *UAW v. Johnson Controls, Inc.*, the Supreme Court unanimously declared unconstitutional Johnson Controls' policy of excluding women of childbearing capacity from jobs in which they would be exposed to lead.

The grounds for barring the women have been that the work involves exposure to lead or other chemicals or radiation that could endanger a fetus, despite the fact that these agents also put men's reproductive processes, and specifically sperm, at risk. And these situations have only occurred relative to higher-paying jobs, traditionally occupied by men, to which women have been newcomers. Comparable concerns have not been raised about women employed in traditionally female jobs in which they are routinely exposed to hazardous chemicals or radiation, such as surgical operating room or x-ray technician, nurse, beautician, or indeed, clerical or domestic worker. Whether the women are planning to have children appears to be irrelevant. Rather, fertile women, as a class, are always considered "potentially pregnant." This is just one more way to keep women out of higher-paying jobs by dressing up sex discrimination as fetal protection. Of course, it also enhances the status of the fetus as a person, while relegating all women, pregnant or not, to the status of fetal carriers.

These kinds of "protections" make no sense from the viewpoint of health, because any substance that endangers a fetus is also dangerous for workers—female *and* male. But it is cheaper for companies to fire "potentially pregnant" workers (which means any woman who cannot prove she is infertile) than to clean up the workplace so that it becomes safe for everyone. Employers claim they are barring women because they are afraid of lawsuits should a worker whose baby is born with a disability, claim that disability was brought on by workplace exposure. But, in fact, no such suit has ever been filed and, considering the problems Vietnam veterans have experienced in suits claiming reproductive damages from exposure to Agent Orange and farm workers from exposure to toxic pesticides, such a suit is not likely to present a major risk to employers.

WHY?

So, why are these various fetal protection activities happening and why only in the United States? Indeed, why do many cities and states post warnings in bars and subways, now also appearing on liquor bottles, that read: "Warning! Drinking alcoholic beverages during pregnancy can cause birth defects"? (Note: any alcoholic beverage, no specification of how much or of alcohol content, and no mention of possible detrimental effects on sperm.) No doubt, the antiabortion movement has helped raise "the fetus" to mythic proportions. Perhaps also prenatal technologies, especially ultrasound imaging, have made fetuses seem more real than before. Not so long ago, physicians could find out about a fetus's health only by touching or listening to a pregnant woman's distended belly. Now, in the minds of many people, fetuses have an identity separate from that of the woman whose body harbors them, since it is not unusual for their future parents to know their sex and expected health status.

But that doesn't explain why these activities are peculiar to the United States. Europeans often assume that anything that is accepted in the United States today will be accepted in Europe tomorrow —or, if not tomorrow, the next day. But pregnancy is not like Coca-Cola. It is embedded in culture and framed by a network of economic and social policies. We cannot understand the profound differences between the ways pregnant women are regarded here and in other Western countries unless we face the fact that this country alone among industrialized nations has no coherent programs of health insurance, social and economic supports for pregnant women, maternal and child care, and protection of workers' rights. This has been true since the beginning of this century, but the situation has been aggravated since the dismemberment of the, however meager, social policies that existed before the Reagan era. Recent pronouncements by "drug czar" William Bennett and Secretary of Health and Human Services Louis Sullivan, urging that drug use during pregnancy be taken as prima facie evidence of child abuse, are among the ways the administration is shifting blame for the disastrous economic and social policies that have resulted in huge increases in poverty, homelessness, and unprecedented levels of drug use onto the victims of these policies.

While the economic circumstances of women and children, and especially those of color, are deteriorating and disparities in access to services and in infant mortality rates are increasing, what a fine

trick it is to individualize these conditions and blame women for selfishly putting their fetuses at risk. Yet taking women to court for fetal endangerment creates more low-income women and more babies that will be warehoused in hospitals or shuttled among an insufficient number of adequate foster homes by overloaded social-service systems. These are not solutions. They are merely ways of diverting attention from the enormous systemic problems that have been aggravated by the Reagan-Bush years and of shifting blame for the consequences onto the most vulnerable people.

The editorial in the June [1990] issue of the *American Journal of Public Health* (Vol. 80, No. 6) calls attention to the longstanding correlation of birthweight with parental income and living environment, regardless of maternal age, education, or marital status. The author points out that although U.S. infant mortality has declined since the 1940s, the overall decline slowed during the conservative Eisenhower and Reagan-Bush years. He also shows that, though infant mortality has gone down overall since 1947, Black/white infant mortality *ratios* have risen from 1.61 in 1947 to 2.08 in 1987 (where race, as usual, is to be interpreted as an indicator of the range of disadvantages that result from racism and not as a biological signifier).

Again and again, studies have documented the deleterious effects of adverse economic and social conditions on maternal and infant health. But it continues to be far easier to get money for yet another study than for the policies and programs that could ameliorate or, indeed, eliminate the dismal conditions that jeopardize the health and welfare of women and children.

WHAT TO DO?

We have to take whatever political actions we can to support the efforts of various community organizations and to pressure government agencies at all levels to provide the economic, social, and educational supports that will let women and children live *above* the poverty level, not below it. We need what other industrialized nations have: adequate education, job security, proper nutrition, subsidized housing, universal health care, accessible drug-treatment programs, and so on. The lack of these is responsible for the disproportionate U.S. infant mortality and disability rates, not women's neglectful behavior during pregnancy.

A friend recently suggested that, rather than being sued, pregnant women should sue in the name of "the fetus" for access to the economic, social, and health measures that are necessary for successful pregnancy outcomes. Of course, this concept suffers from the fact that it, too, makes the fetus a person. Furthermore, such suits probably would not hold up in court, since, while the U.S. Constitution guarantees certain freedoms and rights, it does not guarantee the economic and social conditions necessary for everyone to be able to exercise them. Despite this, a well-orchestrated campaign of this sort could educate and politicize people about the shallowness and hypocrisy of the government's supposed efforts at fetal protection, and so could be used to rally support for the kinds of measures that can improve the needlessly dismal economic and social circumstances in which large sectors of the U.S. population live.   [1990]

 87

Killing the Black Body

DOROTHY ROBERTS

The painful, patient, and silent toil of mothers to gain a fee simple title to the bodies of their daughters, the despairing fight, as of an entrapped tigress, to keep hallowed their own persons, would furnish material for epics.
—Anna Julia Cooper, 1893[1]

In 1989, officials in Charleston, South Carolina, initiated a policy of arresting pregnant women whose prenatal tests revealed they were smoking crack. In some cases, a team of police tracked down expectant mothers in the city's poorest neighborhoods. In others, officers invaded the maternity ward to haul away patients in handcuffs and leg irons, hours after giving birth. One woman spent the final weeks of pregnancy detained in a dingy cell in the Charleston County Jail. When she went into labor, she was transported in chains to the hospital, and remained shackled to the bed during the entire delivery. All but one of the four dozen women arrested for prenatal crimes in Charleston were Black.

We are in the midst of an explosion of rhetoric and policies that degrade Black women's reproductive decisions. Poor Black mothers are blamed for perpetuating social problems by transmitting defective genes, irreparable crack damage, and a deviant lifestyle to their children. A controversial editorial in the *Philadelphia Inquirer* suggested coerced contraception as a solution to the Black underclass. Noting that "[t]he main reason more black children are living in poverty is that the people having the most children are the ones least capable of supporting them," the editorial proposed reducing the number of children born to poor Black women by implanting them with the long-acting contraceptive Norplant. This thinking was supported by the best-selling book *The Bell Curve*, which claims that social disparities stem from the higher fertility rates of genetically less intelligent groups, including Blacks.

Along with this disparagement of Black motherhood, policymakers have initiated a new wave of reproductive regulation. The targeting of Black women who use drugs during pregnancy is only one example. State legislatures across the country are considering measures designed to keep women on welfare from having babies—a goal also advanced by Newt Gingrich's Contract with America and then incorporated in the [1996] federal welfare law. The plans range from denying benefits to children born to welfare mothers to mandatory insertion of Norplant as a condition of receiving aid. Many family-planning clinics, with the support of Medicaid, are already encouraging young Black women to keep the risky device implanted in their arms. The emerging agenda is reminiscent of government-sponsored programs as late as the 1970s that coerced poor Black women by the thousands into being sterilized. Meanwhile, a fertility business devoted to helping white middle-class couples to have children is booming.

How can we possibly confront racial injustice in

America without tackling this assault on Black women's procreative freedom? How can we possibly talk about reproductive health policy without addressing race, as well as gender? Yet books on racial justice tend to neglect the subject of reproductive rights; and books on reproductive freedom tend to neglect the influence of race. Few, if any, have addressed the many dimensions of governmental regulation of Black women's childbearing or the impact this repression has had on the way Americans think about reproductive liberty.

The story I tell about reproductive rights differs dramatically from the standard one. In contrast to the account of American women's increasing control over their reproductive decisions, centered on the right to an abortion, I describe a long experience of dehumanizing attempts to control Black women's reproductive lives. The systematic, institutionalized denial of reproductive freedom has uniquely marked Black women's history in America. Considering this history—from slave masters' economic stake in bonded women's fertility to the racist strains of early birth control policy to sterilization abuse of Black women during the 1960s and 1970s to the current campaign to inject Norplant and Depo-Provera in the arms of Black teenagers and welfare mothers—paints a powerful picture of the link between race and reproductive freedom in America.

Several years ago I spoke at a forum in a neighborhood church entitled "Civil Rights Under Attack: Recent Supreme Court Decisions," sponsored by several civil rights organizations. I chose to focus on how the Supreme Court's decision in *Webster v. Reproductive Health Services,* which weakened the holding in *Roe v. Wade* and denied women a right to abortion in publicly funded hospitals, hurt Black women. I linked the decision to a series of current attacks on Black women's reproductive autonomy, including the growing trend to prosecute poor Black mothers for smoking crack while pregnant. When it came time for questions, I was immediately assailed by a man in the audience for risking solidarity around racial issues by interjecting the controversial issue of reproduction. He thought it was dangerous to mention the word "abortion." He said that re-

productive rights was a "white woman's issue," and he advised me to stick to traditional civil rights concerns, such as affirmative action, voting rights, and criminal justice.

While this man felt that the civil rights agenda should leave out reproductive health concerns, the mainstream reproductive rights agenda has neglected Black women's concerns. Public and scholarly debate about reproductive freedom has centered on abortion, often ignoring other important reproductive health policies that are most likely to affect Black women. Yet I came to grasp the importance of women's reproductive autonomy, not from the mainstream abortion rights movement, but from studying the lives of slave women, like those described by Anna Julia Cooper, who fought to retain control over their reproductive lives. The feminist focus on gender and identification of male domination as the source of reproductive repression often overlooks the importance of racism in shaping our understanding of reproductive liberty and the degree of "choice" that women really have.

I want to convince readers that reproduction is an important topic and that it is especially important to Black people. It is important not only because the policies I discuss keep Black women from having children but because these policies persuade people that racial inequality is perpetuated by Black people themselves. The belief that Black procreation is the problem remains a major barrier to radical change in America. It is my hope that by exposing its multiple reincarnations, [I] will help to put this dangerous fallacy to rest. I also want to convince readers to think about reproduction in a new way. These policies affect not only Black Americans but also the very meaning of reproductive freedom.

My objective is to place these issues in their broader political context by exploring how the denial of Black reproductive autonomy serves the interests of white supremacy. I am also interested in the way in which the dominant understanding of reproductive rights has been shaped by racist assumptions about Black procreation. Three central themes, then, run through the history of Black women's reproductive lives. The first is that *regulating*

Black women's reproductive decisions has been a central aspect of racial oppression in America. Not only do these policies injure individual Black women, but they also are a principal means of justifying the perpetuation of a racist social structure. Second, *the control of Black women's reproduction has shaped the meaning of reproductive liberty in America.* The traditional understanding of reproductive freedom has had to accommodate practices that blatantly deny Black women control over critical decisions about their bodies. Highlighting the racial dimensions of contemporary debates such as welfare reform, the safety of Norplant, public funding of abortion, and the morality of new reproductive technologies is like shaking up a kaleidoscope and taking another look.

Finally, in light of the first two themes, *we need to reconsider the meaning of reproductive liberty to take into account its relationship to racial oppression.* While Black women's stories are sometimes inserted as an aside in deliberations about reproductive issues, I place them at the center of this reconstructive project. How does Black women's experience change the current interpretation of reproductive freedom? The dominant notion of reproductive liberty is flawed in several ways. It is limited by the liberal ideals of individual autonomy and freedom from government interference; it is primarily concerned with the interests of white, middle-class women; and it is focused on the right to abortion. The full extent of many Americans' conception of reproductive freedom is the Constitution's protection against laws that ban abortion. I suggest an expanded and less individualistic conception of reproductive liberty that recognizes control of reproduction as a critical means of racial oppression and liberation in America. I do not deny the importance of autonomy over one's own reproductive life, but I also recognize that reproductive policy affects the status of entire groups. Reproductive liberty must encompass more than the protection of an individual woman's choice to end her pregnancy. It must encompass the full range of procreative activities, including the ability to bear a child, and it must acknowledge that we make reproductive decisions within a social context, including inequalities of wealth and power. *Re-productive freedom is a matter of social justice,* not individual choice.   [1997]

NOTES

1. Quoted in Bert James Loewenberg and Ruth Bogin, eds., *Black Women in Nineteenth-Century American Life* (University Park: Pennsylvania State University Press, 1976), p. 329. Free Black women purchased their daughters and sisters from white slave masters to enable them to escape sexual abuse. A fee simple title gives the holder absolute ownership of property.

 88

Developing a Reproductive Rights Agenda for the Next Century

KATHRYN KOLBERT

This is a call for a reproductive rights agenda for the next century. It suggests a process for developing a comprehensive approach to reproductive rights issues and outlines an agenda that can serve as a starting point for further discussions. Defining our goals is essential to achieving them. By taking the time now to articulate our vision of the future and grapple with the many hard questions that surround reproduction—questions about sexuality, childbearing, and parenting—we can develop and build a consensus about the basic premises of our work. We will then be better able to set priorities and develop collective strategies to achieve our goals.

1. FREEDOM AND LEGAL RIGHTS TO MAKE VOLUNTARY DECISIONS

Our law[s] and social institutions must enable women to make voluntary, thoughtful, and deliberate choices about their own sexuality, childbearing, and parenting and must respect the decisions that women make for themselves and their families.

All persons must have the legal right to make voluntary and informed decisions. Our legal system cannot be used to deprive women of equal access to a full range of reproductive options. Nor can it be used to coerce women's reproductive behavior or choices, regardless of age, ancestry, creed, disability, economic status, marital status, national origin, parental status, race, sex, or sexual orientation.

2. COMPREHENSIVE, QUALITY, AND AFFORDABLE HEALTH CARE AND HUMAN SERVICES

A. A Full Range of Reproductive Options

Women must have access to the full range of safe, effective, and affordable birth control methods, and medical research must develop better, safer methods. Men as well as women must assume responsibility for birth control, and technologies must be developed that will enable them to do so.

Women who find themselves pregnant must have access to quality counseling to determine their reproductive choices. If they choose to terminate their pregnancies, they must have access to all safe and affordable abortion methods and related health services at or near their homes or jobs.

Women who choose to carry a pregnancy to term must have access to quality prenatal care, genetic screening and counseling, childbirth and postpartum care, and pediatric care for their children.

Pregnant women, especially poor women and women in Black, Hispanic, and Native American communities who are experiencing a crisis of drug and alcohol abuse, must be provided reproductive health, maternity, and addiction services in an environment that is supportive and free of stigma. They must be fully informed of the risks to themselves and their infants in a way that is caring and nonpunitive and that helps them to deal with additional problems of poverty, poor housing, and male violence.

All women must have access to confidential and quality care for sexually transmitted diseases. Women who are HIV positive or at risk for AIDS who are or may become pregnant have the same right to noncoercive counseling and choice as women with other disabilities or possible fetal impairments. AIDS testing, like prenatal diagnosis, should be offered on an anonymous or confidential and voluntary basis and within a program of counseling and education that respects all persons' rights to express their sexuality.

B. Comprehensive Care

Because reproductive choice includes the ability to care for as well as bear children, comprehensive health care and human services must be available to all families. Whether offered through public or private health programs, the services must be physically accessible—to disabled and rural women, to those dependent on public transportation, to those who work nights—and must be affordable to all.

C. Safe and Quality Care

Health and human services including all reproductive health services should focus on health, wellness, and the prevention of problems, as well as on the cure and amelioration of problems, and should be provided in a culturally supportive manner, in an environment that is free from violence, deception, and fraud. Women should define their own needs and be enabled through the use of these services to make positive changes in their lives.

Medical practitioners must not adopt unnecessary or invasive practices that endanger women's lives or health and must not use their power or authority to coerce reproductive decisions. For example, procedures such as sterilization, hysterectomy, amniocentesis, ultrasound, Caesarean section, or electronic fetal monitoring should be used only when medically appropriate. To prevent further medical abuse, the crisis in malpractice and liability insurance which has forced medical practitioners to adopt unnecessary or invasive practices in order to protect against legal liability must be addressed without leaving women unprotected.

D. Informed Consent and Informed Refusal

Principles of informed consent and informed refusal must be an intrinsic part of the decision making process and must be backed up by supportive counseling. Only when women have full knowledge about the ramifications of accepting or rejecting a particular health option, including explanations of medical procedures and their risks and benefits in understandable terms in the woman's own language, can decisions be voluntary. At the same time, women must have the option of refusing particular types of information—e.g., the sex of the child after amniocentesis. In addition, informed consent must not become a pretext for harassment or discouragement of a particular reproductive choice, such as abortion or sterilization.

3. SEXUALITY, REPRODUCTIVE, AND LIFE SKILL EDUCATION

Women, particularly teenage women, often become pregnant because they lack essential knowledge about sex, pregnancy, and contraception. Persons of all ages must have sufficient information about their sexuality and reproductive health to make intelligent decisions about sexuality, childbearing, and parenting. Information about how their bodies work, varied forms of sexuality, contraceptives, and sexually transmitted diseases must be provided to all persons at accessible locations, in a manner that is understandable and age-appropriate. Men as well as women must be taught that they have equal responsibility to be well informed about and to participate fully in choices related to sexual behavior, reproduction, and parenting.

It is especially important that women and men should be fully informed about the risks and pathology of AIDS and the necessity of using condoms or other "safe sex" practices. Public education campaigns to prevent the spread of HIV should be administered in a context that respects all persons' needs to express their sexuality, both inside and outside the traditional framework of marriage and heterosexuality.

But education about sexuality and reproduction is only a part of the solution. Women, especially young women, often choose to become mothers because they have no realistic possibilities of advancement in society. Our educational system must provide women with the opportunity to set ambitious goals for their future, and the background to make these goals a reality, enabling women to choose motherhood when it is the best choice for them.

4. FREEDOM TO EXPRESS ONE'S SEXUALITY, AND TO ADOPT VARIED FAMILY ARRANGEMENTS OR LIFESTYLES

If women and men are coerced or socialized into heterosexual relationships, or if childbearing or childrearing is permissible only within heterosexual relationships, then people's ability to make intimate decisions about reproduction, as well as about sexuality and parenting, is constrained. Society must not discriminate against, stigmatize, or penalize persons on the basis of their sexuality or sexual preference. Moreover, varied forms of sexual expression including heterosexuality, bisexuality, and homosexuality must be accepted as normal human responses, with positive meaning and value.

Women must be free to say no to sexuality, childbearing, and parenting as they are to choose these options. Women must be free to express their sexuality in whatever noncoercive forms they choose, without recriminations, without effect on their value in our society or their self-esteem, and without fear of becoming pregnant if they do not wish to be so.

Varied forms of family and living arrangements must be acceptable choices. When women choose to parent outside of marriage, or to live collectively or inter-generationally, these choices must be respected. The legal barriers to and social stigma of unwed parenthood, inter-racial childbearing, or lesbian motherhood must be eliminated if true reproductive choice for all women is to be an option. Moreover, since pressure to have children is often brought about because there are few other acceptable adult-child relationships, we must encourage alternative forms of adult-child interaction.

5. ECONOMIC EQUITY AND REPRODUCTION

In order that all persons have equal opportunity to become parents, they must have the means to do so.

The economic barriers to alternative forms of reproduction, such as the cost of adoption, donor insemination, in vitro fertilization, or embryo transfer must be lessened for low-income women through fee reduction or subsidies.

If we want a society in which children are truly an option, women must have the economic means to raise their children—to provide adequate food, clothing, and shelter, and quality child care and education. We must work to eliminate the feminization of poverty that today so limits women's reproductive options and work to create jobs and a welfare system that afford dignity to all and which is free from coercive childbearing policies. Without an economy and social services that support women, women are unable to support their children and families; responsible parenting is possible only in a society that provides the necessary resources for parents.

Public policies must be enacted that will ease the burdens of working parents, caught between responsibilities of job and home. In addition to quality, affordable child care services, a reproductive rights agenda requires gender-neutral pregnancy and child care leave provisions and flexible work schedules available without penalty to fathers as well as mothers. To make these provisions available to all working parents and not just the most privileged, leave time must be paid. Corporate and governmental employers should be encouraged to initiate internal education programs, similar to those currently under way regarding sexual harassment, to change employee attitudes about male and same-sex partner participation in prenatal and child care tasks.

6. FREEDOM FROM VIOLENCE

Because fear of violence by a spouse or partner and fear of sexual assault limit everyone's ability to make intimate decisions, all persons must be free to choose whether, when, and with whom they have sex and have children, and to raise their children without fear of sexual assault, abuse, violence, or harassment in their homes, on the streets, or at their jobs.

7. FREEDOM FROM REPRODUCTIVE HAZARDS

All persons must be free from reproductive hazards within the environment, in their homes, and at their workplaces. Rather than attempting to repair the effects of reproductive hazards by treating infertility or disease or by banning fertile women from hazardous worksites (and consequently from higher paying jobs), we must eliminate the hazards.

8. FAMILY LAW AND SERVICES

In order to enable all persons to freely form the arrangements in which they parent, they must be able to establish and terminate these arrangements without economic and social penalty. Fair and equitable marriage, domestic partnership, divorce, child support, and child custody laws must be available and enforceable by women whose marriage or other family arrangements have dissolved or proven inadequate. In the event of the death or disability of both of a child's parents, governmental and community resources must provide for the well-being of the child. In the event of child abuse or neglect, governmental and community resources must provide necessary medical, social, and legal services to keep families together.

9. POLITICAL PARTICIPATION

All persons must have the full right to express their views and, through organized, collective, and nonviolent action, to work actively for positive, systematic changes that will guarantee reproductive choice. Women must have the opportunity to be involved at all levels of the political process and within all political parties and be encouraged to take positions of leadership.   [1998]

PART VI

The Differences Among Us: Divisions and Connections

We are encouraged, in our society, to see ourselves as individuals, whose progress in the world is determined by our own merits and efforts. As we have seen, however, the deeply rooted gender bias that shapes our institutions and culture stunts our possibilities as women. Gender, however, is only one of many systems of inequality that structure our institutions and shape our experience. As Lee Bell has pointed out,

> One of the privileges of dominant group status is the luxury to see oneself as an individual. A white man, for example, is rarely defined by whiteness or maleness. If he does well on his job, he is acknowledged as a highly qualified individual. If he does poorly, the blame is attributed to him alone. Those in subordinated groups, however, can never fully escape being defined by their social group memberships. A Puerto Rican woman in the U.S. mainland, for example, may wish to be viewed as an individual and acknowledged for her personal talents and abilities. Yet she can never fully escape the dominant society's assumptions about her racial/ethnic group, language, and gender. If she excels in her work, she may be seen as atypical or exceptional. If she does poorly, she may be seen as representative of the limitations of the group. In either case, she rises or falls not on the basis of individual qualities alone, but always also partly as a member of her group(s).[1]

As we can see from this example, a woman who is also a member of another subordinate group is affected simultaneously by multiple identities that interact with each other. Some women are limited by oppression and concurrently benefit from advantages. For example, an affluent African-American woman will gain from the privileges of social class while she simultaneously faces discrimination because of her race and sex. The ways that race and gender discrimination play out in the life of a poor African-American woman will be very different. Similarly, a white lesbian, while enduring the discrimination of a heterosexist society, benefits from being white in a racist culture. Jewish women benefit from white privilege while sometimes being subject to anti-Semitism. By deepening our understanding of various forms of oppression and privilege and the ways they operate in women's lives, we can better address the needs of all women, draw on our various resources, and work together to develop an inclusive feminist vision. Unless we eradicate all forms of domination, we will not be able to create a world in which all women can be free to determine their lives.

Why, many people ask, is it necessary to focus on difference? Why can't we focus on our common humanity or our common experiences as women? In a society in which some group's interests, norms, and values are dominant, suppressing difference means that the experience of people who are not among the dominant group is rendered invisible. In the United States, male, white, heterosexual, middle-class, youthful, and able-bodied norms have been dominant, and other people's experience is marginalized.

---

[1]Lee Anne Bell, "Theoretical Perspectives for Social Justice Education," in *Teaching Diversity and Social Justice, A Sourcebook.* Maurianne Adams, Lee Anne Bell, and Pat Griffin, eds. (New York: Routledge, 1997).

Tightly interwoven in the fabric of our society, inequalities of power and re-sources and discriminatory attitudes create and sustain various systems of dominance and subordination. Laws and practices have structured our various institutions to accord advantages to dominant groups and deny them to members of subordinate groups. Discriminatory attitudes and ideas justify and perpetuate these inequalities. In *The Second Sex,* her pathbreaking book about the subordination of women, Si-mone de Beauvoir suggested that dominant groups tend to see themselves as the sub-ject relegating subordinate groups to the status of "other," inessential, marginal and deviant. The media, literature, language, and prevailing attitudes of the culture de-pict the dominant groups as representing the universal human. Stereotypes of sub-ordinate groups rob members of their individuality, even when they are ostensibly positive—for example, the idea that old women are all grandmotherly, that African-American women are all strong, that Native American women are all spiritual.

This part focuses particularly on the effects of race, class, sexual orientation, and age on women's experience and relationships among women. It examines the ways institutional discrimination, as well as pervasive prejudice, can prevent us from understanding the experiences we have in common and appreciating the differences among us as a resource. Some of the articles in this part reveal these divisions by fo-cusing on the often painful dynamics in our daily lives that reinforce them. Because the barriers between women are hardened by ignorance, Part VI includes a large number of first-person and fictional accounts that present women's experiences through their own eyes.

Racism affects all of us, influencing the way we relate to each other and the way we see the world. Because our society marginalizes people of color, white people often think their experience is universal and don't recognize or value other people's activities, needs, or contributions. Adrienne Rich, in an essay called "Disloyal to Civilization," describes what she calls white "solipsism." This, she argues, is "not the consciously held *belief* that one race is inherently superior to all others, but a tunnel-vision which simply does not see non-white experience or existence as pre-cious or significant, unless in spasmodic, impotent guilt reflexes . . ." She argues that to get beyond this, white women need to listen closely to what the "politics of skin color" have meant to women of color.[2] This would involve understanding the ways that racism has kept women from working effectively against sexism, such as when women excluded African-American women from the early twentieth-century suffrage organizations in order to avoid alienating white racist Southerners.

The class system has functioned in similar ways. Economic inequality both shapes our social institutions and is reinforced by them. For example, studies have shown that students from well-funded school districts perform better than those from poorly funded school districts, and that academic achievement translates into differences in skill level and employability. In 1997, the average school in a wealthy

---

[2] Adrienne Rich, "Disloyal to Civilization," in *Lies, Secrets and Silence,* pp. 306 and 307.

district received 24% more funding than the average school in a poor district, and in some states the disparity is even wider.[3]

Women who have greater access to education, health care, employment opportunities, and other resources have sometimes worked for their own advancement, excluding and ignoring poor women. For example, middle- and upper-class women in Puerto Rico in the 1920s advanced a law which gave the right to vote only to literate women over 21, excluding thousands of illiterate women even though many of them had been working for decades to win suffrage. Today, defending the legal right to abortion without also demanding *access* to abortion for women who depend on welfare and public health clinics would sacrifice the reproductive rights of countless women. In the past 20 years, increasing numbers of women in the U.S. have entered previously male-dominated professions such as business, law, and medicine, yet large numbers of women continue to work in dead-end, low-wage jobs, thus widening class divisions.

Prejudice and discrimination against lesbians in our culture are a reflection of what Adrienne Rich has called "compulsory heterosexuality," a complex web of laws, practices, and attitudes that enforce heterosexuality as a norm and render love relationships between people of the same sex "deviant."[4] As a result of institutional discrimination against lesbians and gay men—sometimes called heterosexism—lesbian mothers have been denied custody of their children, lesbian partners cannot always get health coverage for each other, and lesbians have been fired from jobs because of their sexual orientation. Because of the heavy sanctions, many lesbians have hidden their sexual orientation from employers, family, and friends, and prejudice thrives in an atmosphere in which lesbian lives are hidden. We rarely learn about the rich history of women who have chosen to create lives with each other. As a result, myths and misconceptions about lesbians are numerous in our culture.

Taboos against love between women have constrained the lives of all women. Fear of being labeled a lesbian often deters women from acting and speaking freely. For example, women have sometimes been afraid to develop close friendships because of the fear of being labeled a lesbian, and have sometimes been hesitant to participate in activities that violate the norms of "femininity." As long as the accusation "what are you, some kind of dyke?" still has the power to intimidate women, no woman can be free. Freedom to love whomever we choose is a central ingredient of feminism.

For women in our society, aging brings with it a cluster of social taboos and institutional inequities that we call ageism. As Susan Sontag has pointed out, "for a woman to be obliged to state her age, after 'a certain age,' is always a miniature ordeal." Once she passes that certain age, Sontag argues, a woman's age is "some-

---

[3] United States General Accounting Office Report Letter: 1
[4] Adrienne Rich, "Compulsory Heterosexuality and Lesbian Existence," *Signs*, 5(4), pp. 631–660.

thing of a dirty secret."[5] While aging men are often considered "distinguished," women are offered an array of camouflage products—cosmetics, surgery, and hair colorings—to prevent them from being seen as old in a culture that equates female beauty with youthfulness. As Cynthia Rich points out, even language trivializes old women's actions. While usually not meant maliciously, expressions such as "little old lady" demean and belittle old women.

Because of the disadvantaged position of women in the work force and the lack of financial compensation for women's work in the home, far more women over 65 live in poverty than their male contemporaries. Women living alone are disproportionately represented among the elderly poor, and their poverty often results in inadequate health care.

Improving the position of all women in the work force will address some of these problems, but changes in social policy are required to provide adequate health care and pensions for people who have spent much of their lives outside the work force, and to ensure that affordable housing is available for the thousands of old women living alone.

Becoming aware of the institutional inequities in our society encourages us to challenge what Peggy McIntosh has described as "the myth of meritocracy," the belief that one's success is purely the result of one's own abilities and efforts, unaffected by the advantages or disadvantages that accrue to various social groups. Recognizing the ways that systems of power and privilege enhance the lives of members of advantaged groups can help us to understand better the way they restrict the lives of people without these privileges.

The stories, essays, and poems in this Part address the many dimensions of prejudice and institutional discrimination as they affect women. They also reveal some of the attitudes that have prevented women from honestly addressing the differences among us, such as the assumptions that some people's experience is universal while others is marginal and deviant, the fear of conflict, and the desire to feel safe. By seeing differences from a variety of viewpoints, we can begin to move beyond the distrust of difference that permeates our culture and use our experiences to enrich our analysis of society and understanding of women's lives.

---

[5] Susan Sontag, "The Double Standard of Aging," in *The Other Within Us: Feminist Explorations of Women and Aging.* Marilyn Pearsall, ed. (Boulder: Westview Press, 1997).

Take a Closer Look: Racism in Women's Lives

Racism in our society operates on many levels and implicates all of us, whether we are conscious of it or not. Despite the advances of the civil rights movement, people of color continue to encounter racism both in institutions and among individuals. Because our society remains highly segregated by race and ethnicity, most of us grow up ignorant of the experiences and feelings of other groups of people. Beverly Daniel Tatum's article, which begins this section, explores the meaning of racism for all of us and makes useful distinctions between individual prejudice and racism, the system of advantages and disadvantages based on race that structures our social institutions. Understanding the ways that racism affects us requires us to recognize differences, despite pervasive pressure in our society to ignore them, as described in Adrienne Su's essay, "Codes of Conduct."

Many of the pieces in this section tell of the scars of racism through the eyes of its victims. They enable us to see both the enormously destructive power of racism and the will of the human spirit to resist it. They also reveal various forms that racism can take. The authors of the first two poems demonstrate the ways that racial stereotypes obliterate their individuality. "Take a Closer Look" and the excerpt from Angela Davis's *Autobiography* describe the agony of children trying to develop a sense of themselves in a racist world. While struggling to survive the daily hostility and contempt of white people in the South in the 1940s and 1950s, Davis developed methods of maintaining her dignity and self-respect.

 89

Defining Racism: "Can We Talk?"

BEVERLY DANIEL TATUM

The impact of racism begins early. Even in our preschool years, we are exposed to misinformation about people different from ourselves. Many of us grew up in neighborhoods where we had limited opportunities to interact with people different from our own families. When I ask my college students,

"How many of you grew up in neighborhoods where most of the people were from the same racial group as your own?" almost every hand goes up. There is still a great deal of social segregation in our communities. Consequently, most of the early information we receive about "others"—people racially, religiously, or socioeconomically different from ourselves—does not come as the result of firsthand experience. The secondhand information we do receive has often been distorted, shaped by cultural stereotypes, and left incomplete.

Some examples will highlight this process. Several years ago one of my students conducted a research project investigating preschoolers' conceptions of Native Americans.[1] Using children at a local day care center as her participants, she asked these three- and four-year-olds to draw a picture of a Native American. Most children were stumped by her request. They didn't know what a Native American was. But when she rephrased the question and asked them to draw a picture of an Indian, they readily complied. Almost every picture included one central feature: feathers. In fact, many of them also included a weapon—a knife or tomahawk—and depicted the person in violent or aggressive terms. Though this group of children, almost all of whom were White, did not live near a large Native American population and probably had had little if any personal interaction with American Indians, they all had internalized an image of what Indians were like. How did they know? Cartoon images, in particular the Disney movie *Peter Pan,* were cited by the children as their number-one source of information. At the age of three, these children already had a set of stereotypes in place. Though I would not describe three-year-olds as prejudiced, the stereotypes to which they have been exposed become the foundation for the adult prejudices so many of us have.

Sometimes the assumptions we make about others come not from what we have been told or what we have seen on television or in books, but rather from what we have *not* been told. The distortion of historical information about people of color leads young people (and older people, too) to make assumptions that may go unchallenged for a long time. Consider this conversation between two White students following a discussion about the cultural transmission of racism:

"Yeah, I just found out that Cleopatra was actually a Black woman."

"What?"

The first student went on to explain her newly learned information. The second student exclaimed in disbelief, "That can't be true. Cleopatra was beautiful!"

What had this young woman learned about who in our society is considered beautiful and who is not? Had she conjured up images of Elizabeth Taylor when she thought of Cleopatra? The new information her classmate had shared and her own deeply ingrained assumptions about who is beautiful and who is not were too incongruous to allow her to assimilate the information at that moment.

Omitted information can have similar effects. For example, another young woman, preparing to be a high school English teacher, expressed her dismay that she had never learned about any Black authors in any of her English courses. How was she to teach about them to her future students when she hadn't learned about them herself? A White male student in the class responded to this discussion with frustration in his response journal, writing "It's not my fault that Blacks don't write books." Had one of his elementary, high school, or college teachers ever told him that there were no Black writers? Probably not. Yet because he had never been exposed to Black authors, he had drawn his own conclusions that there were none.

Stereotypes, omissions, and distortions all contribute to the development of prejudice. *Prejudice* is a preconceived judgment or opinion, usually based on limited information. I assume that we all have prejudices, not because we want them, but simply because we are so continually exposed to misinformation about others. Though I have often heard students or workshop participants describe someone as not having "a prejudiced bone in his body," I usually suggest they look again. Prejudice is one of the inescapable consequences of living in a racist society. Cultural racism—the cultural images and messages that affirm the assumed superiority of Whites and the assumed inferiority of people of color—is like smog in the air. Sometimes it is so thick it is visible, other times it is less apparent, but always, day in and day out, we are breathing it in. None of us would introduce ourselves as "smog-breathers" (and most of us don't want to be described as prejudiced), but if we live in a smoggy place, how can we avoid breathing the air? If we live in an environment in which we are bombarded with stereotypical images in the media, are frequently exposed to the ethnic jokes of friends and family members, and are rarely informed of the accomplishments of oppressed groups, we will develop the negative categorizations of those groups that form the basis of prejudice.

People of color as well as Whites develop these categorizations. Even a member of the stereotyped group may internalize the stereotypical categories about his or her own group to some degree. In fact, this process happens so frequently that it has a name, *internalized oppression*.

Certainly some people are more prejudiced than others, actively embracing and perpetuating negative and hateful images of those who are different from themselves. When we claim to be free of prejudice, perhaps what we are really saying is that we are not hatemongers. But none of us is completely innocent. Prejudice is an integral part of our socialization, and it is not our fault. Just as the preschoolers my student interviewed are not to blame for the negative messages they internalized, we are not at fault for the stereotypes, distortions, and omissions that shaped our thinking as we grew up.

To say that it is not our fault does not relieve us of responsibility, however. We may not have polluted the air, but we need to take responsibility, along with others, for cleaning it up. Each of us needs to look at our own behavior. Am I perpetuating and reinforcing the negative messages so pervasive in our culture, or am I seeking to challenge them? If I have not been exposed to positive images of marginalized groups, am I seeking them out, expanding my own knowledge base for myself and my children? Am I acknowledging and examining my own prejudices, my own rigid categorizations of others, thereby minimizing the adverse impact they might have on my interactions with those I have categorized? Unless we engage in these and other conscious acts of reflection and reeducation, we easily repeat the process with our children. We teach what we were taught. The unexamined prejudices of the parents are passed on to the children. It is not our fault, but it is our responsibility to interrupt this cycle.

RACISM: A SYSTEM OF ADVANTAGE BASED ON RACE

Many people use the terms *prejudice* and *racism* interchangeably. I do not, and I think it is important to make a distinction. In his book *Portraits of White Racism*, David Wellman argues convincingly that limiting our understanding of racism to prejudice does not offer a sufficient explanation for the persistence of racism. He defines racism as a "system of advantage based on race."[2] In illustrating this definition, he provides example after example of how Whites defend their racial advantage—access to better schools, housing, jobs—even when they do not embrace overtly prejudicial thinking. Racism cannot be fully explained as an expression of prejudice alone.

This definition of racism is useful because it allows us to see that racism, like other forms of oppression, is not only a personal ideology based on racial prejudice, but a *system* involving cultural messages and institutional policies and practices as well as the beliefs and actions of individuals. In the context of the United States, this system clearly operates to the advantage of Whites and to the disadvantage of people of color. Another related definition of racism, commonly used by antiracist educators and consultants, is "prejudice plus power." Racial prejudice when combined with social power—access to social, cultural, and economic resources and decision-making—leads to the institutionalization of racist policies and practices. While I think this definition also captures the idea that racism is more than individual beliefs and attitudes, I prefer Wellman's definition because the idea of systematic advantage and disadvantage is critical to an understanding of how racism operates in American society.

In addition, I find that many of my White students and workshop participants do not feel powerful. Defining racism as prejudice plus power has little personal relevance. For some, their response to this definition is the following: "I'm not really prejudiced, and I have no power, so racism has nothing to do with me." However, most White people, if they are really being honest with themselves, can see that there are advantages to being White in the United States. Despite the current rhetoric about affirmative action and "reverse racism," every social indicator, from salary to life expectancy, reveals the advantages of being White.[3]

The systematic advantages of being White are often referred to as White privilege. In a now well-known article, "White Privilege: Unpacking the Invisible Knapsack," Peggy McIntosh, a White feminist scholar, identified a long list of societal privileges that she received simply because she was White.[4] She did not ask for them, and it is important to note that she hadn't always noticed that she was receiving them. They included major and minor advantages. Of course she enjoyed greater access to jobs and housing. But she also was able to shop in department stores without being followed by suspicious salespeople and could always find appropriate hair care products and makeup in any drugstore. She could send her child to school confident that the teacher would not discriminate against him on the basis of race. She could also be late for meetings, and talk with her mouth full, fairly confident that these behaviors would not be attributed to the fact that she was White. She could express an opinion in a meeting or in print and not have it labeled the "White" viewpoint. In other words, she was more often than not viewed as an individual, rather than as a member of a racial group.

The article rings true for most White readers, many of whom may have never considered the benefits of being White. It's one thing to have enough awareness of racism to describe the ways that people of color are disadvantaged by it. But this new understanding of racism is more elusive. In very concrete terms, it means that if a person of color is the victim of housing discrimination, the apartment that would otherwise have been rented to that person of color is still available for a White person. The White tenant is, knowingly or unknowingly, the beneficiary of racism, a system of advantage based on race. The unsuspecting tenant is not to blame for the prior discrimination, but she benefits from it anyway.

For many Whites, this new awareness of the benefits of a racist system elicits considerable pain, often accompanied by feelings of anger and guilt. These uncomfortable emotions can hinder further discussion. We all like to think that we deserve the good things we have received, and that others, too, get what they deserve. Social psychologists call this tendency a "belief in a just world."[5] Racism directly contradicts such notions of justice.

Understanding racism as a system of avantage based on race is antithetical to traditional notions of an American meritocracy. For those who have internalized this myth, this definition generates considerable discomfort. It is more comfortable simply to think of racism as a particular form of prejudice. Notions of power or privilege do not have to be addressed when our understanding of racism is constructed in that way.

The discomfort generated when a systemic definition of racism is introduced is usually quite visible in the workshops I lead. Someone in the group is usually quick to point out that this is not the definition you will find in most dictionaries. I reply, "Who wrote the dictionary?" I am not being facetious with this response. Whose interests are served by a "prejudice only" definition of racism? It is important to understand that the system of advantage is perpetuated when we do not acknowledge its existence.

RACISM: FOR WHITES ONLY?

Frequently someone will say, "You keep talking about White people. People of color can be racist, too." I once asked a White teacher what it would mean to her if a student or parent of color accused her of being racist. She said she would feel as though she had been punched in the stomach or called a "low-life scum." She is not alone in this feeling. The word *racist* holds a lot of emotional power. For many White people, to be called racist is the ultimate insult. The idea that this term might only be applied to Whites becomes highly problematic for after all, can't people of color be "low-life scum" too?

Of course, people of any racial group can hold hateful attitudes and behave in racially discriminatory and bigoted ways. We can all cite examples of horrible hate crimes which have been perpetrated by people of color as well as Whites. Hateful behavior is hateful behavior no matter who does it. But when I am asked, "Can people of color be racist?" I reply, "The answer depends on your definition of racism." If one defines racism as racial prejudice, the answer is yes. People of color can and do have racial prejudices. However, if one defines racism as a system of advantage based on race, the answer is no. People of color are not racist because they do not systematically benefit from racism. And equally important, there is no systematic cultural and institutional support or sanction for the racial bigotry of people of color. In my view, reserving the term *racist* only for behaviors committed by Whites in the context of a White-dominated society is a way of acknowledging the ever-present power differential afforded Whites by the culture and institutions that make up the system of advantage and continue to reinforce notions of White superiority. (Using the same logic, I reserve the word *sexist* for men. Though women can and do have gender-based prejudices, only men systematically benefit from sexism.)

Despite my best efforts to explain my thinking on this point, there are some who will be troubled, perhaps even incensed, by my response. To call the racially motivated acts of a person of color acts of racial bigotry and to describe similar acts committed by Whites as racist will make no sense to some people, including some people of color. To those, I will respectfully say, "We can agree to disagree." At moments like these, it is not agreement that is essential, but clarity. Even if you don't like the definition of racism I am using, hopefully you are now clear about what it is. If I also understand how you are using the term, our conversation can continue—despite our disagreement.

Another provocative question I'm often asked is "Are you saying all Whites are racist?" When asked this question, I again remember that White teacher's response, and I am conscious that perhaps the question I am really being asked is, "Are you saying all Whites are bad people?" The answer to that question is of course not. However, all White people, intentionally or unintentionally, do benefit from racism. A more relevant question is what are White people as individuals doing to interrupt racism? For many White people, the image of a racist is a hood-wearing Klan member or a name-calling Archie Bunker figure. These images represent what might be called *active racism*, blatant, intentional acts of racial bigotry and discrimination. *Passive racism* is more subtle and can be seen in the collusion of laughing when a racist joke is told, of letting exclusionary hiring practices go unchallenged, of accepting as appropriate the omissions of people of color from the curriculum, and of avoiding difficult race-related issues. Because racism is so ingrained in

the fabric of American institutions, it is easily self-perpetuating.[6] All that is required to maintain it is business as usual.

I sometimes visualize the ongoing cycle of racism as a moving walkway at the airport. Active racist behavior is equivalent to walking fast on the conveyor belt. The person engaged in active racist behavior has identified with the ideology of White supremacy and is moving with it. Passive racist behavior is equivalent to standing still on the walkway. No overt effort is being made, but the conveyor belt moves the bystanders along to the same destination as those who are actively walking. Some of the bystanders may feel the motion of the conveyor belt, see the active racists ahead of them, and choose to turn around, unwilling to go to the same destination as the White supremacists. But unless they are walking actively in the opposite direction at a speed faster than the conveyor belt—unless they are actively antiracist—they will find themselves carried along with the others.

So, not all Whites are actively racist. Many are passively racist. Some, though not enough, are actively antiracist. The relevant question is not whether all Whites are racist, but how we can move more White people from a position of active or passive racism to one of active antiracism? The task of interrupting racism is obviously not the task of Whites alone. But the fact of White privilege means that Whites have greater access to the societal institutions in need of transformation. To whom much is given, much is required.

It is important to acknowledge that while all Whites benefit from racism, they do not all benefit equally. Other factors, such as socioeconomic status, gender, age, religious affiliation, sexual orientation, mental and physical ability, also play a role in our access to social influence and power. A White woman on welfare is not privileged to the same extent as a wealthy White heterosexual man. In her case, the systematic disadvantages of sexism and classism intersect with her White privilege, but the privilege is still there. This point was brought home to me in a 1994 study conducted by a Mount Holyoke graduate student, Phyllis Wentworth.[7] Wentworth interviewed a group of female college students, who were both older than their peers and were the first members of their families to attend college, about the pathways that led them to college. All of the women interviewed were White, from working-class backgrounds, from families where women were expected to graduate from high school and get married or get a job. Several had experienced abusive relationships and other personal difficulties prior to coming to college. Yet their experiences were punctuated by "good luck" stories of apartments obtained without a deposit, good jobs offered without experience or extensive reference checks, and encouragement provided by willing mentors. While the women acknowledged their good fortune, none of them discussed their Whiteness. They had not considered the possibility that being White had worked in their favor and helped give them the benefit of the doubt at critical junctures. This study clearly showed that even under difficult circumstances, White privilege was still operating.

It is also true that not all people of color are equally targeted by racism. We all have multiple identities that shape our experience. I can describe myself as a light-skinned, well-educated, heterosexual, able-bodied, Christian African American woman raised in a middle-class suburb. As an African American woman, I am systematically disadvantaged by race and by gender, but I systematically receive benefits in the other categories, which then mediate my experience of racism and sexism. When one is targeted by multiple isms—racism, sexism, classism, heterosexism, ableism, anti-Semitism, ageism—in whatever combination, the effect is intensified. The particular combination of racism and classism in many communities of color is life-threatening. Nonetheless, when I, the middle-class Black mother of two sons, read another story about a Black man's unlucky encounter with a White police officer's deadly force, I am reminded that racism by itself can kill.   [1997]

NOTES

1. Approximately 75 percent of all Black college students attend predominantly White colleges. For a discussion of Black college attendance and retention at White colleges in comparison to historically Black colleges, see W. R. Allen, "The color of success: African-American college stu-

dent outcomes at predominantly White and historically Black public colleges and universities," *Harvard Educational Review* 62, no. 1 (1992): 26–44.

2. For a detailed account and many more examples of campus racism, see J. R. Feagin and M. P. Sikes, *Living with racism: The Black middle-class experience* (Boston: Beacon Press, 1994), ch. 3.

3. Many researchers have reported similar findings. For more information, see J. Fleming, *Blacks in college* (San Francisco: Jossey-Bass, 1984). See also W. R. Allen, E. G. Epp, and N. Z. Haniff (Eds.), *College in Black and White: African American students in predominantly White and historically Black public universities* (Albany: State University of New York Press, 1991).

4. W. R. Allen, "The color of success," pp. 39–40. The National Study of Black College Students (NSBCS) surveyed more than twenty-five hundred Black college students attending a total of sixteen public universities (eight predominantly White and eight historically Black) about their college experiences and outcomes.

5. For a discussion of White students' responses to learning about the racial identity development process of students of color, see B. D. Tatum, "Talking about race, learning about racism."

6. Haley and Malcolm X, *The Autobiography of Malcolm X,* p. 174.

7. M. E. Dyson, *Race rules: Navigating the color line* (Boston: Beacon Press, 1996), p. 151.

 90

Codes of Conduct

ADRIENNE SU

In the South, where I grew up, the people have an unspoken agreement. Reality is what everyone says it is. The agreement is meant to protect others from any perceived slight. It can be as innocuous as complimenting an ugly outfit, but among the truly polite, you could walk into church with a horse instead of your husband, and everyone would not only fail to notice anything wrong but also exclaim, "What a beautiful hat you have on! And Harry is looking so well! The two of you must come over for dinner sometime." By the end of the day, you'd actually believe that the horse was a man.

In the third grade, some friends and I often re-enacted scenes from "Little House on the Prairie." My blonde friend played Mary because of the color of her hair. Another played Carrie, the youngest sister, because she was the youngest. I played Laura, "because you have dark hair," the others explained. Nobody ever pointed out that I did not in the slightest resemble a white Midwestern girl with freckles and brown pigtails. To suggest that perhaps I looked more like the long-lost daughter of a railroad worker of that time was to suggest that I looked different from my friends, and that simply was not done.

Not that the subject never came up—there might be a snack in my lunch that the other kids thought was strange, or a teacher might discreetly ask me about the trip my father took shortly after Nixon's visit opened China to the U.S. But most of the time, there was no language for addressing what made me different. No one asked me about Chinese culture or how to say things in Chinese, which I didn't know, anyway. Questions of the sort were considered rude, a way of pointing out that I looked Chinese, rather than like the Southern gal I was.

This doesn't sound too serious—just a form of Southern gentility. But imagine living your whole life in an environment where everyone says that a cat is a dog, all the time. Your perception of animals changes. You see a cat racing up a tree and remark, "My, that dog is a good climber." You hear a plaintive meow from outside and put a beef bone in the backyard. And when you yourself are a cat in this world, you grow to think you are a dog.

This is fine until you leave this world—and go to a land known as the North, where people not only recognize cathood but celebrate it. They form alliances to preserve feline culture, holding fish dinners and mouse-catching lectures. They hold cat networking activities and cat social events—even writers' conferences for cats who have a way with words. For the cat who's lived her whole life thinking she's a dog, this can come as a bit of a shock.

Up North, in college, I'd find myself in a group of Chinese Americans and think, Hey, I'm surrounded! before realizing that I blended in. I'd go to a gathering of Chinese students and wait to be discovered and thrown out. Talking with my Korean-American roommate, I found that I wasn't the only one whose lack of interest in math and science was seen as a possible birth defect.

One day, when I referred to myself as "Oriental," everyone in the room—white, Korean, Hispanic—pounced on me.

"It's Asian," they cried. "Oriental is offensive."

That was how I learned that there was a vocabulary for a long-unnamed aspect of my life. My visceral feelings of family obligation were known as filial piety, or, as my roommate and I described it, Asian guilt. My parents' unwillingness to contradict their friends was an act of saving face for all. And the melodramatic struggles to pay for dinner were not earnest fights but the desire to avoid guanxi, or obligation, to the other party.

I went home using not the big words of a kid home from college, but ordinary words for things that were familiar, in fact mundane, to my parents.

"I think we're making an unbalanced dinner," I said, peering into a beef stew. "Too many hot element ingredients, too few cold elements. Maybe—"

My mother, absorbed in The Wall Street Journal, waved a dismissive hand. My father, opening his mail, murmured, "Whatever." My brother, who was getting ready for hockey practice, was already out the door.

The next evening, I visited my best friend, the one who'd played Carrie, and sat down to my zillionth Southern dinner with her family.

"What classes are you taking?" her mother asked.

"I'm taking Chinese, so I can eavesdrop on my parents," I said, "and a course in East Asian religions—"

"What kind of job do you plan to get with that?" my friend's father joked.

"I just want to know enough to be able to talk to my relatives in China," I said. "To find out who I really am."

What happened next was very strange. You could hear a crumb of cornbread drop. My friend's house had always been a second home to me, as mine was to her, but on this topic, her family, unlike mine, was stuck. And it was my fault: I had carelessly dragged the conversation into never-never land, the land of what made me different.

During that frozen silence, I busied myself eating. Then I heard myself say:

"These mashed potatoes are wonderful! I've been

so homesick for them. Up North, people just don't know how to cook."

My friend's mother urged me to have more. My friend's father passed the gravy and made a joke about Yankees. And instantly, my friend and I were eight years old again and digging into our plates, ravenous as puppies, because we were growing so fast.

[1997]

🌿 91

Salad

JANICE MIRIKITANI

The woman
did not mean to
offend me,

her blue eyes
blinking
at the glint
of my blade,

as I cut
precisely
like magic
the cucumber in
exact, even,
quick slices.

Do you orientals
do everything
so neatly?   [1982]

🌿 92

I Am Not Your Princess

CHRYSTOS

especially for Dee Johnson

Sandpaper between two cultures which tear one
    another apart I'm not

a means by which you can reach spiritual under-
    standing or even
learn to do beadwork
I'm only willing to tell you how to make fry bread
1 cup flour, spoon of salt, spoon of baking powder
Stir   Add milk or water or beer until it holds
    together
Slap each piece into rounds   Let rest
Fry in hot grease until golden
This is Indian food only if you know that Indian is
    a government word
which has nothing to do with our names for
    ourselves
I won't chant for you
I admit no spirituality to you
I will not sweat with you or ease your guilt with
    fine turtle tales
I will not wear dancing clothes to read poetry
    or explain hardly anything at all
I don't think your attempts to understand us
    are going to work so I'd rather
you left us in whatever peace we can still
    scramble up
after all you continue to do
If you send me one more damn flyer about how
    to heal myself for $300
with special feminist counseling I'll probably set
    fire to something
If you tell me one more time that I'm wise I'll
    throw up on you
Look at me
See my confusion   loneliness   fear   worrying
    about all our struggles to keep
what little is left for us
Look at my heart   not your fantasies
Please don't ever again tell me about your
    Cherokee great-great grandmother
Don't assume I know every other Native Activist in
    the world personally
That I even know the names of all the tribes
or can pronounce names I've never heard
or that I'm expert at the peyote stitch
If you ever
again tell me
how strong I am
I'll lay down on the ground & moan so you'll see

at last   my human weakness   like your own
I'm not strong   I'm scraped
I'm blessed with life while so many I've known
    are dead
I have work to do   dishes to wash   a house to
    clean   There is no magic
See my simple cracked hands which have washed
    the same things you wash
See my eyes dark with fear in a house by myself
    late at night
See that to pity me or to adore me are the same
1 cup flour, spoon of salt, spoon of baking powder
    & liquid to hold
remember this is only my recipe   There are many
    others
Let me rest
here
at least   [1987]

 93

Take a Closer Look

CARRIE CASTRO

Can you see as you
take a closer look
beyond how I appear
to be so self assured
of who I am.
My name alone
    morena
does not reveal
the inner thoughts
of uneasiness
I sometimes feel.

Let me take you
back
to a time
when I was young
and didn't understand
the significance

of colored skins
when I didn't realize
they made a difference.

Back
to a time
when I became
aware of the division
some say existed
between those born
here and those who
come from "over there,"
we made the difference.

Back
to a time
when I grew older
and longed to be
someone else
instead of "me"
because I didn't feel
that was good enough,
I made the difference.

Take a closer look
because inside
my insecurities
you will find
that the reasons
arise from the
cobwebbed minds
of those who cannot see
any beauty in faces
darker than their own.   [1980]

 94

An Autobiography (excerpt)

ANGELA DAVIS

The big white house on top of the hill was not far
from our old neighborhood, but the distance could
not be measured in blocks. The government hous-

ing project on Eighth Avenue where we lived before was a crowded street of little red brick structures —no one of which was different from the other. Only rarely did the cement surrounding these brick huts break open and show patches of green. Without space or earth, nothing could be planted to bear fruit or blossoms. But friends were there—and friendliness.

In 1948 we moved out of the projects in Birmingham, Alabama, to the large wooden house on Center Street. My parents still live there. Because of its steeples and gables and peeling paint, the house was said to be haunted. There were wild woods in back with fig trees, blackberry patches and great wild cherry trees. On one side of the house was a huge Cigar tree. There was space here and no cement. The street itself was a strip of orange-red Alabama clay. It was the most conspicuous house in the neighborhood—not only because of its curious architecture but because, for blocks around, it was the only house not teeming inside with white hostility. We were the first Black family to move into that area, and the white people believed that we were in the vanguard of a mass invasion.

At the age of four I was aware that the people across the street were different—without yet being able to trace their alien nature to the color of their skin. What made them different from our neighbors in the projects was the frown on their faces, the way they stood a hundred feet away and glared at us, their refusal to speak when we said "Good afternoon." An elderly couple across the street, the Montees, sat on their porch all the time, their eyes heavy with belligerence.

Almost immediately after we moved there the white people got together and decided on a border line between them and us. Center Street became the line of demarcation. Provided that we stayed on "our" side of the line (the east side) they let it be known we would be left in peace. If we ever crossed over to their side, war would be declared. Guns were hidden in our house and vigilance was constant.

Fifty or so yards from this hatred, we went about our daily lives. My mother, on leave from her teaching job, took care of my younger brother Benny, while waiting to give birth to another child, my sister Fania. My father drove his old orange van to the service station each morning after dropping me off at nursery school. It was next door to the Children's Home Hospital—an old wooden building where I was born and where, at two, I had my tonsils removed. I was fascinated by the people dressed in white and tried to spend more time at the hospital than at the nursery. I had made up my mind that I was going to be a doctor—a children's doctor.

Shortly after we moved to the hill, white people began moving out of the neighborhood and Black families were moving in, buying old houses and building new ones. A Black minister and his wife, the Deyaberts, crossed into white territory, buying the house right next to the Montees, the people with the hateful eyes.

It was evening in the spring of 1949. I was in the bathroom washing my white shoelaces for Sunday School the next morning when an explosion a hundred times louder than the loudest, most frightening thunderclap I had ever heard shook our house. Medicine bottles fell off the shelves, shattering all around me. The floor seemed to slip away from my feet as I raced into the kitchen and my frightened mother's arms.

Crowds of angry Black people came up the hill and stood on "our" side, staring at the bombed-out ruins of the Deyaberts' house. Far into the night they spoke of death, of white hatred, death, white people, and more death. But of their own fear they said nothing. Apparently it did not exist, for Black families continued to move in. The bombings were such a constant response that soon our neighborhood became known as Dynamite Hill.

The more steeped in violence our environment became, the more determined my father and mother were that I, the first-born, learn that the battle of white against Black was not written into the nature of things. On the contrary, my mother always said, love had been ordained by God. White people's hatred of us was neither natural nor eternal. She knew that whenever I answered the telephone and called to her, "Mommy, a white lady wants to talk to you," I was doing more than describing the curious drawl.

Every time I said "white lady" or "white man" anger clung to my words. My mother tried to erase the anger with reasonableness. Her experiences had included contacts with white people seriously committed to improving race relations. Though she had grown up in rural Alabama, she had become involved, as a college student, in anti-racist movements. She had worked to free the Scottsboro Boys and there had been whites—some of them Communists—in that struggle. Through her own political work, she had learned that it was possible for white people to walk out of their skin and respond with the integrity of human beings. She tried hard to make her little girl—so full of hatred and confusion—see white people not so much as what they were as in terms of their potential. She did not want me to think of the guns hidden in drawers or the weeping black woman who had come screaming to our door for help, but of a future world of harmony and equality. I didn't know what she was talking about.

When Black families had moved up on the hill in sufficient numbers for me to have a group of friends, we developed our own means of defending our egos. Our weapon was the word. We would gather on my front lawn, wait for a car of white people to pass by and shout the worst epithets for white people we knew: Cracker. Redneck. Then we would laugh hysterically at the startled expressions on their faces. I hid this pastime from my parents. They could not know how important it was for me, and for all of us who had just discovered racism, to find ways of maintaining our dignity.   [1974]

The Legacy of Class

In the United States, people do not talk about class very much. Nevertheless, most people are very aware of class differences as they manifest themselves in the way people look, talk, and move through the world, and this awareness affects the way we relate to each other. As Donna Langston explains in "Tired of Playing Monopoly?" our class backgrounds have a powerful effect on our values, the ways we see ourselves, and the choices we have in our lives. For example, women who grew up in middle-class homes often saw work outside the home as a form of liberation, while women in poor and working-class families have always worked, often at alienating, dead-end jobs.

This section includes stories and essays that explore the meaning of class in women's lives. Dorothy Allison and Kendall Johnson describe the vast distance between the social and cultural realities of middle-class and poor people. For Bernice Mennis, being Jewish and working class are closely intertwined in her recollections of making sense of a world in which she often felt different.

The feminist ideal of sisterhood among women is often challenged by class divisions. In "Sisters," both women are African American, united by the racism and sexism in their lives but divided by social class. Jealousy, competition, and the belief that one can make it on one's own if one is "tough enough" keep them from offering each other the support they each desperately need. In Toi Derricotte's poem, Grace Paley, a well-known North American writer, reaches across class differences with a small act of consideration.

95

Tired of Playing Monopoly?

DONNA LANGSTON

I. Magnin, Nordstrom, The Bon, Sears, Penneys, K mart, Goodwill, Salvation Army. If the order of this list of stores makes any sense to you, then we've begun to deal with the first question which inevitably arises in any discussion of class here in the U.S.— huh? Unlike our European allies, we in the U.S. are reluctant to recognize class differences. This denial of class divisions functions to reinforce ruling class control and domination. America is, after all, the supposed land of equal opportunity where, if you just work hard enough, you can get ahead, pull yourself up by your bootstraps. What the old bootstraps theory overlooks is that some were born with silver shoe horns. Female-headed households, communities of color, the elderly, disabled and children find themselves, disproportionately, living in poverty. If hard work were the sole determinant of your ability to support yourself and your family, surely we'd have a different outcome for many in our society. We also, however, believe in luck and, on closer examination, it certainly is quite a coincidence that the "unlucky" come from certain race, gender and class backgrounds. In order to perpetuate racist, sexist and classist outcomes, we also have to believe that the current economic distribution is unchangeable, has always existed, and probably exists in this form throughout the known universe, i.e., it's "natural." Some people explain or try to account for poverty or class position by focusing on the personal and moral merits of an individual. If people are poor, then it's something they did or didn't do; they were lazy, unlucky, didn't try hard enough, etc. This has the familiar ring of blaming the victims. Alternative explanations focus on the ways in which poverty and class position are due to structural, systematic, institutionalized economic and political power relations. These power relations are based firmly on dynamics such as race, gender, and class.

In the myth of the classless society, ambition and intelligence alone are responsible for success. The myth conceals the existence of a class society, which serves many functions. One of the main ways it keeps the working-class and poor locked into a class-based system in a position of servitude is by cruelly creating false hope. It perpetuates the false hope among the working-class and poor that they can have different opportunities in life. The hope that they can escape the fate that awaits them due to the class position they were born into. Another way the rags-to-riches myth is perpetuated is by creating enough visible tokens so that oppressed persons believe they, too, can get ahead. The creation of hope through tokenism keeps a hierarchical structure in place and lays the blame for not succeeding on those who don't. This keeps us from resisting and changing the class-based system. Instead, we accept it as inevitable, something we just have to live with. If oppressed people believe in equality of opportunity, then they won't develop class consciousness and will internalize the blame for their economic position. If the working-class and poor do not recognize the way false hope is used to control them, they won't get a chance to control their lives by acknowledging their class position, by claiming that identity and taking action as a group.

The myth also keeps the middle class and upper class entrenched in the privileges awarded in a class-based system. It reinforces middle- and upper-class beliefs in their own superiority. If we believe that anyone in society really can get ahead, then middle- and upper-class status and privileges must be deserved, due to personal merits, and enjoyed—and defended at all costs. According to this viewpoint, poverty is regrettable but acceptable, just the outcome of a fair game: "There have always been poor people, and there always will be."

Class is more than just the amount of money you have; it's also the presence of economic security. For the working class and poor, working and eating are matters of survival, not taste. However, while one's class status can be defined in important ways in terms of monetary income, class is also a whole lot more—specifically, class is also culture. As a result of the class you are born into and raised in, class is your understanding of the world and where you fit in; it's composed of ideas, behavior, attitudes, values, and language; class is how you think, feel, act, look, dress, talk, move, walk; class is what stores you shop at, restaurants you eat in; class is the schools you attend, the education you attain; class is the very jobs you will work at throughout your adult life. Class even determines when we marry and become mothers. Working-class women become mothers long before middle-class women receive their bachelor's degrees. We experience class at every level of our lives; class is who our friends are, where we live and work even what kind of car we drive, if we own one, and what kind of health care we receive, if any. Have I left anything out? In other words, class is socially constructed and all-encompassing. When we experience classism, it will be because of our lack of money (i.e., choices and power in this society) and because of the way we talk, think, act, move—because of our culture.

Class affects what we perceive as and what we have available to us as choices. Upon graduation from high school, I was awarded a scholarship to attend any college, private or public, in the state of California. Yet it never occurred to me or my family that it made any difference which college you went to. I ended up just going to a small college in my town. It never would have occurred to me to move away from my family for school, because no one ever had and no one would. I was the first person in my family to go to college. I had to figure out from reading college catalogs how to apply—no one in my family could have sat down and said, "Well, you take this test and then you really should think about . . ." Although tests and high school performance had shown I had the ability to pick up white middle-class lingo, I still had quite an adjustment to make —it was lonely and isolating in college. I lost my friends from high school—they were at the community college, vo-tech school, working, or married. I lasted a year and a half in this foreign environment before I quit college, married a factory worker, had a baby and resumed living in a community I knew. One middle-class friend in college had asked if I'd like to travel to Europe with her. Her father was a college professor and people in her family had actually travelled there. My family had seldom been able to take a vacation at all. A couple of times my parents were able—by saving all year—to take the family over to the coast on their annual two-week vacation. I'd seen the time and energy my parents invested in trying to take a family vacation to some place a few hours away; the idea of how anybody ever got to Europe was beyond me.

If class is more than simple economic status but one's cultural background, as well, what happens if you're born and raised middle-class, but spend some of your adult life with earnings below a middle-class income bracket—are you then working-class? Probably not. If your economic position changes, you still have the language, behavior, educational background, etc., of the middle class, which you can bank on. You will always have choices. Men who consciously try to refuse male privilege are still male; whites who want to challenge white privilege are still white. I think those who come from middle-class backgrounds need to recognize that their class privilege does not float out with the rinse water. Middle-class people can exert incredible power just by being nice and polite. The middle-class way of doing things is the standard—they're always right, just by being themselves. Beware of middle-class people who deny their privilege. Many people have times when they struggle to get shoes for the kids, when budgets are tight, etc. This isn't the same as long-term economic conditions without choices. Being

working-class is also generational. Examine your family's history of education, work, and standard of living. It may not be a coincidence that you share the same class status as your parents and grandparents. If your grandparents were professionals, or your parents were professionals, it's much more likely you'll be able to grow up to become a yuppie, if your heart so desires, or even if you don't think about it.

How about if you're born and raised poor or working-class, yet through struggle, usually through education, you manage to achieve a different economic level: do you become middle class? Can you pass? I think some working class people may successfully assimilate into the middle class by learning to dress, talk, and act middle-class—to accept and adopt the middle-class way of doing things. It all depends on how far they're able to go. To succeed in the middle-class world means facing great pressures to abandon working-class friends and ways.

Contrary to our stereotype of the working class —white guys in overalls—the working class is not homogeneous in terms of race or gender. If you are a person of color, if you live in a female-headed household, you are much more likely to be working-class or poor. The experience of Black, Latino, American Indian or Asian American working classes will differ significantly from the white working classes, which have traditionally been able to rely on white privilege to provide a more elite position within the working class. Working-class people are often grouped together and stereotyped, but distinctions can be made among the working-class, working-poor and poor. Many working-class families are supported by unionized workers who possess marketable skills. Most working-poor families are supported by non-unionized, unskilled men and women. Many poor families are dependent on welfare for their income.

Attacks on the welfare system and those who live on welfare are a good example of classism in action. We have a "dual welfare" system in this country whereby welfare for the rich in the form of tax-free capital gain, guaranteed loans, oil depletion allowances, etc., is not recognized as welfare. Almost everyone in America is on some type of welfare; but, if you're rich, it's in the form of tax deductions for "business" meals and entertainment, and if you're poor, it's in the form of food stamps. The difference is the stigma and humiliation connected to welfare for the poor, as compared to welfare for the rich, which is called "incentives." Ninety-three percent of welfare recipients are women. A common focal point for complaints about "welfare" is the belief that most welfare recipients are cheaters—goodness knows there are no middle-class income tax cheaters out there. Imagine focusing the same anger and energy on the way corporations and big business cheat on their tax revenues. Now, there would be some dollars worth quibbling about. The "dual welfare" system also assigns a different degree of stigma to programs that benefit women and children and programs whose recipients are primarily male, such as veterans' benefits. The implicit assumption is that mothers who raise children do not work and therefore are not deserving of their daily bread crumbs.

Working-class women's critiques have focused on the following issues:

Education: White middle-class professionals have used academic jargon to rationalize and justify classism. The whole structure of education is a classist system. Schools in every town reflect class divisions: like the store list at the beginning of this article, you can list schools in your town by what classes of kids attend, and in most cities you can also list by race. The classist system is perpetuated in schools with the tracking system, whereby the "dumbs" are tracked into homemaking, shop courses and vocational school futures, while the "smarts" end up in advanced math, science, literature, and college-prep courses. If we examine these groups carefully, the coincidence of poor and working-class backgrounds with "dumbs" is rather alarming. The standard measurement of supposed intelligence is white middle-class English. If you're other than white middle-class, you have to become bilingual to succeed in the educational system. If you're white middle-class, you only need the language and writing skills you were raised with, since they're the standard. To do well in society presupposes middle-class background, experiences and learning for everyone. The tracking system separates those from the working class who can potentially assimilate to the middle

class from all our friends, and labels us "college bound."

After high school, you go on to vocational school, community college, or college—public or private—according to your class position. Apart from the few who break into middle-class schools, the classist stereotyping of the working class as being dumb and inarticulate tracks most into vocational and low-skilled jobs. A few of us are allowed to slip through to reinforce the idea that equal opportunity exists. But for most, class position is destiny—determining our educational attainment and employment. Since we must overall abide by middle-class rules to succeed, the assumption is that we go to college in order to "better ourselves"—i.e., become more like them. I suppose it's assumed we have "yuppie envy" and desire nothing more than to be upwardly mobile individuals. It's assumed that we want to fit into their world. But many of us remain connected to our communities and families. Becoming college-educated doesn't mean we have to, or want to, erase our first and natural language and value system. It's important for many of us to remain in and return to our communities to work, live, and stay sane.

Jobs: Middle-class people have the privilege of choosing careers. They can decide which jobs they want to work, according to their moral or political commitments, needs for challenge or creativity. This is a privilege denied the working-class and poor, whose work is a means of survival, not choice. Working-class women have seldom had the luxury of choosing between work in the home or market. We've generally done both, with little ability to purchase services to help with this double burden. Middle- and upper-class women can often hire other women to clean their houses, take care of their children, and cook their meals. Guess what class and race those "other" women are? Working a double or triple day is common for working-class women. Only middle-class women have an array of choices such as: parents put you through school, then you choose a career, then you choose when and if to have babies, then you choose a support system of working-class women to take care of your kids and house if you choose to resume your career. After the birth of my second child, I was working two part-time jobs—one loading trucks at night—and going to school during the days. While I was quite privileged because I could take my colicky infant with me to classes and the day-time job, I was in a state of continuous semi-consciousness. I had to work to support my family; the only choice I had was between school or sleep: Sleep became a privilege. A white middle-class feminist instructor at the university suggested to me, all sympathetically, that I ought to hire someone to clean my house and watch the baby. Her suggestion was totally out of my reality, both economically and socially. I'd worked for years cleaning other people's houses. Hiring a working-class woman to do the shit work is a middle-class woman's solution to any dilemma which her privileges, such as a career, may present her.

Individualism: Preoccupation with one's self—one's body, looks, relationships—is a luxury working-class women can't afford. Making an occupation out of taking care of yourself through therapy, aerobics, jogging, dressing for success, gourmet meals and proper nutrition, etc., may be responses that are directly rooted in privilege. The middle-class have the leisure time to be preoccupied with their own problems, such as their waistlines, planning their vacations, coordinating their wardrobes, or dealing with what their mother said to them when they were five—my!

The white middle-class women's movement has been patronizing to working-class women. Its supporters think we don't understand sexism. The idea of women as passive, weak creatures totally discounts the strength, self-dependence and interdependence necessary to survive as working-class and poor women. My mother and her friends always had a less-than-passive, less-than-enamoured attitude toward their spouses, male bosses, and men in general. I know from listening to their conversations, jokes and what they passed on to us, their daughters, as folklore. When I was five years old, my mother told me about how Aunt Betty had hit Uncle Ernie over the head with a skillet and knocked him out because he was raising his hand to hit her, and how he's never even thought about doing it since. This story was told to me with a good amount of glee and laughter. All the men in the neighborhood were told

of the event as an example of what was a very acceptable response in the women's community for that type of male behavior. We kids in the neighborhood grew up with these stories of women giving husbands, bosses, the welfare system, schools, unions and men in general—hell, whenever they deserved it. For me there were many role models of women taking action, control and resisting what was supposed to be their lot.   [1988]

 96

Context

DOROTHY ALLISON

One summer, almost ten years ago, I brought my lover down to Greenville to visit my aunt Dot and the rest of my mama's family. We took our time getting there, spending one day in D.C. and another in Durham. I even thought about suggesting a side trip over to the Smoky Mountains, until I realized the reason I was thinking about that was that I was afraid. It was not my family I feared. It was my lover. I was afraid to take my lover home with me because of what I might see in her face once she had spent some time with my aunt, met a few of my uncles, and tried to talk to any of my cousins. I was afraid of the distance, the fear, or the contempt that I imagined could suddenly appear between us. I was afraid that she might see me though new eyes, hateful eyes, the eyes of someone who suddenly knew fully how different we were. My aunts' distance, my cousins' fear, or my uncles' contempt seemed much less threatening.

I was right to worry. My lover did indeed see me with new eyes, though it turned out that she was more afraid of my distancing myself from her than of her fear and discomfort coming between us. What I saw in her face after the first day in South Carolina was nothing I had expected. Her features were marked with a kind of tenuous awe, confusion, uncertainty, and shame. All she could say was that she hadn't been prepared. My aunt Dot had welcomed her, served ice tea in a tall glass, and made her sit in the best seat at the kitchen table, the one near the window where my uncle's cigarette smoke wouldn't bother her. But my lover had barely spoken.

"It's a kind of a dialect, isn't it," she said to me in the motel that night. "I couldn't understand one word in four of anything your aunt said." I looked at her. Aunt Dot's accent was pronounced, but I had never thought of it as a dialect. It was just that she hadn't ever been out of Greenville County. She had a television, but it was for the kids in the living room. My aunt lived her life at that kitchen table.

My lover leaned into my shoulder so that her cheek rested against my collar bone. "I thought I knew what it would be like—your family, Greenville. You told me so many stories. But the words . . ." She lifted her hand palm up into the air and flexed the fingers as if she were reaching for an idea.

"I don't know," she said. "I thought I understood what you meant when you said 'working class' but I just didn't have a context."

I lay still. Although the motel air conditioner was working hard, I could smell the steamy moist heat from outside. It was slipping in around the edges of the door and windows, a swampy earth-rich smell that reminded me of being ten years old and climbing down to sleep on the floor with my sisters, hoping it would be a little cooler there. We had never owned an air conditioner, never stayed in a motel, never eaten in a restaurant where my mother did not work. Context. I breathed in the damp metallic air-conditioner smell and remembered Folly Beach.

When I was about eight my stepfather drove us there, down the road from Charleston, and all five of us stayed in one room that had been arranged for us by a friend of his at work. It wasn't a motel. It was a guesthouse, and the lady who managed it didn't seem too happy that we showed up for a room someone else had already paid for. I slept in a fold-up cot that kept threatening to collapse in the night. My sisters slept together in the bed across from the one my parents shared. My mama cooked on a two-burner stove to save us the cost of eating out, and our greatest treat was take-out food—fried fish my stepfather swore was bad and hamburgers from the same place

that sold the fish. We were in awe of the outdoor shower under the stairs where we were expected to rinse off the sand we picked up on the beach. We longed to be able to rent one of the rafts, umbrellas, and bicycles you could get on the beach. But my stepfather insisted all that stuff was listed at robbery rates and cursed the men to who tried to tempt us with it. That didn't matter to us. We were overcome with the sheer freedom of being on a real vacation in a semi-public place all the time where my stepfather had to watch his temper, and of running everywhere in bathing suits and flip-flops.

We were there a week. Twice my stepfather sent us to the beach while he and Mama stayed in the room. We took the opportunity to follow other families around, to listen to fathers praising their sons and watch mothers blushing with pride at how people looked at their girls. We listened to accents and studied picnic menus. Everyone was strange and wonderful, on vacation.

My stepfather lost his temper only once on that trip. He was horrified at the prices in the souvenir shops and made us keep our hands in our pockets.

"Jew bastards will charge me if you break anything," he cursed.

I flinched at his words and then realized that the man behind the counter heard him. I saw his blush and outrage as his eyes followed my stepfather's movement toward the door. Then I saw his eyes flicker over to me and my sisters, registering the same contempt with which he had looked at my stepfather. Heat flamed in my neck and I wanted to apologize—to tell him we were not like our stepfather—but I could do nothing. I couldn't speak a word to him in front of my stepfather, and if I had, why would he have believed me? Remember this, I thought. Don't go deaf and blind to what this feels like, remember it. I gritted my teeth and kept my head up, looked that man in the face and mouthed, "I'm sorry," but I could not tell if he understood me.

What context did he have for people like us?

After my lover fell asleep that first night in Greenville, I lay awake a long time thinking. My lover was a Yankee girl from a good family, who had spent the summers of her childhood on the Jersey Shore. I had gone there with her, walked with her on the beaches of her memory, wide and flat and grey-white, so clear I felt intimidated. Seeing where she had grown up, meeting some of her family, I had understood her better, seen where some of her fear came from, and her pride. What had she understood about me today? I wondered.

I turned my head to the side to look at her sleep, her mouth soft against my skin. Her hair was dark and shiny, her teeth straight and white. I wondered what she would have thought of Folly Beach, the poor man's Jersey Shore, or of us if she could have seen us there. I burned with old shame and then stubbornly shook it off.

Context is so little to share, and so vital.　[1994]

🌱 97

Sisters

BARBARA NEELY

. . . and are we not one
daughter of the same dark mother's child
breathing one breath from a multitude of mouths . . .
　—from the Sisterhood Song of the Yenga Nation

The offices of Carstairs and Carstairs Management Consultants had that hushed, forbidden air of after five o'clock. No light shone from beneath any of the office doors bordering the central typing pool which was also deserted, except for the new cleaning woman working her way among the desks. Lorisa was the last of the office staff to leave. She'd pushed the button for the elevator before she remembered the notes on Wider Housewares she wanted to look over before tomorrow morning's meeting. She turned and took a shortcut through the typing pool to her office.

"Good evening," she said to the grey uniform-clad back of the cleaning woman as the woman reached down to pick up a wastebasket. Lorisa automatically put on her polite, remote smile, the one that matched the distance in her tone, while she waited for the woman to move out of her way.

Jackie turned with the wastebasket still in her hand and let her eyes roam so slowly over the woman who'd spoken to her that she might have been looking for something in particular. Then she nodded, briefly, curtly, before turning, lifting the basket and dashing its contents into the rolling bin she pushed along ahead of her. Only then did she step aside.

Lorisa hurried into her office, careful not to slam the door and show her irritation. Where did they find the cleaning staff, the asylum for the criminally insane? The woman had given her a look cold enough to cut stone and barely acknowledged her greeting —as though she were not worth the time it took to be pleasant. She, who was always careful to speak to the gum-chewing black girls who worked in the mail room, the old man who shined shoes in the lobby, the newspaper man and any other of her people she met in the building who did menial work. None of them had ever been anything but equally polite to her. She had noticed the shoeshine man always had something pleasant to say to the mailroom girls and only a "Good day" to her. But considering the difference in their positions, his reticence with her seemed only natural and nothing like the attitude of the cleaning woman.

Although she'd only returned for her notes, she found herself moving papers from one side of her desk to the other, making a list of small tasks for tomorrow, staving off the moment when she would have to confront the cleaning woman once again. But Lorisa realized it wasn't the woman's curt nod or the slowness with which she'd moved aside that made her reluctant to leave her office. It was those eyes. Big, black, dense eyes with something knowing in them—something that had made her feel as though her loneliness and her fear of it, her growing uneasiness about her job, the disturbing hollowness where pleasure in her comfortable life should be, and all her other fears and flaws were as visible to the cleaning woman as so many wrinkles and smudges on her dress. When their eyes had met, the sense of secret knowledge already shared had filled her with an almost overwhelming desire to say something, to explain something about a part of herself she couldn't name. The woman's look of cold disdain had only corroborated her feeling of having been revealed and found wanting. "Your shit ain't so hot, honey, and you know it," the woman's eyes seemed to say. It didn't occur to Lorisa that the way she'd spoken to the cleaning woman could have anything to do with the woman's response. She was tired, with too much work and too little rest. And she was always over-imaginative when her period was about to start. She forced herself to open the door to her office and was nearly lightheaded with relief to find the cleaning woman nowhere in sight.

In the descending elevator, she realized that the term "cleaning woman" rang false against the face and figure she'd just encountered. Cleaning women were fat and full of quiet kindness and mother wit. They were not women who looked to be in their late twenties—her own age—with faces strong and proud as her own. They didn't have lean, hard-muscled arms and eyes like onyx marbles. She remembered her grandmother, her father's squat, black, broad-nosed mother who had cooked and cleaned for white people all of her life. On those rare occasions when Lorisa's mother had consented to a visit from her mother-in-law, or, rarer still, when the family paid the older woman a visit in North Carolina, Grandmother would wait on everyone. She would slip into your room while you were in the bathroom in the morning and make your bed, hang up your clothes, and spirit away anything that looked the least bit in need of mending, washing, or pressing. But her dedication didn't earn her much praise.

"Young black girls learn enough about being mammies without your mother to set an example," Lorisa had once heard her mother say to her father. Her mother was explaining why it was impossible for Lorisa to spend part of her summer with her grandmother, despite Lorisa's and her grandmother's wishes. She'd been sent to camp instead, a camp at which, she remembered now, the white kids had called her and the three other black girls "niggers" and put spiders in their beds. As she crossed the lobby, it occurred to her that her grandmother had once been young, just like the woman cleaning the typing pool. Had there been fire in her grandmother's eyes, too, when she was young? Had she spit in the white folks soup, the way the slaves used

to do? How long did it take to make a *real* cleaning woman?

* * *

Jackie banged another wastebasket against her bin with such vigor she left a dent in the basket. What had made her act like that? She slammed the basket down beside the desk and moved on to the next one. The woman was only trying to be polite. But a mean, evil rage had risen up at the very sight of her—walking around like she owned the place, having her own office. And those shoes! She must have paid a hundred dollars for them shoes! Who'd she think she was? Jackie dumped the last basket and began dry mopping the floor with an over-sized dust-mop. A college education didn't give her the right to give nobody that uptight little greeting, like an icicle down somebody's back, she thought. She'd run into three or four other black women with really good jobs in other buildings where she cleaned. A couple of them had had that air of doing you a favor when they spoke to you, too. But they'd been light-skinned and looked like models, which somehow made their hinctiness less personal. This woman's smooth dark face and big round eyes reminded Jackie of a girl she'd hung out with in school; and she had a cousin with the same big legs and small waist. She didn't need for no plain ole everyday-looking black woman to speak to her because she thought she ought to. She got more than enough of being practically patted on her head, if not her behind, from the phony whites she worked for. She wasn't taking that stuff from one of her own, too!

She let her mind slip into a replay of her latest run-in with her snooty white supervisor in which she'd once again had to point out that she only gave respect when she got it. She was hoping to draw a parallel between the two situations and thereby relieve herself of the knowledge that in the moment when she'd first seen the woman standing there—as crisp and unused as a new dollar bill, as far removed from emptying other people's wastebaskets as a black woman was likely to get—she had been struck dumb by jealousy. She swung the mop in wide arcs, putting more energy into the chore than was called for.

She was just finishing up the Men's Room when she heard the elevator bell. When she left the bathroom no light showed from beneath the woman's door. Although she'd already cleaned the private offices, Jackie crossed the typing pool and tiptoed into the woman's office. She stood in the middle of the room. Light from the street below made turning on the overhead light unnecessary. A hint of some peppery perfume lingered in the air, like a shadow of the woman who worked there. It was a good-sized office, with a beige leather sofa under an abstract painting in shades of blues and brown; a glass and chrome coffee table with dried flowers in a bowl. A big, shiny, wooden desk.

Jackie ran her fingers along the edge of the desk as she walked slowly round it. She stood in front of the leather desk chair and placed the fingertips of both hands lightly on the desk. She leaned forward and looked toward the sofa as though addressing an invisible client or underling. Then she sat—not as she usually sat, with a sigh of relief at getting off her feet as she plopped solidly down. She sat slowly, her head held high, her back straight. In her imagination, she wore Lorisa's raw silk shirtwaist and turquoise beads. Gold glistened at her ears and on her small, manicured hands. Her hair was long and pulled back into a sleek chignon. The desk hid her suddenly corn-free feet, sporting one hundred dollar shoes. And she knew things—math, the meaning of big words, what to tell other people to do . . . things that meant you were closer to being the boss than to being bossed.

Once, so long ago it seemed like the beginning of time, she'd thought she might be something— nothing grand enough for an office like this. Being a secretary is what she'd dreamed about: dressing real neat, walking with her legs close together, in that switchy way secretaries always had on TV, typing and filing and so forth. She must have been about ten years old when she'd hoped for that, not old enough to know that chubby-butt, black-skinned, unwed mothers with GED diplomas and short, nappy hair didn't get jobs as downtown secretaries or very much else, besides floor-moppers or whores, unless they had a college education. She'd had to

drop out of school to take care of her son. She'd never considered marrying Carl's father and he had never asked if she wanted to get married. They were both fifteen and had only had sex twice. Since then, it seemed she only met two kinds of men—those she didn't like who liked her and those she liked who weren't interested in her. Her marriage dream was no more real than any of her other dreams. She lifted a slim, black pen from its desk holder, shined it on the edge of the apron she wore over her uniform, and quickly replaced it.

But hadn't she at least suspected, even back when she was ten and still dreaming about secretarial school and happy-ever-after, that this was what her life was going to be—just what her mother's life had been and that of all her girlfriends who were not in jail or on dope or working themselves to death for some pimp or factory owner? Hadn't she known that questions like: "And what do you want to be when you grow up, little girl?" were only grown-ups' way of not talking to her, since they already knew the limits of her life?

A longing beyond words welled up from her core and threatened to escape into a moan so deep and so wrenching its gathering made her suddenly short of breath. She rose quickly from the chair and headed for the door.

What happened to the part of yourself that dreams and hopes, she wondered. Was it just a phase of growing up, to believe you might amount to something, might do something with your life besides have babies and be poor? And how come some people got to have their dreams come true and others didn't?

* * *

Lorisa lay with her head thrown back against the edge of the high steel tub, droplets from the swirling water gently splashing her face, tightening the skin across her forehead. She stopped by the spa for a whirlpool bath and fifteen minutes in the steam room every day after work. As a reward, she told herself, without thinking about what there was about her work that warranted rewarding. She shifted her weight, careful to keep her feet from the sucking pipe that pulled the water in and forced it out to knead and pummel her muscles, dissolving the tension across her shoulders. But not quite.

Jim Daily's face rose behind her eyelids—a pale, oval moon altering the landscape of her leisure with its sickly light. She pressed her eyelids down as hard as possible, but Daily's face remained.

"You notice how much she looks like the maid in that cleanser commercial? You know the one I mean," he'd gone on to whoever was in earshot, to whoever would listen, as he'd circled her, trapped her with his penetrating voice. "Go ahead," he told her, "Put your hand on your hip and say, 'Look, chile!'" He'd transformed his voice into a throaty falsetto. His pale blue gaze had pinned her to the spot where she stood, like a spotlight, as he'd waited for her to perform, to act like some nigger clown in some minstrel show. All in fun, of course; just joking, of course; no offense intended, of course. A hot flush of shame had warmed her cheeks. Is that how she looked to him, to them? she'd wondered, searching her mind for real similarities between herself and the commercial caricature of whom Daily spoke, even though she knew in her heart that he never saw her, that all black women's faces were most likely one to him.

Lorisa tried to let go of the memory, to give herself over to the soothing water, but her back was stiff now, her tongue pressed too firmly to the roof of her mouth behind tightly clenched teeth. All the rage she couldn't let herself release at the time came rolling to the surface in a flood of scenes in which she said all the things she might have said to him, if she'd had the luxury of saying and acting as she pleased—like the cleaning woman in her office. She saw herself putting her hand on her hip and telling Daily what an ignorant, racist dog he was. A stiletto-thin smile curved her lips at the thought of how he would have looked, standing there with his face gone purple and his whiny nasal voice finally silenced.

Of course, from Daily's point of view, from the firm's point of view, she would only have proved conclusively that all blacks were belligerent and had no sense of proportion, none of the civilizing ability to laugh at themselves. And, of course, she would have lost her job. Daily was slightly senior to her. He was also a white male in a white male firm where she,

and the two white women consultants, did everything they could to distract attention from the fact that they were not biologically certified for the old boys' club. And Lorisa knew she was on even shakier ground than the white women on staff.

She was the one who got the smallest and most mundane clients with whom to work. It was her ideas that were always somehow attributed to someone else. She was invariably the last to know about changes in the firm's policies or procedures and office gossip was stone cold by the time she heard it. For a while, she'd been fairly successful at convincing herself all this was due to her being a very junior member of the staff, that race had nothing to do with it. Of course, she realized, with the seventh sense of a colored person in a white society, which members of the firm hated her silently and politely because of her color. Daily was not alone in his racism and he was probably less dangerous, with his overt ignorance, than the quiet haters. But they were individuals. The firm was different. The firm was only interested in making all the money it could. It didn't really care who did the work. Wasn't that what she'd been taught in her college economics courses? But more and more, as men with less seniority and skills than she were given serious responsibilities, she was increasingly unable to plaster over the cracks in the theory that the firm was somehow different from the individuals of which it is composed. More and more she was forced to accept the very good possibility that she'd been hired as a token and would be kept as a company pet, as long as she behaved herself . . . or until some other type of token/pet became more fashionable.

It seemed ironic that in college she'd been one of the black students most involved in trying to better race relations. She'd helped organize integrated retreats and participated in race workshops. She'd done her personal share by rooming with a white girl who became her best friend, costing her what few black girlfriends she'd had on campus. She could almost count the number of dates she'd had on one hand. There were only a few black boys on campus to begin with and a third of them were more interested in her white roommate or light-skinned colored girls than they'd been in the likes of her.

Those who had dated her had done so only once and spread the word that she was "lame," and "cold." She quickly evaded the thought that her love life hadn't improved appreciably since college. Back then, there were times when she had felt more comfortable with some of the white kids than she had with some of the black ones, although she'd denied this vehemently when a black girl accused her of it. And she'd originally liked being the only black at Carstairs and Carstairs. She'd thought she'd have more of a chance to get ahead on her own, without other blacks and their problems and claims to her allegiance.

"We're so proud of our Lorisa," her mother's prim school teacher's voice repeated inside Lorisa's head. The occasion had been a family dinner honoring Lorisa's completion of graduate school and the job offer from Carstairs. "Yes, indeed," her mother had gone on, "Lorisa is a fine example of what a young colored woman can do, if she just puts all this race and sex mess behind her and steps boldly, acts forcefully on her own behalf."

Lorisa wondered what her mother would say if she knew how often her daughter longed for just one pair of dark eyes in one brown face in which to see herself mirrored and know herself whole in moments when she was erased by her co-workers' assumptions about her ability or brains based on her color, not to mention her sex. It was only now that she, herself, realized how much she needed for that brown face to belong to a woman. How long had it been since she'd had one of those I-can-tell-you-cause-you're-just-like-me talks that she remembered from her late childhood and early teens? But that was before she and her girlfriends had been made to understand the ways in which they were destined to compete and to apprehend the generally accepted fact that women could not be trusted.

Still, she'd been smart to keep her mouth shut with Daily. The economy wasn't all that good and lots of companies were no longer interested in trying to incorporate blacks. She could have opened her mouth and ended up with nothing more than her pride. No job. No money. No future. She picked at the possibility like a worrisome scab, imagining herself unable to pay the rent on her newly furnished and decorated apartment or meet the payments on her new car, living a life of frozen fish sticks and cheap pantyhose in a roach-ridden apartment. She saw herself clerking in a supermarket or department store, waiting on people who had once waited on her. Or worse. The face of the cleaning woman from her office replaced Daily's in her mind's eye—the woman's scowl, her hands in cheap rubber gloves, her eyes showing something hot and unsettling, like the first glow of an eruption-bound volcano.

They said it wasn't like the old days. Nowadays, blacks could do anything whites could do. Hadn't a black man gone into space? Hadn't a black woman been named Miss America? Then why was it, she wondered, that the minute she began to contemplate being out of work and what would be available to her, it was only work near the bottom that she expected to find? It was as though her degrees, her experience and skills would amount to nothing, once she descended into the ranks of the black unemployed.

But she was not going to be unemployed. She was not going to be on the outside. She was from a family of achievers. Her father was the first black to get an engineering degree from his alma mater. Her mother had been named best teacher by the local parent-teacher's association for three years in a row. How could she ever explain getting fired to them? Or to members of the black business women's association she'd recently joined? No. She intended to stay right where she was and prove to Carstairs and Carstairs that she was just as dedicated to profit margins and sales, just as adept at sniffing out a rival's weakness and moving in for the kill, just as practiced in the fine art of kissing her superior's ass, as any white boy they could find. She rose quickly from the tub and snatched her towel off the rack, irritated that relaxation had once again eluded her.

* * *

The room was starting to have that acrid, funky odor of people in danger of losing their last dime. Jackie looked around the card table. Light bounced off Big Red's freckled forehead; his belly was a half-submerged beach ball bobbing above the table. Mabel's lips were pressed near to disappearance. It was a look she'd wear as long as there were cards on the table. Her gambling mask, she called it. Bernice was half drunk. Jackie hated playing cards with drunks. They either knocked over a drink and soaked the cards, or started some shit with one of the other players. Bernice had already signified to Alma about the whereabouts and doings of Alma's old man, Rickie, a good-looking Puerto Rican with a Jones for blue-black thighs. Ramrod Slim sat just like his name. His color and the millions of tiny wrinkles on his face reminded Jackie of raisins and prunes.

Jackie riveted her eyes and attention on Slim's hands as he passed out the cards. The hand he dealt her was as indifferent as all the other hands she'd been dealt tonight. Sweat formed a film separating her fingers from the cards. Oh Jesus! If she could just win a couple of hands, win just enough to pay on Carl's dental bill so the dentist would adjust the child's braces. She gritted her teeth at the memory of the note Carl had brought home when he went for his last visit, a note saying he shouldn't return without at least a fifty-dollar payment. Bastard! Honky bastard! All they ever cared about was money. But, of course, it was more than the dentist's money she needed now.

When she'd decided to get in the game, she'd told herself she had twelve dollars' card-playing money. If she lost it, she would leave the game and not have lost anything other than the little bit of extra money she had left over from her bills and other necessities. If she won, there'd be money for the dentist and the shoes she needed so badly. She'd found a quarter on the way to work—a sure sign of luck.

But not only had she lost her twelve dollars, she'd also lost her light bill money, all of her carfare for next week and was now in danger of losing part of her grocery money. She gripped her cards and plucked. Damn! Shit on top of shit. She wasn't hardly in the way of winning this hand. She longed for a drink to take away the taste of defeat, to drown the knowledge of once again having made the wrong decision, taken the wrong risk. She would have to get some money from somewhere. She let her mind run over her list of friends in order of the likelihood of their being able to lend her something and was further disheartened. Almost everybody she knew was either laid off or about to be. Those who were

working steady were in debt and had kids to feed, too. She didn't have a man at the moment. The last one had borrowed twenty-five dollars from her and disappeared. But she would have to find the money somewhere, somehow. She wondered what it would be like to be able to lose this little bit of cash—not much more than a pair of those alligator pumps that woman had worn in the building where she'd cleaned yesterday. She tried to make space in her anxious mind in which to imagine having enough money not to constantly be concerned about it.

"Girl! Is you gonna play cards or daydream?" Big Red grumbled.

Jackie made a desultory play, waited for her inevitable loss, indifferent to whom the winner might be.

* * *

The Carstairs were consummate party givers. They liked entertaining. They liked the accolades providing lavish amounts of expensive food and drink brought them. It was what they did instead of donating to charity. Mr. Carstairs invariably invited all the professional members of the firm and made no secret of how much pleasure it gave him when they were all in attendance. As usual, on party nights, the front door of the Carstairs' twenty-room country place was wide open. A jumble of voices underscored the music that danced out to meet Lorisa as she walked slowly up the front steps.

She hoped it would be different this time. Perhaps, just this once, they would not all turn toward her when she first entered the room and leave her feeling blotted out by their blank, collective stare. She could have made it easier on herself by bringing a date, but she didn't know a man she disliked and trusted enough to subject to one of the Carstairs' parties, or a man who liked her well enough to make the sacrifice. Nevertheless, she attended all the Carstairs' parties, always leaving just as someone started banging out "Dixie" on the piano or telling the latest Jewish, Polish, or gay joke. She knew who would be the butt of the next go-round.

But tonight, she would do more than put in a respectful appearance. Tonight she would prove she was prepared to make whatever sacrifice necessary to play on the team. For she'd decided that it was her non-team player behavior—her inability to laugh at a good joke, no matter who was the butt of it; her momentary appearances at office social functions; her inability to make other staff accept that she was no different from them in any way that counted —that kept her from total acceptance into the firm. Tonight, she would break through the opaque bubble that seemed to keep her from being seen or heard, making her as murky to the whites on staff as they were to her.

After the usual genuflection before the Carstairs and the obligatory exchange of comments about how very glad they were she could come and how pleased she was to be there, Lorisa ordered a stiff drink from the barman and began to circulate with determination. She stopped at one small grouping after another, asking about wives and children, looking interested in golf scores, remaining noncommittal on the issues of busing and affirmative action until her tongue felt swollen, her lips parched and stretched beyond recovery. And still she pressed on: dancing with Bill Steele; laughing at Daily's tasteless joke about a crippled child; listening to Mrs. Carstairs reminisce about Annie Lee, the dear, dead, colored woman who had raised her, while her mama languished on a chaise lounge with a twenty-year-old migraine. And still she pressed on.

And she thought she made her point. She was sure she saw some of them, the ones who counted —the ones who watched the junior staff for signs of weakness or leadership—smile in her direction, nodding their heads as though dispensing a blessing when she caught their eye. Her success was clear in the gentle hug from Mrs. Carstairs, a sign of approval that all the women in the office had come to covet. It was this sense of having proved herself worthy that made her decide to speak to Jill Franklin.

She'd had no intention of trying to enlist anyone in the firm in her struggles with Daily. While she felt one or two of them—including Jill—might be sympathetic, none of them had ever attempted to intervene on her behalf or had even shown overt empathy for her. But the flush of acceptance made her feel as though she had a right to make requests of staff, just like any other member of the firm. She'd been talk-

ing to Jill and Ken Horton, whose offices bordered her own, about baseball, until Ken's wife dragged him away. For a few moments, both of the women were quiet. Lorisa gathered strength from the silence, then spoke.

"Listen, Jill, I need to ask you something. You've been working with Jim Daily for a while, now. And you seem to know him well, get along with him. Tell me, is there anything I can do to make him stop?"

"Stop what?" Jill's voice was full of innocent curiosity, her face bland as milk.

For the first time, since she'd arrived at the party, Lorisa looked someone directly in the eye. Jill's eyes had that same blue distance she saw in Daily's eyes.

"Stop . . ." she began, searching desperately for something safe to say to cover her error.

"Hey, you two! This is a party, come out of that corner!" Somebody Lorisa didn't recognize grabbed Jill's hand and pulled her out to the patio where some people were dancing. Lorisa went in search of the Carstairs and made her good-nights.

* * *

Jackie spotted Mr. Gus as soon as she pushed open the door. He was where she'd expected him to be this time of evening: on his favorite stool near the far end of the bar, away from the juke box in the front of the long room, but not too close to the bathrooms at the back.

"Hey, Miz Pretty." Harold rubbed his grungy bar cloth in a circle and gave her a wink. Cissy and her old man, Juice (so called for his love of it), sat in a booth opposite the bar and stared past each other. Miz Hazel, who ran the newspaper stand, nursed a mug of beer and half a shot of something while she and Harold watched a baseball game on the portable TV at their end of the bar. Jackie was glad for the game. Talking to Mr. Gus would be easier than if the juke box was going. And she did have to talk to Mr. Gus. She'd tried all her girlfriends, her mother and even her hairdresser. Everyone was broke as she was. Mr. Gus was her last hope. She stopped thinking about all the years she'd promised herself that no matter how broke she got, she wouldn't turn to this sly, old brown coot.

She slid onto a stool three up from Mr. Gus and

told Harold to bring her a vodka and orange juice. She glanced at Mr. Gus in the long mirror hanging behind the rows of bottles in front of her. He was looking at the newspaper lying on the bar beside his glass. He didn't lean over the paper, the way most people would. He sat with his back straight, his head slightly inclined, his folded hands resting on the edge of the bar in front of his drink. The white of his shirt glistened in the blue bar light. She had never seen him without shirt and tie, despite the fact that he wore a uniform at work, just like her.

"How you doin', Mr. Gus?"

He looked up as though surprised to find her there, as though he hadn't seen her from the moment she stepped in the door, as though he hadn't been waiting for her since she was a little girl. Mr. Gus was a neighborhood institution. Being a man who understood the economic realities of most black women's lives, he'd cultivated two generations of little girls and was working on a third generation. He took them for rides in his car, gave them candy—all on the up and up, of course. He would never touch a child. He got a portion of his pleasure from waiting, anticipating. Many of Jackie's little playmates had come to learn they could depend on their old friend, nice Mr. Gus, for treats in their adult lives, too. Only now the candy was cash and the price was higher than a "Thank you, Mr. Gus." But despite the fact that she made next-to-no salary and had a child to raise, Jackie had never come around. Until now. Mr. Gus smiled.

"Anything in the paper about that boy who got shot on Franklin Street, last night?" Jackie craned her neck in his direction, her eyes seeming to search the front page of the paper, her chest thrust forward, in her low-cut sweater. She skipped her behind over the barstools between them, still pretending to be intent upon the headlines. But she was mindful of the cat-with-cream smile on his face. It was a smile that made her sure he knew why she was there; that he had sensed, in that special way some men have, that she was vulnerable, could be run to ground like a wounded doe.

She hadn't meant to drink so much, but Mr. Gus was generous. And he was an excellent listener.

There was something about his attitude, his stillness and sympathetic expression that allowed women to tell him things they wouldn't reveal to their best friends. They told their men's secrets, what they had dreamed about the night before and anything else that was on their minds, as though injected with a truth-inducing drug. To many women, what was a little sex for badly needed cash, after this kind of intimacy? It was a line of thinking Mr. Gus encouraged.

And so, Jackie had rattled on about her lousy job and what her supervisor had said to her and how hard it was trying to raise a boy alone. Mr. Gus nodded and tsked, asked a question or two to prime the pump when she hesitated, ordered more drinks and waited for the beg, the plea. And, of course, the payback.

But in the end, Jackie couldn't do it. She told him how badly Carl needed his braces adjusted and what a fool she'd been to lose her carfare and light bill money in a card game. But when it came to asking him could he see his way clear to let her have seventy-five or even fifty dollars, the same hard glint in his eye that had put her off as a child made her hold her tongue. She did try to get him to say his lines—to ask why she sighed so forlornly, or what she meant when she said, in that frightened voice, that she didn't know what she was going to do. But Mr. Gus refused to play. He wanted the beg. He'd been waiting for it for a long, long time.

They left the bar together. Jackie now a little rocky on her feet, Mr. Gus unwilling to lose when he was so very close. He took her up to his place for one last drink. The smell of old men's undershirts sobered her a bit.

"I sure hate to see you in such a bad way," he said as she sat at his kitchen table trying to adjust her breathing to the bad air.

"Course, you coulda had all I got." He poured another dollop of Seagrams in her jelly glass. Jackie quickly drank it down.

"I don't know why you always been so mean to me, Miz Jackie." He rose and walked to stand behind her chair, kneading her left shoulder with pudgy fingers that radiated damp heat, like a moist heat pad. She willed herself not to pull her shoulder away. He breathed like a cat purring.

"Why you so mean, Miz Jackie?" He spoke in a wheedling, whiny tone, as though he, not she, were on the beg.

"You know Mr. Gus ain't gon let you and little Carl go wanting. Don't you know that, now?" He crept closer to the back of her chair, still moving his fingers in damp slow circles.

"I got me a little piece of money, right here in the bedroom; and I want you to have it."

* * *

At first, Lorisa had considered it a sign of her growing esteem among her superiors that she was chosen to take Stanley Wider, of Wider Housewares, to dinner for a preliminary discussion about his signing a contract with the firm. She was so grateful for any indication of growing favor that it hadn't occurred to her to wonder why she, a junior member of the firm, with no real experience with prestigious clients, should be given this plum. The Wider account had the potential for being very big, very important to the career of whoever pulled him in. Now that dinner with Wider was nearly over, Lorisa understood why she'd been chosen.

Mr. Wider was what the women in the office called "a lunch man"—a client who turned into a sex fiend after dark and could, therefore, only be talked to over lunch. Looking at him, anyone would think he was a kindly, trustworthy genteel man— like Walter Cronkite. Only his eyes and his words told the truth about him. She smiled up from her Peach Melba into his lean, clean-shaven face to find his eyes once again caressing her breasts. He smiled sheepishly, boyishly, when he realized he'd been caught. But his eyes remained cold and hard.

Ralph Wider was a serious pursuer of young corporate women on the rise. In the sixties, when women began pressuring for more room at the top, he'd been bitterly against the idea. But a chance encounter with an extremely ambitious female sales representative had shown him the benefits of affirmative action. In his analysis, women in business fell into two categories: those who were confident and competent enough to know they didn't need to take their panties down to do business; and those who could be convinced that in at least his case, a little sex would get them more business than a lot of facts. He didn't meet many black ones and the ones he met were always smart. He figured they had to be to get high enough to deal with him. But he had a fairly good record of convincing category-one women to slip down a notch. The challenge added spice to his business dealings.

"We're very excited about the possibility of working with your people," Lorisa began, trying once again to introduce the reason for their having dinner together. "We think we can . . ."

"You know, I've always admired black women. You all are so . . . so uninhibited." He stretched the last word out into an obscenity. "I bet you can be a very friendly young lady, when you want to be."

This man is important, not just to the firm, but to my career, Lorisa reminded herself before she spoke.

"I'm afraid I've never been particularly famous for my friendliness, Mr. Wider, but I am a first rate efficiency specialist and I've got some ideas about how to increase . . ."

He lifted his glass in a toast as she spoke. "To freedom" he said with a sly grin.

Twice more she tried to raise the subject of business. Each time he countered with another invitation to spend a weekend on his boat or take a ride in his plane, or have dinner with him in his hotel room the following night.

She knew what she should say to him. She'd practiced gently and firmly explaining that she did not appreciate passes as a part of her work. But she'd never had occasion to use that speech, before. And this man had the power to greatly improve her position in the firm, simply by what he said about their evening together.

"Excuse me," she said between dessert and cognac. She could feel his eyes poking at her behind as she headed for the Ladies Room.

She wrapped wet paper towels around her neck, careful not to dampen her blouse and held her wrists under the cold water tap to calm herself. Tears quickened in her eyes at the sudden desire to tell some woman her woes; to explain about *him* being out there waiting for her and what ought she to do. Somebody deep inside urged her to go out there, pour a glass of ice water in his lap and run like hell—the same someone who'd urged her to talk to Daily as though he had a tail; the same someone who'd urged her to major in archeology instead of business and to stop smiling at white people, at least on weekends. But she was no fool. She wanted the Wider account and the prestige of getting it. She wanted her salary, her vacations, her car. She wanted to prove she was just as good as anybody else in the firm. At the moment, she just didn't know why she needed to prove it.

Lorisa dried her hands, checked her make-up and straightened her shoulders. She couldn't come apart now. She couldn't let them think she was incapable of handling any task the firm gave her. For all she knew, she was being tested. She brushed at her hair and willed that frightened look out of her eyes. I have a contract to get, she told herself as she opened the door.

She stared at his slim, distinguished figure as she crossed the room. So deceiving, she thought, like a bright shiny apple turned to maggotty mush on the inside. But if she could just get him to agree to look at the prospectus. He rose as she returned to her seat.

"I mean it, little lady," he said as he sat down, "I think you're really something special. I'm sure I can do business with you!" he added with a smile as his leg brushed hers beneath the table.

* * *

If there'd been any way for Lorisa to avoid getting on the elevator with Jackie, she'd have done so. If there'd been other people she'd have had no hesitation about getting on. Other people would have kept her from speaking, as she now feared she might. She didn't look at the woman as she entered the elevator, but she didn't need to. She remembered those eyes. The elevator doors hissed shut before her. The lobby button was already lit so she had only to stand there. She kept her eyes straight ahead and wondered if the elevator always moved this slowly or if the

damned thing was going to stall, leaving them alone together for the rest of the night.

Jackie studied Lorisa's back and tried to get up the courage to say something. This was the first time she'd seen the woman since their encounter a couple of evenings ago. She still felt bad about how she'd responded. She wanted to apologize, maybe even change her luck by doing so.

"I'm real sorry for the way I acted the other day. Let me buy you a drink to make up for it," she practiced in her head, even though she didn't have enough money to buy herself a drink. She saw the two of them walking down the street to Libby's Place where she knew she could buy a round or two on credit. They would sit in a booth near the back. The juke box would be off, so the place would be quiet enough for talk. The woman would buy her a drink in return and they would talk about what they needed to talk about. Wasn't no black woman's life without something that needed talking about. But none of that was really going to happen. She could tell from the way the woman stood that she didn't want to be bothered.

As the elevator reached the lower floors, Lorisa reached in her pocket, pulled out her leather driving gloves and smoothed them on over long, slim fingers. She tried to keep her attention focused on what she was doing and away from her urge to somehow make herself acceptable to the woman standing behind her.

"Girl, you sure are evil!" she heard herself saying in a way that smacked of respect for the woman's willingness to give her economic betters hell. She saw them walking out of the building together. She would tell the woman her name and offer her a lift. Their talk in the car would be slow but easy. They might discover they liked one another.

But, of course, that whole scene was irrational. Why should she take a chance on being insulted again? Why should it make any difference to her whether this woman considered her somebody worth being pleasant to? She pressed her lips firmly together as the elevator finally slid to a stop. She stepped quickly forward and brisk-stepped her way to the other door, trying to put as much distance between herself and the cleaning woman as possible, before she did something she would regret.

After all, it wasn't as though they had anything in common.   [1985]

98

Jewish and Working Class

BERNICE MENNIS

When I was called to speak at this conference about working-class experience, my immediate reaction was: "No, get someone else." One voice said: "I have nothing worthwhile to say." A second voice said: "I was not born poor. I always ate well. I never felt deprived. I have not suffered enough to be on this panel." Both voices silenced me. The first came from my class background—a diminished sense of competence, ability, control, power. ("Who are you anyway? You have nothing to say. No one cares or will listen.") The second, the guilt voice, comes from a strange combination of my Jewishness, my fear of anti-Semitism, my own psychological reaction to my own deprivations: a denial of my own pain if someone else seems to suffer more.

Economic class has been a matter of both shame and pride for me, depending on the value judgments of the community with which I identified. The economic class reality has always remained the same: My father had a very small outdoor tomato and banana stand and a small cellar for ripening the fruit. Until he was 68, he worked twelve hours a day, six days a week, with one week vacation. Although he worked hard and supported our family well, my father did not feel proud of his work, did not affirm his strength. Instead, he was ashamed to have me visit his fruit stand; he saw his work as dirty, himself as an "ignorant greenhorn." The legacy of class.

And I accepted and echoed back his shame. In elementary school, when we had to go around and

say what work our parents did, I repeated my father's euphemistic words: "My father sells wholesale and retail fruits and vegetables." It's interesting that later, when I was involved in political actions, my shame turned to pride of that same class background. The poorer one was born, the better, the more credit.

Both reactions—shame and pride—are based on a false assumption that one has control and responsibility for what one is born into. (Society—those in power, institutions—is responsible for people being born into conditions of economic limitation and suffering, for racism and classism. But as individuals we do not choose our birth.) That blame/credit often prevents us from seeing clearly the actual effects of growing up in a certain class: what it allows, what it inhibits, blocks, destroys. Also, if we take credit for what is out of our control, we sometimes do not take sufficient credit and responsibility for what is in our control: our consciousness, our actions, how we shape our lives.

What becomes difficult immediately in trying to understand class background is how it becomes hopelessly entangled with other issues: the fact that my father was an immigrant who spoke with a strong accent, never felt competent to write in English, always felt a great sense of self-shame that he projected onto his children; that my father had witnessed pogroms and daily anti-Semitism in his tiny *shtetl* in Russia, that we were Jewish, that the Holocaust occurred; that neither of my parents went to school beyond junior high school; that I was the younger daughter, the "good" child who accepted almost everything without complaining or acknowledging pain; that my sister and I experienced our worlds very differently and responded in almost opposite ways. It's difficult to sort out class, to see clearly. . . .

Feelings of poverty or wealth are based on one's experiences and where one falls on the economic spectrum. The economic class and the conditions we grow up under are very real, objective, but how we label and see those circumstances is relative, shaped by what we see outside ourselves. Growing up in the Pelham Parkway–Lydig Avenue area of the Bronx, I heard my circumstances echoed everywhere: Everyone's parents spoke Yiddish and had accents; they all spoke loudly and with their hands; few were educated beyond junior high school; no one dressed stylishly or went to restaurants (except for special occasions) or had fancy cars or dishwashers or clothes washers. (Our apartment building had, and still has, only one washing machine for 48 apartments. The lineup of baskets began early in the morning. My mother and I hung the clothes on the roof.) We ate good kosher food and fresh fruits and vegetables (from my uncle's stand). My mother sewed our clothes or we would shop in Alexander's and look for bargains (clothes with the manufacturers' tags removed). Clothes were passed between sisters, cousins, neighbors. I never felt poor or deprived. I had no other perspective, no other reality from which to judge our life.

When I went to the World's Fair and watched the G.E. exhibit of "Our Changing World," I remember being surprised that what I believed was a modern-day kitchen—an exact duplicate of our kitchen at home—was the kitchen of the '40s. When I received a fellowship for graduate school, I was surprised to discover I was eligible for the maximum grant because my parents' income fell in the lowest income category. I was surprised when I met friends whose parents talked about books and psychology and art, when I met people who noticed labels and brand names and talked about clothes and cars (but never mentioned costs and money).

What I also didn't see or appreciate was all the work and struggle of my parents to maintain and nourish us, work done silently and without any credit for many years. A few years ago I wrote a poem called "The Miracle" about my mother and her skilled unacknowledged work.

Clearly our assumptions, expectations, and hopes are unconsciously shaped by our class backgrounds. At a very young age I learned to want only what my parents could afford. It was a good survival mechanism that allowed me never to feel deprived or denied. At a later age, when I would read in natural history books about the "immortal species," the les-

son was reaffirmed: The key to survival was always to become smaller, to minimize needs. Those species that had become dependent on more luxuriant conditions perished during hard times. Those used to less survived.

There is something powerful about surviving by adapting to little. The power comes from an independence of need, an instinct that allows us to get by. But it is a defense, and, like any defense, its main fault was that it never allowed me to feel the edge of my own desires, pains, deprivations. I defined my needs by what was available. Even now I tend to minimize my needs, to never feel deprived—a legacy of my class background.

Class background reveals itself in little ways. Around food, for example. My family would sip their soup loudly, putting mouth close to bowl. We would put containers directly on the table and never use a butter dish. We would suck bone marrow with gusto, pick up chicken bones with our hands, crunch them with our teeth, and leave little slivers on our otherwise empty plates. We would talk loudly and argue politics over supper. Only later did I become conscious of the judgment of others about certain behavior, ways of eating, talking, walking, dressing, being. Polite etiquette struck me as a bit absurd, as if hunger were uncivilized: the delicate portions, the morsels left on the plate, the proper use of knife and fork, the spoon seeming to go in the opposite direction of the mouth. The more remote one was from basic needs, the higher one's class status. I usually was unconscious of the "proper behavior": I did not notice. But if I ever felt the eye of judgment, my first tendency would be to exaggerate my "grossness" in order to show the absurdity of others' snobbish judgments. I would deny that that judgment had any effect other than anger. But I now realize that all judgment has effect. Some of my negative self-image as *klutz, nebbish,* ugly, unsophisticated is a direct result of the reflection I saw in the judging, sophisticated eye of the upper class.

Lack of education and lack of money made for an insecurity and fear of doing almost anything, a fear tremendously compounded by anti-Semitism and World War II. My parents were afraid to take any risks—from both a conviction of their own incompetence and a fear that doing anything big, having any visibility, would place them in danger. From them I inherited a fear that if I touched something, did anything, I would make matters worse. There was an incredible nervousness in my home around fixing anything, buying anything big, filling out any forms. My mother still calls me to complete forms for her. When my father was sick, my parents needed me to translate everything the doctor said, not because they did not understand him, but because their fear stopped them from listening when anyone very educated or in authority spoke.

I did not inherit the fear of those in authority. In fact, my observation of people's condescension, use of authority, and misuse of power helped shape my politics at a young age. I identified with the underdog, was angry at the bully, fought against the misuse of power. But I did inherit their fear of taking risks, of doing anything big, of trying anything new. I have trouble with paper forms; I've never been able to write a grant proposal; I have no credit cards. I sometimes seek invisibility as a form of safety.

For poorer people, for people who experience prejudice, there is a strong feeling that one has no power, no ability to affect or control one's environment. For nine years my family and I lived in a very small three-room apartment; my sister and I had no bedroom of our own. When we moved from the fifth floor to the sixth, we got a tiny room just big enough for two beds and a cabinet. I never thought to put up a picture, to choose a room color or a bedspread. I had no notion of control over private space, of shaping my environment.

That feeling of lack of control over one's environment, of no right to one's own space, was psychologically intensified by my parents' experiences of anti-Semitism and by the Holocaust. These fostered a deep sense of powerlessness and vulnerability and, on an even more basic level, a doubt whether we really had a right to exist on this earth.

In college I took a modern dance class. A group of us began "dancing" by caving in on ourselves, slinking around the side walls of the gym. I remember the teacher saying that to dance one needed to be able to open one's arms and declare the beauty of one's being, to take up one's space on the dance floor: to say "I am here." For many women who experience poverty and prejudice this kind of self-assertion feels foreign, impossible, dangerous. One of the unconscious effects of being born wealthy is a natural sense of one's right to be here on this earth, an essential grace that comes from the feeling of belonging. (The danger, of course, is that wealthier people often take up too much space. They do not see the others crushed under their wide flinging steps.) Where the poorer person's danger is the self-consciousness that shrinks us into invisibility, the wealthier one's is the unconscious arrogance that inflates.

But what happens when one feels self-conscious and small and is seen as large, wealthy, powerful, controlling? At a young age, I knew the anti-Semitic portrait of the wealthy, exploitative Jew. I also knew that I did not feel powerful or controlling. My parents and I felt powerless, fearful, vulnerable. We owned nothing. All my parents saved, after working fifty years, would not equal the cost of one year of college today. What does it mean to have others' definition of one's reality so vastly different from one's experience of it? The effects are confusion, anger, entrapment. I lost touch with what was real, what my own experiences really were.

As a political person I felt particularly vulnerable to the hated image of "the Jew." I knew it was a stereotype and not my experience or the experience of the Jews I grew up with—but it still made me feel guilt, not pride, for any success I did have, for any rise in status. If the stereotype said "Jews have everything," the only way I could avoid that stereotype would be to have nothing. If you are poor, you are not a Jew. If you are successful, you are a bad Jew. The trap.

The economic and professional success of many second-generation Jews became tinged for me, as if we had done something wrong. To feel bad about achievement, to hold back one's power, is very destructive. My aunts and uncles, my parents, my friends' parents all had little education and little money. Yet we—my cousins, my sister, my friends

—not only went to college, but even to graduate school and law school. I was speaking the other day with my aunt, who was saying what a miracle it was that her four children were all professionals and she was poor and uneducated. But the miracle was not really a miracle at all. It was the result of parents who saw education as very, very important—as a way out of the entrapment of class and prejudice. It was the result of parents who worked desperately hard so that their children could have that way out. It was a City College system in New York City that provided completely free education while we worked and lived at home.

In one generation we created an incredible economic, class, professional, and educational distance between ourselves and our parents. The danger of this success is that we forget the material soil that nourished us, the hard work that propped us up; that we lose our consciousness of the harm and evil of condescension, exploitation, oppression, the pain of being made to feel inferior and invisible. Anzia Yezierska, a Jewish immigrant writer, says "Education without a heart is a curse." But to keep that consciousness and that heart and to be able to step onto the dance floor of life and say "I am here," reflecting back to our parents the beauty and strength we inherited from them, that would be a very real "miracle" indeed.   [1987]

 99

Poverty, Hopelessness and Hope

KENDALL A. JOHNSON

I know that I'm one of the lucky ones. I have a law school education, my ticket into the professional middle class. It's been almost a lifetime since those days of picking fruit and vegetables in the deep south, or freezing without heat or running water in a trailer in upstate New York. It sounds like an American dream, and surely it is, but the odds are against

most poor people and they don't make it out. Although I'm truly grateful that I was one of those who did, it saddens me to know that in a wealthy country like ours, most poor people will remain in poverty regardless of their personal efforts to rise above it.

During my early childhood things seemed hopeless. The daily struggles to survive took priority over everything else. In my family working in the fields for money to eat was more important than going to school. Baby sitting for the little ones so the older ones could work also took priority over school. By the time I realized the importance of education, the immediate struggle to survive was pulling me in the opposite direction. I'm sure that many poor children face this dilemma. Unfortunately, most of them succumb to the pressure and drop out.

Some of the most damning social messages received by poor children are during early childhood education. For me, elementary school was a humiliating experience. I remember feeling inferior, stupid, dirty, ugly and hated. In the early years we often found ourselves homeless, so we were always moving around and I attended several different schools in a short time. Being a new kid was bad enough, but being poor and dirty made us additional targets for ridicule by teachers, school administrators and students alike. To further aggravate the situation, we were absent a lot, which made it almost impossible to keep up with grade level.

Under these circumstances, it was hard to feel positive about school. My self-esteem was constantly under attack. I always felt self-conscious and I was aware of the differences between my family and the others who were better off. Furthermore, my mother and older siblings believed that everybody and everything was against us. At the time it was easy to understand why they thought that way. I used to think that the easiest way to cope with the humiliation and maintain some dignity was to fight with the other kids who picked on us. At the time, I believed that if I were tough and fought back, then I could be proud of myself. It seemed easier and it hurt a lot less than quietly swallowing my shame. This of course led to disciplinary problems with the schools, and it wasn't long before I learned that fighting only made things worse. Most of my brothers and sisters never learned this lesson and continued to get in trouble for fighting in school. I think this is partially why so many boys from poor families are labeled as behavior problems and placed in smaller special education classrooms where school administrators feel they can be more easily controlled.

Girls from poor families are less likely to be tracked in this manner because they are less likely to fight back, but the devastation to their self-esteem is notable. Girls in this situation often try to disappear. They sit in the back of the classroom praying that they won't be called on or even noticed. They skip school on days they have gym class so they won't be embarrassed because they don't have appropriate gym clothes or clean socks and underwear. They avoid participating in school activities and seek out a small group of other girls to hang around with from similar backgrounds. I did this for awhile myself. Most of these girls, if they don't drop out of school to have babies, are tracked into vocational studies such as home economics, cosmetology, and non-college bound mathematics and health sciences.

For me high school was very different. I was the only poor kid in my class taking chemistry, trigonometry, and physics, along with the other college bound courses. Although I was very isolated, I understood how poor children were tracked and I took extreme measures to ensure that I wouldn't be. As soon as I was old enough, I worked after school in the packinghouses packing the fruit and vegetables, instead of picking them during school hours. I fought with my mother to let me go to school, rather than baby-sit. I sought out supportive teachers to mentor me and I always carried my schoolbooks home so if I missed school for a few days I could keep up.

I remember thinking, I'm only a kid and I still have a chance. I'm going to be different. If I stay in school and study hard maybe I can go to college. If I go to college, I won't have to stay poor for the rest of my life. This underlying belief fueled my desire for education as a means to escape the poverty. From the time I was 13 years old through my college career, I would recite this line of reasoning to myself. It kept me focused and gave me the inspiration to remain disciplined. I learned to draw strength from struggle. I was determined to walk the moral high ground. I believed that struggle made one a better person than if things came easy. I told myself this as a source of inspiration during hard times. It got to the point where I believed it, which helped me make it through. Ultimately, my strategies worked and law school was the icing on the cake.

By the time I actually made it to college, I felt a lot of guilt associated with leaving my family behind to pursue my own career. One of the hardest things to watch was the hopes and dreams of my siblings and friends turn to defeat and despair, while my own future looked brighter and brighter with each year of college or law school completed. When I'd go home, all I heard about was everyone's problems and how lucky I was to have gotten out.

At the time I was still broke, living on student loans and part-time waitress jobs, while keeping my eye on the prize. But my family didn't see it that way. I was already well off in their eyes. I had made it. The goal that I was trying to achieve was within my grasp and they saw no distinction between working towards it and having already achieved it. I often thought that they credited my success to luck, as though I personally had little to do with it. I felt like they thought that somehow I was bestowed with the power to change things for all of us, but refused to do so for them. This exacerbated their growing resentment towards me and my feelings of guilt. I knew on some level that regardless of my personal struggles, I was luckier. My future was full of promise, while theirs were not. I felt guilty that I couldn't save them and they didn't understand that I was still struggling to save myself.

Furthermore, by that time most of my daily life was spent with educated middle-class people and I was becoming exposed to different values and belief systems. The cultural divide widened and pretty soon it got harder and harder to find things in common with most of my siblings and former community. Before long, the day to day things that we had in common were reduced to memories. This too became a source of guilt. I wanted to romanticize the struggle and some of the values prevalent among poor people in an effort to hang on to my roots and to maintain a connection with those from whom I came.

I wanted to be proud of my accomplishments and I wanted my family to be proud of me as well. But I knew that on several levels they resented me. On the one hand they are proud of my accomplishments, but on the other hand they resented me for what they perceived was my acquisition of middle class values that they found so repressive. It was as though I had become the enemy, the oppressor. I think they thought that I blamed them for being poor. It was like I had become one of those school administrators of my childhood who looked down on us as though we were trash that would never amount to anything.

Moreover, this new value system that I had learned at college was inconsistent with theirs. They had this "us versus them" mentality and I no longer did. Furthermore, in their eyes I had become one of "them." I had become someone to fear. Like the school administrator, I too had the power to have their children taken away. The ignorance, the violence, and the other dysfunctional behaviors were all things that I had openly rejected and they saw my rejection of these things as a rejection of them. In their view, I denied their struggle and thought that I was better than they were.

The truth is, I rejected the ignorance, the violence, and the despair, but I don't reject the people or their struggle. I know that poor people's hardships are genuine and that most people can't overcome them. I'm a realist and I see the real-life obstacles that stand in their way. But I also understand that if you give up and stop trying, you will never succeed.

The prejudice against poor people by the larger society creates additional barriers, which perpetuate poverty. Poor people live such miserable stressed-out lives that they become depressed after struggling for a better life to no avail. They are routinely abused by welfare workers when applying for assistance, which negatively affects their self-esteem, causing undue anxiety, frustration and even major depression. Negotiating the welfare system is a difficult and humiliating experience, and anyone who has done it will tell you the same. The system is designed to discourage and disqualify people from receiving benefits, rather than helping them. Emotionally abusing

applicants and recipients is the most obvious tactic used in this endeavor. Baseless denials and cutoffs of benefits are another. Poor people often go without basic essentials for months at a time while waiting for benefits to be issued or restored. Their bills go unpaid and many of them experience eviction from their housing, even though they have complied with every request that the welfare agency has asked of them.

The working poor are exploited by employers and often have the limited choices of working for unlivable wages without medical benefits or pension plans, or bowing their heads in shame and enduring the abuse of the welfare system in order to get the assistance they need. Most people receiving public assistance work and make so little money on their jobs that they need additional assistance in order to survive.

Most poor people are women and children. And as we already know working women earn significantly less money then men. They are also significantly less likely to abandon their children. As a result, they are left with the sole physical and financial responsibilities for their children, on about two-thirds of a man's paycheck. Although state welfare plans provide child-support collection departments, the onus of locating the fathers and their resources is generally placed on the shoulders of the women, who are often denied benefits by welfare agencies for not having the relevant information.

After being defeated at every turn, depression and despair are inevitable. Hope turns to hopelessness, which is often misinterpreted as laziness. The more sympathetic middle-class experts refer to this hopelessness as learned helplessness, as though it were phenomena endemic to the poor. I think that it is a perfectly normal response to the circumstances that poor people face. Although it's not a particularly healthy one, neither are the circumstances.

I think that a significant factor in overcoming poverty is struggling against crippling hopelessness and despair. The ability to fight against the overwhelming tide may be the single most important ingredient in actually escaping the cycle. The belief that one has the individual power to change her life against the odds, to me was essential. Although this belief may not be enough for most people, I can't imagine having ever succeeded without it.

I realize that faith and hard work alone are usually not enough, and I acknowledge that coming from a rich first-world country gave me advantages and opportunities that otherwise wouldn't have been available to me. There is no doubt in my mind that there is an element of luck involved. But it is often that luck coupled with the sheer determination of the individual that can sometimes make the difference.

Over the years I have learned that I cannot control what my family thinks. But my guilt for having left them behind has never completely subsided. As time has passed it has gotten easier since many of my family elders have passed away. But it's still painful to witness my siblings aging so quickly, and to watch their children as defeated by poverty as they were.

I guess that part of my sadness stems from the fact that I know that most poor people are not responsible for their poverty and that contrary to common beliefs, they personally have little power to change their situation. In a capitalist system like ours, poverty is inevitable regardless of how rich the country is. Corporate America benefits from the fact that there are no Federal laws guaranteeing workers a livable and fair wage that corresponds with inflation and cost of living. Under this system, it is no surprise that it is those already burdened with sexism and/or racism who are most likely to fall to the bottom of the economic scale.

I make it a point to remind myself of how lucky I am. And I believe that those of us who become educated and escape the traps of poverty have a responsibility to those less fortunate. This sense of duty was ingrained in me, and it is one of those values that I learned from my family that I choose to keep. My family always expected my help, and I felt a responsibility to provide it. Unfortunately, I was unable to cure the ills causing their poverty, and I don't think that I will ever completely get over it.

I cope with my guilt in part by dedicating my professional career to providing legal services to the poor. For the past ten years I have fought in the civil courts to provide affordable housing for poor women and children in New York City. Unfortunately, I often feel like my services are accomplishing little more than putting a band-aid on a hemorrhage. Even so, I take solace in the fact that each time I save a poor family from eviction, I make a difference in their individual lives. I think to myself, maybe the kids can stay in the same school a little longer. And maybe one of those kids will find the will and determination along with a little luck to overcome her adversity.   [2002]

100

Grace Paley Reading

TOI DERRICOTTE

Finally, the audience gets
restless, & they send me
to hunt for Grace. I find her
backing out of the bathroom, bending
over, wiping up her footprints
as she goes with a little
sheet of toilet paper, explaining,
"In some places, after the lady mops, the bosses
    come to check on her.
I just don't want them to think
she didn't do her job."   [1997]

"Are You Some Kind of Dyke?"
The Perils of Heterosexism

Attitudes toward lesbians vary across culture and have changed over time. In the United States, loving sensual relationships between women were not seen as deviant in the seventeenth through nineteenth centuries; it was women who passed as men who were punished. In the late nineteenth century medical experts began to define lesbianism as an illness, and close connections among women became suspect. After World War II the taboos against lesbianism became extremely powerful, resulting in the erasure of lesbian experience from history; discrimination against lesbians in social, political, and economic institutions; and the proliferation of prejudices, misconceptions, and myths about lesbian life.

The essays and short story in this section examine the consequences of heterosexism for all women, exploring the ways that heterosexuality is enforced through prejudice, fear, and the denial of resources to lesbian couples. Suzanne Pharr demonstates that homophobia, the fear of homosexuality, and heterosexism—the assumption that heterosexuality is a superior way of life—are used to prevent all women from challenging sexism. In "Cat," love between two young girls feels natural to them until the prejudice of adults destroys it. Carla Trujillo describes the ways that Chicana lesbians are threatening to the established power relations in the Chicano community and urges Chicanas to recognize the commonalities among lesbian and heterosexual women.

Because of the hostility and bigotry lesbians face, coming out is a difficult process for both lesbians and their children. In some situations, being open about being a lesbian entails serious risks. For both Jewelle Gomez and Megan McGuire, however, relationships with friends and family were strengthened when they were open about their lives.

101

Homophobia and Sexism

SUZANNE PHARR

Homophobia works effectively as a weapon of sexism because it is joined with a powerful arm, heterosexism. Heterosexism creates the climate for homophobia with its assumption that the world is and must be heterosexual and its display of power and privilege as the norm. Heterosexism is the systemic display of homophobia in the institutions of society. Heterosexism and homophobia work together to enforce compulsory heterosexuality and that bastion of patriarchal power, the nuclear family. The central focus of the rightwing attack against women's liberation is that women's equality, women's self-determination, women's control of our own bodies and lives will damage what they see as the crucial societal institution, the nuclear family. The attack has been led by fundamentalist ministers across the country. The two areas they have focused on most consistently are abortion and homosexuality, and their passion has led them to bomb women's clinics and to recommend deprogramming for homosexuals and establishing camps to quarantine people with AIDS. To resist marriage and/or heterosexuality is to risk severe punishment and loss.

It is not by chance that when children approach puberty and increased sexual awareness they begin to taunt each other by calling these names: "queer," "faggot," "pervert." It is at puberty that the full force of society's pressure to conform to heterosexuality and prepare for marriage is brought to bear. Children know what we have taught them, and we have given clear messages that those who deviate from standard expectations are to be made to get back in line. The best controlling tactic at puberty is to be treated as an outsider, to be ostracized at a time when it feels most vital to be accepted. Those who are different must be made to suffer loss. It is also at puberty that misogyny begins to be more apparent, and girls are pressured to conform to societal norms that do not permit them to realize their full potential. It is at this time that their academic achievements begin to decrease as they are coerced into compulsory heterosexuality and trained for dependency upon a man, that is, for economic survival.

There was a time when the two most condemning accusations against a woman meant to ostracize and disempower her were "whore" and "lesbian." The sexual revolution and changing attitudes about heterosexual behavior may have led to some lessening of the power of the word *whore,* though it still has strength as a threat to sexual property and prostitutes are stigmatized and abused. However, the word *lesbian* is still fully charged and carries with it the full threat of loss of power and privilege, the threat of being cut asunder, abandoned, and left outside society's protection.

To be a lesbian is to be *perceived* as someone who has stepped out of line, who has moved out of sexual/economic dependence on a male, who is woman-identified. A lesbian is perceived as someone who can live without a man, and who is therefore (however illogically) against men. A lesbian is perceived as being outside the acceptable, routinized order of things. She is seen as someone who has no societal institutions to protect her and who is not privileged to the protection of individual males. Many heterosexual women see her as someone who stands in contradiction to the sacrifices they have made to conform to compulsory heterosexuality. A lesbian is perceived as a threat to the nuclear family, to male dominance and control, to the very heart of sexism.

Gay men are perceived also as a threat to male dominance and control, and the homophobia expressed against them has the same roots in sexism as does homophobia against lesbians. Visible gay men are the objects of extreme hatred and fear by heterosexual men because their breaking ranks with male heterosexual solidarity is seen as a damaging rent in the very fabric of sexism. They are seen as betrayers, as traitors who must be punished and eliminated. In the beating and killing of gay men we see clear evidence of this hatred. When we see the fierce homophobia expressed toward gay men, we can begin to understand the ways sexism also affects males through imposing rigid, dehumanizing gender roles on them. The two circumstances in which it is legitimate for men to be openly physically affectionate with one another are in competitive sports and in the crisis of war. For many men, these two experiences are the highlights of their lives, and they think of them again and again with nostalgia. War and sports offer a cover of all-male safety and dominance to keep away the notion of affectionate openness being identified with homosexuality. When gay men break ranks with male roles through bonding and affection outside the arenas of war and sports, they are perceived as not being "real men," that is, as being identified with women, the weaker sex that must be dominated and that over the centuries has been the object of male hatred and abuse. Misogyny gets transferred to gay men with a vengeance and is increased by the fear that their sexual identity and behavior will bring down the entire system of male dominance and compulsory heterosexuality.

If lesbians are established as threats to the status quo, as outcasts who must be punished, homophobia can wield its power over all women through lesbian baiting. Lesbian baiting is an attempt to control women by labeling us as lesbians because our behavior is not acceptable, that is, when we are being independent, going our own way, living whole lives, fighting for our rights, demanding equal pay, saying no to violence, being self-assertive, bonding with and loving the company of women, assuming the right to our bodies, insisting upon our own authority, making changes that include us in society's decision-making; lesbian baiting occurs when women are called lesbians because we resist male dominance and control. And it has little or nothing to do with one's sexual identity.

To be named as lesbian threatens all women, not just lesbians, with great loss. And any woman who steps out of role risks being called a lesbian. To understand how this is a threat to all women, one must understand that any woman can be called a lesbian and there is no real way she can defend herself: there is no way to credential one's sexuality. ("The Children's Hour," a Lillian Hellman play, makes this point when a student asserts two teachers are lesbians and they have no way to disprove it.) She may be married or divorced, have children, dress in the most feminine manner, have sex with men, be celibate—but there are lesbians who do all those things. *Lesbians look like all women and all women look like lesbians.* There is no guaranteed method of identification, and as we all know, sexual identity can be kept hidden. (The same is true for men. There is no way to prove their sexual identity, though many go to extremes to prove heterosexuality.) Also, women are not necessarily born lesbian. Some seem to be, but others become lesbians later in life after having lived heterosexual lives. Lesbian baiting of heterosexual women would not work if there were a definitive way to identify lesbians (or heterosexuals).

We have yet to understand clearly how sexual identity develops. And this is disturbing to some people, especially those who are determined to discover how lesbian and gay identity is formed so that they will know where to start in eliminating it. (Isn't it odd that there is so little concern about discovering the causes of heterosexuality?) There are many theories: genetic makeup, hormones, socialization,

environment, etc. But there is no conclusive evidence that indicates that heterosexuality comes from one process and homosexuality from another.

We do know, however, that sexual identity can be in flux, and we know that sexual identity means more than just the gender of people one is attracted to and has sex with. To be a lesbian has as many ramifications as for a woman to be heterosexual. It is more than sex, more than just the bedroom issue many would like to make it: it is a woman-centered life with all the social interconnections that entails. Some lesbians are in long-term relationships, some in short-term ones, some date, some are celibate, some are married to men, some remain as separate as possible from men, some have children by men, some by alternative insemination, some seem "feminine" by societal standards, some "masculine," some are doctors, lawyers and ministers, some laborers, housewives and writers: what all share in common is a sexual/affectional identity that focuses on women in its attractions and social relationships.

If lesbians are simply women with a particular sexual identity who look and act like all women, then the major difference in living out a lesbian sexual identity as opposed to a heterosexual identity is that as lesbians we live in a homophobic world that threatens and imposes damaging loss on us for being *who we are,* for choosing to live whole lives. Homophobic people often assert that homosexuals have the choice of not being homosexual; that is, we don't have to act out our sexual identity. In that case, I want to hear heterosexuals talk about their willingness not to act out their sexual identity, including not just sexual activity but heterosexual social interconnections and heterosexual privilege. It is a question of wholeness. It is very difficult for one to be denied the life of a sexual being, whether expressed in sex or in physical affection, and to feel complete, whole. For our loving relationships with humans feed the life of the spirit and enable us to overcome our basic isolation and to be interconnected with humankind.

If, then, any woman can be named a lesbian and be threatened with terrible losses, what is it she fears? Are these fears real? Being vulnerable to a homophobic world can lead to these losses:

- *Employment.* The loss of job leads us right back to the economic connection to sexism. This fear of job loss exists for almost every lesbian except perhaps those who are self-employed or in a business that does not require societal approval. Consider how many businesses or organizations you know that will hire and protect people who are openly gay or lesbian.
- *Family.* Their approval, acceptance, love.
- *Children.* Many lesbians and gay men have children, but very, very few gain custody in court challenges, even if the other parent is a known abuser. Other children may be kept away from us as though gays and lesbians are abusers. There are written and unwritten laws prohibiting lesbians and gays from being foster parents or from adopting children. There is an irrational fear that children in contact with lesbians and gays will become homosexual through influence or that they will be sexually abused. Despite our knowing that 95 percent of those who sexually abuse children are heterosexual men, there are no policies keeping heterosexual men from teaching or working with children, yet in almost every school system in America, visibly gay men and lesbians are not hired through either written or unwritten laws.
- *Heterosexual privilege and protection.* No institutions, other than those created by lesbians and gays —such as the Metropolitan Community Church, some counseling centers, political organizations such as the National Gay and Lesbian Task Force, the National Coalition of Black Lesbians and Gays, the Lambda Legal Defense and Education Fund, etc.,—affirm homosexuality and offer protection. Affirmation and protection cannot be gained from the criminal justice system, mainstream churches, educational institutions, the government.
- *Safety.* There is nowhere to turn for safety from physical and verbal attacks because the norm presently in this country is that it is acceptable to be overtly homophobic. Gay men are beaten on the streets; lesbians are kidnapped and "deprogrammed." The National Gay and Lesbian Task Force, in an extended study, has documented violence against lesbians and gay men and noted the inadequate response of the criminal justice system.

One of the major differences between homophobia/heterosexism and racism and sexism is that because of the Civil Rights Movement and the women's movement racism and sexism are expressed more covertly (though with great harm); because there has not been a major, visible lesbian and gay movement, it is permissible to be overtly homophobic in any institution or public forum. Churches spew forth homophobia in the same way they did racism prior to the Civil Rights Movement. Few laws are in place to protect lesbians and gay men, and the criminal justice system is wracked with homophobia.

- *Mental health.* An overtly homophobic world in which there is full permission to treat lesbians and gay men with cruelty makes it difficult for lesbians and gay men to maintain a strong sense of well-being and self-esteem. Many lesbians and gay men are beaten, raped, killed, subjected to aversion therapy, or put in mental institutions. The impact of such hatred and negativity can lead one to depression and, in some cases, to suicide. The toll on the gay and lesbian community is devastating.
- *Community.* There is rejection by those who live in homophobic fear, those who are afraid of association with lesbians and gay men. For many in the gay and lesbian community, there is a loss of public acceptance, a loss of allies, a loss of place and belonging.
- *Credibility.* This fear is large for many people: the fear that they will no longer be respected, listened to, honored, believed. They fear they will be social outcasts.

The list goes on and on. But any one of these essential components of a full life is large enough to make one deeply fear its loss. A black woman once said to me in a workshop, "When I fought for Civil Rights, I always had my family and community to fall back on even when they didn't fully understand or accept what I was doing. I don't know if I could have borne losing them. And you people don't have either with you. It takes my breath away."

What does a woman have to do to get called a lesbian? Almost anything, sometimes nothing at all, but certainly anything that threatens the status quo, anything that steps out of role, anything that asserts the rights of women, anything that doesn't indicate submission and subordination. Assertiveness, standing up for oneself, asking for more pay, better working conditions, training for and accepting a nontraditional (you mean a man's?) job, enjoying the company of women, being financially independent, being in control of one's life, depending first and foremost upon oneself, thinking that one can do whatever needs to be done, but above all, working for the rights and equality of women.

In the backlash to the gains of the women's liberation movement, there has been an increased effort to keep definitions man-centered. Therefore, to work on behalf of women must mean to work against men. To love women must mean that one hates men. A very effective attack has been made against the word *feminist* to make it a derogatory word. In current backlash usage, *feminist* equals *man-hater* which equals *lesbian*. This formula is created in the hope that women will be frightened away from their work on behalf of women. Consequently, we now have women who believe in the rights of women and work for those rights while from fear deny that they are feminists, or refuse to use the word because it is so "abrasive."

So what does one do in an effort to keep from being called a lesbian? She steps back into line, into the role that is demanded of her, tries to behave in such a way that doesn't threaten the status of men, and if she works for women's rights, she begins modifying that work. When women's organizations begin doing significant social change work, they inevitably are lesbian-baited; that is, funders or institutions or community members tell us that they can't work with us because of our "man-hating attitudes" or the presence of lesbians. We are called too strident, told we are making enemies, not doing good.

The battered women's movement has seen this kind of attack: the pressure has been to provide services only, without analysis of the causes of violence against women and strategies for ending it. To provide only services without political analysis or direct action is to be in an approved "helping" role; to analyze the causes of violence against women is to begin the work toward changing an entire system of power and control. It is when we do the latter that we are threatened with the label of man-hater or lesbian. For my politics, if a women's social change organization has not been labeled lesbian or communist, it is probably not doing significant work; it is only "making nice."

Women in many of these organizations, out of fear of all the losses we are threatened with, begin to modify our work to make it more acceptable and less threatening to the male-dominated society which we originally set out to change. The work can no longer be radical (going to the root cause of the problem) but instead must be reforming, working only on the symptoms and not the cause. Real change for women becomes thwarted and stopped. The word *lesbian* is instilled with the power to halt our work and control our lives. And we give it its power with our fear.   [1988]

🌿 102

Cat

JULIE BLACKWOMON

It is three days after my twelfth birthday and my mother is sitting beside me on the edge of my bed. She is holding a box of sanitary napkins and a little booklet that reads "What Every Young Girl Should Know" and telling me for the third straight year that I am to read the book and keep the pads hidden from the sight of Daddy and Leroy. I am hardly listening. I am sneaking furtive glances out the window and patiently waiting for her to finish so I can meet the boys out on the lot for our softball game.

My mother is saying, "Look, you've thrown your pretty dress on the floor." She is bending down to pick it up. It is a white flared dress with large yellow flowers. Daddy bought it for my birthday. I am remembering the party, the coconut cake with the twelve ballerinas holding twelve pink candles. Momma had straightened my hair but refused to

wave it tight to my head so it would look like a process, the way I usually wear it. Instead she has fluffed
up the curls like she does my sister Dee Dee's hair.
Momma is serving punch in a white apron or just
standing around with her hands in the pockets.
When she catches my eye she motions with her head
for me to go over and talk with the other girls who
are standing in a cluster around the record player. I
smile nervously back at her, but remain where I am.
My friends are all acting strange. Leroy, my brother
and very best friend, has been stuck up under Die-
dra Young all evening, and Raymond and Zip-Zip
are out on the back steps giggling with Peggy and
Sharon. Jeffrey teases me about my knobby black
knees under my new dress until I threaten to punch
him in the mouth. I wander out to the kitchen to
play with Fluffy, our cat, until Momma misses me
and comes to drag me back to the party.

Now, sitting on my bed with Momma, she is
saying she will have to get me a training bra. I self-
consciously reach up and touch my breasts, then jerk
my hands down again. I hate them. I'm always hurting them when I bump into things and now when I
fight I not only have to protect my face and head I
have to worry about getting hit in the breast too.

"Momma, can I go now? I gotta pitch today," I
say. Momma puts her arm around my shoulder and
pulls me closer to her. "Sugar, you've got to stop
playing with those boys all the time; why don't you
go play with Sheila, that nice young girl who's staying with the Jenkins?"

"But I don't know her."

"Well, you can get to know her. She's a nice girl
and she doesn't know anybody. You can introduce
her to the rest of the girls."

"But Dee Dee know them better than I do."

"Yeah, sugar, but Sheila doesn't have any girlfriends and you don't either, so you could be friends
with each other."

I pull away from her. "I got friends," I say. I'm
getting annoyed with the conversation, I want to go
out and play. I get up and walk over to the window
and stand there with my back to her.

"O.K.," Momma says finally, "but I've invited
the Jenkins over for lunch Sunday and if you want

to be friends with Sheila fine, if not . . ." She shrugs
her shoulders.

"You gonna make Dee Dee be there too?"

"Yup."

"Can we invite Zip-Zip and Jeffrey?"

She hesitates a moment. ". . . Maybe next time."

"O.K., can I go now?" I am inching towards the
door.

"All right, scoot." She pats me on the butt as
I pass her. I am running down the steps, jumping
over the last two. Dee Dee, who has been listening
at the door, says, "Can I go with you, Cat?"

"No."

"Why not?"

"'Cause you can't."

I reach the vacant lot where we play ball. There
is no game today. The boys are busy gathering ammunition—dirt clods, rocks, bottles—for the fight
with the white boys from across the tracks.

Dee Dee whines to Leroy: "Leroy, I wanna go."

"You can't," Leroy says.

"How come?"

"'Cause you're too young."

"I'm just as old as Jeffrey!"

"You can't go," Leroy says, ". . . besides you're
a girl."

"Cat's a girl," she says indignantly.

We all ignore her. We are gathering sticks and
rocks and throwing them into an empty milk crate.

"How come I can't go? Huh? How come?" Nobody answers her. We are all walking across the lot.
Raymond and Leroy are carrying the ammunition;
Dee Dee is standing where we left her, yelling, "I'm
gonna tell Momma what you're up to! I'm gonna tell
you going cross the tracks to fight with those white
boys." Then, after a moment or two: ". . . And Cat's
got Kotex in her dresser drawer!" My neck burns
but I keep walking.

I am sixteen years old and sitting in Sheila's dining
room. We are playing checkers and I am losing and
not minding at all. Her cousin Bob comes in. He is
stationed in Georgia and on leave from the army.
He says hi to Sheila, ignores me completely and
walks through to the back with his green duffel bag

in his left hand. His voice drifts in from the kitchen, "Where'd the little bulldagger come from?" Sheila springs back from the table so fast her chair overturns. She yells in the kitchen doorway, "You shut your nasty mouth, Bob Jenkins!" The next day we are supposed to make cookies for her aunt's birthday but she calls to suggest we do it over my house instead. I do not go back over Sheila's again unless Dee Dee is with me, or there is no one home.

We are in Fairmount Park within some semienclosed shrubbery. Sheila and I are lying on our backs on an old army blanket. We look like Siamese twins joined together at the head. The sky is blue above us and I am chewing on the straw that came with my coke.

"Cat, tell me again how you used to almost be late for school all the time 'cause you used to be waiting for me to come out of my house so we could walk to school together," Sheila says.

"I've told you three thousand times already."

"Well, tell me again, I like to hear it."

"If you hadn't been peeping from behind the curtains yourself and waiting for *me* to come out we'd both have gotten to school on time."

She laughs softly, then turns over on her stomach.

"I want a kiss," she says.

I lean up on my elbow, check around to make sure nobody's peeping through the bushes then turn and press my lips to hers. After a few seconds she pulls away. "Man, Cat, I never felt this way about anybody before."

"Me neither." I reach over and touch her hand. We kiss again, briefly, our lips just touching. Then we turn and lie as we were before but continue holding hands.

"Cat?"

"Yeah?"

"I think I'm in love."

"Me too."

She squeezes my hand. I squeeze hers back.

"What would you do if Bob came by and saw us now?" Sheila asks.

"What would you do?"

"I don't know. I'd just say hi, I guess."

"Then I would too," I say.

The sun has moved and is now shining directly over us. I cover my eyes with my arm.

"Bob would say we're both bulldaggers," Sheila says after a while.

"Yeah, I guess he would," I say.

"We aren't bulldaggers, are we, Cat?"

"No, bulldaggers want to be men and we don't want to be men, right?"

"Right, we just love each other and there's nothing wrong with loving someone."

"Yeah and nobody can choose who you fall in love with."

"Right."

Sheila and I are in her bedroom; her uncle is standing over the bed shouting, "What the hell's going on here?" He is home from work early. Sheila and I scramble for the sheet and clutch it across our bodies. I am waiting for her uncle to leave so I can get up and dressed, but he just stands there staring, thunder in his face. Finally I release my end of the sheet and scramble to the foot of the bed. Sheila's stockings are entwined in my blouse. I cram panties into my pocket and pull blue jeans over naked, ashen legs. I am trembling. Her uncle's eyes follow me around the room like harsh spotlights.

Later at my house, Momma, Daddy and I are in the dining room. Leroy and Dee Dee are in their rooms, the doors are shut tight; they've been ordered not to open them. My mother sits on the couch wringing her hands. I sit stiffly forward on the edge of a straight backed chair. My head down. My teeth clenched. My father stomps back and forth across the floor, his hands first behind him, holding each other at the butt, then gesturing out in front of him. He is asking, "What's this I hear about you being in bed with the Jenkins girl?" I sit still on the edge of my chair, looking straight ahead.

"I'm talking to you, Catherine!" His voice is booming to the rafters, I'm sure the neighbors hear. It is dark outside and a slight breeze puffs out the window curtains. I am holding a spool of thread that had been on the table. I am squeezing it in my hands, the round edges intrude into my palms. I continue to squeeze.

"You hear me talking to you, girl?" He is standing directly over me now, his voice reverberates in my ear. I squeeze the spool of thread and stare at a spider-shaped crack in the wall above the light switch. There is an itch on my left leg, below my knee. I do not scratch. Dogs bark in the backyards and one of the Williams kids is getting a spanking. I hear the strap fall, a child wailing, and an angry female voice.

My father is saying, "Look, you'd better say something, you brazen heifer!" He jerks my head around to face him. I yank it back to stare at the crack in the wall.

"You're lucky Tom Jenkins didn't have you arrested—forcing yourself on that girl like that. . . ."

"What? What? What force? Sheila didn't say I forced her to do anything!"

"If you didn't force her, then what happened?"

"Sheila didn't say that! She didn't say it! Mr. Jenkins must have said it!" I am on my feet and trembling, and screaming at the top of my lungs.

"Then what did happen?" my father screams back at me. I sit back down in the chair and again stare at the crack in the wall over the light switch. Trying to concentrate on it, blot out my father's voice. I cannot. I get up and run to the chair where my mother sits. I am pulling on her arm. "Momma, Sheila didn't say that, did she? She didn't say I forced her?"

Momma sits there biting on her bottom lip and wringing her hands. She does not look at me. She lays her hand on my head and does not speak. My father grabs my arm and yanks me away. I am enveloped in his sour breath as he shouts, "Look, I'm a man of God and don't you dare doubt my word!" I yank my arm from his grip and run towards the steps, toward the safety of my bedroom.

"I haven't dismissed you!" I hear my father's footsteps behind me. He grabs me by my tee shirt and swings me around. I lose my footing and fall at the bottom of the steps.

"Arthur, Arthur!" My mother is running behind us. My father's knee is in my chest; he is yelling in a hoarse angry voice, "Catherine Johnson, I have one more thing to say to you, then we needn't discuss it anymore, but you listen carefully because I mean every word I say: There will be no bulldaggers in my house, do you understand me? THERE WILL BE NO BULLDAGGERS IN MY HOUSE!"

I am sitting beside Sheila on a bench in Fairmount Park; we are within walking distance of the spot where we used to meet with our lunch on Daddy's old army blanket. The grass is completely green except for one long crooked brown streak where the boys trampled a short cut to the basketball court. The leaves are green too, save for one or two brown and yellow ones beneath the bench at our feet. Sheila's head is bent.

"I'm sorry," she is saying. She is picking minute pieces of lint from a black skirt. "I'm really sorry but you don't know how my uncle is when he gets mad." I am silent. I am watching three boys play basketball on the court about twenty yards away. A tall white kid leaps up and dunks the ball.

"I just didn't know what else to do," Sheila continues. "I was scared and Uncle Jim kept saying, 'She made you do it, didn't she? She made you do it, didn't she?' And before I knew it, I'd said 'yes'." A short black kid knocks the ball out of bounds and a fat boy in a green shirt darts out to retrieve it.

"Cathy?" Her hand is on my forearm and I turn to look her full in the face. "I'm sorry, Cat, I just didn't know what else to do." I turn again towards the basketball court. The tall white boy is holding the ball under his arm and shaking the hand of a short kid. The fat boy in the green sweat shirt is pulling a navy blue poncho on over his head.

"Cathy, please?" Sheila is saying. I turn to look her full in the face. "It's all right, Sheila, it's all right." It is getting windy. The basketball court empties and Sheila asks if I'll meet her at our spot next Saturday. I lie and say yes. She checks to make sure no one's looking, pecks me on the cheek, then gets up to leave. I sit watching the empty basketball court for a long time, then I get up and take the long way home.

[1983]

✹ 103

Chicana Lesbians: Fear and Loathing in the Chicano Community

CARLA TRUJILLO

The vast majority of Chicano heterosexuals perceive Chicana lesbians as a threat to the community. Homophobia, that is, irrational fear of gay or lesbian people and/or behaviors, accounts, in part, for the heterosexist response to the lesbian community. However, I argue that Chicana lesbians are perceived as a greater threat to the Chicano community because their existence disrupts the established order of male dominance, and raises the consciousness of many Chicanas regarding their own independence and control. Some writers have addressed these topics[1]; however, an analysis of the complexities of lesbian existence alongside this perceived threat has not been undertaken. While this essay is by no means complete, it attempts to elucidate the underlying basis of these fears which, in the very act of the lesbian existence, disrupt the established norm of patriarchal oppression.

SEXUALITY

As lesbians, our sexuality becomes the focal issue of dissent. The majority of Chicanas, both lesbian and heterosexual, are taught that our sexuality must conform to certain modes of behavior. Our culture voices shame upon us if we go beyond the criteria of passivity and repression, or doubts in our virtue if we refuse.[2] We, as women, are taught to suppress our sexual desires and needs by conceding all pleasure to the male. As Chicanas, we are commonly led to believe that even talking about our participation and satisfaction in sex is taboo. Moreover, we (as well as most women in the United States) learn to hate our bodies, and usually possess little knowledge of them. Lourdes Arguelles did a survey on the sexuality of 373 immigrant Latinas and found that over half of the women possessed little knowledge of their reproductive systems or their own physiology. Most remarked they "just didn't look down there."[3]

Not loving our bodies affects how we perceive ourselves as sexual beings. As lesbians, however, we have no choice but to confront our sexuality before we can confront our lesbianism. Thus the commonly held viewpoint among heterosexuals that we are "defined by our sexuality" is, in a way, partially true. If we did not bring our sexuality into consciousness, we would not be able to confront ourselves and come out.

After confronting and then acknowledging our attraction, we must, in turn, learn to reclaim that what we're told is bad, wrong, dirty, and taboo— namely our bodies, and our freedom to express ourselves in them. Too often we internalize the homophobia and sexism of the larger society, as well as that of our own culture, which attempts to keep us from loving ourselves. As Norma Alarcón states, "[Chicana lesbians] must act to negate the negation."[4] A Chicana lesbian must learn to love herself, both as a woman and a sexual being, before she can love another. Loving another woman not only validates one's own sexuality, but also that of the other woman, by the very act of loving. Understanding this, a student in a workshop that Cherríe Moraga and I conducted on lesbian sexuality stated, "Now I get it. Not only do you have to learn to love your own vagina, but someone else's too."[5] It is only then that the subsequent experiences of love and commitment, passion and remorse can also become our dilemmas, much like those of everyone else. The effort to consciously reclaim our sexual selves forces Chicanas to either confront their own sexuality or, in refusing, castigate lesbians as *vendidas** to the race, blasphemers to the church, atrocities against nature, or some combination.

IDENTIFICATION

For many Chicanas, our identification as women, that is, as complete women, comes from the belief that we need to be connected to a man.[6] Ridding

_____

*traitors.

ourselves of this parasitic identification is not always easy, for we grow up, as my Chicana students have pointed out, defined in a male context: daddy's girl, some guy's girlfriend, wife, or mother. Vying for a man's attention compromises our own personal and intellectual development. We exist in a patriarchal society that undervalues women.[7] We are socialized to undervalue ourselves, as well as anything associated with the concept of self. Our voice is considered less significant, our needs and desires secondary. As the Chicanas in the MALCS workshop indicated,[8] our toleration of unjust behavior from men, the church, the established order, is considered an attribute. How much pain can we bear in the here-and-now so that we may be better served in the afterlife? Martyrdom, the cloth of denial, transposes itself into a gown of cultural beauty.

Yet, an alliance with a man grants a woman heterosexual privileges, many of which are reified by the law, the church, our families and, of course, "la causa." Women who partake in the privileges of male sexual alliance may often do so at the cost of their own sense of self, since they must often subvert their needs, voice, intellect, and personal development in these alliances. These are the conditional contradictions commonly prescribed for women by the patriarchy in our culture and in the larger society. Historically, women have been viewed as property.[9] Though some laws have changed, ideologically little else has. Upon marriage, a father feels he can relinquish "ownership" and "responsibility" of his daughter to her husband. The Chicana feminist who confronts this subversion, and critiques the sexism of the Chicano community, will be called *vendida* if she finds the "male defined and often anti-feminist" values of the community difficult to accept.[10]

The behaviors necessary in the "act of pursuing a man" often generate competition among women, leading to betrayal of one another.[11] When a woman's sense of identity is tied to that of a man, she is dependent on this relationship for her own self-worth. Thus, she must compete with other women for his attention. When the attention is then acknowledged and returned, she must work to ensure that it is maintained. Ensuring the protection of this precious commodity generates suspicion among women, particularly single, unattached women. Since we're all taught to vie for a man's attention, we become, in a sense, sexual suspects to one another. The responsibility is placed entirely upon the woman with little thought given to the suspected infidelity of the man.

We should ask what role the man places himself in regarding his support of these behaviors. After all, the woman is commonly viewed as his possession. Hence, in the typical heterosexual relationship both parties are abetting the other, each in a quest that does not improve the status of the woman (nor, in my view, that of the man), nor the consciousness of either of them.

How does the Chicana lesbian fit into this picture? Realistically, she doesn't. As a lesbian she does many things simultaneously: she rejects "compulsory heterosexuality";[12] she refuses to partake in the "game" of competition for men; she confronts her own sexuality; and she challenges the norms placed upon her by culture and society, whose desire is to subvert her into proper roles and places. This is done, whether consciously or unconsciously, by the very aspect of her existence. In the course of conducting many workshops on lesbian sexuality, Chicana heterosexuals have often indicated to me that they do not associate with lesbians, since it could be assumed that either (1) they, too, must be lesbians, or (2) if they're not, they must be selling out to Anglo culture, since it is implied that Chicana lesbians do and thus any association with lesbians implicates them as well. This equivocation of sexual practice and cultural alliance is a retrograde ideology, quite possibly originating from the point of view that the only way to uplift the species is to propagate it. Thus, homosexuality is seen as "counter-revolutionary."

Heterosexual Chicanas need not be passive victims of the cultural onslaught of social control. If anything, Chicanas are usually the backbone of every *familia,* for it is their strength and self-sacrifice which often keeps the family going. While heterosexual Chicanas have a choice about how they want to live their lives (read: how they choose to form their identities[13]), Chicana lesbians have very little choice, because their quest for self-identification comes with the territory. This is why "coming out" can be a major source of pain for Chicana lesbians, since the basic fear of rejection by family and community is paramount.[14] For our own survival, Chicana lesbians must continually embark on the creation or modification of our own *familia,* since this institution, as traditionally constructed, may be non-supportive of the Chicana lesbian existence.[15]

MOTHERHOOD

The point of view that we are not complete human beings unless we are attached to a male is further promoted by the attitude that we are incomplete as women unless we become mothers. Many Chicanas are socialized to believe that our chief purpose in life is raising children.[16] Not denying the fact that motherhood can be a beautiful experience, it becomes, rather, one of the few experiences not only supported [by] but expected in a traditional Chicano community. Historically, in dual-headed households, Chicanas (as well as other women) were relegated to the tasks of home care and child rearing, while the men took on the task of earning the family's income.[17] Economic need, rather than feminist consciousness, has been the primary reason for the change to two-income households. Nevertheless, for many Chicanas, motherhood is still seen by our culture as the final act in establishing our "womanhood."

Motherhood among Chicana lesbians does exist. Many lesbians are mothers as by-products of divorce, earlier liaisons with men, or through artificial insemination. Anecdotal evidence I have obtained from many Chicana lesbians in the community indicates that lesbians who choose to become mothers in our culture are seen as aberrations of the traditional concept of motherhood, which stresses male-female partnership. Choosing to become a mother via alternative methods of insemination, or even adopting children, radically departs from society's view that lesbians and gay men cannot "successfully" raise children. Therefore, this poses another threat to the Chicano community, since Chicana lesbians are perceived as failing to partake in one of their chief obligations in life.

RELIGION

Religion, based on the tradition of patriarchal control and sexual, emotional, and psychological repression, has historically been a dual means of hope for a better afterlife and social control in the present one. Personified by the Virgen de Guadalupe, the concept of motherhood and martyrdom go hand in hand in the Catholic religion. Nevertheless, as we are all aware, religion powerfully affects our belief systems concerning life and living. Since the Pope does not advocate a homosexual lifestyle,[18] lesbians and gay men are not given sanction by the largely Catholic Chicano community—hence, fulfilling our final threat to the established order. Chicana lesbians who confront their homosexuality must, in turn, confront (for those raised in religious households) religion, bringing to resolution some compromise of religious doctrine and personal lifestyle. Many choose to alter, modify, or abandon religion, since it is difficult to advocate something which condemns our existence. This exacerbates a sense of alienation for Chicana lesbians who feel they cannot wholly participate in a traditional religion.

In sum, Chicana lesbians pose a threat to the Chicano community for a variety of reasons, primarily because they threaten the established social hierarchy of patriarchal control. In order to "come-out," Chicana lesbians must confront their sexuality, therefore bringing a taboo subject to consciousness. By necessity, they must learn to love their bodies, for it is also another woman's body which becomes the object of love. Their identities as people alter and become independent of men; hence there is no need to submit to, or perform the necessary behaviors that cater to wooing, the male ego. Lesbians (and other feminist women) would expect to treat and be treated by men as equals. Men who have traditionally interacted with women on the basis of their gender (read: femininity) first, and their brains second, are commonly left confused when the lesbian (or feminist) fails to respond to the established pecking order.

Motherhood, seen as exemplifying the final act of our existence as women, is practiced by lesbians, but usually without societal or cultural permission. Not only is it believed that lesbians cannot become mothers (hence, not fulfilling our established purpose as women), but if we do, we morally threaten the concept of motherhood as a sanctified entity, since lesbianism doesn't fit into its religious or cultural confines. Lastly, religion, which does not support the homosexual lifestyle, seeks to repudiate us as sinners if we are "practicing," and only tolerable if not. For her personal and psychological survival, the Chicana lesbian must confront and bring to resolution these established cultural and societal conflicts. These "confrontations" go against many of the values of the Chicano community, since they pose a threat to the established order of male control. Our very existence challenges this order, and in some cases challenges the oftentimes ideologically oppressive attitudes toward women.

It is widely assumed that lesbians and heterosexual women are in two completely different enclaves in regard to the type and manner of the oppression they must contend with. As illustrated earlier in this essay, this indeed, may be true. There do exist, however, different levels of patriarchal oppression which affect all of us as women, and when combined inhibit our collective liberation. If we, as lesbian and heterosexual Chicanas, can open our eyes and look at all that we share as women, we might find commonalities even among our differences. First and foremost among them is the status of *woman*. Uttered under any breath, it implies subservience; cast to a lower position not only in society, but in our own culture as well.

Secondly, the universal of the body. We are all female and subject to the same violations as any woman in society. We must contend with the daily threat of rape, molestation, and harassment—violations which affect all of us as women, lesbian or not.

As indicated earlier, our sexuality is suppressed by our culture—relegated to secrecy or embarrassment, implicating us as wrongful women if we profess to fulfill ourselves sexually. Most of us still grow up inculcated with the dichotomy of the "good girl–bad girl" syndrome. With virtue considered as the most admirable quality, it's easy to understand

which we choose to partake. This generates a cloud of secrecy around any sexual activity, and leads, I am convinced, to our extremely high teenage pregnancy rate, simply because our families refuse to acknowledge the possibility that young women may be sexually active before marriage.

We are taught to undervalue our needs and voices. Our opinions, viewpoints, and expertise are considered secondary to those of males—even if we are more highly trained. Time and again, I have seen otherwise sensible men insult the character of a woman when they are unable to belittle her intellectual capacities.[19] Character assassinations are commonly disguised in the familiar "*vendida* to the race" format. Common it seems, because it functions as the ultimate insult to any conscientious *politica*. Because many of us are taught that our opinions matter little, we have difficulty at times, raising them. We don't trust what we think, or believe in our merits. Unless we are encouraged to do so, we have difficulty thinking independently of male opinion. Chicanas must be constantly encouraged to speak up, to voice their opinions, particularly in areas where no encouragement has ever been provided.

As Chicanas (and Chicanos), most of us are subject to the effects of growing up in a culture besieged by poverty and all the consequences of it: lack of education, insufficient political power and health care, disease and drugs. We are all subject to the effects of a society that is racist, classist and homophobic, as well as sexist, and patriarchally dominant. Colonization has imposed itself and affected the disbursement of status and the collective rights of us as individuals. Chicanas are placed in this order at a lower position, ensconced within a tight boundary which limits our voices, our bodies, and our brains. In classic dissonant fashion, many of us become complicit in this (since our survival often depends on it) and end up rationalizing our very own limitations.

The collective liberation of people begins with the collective liberation of half its constituency—namely women. The view that our hierarchical society places Chicanos at a lower point, and they in turn must place Chicanas lower still, is outmoded and politically destructive. Women can no longer be relegated to supporting roles. Assuaging delicate male egos as a means of establishing our identities is retrograde and subversive to our own identities as women. Chicanas, both lesbian and heterosexual, have a dual purpose ahead of us. We must fight for our own voices as women, since this will ultimately serve to uplift us as a people.   [1991]

NOTES

1. Cherríe Moraga, *Loving in the War Years: Lo que nunca pasó por sus labios* (Boston: South End Press, 1983), 103, 105, 111, 112, 117.
2. See Ana Castillo's essay on sexuality: "La Macha: Toward a Beautiful Whole Self" in *Chicana Lesbians: The Girls Our Mothers Warned Us About*, ed. Carla Trujillo (Berkeley: Third Woman Press, 1991). Also see *The Sexuality of Latinas, Third Woman* 4 (1989).
3. Lourdes Arguelles, "A Survey of Latina Immigrant Sexuality," presented at the National Association for Chicano Studies Conference, Albuquerque, New Mexico, March 29–April 1, 1990.
4. Norma Alarcón, personal communication, MALCS (Mujeres Activas en Letras y Cambio Social) Summer Research Institute, University of California, Los Angeles, August 3–6, 1990.
5. Chicana Leadership Conference, Workshop on Chicana lesbians, University of California, Berkeley, Feb. 8–10, 1990.
6. This was spoken of in great detail in a workshop on Chicana Empowerment and Oppression by Yvette Flores Ortiz at the MALCS, 1990.
7. There are multitudes of feminist books and periodicals which attest to the subordinate position of women in society. Listing them is beyond the scope of this essay.
8. Yvette Flores Ortiz, MALCS, 1990.
9. Peggy R. Sanday, "Female Status in the Public Domain," in *Women, Culture & Society,* eds. Michelle Rosaldo and Louise Lamphere (Stanford: Stanford University Press, 1974), 189–206.
10. *Loving in the War Years,* 113.
11. See Ana Castillo's "La Macha: Toward a Beautiful Whole Self." See also *Loving in the War Years,* 136.
12. Adrienne Rich, "Compulsory Heterosexuality and Lesbian Existence," in *Women: Sex and Sexuality,* eds. Catharine R. Stimpson and Ethel Spector Person (Chicago: University of Chicago Press, 1980), 62–91.
13. As Moraga states, "only the woman intent on the approval can be affected by the disapproval," *Loving in the War Years,* 103.
14. Rejection by family and community is also an issue for gay men; however, their situation is muddied by the concomitant loss of power.
15. Cherríe Moraga attests to the necessity of Chicanas needing to "make *familia* from scratch" in *Giving Up the Ghost* (Los Angeles: West End Press, 1986), 58.
16. *Loving in the War Years,* 113.
17. Karen Sacks, "Engels Revisited: Women, the Organization of Production and Private Property" in *Women, Culture & Society,* 207–222.
18. Joseph Cardinal Ratzinger, Prefect, and Alberto Bouone, Titular Archbishop of Caesarea in Numedia, Secretary, "Letter to the Bishops of the Catholic Church in the Pastoral Care of Homosexual Persons," October 1, 1986. Approved by Pope John Paul II, adopted in an ordinary session of the Congregation for the Doctrine of Faith and ordered published. Reprinted in *The Vatican and Homosexuality,* eds. Jeannine Gramick and Pat Furey (New York: Crossroad Publishing Co., 1988), 1–10.
19. This occurred often to the women MeChA (Movimiento Estudiantil Chicano de Aztlán) leaders who were on the Berkeley campus between 1985 and 1989. It also occurred to a Chicana panel member during a 1990 National Association for Chicano Studies presentation, when a Chicano discussant disagreed with the recommendations based on her research.

🌿 104

Livin' in a Gay Family

MEGAN MCGUIRE

Homosexuality first entered my life when I was twelve years old. The words fag, queer, dyke, and homo were used all around me. I even used them. These words were used to disrespect someone. If you were a fag, you were an outcast or someone others didn't like. In the fall of my seventh-grade year, I began to fear those words and hate people who identified with those words.

And then my mother told me she was gay. She came out. She was a dyke, a fag, a queer. My mother was one of "those" people. I couldn't let any of my friends know. I was afraid they would not like me or that my classmates would beat me up. I wouldn't let anyone know that the other woman, Barb, who was living in my house, was my other mother. I hadn't known about my mom's sexuality until one day when I went into her bedroom and asked "Mom, are you gay?" She told me that she was gay. I became really upset and decided for myself that she was straight. I never gave myself time to think, what if my mom was in fact gay? Then it sunk in. My mom was gay. I cried and got really angry. I wanted to know why she was putting my brother and me into a situation where we had to be secretive about our family. For five years I lived with the secret. It caused me to lie, be angry, and be sad. No one I knew could know that I was living in a gay family.

The first four years my mom was "out" was a very lonely time for me. When I moved up to Boston from Washington, DC, in 1990, I was in a new city, a new school, and a new life. I made friends. I wanted to be liked, so all I could do was laugh at the jokes my friends made about gays. The people I called my "friends" were not people I wanted to be my friends. I hadn't figured out how to make real friends whom I could trust with the secret. I wasn't ready to tell anybody about my family because I wasn't ready to deal with it myself. I was very lonely and depressed, so I occupied myself playing soccer and sitting in front of the TV.

When I entered high school, I played three sports and joined several clubs. I didn't make time to find a group of people who would give me support. Because I was participating in all of these activities, people got to know me and my face became well recognized. I was an active student who pushed for change in student government and played in almost every female volleyball, basketball, and softball game. I felt the pressure to keep the secret a secret. I thought that all the popularity I had gained and the friends I had made would end if people knew my mom was gay.

Despite my social success, I spent most of the time hiding who I was, who my family was, and making up lies. My brother and I would take the "gay" literature and hide it when our friends came over, and we would turn over pictures of Barb and mom together, so they could not be seen. Once my brother told a friend that our car was a used car and that we hadn't had time to take the pink triangle off the back windshield. We didn't have people spend the night to avoid the possibility that they might ask "the question." We lived like this for almost three-and-one-half years. Then we moved into a house that had a basement apartment where, we told our friends, Barb lived. It was really a guest room and an office for my mom and Barb.

In the middle of my sophomore year, I finally made a best friend. I didn't tell her anything and she never asked, even when she spent the night. I guess we adopted the "don't ask, don't tell" policy. She knew Barb and Jean as my mothers. I never had to lie to her, but I didn't talk to her about my family until two years later. By the end of my sophomore year I still had this really good friend, which felt like a record for me.

The same year I was asked to be a peer leader. I told one of the coordinators, who happend to be gay, that my mom was gay. He helped me understand that if people didn't like me because of my mom's sexual orientation, they weren't worth my time. I got involved in fighting homophobia. I decided to get educated, so I attended workshops and became more confident about who I am and who my mom is. I attacked homophobic remarks and started to educate others about homophobia.

But I still had not told people how homophobia affected my life. I had not told people that when I sit in the back of the bus coming back from a game and listen to the team talk about what they think of gay people and the children of those gay people, my stomach turns into a big knot. Even though my mom sat me down and told me that it wasn't fair to myself and to the people I was educating to keep silent, I was not ready to talk about my family, since I still didn't have the peer support I wanted and needed.

During the summer following my sophomore year, things went really well. I finally told someone I met at summer camp that my mother was gay. She was a person I will never forget. First she told me she was gay, and then I told her about my family. It was a relief; she didn't assume or judge. I guess telling her was easier than telling others because she was gay, but it was a tremendous relief. I came back from camp really happy and ready to speak at the national coming out day at my school.

There was one problem. My brother was entering his freshman year at my school and he was not ready for me to speak. He wanted me to stay silent about our family. I told him for that year I wouldn't speak, but the next year I would and that I would not lie to anyone anymore. I mentored a freshman health class, and then I understood why my brother asked me not to speak. I realized that, because of the ninth graders' relative immaturity about sexuality, he would have been harassed for the whole year. So I tried to make it safe for him. I educated the class I mentored about homophobia; his friends were in the class. His friends were now my friends and my friends were his, so we both were building a group we could feel comfortable in.

During February I met a person who helped me take the first steps to tell my friends. He asked the "question." He asked if Barb was my mom's girl-friend and I told him, "Ya, she is." Eventually I told my close friends that my mother was gay. I found out they already knew and they thought it was not an issue. Then in May, a reporter from our city's news-paper asked to interview me about growing up in a gay family. There was a photo exhibit of gay fami-lies on display at one of the local elementary schools, and the paper wanted a youth to talk about the is-sues the show raised.

At the end of May, my story was on the front page of the *Cambridge Chronicle*.[1] I told the city that I'm proud of my family and if people have a prob-lem with it, they should keep it their problem. I wanted people to know I felt I had betrayed my fam-ily by lying, and it was time for me to be honest about being a child of lesbian moms. A week later I spoke in front of a group of a hundred students, parents, staff, and city officials, telling them that words like fag, queer, dyke, and homo are words that hurt. Not only do these words hurt gay men and women, but also their families and children, and we should not tolerate words that hurt and cause hatred. I contin-ued to speak in some classes at my school, explain-ing what my life has been like holding in a secret that really shouldn't have had to be a secret.

Since the *Chronicle* article was published, people have asked me two questions. The first is, "Are you gay?" I choose not to answer this question. As teen-agers most of us can't explain the feelings going on in our minds and bodies, whether they are for a per-son of the same sex or the opposite sex. The second question is, "Why are you making a big deal about telling people about your family?" The answer is that it is a big deal for me. Once the article hit the stands I felt a huge relief; it was like a big splinter had been pulled out of me.

I always wanted to know someone who was older who had gay parents and was out about it. I haven't found someone like this. I want to be that someone for other kids, so children of gay men and women don't have to feel afraid to be true to themselves.

I've helped my brother. I know he will never say, "Thank you; OK, I'm glad I don't have to hide and lie anymore," but I know he is relieved. After the article was published, a kid who played hockey with my brother came up to him and said, "I saw the ar-ticle you fucking fag." My brother said, "Fuck you" and walked away. All of his friends and my friends are cool with it, and they know Barb and my mom as our mothers who are both raising us.

I'm going to enter my last year of high school be-ing able to answer questions about who Barb is, and who my family is, without lying.   [1996]

🌿 105

I Lost It at the Movies

JEWELLE GOMEZ

My grandmother, Lydia, and my mother, Dolores, were both talking to me from their bathroom stalls in the Times Square movie theater. I was washing butter from my hands at the sink and didn't think it at all odd. The people in my family are always talk-ing; conversation is a life force in our existence. My great-grandmother, Grace, would narrate her life story from 7:00 A.M. until we went to bed at night. The only break was when we were reading or the reverential periods when we sat looking out of our tenement windows, observing the neighborhood, which we naturally talked about later.

---

[1] Amy Miller, "Gay Photo Exhibit Causes Stir at High School," *Cambridge Chronicle*, May 25, 1995, p. 1.

So it was not odd that Lydia and Dolores talked non-stop from their stalls, oblivious to everyone except us. I hadn't expected it to happen there, though. I hadn't really expected an "it" to happen at all. To be a lesbian was part of who I was, like being left-handed—even when I'd slept with men. When my great-grandmother asked me in the last days of her life if I would be marrying my college boyfriend I said yes, knowing I would not, knowing I was a lesbian.

It seemed a fact that needed no expression. Even my first encounter with the word "bulldagger" was not charged with emotional conflict. As a teen in the 1960s my grandmother told a story about a particular building in our Boston neighborhood that had gone to seed. She described the building's past through the experience of a party she'd attended there thirty years before. The best part of the evening had been a woman she'd met and danced with. Lydia had been a professional dancer and singer on the black theater circuit; to dance with women was who she was. They'd danced, then the woman walked her home and asked her out. I heard the delicacy my grandmother searched for even in her retelling of how she'd explained to the "bulldagger," as she called her, that she liked her fine but she was more interested in men. I was struck with how careful my grandmother had been to make it clear to that woman (and in effect to me) that there was no offense taken in her attentions, that she just didn't "go that way," as they used to say. I was so happy at thirteen to have a word for what I knew myself to be. The word was mysterious and curious, as if from a new language that used some other alphabet which left nothing to cling to when touching its curves and crevices. But still a word existed and my grandmother was not flinching in using it. In fact she'd smiled at the good heart and good looks of the bulldagger who'd asked her.

Once I had the knowledge of a word and a sense of its importance to me, I didn't feel the need to explain, confess, or define my identity as a lesbian. The process of reclaiming my ethnic identity in this country was already all-consuming. Later, of course, in moments of glorious self-righteousness, I did make declarations. But they were not usually ones I

had to make. Mostly they were a testing of the waters. A preparation for the rest of the world which, unlike my grandmother, might not have a grounding in what true love is about. My first lover, the woman who'd been in my bed once a week most of our high school years, finally married. I told her with my poems that I was a lesbian. She was not afraid to ask if what she'd read was about her, about my love for her. So there, amidst her growing children, errant husband, and bowling trophies I said yes, the poems were about her and my love for her, a love I'd always regret relinquishing to her reflexive obeisance to tradition. She did not flinch either. We still get drunk together when I go home to Boston.

During the 1970s I focused less on career than on how to eat and be creative at the same time. Graduate school and a string of non-traditional jobs (stage manager, mid-town messenger, etc.) left me so busy I had no time to think about my identity. It was a long time before I made the connection between my desire, my isolation, and the difficulty I had with my writing. I thought of myself as a lesbian between girlfriends—except the between had lasted five years. After some anxiety and frustration I deliberately set about meeting women. Actually, I knew many women, including my closest friend at the time, another black woman also in the theatre. She became uncharacteristically obtuse when I tried to open up and explain my frustration at going to the many parties we attended and being too afraid to approach women I was attracted to, certain I would be rejected either because the women were straight and horrified or gay and terrified of being exposed. For my friend theoretical homosexuality was acceptable, even trendy. Any uncomfortable experience was irrelevant to her. She was impatient and unsympathetic. I drifted away from her in pursuit of the women's community, a phrase that was not in my vocabulary yet, but I knew it was something more than just "women." I fell into that community by connecting with other women writers, and that helped me to focus on my writing and on my social life as a lesbian.

Still, none of my experiences demanded that I bare my soul. I remained honest but not explicit. Expediency, diplomacy, discretion, are all words that come to mind now. At that time I knew no political framework through which to filter my experience. I was more preoccupied with the Attica riots than with Stonewall. The media helped to focus our attentions within a proscribed spectrum and obscure the connections between the issues. I worried about who would shelter Angela Davis, but the concept of sexual politics was remote and theoretical.

I'm not certain exactly when and where the theory and reality converged.

Being a black woman and a lesbian unexpectedly blended like that famous scene in Ingmar Bergman's film *Persona*. The different faces came together as one, and my desire became part of my heritage, my skin, my perspective, my politics, and my future. And I felt sure that it had been my past that helped make the future possible. The women in my family had acted as if their lives were meaningful. Their lives were art. To be a lesbian among them was to be an artist. Perhaps the convergence came when I saw the faces of my great-grandmother, grandmother, and mother in those of the community of women I finally connected with. There was the same adventurous glint in their eyes; the same determined step; the penchant for breaking into song and for not waiting for anyone to take care of them.

I need not pretend to be other than who I was with any of these women. But did I need to declare it? During the holidays when I brought home best friends or lovers my family always welcomed us warmly, clasping us to their magnificent bosoms. Yet there was always an element of silence in our neighborhood, and surprisingly enough in our family, that was disturbing to me. Among the regulars in my father, Duke's, bar, was Maurice. He was eccentric, flamboyant, and still ordinary. He was accorded the same respect by neighborhood children as every other adult. His indiscretions took their place comfortably among the cyclical, Saturday night, man/woman scandals of our neighborhood. I regret never having asked my father how Maurice and he had become friends.

Soon I felt the discomforting silence pressing against my life more persistently. During visits home to Boston it no longer sufficed that Lydia and Dolores were loving and kind to the "friend" I brought

home. Maybe it was just my getting older. Living in New York City at the age of thirty in 1980, there was little I kept deliberately hidden from anyone. The genteel silence that hovered around me when I entered our home was palpable but I was unsure whether it was already there when I arrived or if I carried it home within myself. It cut me off from what I knew was a kind of fulfillment available only from my family. The lifeline from Grace, to Lydia, to Dolores, to Jewelle was a strong one. We were bound by so many things, not the least of which was looking so much alike. I was not willing to be orphaned by silence.

If the idea of cathedral weddings and station wagons held no appeal for me, the concept of an extended family was certainly important. But my efforts were stunted by our inability to talk about the life I was creating for myself, for all of us. It felt all the more foolish because I thought I knew how my family would react. I was confident they would respond with their customary aplomb just as they had when I'd first had my hair cut as an Afro (which they hated) or when I brought home friends who were vegetarians (which they found curious). While we had disagreed over some issues, like the fight my mother and I had over Vietnam when I was nineteen, always when the deal went down we sided with each other. Somewhere deep inside I think I believed that neither my grandmother nor my mother would ever censure my choices. Neither had actually raised me; my great-grandmother had done that, and she had been a steely barricade against any encroachment on our personal freedoms and she'd never disapproved out loud of anything I'd done.

But it was not enough to have an unabashed admiration for these women. It is one thing to have pride in how they'd so graciously survived in spite of the odds against them. It was something else to be standing in a Times Square movie theater faced with the chance to say "it" out loud and risk the loss of their brilliant and benevolent smiles.

My mother had started reading the graffiti written on the wall of the bathroom stall. We hooted at each of her dramatic renderings. Then she said (not breaking her rhythm since we all know timing is everything), "Here's one I haven't seen before—

'DYKES UNITE'." There was that profound silence again, as if the frames of my life had ground to a halt. We were in a freeze-frame and options played themselves out in my head in rapid succession: Say nothing? Say something? Say what?

I laughed and said, "Yeah, but have you seen the rubber stamp on my desk at home?"

"No," said my mother with a slight bit of puzzlement. "What does it say?"

"I saw it," my grandmother called out from her stall. "It says: 'Lesbian Money!'"

"What?"

"*Lesbian Money,*" Lydia repeated.

"I just stamp it on my big bills," I said tentatively, and we all screamed with laughter. The other woman at the sinks tried to pretend we didn't exist.

Since then there has been little discussion. There have been some moments of awkwardness, usually in social situations where they feel uncertain. Although we have not explored the "it," the shift in our relationship is clear. When I go home it is with my lover and she is received as such. I was lucky. My family was as relieved as I to finally know who I was.   [1990]

Older, Wiser, and Marginalized: Ageism in Women's Lives

Although everyone hopes to live to old age, our society devalues and marginalizes older people, particularly older women who are no longer attractive in the eyes of a youth-obsessed culture. We begin with an overview of the economic, social, and health concerns of older women that documents the harsh realities of many older women's lives. Written by the advocacy group Older Women's League, this essay describes the ways that discriminatory social policy has resulted in economic insecurity and inadequate health care for many older women. The Older Women's League advocates a national universal health care system, reform of the Social Security System, an end to discriminatory workplace practices, and government programs to provide affordable housing for older women.

Cynthia Rich's discussion of the way the media treated an attempt by a group of old women to get better security in their building reveals the power of stereotypes to trivialize old women. The brave effort of this group of African-American women, "their eyes flashing with anger," to stand up for themselves was transformed by newspaper coverage into a sweet tableau of little old ladies pleading for help. Rich explores the fear and contempt with which old women have been held in our culture and warns younger women of the dangers of being divided from older women.

Older women are often torn between their desire for independence and their physical fragility. In the concluding poem in this chapter, Anna Marie Quevedo describes her grandmother's vulnerability in a large city without an effective and genuine support system.

✿ 106

Older Women: The Realities

OLDER WOMEN'S LEAGUE

Today in America, the average woman age 65 and over lives six years longer than the average man. As a result, she is typically widowed and living alone. She struggles to make ends meet on a limited annual income of $15,615 (compared to an average of $29,171 for men). During her lifetime, she probably spent about 17 years caring for children and 18 years caring for elderly parents. Because of this caregiving, she spent 14 years out of the work force. Even when caregiving didn't stop her from working altogether, it still affected her work pattern and, history shows, dramatically lowered her lifetime earnings. Her retirement income is also smaller because she probably didn't receive a pension, and was paid less than the average man. As a result, she receives lower Social Security benefits.

Because her retirement income is smaller, she spends a higher proportion of her income on housing costs—leaving less for other vital necessities such as utilities, rising medical costs, food, and transportation. In fact, the average older woman spends almost 30 percent of her income on housing. If she is African American or Latina, she spends half or more of her income on housing-related costs.

The average older woman in America spends a larger portion of her retirement income on health care. She likely has two or more chronic illnesses, which probably require the use of prescription drugs. Medicare does not cover the cost of most prescription drugs, and it is unlikely she has any supplemental insurance to make up the difference. All told, the average woman on Medicare spends 20 percent more on prescription drugs than the average man—largely because of her greater longevity but also due to her tendency towards chronic illness.

As she ages, her chronic conditions become more prevalent. As a result, the chances are very good she will need some type of long-term care services. Ironically, she was probably a caregiver for her own parents and perhaps her spouse as well. When she needs care herself, she will likely begin with home health services, but could very well end up in a skilled nursing facility. The typical nursing home resident is a woman, 75 years of age or older, who enters a nursing home because her caregiving needs can no longer be met in the community.

Growing old in America is very different for women than it is for men. Race and ethnicity, family and work arrangements, and economic resources are the primary influences in the quality of older women's lives. The economic status of older women reflects their life patterns, including education, employment history, and marital status. It is often an extension of the problems and choices women dealt with earlier in their lives. And it is a reflection of a retirement system that does not respond to women's needs.

POVERTY: A GENDERED PERSPECTIVE

Overall, women are far more likely to live in poverty than men, but this is especially true for women as they age. As women get older, they often get poorer. With a poverty rate of 12 percent (compared to 7 percent for men), women over age 65 account for more than 70 percent of older adults living in poverty. Women of color fare the worst in retirement. Twenty-five percent of Latinas and 30 percent of African-American women over age 65 live in poverty, compared to 11 percent of white women. For older women, poverty began long ago when they first entered the work force. It began with the realities that shape women's lives early on: the reality of the wage gap, the reality of caregiving, and the reality of part-time jobs that offer few benefits, especially pensions.

Reality: *Women earn less.* The economic chasm that is evident between women and men during their work lives grows much larger during retirement years. Women still earn only 73 percent of what men earn. The pay gap only increases with age. For workers aged 45–54 (a peak earning period), women's earnings are only 71 percent of men's, and among workers aged 55–64, women earn only 68 percent of what men earn. African-American women earn only 64 percent and Latinas earn an astounding 52 percent of what white men earn. The wage gap ensures that the average woman will consistently have a lower retirement income than the average man. Over a lifetime, the wage gap adds up to about $250,000 less in earnings for a woman to invest in her retirement.

Reality: *Women are America's caregivers, and they pay for it in retirement.* As in many other facets of life, gender makes a difference when it comes to informal caregiving. The one common denominator to all forms of caregiving, both paid and unpaid, is that women do the vast majority of the work. Caregiving can be an economic disaster for women and is one of the largest barriers to their retirement security. Because of caregiving, women often take more flexible, lower-wage jobs with few benefits, or stop working altogether. As a result of caregiving, women lose an average of $550,000 in lifetime wage wealth and about $2,100 annually in already desperately needed Social Security payments.

Reality: *Most women don't have income from pensions or savings.* The part-time work that allows women to be caregivers is usually low-wage with few benefits, especially pensions. Women are about half as likely as men to receive pension income, and when they do, the benefit is only about half that of the benefit men receive. When it comes to savings, women don't fare well in general. Women's lower wages prevent them from preparing adequately for retirement. You can't save what you don't earn, and the impact of wage discrimination doesn't end when the job does.

Reality: *Women live longer.* Women live an average of six years longer than men. A longer life expectancy affects all aspects of an older woman's life, especially in relation to retirement income. Marital status, for example, is one of the most important factors in determining economic independence and support in old age. Older women are three times more likely to lose their spouse than men, and this rate only increases as women age. Many women are only a man away from poverty. More than half of elderly widows now living in poverty were not poor before the death of their husbands. The longer women live, the harder it becomes to financially support their growing needs.

The challenges women face and the decisions they make upon entering the work force have serious consequences for their economic well-being in old age. Simply put: non-entry or late entry into the job market, job interruptions, and temporary or part-time employment characterize most women's work history. Many younger women believe this is a problem of the past. But almost two-thirds of women today have the same kinds of jobs that women have traditionally held: sales, clerical, and retail—low-wage positions that frequently offer no benefits. And they hold those jobs for the same reasons: the need to move in and out of the work force to care for family, partners, and friends.

OWL believes that this legacy of poverty does not need to be passed from mothers to daughters and on to granddaughters. We understand the faults and biases of the structure of the U.S. retirement system, which is based on male work and life patterns. We believe that we need to make changes to that structure. Meanwhile, it is possible for some women to break the cycle of poverty that haunts older women

by understanding the impact of the decisions they make during their work lives.

SOCIAL SECURITY: WOMEN'S STAKE

Social Security is much more than a retirement plan. It is the heart of our nation's social insurance program, providing universal coverage for workers and their families through a pooling of resources that guarantees benefits to all who qualify. One leg of the mythical three-legged stool of retirement income, Social Security benefits were designed to be complemented by both pension benefits and personal savings to produce a substantial nest egg for retirement. Unfortunately for many women, Social Security is all they have.

Women are the face of Social Security. Women represent 60 percent of all Social Security recipients at age 65 and 72 percent of all recipients by age 85. By and large, it is women who represent Social Security beneficiaries, and it is women who have the largest stake in the continued success of this important program.

Women depend on Social Security. Because women earn less, are half as likely to have pension income, and live longer, they are especially dependent on Social Security as a stable source of income in retirement. More than any other group, women count on Social Security. Without it, 52 percent of white women, 65 percent of African-American women, and 61 percent of Latinas over age 65 would be poor.

The Social Security program can be improved. The Social Security system still best serves the traditional family: a paid worker (usually the husband), an unpaid homemaker (usually the wife), and children. Today, however, most American families do not fit that profile, and even fewer will in the future. Most of all, the program should better reflect the reality of women's lives.

Privatization simply won't work for women. Proposals for privatization recommend diverting some or all of current Social Security taxes into individual private accounts. A system of private accounts would disadvantage women from the onset. Because women earn only 73 percent of what white men earn and often take time out of the workforce for caregiving, they would start off with much less to invest. Women would also lose the often desperately needed, progressive cost-of-living increases (COLA) built into the current Social Security program, and—because of their longevity—face the very real possibility of outliving their assets. Private accounts are not a guaranteed, lifetime benefit like Social Security—when the money runs out, it's gone.

If it doesn't work for women, it doesn't work. Privatized accounts undermine the promise that Social Security has offered to Americans for 67 years. By allowing individuals to withhold part of their contributions, the financial viability of the entire system will suffer, and its social insurance principles will be undermined.

The reality is that young or old, poor or near poor, today in America, women depend on Social Security. Across the generations, it has been there as a constant source of needed retirement income. It has been there for grandmothers, mothers, sisters, and daughters, and we hope it will continue to be there. Millions of older women depend on this program for their livelihood. It is the cornerstone of their retirement income, it is their insurance against disability and the death of a spouse, it is their guarantee, and it is their earned right.

MEDICARE: WHY WOMEN CARE

The typical Medicare recipient is a woman. She's outlived her spouse, she's divorced, (or, increasingly, she's never been married), and because she's alone, she's more likely than a man to be living in poverty. She suffers from a long-term chronic illness—arthritis, osteoporosis, diabetes—and, chances are, she suffers from more than one. She spends an average of $218 a month on prescription drugs and supplemental insurance. And although she may be living in her own home today, her poor health and the lack of help in managing her daily affairs will probably require her to seek long-term care—paid for by Medicaid—tomorrow.

Preserving Medicare is a uniquely important issue for women. At all age groups over age 65, women outnumber men in the Medicare program. Almost six in ten (58 percent) of those on Medicare at age 65 are women. By age 85, women outnumber men in the Medicare program by more than two to one. Over time, the proportion of Medicare beneficiaries who are women will only increase. More and more, the face of Medicare is a woman's face.

Women need protection from high out-of-pocket expenses. Because older women are more likely to live in poverty, they are more likely to face financial barriers to health care, and they spend a greater portion of their income on health care. The average woman spends 22 percent of her income on out-of-pocket health care services—including prescription drugs and supplemental insurance. The older and poorer the woman, the higher her out-of-pocket health care costs.

Women need a prescription drug benefit. Women need a universal, comprehensive, and voluntary prescription drug benefit that is a part of the Medicare program. Except for those individuals enrolled in Medicare managed care, Medicare does not cover prescription drugs unless they are used in a hospital or other health care institution. Almost eight out of ten women on Medicare use prescription drugs regularly and most pay for these medications out-of-pocket. On average, women's overall out-of-pocket spending for prescription drugs is higher than their male counterparts.

Women need sufficient support for long-term health care. For women, a particularly glaring gap in Medicare is the absence of long-term care coverage. With more chronic and disabling conditions, longer life-spans, and a greater likelihood of being alone, women are more likely than men to have long-term care needs and to use long-term care services. Women account for more than 60 percent of people who receive home health services through Medicare. And over two-thirds of the residents in nursing homes are women.

Medicare is a women's issue. It provides a health and financial safety net for 20 million American women, regardless of health history, health status, employment status, or income. Women's longer lives, lower incomes in retirement, and higher rates of chronic illness make protection against the high cost of health care that Medicare provides especially critical for women. If Medicare does not work for women, then it doesn't work for the majority of Medicare beneficiaries. If it is not affordable for women, it cannot protect the elderly against the high cost of health care. If Medicare-covered services do not reflect the changing medical practice, then the program will become increasingly irrelevant for all. Medicare must be strengthened and preserved for the millions of Americans who are retired or looking forward to retirement and adjusted to better respond to women and their health needs.

THE HOMEFRONT: HOUSING AND OLDER WOMEN

As American women age, the vital need for affordable, quality housing alternatives is increasingly important. Older women are more likely to be poor, living alone, and in need of care services. Where she lives can have a tremendous impact on a woman's well-being and independence in her later years. Unfortunately, women over 65 have difficulty finding and maintaining housing that is both affordable and meets their needs. Whether they are fleeing domestic violence, recovering from divorce, or looking for adequate housing to accommodate their physical conditions, older women often face discrimination, homelessness, and a housing market that does not respond to their needs.

Older women often live alone. Of the more than 9 million older persons living alone in the United States, 80 percent are women. Women living alone face increased economic hardships and social isolation, which has a devastating impact on their overall welfare. As single householders, older women spend a disproportionate amount of their income on housing-related costs. Housing tends to represent one of their greatest expenses, since older women typically maintain smaller incomes and receive fewer benefits than men. Women living alone often live in poverty.

Affordable housing has become increasingly scarce. Whether they rent or own, most older women have difficulty affording a home. The economic, social, and physical challenges older women face are only exacerbated by the current housing crisis. Today's housing market has become increasingly vol-

atile with dramatic declines in affordable housing, along with rental costs that continue to increase faster than income levels for many American households. Many older women struggle to compete for a decreasing supply of affordable housing on the private market.

Older women need community assistance. By 2020, women will represent 85 percent of older persons living alone. As women live longer, services to provide a continuum of care can no longer include just shelter. Along with the development of chronic conditions and disability, women will face increased risks of living in isolation. The need for community-based assistance programs to help older women maintain their independence is apparent. Such programs would include personal care services, transportation services, assistance with daily and household tasks, and structured social activities.

Older women depend on housing assistance. Many older Americans, especially women, count on housing assistance. The typical Section 202 housing assistance resident is a seventy-five year old woman living alone with an income of less than $10,000. However, low-income housing assistance is limited. Unfortunately, federal support for housing assistance should be much stronger, and many of the most vulnerable low-income renters spend years in vain, waiting for rental housing assistance.

Because of their longer life expectancy, higher poverty rates, and greater tendency for chronic medical conditions, women have special housing needs —housing needs that are not being especially addressed. Women need access to affordable and safe housing. Women need access to community care services, and women need the opportunity to live their longer lives in the comfort of a secure home.

As the only national grassroots membership organization to focus solely on issues unique to women as they age, OWL strives to improve the status and quality of life for midlife and older women. OWL is a non-profit, non-partisan organization that accomplishes its work through research, education, and advocacy activities conducted through a chapter network. Now in its 22nd year, OWL provides a strong and effective voice for the more than 58 million women age 40 and over in America.   [2002]

✤ 107

The Women in the Tower

CYNTHIA RICH

In April 1982 a group of Black women demand a meeting with the Boston Housing Authority. They are women between the ages of sixty-six and eighty-one. Their lives, in the "housing tower for the elderly" where they live, are in continual danger. "You're afraid to get on the elevator and you're afraid to get off," says Mamie Buggs, sixty-six. Odella Keenan, sixty-nine, is wakened in the nights by men pounding on her apartment door. Katherine Jefferson, eighty-one, put three locks on her door, but "I've come back to my apartment and found a group of men there eating my food."

The menace, the violence, is nothing new, they say. They have reported it before, but lately it has become intolerable. There are pictures in the *Boston Globe* of three of the women, and their eyes flash with anger. "We pay our rent, and we're entitled to some security," says Mamie Buggs. Two weeks ago, a man attacked and beat up Ida Burres, seventy-five, in the recreation room. Her head wound required forty stitches.

"I understand your desire for permanent security," says Lewis Spence, the BHA representative. "But I can't figure out any way that the BHA is going to be offering 24-hour security in an elderly development." He is a white man, probably in his thirties. His picture is much larger than the pictures of the women.

The headline in the *Boston Globe* reads, "Elderly in Roxbury building plead with BHA for 24-hour security." Ida Burres is described in the story as "a feisty, sparrow-like woman with well-cared-for gray hair, cafe au lait skin and a lilting voice." The byline reads "Viola Osgood."

I feel that in my lifetime I will not get to the bottom of this story, of these pictures, of these words.

Feisty, sparrow-like, well-cared-for gray hair, cafe au lait skin, lilting voice.

Feisty. Touchy, excitable, quarrelsome, like a mongrel dog. "Feisty" is the standard word in newspaper speak for an old person who says what she thinks. As you grow older, the younger person sees your strongly felt convictions or your protest against an intolerable life situation as an amusing overreaction, a defect of personality common to mongrels and old people. To insist that you are a person deepens the stigma of your Otherness. Your protest is not a specific, legitimate response to an outside threat. It is a generic and arbitrary quirkiness, coming from the queer stuff within yourself—sometimes annoying, sometimes quaint or even endearing, never, never to be responded to seriously.

Sparrow-like. Imagine for a moment that you have confronted those who have power over you, demanding that they do something to end the terror of your days and nights. You and other women have organized a meeting of protest. You have called the press. Imagine then opening the newspaper and seeing yourself described as "sparrow-like." That is no simple indignity, no mere humiliation. The fact that you can be described as "sparrow-like" is in part why you live in the tower, why nobody attends. Because you do not look like a natural person—that is, a young or middle-aged person—you look like a sparrow. The real sparrow is, after all, a sparrow and is seen merely as homely, but a woman who is sparrow-like is unnatural and ugly.

A white widow tells of smiling at a group of small children on the street and one of them saying, "You're ugly, ugly, ugly." It is what society has imprinted on that child's mind: to be old, and to look old, is to be ugly, so ugly that you do not deserve to live. Crow's feet. Liver spots. The media: "I'm going to wash that gray right out of my hair and wash in my 'natural' color." "Get rid of those unsightly spots." And if you were raised to believe that old is ugly, you play strange tricks in your own head. An upper middle class white woman, a woman with courage and zest for life, writes in 1982: "When we love we do not see our mates as the young view us —wrinkled, misshapen, unattractive." But then she continues: "We still retain, somewhere, the *memory* of one another as beautiful and lustful, and we see each other at our *once-best.*"

Old is ugly and unnatural in a society where power is male-defined, powerlessness disgraceful.

A society where natural death is dreaded and concealed, while unnatural death is courted and glorified. But old is ugliest for women. A white woman newscaster in her forties remarks to a sportscaster who is celebrating his sixtieth birthday: "What women really resent about men is that *you* get more attractive as you get older." A man is as old as he feels, a woman as old as she looks. You're ugly, ugly, ugly.

Aging has a special stigma for women. When our wombs are no longer ready for procreation, when our vaginas are no longer tight, when we no longer serve men, we are unnatural and ugly. In medical school terminology, we are a "crock"; in the language of the street, we are an "old bag." The Sanskrit word for widow is "empty." But there is more than that.

Sparrow-like. The association of the old woman with a bird runs deep in the male unconscious. Apparently, it flows back to a time when men acknowledged their awe of what they were outsiders to—the interconnected, inseparable mysteries of life and death, self and other, darkness and light. Life begins in genital darkness, comes into light, and returns to darkness as death. The child in the woman's body is both self and other. The power to offer the breast is the power to withhold it. The Yes and the No are inextricable. In the beginning was the Great Mother, mysteriously, powerfully connected to the wholeness of Nature and her indivisible Yeses and Nos. But for those outside the process, the oneness was baffling and intolerable, and the Great Mother was split. Men attempted to divide what they could not control—nature and women's relationship to it. The Great Mother was polarized into separate goddesses or into diametrically opposed aspects of a single goddess. The Good Mother and the Terrible Mother. The Good Mother created life, spread her bounty outward, fertilized the crops, nourished and protected, created healing potions. The Terrible Mother, the original old Witch, dealt in danger and destruction, devoured children as food for herself, concocted poisons. Wombs ≠ tomb, light ≠ darkness, other ≠ self. A world of connectedness was split down the middle.

The Terrible Mother was identified with the winged creatures that feed on mammals: vultures, ravens, owls, crows, bats. Her images in the earliest known culture of India show her as old, birdlike, hideous: "Hooded with a coif or shawl, they have high, smooth foreheads above their staring circular eye holes, their owl-beak nose and grim slit mouth. The result is terrifying . . . the face is a grinning skull."

Unable to partake of the mystery of wholeness represented by the Great Mother, men first divided her, then wrested more and more control of her divided powers. The powerful Good Mother—bounteous life-giver, creator and nurturer of others—became the custodian of children who "belong" to the man or the male state. She can no longer even bear "his" child without the guiding forceps or scalpel of a man. She is the quotidian cook (men are the great chefs) who eats only after she has served others. She is the passive dispenser—as nurse, mother, wife—of the "miracles" of modern medicine created by the brilliance of man.

The Terrible Mother—the "old Woman of the West," guardian of the dead—represented men's fear of the powerful aspect of woman as intimate not only with the mysteries of birth but also of death. Today men are the specialists of death—despite a recent study that suggests that men face natural death with much more anxiety than women do. Today male doctors oversee dying, male priests and rabbis perform the rituals of death, and even the active role of laying out the dead no longer belongs to woman (now the work of male undertakers). Woman is only the passive mourner, the helpless griever. And it is men who vie with each other to invent technologies that can bring about total death and destruction.

The Terrible Mother—the vulture or owl feeding on others—represented the fear of death, but also the fear of woman as existing not only to create and nurture others but to create and nurture her Self. Indeed, the aging woman's body is a clear reminder that women have a self that exists not only for others; it descends into her pelvis as if to claim the womb-space for its own. Woman's Self—her meeting of her own needs, seen by men as destructive and threatening—has been punished and repressed, branded "unnatural" and "unwomanly."

In this century, in rural China, they had a practice called "sunning the jinx." If a child died, or there was some similar misfortune, it was seen as the work of a jinx. The jinx was always an old, poor woman, and she was exposed to the searing heat of the summer sun until she confessed. Like the witches burned throughout Europe in the fifteenth to seventeenth centuries, she was tortured by doublethink. If she died without confessing, they had eliminated the jinx. If she confessed her evil powers, she was left in the sun for three more days to "cure her." In Bali today, the Terrible Mother lingers on in magic plays as Ranga, the witch who eats children, "a huge old woman with drooping breasts and a mat of white hair that comes down to her feet." It is a man who plays her part, and he must be old since only an old man can avoid the evil spirit of the Terrible Mother.

In present-day white culture, men's fear of the Terrible Mother is managed by denial: by insisting on the powerlessness of the old woman, her harmless absurdity and irrelevance. The dread of her power lingers, reduced to farce—as in the Hansel and Gretel story of the old witch about to devour the children until the boy destroys her, or in the comic juxtaposition of Arsenic and Old Lace. The image of her winged power persists, totally trivialized, in the silly witch flying on her broomstick, and in "old bat," "old biddy," "old hen," "old crow," "crow's feet," "old harpy." Until, in April of 1982, an old woman's self-affirmation, her rage at her disempowerment, her determination to die naturally and not at the hands of men, can be diminished to feistiness, and she can be perceived as sparrow-like.

Sparrow-like. Writing for white men, did Viola Osgood unconsciously wish to say, "Ida Burres is not a selfish vulture—even though she is doing what old women are not meant to do, speak for their own interests (not their children's or grandchildren's but their own). She is an innocent sparrow, frail and helpless"? Or had she herself so incorporated that

demeaning image—sparrow-like—that she saw Ida Burres through those eyes? Or both?

Well-cared-for gray hair. Is that about race? About class? An attempt to dispel the notion that a poor Black woman is unkempt? Would Viola Osgood describe a Black welfare mother in terms of her "well-groomed afro"? Or does she mean to dispel the notion that this *old* woman is unkempt? Only the young can afford to be careless about their hair, their dress. The care that the old woman takes with her appearance is not merely to reduce the stigma of ugly; often it is her most essential tactic for survival: it signals to the person who sees her, I am old, but I am not senile. My hair is gray but it is well-cared-for. Because to be old is to be guilty of craziness and incapacity unless proven otherwise.

Cafe au lait skin. Race? Class? Age? Not dark black like Katherine Jefferson, but blackness mitigated. White male reader, who has the power to save these women's lives, you can't dismiss her as Black, poor, old. She is almost all right, she is almost white. She is Black and old, but she has something in common with the young mulatto woman whose skin you have sometimes found exotic and sensual. And she is not the power of darkness that you fear in the Terrible Mother.

A lilting voice. I try to read these words in a lilting voice: "I almost got my eyes knocked out. A crazy guy just came in here and knocked me down and hit me in the face. We need security." These words do not lilt to me. A woman is making a demand, speaking truth to power, affirming her right to live —Black, Old, Poor, Woman. Is the "lilting" to say, "Although her words are strong, although she is bonding with other women, she is not tough and dykey"? Is the "lilting" to say, "Although she is sparrowlike, although she is gray-haired, something of the mannerisms you find pleasing in young women remain, so do not ignore her as you routinely do old women"?

I write this not knowing whether Viola Osgood is Black or white. I know that she is a woman. And I know that it matters whether she is Black or white, that this is not a case of one size fits all. But I know that Black or white, any woman who writes news articles for the *Globe,* or for any mainstream newspaper, is mandated to write to white men, in white men's language. That any messages to women, Black or white, which challenge white men's thinking can at best only be conveyed covertly, subversively. That any messages of appeal to those white men must be phrased in ways that do not seriously threaten their assumptions, and that such language itself perpetuates the power men have assumed for themselves. And I know that Black or white, ageism blows in the wind around us and certainly through the offices of the *Globe.* I write this guessing that Viola Osgood is Black, because she has known that the story is important, cared enough to make sure the photographer was there. I write this guessing that the story might never have found its way into the *Globe* unless through a Black reporter. Later, I find out that she is Black, thirty-five.

And I think that Viola Osgood has her own story to tell. I think that I, white Jewish woman of fifty, still sorting through to find the realities beneath the lies, denials and ignorance of my lifetime of segregations, cannot write this essay. I think that even when we try to cross the lines meant to separate us as women— old and young, Black and white, Jew and non-Jew —the seeds of division cling to our clothes. And I think this must be true of what I write now. But we cannot stop crossing, we cannot stop writing.

Elderly in Roxbury building plead with BHA for 24-hour security. Doubtless, Viola Osgood did not write the headline. Ten words and it contains two lies—lies that routinely obscure the struggles of old women. *Elderly.* This is not a story of elderly people, it is the story of old women, Black old women. Three-fifths of the "elderly" are women; almost all of the residents of this tower are women. An old woman has half the income of an old man. One out of three widows—women without the immediate presence of a man—lives below the official poverty line, and most women live one third of their lives as widows. In the United States, as throughout the world, old women are the poorest of the poor. Seven percent of old white men live in poverty, forty-seven percent of old Black women. "The Elderly," "Old

People," "Senior Citizens," are inclusive words that blot out these differences. Old women are twice unseen—unseen because they are old, unseen because they are women. Black old women are thrice unseen. "Elderly" conveniently clouds the realities of power and economics. It clouds the convergence of racial hatred and fear, hatred and fear of the aged, hatred and fear of women. It also clouds the power of female bonding, of these women in the tower who are acting together as women for women.

Plead. Nothing that these women say, nothing in their photographs, suggests pleading. These women are angry, and if one can demand where there is no leverage—and one can—they are demanding. They are demanding their lives, to which they know full well they have a right. Their anger is clear, direct, unwavering. "Pleading" erases the force of their confrontation. It allows us to continue to think of old women, if we think of them at all, as meek, cowed, to be pitied, occasionally as amusingly "feisty," but not as outraged, outrageous women. Old women's anger is denied, tamed, drugged, infantilized, trivialized. And yet anger in an old woman is a remarkable act of bravery, so dangerous is her world, and her status in that world so marginal, precarious. Her anger is an act of insubordination—the refusal to accept her subordinate status even when everyone, children, men, younger women, and often other older women, assumes it. "We pay our rent, and we're entitled to some security." When will a headline tell the truth: Old, Black, poor women confront the BHA demanding 24-hour security?

The housing tower for the elderly. A tall building filled with women, courageous women who bond together, but who with every year are less able to defend themselves against male attack. A tower of women under siege. A ghetto within a ghetto. The white male solution to the "problem of the elderly" is to isolate the Terrible Mother.

That tower, however, is not simply architectural. Nor is the male violence an "inner city problem." Ten days later, in nearby Stoughton, a man will have beaten to death an eighty-seven-year-old white woman, leaving her body with "multiple blunt injuries around her face, head, and shoulders." This woman was not living in a housing tower for the elderly. She lived in the house where she was born. "She was very, very spry. She worked in her garden a lot and she drove her own car," reports a neighbor. She had the advantages of race, class, a small home of her own, a car of her own. Nor did she turn away from a world that rejects and demeans old women ("spry," like "feisty," is a segregating and demeaning word). At the time of her murder, she was involved in planning the anniversary celebration at her parish.

Yet she was dead for a week before anyone found her body. Why? The reporter finds it perfectly natural. "She outlived her contemporaries and her circle of immediate relatives." Of course. How natural. Unless we remember de Beauvoir: "One of the ruses of oppression is to camouflage itself behind a natural situation since, after all, one cannot revolt against nature."* How natural that young people, or even the middle aged, should have nothing in common with an old woman. Unthinkable that she should have formed friendships with anyone who was not in her or his seventies or eighties or nineties. It is natural that without family, who must tolerate the stigma, or other old people who share the stigma, she would have no close ties. And it is natural that no woman, old or young, anywhere in the world, should be safe from male violence.

But it is not natural. It is not natural, and it is dangerous, for younger women to be divided as by a taboo from old women—to live in our own shaky towers of youth. It is intended, but it is not natural that we be ashamed of, dissociated from, our future selves, sharing men's loathing for the women we are daily becoming. It is intended, but it is not natural that we be kept ignorant of our deep bonds with old women. And it is not natural that today, as we reconnect with each other, old women are still an absence for younger women.

As a child—a golden-haired Jew in the segregated South while the barbed wire was going up around

the Warsaw ghetto—I was given fairy tales to read. Among them, the story of Rapunzel, the golden-haired young woman confined to a tower by an old witch until she was rescued by a young prince. My hair darkened and now it is light again with gray. I know that I have been made to live unnaturally in a tower for most of my fifty years. My knowledge of my history—as a woman, as a lesbian, as a light-skinned woman in a world of dark-skinned women, as the Other in a Jew-hating world—shut out. My knowledge of my future—as an old woman—shut out.

Today I reject those mythic opposites: young/old, light/darkness, life/death, other/self, Rapunzel/Witch, Good Mother/Terrible Mother. As I listen to the voices of the old women of Warren Tower, and of my aging self, I know that I have always been aging, always been dying. Those voices speak of wholeness: To nurture Self = to defy those who endanger that Self. To declare the I of my unique existence = to assert the We of my connections with other women. To accept the absolute rightness of my natural death = to defend the absolute value of my life. To affirm the mystery of my daily dying and the mystery of my daily living = to challenge men's violent cheapening of both.

But I cannot hear these voices clearly if I am still afraid of the old witch, the Terrible Mother in myself, or if I am estranged from the real old women of this world. For it is not the wicked witch who keeps Rapunzel in her tower. It is the prince and our divided selves.

Note: There was no follow-up article on the women of the tower, but Ida Burres, Mamie Buggs, Mary Gordon, Katherine Jefferson, Odella Keenan, and the other women of Warren Tower, did win what they consider to be adequate security—"of course, it is never all that you could wish," said Vallie Burton, President of the Warren Tower Association. They won because of their own bonding, their demands, and also, no doubt, because of Viola Osgood.

[1983]

---

*Simone de Beauvoir, *The Ethics of Ambiguity* (New York: Citadel, 1948), p. 83.

108

The Day Nani Fell and I Wasn't There to Catch Her

ANNA MARIE QUEVEDO

Nana
lives alone in Echo Park
  Allison Street
one block above the Sunset

Sundays
before glaucoma clouded eyes
ruined her independence
she went to mass

sometimes at La Placita
once in awhile Saint Vibiana's
occasionally Saint Anthony's
every single Sunday
every novena Friday

my nana
at the bus stop

waiting patiently for the #10 going downtown
arriving amid clouds of stinking gasoline fumes

    (she'd complain to me
      "Los Angeles is an ugly city"
      she wished she'd never left Silver.)

after church
shopping at the Grand Central
another walk to the bus stop
#28 going home

suddenly she stumbled!
hand stretched out to break the fall
too late
collarbone snapped, shoulder blade broken
downtown L.A. strangers hardly noticed

Nana
went to a medi-cal hungry doctor
told her it was only a sprain and didn't set it
now her shoulder is slumped
her arm permanently crippled

in Silver City someone would have softened the fall
[1982]

Understanding and Valuing Difference

The first step in bridging the differences among us is to broaden our view of female experience in order to understand the complex ways in which various forms of discrimination and prejudice affect the lives of different groups of women. We hope the previous sections of this Part have been useful in this enterprise. In an effort to deepen their understanding of divisions among women, women have also found it useful to reexamine their own experience with a view to understanding how it has been affected by various systems of domination. Peggy McIntosh, recognizing that being white has given her unearned advantages in a racist society, struggles to look at these advantages from the point of view of people who do not share them. Understanding these advantages can enable those of us who benefit from them to better support the struggles of those people who are disadvantaged by systems of unequal power and privilege.

In her influential essay "Age, Race, Class, and Sex: Women Redefining Difference," Audre Lorde, a black lesbian writer who died of cancer in 1993, warns us of the dangers of ignoring difference, and urges us to work harder with ourselves and each other to ensure that our differences, rather than dividing us, will enrich our struggle and our vision.

Groups of people who feel embattled in our society often work to claim their own identity and create communities of support. These communities generate a culture that challenges dominant ideas and enables group members to experience a sense of solidarity. Sometimes this can be a source of tension for women like Beverly Yuen Thompson and Lisa Suhair Majaj who felt they did not wholly fit into the prevailing categories, or available identity-based groups. "Who will be loyal to me?" Thompson asks as she negotiates her bicultural and bisexual identity. As a Palestinian American, Majaj does not feel that her "identities can be neatly divided" but instead experiences them as a complex and shifting web.

The complex web of identity will include different strands of experience for women of various racial backgrounds. For example, while Thompson "didn't consider race" most of the time she was growing up, women who are part African American would be much more likely to be conscious of race in their everyday lives.

In "Friday Night," the concluding poem in this chapter, one woman reaches out to another, conscious both of what they share and of the different cultures they each bring to their friendship.

🌿 109

White Privilege: Unpacking the Invisible Knapsack

PEGGY MCINTOSH

Through work to bring materials from Women's Studies into the rest of the curriculum, I have often noticed men's unwillingness to grant that they are over-privileged, even though they may grant that women are disadvantaged. They may say they will work to improve women's status, in the society, the university, or the curriculum, but they can't or won't support the idea of lessening men's. Denials which amount to taboos surround the subject of advantages which men gain from women's disadvantages. These denials protect male privilege from being fully acknowledged, lessened or ended.

Thinking through unacknowledged male privilege as a phenomenon, I realized that since hierarchies in our society are interlocking, there was most likely a phenomenon of white privilege which was similarly denied and protected. As a white person, I realized I had been taught about racism as something which puts others at a disadvantage, but had been taught not to see one of its corollary aspects, white privilege, which puts me at an advantage.

I think whites are carefully taught not to recognize white privilege, as males are taught not to recognize male privilege. So I have begun in an untutored way to ask what it is like to have white privilege. I have come to see white privilege as an invisible package of unearned assets which I can count on cashing in each day, but about which I was 'meant' to remain oblivious. White privilege is like an invisible weightless knapsack of special provisions, maps, passports, codebooks, visas, clothes, tools and blank checks.

Describing white privilege makes one newly accountable. As we in Women's Studies work to reveal male privilege and ask men to give up some of their power, so one who writes about having white privilege must ask, "Having described it, what will I do to lessen or end it?"

After I realized the extent to which men work from a base of unacknowledged privilege, I understood that much of their oppressiveness was unconscious. Then I remembered the frequent charges from women of color that white women whom they encounter are oppressive. I began to understand why we are justly seen as oppressive, even when we don't see ourselves that way. I began to count the ways in which I enjoy unearned skin privilege and have been conditioned into oblivion about its existence.

My schooling gave me no training in seeing myself as an oppressor, as an unfairly advantaged person, or as a participant in a damaged culture. I was taught to see myself as an individual whose moral state depended on her individual moral will. My schooling followed the pattern my colleague Elizabeth Minnich has pointed out: whites are taught to think of their lives as morally neutral, normative, and average, and also ideal, so that when we work to benefit others, this is seen as work which will allow "them" to be more like "us."

I decided to try to work on myself at least by identifying some of the daily effects of white privilege in my life. I have chosen those conditions which I think in my case *attach somewhat more to skin-color privilege* than to class, religion, ethnic status, or geographical location, though of course all these other factors are intricately intertwined. As far as I can see, my African American co-workers, friends and acquaintances with whom I come into daily or frequent contact in this particular time, place, and line of work cannot count on most of these conditions.

1. I can if I wish arrange to be in the company of people of my race most of the time.
2. If I should need to move, I can be pretty sure of renting or purchasing housing in an area which I can afford and in which I would want to live.
3. I can be pretty sure that my neighbors in such a location will be neutral or pleasant to me.
4. I can go shopping alone most of the time, pretty well assured that I will not be followed or harassed.

5. I can turn on the television or open to the front page of the paper and see people of my race widely represented.

6. When I am told about our national heritage or about "civilization," I am shown that people of my color made it what it is.

7. I can be sure that my children will be given curricular materials that testify to the existence of their race.

8. If I want to, I can be pretty sure of finding a publisher for this piece on white privilege.

9. I can go into a music shop and count on finding the music of my race represented, into a supermarket and find the staple foods which fit with my cultural traditions, into a hairdresser's shop and find someone who can cut my hair.

10. Whether I use checks, credit cards, or cash, I can count on my skin color not to work against the appearance of financial reliability.

11. I can arrange to protect my children most of the time from people who might not like them.

12. I can swear, or dress in second hand clothes, or not answer letters, without having people attribute these choices to the bad morals, the poverty, or the illiteracy of my race.

13. I can speak in public to a powerful male group without putting my race on trial.

14. I can do well in a challenging situation without being called a credit to my race.

15. I am never asked to speak for all the people of my racial group.

16. I can remain oblivious of the language and customs of persons of color who constitute the world's majority without feeling in my culture any penalty for such oblivion.

17. I can criticize our government and talk about how much I fear its policies and behavior without being seen as a cultural outsider.

18. I can be pretty sure that if I ask to talk to "the person in charge," I will be facing a person of my race.

19. If a traffic cop pulls me over or if the IRS audits my tax return, I can be sure I haven't been singled out because of my race.

20. I can easily buy posters, postcards, picture books, greeting cards, dolls, toys, and children's magazines featuring people of my race.

21. I can go home from most meetings of organizations I belong to feeling somewhat tied in, rather than isolated, out-of-place, outnumbered, unheard, held at a distance, or feared.

22. I can take a job with an affirmative action employer without having co-workers on the job suspect that I got it because of race.

23. I can choose public accommodation without fearing that people of my race cannot get in or will be mistreated in the places I have chosen.

24. I can be sure that if I need legal or medical help, my race will not work against me.

25. If my day, week, or year is going badly, I need not ask of each negative episode or situation whether it has racial overtones.

26. I can choose blemish cover or bandages in "flesh" color and have them more or less match my skin.

I repeatedly forgot each of the realizations on this list until I wrote it down. For me white privilege has turned out to be an elusive and fugitive subject. The pressure to avoid it is great, for in facing it I must give up the myth of meritocracy. If these things are true, this is not such a free country; one's life is not what one makes it; many doors open for certain people through no virtues of their own.

In unpacking this invisible backpack of white privilege, I have listed conditions of daily experience which I once took for granted. Nor did I think of any of these perquisites as bad for the holder. I now think that we need a more finely differentiated taxonomy of privilege, for some of these varieties are only what one would want for everyone in a just society, and others give licence to be ignorant, oblivious, arrogant and destructive.

I see a pattern running through the matrix of white privilege, a pattern of assumptions which were passed on to me as a white person. There was one main piece of cultural turf; it was my own turf, and I was among those who could control the turf. *My skin color was an asset for any move I was educated to want to make.* I could think of myself as belonging in major ways, and of making social systems work for me. I could freely disparage, fear, neglect, or be oblivious to anything outside of the dominant cultural forms. Being of the main culture, I could also criticize it fairly freely.

In proportion as my racial group was being made confident, comfortable, and oblivious, other groups were likely being made inconfident, uncomfortable, and alienated. Whiteness protected me from many kinds of hostility, distress, and violence, which I was being subtly trained to visit in turn upon people of color.

For this reason, the word "privilege" now seems to me misleading. We usually think of privilege as being a favored state, whether earned or conferred by birth or luck. Yet some of the conditions I have described here work to systematically overempower certain groups. Such privilege simply *confers dominance* because of one's race or sex.

I want, then, to distinguish between earned strength and unearned power conferred systematically. Power from unearned privilege can look like strength when it is in fact permission to escape or to dominate. But not all of the privileges on my list are inevitably damaging. Some, like the expectation that neighbors will be decent to you, or that your race will not count against you in court, should be the norm in a just society. Others, like the privilege to ignore less powerful people, distort the humanity of the holders as well as the ignored groups.

We might at least start by distinguishing between positive advantages which we can work to spread, and negative types of advantages which unless rejected will always reinforce our present hierarchies. For example, the feeling that one belongs within the human circle, as Native Americans say, should not be seen as privilege for a few. Ideally it is an *unearned entitlement*. At present, since only a few have it, it is an *unearned advantage* for them. This paper results from a process of coming to see that some of the power which I originally saw as attendant on being a human being in the U.S. consisted in *unearned advantage* and *conferred dominance*.

I have met very few men who are truly distressed about systemic, unearned male advantage and conferred dominance. And so one question for me and others like me is whether we will be like them, or whether we will get truly distressed, even outraged, about unearned race advantage and conferred dominance and if so, what we will do to lessen them. In any case, we need to do more work in identifying how they actually affect our daily lives. Many, perhaps most, of our white students in the U.S. think that racism doesn't affect them because they are not people of color; they do not see "whiteness" as a racial identity. In addition, since race and sex are not the only advantaging systems at work, we need similarly to examine the daily experience of having age advantage, or ethnic advantage, or physical ability, or advantage related to nationality, religion, or sexual orientation.

Difficulties and dangers surrounding the task of finding parallels are many. Since racism, sexism, and heterosexism are not the same, the advantaging associated with them should not be seen as the same. In addition, it is hard to disentangle aspects of unearned advantage which rest more on social class, economic class, race, religion, sex and ethnic identity than on other factors. Still, all of the oppressions are interlocking, as the Combahee River Collective Statement of 1977 continues to remind us eloquently.

One factor seems clear about all of the interlocking oppressions. They take both active forms which we can see and embedded forms which as a member of the dominant group one is taught not to see. In my class and place, I did not see myself as a racist because I was taught to recognize racism only in individual acts of meanness by members of my group, never in invisible systems conferring unsought racial dominance on my group from birth.

Disapproving of the systems won't be enough to change them. I was taught to think that racism could end if white individuals changed their attitudes. [But] a "white" skin in the United States opens many doors for whites whether or not we approve of the way dominance has been conferred on us. Individual acts can palliate, but cannot end, these problems.

To redesign social systems we need first to acknowledge their colossal unseen dimensions. The silences and denials surrounding privilege are the key political tool here. They keep the thinking about equality or equity incomplete, protecting unearned advantage and conferred dominance by making these taboo subjects. Most talk by whites about equal opportunity seems to me now to be about equal opportunity to try to get into a position of dominance while denying that *systems* of dominance exist.

It seems to me that obliviousness about white advantage, like obliviousness about male advantage, is kept strongly inculturated in the United States so as to maintain the myth of meritocracy, the myth that democratic choice is equally available to all. Keeping most people unaware that freedom of confident action is there for just a small number of people props up those in power, and serves to keep power in the hands of the same groups that have most of it already.

Though systematic change takes many decades, there are pressing questions for me and I imagine for some others like me if we raise our daily consciousness on the perquisites of being light-skinned. What will we do with such knowledge? As we know from watching men, it is an open question whether we will choose to use unearned advantage to weaken hidden systems of advantage, and whether we will use any of our arbitrarily awarded power to try to reconstruct power systems on a broader base.

[1989]

🌿 110

*Age, Race, Class, and Sex: Women Redefining Difference**

AUDRE LORDE

Much of Western European history conditions us to see human differences in simplistic opposition to each other: dominant/subordinate, good/bad, up/down, superior/inferior. In a society where the good

---

*Paper delivered at the Copeland Colloquium, Amherst College, April 1980.

is defined in terms of profit rather than in terms of human need, there must always be some group of people who, through systematized oppression, can be made to feel surplus, to occupy the place of dehumanized inferior. Within this society, that group is made up of Black and Third World people, working-class people, older people, and women.

As a forty-nine-year-old Black lesbian feminist socialist mother of two, including one boy, and a member of an interracial couple, I usually find myself a part of some group defined as other, deviant, inferior, or just plain wrong. Traditionally, in american society, it is the members of oppressed, objectified groups who are expected to stretch out and bridge the gap between the actualities of our lives and the consciousness of our oppressor. For in order to survive, those of us for whom oppression is as american as apple pie have always had to be watchers, to become familiar with the language and manners of the oppressor, even sometimes adopting them for some illusion of protection. Whenever the need for some pretense of communication arises, those who profit from our oppression call upon us to share our knowledge with them. In other words, it is the responsibility of the oppressed to teach the oppressors their mistakes. I am responsible for educating teachers who dismiss my children's culture in school. Black and Third World people are expected to educate white people as to our humanity. Women are expected to educate men. Lesbians and gay men are expected to educate the heterosexual world. The oppressors maintain their position and evade responsibility for their own actions. There is a constant drain of energy which might be better used in redefining ourselves and devising realistic scenarios for altering the present and constructing the future.

Institutionalized rejection of difference is an absolute necessity in a profit economy which needs outsiders as surplus people. As members of such an economy, we have *all* been programmed to respond to the human differences between us with fear and loathing and to handle that difference in one of three ways: ignore it, and if that is not possible, copy it if we think it is dominant, or destroy it if we think it is subordinate. But we have no patterns for relating across our human differences as equals. As a result, those differences have been misnamed and misused in the service of separation and confusion.

Certainly there are very real differences between us of race, age, and sex. But it is not those differences between us that are separating us. It is rather our refusal to recognize those differences, and to examine the distortions which result from our misnaming them and their effects upon human behavior and expectation.

Racism, the belief in the inherent superiority of one race over all others and thereby the right to dominance. Sexism, the belief in the inherent superiority of one sex over the other and thereby the right to dominance. Ageism. Heterosexism. Elitism. Classism.

It is a lifetime pursuit for each one of us to extract these distortions from our living at the same time as we recognize, reclaim, and define those differences upon which they are imposed. For we have all been raised in a society where those distortions were endemic within our living. Too often, we pour the energy needed for recognizing and exploring difference into pretending those differences are insurmountable barriers, or that they do not exist at all. This results in a voluntary isolation, or false and treacherous connections. Either way, we do not develop tools for using human difference as a springboard for creative change within our lives. We speak not of human difference, but of human deviance.

Somewhere, on the edge of consciousness, there is what I call a *mythical norm,* which each one of us within our hearts knows "that is not me." In america, this norm is usually defined as white, thin, male, young, heterosexual, christian, and financially secure. It is with this mythical norm that the trappings of power reside within this society. Those of us who stand outside that power often identify one way in which we are different, and we assume that to be the primary cause of all oppression, forgetting other distortions around difference, some of which we ourselves may be practicing. By and large within the women's movement today, white women focus upon their oppression as women and ignore differences of race, sexual preference, class, and age. There is a pretense to a homogeneity of experience covered by the word *sisterhood* that does not in fact exist.

Unacknowledged class differences rob women of each others' energy and creative insight. Recently a women's magazine collective made the decision for one issue to print only prose, saying poetry was a less "rigorous" or "serious" art form. Yet even the form our creativity takes is often a class issue. Of all the art forms, poetry is the most economical. It is the one which is the most secret, which requires the least physical labor, the least material, and the one which can be done between shifts, in the hospital pantry, on the subway, and on scraps of surplus paper. Over the last few years, writing a novel on tight finances, I came to appreciate the enormous differences in the material demands between poetry and prose. As we reclaim our literature, poetry has been the major voice of poor, working class, and Colored women. A room of one's own may be a necessity for writing prose, but so are reams of paper, a typewriter, and plenty of time. The actual requirements to produce the visual arts also help determine, along class lines, whose art is whose. In this day of inflated prices for material, who are our sculptors, our painters, our photographers? When we speak of a broadly based women's culture, we need to be aware of the effect of class and economic differences on the supplies available for producing art.

As we move toward creating a society within which we can each flourish, ageism is another distortion of relationship which interferes without vision. By ignoring the past, we are encouraged to repeat its mistakes. The "generation gap" is an important social tool for any repressive society. If the younger members of a community view the older members as contemptible or suspect or excess, they will never be able to join hands and examine the living memories of the community, nor ask the all important question, "Why?" This gives rise to a historical amnesia that keeps us working to invent the wheel every time we have to go to the store for bread.

We find ourselves having to repeat and relearn the same old lessons over and over that our mothers did because we do not pass on what we have learned, or because we are unable to listen. For instance, how many times has this all been said before? For another, who would have believed that once again our daughters are allowing their bodies to be hampered and purgatoried by girdles and high heels and hobble skirts?

Ignoring the differences of race between women and the implications of those differences presents the most serious threat to the mobilization of women's joint power.

As white women ignore their built-in privilege of whiteness and define *woman* in terms of their own experience alone, then women of Color become "other," the outsider whose experience and tradition is too "alien" to comprehend. An example of this is the signal absence of the experience of women of Color as a resource for women's studies courses. The literature of women of Color is seldom included in women's literature courses and almost never in other literature courses, nor in women's studies as a whole. All too often, the excuse given is that the literatures of women of Color can only be taught by Colored women, or that they are too difficult to understand, or that classes cannot "get into" them because they come out of experiences that are "too different." I have heard this argument presented by white women of otherwise quite clear intelligence, women who seem to have no trouble at all teaching and reviewing work that comes out of the vastly different experiences of Shakespeare, Molière, Dostoyefsky, and Aristophanes. Surely there must be some other explanation.

This is a very complex question, but I believe one of the reasons white women have such difficulty reading Black women's work is because of their reluctance to see Black women as women and different from themselves. To examine Black women's literature effectively requires that we be seen as whole people in our actual complexities—as individuals, as women, as human—rather than as one of those problematic but familiar stereotypes provided in this society in place of genuine images of Black women. And I believe this holds true for the literatures of other women of Color who are not Black.

The literatures of all women of Color recreate the textures of our lives, and many white women are heavily invested in ignoring the real differences. For as long as any difference between us means one of us must be inferior, then the recognition of any difference must be fraught with guilt. To allow women of Color to step out of stereotypes is too guilt provoking, for it threatens the complacency of those women who view oppression only in terms of sex.

Refusing to recognize difference makes it impossible to see the different problems and pitfalls facing us as women.

Thus, in a patriarchal power system where white-skin privilege is a major prop, the entrapments used to neutralize Black women and white women are not the same. For example, it is easy for Black women to be used by the power structure against Black men, not because they are men, but because they are Black. Therefore, for Black women, it is necessary at all times to separate the needs of the oppressor from our own legitimate conflicts within our communities. This same problem does not exist for white women. Black women and men have shared racist oppression and still share it, although in different ways. Out of that shared oppression we have developed joint defenses and joint vulnerabilities to each other that are not duplicated in the white community, with the exception of the relationship between Jewish women and Jewish men.

On the other hand, white women face the pitfall of being seduced into joining the oppressor under the pretense of sharing power. This possibility does not exist in the same way for women of Color. The tokenism that is sometimes extended to us is not an invitation to join power; our racial "otherness" is a visible reality that makes that quite clear. For white women there is a wider range of pretended choices and rewards for identifying with patriarchal power and its tools.

Today, with the defeat of ERA, the tightening economy, and increased conservatism, it is easier once again for white women to believe the dangerous fantasy that if you are good enough, pretty enough, sweet enough, quiet enough, teach the children to behave, hate the right people, and marry the right men, then you will be allowed to co-exist with patriarchy in relative peace, at least until a man needs your job or the neighborhood rapist happens along. And true, unless one lives and loves in the trenches it is difficult to remember that the war against dehumanization is ceaseless.

But Black women and our children know the fabric of our lives is stitched with violence and with hatred, that there is no rest. We do not deal with it only on the picket lines, or in dark midnight alleys, or in the places where we dare to verbalize our resistance. For us, increasingly, violence weaves through the daily tissues of our living—in the supermarket, in the classroom, in the elevator, in the clinic and the schoolyard, from the plumber, the baker, the saleswoman, the bus driver, the bank teller, the waitress who does not serve us.

Some problems we share as women, some we do not. You fear your children will grow up to join the patriarchy and testify against you, we fear our children will be dragged from a car and shot down in the street, and you will turn your backs upon the reasons they are dying.

The threat of difference has been no less blinding to people of Color. Those of us who are Black must see that the reality of our lives and our struggle does not make us immune to the errors of ignoring and misnaming difference. Within Black communities where racism is a living reality, differences among us often seem dangerous and suspect. The need for unity is often misnamed as a need for homogeneity, and a Black feminist vision mistaken for betrayal of our common interests as a people. Because of the continuous battle against racial erasure that Black women and Black men share, some Black women still refuse to recognize that we are also oppressed as women, and that sexual hostility against Black women is practiced not only by the white racist society, but implemented within our Black communities as well. It is a disease striking the heart of Black nationhood, and silence will not make it disappear. Exacerbated by racism and the pressures of powerlessness, violence against Black women and children often becomes a standard within our communities, one by which manliness can be measured. But these women-hating acts are rarely discussed as crimes against Black women.

As a group, women of Color are the lowest paid wage earners in America. We are the primary targets of abortion and sterilization abuse, here and abroad. In certain parts of Africa, small girls are still being sewed shut between their legs to keep them docile and for men's pleasure. This is known as female circumcision, and it is not a cultural affair as the late Jomo Kenyatta insisted, it is a crime against Black women.

Black women's literature is full of the pain of frequent assault, not only by a racist patriarchy, but also by Black men. Yet the necessity for and history of shared battle have made us, Black women, particularly vulnerable to the false accusation that antisexist is anti-Black. Meanwhile, womanhating as a recourse of the powerless is sapping strength from Black communities, and our very lives. Rape is on the increase, reported and unreported, and rape is not aggressive sexuality, it is sexualized aggression. As Kalamu ya Salaam, a Black male writer points out, "As long as male domination exists, rape will exist. Only women revolting and men made conscious of their responsibility to fight sexism can collectively stop rape." *

Differences between ourselves as Black women are also being misnamed and used to separate us from one another. As a Black lesbian feminist comfortable with the many different ingredients of my identity, and a woman committed to racial and sexual freedom from oppression, I find I am constantly being encouraged to pluck out some one aspect of myself and present this as the meaningful whole, eclipsing or denying the other parts of self. But this is a destructive and fragmenting way to live. My fullest concentration of energy is available to me only when I integrate all the parts of who I am, openly, allowing power from particular sources of my living to flow back and forth freely through all my different selves, without the restrictions of externally imposed definition. Only then can I bring myself and my energies as a whole to the service of those struggles which I embrace as part of my living.

---

*From "Rape: A Radical Analysis, An African-American Perspective" by Kalamu ya Salaam in *Black Books Bulletin*, vol. 6, no. 4 (1980).

A fear of lesbians, or of being accused of being a lesbian, has led many Black women into testifying against themselves. It has led some of us into destructive alliances, and others into despair and isolation. In the white women's communities, heterosexism is sometimes a result of identifying with the white patriarchy, a rejection of that interdependence between women-identified women which allows the self to be, rather than to be used in the service of men. Sometimes it reflects a die-hard belief in the protective coloration of heterosexual relationships, sometimes a self-hate which all women have to fight against, taught us from birth.

Although elements of these attitudes exist for all women, there are particular resonances of heterosexism and homophobia among Black women. Despite the fact that woman-bonding has a long and honorable history in the African and African-american communities, and despite the knowledge and accomplishments of many strong and creative women-identified Black women in the political, social and cultural fields, heterosexual Black women often tend to ignore or discount the existence and work of Black lesbians. Part of this attitude has come from an understandable terror of Black male attack within the close confines of Black society, where the punishment for any female self-assertion is still to be accused of being a lesbian and therefore unworthy of the attention or support of the scarce Black male. But part of this need to misname and ignore Black lesbians comes from a very real fear that openly women-identified Black women who are no longer dependent upon men for their self-definition may well reorder our whole concept of social relationships.

Black women who once insisted that lesbianism was a white woman's problem now insist that Black lesbians are a threat to Black nationhood, are consorting with the enemy, are basically un-Black. These accusations, coming from the very women to whom we look for deep and real understanding, have served to keep many Black lesbians in hiding, caught between the racism of white women and the homophobia of their sisters. Often, their work has been ignored, trivialized, or misnamed, as with the work of Angelina Grimke, Alice Dunbar-Nelson, Lorraine Hansberry. Yet women-bonded women have always been some part of the power of Black communities, from our unmarried aunts to the amazons of Dahomey.

And it is certainly not Black lesbians who are assaulting women and raping children and grandmothers on the streets of our communities.

Across this country, as in Boston during the spring of 1979 following the unsolved murders of twelve Black women, Black lesbians are spearheading movements against violence against Black women.

What are the particular details within each of our lives that can be scrutinized and altered to help bring about change? How do we redefine difference for all women? It is not our differences which separate women, but our reluctance to recognize those differences and to deal effectively with the distortions which have resulted from the ignoring and misnaming of those differences.

As a tool of social control, women have been encouraged to recognize only one area of human difference as legitimate, those differences which exist between women and men. And we have learned to deal across those differences with the urgency of all oppressed subordinates. All of us have had to learn to live or work or coexist with men, from our fathers on. We have recognized and negotiated these differences, even when this recognition only continued the old dominant/subordinate mode of human relationship, where the oppressed must recognize the masters' difference in order to survive.

But our future survival is predicated upon our ability to relate within equality. As women, we must root out internalized patterns of oppression within ourselves if we are to move beyond the most superficial aspects of social change. Now we must recognize differences among women who are our equals, neither inferior nor superior, and devise ways to use each other's difference to enrich our visions and our joint struggles.

The future of our earth may depend upon the ability of all women to identify and develop new definitions of power and new patterns of relating across

Beside My Sister, Facing the Enemy

MARI MATSUDA

Haunani-Kay Trask recounts the dispossession of Native Hawaiian people—their land-lessness, poverty, unemployment, imprisonment, rates of disease, and illiteracy. Trask speaks of the *haole* (Caucasian) colonizers who removed the Hawaiian government by force, leaving wounds in the native population that have never healed. Expressing outrage at the haole-backed takeover of Hawai'i has earned Trask the reputation of "haole-hater." She speaks out in the press. She writes. She debates. Trask is constantly engaged in dialogue with the haole. She works with whites in coalition on a variety of issues, from nuclear testing in the Pacific, to South African divestment, to degradation of the environment through geothermal development.

I have heard people say of Professor Trask, "She would be much more effective if she weren't so angry," as though they expect a Native Hawaiian feminist to work in coalition without anger. There is a politics of anger: who is allowed to get angry, whose anger goes unseen, and who seems angry when they are not.

Once, when I intended to compliment an African-American woman on a powerful speech she had made, I said: "I admire your ability to express anger." She looked at me coolly and replied, "I was not angry. If I were angry I would not be speaking here." Another African-American friend of mine jumped into the conversation. "I'm disappointed in you," she said. "This is what always happens to us when a Black woman speaks her mind. Someone calls us angry."

I remember this exchange because it was an uncomfortable one for me, and because it was a moment of learning. Talking across differences, my colleague told me that if she were hatefully angry, beyond hope of coalition, she would not talk. In this light, Professor Trask's strong words are acts of engagement, not estrangement.

Would Professor Trask be more effective if she were less angry? There is a cost to speaking without anger of the deaths and dislocation that native Hawaiians suffered in post-contact Hawai'i. On the simple, communicative level, failure to express the pain created by this legacy obscures the depth of one's feeling and discounts the subordination experienced by one's community. More significantly, the use of polite, rational tones when one is feeling violation is a betrayal of the self.

Professor Trask's many white and Asian colleagues who choose to remain in the room when she speaks in tones of outrage about the destruction of Hawaiian lives, land, and culture inevitably find their understanding greatly enriched. The discomfort brings with it an opportunity for learning. As a third-generation Japanese-American, I have felt the discomfort and benefitted from the learning when Professor Trask criticizes the role of immigrants in displacing Native Hawaiians. The choice is mine to remain in the conversation, discussing (sometimes with acrimony) the role of colonialism in bringing my peasant ancestors eastward from Asia to work on land that once belonged to indigenous peoples of Hawai'i and North America.

I could shelter myself from conflict by leaving the conversation, but I have come to believe that the comfort we feel when we avoid hard conversations is a dangerous comfort, one that seduces us into ignorance about the experiences of others and about the full meaning of our own lives.

difference. The old definitions have not served us, nor the earth that supports us. The old patterns, no matter how cleverly rearranged to imitate progress, still condemn us to cosmetically altered repetitions of the same old exchanges, the same old guilt, hatred, recrimination, lamentation, and suspicion.

For we have, built into all of us, old blueprints of expectations and response, old structures of oppression, and these must be altered at the same time as we alter the living conditions which are a result of those structures. For the master's tools will never dismantle the master's house.

As Paulo Freire shows so well in *The Pedagogy of the Oppressed,** the true focus of revolutionary change is never merely the oppressive situations which we seek to escape, but that piece of the oppressor which is planted deep within each of us, and which knows only the oppressors' tactics, the oppressors' relationships.

Change means growth, and growth can be painful. But we sharpen self-definition by exposing the self in work and struggle together with those whom we define as different from ourselves, although sharing the same goals. For Black and white, old and young, lesbian and heterosexual women alike, this can mean new paths to our survival.

We have chosen each other
and the edge of each others battles
the war is the same
if we lose
someday women's blood will congeal
upon a dead planet
if we win
there is no telling
we seek beyond history
for a new and more possible meeting.†   [1980]

---

*Seabury Press, New York, 1970
†From "Ourlines," unpublished poem.

111

Fence Sitters, Switch Hitters, and Bi-Bi Girls: An Exploration of Hapa and Bisexual Identities

BEVERLY YUEN THOMPSON

I had been wondering about taking part in a student theatre project about being Asian American, and I said to Tommy, "The thing is, I don't feel as though I've really lived the . . . Asian American experience." (Whatever I thought that was.)

Tommy kind of looked at me. And he said, "But, Claire, you are Asian American. So whatever experience you have lived, that is the Asian American experience."

I have never forgotten that.

—Claire Huang Kinsley, "Questions People Have Asked Me. Questions I Have Asked Myself"

Claire Huang Kinsley articulates a common sentiment among multiracial Asian Americans regarding their racial and ethnic identity: She describes the reaction that her mixed heritage has provoked from Asians and Anglos, both of whom frequently view her as the "other." In response to these reactions, her faith in her racial identity has been shaken, and she feels unable to identify herself—fearful of being alienated for choosing either her Chinese or Anglo heritage, or both. Although she knows that she is mixed race, the question that still plagues her is whether or not she is included in the term "Asian American." [1]

When I first read Kinsley's article, I was elated to find recognition of a biracial Asian American experience that resembled my own. I have a Chinese mother and an Anglo-American father, as does she, and I am constantly confronted with questions about my ethnic background from curious individuals. Like Kinsley, I also question my ability to call myself Asian American because of my mixed heritage. However, in addition to my mixed heritage, I am also bisexual, which brings with it additional complications and permutations around my identity formation and self-understanding. The process of identity formation, especially of multiple identities, is complex and lifelong, and my experiences have been no exception.

Though I have always understood that I was mixed race, a true understanding of what this meant in terms of my self-understanding and my relation to the dominant culture and Asian American communities did not develop until I was much older. My first exposure to the political side of identity politics came at the ages of fourteen and fifteen when I began to develop a feminist understanding of the world around me. Then, at seventeen, I first began to call myself bisexual after two years of questioning my sexuality and believing that the only options that were available were either a lesbian or straight identity. Finally at the age of nineteen I began to uncover the history of Asians in America through my college course work and developed a newfound understanding of my racial identity and its political implications. Yet, as is usually the case, this process was never as linear as it may sound.

Growing up, I was very aware that I was both Chinese and white—but I did not possess a term or racial category that recognized my position. Instead of creating or claiming a category that would accommodate me, I was left in confusion. How was it possible that I existed outside of the racial order of the census forms in my grade school, and what would I have to do in order to correctly fill in the answer to my racial puzzle? This confusion led to great discussions with my father about how I should identify myself. Well-meaning as he was, the only answer that he could arrive at was to choose between the two. This answer did not satisfy me because it would imply that I would be choosing between my parents —a choice I could not make.

Multiracials of Asian descent have a variety of choices available for self-identification; however, this "choice" may become obscured by others who may be quick to categorize based upon their own monoracial template of racial understanding. Physical traits are frequently scrutinized as ethnic signifiers, and one's mixed-race identity may not be accepted by outsiders. Maria P. P. Root elaborates:

To assume that the biracial person will racially identify with how they look is presumptive, but pervasive. Besides, the biracial person is perceived differently by different people. Many persons make the mistake of thinking the biracial person is fortunate to have a choice; however, the reality is that the biracial person has to fight very hard to exercise choices that are not congruent with how they may be visually or emotionally perceived.[2]

Biracials and multiracials, then, develop a racial identity that risks criticism or denial from others; this influences the ways in which they self-identify, which may change in different contexts. When faced with the "What are you?" question, multiracials may try and consider what the person is really asking and respond accordingly. Racial fluidity is difficult to "see" in a world constructed by mutually exclusive categories based on a black–white dichotomy.

When I was growing up in white-dominated Spokane, Washington, I spent most of my childhood, like most children, trying to fit in. My racial identity would raise its head occasionally, but most of the time I did not consider race. However, I did spend a great deal of energy rejecting my Chinese heritage, which I thought would certainly differentiate me from my white classmates. I would not allow my mother to teach me Chinese, which she attempted to do; I made fun of the Chinese food in the restaurants where she would take us; and I identified more and more with my father, whose side I would take when he belittled my mother's culture and "superstitions." I thought that if I did not speak Chinese then I could use that as proof that I really was white like everyone else. However, when we did end up in Seattle's Chinatown on vacation, I was secretly proud and impressed that my mother could speak in Chinese to the waitresses and would beg her to do so.

When my racial identity was used against me by my peers in school, it was an upsetting experience. One day in my grade school the other children began teasing me and a classmate, Michael, who was Chinese. Based on our racial similarities, they joked that we were dating. I was horrified to have my classmates group me with this Chinese boy. I took offense, and from that moment on I tried to distance myself from Michael. I thought that if I were friends with him then the Chinese in me would be brought to the surface—made more obvious—and that would be the reason we were friends. There were only three Asians in my grade school, and we were two of them; the only other was my best friend, Cassie, who was also hapa, or of mixed Asian/Pacific Islander descent.[3] Cassie had a white mother and a Japanese father who owned a Japanese restaurant downtown and was therefore never around her house at the same time as any of her friends. She passed as white and, without her father around to connote her Japanese ancestry, her identity was never at issue. Curiously, never once in my eight-year friendship with her did we ever discuss our similar racial identities.

When a few years later I began reading feminist books, I developed a feminist consciousness that consumed all aspects of my life. It fundamentally changed the way I understood myself and the world around me. I was ignited and passionate, seeking out feminist organizations where I could take part in concrete actions around my political philosophy. Yet the literature I read lacked a racial analysis, and this carried over into my developing consciousness. I had moved to Seattle to attend college, and I became active with NOW, Clinic Defense Project, a youth socialist organization, and a queer youth group based in Spokane. I traveled between Seattle and Spokane a great deal and was politically active in both cities. I began to meet many people whose politics and sexual orientation were diverse, and I questioned my own long-held beliefs. My new roommate came out as a lesbian, and we learned a great deal about each other through that experience. She was also a hapa—mixed Hawaiian, Filipina, and white —and she would attempt to engage in racial identity conversations, but that topic did not hold me as much as discussions of politics and sexuality. I had begun to question my sexual orientation: I no longer proclaimed myself heterosexual, yet neither did I adopt a lesbian identity.

As I had years earlier agonized between the choice of seeing myself as Chinese or white, I now agonized between the choice of lesbian or straight. I knew that neither choice represented my feelings, yet I could not comprehend another option.

The messages that I received from both the lesbian community and dominant straight society were the same: choose. When I was in college, at around the age of seventeen, I realized that bisexuality existed as an option, and immediately I knew that was the identity that most accurately described who I felt I was. But I also knew that claiming a bisexual identity would be a hardship because others would analyze me through their monosexual template of understanding. Indeed I ran across many people who demanded to know, "Which do you really like better, boys or girls?" This question reminded me of how my ethnic identity had often elicited the query, "What are you?" People were again confused. Now both my racial and sexual identity crossed lines of demarcation, enacting border-crossings that people have assumed are unnatural and problematic.

Root suggests that the "racially mixed woman may be more open to exploring sexual orientation" because of their lived experience of understanding racial identity as complex. Therefore, this understanding of racial identity may "transfer over to viewing sexual orientation as flexible and sexual identity as mutable."[4] Throughout my life I have had to explain my racial identity instead of having an easy and ready-made label like most monoracials. Yet, besides the occasional difficulty of explaining my race, I also enjoyed being more than one, having more options, and enjoying the benefit of traveling in more than one group. Now with my emerging sexuality, bisexuality seemed the natural conclusion. Already I was racially mixed and therefore I could understand the meaning of a bisexual identity in my own life. Somehow it all came together in a complementary fashion.

After I had come out as bisexual I began to embrace my Asian heritage and accept it back into my life. I was in my senior year at Eastern Washington University, and I began to focus my research on Asian American women and their history. Yet, it was not until I went to graduate school in women's studies at San Diego State University that I gained greater exposure to Asian American culture and history. It was an awakening that I compare to the development of my feminist consciousness. I was both excited to find the material and angered that it had taken so long to discover Asian American history. I wrote on the Japanese internment, studied Chinese American history, and read every Asian American studies book I could find.

Slowly I discovered that, although I could relate to some of the issues and material, my reality as a young bisexual hapa woman was not being addressed. I began to question the place of the multiracial Asian in the academic fields of ethnic studies and women's studies. Ethnic studies seemed to focus overwhelmingly on families that fit a specific model—namely, a heterosexual family made up of two immigrant parents of the same ethnicity and the conflicts their children face negotiating between their Asian parents and Anglo society. In women's studies, there was an awareness and commentary on race and difference among women, but that usually focused on the black–white racial dichotomy; Asian American women were rarely mentioned. Where was I to find myself represented in academic theory that claimed to represent women and racial minorities? As I studied further, however, I became aware that I was not the only one grappling with these issues: There were hapa groups forming around the country as well as magazines and books that were addressing this issue and demanding acceptance within the Asian American community and academy.[5]

My challenge in graduate school, as I saw it, was to explore where I could find myself reflected, with all my complexity, in the literature of ethnic studies and women's studies. As Dana Y. Takagi suggests, it is crucial to recognize "different sexual practices and identities that also claim the label Asian American" in order to begin to challenge notions of identity that have, in the past, been accepted "unproblematically and uncritically in Asian American Studies."[6] Within the "Asian American experience" there is a great deal of diversity that has thus far remained underexplored. Issues of interracial relationships, transracial adoption, biracial identity, and queer identity have remained marginalized and considered exceptions to an unspoken norm of Asian American identity. David Eng and Alice Horn believe it is imperative "to recognize that Asian Americans are never purely, or merely, racial subjects" and to dissolve any rigid or monolithic definitions.[7] Once

monolithic norms are instituted, diversity and complexity are shut out and remain excluded.

I have seen these norms instituted in a variety of ways within identity-based groups in my experiences. Organizations and literature on identity deemphasize aspects that are not considered directly related to the main unifying force they address. I have found myself continuing this silence when in group situations because of the offhanded manner in which comments regarding these other aspects are received. For example, I have usually found myself to be the only Asian American in queer organizations; therefore I feel uncomfortable bringing attention to racial issues because this would presumably turn me into both an object of curiosity and an educator. I prefer to discuss racial issues with others who have similar experiences so that we can share on an equal basis and validate each other in respectful and mutual ways. At the same time, when I am in organizations that focus on racial identity, I also feel silence around sexual identity because, again, I do not want to position myself as an object or educator. In other words, I do not want to detract from my connection with others. Unfortunately, connection is usually based on one issue with other aspects of identity being minimized instead of validated.[8]

Segregating multiple identities in theories of race and gender results in fracturing self-understanding—separating one's gender from race and sexuality. This segregation is also an impossibility: At any moment we inhabit all of our identities and may face discrimination on any or all levels. It is a painful experience to seek out a community based on race, gender, or sexuality only to have other identities denied and rejected. As Karen Maeda Allman reasons, "Mixed-race lesbians may be suspicious of any kind of identity politics based on single-group membership, whether based on race, gender, or sexual orientation. Too many opportunities exist to exclude us, to declare us as suspect others."[9] When people of color come out as queer, race is an important consideration. Rejection from one's racial/ethnic community based on homophobia, and from the queer community based on racism, is a very real consequence that may bar individuals from true acceptance in any specific community. As a hapa bisexual,

I am constantly seeking out inclusion and acceptance of my sexuality in the Asian American community as well as acceptance of my racial identity in the bisexual and queer community.

Paula C. Rust comments that "a positive integration of one's racial, ethnic, or class identity with one's sexual identity is greatly facilitated by support from others who share an individual's particular constellation of identities."[10] The first time I experienced being around others with my "constellation of identities" was when I attended the second national conference of the Asian and Pacific-Islander Lesbian and Bisexual Women's Network at UCLA in July of 1998. One of the workshops at this conference was titled "Mixed Girls in the Mix: Hapas, Mixed Breeds, and Other Racial Misfits." Attending this session was a homecoming for me. Never before had I sat in a room filled with hapas who were both bisexual and lesbian. Of the twenty-plus attendees at the workshop, there was a vast array of racial and ethnic diversity. Half of the women were Asian and white, while the other half of the room represented a great diversity of mixed-race hapa women. We explored and discussed numerous issues, and for many of us it was an amazing and eye-opening experience merely to be around other women with whom we had so much in common—and yet still so much in difference. The workshop went overtime, making it very evident that this group needed more time together. Therefore the group decided to create a hapa caucus. Later that evening when the caucuses met, some of the women chose to go to the caucus groups of their ethnicities and some returned to the hapa caucuses; we again had to choose between identifying as hapa over our monoethnic options.

I met several women in this newly formed caucus who also identified as both biracial and bisexual. When I mentioned that I was doing research on biracial and bisexual Asian women, one of the women exclaimed, "The bi-bi girls!" and went on to explain that she herself was a "bi-bi girl" as were some of her friends. I was overflowing with excitement to meet someone who shared my same "constellation of identities" and had even coined a term for this identity.

Rust speaks to this topic of the "bi-bi" identity:

Many bisexuals of mixed race or ethnicity feel a comfortable resonance between their mixed heritage and their bisexuality. In a society where both racial-ethnic and sexual categories are highly elaborated, individuals of mixed heritage or who are bisexual find themselves straddling categories that are socially constructed as distinct from one another.[11]

Rust captures the ideological and theoretical similarities of bisexual and multiracial identities in this passage, echoing my own experiences of these two identities. Because of the exclusion bisexuals and biracials experience in monoracial and monosexual communities, different responses result when these mixed identities come together in the same individual. For some, this combination brings a sense of familiarity, of being once again outside of the box, of confusing people. Others, however, may be disappointed that they are again marginalized, unwilling to deal with further oppression.

When I think that I must choose between another set of boxes—straight or lesbian—I feel the same pressure and the same inability as I felt choosing between white and Chinese, between my mother and my father. My choice was made for me. It was written on my skin; my face and gestures reflect both parents who made me. And the choice of who I love is decided for me: I love both my mother and my father and will never deny love and acceptance for someone based on their gender or race. Marian M. Sciachitano believes that "taking up a bicultural and biracial politics of difference" means accepting "the contradictions, the uneasiness, and the ambiguity" of such an identity, which may also apply to a bisexual label and the interaction of the two.[12] Yet the contradictions, uneasiness, and ambiguity are imposed from the outside and arise when I must fit myself into the established mutually exclusive order. For myself, I find comfort in the middle ground, in the ability to transgress and question lines of demarcation and challenge systematic segregation.

I am hapa because I am the descendent of two cultures, two languages, and two people who came together across these boundaries. I am firmly located in the late twentieth century in the United States where interracial marriages have only been legal for a generation. I am one of many people who are hapa, Amerasian, mixed breeds, and mutts. I am constantly called Japanese, Korean, Chinese, Oriental. I am comfortable in other people's discomfort. I am hurt that I denied my mother a proper place in my life. She has divorced my father and has gone to live with Chinese female friends from her childhood, her other life within which I will never be truly included. When I visit her I am left out of the conversation, but the sound of Cantonese soothes me. Sometimes when I pay attention I realize that I am able to follow their body language and remember some Chinese words, but it is the English phrases that are a part of their Chinese American vocabulary that always give me the final gist. I am loyal to my Chinese heritage, I am loyal to my white heritage, and I am loyal to my antiracist beliefs.

I am bisexual because I recognize that both women and men have contributed to my life and I want the freedom to choose a partner based on a person's integrity rather than on genitalia. I am firmly located not only in a time when queer people are oppressed but also in a time when a vital queer community has developed that gives me the ability to understand what that identity means. I am one of many people who are bisexual, queer, fence sitters, and switch hitters. I am called queer, dyke, straight. I am comfortable in other people's discomfort. I am loyal to my love for women, I am loyal to my love for men, and I am loyal to my beliefs in feminism and antiheterosexism.

The question that still lingers in my mind is who will be loyal to me? Which group/community/movement(s) will claim me as their member and comrade? I want to see a movement against oppression that does not trivialize or deny me any aspect of my identity, that recognizes the interconnectedness of my sexuality, race, gender, and politics. I am one of many people whose fight against oppression does not end with their gender, race, or sexuality alone. I am reminded of the words of Teresa Kay Williams:

> One day, the debate on passing will become obsolete (will pass), when Asian-descent multiracials can express the full range of their humanity in which boundaries of race, ethnicity; nation, class, gender,

sexuality, body, and language can be crossed and transgressed without judgement, without scorn, and without detriment.[13]

I find a great deal of comfort reading these words by authors whose identities are similar to my own. I know that I am not alone in this world that consistently tries to deny the existence of multiracials and bisexuals. Merely by existing I am challenging stereotypes and the status quo. This battle against racism, sexism, and bi/homophobia is being fought on many fronts by people who are like me, people who have my back.   [2000]

NOTES

1. Claire Huang Kinsley, "Questions People Have Asked Me. Questions I Have Asked Myself," in *Miscegenation Blues: Voices of Mixed Race Women,* ed. Carol Camper (Toronto: Sister Vision Press, 1994), pp. 113–32.
2. Maria P. P. Root, "Resolving 'Other' Status: Identity Development of Biracial Individuals," in *Diversity and Complexity in Feminist Therapy,* ed. Laura S. Brown and Maria P. P. Root (New York: Harrington Park Press, 1990), p. 197, original emphasis.
3. A term of Hawaiian origin, hapa haole literally means "half outsider" or half white. Although it was originally used as an insult, it is currently being used on the mainland by Asian/Pacific Islanders as a positive term designating those who are mixed race of Asian/Pacific Islander descent.
4. Root, "Resolving 'Other' Status," p. 185, original emphasis.
5. Overwhelmingly I find that Asian American literature does not mention nonheterosexual identities, which continues to promote invisibility for queer Asians. A few notable exceptions are Russel Leong, ed., *Asian American Sexualities: Dimensions of the Gay and Lesbian Experience* (New York: Routledge, 1996); Sharon Lim-Hing, ed., *The Very Inside: An Anthology of Writings by Asian and Pacific Islander Lesbian and Bisexual Women* (Toronto: Sister Vision Press, 1994); and David L. Eng and Alice Y. Hom, eds., *Q & A: Queer in Asian America* (Philadelphia: Temple University Press, 1998).
6. Dana Y. Takagi, "Maiden Voyage: Excursion into Sexuality and Identity Politics in Asian America," *Amerasia Journal* 20:1 (1994), p. 2.
7. David L. Eng and Alice Y. Hom, "Introduction: Q & A: Notes on a Queer Asian America," in Eng and Hom, Q & A, p. 3.
8. I did discover, however, an emerging discussion on multiple identities and their necessary inclusion in feminist research. Through such books as Gloria Anzaldua, ed., *Making Face, Making Soul/Haciendo Caras: Creative and Critical Perspectives by Feminists of Color* (San Francisco: Aunt Lute, 1990); Gloria Anzaldua and Cherrie Moraga, *This Bridge Called My Back: Writings by Radical Women of Color* (Watertown, Mass.: Persephone Press, 1981); and

Asian Women United of California, ed., *Making Waves: An Anthology of Writings By and About Asian American Women* (Boston: Beacon Press, 1989), the voices of women of color and lesbians are emerging. Indeed, the postmodern phase we are in has pushed the concept of difference to buzz word status. Yet, although frequently mentioned, difference is yet to be completely integrated.

9. Karen Maeda Allman, "(Un)Natural Boundaries: Mixed Race, Gender, and Sexuality," in *The Multiracial Experience: Racial Borders as the New Frontier,* ed. Maria P. P. Root (Thousand Oaks, Calif.: Sage, 1996), p. 287, emphasis original.

10. Paula C. Rust, "Managing Multiple Identities: Diversity Among Bisexual Women and Men," in *Bisexualilty: The Psychology and Politics of an Invisible Minority,* ed. Beth A. Firestein (Thousand Oaks, Calif.: Sage, 1996), p. 254.

11. Rust, "Managing Multiple Identities," pp. 69–70.

12. Marian M. Sciachitano, "Claiming a Politics of Biracial Asian American Difference," in *A Gathering of Voices on the Asian American Experience,* ed. Annette White-Parks et al. (Fort Atkinson, Wis.: Highsmith Press, 1994), p. 52.

13. Teresa Kay Williams, "Race-ing and Being Raced: The Critical Interrogation of 'Passing,'" *Amerasia Journal* 23:1 (1997), p. 64.

✤ 112

Boundaries: Arab/American

LISA SUHAIR MAJAJ

One evening a number of years ago, at a workshop on racism, I became aware—in one of those moments of realization that is not a definitive falling into place, but instead a slow groundswell of understanding—of the ways in which I experience my identity as not merely complex, but rather an uninterpretable excess.

Workshop participants were asked to group ourselves in the center of the room. As the facilitator called out a series of categories, we crossed to one side of the room or the other, according to our self-identification: white or person of color, heterosexual or lesbian/bisexual, middle/upper-class or working-class, born in the United States or in another country, at least one college-educated parent or parents

with no higher education, English as a native language or a second language. Although I am used to thinking of myself in terms of marginality and difference, I found myself, time after time, on the mainstream side of the room. White (as I called myself for lack of a more appropriate category), heterosexual, middle-class, born in the United States to a college-educated parent, a native speaker of English, I seemed to be part of America's presumed majority.

I learned a great deal that night about how much I take for granted those aspects of my life which locate me in a privileged sphere. It is a lesson of which I remain acutely conscious, and for which I am grateful. But looking across the room at the cluster of women representing what American society understands as "other," I was disconcerted by the lack of fit between the definitions offered that evening and my personal reality. Born in the United States, I have nonetheless lived much of my life outside it, in Jordan and Lebanon. My father was college-educated and middle-class, but Palestinian—hardly an identity suggestive of inclusion in mainstream American society. I considered myself white: my olive-tinged skin, while an asset in terms of acquiring a ready tan, did not seem a dramatic marker of difference. But I have received enough comments on my skin tone to make me aware that this is not entirely a neutral issue—and as I have learned the history of colonialism in the Arab world, I have come to understand the ways in which even light-skinned Arabs are people of color. Native speaker of English, I grew up alienated from the linguistic medium —Arabic—that swirled around me, living a life in some ways as marginal as that of a non-English speaker in the United States. Although I do not think of myself as having an accent, I have more than once been assumed to be foreign; I speak with an intonation acquired from the British-inflected Jordanian English that delineated my childhood, or from years of the careful enunciation one adopts when addressing non-native speakers. I have been the target of various forms of harassment specifically linked to my Arab identity, from hostile comments to threatening phone calls, racist mail, and destruction of property. I have feared physical assault when wearing something that identifies me as an Arab. And so, standing on the majority side of the room that evening, observing the discrepancy between the facts of my life and the available categories of inclusion and exclusion, I could not help but wonder whether these categories are insufficient, or insufficiently nuanced. . . .

I discovered soon enough that being Arab in the United States—worse, being Palestinian—offers little in the way of reassurance. My hopeful belief that moving to the United States would be a homecoming was quickly shaken. Once I claimed a past, spoke my history, told my name, the walls of incomprehension and hostility rose, brick by brick: un-funny "ethnic" jokes, jibes about terrorists and kalashnikovs, about veiled women and camels; or worse, the shifts to other subjects. Searching for images of my Arab self in American culture I found only unrecognizable stereotypes. In the face of such incomprehension I could say nothing.

But I have grown weary of my silence and paranoia; my fear that if I wear a Palestinian emblem, a *kaffiyeh,* use my few words of Arabic, say my name and where I am from, I will open myself to suspicion or hatred. 1 am tired of being afraid to speak who I am: American and Palestinian, not merely half of one thing and half of another, but both at once— and in that inexplicable melding that occurs when two cultures come together, not quite either, so that neither American nor Arab find themselves fully reflected in me, nor I in them.

Perhaps it should not have surprised me to cross and recross that room of divisions and find myself nowhere. . . .

* * *

In my experience cultural marginality has been among the most painful of alienations. My childhood desire, often desperate, was not so much to be a particular nationality, to be American or Arab, but to be wholly one thing or another: to be *something* that I and the rest of the world could understand, categorize, label, predict. Although I spent years struggling to define my personal politics of location, I remained situated somewhere between Arab and American cultures—never quite rooted in either, always constrained by both. My sense of liminality

grew as I became more aware of the rigid nature of definitions: Arab culture simultaneously claimed and excluded me, while the American identity I longed for retreated inexorably from my grasp.

My experiences in the United States in many ways reinforced this sense of exclusion. Upon arriving in Michigan for graduate school, after four years at the American University of Beirut during which both my American and Palestinian identities had been inevitably politicized, I yearned, yet again, for the simplicity of belonging. Consciously drawing as little attention as possible to my name, my family, my background, I avoided Middle Eastern organizations, and made no Arab friends at all. A few days after my arrival in the United States, when a man asked me provocatively why I wore a "map of Israel" around my neck, I answered briefly that it was a map of historic Palestine and then retreated from his attempts to draw me into debate, shrinking deep into a cocoon of silence.

"Passing demands a desire to become invisible," writes Michelle Cliff. "A ghost-life. An ignorance of connections."* While the incidents that first made me afraid to reveal myself in the United States were minor—pointed questions, sidelong glances, awkward silences—they were enough to thrust me firmly back into a desire for invisibility. I sought anonymity, as if trying to erode the connections that had brought me, juncture by juncture, to where and who I was, the product of histories I could no more undo than I could undo my bone structure.

But passing, as I was to learn, wreaks implicit violence upon the lived reality of our experiences. "Passing demands quiet," Cliff warns. "And from that quiet—silence." I have learned to understand silence as something insidious. As a child, lost between the contradictory demands of the worlds I moved between, I claimed silence as a tool of survival; I honed it still further in my American context. What I did not then realize was that silence, with time, atrophies the voice—a loss with such grave consequences that it is a form of dispossession. Silence made it possible for me to blend into my sur-

---

*Michelle Cliff, *Claiming an Identity They Taught Me to Despise* (Watertown, MA: Persephone Press, 1980), 5.

roundings, chameleon-like; it enabled me to absorb without self-revelation what I needed to know. But its implications were disastrous. Silence wrapped itself around my limbs like cotton wool, wound itself into my ears and eyes, filled my mouth and muffled my throat. I do not know at what point I began to choke. Perhaps there was never a single incident, just a slow deposition of sediment over time. Until one day, retching, I spat out some unnameable substance. And I attempted to speak.

By this time I was beginning to claim the tools of feminism. In Beirut I had pored over a copy of *The Feminine Mystique,* startled by the wave of recognition it evoked. Later, graduate school exposed me to the analytical training and the affirmation of voice that I had been lacking. Although I eventually discovered its cultural insensibilities, American feminism enabled me to begin interrogating the entanglement of gender and culture in a search for my own definitions. While much in my experience had tempted me to reject Arab culture as misogynist, my growing awareness of the ways in which my experiences represented not Arab culture *per se,* but a conflicted interaction between Arab and American, led me to explore my Palestinian background for positive symbols, not just nationalistic but gendered, on which to draw for identification and strength.

This exploration reinforced my acute awareness of the representation and misrepresentation of Arab culture in the United States. There are ways in which Palestinian women escape the typical stereotypes of Arab women—exotic, sensualized, victimized—only to be laden with the more male-coded, or perhaps merely generic, images of irrational terrorists and pathetic refugees. But none of these images reflect the Arab women I know: my widowed Palestinian grandmother, who raised three boys and buried two girls, raising two grandchildren as well after their mother was killed by a Zionist group's bomb, whose strength and independence people still speak of with awe; or my Lebanese aunt, a skilled nurse, who ran a Jerusalem hospital ward for years, raised four children, gracefully met the social requirements of her husband's busy political and medical careers, and now directs a center for disabled children. My increasing anger at the portrayal of the Middle East

as a chaotic realm outside the boundaries of rational Western comprehension, and a slowly developing confidence in my own political and cultural knowledge, came together with my burgeoning feminism to make possible an articulation that, although tentative, was more empowering than anything I had experienced.

At some point I began to feel anger. At the jokes about *kalashnikovs* in my backpack, grenades in my purse. At the sheer amazement of a woman who asked my mother, "But why did you marry a terrorist?" At an acquaintance's incredulous look when I spoke of Arab feminism. At the comments that it must be dangerous to live in Jordan "because of all the terrorism." At the college professor who did not believe that Arabs could be Christians. At the knowledge that when I posted announcements of Arab cultural events on campus they would be torn down moments later. At the look of shock and dismay, quickly masked, on the face of a new acquaintance just learning of my Palestinian background. At the startled response of someone who, having assumed my Arab name to be my spouse's, learned that I chose to keep an *Arab* name. At the conversations in which I am forced to explain that Palestinians do indeed exist; that they claim a long history in Palestine.

And with the anger has come fear. Of the unknown person in my apartment building who intercepted packages I had ordered from an Arab-American organization, strewing their contents, defaced with obscenities, at my door. Of the hostility of airport security personnel once they know my destination or origin point: the overly thorough searches, the insistent questions. Of the anonymous person who dialed my home after I was interviewed by my local paper, shouting "Death to Palestinians!" Of the unsigned, racist mail. Of the mysterious hit-and-run driver who smashed my car as it was parked on a quiet residential street, a Palestine emblem clearly visible through the window of the car door.

Such actions inscribe their subjects within a singular, predetermined identity, and often elicit responses validating precisely this identity. However, such exclusionary identification remains, finally untenable. During the Gulf War a radio commentator proclaimed, "In war there are no hyphenated Americans, just Americans and non-Americans." It is a familiar, and chilling, sentiment: Japanese-Americans in particular can speak to its implications. But what is to become of those of us in-between, those of us who are neither "just" Americans, nor "just" non-Americans? I could say that I opposed the Gulf War as a human being first, as an American second, and only third as a Palestinian. But in fact my identities cannot be so neatly divided. I am never just an American, any more than I am just a Palestinian. Yet I am not therefore any less of an American, or less of a Palestinian. As I was rarely given the choice in the Middle East to claim or not claim my American identity, so I am not often given the choice in my American context to be or not to be Palestinian. At best I can attempt to pass, suppressing my identity and resorting to silence. And when this strategy fails—*or when I reject it*—then I am forced to take responsibility for *both* American and Palestinian histories in their contradictory entireties—histories articulated through idealism, but resorting too often to violence. And in so doing I come to a fuller understanding of the contradictions, the excesses, which spill over the neat boundaries within which I am often expected to, and sometimes long to, reside. . . .

* * *

. . . I claim the identity "Arab-American" not as a heritage passed from generation to generation, but rather as an on-going negotiation of difference. My parents articulated their relationship oppositionally, assumptions colliding as they confronted each other's cultural boundaries. Child of their contradictions, I seek to transform that conflict into a constant motion testing the lines that encircle and embrace me, protect and imprison me. I am caught within a web: lines fade and reappear, forming intricate patterns, a maze. I live at borders that are always overdetermined, constantly shifting. Gripped by the logic of translation, I still long to find my reflection on either side of the cultural divide. But the infinitely more complex web of music beckons, speaking beyond, translation. Who can say how this will end?

[1994]

 113

Friday Night

LINDA HOGAN

Sometimes I see a light in her kitchen
that almost touches mine,
and her shadow falls straight
through trees and peppermint
and lies down at my door
like it wants to come in.

Never mind that on Friday nights
she slumps out her own torn screen
and lies down crying on the stoop.
And don't ask about the reasons;
she pays her penalties for weeping.
Emergency Room:
Eighty dollars to knock a woman out.
And there are laughing red-faced neighbor men
who put down their hammers
to phone the county.
Her crying tries them all.
Don't ask for reasons
why they do not collapse
outside their own tight jawbones
or the rooms they build
a tooth and nail at a time.

Never mind she's Mexican
and I'm Indian
and we have both replaced the words
to the national anthem with our own.
Or that her house smells of fried tortillas
and mine of Itchko and sassafras.

Tonight she was weeping in the safety of moonlight
and red maples.
I took her a cup of peppermint tea,
and honey,
it was fine blue china
with marigolds growing inside the curves.
In the dark, under the praying mimosa
we sat smoking little caves of tobacco light,
me and the *Señora of Hysteria,* who said
Peppermint is every bit as good as the ambulance.
And I said, Yes. It is home grown.   [1985]

PART VII

Violence Against Women

In the past 20 years, research on violence against women has demonstrated that women of all backgrounds have experienced violence, often at the hands of men they love. In fact, the far-ranging physical and emotional consequences of violence against women make it a major public health and criminal justice concern in the United States.[1] Whether in the form of rape, domestic violence, or childhood sexual abuse, violence against women represents an abuse of power in a misogynist culture. When violence occurs in the family, as in the case of domestic violence and incest, a cloak of privacy surrounds it, frequently silencing its victims. The feminist insistence on the political nature of private life enabled women to talk about the experience of violence, revealing how widespread it was and shattering the myths surrounding it.

The roots of domestic violence, also referred to as "intimate partner violence," lie in the soil of the patriarchal family. The belief that wives are the possessions of a male "head of household" who should control the behavior of all other family members is deeply embedded in social traditions. Women's disadvantaged position in the work force and their continued responsibility for child raising reinforce their economic dependence on their husbands and partners, thereby making it difficult for women to leave abusive relationships. For years, domestic violence eluded the criminal justice system because police were reluctant to interfere in family life. Women who have been trained all their lives to believe that they should accommodate to men's needs and fix any problems that arise in their relationships are often trapped in violent relationships by their own feelings of guilt and shame. Many women in abusive relationships have ambivalent feelings about their abuser. On the one hand, they can genuinely feel positively toward him when "things are going well," but feel angry and betrayed when he is assaulting them.

In the past three decades, women have organized to make the criminal justice system more effective in dealing with domestic violence by educating police and changing laws to ensure that women get the protection they need from law enforcement agencies. Women have also organized a network of shelters and "safe houses" for women who are fleeing abusive relationships. However, these shelters can only temporarily house a small fraction of those who need them. In 1996, the trial of O.J. Simpson, a star football player charged with the murder of his wife Nicole Simpson, focused the country's attention on the prevalence of domestic violence as evidence of Simpson's violent treatment of Nicole surfaced during the trial. Violence against women is more openly discussed than it has been in the recent past, and victims today are more likely to know where to turn for help. Despite these advances, however, violence remains a part of the lives of far too many women and their children; recent statistics indicate that approximately 1.3 million U.S. women are physically assaulted by an intimate partner annually.[2]

---

[1] Patricia Tjaden and Nancy Thoennes, "Full Report of the Prevalence, Incidence, and Consequences of Violence Against Women." U.S. Department of Justice NCJ 183781, November 2000.
[2] Ibid.

Sexual violence affects the lives of all women. Fear of rape shapes women's behavior from girlhood, restricting their movement and limiting their freedom. But despite the precautions women learn to take, thousands of women and girls are raped and molested each year. A national survey of women in the United States 18 years and older found that one of six women has been a victim of attempted or completed rape. Additionally, it was estimated that 876,064 women are raped each year in the United States—and the majority of them were raped by men they knew (present or former spouse, boyfriend, or date).[3] Rape, however, is a grossly underreported crime. The FBI estimates that only about 16% of all rapes are reported. In 2000, 90,186 forcible rapes were reported to the FBI (32 per 100,000 women), representing the first increase since 1992.[4] Overall, researchers acknowledge the difficulty in accurately assessing the prevalence of rape, and suggest that depending on how rape is defined, somewhere between 20% and 27% of women have reported being victims of rape or attempted rape.[5]

In spite of its pervasiveness, women's experience of sexual violence was, until the 1980s, rarely discussed in public. In 1971 Susan Griffin's article, "Rape: The All-American Crime," broke the silence about rape and called attention to the ways that images of sexual violence pervade Western culture. Susan Brownmiller's comprehensive study, *Against Our Will*, continued this investigation, tracing the history of rape in Western culture and demonstrating that, far from being a problem of individual psychopaths, sexual violence against women has been reinforced by our legal and criminal justice system, as well as by prevailing ideas about gender and sexuality.[6] The belief that women are the sexual property of men is still alive today, embodied in the legal statutes of the thirty-three states in which it is legal for a man to rape his wife in some situations.[7] The notion that women are responsible for male sexual behavior is reflected in the humiliating questions rape victims are often asked about their sexual histories, and contributes to the low rate of conviction in rape trials. Such victim-blaming occurs not only in the courtroom, but also in everyday discourse, making it difficult for many rape survivors to come forward and press charges against their attackers.

Racism has shaped the experience of rape in this culture, from the systematic rape of enslaved African-American women to the false charges of rape that were used as a pretense for lynching African-American men in the South in the early twentieth century. African-American rape victims are less frequently believed by white juries, and African-American men are more frequently convicted. The popular myth of the black rapist clouds the realities that most rapes are committed by

---

[3] Ibid.
[4] FBI Uniform Crime Reports, Forcible Rape, 2000.
[5] Maria Bevacqua, *Rape on the Public Agenda: Feminism and the Politics of Sexual Assault.* (Boston: Northeastern University Press, 2000).
[6] Susan Brownmiller, *Against Our Will: Men, Women and Rape.* (New York: Simon and Schuster, 1975).
[7] ViolenceAgainstWomen.net

men who are the same race as their victims, and that the majority of men arrested for rape in 2000 were white.[8]

Among the myriad misconceptions that surround the subject of rape is the notion that most rapes are committed by strangers. In fact, researchers estimate that between 60% and 80% of all rapes are acquaintance rapes, many of which occur in dating situations. The traditions of sexual conquest in which women are seen as sexual objects and male sexuality is assumed to be uncontrollable make it particularly difficult for the victims of date rape to speak out and be taken seriously. Male culture on college campuses, particularly in fraternities, has encouraged the treatment of women as sexual prey and celebrated male lust and sexual prowess. More recently, the proliferation of drug-induced rape via Rohypnol, the "date rape drug," has increased women's fears of acquaintance rape. Wherever it occurs, rape is a powerful expression of women's subordinate status. To combat it demands asserting that women have a right to say no to unwanted sex and to be seen as sexual actors, not objects.

The sexual abuse of young girls by a trusted adult is another form of sexual violence that has surfaced in shocking proportions in recent years. Researchers estimate that one in four girls is a victim of childhood sexual abuse. Girls are often painfully confused when molested by an adult from whom they crave attention and approval. Feelings of betrayal often follow young women into adulthood, as they attempt to deal with the emotional consequences of abuse. Like the other forms of sexual violence, the molestation of girl children is an egregious violation of female bodily integrity, and a cruel, abusive exercise of power.

Because they confront us with some of the most horrifying consequences of sexism, the essays and stories in this Part are very upsetting. However, only by acknowledging the contempt with which women and girls have often been treated can we begin to take action to address violence against women, thereby initiating a major shift in how our society views girls and women.

---

[8]FBI Uniform Crime Reports, Forcible Rape, 2000.

Violence Against Women in Intimate Relationships

Physical violence directed at women by their intimate partners has made the home a frightening and dangerous place for the millions of women who are abused each year. Myths and misconceptions prevent many people from understanding the experiences of battered women and the reasons that they stay in abusive relationships. Many assume that "if it really was that bad" abused women would leave the relationship. Others think that "if she learned to stay out of the way, she wouldn't get hurt." These myths are dangerous, setting the stage for social acceptance of violence against women. The reality is that social and economic realities deter battered women from picking up and leaving abusive relationships. This section begins with Ann Jones's overview of violence against women in the home, as well as in dating relationships, and suggests steps that our society must take to end it. She stresses the connections among the political, social, and economic changes necessary to reduce violence against women.

Fear of social judgment and shame often prevent many battered women from speaking out about their lives, thereby gaining support and possibly changing their relationships. They are often trapped in a nightmarish cycle of abuse and apologies, and tiptoe around their partner in fear that he might strike out. "A Letter from a Battered Wife" is a personal account of a young wife who has been severely beaten by her husband throughout their marriage. Although this letter was written almost 20 years ago, it is still, unfortunately, an accurate depiction of intimate partner violence. In "Countdown," Lanette Fisher-Hertz tells the story of Cassie, a young girl who watches her mother's attempts to steer clear of her boyfriend's angry outbursts. Mitsuye Yamada also shares the terror of living with her abuser. In "La Princesa," a Chicana feminist in graduate school looks back on an abusive relationship and realizes that "earned privileges . . . only buy us time." Written by women of different cultural backgrounds, these accounts reveal that all too often society tacitly condones violence against women in intimate relationships. Margaretta Wan Ling and Cheng Imm Tan discuss the experiences of Asian-American women who face numerous obstacles at shelters for battered women and law enforcement agencies, and those imposed by the traditions of their own cultures. While these examples highlight the interaction of racism and sexism in the lives of women of color, they also demonstrate that all battered women confront similar issues and share common experiences.

🦎 114

Battering:
Who's Going to Stop It?

ANN JONES

"He's fucking going nuts . . . ," Nicole Brown Simpson told a police dispatcher on October 25, 1993. Eight months later, after O. J. Simpson was arrested for the murder of his ex-wife and her friend Ronald Goldman, that 911-call was played and replayed on television and radio, plunging startled Americans into the midst of a typical terrifying incident of what we lamely call "domestic" violence. Previously, both O. J. Simpson and Jon Russo, vice president of the Hertz Corporation, which retained Simpson as its spokesman even after he pleaded no contest to assaulting Nicole in 1989, had described O. J.'s wife beating as a private "family matter" of no significance.

The press calls O. J. Simpson the most famous American ever charged with murder, but he's certainly not the first celebrity to be a batterer, or even to be implicated in homicide. In fact, the list of celebrity batterers from the sports world alone is a long one which includes boxer Sugar Ray Leonard, baseball star Daryl Strawberry, former University of Alabama basketball coach Wimp Sanderson, former heavyweight champ Mike Tyson (cited by then-wife Robin Givens and subsequently convicted of raping Miss Black Rhode Island), California Angels pitcher Donnie Moore (who shot and wounded his estranged wife, Tonya, before killing himself in 1989), and Philadelphia Eagles defensive lineman Blenda Gay (stabbed to death in 1976 by his battered wife, Roxanne, who said she acted in self-defense).

The list of entertainers named as batterers is also lengthy and star-studded. Tina Turner reported in her autobiography that husband Ike abused her for years. Ali MacGraw described the violent assaults of Steve McQueen. Sheila Ryan sued her then-husband James Caan in 1980, alleging that he'd beaten her. Madonna accused Sean Penn, and

Daryl Hannah named Jackson Browne. Such incidents make titillating copy for scandal sheets and tabloid TV.

And such incidents continue to be commonplace —as all-American as football—precisely because so many people still think of battering as, in O. J.'s words, "no big deal." But when America listened last June to that 911-tape, eavesdropping on the private, violent raging of the man publicly known as the cool, affable Juice, anyone could hear that what Nicole Brown was up against was a very big deal indeed. For the first time, Americans could hear for themselves the terror that millions of American women live with every day.

That terror begins with small, private, seemingly ordinary offenses. Take this list of complaints logged in a single week by the security office of one small institution. One woman harassed by "unwanted attention" from a man. One woman "annoyed" at finding "obscene photographs" in her desk. Two women "annoyed" by obscene phone calls from men. One woman sexually assaulted in her living quarters by a male acquaintance. One woman stalked by a man in violation of a restraining order.

Routine offenses? You bet. And they're increasingly common—not just because women are fed up with such behavior and reporting it more often, but because these days there's more and worse to report.

What makes this particular list of complaints noteworthy is that it comes from the security office at a small New England college—the sort of place where old stone buildings surround a quadrangle shaded by ancient trees. The sort of place where parents who can afford it send their daughters to be *safe* from the dangers of the "real" world, safe from violence and violent men.

These days, however, there seems to be no safe haven. Not in exclusive Brentwood. Not even on the picture-perfect college campus. Violence, which has always struck women of every social class and race, seems to be aimed increasingly at the young.

Last year, at Mount Holyoke College—the oldest women's college in the country—the student newspaper carried the front page headline: "Domestic

Violence on the Rise." Reported cases of "domestic" violence were increasing all across the country, according to student reporter Gretchen Hitchner—and on the Mount Holyoke campus as well. "There are five or six students on campus who have obtained stay-away orders," Hitchner reported.

Beyond the boundaries of the campus, the statistics grew much worse. Statewide, in Massachusetts in 1991, a woman was murdered by a current or former husband or boyfriend every twenty days. By 1993, such a murder occurred once every eight days. Among the dead: Tara Hartnett, a twenty-one-year-old senior psychology major at the nearby University of Massachusetts at Amherst. In February 1993, Tara Hartnett had obtained a restraining order against James Cyr, Jr., her former boyfriend and the father of her eleven-month-old daughter. In March, when Hartnett's roommates were away on spring break, Cyr broke in, stabbed Hartnett, set the house on fire, and left her to die of smoke inhalation.

"Incidents" like the murder of Tara Hartnett happen all the time. Every day, in fact, four or five women die in the United States at the hands of their current or former husbands or boyfriends. But recently feminists (like me) who call attention to these crimes have been taking a lot of heat for perpetuating the image of women as "victims." Critics charge that "victim feminists" exaggerate the dangers women face in male violence. Katie Roiphe, for example, suggests in her book *The Morning After* that most alleged cases of date rape involve nothing more than second thoughts by daylight after bad sex the night before. Battering, according to the critics, is nothing that any woman with moderate self-esteem and a bus token can't escape. What prevents women from exercising our full female power and strength, some say, is not male violence but the *fear* of violence induced by fuddy-duddy feminists who see all women as victims.

Could it be true that the apparent crime wave against women, on campus and off, is only a delusion of paranoid radical feminists? Is it real violence that keeps women down, or only feminists' hysterical perceptions that hamper us?

In Canada, where the same questions were raised, Statistics Canada attempted to find out by interviewing 12,300 women nationwide in the most comprehensive study of violence against women ever undertaken. The results were worse than expected. They showed violence against women to be far more common than earlier, smaller scale studies had indicated. They revealed that more than half of Canadian women (51 percent) have been physically or sexually assaulted at least once in their adult lives. And more than half of those women said they'd been attacked by dates, boyfriends, husbands, friends, family members, or other men familiar to them. One in ten Canadian women, or one million, had been attacked in the past year.

These figures apply only to Canada, but considering that the United States is a more violent culture all around, it's unlikely that women in the United States are any safer from attack. In fact, battering alone is now the single leading cause of injury to women in the United States. A million women every year visit physicians and hospital emergency rooms for treatment of battering injuries. The National Centers for Disease Control identify battering as a leading cause of the spread of HIV and AIDS, as countless batterers force "their" women into unprotected sex. The American Medical Association reports that 38 percent of obstetric patients are battered during pregnancy, and studies name battering during pregnancy a cause of birth defects and infant mortality.

Survivors confirm that a man often begins to batter during a woman's first pregnancy, when she is most vulnerable and least able to pack up and move. Marie's husband, a lawyer, beat her so severely during her seventh month that she went into labor. He then ripped out the phone, locked her in a second-floor bedroom, and left the house. She barely survived, and the little boy she bore that day has always been small and frail. Carol miscarried after her husband knocked her down and kicked her repeatedly in the belly. He threatened to kill her if she tried to leave. When she became pregnant again, he beat her again, saying "I'm going to kill that baby and you, too." Instead, she killed him with his own gun and was sentenced to twenty years in prison, where she bore her child and gave it up for adoption. Jean left her husband after he repeatedly punched her in the belly while she was pregnant. Later, when a doctor told Jean that her daughter had epilepsy, he asked if Jean had suffered a fall or an "accident" of any kind during pregnancy. Now that her daughter is in college and still suffering seizures, Jean says, "I only lived with that man for a year, but he casts his shadow over every day of my life, and my daughter's, too."

Millions of women live with such consequences of male violence, but it's not surprising that many choose another way out. Battering is cited as a contributing factor in a quarter of all suicide attempts by women, and half of all suicide attempts by black women. At least 50 percent of homeless women and children in the United States are in flight from male violence. Only a few years ago the FBI reported that in the United States a man beats a woman every eighteen seconds. By 1989, the figure was fifteen seconds. Now it's twelve.

Some people take those facts and statistics at face value to mean that male violence is on the rise; while others argue that what's increasing is merely the *reporting* of violence. But no matter how you interpret the numbers, it's clear that male violence is not going *down*.

As crime statistics go, homicide figures are most likely to be accurate, for the simple reason that homicides produce corpses—hard to hide and easy to count. Homicide figures all across the country —like those in Massachusetts—indicate so clearly that violence against women is on the rise that some sociologists have coined a new term for a common crime: "femicide." The FBI estimates that every year men murder about three thousand wives and girlfriends. The conclusion is inescapable: male violence against women is *real*. And it is widespread.

Such violence was once thought of as the plague of married women, but battering, like date rape, affects young, single women as well. In its recent study, Statistics Canada found that a disproportionate number of women reporting physical or sexual assault were young. Women ages eighteen to twenty-four were more than twice as likely as older women to report violence in the year preceding the study;

27 percent of them had been attacked in the past year. In the United States, the first study of "premarital abuse," conduced in 1985, reported that one in five college students was the victim of "physical aggression," ranging from slapping and hitting to "more life threatening violence." When a guy who'd had too much to drink offered Sarah a ride home from a fraternity party, she turned him down and advised him not to drive. He waited for her outside and beat her up—to "teach the bitch a lesson," he said. Susan went home for her first break from college and told her hometown boyfriend that she wanted to date at school. In response, he deliberately pulled out clumps of her hair, broke her arm, and drove her car into a tree. After Bonnie broke up with a possessive guy she'd been dating at college, he sneaked into her home at night and smashed in her head with a hatchet. Typically, guys like this think they're *entitled* to get their way, by any means necessary. Resorting to violence seems justified to them. They think they've done nothing wrong—or at least no more than she *asked* for.

Even high school boys are acting out the macho myth. A study of white middle-class high school juniors and seniors found that roughly one in four had some experience of dating violence, either as victim or perpetrator. In another study one in three teenage girls reported being subjected to physical violence by a date. After reviewing many such studies of high school and college students, Barrie Levy, author of *In Love and In Danger: A Teen's Guide to Breaking Free of Abusive Relationships,* reports that "an average of twenty-eight percent of the students experienced violence in a dating relationship. That is more than one in every four students." Male counselors who work with wife beaters confirm that many older batterers first began to use violence as teenagers, against their dates.

That doesn't mean that violence against young women is just "kid's stuff." According to the FBI, 20 percent of women murdered in the United States are between the ages of fifteen and twenty-four. Recently a high school boy in Texas shot his girlfriend for being "unfaithful," and for good measure he killed her best friend, too. Former police officer Barbara Arrighi, who has witnessed increased date rape, battering, and stalking among college students as assistant director for public safety at Mount Holyoke College, bluntly sums up the situation: "Anyone who doesn't believe America has a serious problem with violence against young women," she says, "is living in Lalaland."

Some who've studied dating violence say young women may be more vulnerable to male aggression because they believe so innocently in "true love." Schooled by romance novels and rock videos, which typically mingle sex and violence, they're more likely to mistake jealousy, possessiveness, control, and even physical or sexual assault for passion and commitment. In fact, in some surveys of college dating, about one-third of students interviewed reported that their relationships *improved* after violence—although most of the students who said so were men.

Consider the case of Kristin Lardner who was twenty-one in 1992 when her ex-boyfriend Michael Cartier gunned her down on a Boston street, then later shot himself. Kristin Lardner herself was scared to death of Michael Cartier, a man she had dated for only two months; and she did just what abused women are supposed to do. She stopped dating Cartier the first time he hit her; and when he followed her, knocked her down in the street, and kicked her unconscious, she got a restraining order against him. But even after she was murdered, Lardner's roommate and best friend still bought the "romantic" view of Michael Cartier's violence. She told reporters that Lardner had "cared" about Cartier, and "she was the only one who ever did. That's what pushed him over the edge . . . when he lost her."

Young men, too, buy into this romantic scenario. One of Michael Cartier's male friends commented after the murder: "He loved her a lot and it was probably a crime of passion. He didn't do it because he's nuts," the friend said. "He was in love."

But Cartier's former girlfriend, Rose Ryan, also talked to reporters, and what she had to say put Michael Cartier's "love" in a new light. She had cared about Cartier, too, she said, and for months she had tried to make him happy with love and kindness and Christmas presents, even after he started to abuse her. It didn't work. Finally, after he attacked her

with scissors, she brought assault charges against him and got him jailed for six months. Then, after Cartier murdered Kristin Lardner, Rose Ryan spoke about his "lovemaking." "After he hit me several times in the head," she said, "he started to cry." He would say, "I'm so sorry. I always hit people I love." And the clincher: "My mother, she never loved me. You're the only one."

It's a familiar part of the batterer's control technique, that message. And it often works because it appeals at once to a woman's compassion and her power, snaring her in a web of "love" and "violence" as two contradictory concepts become inextricably entwined. It leads some women to reinterpret a boyfriend's violent behavior as passion. It leads some—like Rose Ryan for a while—to forgive and try to help a batterer to change. Attorney Lynne Gold-Birkin, founder of the American Bar Association's Committee on Domestic Violence and chair of the ABA's family law section, recently pointed out on ABC's *This Week with David Brinkley* that many married women subjected to abuse don't walk out at once "because they don't want the marriage to end; they want him to stop beating them." But in the end, as the story of Kristin Lardner shows, even a woman who tolerates no violence at all is not safe from it.

To find an explanation for the high rate of male violence against young women, we have to look to the source: to men. Many people still mistakenly believe that batterers are somehow different from ordinary men—that they are "crazy" men with short fuses who "lose control" of themselves and blow up, especially when under the influence of drink or drugs. But those who counsel batterers say that just the reverse is true: the battering man is perfectly in control of himself—and of the woman he batters. That, after all, is the purpose of battering. A man—of any age—threatens, intimidates, abuses, and batters a woman to make her do what he wants. It works. He gets his way, and as a bonus he gets a heady rush of experiencing his own power. As one reformed eighteen-year-old guy put it: "I enjoyed intimidating people." David Adams, director of Emerge, a Boston counseling program for batterers, points out that the same man who says he "loses control" of his temper with "his" woman will be perfectly calm when the police arrive. "Clearly he knows what he's doing," Adams says. "He's making rational choices about how to act with whom—on the basis of what he can get away with."

It's likely, then, that young women—even young women "in love"—get battered for the same reason older women get battered. Namely, they have minds of their own. They want to do what *they* want. Battered women are often mistakenly thought of as "passive" or "helpless" because some of them look that way *after* they've been beaten into submission and made hostage to terror. Their inability to escape is the *result* of battering, not its cause. According to one study, three out of four battering victims are actually single or separated women trying to get free of men who won't let them go. They are not merely victims; they are the resistance. But they are almost entirely on their own.

How can we help women get free of this violence? That's the question that survivors of battering and their advocates have been grappling with for twenty years. And they've done a phenomenal job. Never before in history has there been such an organization of crime victims united to rescue other victims and prevent further crimes. Although battered women's shelters are still so overburdened that they must turn away more women than they take in, they have provided safe haven over the years for millions of women and their children. Undoubtedly, they have saved thousands of lives.

In addition, the battered women's movement has brought battering out of the private household and into the spotlight of public debate. There it has raised a much harder question: how can we make men stop their violence? To that end, the battered women's movement has pushed for—and achieved—big changes in legislation, public policy, and law enforcement. The Violence against Women Act, passed by Congress in 1994, is only one recent example. This bill correctly considers male violence against women as a violation of women's civil rights and provides a wide range of legal remedies for women.

But what's needed is a national campaign to go after the men at fault. Experts such as Susan Schechter, author of *Women and Male Violence,* say that men continue to use violence to get their way *because they can.* Nobody stops them. There's no reason for a man who uses violence to change his behavior unless he begins to suffer some real consequences, some punishment that drives home strong social and legal prohibitions against battering. In the short run, the most effective way to protect women and children, save lives, and cut down violence is to treat assault as the crime it is: to arrest batterers and send them to jail.

Usually, that's not what happens. Right now, most batterers suffer *no* social or legal consequences at all for their criminal behavior. Although police in most states and localities are now authorized to arrest batterers, many police departments still don't enforce the law. If police do make arrests, prosecutors commonly fail to prosecute. And if batterers are convicted, judges often release them—or worse, order them into marital counseling *with* the women they've assaulted. Many men are required to attend a few weekly sessions of a therapeutic support group where they shoot the breeze with other batterers, after which their crime is erased from the record books. (Counselors like David Adams who lead such groups are the first to say that the groups don't work.) One 1991 study found that among assaultive men arrested, prosecuted, convicted, and sentenced, less than 1 percent (0.9 percent) served any time in jail. The average batterer taken into custody by police is held less than two hours. He walks away laughing at his victim and at the police as well.

Even men convicted of near-fatal attacks upon their girlfriends or wives are likely to draw light sentences or be released on probation with plenty of opportunity to finish the job. The husband of Burnadette Barnes, for example, shot her in the head while she slept, served three months in prison for the offense, and was released to threaten her again. Desperate, Burnadette Barnes hired a man to kill her husband. She was convicted of murder and conspiracy to murder and sentenced to life in prison.

In Michigan, police officer Clarence Ratliff shot and killed his estranged wife, Carol Irons, who incidentally was the youngest woman ever appointed to the Michigan bench. (As a judge she was known to treat domestic violence cases seriously.) When the police tried to arrest Ratliff, he squeezed off a few wild shots before he surrendered. For killing his wife, Ratliff got ten to fifteen years; for shooting at the cops, two life terms plus some additional shorter terms for using a firearm.

Such cases make clear that in the scales of American justice men weigh more than women. Assaulting a man is a serious crime, but assaulting a woman or even killing her—well, that's not so bad.

We can do better. Thanks to the battered women's movement, we now know that any social, economic, or political development that counteracts sexism and promotes sex equality helps in the long run to eliminate violence by reducing the power men hold, individually and institutionally, over women. We now know that all the institutions to which battered women and children are likely to turn for help— hospitals, mental health facilities, social welfare services, child protective services, police departments, civil and criminal courts, schools, churches—must join a *concerted* effort to prevent violence before it occurs and stop it when it does. They must stand ready to defend the constitutional right that belongs to all women—(though no one ever speaks of it): the right to be free from bodily harm.

That's where college can set a good example for the rest of society. While public officials often seem to accept violence against women as an inevitable social problem, colleges can't afford to. They're obliged to keep their students safe. Mount Holyoke's Barbara Arrighi says,

> We've had to work at safety, but as a closed, self-contained system we have advantages over the big world. If one of our students is victimized, she finds a whole slew of helpers available right away— campus and city police, medical services, housing authorities, counselors, chaplains, academic deans. We'll ban offenders from the campus under trespass orders. We'll make arrests. We'll connect her to the county prosecutor's victim/witness assistance program. We'll go to court with her. We'll help her get a protective order or file a civil complaint. We take these things seriously, we don't try to pin the blame on her, and we don't fool around.

What Arrighi describes is the way the system ought to work in every community.

As things stand now, it's still up to women to make the system respond—and too often, on a case-by-case basis. It takes time, money, courage, and determination to get a result that looks like justice. Take the case of Stephanie Cain, for example. A college student, she had dated Elton "Tony" Ekstrom III for nine months. Then, during the course of one hour on the night of April 28, 1992, he beat her up. He punched and kicked her repeatedly, leaving her with a fractured nose and a face nearly unrecognizable to those who saw her immediately following the attack. Afterward, she said, she lost confidence and mistrusted people. She suffered seizures and had to drop out of college. Major surgery to reconstruct her nose permanently altered her appearance.

Ekstrom was arrested and charged with assault and battery with a dangerous weapon: his foot. But Stephanie Cain wasn't permitted to tell her story in court, for Ekstrom never went to trial. Instead he was allowed to plead guilty to a reduced charge of assault and battery. The judge gave him a two-year suspended sentence, and Ekstrom walked away— still thinking he'd done nothing wrong.

That result upset Stephanie Cain. Worried that Ekstrom might do the same thing to another woman, she decided to sue him for the damage he'd done. In December 1992, when she was back in college finishing her degree, she finally got her day in court. "The best part," she said, "was looking right at him, knowing I wasn't afraid of him anymore." After hearing her story, the jury awarded Cain and her parents $153,000 in damages for her injuries, medical expenses, and emotional distress. At last Ekstrom was to pay a price for his criminal act, as a civil court jury compensated Stephanie Cain for a crime the criminal court had failed to punish. "Every time I look in the mirror," Cain said, "I'm reminded of what happened. There's no reason he should just forget it."

The victory she won was a victory for all women. But it shouldn't have been that hard. And she shouldn't have had to fight for justice all by herself.

[1996]

 115

A Letter From a Battered Wife

DEL MARTIN

A friend of mine received the following letter after discussing wife-beating at a public meeting.

I am in my thirties and so is my husband. I have a high school diploma and am presently attending a local college, trying to obtain the additional education I need. My husband is a college graduate and a professional in his field. We are both attractive and, for the most part, respected and well-liked. We have four children and live in a middle-class home with all the comforts we could possibly want.

I have everything, except life without fear.

For most of my married life I have been periodically beaten by my husband. What do I mean by "beaten"? I mean that parts of my body have been hit violently and repeatedly, and that painful bruises, swelling, bleeding wounds, unconsciousness, and combinations of these things have resulted.

Beating should be distinguished from all other kinds of physical abuse—including being hit and shoved around. When I say my husband threatens me with abuse I do not mean he warns me that he may lose control. I mean that he shakes a fist against my face or nose, makes punching-bag jabs at my shoulder, or makes similar gestures which may quickly turn into a full-fledged beating.

I have had glasses thrown at me. I have been kicked in the abdomen when I was visibly pregnant. I have been kicked off the bed and hit while lying on the floor—again, while I was pregnant. I have been whipped, kicked and thrown, picked up again and thrown down again. I have been punched and kicked in the head, chest, face, and abdomen more times than I can count.

I have been slapped for saying something about politics, for having a different view about religion, for swearing, for crying, for wanting to have intercourse. I have been threatened when I wouldn't do something he told me to do. I have been threatened when he's had a bad day and when he's had a good day.

I have been threatened, slapped, and beaten after stating bitterly that I didn't like what he was doing with another woman.

After each beating my husband has left the house and remained away for a few days.

Few people have ever seen my black and blue face or swollen lips because I have always stayed indoors afterwards, feeling ashamed. I was never able to drive following one of these beatings, so I could not get myself to a hospital for care. I could never have left my young children alone, even if I could have driven a car.

Hysteria inevitably sets in after a beating. This hysteria—the shaking and crying and mumbling—is not accepted by anyone, so there has never been anyone to call.

My husband on a few occasions did phone a day or so later so we could agree on an excuse I would use for returning to work, the grocery store, the dentist appointment, and so on. I used the excuses—a car accident, oral surgery, things like that.

Now, the first response to this story, which I myself think of, will be "Why didn't you seek help?"

I did. Early on in our marriage I went to a clergyman who, after a few visits, told me that my husband meant no real harm, that he was just confused and felt insecure. I was encouraged to be more tolerant and understanding. Most important, I was told to forgive him the beatings just as Christ had forgiven me from the cross. I did that, too.

Things continued. Next time I turned to the doctor. I was given little pills to relax me and told to take things a little easier. I was just too nervous.

I turned to a friend, and when her husband found out, he accused me of either making things up or exaggerating the situation. She didn't, but she could no longer really help me. Just by believing me she was made to feel disloyal.

I turned to a professional family guidance agency. I was told there that my husband needed help and that I should find a way to control the incidents. I couldn't control the beatings—that was the whole point of my seeking help. At the agency I found I had to defend myself against the suspicion that I wanted to be hit, that I invited the beatings. Good God! Did the Jews invite themselves to be slaughtered in Germany?

I did go to two more doctors. One asked me what I had done to provoke my husband. The other asked if we had made up yet.

I called the police one time. They not only did not respond to the call, they called several hours later to ask if things had "settled down." I could have been dead by then!

I have nowhere to go if it happens again. No one wants to take in a woman with four children. Even if there were someone kind enough to care, no one wants to become involved in what is commonly referred to as a "domestic situation."

Everyone I have gone to for help has somehow wanted to blame me and vindicate my husband. I can see it lying there between their words and at the end of their sentences. The clergyman, the doctor, the counselor, my friend's husband, the police—all of them have found a way to vindicate my husband.

No one has to "provoke" a wife-beater. He will strike out when he's ready and for whatever reason he has at the moment.

I may be his excuse, but I have never been the reason.

I know that I do not want to be hit. I know, too, that I will be beaten again unless I can find a way out for myself and my children. I am terrified for them also.

As a married woman I have no recourse but to remain in the situation which is causing me to be painfully abused. I have suffered physical and emotional battering and spiritual rape because the social structure of my world says I cannot do anything about a man who wants to beat me. . . . But staying with my husband means that my children must be subjected to the emotional battering caused when they see their mother's beaten face or hear her screams in the middle of the night.

I know that I have to get out. But when you have nowhere to go, you know that you must go on your own and expect no support. I have to be ready for that. I have to be ready to support myself and the children completely, and still provide a decent environment for them. I pray that I can do that before I am murdered in my own home.

I have learned that no one believes me and that I cannot depend upon any outside help. All I have left is the hope that I can get away before it is too late.

I have learned also that the doctors, the police, the clergy, and my friends will excuse my husband for distorting my face, but won't forgive me for looking bruised and broken. The greatest tragedy is that I am still praying, and there is not a human person to listen.

Being beaten is a terrible thing; it is most terrible of all if you are not equipped to fight back. I recall an occasion when I tried to defend myself and actually tore my husband's shirt. Later, he showed it to a relative as proof that I had done something terribly wrong. The fact that at that moment I had several raised spots on my head hidden by my hair, a swollen lip that was bleeding, and a severely damaged cheek with a blood clot that caused a permanent dimple didn't matter to him. What mattered was that I tore his shirt! That I tore it in self-defense didn't mean anything to him.

My situation is so untenable I would guess that anyone who has not experienced one like it would find it incomprehensible. I find it difficult to believe myself.

It must be pointed out that while a husband can beat, slap, or threaten his wife, there are "good days." These days tend to wear away the effects of the beating. They tend to cause the wife to put aside the traumas and look to the good—first, because there is nothing else to do; second, because there is nowhere and no one to turn to; and third, because the defeat is the beating and the hope is that it will not happen again. A loving woman like myself always hopes that it will not happen again. When it does, she simply hopes again, until it becomes obvious after a third beating that there is no hope. That is when she turns outward for help to find an answer. When that help is denied, she either resigns herself to the situation she is in or pulls herself together and starts making plans for a future life that includes only herself and her children.

For many the third beating may be too late. Several of the times I have been abused I have been amazed that I have remained alive. Imagine that I have been thrown to a very hard slate floor several times, kicked in the abdomen, the head, and the chest, and still remained alive!

What determines who is lucky and who isn't? I could have been dead a long time ago had I been hit the wrong way. My baby could have been killed or deformed had I been kicked the wrong way. What saved me?

I don't know. I only know that it has happened and that each night I dread the final blow that will kill me and leave my children motherless. I hope I can hang on until I complete my education, get a good job, and become self-sufficient enough to care for my children on my own.   [1983]

🌿 116

The Club

MITSUYE YAMADA

He beat me with the hem of a kimono
worn by a Japanese woman
this prized
painted
wooden statue
carved to perfection
in Japan or maybe Hong Kong.

She was usually on display
in our living room atop his bookshelf
among his other overseas treasures
I was never to touch.
She posed there most of the day
her head tilted

her chin resting lightly
on the white pointed fingertips
of her right hand
her black hair
piled high on her head
her long slim neck bared
to her shoulders.
An invisible hand
under the full sleeve
clasped her kimono
close to her body
its hem flared
gracefully around her feet.

That hem
made fluted red marks
on these freckled arms
my shoulders
my back.

That head
inside his fist
made camel
bumps
on his knuckles.
I prayed for her
that her pencil thin neck
would not snap
or his rage would be unendurable.
She held fast for me
didn't even chip or crack.

One day, we were talking
as we often did the morning after.
Well, my sloe-eyed beauty, I said
have you served him enough?
I dared to pick her up with one hand
I held her gently by the flowing robe
around her slender legs.
She felt lighter than I had imagined.
I stroked her cold thighs
with the tips of my fingers
and felt a slight tremor.

I carried her into the kitchen and wrapped her
in two sheets of paper towels
We're leaving
I whispered

you and I
together.

I placed her
between my clothes in my packed suitcase.
That is how we left him
forever.   [1989]

🌿 117

Countdown

LANETTE FISHER-HERTZ

It was almost time for a beating.

The withering Ft. Lauderdale heat had stopped even the palm tree leaves around their apartment complex from moving, but Cassie could see her mother getting jumpier and more frantically active each day. She'd started cleaning the house with extra vigor, cooking Crew's favorite dinners—Shepherd's pie, meatloaf with gravy and whipped potatoes, bloody steak with rice and green beans—and wearing clothes that would not provoke him. As if that were possible. Loose, high-collared tops and baggy slacks. No heels. Very little make-up.

Her mother's efforts, Cassie knew, demanded precise balancing, because too little make-up—or clothes that made her look shapeless—would also be a mistake, as they'd learned the last time.

"What are you trying—to embarrass me?" Crew had hissed, watching Sandra, Cassie's mom, get dressed for his softball game. "You want to make everyone think I can't get a good-looking woman? Jesus, what a slob. Get in there and make yourself look halfway decent, for Christ's sake."

That had been three months ago, when it was still cool enough to play softball or run around playing tag on the adjacent field. Sandra's outfit hadn't mattered much, after all, because that night after the softball game, Crew had twisted her arm out of its shoulder socket—and then made her wait a whole day cradling it in her lap before he let her go to the hospital. But ever since they'd moved back in with him, Sandra kept picking each day's outfit with extra care anyway, acting as if it mattered.

Now, with the July sun unrelenting, Cassie stayed in her room as much as possible, building an entire Barbie city out of cardboard boxes she'd begged from the liquor store around the corner. Barbie's dream house. Barbie's medical center. Barbie's school. Barbie's stables, filled with cardboard horses she traced and cut. Using a shoe box, scissors and red markers, she'd even constructed a Barbie convertible, scotch-taping on the black construction-paper tires. She could sit Barbie inside it and drag it across the green shag carpeting, which looked like grass from a sweeter place than Florida. She made driving noises as Barbie dashed confidently around her cardboard city, her cornsilk hair swinging. Cassie, who was 11, was glad she and Barbie didn't have to worry about their wardrobes as much as her mother did. They looked the same in pretty much everything they put on.

Cassie used to have all the Barbie toys, the real ones, made from shiny, colorful plastic, many of them acquired before her father had walked out, leaving Sandra, he said—but leaving, Cassie, too, as it turned out. Cassie's Barbie dream house, a Christmas gift from Crew the year she was nine, even had lights that turned on in the bedroom and kitchen until the batteries wore out. She'd had more than a dozen Barbies, too, and six plastic horses, one with high-stepping legs that pranced when you pumped its tail. But Cassie's mother had made her leave everything the last time they ran away from Crew—so now all she had was the one Barbie, one Ken and one Skipper.

When Sandra met Crew, he gave her just the attention she needed—plus, he was the one customer at the bar who over-tipped without ever trying to grab a piece of her, she told Cassie.

Sandra tried describing him to Cassie, who was seven. "He makes me believe in the ending of all your fairy tales," she said, and Cassie pictured him, a prince in tights, and was surprised when he showed up in shorts and a Budweiser T-shirt.

He'd been nice to Cassie, though; when Sandra brought him to meet her, he had magic tricks in his pockets, and all afternoon he kept making them laugh with surprise, pulling quarters out of their ears, guessing the cards they'd picked, making things disappear.

"We're moving in with him," Sandra announced that night, and Cassie was delighted, imagining every day like a carnival.

Over the past four years, she'd learned summers with Crew were the worst, because she couldn't go to school every day—and this summer, she hadn't lived in the neighborhood long enough to make any friends. Crew's temper was hotter in summer, and Cassie and her mother strained to keep him cool, running the air conditioners at full blast, bringing him freezing cold beers, the ice chips still sweating down the sides of the bottles. Once, when Crew seemed in one of his darkest moods ever, Cassie had folded a piece of science-project poster paper into a giant accordion fan and sat on the coffee table in front of him fanning him like the little black girls in *Gone With the Wind* had fanned the white ladies during nap time at Twelve Oaks. Cassie loved how special she'd felt when she'd seen Crew smile and relax, his head tipping back against the couch, his hand loosening around the neck of the beer as she waved her arms up and down in front of him.

"What a good girl you are," he told her. She lived for days in the glow of those words—and kept trying to think up new ways to get him to repeat them.

"Be good, please," her mother begged now, every day, when Crew was due home from work. "He's going through a rough time, and the last thing he needs is for us to get on his nerves."

Cassie did her best. She drew him cards, love notes that she left on his dinner plate so he'd see them first thing when he came home. "Dear Daddy," she wrote, even though he wasn't her real father. When he was being nice, she liked to pretend he was her daddy—and he seemed to like it, too, when he was in a good mood. Her own daddy hadn't seen her in four years, so she didn't even feel guilty when she wrote to Crew: "You are the best Daddy!!! Thanks for taking us out on the boat ride last week. You are so nice!!! I love you!!!! Love, Cassie." She made the "o" and the "v" in the word love look like little

hearts, and she drew flowery borders all over the paper.

Cassie's mother had a permanent worried expression on her face as the days ticked by. Cassie thought there ought to be a countdown to the beatings, like the one they had for the NASA launch her fourth grade class had attended. Except at NASA, each mission was precisely planned, with an entire team swarming like ants all over the launch pad checking everywhere for any sign of trouble that might force them to abort. She didn't think Crew planned anything quite that carefully, and she couldn't see any way to stop what was coming—no control tower to which she could signal for help. She could just feel the beating approaching, like a camera moving in for a close-up, one frame at a time.

Cassie wondered why they never ran away *before* a beating. Her mom seemed to know it was coming as much as Cassie did—so how come they only packed up and snuck onto a Greyhound bus while Crew was at work *after* her mom was all beat up?

One afternoon, helping her mom set the table, Cassie tried to suggest an escape plan.

"Mom? Maybe we should just go visit Grandma for a while now?" Cassie said, her tongue licking the dry corners of her mouth. "I was thinking it's almost Grandma's birthday anyway, and school doesn't start for another month, and Crew seems like maybe he could use a little break—"

"That's just why we're not leaving!" she scolded, as if Cassie were the worst kind of traitor. "How do you think Crew would feel if we left him all alone right when he's going through this rough time?" She folded paper napkins next to each of their plates.

"Well, I don't know," Cassie said sulkily, pouring the Kool-Aid she'd mixed that morning. "I don't think we seem to be helping him much."

"Well then," Cassie's mother said briskly, pushing her hair back out of her face, "we need to try a little harder, that's all. He—he's better, Cassie, he really is; you have to have a little faith. He got counseling after the last time, and he hasn't laid a hand on me since we came back. He doesn't want to lose us; we just have to believe in him. No one's ever believed in him before. Now, how do I look?"

Cassie squinted and tried to see her as Crew would. Snug jeans, but long blouse that covered her curves, pale lipstick and eye shadow, long brown hair, smoothly combed, with the blonde streaks in front teased back a bit.

"Nice," Cassie assured her. "Wanna play rummy before he comes home?"

Cassie's mom glanced nervously at the clock. "Maybe one quick game," she said, "but I'm cooking, so we have to hurry."

Cassie dealt as fast as she could, her fingers struggling to shuffle the cards, which stuck together from the humidity, even in the chilled apartment. How could you make rummy fast? Either you got the cards or you didn't. She was waiting for a king when they heard Crew coming down the apartment hall, his marina keys swinging from the chain he wore on his belt.

"Stop!" her mother barked, as if Cassie were picking her nose instead of reaching for a card. They both jumped up guiltily from the coffee table and started moving toward the kitchen as the front door swung open.

Crew was smiling when he came in, his sunburned face even redder than usual, his big teeth showing under his moustache. He always looked happy when he came in. No matter how many times she saw his mood switch fast as a slammed-shut book, Cassie still felt hopeful every time she saw him looking so glad to see them.

"Ladies!" he greeted them, scooping Sandra around the waist and giving her a big sloppy kiss. Usually kisses like that meant he'd stopped already for a beer or two at the bar at the marina—so Cassie started into the kitchen to get him another one.

Crew's look turned menacing. "Don't you even say hello, Miss Priss?" he asked her. His jeans had dark oil stains on the sides, as if he'd been rubbing his hands on his hips a lot while he worked on the boat engines. She hoped he hadn't run into an engine he couldn't fix today, or worse, gotten chewed out by his boss. Sometimes when he was extra dirty it meant he'd had a great day, just him and the engines, tinkering in the sun all day, maybe even finding time for a joint at lunch. Other times it meant

he'd been worked like a dog and treated like shit and had engine grease spilled all over him and would be looking for someone to blame. Cassie wished he wore a sign when he came home so she could tell what to expect.

"I was—" she started, then stopped. "Sorry. Hi, Daddy!" She kind of waved at him, her tongue working against the side of her mouth, where sometimes she licked until she made sores.

"You want to get me a beer, Miss Priss?" he asked her. "Or are you two ladies of leisure too liberated for that?" He glanced at their card game, their hands face down on the coffee table, as if he were gesturing to Exhibit A. They both knew what he meant. That they were lazy. That only he worked, while they sat around being taken care of by him.

Actually, Sandra still worked, too, as a waitress, but she did a midnight to 6 A.M. shift so that she was always there with Crew in the evenings. He constantly needled her about how lucky she was to have her days free while he slaved in the hot sun, even though lots of times Cassie knew her mother was so tired she just started crying, slumped over the wheel of her car, or worse, right in the supermarket where everyone could see her.

While Cassie was in the kitchen, she could hear Crew kissing her mother. He was making loud slurping noises that made Cassie's throat tighten. She had tried kissing a boy once, in fifth grade last year, but it had been a papery, dry affair, very sweet, his mouth tasting faintly of Bubble Yum. She and her friend Dineen had pretended once to French kiss, too, poking their tongues in one another's mouths, and the sensation had been so disgusting she'd wondered how adults ever came to like it. Crew kissed and touched her mother constantly, which Sandra explained was because Crew hadn't gotten any affection as a child—though Cassie couldn't see how that kind of slobbering was going to make up for the fact that Crew had grown up with a scared mother and a dad who used to beat him with a pipe.

When she came out with the beer, Crew was dragging her mom toward their bedroom. Sandra looked back at Cassie apologetically. "Can you keep an eye on the dinner, honey?"

"Is that all you can think about?" Crew growled against the side of her mother's throat. "Stop being such a damned drudge. Live a little!" He pulled Sandra by the hand and left Cassie standing in the middle of the living room, holding the open beer. She'd been proud she'd been able to use the bottle opener, but he hadn't noticed.

When she started to hear noises—her mother's low moans, Crew's louder voice barking something Cassie couldn't make out—Cassie decided to go outside. She didn't know a living soul here except for the old woman down the hall, Mrs. Levinsky, who had been brave enough to bang on their door and tell Crew to "cool his jets" one day when she'd heard him screaming at them. Sandra had told Mrs. Levinsky everything was fine, they were all just fine, but Mrs. Levinsky was still always asking Cassie how things were, in urgent whispers, any time she saw her alone in the hall. Cassie wanted to visit Mrs. Levinsky now, but Crew called her a dried up old bitch, and Cassie knew he'd be furious if he found her there.

Instead, she came down the stairwell and stepped outside, where the fierce, hot air and burning sunshine made her eyes water. It had been days since she'd been out of doors, so she was surprised to find that even in the heat, there were some kids playing dodgeball across the street. She stood for a minute staring at them, shielding her face from the glare, hoping they'd invite her to join them.

"Can I play?" she called after a few minutes, her voice too low to carry. Then again, louder, moving quickly across the street with her eyes fixed on the ball for bravery: "Hey, can I play?"

The kids turned to look at her, and for a moment, she didn't understand the expressions she saw —the way their faces turned from guarded to horrified. When she heard one of them scream, it was too late. The car she hadn't even noticed coming hit her full on, a giant faded blue hood tossing her up, up, as if pushing her on her way into their game. Then the ground where they'd been playing was rushing at her, very fast and black, a blur of unyielding space that sent the kids running and shattered her when she hit.

When her eyes opened, she could see the dodge ball, lying in a red puddle near her head. There were sirens approaching, and somewhere nearby, a sobbing, screaming woman who said over and over, accusingly, "You came out of nowhere! Nowhere!" And there were kids all around her, their faces wide with interest.

"The dinner's burning," she told someone, but no one seemed to hear.

Two paramedics in dark blue rushed through everyone, parting the children like air and crouching purposefully beside her. "Don't even try to move," ordered one of them, a tall, thin man whose body provided merciful shade. Cassie was so relieved, she peed on herself—though her pants already felt so wet, she couldn't be sure. When he asked her name, she told him gratefully, feeling in good hands.

"Where do you live?" asked the other paramedic, a little blonde woman with a deep tan. "Where are your parents?" As they spoke to her, they were surrounding her with equipment: boards, bottles, straps, tearing paper off of sterile bandages and needles.

Cassie started to blubber, which made it hard for her to breathe. "Please don't tell," she said. "Can someone check the dinner? I'm supposed to be watching it."

The paramedics exchanged glances, and the woman answered first: "I can check it. What apartment are you in?"

Cassie tried to point, but found she'd been strapped to a board, her wrists secured. She realized she didn't know the address. The paramedics followed her glance to the building.

"Apartment 2D," she told them—surprising herself by directing them to Mrs. Levinsky's apartment. She wanted her mother, but Crew hated when Cassie got sick, so she couldn't even imagine how enraged he'd be that she'd gotten herself hit by a car. She also knew he hated to be interrupted. She thought he'd take the news better from Mrs. Levinsky, who seemed to intimidate him, whatever he said behind her back.

"OK," said the blonde. "Somebody get a cop over there to 2D and tell the parents we've taken their little girl to Ft. Lauderdale General." The two of them were lifting her on the board as easily as if she weighed nothing, moving her smoothly into the ambulance.

"Am I going to die?" she asked the one who folded his body into the back with her.

He smiled reassuringly. "No way, Cassie. I've never lost a patient."

"Maybe I'll be first," she said hopefully, and closed her eyes.

In the hospital, when she woke up, everything hurt, and her throat felt stuffed with ground glass. Her mom and Crew were standing by the foot of the bed, murmuring, Crew's arm around Sandra. Cassie could feel immobilizing casts on what seemed to be every inch of her. Before they noticed she was awake, she wanted to ask for water, but she remembered when she'd had a fever last year, how she'd called out from her bed for a drink, and Crew had come in and thrown a glass of ice water straight into her face.

"You want water?" he'd asked, his head and body backlit by the hall light coming in through her open door. "You think nothing of interrupting people's sleep because you're so thirsty? Here's your fucking water."

So now she lay still, hoping her mother would look over and notice how chapped and puffy her mouth was.

She fell back asleep and awoke to feel her mother's hand on her face, soft and cool as the petals Cassie had picked for Crew last month for Father's Day.

"Cassie, love!" her mother said when she saw her eyes open. She bent low to drop tiny kisses all over Cassie's scratched and throbbing face. "Thank god, thank god. You're going to be fine." Her voice, though, was more soothing than the expression Cassie could see underneath. *You've gotten us in trouble,* she thought her mother's eyes said.

"Mommy!" Cassie pleaded, tears she couldn't move a hand to catch sliding sideways from her eyes. "I'm so sorry. I didn't mean to."

"Of course, of course," her mom soothed. "It was just an accident. And thank god you're going to be OK, completely OK."

"You never look where you're going," Crew added —but his tone was mild, affectionate, as if he were describing an endearing quality. He smiled at Cassie lovingly and stroked Sandra's hair: "We're just going to have to keep a better eye on you from now on, Princess. Those cops and Mrs. Levinsky wondered if you'd been abused, because of the way you lay there carrying on about the dinner, but we told them you always did just have too much on your mind for a kid your age. Come *on,* Cassie—did you really think we might care about the dinner when you had five broken bones and needed a blood transfusion? Jesus, hon, don't you know we love you?"

Cassie stared at him hopefully, half-ashamed for having doubted it.

"Your mom and I gave blood for you," said Crew, extending his arm so she could see the Band-aid inside his elbow. "And you know what a baby I am about needles—so just remember *that* next time you forget how much we love you."

"It was an accident," repeated Sandra, her fingers still stroking Cassie's forehead. "It was just an accident."

And suddenly Cassie understood, recognizing those words as the same ones her mother repeated after each beating. It was always an accident, whatever befell them. And now her own accident was going to take the place of the one that had been coming. Her own bandages and blood and casts would be enough. Her mother would be spared. Cassie had rescued her at last.

Now Crew would be kind, bring them presents and take them out for McDonald's and boat races, play board games and make up silly songs, compliment them lavishly, turn sweetly sentimental when he drank, instead of surly. He would give them hope again, just as he had after every other accident. All Cassie had to do was keep quiet, believe in him again, let him love her. She felt a surge of power, knowing how eager he was to please her, even if only for this moment.

"I'm thirsty," Cassie announced, her tears dried —and she didn't even flinch when Crew cupped the back of her bandaged head and held the glass tenderly to her mouth. [2002]

🌿 118

La Princesa

LATINA ANÓNIMA

His car pulled into the driveway. I was crouching behind my neighbor's car, waiting for him to enter the house. As soon as I heard the door slam shut, my heart racing, I ran to the end of the block. I remember feeling the wind in my face and my backpack, carrying students' exams, slumped against my right shoulder. All my senses were alert. It was past dusk and all I could think of was "Where can I go?"

I spotted a bus and jumped on it, shaking, as I slipped some coins into the box, trying to pretend —that everything was fine.

I had finally left him for good. Memories jarred my otherwise numb state.

It was Christmas Eve. We were celebrating it quietly, with a roaring fire, a small "charlie brown" kind of tree, and an abundance of gifts to exchange. I opened package after package—of clothes he had picked out for me. Meanwhile, I lost count of his drinks. Later that evening, I soaked the sleeve of my new coat, stained with blood from the busted lip he had added to my evening's "gifts." I wondered how I would hide the bruises on my left temple and the cuts on the lower left corner of my lip from the friends coming over the next day for tamales. I remember, most of all, looking in the mirror the next morning, not recognizing my own eyes. They were completely vacant of all emotion.

As the bus made stop after stop, I remembered the two years' worth of incidents, apology after apology, promise after promise. I clung to the memory of when I finally snapped, of the moment I knew I would *plan my escape*. It was toward the end of the relationship. By this time I was getting "bold," verbally challenging him when he questioned me, not caring if what I said provoked him. By that time I had finally figured out that no matter what I did, he would find reason for violence.

I entered the house, carrying bags of groceries, placing them on the table. He questioned me, asking me why I had gotten the wrong kind of sausage. He had asked for hot links and I had bought Italian sausage. He wanted me to return to the store and get the ones he wanted. I didn't like the fact that his tone of voice was in the form of an order. "Go back to the store and get the RIGHT kind," he screamed. I refused and told him, "I'm not going." He shoved me, from one room to another, beginning his tirade of intimidation. When we entered the living room, he pushed me to the floor. I feigned that he had hurt my back, as a way of keeping him from continuing. Not knowing whether he had really hurt me, he kicked me. He kicked me while I was down on the floor. I was no better than a dog. That's when I snapped.

That's when I knew that whatever it took I would leave this animal and keep him out of my life forever.

Over the next few months, as I recovered in the safety of my mother's home, I kept asking myself, How could this happen to me? Only a few years before, I had been special. My picture made Spanish-speaking newspapers, announcing my fellowship award to attend graduate school. My entire history, up until this point, had been laced with validation, awards, and recognition for my academic achievements. And at home, I had been loved and cherished. How could I have reached the point that I would accept the slightest form of physical or emotional violence to my person? The question remains today.

As I sought ways to heal and understand, I did what every good academic does. I went to the library. I punched in the words "battery," "domestic violence," and "women" into the computer. Based on her research and interviews in *The Battered Woman*, Lenore Walker developed a typology of characteristics and types of women who tend to become victims of domestic violence. In these pages, I found a description of "the princess syndrome." The princess, Walker explains, is shocked by her confrontation with violence. So sheltered, protected, and revered has she been and so unexposed to any kind of violence in her life that when she encounters someone violent, she is in a state of shock. With no experience of invalidation and feeling intense personal criticism for the first time in her life, the princess believes she can "do right" by the perpetrator and change his opinion of her. Like the other types

Violence in Intimate Relationships: a Feminist Perspective

BELL HOOKS

Given the nature of patriarchy, it has been necessary for feminists to focus on extreme cases to make people confront the issue, and acknowledge it to be serious and relevant. Unfortunately, an exclusive focus on extreme cases can and does lead us to ignore the more frequent, more common, yet less extreme case of occasional hitting. Women are also less likely to acknowledge occasional hitting for fear that they will then be seen as someone who is in a bad relationship or someone whose life is out of control. Currently, the literature about male violence against women identifies the physically abused woman as a "battered woman." While it has been important to have an accessible terminology to draw attention to the issue of male violence against women, the terms used reflect biases because they call attention to only one type of violence in intimate relationships. The term "battered woman" is problematical. It is not a term that emerged from feminist work on male violence against women; it was already used by psychologists and sociologists in the literature on domestic violence. This label "battered woman" places primary emphasis on physical assaults that are continuous, repeated, and unrelenting. The focus is on extreme violence, with little effort to link these cases with the everyday acceptance within intimate relationships of physical abuse that is not extreme, that may not be repeated. Yet these lesser forms of physical abuse damage individuals psychologically and, if not properly addressed and recovered from, can set the stage for more extreme incidents.

Most importantly, the term "battered woman" is used as though it constitutes a separate and unique category of womanness, as though it is an identity, a mark that sets one apart rather than being simply a descriptive term. It is as though the experience of being repeatedly violently hit is the sole defining characteristic of a woman's identity and all other aspects of who she is and what her experience has been are submerged.

. . . Women who are hit once by men in their lives, and women who are hit repeatedly do not want to be placed in the category of "battered woman" because it is a label that appears to strip us of dignity, to deny that there has been any integrity in the relationships we are in. A person physically assaulted by a stranger or a casual friend with whom they are not intimate may be hit once or repeatedly but they do not have to be placed into a category before doctors, lawyers, family, counselors, etc. take their problem seriously. Again, it must be stated that establishing categories and terminology has been part of the effort to draw public attention to the seriousness of male violence against women in intimate relationships. Even though the use of convenient labels and categories has made it easier to identify problems of physical abuse, it does not mean the terminology should not be critiqued from a feminist perspective and changed if necessary.

of women, she endures all the typical cycles before leaving the batterer.

With hindsight, in contextualizing my circumstances, it would be an understatement to say that there were competing tensions in my life at the time. They culminated to create ripe conditions—even for a former homecoming "princess," literally—to enter and come to know a sphere of violence far too many women experience. Ideologically, I had failed to reconcile the family expectation that I marry and have children with my pursuit of an advanced degree and my identity as a Chicana feminist (the ironies prevail). I thought I could have both. Hence, when I connected with this man I was still trying to be a "good girl" and find that husband everyone expected. Yet I was in a graduate program that was brutally competitive, alienating, and disempowering. Looking back, I realize that my self-esteem was at an all-time low with respect to my graduate studies and that I was no longer looking to the institution, or academic processes, to nourish my sense of self. Thus, it was no surprise that when I met this man I foolishly looked to him as someone who would make me feel that I was special.

During pensive moments, I've developed a theory for *princesas* of color. *Earned privileges* in a given life cycle only buy us time. The structures of subordination will get even the achievers. Those who think they might have escaped find themselves— like countless other *princesas* of color—treated just as women. Today the memories of this time in my life seem surreal. I do not identify, much less connect, with the experiences I've just recounted. It's as if they belong to someone else. But they don't, and instead they are tucked away in what I like to call my *caja de llagas*, my box of scars. I do, however, use the memories to move myself into using my voice. By remembering the contents, I remember to speak.

[2001]

🌿 119

Holding Up More Than Half the Heavens

MARGARETTA WAN LIN
and CHENG IMM TAN

Because of the barriers of language, culture, and economic disparities and the vagaries of racism and sexism, Asian Pacific American (APA) victims of domestic violence suffer revictimization at the hands of institutions designed to serve battered women. According to the 1990 U.S. Census, Asians and Pacific Islanders are the fastest growing minority group, totalling nearly seven million. And yet, in the entire United States only two shelters exist for APA women, one safe-home network and one advocacy group that provides culturally sensitive programs and counseling.[1] Of the domestic violence resources available—police, shelters, hotlines, human services programs—few have staff who speak Asian Pacific languages. Given the highly sensitive nature of addressing domestic violence, it is unacceptable not to have linguistically accessible resources. The language barrier, in effect, shuts out most refugee and immigrant women. In addition, many battered women's shelters turn away APA women because of language and cultural difficulties or sheer racism. Economic concerns present yet another obstacle. Most women who are victims of domestic violence do not have control of the family's money. Many leave their homes with little besides the clothes on their backs. This means that many battered APA women who have gathered up the strength and courage to flee the violence in their homes must then return there because they have no other viable options. Legal protection is also often both inaccessible because of cultural and linguistic barriers and unavailable because of institutionalized racism and sexism. There are too many examples of the revictimization of battered APA women by institutionalized forces; it would require another whole book just to document the abuses we have seen. Consider the story of Ling.

One evening as Ling was cleaning some fish for dinner her husband, who had beaten her repeatedly for the past eight years, and had given her concussions, a broken hip, and a broken jaw, began to pick a fight. Ling did not answer any of his accusations and her enduring silence made him even angrier. He picked up a chair to strike her. She sidestepped the impending blow and screamed at him to stop. The chair broke against the door and he lunged at her, more enraged than before. Ling tried to ward him off by waving the knife that she had been using to clean the fish for dinner that evening. He continued to lunge at her and in attempting to get the knife, fell upon the knife and cut himself. He continued to strike out at Ling.

Terrified, Ling ran to a nearby store to call the police. When the police came, her husband who spoke good English, accused Ling of attacking him. Ling's English was not enough to defend herself. The police whom she called arrested Ling and put her in jail. They set her bond at $2,500. The case against Ling is still pending. This is how our justice system works to protect battered women.

THE PRIMACY OF FEAR OF RACIST ATTACKS, THE SACRIFICE OF OUR SISTERS

Within each ethnic group, male control and domestic violence take on culturally specific expressions. APA communities have tolerated and overlooked domestic violence for some of the same reasons that mainstream society has tolerated and overlooked it for so long—the unquestioning acceptance of patriarchy, of male control and privilege. Some APA activists worry that bringing domestic violence into the open will confirm negative stereotypes about the community, and further fuel the fires of anti-Asian sentiment. To expose the problem within APA communities is not a statement about the greater violence or misogyny in Asian Pacific culture. Instead, the sad reality is that Asian men, like all other men, live in a male-dominated culture that views women

as property, objects they must control and possess. Compounding this reality, or underlying it, are cultures that view violence as an acceptable solution to problems.

As a reaction to the pervasive racism and cultural imperialism that threaten to undermine our cultural integrity, APA activists and community leaders have been reluctant to look self-critically at traditional misogynistic attitudes and practices for fear that it would reinforce racist stereotypes about Asian Pacific Americans. This attitude of denial, however, does not keep racism at bay. Instead, it is at odds with cherished notions of our rights as humans and citizens.

The same reasons that inspire the unequivocal and emphatic support of APA activists to identify crimes motivated by race, color, and/or national origin as hate crimes hold for crimes motivated by gender. As with crimes of racist hate, statistics on domestic violence are inadequate; elected officials will not fund programs until we fully document the violence; keeping such statistics would encourage more public awareness and debate on the crimes.

While there is an emerging effort on the part of APA women activists to include domestic violence as a hate crime, APA civil rights and advocacy groups have not supported their work. We believe that along with sexist motivations, fear of betraying our brothers, of adding to their oppression, plays a role in the glaring absence of their support. Such fear causes APA activists to overlook and ignore domestic violence. It has meant sacrificing the lives of our sisters.

A heinous example of this is Dong Lu Chen's murder of his wife, Jian Wan Chen, and his successful use of the cultural defense. On September 7, 1987, Jian Wan Chen's husband smashed her skull in with a claw hammer after she allegedly admitted to having an affair. Chen's teenage son discovered her body in the family's Brooklyn apartment. The trial judge sentenced Dong to five years probation on a reduced manslaughter charge after concluding, based on the testimony of an anthropologist, that Dong was driven to violence by traditional Chinese values about adultery and loss of manhood. APA activists came out in support of the cultural defense as a necessary tool to protect immigrants in U.S. courtrooms.

Does this mean that Jian Wan Chen's immigrant status is negligible, or that such activists believe that Asian men are traditionally more violent and misogynistic than their white counterparts? Does it mean that the status of Jian Wan Chen as an Asian sister, as a human being, is negligible when weighed against the crime of her husband? And what are the repercussions of such outrage? Domestic violence counselors have reported that the case has convinced many battered APA women that they have no protection, period. As for the lawyers, they feel "empowered" to use the cultural defense at any opportunity.[2] What does this say about our society, about our value of human life, about our perception of justice?

The fear of racist attacks on our cultures and communities is so pervasive and deep that it has frustrated our attempts at addressing domestic violence in APA communities. When we first started addressing such issues in the Boston area, we received harassing calls, our tires were slashed, threats and accusations were made that we were family-wreckers. This fear and anger from the APA community have also compromised our strategies in responding to domestic violence. Activists and community leaders have advocated treatments that do not threaten traditional beliefs and practices, such as mediation, family counseling, and elder intervention. Such measures, however, do not address the underlying attitudes and institutions that uphold violence against APA women and children.

OUR STRUGGLE TOGETHER

Domestic violence demeans and destroys our communities more than any other violence perpetuated on us. It is not an isolated issue. It is not a private family affair protected by the rights of privacy. It is a violent crime of hate that attacks the very fiber of our collective health and we should treat it as such. Symptoms of the sickness spill beyond the confines of the home and taint our participation in the community, our performances in jobs and schools, our personal relationships. It harms every aspect of our lives and the lives that we touch. Because it is premised on unequal relationships and because of its destructive and often fatal impact, domestic violence is not suitable for internal solutions nor should the rights of privacy protect it.

The power to define domestic violence, to give credence to its reality, means much more than validating the experiences of battered women and children. Recognizing the critical dimensions of domestic violence in APA communities translates into accessing resources for dealing with the symptoms, such as making local community health clinics and doctors aware of and able to treat the problems, providing multilingual and multicultural services, and making outside funding sources available to shelters and programs. It means community pressure—saying that domestic violence is unacceptable, that we can no longer sweep it under the proverbial rug or sanction it with patriarchal/misogynist sayings. It means, most of all, empowering victims: stopping the internalization of blame, recognizing their agency to leave, and reaching the empowerment to heal and realize their potentials as humans.

We Asian Pacific Americans in control of our destinies, who are concerned about the well-being of our families and our communities, we must be the ones to break the silence.

Our challenge as leaders and activists in our communities is to strategize ways we can work together to address domestic violence in our own communities. We need to examine and change the underlying attitudes and structures within our communities that maintain violence against women and children. We need to focus on both intervention and prevention. We need to work together on outreach and education to make our communities aware of domestic violence issues and to create intolerance to violence against women and children.

Those of us who work in community health and social services agencies must make information on domestic violence available. We need to have in-house training sessions for our staff so they will understand the seriousness of the problem and know, at the very least, how to approach suspected victims of domestic violence to offer information and resources. We need to take on the responsibility and be the vehicle for change. We need to begin to collect data on domestic violence. As long as no data exist, government agencies at all levels can deny the problem and we will continue to lack the political leverage to advocate for appropriate services.

We need to push for multilingual and multicultural services in the human service, legal, and law enforcement systems so that they do not overlook or underserve the needs of Asian Pacific Americans. We need ethnically specific services like Asian women's shelters and resources that are culturally sensitive and appropriate but also connected to the larger resources. Lack of access to services places the lives of Asian Pacific American women and children at unnecessary risk.

Most of all, we need to go inward, deep within, to examine the effects of domestic violence on our persons, to get rid of the shame and blame we feel as victims, to recognize our responsibility and agency for change if we are perpetrators of the violence, to heal the wounds that keep us silent and complicit.

[1994]

NOTES

1. Centers in San Francisco, Los Angeles, and New York City provide programs for Chinese, Korean, Philippine, Japanese, Indonesian, Laotian, Vietnamese, and Cambodian women, and are staffed with multilingual abuse-hotlines. A program in Boston provides counseling and advocacy services for Vietnamese, Cambodian, and Chinese women. Bilingual hotlines are available for Koreans in Honolulu and Chicago and for Indians in New Brunswick, New Jersey.
2. Alexis Jetter, "Fear is Legacy of Wife Killing in Chinatown," *Newsday,* November 26, 1989.

Sexual Violence and Rape

Sexual violence against women and girls, like battering, is surrounded by images and myths that mask the realities of assaulted women's lives. Whether or not a woman has personally experienced sexual assault, the threat of violence shadows all women's lives.

Recently many young women have begun to speak out about the climate of sexual intimidation that pervades high school social life. Athena Devlin and Pamela Fletcher write about the sexual assault and coercion of girls, pointing out the ways that "the silence between them" perpetuated their powerlessness. After describing the many instances in her life in which no one challenged the sexual assault of girls and young women, Fletcher invites us to envision a time when women are "connected to each other, when we no longer feel the need and desire to conspire with men against each other in order to survive in a misogynist, violent culture."

Susan Griffin's 1971 article drew rape out of the realm of inexplicable atrocities and placed it squarely in the context of a patriarchal society. It generated a good deal of analysis about the connection between rape and prevailing ideas about women, men, and sexuality. This analysis has led more recently to movements against marital and acquaintance rape. Rape is an abuse of power that is expressed through sexual violence. Many misconceptions about rape suggest that assaulted women somehow "provoked" their attackers into raping them, either verbally or by seductive dress and demeanor. As Ntozake Shange's poem shows, the irrational violence of rape occurs "with no immediate cause."

While stranger rape and acquaintance rape are similar, they differ in significant ways. Perhaps the most notable characteristic of acquaintance rape is the betrayal of trust experienced by a woman when someone she knows, and may care about, rapes her. Peggy Reeves Sanday surveys studies of acquaintance rape on college campuses and its impact on women. In doing so, she confronts the myths about acquaintance rape that prevent many women from naming coercive sexual experiences as rape.

120

Rape:
The All-American Crime

SUSAN GRIFFIN

I

I have never been free of the fear of rape. From a very early age I, like most women, have thought of rape as part of my natural environment—something to be feared and prayed against like fire or lightning. I never asked why men raped; I simply thought it one of the many mysteries of human nature.

I was, however, curious enough about the violent side of humanity to read every crime magazine I was able to ferret away from my grandfather. Each issue featured at least one "sex crime," with pictures of a victim, usually in a pearl necklace, and of the ditch or the orchard where her body was found. I was never certain why the victims were always women, nor what the motives of the murderer were, but I did guess that the world was not a safe place for women. I observed that my grandmother was meticulous about locks, and quick to draw the shades before anyone removed so much as a shoe. I sensed that danger lurked outside.

At the age of eight, my suspicions were confirmed. My grandmother took me to the back of the house where the men wouldn't hear, and told me that strange men wanted to do harm to little girls. I learned not to walk on dark streets, not to talk to strangers, or get into strange cars, to lock doors, and to be modest. She never explained why a man would want to harm a little girl, and I never asked.

If I thought for a while that my grandmother's fears were imaginary, the illusion was brief. That year, on the way home from school, a schoolmate a few years older than I tried to rape me. Later, in an obscure aisle of the local library (while I was reading *Freddy the Pig*) I turned to discover a man exposing himself. Then, the friendly man around the corner was arrested for child molesting.

My initiation to sexuality was typical. Every woman has similar stories to tell—the first man who attacked her may have been a neighbor, a family friend, an uncle, her doctor, or perhaps her own father. And women who grow up in New York City always have tales about the subway. . . .

When I was very young, my image of the "sexual offender" was a nightmarish amalgamation of the bogey man and Captain Hook: he wore a black cape, and he cackled. As I matured, so did my image of the rapist. Born into the psychoanalytic age, I tried to "understand" the rapist. Rape, I came to believe, was only one of many unfortunate evils produced by sexual repression. Reasoning by tautology, I concluded that any man who would rape a woman must be out of his mind.

Yet, though the theory that rapists are insane is a popular one, this belief has no basis in fact. According to Professor Menachem Amir's study of 646 rape cases in Philadelphia, *Patterns in Forcible Rape*, men who rape are not abnormal. Amir writes, "Studies indicate that sex offenders do not constitute a unique or psychopathological type; nor are they as a group invariably more disturbed than the control groups to which they are compared." Alan Taylor, a parole officer who has worked with rapists in the prison facilities at San Luis Obispo, California, stated the question in plainer language, "Those men were the most normal men there. They had a lot of hang-ups, but they were the same hang-ups as men walking out on the street."

Another canon in the apologetics of rape is that, if it were not for learned social controls, all men would rape. Rape is held to be natural behavior, and not to rape must be learned. But in truth rape is not universal to the human species. Moreover, studies of rape in our culture reveal that far from being impulsive behavior, most rape is planned. Professor Amir's study reveals that in cases of group rape (the "gangbang" of masculine slang), 90 percent of the rapes were planned; in pair rapes, 83 percent of the rapes were planned; and in single rapes, 58 percent were planned. These figures should significantly discredit the image of the rapist as a man who is suddenly overcome by sexual needs society does not allow him to fulfill.

Far from the social control of rape being learned,

comparisons with other cultures lead one to suspect that, in our society, it is rape itself that is learned. (The fact that rape is against the law should not be considered proof that rape is not in fact encouraged as part of our culture.)

This culture's concept of rape as an illegal, but still understandable, form of behavior is not a universal one. In her study *Sex and Temperament,* Margaret Mead describes a society that does not share our views. The Arapesh do not ". . . have any conception of the male nature that might make rape understandable to them." Indeed our interpretation of rape is a product of our conception of the nature of male sexuality. A common retort to the question, why don't women rape men, is the myth that men have greater sexual needs, that their sexuality is more urgent than women's. And it is the nature of human beings to want to live up to what is expected of them.

And this same culture which expects aggression from the male expects passivity from the female. Conveniently, the companion myth about the nature of female sexuality is that all women secretly want to be raped. Lurking beneath her modest female exterior is a subconscious desire to be ravished. The following description of a stag movie, written by Brenda Starr in Los Angeles' underground paper, *Everywoman,* typifies this male fantasy. The movie "showed a woman in her underclothes reading on her bed. She is interrupted by a rapist with a knife. He immediately wins her over with his charm and they get busy sucking and fucking." An advertisement in the *Berkeley Barb* reads, "Now as all women know from their daydreams, rape has a lot of advantages. Best of all it's so simple. No preparation necessary, no planning ahead of time, no wondering if you should or shouldn't; just whang! bang!" Thanks to Masters and Johnson even the scientific canon recognizes that for the female, "whang! bang!" can scarcely be described as pleasurable.

Still, the male psyche persists in believing that, protestations and struggles to the contrary, deep inside her mysterious feminine soul, the female victim has wished for her own fate. A young woman who was raped by the husband of a friend said that days after the incident the man returned to her home, pounded on the door and screamed to her, "Jane, Jane. You loved it. You know you loved it."

The theory that women like being raped extends itself by deduction into the proposition that most or much of rape is provoked by the victim. But this too is only myth. Though provocation, considered a mitigating factor in a court of law, may consist of only "a gesture," according to the Federal Commission on Crimes of Violence, only 4 percent of reported rapes involved any precipitative behavior by the woman.

The notion that rape is enjoyed by the victim is also convenient for the man who, though he would not commit forcible rape, enjoys the idea of its existence, as if rape confirms that enormous sexual potency which he secretly knows to be his own. It is for the pleasure of the armchair rapist that detailed accounts of violent rapes exist in the media. Indeed, many men appear to take sexual pleasure from nearly all forms of violence. Whatever the motivation, male sexuality and violence in our culture seem to be inseparable. James Bond alternately whips out his revolver and his cock, and though there is no known connection between the skills of gun-fighting and love-making, pacifism seems suspiciously effeminate. . . .

In the spectrum of male behavior, rape, the perfect combination of sex and violence, is the penultimate act. Erotic pleasure cannot be separated from culture, and in our culture male eroticism is wedded to power. Not only should a man be taller and stronger than a female in the perfect love-match, but he must also demonstrate his superior strength in gestures of dominance which are perceived as amorous. Though the law attempts to make a clear division between rape and sexual intercourse, in fact the courts find it difficult to distinguish between a case where the decision to copulate was mutual and one where a man forced himself upon his partner.

The scenario is even further complicated by the expectation that, not only does a woman mean "yes" when she says "no," but that a really decent woman ought to begin by saying "no," and then be led down the primrose path to acquiescence. Ovid, the author of Western Civilization's most celebrated sex-manual, makes this expectation perfectly clear:

> . . . and when I beg you to say "yes," say "no." Then let me lie outside your bolted door. . . . So Love grows strong. . . .

That the basic elements of rape are involved in all heterosexual relationships may explain why men often identify with the offender in this crime. But to regard the rapist as the victim, a man driven by his inherent sexual needs to take what will not be given him, reveals a basic ignorance of sexual politics. For in our culture heterosexual love finds an erotic expression through male dominance and female submission. A man who derives pleasure from raping a woman clearly must enjoy force and dominance as much or more than the simple pleasures of the flesh. Coitus cannot be experienced in isolation. The weather, the state of the nation, the level of sugar in the blood—all will affect a man's ability to achieve orgasm. If a man can achieve sexual pleasure after terrorizing and humiliating the object of his passion, and in fact while inflicting pain upon her, one must assume he derives pleasure directly from terrorizing, humiliating and harming a woman. According to Amir's study of forcible rape, on a statistical average the man who has been convicted of rape was found to have a normal sexual personality, tending to be different from the normal, well-adjusted male only in having a greater tendency to express violence and rage.

And if the professional rapist is to be separated from the average dominant heterosexual, it may be mainly a quantitative difference. For the existence of rape as an index to masculinity is not entirely metaphorical. Though this measure of masculinity seems to be more publicly exhibited among "bad boys" or aging bikers who practice sexual initiation through group rape, in fact, "good boys" engage in the same rites to prove their manhood. In Stockton, a small town in California which epitomizes silent-majority America, a bachelor party was given last summer for a young man about to be married. A woman was hired to dance "topless" for the amusement of the guests. At the high point of the evening the bridegroom-to-be dragged the woman into a bedroom. No move was made by any of his companions to stop what was clearly going to be an attempted rape. Far from it. As the woman described, "I tried to keep him away—told him of my *herpes genitalis,* et cetera, but he couldn't face the guys if he didn't screw me." After the bridegroom had finished raping the woman and returned with her to the party, far from chastising him, his friends heckled the woman and covered her with wine.

It was fortunate for the dancer that the bridegroom's friends did not follow him into the bedroom for, though one might suppose that in group rape, since the victim is outnumbered, less force would be inflicted on her, in fact, Amir's studies indicate, "the most excessive degrees of violence occurred in group rape." Far from discouraging violence, the presence of other men may in fact encourage sadism, and even cause the behavior. In an unpublished study of group rape by Gilbert Geis and Duncan Chappell, the authors refer to a study by W. H. Blanchard which relates, "The leader of the male group . . . apparently precipitated and maintained the activity, despite misgivings, because of a need to fulfill the role that the other two men had assigned to him. 'I was scared when it began to happen,' he says. 'I wanted to leave but I didn't want to say it to the other guys—you know—that I was scared.'"

Thus it becomes clear that not only does our culture teach men the rudiments of rape, but society, or more specifically other men, encourage the practice of it.

II

Every man I meet wants to protect me. Can't figure out what from.

—Mae West

. . . According to the male mythology which defines and perpetuates rape, it is an animal instinct inherent in the male. The story goes that sometime in our pre-historical past, the male, more hirsute and burly than today's counterparts, roamed about an uncivilized landscape until he found a desirable female. (Oddly enough, this female is *not* pictured as more muscular than the modern woman.) Her mate does not bother with courtship. He simply grabs her by the hair and drags her to the closest cave. Presumably, one of the major advantages of modern civilization for the female has been the civilizing of the male. We call it chivalry.

But women do not get chivalry for free. According to the logic of sexual politics, we too have to civilize our behavior. (Enter chastity. Enter virginity. Enter monogamy.) For the female, civilized behavior means chastity before marriage and faithfulness within it. Chivalrous behavior in the male is supposed to protect that chastity from involuntary defilement. The fly in the ointment of this otherwise peaceful system is the fallen woman. She does not behave. And therefore she does not deserve protection. Or, to use another argument, a major tenet of the same value system: what has once been defiled cannot again be violated. One begins to suspect that it is the behavior of the fallen woman, and not that of the male, that civilization aims to control.

The assumption that a woman who does not respect the double standard deserves whatever she gets (or at the very least "asks for it") operates in the courts today. While in some states a man's previous rape convictions are not considered admissible evidence, the sexual reputation of the rape victim is considered a crucial element of the facts upon which the court must decide innocence or guilt. . . .

According to the double standard, a woman who has had sexual intercourse out of wedlock cannot be raped. Rape is not only a crime of aggression against the body; it is a transgression against chastity as defined by men. When a woman is forced into a sexual relationship, she has, according to the male ethos, been violated. But she is also defiled if she does not behave according to the double standard, by maintaining her chastity, or confining her sexual activities to a monogamous relationship.

One should not assume, however, that a woman can avoid the possibility of rape simply by behaving. Though myth would have it that mainly "bad girls" are raped, this theory has no basis in fact. Available statistics would lead one to believe that a safer course is promiscuity. In a study of rape done in the District of Columbia, it was found that 82 percent of the rape victims had a "good reputation." Even the Police Inspector's advice to stay off the streets is rather useless, for almost half of reported rapes occur in the home of the victim and are committed by a man she has never before seen. Like indiscriminate terrorism, rape can happen to any woman, and few women are ever without this knowledge.

But the courts and the police, both dominated by white males, continue to suspect the rape victim, *sui generis,* of provoking or asking for her own assault. According to Amir's study, the police tend to believe that a woman without a good reputation cannot be raped. The rape victim is usually submitted to countless questions about her own sexual mores and behavior by the police investigator. This preoccupation is partially justified by the legal requirements for prosecution in a rape case. The rape victim must have been penetrated, and she must have made it clear to her assailant that she did not want penetration (unless of course she is unconscious). A refusal to accompany a man to some isolated place to allow him to touch her does not in the eyes of the court, constitute rape. She must have said "no" at the crucial genital moment. And the rape victim, to qualify as such, must also have put up a physical struggle—unless she can prove that to do so would have been to endanger her life.

But the zealous interest the police frequently exhibit in the physical details of a rape case is only partially explained by the requirements of the court. A woman who was raped in Berkeley was asked to tell the story of her rape four different times "right out in the street," while her assailant was escaping. She was then required to submit to a pelvic examination to prove that penetration had taken place. Later, she was taken to the police station where she was asked the same questions again: "Were you forced?" "Did he penetrate?" "Are you sure your life was in danger and you had no other choice?" This woman had been pulled off the street by a man who held a 10-inch knife at her throat and forcibly raped her. She was raped at midnight and was not able to return to her home until five in the morning. Police contacted her twice again in the next week, once by telephone at two in the morning and once at four in the morning. In her words, "The rape was probably the least traumatic incident of the whole evening. If I'm ever raped again, . . . I wouldn't report it to the police because of all the degradation. . . ."

If white women are subjected to unnecessary and often hostile questioning after having been raped, third world women* are often not believed at all. According to the white male ethos (which is not only sexist but racist), third world women are defined from birth as "impure." Thus the white male is provided with a pool of women who are fair game for sexual imperialism. Third world women frequently do not report rape and for good reason. When blues singer Billie Holliday was 10 years old, she was taken off to a local house by a neighbor and raped. Her mother brought the police to rescue her, and she was taken to the local station crying and bleeding:

> When we got there, instead of treating me and Mom like somebody who called the cops for help, they treated me like I'd killed somebody. . . . I guess they had me figured for having enticed this old goat into the whorehouse. . . . All I know for sure is they threw me into a cell . . . a fat white matron . . . saw I was still bleeding, she felt sorry for me and gave me a couple glasses of milk. But nobody else did anything for me except give me filthy looks and snicker to themselves.
>
> After a couple of days in a cell they dragged me into a court. Mr. Dick got sentenced to five years. They sentenced me to a Catholic institution.

Clearly the white man's chivalry is aimed only to protect the chastity of "his" women.

As a final irony, that same system of sexual values from which chivalry is derived has also provided womankind with an unwritten code of behavior, called femininity, which makes a feminine woman the perfect victim of sexual aggression. If being chaste does not ward off the possibility of assault, being feminine certainly increases the chances that it will succeed. To be submissive is to defer to masculine strength; is to lack muscular development or any interest in defending oneself; is to let doors be opened, to have one's arm held when crossing the street. To be feminine is to wear shoes which make it difficult to run; skirts which inhibit one's stride; underclothes which inhibit the circulation. Is it not an intriguing observation that those very clothes which are thought to be flattering to the female and attractive to the male are those which make it impossible for a woman to defend herself against aggression?

Each girl as she grows into womanhood is taught fear. Fear is the form in which the female internalizes both chivalry and the double standard. Since, biologically speaking, women in fact have the same if not greater potential for sexual expression as do men, the woman who is taught that she must behave differently from a man must also learn to distrust her own carnality. She must deny her own feelings and learn not to act from them. She fears herself. This is the essence of passivity, and of course, a woman's passivity is not simply sexual but functions to cripple her from self-expression in every area of her life.

Passivity itself prevents a woman from ever considering her own potential for self-defense and forces her to look to men for protection. The woman is taught fear, but this time fear of the other; and yet her only relief from this fear is to seek out the other. Moreover, the passive woman is taught to regard herself as impotent, unable to act, unable even to perceive, in no way self-sufficient, and, finally, as the object and not the subject of human behavior. It is in this sense that a woman is deprived of the status of a human being. She is not free to be. . . .

III

If the basic social unit is the family, in which the woman is a possession of her husband, the superstructure of society is a male hierarchy, in which men dominate other men (or patriarchal families dominate other patriarchal families). And it is no small irony that, while the very social fabric of our male-dominated culture denies women equal access to political, economic and legal power, the literature, myth and humor of our culture depicts women not only as the power behind the throne, but the real

---

*Editor's note: "Third World" was used to describe women of color in the U.S. at the time this article was written.

source of the oppression of men. The religious version of this fairy tale blames Eve for both carnality and eating of the tree of knowledge, at the same time making her gullible to the obvious devices of a serpent. Adam, of course, is merely the trusting victim of love. Certainly this is a biased story. But no more biased than the one television audiences receive today from the latest slick comedians. Through a media which is owned by men, censored by a State dominated by men, all the evils of this social system which make a man's life unpleasant are blamed upon "the wife." The theory is: were it not for the female who waits and plots to "trap" the male into marriage, modern man would be able to achieve Olympian freedom. She is made the scapegoat for a system which is in fact run by men.

Nowhere is this more clear than in the white racist use of the concept of white womanhood. The white male's open rape of black women, coupled with his overweening concern for the chastity and protection of his wife and daughters, represents an extreme of sexist and racist hypocrisy. While on the one hand she was held up as the standard for purity and virtue, on the other the Southern white woman was never asked if she wanted to be on a pedestal, and in fact any deviance from the male-defined standards for white womanhood was treated severely. (It is a powerful commentary on American racism that the historical role of Blacks as slaves, and thus possessions without power, has robbed black women of legal and economic protection through marriage. Thus black women in Southern society and in the ghettoes of the North have long been easy game for white rapists.) The fear that black men would rape white women was, and is, classic paranoia. Quoting from Ann Breen's unpublished study of racism and sexism in the South *"The New South: White Man's Country,"* Frederick Douglass legitimately points out that, "had the black man wished to rape white women, he had ample opportunity to do so during the civil war when white women, the wives, sisters, daughters and mothers of the rebels, were left in the care of Blacks. But yet not a single act of rape was committed during this time. The Ku Klux Klan, who tarred and feathered black men and lynched them in the honor of the purity of white woman-

hood, also applied tar and feathers to a Southern white woman accused of bigamy, which leads one to suspect that Southern white men were not so much outraged at the violation of the woman as a person, in the few instances where rape was actually committed by black men, but at the violation of his property rights." In the situation where a black man was found to be having sexual relations with a white woman, the white woman could exercise skin-privilege, and claim that she had been raped, in which case the black man was lynched. But if she did not claim rape, she herself was subject to lynching.

In constructing the myth of white womanhood so as to justify the lynching and oppression of black men and women, the white male has created a convenient symbol of his own power which has resulted in black hostility toward the white "bitch," accompanied by an unreasonable fear on the part of many white women of the black rapist. Moreover, it is not surprising that after being told for two centuries that he wants to rape white women, occasionally a black man does actually commit that act. But it is crucial to note that the frequency of this practice is outrageously exaggerated in the white mythos. Ninety percent of reported rape is intra- not inter-racial. . . .

Indeed, the existence of rape in any form is beneficial to the ruling class of white males. For rape is a kind of terrorism which severely limits the freedom of women and makes women dependent on men. Moreover, in the act of rape, the rage that one man may harbor toward another higher in the male hierarchy can be deflected toward a female scapegoat. For every man there is always someone lower on the social scale on whom he can take out his aggressions. And that is any woman alive.

This oppressive attitude towards women finds its institutionalization in the traditional family. For it is assumed that a man "wears the pants" in his family—he exercises the option of rule whenever he so chooses. Not that he makes all the decisions—clearly women make most of the important day-to-day decisions in a family. But when a conflict of interest arises, it is the man's interest which will prevail. His word, in itself, is more powerful. He lords it over his wife in the same way his boss lords it over him, so that the very process of exercising his power becomes as important an act as obtaining whatever it is his power can get for him. This notion of power is key to the male ego in this culture, for the two acceptable measures of masculinity are a man's power over women and his power over other men. A man may boast to his friends that "I have 20 men working for me." It is also aggrandizement of his ego if he has the financial power to clothe his wife in furs and jewels. And, if a man lacks the wherewithal to acquire such power, he can always express his rage through equally masculine activities—rape and theft. Since male society defines the female as a possession, it is not surprising that the felony most often committed together with rape is theft. . . .

―――――――

Rape is an act of aggression in which the victim is denied her self-determination. It is an act of violence which, if not actually followed by beatings or murder, nevertheless always carries with it the threat of death. And finally, rape is a form of mass terrorism, for the victims of rape are chosen indiscriminately, but the propagandists for male supremacy broadcast that it is women who cause rape by being unchaste or in the wrong place at the wrong time— in essence, by behaving as though they were free.

The threat of rape is used to deny women employment. (In California, the Berkeley Public Library, until pushed by the Federal Employment Practices Commission, refused to hire female shelvers because of perverted men in the stacks.) The fear of rape keeps women off the streets at night. Keeps women at home. Keeps women passive and modest for fear that they be thought provocative.

It is part of human dignity to be able to defend oneself, and women are learning. Some women have learned karate; some to shoot guns. And yet we will not be free until the threat of rape and the atmosphere of violence is ended, and to end that the nature of male behavior must change.

But rape is not an isolated act that can be rooted out from patriarchy without ending patriarchy itself. The same men and power structure who victimize women are engaged in the act of raping Vietnam, raping Black people and the very earth we live upon. Rape is a classic act of domination where, in

the words of Kate Millett, "the emotions of hatred, contempt, and the desire to break or violate personality," take place. This breaking of the personality characterizes modern life itself. No simple reforms can eliminate rape. As the symbolic expression of the white male hierarchy, rape is the quintessential act of our civilization, one which, Valerie Solanis warns, is in danger of "humping itself to death."   [1971]

 121

The Shame of Silence

ATHENA DEVLIN

As in every high school, there was in mine a set of especially powerful boys who were "popular." At my school in Texas, they were all football stars. When I was a freshman, and dying to make a good impression, I was invited by one of them to come over to his house to watch television. I don't think I will ever be able to forget (much to my embarrassment these days) how excited I was. By the time I left my house, my room looked like a clothes bomb had exploded in it. I was smiling from ear to ear, probably having visions of becoming a cheerleader. I forgot to ask myself *why* he had called me. I forgot to remember that I was *not* what you would call a popular girl. I rang his doorbell with a pounding heart and ridiculous aspirations. Bill let me in and led me into the living room. There, sitting on couches, were about eight boys. They were all watching a porno film on the VCR. They looked at me with open dislike and said "hi" pretty much in unison. I just stood there, frozen with disappointment while a blond woman acted out ecstasy on the television screen. No one spoke. After what seemed like a very long time, I turned away and walked into the kitchen just off the living room and sat at the table. I was embarrassed by my expectations. I felt like I had forgotten my "place." Now I remembered. I knew why I had been invited over. Bill let me stay in the kitchen by myself for about 20 minutes. When he finally walked in he just looked at me and said "You wanna go outside?"

I said yes because it felt like the only way out. We went out to his back yard; to reclining deck chairs by a lit pool. We started making out. His hands were everywhere, his breath stank. I felt worthless and just let it happen. Then, when he leaned over to get to the hook of my bra, I looked up and there they all were, all eight of them standing on the second floor balcony watching us. I started yelling. Bill didn't say anything. He didn't tell them to go away, he didn't offer me an explanation. I suddenly got the feeling that it had all been planned this way. I was trying to stand and get my shirt back on when Bill took my hand and pulled me behind a fence at the back of the yard. When we got there, he turned and told me he wanted a hand job. I gave him one and left. I felt only one thing, and it wasn't anger; it was shame.

To be a "successful" girl in Highland Park was to be successful with boys. So, undeniably the girls that I grew up with viewed each other as less important than the boys they dated and more often than not, as would-be enemies. Nothing was ever as important as being accepted by men. And this, quite effectively, alienated us from one another. The key to success with boys in my high school was having the right kind of reputation, and reputation for a girl was for the most part focused narrowly on her looks and her sexual life. Importantly, it was the boys who decided what "type" a girl was sexually—which, in a social setting like this one, gave them a lot of power. What put them in this position was exactly that thing the girls lacked: each other. Maybe it was from all those hours of football practice where they had to depend on one another that did it, or maybe it was just because they felt important enough not to seek female approval as desperately as we sought theirs that made some sort of solidarity among them more possible. But in any event, it was to their distinct advantage. For girls, trying to please the powers that be was very confusing because we were supposed to be attractive and sexually exciting in order to be accepted, while simultaneously prudish and innocent. We were supposed to be sweet and deferential towards them but we were also supposed to be able to stop them when they went too far. I suppose I never got that delicate balance down. I got one side of the equation but not the other.

Not surprisingly, then, the shame I felt by having been treated as worthless by boys was something I desperately wanted to *hide*. I had failed, it seemed in the most important way. I never told any of my girl friends about that night and, because of my shame, which covered everything, I wasn't even really aware of my anger, and it certainly did not occur to me to *show* any anger towards these boys. I had never heard a girl publicly denounce a boy for his behavior towards her, though I had seen many a girl be thoroughly disgraced in those hallways of Highland Park High. So, when the story of my night with the football stars got passed along by the boys, the girls who heard about it never tried to comfort me. They whispered about me instead, often to the very boys that had been involved. They were gaining points by disassociating themselves from me, because I was the one at fault. Boys will be boys after all. It's the girls who say yes that were held accountable at my high school—by both sexes.

About six months later when my reputation as a "slut" had been firmly established, I began hanging out with a girl named Cindy who had a similar public identity. Some of the boys from the group that participated in that horrible night often asked us out when their regular girl friends were away or safely tucked behind curfews. I usually said no, although I occasionally agreed because going out with them still felt like a form of acceptance. At least they thought I was pretty enough to make out with. But Cindy went out with them a lot. One Friday night something happened. To this day I do not know what actually went on (no surprise). I just knew she was upset and the following Monday, Will, one of the boys she went out with, started hassling her in the hall. She began to cry in the middle of passing period with everyone staring. Suddenly, and for the first time, I felt incredibly angry and before fear held me back, I began to yell at Will. I don't remember what I said exactly, but it was something to the effect of who did he think he was, and that I thought he was an asshole. I don't think he had ever been so surprised. He stared at me in complete amazement. And so did Cindy. Unfortunately, it didn't take him too long to recover and he told me in a voice loud enough for everyone in the building to hear, that

I was a whore and everyone knew it, that I would sleep with anyone (I was still a virgin at the time), and that I was completely disgusting. The contempt in his voice was incredible. I started to feel ashamed again. One did not have scenes like this at Highland Park. But the surprise was Cindy hated me for it. In her opinion I had done an unforgivable thing in sticking up for her. And, what I learned was that girls didn't want each other's protection because it made them less attractive to boys. They feared focusing on each other too much.

For me, however, this incident was a turning point because afterwards these boys left me alone completely. I was released from the painful confusion of boys wanting me and disliking me at the same time—ignoring me or talking about me behind my back and then calling me up late on Friday night. I had yelled at a football star in front of everyone. That made me completely unacceptable as opposed to only marginally so. People began to make sure they didn't cross my path. I was left alone. Moreover, I was feared. It was then that I began to realize just how much the boys depended on the girls not do anything to defend themselves, that they depended heavily on our passivity. I saw that they lived in fear of us taking action. Any action. And I began to suspect that the isolation I noticed so many of the girls at my high school in Dallas feeling served a purpose useful enough to be a consequence of deliberateness. Still, I never made another scene.

But that was not really the greatest tragedy. Rather it was, and is, that girls grow up not knowing each other very well. And that while going through the same things, they are without both the benefit of each other's comfort and understanding, and more vulnerable to abuse. I am close to only one girl who went to high school with me, and that is probably only because we ended up at the same college. When I told her about writing this essay she told me, for the first time, some of her experiences at Highland Park. They were as tortured and humiliating as mine, but I had never heard her stories before and she had never heard mine. High school obviously wasn't a great experience for either of us, and while we sat there tracing the damage through to our present lives, I desperately wished it had been different.

And it could have been if we could have shaken off the terrible trap of shame and talked about our lives and found ways to support each other. It seems clear to me now that not only were the boys protecting each other, but we girls were protecting the boys through the silence that existed between us. [1992]

122

Whose Body Is It, Anyway?

PAMELA FLETCHER

RAPE

I never heard the word while growing up. Or, if I had, I blocked it out because its meaning was too horrific for my young mind: a stranger, a weapon, a dark place, blood, pain, even death. But I do remember other people's responses to it, especially those of women. I specifically remember hearing about Rachel when I was in high school in the '70s. The story was that she "let" a group of boys "pull a train" on her in the football field one night. I remember the snickers and the looks of disgust of both the girls and the boys around campus. It was common knowledge that nobody with eyes would want to fuck Rachel; she had a face marred by acne and glasses. But, she had *some* body.

While I am writing this essay, I remember the stark sadness and confusion I felt then. This same sadness returns to me now, but I am no longer confused. Then I wondered how she could "do" so many guys and actually like it (!). Then I thought maybe she didn't like it after all, and maybe, just maybe, they made her do it. But the word rape never entered my mind. After all, she knew them, didn't she? There was no weapon, no blood. She survived, didn't she? And, just what was she doing there all by herself, anyway? Now, I know what "pulling a train" is. Now I know they committed a violent crime against her body and her soul. Now I know why she walked around campus with that wounded face, a face that none of us girls wanted to look into because we knew intuitively that we would see a reflection of our own wounded selves. So the other girls did not look into her eyes. They avoided her and talked about her like she was "a bitch in heat." Why else would such a thing have happened to her?

I tried to look into Rachel's eyes because I wanted to know something—what, I didn't know. But she looked down or looked away or laughed like a lunatic, you know, in that eerie, loud, nervous manner that irritated and frightened me because it didn't ring true. Now I wonder if she thought such laughter would mask her pain. It didn't.

PAINFUL SILENCE AND DEEP-SEATED RAGE

I remember another story I heard while I was in college. Larry told me that his close friend, Brenda, let Danny stay over one night in her summer apartment after they had smoked some dope, and he raped her. Larry actually said that word.

"Don't tell anyone," Brenda begged him. "I never should have let him spend the night. I thought he was my friend."

Larry told me not to ever repeat it to anyone else. And, trying to be a loyal girlfriend to him and a loyal friend to Brenda, I didn't say anything. When we saw Danny later at another friend's place, we neither confronted nor ignored him. *We acted as though everything was normal.* I felt agitated and angry. I wondered why Larry didn't say anything to Danny, you know, man-to-man, like: "That shit was not cool, man. Why you go and do somethin' like that to the sista?"

It never occurred to me to say anything to Brenda, because I wasn't supposed to know, or I was supposed to act as though I didn't know, stupid stuff like that. I sat there, disconnected from her, watching her interact with people, Danny among them, acting as though everything was normal.

DENIAL

Since I began writing this essay two months ago, I have had such difficulty thinking about my own related experiences. I hadn't experienced rape. Or, had I? For months, in the hard drive of my subconscious mind, I searched for files that would yield any incidence of sexual violence or sexual terrorism. When

certain memories surfaced, I questioned whether those experiences were "real rapes."

I have some very early recollections that challenge me. Max, my first boyfriend, my childhood sweetheart, tried to pressure me into having sex with him when we were in junior high. Two of my friends, who were the girlfriends of his two closest friends, also tried to pressure me because they were already "doing it" for their "men."

"Don't be a baby," they teased. "Everybody's doing it."

But I wouldn't cave in, and I broke up with Max because he wasn't a decent boy.

A year later, when we reached high school, I went crawling back to Max because I "loved" him and couldn't stand his ignoring me. He stopped ignoring me long enough to pin me up against the locker to kiss me roughly and to suck on my neck long and hard until he produced sore, purple bruises, what we called hickies. I had to hide those hideous marks from my parents by wearing turtleneck sweaters. Those hickies marked me as his property and gave his friends the impression that he had "done" me, even though we hadn't gotten that far yet. We still had to work out the logistics.

I hated when he gave me hickies, and I didn't like his exploring my private places as he emotionally and verbally abused me, telling me I wasn't pretty like Susan: "Why can't you look like her?" And I remember saying something like, "Why don't you go be with her, if that's what you want?" He answered me with a piercing "don't-you-ever-talk-to-me-like-that-again" look, and I never asked again. He continued, however, to ask me the same question.

In my heart, I realized that the way he treated me was wrong because I felt violated; I felt separated from my body, as if it did not belong to me. But at sixteen I didn't know how or what to feel, except that I felt confused and desperately wanted to make sense out of what it meant to be a girl trapped inside a woman's body. Yes, I felt trapped, because I understood that we girls had so much to lose now that we could get pregnant. Life sagged with seriousness. Now everybody kept an eye on us: our parents, the churches, the schools, and the boys. Confusion prevailed. While we were encouraged to have a slight interest in boys (lest we turn out "funny") so that ultimately we could be trained to become good wives, we were instructed directly and indirectly to keep a safe distance away from them.

We liked boys and we thought we wanted love, but what we really wanted as youth was to have some fun, some clean, innocent fun until we got married and gave our virtuous selves to our husbands just as our mothers had done. We female children had inherited this lovely vision from our mothers and from fairy tales. Yet now we know that those visions were not so much what our mothers had experienced, but what they wished they had experienced, and what they wanted for us.

We thought "going with a boy" in the early '70s would be romance-filled fun that involved holding hands, stealing kisses, exchanging class rings, and wearing big lettered sweaters. Maybe it was, for some of us. But I know that many of us suffered at the hands of love.

I soon learned in high school that it was normal to be mistreated by our boyfriends. Why else would none of us admit to each other the abuse we tolerated? These boys "loved" us, so we believed that they were entitled to treat us in any way they chose. We believed that somehow we belonged to them, body and soul. Isn't that what many of the songs on the radio said? And we just knew somehow that if we did give in to them, we deserved whatever happened, and if we didn't give in, we still deserved whatever happened. Such abuse was rampant because we became and remained isolated from each other by hoisting our romances above our friendships.

We didn't define what they did to us as rape, molestation, or sexual abuse. We called it love. We called it love if it happened with our boyfriends, and we called other girls whores and sluts if it happened with someone else's boyfriend or boyfriends, as in the case of Rachel and "the train."

We called it love because we had tasted that sweet taste of pain. Weren't they one and the same?

REALIZATION

One sharp slap from Max one day delivered the good sense I had somehow lost when I got to high school. After that point I refused to be his woman, his property. When I left home for college, I left with the keen awareness that I had better take good care of myself. In my involvement with Max, I had allowed a split to occur between my body and my soul, and I had to work on becoming whole again.

I knew that I was growing stronger (though in silent isolation from other young women and through intense struggle) when I was able to successfully resist being seduced (read: molested) by several college classmates and when I successfully fought off the violent advances and the verbal abuse (what I now recognize as an attempted rape) of someone with whom I had once been sexually intimate.

But how does a woman become strong and whole in a society in which women are not permitted (as if we need permission!) to possess ourselves, to own our very bodies? We females often think we are not entitled to ourselves, and many times we give ourselves away for less than a song. The sad truth of the matter is that this is how we have managed to survive in our male-dominated culture. Yet, in the wise words of the late Audre Lorde, "the Master's tools will never dismantle the Master's house." In other words, as long as we remain disconnected from ourselves and each other and dependent on abusive males, we will remain weak, powerless, and fragmented.

Just imagine how different our lives would be today if we were not injured by internalized misogyny and sexism. Imagine how different our lives would be if we would only open our mouths wide and collectively and loudly confront males and *really* hold them accountable for the violent crimes they perpetrate against females. Imagine how our lives would be if all mothers tell their daughters the truth about romantic love and teach them to love themselves as females, to value and claim their bodies, and to protect themselves against violent and disrespectful males.

What if we girls in junior high and high school believed we deserve respect rather than verbal and sexual abuse from our male classmates? What if we girls in my high school had confronted the gang of boys who raped Rachel that night in the football field twenty years ago, rather than perpetuated that cycle of abuse and shame she suffered? What if Larry and

I had confronted Danny for raping Brenda that summer night in her apartment? What if Brenda had felt safe enough to tell Larry, me, and the police? What if we females believed ourselves and each other to be as important and deserving of our selfhood as we believe males to be? Just imagine.

Envision a time when we women are connected to ourselves and each other, when we no longer feel the need and desire to conspire with men against each other in order to survive in a misogynist, violent culture. We must alter our destructive thinking about being female so that we can begin to accept, love, and cherish our femaleness. It is the essence of our lives.

Readjusting our lens so we can begin to see ourselves and each other as full, capable, and mighty human beings will take as much work as reconstructing our violent society. Neither job is easy, but the conditions and the tasks go hand in hand. Two ways to begin our own transformation are to become physically active in whatever manner we choose so we can take pleasure in fully connecting to ourselves and in growing physically stronger, and to respect, protect, support, and comfort each other. Once we stop denying that our very lives are endangered, we will soon discover that these steps are not only necessary but viable in empowering ourselves and claiming our right to exist as whole human beings in a peaceful, humane world.   [1993]

 123

With No Immediate Cause

NTOZAKE SHANGE

every 3 minutes a woman is beaten
every five minutes a
woman is raped/every ten minutes
a lil girl is molested
yet i rode the subway today
i sat next to an old man who

may have beaten his old wife
3 minutes ago or 3 days/30 years ago
he might have sodomized his
daughter but i sat there
cuz the young men on the train
might beat some young women
later in the day or tomorrow
i might not shut my door fast
enuf/push hard enuf
every 3 minutes it happens
some woman's innocence
rushes to her cheeks/pours from her mouth
like the betsy wetsy dolls have been torn
apart/their mouths
mensis red & split/every
three minutes a shoulder
is jammed through plaster & the oven door/
chairs push thru the rib cage/hot water or
boiling sperm decorate her body
i rode the subway today
& bought a paper from a
man who might
have held his old lady onto
a hot pressing iron/i dont know
maybe he catches lil girls in the
park & rips open their behinds
with steel rods/i cdnt decide
what he might have done i only
know every 3 minutes
every 5 minutes every 10 minutes/so
i bought the paper
looking for the announcement
there has to be an announcement
of the women's bodies found
yesterday/the missing little girl
i sat in a restaurant with my
paper looking for the announcement
a yng man served me coffee
i wondered did he pour the boiling
coffee/on the woman cuz she waz stupid/
did he put the infant girl/in
the coffee pot/with the boiling coffee/cuz she cried
    too much
what exactly did he do with hot coffee
i looked for the announcement

the discovery/of the dismembered
woman's body/the
victims have not all been
identified/today they are
naked & dead/refuse to
testify/one girl out of 10's not
coherent/i took the coffee
& spit it up/i found an
announcement/not the woman's
bloated body in the river/floating
not the child bleeding in the
59th street corridor/not the baby
broken on the floor/
 "there is some concern
 that alleged battered women
 might start to murder their
 husbands & lovers with no
 immediate cause"
i spit up i vomit i am screaming
we all have immediate cause
every 3 minutes
every 5 minutes
every 10 minutes
every day
women's bodies are found
in alleys & bedrooms/at the top of the stairs
before i ride the subway/buy a paper/drink
coffee/i must know/
have you hurt a woman today
did you beat a woman today
throw a child cross a room
 are the lil girl's panties
 in yr pocket
did you hurt a woman today

i have to ask these obscene questions
the authorities require me to
establish
immediate cause

every three minutes
every five minutes
every ten minutes
every day   [1970]

✤ 124

Naming and Studying Acquaintance Rape

PEGGY REEVES SANDAY

When it comes to my masculinity I get very defensive. Because I know that men are admired for having many partners, I set quotas—so many girls in one month. The joy of sex for me is the feeling of acceptance and approval which always goes with having sex with a new person.
      —Male college student[1]

Martha McCluskey went to college during a time when feminist activism for rape reform was well under way, however not yet widely publicized outside scholarly and legal circles. In 1977 she was sexually abused by a group of fraternity brothers while a student at Colby College. At the time, however, Martha thought that being assaulted by "normal white college men . . . was not significant" and she didn't understand it as "real violence." It wasn't until after graduating from Yale Law School that she wrote about the assault in an article in the *Maine Law Review* on "privileged violence in college fraternities."

It happened at the beginning of vacation, when her dorm was nearly empty. As she described it:

I am standing in the hallway looking out the window for my ride home. I turn around and my suitcase is gone; Joe and Bill from down the hall are laughing as they carry it away. I follow them. I hear a door lock behind me. They let go of my suitcase and grab me.

I am lying on the bare linoleum floor of Joe's bedroom. In the room are a group of Lambda Chi and KDR pledges who live on my hall; several of them are football players. Some are sitting on the bed, laughing. Two others are pinning my arms and my legs to the floor. Joe is touching me while the others cheer.

I am a friendly fellow-classmate as I reasonably explain that I'm in a rush to catch a ride, that I'm not in the mood to joke around; that I'd really like them to please cut it out. It takes a few long upside-down seconds before things look different. As I start to scream and fight I feel like I am shattering a world that will not get put back together. They let me go.

Later I don't talk about this, not even to myself. I sit near Joe and Bill in sociology and English classes. I don't talk in class.[2]

Starting in the 1970s, research on acquaintance rape conducted by psychologists, sociologists, and medical researchers began, and by the 1990s a significant body of knowledge on all aspects of sexual assault and abuse had been established. At first the research focused on the annual incidence and lifetime prevalence of acquaintance rape in order to establish the scope of the problem, but soon expanded to include causes, consequences, social and psychological costs, and prevention. The studies operated within the legal definition of rape as sexual intercourse, including oral or anal penetration, due to force, the threat of force, or by taking advantage of a person's incapacity to consent. Most studies focused on the heterosexual rape of females. However, in recent years attention has turned also to the heterosexual and same-sex rape of male victims. Least attention has been given to same-sex rape of women.[3]

THE EARLY STUDIES

Studies making a distinction between jump-from-the-bushes stranger rape and rape involving people who know one another go back at least to the 1950s. In 1952 the *Yale Law Journal* recognized that rape ranges from "brutal attacks familiar to tabloid readers to half won arguments of couples in parked cars." Kalven and Zeisel's distinction between "aggravated" and "simple" rape in their national study of fifties trials was the first to demonstrate that a significant proportion (40 percent) of rape cases going to trial involved acquaintances. Both of these acknowledged that when the parties know one another a conviction is much more difficult. Kalven and Zeisel were able to attribute the difficulty to juror prejudice by showing that judges were much more likely than jurors to believe that the evidence warranted a conviction in cases of simple rape.[4]

The most well-known of the early studies acknowledging the scope of acquaintance rape was authored by sociologist Menachem Amir. Based on an examination of police files of rapes occurring in 1958 and 1960, Amir concluded that rapists are generally "normal" men. About half of all the rapes were committed by men who knew their victims. Only 42 percent of the rapists were complete strangers to their victims, and not all of the victims resisted to the utmost.[5] More than half of the victims were submissive during the rape; about one fifth of the victims put up a strong physical fight; and another quarter actively resisted in some other way, like screaming. Twenty percent of the victims were between the ages of ten and fourteen, and 25 percent between fifteen and nineteen. The younger the victim the less likely she was to resist.[6]

The first widely read feminist studies mentioning acquaintance or date rape were authored by Susan Brownmiller and Diana Russell in the mid-1970s. In her landmark study, *Against Our Will*, Brownmiller is the first to use the term "date rape." The kind of interaction Brownmiller labeled date rape was typical of men and women caught in the double bind of the sexual revolution. Men pressed their advantage thinking that all women now "wanted it," but nice girls hadn't yet learned to make a no stick. Brownmiller phrased the problem as follows:

> In a dating situation an aggressor may press his advantage to the point where pleasantness quickly turns to unpleasantness and more than the woman bargained for, yet social propriety and the strictures of conventional female behavior that dictate politeness and femininity demand that the female gracefully endure, or wriggle away if she can, but a direct confrontation falls outside of the behavioral norms. These are the cases about which the police are wont to say, "She changed her mind afterward," with no recognition that it was only afterward that she dared pull herself together and face up to the fact that she had truly been raped.[7]

Brownmiller's historic contribution to the anti-rape movement is in her valuable analysis of the cultural forces shaping female passivity when confronted with male sexual aggression and her conceptualization of rape as violence. Brownmiller urged a generation of young women to learn to say no and overcome their historical training to be nice. She recognized that date rapes hardly ever get to court and don't look good on paper because the "intangibles of victim behavior . . . present a poor case."[8] These are the kinds of cases that Kalven and Zeisel found usually ended in acquittals. Brownmiller admits that even with her feminist awareness she often feels like shouting, "Idiot, why didn't you see the warning signs earlier?" upon hearing such cases.

Before she began researching rape in the early 1970s, Diana Russell held the "crazed stranger" theory of rape, believing that rape was "an extremely sadistic and deviant act, which could be performed only by crazy or psychopathic people." The idea had never occurred to her that rape by a lover, friend, or colleague was possible. She learned differently in 1971 while she was attending the highly publicized rape trial of Jerry Plotkin in San Francisco. Plotkin was a jeweler accused of abducting a young woman at gunpoint to his swank apartment, where he and three other men raped and forced her to commit various sexual acts.[9]

During the trial, which drew many feminist protestors, Russell began hearing stories from other women who had been raped but who had not reported the rape, fearing the treatment they would probably receive in the courtroom. The outcome of the Plotkin trial was a grim reminder of why so few were willing to report. The jury acquitted Plotkin because of the complainant's prior sex life, which was gone over in minute detail in the courtroom.[10] Convinced of the injustice of the verdict and aware of the need for further education, Russell embarked on a program of research that would produce two of the most important early studies of acquaintance rape.

Russell's first book, *The Politics of Rape*, was based on interviews with ninety women. In chapters titled "Lovers Rape, Too," "Some of Our Best Friends Are Rapists," and "Fathers, Husbands, and Other Rapists," to name just a few, Russell records women's experiences which demonstrate that rape is just as likely to occur between acquaintances as between strangers. The level of force employed during rape ranged from intimidation in some instances to extreme force in others. A typical case is reflected in one woman's statement that she put up as much struggle as she could, but he "used all of his strength, and he was very forceful and kept [her] down."[11]

Another woman, who was raped by a fraternity brother, said she didn't scream because she was afraid he would call his frat brothers and "run a train" on her.[12]

The reasons these women gave for not reporting their experiences reflect the dominant belief that to do so would be embarrassing and useless. The first woman thought about going to the police but decided against it, believing that her accusation of rape would be impossible to prove. The woman who was raped by the frat brother told a close friend but remained silent otherwise, due to depression.[13] Another woman, who had been gang raped after getting into a car, told her brother, who called her a whore. When she told her husband many years later, he started punching her in the head. She never thought of going to the police, for fear of how her parents would react. One by one the women Russell interviewed gave similar reasons for not reporting.[14]

In 1978, Russell conducted a survey in San Francisco of 930 randomly selected women ranging in age from eighteen to eighty. Her results provided a statistical profile of acquaintance-versus-stranger rape in a diverse population of all social classes and racial/ethnic groups. The study followed the legal definition of rape in California and most other states at that time. Questions were asked about experiences of forced, nonconsensual intercourse as well as about experiences of "unwanted" sexual intercourse while asleep, unconscious, drugged, or otherwise helpless. The inclusion of the question about physical helplessness due to alcohol or drugs also was in keeping with the legal definition of rape in California. Russell was very careful to exclude from the rape category any experiences in which women reported *feeling* rather than *being* forced.[15]

Of the 930 women, 24 percent reported at least one completed rape, and 31 percent reported at least one attempted rape.[16] Russell used the term acquaintance rape as an umbrella term to distinguish rapes involving people who know one another from rapes involving strangers. Thirty-five percent of the women in her study experienced rape or attempted rape by an acquaintance (ranging in degrees of intimacy from casual acquaintances to lovers) as compared with 11 percent raped by strangers and 3 percent by relatives (other than husbands or ex-husbands).[17] Only 8 percent of all incidents of rape and attempted rape were reported to the police.[18] These incidents were much more likely to involve strangers than men known to the victim.[19]

Another important early survey was conducted in 1978 by psychologist Mary Koss of nearly four thousand college students at Kent State University, where she taught. As a young psychology professor just starting out in the mid-seventies, Koss had read Susan Brownmiller's book on rape and felt that the next step should be a scientific study of the epidemiology of rape. When she first designed the Kent State study, Koss preferred the label "hidden rape" to "acquaintance rape" because of the growing recognition in law enforcement circles that rape was "the most underreported of major crimes." She chose to study "unacknowledged victims of rape," women who have experienced forced sexual intercourse but do not call it rape.

In criminology terms, the unacknowledged victim is the "safe victim." For law enforcement purposes it is always important to identify the kinds of people most likely to be safe victims in any class of crime so that they can be protected through educational programs informing them of their rights. At the time Koss embarked on the Kent State survey, government estimates suggested that "only 40–50 percent of the rapes that occur each year are reported to the police."[20]

Koss's goal was to determine the prevalence of hidden rape. For the survey, she identified four degrees of sexual aggression ranging from what she called "low sexual victimization" to "high sexual victimization" in order to separate gradations of sexual abuse.[21] The category labeled "high sexual victimization" was the category that Koss defined as rape. It included women who said they had experienced unwanted intercourse or penetration of the mouth or anus from a man or men who used or threatened to use physical force. Koss separated this category of rape victims into two types: women who acknowledged they had been raped and those who did not name what happened to them as rape. Koss found that 13 percent of the women interviewed answered yes to at least one of three questions asking them whether they had experienced forced penetration at any time since the age of fourteen. Only 6 percent of the women interviewed, however, answered yes to the question "Have you ever been raped?"[22]

Less than 5 percent of the men in the study admitted to using force. Those who admitted to using force were remarkably similar to the sexually aggressive men described in Kirkendall's 1961 study of college men. For example, like their 1950s counterparts, the Kent State males expressed attitudes illustrative of the double standard. They were more approving of sexual relationships with prostitutes and more disapproving of sexual freedom for women than the less aggressive men in the study. They preferred traditional women, who were dependent, attention-seeking, and suggestible. Their first experiences with sexual intercourse tended to be unsatisfactory, but they expressed more pride in these experiences than the less aggressive men. When asked if they had sex the first time because it was socially expected, nearly half of the men in the sexually aggressive groups answered yes, as compared with only a quarter of the nonsexually aggressive men.

There were other differences between the types of men in Koss's study reminiscent of Kirkendall's findings. The highly sexually aggressive men were more likely to identify with a male peer culture. More were likely to be in fraternities than those reporting no or low sexual aggression. They were more insensitive to the woman's resistance and more likely to think that sexual aggression was normal sexual behavior, part of the game that had to be played with women. They believed that a woman would be only moderately offended if a man forced his way into her house after a date or forced his attentions in other ways.[23]

RECENT STUDIES

To see whether she could replicate her Kent State findings in a nationwide sample, Koss joined with *Ms.* magazine in a 1985 survey of 6,159 students on thirty-two college campuses. The results of this survey would play a significant role in stepping up anti-rape activism on college campuses, and in inspiring the campus section of the Violence Against Women Act, which would be introduced into Congress five years later.

The survey questions were similar to those Koss used in the Kent State study. This time, however, she included a question about unwanted sexual intercourse that occurred because of the effects of alcohol or drugs. The results showed the extent to which sexual behavior in a college population had changed since Kinsey's male and female studies in the 1940s and 1950s. For example, the percentages of college-age males who were having sexual intercourse rose from 44 percent, reported by Kinsey, to 75 percent, reported by Koss in the 1980s. For college-age females, the percentages changed from 20 percent, reported by Kinsey, to 69 percent, reported by Koss.[24] Morton Hunt, who conducted a survey of the sexual behavior of two thousand individuals in twenty-four cities in 1972, found a similar increase for college men, but a less marked increase for college women.[25]

The results of Koss's national study were widely disseminated and quoted after publication in the *Journal of Consulting and Clinical Psychology* in 1987.[26] Robin Warshaw's *I Never Called It Rape,* the first major book on acquaintance rape, was based on Koss's study. Warshaw reported that one in four women surveyed were victims of rape or attempted rape, 84 percent of those raped knew their attacker, and that 57 percent of the rapes happened on dates.[27] The women thought that most of their offenders (73 percent) were drinking or using drugs at the time of the assault, and 55 percent admitted to using intoxicants themselves. Most of the women thought that they had made their nonconsent "quite" clear and that the offender used "quite a bit" of force. They resisted by using reasoning (84 percent) and physical struggle (70 percent).[28] Only one quarter (27 percent) of the rape victims acknowledged themselves as such. Five percent reported their rapes to the police. Although many women did not call it rape, Koss reported that "the great majority of rape victims conceptualized their experience in highly negative terms and felt victimized whether or not they realized that legal standards for rape had been met."[29]

The results for the men were similar to what Koss had found at Kent State. One quarter of the men reported involvement in some form of sexual aggression, ranging from unwanted touching to rape. Three percent admitted to attempted rape and 4.4 percent to rape.[30] A high percentage of the males did not name their use of force as rape. Eighty-eight percent said it was definitely *not* rape. Forty-seven percent said they would do the same thing again.[31]

Koss's findings that men viewed the use of force as normal were corroborated by other surveys conducted on college campuses. For example, one study cited by Russell found that 35 percent of the males questioned about the likelihood that they would rape said they might if they could get away with it. When asked whether they would force a female to do something sexual she really did not want to do, 60 percent of the males indicated in a third college study that they might, "given the right circumstances."[32]

Convicted rapists hold similar beliefs. In a study of 114 rapists, Diana Scully found that many either denied that the sexual activity for which they were convicted was rape, or they claimed it hadn't happened. One told her the sexual activity for which he was convicted was "just fucking." Other rapists told her that men rape because they have learned that in America they can get away with it because victims don't report. Almost none of the convicts she interviewed thought they would go to prison. Most of them perceived rape as a rewarding, low-risk act.[33]

Since the early studies conducted by Koss and Russell, a number of additional scientifically designed research studies conducted on campuses in various states and in various communities reveal that an average of between 13 percent and 25 percent of the participating females respond affirmatively to questions asking if they had ever been penetrated against their consent by a male who used force, threatened to use force, or took advantage of them when they were incapacitated with alcohol or other drugs.[34] A more recent national study, published in 1992 by the National Victim Center, defined rape more narrowly by leaving alcohol and drugs out of the picture. Thirteen percent of this national sample of a cross-section of women reported having been victims of at least one completed rape in their life-times. Most of these women had been raped by someone they knew.[35]

ACQUAINTANCE GANG RAPE

In the 1980s quite a few cases of acquaintance gang rape were reported around the country. In the *Ms.* article announcing the results of Koss's Kent State study, Karen Barrett describes an incident that took place at Duke University in the Beta Phi Zeta fraternity. A woman had gotten very drunk and passed out. Men lined up outside the door yelling, "Train!" Although the woman did not press charges, saying that she had been a willing participant, Duke moved against the fraternity after it was discovered that senior members had assigned a pledge the task of "finding a drunk woman for a gang bang."[36]

In Koss's national study she found that 16 percent of the male students who admitted rape, and 10 percent of those who admitted attempting a rape, took part in episodes involving more than one attacker.[37] In 1985 Julie Ehrhart and Bernice Sandler wrote a report for the Association of American Colleges describing such incidents. They found a common pattern. When a vulnerable young woman is high on drugs, drunk, or too weak to protest, she becomes a target for a train. In some cases her drinks might have been spiked with alcohol without her knowledge. When she is approached by several men in a locked room, she reacts with confusion and panic. As many as two to eleven or more men might have sex with her.[38]

In a survey of twenty-four documented cases of alleged college gang rape reported during the 1980s, psychologist Chris O'Sullivan found that thirteen were perpetrated by fraternity men, nine by groups of athletes, and two by men unaffiliated with any group. Nineteen of the cases were reported to the police. In eleven cases, the men pleaded guilty to lesser charges. In five of the six cases that went to trial, all of the men were acquitted. The only finding of "guilty" in the twenty-four cases she studied involved black defendants on football scholarships.[39]

In 1983, I began hearing stories describing gang rape on college campuses in several parts of the country. One such incident became the focus of my book *Fraternity Gang Rape*. The incident was brought to my attention by a student, whom I called Laurel in the book. Laurel alleged that she was raped at a fraternity party when she was drunk and too high on LSD to know what was happening. The local district attorney for sex crimes, William Heinman, concluded that a gang rape had occurred because from his investigation of Laurel's state during the party, "there was no evidence that she was lucid" and able to give consent. When her behavior was described to Judge Lois Forer, she also concluded that Laurel was "incapable of giving consent."[40]

The brothers claimed that Laurel had lured them into what they called an "express." Reporting the party activities that night, they posted the following statement on their bulletin board a few days later:

> Things are looking up for the [name of fraternity] sisters program. A prospective leader for the group spent some time interviewing several [brothers] this past Thursday and Friday. Possible names for the little sisters include [the] "little wenches" and "the [name of fraternity] express."[41]

One of the boys involved in the act, who lost his virginity that night, said that he thought what happened was normal sexual behavior, even though the trauma experienced by Laurel sent her to a hospital for a long period of recovery and kept her out of school for two years. He explained his behavior by referring to the pornography he and his brothers watched together at the house. "Pulling train," as they called it, didn't seem odd to him because "it's something that you see and hear about all the time."[42]

Another brother talked at length with me about what he thought happened. Tom [pseudonym] was adamant that it was not rape because Laurel did not name it rape at first. It was only later that she called it rape after talking to campus feminists, he said. He suggested that the real problem was "her sexual identity confusion" and that both men and women who are sexually confused indulge in casual sex. According to Tom, a lot of guys "engage in promiscuous sex to establish their sexuality," because male sexual identity is based on sexual performance. The male ego is built on sexual conquests as a way of gaining respect from other men. For men, he said, there was lots of peer pressure to be sexually successful.[43]

When I asked Tom about Laurel's bruises, he admitted that she had been bruised that night because she had taken acid and was dancing wildly. He added that sex always involves some degree of force, which also explained the bruises. He went on to say that "subconsciously women are mad that they are subordinate in sex and are the objects of force."[44]

[1996]

NOTES

1. Interview with anonymous college student, spring 1984.
2. McCluskey (1992:261–62).
3. For an excellent summary of studies of the heterosexual and homosexual assault of male victims, see Struckman-Johnson (1991:192–213).

   For another source see Hickson et al. (1994), which describes a study of 930 homosexually active men living in England and Wales in which 27.6 percent said they had been sexually assaulted or had had sex against their will. Some of these men reported being abused by women assailants. Another source on male-male acquaintance rape is Mezey and King (1992).

   For a study of partner abuse in lesbian relationships see Renzetti (1992).
4. Kalven and Zeisel (1966:254).
5. Amir (1971). See LeGrand (1973:922–23) on Amir and for other studies on proportion of stranger to acquaintance rape cases.

   For still another study see Prentky, Burgess, and Carter (1986:73–98). These authors state that a sample of sixteen studies showed that the incidence of stranger rape ranged from 26 percent to 91 percent.
6. Amir (1971:245) and LeGrand (1973:922–24).
7. Brownmiller (1975:257).
8. Ibid.
9. Russell (1984a:11). First published in 1974.
10. Ibid., p. 12.
11. Ibid., p. 102.
12. Ibid., p. 136. A "train" is a sexual ritual in which a number of men line up to rape a woman in succession. See Sanday (1990) for a discussion of trains.
13. Ibid., pp. 107; 137.
14. Ibid., pp. 31–34.
15. Russell (1984b:34; 37–38).
16. Ibid., p. 35.
17. Ibid., p. 59.
18. Ibid., pp. 35–36.
19. Ibid., pp. 96–97; 284.
20. Koss (1985:194).
21. The kind of behavior Brownmiller (1975:257) called date rape (see discussion in the text) corresponded to Koss's (1985:196) "low sexual victimization" category, which Koss does not label rape.
22. Two of the three questions used to determine the 13 percent asked whether actual or threatened physical force had been used in nonconsensual intercourse. The third question asked whether oral or anal intercourse or penetration with an object through the use of force or threat of force had been used in nonconsensual intercourse. Koss (1981: Table 4, p. 51). See also Koss and Oros (1982:455–57).
23. Koss (1981:21–27).
24. For Kinsey data see Kinsey (1953:330–31; 1948:348). From Koss's data, which she supplied to me, I calculated results from the responses to the question: "Have you ever willingly had sexual intercourse with a member of the opposite sex?" The percentages refer to those answering yes.
25. Hunt (1974:149–53).
26. For the first published version see Koss, Gidycz, and Wisniewski (1987:162–70).
27. Warshaw (1988:11). See also Koss (1988:15–16).
28. Koss (1988:15–16).
29. Koss (1992a:122–26). For more discussion of these statistics and how they were used in the backlash against Koss, see Chapter 11.
30. One and a half percent of the men said they had forced a woman into intercourse, oral or anal penetration, or penetration with objects by using threats or physical force, 4 percent of the men said they had intercourse with an unwilling woman by giving her drugs or alcohol. See Koss (1988:8).
31. Koss (1988:18–19).
32. Malamuth study summarized by Russell (1984b:159); Briere study in Russell (1984b:64). See also Malamuth (1981:138–157).
33. Scully (1990:27–28; 159; 163).
34. For a summary of these studies and others, see Koss and Cook (1993:110). For further discussion of acquaintance rape statistics, see Chapter 11.
35. For a summary of many studies, see Koss (1993:1,062–9). For the 1992 national study on rape, see National Victim Center (1992). Koss found that 16 percent of the women in her national sample said they had experienced nonconsensual sex due to a man's force, threat of force, or use of alcohol. When Koss excluded the question about alcohol, this figure was reduced to 11 percent; see Koss and Cook (1993:106).
36. Barrett (1982:50–51).
37. Warshaw (1988:101).
38. See discussion in Sanday (1990:1–2). See also Ehrhart and Sandler (1985).
39. O'Sullivan (1991:144; 151).
40. Sanday (1990:74–75).
41. Ibid., pp. 5–7.
42. Ibid., p. 34.
43. Ibid., pp. 71–72.
44. Ibid., p. 72.

Incestuous Sexual Abuse

The sexual abuse of a girl by a relative or close family friend has been shrouded in secrecy, even though it occurs to approximately one out of four girls. Incestuous sexual abuse challenges the assumption that safety, love, and trust can be found in the family. The pieces in this section address this issue from several perspectives. Lanette Fisher-Hertz provides an analysis of the extent to which child sexual abuse laws essentially protect abusers while they place the burden of prevention on children. Fisher-Hertz reports that in many states, the average penalty for a pedophile is lighter if he abuses his own child rather than a child outside of the family. According to Fisher-Hertz, this reality reflects the extent to which a "system of collusion—however unintentionally—works to perpetuate male sexual violence."

Little girls who are sexually abused experience many long-lasting effects, as well as immediate ones such as the loss of innocence and sense of safety. Peri Rainbow shares her compelling personal account of recovering from childhood incest. Recovering the long-buried memories and learning about their effects on her enabled Rainbow to understand and change her own destructive emotional patterns. Ruth Innes recalls that when her abuse occurred, she no longer felt safe while playing on the hill with her make-believe fairy friends. In "Fairy Summer—Or How I Learned to Wash the Dishes," Innes details her transition from a girl-child who believed in the magic of fairies one summer to a girl who washed dishes and feared the possibility of abuse the next summer.

This section closes with "Bubba Esther, 1888," a poem recounting a grandmother's experience of incest 80 years earlier. Her words remind us that although our society is often silent about childhood sexual abuse, it has long affected the lives of girls and women, who often carry the pain within them throughout their lives.

🦎 125

Protecting Male Abusers and Punishing the Women Who Confront Them: The Current Status of Child-Sex Abuse in America

LANETTE FISHER-HERTZ

In my second month as executive director of the Child Abuse Prevention Center in Dutchess County, New York, a team of sexual-abuse investigators walked into my office flush with triumph. They had obtained a signed confession from a 38-year-old man, Carmine Fowler, who had repeatedly raped and sodomized his eighth-grade daughter, Melanie, during the summer of 2000.[1] The team was thrilled to have persuaded Carmine to "tell his side of the story" since confessions are usually the only means of obtaining a felony conviction for sexual abuse of a minor. (A child's testimony alone is considered insufficient evidence for an indictment.) In this case, our burly male investigator had assured Carmine that he understood perfectly how provocative young girls could be—which was, apparently, all the macho encouragement Carmine needed. As he and the investigator shared coffee at Fowler's kitchen table, Carmine earnestly explained that he had engaged in oral, anal and vaginal sex with his 14-year-old daughter because "she was getting older," and he "didn't want her learning about this kind of stuff from a stranger." By the time Carmine was done explaining himself, the team had enough information to file a 23-count indictment.

Because I was new to the field of child sexual abuse, I had naïve hopes that justice would be served in this case. Instead, I soon learned that because Melanie was over 13 years of age and had "consented" to have sex with her father (inasmuch as any child can "consent" to her own abuse), statutory rape laws did not protect her.[2] Additionally, because Melanie was sexually assaulted by her own father, he could only be charged with E felonies, which carry the lightest sentences. Before long, Melanie was estranged from her entire family, had been moved away from all her friends and was placed many miles from the small-town school district where she had lived all her life. She has since been consigned to spend her adolescence in a juvenile detention center with other "delinquent" teens.[3]

Meanwhile, Carmine continues to enjoy the full support of his extended family, several of whom borrowed money against their mortgages to help cover his legal expenses. He plea-bargained his case down to two counts of sodomy and was eligible for parole the following summer, with a likely release date of summer 2002. Melanie's mother, Jennifer, who had been 14 years old when Carmine, then 21, impregnated her (an act that is, in itself, a seldom-prosecuted felony), was also convicted of sodomy for participating in Melanie's molestation; her defense that Carmine had forced her to participate after years of violent abuse was dismissed, and she received the same sentence as her husband.[4]

---

[1] Although I regret protecting the identity of a single rapist, I have changed names and minor, identifying details about each case in order to protect the identities of the abuse survivors. No girl should ever be ashamed to have survived sexual assault, but too often, girls and women are still treated as if they have done something shameful simply by naming the acts that have been perpetrated upon them.

[2] Historically, daughters, like wives, were considered their father's property—and rape laws were only enacted to protect men's financial interests in them. One legacy of this legal doctrine is that most statutory rape laws only apply to men who have sex with girls who are *not* family members. In February, 2001, New York updated its statutory rape laws so that anyone over 21 who has sex with anyone 16 or younger is now committing a felony—but the year before, Fowler's penetration of his daughter was not considered a felony because he had not used force.

[3] Approximately half the time, the abused child—and not the abuser—is removed from home (Russell, & Bolen, 2000). Finding foster placements for teens is difficult, and many abused girls wind up in group homes or institutional settings designed for criminals.

[4] According to Jacobs (1994), at least 20 percent of incest survivors "had witnessed a life-threatening attack on [their] mothers by the perpetrator. These findings suggest that incest is often part of a culture of violence that pervades the family."

The case was considered a major victory for our Child Abuse Prevention Center, garnering two felony convictions and sentences of record length. I struggled to understand why even this light sentence was considered an exceptionally good outcome given the horror I elicited when I spoke of these crimes in public.

"The girl was over 13, and she was no angel,"[5] one attorney explained. "Plus no force was used, which means some of these crimes may not qualify as felonies. But the bottom line is: judges hate to give any jail time when it's a family matter. This is a good outcome, believe me."[6]

I had trouble understanding this at first; why *wouldn't* judges want to imprison men who raped young girls? Politically, going after child rapists seems like a smart move. Yet the more familiar I became with the system, the less I could avoid acknowledging its function: The legal, social and family institutions surrounding child sexual abuse discourage the reporting and prosecuting of intrafamilial sexual assault. Sexual abuse by strangers is treated somewhat more seriously, but fathers or father-figures, including uncles, grandfathers, and stepfathers, account for 33 to 50 percent of girls' abuse and acquaintances for another 40 percent (Levesque, 1999). Even when the abuse is perpetrated by strangers, most men's sex crimes are unreported.

In a long-range study of 648 cases of child sexual abuse, only five percent were ever reported to the police—even though nearly one-third of victims knew their perpetrators had sexually abused other relatives (Russell, 1986). A 1988 Harvard study found 75 percent of children who reported sexual abuse by a divorced or separated parent were not believed by authorities (Armstrong, 1994). Our increased awareness has had almost no impact on conviction rates: A study of 173 men charged with child sexual abuse found just two percent were found

guilty as charged, while fewer than five served a sentence longer than one year (DeFrancis, 1969). The total conviction rate in Russell's long-term study of 648 abuse cases was one percent (Russell, 1986).

Even the few men who are convicted *spend no time in jail in a majority of cases*—with probation and counseling the routine recommendations. In many states, because the penalty for incest is lighter than the penalty for sexually abusing a child outside of one's family, defense attorneys often invoke the "incest loophole," in which sex offenders are charged with the "lesser" crime of incest. In the interests of "preserving the family," which is federally mandated as the primary goal for nearly all child abuse cases, most men charged with a criminal count of sexual abuse are given a deferred sentence and referred for "rehabilitation" (Russell, 1986).

According to the U.S. Department of Justice, 60 percent of the nation's convicted sex offenders —two-thirds of whom report that their victims were minors—are currently on parole or probation. Nearly 40 percent of their victims were under the age of 12.[7] These statistics make clear that the system functions to protect men (approximately 95% of sexual abusers are male) while punishing women and girls, who are one and a half to three times more likely than boys to be the victims of sexual assault (Finkelhor, 1981, Levesque, 1999). In national surveys, between 15% and 33% of women say they have been sexually abused (if surveys are conducted by researchers who establish one-on-one rapport, the percentage of women reporting a history of sexual abuse is higher).[8] *The Na-*

In the Fowler case, Carmine had a history of violence but had never been prosecuted for it.

[5] Sex abuse victims were often labeled promiscuous by caseworkers and district attorneys, particularly if the girls were victimized more than once.

[6] Local attorneys refused to speak on the record about any judge.

[7] A Bureau of Justice Statistics report available online, *http://www.ojp.usdoj.gov/bjs/pub/press/soo.pr,* notes that in 1997, an estimated 134,000 convicted offenders were under conditional supervision in communities throughout the United States. The report also noted that approximately 8 percent of rapists released from prison are rearrested for a new rape within three years. Data were unavailable for other sex offenses in this report.

[8] Feminist research often involves smaller samples to allow for more in-depth, personal interviews conducted by supportive clinicians who engage in extensive dialogue with interview subjects. The trust and rapport that is established during these more intimate interviews often elicits findings of a greater incidence of violence against women. The historical silence surrounding sexual violence against women creates an additional

tional Women's Study reported in 1992 that rape in the United States is "a tragedy of youth," with two-thirds of all rapes taking place during childhood or adolescence.[9]

Although all sexual assaults are seriously under-reported, child sexual abuse may be the least reported of all. Sudden, violent sexual attacks by strangers, particularly attacks that cause visible injuries to the victims are most likely to be reported to police, presumably because officials are more likely to regard injured victims as credible (Gilmartin, 1994). Since a majority of child sexual abuse is perpetrated by trusted authority figures who use bribery, coercion, emotional manipulation, threats and other non-violent methods to induce their young victims to cooperate, few child-sexual abuse victims fit the category of those most likely to be believed when they disclose. Additionally, children may suppress conscious recollection of the abuse for weeks, months or years—or may be frightened by threats or the fear that they will destroy their families if they tell. Finally, parents who do discover their children have been sexually abused may choose to handle the matter without police involvement.

During the year in which I led the local Child Abuse Prevention Center, the gendered nature of child sexual abuse was rarely discussed. Instead, the unrelenting nature of male sexual violence was often masked behind attempts to prove that there are probably a great many, as-yet-undiscovered, *female* sexual offenders. Multiple studies have been done, but none has shown women sexually abusing children in large numbers. The small percent of women who have been found to be sexually abusive have

most often been accomplices of men (Wurtele & Miller-Perrin, 1992). According to Russell (1986):

> "The truth that must be faced is that this culture's notion of masculinity—particularly as it is applied to male sexuality—predisposes men to violence, to rape, to sexually harass, and to sexually abuse children.... If this culture considered it unmasculine for men to want sexual or romantic relationships with partners who are not their equals—partners who are younger, more innocent, vulnerable, less powerful, deferential, and uncritical—then the prevalence of child sexual abuse would also be likely to decline."

Instead, law enforcement officers and child-abuse investigators, while usually well-intentioned, frequently expressed the larger society's victim-blaming and mother-blaming sentiments. Mothers are often threatened with loss of custody because their husbands or boyfriends molested their daughters—a threat that ironically mimics the threats these women hear from abusive men who warn they will take away the woman's kids (or cause them to be taken by the state) if the man's authority is challenged (Barker, 2001).

Even girls themselves are often angrier at their mothers for failing to protect them than they are at the father-figures who abused them. Meiselman (1978) found that in adulthood, 60 percent of incest survivors had at least somewhat forgiven their fathers, but 60 percent still had strong negative feelings toward their mothers—even though 75 to 95% of mothers are unaware of the abuse and, when told, support their daughters.

Daughters' attitudes reflect those of the larger society, in which mother-blame has long been part of our cultural response to incest (Russell & Bolen, 2000). Theorists claimed men molested their daughters because of the failings of their wives, who were said to be disabled, alcoholic, frigid, rejecting or otherwise not fulfilling their wifely duties. More recently, the "dysfunctional family" is treated collectively, with an emphasis on helping mothers realize how they have "enabled" abusive behavior. Mothers whose daughters have been victimized are often mandated to attend workshops to help them understand the role they played in allowing their daughters to be molested. Fathers or stepfathers may also

---

challenge for interviewers, who may not get the full story in a first interview. Kelly (1988), for example, conducted multiple interviews with 60 women and reported that "almost 75 per cent . . . remembered additional incidents of sexual violence or aspects of incidents . . . between the original interview and the follow-up."

[9] *Rape In America*, a 1992 report by the National Victim Center based on a National Institute of Drug Abuse-funded survey of a national probability sample of 4,008 adult American women. Findings included: "29 percent of all rapes happened before the victim was age 11, and an additional 32 percent happened between the ages of 11 and 17—with 22 percent occurring between the ages of 18 and 24."

be mandated to attend such programs—but if they are willing to walk away without further contact with their daughters (as many are), they can often avoid treatment altogether.

Most states have now created statutes that penalize mothers as severely for "failure to protect" a child from sexual assault as they penalize men for actually committing aggravated rape or sexual battery on a child (National Clearinghouse on Child Abuse and Neglect, 2000). In reality, because the criminal burden of proof is so high, mothers are *more often* penalized by social service agencies and family court systems for "failure to protect" than fathers are charged with the actual sexual abuse from which the mothers "failed" to protect them. In fact, some judges appear *more* likely to grant custody to fathers who *have* been accused of sexual abuse.

Mothers who refused to return their children to their abusers have often been jailed or forced into hiding with their children. Battered women, whose children are at increased risk of sexual abuse, also find that when they turn to police or social service agencies for help, they are often put on trial themselves. Marna Tucker, Washington, D.C. chair of the Mayor's Commission on Violence Against Women, notes, "If women say the wrong thing and it appears they did not protect their children adequately, they can have their kids taken away from them or be subject to prosecution for failure to protect." During an 18-month period in that city in 2000 and 2001, 66 women who sought shelter from domestic violence wound up having their own parenting investigated by Child and Family Services workers.

Cultural, racial and class divisions also lead to misperceptions about the scope and extent of the problem—and in some cases leave women torn between their desire to protect their communities and their desire to protect their daughters. Women who are members of marginalized communities may have valid reasons to distrust law enforcement officials and be reluctant to fuel perceptions that their men are deviant or criminal. Although the majority of mothers of color do believe and support their daughters' disclosures, launching a child sexual abuse investigation forces women to rely on social-service workers they may previously have viewed as the enemy—and with good reason. Black women who involved state child-protection agencies reported feeling "disempowered and devalued" (Bernard, 1997). When impoverished women call upon the system for help, they run the greatest risk of having their daughters removed from them: Children whose parents have a family income of $15,000 or less are 22 times as likely to be removed from their mothers as children in households with incomes above $30,000 (Sedlak & Broadhurst, 1996).

The innate, human desire to believe that the world is fair and that bad things only happen to people who behave badly makes us *want* to attribute at least some blame to mothers—and even to the child victims of sexual abuse (Lerner, 1980). Undergraduate students—a group still young enough to hope the world is as fair as they want it to be—are among those most likely to blame victims of hypothetical child sexual abuse cases. Given a scenario in which a little girl behaved as most incest victims do—which is to say she lay there in a state of bewilderment or disassociation while the abuse took place—many students insisted the little girl "should have resisted;" a full third said the incest was the girl's fault (Waterman & Foss-Goodman, 1984). In follow-up studies, in which subjects were presented with a similar hypothetical case of an "average" victim—a 10-year-old girl being molested by her father—even some teachers (16 percent), school psychologists (8 percent), and other mandated-reporters (those who are obligated by law to report suspicions of sexual abuse) attributed some blame to the victim for not actively resisting her abuser. These and other studies found that the more traditional one's beliefs are about gender roles, the more likely one is to blame the victim (Ford, Schindler & Medway, 1999).

Low arrest and conviction rates for male sexual abusers, systematic and institutionalized blaming of mothers and victims, and our collective, shamed silence regarding individual cases in families and communities have contributed to escalating numbers of sexual assaults on young girls (Russell & Bolen, 2000). Given the ubiquitousness of cultural

Toward a Black Feminist Understanding of Child Sexual Abuse

MELBA WILSON

Sexual harassment, violence and exploitation of women transcends class and race boundaries. Black and white men, regardless of their class position, align with each other on the basis of shared sexism. The consequences of this for black communities are that black men who are victimised by racism in common with black women also collude, as males, to oppress black women in a sexist way.

This belies a failure to understand the dynamics of class structures which seek to undermine the cohesion of black communities. Some black men (and it is my argument that it is mainly these men who sexually abuse black girls and women) fail to make the connection between racism and sexism. They play out their sexist and sexualised aggression with black girls/women as the losers. Black men who commit sexual abuse against children devalue us as a community of people and undermine attempts to throw off stereotypes and work toward shared and equitable solutions for all.

The sexism of some black men and the racism of white society results in a reluctance by some black women survivors of incest and CSA to name their abusers and therein take control of their lives. If a woman does take action, and goes to the police, for example, she is likely to be condemned by her own community for betrayal and to have her own sexuality called into question by the wider community, thus reinforcing the stereotypes. If she doesn't, she is left with maintaining the silence which gives tacit approval to the abuse, and thus undervalues her own worth as a participating and *equal* member of the community.

I view the task of black feminists as being to work toward overcoming this compulsion to blame black women for their own abuse. It is a struggle which must make us question any knee-jerk tendency to treat women as mindless objects or body parts. As black women, we should be arguing for a respect which recognises the mutual right of black women and black men to break free of the confines laid down by others; confines which have conspired to keep us all victims, by dividing one from the other. My argument is for the right to live our lives unfettered, and on our own terms; with the roles we occupy being roles that are defined by ourselves.

messages promoting male sexual power (including websites urging viewers to "CUM SEE FATHER-DAUGHTER INCEST AT ITS HOTTEST!"), good-intentioned men may feel proud simply to have avoided taking part in any acts of sexual violence. Unfortunately, the ways in which we perpetuate sexual abuse are often subtler than that. If, for example, a girl sees her father consume pornography—or react salaciously to pornographic images of teenagers in pop culture—she receives a clear message that *her* value as a sex object exists not only "out there" in the wide world, but also at home, where her earliest self-images are formed.

As women make political gains, public representations increasingly reduce women to the status of sexual objects—and incidents of male violence and child molestation rise. The current (supposedly non-pornographic) hypersexualization of young girls is creating a similar sense of confusion among girls and women—as well as among men and boys. Even non-abusive fathers find themselves saturated with increasingly sexualized images of young girls —and fewer and fewer safe points of connection in their daughters' lives. To build real relationships and strong girls, fathers need to stop demonstrating their desire to possess and objectify girls' bodies (a desire they unwittingly demonstrate every time they whistle at a young girl on TV, for example). They also must demonstrate that they *do* value autonomy in girls, including sexual autonomy in their own daughters—along with high spirits, athleticism, a fierce intellect, strength of character, and righteous anger. In sum, they need to reject rigid gender stereotyping and admire all that is the antithesis of the passive, obedient "perfect victim." And mothers need to be empowered—socially and economically—to do the same. If we ignore the dynamics that empower abusers, we will be addressing sexual violence in a vacuum.

To effect real change, we need to speak plainly to the men in our lives about the fear in ours—and to keep speaking until they are as horrified by the preponderance of male sexual violence as we are. (We'll know they've heard us when they stop telling us to just relax.) If there's a child molester in our lives, we must stop protecting him with our silence —and encourage every woman who confides her own dark secrets to do the same. We need to name and publicly shame every perpetrator we know— from the corporate manager getting his R&R with a 12-year-old in Bangkok to the online pal we discover using child porn to the elderly uncle who held us too hard on his lap and still makes girls squirm at family gatherings. Finally, we need to celebrate the courage of the children who endured these sexual atrocities—by letting them know we believe them and are proud of them for speaking out—and that they were not responsible for their abuse. We need to make girls glad, not regretful, when they tell.

Finally, speak-outs among women, in which we reveal to one another the extent of the violence in our lives, are an important first step—but we cannot take back the night until the men assaulting us are dragged out into the daylight. Our collective, unashamed admissions and unified demands for justice are needed to end sexual terrorism in our lives —and in the lives of all the lost girls and boys currently enduring lives of sexual slavery around the world. Our vibrant, sexually alive bodies, and the beautiful hopeful bodies of all our children, deserve nothing less.   [2002]

WORKS CITED

Armstrong, Louise. *Rocking the Cradle of Sexual Politics: What Happened When Women Said Incest.* Reading, MA: Addison-Wesley Publishing Co. 1994.

Barker, Karlyn. "Policy Turns the Abused into Suspects: Mothers Find Seeking Help Can Backfire." *The Washington Post.* 12/26/01.B1-B4.

Barry, Kathleen. *The Prostitution of Sexuality.* NY: New York University Press, 1995.

Berger, Leslie Beth. *Incest, Work and Women: Understanding Consequences of Incest on Women's Careers, Work and Dreams.* Springfield, IL: Charles C. Thomas, 1998.

Bernard, Claudia. "Black Mothers' Emotional and Behavioral Responses to the Sexual Abuse of Their Children." *Out of the Darkness: Contemporary Perspectives on Family Violence.* Kaufman, Glenda and Jana L. Jasinski, Eds. Thousand Oaks, CA: Sage, 1997: 80–94.

DeFrancis, Vincent. *Protecting the Child Victim of Sex Crimes Committed by Adults.* Denver: American Humane Society: 1969.

Finkelhor, David. *Sexually Abused Children.* NY: The Free Press, 1981.

Ford, Harriett, Claudia B. Schindler, and Frederic J. Medway. "School Professionals' Attributions of Blame for Child Sexual Abuse." *Journal of School Psychology,* Vol. 39, No. 1 (2001): 25–44.

Gilmartin, Pat. *Rape, Incest, and Child Sexual Abuse: Consequences and Recovery.* NY & London: Garland, 1994.

Herman, Judith Lewis. *Father-Daughter Incest.* Cambridge, MA: Harvard University Press, 1981.

Itzen, Catherine. "Pornography and the Organization of Intra- and Extrafamilial Child Sexual Abuse." *Out of the Darkness.* Glenda Kaufman and Jana Jasinski, eds. pp. 58–79.

Jacobs, Janet Liebman. *Victimized Daughters: Incest and the Development of the Female Self.* NY & London: Routledge, 1994.

Kelly, Liz. *Surviving Sexual Violence.* Minneapolis: University of Minnesota Press, 1988.

Lerner, Melvin. *The Belief in a Just World: A Fundamental Delusion.* NY: Plenum, 1980.

Levesque, Roger J.R. *Sexual Abuse of Children: A Human Rights Perspective.* Bloomington and Indianapolis: Indiana University Press, 1999.

Meiselman, Karen. *Incest: A Psychological Study of Causes and Effects, with Treatment Recommendations.* San Francisco: Josey-Bass, 1978.

Mrazek, Patricia Beezley and C. Henry Kempe, Eds. *Sexually*

Abused Children and Their Families. Oxford: Pergamon Press, 1987.

"Pedophile Priest: A Shameful Silence." *The Week: The Best of the U.S. and International Media*. February 1, 2001.

Rosen, Leora N. and Michelle Etlin. *The Hostage Child: Sex Abuse Allegations in Custody Disputes*. Bloomington & Indianapolis: Indiana University Press, 1996.

Rape In America, a 1992 report by the National Victim Center. Cited in "The Scope of Violent Crime and Victimization." http://www.ojp.usdoj.gov/ovc/assist/nvaa/ch01scope.htm

Romero, Mary & Abigail J. Stewart, eds. *Women's Untold Stories: Breaking Silence, Talking Back, Voicing Complexity*. NY: Routledge, 1999.

Russell, Diana E. H. and Rebecca M. Bolen. *The Epidemic of Rape and Child Sexual Abuse in the United States*. Thousand Oaks, CA: Sage Publications, 2000.

Russell, Diana. *The Secret Trauma: Incest in the Lives of Girls and Women*. NY: Basic Books Inc., 1986.

———. *Sexual Exploitation*. Beverly Hills, CA: Sage, 1984.

Sedlak, Andrea J. and Broadhurst, Diane D. The Third National Incidence Study of Child Abuse and Neglect (NIS-3): Final Report. Washington, D.C.: U.S. Department of Health and Human Services, Government Printing Office, 1996.

Tower, Cynthia Crosson. *Secret Scars: A Guide for Survivors of Child Sexual Abuse*. NY: Penguin, 1988.

Walker, Lenore E.A., *Handbook on Sexual Abuse of Children*. NY: Springer Publishing Co., 1988.

Waterman, C.K. & Foss-Goodman, D. "Child molesting: Variables Relating to Attribution of Fault to Victims, Offenders, and Non-participating Parents." *The Journal of Sex Research*, 20 (1984): 329–349.

Wurtele, Sandy K. and Cindy L. Miller-Perrin. *Preventing Child Sexual Abuse: Sharing the Responsibility*. Lincoln: University of Nebraska Press, 1992.

🌿 126

Making Sense of the Experience of Incest Survivors

PERI L. RAINBOW

I grew into adulthood with lingering questions about my past. Mostly, I wondered why I couldn't remember anything that happened to me before my parents' divorce, when I was twelve. I wasn't quite sure what I was supposed to remember, and I cautiously asked friends about their childhood memories. "Do you remember when you were seven years old, or eight, or six?" I'd listen to the details my friends remembered, not just special occasions like birthdays or holidays, but daily occurrences and what it felt like to be a child, and I'd wonder why I didn't know this about my life. I never let anyone know why I was asking and never revealed my own gaps. I didn't understand why, but I felt ashamed about not remembering. I did have what I call "Kodak memories." I would look at a childhood picture and repeat stories that were told to me about those times, vaguely sensing familiarity. But I felt no real connection with the child in the photograph. It was as if I was looking into the eyes of a stranger. Some unknown child stared back at me. Although I knew intellectually that the child was me, I felt deep inside that I was someone different. I didn't know then that the sexual abuse I had suffered was too painful to remember and that by blocking it out, I had also blocked out the memories of my childhood. I couldn't remember what being a child actually felt like. Feeling and knowing were to remain separate and distinct experiences for me for a long time to come.

I was a daring and promiscuous adolescent. At age fourteen, I had my first consensual sexual experience, and I also began to experiment with drugs. The fear and anticipation I felt when taking risks were uncannily familiar. So was sexual stimulation, and I found some comfort in this familiarity. Something about these experiences, though, while familiar and therefore comforting, also felt unsatisfying and vaguely frightening.

I spent my adolescence escaping life and my feelings about it, through chemicals, sex, and music. I was fortunate to connect with people (friends my own age and older) who were able to keep me relatively safe, despite my muted awareness. I was, however, raped by a "friend" at age fifteen and molested by my mother's (male) partner at around the same time. I dismissed these incidents as insignificant and my fault. Actually, I didn't think about these incidents or define them as sexual assaults until my first college women's studies course. Instead of attending to the life my mother provided, I created my own "family" and spent a lot of time away from home. I was introduced to Jerry Garcia and the Grateful Dead at age fourteen, and their world—concert touring, LSD, marijuana, and sex—became my own. My friends and acquaintances became my family. They kept me distant from the pain buried inside, and perhaps in some ways they gave me the love that I needed to survive. I found solace in my head, using drugs to stay there, and found love through sex, using my body to feel wanted. I didn't understand then how significant this separation was and how I was doing exactly what I had learned to do as a child to survive the incest. I survived without feeling very much for many years. I was blessed with a fair amount of intelligence, and that, coupled with charm and an air of aloofness possible for one who rarely feels, enabled me to do well in high school.

I took these patterns (survival skills) with me to college and spent the first two years experimenting with drugs and men. I barely passed my classes, as I was rarely if ever fully present at any point during that time. Toward the end of my sophomore year, an incident occurred that I was absolutely unprepared for. I was working at a vacation resort to support myself through college. One day, as I was working by the swimming pool giving out sporting equipment, I looked up and saw Bill, my father's best friend. He had been my music teacher, my caretaker, my "uncle"; he was family. A flood of physical and emotional feelings engulfed me when I recognized him. I was repulsed and terrified, and I was confused, as I could not explain any of this. My body reacted to these feelings as if it were a completely separate entity. I choked. I couldn't breathe and gasped for air, immediately hyperventilating. I felt excruciating pain in my stomach and in my vagina. I doubled over, vomited, and began to cry uncontrollably. It was as if something horrible was happening to my body, only right then and there, nothing was. As soon as I could, I locked myself in the equipment hut and rocked myself to safety. Although my mind had no memory of the sexual abuse, my body remembered.

That first flashback set in motion a process in which I have been involved, both consciously and subconsciously, ever since. In the many flashbacks that followed, remnants of the past would surface, sometimes like torn pieces of still photos stored in my brain, other times like a flood. With each flashback I was thrown into the past, and I felt the terror and the pain I must have known as a little girl. I was fortunate that these experiences lasted only seconds or moments, but from each one I emerged frightened and confused. Memories would also surface, not only of the abuse but also of happy times in my childhood, times I had not previously recalled. During flashbacks, I felt as if I were occupying the past. I was fully conscious of the present during the memories and simply took a mental note of their surfacing. I am still aware when new memories surface and always declare it out loud. At one point I wrote down everything I remembered, good and bad, as I feared that I would forget again. I now know that once the mind releases these things, they are back forever. Survivors remember when our minds are convinced that our bodies can tolerate the pain of knowing. Once we know, we know. It's interesting to me that the memories of the abuse, although confusing, did not surprise me. Somewhere inside I had always known. Knowing and believing, however, are two very different things.

What happened for me next further confused me and made it difficult for me to trust my judgment. I told my mother. I said, "I think Bill did something to me." She said, "Oh, don't be ridiculous—you just never liked him." It felt like my head was about to pop off my shoulders. I felt invisible, and for a moment I believed her. "I must be crazy" was what went through my mind, but then quickly, perhaps because of the vividness of my recent emotions, I thought, "No way." I did not, however, try to convince my mother of what I barely knew myself. It wasn't until four years later, when Bill's picture appeared in a local paper as he was being led away by police for molesting a little girl, that my mother believed me. Interestingly, that arrest cracked my mother's own wall of denial, and she remembered that Bill had been arrested at least once before, when I was about seven years old. He had exposed himself to a group of young campers near the place where our families spent our summers. It is the place where my most severe memories of abuse are from.

Once I began to believe that something actually did happen to me, the memories and flashbacks, as vague and disjointed as they were, became more disturbing. Now that my body was mine, it felt like it was betraying me. I felt crazy. I had difficulty being alone and difficulty being with others. Drugs helped to numb the pain but also interfered with my ability to function as a college student. I took a leave from school and left the state for several months, most of which was spent in a marijuana fog.

I returned to college believing more than ever that I had experienced something horrible involving Bill but ready to focus on something outside myself. My memories were still vague, and perhaps shifting my focus was a much needed distraction. I also believed that because of my own suffering, my college education, and my newly recognized class privilege that I could and ought to help others. I had always wanted to work in human services. I felt comfortable with pain and suffering and, as I could not touch my own, felt passionate about the suffering of others. I had declared a sociology major early on in my college career. After my hiatus, I stumbled upon an elective that was cross-listed with the Women's Studies Program. The course, entitled "Violence Against Women in the U.S.," was taught by a soft-spoken, even-tempered, radical feminist named Alice Fix. In this class, I realized that it was not my fault that a "friend" forced me to have intercourse against my will, despite the fact that I had invited him to my room. Redefining and clarifying that experience from my adolescence helped me to better understand my connection to suffering. Although I still didn't really know what had happened to me as a child, I did know that at age fifteen, Greg's behavior was not unfamiliar. The more I learned about other women's experiences, with sexual violence in particular and life in general, the more I felt a bond with other women. Like the survivors I work with in group therapy, I began to experience women's power. I learned about resistance and survival and became aware of my own.

It would be wonderful to say that my healing began there and progressed upwardly thereafter; however, healing from trauma does not work that way. Survivors take "baby steps" and often pace themselves so as not to be overwhelmed. I slowed down

the process of recognizing my childhood abuse by doing what I had always done so skillfully: I split myself in two. I separated my mind (knowledge) from my body (feelings) as a child. I reentered a familiar dissociated state of being. Intellectually, I became passionate about feminism and learning about women's lives. I became politically active, joining organizations, demonstrating, educating others about violence against women. I worked at a shelter for battered women and became the director of a women's crisis center. I was a leader, using my head to guide me. My body, however, stayed in what was familiar and unsafe.

I struggled for two years to maintain this dichotomy. Feminism tugged at my body. The personal, after all, is the political, and I had difficulty keeping my body, my heart, distant from the lives of other women. I had, throughout my life, often found my body at risk from others and even tried on several occasions to take my own life as well. Now, I was meeting other women who did so too, and as we learned more about and valued each other, it didn't seem to make much sense. It took nearly dying at the hands of my partner, however, and a radical intervention by a women's studies professor to move me to take action on my own behalf. I left the abusive relationship and began therapy. I also pursued my professional development in a more focused way.

Through my study of sexual abuse I learned about the dissociative process and became determined to share this knowledge with others. I wanted survivors and those who care about us to know that the residual effects, those "crazy" thoughts and behaviors, make perfect sense and that there is hope for recovery. It was knowledge and feelings together, perhaps in sync for me for the first time, that convinced me to continue on this path. The emotions I felt were connected not only to my own experience as a victim but to the courage of millions of survivors, who have struggled to understand and improve the quality of their lives. My feminist beliefs gave me faith in the possibility of change and appreciation for passion as a wonderfully powerful force.

As a budding feminist therapist, I recognized the misogyny inherent in men's abuse of women and children. I believe that the sexist socialization of men plays an important role in this. I also believe that as a feminist, it is my responsibility to take action. And so, I have proceeded to learn and to share, helping others to understand and heal.

Bennett Braun's work on traumatic memory helped me to understand what I and millions of trauma survivors have experienced. He uses the levels of the "BASK" Model of Dissociation (behavior, affect, sensation, and knowledge) to suggest that when a traumatic event occurs, it is often fragmented by the brain and stored separately on each of these levels. One level—for example, knowledge of an event—may be accessible to one's consciousness.[1] I knew that those childhood pictures were of me; however, sensation, feelings related to the event, were not available. I could not recall what it felt like to be her. The process by which one's brain separates these levels is called dissociation. A person may dissociate from the past, such as I did regarding my experience with childhood. or may dissociate in the present, such as not feeling events currently occurring. I, like many survivors, incorporated dissociation into my functioning as a child, so that I could avoid feeling and reliving painful events. As they were happening, the sensations were stored in one place and the knowledge in another. Both levels remained distant from my consciousness; the knowledge, however, was closer to the surface. Also like many survivors, I experience current dissociation. When a trauma survivor is in what is perceived to be an unsafe situation, she or he may describe feeling nothing or numb or might lose conscious knowledge and therefore not recall what she or he did during that particular time period. Dissociation is a common protective mechanism that shields the survivor from events or memories of events too painful to feel. When controlled, it is a remarkable tool a survivor might use to get through uncomfortable situations. Taking control, learning to ground oneself

to the present, is an important part of the healing process. It is initially a difficult concept to internalize, since dissociation first occurred automatically.

I also learned that seeing the man who abused me triggered the instant recall that occurred in my body and that my response was a common reaction to the surfacing of a traumatic memory. Since I was still so psychologically defended, so unsafe, and therefore not ready to access the memory cognitively, my mind kept part of it buried. After seeing my perpetrator, however, my body no longer could do so. Unlike a typical memory, though, in which you know that this thing happened in the past, an abreaction or flashback feels as if it's occurring in the present. I felt like I was back there, and my body was responding to an assault. I felt the physical pain, the terror, and the disgust. I was, for those moments, approximately six years old.

Survivors of trauma experience many forms of dissociation when memories of the past are triggered; a smell, a sound, a color, a person, a type of food—anything can trigger a memory. Flashbacks can be as dangerous as any form of dissociation, since one loses consciousness of the present while it's happening. For a few seconds, a few minutes, perhaps a few days, a survivor might be responding to the past, not the present. This is a confusing state of consciousness and easy to mistrust. It mimics the state of mind of an incest victim, who is often disbelieved and made to feel that her true reality is not possible.

As I reflect on my own healing process and the healing of the hundreds of survivors I have known, I find it perfectly understandable that so many deny that the abuse ever really happened. The survivors I have known are not anxious to identify as such. Why would anyone want to believe that the person or persons who were supposed to love and protect them brutalized them instead? And because our society has denied the existence of incest from the time of the subject's first public appearance, denial is institutionally supported. In her invaluable book entitled *Trauma and Recovery,* Judith Herman explains how Sigmund Freud, the "father" of psychoanalysis,

---

[1] B. G. Braun, "The BASK Model of Dissociation," *Dissociation* 1 (1) (1988), 5.

identified childhood sexual abuse at the root of the hysterical symptoms of his adult female patients.[2] Freud, however, ensconced as he was in the upper-middle-class life of Vienna, was unwilling to confront what Herman calls the "radical social implications" of his theory about the origins of female hysteria—that incestuous abuse was widespread even among the middle class. Unwilling to risk the derision of his colleagues and the possible loss of financial support for his work, Freud reinterpreted his patients' stories as fantasies resulting from an unsatisfied and immature desire to have sex with their fathers. By defining his female patients as hysterical liars, Freud laid the foundation for the future of medical and psychiatric treatment of women and the pervasive belief in the dishonest, immature, and pathologically sexual nature of women and children. With this one decision, Freud laid the groundwork for the institutional denial of the abuse of female children by adult men.

Survivors of sexual abuse also learn to mistrust their own judgments and perceptions and often have difficulty trusting other people. In addition survivors often have difficulty expressing anger and engaging in sexual intimacy. As survivors often associate anger with violence (a logical connection for many), the notion of expressing anger is terrifying. Some survivors cannot imagine expressing anger without hurting themselves or someone else, and many often do. For some, getting in touch with their anger means allowing years of rage to surface, and that kind of explosion seems deadly. It is as if one has been sitting on top of an active volcano, and moving from that spot will result in a cascade of hot lava that could carry anyone in its path very far away. Learning to own one's anger, understand one's rage, and express these emotions safety are important parts of the healing process. With guidance, survivors have developed quite remarkable ways of safely releasing rage and finding support from the people they love to deal with the frightening intensity of these emotions.

Sexual intimacy, understandably, is also problematic for many survivors. When control of one's body was taken and exploited for another's pleasure, it is difficult to find physical closeness with another person pleasurable. Sometimes survivors feel betrayed by their own bodies because they remember feeing pleasurable sensations stimulated by an abuser. Survivors frequently avoid sexual intimacy. Some dissociate, so as to maintain a relationship without actually feeling anything. Others equate sex with love and, as they have been taught and as I did, use their bodies to feel a sense of self-worth. Unfortunately, each of these scenarios can have negative and often dangerous consequences. Survivors need to find safe consensual situations in which to experience sexual pleasure and to develop boundaries. This work, like the rest, involves trust and time.

Survivors who have experienced healing and worked to move beyond their victimization have chosen to live life with full awareness. Moving on means accepting what has happened and its effects and living life to its fullest despite the difficulties. It means using newly identified skills to improve the quality of one's life and acknowledging the support of others. Although some would argue that forgiveness is essential to healing, I believe that some things are simply unforgivable. I do not forgive the man who forced himself on me again and again, throughout my childhood. For me, forgiveness came in forgiving myself, for not being good enough, pretty enough, smart enough, to have the kind of love I had always wanted. It also came for me in forgiving my mother who, although not the perfect parent, did all she knew how to do. I believe she did the best she could, and I have been truly blessed with the opportunity to build a solid relationship with her. I have also been blessed with the chance to make a contribution to the lives of incest survivors. I am committed to sharing my knowledge with others and to working for change. As a psychotherapist, a teacher, a friend, and a lover, I use my skills every day. I believe, however, that real change—an end to sexual

---

[2] J. L. Herman, *Trauma and Recovery* (New York: HarperCollins, 1992), pp. 13–14.

violence—will only come through transforming the institutions of our society that support and perpetuate it: the media, which surround us with objectified female bodies; the medical system, which denies and pathologizes women's pain; the legal system, which claims to seek truth while ignoring women's realities; the institutions of family and religion, which are traditionally organized to repress women and every other place in society where women are devalued and men are taught that true masculinity, an ideal to strive for, is defined by one's ability to gain power over others, by any means possible. My abuser no longer controls my life, but I am bombarded with messages daily that reinforce my vulnerability as a woman. I am determined to control my own life, in spite of these messages, and to use my power to promote change. I know that this work is not easy. I know that I am not alone. I honor each day as an accomplishment.   [1999]

127

Fairy Summer — Or How I Learned To Wash Dishes

RUTH INNES

I didn't want to take the man up the hill with me. I didn't want to show him where I played. But he asked very nicely and I was afraid to be rude. No one had ever taught me that a child could say no when a grownup asked for something.

My grandparents had a restaurant and lived in the apartment above it. One summer, when I was five years old, grandma and grandpa took a trip to Sweden so my mother ran the restaurant for them. To make it easier, my parents moved from our house to the living quarters above the restaurant.

There wasn't anyone for me to play with around the restaurant, but I had always been a solitary child and liked playing alone. My favorite place to play was up on the hill behind the restaurant. There was a little spring up there which made even the hottest

day seem cool. I was sure the fairies came there to drink and I spent hours making fairy houses with the softest of mosses for their carpets and beds, pretty pebbles for their chairs and tables, and flower petals for bedclothes and tablecloths. The nooks at the roots of the big hemlock trees were wonderful spots for fairy houses, and damp earth from around the spring made good stout walls to keep the fairies safe while they slept. Sometimes, when I inspected the houses early in the morning, there were definite signs that the fairies had been there—a tantalizing footstep in the moss or a bit of dust from the fairy wings left on the furniture. I shivered with delight and carefully smoothed out the moss and dusted the furniture.

I hated the days when it rained and I had to stay inside to play. Those days I spent a lot of time at the kitchen table cutting out paper dolls and peeking into the bar that stretched across the restaurant, watching the men who sat there drinking beer. Most of those men worked for the lumber company that was sporadically cutting timber around town. When they weren't actually in the woods working, those men seemed to be sitting at our bar drinking beer. They worked in the woods and they drank beer, which made them hiccup a lot, so it seemed very logical to me that they were called woodhicks.

Some of the woodhicks fussed over me, asking dumb questions about how old I was and where I got my rosy cheeks. I didn't want to talk to them but mother and dad always told me to be polite. So when one of the woodhicks stopped me as I was about to start up the hill and asked me to take him along, I didn't know what to say. I didn't want to, but I didn't want to offend him either. I can still remember his beery breath in my face as he coaxed, "Come on, show me where you play, pretty please."

"You wouldn't like it up there," I finally told him. "And besides, your feet are too big and you might step on a fairy."

"I'll be very careful where I put my feet . . . I'll walk softly," he persisted.

Reluctantly I started up the path with the man close behind me. I went as fast as I could, hoping that after I showed him he'd go back down to the bar.

We hadn't gone very far when he suggested we sit down. "No," I protested, "this is not up the hill yet. This is just the path. You said you wanted to see."

"What's the hurry? I need to rest a little," the man said, sitting down by a fallen log. "Come sit with me . . . we both need to rest."

I was puzzled. This man worked in the woods all day. Surely he could walk further than that without being tired. Still at a loss as to the proper thing to do, I finally sat down beside him. He immediately put one arm around my waist and pulled me close to him. He put his other hand on my knee and pretended to brush off a bit of dirt. "Oops," he said, as the dirt turned out to be a scab, and then he quickly moved his hand up my leg and under my shorts to stroke the crotch of my panties. His sour breath was in my face again and he began to lean over me even closer. I didn't know why, but I knew something was wrong and I broke away from him and ran down the hill as fast as I could.

"Here now, come back girlie, I won't hurt you," he called after me, but I kept running.

Down at the restaurant I rushed into the kitchen bathroom and hid behind the door. I didn't dare shut the door because that meant the bathroom was in use and I didn't want anyone to know I was in there. I was afraid that the man might come looking for me and someone would tell him where I was. I hid behind that door for what seemed like a long time; I kept peeking through the crack the door made where it was hinged to the wall, but I couldn't see very much. I thought that if he appeared in the narrow view I'd slam and lock the door.

Mother finally came in to use the bathroom and discovered me cowering behind the door.

"What are you doing in here?" she asked, looking at me curiously.

"Nothing," I answered, "just hiding."

"Who are you hiding from?" Mother demanded.

"That man," I said.

"What man?"

"That woodhick I ran away from."

"Tell me exactly what you're talking about."

So I told mother about the woodhick who asked so politely for me to take him up the hill and how I was afraid to be rude so I'd started up the hill with him but then ran away from him.

"What did he do to you?" Mother insisted on knowing.

"He felt my panties," I admitted, feeling ashamed.

Mother rushed out of the bathroom and into the restaurant searching for that man, but he wasn't there. When she came back to the bathroom I knew she was very angry and she said to me, "Don't you ever do that again!"

I started to cry. Mother dropped to her knees and put her arms around me. She explained that she wasn't angry at me, but at the man, that she only meant I should never go anywhere with anyone again but come and tell her if anyone even suggested it. In spite of her reassurances I felt that I had done something wrong.

The rest of the summer was ruined for me. Up the hill was a dangerous place to go. What if the man was up there waiting for me? Or what if he came up while I was there and wanted to touch me again? I stayed away from the hill and, because I hung around the kitchen at the restaurant so much, mother decided I might as well learn how to wash dishes. By the next summer I didn't believe in fairies any more.   [1992]

 128

Bubba* Esther, 1888

RUTH WHITMAN

She was still upset,
she wanted to tell me,
she kept remembering
his terrible hands:

> how she came, a young girl
> of seventeen, a freckled
> fairskinned Jew from Kovno

———————

*grandma

to Hamburg with her uncle
and stayed in an old house
and waited while he bought
the steamship tickets
so they could sail to America

and how he came into her room
sat down on the bed, touched
her waist, took her by the
breast, said for a kiss
she could have her ticket,

her skirts were rumpled, her
petticoat torn, his teeth were
broken, his breath full of
onions, she was ashamed

still ashamed, lying
eighty years later
in the hospital bed,
trying to tell me,
trembling, weeping with anger   [1980]

PART VIII

Changing Our World

Throughout history women have worked to improve their lives in the workplace, in schools, and in communities. While changing the position of women in our society can seem like an overwhelming task, women have, in fact, made significant progress when they have organized. By articulating a critique of male domination and demanding the inclusion of women in social and political life, feminist movements have been crucial in accomplishing these changes. By thus changing the environment, organized feminism has supported and inspired women's efforts to work on their own behalf wherever they are. This Part, therefore, begins with a brief survey of what historians often refer to as the first and second waves of feminism in the U.S.

The metaphor of waves has been the subject of a lively debate among historians. Research has shown that the periods before and between waves should not be seen as periods of dormancy because, while feminism may not have been as visible, many important efforts to challenge male domination occurred in various contexts. Yet the periods of mass mobilization that have been identified as waves, while they built on the groundwork laid by earlier efforts, accelerated the pace of change, created major shifts in popular consciousness, engaged large numbers of women in various feminist activities, and had profound effects on countless women's lives. Bearing in mind that feminist activity has taken a variety of forms throughout history, we examine the movements identified as the first and second waves of feminism looking at both the strengths and weaknesses, so that knowledge of the past can inform our efforts to improve the position of women in the present.

The first wave of feminism, which emerged in the 1840s, began with a broad-ranging critique of women's social, political, and economic position in society as expressed by the Resolutions of the Seneca Falls Convention. Much of this initial breadth, however, was lost as the movement narrowed to focus on achieving the right to vote. The second wave of feminism that emerged in the 1960s reengaged many of these issues, developing a critique of the politics of personal life through a process that came to be called consciousness raising, an examination of one's personal life through feminist lenses.

Throughout the next three decades the movement grew and challenged the subordination of women in a wide variety of arenas. While the achievements of the feminist movement have been impressive, however, the goal of creating a society in which women are able to participate fully in all aspects of social, economic, and political life is still unrealized. In the midst of the process of approaching this goal, a multilayered assault against feminism was launched. In the 1980s the "new right," a coalition of conservative and religious organizations, mounted an offensive against women's rights and has succeeded in restricting women's reproductive freedom, diluting affirmative action programs, and preventing the passage of the Equal Rights Amendment. Most people in our country favor equal rights and reproductive freedom for women, but they have not been sufficiently organized to prevent the erosion of many of the accomplishments of the previous decade. While there was still a great deal of support for the general goals of feminism, many women hesitated to identify themselves with the feminist movement. "I'm not a feminist, but," a refrain of the 1980s, represented the success of a media attack on feminism that Susan Faludi exposed in her best-selling book *Backlash*.

Nevertheless, feminism has not disappeared but continues to grow, taking new forms as it tackles new problems. Women throughout the world are organizing on their own behalf, and in the last 25 years a global feminist movement has developed which has insisted that women's rights are human rights. Women throughout the world are organizing against violence against women and the international sex trade, demanding women's reproductive rights, working to enhance women's economic independence and to improve women's education, demanding increased political rights for women, and challenging the rise of fundamentalism. Western (sometimes called northern) feminists meeting with women in Africa, Asia, the Middle East, and Latin America (sometimes called southern) have realized that feminism must encompass survival issues, such as access to food and water in order to support women's struggles for self-determination. In past years, feminists seeking to connect women of various countries have established transnational organizations, sponsored international conferences, and promoted education about women's issues in various parts of the world. Such networks increase the possibility of cooperative action across national boundaries. A global feminist movement can challenge what Charlotte Bunch calls the "dynamic of domination embedded in male violence" by working against militarism, racism, and sexism wherever they exist.

Activists throughout the world have challenged international financial institutions such as the International Monetary Fund and the World Bank, whose policies have had harmful effects on women. For example, in order to ensure that countries that owe money to financial institutions can pay off their debt, Structural Adjustment Programs were imposed on many countries in the developing world. These programs have resulted in cutting back social services and pushing countries to develop export-oriented industries in which hundreds of thousands of young women work for low wages under intolerable working conditions. Since many of these factories are subcontracted by U.S.-based corporations such as The Gap, Wal-Mart, and Nike, an anti-sweatshop movement has developed in the United States. Students have played an important role in this movement by insisting that their campuses refuse to buy school apparel from corporations that have not agreed to guarantee their workers basic human rights.

In the past decade, there have been signs of another revival of feminist energy in the United States. The massive increase in wage-earning mothers in the last two decades is heightening awareness of the need for public policy changes that will support women and their families; the reproductive rights movement has been reinvigorated in response to the anti-abortion decisions of the Supreme Court; and women are running for office with money raised by feminist fundraising efforts.

A third wave of American feminism is beginning to take shape. Leslie Heywood and Jennifer Drake, two women who describe themselves as third-wave feminists, see their movement as combining "elements of second-wave critique of beauty and culture, sexual abuse, and power structures, while it also acknowledges and makes use of the pleasure, danger, and defining power of those structures."[1] Women singers are introducing passionate feminist lyrics into popular music, and young women are producing "zines" that express anger at the pressures on young girls to conform to media-inspired images of femininity and outrage at violence against women. Young women are also using the Internet to organize and network around a wide variety of issues. Young feminists have reclaimed the word "girl," which second-wave feminists found demeaning, infusing it with a new spirit of independence, defiance, and female solidarity. In *Manifesta: Young Women, Feminism and the Future,* Amy Richards and Jennifer Baumgardner describe third-wave feminism as building on the accomplishments of earlier feminists, addressing the obstacles that continue to keep women subordinate. They see third-wave feminist activism as encompassing a range of activities from "the single mother who organizes the baby-sitting chain on Election Day so that all the housebound mothers can vote" to mass demonstrations against unfair policies and practices.[2]

One of the strengths of contemporary feminism is its multi-issue approach. As women confront sexism in different situations, new issues emerge and our understanding of women's experience deepens. The final section of this Part includes descriptions of women organizing in various contexts from the 1970s to the 2000s. They tell stories of women who, inspired by the growing legitimacy of feminist concerns, refused to accept unfair treatment or who perceived a problem and decided to do something about it. In all of these organizing efforts, consciousness raising was a crucial ingredient since women needed to talk to each other about their experience in order to develop strategy. In some situations, such as women dealing with AIDS in prison, breaking the silence in itself makes an enormous difference. These stories demonstrate that, despite the media proclamations, feminism did not die in the 1980s; it lived in the many efforts of women organizing around specific issues on both a national and local level.

The final selections address current feminist activism. As women develop strategies and tactics to address current issues, they are reviving methods such as civil disobedience and developing new approaches to change. Young women bring a fresh perspective to feminism as they grew up in a world in which feminist ideas and language were an integral part of our culture, even though much work needs to be done to achieve feminist goals.

---

[1] Leslie Heywood and Jennifer Drake, "Introduction," in *Third Wave Agenda: Being Feminist, Doing Feminism,* Leslie Heywood and Jennifer Drake, eds. (Minneapolis: University of Minnesota Press, 1997), p. 3.
[2] Amy Richards and Jennifer Baumgardner, *Manifesta: Young Women, Feminism and the Future* (New York: Farrar, Strauss and Giroux, 2000).

Feminism as a Social Movement

We discussed feminist *ideas* earlier in this book, but we turn in this section to a consideration of feminism as a *social movement,* beginning with a brief history of feminism in the United States from 1848 to 1990 and documents from the first and second wave of feminism. The first document was signed by the people who gathered at the first women's rights convention in Seneca Falls, New York, in 1848 and describes the wide range of issues they discussed. It is useful to think about the extent to which the goals of the Seneca Falls convention have been achieved and what issues seem most resistant to change.

Three years later, Sojourner Truth addressed a women's rights convention in Akron, Ohio. The speech that she made was popularized by Frances Gage, who wrote it down 12 years after it was given, and differed significantly from the version that was reported at the time. The Gage version, featuring the refrain "Ain't I a Woman," became a rallying cry for the feminist movement, but historians believe that the newspaper version was closer to her actual words. We present first the speech reported in the *Salem Anti-Slavery Bugle* in 1851 that historian Nell Painter has recovered in her biographical work on Sojourner Truth; we follow this with Frances Gage's version.

The third document was written in the early days of the second wave of feminism. It describes the evolution of consciousness raising as a technique for understanding women's oppression, an important source of insight for women's liberation activists in the 1960s and 1970s. The insights that emerged in consciousness raising often laid the foundation for action projects. As women talked about their bodies, for example, they confronted their own woeful ignorance, a legacy of years of secrecy and shame. Convinced that knowledge was an essential ingredient of controlling one's own body, they determined to teach themselves and each other about women's physiology. Susan Brownmiller tells the story of the Boston Women's Health Book Collective, which emerged from this process and produced a book that was on the best-seller list for years, was translated into many languages, and has become a valuable resource for women throughout the world.

In the next four essays, women of color discuss the analysis that emerged from their discussion of the inseparable, multiple oppressions that they encounter. Their writing speaks to the necessity of working against all forms of oppression simultaneously, which involves working with men against racism while challenging their sexism, an often painful process.

The feminism of women of color draws on the day-to-day heroism of mothers and grandmothers, which is embodied for Barbara Smith in Alice Walker's definition of "womanist." Chicana feminists, Alma Garcia explains, have had to struggle against sexist traditions deeply embedded in their culture. In an essay written after attending the founding convention of Ohoyo, a national organization of American Indian women in 1979, Kate Shanley points out that American Indian feminists seek to retain the alternative family forms and communal values of tribal life. As all these selections point out, coalitions among different groups of women can only be meaningful if each group has had a chance to develop its own agenda.

Like any movement that challenges established hierarchies and cherished beliefs, the feminist movement has encountered ridicule and opposition. In her best-selling book *Backlash: The Undeclared War on American Women*, Susan Faludi exposed the media assault on feminism during the 1980s. Faludi argues that the press, TV, movies, and fashion industry have endeavored to convince women to relinquish the struggle for equality and respect by proclaiming that although women have won all the rights they need, it only makes them miserable. In fact, equality has not been achieved, and women are struggling to combine work and family without institutional supports.

Despite the backlash, women throughout the world continue to organize against violence, discrimination, and exploitation. One of the most exciting developments of the 1980s was the networking among women from around the world. Many international organizations have emerged that address violence against women, the role of women in development, and the effect of war on women's lives, and work toward an increase in women's political and economic power around the world. The 1995 conference in Beijing was a watershed event for the emerging global feminist movement, strengthening the international connections among women's groups and laying the groundwork for future activities. One of the major challenges to women around the world is the growth of multinational corporations that move around the world in search of cheap female labor. The athletic footwear industry in particular has become highly profitable by moving its factories to Asia where young women who had been trained to sacrifice themselves for their families' well-being are hired at extremely low wages. In the final essay in this section, Cynthia Enloe describes the resistance of some of these women workers, suggesting ways that women in the United States can support their efforts.

🌿 129

A History of Feminist Movements in the U.S.

AMY KESSELMAN

The history of feminism is a story of ebb and flow. There have been periods when women's issues were on everyone's lips: laws changed, barriers toppled, and a world in which women and men participated equally in all aspects of life seemed to be around the corner. Such periods were often followed by periods of reaction in which feminism was labeled evil and socially destructive, and efforts to achieve equality for women stagnated. While women have worked to improve their lives throughout history in a variety of ways, historians often describe the organized women's movements of the United States as two waves of feminism, since it was these movements that pushed women's issues to the forefront of national politics. Both the first and second waves of U.S. feminism were born in periods of cultural upheaval when many people were engaged in questioning social, cultural and political norms.

The first wave of feminism emerged among women who were active in the reform movements of the 1840s and 1850s. The anti-slavery movement in particular nurtured female organizing efforts and stimulated thinking about the meaning of human rights for women. In 1848 a group of women who had been involved in Quaker and anti-slavery activities organized a convention at Seneca Falls, New York to "discuss the social, civil and religious rights of women."[1] About 300 people gathered, and adopted a series of resolutions drafted by Elizabeth Cady Stanton calling for an end to the subordination of women in all areas of life. While both women and men attended this convention, the speeches and resolutions made it clear, in the words of Elizabeth Cady Stanton, "that woman herself must do this work; for woman alone can understand the height, the depth, the length and the breadth of her deg-

radation."[2] Women's rights conventions were held yearly after this and women all over the country engaged in efforts to change unjust laws, improve the education of women, and eliminate the barriers to women's participation in public life.

While the leadership of the women's rights movement was predominantly white, there were several prominent African-American women who worked for the emancipation of both African Americans and women. Maria Stewart of Boston was one of the first women to speak in public to groups of women and men, urging African-American women to become economically independent. Sojourner Truth, a spellbinding orator, spoke at women's rights and anti-slavery meetings of the connection between freedom for women and emancipation of enslaved African Americans. After the Civil War Mary Ann Shadd Cary argued that Black women were eligible to vote under the Fourteenth Amendment and successfully registered to vote in 1871. Frances Ellen Watkins Harpur, a poet and lecturer, spoke frequently at women's rights conventions as a voice for black women.

At first obtaining the right to vote was but one of the many goals of the women's rights movement, but by the end of the Civil War, it became the primary focus of the movement, since women's rights activists believed that winning suffrage was a necessary tool for the achievement of all other aspects of women's emancipation. Women worked state by state to obtain the right to vote and by 1900 had achieved suffrage in several Western states. After the turn of the century, a new generation of women suffragists renewed the effort to pass a national amendment to the Constitution granting women the right to vote.

The focus on suffrage had advantages and disadvantages. It was a concrete reform that could be used to mobilize women and it symbolized, perhaps more than anything else, the participation of women as individuals in public life. On the other hand, winning the right to vote required gaining the approval of male voters and politicians. Women suffragists often adopted whatever arguments they felt were necessary to persuade those in power that it was in their interest to grant women the right to vote. They often invoked traditional gender roles as they campaigned for the vote, urging for example that women would "sew the seams and cook the meals; to vote won't take us long."[3]

Suffragist pragmatism also intensified the racism, nativism and class bias of the white, native-born leadership of the major suffrage organizations. In the late nineteenth and early twentieth centuries, immigrants poured into the United States, radically changing the social, economic and political landscape. The rhetoric of women's suffrage leadership often reflected the bias of white, native-born citizens against these new Americans. Carrie Chapman Catt, for example, who became president of the National American Woman Suffrage Association, warned against "the danger of the ignorant foreign vote which was sought to be brought up by each party . . ." Urging literacy requirements, she concluded that the best solution would be to "cut off the vote of the slums and give it to the women . . ."[4]

Similarly Southern white suffragists were willing to invoke racism to further their cause, arguing that the enfranchisement of white women would help to sustain white supremacy in the South. When the NAWSA voted in 1903 to allow state chapters to determine their own membership it gave tacit approval to Southern racism since Southern clubs excluded African-American women and often argued that suffrage be granted only to those who met property or literacy requirements.

Despite the racism of white women's suffrage organizations, African-American women were actively involved in efforts to gain the right to vote in the early twentieth century, organizing Black women's suffrage clubs throughout the United States. "If white women needed the vote to acquire advantages and protection of their rights, then black women needed the vote even more so" argued Adella Hunt Logan, a member of the Tuskegee Woman's Club.[5] The National American Woman Suffrage Association, however, was engaged in efforts to get the woman suffrage amendment passed by a U.S. Senate dominated by white Southern men. As a result they were less than hospitable to African-American women's groups that wanted to affiliate, arguing that

they should resubmit their application after the vote was won.

While the women's suffrage movement was focused on the single issue of winning the right to vote, the late nineteenth and early twentieth century saw the flowering of many different efforts by women to improve their lives and the lives of others. Margaret Sanger, Emma Goldman and others led a movement to make birth control legal and available to all women. Ida B. Wells initiated a crusade against lynching, a source of terror among black people during this period. Black and white women educators worked to expand women's educational opportunities and women labor activists organized to improve the wages and working conditions of the wage-earning women who worked in factories, stores and offices.

Attitudes towards women's capabilities began to shift and the image of the "new woman" of the early twentieth century embodied self-reliance and involvement with the world. It was during this period that the term *feminism* was introduced by women who believed women's emancipation required deeper changes than the right to vote. They argued for the full integration of women into social, political and economic life. While suffragists often argued for the right to vote in the name of women's traditional roles, claiming that women's propensity for nurturance and housekeeping would be useful in the public world, feminists renounced self-sacrifice in favor of self-development. At a 1914 meeting entitled "What is Feminism?" Mary Jenny Howe stated: "We want simply to be ourselves . . . not just our little female selves but our whole big human selves."[6]

Women of color saw the connections among various forms of oppression. Anna Cooper, an African-American woman, pointed out in her address to the World's Congress of Representative Women in 1896:

> Not till . . . race, color, sex and condition are seen as accidents, and not the substance of life . . . not till then is woman's lesson taught and woman's cause won—not the white woman's, nor the black woman's nor the red woman's, but the cause of every man and every woman who has writhed silently under a

mighty wrong. Woman's wrongs are thus indissolubly linked with all undefended woe, and the acquirement of her "rights" will mean the final triumph of all right over might.[7]

Socialists like Charlotte Perkins Gilman suggested that women's emancipation required the elimination of private housekeeping in favor of community kitchens and child care centers. "If there should be built and opened," Gilman argued,

> in any of our large cities today a commodious and well served apartment house for professional women with families, it would be filled at once. The apartments would be without kitchens; but there would be a kitchen belonging to the house from which meals could be served to the families in their rooms or in a common dining room, as preferred. It would be a home where the cleaning was done by efficient workers, not hired separately by the families, but engaged by the manager of the establishment; and a roof-garden, day nursery and kindergarten under well-trained professional nurses and teachers would insure proper care of the children.[8]

After 72 years of work the women's suffrage amendment was ratified by the states in 1920. In the decades that followed, the women's movement shrank in numbers and influence and those women who remained active were divided about the best way to improve women's lives. While the Constitution now gave all citizens the right to vote, African Americans of both sexes had been disenfranchised in the South by racist violence and state laws. While magazines and newspapers often proclaimed that women's equality had been achieved, many barriers to women's full participation in the workplace, in politics, and in cultural and social life remained intact. Feminism fell into disrepute, conjuring up images of fanatic women out to spoil men's fun. When the depression of the 1930s created massive unemployment, women wage earners were regarded with suspicion, further intensifying anti-feminist sentiment. By the post–World War II era a resurgence of the cult of domesticity denigrated female ambition, even though large numbers of women were working for wages. While there were groups of women who remained active on behalf of women, laying the groundwork for the future resurgence of feminism,

feminism itself was demonized in the popular culture. In the 1960s when women again began to rebel against their subordinate status, the first wave of feminism was a distant memory; recovering its history was an important ingredient in developing a new movement for the liberation of women.

What lessons can we learn from the rise and fall of the first wave of women's rights activism in the United States? Winning the right to vote, a seemingly basic democratic right, took almost a century to accomplish and required an enormous amount of brilliant organizing, writing and speaking. The benefit of hindsight, however, allows us to see that a great deal was sacrificed to achieve this goal. The capitulation of the suffrage movement to racism and prejudice against immigrants meant that it spoke for a narrow segment of women. Its failure to challenge the division between men's and women's worlds meant that when it won the right to vote, many forms of sexism remained. The suffrage movement demonstrates the perils of focusing exclusively on one goal, deferring others until it is achieved.

The second wave of feminism developed among different groups of women whose combined resources and insights augmented its power. The equal rights segment of the movement originated among women working within government agencies who were frustrated by the slow pace of change. They founded the National Organization for Women (NOW) in 1966 to work for equality in work, education and politics. One of NOW's founders, Betty Friedan, was the author of the influential best seller *The Feminine Mystique,* which described the frustrations of college-educated suburban housewives and argued that women should be encouraged to pursue careers as well as motherhood.

The tensions that were building in the lives of women in the 1950s and 1960s, however, went beyond the need for work outside the home; they had to do with the devaluation of women in everyday life, sexual objectification, the violence against women that permeated society, and the socialization of women to meet the needs of men. These aspects of sexism were so tightly woven into the fabric of United States culture that they were taken for granted and rarely discussed. Young women who had been involved in the social movements for peace and justice in the 1960s were able to bring these issues into the open. These young women called themselves "women's liberation," and argued for radical changes in the political, social and economic institutions of our society. Accustomed to being on the fringes of respectability, they were willing to talk about subjects that were previously hidden and analyze their own lives for insights about the nature of women's oppression, a process that came to be known as consciousness raising. As women began to talk about their childhood, their sexual lives, their feelings about being female, their work and school experiences, and their experience of male violence, the contours of feminist theory emerged. One member of a consciousness raising group remembers:

> We would take some piece of experience, that it had never occurred to me at least to think about differently, and talk about it. Like . . . High School, and the importance of having boobs, and what it was like to be smart, and . . . whether you could major in Math or Science—the things which are now canons of the faith. So we would look at one another and say, "well, I remember" and kind of piece it together like that. "The way that I felt about this was . . ." The experience that captured that best for me was one day looking at the front page of the newspaper and there was not a single woman's name on it—and I had been reading the newspaper all my life and I had never noticed that. It was like that. And this light; I mean it was literally like someone had screwed in a light bulb. And all of a sudden I had a set of lenses for looking at the world, that I hadn't had before, and the whole world looked different through them.[9]

While the analysis that emerged from consciousness raising was often presented as applicable to all women, it reflected the experience of the white middle-class women who dominated most of the early groups. Women within the Black, Chicano, Asian and American Indian movements of the late 60s and 70s were questioning the sexism within their own movements, often encountering resistance from movement men. While some of the ideas being articulated by white feminists resonated in the lives of women of color, others were alien to their experience. In groups of their own, women of color broke traditional silences and generated a feminist analysis that spoke to their experience and recognized the interaction of racism and sexism in their lives. In an Asian women's group in the early 1970s, for example, Miya Iwataki remembers

> Women began talking about years of scotch-taping eyelids to create a double eyelid fold and then carefully painting it over with Maybelline eyeliner. Women began to break through years of checking out each other as competition for Asian men; of fearing being found out that one was not a virgin; or having to be anything but a "natural woman."[10]

For the women who were reinventing feminism, the rediscovery of a history of feminist thought and practice was enormously exhilarating; it reconfirmed their belief in the necessity and possibility of changing women's position at a time when women's liberation activists were being ridiculed and discounted. Members of a Chicana women's group in 1971, for example, were delighted to discover a women's organization that published a newspaper called "Hijas de Cuahtemac" during the 1910 Mexican Revolution, and they decided to use the same name for their own group. Anna Nieto-Gomez, one of the members, remembers

> . . . it was like I had been in a cave and someone has just lit the candle. I [suddenly] realized how important it was to read about your own kind, the women of your own culture, or your own historical heritage, doing the things that you were doing. [It] re-affirmed and validated that you're not a strange, alien person, that what you're doing is not only normal but a part of your history.[11]

The interaction of the various groups of women strengthened the feminist movement. NOW broadened its agenda to include the issues raised by "women's liberation," recognizing that the achievement of equality would require deep systemic changes in the relationship between home and family and the concepts of "femininity" and "masculinity." While women's liberation groups were generating analysis and challenging long-held assumptions, NOW provided concrete strategies for implementing these ideas, such as litigation against discriminatory corporations and efforts to change laws governing rape, violence and divorce.

As different groups of women developed feminist analysis to address their experience, feminism grew deeper and broader. This process was not always without friction, as groups who felt their needs were being ignored confronted the leadership of feminist organizations. After several stormy meetings NOW included the protection of lesbian rights in its agenda. Women of color reshaped feminist analysis to address their experience and challenged feminist organizations to work against racism and develop an "inclusive sisterhood."[12]

Feminists accomplished a great deal in a short period of time. Ridiculed at first by the media, they quickly changed public consciousness about a host of issues from rape to employment discrimination. Feminists worked in a variety of ways to change laws, attitudes, practices and institutions. NOW and other equal rights groups challenged segregated want ads, sued hundreds of major corporations for sex discrimination, and lobbied in state legislatures to change laws about rape, domestic violence, divorce and employment. Women working outside the system established battered women's shelters, rape crisis centers, and feminist health clinics. Feminists inside the university created women's studies programs and engaged in research about women in various disciplines. Throughout the 1970s and 80s countless women made individual changes in their lives, going back to school or waged work, leaving oppressive marriages, developing emotional and sexual relationships with other women, working to develop relationships of mutuality and respect with men.

Since reproductive freedom was clearly central to women's efforts to participate fully and equally in society, feminists throughout the country united in efforts to repeal abortion laws, reinvigorating an abortion reform movement that had been active throughout the 1960s. While a few states legalized abortion in the early 1970s, most state legislatures were resistant to efforts to decriminalize abortion, so women throughout the country filed suits against state laws that made abortion illegal. The suit against the Texas abortion statute, *Roe v. Wade,* made its way to the Supreme Court, which legalized abortion in its landmark decision in 1973.

Many feminists felt that the effort to end sex discrimination would be substantially enhanced by a federal amendment guaranteeing equal rights to women. In 1972 an equal rights amendment was passed by the U.S. Congress, which proclaimed "equality of rights under the laws shall not be denied or abridged by the U.S. or by any State on account of sex." The amendment was then sent on to be ratified by the states and was quickly approved in the legislatures of 34 of the 38 states required for final passage. It stalled, however, in fourteen states in which a new coalition of conservative organizations mobilized to defeat it. Charging that the equal rights amendment and the feminist revolution that it came to symbolize would undermine traditional values and deprive women of the protections they have as wives and mothers, opponents of the ERA enlisted women in their anti-ERA campaign. Mormon and evangelical religious organizations poured resources into efforts to defeat the ERA. Their rhetoric tapped into anxiety about changes in the division of labor, sexuality, and the family, and galvanized a new anti-feminist coalition that opposed the ERA, the legalization of abortion, and other feminist reforms. When the deadline for ratification arrived in 1982, the ERA had not passed in enough states for ratification.

The ascendancy of the right wing in the Republican Party in the 1980s further enhanced the power of the new right assault, and many of the gains of the 1970s were seriously threatened. The second wave of feminism, however, left an indelible imprint on American society. While the momentum may have slowed, millions of women's lives have been changed, and cherished assumptions about gender, sexuality, work and family have been deeply shaken. Although women remain a minority in positions of political power, their voices are being heard more clearly on public policy issues. Integrating feminist approaches to these issues into public policy will require continued pressure on centers of political power.   [2002]

NOTES

1. Eleanor Flexner, *Century of Struggle: The Woman's Rights Movement in the United States* (Cambridge, MA: Harvard University Press, 1970), p. 74.

2. Flexner, p. 77

3. Getting E. Knight and S. Julty, "Getting out the Vote" in *Songs of the Suffragettes,* Phonograph Record No. FH 5281, Folkways, 1958.

4. Quoted in Aileen Kraditor, *The Ideas of the Women's Suffrage Movement 1890–1920* (New York: Norton, 1981), p. 125.

5. Quoted in Paula Giddings, *When and Where I Enter: The Impact of Black Women on Race and Sex in America* (New York: William Morrow, 1984), p. 121.

6. Quoted in Nancy Cott, *The Grounding of Modern Feminism* (New Haven, CT: Yale University Press, 1987), p. 39.

7. Quoted in Elsa Barkley Brown, "Maggie Lena Walker and the Independent Order of St. Luke," *Signs* 14 (Spring, 1989), p. 614.

8. Charlotte Perkins Gilman, "Women in Economics," in Alice Rossi ed., *The Feminist Papers* (Boston: 9#3 [Northeastern University Press, 1988]), p. 592.

9. Elizabeth Gilbertson, Interview with author, July 6, 1991.

10. Quoted in Sherna Gluck, "Whose Feminism, Whose History?: Reflections on Excavating the History of (the) U.S. Women's Movement(s)," Nancy Naples, ed. *Community Activism and Feminist Politics* (New York: Routledge, 1998), p. 40.

11. Gluck, p. 39.

12. Bonnie Thornton Dill, "Race, Class and Gender: Prospects for an Inclusive Sisterhood," *Feminist Studies,* Vol. 9, no. 1 (Spring, 1983), p. 131.

SOURCES

Barkley Brown, Elsa, "Womanist Consciousness: Maggie Lena Walker and the Independent Order of St. Luke," *Signs* 14(3), 1989.

Cott, Nancy, *The Grounding of Modern Feminism.* New Haven: Yale University Press, 1987.

Dill, Bonnie Thornton, "Race, Class and Gender: Prospects for an Inclusive Sisterhood," *Feminist Studies* 9:1, 1984 (Spring, 1983), p. 131–150.

DuBois, Ellen Carol, *Woman Suffrage and Women's Rights.* New York: New York University Press, 1998.

Evans, Sara, *Personal Politics: The Roots of Women's Liberation in the Civil Rights Movement and the New Left.* New York: Knopf, 1979.

Flexner, Eleanor, *Century of Struggle: The Woman's Rights Movement in the United States.* Cambridge: Harvard University Press, 1970.

Friedan, Betty, *The Feminine Mystique.* New York: Norton, 1963.

Giddings, Paula, *When and Where I Enter.* New York: William Morrow, 1984.

Gilman, Charlotte Perkins. "Women and Economics," in *The Feminist Papers,* ed. Rossi, Alice. Boston: Northeastern University Press, 1988.

Gluck, Sherna. "Whose Feminism, Whose History?: Reflec-
tions on Excavating the History of (the) U.S. Women's Movement(s), ed. Naples, Nancy. *Community Activism and Feminist Politics.* New York: Routledge, 1998.

Hoff-Wilson, Joan, ed. *Rights of Passage: the Past and Future of the Equal Rights Amendment.* Bloomington: Indiana University Press, 1986.

Knight, E. and Julty, S. "Getting Out the Vote" in *Songs of the Suffragettes.* Phonograph Record #FH 5281, Folkways, 1958.

Kraditor, Aileen, *The Ideas of the Women's Suffrage Movement 1890–1920.* New York: Norton, 1981.

Rosen, Ruth, *The World Split Open: How the Modern Women's Movement Changed America.* New York: Viking, 2000.

 130

The Seneca Falls Women's Rights Convention, 1848

"DECLARATION OF SENTIMENTS"

When, in the course of human events, it becomes necessary for one portion of the family of man to assume among the people of the earth a position different from that which they have hitherto occupied, but one to which the laws of nature and of nature's God entitle them, a decent respect to the opinions of mankind requires that they should declare the causes that impel them to such a course.

We hold these truths to be self-evident: that all men and women are created equal; that they are endowed by their Creator with certain inalienable rights; that among these are life, liberty, and the pursuit of happiness; that to secure these rights governments are instituted, deriving their just powers from the consent of the governed. Whenever any form of government becomes destructive of these ends, it is the right of those who suffer from it to refuse allegiance to it, and to insist upon the institution of a new government, laying its foundation on such principles, and organizing its powers in such form, as to them shall seem most likely to effect their safety and happiness. Prudence indeed, will dictate that governments long established should not be changed for light and transient causes; and accordingly all experience hath shown that mankind are more disposed to suffer, while evils are sufferable, than to right themselves by abolishing the forms to which they were accustomed. But when a long train of abuses and usurpations, pursuing invariably the same object evinces a design to reduce them under absolute despotism, it is their duty to throw off such government, and to provide new guards for their future security. Such has been the patient sufferance of the women under this government, and such is now the necessity which constrains them to demand the equal station to which they are entitled.

The history of mankind is a history of repeated injuries and usurpations on the part of man toward woman, having in direct object the establishment of an absolute tyranny over her. To prove this, let facts be submitted to a candid world.

He has never permitted her to exercise her inalienable right to the elective franchise.

He has compelled her to submit to laws, in the formation of which she had no voice.

He has withheld from her rights which are given to the most ignorant and degraded men—both natives and foreigners.

Having deprived her of this first right of a citizen, the elective franchise, thereby leaving her without representation in the halls of legislation, he has oppressed her on all sides.

He has made her, if married, in the eye of the law, civilly dead.

He has taken from her all right in property, even to the wages she earns.

He has made her, morally, an irresponsible being, as she can commit many crimes with impunity, provided they be done in the presence of her husband. In the covenant of marriage, she is compelled to promise obedience to her husband, he becoming, to all intents and purposes, her master—the law giving him power to deprive her of her liberty, and to administer chastisement.

He has so framed the laws of divorce, as to what shall be the proper causes, and in case of separation, to whom the guardianship of the children shall be given, as to be wholly regardless of the happiness of women—the law, in all cases, going upon a false supposition of the supremacy of man, and giving all power into his hands.

After depriving her of all rights as a married woman, if single, and the owner of property, he has taxed her to support a government which recognizes her only when her property can be made profitable to it.

He has monopolized nearly all the profitable employments, and from those she is permitted to follow, she receives but a scanty remuneration. He closes against her all the avenues to wealth and distinction which he considers most honorable to himself. As a teacher of theology, medicine, or law, she is not known.

He has denied her the facilities for obtaining a thorough education, all colleges being closed against her.

He allows her in Church, as well as State, but a subordinate position, claiming Apostolic authority for her exclusion from the ministry, and, with some exceptions, from any public participation in the affairs of the Church.

He has created a false public sentiment by giving to the world a different code of morals for men and women, by which moral delinquencies which exclude women from society, are not only tolerated, but deemed of little account in man.

He has usurped the prerogative of Jehovah himself, claiming it as his right to assign for her a sphere of action, when that belongs to her conscience and to her God.

He has endeavored, in every way that he could, to destroy her confidence in her own powers, to lessen her self-respect, and to make her willing to lead a dependent and abject life.

Now, in view of this entire disfranchisement of one-half the people of this country, their social and religious degradation—in view of the unjust laws above mentioned, and because women do feel themselves aggrieved, oppressed, and fraudulently deprived of their most sacred rights, we insist that they have immediate admission to all the rights and privileges which belong to them as citizens of the United States.

In entering upon the great work before us, we anticipate no small amount of misconception, misrepresentation, and ridicule; but we shall use every instrumentality within our power to effect our object. We shall employ agents, circulate tracts, petition the State and National legislatures, and endeavor to enlist the pulpit and the press in our behalf. We hope this Convention will be followed by a series of Conventions embracing every part of the country.

SENECA FALLS RESOLUTIONS

Whereas, The great precept of nature is conceded to be, that "man shall pursue his own true and substantial happiness." Blackstone in his Commentaries remarks, that this law of Nature being coeval with mankind, and dictated by God himself, is of course superior in obligation to any other. It is binding over all the globe, in all countries and at all times; no human laws are of any validity if contrary to this, and such of them as are valid, derive all their force, and all their validity, and all their authority, mediately and immediately, from this original; therefore,

Resolved, That such laws as conflict, in any way, with the true and substantial happiness of woman, are contrary to the great precept of nature and of no validity, for this is "superior in obligation to any other."

Resolved, That all laws which prevent woman from occupying such a station in society as her conscience shall dictate, or which place her in a position inferior to that of man, are contrary to the great precept of nature, and therefore of no force or authority.

Resolved, That woman is man's equal—was intended to be so by the Creator, and the highest good of the race demands that she should be recognized as such.

Resolved, That the women of this country ought to be enlightened in regard to the laws under which they live, that they may no longer publish their degradation by declaring themselves satisfied with their present position, nor their ignorance, by asserting that they have all the rights they want.

Resolved, That inasmuch as man, while claiming for himself intellectual superiority, does accord to woman moral superiority, it is pre-eminently his duty to encourage her to speak and teach, as she has an opportunity, in all religious assemblies.

Resolved, That the same amount of virtue, delicacy, and refinement of behavior that is required of woman in the social state, should also be required of man, and the same transgressions should be visited with equal severity on both man and woman.

Resolved, That the objection of indelicacy and impropriety, which is so often brought against woman when she addresses a public audience, comes with a very ill-grace from those who encourage, by their attendance, her appearance on the stage, in the concert, or in feats of the circus.

Resolved, That woman has too long rested satisfied in the circumscribed limits which corrupt customs and a perverted application of the Scriptures have marked out for her, and that it is time she should move in the enlarged sphere which her great Creator has assigned her.

Resolved, That it is the duty of the women of this country to secure to themselves their sacred right to the elective franchise.

Resolved, That the equality of human rights results necessarily from the fact of the identity of the race in capabilities and responsibilities.

Resolved, therefore, That, being invested by the Creator with the same capabilities, and the same consciousness of responsibility for their exercise, it is demonstrably the right and duty of woman, equally with man, to promote every righteous cause by every righteous means; and especially in regard to the great subjects of morals and religion, it is self-evidently her right to participate with her brother in teaching them, both in private and in public, by writing and by speaking, by any instrumentalities proper to be used, and in any assemblies proper to be held; and this being a self-evident truth growing out of the divinely implanted principles of human nature, any custom or authority adverse to it, whether modern or wearing the hoary sanction of antiquity, is to be regarded as a self-evident falsehood, and at war with mankind.

Resolved, That the speedy success of our cause depends upon the zealous and untiring efforts of both men and women, for the overthrow of the monopoly of the pulpit, and for the securing to women an equal participation with men in the various trades, professions, and commerce.   [1848]

🌿 131

Sojourner Truth's Defense of the Rights of Women

Sojourner Truth was born into slavery in Ulster County, New York, in about 1797 (the exact date of her birth is uncertain). After her escape from slavery she became involved in several of the religious and political movements of her day. Changing her name from Isabella to Sojourner Truth, she traveled widely, speaking eloquently against slavery, for women's rights, and about her vision of a kind and loving God. She died in Battle Creek, Michigan, in 1883.

At the 1851 Women's Rights Convention in Akron, Ohio, Sojourner Truth gave a stirring speech on women's rights. Below are two versions: a contemporary newspaper account and the reminiscences of Frances Gage, a prominant white suffragist. (We have dropped the dialect Gage used to record Sojourner Truth's words.)

THE ANTI-SLAVERY BUGLE

One of the most unique and interesting speeches of the Convention was made by Sojourner Truth, an emancipated slave. It is impossible to transfer it to paper, or convey any adequate idea of the effect it produced upon the audience. Those only can appreciate it who saw her powerful form, her whole-souled, earnest gestures, and listened to her strong and truthful tones. She came forward to the platform and addressing the President said with great simplicity:

> May I say a few words? Receiving an affirmative answer, she proceeded; I want to say a few words about this matter. I am a woman's rights. [*sic*] I have as much muscle as any man, and can do as much work as any man. I have plowed and reaped and husked and chopped and mowed, and can any man do more than that? I have heard much about the sexes being equal; I can carry as much as any man, and can eat as much too, if I can get it. I am as strong as any man that is now. As for intellect, all I can say is, if a woman have a pint and man a quart—why cant she have her little pint full? You need not be afraid to give us our rights for fear we will take too much,—for we cant take more than our pint'll hold. The poor men seem to be all in confusion, and dont know what to do. Why children, if you have woman's rights give it to her and you will feel better. You will have your own rights, and they wont be so much trouble. I cant read, but I can hear. I have heard the bible and have

learned that Eve caused man to sin. Well if woman upset the world, do give her a chance to set it right side up again. The Lady has spoken about Jesus, how he never spurned woman from him, and she was right. When Lazarus died, Mary and Martha came to him with faith and love and besought him to raise their brother. And Jesus wept—and Lazarus came forth. And how came Jesus into the world? Through God who created him and woman who bore him. Man, where is your part? But the women are coming up blessed be God and a few of the man are coming up with them. But man is in a tight place, the poor slave is on him, woman is coming on him, and he is surely between a hawk and a buzzard.

[1851]

FRANCES GAGE'S REMINISCENCES

The second day the work waxed warm. Methodist, Baptist, Episcopal, Presbyterian, and Universalist ministers came in to hear and discuss the resolutions presented. One claimed superior rights and privileges for man, on the ground of "superior intellect"; another, because of the "manhood of Christ; if God had desired the equality of woman, He would have given some token of His will through the birth, life, and death of the Saviour." Another gave us a theological view of the "sin of our first mother."

There were very few women in those days who dared to "speak in meeting"; and the august teachers of the people were seemingly getting the better of us, while the boys in the galleries, and the sneerers among the pews, were hugely enjoying the discomfiture, as they supposed, of the "strong-minded." Some of the tender-skinned friends were on the point of losing dignity, and the atmosphere betokened a storm. When, slowly from her seat in the corner rose Sojourner Truth, who, till now, had scarcely lifted her head. "Don't let her speak!" gasped half a dozen in my ear. She moved slowly and solemnly to the front, laid her old bonnet at her feet, and turned her great speaking eyes to me. There was a hissing sound of disapprobation above and below. I rose and announced "Sojourner Truth," and begged the audience to keep silence for a few moments. The tumult subsided at once, and every eye was fixed on this almost Amazon form, which stood nearly six feet high, head erect, and eyes piercing the upper air like one in a dream. At her first word there was a profound hush. She spoke in deep tones, which, though not loud, reached every ear in the house, and away through the throng at the doors and windows.

"Well, children, where there is so much racket there must be something out of kilter. I think that 'twixt the Negroes of the South and the women at the north all talking about rights, the white men will be in a fix pretty soon. But what's all this here talking about?

"That man over there says that women need to be helped into carriages, and lifted over ditches and to have the best place everywhere. Nobody ever helps me into carriages, or over mudpuddles, or gives me any best place!" And raising herself to her full height, and her voice to a pitch like rolling thunder, she asked, "And ar'n't I a woman? I could work as much and eat as much as a man—when I could get it—and bear the lash as well! And ar'n't I a woman? I have borne thirteen children, and seen them almost all sold off to slavery, and when I cried out with my mother's grief, none but Jesus heard me! And ar'n't I a woman?

"Then they talk about this thing in the head; what this they call it?" ("Intellect" whispered some one near.) "That's it, honey. What's that got to do with women's rights or Negroes? If my cup won't hold but a pint, and your holds a quart, wouldn't you be mean not to let me have my little half-measure full?" And she pointed her significant finger, and sent a keen glance at the minister who had made the argument. The cheering was long and loud.

"Then that little man in black there, he says women can't have as much rights as men, 'cause Christ wasn't a woman! Where did your Christ come from?" Rolling thunder couldn't have stilled that crowd, as did those deep, wonderful tones, as she stood there with outstretched arms and eyes of fire. Raising her voice still louder, she repeated, "Where did your Christ come from? From God and a woman! Man had nothing to do with him." Oh, what a rebuke that was to that little man.

Turning again to another objector, she took up the defense of Mother Eve, I cannot follow her

through it all. It was pointed, and witty and solemn; eliciting at almost every sentence deafening applause; and she ended by asserting: "If the first woman God ever made was strong enough to turn the world upside down all alone, these women together" (and she glanced her eye over the platform) "ought to be able to turn it back, and get it right side up again! And now they are asking to do it, the men better let them. Obliged to you for hearing me, and now old Sojourner has got nothing more to say."

Amid roars of applause, she returned to her corner, leaving more than one of us with streaming eyes, and hearts beating with gratitude. She had taken us up in her strong arms and carried us safely over the slough of difficulty turning the whole tide in our favor.   [1863]

🌿 132

Consciousness Raising: A Radical Weapon

KATHIE SARACHILD

From a talk given to the First National Conference of Stewardesses for Women's Rights in New York City, March 12, 1973.

To be able to understand what feminist consciousness-raising is all about, it is important to remember that it began as a program among women who all considered themselves radicals.

Before we go any further, let's examine the word "radical." It is a word that is often used to suggest extremist, but actually it doesn't mean that. The dictionary says radical means root, coming from the Latin word for root. And that is what we meant by calling ourselves radicals. We were interested in getting to the roots of problems in society. You might say we wanted to pull up weeds in the garden by their roots, not just pick off the leaves at the top to make things momentarily look good. Women's Liberation was started by women who considered themselves radicals in this sense.

Our aim in forming a women's liberation group

was to start a *mass movement of women* to put an end to the barriers of segregation and discrimination based on sex. We knew radical thinking and radical action would be necessary to do this. We also believed it necessary to form Women's Liberation groups which excluded men from their meetings.

In order to have a radical approach, to get to the root, it seemed logical that we had to study the situation of women, not just take random action. How best to do this came up in the women's liberation group I was in—New York Radical Women, one of the first in the country—shortly after the group had formed. We were planning our first public action and wandered into a discussion about what to do next. One woman in the group, Ann Forer, spoke up: "I think we have a lot more to do just in the area of raising our consciousness," she said. "Raising consciousness?" I wondered what she meant by that. I'd never heard it applied to women before.

"I've only begun thinking about women as an oppressed group," she continued, "and each day, I'm still learning more about it—my consciousness gets higher."

Now I didn't consider that I had just started thinking about the oppression of women. In fact, I thought of myself as having done lots of thinking about it for quite a while, and lots of reading, too. But then Ann went on to give an example of something she'd noticed that turned out to be a deeper way of seeing it for me, too.

"I think a lot about being attractive," Ann said. "People don't find the real self of a woman attractive." And then she went on to give some examples. And I just sat there listening to her describe all the false ways women have to act: playing dumb, always being agreeable, always being nice, not to mention what we had to do to our bodies with the clothes and shoes we wore, the diets we had to go through, going blind not wearing glasses, all because men didn't find our real selves, our human freedom, our basic humanity "attractive." And I realized I still could learn a lot about how to understand and describe the particular oppression of women in ways that could reach other women in the way this had just reached me. The whole group was moved as I was, and we decided on the spot that what we needed—in the words Ann used—was to "raise our consciousness some more."

At the next meeting there was an argument in the group about how to do this. One woman—Peggy Dobbins—said that what she wanted to do was make a very intensive study of all the literature on the question of whether there really were any biological differences between men and women. I found myself angered by that idea.

"I think it would be a waste of time," I said. "For every scientific study we quote, the opposition can find their scientific studies to quote. Besides, the question is what *we* want to be, what we think we are, not what some authorities in the name of science are arguing over what we are. It is scientifically impossible to tell what the biological differences are between men and women—if there are any besides the obvious physical ones—until all the social and political factors applying to men and women are equal. Everything we have to know, have to prove, we can get from the realities of our own lives. For instance, on the subject of women's intelligence. We know from our own experience that women play dumb for men because, if we're too smart, men won't like us. I know, because I've done it. We've all done it. Therefore, we can simply deduce that women are smarter than men are aware of, and smarter than all those people who make studies are aware of, and that there are a lot of women around who are a lot smarter than they look and smarter than anybody but themselves and maybe a few of their friends know."

In the end the group decided to raise its consciousness by studying women's lives by topics like childhood, jobs, motherhood, etc. We'd do any outside reading we wanted to and thought was important. But our starting point for discussion, as well as our test of the accuracy of what any of the books said, would be the actual experience we had in these areas. One of the questions, suggested by Ann Forer, we would bring at all times to our studies would be—who and what has an *interest* in maintaining the oppression in our lives. The kind of actions the group should engage in, at this point, we decided—acting on an idea of Carol Hanisch, another woman in the group—would be consciousness-raising actions . . . actions brought to the public for the specific purpose of challenging old ideas and raising new ones, the very same issues of feminism we were studying ourselves. Our role was not to be a "service organization," we decided, nor a large "membership organization." What we were talking about being was, in effect, Carol explained, a "zap" action, political agitation and education group something like what the Student Non-Violent Coordinating Committee (S.N.C.C.) had been. We would be the first to dare to say and do the undareable, what women really felt and wanted. The first job now was to raise awareness and un derstanding, our own and others —awareness that would prompt people to organize and to act on a mass scale.

The decision to emphasize our own feelings and experiences as women and to test all generalizations and reading we did by our own experience was actually the scientific method of research. We were in effect repeating the 17th century challenge of science to scholasticism: "study nature, not books," and put all theories to the test of living practice and action. It was also a method of radical organizing tested by other revolutions. We were applying to women and to ourselves as women's liberation organizers the practice a number of us had learned as organizers in the civil rights movement in the South in the early 1960's.

Consciousness-raising—studying the whole gamut of women's lives, starting with the full reality of one's own—would also be a way of keeping the movement radical by preventing it from getting sidetracked into single issue reforms and single issue organizing. It would be a way of carrying theory about women further than it had ever been carried before, as the groundwork for achieving a radical solution for women as yet attained nowhere.

It seemed clear that knowing how our own lives related to the general condition of women would make us better fighters on behalf of women as a whole. We felt that all women would have to see the fight of women as their own, not as something just to help "other women," that they would have to see this truth about their own lives before they would fight in a radical way for anyone. "Go fight your own oppressors," Stokely Carmichael had said to the white civil rights workers when the black power movement began. "You don't get radicalized fighting other people's battles," as Beverly Jones, author of the pioneering essay, "Toward a Female Liberation Movement," put it.   [1973]

 133

The Boston Women's Health Book Collective

SUSAN BROWNMILLER

Collective was always a word with variable meanings in women's liberation. The utopian desire to submerge individual ego for the greater political good led to a range of experiments in the sixties and seventies such as fitful stabs at group writing and the founding of communal houses where personal lives intermingled at every conceivable level and food, clothes, and money were shared. Of all the experiments, foolish and grand, that marked the era, I can say without fear of contradiction that the Boston Women's Health Book Collective stands as an unqualified success. It became the heroic lifetime achievement for the twelve relatively unknown women who wrote and edited the feminist classic *Our Bodies, Ourselves.*

Nancy Hawley had grown up in radical politics. Her mother had been in the Communist Party, and Nancy herself was a charter member of the Students for a Democratic Society at the University of Michigan. After an inspiring conversation in 1968 with her old chum Kathie Amatniek, she started one of the first consciousness-raising groups in Cambridge, enlisting the young mothers in her child's cooperative play group. Happily pregnant again, she attended the stormy Thanksgiving conference in Lake Villa, Illinois, but unlike Amatniek, Charlotte Bunch, and many others, Hawley came away from it euphoric. A heated discussion on motherhood led by Shulamith Firestone, who said that pregnancy was barbaric and women would be equal only when science offered technological alternatives to biological reproduction, left her convinced that the movement needed her input.

In May 1969, a month after giving birth, Hawley chaired an overflowing workshop called "Women and Their Bodies" at a New England regional conference on women's liberation. (This was the Mother's Day weekend conference at Emmanuel College in Boston, which led to the founding of the socialist-feminist Bread and Roses and where Cell Sixteen gave a rousing karate demonstration.) Summoning an incident fresh in her mind, Hawley opened her workshop by reporting a glib, sexist remark by her obstetrician. "He said," she recalls, "that he was going to sew me up real tight so there would be more sexual pleasure for my husband." Hawley's report, and her outrage, unleashed a freewheeling exchange on patronizing male doctors, childbirth, orgasm, contraception, and abortion that was so voluble and intense nobody wanted to go home.

"Everybody had a doctor story," exclaims Paula Doress, who was scheduled to give birth two weeks later. "We put aside our prepared papers and did consciousness raising."

Vilunya Diskin, in another workshop, received an excited report from Hawley that night. Diskin had survived the Holocaust by being placed with a Polish family. As a young married woman in Boston, she had undergone two traumatic childbirths with severe complications. Her first baby lived, but she had lost her second to hyaline membrane, a lung disease that the hospital had failed to monitor in time. "I was solidly middle-class and well educated, and my health care had been appalling," she says. "So I could imagine what it was like for others without my resources."

A fluid core of activists from the Emmanuel conference agreed to continue meeting in order to compile a list of doctors they felt they could trust. They resolved as well to take the "Women and Their Bodies" workshop into the community, wherever they could find free space in church basements and nursery schools. "Our idea," says Diskin, "was to go out in pairs. We hoped that the women who attended the workshop would then go on and give it themselves."

To the core group's bewilderment, the doctors list kept dwindling. Every time it got up to four seemingly solid, unimpeachable names, somebody new showed up to exclaim, "Oh, do I have a story about *him!*" But the workshop project soared. As the summer turned into fall, the women amassed enough hard medical information and the confidence to borrow a lounge at MIT for a 12-session course. Venereal disease and "Women, Medicine and Capitalism" were added to the program.

Ruth Bell, a stranger to Boston, went to the course at MIT in an oversized pair of "Oshkosh, by Gosh" denim overalls, her maternity outfit. "Fifty women were talking about their lives, their sexuality, their feelings," she remembers. "I raised my hand and said, 'I'm pregnant for the first time and I don't know much about this and I'm having nightmares.' Three or four other women got up and said 'That happened to me, too. Let's meet after and talk about it and maybe we can figure something out.' That's how it was. Somebody had a concern, she raised her hand, and three or four others said, 'Boy, that happened to me, too.'"

Joan Ditzion, married to a Harvard medical student and debating whether to have kids, was transfixed by a large, detailed drawing of a vagina with labia and clitoris that the women had placed on an easel. "I'd only seen pictures like that in my husband's textbooks. These women were speaking so easily, without shame. I got my first sense that women could own our own anatomy."

Wendy Sanford, born into an upper-class Republican family, was battling depression after her son's birth. Her friend Esther Rome, a follower of Jewish Orthodox traditions, dragged her to the second MIT session. Previously Wendy had kept her distance from political groups. "I walked into the lounge," she recalls, "and they were talking about masturbation. I didn't say a word. I was shocked; I was fascinated. At a later session someone gave a breastfeeding demonstration. That didn't shock me —I'd been doing it—but then we broke down into small groups. I had never 'broken down into a small group' in my life. In my group people started talking about postpartum depression. In that one 45-minute period I realized that what I'd been blaming myself for, and what my husband had blamed me for, wasn't my personal deficiency. It was a combination of physiological things and a real societal thing, isolation. That realization was one of those moments that makes you a feminist forever."

Ruth Bell gave birth to her daughter in the middle of the course and returned to become "a second-stage original member" of the amorphous collective, along with Joan Ditzion and a renewed, reenergized Wendy Sanford. "There was an open invitation to anyone who wanted to help revise the course notes into a more formal packet," Bell remembers. "If you wanted to work on writing, you'd pair or triple up with people who could do research."

"We had to get hold of good medical texts," says Paula Doress, "so we borrowed student cards to get into Countway, the Harvard Medical School library. It was very eye-opening to realize that we could understand the latinized words."

"Then we'd stand up at a meeting and read what we had written," Ruth Bell continues. "People would make notes. Somebody would raise a hand and say, 'I think you should add this sentence' or 'You need a comma here.' This was how the first editing got done."

Duplicated packets of the course material were making their way around the country. Closer to home, somebody contacted the New England Free Press, a leftist mail-order collective in downtown Boston. "Basically they were a bunch of men, conventionally Marxist, who printed and sold pamphlets at 10 to 25 cents," Jane Pincus sums up. "They didn't see us as political." The mail-order collective grudgingly agreed to publish and distribute the health course papers if the women paid their own printing costs. "So we raised $1,500 from our parents and friends," Pincus relates. "And then we had to hire somebody to send out the orders because the demand was so great."

Five thousand stapled copies of "Women and Their Bodies" on newsprint paper with amateur photos and homey line drawings rolled off the press in December 1970 bearing a cover price of 75 cents. The blunt 136-page assault on the paternalism of the medical establishment that juxtaposed personal narratives with plainspoken prescriptives immediately sold out. A second edition of 15,000 copies, with the price lowered to 35 cents, bore an important change. In one of those Eureka moments, somebody had exclaimed, "Hey, it isn't women and *their* bodies—it's us and our bodies. *Our Bodies, Ourselves.*"

Women's centers in big cities and college towns were thirsting for practical information and new ways to organize. The Boston collective's handbook with its simple directive, "You can substitute the experience in your city or state here," fit the bill. Subsequent press runs for *Our Bodies, Ourselves* were upped to 25,000 in an attempt to satisfy the demand. Three printings in 1971 were followed by six printings in 1972.

"We are working on revisions," the collective declared. "We want to add chapters on menopause and getting older and attitudes toward children, etc., etc., but we haven't had time." There was no shortage of feedback. "The first edition was weak on the dangers of high-dose estrogen oral contraceptives," Barbara Seaman remembers. She mailed the women a copy of her book, *The Doctors' Case Against the Pill*, and was gratified to see that the next edition reflected her concern. "A woman in Iowa wrote in and said, 'You didn't mention ectopic pregnancy,'" remembers Jane Pincus. "And we said 'Great, write about it and we'll put it in.' This is really how the book evolved."

It was only a matter of time before the big guns in New York publishing got wind of the phenomenal underground success. In the fall of 1972 they came courting with offers of a modest advance. Jonathan Dolger at Simon & Schuster had roomed with Jane Pincus's husband at college, but Charlotte Mayerson at Random House possessed what looked like an insurmountable advantage. "Charlotte was a she, and I was not," says Dolger. "They wanted a woman to edit their book and in truth, we didn't have many women at S & S in those days." Dolger asked Alice Mayhew, a recent arrival, to accompany him to Boston.

Dressed in army fatigues and work boots, the collective grilled the two editors about their intentions. While Dolger quaked in his business suit, Mayhew brusquely got down to business. "I got the impression they were all married to professors at MIT and Harvard," she remembers, not far off the mark. The following evening it was Mayerson's turn to present her case.

For the first time in their experience as a working collective, the women were unable to reach a consensus. They felt a sisterly bond with Mayerson, and indeed they would work with her on later projects, but she would not get the best-selling *Our Bodies, Ourselves.* Random House was owned at the time by RCA, a conglomerate with huge government defense contracts, rendering it complicitous in the war machine. An independent company and seemingly purer, Simon & Schuster won the agonizing vote by a narrow margin.

Freezing their ranks, the women incorporated as a nonprofit foundation. One member, suddenly desirous of a change in lifestyle, split for Toronto. The last to come aboard were Judy Norsigian, their "baby" at 23, and Norma Swenson, their "old lady" at 40. Norsigian and Swenson were to become the public face of the collective over the years.

When news of the commercial sale appeared in the penultimate *New England Free Press,* the mail-order leftists commandeered a page of their own to cry foul, warning that a capitalist publisher would impede the building of socialist consciousness. The women dodged the ideological brickbats as best they could while they readied their beloved creation for its aboveground debut. "Everything had to be decided by consensus," Mayhew remembers. "It took a long time. But we knew they were in touch with a generation of young women who wanted to be talked to straightforwardly. We would have been dopey to interfere."

Rape, an emerging issue for feminists, became a chapter in the handsome, large-format 1973 Simon & Schuster *Our Bodies, Ourselves.* Judy Norsigian, a veteran of the commune movement, wrote a chapter on nutrition. Mindful of the rising tide of lesbian consciousness, the women sent out a call for the appropriate expertise. A Boston gay women's collective produced "In Amerika They Call Us Dykes," insisting on anonymity and complete editorial con-

trol of the pages. Continuing the policy started in the first newsprint edition, the illustrations for the aboveground *Our Bodies, Ourselves* included many line drawings and photographs of African-American women. A sharp dig at the U.S. military presence in Vietnam survived in the aboveground edition (the context was venereal disease), but the proviso "Don't forget that Ortho and Tampax are capitalist organizations pushing their own products for profits" got axed. "Women, Medicine and Capitalism," a lengthy polemic, shrank to an unrecognizable paragraph in "Women and Health Care" amid the nitty-gritty on yeast infections, cystitis, and crabs. Softer rhetoric was a collective decision, in line with the women's desires to reach the mainstream and include more facts, but they resisted the ladylike language a copy editor they nicknamed Blue Pencil wished to impose. "Where we wrote *pee,*" says Jane Pincus, "Blue Pencil changed it to *urinate.* We changed it right back."

Our Bodies, Ourselves sold more than a million copies and earned more than a half million dollars in royalties for the collective in its first five years of commercial distribution. More important, it became the premier sourcebook for a generation of sexually active young women across all lines of race and class. It was deeply discounted or given out free at birth control clinics, and it found an audience among hard-to-reach teenagers when it was adopted as a teaching tool in hundreds of high school sex education programs. The royalty money was dispersed to movement projects except for the pittance paid to the staff people, chiefly Norsigian, Swenson, and Rome. By the latter part of the 1970s, the collective, which convened periodically to work on updated editions, had witnessed four divorces and three second marriages. A few members left the Boston area with their husbands, and one discovered her lesbian identity. All told, the women reared nearly two dozen children. "People used to come from overseas and ask to the see the house where the collective lived," says Norma Swenson. "I think they were disappointed to find that we led individual lives."   [1998]

🌿 134

Introduction to Home Girls: A Black Feminist Anthology

BARBARA SMITH

Black women as a group have never been fools. We couldn't afford to be. Yet in the last two decades many of us have been deterred from identifying with a liberation struggle which might say significant things to women like ourselves, women who believe that we were put here for a purpose in our own right, women who are usually not afraid to struggle.

Although our involvement has increased considerably in recent years, there are countless reasons why Black and other Third World women have not identified with contemporary feminism in large numbers.[1] The racism of white women in the women's movement has certainly been a major factor. The powers-that-be are also aware that a movement of progressive Third World women in this country would alter life as we know it. As a result there has been a concerted effort to keep women of color from organizing autonomously and from organizing with other women around women's political issues. Third World men, desiring to maintain power over "their women" at all costs, have been among the most willing reinforcers of the fears and myths about the women's movement, attempting to scare us away from figuring things out for ourselves.

It is fascinating to look at various kinds of media from the late 1960s and early 1970s, when feminism was making its great initial impact, in order to see what Black men, Native American men, Asian American men, Latino men, and white men were saying about the irrelevance of "women's lib" to women of color. White men and Third World men, ranging from conservatives to radicals, pointed to the seeming lack of participation of women of color in the movement in order to discredit it and to undermine the efforts of the movement as a whole. All kinds of men were running scared because they knew that if the women in their midst were changing, they were going to have to change too. In 1976 I wrote:

> Feminism is potentially the most threatening of movements to Black and other Third World people because it makes it absolutely essential that we examine the way we live, how we treat each other, and what we believe. It calls into question the most basic assumption about our existence and this is the idea that biological, i.e., sexual identity determines all, that it is the rationale for power relationships as well as for all other levels of human identity and action. An irony is that among Third World people biological determinism is rejected and fought against when it is applied to race, but generally unquestioned when it applies to sex.[2]

In reaction to the "threat" of such change, Black men, with the collaboration of some Black women, developed a set of myths to divert Black women from our own freedom.

MYTHS

Myth No. 1: The Black woman is already liberated. This myth confuses liberation with the fact that Black women have had to take on responsibilities that our oppression gives us no choice but to handle. This is an insidious, but widespread myth that many Black women have believed themselves. Heading families, working outside the home, not building lives or expectations dependent on males, seldom being sheltered or pampered as women, Black women have known that their lives in some ways incorporated goals that white middle-class women were striving for, but race and class privilege, of course, reshaped the meaning of those goals profoundly. As W.E.B. DuBois said so long ago about Black women: ". . . our women in black had freedom contemptuously thrust upon them."[3] Of all the people here, women of color generally have the fewest choices about the circumstances of their lives. An ability to cope under the worst conditions is not liberation, although our spiritual capacities have often made it look like a life. Black men didn't say anything about how poverty, unequal pay, no childcare, violence of every kind including battering, rape, and sterilization abuse, translated into "liberation."

Underlying this myth is the assumption that Black women are towers of strength who neither feel nor need what other human beings do, either emotionally or materially. White male social scientists, particularly Daniel P. Moynihan with his "matriarchy theory," further reinforce distortions concerning Black women's actual status. A song inspired by their mothers and sung by Sweet Honey in the Rock, "Oughta Be A Woman," lyrics by June Jordan and music by Bernice Johnson Reagon, responds succinctly to the insensitivity of the myth that Black women are already liberated and illustrates the home-based concerns of Black feminism:

OUGHTA BE A WOMAN

Washing the floors to send you to college
Staying at home so you can feel safe
What do you think is the soul of her knowledge
What do you think that makes her feel safe

Biting her lips and lowering her eyes
To make sure there's food on the table
What do you think would be her surprise
If the world was as willing as she's able

Hugging herself in an old kitchen chair
She listens to your hurt and your rage
What do you think she knows of despair
What is the aching of age

The fathers, the children, the brothers
Turn to her and everybody white turns to her
What about her turning around
Alone in the everyday light

There oughta be a woman can break
Down, sit down, break down, sit down
Like everybody else call it quits on Mondays
Blues on Tuesdays, sleep until Sunday
Down, sit down, break down, sit down

A way outa no way is flesh outa flesh
Courage that cries out at night
A way outa no way is flesh outa flesh

Bravery kept outa sight
A way outa no way is too much to ask
Too much of a task for any one woman[4]

Myth No. 2: Racism is the primary (or only) oppression Black women have to confront. (Once we get that taken care of, then Black women, men, and children will all flourish. Or as Ms. Luisah Teish writes, we can look forward to being "the property of powerful men.")[5]

This myth goes hand in hand with the one that the Black woman is already liberated. The notion that struggling against or eliminating racism will completely alleviate Black women's problems does not take into account the way that sexual oppression cuts across all racial, nationality, age, religious, ethnic, and class groupings. Afro-Americans are no exception.

It also does not take into account how oppression operates. Every generation of Black people, up until now, has had to face the reality that no matter how hard we work we will probably not see the end of racism in our lifetimes. Yet many of us keep faith and try to do all we can to make change now. If we have to wait for racism to be obliterated *before* we can begin to address sexism, we will be waiting for a long time. Denying that sexual oppression exists or requiring that we wait to bring it up until racism, or in some cases capitalism, is toppled, is a bankrupt position. A Black feminist perspective has no use for ranking oppressions, but instead demonstrates the simultaneity of oppressions as they affect Third World women's lives.

Myth No. 3: Feminism is nothing but man-hating. (And men have never done anything that would legitimately inspire hatred.)

It is important to make a distinction between attacking institutionalized, systematic oppression (the goal of any serious progressive movement) and attacking men as individuals. Unfortunately, some of the most widely distributed writing about Black women's issues has not made this distinction sufficiently clear. Our issues have not been concisely defined in these writings, causing much adverse reaction and confusion about what Black feminism really is.[6]

This myth is one of the silliest and at the same time one of the most dangerous. Anti-feminists are incapable of making a distinction between being critically opposed to sexual oppression and simply hating men. Women's desire for fairness and safety in our lives does not necessitate hating men. Trying to educate and inform men about how their feet are planted on our necks doesn't translate into hatred either. Centuries of anti-racist struggle by various people of color are not reduced, except by racists, to our merely hating white people. If anything it seems that the opposite is true. People of color know that white people have abused us unmercifully and it is only sane for us to try to change that treatment by every means possible.

Likewise the bodies of murdered women are strewn across the landscape of this country. Rape is a national pastime, a form of torture visited upon all girls and women, from babies to the aged. One out of three women in the U.S. will be raped during her lifetime. Battering and incest, those home-based crimes, are pandemic. Murder, of course, is men's ultimate violent "solution." And if you're thinking as you read this that I'm exaggerating, please go get today's newspaper and verify the facts. If anything is going down here it's woman-hatred, not man-hatred, a war against women. But wanting to end this war still doesn't equal man-hating. The feminist movement and the anti-racist movement have in common trying to ensure decent human life. Opposition to either movement aligns one with the most reactionary elements in American society.

Myth No. 4: Women's issues are narrow, apolitical concerns. People of color need to deal with the "larger struggle." This myth once again characterizes women's oppression as not particularly serious, and by no means a matter of life and death. I have often wished I could spread the word that a movement committed to fighting sexual, racial, economic, and heterosexist oppression, not to mention one which opposes imperialism, anti-Semitism, the oppressions visited upon the physically disabled, the old and the young, at the same time that it challenges militarism and imminent nuclear destruction is the very opposite of narrow. All segments of the women's movement have not dealt with all of these issues, but neither have all segments of Black people. This myth is plausible when the women's move-

ment is equated only with its most bourgeois and reformist elements. The most progressive sectors of the feminist movement, which includes some radical white women, have taken the above issues, and many more, quite seriously. Third World women have been the most consistent in defining our politics broadly. Why is it that feminism is considered "white-minded" and "narrow" while socialism or Marxism, from verifiably white origins, is legitimately embraced by Third World male politicos, without their having their identity credentials questioned for a minute?

Myth No. 5: Those feminists are nothing but Lesbians. This may be the most pernicious myth of all and it is essential to understand that the distortion lies in the phrase "nothing but" and not in the identification Lesbian. "Nothing but" reduces Lesbians to a category of beings deserving of only the most violent attack, a category totally alien from "decent" Black folks, i.e., not your sisters, mothers, daughters, aunts, and cousins, but bizarre outsiders like no one you know or *ever* knew.

Many of the most committed and outspoken feminists of color have been and are Lesbians. Since many of us are also radicals, our politics, as indicated by the issues merely outlined above, encompass all people. We're also as Black as we ever were. (I always find it fascinating, for example, that many of the Black Lesbian-feminists I know still wear their hair natural, indicating that for us it was more than a "style.") Black feminism and Black Lesbianism are not interchangeable. Feminism is a political movement and many Lesbians are not feminists. Although it is also true that many Black feminists are not Lesbians, this myth has acted as an accusation and a deterrent to keep non-Lesbian Black feminists from manifesting themselves, for fear it will be hurled against them.

Fortunately this is changing. Personally, I have seen increasing evidence that many Black women of whatever sexual preference are more concerned with exploring and ending our oppression than they are committed to being either homophobic or sexually separatist. Direct historical precedent exists for such commitments. In 1957, Black playwright and activist Lorraine Hansberry wrote the following in a letter to *The Ladder,* an early Lesbian periodical:

> I think it is about time that equipped women began to take on some of the ethical questions which a male-dominated culture has produced and dissect and analyze them quite to pieces in a serious fashion. It is time that "half the human race" had something to say about the nature of its existence. Otherwise—without revised basic thinking—the woman intellectual is likely to find herself trying to draw conclusions—moral conclusions—based on acceptance of a social moral superstructure which has never admitted to the equality of women and is therefore immoral itself. As per marriage, as per sexual practices, as per the rearing of children, etc. In this kind of work there may be women to emerge who will be able to formulate a new and possible concept that homosexual persecution and condemnation has at its roots not only social ignorance, but a philosophically active anti-feminist dogma.[7]

I would like a lot more people to be aware that Lorraine Hansberry, one of our most respected artists and thinkers, was asking in a Lesbian context some of the same questions we are asking today, and for which we have been so maligned.

Black heterosexuals' panic about the existence of both Black Lesbians and Black gay men is a problem that they have to deal with themselves. A first step would be for them to better understand their own heterosexuality, which need not be defined by attacking everybody who is not heterosexual.

HOME TRUTHS

Above are some of the myths that have plagued Black feminism. The truth is that there is a vital movement of women of color in this country. Despite continual resistance to women of color defining our specific issues and organizing around them, it is safe to say in 1982 that we have a movement of our own. I have been involved in building that movement since 1973. It has been a struggle every step of the way and I feel we are still in just the beginning stages of developing a workable politics and practice. Yet the feminism of women of color, particularly of Afro-American women, has wrought many changes during these years, has had both ob-

vious and unrecognized impact upon the development of other political groupings and upon the lives and hopes of countless women.

The very nature of radical thought and action is that it has exponentially far-reaching results. But because all forms of media ignore Black women, in particular Black feminists, and because we have no widely distributed communication mechanisms of our own, few know the details of what we have accomplished. One of the purposes of *Home Girls* is to get the word out about Black feminism to the people who need it most: Black people in the U.S., the Caribbean, Latin America, Africa—everywhere. It is not possible for a single introduction or a single book to encompass all of what Black feminism is, but there is basic information I want every reader to have about the meaning of Black feminism as I have lived and understood it.

In 1977, a Black feminist organization in Boston of which I was a member from its founding in 1974, the Combahee River Collective, drafted a political statement for our own use and for inclusion in Zillah Eisenstein's anthology, *Capitalist Patriarchy and the Case for Socialist Feminism*. In our opening paragraph we wrote:

> The most general statement of our politics at the present time would be that we are actively committed to struggling against racial, sexual, heterosexual, and class oppression and see as our particular task the development of integrated analysis and practice based upon the fact that the major systems of oppression are interlocking. The synthesis of these oppressions creates the conditions of our lives. As Black women we see Black feminism as the logical political movement to combat the manifold and simultaneous oppressions that all women of color face.

The concept of the simultaneity of oppression is still the crux of a Black feminist understanding of political reality and, I believe, one of the most significant ideological contributions of Black feminist thought.

We examined our own lives and found that everything out there was kicking our behinds—race, class, sex, and homophobia. We saw no reason to rank oppressions, or, as many forces in the Black community would have us do, to pretend that sexism, among all the "isms," was not happening to us. Black feminists' efforts to comprehend the complexity of our situation as it was actually occurring, almost immediately began to deflate some of the cherished myths about Black womanhood, for example, that we are "castrating matriarchs" or that we are more economically privileged than Black men. Although we made use of the insights of other political ideologies, such as socialism, we added an element that has often been missing from the theory of others: what oppression is comprised of on a day-to-day basis, or as Black feminist musician Linda Tillery sings, ". . . what it's really like/To live this life of triple jeopardy."[8]

This multi-issued approach to politics has probably been most often used by other women of color who face very similar dynamics, at least as far as institutionalized oppression is concerned. It has also altered the women's movement as a whole. As a result of Third World feminist organizing, the women's movement now takes much more seriously the necessity for a multi-issued strategy for challenging women's oppression. The more progressive elements of the left have also begun to recognize that the promotion of sexism and homophobia within their ranks, besides being ethically unconscionable, ultimately undermines their ability to organize. Even a few Third World organizations have begun to include the challenging of women's and gay oppression on their public agendas.

Approaching politics with a comprehension of the simultaneity of oppressions has helped to create a political atmosphere particularly conducive to coalition building. Among all feminists, Third World women have undoubtedly felt most viscerally the need for linking struggles and have also been most capable of forging such coalitions. A commitment to principled coalitions, based not upon expediency, but upon our actual need for each other is a second major contribution of Black feminist struggle. Many contributors to *Home Girls* write out of a sense of our ultimate interdependence. Bernice Johnson Reagon's essay, "Coalition Politics: Turning the Century," should be particularly noted. She writes:

You don't go into coalition because you just *like* it. The only reason you would consider trying to team up with somebody who could possibly kill you, is because that's the only way you can figure you can stay alive. . . . Most of the time you feel threatened to the core and if you don't you're not really doing no coalescing.

The necessity for coalitions has pushed many groups to rigorously examine the attitudes and ignorance within themselves which prevent coalitions from succeeding. Most notably, there has been the commitment of some white feminists to make racism a priority issue within the women's movement, to take responsibility for their racism as individuals, and to do antiracist organizing in coalition with other groups. Because I have written and spoken about racism during my entire involvement as a feminist and have also presented workshops on racism for white women's organizations for several years during the 1970s, I have not only seen that there are white women who are fully committed to eradicating racism, but that new understandings of racial politics have evolved from feminism, which other progressive people would do well to comprehend.[9]

Having begun my political life in the Civil Rights movement and having seen the Black liberation movement virtually destroyed by the white power structure, I have been encouraged in recent years that women can be a significant force for bringing about racial change in a way that unites oppressions instead of isolating them. At the same time the percentage of white feminists who are concerned about racism is still a minority of the movement, and even within this minority those who are personally sensitive and completely serious about formulating an *activist* challenge to racism are fewer still. Because I have usually worked with politically radical feminists, I know that there are indeed white women worth building coalitions with, at the same time that there are apolitical, even reactionary, women who take the name of feminism in vain.

One of the greatest gifts of Black feminism to ourselves has been to make it a little easier simply to *be* Black and female. A Black feminist analysis has enabled us to understand that we are not hated and abused because there is something wrong with us, but because our status and treatment is absolutely prescribed by the racist, misogynistic system under which we live. There is not a Black woman in this country who has not, at some time, internalized and been deeply scarred by the hateful propaganda about us. There is not a Black woman in America who has not felt, at least once, like "the mule of the world," to use Zora Neale Hurston's still apt phrase.[10] Until Black feminism, very few people besides Black women actually cared about or took seriously the demoralization of being female *and* colored *and* poor *and* hated.

When I was growing up, despite my family's efforts to explain, or at least describe, attitudes prevalent in the outside world, I often thought that there was something fundamentally wrong with me because it was obvious that me and everybody like me was held in such contempt. The cold eyes of certain white teachers in school, the Black men who yelled from cars as Beverly and I stood waiting for the bus, convinced me that I must have done something horrible. How was I to know that racism and sexism had formed a blueprint for my mistreatment long before I had ever arrived here? As with most Black women, others' hatred of me became self-hatred, which has diminished over the years, but has by no means disappeared. Black feminism has, for me and for so many others, given us the tools to finally comprehend that it is not something we have done that has heaped this psychic violence and material abuse upon us, but the very fact that, because of who we are, we are multiply oppressed. Unlike any other movement, Black feminism provides the theory that clarifies the nature of Black women's experience, makes possible positive support from other Black women, and encourages political action that will change the very system that has put us down.   [1983]

NOTES

1. The terms Third World women and women of color are used here to designate Native American, Asian-American, Latina, and Afro-American women in the U.S. and the indigenous peoples of Third World countries wherever they may live. Both the terms Third World women and women of color apply to Black American women. At times in the introduction Black women are specifically designated as Black or Afro-American and at other times the terms women of color and Third World women are used to refer to women of color as a whole.

2. Smith, Barbara. "Notes for Yet Another Paper on Black Feminism, or Will the Real Enemy Please Stand Up?" in *Conditions: Five, The Black Women's Issue,* eds. Bethel & Smith. Vol. 2, No. 2 (Autumn, 1979), p. 124.

3. DuBois, W.E.B. *Darkwater, Voices from Within the Veil,* New York: AMS Press, 1969, p. 185.

4. Jordan, June & Bernice Johnson Reagon. "Oughta Be A Woman," *Good News,* Chicago: Flying Fish Records, 1981, Songtalk Publishing Co. Quoted by permission.

5. Teish, Luisah. "Women's Spirituality: A Household Act," in *Home Girls,* ed. Smith. Watertown: Persephone Press, Inc., 1983. All subsequent references to work in *Home Girls* will not be cited.

6. See Linda C. Powell's review of Michele Wallace's *Black Macho and the Myth of the Super Woman* ("Black Macho and Black Feminism") in this volume and my review of Bell Hooks' (Gloria Watkins) *Ain't I A Woman: Black Women and Feminism* in *The New Women's Times Feminist Review,* Vol. 9, no. 24 (November, 1982), pp. 10, 11, 18, 19 & 20 and in *The Black Scholar,* Vol. 14, No. 1 (January/February 1983), pp. 38–45.

7. Quoted from *Gay American History: Lesbians and Gay Men in the U.S.A.,* ed. Jonathan Katz. New York: T. Y. Crowell, 1976, p. 425. Also see Adrienne Rich's "The Problem with Lorraine Hansberry," in "Lorraine Hansberry: Art of Thunder, Vision of Light," *Freedomways,* Vol. 19, No. 4, 1979, pp. 247–255 for more material about her woman-identification.

8. Tillery, Linda. "Freedom Time," *Linda Tillery,* Oakland: Olivia Records, 1977, Tuizer Music.

9. Some useful articles on racism by white feminists are Elly Bulkin's "Racism and Writing: Some Implications for White Lesbian Critics." *Sinister Wisdom* 13 (Spring, 1980), pp. 3–22; Minnie Bruce Pratt's "Rebellion." *Feminary,* Vol. 11, Nos. 1 & 2 (1980), pp. 6–20; and Adrienne Rich's "Disloyal to Civilization: Feminism, Racism, Gynephobia." *On Lies, Secrets and Silence: Selected Prose 1966–1978.* New York: W. W. Norton, 1979, pp. 275–310.

10. Hurston, Zora Neale. *Their Eyes Were Watching God.* Urbana: University of Illinois, 1937, 1978, p. 29.

135

The Development of Chicana Feminist Discourse

ALMA M. GARCIA

Between 1970 and 1980, a Chicana feminist movement developed in the United States that addressed the specific issues that affected Chicanas as women of color. During the 1960s, the Chicano movement, characterized by a politics of protest, came into being, and focused on a wide range of issues: social justice, equality, educational reforms, and political and economic self-determination for Chicano communities in the United States.[1] Various struggles evolved within the Chicano movement: the United Farmworkers' unionization efforts;[2] the New Mexico Land Grant movement;[3] the Colorado-based Crusade for Justice;[4] the Chicano student movement;[5] and the Raza Unida Party.[6]

ORIGINS OF CHICANA FEMINISM

Rowbotham argues that women may develop a feminist consciousness as a result of their experiences with sexism in revolutionary struggles or mass social movements.[7] Chicana feminists began the search for a "room of their own" by assessing their participation within the Chicano movement. Their feminist consciousness emerged from a struggle for equality with Chicano men and from a reassessment of the role of the family as a means of resistance to oppressive societal conditions.

Historically, as well as during the 1960s and 1970s, the Chicano family represented a source of cultural and political resistance to the various types of discrimination experienced in the American society.[8] At the cultural level, the movement emphasized the need to safeguard the value of family loyalty. At the political level, the Chicano movement used the family as a strategic organizational tool for protest activities.

As women began to question their traditional female roles,[9] dramatic changes in the structure of Chicano families occurred. Thus, a Chicana feminist movement originated from the nationalist Chicano struggle: Rowbotham refers to such a feminist movement as "a colony within a colony."[10] But as the Chicano movement developed during the 1970s, Chicana feminists began to draw up their own political agenda and entered into a dialogue with the movement that explicitly reflected their struggles to secure a room of their own within it.

CHICANA FEMINISM AND CULTURAL NATIONALISM

During the 1960s and 1970s, Chicana feminists responded to the criticism that Chicano cultural nationalism and feminism were irreconcilable. Cultural nationalism represented a major, but not monolithic, component of the Chicano movement. It emphasized cultural pride, resistance, and survival within an Anglo-dominated nation-state. Thus, cultural nationalism shaped the political direction of the Chicano social protest movement. Sharing ideological roots with Black cultural nationalism, Chicanismo, as Chicano cultural nationalism became known, advocated a movement of cultural renaissance and resistance within Chicano communities throughout the United States. Chicanismo emphasized Mexican cultural pride as a source of political unity and strength capable of mobilizing Chicanos as an oppositional political group within the dominant American political landscape. Thus, Chicanismo provided a framework for the development of a collective ethnic consciousness—the essence of any nationalist ideology—that challenged the ideological hegemony of Anglo America. Moreover, Chicano cultural nationalism situated the sociohistorical experiences of Chicanos within a theoretical model of internal colonialism. Chicano communities were analyzed as ethnic "nations" existing under direct exploitation by the dominant society. "Nationalism, therefore, was to be the common denominator for uniting all Mexican Americans and making possible effective political mobilization."[11]

One source of ideological disagreement between Chicana feminism and this cultural nationalist ideology was cultural survival. Many Chicana feminists believed that a focus on cultural survival did not acknowledge the need to alter male-female relations within Chicano communities. For example, Chicana feminists criticized the notion of the "ideal Chicana" that glorified Chicanas as strong, long-suffering women who had endured and kept Chicano culture and the family intact. To Chicana feminists, this concept represented an obstacle to the redefinition of gender roles. Nieto Gomez stated:

> Some Chicanas are praised as they emulate the sanctified example set by [the Virgin] Mary. The woman par excellence is mother and wife. She is to love and support her husband and to nurture and teach her children. Thus, may she gain fulfillment as a woman. For a Chicana bent upon fulfillment of her personhood, this restricted perspective of her role as a woman is not only inadequate but crippling.[12]

Chicana feminists were also skeptical about the cultural nationalist interpretation of machismo. Such an interpretation viewed machismo as an ideological tool used by the dominant Anglo society to justify the inequalities experienced by Chicanos. According to this interpretation, the relationship between Chicanos and the larger society was that of an internal colony dominated and exploited by the capitalist economy.[13] Machismo, like other cultural traits, was blamed by Anglos for blocking Chicanos from succeeding in the American society. In reality, the economic structure and colony-like exploitation were to blame.

Some Chicana feminists agreed with this analysis of machismo, asserting that a mutually reinforcing relationship existed between internal colonialism and the development of the myth of machismo. According to Sosa Riddell, machismo was a myth "propagated by subjugators and colonizers, which created damaging stereotypes of Mexican/Chicano males."[14] As a type of social control imposed by the dominant society the myth of machismo distorted gender relations within Chicano communities, creating stereotypes of Chicanas as passive and docile

women. As Nieto concluded: "Although the term 'machismo' is correctly denounced by all because it stereotypes the Latin man . . . it does a great disservice to both men and women. Chicano and Chicana alike must be free to seek their own individual fulfillment."[15]

Some Chicana feminists criticized the myth of machismo used by the dominant society to legitimate racial inequality, but others moved beyond this level of analysis to distinguish between the machismo that oppressed both men and women and the sexism in Chicano communities in general, and the Chicano movement in particular, that oppressed Chicana women.[16] According to Vidal, the origins of a Chicana feminist consciousness were prompted by the sexist attitudes and behavior of Chicano males, which constituted a "serious obstacle to women anxious to play a role in the struggle for Chicana liberation."[17]

Furthermore, many Chicana feminists disagreed with the cultural nationalist view that machismo could be a positive value within a Chicano cultural value system. They challenged the notion that machismo was a source of masculine pride for Chicanos and therefore a defense mechanism against the dominant society's racism. Chicana feminists called for changes in the ideologies responsible for distorting relations between women and men. One such change was to modify the cultural nationalist position that looked upon machismo as a source of cultural pride.

Chicana feminists called for a focus on the universal aspects of sexism that shape gender relations in both Anglo and Chicano culture. Although they acknowledged the economic exploitation of all Chicanos, they outlined the double exploitation experienced by Chicanas. Sosa Riddell concluded: "It was when Chicanas began to seek work outside of the family groups that sexism became a key factor of oppression along with racism."[18] Francisca Flores summarized some of the consequences of sexism:

> It is not surprising that more and more Chicanas are forced to go to work in order to supplement the family income. The children are farmed out to a rela-

tive to baby-sit with them, and since these women are employed in the lower income jobs, the extra pressure placed on them can become unbearable.[19]

CHICANA FEMINISM AND FEMINIST BAITING

The systematic analysis by Chicana feminists of the impact of racism and sexism on Chicanas within American society and, above all, within the Chicano movement was often misunderstood as a threat to the political unity of the Chicano movement. But Marta Cotera, a leading voice of Chicana feminism, pointed out:

> The aggregate cultural values we [Chicanas] share can also work to our benefit if we choose to scrutinize our cultural traditions, isolate the positive attributes and interpret them for the benefit of women. It's unreal that Hispanas have been browbeaten for so long about our so-called conservative (meaning reactionary) culture. It's also unreal that we have let men interpret culture only as those practices and attitudes that determine who does the dishes around the house. We as women also have the right to interpret and define the philosophical and religious traditions beneficial to us within our culture, and which we have inherited as our tradition. To do this, we must become both conversant with our history and philosophical evolution, and analytical about the institutional and behavioral manifestations of the same.[20]

Such Chicana feminists were attacked for developing a "divisive ideology"—a feminist ideology that was frequently viewed as a threat to the Chicano movement as a whole. As Chicana feminists examined their roles as women activists within the Chicano movement, an ideological split developed. One group saw itself as "loyalists" who believed that the Chicano movement did not have to deal with sexual inequities because Chicano men as well as Chicano women experienced racial oppression. According to Nieto Gomez, who was not a loyalist, their belief was that if men oppress women, it is not the men's fault but rather that of the system.[21]

Even if such a problem existed, and they did not believe that it did, the loyalists maintained that such a matter would best be resolved internally, within the Chicano movement. They denounced the formation of a separate Chicana feminist movement on the grounds that it was a politically dangerous strategy, perhaps Anglo-inspired. Such a movement would undermine the unity of the Chicano movement by raising an issue that was not seen as central. Loyalists viewed racism as the most important issue within the Chicano movement. Nieto Gomez quotes one such loyalist:

> I am concerned with the direction that the Chicanas are taking in the movement. The words such as liberation, sexism, male chauvinism, etc., were prevalent. The terms mentioned above plus the theme of individualism is a concept of the Anglo society; terms prevalent in the Anglo women's movement. The familia has always been our strength in our culture. But it seems evident . . . that you [Chicana feminists] are not concerned with the familia, but are influenced by the Anglo woman's movement.[22]

Chicana feminists were also accused of undermining the values associated with Chicano culture. Loyalists saw the Chicana feminist movement as an "anti-family, anti-cultural, anti-man and therefore an anti-Chicano movement."[23] Feminism was, above all, believed to be an individualistic search for identity that detracted from the Chicano movement's "real" issues, such as racism. Nieto Gomez quotes a loyalist: "And since when does a Chicana need identity? If you are a real Chicana then no one regardless of the degrees needs to tell you about it. The only ones who need identity are the vendidas, the falsas, and the opportunists."[24]

The ideological conflicts between Chicana feminists and loyalists persisted throughout the 1970s, exacerbated during various Chicana conferences. At times, such confrontations served to increase Chicana feminist activity that challenged the loyalists' attacks, yet these attacks also served to suppress feminist activities.

Chicana feminists as well as Chicana feminist lesbians continued to be labeled *vendidas*, or "sellouts." Chicana loyalists continued to view Chicana feminism as associated not only with melting into white society but, more seriously, with dividing the Chicano movement. Similarly, many Chicano males were convinced that Chicana feminism was a divisive ideology incompatible with Chicano cultural nationalism. Nieto Gomez said that "[with] respect to [the] Chicana feminist, their credibility is reduced when they are associated with [feminism] and white women." She added that as a result, Chicana feminists often faced harassment and ostracism within the Chicano movement.[25] Similarly, Cotera stated that Chicanas "are suspected of assimilating into the feminist ideology of an alien [white] culture that actively seeks our cultural domination."[26]

Chicana feminists responded quickly and often vehemently to such charges. Flores answered, in an editorial, that birth control, abortion, and sex education are not merely "white issues." Reacting to the accusation that feminists were responsible for the "betrayal of [Chicano] culture and heritage," Flores said, "Our culture hell"—a phrase that became a dramatic slogan of the Chicana feminist movement.[27]

Chicana feminists' defense throughout the 1970s against those declaring that a feminist movement was divisive for the Chicano movement was to reassess their roles within the Chicano movement and to call for an end to male domination. Their challenges of traditional gender roles represented a means to achieve equality.[28] To increase the participation of and opportunities for women in the Chicano movement, feminists agreed that both Chicanos and Chicanas had to address the issue of gender inequality.[29] Furthermore, Chicana feminists argued that the resistance that they encountered reflected the existence of sexism on the part of Chicano males and the antifeminist attitudes of the Chicana loyalists. Nieto Gomez, in reviewing the experiences of Chicana feminists in the Chicano movement, concluded that Chicanas "involved in discussing and applying the women's question have been ostracized, isolated and ignored." She argued that "in organizations where cultural nationalism is extremely strong, Chicana feminists experience intense harassment and ostracism."[30] Black and Asian American women also faced severe criticism as they pursued feminist issues in their own communities. Indeed, as their participation in collective efforts to end racial oppression increased, so did their confrontations with sexism.[31]

CHICANA FEMINISTS AND WHITE FEMINISTS

The historical relationship between Chicana feminists and white feminists developed along problematic, if not contentious, lines. A major ideological tension between them involved the analysis by Chicana feminists of their experiences as both women and members of an ethnic community. Although Chicana feminists were critical of the patriarchal tendencies within the Chicano cultural nationalist movement, their feminist writings reveal a constant focus on the nature and consequences of racism on their daily lives, as well as on the role of a modified nationalist response as a form of resistance against the pernicious effects of racism.

Chicana feminists struggled to develop a feminist ideology that would successfully integrate race and gender as analytical tools. Feminism and nationalism were seen as political ideologies that could complement each other and, therefore, provide a more sharply focused view of the structural conditions of inequality experienced by Chicanas in American society. To the extent that Chicana feminists viewed the white feminist movement as incapable of integrating women of color and their nationalist struggles, political coalitions between the two groups appeared impossible. Nevertheless, Chicana feminists engaged in an ideological dialogue with white feminists.

Several issues made coalition-building difficult. First, Chicana feminists criticized what they considered to be a cornerstone of white feminist thought: an emphasis on gender oppression to explain the life circumstances of women. Chicana feminists believed that the white feminist movement overlooked the effects of racial oppression experienced by Chicanas and other women of color. Thus, Del Castillo maintained that the Chicana feminist movement was "different primarily because we are [racially] oppressed people."[32] In addition, Chicana feminists criticized white feminists who believed that a general women's movement would be able to overcome racial differences among women. Chicanas interpreted this as a failure by the white feminist movement to deal with racism. Without the incorporation of an analysis of racial oppression to explain the experiences of Chicanas as well as other women of color, a coalition with white feminists would be highly unlikely.[33] Longeaux y Vasquez concluded: "We must have a clearer vision of our plight and certainly we cannot blame our men for the oppression of the women."[34]

Chicana feminists adopted an analysis that began with race as a critical variable in interpreting the experiences of Chicano communities in the United States. They expanded this analysis by identifying gender as a variable interconnected with race in analyzing the specific daily life circumstances of Chicanas in Chicano communities. They did not view women's struggles as secondary to the nationalist movement but argued instead for an analysis of race and gender as multiple sources of oppression.[35] Thus, Chicana feminism went beyond the limits of an exclusively racial theory of oppression that tended to overlook gender and also beyond the limits of a theory of oppression based exclusively on gender that tended to overlook race.

A second factor preventing an alliance between Chicana feminists and white feminists was the middle-class orientation of white feminists. Throughout the 1970s Chicana feminists viewed the white feminist movement as a middle-class movement.[36] In contrast, they viewed the Chicano movement in general as a working-class movement. They repeatedly made reference to the difference, and many began their works with a section dissociating themselves from the "women's liberation movement." Chicana feminists as activists in the broader Chicano movement identified as major struggles the farmworkers' movement, welfare rights, undocumented workers, and prisoners' rights. Such issues were seen as far removed from the demands of the white feminist movement, and Chicana feminists could not get white feminist organizations to deal with them.[37]

White feminist organizations were also accused of being exclusionary, patronizing, or racist in their dealings with Chicanas and other women of color. Cotera states:

> Minority women could fill volumes with examples of put-downs, put-ons, and out-and-out racism shown to them by the leadership in the [white feminist] movement. There are three major problem areas in the minority-majority relationship in the movement: (1) paternalism or maternalism, (2) extremely limited opportunities for minority women . . . , (3) outright discrimination against minority women in the movement.[38]

Chicana feminists continued to stress the importance of developing autonomous feminist organizations that would address the struggles of Chicanas as members of an ethnic minority and as women. Rather than attempt to overcome the obstacles to coalition-building between Chicana feminists and white feminists, Chicanas called for autonomous feminist organizations for all women of color.[39] Chicana feminists believed that sisterhood was indeed powerful but only to the extent that racial and class differences were understood and, above all, respected. Nieto concludes: "The Chicana must demand that dignity and respect within the women's rights movement which allows her to practice feminism within the context of her own culture. . . . Her approaches to feminism must be drawn from her own world."[40]

CHICANA FEMINISM: AN EVOLVING FUTURE

Chicana feminists, like Black, Asian American, and Native American feminists, experience specific life conditions that are distinct from those of white feminists. Socioeconomic and cultural differences in Chicano communities directly shaped the development of Chicana feminism and the relationship between Chicana feminists and feminists of other racial and ethnic groups, including white feminists. Future dialogue among all feminists will require a shared understanding of the existing differences as well as of the similarities. Like other women of color, Chicana feminists must address issues that specifically affect them as women of color. In addition, Chicana feminists must address issues that have particular impact on Chicano communities, such as poverty, limited opportunities for higher education, high school dropouts, health care, bilingual education, immigration reform, prison reform, welfare, and recently, United States policies in Central America.

At the academic level, an increasing number of Chicana feminists continue to join in a collective effort to carry on the feminist legacy inherited from the 1970s. In June 1982 a group of Chicana academics organized the national feminist organization Mujeres Activas en Letras y Cambio Social (MALCS) in order to build a support network for Chicana professors, undergraduates, and graduate students. The organization's major goal is to fight the race, class, and gender oppression facing Chicanas in institutions of higher education. In addition, MALCS aim to bridge the gap between academic work and the Chicano community.

In 1984 the national conference of the National Association for Chicano Studies (NACS), held in Austin, Texas, adopted the theme *"Voces de la Mujer"* in response to demands from the Chicana Caucus. As a result, for the first time since its founding in 1972, the NACS national conference addressed the issue of women. Compared with past conferences, a large number of Chicanas participated by presenting their research and chairing and moderating panels. A plenary session addressed the gender inequality in higher education and within NACS. And at the business meeting, sexism within NACS was again seriously debated because it continues to be one of the "unsettled issues" of concern to Chicana feminists. A significant outcome of the conference was that its published proceedings that year were the first to be devoted to Chicanas and Mexicanas.[41]

Chicana feminists continue to raise critical issues concerning the nature of the oppression experienced by Chicanas and other women of color. They, like African American, Asian American, and Native American feminists, focus on the consequences of the intersection of race, class, and gender in the daily lives of women in American society. Chicana feminists have adopted a theoretical perspective that em-phasizes the simultaneous impact of these critical variables for women of color.[42]

Chicana feminists have emphasized that Chicanas have made few gains in comparison to white men and women, as well as Chicano men, in terms of labor-force participation, income, education levels, rates of poverty, and other socioeconomic status indicators. Over the past forty years, Chicanas have made only small occupational moves from low-pay unskilled jobs to higher-pay skilled and semiprofessional employment. Studies indicate that about 66 percent remain occupationally segregated in such low-paying jobs as sales, clerical, service, and factory work. Further, Chicanas experience major social-structural constraints that limit their upward social mobility.[43] Less than 15 percent of all Chicanas have entered the occupational ranks of professionals, educational administrators, and business managers. In addition, Chicano families had approximately two-thirds of the family income of non-Hispanic families —approximately the same as ten years ago—and about 46 percent of families headed by Chicanas had incomes below the poverty level.

Chicana feminists are also concerned about Chicano schooling; the persistently low levels of educational attainment are deemed to be evidence of the role of race, class, and gender stratification in reinforcing and perpetuating inequalities. Chicanas, as well as all Latinas, have shockingly high dropout rates, with the not surprising consequence that Chicanas are scarce in the halls of academe.[44] According to one of the few studies on Chicanas in higher education, "of all the major population groups, Mexican American females are the poorest and the most underrepresented in higher education."[45]

Despite the limited numbers of Chicana academics, Chicana feminist discourse has developed within the academy as Chicana feminists have entered into specific dialogues with other feminists. Chicanas have criticized feminist scholarship for the exclusionary practices that have resulted from the discipline's limited attention to differences among women relating to race, ethnicity, class, and sexual preference.[46] Interestingly, Chicana feminists are also critical of Chicano studies and ethnic studies scholarship, which have too often lacked a systematic gender analysis.[47] As a result, Chicana feminist discourse is integrating the experiences of Chicanas within these academic disciplines. Chicana feminist scholars advocate restructuring the academy in order to integrate the "new knowledge" about women,[48] in this case, Chicanas. Indeed, Chicana feminist scholarship "came of age" in the 1990s, with publication of a variety of anthologies written by and about Chicanas.[49]

Chicana feminist scholars are revitalizing the fields of Chicano studies, ethnic studies, and women's studies. Indeed, many of them argue that their writings are creating a separate, interdisciplinary field: Chicana studies.

Sociologist Denise Segura reflects on the different approaches found among Chicana feminist scholars:

> There are several types of Chicana scholarship. One type tries to connect research on Chicanas to mainstream frameworks in the respective fields; another type tries to develop an understanding of the status and oppression of Chicanas, using feminist frameworks as points of departure; another type, connected to postmodernist frameworks, tries to get away from all mainstream thought. It begins with Chicanas as a point of departure and builds from there an understanding of their uniqueness as well as their commonalities with other oppressed peoples in this society.[50]

In their study of Chicana feminism among Chicanas in higher education and Chicana white-collar workers, Pesquera and Segura found that Chicana feminism is not ideologically monolithic. Pesquera and Segura documented the emergence of ideologically divergent strands of Chicana feminism based on the social positioning of specific groups of Chicanas.[51] A future task for Chicana feminist scholars will be to explore further the dynamic interaction of cross-cutting memberships based on class, education, sexual orientation, and other critical variables in order to understand better the continued development of Chicana feminist discourse in the twenty-first century.

Chicana scholars are truly moving in new direc-tions. Chicana feminist writings represent the accumulated maturity of an intellectual tradition rooted in the political activism of the 1960s. Nevertheless, Chicana feminists, like other feminist women of color, continue to join their intellectual discourse with their political activism. Indeed, each informs the other. Pesquera and Segura succinctly characterize the major underlying force of Chicana feminist discourse as a

> Chicana critique of cultural, political and economic conditions in the United States. It is influenced by the tradition of advocacy scholarship, which challenges the claims of objectivity and links research to community concerns and social change. It is driven by a passion to place the Chicana, as speaking subject, at the center of intellectual discourse.[52]

The voices of Chicana feminists will continue to resonate as the next century approaches. Their struggles and triumphs will continue to shape the ideological direction of American feminism and future generations of feminists. [1997]

NOTES

1. Mario Barrera, "The Study of Politics and the Chicano," *Aztlan* 5 (1976): 9–26; Carlos Munoz, Jr., "The Politics of Protest and Liberation: A Case Study of Repression and Cooptation," *Aztlan* 5 (1974): 119–141; Armando Navarro, "The Evolution of Chicano Politics," *Aztlan* 5 (1974): 57–84.
2. John Dunne, *Delano: The Story of the California Grape Strike* (New York: Straus, 1967); Sam Kushner, *Long Road to Delano* (New York: International, 1975); Eugene Nelson, *Huelga: The First 100 Days* (Delano, CA: Farm Workers Press, 1966).
3. Peter Nabokov, *Tijerina and the Courthouse Raid* (Albuquerque: University of New Mexico Press, 1969).
4. Tony Castro, *Chicano Power* (New York: Saturday Review Press, 1974): Matt Meier and Feliciano Rivera, *The Chicanos* (New York: Hill & Wang, 1972).
5. F. Chris Garcia and Rudolpho O. de la Garza, *The Chicano Political Experience* (North Scituate, MA: Duxbury, 1977).
6. John Shockley, *Chicano Revolt in a Texas Town* (South Bend: University of Notre Dame Press, 1974).
7. Sheila Rowbotham, *Women, Resistance and Revolution: A History of Women and Revolution in the Modern World* (New York: Vintage, 1974).
8. Maxine Baca Zinn, "Political Familism: Toward Sex Role Equality in Chicano Families," *Aztlan* 6 (1977): 13–27.
9. Ibid.
10. Rowbotham, *Women, Resistance and Revolution,* p. 206.

11. Carlos Munoz, Jr., *Youth, Identity, Power: The Chicano Movement* (New York: Verso, 1989), p. 77.
12. Ibid., p. 4.
13. Tomas Almaguer, "Historical Notes on Chicano Oppression," *Aztlan* 5 (1974): 27–56; Mario Barrera, *Race and Class in the Southwest* (Notre Dame: University of Notre Dame Press, 1979).
14. Adaljiza Sosa Riddell, "Chicanas en el Movimiento," *Aztlan* 5 (1974): 159.
15. Nieto Gomez, "Chicanas Identify," p. 4.
16. Henri Chavez, "The Chicanas," *Regeneracion* 1 (1971): 14; Marta Cotera, *The Chicana Feminist* (Austin, TX: Austin Information Systems Development, 1977); Marta Cotera, "Feminism: the Chicana and Anglo Versions: An Historical Analysis," in *Twice a Minority: Mexican American Women*, ed. Margarita Melville (St. Louis, MO: C. V. Mosby, 1980), pp. 217–234; Adelaida Del Castillo, "La Vision Chicana," *La Gente* 8 (1974): p. 8; Evelina Marquez and Margarita Ramirez, "Women's Task Is to Gain Liberation," in *Essays on La Mujer*, ed. Rosaura Sanchez and Rosa Martinez Cruz (Los Angeles: UCLA Chicano Studies Center, 1977), pp. 188–194; Riddell, "Chicanas en el Movimiento"; Maxine Baca Zinn, "Chicanas: Power and Control in the Domestic Sphere," *De Colores* 2 no. 3, (1975): 19–31.
17. Mirta Vidal, "New Voice of La Raza: Chicanas Speak Out," *International Socialist Review* 32 (1971): 8.
18. Riddell, "Chicanas en el Movimiento," p. 159.
19. Francisca Flores, "Conference of Mexican Women: Un Remolina," *Regeneracion*, no. 1 (1971): 4.
20. Cotera, *The Chicana Feminist*, p. 9.
21. Anna Gomez Nieto, "La Feminista," *Encuentro Remenil* 1 (1973): 34–47, lt p. 35.
22. Ibid.
23. Ibid.
24. Ibid.
25. Anna Gomez Nieto, "Sexism in the Movement," *La Gente* 6, no. 4 (1976): 10.
26. Cotera 1977, p. 30.
27. Flores, "Conference of Mexican Women," p. 1.
28. Enriqueta Longeaux y Vasquez, "The Woman of La Raza," *El Grito del Norte* (November 1969): 12. Also, Enriqueta Longeaux y Vasquez, "La Chicana: Let's Build a New Life," *El Grito del Norte* 2 (November 1969): 11.
29. Evey Chapa, "Report from the National Women's Political Caucus," *Magazin* 11 (1973); 37–39; Chavez, "The Chicanas"; Del Castillo, "La Vision Chicana"; Cotera, *The Chicana Feminist*; Dorinda Moreno, "The Image of the Chicana and the La Raza Woman," *Caracol* 2 (1979): 14–15.
30. Nieto, "La Feminista," p. 31.
31. Chow, "The Development of Feminist Consciousness," p. 288; hooks, *Ain't I a Woman*; White, "Listening to the Voices of Black Feminism."
32. Del Castillo, "La Vision Chicana," p. 8.
33. Chapa, "Report from the National Women's Political Caucus"; Cotera, *The Chicana Feminist*; Nieto Gomez, "La Feminista"; Longeaux y Vasquez, "Soy Chicana Primera."
34. Longeaux y Vasquez, "Soy Chicana Primera."
35. Cotera, *The Chicana Feminist*.
36. Chapa, "Report from the National Women's Political Caucus"; Cotera, *The Chicana Feminist*; Longeaux y Vasquez, "Soy Chicana Primero"; Martinez, "The Chicana"; Nieto, "The Chicana and the Women's Rights Movement"; Orozco, "La Chicana and 'Women's Liberation.'"
37. Cotera, *The Chicana Feminist*.
38. Cotera, "Feminism," p. 227.
39. Cotera, *The Chicana Feminist*; Sylvia Gonzalez, "Toward a Feminist Pedagogy for Chicana Self-Actualization," *Frontiers* 5 (1980): 48–51; Consuelo Nieto, "Consuelo Nieto on the Women's Movement," *Interracial Books for Children,*" *Bulletin* 5, no. 4 (1975).
40. Consuelo Nieto, "The Chicana and the Women's Rights Movement"; *La Luz*, September 3, 1974, p. 4.
41. Cordova et al., *Chicana Voices*.
42. Moraga and Anzaldua, *This Bridge Called My Back*; Moraga, "La Guera"; hooks, *Feminist Theory*; Alma Garcia, "Studying Chicanas" in *Chicana Voices*, Teresa Cordova et al. (Austin, Texas; Center for Mexican American Studies, 1986); Gloria Anzaldua, *Borderlands/La Frontera: The New Mestiza* (San Francisco: Aunt Lute Press, 1987); Gloria Anzaldua, *Making Face, Making Sant —Haciendo Caras: Creative and Critical Perspectives by Feminists of Color* (San Francisco: Aunt Lute Press, 1990).
43. Denise Segura, "Chicana and Mexican Immigrant Women at Work: Impact of Class, Race, and Gender on Occupational Mobility," *Gender and Society* 3 (1989): 37–52; Mary Romero, *Maid in the U.S.A.* (New York: Routledge, 1992).
44. Christine Marie Sierra, "The University Setting Reinforces Inequality," in Cordova et al., *Chicana Voices*, pp. 5–7; Orozco, "La Chicana and 'Women's Liberation'"; Denise Segura, "Chicanas and Triple Oppression in the Labor Force," in Cordova et al., *Chicana Voices*, pp. 47–65; Denise Segura, "Slipping Through the Cracks: Dilemmas in Chicana Education," in *Building with Our Hands*, ed. Adeala de la Torre and Beatrice Pesquera (Berkeley: University of California Press, 1993).
45. Maria Chacon, *Chicanas in Post-Secondary Education* (Stanford: Stanford University Press, 1982).
46. Maxine Baca Zinn, Lynn Weber Cannon, Elizabeth Higginbotham, and Bonnie Thornton Dill, "The Cost of Exclusionary Practices in Women's Studies," *Signs* 11 (1986): 290–302.
47. Mujeres en Marcha, *Chicanas in the 80s: Unsettled Issues* (Berkeley: Chicano Studies Publication Unit, 1983); Orozco, "La Chicana and 'Women's Liberation'"; Norma Alarcon, "The Theoretical Subject(s) of This Bridge Called My Back and Anglo American Feminism," in *Criticism in the Borderlands: Studies in Chicano Literature, Culture and Ideology*, ed. Hector Calderon and Jose David Saldivar (Durham: Duke University Press, 1991); Alma Garcia, "Chicano Studies and 'La Chicana' Courses: Curriculum Options and Reforms," in *Community Empowerment and Chicano Scholarship:*

Selected Proceedings of National Association of Chicano Studies, 1992.

48. Joan Wallach Scott, *Gender and Politics in History* (New York: Columbia University Press, 1988).

49. Adeala de la Torre and Beatrice Pesquera, eds., *Building with Our Hands* (Berkeley: University of California Press, 1993); Tey Diana Rebolledo and Eliana S. Rivero, *Infinite Divisions: An Anthology of Chicana Literature* (Tucson: University of Arizona Press, 1993); Norma Alarcon et al., *Chicana Critical Issues* (Berkeley: Third World Press, 1993).

50. Segura, quoted in *Building With Our Hands*, p. 6.

51. Beatriz M. Pesquera and Denise M. Segura, "There Is No Going Back: Chicanas and Feminism," in *Chicana Critical Issues*, ed. Norma Alarcon (Berkeley: Third Woman Press, 1993), pp. 95–115.

52. Ibid., p. 1.

 136

Thoughts on Indian Feminism

KATE SHANLEY

Attending the Ohoyo conference in Grand Forks, North Dakota was a returning home for me in a spiritual sense—taking my place beside other Indian women, and an actual sense—being with my relatives and loved ones after finally finishing my pre-doctoral requirements at the university. Although I have been a full-time student for the past six years, I brought to the academic experience many years in the workaday world as a mother, registered nurse, volunteer tutor, social worker aide, and high school outreach worker. What I am offering in this article are my thoughts as an Indian woman on feminism. Mine is a political perspective that seeks to re-view the real-life positions of women in relation to the theories that attempt to address the needs of those women.

Issues such as equal pay for equal work, child health and welfare, and a woman's right to make her own choices regarding contraceptive use, sterilization and abortion—key issues to the majority women's movement—affect Indian women as well; however, equality *per se,* may have a different meaning

for Indian women and Indian people. That difference begins with personal and tribal sovereignty—the right to be legally recognized as peoples empowered to determine our own destinies. Thus, the Indian women's movement seeks equality in two ways that do not concern mainstream women: (1) on the individual level, the Indian woman struggles to promote the survival of a social structure whose organizational principles represent notions of family different from those of the mainstream; and (2) on the societal level, the People seek sovereignty as a people in order to maintain a vital legal and spiritual connection to the land, in order to *survive* as a people.

The nuclear family has little relevance to Indian women; in fact, in many ways, mainstream feminists now are striving to redefine family and community in a way that Indian women have long known. The American lifestyle from which white middle-class women are fighting to free themselves, has not taken hold in Indian communities. Tribal and communal values have survived after four hundred years of colonial oppression.

It may be that the desire on the part of mainstream feminists to include Indian women, however sincere, represents tokenism just now, because too often Indian people, by being thought of as spiritual "mascots" to the American endeavor, are seen more as artifacts than a real people able to speak for ourselves. Given the public's general ignorance about Indian people, in other words, it is possible that Indian people's real-life concerns are not relevant to the mainstream feminist movement in a way that constitutes anything more than a "representative" facade. Charges against the women's movement of heterosexism and racism abound these days; it is not my intention to add to them except to stress that we must all be vigilant in examining the underlying assumptions that motivate us. Internalization of negative (that is, sexist and racist) attitudes towards ourselves and others can and quite often does result from colonialist (white patriarchal) oppression. It is more useful to attack the systems that keep us ignorant of each other's histories.

The other way in which the Indian women's movement differs in emphasis from the majority women's movement, lies in the importance Indian people place on tribal sovereignty—it is the single most pressing political issue in Indian country today. For Indian people to survive culturally as well as materially, many battles must be fought and won in the courts of law, precisely because it is the legal recognition that enables Indian people to govern ourselves according to our own world view—a world view that is antithetical to the *wasicu* (the Lakota term for "takers of the fat") definition of progress. Equality for Indian women within tribal communities, therefore, holds more significance than equality in terms of the general rubric "American."

Up to now I have been referring to the women's movement as though it were a single, well-defined organization. It is not. Perhaps in many ways socialist feminists hold views similar to the views of many Indian people regarding private property and the nuclear family. Certainly, there are some Indian people who are capitalistic. The point I would like to stress, however, is that rather than seeing differences according to a hierarchy of oppressions (white over Indian, male over female), we must practice a politics that allows for diversity in cultural identity as well as in sexual identity.

The word "feminism" has special meanings to Indian women, including the idea of promoting the continuity of tradition, and consequently, pursuing the recognition of tribal sovereignty. Even so, Indian feminists are united with mainstream feminists in outrage against woman and child battering, sexist employment and educational practices, and in many other social concerns. Just as sovereignty cannot be granted but *must be recognized* as an inherent right to self-determination, so Indian feminism must also be recognized as powerful in its own terms, in its own right.

Feminism becomes an incredibly powerful term when it incorporates diversity—not as a superficial political position, but as a practice. The women's movement and the Indian movement for sovereignty suffer similar trivialization, because narrow factions turn ignorance to their own benefit so that they can exploit human beings and the lands they live on for corporate profit. The time has come for Indian women and Indian people to be known on our own

terms. This nuclear age demands new terms of communication for all people. Our survival depends on it. Peace.   [1984]

 137

Presenting the Blue Goddess: Toward a National Pan-Asian Feminist Agenda

SONIA SHAH

We all laughed sheepishly about how we used to dismiss the South Asian women in our lives as doormats irrelevant to our feminist lives. For most of us in that fledgling South Asian American women's group in Boston, either white feminists or black feminists had inspired us to find our Asian feminist heritage. Yet neither movement had really prepared us for actually finding any. The way either group defined feminism did not, could not, define our South Asian feminist heritages. That, for most of us, consisted of feisty immigrant mothers, ball-breaking grandmothers, Kali-worship (Kali is the blue goddess who sprang whole from another woman and who symbolizes "shakti"—Hindi for womanpower), social activist aunts, freedom-fighting/Gandhian great-aunts. In many ways, white feminism, with its "personal is political" maxim and its emphasis on building sisterhood and consciousness raising, had brought us together. Black feminism, on the other hand, had taught us that we could expect more—that feminism can incorporate a race analysis. Yet, while both movements spurred us to organize, neither included our South Asian American agendas —battery of immigrant women, the ghettoization of the Indian community, cultural discrimination, and bicultural history and identity.

I felt we were starting anew, starting to define a South Asian American feminism that no one had articulated yet. As I began to reach out to other Asian

American women's groups over the years and for this chapter, however, that sense faded a bit. Asian American women have been organizing themselves for decades, with much to show for it.

Our shakti hasn't yet expressed itself on a national stage accessible to all our sisters. But we are entering a moment in our organizing when we will soon be able to create a distinctly Asian American feminism, one that will be able to cross the class and culture lines that currently divide us.

The first wave of Asian women's organizing, born of the women's liberation and civil rights movements of the 1960s, established groups like Asian Women United in San Francisco, Asian Sisters in Action in Boston, and other more informal networks of primarily professional, East Asian American women. They focused on empowering Asian women economically and socially and accessing political power. Asian Women United, for example, has produced videos like *Silk Wings,* which describes Asian women in nontraditional jobs, and books like *Making Waves,* an anthology of Asian American women's writing.

In contrast, the second wave of organizing, politicized by the 1980s multicultural movements, includes the many ethnically specific women's groups that tend to start out as support networks, some later becoming active in the battered women's movement (like Manavi in New Jersey, Sneha in Hartford, and the New York Asian Women's Center, which offer battery hotlines and shelter for Asian women) and others working in the women-of-color and lesbian/gay liberation movements. Culturally, these groups are Korean, Indian, Cambodian, Filipina, and from other more recently arrived immigrant groups who may not have felt part of the more established, primarily East Asian women's networks. These different groups are divided by generation, by culture, and by geographic location. Anna Rhee, a cofounder of the Washington Alliance of Korean American Women (WAKAW), a group of mostly 1.5 generation (those who emigrated to the United States in early adulthood) and second-generation Korean American women, with an average age of twenty-seven to twenty-eight, says she felt "we were starting anew, because of the focus on English speak-

ing Korean women, which was different from any other group we had seen." WAKAW, like many similar groups, started as a support group, but has since evolved into activism, with voter registration and other projects.

Talking to various Asian American women activists, I was inspired by the many projects they have undertaken, and impressed with the overwhelming sense women had that the Asian American women's community today stands at a crossroads and has great potential. The New York Asian Women's Center, which runs several programs fighting violence against Asian women, just celebrated its tenth birthday. The Pacific Asian American Women's Bay Area Coalition honors Asian American women with Woman Warrior (á la Maxine Hong Kingston's novel) leadership awards, catapulting their honorees on to other accolades. Indian Subcontinent Women's Alliance for Action (ISWAA) in Boston just assembled a grassroots arts exhibit of works by and for South Asian women. Asian Women United, in addition to several other videos, is working on a video of Asian American visual artists. The Washington Alliance for Korean American women is taking oral histories of Korean mothers and daughters. Everyone has a story of another group starting up, another exciting Asian American woman activist.

So far, Asian American women activists have used two general organizing models. The first is based on the fact that Asian women need each other to overcome the violence, isolation, and powerlessness of their lives; no one else can or will be able to help us but each other. The groups that come together on this basis focus on the immediate needs of the community: housing battered women, finding homes for abandoned women and children, providing legal advocacy for refugee women, and so forth.

The second model is based on shared identity and the realization that both Asian and U.S. mainstream cultures make Asian American women invisible. The groups that come together on this basis work on articulating anger about racism and sexism, like other women of color groups, but also on fighting the omnipresent and seductive pressure to assimilate, within ourselves and for our sisters.

Today, our numbers are exploding, in our immigrant communities and their children, and subsequently, in our activist communities. Our writers, poets, artists, and filmmakers are coming of age. Our activist voices against anti-Asian violence, battery, and racism are gaining legal, political, and social notice. We still have much ground to cover in influencing mainstream culture: we must throw those exoticizing books about Asian women off the shelf and replace them with a slew of works on pan-Asian feminism; women of color putting together collections of radical essays must be able to "find" Asian American feminists; *Ms.* magazine must offer more than a colorful photo of an Indian mother and daughter with less than three lines about them in a related cover article; critics must stop touting Asian American women's fiction as "exotic treasures"; Fifth Avenue advertising executives must stop producing ads that exploit tired stereotypes of Asian female "exotic beauty" and "humble modesty" with images of silky black hair and Asian women demurely tucking tampons into their pockets.

Our movement faces crucial internal challenges as well. Longtime Asian American feminist activists, such as Helen Zia, a contributing editor to *Ms.*, wonder, "What makes us different from white feminists or black feminists? What can we bring to the table?" and complain that "these questions haven't really been developed yet." Others, such as Jackie Church, a Japanese American activist, state that "there just aren't enough Asian American feminists who aren't doing five different things at once."

On the one hand, our national Asian women's groups, while inclusive across Asian ethnicities, haven't yet developed an Asian feminism *different* from black or white feminism. On the other, our ethnically specific groups, while emotionally resonant and culturally specific, are still remote and inaccessible to many of our sisters.

The movements of the 1960s colluded with the mainstream in defining racism in black and white terms; racism is still defined as discrimination based on skin color, that is, race. They also, to some extent, elevated racism, defined in this way, to the top of layers of oppression. This narrow definition has distorted mainstream perception of anti-Asian racism and even our perception of ourselves—as either nonvictims of racism or victims of racism based on skin color. By these assumptions, an Indian assaulted because she "dresses weird" is not a victim of racism; a Chinese shopkeeper harassed because she has a "funny accent" is not a victim of racism. Mainstream culture finds neither of these incidents as disturbing, unacceptable, or even downright "evil" as racism. By this definition, one must be in either the black or white camp to even speak about racism, and we are expected to forget ourselves. Whites try to convince us we are really *more like them;* depending on our degree of sensitivity toward racist injustice, we try to persuade blacks that we are more like them.

For example, many Asian American women have described Asian women's experience of racism as a result of stereotypes about "exotica" and "china dolls," two stereotypes based on our looking different from white people. But our experiences of racism go far beyond that. Rather than subvert the definition of racism itself, or uncover new layers of oppression just as unacceptable and pernicious as racism but based on what I call cultural discrimination, we have attempted to fit our experience of discrimination into the given definition. We too assume that racism is the worst kind of oppression, by emphasizing that racism against us is based on skin color and racial differences. Indeed, when we forged our first wave of women's movement, solidarity with other people of color whose activism revolved around black/white paradigms of oppression was a matter of survival. And organizing around racially based oppressions served as common ground for all ethnic Asians.

Yet our experiences of oppression are, in many qualitative ways, different from those of black and white people. For me, the experience of "otherness," the formative discrimination in my life, has resulted from culturally different (not necessarily racially different) people thinking they were culturally central: thinking that *my* house smelled funny, that *my* mother talked weird, that *my* habits were strange. They were normal; I wasn't.

Today, a more sophisticated understanding of oppression is emanating from all people of color groups. The Los Angeles riots, among other ethnic conflicts, unmasked to belated national attention the reality of an ethnic conflict (between blacks and browns, as well as between the white power structure and oppressed people of color) impossible to explain away simply as white-against-black racism. Multicultural movements and growing internationalism have raised questions about our hierarchy of oppressions. Asian American men and women activists are beginning to create legal and social definitions of cultural discrimination. Our movement can march beyond black/white paradigms that were once useful, and start to highlight cultural discrimination—our peculiar blend of cultural and sexist oppression based on our accents, our clothes, our foods, our values, and our commitments. When we do this successfully, we will have not just laid a common ground for all ethnic Asian women for the practical goal of gaining power, we will have taken an important political step toward understanding and, from there, struggling against the many layers of oppression.   [1997]

🌿 138

Blame It on Feminism

SUSAN FALUDI

To be a woman in America at the close of the 20th century—what good fortune. That's what we keep hearing, anyway. The barricades have fallen, politicians assure us. Women have "made it," Madison Avenue cheers. Women's fight for equality has "largely been won," *Time* magazine announces. Enroll at any university, join any law firm, apply for credit at any bank. Women have so many opportunities now, corporate leaders say, that we don't really need equal opportunity policies. Women are so equal now, lawmakers say, that we no longer need an Equal Rights Amendment. Women have "so much," former President Ronald Reagan says, that the White House no longer needs to appoint them to higher office. Even American Express ads are saluting a woman's freedom to charge it. At last, women have received their full citizenship papers.

And yet . . .

Behind this celebration of the American woman's victory, behind the news, cheerfully and endlessly repeated, that the struggle for women's rights is won, another message flashes. You may be free and equal now, it says to women, but you have never been more miserable.

This bulletin of despair is posted everywhere—at the newsstand, on the TV set, at the movies, in advertisements and doctors' offices and academic journals. Professional women are suffering "burnout" and succumbing to an "infertility epidemic." Single women are grieving from a "man shortage." The *New York Times* reports: Childless women are "depressed and confused" and their ranks are swelling. *Newsweek* says: Unwed women are "hysterical" and crumbling under a "profound crisis of confidence." The health advice manuals inform: High-powered career women are stricken with unprecedented outbreaks of "stress-induced disorders," hair loss, bad nerves, alcoholism, and even heart attacks. The psychology books advise: Independent women's loneliness represents "a major mental health problem today." Even founding feminist Betty Friedan has been spreading the word: she warns that women now suffer from a new identity crisis and "new 'problems that have no name.'"

How can American women be in so much trouble at the same time that they are supposed to be so blessed? If the status of women has never been higher, why is their emotional state so low? If women got what they asked for, what could possibly be the matter now?

The prevailing wisdom of the past decade has supported one, and only one, answer to this riddle: it must be all that equality that's causing all that pain. Women are unhappy precisely *because* they are free. Women are enslaved by their own liberation. They have grabbed at the gold ring of independence, only to miss the one ring that really matters. They have gained control of their fertility, only to destroy it. They have pursued their own professional dreams—and lost out on the greatest female adventure. The women's movement, as we are told time and again, has proved women's own worst enemy.

"In dispensing its spoils, women's liberation has given my generation high incomes, our own cigarette, the option of single parenthood, rape crisis centers, personal lines of credit, free love, and female gynecologists," Mona Charen, a young law student, writes in the *National Review,* in an article titled "The Feminist Mistake." "In return it has effectively robbed us of one thing upon which the happiness of most women rests—men." The *National Review* is a conservative publication, but such charges against the women's movement are not confined to its pages. "Our generation was the human sacrifice" to the women's movement, *Los Angeles Times* feature writer Elizabeth Mehren contends in a *Time* cover story. Baby-boom women like her, she says, have been duped by feminism: "We believed the rhetoric." In *Newsweek,* writer Kay Ebeling dubs feminism "the Great Experiment That Failed" and asserts "women in my generation, its perpetrators, are the casualties." Even the beauty magazines are saying it: *Harper's Bazaar* accuses the women's movement of having "lost us [women] ground instead of gaining it."

In the last decade, publications from the *New York Times* to *Vanity Fair* to the *Nation* have issued a steady stream of indictments against the women's movement, with such headlines as WHEN FEMINISM FAILED or THE AWFUL TRUTH ABOUT WOMEN'S LIB. They hold the campaign for women's equality responsible for nearly every woe besetting women, from mental depression to meager savings accounts, from teenage suicides to eating disorders to bad complexions. The "Today" show says women's liberation is to blame for bag ladies. A guest columnist in the *Baltimore Sun* even proposes that feminists produced the rise in slasher movies. By making the "violence" of abortion more acceptable, the author reasons, women's rights activists made it all right to show graphic murders on screen.

At the same time, other outlets of popular culture have been forging the same connection: in Hollywood films, of which *Fatal Attraction* is only the most famous, emancipated women with condominiums of their own slink wild-eyed between bare walls, paying for their liberty with an empty bed, a barren womb. "My biological clock is ticking so loud it keeps me awake at night," Sally Field cries in the film *Surrender,* as, in an all too common transformation in the cinema of the '80s, an actress who once played scrappy working heroines is now showcased groveling for a groom. In prime-time television shows, from "thirtysomething" to "Family Man," single, professional, and feminist women are humiliated, turned into harpies, or hit by nervous breakdowns; the wise ones recant their independent ways by the closing sequence. In popular novels, from Gail Parent's *A Sign of the Eighties* to Stephen King's *Misery,* unwed women shrink to sniveling spinsters or inflate to fire-breathing she-devils; renouncing all aspirations but marriage, they beg for wedding bands from strangers or swing axes at reluctant bachelors. We "blew it by waiting," a typically remorseful careerist sobs in Freda Bright's *Singular Women;* she and her sister professionals are "condemned to be childless forever." Even Erica Jong's high-flying independent heroine literally crashes by the end of the decade, as the author supplants *Fear of Flying*'s saucy Isadora Wing, a symbol of female sexual emancipation in the '70s, with an embittered careerist-turned-recovering-"co-dependent" in *Any Woman's Blues*—a book that is intended, as the narrator bluntly states, "to demonstrate what a deadend the so-called sexual revolution had become, and how desperate so-called free women were in the last few years of our decadent epoch."

Popular psychology manuals peddle the same diagnosis for contemporary female distress. "Feminism, having promised her a stronger sense of her own identity, has given her little more than an identity *crisis,*" the best-selling advice manual *Being a Woman* asserts. The authors of the era's self-help classic *Smart Women/Foolish Choices* proclaim that women's distress was "an unfortunate consequence of feminism," because "it created a myth among women that the apex of self-realization could be achieved only through autonomy, independence, and career."

Finally, some "liberated" women themselves have joined the lamentations. In confessional accounts, works that invariably receive a hearty greeting from the publishing industry, "recovering Superwomen" tell all. In *The Cost of Loving: Women and the New Fear of Intimacy,* Megan Marshall, a Harvard-pedigreed writer, asserts that the feminist "Myth of Independence" has turned her generation into unloved and unhappy fast-trackers, "dehumanized" by careers and "uncertain of their gender identity." Other diaries of mad Superwomen charge that "the hardcore feminist viewpoint," as one of them puts it, has relegated educated executive achievers to solitary nights of frozen dinners and closet drinking. The triumph of equality, they report, has merely given women hives, stomach cramps, eye-twitching disorders, even comas.

But what "equality" are all these authorities talking about?

If American women are so equal, why do they represent two-thirds of all poor adults? Why are more than 80 percent of full-time working women making less than $20,000 a year, nearly double the male rate? Why are they still far more likely than men to live in poor housing and receive no health insurance, and twice as likely to draw no pension? Why does the average working woman's salary still lag as far behind the average man's as it did twenty years ago? Why does the average female college graduate today earn less than a man with no more than a high school diploma (just as she did in the '50s)—and why does the average female high school graduate today earn less than a male high school dropout? Why do American women, in fact, face the worst gender-based pay gap in the developed world?

If women have "made it," then why are nearly 80 percent of working women still stuck in traditional "female" jobs—as secretaries, administrative "support" workers and salesclerks? And, conversely, why are they less than 8 percent of all federal and state judges, less than 6 percent of all law partners, and less than one half of 1 percent of top corporate managers? Why are there only three female state governors, two female U.S. senators, and two Fortune 500 chief executives? Why are only nineteen of the four thousand corporate officers and directors

women—and why do more than half the boards of Fortune companies still lack even one female member?

If women "have it all," then why don't they have the most basic requirements to achieve equality in the work force? Unlike virtually all other industrialized nations, the U.S. government still has no family-leave and child care programs—and more than 99 percent of American private employers don't offer child care either. Though business leaders say they are aware of and deplore sex discrimination, corporate America has yet to make an honest effort toward eradicating it. In a 1990 national poll of chief executives at Fortune 1000 companies, more than 80 percent acknowledged that discrimination impedes female employees' progress—yet, less than 1 percent of these same companies regarded *remedying* sex discrimination as a goal that their personnel departments should pursue. In fact, when the companies' human resource officers were asked to rate their department's priorities, women's advancement ranked last.

If women are so "free," why are their reproductive freedoms in greater jeopardy today than a decade earlier? Why do women who want to postpone childbearing now have fewer options than ten years ago? The availability of different forms of contraception has declined, research for new birth control has virtually halted, new laws restricting abortion —or even *information* about abortion—for young and poor women have been passed, and the U.S. Supreme Court has shown little ardor in defending the right it granted in 1973.

The word may be that women have been "liberated," but women themselves seem to feel otherwise. Repeatedly in national surveys, majorities of women say they are still far from equality. Nearly 70 percent of women polled by the *New York Times* in 1989 said the movement for women's rights had only just begun. Most women in the 1990 Virginia Slims opinion poll agreed with the statement that conditions for their sex in American society had improved "a little, not a lot." In poll after poll in the decade, overwhelming majorities of women said they needed equal pay and equal job opportunities, they needed an Equal Rights Amendment, they needed the right to an abortion without government interference, they needed a federal law guaranteeing maternity leave, they needed decent child care services. They have none of these. So how exactly have we "won" the war for women's rights?

Seen against this background, the much bally-hooed claim that feminism is responsible for making women miserable becomes absurd—and irrelevant. The afflictions ascribed to feminism are all myths. From "the man shortage" to "the infertility epidemic" to "female burnout" to "toxic day care," these so-called female crises have had their origins not in the actual conditions of women's lives but rather in a closed system that starts and ends in the media, popular culture, and advertising—an endless feedback loop that perpetuates and exaggerates its own false images of womanhood.

Women themselves don't single out the women's movement as the source of their misery. To the contrary, in national surveys 75 to 95 percent of women credit the feminist campaign with *improving* their lives, and a similar proportion say that the women's movement should keep pushing for change. Less than 8 percent think the women's movement might have actually made their lot worse.

* * *

What actually is troubling the American female population, then? If the many ponderers of the Woman Question really wanted to know, they might have asked their subjects. In public opinion surveys, women consistently rank their own *inequality,* at work and at home, among their most urgent concerns. Over and over, women complain to pollsters about a lack of economic, not marital, opportunities; they protest that working men, not working women, fail to spend time in the nursery and the kitchen. The Roper Organization's survey analysts find that men's opposition to equality is "a major cause of resentment and stress" and "a major irritant for most women today." It is justice for their gender, not wedding rings and bassinets, that women believe to be in desperately short supply. When the *New York Times* polled women in 1989 about "the most important problem facing women today," job discrimination was the overwhelming winner; none of the crises the media and popular culture had so assidu-

ously promoted even made the charts. In the 1990 Virginia Slims poll, women were most upset by their lack of money, followed by the refusal of their men to shoulder child care and domestic duties. By contrast, when the women were asked where the quest for a husband or the desire to hold a "less pressured" job or to stay at home ranked on their list of concerns, they placed them at the bottom.

As the last decade ran its course, women's unhappiness with inequality only mounted. In national polls, the ranks of women protesting discriminatory treatment in business, political, and personal life climbed sharply. The proportion of women complaining of unequal employment opportunities jumped more than ten points from the '70s, and the number of women complaining of unequal barriers to job advancement climbed even higher. By the end of the decade, 80 percent to 95 percent of women said they suffered from job discrimination and unequal pay. Sex discrimination charges filed with the Equal Employment Opportunity Commission rose nearly 25 percent in the Reagan years, and charges of general harassment directed at working women climbed 208 percent. In the decade, complaints of sexual harassment jumped 70 percent. At home, a much increased proportion of women complained to pollsters of male mistreatment, unequal relationships, and male efforts to, in the words of the Virginia Slims poll, "keep women down." The share of women in the Roper surveys who agreed that men were "basically kind, gentle, and thoughtful" fell from almost 70 percent in 1970 to 50 percent by 1990. And outside their homes, women felt more threatened, too: in the 1990 Virginia Slims poll, 72 percent of women said they felt "more afraid and uneasy on the streets today" than they did a few years ago. Lest this be attributed only to a general rise in criminal activity, by contrast only 49 percent of men felt this way.

The truth is that the 1980s saw a powerful counter-assault on women's rights, a backlash, an attempt to retract the handful of small and hard-won victories that the feminist movement did manage to win for women. This counterassault is largely insidious: in a kind of pop-culture version of the Big Lie, it stands the truth boldly on its head and proclaims that the very steps that have elevated women's position have actually led to their downfall.

The backlash is at once sophisticated and banal, deceptively "progressive" and proudly backward. It deploys both the "new" findings of "scientific research" and the dime-store moralism of yesteryear; it turns into media sound bites both the glib pronouncements of pop-psych trend-watchers and the frenzied rhetoric of New Right preachers. The backlash has succeeded in framing virtually the whole issue of women's rights in its own language. Just as Reaganism shifted political discourse far to the right and demonized liberalism, so the backlash convinced the public that women's "liberation" was the true contemporary American scourge—the source of an endless laundry list of personal, social, and economic problems.

But what has made women unhappy in the last decade is not their "equality"—which they don't yet have—but the rising pressure to halt, and even reverse, women's quest for that equality. The "man shortage" and the "infertility epidemic" are not the price of liberation; in fact, they do not even exist. But these chimeras are the chisels of a society-wide backlash. They are part of a relentless whittling-down process—much of it amounting to outright propaganda—that has served to stir women's private anxieties and break their political wills. Identifying feminism as women's enemy only furthers the ends of a backlash against women's equality, simultaneously deflecting attention from the backlash's central role and recruiting women to attack their own cause.

Some social observers may well ask whether the current pressures on women actually constitute a backlash—or just a continuation of American society's long-standing resistance to women's rights. Certainly hostility to female independence has always been with us. But if fear and loathing of feminism is a sort of perpetual viral condition in our culture, it is not always in an acute stage; its symptoms subside and resurface periodically. And it is these episodes of resurgence, such as the one we face now, that can accurately be termed "backlashes" to women's advancement. If we trace these occurrences in American history, we find such flare-ups are hardly

random; they have always been triggered by the perception—accurate or not—that women are making great strides. These outbreaks are backlashes because they have always arisen in reaction to women's "progress," caused not simply by a bedrock of misogyny but by the specific efforts of contemporary women to improve their status, efforts that have been interpreted time and again by men—especially men grappling with real threats to their economic and social well-being on other fronts—as spelling their own masculine doom.

The most recent round of backlash first surfaced in the late '70s on the fringes, among the evangelical right. By the early '80s, the fundamentalist ideology had shouldered its way into the White House. By the mid-'80s, as resistance to women's rights acquired political and social acceptability, it passed into the popular culture. And in every case, the timing coincided with signs that women were believed to be on the verge of breakthrough.

Just when women's quest for equal rights seemed closest to achieving its objectives, the backlash struck it down. Just when a "gender gap" at the voting booth surfaced in 1980, and women in politics began to talk of capitalizing on it, the Republican party elevated Ronald Reagan and both political parties began to shunt women's rights off their platforms. Just when support for feminism and the Equal Rights Amendment reached a record high in 1981, the amendment was defeated the following year. Just when women were starting to mobilize against battering and sexual assaults, the federal government stalled funding for battered-women's programs, defeated bills to fund shelters, and shut down its Office of Domestic Violence—only two years after opening it in 1979. Just when record numbers of younger women were supporting feminist goals in the mid-'80s (more of them, in fact, than older women) and a majority of all women were calling themselves feminists, the media declared the advent of a younger "postfeminist generation" that supposedly reviled the women's movement. Just when women racked up their largest percentage ever supporting the right to abortion, the U.S. Supreme Court moved toward reconsidering it.

In other words, the antifeminist backlash has been

set off not by women's achievement of full equality but by the increased possibility that they might win it. It is a preemptive strike that stops women long before they reach the finish line. "A backlash may be an indication that women really have had an effect," feminist psychiatrist Dr. Jean Baker Miller has written, "but backlashes occur when advances have been small, before changes are sufficient to help many people. . . . It is almost as if the leaders of backlashes use the fear of change as a threat before major change has occurred." In the last decade, some women did make substantial advances before the backlash hit, but millions of others were left behind, stranded. Some women now enjoy the right to legal abortion—but not the 44 million women, from the indigent to the military work force, who depend on the federal government for their medical care. Some women can now walk into high-paying professional careers—but not the more than 19 million still in the typing pools or behind the department store sales counters. (Contrary to popular myth about the "have-it-all" baby-boom women, the largest percentage of women in this generation remain typists and clerks.)

As the backlash has gathered force, it has cut off the few from the many—and the few women who have advanced seek to prove, as a social survival tactic, that they aren't so interested in advancement after all. Some of them parade their defection from the women's movement, while their working-class peers founder and cling to the splintered remains of the feminist cause. While a very few affluent and celebrity women who are showcased in news articles boast about having "found my niche as Mrs. Andy Mill" and going home to "bake bread," the many working-class women appeal for their economic rights—flocking to unions in record numbers, striking on their own for pay equity and establishing their own fledgling groups for working women's rights. In 1986, while 41 percent of upper-income women were claiming in the Gallup poll that they were not feminists, only 26 percent of low-income women were making the same claim.

* * *

Backlash happens to be the title of a 1947 Hollywood movie in which a man frames his wife for a murder he's committed. The backlash against women's rights works in much the same way: its rhetoric charges feminists with all the crimes it perpetrates. The backlash line blames the women's movement for the "feminization of poverty"—while the backlash's own instigators in Washington pushed through the budget cuts that helped impoverish millions of women, fought pay equity proposals, and undermined equal opportunity laws. The backlash line claims the women's movement cares nothing for children's rights—while its own representatives in the capital and state legislatures have blocked one bill after another to improve child care, slashed billions of dollars in federal aid for children, and relaxed state licensing standards for day care centers. The backlash line accuses the women's movement of creating a generation of unhappy single and childless women—but its purveyors in the media are the ones guilty of making single and childless women feel like circus freaks.

To blame feminism for women's "lesser life" is to miss entirely the point of feminism, which is to win women a wider range of experience. Feminism remains a pretty simple concept, despite repeated—and enormously effective—efforts to dress it up in greasepaint and turn its proponents into gargoyles. As Rebecca West wrote sardonically in 1913, "I myself have never been able to find out precisely what feminism is: I only know that people call me a feminist whenever I express sentiments that differentiate me from a doormat."

The meaning of the word "feminist" has not really changed since it first appeared in a book review in the *Athenaeum* of April 27, 1895, describing a woman who "has in her the capacity of fighting her way back to independence." It is the basic proposition that, as Nora put it in Ibsen's *A Doll's House* a century ago, "Before everything else I'm a human being." It is the simply worded sign hoisted by a little girl in the 1970 Women's Strike for Equality: I AM NOT A BARBIE DOLL. Feminism asks the world to recognize at long last that women aren't decorative ornaments, worthy vessels, members of a "special-interest group." They are half (in fact, now more than half) of the national population, and just as deserving of rights and opportunities, just as capable of participating in the world's events, as the other half. Feminism's agenda is basic: It asks that women not be forced to "choose" between public justice and private happiness. It asks that women be free to define themselves—instead of having their identity defined for them, time and again, by their culture and their men.

The fact that these are still such incendiary notions should tell us that American women have a way to go before they enter the promised land of equality.

[1991]

NOTES

542   Women's fight for . . . : Nancy Gibbs, "The Dreams of Youth," *Time,* Special Issue: "Women: The Road Ahead," Fall 1990, p. 12.

542   Women have "so much" . . . : Eleanor Smeal, *Why and How Women Will Elect the Next President* (New York: Harper & Row, 1984), p. 56.

542   The *New York Times* reports . . . : Georgia Dullea, "Women Reconsider Childbearing Over 30," *New York Times,* Feb. 25, 1982, p. C1.

542   *Newsweek* says: Unwed women . . . : Eloise Salholz, "The Marriage Crunch," *Newsweek,* June 2, 1986, p. 55.

542   The health advice manuals . . . : See, for example, Dr. Herbert J. Freudenberger and Gail North, *Women's Burnout* (New York: Viking Penguin, 1985); Marjorie Hansen Shaevitz, *The Superwoman Syndrome* (New York: Warner Books, 1984); Harriet Braiker, *The Type E Woman* (New York: Dodd, Mead, 1986); Donald Morse and M. Lawrence Furst, *Women Under Stress* (New York: Van Nostrand Reinhold Co., 1982); Georgia Witkin-Lanoil, *The Female Stress Syndrome* (New York: Newmarket Press, 1984).

542   The psychology books . . . : Dr. Stephen and Susan Price, *No More Lonely Nights: Overcoming the Hidden Fears That Keep You from Getting Married* (New York: G. P. Putnam's Sons, 1988), p. 19.

542   Even founding feminist Betty Friedan . . . : Betty Friedan, *The Second Stage* (New York: Summit Books, 1981), p. 9.

543   "In dispensing its spoils . . .": Mona Charen, "The Feminist Mistake," *National Review,* March 23, 1984, p. 24.

543   "Our generation was the human sacrifice . . .": Claudia Wallis, "Women Face the '90s," *Time,* Dec. 4, 1989, p. 82.

543   In *Newsweek,* writer . . . : Kay Ebeling, "The Failure of Feminism," *Newsweek,* Nov. 19, 1990, p. 9.

543   Even the beauty magazines . . . : Marilyn Webb, "His Fault Divorce," *Harper's Bazaar,* Aug. 1988, p. 156.

543   In the last decade . . . : Mary Anne Dolan, "When Feminism Failed," *The New York Times Magazine,* June 26, 1988, p. 21; Erica Jong, "The Awful Truth About Women's Liberation," *Vanity Fair,* April 1986, p. 92.

543   The "Today" show . . . : Jane Birnbaum, "The Dark Side of Women's Liberation," *Los Angeles Herald Examiner,* May 24, 1986.

543   A guest columnist . . . : Robert J. Hooper, "Slasher Movies Owe Success to Abortion" (originally printed in the *Baltimore Sun*), *Minneapolis Star Tribune,* Feb. 1, 1990, p. 17A.

543   In popular novels . . . : Gail Parent, *A Sign of the Eighties* (New York: G. P. Putnam's Sons, 1987); Stephen King, *Misery* (New York: Viking, 1987).

543   We "blew it by . . .": Freda Bright, *Singular Women* (New York: Bantam Books, 1988), p. 12.

543   Even Erica Jong's . . . : Erica Jong, *Any Woman's Blues* (New York: Harper & Row, 1989) pp. 2–3. A new generation of young "post-feminist" female writers, such as Mary Gaitskill and Susan Minot, also produced a bumper crop of grim-faced unwed heroines. These passive and masochistic "girls" wandered the city zombie-like; they came alive and took action only in seeking out male abuse. For a good analysis of this genre, see James Wolcott, "The Good-Bad Girls," *Vanity Fair,* Dec. 1988, p. 43.

543   "Feminism, having promised her . . .": Dr. Toni Grant, *Being a Woman: Fulfilling Your Femininity and Finding Love* (New York: Random House, 1988), p. 25.

543   The authors of . . . : Dr. Connell Cowan and Dr. Melvyn Kinder, *Smart Women/Foolish Choices* (New York: New American Library, 1985) p. 16.

544   In *The Cost of Loving* . . . : Megan Marshall, *The Cost of Loving: Women and the New Fear of Intimacy* (New York: G. P. Putnam's Sons, 1984), p. 218.

544   Other diaries of . . . : Hilary Cosell, *Woman on a Seesaw: The Ups and Downs of Making It* (New York: G. P. Putnam's Sons, 1985); Deborah Fallows, *A Mother's Work* (Boston: Houghton Mifflin, 1985); Carol Osborn, *Enough is Enough* (New York: Pocket Books, 1986); Susan Bakos, *This Wasn't Supposed to Happen* (New York: Continuum, 1985). Even when the women aren't really renouncing their liberation, their publishers promote the texts as if they were. Mary Kay Blakely's *Wake Me When It's Over* (New York: Random House, 1989), an account of the author's diabetes-induced coma, is billed on the dust jacket as "a chilling memoir in which a working supermom exceeds her limit and discovers the thin line between sanity and lunacy and between life and death."

544   If American women are so equal . . . : "Money, Income and Poverty Status in the U.S.," 1989, Current Population Reports, U.S. Bureau of the Census, Department of Commerce, Series P-60, #168.

544   Why are they still . . . : Cushing N. Dolbeare and Anne J. Stone, "Women and Affordable Housing," *The American Woman 1990–91: A Status Report,* ed. by Sara E. Rix (W. W. Norton & Co., 1990) p. 106; Newton, "Pension Coverage," p. 268; "1990 Profile," 9 to 5/ National Association of Working Women; Salaried and Professional Women's Commission Report, 1989, p. 2.

544   Why does the average . . . : "Briefing Paper on the Wage Gap," National Committee on Pay Equity, p. 3; "Average Earnings of Year-Round, Full-Time Workers

by Sex and Educational Attainment," 1987, U.S. Bureau of the Census, February 1989, cited in *The American Woman 1990–91*, p. 392.

544 If women have "made it," then . . . : Susanna Downie, "Decade of Achievement, 1977–1987," The National Women's Conference Center, May 1988, p. 35; statistics from 9 to 5/National Association of Working Women.

544 And, conversely . . . : Statistics from Women's Research & Education Institute, U.S. Bureau of the Census, U.S. Bureau of Labor Statistics, Catalyst, Center for the American Woman and Politics. See also *The American Woman 1990–91*, p. 359; Deborah L. Rhode, "Perspectives on Professional Women," *Stanford Law Review*, 40, no. 5 (May 1988): 1178–79; Anne Jardim and Margaret Hennig, "The Last Barrier," *Working Woman*, Nov. 1990, p. 130; Jaclyn Fierman, "Why Women Still Don't Hit the Top," *Fortune*, July 30, 1990, p. 40.

544 Unlike virtually . . . : "1990 Profile," 9 to 5/National Association of Working Women; Bureau of Labor Statistics, 1987 survey of nation's employers. See also "Who Gives and Who Gets," *American Demographics*, May 1988, p. 16; "Children and Families: Public Policies and Outcomes, A Fact Sheet of International Comparisons," U.S. House of Representatives, Select Committee on Children, Youth and Families.

544 In a 1990 national poll . . . : "Women in Corporate Management," national poll of Fortune 1000 companies by Catalust, 1990.

544 Why do women who want . . . : Data from Alan Guttmacher Institute.

544 Nearly 70 percent . . . : E. J. Dionne, Jr., "Struggle for Work and Family Fueling Women's Movement," *New York Times*, Aug. 22, 1989, p. A1. The Yankelovich Clancy Shulman poll (Oct. 23–25, 1989, for *Time/CNN*) and the 1990 Virginia Slims Opinion Poll (The Roper Organization Inc., 1990) found similarly large majorities of women who said that they needed a strong women's movement to keep pushing for change.

544 Most women in the . . . : The 1990 Virginia Slims Opinion Poll, The Roper Organization, Inc., pp. 8, 18.

544 In poll after . . . : The Louis Harris Poll, 1984, found 64 percent of women wanted the Equal Rights Amendment and 65 percent favored affirmative action. Similar results emerged from the national *Woman's Day* poll (Feb. 17, 1984) by *Woman's Day* and Wellesley College Center for Research on Women, which emphasized middle-American conventional women (80 percent were mothers and 30 percent were full-time homemakers). The *Woman's Day* poll found a majority of women, from all economic classes, seeking a wide range of women's rights. For instance, 68 percent of the women said they wanted the ERA, 79 percent supported a woman's right to choose an abortion, and 61 percent favored a federally subsidized national childcare program. Mark Clements Research Inc.'s Annual Study of Women's Attitudes found in 1987 that 87 percent of women wanted a federal law guaranteeing maternity leave and about 94 percent said that more

child care should be available. (In addition, 86 percent wanted a federal law enforcing the payment of child support.) The Louis Harris Poll found 80 percent of women calling for the creation of more day-care centers. See *The Eleanor Smeal Report*, June 28, 1984, p. 3; Warren T. Brookes, "Day Care: Is It a Real Crisis or a War Over Political Turf?" *San Francisco Chronicle*, April 27, 1988, p. 6; Louis Harris, *Inside America* (New York: Vintage Books, 1987), p. 96.

545 To the contrary . . . : In the 1989 *Time/CNN* poll, 94 percent of women polled said the movement made them more independent; 82 percent said it is still improving women's lives. Only 8 percent said it may have made their lives worse. A 1986 *Newsweek* Gallup poll found that 56 percent of women identified themselves as "feminists," and only 4 percent described themselves as "anti-feminists."

545 In public opinion . . . : In the Annual Study of Women's Attitudes (1988, Mark Clements Research), when women were asked, "What makes you angry?" they picked three items as their top concerns: poverty, crime, and their own inequality. In the 1989 *New York Times* Poll, when women were asked what was the most important problem facing women today, job inequality ranked first.

545 The Roper Organization's . . . : Bickley Townsend and Kathleen O'Neil, "American Women Get Mad," *American Demographics*, Aug. 1990, p. 26.

545 When the *New York Times* . . . : Dionne, "Struggle for Work and Family," p. A14.

545 In the 1990 . . . : 1990 Virginia Slims Opinion Poll, pp. 29–30, 32.

545 In national polls . . . : Data from Roper Organization and Louis Harris polls. The 1990 Roper survey found most women reporting that things had "gotten worse" in the home and that men were more eager "to keep women down": See 1990 Virginia Slims Opinion Poll, pp. 18, 21, 54. The Gallup Organization polls charted an 8 percent increase in job discrimination complaints from women between 1975 and 1982. Mark Clements Research's 1987 Women's Views Survey (commissioned by *Glamour* magazine) found that on the matter of women's inequality, "more women feel there is a problem today." Reports of wage discrimination, the survey noted, had jumped from 76 percent in 1982 to 85 percent in 1988. (See "How Women's Minds Have Changed in the Last Five Years," *Glamour*, Jan. 1987, p. 168.) The annual surveys by Mark Clements Research also find huge and increasing majorities of women complaining of unequal treatment in hiring, advancement, and opportunities in both corporate and political life. (In 1987, only 30 percent of women believed they got equal treatment with men when being considered for financial credit.) A *Time* 1989 poll found 94 percent of women complaining of unequal pay, 82 percent of job discrimination.

545 Sex discrimination charges . . . : Statistics from U.S. Equal Employment Opportunity Commission, "National Database: Charge Receipt Listing," 1982–88; "Sexual Harassment," 1981–89.

545   At home, a much increased . . . : Townsend and O'Neil, "American Women Get Mad," p. 28.

545   And outside their . . . : 1990 Virginia Slims Opinion Poll, p. 38.

546   Just when women . . . : "Inequality of Sacrifice," p. 23.

546   Just when record numbers . . . : A 1986 Gallup poll conducted for *Newsweek* found a majority of women described themselves as feminists and only 4 percent said they were "antifeminists." While large majorities of women throughout the '80s kept on favoring the full feminist agenda (from the ERA to legal abortion), the proportion of women who were willing publicly to call themselves feminists dropped off suddenly in the late '80s, after the mass media declared feminism the "F-word." By 1989, only one in three women were calling themselves feminists in the polls. Nonetheless, the pattern of younger women espousing the most pro-feminist sentiments continued throughout the decade. In the 1989 Yankelovich poll for *Time*/CNN, for example, 76 percent of women in their teens and 71 percent of women in their twenties said they believed feminists spoke for the average American woman, compared with 59 percent of women in their thirties. Asked the same question about the National Organization for Women, the gap appeared again: 83 percent of women in their teens and 72 percent of women in their twenties said NOW was in touch with the average woman, compared with 65 percent of women in their thirties. See Downie, "Decade of Achievement," p. 1; 1986 Gallup/*Newsweek* poll; 1989 Yankelovich/*Time*/CNN poll.

547   "A backlash may be an indication that . . .": Dr. Jean Baker Miller, *Toward a New Psychology of Women* (Boston: Beacon Press, 1976), pp. xv–xvi.

547   Some women now . . . : Kate Michelman, "20 Years Defending Choice, 1969–1988," National Abortion Rights Action League, p. 4.

547   Some women can now . . . : "Employment and Earnings," Current Population Survey, Table 22, Bureau of Labor Statistics, U.S. Department of Labor.

547   (Contrary to popular myth . . .): Cheryl Russell, *100 Predictions for the Baby Boom* (New York: Plenum Press, 1987), p. 64.

547   While a very few . . . : "A New Kind of Love Match," *Newsweek,* Sept. 4, 1989, p. 73; Barbara Hetzer, "Superwoman Goes Home," *Fortune,* Aug. 18, 1986, p. 20; "Facts on Working Women," Aug. 1989, Women's Bureau, U.S. Department of Labor, no. 89—2; and data from the Coalition of Labor Union Women and Amalgamated Clothing and Textile Workers Union. The surge of women joining unions in the late '80s was so great that it single-handedly halted the ten-year decline in union membership. Black women joined unions at the greatest rate. Women led strikes around the country, from the Yale University administrative staffs to the Daughters of Mother Jones in Virginia (who were instrumental in the Pittston coal labor battle) to the Delta Pride catfish plant processors in Mississippi (where women organized the largest strike by black workers ever in the state, lodging a protest against a plant that paid its mostly female employees poverty wages, punished them if they skinned less than 24,000 fish a day,

and limited them to six timed bathroom breaks a week). See Tony Freemantle, "Weary Strikers Hold Out in Battle of Pay Principle," *Houston Chronicle,* Dec. 2, 1990, p. 1A; Peter T. Kilborn, "Labor Fight on a Catfish 'Plantation,'" *The News and Observer,* Dec. 16, 1990, p. J2.

547   In 1986, while . . . : 1986 Gallup Poll; Barbara Ehrenreich, "The Next Wave," *Ms.,* July/August 1987, p. 166; Sarah Harder, "Flourishing in the Mainstream: The U.S. Women's Movement Today," *The American Woman 1990–91,* p. 281. Also see 1989 Yankelovich Poll: 71 percent of black women said feminists have been helpful to women, compared with 61 percent of white women. A 1987 poll by the National Women's Conference Commission found that 65 percent of black women called themselves feminists, compared with 56 percent of white women.

547   The backlash line claims . . . : Data from Children's Defense Fund. See also Ellen Wojahm, "Who's Minding the Kids?" *Savvy,* Oct. 1987, p. 16; "Child Care: The Time is Now," Children's Defense Fund, 1987, pp. 8–10.

547   "I myself . . .": Rebecca West, *The Clarion,* Nov. 14, 1913, cited in Cheris Kramarae and Paula A. Treichler, *A Feminist Dictionary* (London: Pandora Press, 1985) p. 160.

547   The meaning of the word "feminist" . . . : *The Feminist Papers: From Adams to de Beauvoir,* ed. by Alice S. Rossi (New York: Bantam Books, 1973), p. xiii. For discussion of historical origins of term feminism, see Karen Offen, "Defining Feminism: A Comparative Historical Approach," in *Signs: Journal of Women in Culture and Society,* 1988, 14, no. 1, pp. 119–57.

547   I AM NOT A BARBIE DOLL . . . : Carol Hymowitz and Michaele Weissman, *A History of Women in America* (New York: Bantam Books, 1978), p. 341.

139

Bringing the Global Home

CHARLOTTE BUNCH

One of the most exciting world developments today is the emergence of feminism all over the globe. Women of almost every culture, color, and class are claiming feminism for themselves. Indigenous movements are developing that address the specific regional concerns of women's lives and that expand the definition of what feminism means and can do in the future.

This growth of feminism provides both the challenge and the opportunity for a truly global women's movement to emerge in the 1980s. But a global movement involves more than just the separate development of feminism in each region, as exciting and important as that is. Global feminism also requires that we learn from each other and develop a global perspective within each of our movements. It means expansion of our understandings of feminism and changes in our work, as we respond to the ideas and challenges of women with different perspectives. It means discovering what other perspectives and movements mean to our own local setting. Any struggle for change in the late-twentieth century must have a global consciousness since the world operates and controls our lives internationally already. The strength of feminism has been and still is in its decentralized grass-roots nature, but for that strength to be most effective, we must base our local and national actions on a world view that incorporates the global context of our lives. This is the challenge of bringing the global home.

A global feminist perspective on patriarchy worldwide also illustrates how issues are interconnected, not separate isolated phenomena competing for our attention. This involves connections among each aspect of women's oppression and of that subordination to the socioeconomic conditions of society, as well as between local problems and global realities.

To develop global feminism today is not a luxury —it requires going to the heart of the problems in our world and looking at nothing less than the threats to the very survival of the planet. We are standing on a precipice facing such possibilities as nuclear destruction, worldwide famine and depletion of our natural resources, industrial contamination, and death in many forms. These are the fruits of a world ruled by the patriarchal mode—of what I call the "dynamic of domination," in which profits and property have priority over people, and where fear and hatred of differences have prevented a celebration of and learning from our diversity.

Feminists are part of a world struggle that is taking place today over the direction that the future will take. Crucial choices are being made about the very possibilities for life in the twenty-first century —from macro-level decisions about control over resources and weapons to micro-level decisions about control over individual reproduction and sexuality. At this juncture in history, feminism is perhaps the most important force for change that can begin to reverse the dynamic of patriarchal domination by challenging and transforming the way in which humans look at ourselves in relation to each other and to the world.

A GLOBAL VIEW OF FEMINISM

The excitement and urgency of issues of global feminism were brought home to me at a Workshop on Feminist Ideology and Structures sponsored by the Asian and Pacific Centre for Women and Development in Bangkok in 1979. Women from each region presented what they were doing in relation to the themes of the UN Decade for Women. In doing this, we realized the importance of the international male-dominated media in influencing what we knew and thought about each other before we came to Bangkok.

We saw how the media has made the women's movement and feminism appear trivial, silly, selfish, naïve, and/or crazy in the industrialized countries while practically denying its existence in the Third World. Western feminists have been portrayed as concerned only with burning bras, having sex, hating men, and/or getting to be head of General Motors. Such stereotypes ignore the work of most feminists and distort even the few activities the media do report. So, for example, basic political points that women have tried to communicate—about what it means to love ourselves in a woman-hating society —get twisted into a focus on "hating" men. Or those demonstrations that did discard high-heeled shoes, makeup, or bras, as symbolic of male control over women's self-definition and mobility, have been stripped of their political content.

Thus, women who feel that their priorities are survival issues of food or housing are led to think that Western feminists are not concerned with these matters. Similarly, media attempts to portray all feminists as a privileged elite within each country seek to isolate us from other women. The real strength of feminism can be seen best in the fact that more and more women come to embrace it in spite of the overwhelming effort that has gone into distorting it and trying to keep women away.

By acknowledging the power of the media's distortion of feminism at the Bangkok workshop, we were able to see the importance of defining it clearly for ourselves. Our definition brought together the right of every woman to equity, dignity, and freedom of choice through the power to control her own life and the removal of all forms of inequalities and oppression in society. We saw feminism as a world view that has an impact on all aspects of life, and affirmed the broad context of the assertion that the "personal is political." This is to say that the individual aspects of oppression and change are not separate from the need for political and institutional change.

Through our discussion, we were able to agree on the use of this concept of feminism to describe women's struggles. While some had reservations about using the word "feminism," we chose not to allow media or government distortions to scare us away from it. As one Asian pointed out, if we shied away from the term, we would simply be attacked or ridiculed for other actions or words, since those who opposed us were against what we sought for women and the world and not really concerned with our language.

In Copenhagen at the 1980 NGO Forum, the conference newspaper came out with a quote-of-the-day from a Western feminist that read: "To talk feminism to a woman who has no water, no home, and no food is to talk nonsense." Many of us felt that the quote posed a crucial challenge to feminists. We passed out a leaflet, "What Is Feminism?," describing it as a perspective on the world that would address such issues, and we invited women to a special session on the topic. Over three hundred women from diverse regions gathered to debate what feminism really means to us and how that has been distorted by the media and even within our own movements.

The second challenge we saw in the quote was that if it were true and feminists did not speak to such issues, then we would indeed be irrelevant to many women. We therefore discussed the importance of a feminist approach to development—one that both addresses how to make home, food, and water available to all and extends beyond equating "development" with industrialization. Terms like "developing nations" are suspect and patronizing. While we need to look at the real material needs of all people from a feminist perspective, we can hardly call any countries "developed." For this reason, while I find all labels that generalize about diverse parts of the world problematic, I use "Western" or "industrialized" and "Third World," rather than "developing" and "developed."

Recently at a meeting in New York, I saw another example of confusion about the meaning of feminism. Two women who had just engaged in civil disobedience against nuclear weapons were discussing feminism as the motivating force behind their actions, when a man jumped up impatiently objecting, "But I thought this meeting was about disarmament, not feminism." It was the equivalent of "to talk feminism in the face of nuclear destruction is to talk nonsense." Such attitudes portray feminism as a luxury of secondary concern and thus both dismiss female experience as unimportant and limit our politics. They fundamentally misconstrue feminism as about "women's issues" rather than as a political perspective on life.

Seeing feminism as a transformational view is crucial to a global perspective. But to adopt a global outlook does not mean, as some feminists fear and male politicos often demand, that we abandon working on the "women's issues" that we fought to put on the political agenda. Nor does it imply setting aside our analysis of sexual politics. Rather it requires that we take what we have learned about sexual politics and use feminist theory to expose the connections between the "women's issues" and other world questions. In this way, we demonstrate our point that all issues are women's issues and need feminist analysis. For example, we must show how a society that tacitly sanctions male violence against women and children, whether incest and battery at home, rape on the streets, or sexual harassment on the job, is bound to produce people who are militaristic and believe in their right to dominate others on the basis of other differences such as skin color or nationality. Or we can point out how the heterosexist assumption that every "good" woman wants to and eventually will be supported by a man fuels the economic policies that have produced the feminization of poverty worldwide. This refusal to accept a woman who lives without a man as fully human thus allows policy makers to propose such ideas as keeping welfare payments or even job opportunities for single mothers limited since they "contribute to the destruction of the family."

The examples are endless. The task is not one of changing our issues but of expanding the frameworks from which we understand our work. It means taking what we have learned in working on "women's issues" and relating that to other areas, demanding that these not be seen as competing but as enabling us to bring about more profound change. To use the illustration above, to seek to end militarism without also ending the dynamic of domination embedded in male violence at home would be futile. And so, too, the reverse: we will never fully end male violence against individual women unless we also stop celebrating the organized violence of war as manly and appropriate behavior.

MAKING CONNECTIONS

The interconnectedness of the economic and sexual exploitation of women with militarism and racism is well illustrated in the area of forced prostitution and female sexual slavery. It is impossible to work on one aspect of this issue without confronting the whole socioeconomic context of women's lives. For example, females in India who are forced into prostitution are often either sold by poverty-stricken families for whom a girl child is considered a liability, or they have sought to escape arranged marriages they find intolerable. In the United States, many girls led into forced prostitution are teenage runaways who were victims of sexual or physical abuse at home, and for whom there are no jobs, services, or safe places to live.

In parts of Southeast Asia, many women face the limited economic options of rural poverty; joining assembly lines that pay poorly, destroy eyesight, and often discard workers over thirty; or of entering

the "entertainment industry." In Thailand and the Philippines, national economies dependent on prostitution resulted from U.S. military brothels during the Vietnam War. When that demand decreased, prostitution was channeled into sex tourism—the organized multimillion-dollar transnational business of systematically selling women's bodies as part of packaged tours, which feeds numerous middlemen and brings foreign capital into the country. In all these situations, the patriarchal beliefs that men have the right to women's bodies, and that "other" races or "lower" classes are subhuman, underlie the abuse women endure.

Feminists organizing against these practices must link their various aspects. Thus, for example, women have simultaneously protested against sex tourism and militarism, created refuges for individual victims who escape, and sought to help women develop skills in order to gain more control over their lives. Japanese businesses pioneered the development of sex tourism. Feminists in Japan pioneered the opposition to this traffic. They work with Southeast Asian women to expose and shame the Japanese government and the businesses involved in an effort to cut down on the trade from their end.

On the international level, it is clear that female sexual slavery, forced prostitution, and violence against women operate across national boundaries and are political and human rights abuses of great magnitude. Yet, the male-defined human rights community by-and-large refuses to see any but the most narrowly defined cases of slavery or "political" torture as their domain. We must ask what is it when a woman faces death at the hands of her family to save its honor because she was raped? What is it when two young lesbians commit suicide together rather than be forced into unwanted marriages? What is it when a woman trafficked out of her country does not try to escape because she knows she will be returned by the police and beaten or deported? An understanding of sexual politics reveals all these and many more situations to be political human-rights violations deserving asylum, refugee status, and the help that other political victims are granted. As limited as human rights are in our world, we must demand at least that basic recognition for such women, while we seek to expand concern for human rights generally.

In these areas as well as others, feminists are creating new interpretations and approaches—to human rights, to development, to community and family, to conflict resolution, and so on. From local to global interaction, we must create alternative visions of how we can live in the world based on women's experiences and needs in the here-and-now.

LEARNING FROM DIVERSITY

In sharing experiences and visions across national and cultural lines, feminists are inspired by what others are doing. But we are also confronted with the real differences among us. On the one hand, our diversity is our strength. It makes it possible for us to imagine more possibilities and to draw upon a wider range of women's experiences. On the other hand, differences can also divide us if we do not take seriously the variations on female oppression that women suffer according to race, class, ethnicity, religion, sexual preference, age, nationality, physical disability, and so on. These are not simply added onto the oppression of women by sex, but shape the forms by which we experience that subordination. Thus, we cannot simply add up the types of oppression that a woman suffers one-by-one as independent factors but must look at how they are interrelated.

If we take this approach, we should be more capable of breaking down the ways in which difference itself separates people. Patriarchal society is constructed on a model of domination by which each group is assigned a place in the hierarchy according to various differences, and then allocated power or privileges based on that position. In this way, difference becomes threatening because it involves winning or losing one's position/privileges. If we eliminated the assignment of power and privilege according to difference, we could perhaps begin to enjoy real choices of style and variations of culture as offering more creative possibilities in life.

The world has been torn apart by various male divisions and conflicts for thousands of years and we should not assume that women can overcome and solve in a short time what patriarchy has so intricately conceived. The oppressions, resentments, fears, and patterns of behavior that have developed due to racism, classism, nationalism, and sexism, are very deep. We cannot just wish them away with our desire for women to transcend differences. Above all, we do not overcome differences by denying them or downplaying their effects on us—especially when the one denying is in the position of privilege.

A white woman can only legitimately talk about overcoming differences of race if she struggles to understand racism both as it affects her personally and as she affects it politically. A heterosexual can get beyond the divisions of sexual preference only by learning about both the oppression of lesbians and by acknowledging the insights that come from that orientation. A U.S. American must understand the effects of colonialism before she can hope for unity with women beyond national boundaries. Too often the call to transcend differences has been a call to ignore them at the expense of the oppressed. This cannot be the route of global feminism. We can only hope to chart a path beyond male divisions by walking through them and taking seriously their detrimental effects on us as women. This examination of and effort to eliminate other aspects of oppression does not come before or after working on sexism—it is simultaneous.

A crucial part of this process is understanding that reality does not look the same from different people's perspectives. It is not surprising that one way that feminists have come to understand about differences has been through the love of a person from another culture or race. It takes persistence and motivation—which love often engenders—to get beyond one's ethnocentric assumptions and really learn about other perspectives. In this process and while seeking to eliminate oppression, we also discover new possibilities and insights that come from the experience and survival of other peoples.

In considering what diversity means for a global movement, one of the most difficult areas for feminists is culture. In general, we affirm cultural diversity and the variety it brings to our lives. Yet, almost all existing cultures today are male-dominated. We know the horrors male powers have wrought over the centuries in imposing one cultural standard over another. Popular opposition to such imposition has often included affirmation of traditional cultures. Certainly none of our cultures can claim to have the answers to women's liberation since we are oppressed in all of them.

We must face the fact that in some instances male powers are justifying the continuation or advocating the adoption of practices oppressive to women by labeling them "cultural" and/or "resistance to Western influence." Feminists must refuse to accept *any* forms of domination of women—whether in the name of tradition or in the name of modernization. This is just the same as refusing to accept racial discrimination in the name of "culture," whether in the South of the USA or in South Africa. Feminists are seeking new models for society that allow for diversity while not accepting the domination of any group. For this, women in each culture must sort out what is best from their own culture and what is oppressive. Through our contact with each other, we can then challenge ethnocentric biases and move beyond the unconscious cultural assumptions inherent in our thinking.

In taking into account and challenging the various forms of domination in the world, we do not necessarily accept existing male theories about or solutions to them. We must always have a woman-identified approach—that is, one of seeking to identify with women's situations rather than accepting male definitions of reality. Such a process enables us to distinguish what is useful from male theories and to see where feminist approaches are being or need to be applied to issues such as race, class, and culture. Further, in a world so saturated with woman-hating, it is through woman-identification, which involves profoundly learning to love women and to listen for women's authentic perspectives, that we can make breakthroughs in these areas.

We confront a similar dilemma when examining nationalism. From a feminist perspective, I see nationalism as the ultimate expression of the patriarchal dynamic of domination—where groups battle for control over geographic territory, and justify violence and aggression in the name of national security. Therefore I prefer the term "global" to "international" because I see feminism as a movement among peoples beyond national boundaries and not among nation-states. Yet, nationalism has also symbolized the struggle of oppressed peoples against the control of other nations. And many attempts to go beyond nationalism have simply been supranational empire-building, such as the idea of turning Africans into "Frenchmen." Further, in the context of increasing global control over us all by transnational corporations, many see nationalism as a form of resistance. In seeking to be global, feminists must therefore find ways to transcend patriarchal nationalism without demanding sameness, and while still preserving means of identity and culture that are not based on domination.

THINK GLOBALLY, ACT LOCALLY

A major obstacle that feminists face in seeking to be global is our lack of control over the resources necessary for maintaining greater contact worldwide. It takes time and money as well as energy and commitment to overcome the problems of distance, language, and culture. Feminists have little control over existing institutions with global networks, such as the media, churches, universities, and the state, but sometimes we must utilize such networks even as we try to set up our own.

Since feminists have limited resources for global travel and communication, it is vital that we learn how to be global in consciousness while taking action locally. For this, we must resist the tendency to separate "international" work into a specialized category of political activity that is often viewed as inaccessible to most women. This tendency reflects a hierarchical mode in which the "world level" is viewed as above the "local level." For those whose work focuses primarily on the global aspects of issues, the challenge is not to lose touch with the local arena on which any effective movement is based. For those whose work is focused locally, the challenge is to develop a global perspective that informs local work. For all of us, the central question is to understand how the issues of women all over the world are interrelated and to discern what that means specifically in each setting.

Global interaction is not something that we choose to do or not to do. It is something in which we are already participating. All we choose is whether to be aware of it or not, whether to try to understand it and how that affects our actions. For citizens of the U.S., we begin our global consciousness with awareness of the impact that our country's policies have on other people's daily lives. I learned in the antiwar movement that often the most useful thing that we can do for people elsewhere is to make changes in the U.S. and in how it exercises power in the world.

There are many well-known issues such as military aggression, foreign aid and trade policies, or the possibility of worldwide destruction through nuclear weapons or chemical contamination that we see as global. But there are numerous less obvious illustrations of global interrelatedness, from the present world economy where women are manipulated as an international cheap labor pool to the traffic in women's bodies for forced prostitution. Therefore, any attempt we make to deal with the needs of women in the U.S., such as employment, must examine the global context of the problem. In this instance, that means understanding how multinational corporations move their plants from country to country or state to state, exploiting female poverty and discouraging unionization by threatening to move again. We must use global strategies, such as that proposed by one group on the Texas-Mexico border advocating an international bill of rights for women workers as a way to organize together for basic standards for all. In a world where global forces affect us daily, it is neither possible nor conscionable to achieve a feminist utopia in one country alone. . . .

A MATTER OF PERSPECTIVE

Beyond techniques and information, the primary task remains one of attitude, approach, and perspective. The point is not that we necessarily change the focus of our work but that we make connections that help to bring its global aspects to consciousness—in our programs, our slogans, our publications, and our conversations with other women. It is when we try to make a hierarchy of issues, keeping them sep-

arate and denying the importance of some in order to address others, that we are all defeated.

To use a previous example, if I cannot develop an analysis and discuss openly the ways in which heterosexism supports the international feminization of poverty, without having some women's homophobia prevent them from utilizing this insight, or without having some lesbians fear that I have abandoned "their issue" by working more on global poverty, then work in both areas is diminished. I believe that the path to effective global feminist theory and action is not through denial of any issue or analysis but through listening, questioning, struggling, and seeking to make connections among them.

To work locally with a global perspective does require stretching feminism, not to abandon its insights but to shed its cultural biases, and thus to expand its capacity to reach all people. In this process, we risk what seems certain at home by taking it into the world and having it change through interaction with other realities and perceptions. It can be frightening. But if we have confidence in ourselves and in the feminist process, it can also be exciting. It can mean the growth of a more effective feminism with a greater ability to address the world and to bring change. If we fail to take these risks and ignore the global dimensions of our lives, we lose possibilities for individual growth and we doom feminism to a less effective role in the world struggle over the direction of the twenty-first century.

My visions of global feminism are grand, perhaps even grandiose. But the state of the world today demands that women become less modest and dream/plan/act/risk on a larger scale. At the same time, the realization of global visions can only be achieved through the everyday lives and action of women locally. It depends on women deciding to shape their own destiny, claiming their right to the world, and exercising their responsibility to make it in some way, large or small, a better place for all. As more women do this with a growing world perspective and sense of connection to others, we can say that feminism is meeting the challenge of bringing the global home.   [1987]

🪶 140

Advancing Women's Rights: Beijing '95 and After

CHARLOTTE BUNCH and SUSANA FRIED

This article assesses progress in the acceptance of women's rights as human rights within the context of the UN World Conference on Women in Beijing in 1995 and its review (Beijing + 5) in 2000. The Beijing Conference was the culmination of a global campaign for the affirmation of the human rights of women. In the years since 1995, women activists around the world have worked for the implementation of the commitments made in Beijing and to further develop policies at all levels that will help to realize concretely the human rights of women in all our diversity.

The first section of this article analyzes both the gains and the limitations of the Beijing Platform and women's organizing for it in terms of women's human rights. The second section, written by Charlotte Bunch, evaluates the review process at Beijing Plus 5 including the influence of the backlash that developed after the Beijing conference and feminists' response to it.

The Fourth World Conference on Women in Beijing established clearly that women are a global force for the twenty-first century and that women's human rights are central to women's leadership for the future. Women's rights as human rights permeated debates and delegates' speeches at the official UN intergovernmental conference as well as at the parallel Non-Governmental Organization (NGO) Forum held some thirty miles away in Huairou, where it was a palpable presence in many sessions. The combined effect of these activities was a groundswell of support for making the entire Platform an affirmation of the human rights of women, including women's rights to education, health, and freedom from violence, as well as to the exercise of citizenship in all its manifestations. Previous UN women's conferences were seen as primarily about women and development or even women's rights, but not about the concept of human rights as it applies to women.

This report assesses the Beijing Declaration and Platform for Action, which came out of the governmental conference, focusing on its implications for women's human rights advocacy. The conference was mandated to produce a consensus "platform" that would implement the goals set forth in the "Forward-Looking Strategies" from the 1985 Nairobi World Conference on Women and advance the 1995 conference theme of "Action for Equality, Development, and Peace." More than four thousand NGO delegates accredited to the governmental conference worked to influence the document's articulation of the conditions faced by women worldwide as well as the content of the strategies proposed.

In the context of such international UN meetings, controversies over language are debates about the direction of governmental policy. If the agreements that result from these meetings are to be meaningful beyond the moment, attention must be paid to the details of the compromises, as well as to the subtextual disputes they represent. These documents address several aspects of international debates over gender roles, including (1) ways in which feminist language and concepts are beginning to inform public policy, (2) instances in which these concepts are deployed to undermine feminist goals, (3) cases in which the links between feminist theoretical analyses and political practices are weak, and (4) spaces where the political attention of women's movements must be focused in a more concerted fashion.

An important caveat to be made about documents that come out of UN conferences is that they are consensus based, which means that often the lowest common denominator prevails, and, therefore, weak language may emerge from the most contentious and passionate debates. Nevertheless, getting reluctant governments even to agree to weak text when it represents an advancement over their prior positions can be important. Further, these documents and programs of action do not have the status of international law. Instead, they carry political and moral weight as policy guidelines for the UN, governments, and other international organizations.

To use these documents effectively, they must be approached as statements of best intentions and commitments to which organized groups can seek to hold governments and the UN accountable.

Overall, the Beijing Platform for Action is a positive affirmation of women's human rights in many areas. It demands the economic and political empowerment of women and calls for more active intervention by governments on behalf of women's equality. The successes that women achieved in this process have been long in the making. They grow out of many decades of women's organizing generally, and specifically out of twenty years of attention to women at the UN, and four years of women's explicit and increasing participation as an organized force in UN intergovernmental conferences addressing major global concerns, such as the environment (Rio de Janeiro, 1992), human rights (Vienna, 1993), population and development (Cairo, 1994), and social development (Copenhagen, 1995). This has resulted in increasingly sophisticated lobbying of governmental delegates by women whose efforts are based on years of working to build international feminist strategies around common concerns, such as reproductive rights and violence against women. Networking among women prior to the Beijing conference produced effective cross-cultural alliances and led to significant collaboration between women on government delegations, in the UN and in NGO caucuses.

The Platform for Action outlines action for the human rights of women in twelve interrelated critical areas, from poverty and education to violence and the media. In spite of concerted attempts by religious fundamentalists and secular conservatives to narrow the reach of human rights, women's rights are framed throughout the Platform as indivisible, universal, and inalienable human rights. Such an understanding can be transformed into human rights practices—reaffirming women's rights to literacy, food, and housing, along with their rights to freedom of association and speech and to live free of violence, enslavement, or torture.

Yet, while the Platform clearly moves in the direction of advancing women's rights as human rights, it also reflects contentious debate about women's role in society and the construction of gender. The subtext to the Platform was the ongoing controversy about feminism and gender roles. For instance, one of the hottest debates in the final preparatory meeting was over the use of the term *gender* in the draft Platform. The Vatican and a few states argued against using *gender* at all unless it was explicitly tied to the "natural" biological roles of the sexes. When its efforts failed, the Holy See noted in its final statement to the conference that its members understood the term *gender* to be "grounded in biological sexual identity, male or female. . . . The Holy See thus excludes dubious interpretations based on world views which assert that sexual identity can be adapted indefinitely to suit new and different purposes." [1]

Some major controversies illustrate what women gained and the limitations of the Platform for Action. For example, in the contested area of sexual rights, many thought governments would not accept this language, and the phrase *sexual rights* per se was rejected. However, these boundaries were expanded in the health section of the Platform, which states in paragraph 97 that "the human rights of women include their right to have control over and decide freely and responsibly on matters related to their sexuality, including sexual and reproductive health, free of coercion, discrimination and violence." Similarly, explicit support for the rights of lesbians and the term *sexual orientation* were excluded from the Platform in final late-night negotiations. Nevertheless, the door was opened with this first open discussion of the issue in the UN, which also exposed the virulence of homophobia among those who manipulate it to oppose women's rights generally. At least some governments in each region of the world supported the need to include sexual orientation as deserving of protection from discrimination, and a number stated that their interpretation of the prohibition against discrimination on the basis of "other" status in several human rights treaties applies to lesbians and gays.

Another major debate centered on the term *uni-*

---

[1] United Nations, *UN Report of the Fourth World Conference on Women* (New York: United Nations, 1995), 165.

versal and the use of religion and culture to limit women's human rights. Women sought to maintain the 1993 Vienna World Conference on Human Rights recognition that women's human rights are universal, inalienable, indivisible, and interdependent. The Vatican, some Islamist governments, and a few other states overtly attempted unsuccessfully to limit the extent of universal application of women's human rights. However, they used this debate to claim that there is a feminist imperialism that reflects disrespect for religion and culture, an overzealous individualism, and an effort to impose Western values that destroy the family and local communities. Nineteen states entered reservations to text in the Platform that was not in conformity with Islamic law or traditional religious interpretations, particularly references to reproductive health and rights, inheritance, sexuality, and abortion. This is not a new debate, but women need to learn better how to argue for universality of rights without implying homogenization, especially around religion and culture, which can be positive for some women.

Human rights is not a static concept; it has varying meanings depending on a range of political, intellectual, and cultural traditions. Often in international organizing women speak of "culture" and national sovereignty in debates over human rights only as negative influences because they are so often used as excuses to deny women's rights. However, culture is constructed in many ways and exists not only as hegemonic culture but also as alternative cultures, oppositional cultures, and cultures of resistance. Women must create a more nuanced conversation that can address the tension between calls for recognizing the universality of women's human rights and the respect for and nurturance of local cultures and oppositional strategies. This entails women's defining the terms of debate and of culture themselves rather than letting the debate be defined by others.

The movement for women's human rights has sought to be a partial answer to this tension. In contrast to organizing that emphasizes categories of difference or identity, which were also well represented at the NGO Forum and government conference, efforts around women's human rights take as their reason for coming together the construction of a common political goal, based on a set of norms or justice, however problematic that may be, rather than a commonality of experience. The coalitions that emerge, then, are politically constructed, rather than determined on the basis of biology, geography, culture, ethnicity, and so on. The potential of such coalitions could be seen at the NGO Forum and in many of the global issue caucuses that lobbied together across geographical lines for more feminist language in the Platform for Action.

This incorporation of women's human rights language and concepts by governments and organizations from all parts of the world and in all manner of ways indicates more than a rhetorical gesture. It represents a shift in analysis that moves beyond single-issue politics or identity-based organizing and enhances women's capacity to build global alliances based on collective political goals and a common agenda. Moreover, because human rights is a language that has legitimacy among many individuals and governments, the appeal to human rights agreements and international norms can fortify women's organizing.

However, realization of the potential we viewed in Beijing requires vigorous leadership and a willingness to engage in open and often difficult political dialogue across many differences that tend to divide women. It also demands that women become politically active in local communities, in national political contests, and in international debates in the effort to reshape the terms of debate for the twenty-first century. The Beijing Platform for Action can be a vital tool in this process as it provides an affirmation of women's rights as human rights and outlines many of the actions necessary to realize women's empowerment. But how far the Platform and the concept of women's human rights will take women depends on whether women are able to use them to further their efforts to influence policy and action at all levels from the global to the local.

WOMEN'S HUMAN RIGHTS FIVE YEARS AFTER BEIJING

One of the most remarkable achievements of the last forty years has been the widespread growth of women's movements around the world and the ways in which feminist questions have altered roles, relationships, and public debates in almost every corner of the globe. While this clearly remains an unfinished revolution, it is these changes and the backlash against them that provide the framework for assessing the significance and outcome of the Beijing + 5 Review. We must place this, at times frustrating, review process in the larger context of women's organizing, particularly around the United Nations World Conferences over the past quarter-of-a-century.

Since the late 1960s, and with added impetus from the 1975 International Women's Year World Conference in Mexico City, women have been raising consciousness about their status in every region of the world. Women have put dozens of new issues on the world's agenda as well as sought to alter the way in which many global questions are viewed. Women are now on the agenda worldwide in every field of study and in every area of public life. Abuses and neglect that once were ignored as routine are now being challenged, and that is major progress. The proof of change is the list of fights we are waging: against domestic violence, marital rape, incest, genital mutilation, sexual harassment, enforced heterosexuality, forced pregnancy, femicide, trafficking in humans, and every kind of humiliation we once were told was just life, just a woman's lot. We are fighting for women's rights to education, to reproductive and other health care choices, to property, land, and inheritance, to political participation, equal pay, and an equal voice in decision-making on all issues. All of these inalienable rights were once denied us without a second thought. Not only are we now on the agenda, we are working to transform that agenda. The fact that there is opposition to a movement for such basic changes should not, therefore, come as a surprise.

In the decade between the 1985 Third World Conference on Women in Nairobi and the 1995 Fourth World Conference in Beijing, women's networks formed regionally and globally that succeeded in advancing women's voices and perspectives on global issues in many arenas. Among the most visible of these efforts has been women's organizing to put gender on the agenda at UN World Conferences in the 1990s, from the Earth Summit in Rio (1992) to the Human Rights Conference in Vienna (1993), the Cairo International Conference on Population and Development (1994), the Copenhagen Summit for Social Development (1995), the Habitat Conference in Istanbul (1996), and the World Food Summit in Rome (1997). These efforts have established women as a global force in some areas and demonstrated our potential in others.

The Beijing Women's Conference was a high point in this process with more people attending both the inter-governmental proceedings and the parallel NGO Forum than any other UN World Conference to date—in spite of efforts by some to boycott and by the Chinese government to discourage NGO participation. In Beijing, 189 governments made a broad range of promises to uphold the human rights of the three billion people who are female. The *Beijing Platform for Action* was a veritable referendum on the human rights of women in twelve critical areas of concern ranging from socio-economic rights, like poverty and education, to political participation and newer areas of acknowledged human rights abuse, such as violence against women at home and in armed conflict. Beijing firmly established that women's rights are human rights and that meeting women's needs is central to every nation's progress in economic development and democracy.

As women have become more forceful in the global arena, inevitably, there has been resistance. The backlash against women did not start in the 1990s, but it has grown with the emergence of an unholy alliance of forces that work to defeat women's growing self-determination and political power nationally and internationally. Whether they operate under the guise of Christian, Muslim or other religious fundamentalisms, or as right wing U.S. Republicans or nationalistic forces in ethnic conflicts around the world, they are united in opposition to women's growing strength and advances towards self-determination. Women waged particularly intense battles with them in Cairo and Beijing around the issues of reproductive and sexual rights; and these forces came back with a vengeance in the + 5 reviews of these two pivotal conferences in 1999 and 2000.

WHAT HAPPENED IN THE BEIJING + 5 PROCESS

The United Nations meeting to measure progress five years after the Fourth World Conference on Women became yet another site in the global contest over women's roles and rights. But the tension surrounding the Beijing + 5 process did not come only from the classic "feminist versus fundamentalist" show-down. Since Beijing, the impact of globalization has also exacerbated conflicts between rich and poor nations and increased many states' insecurity about their ability to control their destinies. Advances in international human rights law and increased efforts to hold individuals accountable for war crimes—highlighted by moves toward the creation of an International Criminal Court and the indictment of General Pinochet of Chile—have brought to the surface the tension between the UN's commitment to uphold human rights while, at the same time, respecting national sovereignty. Under the guise of preserving national sovereignty or cultural diversity, some governments have become leery of human rights in general, as well as with regard to women.

As a result of these various factors, the political climate of the UN General Assembly in the fall of 1999 has been described by many as one of the most tense in recent memory. Since the Beijing + 5 Review was a special session of the General Assembly, it fell victim to these tensions as well. The cooperation across geopolitical lines that is necessary for reaching consensus was harder to muster this time than it had been in 1995, and the amount of political capital that most governments were prepared to expend on a review was less than what they had put into the Beijing Conference. Further, most governments were aware of how little progress they had made toward fulfilling the Beijing promises and were reluctant to make more commitments. Even assessing women's status has grown more complex with significant improvements in some areas for some women offset by economic decline and growing violence for others.

Advocates for women's rights entered the Beijing + 5 process seeking a variety of advances for women. Where the *Beijing Platform* was strong in some areas like health and violence against women, the primary goal was to get governments to make more concrete commitments to fulfilling their promises through determining benchmarks, time-bound targets, and dedicated resources. In other areas where the Platform was weaker or had neglected critical issues, the goal was to get additional statements addressing matters like the impact of globalization on women, HIV/AIDS, women and peace-keeping, and issues of racism and discrimination based on sexual orientation, to name but a few. In general, the goal was to use the review process to strengthen governmental commitment and international cooperation aimed at implementing the Platform and the human rights principles embodied in it through spelling out concrete actions that should be taken at all levels—local, national, regional, and international.

However, we often found ourselves reduced to defending the turf gained in Beijing or seemingly only making incremental advances on it. Conservative non-governmental forces, primarily from the religious right wing in North America, were present in large numbers and worked with representatives from a handful of determined and very vocal countries and the Holy See to water down the Beijing commitments, or at least stall any efforts to go forward from them. The uneasy and complex geopolitical climate in the UN seemed to make it difficult to move the process forward. The period from the final preparatory committee in March through most of the Special Session in June was characterized by long, drawn-out and tedious negotiations and stalemate. Finally, the many drafts and re-drafts, and confusion about what kind of document was needed, during the negotiations resulted in a final report that is unwieldy and often hard to follow.

Given the investment that so many women around the world had made in the *Beijing Platform*, it was critical to defend those advances and not lose ground in this highly visible global arena. In the end, the document produced by the Beijing + 5 Process does not retreat and is better than the frustrating process led many of us to believe it would be. Most importantly, the *Beijing Plus Five Political Declaration* reaffirms that governments have the responsibility to implement the *Beijing Platform for Action*, and thus the Platform remains the reference point for governmental commitment to and action on women's rights in all twelve critical areas of concern for the next decade.

While the conservative forces did not succeed in changing the Beijing Platform, they did weaken proposals for actions that governments should undertake at this time to implement it, adding qualifying phrases like "where appropriate," or saying parties should "consider" certain actions rather than calling on them to act. Many specific dates and numerical targets proposed by some governments were removed from the draft, making it harder to measure progress and hold governments accountable to their commitments. Unfortunately, a number of governments who were reluctant to be politically bound to such goals hid behind the more vocal opponents in allowing these proposals to be compromised. As the NGO statement released by the Linkage Caucus on the final day of the special session states: "We regret that there was not enough political will on the part of some governments and the UN system to agree on a stronger document with more concrete benchmarks, numerical goals, timebound targets, indicators, and resources aimed at implementing the Beijing Platform." The document could have been better but it could also have been a great deal worse. It does include strong stands against trafficking in women and girls, against domestic violence—including marital rape—and against so-called "honor killings." It demands that more attention be devoted to combating racism, to the ways that globalization adversely affects women, and to the devastating HIV-AIDS epidemic. It makes maternal mortality a health sector priority and affirms women's hard won goals in the Cairo + 5 review.

Finally, we cannot talk about what happened at Beijing + 5 without noting the ways in which nongovernmental organizations (NGOs) utilized the occasion to engage once more with governments about their responsibilities for upholding the human rights of women. Women, and some men, participated in record numbers during the Review, as they did at the World Conference on Women in Beijing—proving once more that this is an issue central to people's lives and passions. At all four regional meetings, NGOs gathered before and/or during the governmental meetings to lobby delegates and to produce statements on a wide array of concerns. At the Special Session in New York, regional caucuses and international affinity groups formed around specific issues, prepared draft language, and lobbied delegates. Many women from NGOs served on governmental delegations and/or provided technical expertise on gender issues to delegations. Based on the growing NGO experience of the past decade both working at UN conferences and in other international arenas, many of these networks have become effective at forging common positions across various geopolitical lines.

One of the most heartening aspects of this process was the significant presence of young women who organized their own caucuses as well as participated in others. Another important development was the way some NGO Caucuses utilized the occasion not only to address the Beijing + 5 Review but also to garner attention for their concerns from the media and governments as well as the UN. For example, the Caucus on Women and Armed Conflict engaged UN personnel and governments in conversation about women and peace keeping which helped lay the groundwork for the first historic meeting on this topic, which was held by the Security Council in October 2000.

At the national level, most governments felt obliged to meet with NGOs and make reports on what they are doing to implement the *Beijing Platform;* many women engaged governments and others in debates about what needs to be done in their countries to advance women's rights. Over 100 alternative reports prepared by NGOs challenged governments' rosy national reports to the UN by telling the unvarnished truth about what governments have and have not done. In addition to focusing on the debates over the inter-governmental document, women held symposia, workshops, and conferences to share experiences and learn from one another about what has worked and what has not in their own countries. As in Beijing, women used the space provided by the review to network and share strategies across cultural, racial, sexual, national, and other boundaries and to outline some of the challenges ahead in the unfinished agenda of achieving rights and equality for women.

WHAT BEIJING + 5 REVEALED: TOWARDS THE FUTURE

While the processes of the Nairobi and Beijing Women's Conferences were also frustrating at times, they were still high points for the international women's movement in terms of defining and elaborating women's needs and rights and setting standards for what governments should do to advance women's position in the world. The Beijing + 5 Review was inevitably more sobering, as it sought to assess how much had been done towards these lofty goals in a relatively short period of time. It should come as no surprise that the process of implementing these standards and enforcing respect for rights that have been violated around the world for centuries is more difficult.

The challenges of Beijing + 5 were the same ones faced today by women's movements locally and internationally: institutional resistance and backlash, lack of political will, insufficient resources for the task at hand, cultural undertow, and the need for alternative social models and concepts that spell out women's visions for a world without discrimination and violence. It was to address such issues that we chose to hold the Women 2000 Symposium during the Beijing + 5 Process. For, while fighting for words in the inter-governmental document that will maintain official commitment to women's rights as human rights, we also need to look at women's concrete strategies and actions in the world, as they seek to fulfill the promises contained in that language.

The Beijing + 5 process also raised important questions for reflection about working for women's human rights through the United Nations system. It pointed to some of the limitations of this work when governments are not really committed to the words they pen. At the same time, it reminded us of the value of women continuing to use the public space that the UN provides. Many people are looking for better ways for the UN to conduct such reviews since this one, like most of the other "plus five" reviews of this past decade, has proven frustrating. Perhaps processes of such profound transformation as the ones signaled by the UN women's conferences need a longer time frame before a realistic assessment of progress can take place. Another issue left unanswered by this review is whether there will be another world conference on women in the future. This question is now in the hands of the Commission on the Status of Women and the Committee on Economic, Social and Cultural Rights (ECOSOC) who must determine whether to hold such an event in 2005 or at any other point in the coming decade. While the UN is talking about cutting back on holding world conferences, the women's conferences have proven to be a vital impetus for the growth of the women's movement and have provided opportunities—which are still all too rare—for women to meet across national, regional, and cultural lines. Whether in 2005 or later, it seems critical that women maintain the push to hold another such conference within the next decade, both as a global gathering point for women's advocates and as a target that reminds governments of their accountability to their promises to the world's women.

One of the insights that this process has revealed is the importance of human rights mechanisms for women. Indeed, the human rights underpinnings of the *Beijing Platform for Action* came under attack, in part because women have begun to use human rights more effectively over the past decade. Some governments objected to using human rights instruments to guarantee the *Platform*'s promises to women; but if they can deny human rights to women on cultural or national grounds, then the very concept of human rights being universal is undermined. We came away from Beijing + 5 with a document that did not back down on the fundamental truth that women's rights are human rights. However, the attack on this gain reminded us that realizing it is an ongoing work for which we must remain vigilant. It also pointed to the importance of women utilizing the *Convention on the Elimination of All Forms of Discrimination against Women* (CEDAW) and all other human rights treaties which, unlike the *Beijing Plat-*

form, are legally binding obligations on the countries that sign them.

Overall, the global women's movement prevailed in the Beijing + 5 process in spite of frustrations and obstacles. The *Beijing Platform for Action* was reaffirmed and governments once more pledged that it is their responsibility to work for its implementation. While there were not as many specific targets set and resources allocated as many of us sought, there were many concrete advances that women can build on as we work to implement the *Platform* and to hold governments accountable to their commitments to women. The Beijing + 5 Review had its ups and downs, but it provided one more opportunity for public discussion of many issues that affect and concern women. Because of this event, the media has aired issues locally and globally, also demonstrating the importance of women as a constituency for the UN. It is women who have placed women's empowerment and human rights on the world's agenda, utilizing events like the UN World Conferences as well as many other strategies. And it is women who will continue to advance this agenda. This has been yet another moment where women have demonstrated determination in working to realize justice and all human rights for all women in all our diversity.   [1996, 2002]

🌿 141

The Globetrotting Sneaker

CYNTHIA ENLOE

All the "New World Order" really means to corporate giants like athletic shoemakers is that they now have the green light to accelerate long-standing industry practices. In the early 1980s, the field marshals commanding Reebok and Nike, which are both U.S.-based, decided to manufacture most of their sneakers in South Korea and Taiwan, hiring local women. L.A. Gear, Adidas, Fila, and Asics quickly followed their lead. In short time, the coastal city of Pusan, South Korea, became the "sneaker capital of the world." Between 1982 and 1989 the U.S. lost 58,500 footwear jobs to cities like Pusan, which attracted sneaker executives because its location facilitated international transport. More to the point, South Korea's military government had an interest in suppressing labor organizing, and it had a comfortable military alliance with the U.S. Korean women also seemed accepting of Confucian philosophy, which measured a woman's morality by her willingness to work hard for her family's well-being and to acquiesce to her father's and husband's dictates. With their sense of patriotic duty, Korean women seemed the ideal labor force for export-oriented factories.

U.S. and European sneaker company executives were also attracted by the ready supply of eager Korean male entrepreneurs with whom they could make profitable arrangements. This fact was central to Nike's strategy in particular. When they moved their production sites to Asia to lower labor costs, the executives of the Oregon-based company decided to reduce their corporate responsibilities further. Instead of owning factories outright, a more efficient strategy would be to subcontract the manufacturing to wholly foreign-owned—in this case, South Korean—companies. Let them be responsible for workers' health and safety. Let them negotiate with newly emergent unions. Nike would retain control over those parts of sneaker production that gave its officials the greatest professional satisfaction and the ultimate word on the product: design and marketing. Although Nike was following in the footsteps of garment and textile manufacturers, it set the trend for the rest of the athletic footwear industry.

But at the same time, women workers were developing their own strategies. As the South Korean pro-democracy movement grew throughout the 1980s, increasing numbers of women rejected traditional notions of feminine duty. Women began organizing in response to the dangerous working conditions, daily humiliations, and low pay built into their work. Such resistance was profoundly threatening to the government, given the fact that South Korea's emergence as an industrialized "tiger" had depended on

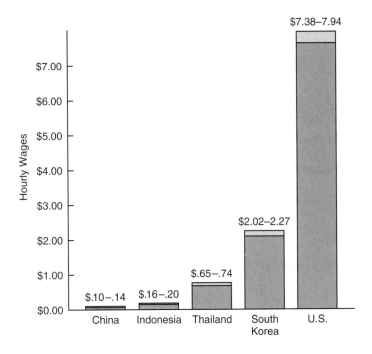

Figure 1 Hourly Wages in Athletic Footwear Factories

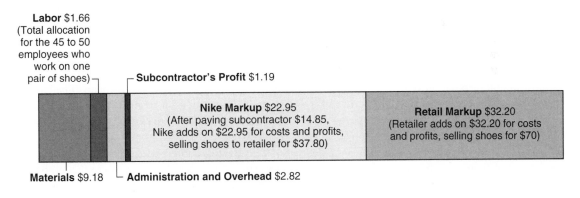

Figure 2 A $70 Pair of Nike Pegasus: Where the Money Goes

women accepting their "role" in growing industries like sneaker manufacture. If women reimagined their lives as daughters, as wives, as workers, as citizens, it wouldn't just rattle their employers; it would shake the very foundations of the whole political system.

At the first sign of trouble, factory managers called in government riot police to break up employees' meetings. Troops sexually assaulted women workers, stripping, fondling, and raping them "as a control mechanism for suppressing women's engagement in the labor movement," reported Jeong-

Lim Nam of Hyosung Women's University in Taegu. It didn't work. It didn't work because the feminist activists in groups like the Korean Women Workers Association (KWWA) helped women understand and deal with the assaults. The KWWA held consciousness-raising sessions in which notions of feminine duty and respectability were tackled along with wages and benefits. They organized independently of the male-led labor unions to ensure that their issues would be taken seriously, in labor negotiations and in the pro-democracy movement as a whole.

The result was that women were at meetings with management, making sure that in addition to issues like long hours and low pay, sexual assault at the hands of managers and health care were on the table. Their activism paid off: in addition to winning the right to organize women's unions, their earnings grew. In 1980, South Korean women in manufacturing jobs earned 45 percent of the wages of their male counterparts; by 1990, they were earning more than 50 percent. Modest though it was, the pay increase was concrete progress, given that the gap between women's and men's manufacturing wages in Japan, Singapore, and Sri Lanka actually *widened* during the 1980s. Last but certainly not least, women's organizing was credited with playing a major role in toppling the country's military regime and forcing open elections in 1987.

Without that special kind of workplace control that only an authoritarian government could offer, sneaker executives knew that it was time to move. In Nike's case, its famous advertising slogan—"Just Do It"—proved truer to its corporate philosophy than its women's "empowerment" ad campaign, designed to rally women's athletic (and consumer) spirit. In response to South Korean women workers' newfound activist self-confidence, the sneaker company and its subcontractors began shutting down a number of their South Korean factories in the late 1980s and early 1990s. After bargaining with government officials in nearby China and Indonesia, many Nike subcontractors set up shop in those countries, while some went to Thailand. China's government remains nominally Communist; Indonesia's ruling generals are staunchly anti-Communist. But both are governed by authoritarian regimes who share the belief that if women can be kept hard at work, low paid, and unorganized, they can serve as a magnet for foreign investors.

Where does all this leave South Korean women —or any woman who is threatened with a factory closure if she demands decent working conditions and a fair wage? They face the dilemma confronted by thousands of women from dozens of countries. The risk of job loss is especially acute in relatively mobile industries; it's easier for a sneaker, garment, or electronics manufacturer to pick up and move than it is for an automaker or a steel producer. In the case of South Korea, poor women had moved from rural villages into the cities searching for jobs to support not only themselves, but parents and siblings. The exodus of manufacturing jobs has forced more women into the growing "entertainment" industry. The kinds of bars and massage parlors offering sexual services that had mushroomed around U.S. military bases during the Cold War have been opening up across the country.

But the reality is that women throughout Asia are organizing, knowing full well the risks involved. Theirs is a long-term view; they are taking direct aim at companies' nomadic advantage, by building links among workers in countries targeted for "development" by multinational corporations. Through sustained grassroots efforts, women are developing the skills and confidence that will make it increasingly difficult to keep their labor cheap. The United Nations conference on women in Beijing, China, was a rare opportunity to expand their cross-border strategizing.

The Beijing conference provided an important opportunity to call world attention to the hypocrisy of the governments and corporations doing business in China. Numerous athletic shoe companies followed Nike in setting up manufacturing sites throughout the country. This included Reebok—a company claiming its share of responsibility for ridding the world of "injustice, poverty, and other ills that gnaw away at the social fabric," according to a statement of corporate principles.

Since 1988, Reebok has been giving out annual human rights awards to dissidents from around the world. But it wasn't until 1992 that the company adopted its own "human rights production standards"—after labor advocates made it known that the quality of life in factories run by its subcontractors was just as dismal as that at most other athletic shoe suppliers in Asia. Reebok's code of conduct, for example, includes a pledge to "seek" those subcontractors who respect workers' rights to organize. The only problem is that independent trade unions are banned in China. Reebok has chosen to ignore that fact, even though Chinese dissidents have been the recipients of the company's own human rights award. As for working conditions, Reebok now says it sends its own inspectors to production sites a couple of times a year. But they have easily "missed" what subcontractors are trying to hide—like 400 young women workers locked at night into an overcrowded dormitory near a Reebok-contracted factory in the town of Zhuhai, as reported last August in the *Asian Wall Street Journal Weekly.*

* * *

Nike's cofounder and CEO Philip Knight has said that he would like the world to think of Nike as "a company with a soul that recognizes the value of human beings." Nike, like Reebok, says it sends in inspectors from time to time to check up on work conditions at its factories; in Indonesia, those factories are run largely by South Korean subcontractors. But according to Donald Katz in a recent book on the company, Nike spokesman Dave Taylor told an in-house newsletter that the factories are "[the subcontractors'] business to run." For the most part, the company relies on regular reports from subcontractors regarding its "Memorandum of Understanding," which managers must sign, promising to impose "local government standards" for wages, working conditions, treatment of workers, and benefits.

In April, the minimum wage in the Indonesian capital of Jakarta will be $1.89 *a day*—among the highest in a country where the minimum wage varies by region. And managers are required to pay only 75 percent of the wage directly; the remainder can be withheld for "benefits." By now, Nike has a well-honed response to growing criticisms of its low-cost labor strategy. Such wages should not be seen as exploitative, says Nike, but rather as the first rung

on the ladder of economic opportunity that Nike has extended to workers with few options. Otherwise, they'd be out "harvesting coconut meat in the tropical sun," wrote Nike spokesman Dusty Kidd, in a letter to the *Utne Reader.* The all-is-relative response craftily shifts attention away from reality: Nike didn't move to Indonesia to help Indonesians; it moved to ensure that its profit margin continues to grow. And that is pretty much guaranteed in a country where "local standards" for wages rarely take a worker over the poverty line. A 1991 survey by the International Labor Organization (ILO) found that 88 percent of women working at the Jakarta minimum wage at the time—slightly less than a dollar a day—were malnourished.

A woman named Riyanti might have been among the workers surveyed by the ILO. Interviewed by the *Boston Globe* in 1991, she told the reporter who had asked about her long hours and low pay: "I'm happy working here. . . . I can make money and I can make friends." But in fact, the reporter discovered that Riyanti had already joined her coworkers in two strikes, the first to force one of Nike's Korean subcontractors to accept a new women's union and the second to compel managers to pay at least the minimum wage. That Riyanti appeared less than forthcoming about her activities isn't surprising. Many Indonesian factories have military men posted in their front offices who find no fault with managers who tape women's mouths shut to keep them from talking among themselves. They and their superiors have a political reach that extends far beyond the barracks. Indonesia has all the makings for a political explosion, especially since the gap between rich and poor is widening into a chasm. It is in this setting that the government has tried to crack down on any independent labor organizing—a policy that Nike has helped to implement. Referring to a recent strike in a Nike-contracted factory, Tony Nava, Nike representative in Indonesia, told the *Chicago Tribune* in November 1994 that the "troublemakers" had been fired. When asked about Nike policy on the issue, spokesman Keith Peters struck a conciliatory note: "If the government were to allow and encourage independent labor organizing, we would be happy to support it."

Indonesian workers' efforts to create unions independent of governmental control were a surprise to shoe companies. Although their moves from South Korea have been immensely profitable [see chart], they do not have the sort of immunity from activism that they had expected. In May 1993, the murder of a female labor activist outside Surabaya set off a storm of local and international protest. Even the U.S. State Department was forced to take note in its 1993 worldwide human rights report, describing a system similar to that which generated South Korea's boom 20 years earlier: severely restricted union organizing, security forces used to break up strikes, low wages for men, lower wages for women—complete with government rhetoric celebrating women's contribution to national development.

Yet when President Clinton visited Indonesia he made only a token effort to address the country's human rights problem. Instead, he touted the benefits of free trade, sounding indeed more enlightened, more in tune with the spirit of the post–Cold War era than do those defenders of protectionist trading policies who coat their rhetoric with "America first" chauvinism. But "free trade" as actually being practiced today is hardly *free* for any workers—in the U.S. or abroad—who have to accept the Indonesian, Chinese, or Korean workplace model as the price of keeping their jobs.

The not-so-new plot of the international trade story has been "divide and rule." If women workers and their government in one country can see that a sneaker company will pick up and leave if their labor demands prove more costly than those in a neighbor country, then women workers will tend to see their neighbors not as regional sisters, but as competitors who can steal their precarious livelihoods. Playing women off against each other is, of course, old hat. Yet it is as essential to international trade politics as is the fine print in GATT.

But women workers allied through networks like the Hong Kong-based Committee for Asian Women are developing their own post–Cold War foreign policy, which means addressing women's needs: how to convince fathers and husbands that a woman going out to organizing meetings at night is not sexually promiscuous; how to develop workplace agendas that respond to family needs; how to work with male unionists who push women's demands to the bottom of their lists; how to build a global movement.

These women refuse to stand in awe of the corporate power of the Nike or Reebok or Adidas executive. Growing numbers of Asian women today have concluded that trade politics have to be understood by women on their own terms. If women in Russia and Eastern Europe can challenge Americanized consumerism, if Asian activists can solidify their alliances, and if U.S. women can join with them by taking on trade politics—the post-Cold War sneaker may be a less comfortable fit in the 1990s.   [1997]

This article draws from the work of South Korean scholars Hyun Sook Kim, Seung-kyung Kim, Katherine Moon, Seungsook Moon, and Jeong-Lim Nam.

Women Organizing: Many Issues, Many Voices

The ideas of feminism have influenced countless women, changing their ideas about themselves and expectations of their future. In their daily lives many women have asserted themselves against woman-hating behavior they encounter in their daily lives. Sonia Sanchez, for example, responded to street harassment with dignity and ingenuity. But ending women's subordination involves more than individual acts. It requires working together to challenge sexist practices and institutions and creating organizations that embody a vision of a more humane and just society. How do people move from a consciousness of injustice to political involvement? Rebecca Walker describes the process by which she commits herself to working politically for women's freedom. Written immediately after the Senate confirmation hearings of Clarence Thomas, the Supreme Court justice who had been accused of sexual harassment by Anita Hill, a former employee, Walker's essay echoes the outrage of many women at what they saw as a vivid enactment of women's political powerlessness. For some young women, like Nell Geiser, activism is becoming a way of life, a way of expressing their political views and sustaining a vision of a more equitable world.

Feminism cannot be located in one central organization. Rather it exists in the myriad groups and organizing projects that women form when they encounter injustice or seek to address unmet needs. We present here four examples of women organizing in various contexts. In each situation, the first step was breaking the silence about women's experience and naming the problems they faced. The ideas and activities of each group reflect their particular needs and perspectives. The women in "Voices" created an organization for women with AIDS in prison in the late 1980s. Their organization was able to make institutional changes while engaged in meeting the needs of women prisoners. African-American feminists in the 1990s organized a series of actions to make a black feminist viewpoint visible on crucial political issues. Korean immigrant women organized in response to the inhumane conditions in their workplace, and college students have organized to challenge the campus culture that encourages acquaintance rape.

We conclude our book with examples of two dimensions of feminist activism. The excerpt from *Manifesta: Young Women, Feminism and the Future* is a call for a political movement that addresses the structural and cultural barriers to women's self-determination, while the personal narratives describe the ways three women have brought the ideas they learned in women's studies into their work lives.

🌿 142

style no. 1

SONIA SANCHEZ

i come from a long line of rough mamas.

so here i was walking down market street. coming out of a city hall meeting. night wind at my back, dressed in my finest. black cashmere coat caressing the rim of my gray suede boots. hat sitting acey duecy. anointing the avenue with my black smell.

and this old dude. red as his car inching its way on the sidewalk. honked his horn. slid his body almost out of his skin. toward me. psst. psst. hey. let's you and me have some fun. psst. psst. c'mon babe. don't you want some of this?

and he pulled his penis out of his pants. held the temporal wonder of men in his hands.

i stopped. looked at him. a memory from deep in the eye. a memory of saturday afternoon moviehouses where knowledge comes with a tremulous cry. old white men. spiderlike. spinning their webs towards young girls legs and out budabbot and loucostello smiles melted. and we moved in the high noon walk of black girls. smelling the breath of an old undertow.

and i saw mama Dixon, dancing on his head. mama Dixon. big loud friend of the family. who stunned us with her curses and liquor. being herself. whose skin breathed hilarious breaths. and i greased my words on her tongue. and she gave them back to me like newly tasted wine.

motha fucka. you even offend the night i said. you look like an old mole coming out of its hole. take yo slimy sat ole ass home. fo you get what's coming to you. and yo generation. ask yo mama to skin you. that is if you have had one cuz anybody ugly as you couldna been born.

and i turned my eyes eastward. toward the garage. waking up the incipient night with my steps. ready for the short days. the wind singing in my veins. [1987]

🌿 143

Becoming the Third Wave

REBECCA WALKER

I am not one of the people who sat transfixed before the television, watching the Senate hearings. I had classes to go to, papers to write, and frankly, the whole thing was too painful. A black man grilled by a panel of white men about his sexual deviance. A black woman claiming harassment and being discredited by other women. . . . I could not bring myself to watch that sensationalized assault [on] the human spirit.

To me, the hearings were not about determining whether or not Clarence Thomas did in fact harass Anita Hill. They were about checking and redefining the extent of women's credibility and power.

Can a woman's experience undermine a man's career? Can a woman's voice, a woman's sense of self-worth and injustice, challenge a structure predicated upon the subjugation of our gender? Anita Hill's testimony threatened to do that and more. If Thomas had not been confirmed, every man in the United States would be at risk. For how many senators never told a sexist joke? How many men have not used their protected male privilege to thwart in some way the influence or ideas of a woman colleague, friend, or relative?

For those whose sense of power is so obviously connected to the health and vigor of the penis, it would have been a metaphoric castration. Of course this is too great a threat.

While some may laud the whole spectacle for the consciousness it raised around sexual harassment, its very real outcome is more informative. He was promoted. She was repudiated. Men were assured of the inviolability of their penis/power. Women were admonished to keep their experiences to themselves.

The backlash against U.S. women is real. As the misconception of equality between the sexes becomes more ubiquitous, so does the attempt to restrict the boundaries of women's personal and political power. Thomas's confirmation, the ultimate rally of support for the male paradigm of harassment, sends a clear message to women: "Shut up! Even if you speak, we will not listen."

I will not be silenced.

I acknowledge the fact that we live under siege. I intend to fight back. I have uncovered and unleashed more repressed anger than I thought possible. For the umpteenth time in my 22 years, I have been radicalized, politicized, shaken awake. I have come to voice again, and this time my voice is not conciliatory.

The night after Thomas' confirmation I ask the man I am intimate with what he thinks of the whole mess. His concern is primarily with Thomas' propensity to demolish civil rights and opportunities for people of color. I launch into a tirade. "When will progressive black men prioritize my rights and wellbeing? When will they stop talking so damn much about 'the race' as if it revolved exclusively around them?" He tells me I wear my emotions on my sleeve. I scream "I need to know, are you with me or are you going to help them try to destroy me?"

A week later I am on a train to New York. A beautiful mother and daughter, both wearing green outfits, sit across the aisle from me. The little girl has tightly plaited braids. Her brown skin is glowing and smooth, her eyes bright as she chatters happily while looking out the window. Two men get on the train and sit directly behind me, shaking my seat as they thud into place. I bury myself in *The Sound and the Fury*. Loudly they begin to talk about women. "Man, I fucked that bitch all night and then I never called her again." "Man, there's lots of girlies over there, you know that ho, live over there by Tyrone? Well, I snatched that shit up."

The mother moves closer to her now quiet daughter. Looking at her small back I can see that she is listening to the men. I am thinking of how I can transform the situation, of all the people in the car whose silence makes us complicit.

Another large man gets on the train. After exchanging loud greetings with the two men, he sits next to me. He tells them he is going to Philadelphia to visit his wife and child. I am suckered into thinking that he is different. Then, "Man, there's a ton

of females in Philly, just waitin' for you to give 'em some." I turn my head and allow the fire in my eyes to burn into him. He takes up two seats and has hands with huge swollen knuckles. I imagine the gold rings on his fingers slamming into my face. He senses something, "What's your name, sweetheart?" The other men lean forward over the seat.

A torrent explodes: "I ain't your sweetheart, I ain't your bitch, I ain't your baby. How dare you have the nerve to sit up here and talk about women that way, and then try to speak to me." The woman/mother chimes in to the beat with claps of sisterhood. The men are momentarily stunned. Then the comeback: "Aw, bitch, don't play that woman shit over here 'cause that's bullshit." He slaps the back of one hand against the palm of the other. I refuse to back down. Words fly.

My instinct kicks in, telling me to get out. "Since I see you all are not going to move, I will." I move to the first car. I am so angry that thoughts of murder, of physically retaliating against them, of separatism, engulf me. I am almost out of body, just shy of being pure force. I am sick of the way women are negated, violated, devalued, ignored. I am livid, unrelenting in my anger at those who invade my space, who wish to take away my rights, who refuse to hear my voice.

As the days pass, I push myself to figure out what it means to be a part of the Third Wave of feminism. I begin to realize that I owe it to myself, to my little sister on the train, to all of the daughters yet to be born, to push beyond my rage and articulate an agenda. After battling with ideas of separatism and militancy, I connect with my own feelings of powerlessness. I realize that I must undergo a transformation if I am truly committed to women's empowerment. My involvement must reach beyond my own voice in discussion, beyond voting, beyond reading feminist theory. My anger and awareness must translate into tangible action.

I am ready to decide, as my mother decided before me, to devote much of my energy to the history, health, and healing of women. Each of my choices will have to hold to my feminist standard of justice.

To be a feminist is to integrate an ideology of

equality and female empowerment into the very fiber of my life. It is to search for personal clarity in the midst of systemic destruction, to join in sisterhood with women when often we are divided, to understand power structures with the intention of challenging them.

While this may sound simple, it is exactly the kind of stand that many of my peers are unwilling to take. So I write this as a plea to all women, especially the women of my generation: Let Thomas' confirmation serve to remind you, as it did me, that the fight is far from over. Let this dismissal of a woman's experience move you to anger. Turn that outrage into political power. Do not vote for them unless they work for us. Do not have sex with them, do not break bread with them, do not nurture them if they don't prioritize our freedom to control our bodies and our lives.

I am not a postfeminism feminist. I am the Third Wave.   [1992]

🌿 144

Why I'm An Activist

NELL GEISER

We entered the fourth small non-profit office of the day and pulled out our notebooks for another meeting. The women of South Asian Women's Empowerment and Resource Alliance (SAWERA) who welcomed us offered Indian sweets and mango juice. Fifteen of us and about eight representatives of SAWERA squeezed into their small space and discussed how domestic abuse affects South Asian women in the Portland area. Nidhi, a junior at the University of Wisconsin at Madison and part of our group, brought up some of her insights as an Indian American. We talked about cultural issues inherent in addressing domestic abuse within South Asian families. And we posed questions about youth outreach and popular education targeting men. The

women who started SAWERA as a grassroots, direct service organization gave us a whirlwind history of the group; then we trooped out the door, down the stairs, and back into our big red van (lovingly dubbed, "The Red Menace").

And what were we, a group of fifteen 16- to 26-year-old women, doing traipsing between non-profit offices and community centers in cities in the Pacific Northwest? We were doing our best to reach out across movements, build bridges between struggles, and get an insider's view of the future of activism. ROAMS—Reaching Out Across Movements—was the title of our 17-day excursion through four states, organized by the Third Wave Foundation based in New York City. We embarked on our journey as a bunch of pretty radical young feminists committed to bringing the concept of young women's leadership in social justice organizing and activism to the forefront of our discussions with grassroots, activist organizations throughout the Northwest.

A NON-TRADITIONAL ROAD TRIP

The ubiquitous question—"Why did you become an activist?"—is easier for me to answer after spending two and a half weeks last summer with those fourteen other women of ROAMS. We slept on the floors of people's houses, on the floors of organizations like Communities Against Rape and Abuse (CARA) in Seattle, and at cheap motels in four states. We spent hours together in the van, discussing revolution vs. reform and the future of campus organizing, listening to music, or just staring out the window at the breathtaking scenes of the Northwest. And then there were the more than forty meetings with progressive organizations ranging from the Community Coalition for Environmental Justice in Seattle to the Women of Color Alliance in Boise, from Danzine, a sexworkers' organizing group in Portland, to WEEL (Working for Equality and Economic Liberation), a welfare rights group in Montana. We gained an understanding of the political climate and social justice struggles of the Northwest that an outsider just can't get except through an extended tour of that complex region.

One of the aims of the trip was to focus the financial resources of the Third Wave Foundation on a philanthropically under-served region. The small, five-year-old foundation offers grants from a few hundred to a few thousand dollars to support grassroots organizing efforts that have young women at the helm. Third Wave is the only national philanthropic organization in the country with a constituency of young women, ages fifteen to thirty. Last year, ROAMS went on its inaugural journey, exploring the rich activism of the Southeast. And next year, Third Wave will fly another multiracial, multi-class, geographically disparate group of women committed to activism and social justice to the Southwest for a nontraditional road trip.

BECOMING MYSELF: ACTIVISM AS A WAY OF LIFE

I am seventeen years old and people do often ask me why I'm an activist. Sometimes I wish it were self-evident that activism is really the only thing worth doing. But usually I explain that I grew up in a social justice–oriented household; I read books about the Civil Rights Movement (I remember being profoundly moved in fourth grade by an autobiography by one of the students who integrated Central High School in Little Rock, Arkansas); I got involved with the Rocky Mountain Peace and Justice Center in 1998 when the U.S. began bombing Iraq and I've valued that steadfast institution and activist community ever since; I co-founded a youth activist zine called *Co•Motion* in the second semester of my freshman year in high school.

Once someone asked me to describe what type of activist I am. I don't really know yet—I'm only seventeen—but there are a few things I'm sure of: I am the type of activist who believes unconditionally in the interconnection of struggles and the power of solidarity. I am the type of activist who shamelessly promotes how fun and powerful activism is so that other kids will consider raising their fists and joining the fight. I am the type of activist who looks to the past and the legacy of social justice struggles in this country and globally for inspiration and strategies to instruct our work today. I am the type of activist who considers how I can be effective—discovering

the power of journalism and grassroots media in building the movement. I am the type of activist who has had an immense amount of privilege as a white, middle-class kid in Boulder, Colorado. This has enabled me to *be* an activist, and to desire greatly to own my privilege and work toward dismantling a system in which privilege and power are unequally distributed.

So, for some, activism is a privilege. Activism can be a desperate measure and a last resort. Activism is a way of thinking about the world that is larger than the American Dream, larger than patriotism, larger than one life or one lifetime. Activism is also the only choice for many brave women and men around the world for whom silence and acquiescence mean the perpetuation of oppression and powerlessness.

FLASHBACK: AN ACTIVIST COMING OF AGE

No cars on the streets. Just helicopters in the sky and police squads on the ground. And puppets. Lots of puppets. Human barricades surrounded the World Bank and International Monetary Fund (IMF) buildings at a police-enforced radius. The atmosphere was festive, but also apprehensive. The streets and the Secret Service were both more formidable in Washington, DC than in Seattle, the site of a massive activist victory in shutting down the meetings of the World Trade Organization in 1999. But we were to be tens of thousands strong that day, and as I emerged from the Metro and walked along the wide avenue I felt jubilant and refreshed.

Three friends and I had spent the previous evening in jail, along with about six hundred others, arrested in a dragnet effort to intimidate the demonstrators and subvert the next day's activities. The DC police put an entire march opposing the Prison Industrial Complex on school buses and in paddy wagons. (Can you say "unconstitutional arrests?") Whether unconstitutional or not, an activist's first arrest is always an important rite of passage, so I was trying to look at the whole situation sort of philosophically. We spent several hours in custody —finger-printed, shoe laces removed, the whole deal. About twenty minors were arrested during the sweep of our march. The girls sat together in a cell at a juvenile detention center, complaining to each other that we might not even get out in time for the big demonstrations the next day.

I was also thinking about how amazingly strong women often are when they undertake jail solidarity actions (jail solidarity is a tactic in which everyone arrested refuses to identify themselves in order to ensure equal treatment for all). A new generation of feminist activists is stepping up to spend a night, or a month, in jail for protesting unjust institutions like the School of the Americas. Based at an army base in Georgia and funded by U.S. tax dollars, the SOA trains Latin American soldiers in counterinsurgency techniques and counts among its graduates hundreds of infamous human rights violators such as Panama dictator Manuel Noriega. Young people are getting arrested for protesting the death penalty and the incarceration of Mumia Abu Jamal, an African-American journalist on death row in Pennsylvania for allegedly killing a Philadelphia police officer nineteen years ago. Many contend that his original trial was riddled with prosecutorial misconduct and that he should receive a new trial. I thought about how more kids are fighting against a severe lack of access to abortion services for young women. And as I sat on a metal bench in that jail cell, I considered the experience of youth of color in Washington, DC as they deal with racist, unconstitutional police practices every day.

The kids arrested that day were lucky. We got out with all charges dropped by midnight. Many of the adults remained on school buses all night, without food or water, plastic handcuffs biting into their wrists. Processing all the arrestees took so long that some weren't released until midday, and all the adults had to pay $50 to plead no contest against manufactured charges.

Of course, the experiences of most people affected by the World Bank and IMF are incomparably worse than an inconvenient arrest on a Saturday night. Both institutions, founded in 1944, have played a lead role in dictating social and economic policy in poor countries for the past twenty years.

They have aimed to keep the world safe for corporate domination. The IMF lends money to governments in Africa, Asia, and Latin America to pay off foreign banks and creditors, while the World Bank focuses on development projects—mostly involving oil exploration and huge dams. The recipients end up with the short end of the deal, however, under Structural Adjustment Programs that prioritize servicing debt over education and social services. Countries pressed by the agendas of the IMF and World Bank have shifted to export-led economies, a system that deprives populations of the means to meet their own basic needs and also despoils local environments.

Multinational corporations end up on top, as they gain greater access to cheap labor and cheaper natural resources. And all of this is deeply connected to women's rights. Women make up the majority of the workers in the sweatshops that manufacture products for Nike and the GAP, women often receive less education than their male counterparts and so have fewer chances to advance, and women are *not* the powerbrokers of the global economy. So it is women around the world who are disproportionately affected by the policies of the IMF, World Bank, and other international economic institutions.

The sun was bright the morning after our brief experience with the Washington, DC criminal justice system. We were just happy to be out in time to take part in a historic day: April 16, 2000. A strong sentiment of solidarity pervaded the blockades, rallies, and marches. All of us in the streets represented the movement insisting that undemocratic institutions would not meet, ever again, without angry, righteous people demanding justice from below. People from India, China, Nigeria, Ecuador, Bolivia, Mexico, students from the United States, the now-famed alliance of Teamsters and Turtles (the coalition between labor and environmentalists that grew out of the protests in Seattle the year before) —everyone gathered to advance a different vision from the one that the IMF and World Bank offered that day. Rather than dams, debt, and corporate-funded destruction, we offered a globalization from the grassroots, a globalization that values humanity and the earth, and refuses the false value of profits for the few and trickle-down economics.

ORGANIZING FOR SOCIAL CHANGE: LESSONS FROM THE FIELD

Activism is not all mass marches and getting arrested. Community organizing is key in building a sustainable movement for democracy and equality. Learning organizing strategies was a big part of the trip I participated in through the Third Wave Foundation. As the fifteen young women of ROAMS traveled through the world of activism in the Northwest during the hot weeks of July and August, it was in grassroots, often youth or community of color-focused, groups that we saw innovation and savvy. Sisters in Action for Power was the first organization our group met with when we arrived in Portland, and they remained one of the most impressive of the entire two and a half week trip. Sisters in Action provided an impressive model of how popular education and community organizing can go hand in hand. And we were lucky that Sisters in Action member Shurnice Davis participated in ROAMS, adding her insight and experience to our discussions of activism throughout the trip through Oregon, Washington, Idaho, and Montana.

Last summer was an exciting time for Sisters. After working tirelessly for three years on a transportation equity campaign, the city's public transportation department, Tri-Met, agreed to provide youth with $16 monthly passes, reduced from $32. The young women, who have been demanding free bus passes for people under 18, say they will not stop with this victory, but that this is a step in the right direction. The root of the problem is the fact that there aren't many yellow school buses traversing the streets of Portland. In fact, Portland, along with Eugene, is exempted from providing school bus service because of its extensive public transportation system.

When Sisters in Action began to look at this issue, they found, through a canvas of 2,000 students and their families, that 11% of public school students sometimes missed school because they didn't have money for the bus. Families have to make choices between lunch money or bus money, and these young women wouldn't stand for this violation of low-income students' right to an education. Besides, they argue, while Portland *could* remedy this problem through a little reallocation of resources, Tri-Met instead spends money on programs that primarily service downtown shoppers, suburban commuters, and business people. Why, they ask, doesn't more money go to servicing the communities most dependent on public transportation?

SMALL VICTORIES AND KEEPING UP THE FIGHT

On the final night of our revolutionary road trip, we were hanging out downstairs at the Seattle hostel when Shurnice got a call. It was one of the organizers with Sisters in Action, telling her that they'd won the campaign. The Transportation Board had voted in their favor that night, and Shurnice was eager to get home so they could celebrate. We all hugged and congratulated her—it was a wonderful, inspiring end to an experience that taught me a great deal about the power and pitfalls of activism.

Surrounded by those other young women, I was convinced that the future of our planet is not quite as precarious as it might seem sometimes. More and more, the youth movement is characterized by a broad and inclusive analysis. Even if young people are lacking in historical and institutional memory, even if we are limited by the prevailing picture of youth as criminals promoted in the mainstream media, we are forging ahead in understanding connections between oppressions and building alliances among different struggles. Corporate exploitation is directly related to the disenfranchisement of women around the world. Wealth inequality feeds the undemocratic political establishment. Oil fuels war. And all of this is increasingly clear to a new youth movement that is coming of age in the years of Clinton, Bush, and "the War on Terror."

So in the end, I have to reiterate that I am an activist because traveling through the Northwest was a lot of fun. The people on that trip felt like exactly the right group with whom to spend many hours in a van: diverse, feminist, politically schooled young women who are out to raise hell. And in the larger scheme of things, the same good times and strong commitment to social justice analysis can co-exist. We simply must continue to question our own privilege, struggle for our own communities, and reach out across movements.   [2002]

🦎 145

Voices

WOMEN OF ACE (AIDS COUNSELING AND EDUCATION), BEDFORD HILLS CORRECTIONAL FACILITY

The authors of this essay are Kathy Boudin, Judy Clark, "D," Katrina Haslip, Maria D. L. Hernandez, Suzanne Kessler, Sonia Perez, Deborah Plunkett, Aida Rivera, Doris Romeo, Carmen Royster, Cathy Salce, Renee Scott, Jenny Serrano, and Pearl Ward.

INTRODUCTION

We are writing about ACE because we feel that it has made a tremendous difference in this prison and could make a difference in other prisons. ACE stands for AIDS Counseling and Education. It is a collective effort by women in Bedford Hills Correctional Facility. This article will reflect that collectivity by being a patchwork quilt of many women's voices.

ACE was started by inmates in 1988 because of the crisis that AIDS was creating in our community. According to a blind study done in the Fall-Winter of 1987–88, almost 20 percent of the women entering the New York state prison system were HIV infected.[1] It is likely to be higher today. In addition, women here have family members who are sick and friends who are dying. People have intense fears of transmission through casual contact because we live so closely together. Women are worried about their children and about having safe sex. All this need and energy led to the creation of ACE.

BEFORE ACE

Prior to the formation of ACE, Bedford was an environment of fear, stigma, lack of information, and evasion. AIDS was a word that was whispered. People had no forum in which to talk about their fears. The doctors and nurses showed their biases. They preferred to just give advice, and many wouldn't touch people because of their own fears. There were several deaths. This inflamed people's fear more. People didn't want to look at their own vulnerability—their IV drug use and unsafe sex.

> I felt very negative about people who I knew were sick. To save face, I spoke to them from afar. I felt that they all should be put into a building by themselves because I heard that people who were healthy could make them sick and so they should get specific care. I figured that I have more time (on my sentence); why should I be isolated? They should be. I felt very negative and it came a lot from fear.[2]

Women at Bedford who are sick are housed in a hospital unit called In Patient Care (IPC). ACE members remember what IPC was like before ACE:

> The IPC area—the infirmary—was horrible before, a place where nobody wanted to be. It was a place to go to die. Before ACE people started going there, it looked like a dungeon. It was unsanitary. Just the look of it made people feel like they were going to die. That was the end.

There was no support system for women who wanted to take the HIV-antibody test:

> I had a friend who tested positive. The doctor told her, you are HIV positive, but that doesn't mean you have AIDS. You shouldn't have sex, or have a baby, and you should avoid stress. Period. No information was given to her. No counseling and support. She freaked out.

THE BEGINNING OF ACE: BREAKING THE SILENCE

Some of us sensed that people needed to talk, but no one would break the silence. Finally, five women got together, and made a proposal to the superintendent:

We said that we ourselves had to help ourselves. We believed that as peers we would be the most effective in education, counseling, and building a community of support. We stated four main goals: to save lives through preventing the spread of HIV; to create more humane conditions for those who are HIV positive; to give support and education to women with fears, questions, and needs related to AIDS; to act as a bridge to community groups to help women as they reenter the community.

The superintendent accepted the proposal. Each of the five women sought out other women in the population who they believed were sensitive and would be interested in breaking the silence. When they reached 35, they stopped and a meeting was called.

BREAKING THE SILENCE CHANGED US: WE BEGAN TO BUILD A COMMUNITY

At that first meeting a sigh of relief was felt and it rippled out. There was a need from so many directions. People went around the table and said why they were there. About the fourth or fifth woman said, "I'm here because I have AIDS." There was an intense silence. It was the first time anyone had said that aloud in a group. By the end of the meeting, several more women had said that they were HIV positive. Breaking the silence, the faith that it took, and the trust it built was really how ACE started.

BREAKING THE SILENCE MEANT SOMETHING SPECIAL TO PWAS

I often ask myself how it is that I came to be open about my status. For me, AIDS had been one of my best kept secrets. It took me approximately 15 months to discuss this issue openly. As if not saying it aloud would make it go away. I watched other people with AIDS (PWAs), who were much more open than I was at the time, reveal to audiences their status/their vulnerability, while sharing from a distance, from silence, every word that was being uttered by them. I wanted to be a part of what they were building, what they were doing, their statement, "I am a PWA," because I was. It was a relief when I said it. I could stop going on with the lie. I could be me. People were supportive and they didn't shun me. And now I can go anywhere and be myself.

SUPPORTING PWAS

PWAs and HIV-positive women are at the heart of our work. ACE believes that everyone facing HIV-related illness is confronting issues of life and death and struggling to survive and thrive.

We had to have some place for PWAs to share their experiences with each other. There have been numerous support groups which allowed us to express things that hadn't been verbalized but that had been on our minds. It was interesting to see that we had similar issues: how to tell significant others, our own vulnerability about being open, living with AIDS. My first group was a mixture of people. Some were recently diagnosed and others had been diagnosed for two years. It was informative and it was emotional. Sometimes we would just come to a meeting and cry. Or we might come there and not even talk about the issue of AIDS and just have a humor session because we are just tired of AIDS.

One of the first things that ACE ever did was to work in IPC.

ACE started going to IPC. We painted, cleaned up, made it look so good that now the women want to stay there. We take care of the girls who are sick, making them feel comfortable and alive. Now, women there know they have a friend. They feel free, they talk, and look forward to visits. They know they're not there to die, not like before.

BEING A BUDDY

I have been involved in ACE for about three years. About a year ago I started visiting the women in IPC. I was really afraid at first. Not afraid of getting sick, but of becoming emotionally involved and then have the women die. At first, I tried to keep my feelings and friendship at a minimum. The more I went, the more I lost this fear. There is one woman I have gotten closer to than the rest. She has been in IPC since I first started going there. We are buddies. For me to be her buddy means unconditionally loving her and accepting her decisions. I go almost every night to IPC. Some nights we just sit there and say nothing. But there is comfort in my presence. She had a stroke before I met her. So there is a lot she cannot do for herself. There are times when I bathe and dress her. Iron her clothes.

I do not think of any of these things as chores. Soon she will be going home. I am overjoyed, but I'm also saddened knowing that I will not see her again. I will miss her hugs, her complaining, and her love. But I would do it all over again and I probably will with someone else.

MEDICAL ADVOCACY

It is obviously a matter of life or death for anyone who is HIV infected to get good medical care and have a good relationship with her health providers. Medical facilities in prisons start out understaffed and ill equipped, and the AIDS crisis escalated these problems enormously. In the 1970s women prisoners here instituted a class action suit, *Todaro v. Ward,* to demand better medical care. Because of that case, the medical facilities and care at Bedford are monitored for the court by an outside expert. That expert issued a report criticizing all aspects of the medical department for being inadequately prepared to meet women's AIDS-related medical needs, and the prison faced a court hearing and possible contempt charges. Under that pressure the state agreed to numerous changes that brought new medical staff and resources, including a full-time medical director, a part-time infectious disease specialist, and more nurses. ACE was able to institute a medical advocacy plan that allowed ACE members to accompany women to their doctor's consultation visit to ensure that nothing was missed. Afterward, there can be a private discussion between the patient and the advocate to clarify matters for the woman, to explore possibilities of treatment, or just to allow the person to express whatever emotions she experienced when she received the news from the doctor.

PEER EDUCATION

Our approach is *peer* education, which we believe is best suited for the task of enabling a community to mobilize itself to deal with AIDS. The people doing the training clearly have a personal stake in the community. The education is for all, in the interests of all. This is communicated from the beginning by the women doing the teaching.

Our peer education takes a problem-posing approach. We present issues as problems facing all

of us, problems to be examined by drawing on the knowledge and experience of the women being trained. What are the issues between a man and a woman, for example, that make it hard for a woman to demand that her man use a condom? Will distributing free needles or advocating bleach kits stop the spread of AIDS among IV drug users?

Our educational work is holistic. Education is not solely a presentation of facts, although that is an important part of the trainers' responsibilities. But what impact do feelings and attitudes have on how people deal with facts? Why would a person who knows that you cannot get AIDS by eating from a PWA's plate still act occasionally as if you could? Why would a person who knows that sex without a condom could be inviting death, not use a condom? For education to be a deep process, it involves understanding the whole person; for education to take root within a community, it means thinking about things on a community, social level.

> Coming to prison, living under these conditions, was scary, and AIDS made it even scarier. I was part of a society that made judgments and had preconceived ideas about the women in prison.

EDUCATING OURSELVES

Workshops

To become members of ACE, women must be educated through a series of eight workshops. We look at how stigma and blame have been associated with diseases throughout history, and how the sexism of this society impacts on women in the AIDS epidemic. We teach about the nature of the virus, strategies for treatment, and holistic approaches. After the eight weeks, we ask who would like to become involved, and then there is a screening process. The Superintendent has final approval. The workshops are followed by more intensive training of women who become members.

Orientation

When women enter the New York state prison system, they must come first to Bedford Hills, where they either stay or move on after several weeks to one of several other women's prisons. ACE members talk with the women when they first arrive.

> We do orientations of 10 to 35 women. We explain to them how you can and cannot get AIDS, about testing and about ACE. Sometimes the crowd is very boisterous and rude. I say "AIDS" and they don't want to hear about it. But those are the ones I try to reach. After orientation is over, the main ones that didn't want to hear about AIDS are the ones who want to talk more and I feel good about that. A lot of times, their loudness is a defense because they are afraid of their own vulnerability. They know that they are at risk for HIV infection because of previous behaviors. After I finish doing orientation, I have a sense of warmth, because I know I made a difference in some of their lives.

Seminars

One of the main ways we interact with our sisters is through seminars. We talk about AIDS issues with groups of women on living units, in classrooms, and in some of the other prison programs such as family violence, drug treatment, and Children's Center.

> The four back buildings are dormitories, each holding 100 women with double bunked beds. We from ACE gather right after count, with our easel and newsprint and magic markers and our three-by-five cards with the information on whatever presentation we're making. We move in twos and threes through the connecting tunnels to the building. When we arrive some of the women are sitting in the rec room, but many others are in their cubicles/cells. They ask why we're here. We look like a traveling troupe— and we've felt like it, not knowing what to expect. Some women are excited that we're going to talk about AIDS. Others say, "forget it," or "fuck you, I've heard enough about it, it's depressing."

But we begin, and people slowly gather.

> We ask the women to help us role-play a situation such as a woman going home from prison, trying to convince her man, who has been taking care of her while she's inside, to use a condom. Then the role-play is analyzed. What problems are encountered and how do we deal with those problems? We try to come up with suggestions that we can see ourselves using in that situation. We talk about the risk of violence.

One of the most immediate problems people have is whether or not to take the HIV-antibody test. We do not push testing. We explain what the test is and have a group discussion of things the women need to consider. A woman may be inclined to get tested, but she needs to know that she is likely to be transferred upstate before the results come back from the lab. The choice is up to her. Toward the end of the seminar, PWAs talk about their experiences living with AIDS.

> When they speak, they bring together everything that we have said. Not only that, but they let people know that living with AIDS is not instant death. It makes people realize why the struggles, working together, and being as one are so important. When I hear the women who are PWAs speak, it makes me realize that I could have been in their shoes, or I could still be, if they hadn't been willing to talk about their risk behaviors and what has happened to them. It gives me the courage to realize that it's not all about me. It's actually about us.

We end each seminar with all the women standing with our arms around each other or holding hands—without any fear of casual contact—singing our theme song, "Sister."[3] We sing, having come to a new place where we are for each other, unified. We all feel some sense of relief and some sense of hope. Talking about AIDS openly has changed how we live. We leave the seminar with the knowledge that we can talk about AIDS and that we're going to be okay. . . .

Counseling

When we conduct the seminars and orientation sessions, women come up to us afterward with personal questions and problems. It could be they are HIV positive, or they are thinking of taking the test, or they have a family member who is sick, or they are thinking about getting involved with someone in a relationship. Sometimes they raise one issue, but underlying it are a lot of other issues they're not yet ready to talk about. Because women know we're in ACE, we're approached in our housing units, at school, on the job, in the mess hall, as we walk from one place to another. Women stop us, needing to talk. We're a haven for women because they know ACE has a principle of confidentiality. Women can trust us not to abuse the information they are sharing with us.

> Peer counseling. I'm just impressed that we can do it. I didn't know what kind of potential we'd have as peers. We talk the language that each of us understands. Even if it's silent, even if it's with our eyes, it's something that each of us seems to understand. I know I wouldn't want someone from the Department of Health who hasn't even taken a Valium to try to educate me about IV drug use. How could they give me helpful hints? I would feel that they are so out of tune with reality that I wouldn't be able to hear them.

A CRISIS AND OPPORTUNITY FOR OUR COMMUNITY

We are a small community and we are so isolated you can feel it—the suffering, the losses, the fears, the anxiety. Out in the street you don't have a community of women affected and living together facing a problem in this same way. We can draw on the particular strengths that women bring: nurturance, caring, and personal openness. So many women prisoners have worked in nursing and old age homes. Yet when they did, they were never given respect. Here these same activities are valued, and the women are told "thank you," and that creates initiative and feelings of self-worth. And ACE helps us to be more self-conscious about a culture of caring that as women we tend to create in our daily lives.

> For the first time in prison I was part of a group that cared about other prisoners in prison. What did that feel like? It felt like I wasn't alone in caring about people, because in this type of setting I was beginning to wonder about people caring.

OUR IMPACT ON WOMEN

We know that we have played a role in communicating information about what is safe and what is not safe in sexual behavior—both between a man and woman and between two women—and we have certainly been able to create open and relaxed discus-

sions about all this. But we know that actually changing behaviors is another leap ahead of us. We are learning that it's not a one-shot deal, that information doesn't equal behavior change, and it's not just an individual thing. Social norms have to change, and this takes time. And when you talk about women having to initiate change you're up against the fact that women don't have that kind of empowerment in this society. Women who have been influenced by ACE have experienced a change in attitude, but it is unclear whether this will translate into behavior change once they leave the prison.

> When I first started taking the workshops I was 100 percent against using condoms. And yet I like anal sex. But now my views are different. We're the bosses of our own bodies. You know, a lot of people say it's a man's world. Well, I can't completely agree.

OUR DIVERSITY IS A STRENGTH

We are a diverse community of women: Black, Latin, and white, and also from countries throughout the world. In ACE there was at first a tendency to deny the differences, maybe out of fear of disunity. Now there is a more explicit consciousness growing that we can affirm our diversity and our commonality because both are important. In the last workshop on women, we broke for a while into three groups —Black, Latina, and white women—to explore the ways AIDS impacted on our particular culture and communities. We are doing more of those kinds of discussions and developing materials that address concerns of specific communities. The Hispanic Sector of ACE is particularly active, conducting seminars in Spanish and holding open meetings for the population to foster Hispanic awareness of AIDS issues.

> The workshops didn't deal enough with different ethnic areas, and being Puerto Rican and half-Indian, some things seemed ridiculous in terms of the Hispanic family. Some of the ways people were talking about sex wouldn't work in a traditional Hispanic family. For example, you can't just tell your husband that he has to wear a condom. Or say to him, "You have to take responsibility." These ap-

"Sister"

CRIS WILLIAMSON

Born of the earth
Child of God
Just one among the family
And you can count on me
To share the load
And I will always help you
Hold burdens
And I will be the one
To help you ease your pain
Lean on me, I am your sister
Believe on me, I am your friend
I will fold you in my arms
Like a white wing dove
Shine in your soul
Your spirit is crying
Born of the earth
Child of God
Just one among the family
And you can count on me
To share the load
And I will always help you
Hold burdens
And I will be the one
To help you ease your pain
Lean on me, I am your sister
Believe on me, I am your friend
Lean on me, I am your sister
Believe on me, I am your friend

proaches could lead to marital rape or abuse. The empowerment of Hispanic women means making sure that their children are brought up.

WORKING IN A PRISON

We have a unique situation at Bedford Hills. We have a prison administration that is supportive of inmates developing a peer-based program to deal with AIDS. However, because we are in a prison there are a lot of constraints and frustrations. Before we had staff persons to supervise us, we could not work out of an office space. That meant that we couldn't see women who wanted to talk on an individual level unless we ran into them in the yard or rec room.

You could be helping someone in IPC take her daily shower; it's taking longer than usual because she is in a lot of pain or she needs to talk, but that's not taken into consideration when the officer tells you that you have to leave immediately because it's "count-time." You could be in the rec room, a large room with a bunch of card tables, loud music, and an officer overseeing groups of women sitting on broken-down chairs. You're talking to a woman in crisis who needs comforting. You reach out to give her a hug and the C.O. may come over to admonish you, "No physical contact, ladies." Or maybe a woman has just tested positive. She's taken her first tentative steps to reach out by talking to someone from ACE and joining a support group. Days after her first meeting, she is transferred to another prison.

It's been difficult to be able to call ourselves counselors and have our work formally acknowledged by the administration. Counseling is usually done by professionals in here because it carries such liability and responsibility. We're struggling for the legitimacy of peer counseling. The reality is that we've been doing it in our daily lives here through informal dialogue. We now have civilian staff to supervise us, and Columbia University will be conducting a certification training program to justify the title "peer counselor."

After working over two years on our own, we are now being funded by a grant from the New York State AIDS Institute, coordinated by Columbia University School of Public Health and by Women and AIDS Resource Network (WARN). The money has allowed hiring staff to work with ACE. ACE began as a totally volunteer inmate organization with no office or materials, operating on a shoestring and scrambling for every meeting. Now we have an office in a prime location of the prison, computers, and a civilian staff responsible for making certain that there is something to show for their salaries. Inmates who used to work whenever they could find the time are now paid 73 cents a day as staff officially assigned to the ACE Center. The crises are no longer centered around the problems of being inside a prison, but more on how to sustain momentum and a real grassroots initiative in the context of a prison. This is a problem faced by many other community organizations when they move past the initial momentum and become more established institutions.

BUILDING A CULTURE OF SURVIVAL

When, in the spring of 1987, we said, "Let's make quilt squares for our sisters who have died," there were more than 15 names. Over the next year we made more and more quilt squares. The deaths took a toll not just on those who knew the women but on all of us. Too many women were dying among us. And, for those who were HIV positive or worried that they might be, each death heightened their own vulnerabilities and fears. We have had to develop ways to let people who are sick know that if they die, their lives will be remembered, they will be honored and celebrated, and they will stay in our hearts.

> I remember our first memorial. Several hundred women contributed money—25 cents, 50 cents, a dollar—for flowers. Both Spanish and Black women sang and in the beginning everyone held hands and sang "That's What Friends Are For," and in the end we sang "Sister." People spoke about what Ro meant to them. Ro had died and we couldn't change that. But we didn't just feel terrible. We felt love and caring and that together we could survive the sadness and loss.
>
> In the streets, funerals were so plastic, but here, people knew that it could be them. It's not just to pay respect. When we sang "Sister," there was a charge between us. Our hands were extended to each other. There was a need for ACE and we could feel it in the air.

It was out of that same need that ACE was formed. It will be out of that same need that ACE will continue to strive to build community and an environment of trust and support. We are all we have—ourselves. If we do not latch on to this hope that has strengthened us and this drive that has broken our silence, we too will suffer and we will remain stigmatized and isolated. Feel our drive in our determination to make changes, and think "community," and make a difference.   [1990]

NOTES

1. Perry F. Smith et al., *Infection Among Women Entering the New York State Correctional System* (1990), unpublished manuscript.
2. All quotations are from the authors' conversations with prisoners at Bedford Hills.
3. By Cris Williamson, from the album *The Changer and the Changed*, Olivia Records, 1975.

146

Black Feminism at Twenty-One: Reflections on the Evolution of a National Community

BARBARA RAMSBY

When Deborah King, Elsa Barkley Brown, and I launched the African-American Women in Defense of Ourselves (AAWIDOO) campaign to protest Clarence Thomas's nomination to the Supreme Court and to highlight the issue of sexual harassment and the media's silencing of black women, we did not talk about our long-term goals. As it turned out, our ideas about where the mobilization was headed and at what pace were quite different, and, after several local branches in Chicago, New York, and Philadelphia failed to sustain themselves without the support of a national body or solidly planted roots, the entire AAWIDOO initiative slowly and quietly faded out of existence. Nevertheless, a collective silence had been broken. Not since the National Black Feminist Organization and its more well-known offshoot, the Combahee River Collective, made their marks in the mid-1970s had black women in the United States organized around a feminist/womanist agenda and made a national public intervention. We raised more than $50,000 in a short time to place ads in the *New York Times* and African-American newspapers around the country, and we compiled a mailing list of over two thousand names, which itself became

a vital resource for subsequent local and national mobilizations. The campaign represented a growing consensus among an often invisible network of activists and intellectuals who at least partly shared a political vision, even if we were not all card-carrying members of any one club.[1]

In 1993, black feminist writer Jill Nelson, activist Gail Garfield, and others organized a series of rallies to protest plans by the predominantly male political establishment of Harlem to give Mike Tyson, a convicted rapist, a hero's welcome after his release from prison. Black feminist activists in Harlem took the principled but unpopular position that rape was both a feminist issue and a black community issue and that, racism within the criminal justice system notwithstanding, rapists could not be celebrated as heroes in our community. The Harlem activists requested the AAWIDOO mailing list to publicize and garner support for their campaign, and AAWIDOO's strategy of buying newspaper ads served as an inspiration and model for St. Louis activists who organized a similar campaign against the exaltation of Tyson in their community.[2]

The growing network of black feminists across the country again became visible in 1995 when the aspiring patriarch of black politics, Nation of Islam minister Louis Farrakhan, convened a gathering of men in the nation's capital to reclaim their rightful places as heads of their families and leaders of the entire black community. Feminist activist and law professor Kimberle Crenshaw organized a national meeting in New York in the spring of 1995 to explore how black feminists should respond to the MMM. We formed an ad hoc committee, issued a public

---

[1] During the MMM mobilization, the *New York Times Magazine* featured a story on black feminism by a novice writer who distorted and obscured more about black feminism than she revealed (Zooks 1995). This type of skewed media coverage reinforces invisibility as much as outright silence does. For more carefully researched studies of black feminism and black women's political activism, see Smith 1983; Giddings 1984; Guy-Sheftall 1995; Collins 1998.

[2] White 1999 provides an excellent detailed analysis of the St. Louis campaign.

statement, and participated in several community forums. Our response to the MMM and the increasing male-centeredness of black politics and community priorities represented a deepening national consensus among black feminists. The black community as a whole was sharply divided over the march, with the majority in support. The issue, for many, was not clear cut: for some, opposing Clarence Thomas's sexism had been easy because there were so many other reasons (having to do with his conservative antiblack politics) to oppose him, but to challenge a charismatic religious icon like Farrakhan or a superstar athlete like Tyson was a different matter altogether. Nevertheless, black feminists once again mobilized on fairly short notice to do precisely that.

The black feminist statement issued on the eve of the MMM, like AAWIDOO's four years earlier, was not a narrow, single-issue document. It outlined both the sexism and unprecedented gender exclusivity of the MMM and also the conservative class message of the march's principal spokesman. A core of activists held several follow-up meetings and a three-day-long retreat to try to map out a way forward after the march. Again, old phone chains from previous mobilizations were activated and relationships reestablished. There was a clear sense of a tangible national constituency. While most of those who participated were college educated and, to a large extent, middle class, we were engaged in many different areas of political work: international human rights; antiviolence; opposition to the prison industrial complex; welfare rights and antipoverty work; civil rights and sexual harassment litigation; alternative media; lesbian, bisexual, gay, and transsexual work; and student organizing. Some of the members of this group, which called itself African-American Agenda 2000, later became key organizers of either the African American Policy Forum or the Feminist Caucus of the Black Radical Congress (two groups that reconnected to work on the Tabitha Walrond case in the summer of 1999).[3] Even though questions of strategy and tactics have divided us at times, our politics keep bringing us back together.

So, what are the politics that unite a disparate cross section of organizers under the rubric of black feminism? Let me first address the method and style of organizing and then, briefly, the ideological content. Over the past decade, the style of black feminist work has represented a democratic impulse within the larger progressive movement, with decentralized mobilization efforts, informal leadership, and flexible structures. This has not always been the most efficient way to organize, but the political benefits have outweighed the inconvenience. Moreover, we have benefited from such organizational structures, which have consisted of less hierarchical steering committees and coordinating groups rather than chairpersons, presidents, and officers in the more common linear fashion. Over the years, black women have evolved organization styles consistent with the specific cultural, economic, and historical realities that have defined our lives. I cannot, within the confines of this article, outline all of the nuanced variations, but one predominant strain is a decentralized, group-centered, grassroots democratic model, best exemplified by the lifelong work of Ella Jo Baker and Septima Poinsette Clark.[4] Given this history, it is not surprising that no single charismatic figure has emerged to personify and symbolize the movement. For example, there is no dark-skinned version of Gloria Steinem or Betty Freidan in black feminist circles; there are no female counterparts to Louis Farrakhan or Jesse Jackson, Sr. in terms of political visibility. Angela Davis, Barbara Smith, and bell hooks are perhaps the most renowned living black feminist personae, but, for different reasons, each has admirably resisted and declined icon status.

But what are the ideological tenets around which

---

[3] Walrond was a young black woman on welfare who, in May 1999, was convicted of negligent homicide for her baby's death. She had attempted unsuccessfully to breast-feed the baby, was not given adequate medical support, and was denied medical treatment for the child a short time before he died because his Medicaid card had not yet arrived in the mail. A coalition of groups supported Walrond's case, citing it as an example of sexism, racism, economic injustice, and the growing emphasis on prisons over social services.

[4] On the democratic character of many of black women's organizing efforts, see Brodkin 1988; Payne 1995; Robnett 1997.

black feminists have organized? Perhaps strongest is the notion that race, class, gender, and sexuality are codependent variables that cannot readily be separated and ranked in scholarship, in political practice, or in lived experience. The main tension within diverse political coalitions has been the tendency to rank different systems of oppression and thus prioritize the liberation agendas of certain groups within the coalition. Because any political agenda that addresses the realities of most African-American women's lives must deal with the four major systems of oppression and exploitation—race, class, gender, and sexuality—black feminist politics radically breaks down the notion of mutually exclusive, competing identities and interests and instead understands identities and political process as organic, fluid, interdependent, dynamic, and historical. The openness of our political processes and the permeability of our multiple identities help create the potential for collaborations that transcend social boundaries and reject elitist criteria for leadership. Instead of policing boundaries, racial or otherwise, black feminists have more often than not penetrated these barriers, expanding the meaning of "we" and "community" in the process.

Contrary to those who argue that black struggles, women's struggles, queer struggles narrow our range of vision and divide us into factions, the radical organizers and theorists within these so-called identity-based movements actually offer the terms for a higher level of unity, integration, and interaction. Radicals within the feminist, lesbigay-trans, and people of color communities generally see fighting against economic exploitation as intimately related to, and inseparable from, the fight against racism, sexism, and heterosexism and as a critical component of their political agenda. Thus, these forces are potentially the connective tissue between various social change movements and constituencies, rather than the wedge that divides them. Nothing embodies this spirit better than the founding statement of the Combahee River Collective, conceived nearly a quarter-century ago by black lesbian feminist activists in Boston, many of whom continue to play central roles in progressive struggles today. It reads: "The most general statement of our politics at the present time would be that we are actively committed to struggling against racial, sexual, heterosexual, and class oppression and see as our particular task the development of integrated analysis and practice based upon the fact that the major systems of oppression are interlocking. The synthesis of these oppressions creates the conditions of our lives" (Combahee River Collective [1977] 1995, 232).

It is no coincidence, then, that black feminist organizers around the country have deeply immersed themselves in struggles that incorporate but are not isolated to gender issues.[5] In the decades since the formation of the short-lived Combahee River Collective, black feminist practice has evolved, not so much reinventing itself as building on the foundational vision, outlined in 1977, of an inclusive, multi-issue political agenda built on a fluid democratic practice. And while we often bemoan the absence of a tangible physical place of our own, black feminists are not invisible, nor have we been effectively silenced. A wealth of scholarship has helped to forge a heterogeneous body of work that explores and debates the applications and interpretations of black feminist political ideology. More important, because of our persistent efforts—the lessons learned, strategies explored, trust established, storms weathered—perhaps now we have the kind of history that can give us greater optimism for the future, optimism that might enable the forging of an independent black feminist organization with links and ties to multiple other oppositional and visionary movements of the twenty-first century. [2000]

REFERENCES

Brodkin, Karen. *Caring by the Hour: Women, Work, and Organizing at Duke Medical Center.* Urbana: University of Illinois Press, 1988.

Collins, Patricia Hill. *Fighting Words: Black Women and the Search for Justice.* Minneapolis: University of Minnesota Press, 1998.

---

[5] For example, Beth Richie's (1995) work on domestic violence has connections with larger antiviolence, antipoverty, and prisoners' rights movements, as does Angela Davis's work on the prison industrial complex. Atlanta-based black feminist Loretta Ross and Washington, D.C.-based organizer and law professor Lisa Crooms have worked on international and domestic human rights projects that incorporate many issues in additon to gender.

Combahee River Collective (Barbara Smith, Beverly Smith, and Demita Frazier). (1977) 1995. "A Black Feminist Statement." In Guy-Sheftall 1995, 232–40.

Giddings, Paula. *When and Where I Enter: The Impact of Black Women on Race and Sex in America.* New York: Morrow, 1989.

Guy-Sheftall, Beverly, ed. *Words of Fire: An Anthology of African-American Feminist Thought.* New York: New Press, 1995.

hooks, bell. *Feminist Theory from Margin to Center.* Boston: South End.

Payne, Charles M. *I've Got the Light of Freedom: The Organizing Tradition and the Mississippi Freedom Struggle.* Berkeley: University of California Press, 1995.

Richie, Beth. *Compelled to Crime: The Gender Entrapment of Battered Black Women.* New York: Routledge, 1995.

Robnett, Belinda. *How Long? How Long? African-American Women in the Struggle for Civil Rights.* New York: Oxford University Press, 1997.

Smith, Barbara. *The Truth That Never Hurts: Writings on Race, Gender, and Freedom.* New Brunswick, N.J.: Rutgers University Press, 1998.

Smith, Barbara, ed. *Home Girls: A Black Feminist Anthology.* New York: Kitchen Table/Women of Color, 1983.

White, Aaronette M. "Talking Feminist, Talking Black: Micromobilization Processes in a Collective Protest against Rape." *Gender & Society* 13(1):77–100, 1999.

Zooks, Krystal Brent. "A Manifesto of Sorts for a New Black Feminist Movement." *New York Times Magazine,* November 12, 1995.

147

"Each Day I Go Home with A New Wound in My Heart"

MIRIAM CHING YOON LOUIE

On June 6, 1998, workers, their supporters, and Korean Immigrant Workers Advocates (KIWA) organizers embarked on a massive march demanding justice for Korean and Latino restaurant workers in Los Angeles' Koreatown. Snaking through minimalls filled with surprised shoppers, the marchers' stomachs soon growled as the mouth-watering smells of *kalbi, bulgogi, kimchee, mae-un tang, dwenjang jikae,* and *pa-chun* wafted out the doors of their favorite restaurants. The march ended in front of the Shogun Sushi Restaurant where workers were paid just $2 an hour. Koreatown restaurant worker Han Hee Jin surged to the front of the rally and delivered a fiery speech. Just a week before, her boss fired her from a *naeng myon* [cold noodle] specialty restaurant when she complained about having to simultaneously wait tables, cook, and wash dishes. Han told the marchers,

> Even though we need each other, owners always treat workers with suspicion. And yet employers want to be treated as Master. Even in a small restaurant, we are always forced to call employers, "Yes, Boss," "Yes, Madam," while we are subjected to degrading comments such as "you are only a servant" or "you are made for carrying a tray all your life" or "you, waitress bitch." After seven years of being subjected to these and more degrading remarks, I stand here today to state that we will not tolerate them anymore.[1]

Han's impassioned appeal signaled a major new twist in a drama unfolding within the emerging Korean community. Despite blacklisting and censorship, women like Han have begun to break the silence and stand up for their rights. Like their Chinese and Mexican counterparts, many Korean immigrant women workers worked in global assembly line, service, and finance industry jobs before coming to the United States. As young women they served as the foot soldiers in South Korea's rapid march to industrialization and Four Dragon status.[2] They labored under the shadow of South Korea's militarized and globalized sex industry and within niches of the informal economy that sprang up from the ruins of their war-ravaged country. After immigrating, many Korean immigrant women found work in factories like those they had worked in at home; others started on the lowest rungs of the service industry, especially within the ethnic enclave economy that mushroomed with the jump in Korean immigration after 1965. Some brought their experiences with the independent workers movement in South Korea. . . .

ORGANIZING WOMEN, RELEASING HAN

Immigrant Korean women workers confronted gender and class oppression not only at their workplaces, but also within their families and the Korean community. In the course of organizing, the women began to develop a women's support network, and incorporate gender-specific education campaigns and services into their organizing work.

Despite Korean women's long work hours in the United States, they are still expected to perform almost all the domestic chores in their homes, while their husbands cope with either long hours or underemployment and a big drop in economic and social status, connections, and stability.[3] This creates a volatile environment in which alcoholism and domestic violence often erupt. A 2000 community needs assessment survey on the problem of domestic violence conducted by Shimtuh, the Korean Domestic Violence Program, found that 42 percent of the 347 respondents said that they knew of a Korean woman who had experienced physical violence from a husband or boyfriend, while 50 percent knew of a Korean woman who had experienced regular emotional abuse, and 33 percent reported that their fathers had hit their mothers at least once.[4]

The combined gender and class oppression women face became evident during a sharing session held in April 1999 among some Korean women workers (who wish to remain anonymous). The women began by drawing charts plotting the highs and lows of their lives. One woman described the collapse of her husband's business, into which she had poured all of her labor and for which she had borrowed money from her family. She told of how her husband then fled to the United States, leaving her to close down the business and pay off its debts by herself. Once she arrived in the United States to start life over again, she found herself having to fight an abusive boss.[5]

Another woman, "Mrs. H.," told of how she and her husband, poor and hungry while struggling to survive in Korea, had planned a family suicide. They would drown themselves by jumping into the river while holding their kids. But she couldn't bear to pass the baby over the fence. Then her husband bolted. She searched for him for days. Since his body never turned up in the river, she began to suspect that he was still alive. He later appeared, and they eventually migrated to the United States with their children. Laughing bitterly and joking to make light of her story, she described how she went through many hardships because of her husband's drinking and gambling and her family's extreme poverty. Later when another woman recounted being beaten black and blue by her husband, Mrs. H. shouted out, "That's why I never left him in spite of everything; he never beat me."[6]

These stories released a flood of pent-up anguish, resentment, and tears, mixed with exclamations of "*sei sang eh!* [what is this world coming to]" and other expressions of shock, sympathy, and support. Sometimes the women's faces glistened with tears; at other moments the room erupted in peals of laughter as they teased each other about the absurdity of it all.

The women workers' consciousness raising session combined popular education methodology and the cathartic release of *han*.[7] *Han* is the Korean term used to describe accumulated suffering, sadness, and hardship. According to psychiatrist Luke Kim, *han* is an "individual and collective emotive state of Koreans, involving feelings of anger, rage, grudge, resignation, hate and revenge. [It is a] form of victimization syndrome of Korean people, with feelings of injustice and indignation suppressed and endured."[8] The "down side" of *han*, is the sadness, oppression, injustice, colonialism, war, tragedy, and cruel twists of fate suffered by Korean people. But the sharing of *han* between the women workers expresses the "up side" of *han*, a socially and culturally shared understanding that acknowledges and articulates Korean women's pent-up suffering, and *therefore*, facilitates and allows for its release through a collective process of support, solidarity, and sisterhood.

JOINING THE MOVEMENT

Korean women workers joined the movement when they reached the point when they could no longer tolerate their bosses' abuses. Some women organized together with their co-workers, while others started out fighting because of an individual grievance. Because of the close-knit character of the Korean community and ethnic enclave, women's decisions to stand up for their rights had immediate consequences. Restaurant owners quickly blacklisted some of the first Korean women restaurant workers who dared speak out. In addition to the bosses' attacks, some women endured censorship from their ministers and the ethnic media, and pressure from worried co-workers and family members who feared they would never be able to work in Koreatown again.

Chu Mi Hee worked at Koreatown's largest restaurant, Siyeon, as a waitress for two years. In 1996, she was fired and blacklisted after participating in a struggle against the boss.

Him dul ot jiyo! [It was a strain, it was very hard] to work there. If things did not go his way, he [the boss] would use his fists. He would kick things, even people. The woman owner was about the same. She didn't use her fists, but she did the same thing with her words. They treated the workers very inhumanely. At first about 36 people worked there. . . . Then they started firing people they didn't like, and also to cut their labor costs. That's when our Mexican *chinku* [friends] started opening relations with KIWA. . . . Without me knowing, the owners found out and fired our Mexican friends.

We wanted to be treated with dignity and not have to work under physical and verbal abuse. Most of the Mexican workers and Korean waitresses united. With KIWA's help, we leafleted the customers. We made a wildcat strike that lasted one hour and demanded that the original promises be kept that the owners made when they opened. . . . I hoped that protesting, passing out leaflets, talking to people, all of these things would bring about good results. I feel that the things we were demanding were very basic. We were not asking for anything outrageous.[9]

After she was fired by Siyeon for fighting for a collective bargaining agreement, she took a new job at a coffee shop called Prince, which was owned by a cousin of one of the Siyeon owners. She was disoriented when Prince's manager and then her minister called her at home.

I was awakened by a phone call from the minister of the church where the manager and I went. The minister said, "I heard that you are suing [Siyeon] on behalf of the workers. How can you do such a childish thing?" The minister said he had gotten a phone call from the [Prince] manager and heard all

about what was going on and that it was hard for me to continue working at [Prince]. Then I knew that I was being blacklisted.

When the Siyeon owner found out that I worked at Prince, he went to the Prince owner and asked, "How can you hire a person like that?" The Prince owner said, "None of your business." But the Prince owner wanted to consult with the manager because she was the one who referred me to Prince. The manager told me, "I'm very disappointed in you. How could you [participate in the Siyeon dispute]? Koreatown is really small. It's going to be hard for you to find another job." I demanded [that she] let me talk to the owner directly. She [the manager] said, "Let's all quit." At that time I felt really disappointed in humanity. After that incident I couldn't go back to church and face the [manager]. I found another job after resting for a while. To find a new job, I had to show my work experience, but to show my experience I had to talk about Siyeon. So I was afraid to go to places to look for work.[10]

The Siyeon workers had successfully negotiated a collective bargaining agreement in February and March of 1996, establishing wage scales, meal times, and the conditions for discharge, but they had to keep fighting for compliance. KIWA helped file lawsuits against the Siyeon and Prince operatives for firing and blacklisting Chu. On February 15, 1997, however, Siyeon went out of business and the case was subsequently dropped.[11]

Paek Young Hee worked 12 hours a day, 6 days a week, but her boss at Ho Dong restaurant blacklisted her for demanding unpaid wages in 1996. As with Chu, the owners association contacted Paek's next boss to get her fired.[12] Luckily, her new boss told her what had happened.

One day when I was working at my new job, the owner called me into the office and asked why did I go against the restaurant where I was fired. I told him that it was only because I was not paid my rightful wage. The owner confessed that he had received a call from the Korean Restaurant Owners Association who told the owner to let me go because I was a troublemaker. But the owner ended up telling me that I was a great worker and that they needed me and were not going to fire me. I am still working at this restaurant now.[13]

Paek weathered a lot of criticism because she spoke up about the wages she was owed and how she was fired and blacklisted.

> I am very grateful because KIWA helps poor people who are powerless. I try to be active and help out all that I can. . . . But I feel a little ashamed. I feel like I have done something that I should not have done. All the people around me are telling me, "Why are you stabbing somebody from your own nationality? If they didn't pay you that well, you should have just accepted it, and left it at that. Why did you have to take these actions?" I tell them, "Why shouldn't I be paid for the work that I did?" But at the same time they give me dirty looks like I did something wrong.
>
> Both my children and my husband were not at all supportive of my actions . . . especially after they saw the news on the TV. The children said that the fact that I came out on TV might have a negative impact on their future as students. My husband was embarrassed because all his co-workers were talking about it. They were saying it was a disgrace. . . . Although I was criticized, . . . I feel that it was not right to let the owner of the restaurant do what she did to me and the other people. I did it to stop her from continuing to do these things to people.[14]

SPEAKING UP FOR THE POWERLESS

Immigrant women workers have said *ka ja!* [let's go!] and begun to write a new chapter in Korean-American history. This story begins with their labor struggles in their homeland and continues in the kitchens, dining rooms, hotels, factories, and on the picket lines of inner city barrios, tossed together like *chap chae* [mixed vegetables and noodles] with their Mexican and Central American immigrant co-workers. They have endured long hours, low wages, sexual harassment, age discrimination, insults, firings, blacklisting, censorship, criticism, and fear. They have been urged to be patient, endure, and keep their mouths shut. Yet these pioneers are taking a stand and beginning to change the climate and thinking within the community, winning respect for women workers' human rights, building multi-racial solidarity, opening up new spaces for democracy, and securing more justice within the Korean and other communities of color within the United States.

The November 14, 1998 community town hall meeting of Koreatown restaurant workers demanding "justice, dignity, and democracy" conveyed a tumultuous mix of images, languages, emotions. An angry gauntlet of restaurant owners taunted all seeking to enter the towering union hall hosting the gathering. The owners' ringleader boasted that he learned how to picket after being picketed by workers and KIWA. Inside the hall the atmosphere was simultaneously welcoming, protective, and edgy as Korean and Mexican restaurant workers delivered testimony to elected officials, government enforcement agencies, Korean, Spanish, and English language press, community supporters, and family members. After describing the abusive behavior by her ex-bosses, Kyung Park said:

> I go home every day with a new wound in my heart because of all the hurtful things that happen at work. I am a wife and mother at home, but at work, I am viewed sometimes as a servant, sometimes as a thief. This is the reality of restaurant workers. Not being able to get paid as we are supposed (to) and suffering through each day facing insults and curses—this is what makes up the lives of restaurant workers in Koreatown. . . . I would like to say to all the government leaders, media, workers, and all the other members of the audience present today: it is very possible that by coming forward today I may face the possibility of losing my job. But I have chosen to come to this gathering today in spite of all that. This is because I believe that unless someone speaks up for the rights of the powerless workers in Koreatown, we would have no choice but to go on living with bruises in our hearts.[15]   [2001]

NOTES

1. Han Hee Jin, Speech delivered in front of Shogun Sushi, Koreatown, Los Angeles, June 6, 1998.
2. Called the "Four Dragons," "Four Tigers," or the East Asian Newly Industrialized Countries (NICs), South Korea, Taiwan, Singapore, and Hong Kong experienced rapid economic growth since the 1960s based on their special relationship with the United States and Japan, and a system of state-directed capitalist development (Bello, Walden and Rosenfeld, 1990) 1–16.
3. See Song and Moon,1998b: 161–173.
4. Shimtuh, 2000. See also Korean American Coalition to End Domestic Abuse, 1999; and Song and Moon, 1998b: 162–163. Song and Moon's 1987 study that found that 60 percent of Korean immigrant women reported having been battered by their spouses.

5. Meeting of Koreatown restaurant workers, April 3, 1999.
6. Meeting of Koreatown restaurant workers, April 3, 1999.
7. Popular education is the process through which people process direct lived experiences as the knowledge base from which to make connections with and analyze broader relations in the society and economy. See Freire, 1990; Bell et al, 1990.
8. Kim, Luke I., 1991, cited in Kim-Goh, 1998:230. The cultural sector of the 1980s *minjung* movement helped reclaim and transform the practice of *kut* and *han puri*, Korean shamanistic exorcism and *han* release rituals, such as those dedicated to the memory of the Comfort Women and the martyrs of the Kwangju Massacre. Luke Kim says that Korean psychotherapists and theologians have grown more interested in exploring the concept of *han* as it sheds light on problems facing their clients and parishioners (Kim, Luke I., 1998:219).
9. Interview with Chu Mi Hee, March 25, 1997.
10. Interview with Chu Mi Hee, March 25, 1997.
11. See Korean Immigrant Workers Advocates, 1997.
12. Korean Immigrant Workers Advocates, 1996.
13. Interview with Paek Young Hee, March 27, 1997.
14. Interview with Paek Young Hee, March 27, 1997.
15. Korean Immigrant Workers Advocates, 1998b.

 148

Just Sex: Students Rewrite the Rules on Sex, Violence and Equality

JODI GOLD and SUSAN VILLARI

Hook-up, mash, fool around, or shag—isn't it all just sex? Sex is no big deal, right? But what if it isn't consensual? Then it is not just sex. Then it is acquaintance rape. In 1989, when I became an antirape educator, I expected to fight rape. I believed that all rape was violence. Rape was not sex. What I found out later was that, yes, rape is violence—but acquaintance rape is also about sex. When I joined the antisexual violence movement, I found women and men like myself trying to navigate the confusing sexual landscape of the late twentieth century. As a result, I spent more time during college talking about sex than having it. . . .

We are often asked why those involved in a movement to end rape spend so much time talking about sex. Didn't the early antirape feminists teach us that

rape is about power and not about sex? Fortunately, they did—and in doing so put a name to a crime against women that at the time most people believed was perpetrated by sociopaths, not their husbands, lovers, and acquaintances. Twenty-five years later, despite tremendous legal and social reform, society still has trouble distinguishing between sex and violence. Efforts to clarify the distinction are labeled as puritanical, radical, and revolutionary.

Start by asking someone the definition of acquaintance rape, and invariably part of the response will include a reference to the infamous gray area, where sexual definitions, rules, and roles are ill defined or never defined. Follow it up with a question about whose responsibility it is to prevent acquaintance rape, and you are barraged with codes of conduct based on gender or the infamous *he said, she said*. The schism between *he said, she said* also defaults to gray, a place where there is still a hesitancy to assign blame or responsibility. It is as if the gray area is a misty fog that descends upon you and impairs your vision and reason. When caught in the gray, you cannot see far in the distance. The fog may be so dense that two rational and intelligent people experience the same event with an opposite understanding of it. The gray area is powerful enough to jam communication channels during a sexual encounter, causing one person to refuse sex while the other person assumes consent. This gray area seeps into our offices and under our bedroom doors. It invades computer monitors and TV screens. The gray area is enlisted when one person's harassment is another person's joke, or when the same photograph is simultaneously defended as free speech and condemned as a hate crime against women.

The search to clear up the gray area has exposed the mainstream of American society to the controversial connection between sex and violence. The late twentieth century may well be remembered for our heated national debates over sexual harassment, acquaintance rape, interpersonal violence, and pornography in both private conversations and in the public arena. From the Clarence Thomas confirmation hearings to the William Kennedy Smith rape trial to Tailhook to Paula Jones's allegations against President Clinton, the relationship between sex and violence has increasingly been framed as an issue of civil rights and equal protection under the law.

Nowhere have the debates been stronger and the voices louder than on college campuses. Since the mid-1980s a campus social movement has been stirring that, at its core, rejects the belief that forced sex is an acceptable rite of passage for women. Outraged by the high incidence of acquaintance rape, students have begun to dismantle the gray by publicly debating issues of sexual consent, social constructions of gender, and equal protection. Using new as well as recycled tactics, students' efforts to rewrite the rules on sex, violence, and gender relations may well be their generation's chief contribution to social change, much like advocating for peace had been for previous generation's.[1]

Women and men who came of age in the 1980s and 1990s were the first generation to be weaned on feminism, civil rights, and the so-called sexual revolution. For the first time women acquired degrees at the same rate as their male counterparts.[2] For many of these women college not only represented greater academic and career opportunities but seemed to afford the same rights as men to experiment both socially and sexually. Unfortunately, the illusion of sexual freedom smacked up against the reality of acquaintance rape, bringing them face-to-face with deeply rooted sexism. In case after case, when women brought charges against the men who raped them, their cases were dismissed as a relationship problem, or they were chastised for daring to enjoy the same freedoms as their male peers. . . .

Although a dramatic shift in public awareness has helped dispel myths about rape, too many people still believe that women provoke and encourage men to rape them by the way they dress and act. Similarly, men are told they are unable to separate their desires from their actions. Once sexually aroused, or so the story goes, men must pursue sex even if it is forced or coerced. So-called sexual liberation has done very little to change the rule that men are still encouraged to be sexual aggressors and women are assigned as gatekeepers to sex. Following this logic, it is not surprising that women are still held accountable for men's sexually aggressive behavior and ultimately for the prevention of rape.

Asking women to "be aware" or assuming that all men are potential rapists is not the answer: At the heart of the student movement is the collective belief that sexual violence is neither inevitable nor inherent. On campuses across the country, students are calling into question traditional notions of masculinity and femininity, particularly because these beliefs often dictate what is considered acceptable behavior, both socially and sexually, for men and women. Listen closely to most conversations about acquaintance rape, and you will more fully understand our deeply entrenched gender and sexual roles. *What did she expect? She had been drinking and she was in his dorm room at two A.M. How can you blame him? He is just like any other red-blooded American male.*

Rigid gender roles hinder women's ability to say yes to sex and men's ability to say or hear no. Men are told that seduction means pushing verbally or physically until you get a yes, or believing that no really means yes. Consequently, verbally coercive sex and legally defined rape are protected under the guise of seduction. Challenging this accepted behavior, campus activists promote consent, not coercion, as sexy. In what many believe to be a *new sexual revolution,* they lend their passion and power to the continuing struggle for gender and sexual equality.

THE OLD, THE NEW, AND THE RECYCLED

Borrowing techniques from previous generations' efforts to raise awareness about sexual violence, today's activists organize Take Back the Night marches, survivor speak-outs, and self-defense workshops. They challenge campus policies and advocate for increased resources for prevention programs and support services. Traditional forms of antirape activism often serve as the catalyst for the institutionalization of programs and services, but much of today's social change efforts include service projects, peer education, and working within the system. . . . By viewing students as the experts, groups like Students against Violence against Women (SAVAW) at Ithaca College, and Auburn Working for Acquaintance Rape Education (AWARE) provide educational workshops where information and statistics on acquaintance rape are disseminated.

More important, these workshops provide a safe place for students to demystify the gray area by exploring how rigid gender roles and power inequities are connected to acquaintance rape. Simple statements such as "Men and women are equally responsible for the prevention of rape," or "It is possible to give nonverbal consent to sex" prompt lively debates on the unwritten rules for "hooking up" and the nonverbal language of sex. Male facilitators will ask other men if it is possible to separate desire from action. Often men genuinely ask, "How can I be sure that I am not raping someone?" Female facilitators will shatter myths about female sexuality and physicality by openly discussing masturbation, orgasm, and how to fight back when in danger. These types of questions and ensuing discussions reveal how disparate socialization is for men and women in this society. Student educators respond by encouraging both men and women to stop and confirm consent if they are receiving mixed messages. In the age of HIV and AIDS students no longer believe that sex must be mysterious and unspoken. More women and men are having sex in college than ever before, but they want it to be fun, safe, and consensual.[3]

RAPE AS A POLITICAL ISSUE

For anyone to appreciate fully the current wave of antirape activism, it's critical to understand the movement's historical foundations. Kate Millett articulated the first feminist analysis of rape in her 1970 book, *Sexual Politics.* The opening lines of her theory of sexual politics begins:

> Coitus can scarcely be said to take place in a vacuum; although of itself it appears a biological and physical activity, it is set so deeply within the larger context of human affairs that it serves as a charged microcosm of the variety of attitudes and values to which culture subscribes.[4]

For Millett politics is defined as "power over," and patriarchy means men's power over women. Therefore, sex is always political in a patriarchy because it reflects the societal inequality between women and men. All sex is not rape, but the power that men have over women and the socialization of

men as aggressor and women as passive cannot be excluded from the bedroom. Following this logic, rape is not aberrant behavior, but a natural extension of a system that must maintain male dominance.

It was acquaintance rape that ignited the rumblings on college campuses in the mid-eighties, but acquaintance rape was not a new phenomenon. Harry Kalven Jr. and Hans Zeisel conducted a study of three thousand trials in the 1960s and found that 40 percent of rapes going to trial involved acquaintances.[5] Menachem Amir examined police files between 1958 and 1960. He concluded that rapists are generally "normal" men. About half of all rapes were committed by men who knew their victims, and not all the victims resisted loudly.[6] It was the radical feminists of the women's liberation movement who recognized the political importance of acquaintance rape. The central revelation of the first speak-out and conference on rape held in 1971 by the New York Radical Feminists was:

> The violent rapist and boyfriend/husband are one. . . . The act of rape is the logical expression of the essential relationship between men and women: It is a matter to be dealt with in feminist terms for feminist liberation.[7]

Susan Brownmiller, in her 1975 *Against Our Will,* was the first to use the phrase "date rape." She documents the history of rape and examines the cultural forces that maintain women as passive and men as aggressive.[8] At the time of publication many believed that a woman could not be raped "against her will," that certainly a woman would fight to the death.

Brownmiller and other radical feminists acknowledged the existence of and political nature of acquaintance rape, but Diana Russell took it one step further in her first book, *The Politics of Rape,* published in 1974. She interviewed ninety rape survivors and one rapist, who was interviewed by a male colleague. Not all the women were raped by acquaintances, but the rapists included lovers, best friends, fathers, and husbands. The goal of her book was to "emphatically contradict the prevalent view of male authors, clinicians, and doctors, that women enjoy being raped."[9] In 1978 Russell conducted a study of acquaintance rape with 930 randomly selected women. She used the California definition of rape, and she excluded those who "felt" raped but were not "forced." Contrary to the Kalven and Zeisel and Amir findings, she discovered that the vast majority of rapes were perpetrated by acquaintances.[10]

Stranger rape was the easiest and most visible issue of the seventies antirape movement. However, radical feminists had been saying all along that the boyfriend and rapist were one. They pursued three avenues of social change: rape prevention, service reform, and legal advocacy. The first rape crisis center in the world was founded by the Bay Area Women against Rape in 1970 in response to the rape of a Berkeley high school student.[11] Within a few months the D.C. Rape Crisis Center was founded, followed by centers in Philadelphia, Ann Arbor, New York, and Pittsburgh. By 1976 there were four hundred autonomous rape crisis centers. The early rape crisis centers were based on feminist organizing principles of working outside the system, disregard for academic "credentials," attention to process, and a commitment to self-help. They saw themselves as alternatives to the criminal justice system, which generally blamed women for being raped. The predominantly women-only volunteers served as escorts for rape victims during encounters with the law enforcement, medical, and legal systems. They demanded respect for women from emergency room personnel and police and supported victims through a self-help form of recovery. Rape crisis center volunteers were committed to social change in the community and on the campus. The first forms of campus antirape activism occurred in concert with the broader rape crisis movement.

THE EARLY CAMPUS CONNECTION

Antirape activism on the college campus is not new. Community rape crisis centers often worked closely with college campuses providing advocacy, support services, self-defense workshops, and an avenue for campus antirape activists. In 1972 a group of residential advisors at the University of Maryland campus responded to a series of gang rapes and abduc-tions by forming one of the first campus-based rape crisis centers.[12] On April 3, 1973, women at the University of Pennsylvania staged a four-day sit-in in reaction to a series of six rapes and the gang rape of two student nurses. They achieved all their demands, which included a women's center whose primary mission was to provide rape crisis services, a women's studies program, and improved security measures on campus.[13] A campus rape at the University of California at Berkeley led to the adoption of sexual assault programming throughout the entire University of California system in 1976. A committee of students and staff at Berkeley argued that the university was "obligated to create as safe an environment as possible" for women and that rape education was missing from the curricula. Remnants of the University of California sexual assault education program still exist today.[14]

Throughout the 1980s the nation witnessed a surge in antirape activism and research. In 1981 Claire Walsh founded Sexual Assault Recovery Services (SARS) at the University of Florida. The following year she and students formed Campus Organized against Rape (COARS), a peer education group that became one of the earliest nationally recognized antirape peer education programs.[15] A 1982 *Ms.* magazine article entitled "Date Rape: A Campus Epidemic," is credited as the first instance of date rape hitting the mainstream media,[16] and research by Dr. Mary Koss would further prove that the biggest threat on campus was not the crazed stranger, but the trusted friend.

Koss began her landmark research at Kent State University in Ohio the same year that Russell conducted her study in California. Koss believed the logical next step after *Against Our Will* was to conduct a comprehensive epidemiological study of acquaintance rape.[17] She started her work at Kent State with a study of college students' experiences with forced sex. Her results were so intriguing that she replicated the study in 1985 with the help of the National Institute of Mental Health and the *Ms.* Foundation. She surveyed 6,159 students at thirty-two campuses. Koss's findings were later translated for a lay audience by journalist Robin Warshaw in her popular book, *I Never Called It Rape.* Koss documented the increased vulnerability of college-age women to acquaintance rape. The research showed that one out of four women in college today are victims of rape or attempted rape, and 84 percent are assaulted by men whom they know. The average age at the time of the rape was 18½ years old for both the perpetrator and victim/survivor.[18]

The most disturbing yet controversial finding was the reluctance of men and women to define their experiences with forced sex as rape. Only one-quarter of the women surveyed whose experience met the legal definition of rape identified their experience as rape. One in twelve men surveyed reported sexually violent behavior, but the majority did not define their behavior as rape. This phenomenon confirmed what radical feminists had been saying all along—that violence against women is so insidious, it has been framed as part of normative sexual behavior.

Prior to 1985 a limited number of schools had policies or programs addressing sexual assault.[19] By the mid-1980s to the early 1990s, a strong catalyst for institutional reform can be attributed to courageous students going public with their assault stories. Our national survey of college campuses demonstrates that 35 percent of policies enacted by 1993 resulted from a high-profile assault case and/or student activism.[20]

For example, in 1983 several Ohio State basketball players were accused of gang rape. By a twist of fate the NCAA basketball tournament was taking place in Columbus that year. With national media attention protesters picketed outside the stadium, and the university president was quick to respond by funding a rape prevention program that continues to be a national leader. The program was founded with a feminist agenda charged with the task of developing culturally specific curricula. Ohio State is one of the rare schools that actually pay graduate students forty dollars an hour to present workshops to the sixty-thousand-student body.[21]

Student protests at the University of Michigan (1985)[22] and the University of Minnesota (1986)[23] resulted in comprehensive campus sexual assault services. In 1987 a landmark case at Carleton College, a prestigious liberal arts school, launched a na-

tional debate when four female students sued their college for not protecting them against the men whom the college knew to be repeat rapists. The women testified that the school was aware of the previous assaults by their rapists and did nothing to prevent these men from attacking them.[24]

During the late 1980s activism not only sparked the development of institutional policies and procedures, but also tested the limits and enforcement of those policies. At Princeton University, in October 1987, protest and outrage at the lack of enforcement of the sexual harassment policy prompted immediate university action. During an annual Take Back the Night event, several march participants were harassed by fellow Princeton students. One man screamed "We can rape whoever we want," while others dropped their trousers and hurled beer at marchers. The protest that followed this event led to the hiring of a sexual assault director, Myra Hindus, whose job was to oversee the university's sexual assault/harassment policies and procedures.[25]

During this time public opinion was also being shaped by the media and entertainment industries. The topic of acquaintance rape was introduced into television and movies via talk-show hosts, daytime soaps, and drama shows. In 1988 Jodie Foster won an academy award for her role as a "bad girl" rape survivor in the film *The Accused*, which was based on a New Bedford, Connecticut, gang rape trial.

WHY HAS THIS ISSUE MOBILIZED COLLEGE STUDENTS TODAY?

Several important factors appear to have set the stage for the current student movement to end sexual and gender-based violence. In addition to the influence of previous social movements on this generation, and a different sense of entitlement, the contemporary campus is a virtual microcosm of a rape-supportive culture. First-year college students of traditional age represent the highest risk group for being involved in a sexual assault either as perpetrators or victim/survivors.[26] Koss's research found that the use of alcohol and other drugs were involved in a majority of rape cases—70 percent of the men involved and 55 percent of the women involved reported drinking or taking drugs prior to the assault.[27]

The use of alcohol and other drugs is perceived as a social lubricant and an easy way to de-stress from academic pressure.

The campus environment is also influenced by powerful male-dominated institutions, such as fraternities, whose rituals encourage hypermasculinity and excessive alcohol use, further adding to the fertile ground for rape to take root in. In 1985 Erhart and Sandler conducted groundbreaking research on the propensity of all-male groups to rape, identifying fraternity culture as conducive to sexual violence.[28] In *Fraternity Gang Rape: Sex, Brotherhood, and Privilege on Campus,* author Peggy Sanday describes what is called "a train"—a sexual ritual in which a number of fraternity men line up to take turns "having sex" with an intoxicated and unwilling female victim. The behavior is described by the participants as normal, "something that you see and hear about all the time."[29] Sanday describes this all-male behavior as homoerotic, and argues that pornography coupled with fraternity culture teaches young men about sex. Athletes who participate in aggressive sports are also at a higher risk for perpetrating sexual violence.[30] It is important to note that *most* athletes and fraternity members do not commit rape. Rather, the odds are greatly increased when excessive alcohol use is coupled with hypermasculine all-male environments whose groups have privilege on campus.

Finally, the work of previous antirape activists and recent legislation have helped to institutionalize sexual assault prevention and support services. The staff who coordinate sexual violence programs, that is, women's center directors and health educators, often got their start in the second wave of the women's movement. Students are often greeted by a generation of sixties and seventies activists firmly rooted in positions of power ready to serve as willing allies. This provides a unique partnership for current student activism. Activist faculty and staff teach students how to organize effectively and also give them access to resources. On the other hand, student activists can push the envelope without fearing loss of employment.

The North American Student Conferences on Campus Sexual Violence, which began in 1992 in Philadelphia, exemplify this unique and effective partnership.[31] Organized by and for students, with significant support from key administrators, the conferences bring together student educators and activists from around the continent. The first conference was originally planned as a regional event, but students were so eager to network and share resources that registrations came in from schools as far away as Oregon, Hawaii, and Alberta, Canada. Py Bateman, feminist self-defense activist and founder of Alternatives to Fear, remarked after her keynote address at this 1992 student conference:

> College students are perfectly placed for social change. They're young and in a position to put pressure on university administration; open to new ideas; and in training for leadership. *The First National Student Conference on Campus Sexual Assault* is a perfect example of the power of students. I have not seen anything like this since the organizing in the 60s.[32]

THE NEW FACE OF STUDENT ACTIVISM

Despite the stereotype that today's college students are apolitical and disengaged, a recent study by Jeanette S. Cureton and Arthur Levine finds that current undergraduates are the most socially active since the 1930s.[33] Social-change efforts on campuses today are often overlooked or misrepresented because twenty-somethings have developed their own style of activism, a style that on the surface sharply contradicts the popular image of a student activist. According to Paul Loeb, author of *Generation at the Crossroads: Apathy and Action on the American Campus:*

> Students have been looking for different ways to voice social concern. They want to act. They want to help. They don't want to deal with complicated issues and factions or the messy contention of politics. Instead they have revived approaches to involvement that focus on individual service . . . yet, the same approaches often lead them back toward larger social change.[34]

By the early 1990s peer education programs addressing sexual violence were being implemented all across the country. Generally, peer educators are trained volunteers, with very few receiving academic or monetary compensation. By 1995, 56 percent of schools surveyed had students facilitating workshops on sexual violence—with one-third of those students being men.[35] Program names such as CORE (Creating a Rape Free Environment), POWER (People out Working Together to End Rape), and STAAR (Students Together Against Acquaintance Rape) reflect the belief that if men and women work together, sexual violence can be prevented. Sharing only a commitment to end sexual violence, educators and activists find themselves in coalitions with people they normally might not associate with. For example, it is not uncommon to see a fraternity brother facilitating a workshop with a self-identified "radical" feminist or an openly gay man working with the president of the campus Republicans. The common experience of sexual violence and its profound impact on a community cross gender, racial, ethnic, and sexual orientation boundaries. This diversity is what strengthens the activists' ability to infiltrate a large cross section of campus. Groups educate in dorm rooms, classrooms, bars, and locker rooms.

Students become involved in antirape work for a variety of reasons. The most common motivation is being or knowing a survivor of sexual assault. Men frequently become involved because a girlfriend discloses being raped. These men focus their anger and accompanying sense of powerlessness into educating other men.

Groups such as Men Acting for Change (Duke University), Men against Rape and Sexism (Iowa State University), and Black Men for the Eradication of Sexism (Morehouse College) often feel equally constrained by rigid gender roles and resent the perception that all men are potential rapists. Omar Freilla, founder of Black Men for the Eradication of Rape and Sexism, comments: "We have discussion groups and talk about what it is, what it means to be a man, and how we were brought up. We are really trying to de-program ourselves."[36]

The issue of deconstructing masculinity is addressed not only in small discussion groups but also in large-scale campus events. Responding to a comment made by journalist Anna Climlin that the "good guys have to stand up and speak out," Rutgers University launched the Real Men of Rutgers

campaign in the spring of 1994. Appealing to men's role in ending sexual violence, Ruth Koenick, coordinator of Sexual Assault Services, and student educators designed a poster that featured photos and quotes from twelve male student leaders nominated by the campus. Each man chosen contributed his opinion on how violence could be prevented within his own student community. Posters hung prominently in all major offices and buildings on campus.[37]

At Ohio State University, contributor Michael Scarce, then coordinator of the Rape Education and Prevention Program, placed placards above men's urinals on campus that read, "In your hands, you hold the power to stop rape."[38]

SEXUAL POLITICS ROCK THE NATION

According to educator and author Michael Kimmel, the early 1990s may well be remembered as the "decade in which America took a crash course on male sexuality,"[39] with the media not only highlighting high-profile celebrity cases but also bringing national attention to activist strategies happening locally on campuses. Responding to the national attention directed toward Brown University in 1990, contributor Jesselyn Brown writes "you know something has touched a nerve when it manages to get lambasted by feminists, antifeminists, and establishment organs alike." Frustrated by a judicial system that continually dismissed sexual assault cases, women at Brown used their speech to protect their fellow students. To have their speech heard, four Brown women generated a conversation on a centrally located women's bathroom stall, which eventually became known on campus as the "rape list." This simple act caused an uproar across the nation, with administrators denouncing the list as "anti-male" and referring to the women as "Magic Marker terrorists." Jesselyn Brown argues that when women were sexually assaulted on her campus, the cases were dismissed as trivial; yet when women wrote names of men who assaulted them, using their freedom of speech, it was immediately viewed as an infringement of the men's rights.

During the same time period the issue of how to negotiate consensual sex brought national media attention to the campus of Antioch College. Initiated by activist students, the now infamous Sexual Offense Policy at Antioch College requires "willing and verbal" consent for each sexual act. Despite the fact that this policy was supported by the majority of students, it was criticized by outsiders as "sexual correctness" and "courtship management," and it even ended up being spoofed on an episode of *Saturday Night Live*. Andy Abrams, who has been humorously referred to as the Antioch poster boy, believes that asking for consent is not only sexy, but smart. "If you don't talk, then all you got is guesswork."

As we watched in horror the interrogation of Anita Hill, Congress was busy debating antirape legislation. The early 1990s would see the passage of the Campus Security Bill and the Student Right to Know Act, the Ramstead Amendment, and the introduction of the Violence against Women Bill.

LAPTOPS, CELL PHONES, AND THE INTERNET

The use of new technology such as the Internet and E-mail not only helped effectively organize students involved in the movement to end sexual violence but also contributed to a new round of debates over free speech.

In 1995, when Cornell male students E-mailed over the Internet "Top 75 Reasons Women (Bitches) Should Not Have Freedom of Speech," angry students from across the country flooded Cornell's E-mail system, eventually causing it to shut down temporarily.[40]

During the planning stages for the First Canadian Student Conference on Campus Sexual Violence at the University of Alberta in Edmonton in 1998, the Canadian Post Office went on strike. Amber Dean, student coordinator of the conference, quickly turned to electronic means to organize the conference, effectively using E-mail to communicate with conference participants and register students on-line.

As we move into the twenty-first century, the impact of this campus movement remains to be seen. The student movement continues to be strong and vibrant, with the North American Student Conferences on Campus Sexual Violence and its spon-

soring organization, SpeakOut, looking forward to hosting their eighth year of annual conferences in the year 2000.   [2000]

NOTES

1. Sarah Ferguson, "Sex on Campus: How Making Love Became the Vietnam of the Nineties," *Village Voice*, April 1991, p. 9.
2. *The American Woman 1996-97, Woman and Work* (New York: W. W. Norton, 1996), p. 269.
3. Peggy Sanday, *Woman Scorned: Acquaintance Rape on Trial* (New York: Doubleday, 1996), pp. 191–92.
4. Kate Millett, *Sexual Politics* (New York: Simon and Schuster, 1990), p. 23.
5. Harry Kalven Jr. and Hans Zeisel, *The American Jury* (Boston: Little, Brown, 1966), p. 254. See also Peggy Sanday, *Woman Scorned* for complete history of acquaintance rape, pp. 184–207.
6. Menachem Amir, *Patterns in Forcible Rape* (Chicago: University of Chicago Press, 1971), p. 245.
7. Redstockings of the Women's Liberation Movement, *Feminist Revolution* (New York: Random House, 1975), p. 141.
8. Susan Brownmiller, *Against Our Will: Men, Women and Rape* (New York: Ballantine Books, 1975), p. 257.
9. Diana Russell, *The Politics of Rape*, 2d ed. (New York: Stein and Day, 1984), p. 13.
10. Russell, *Politics of Rape*, p. 59.
11. Sharon Sayles, "Ten Years: 1972–1982: Working against Sexual Assault," Archives of the National Coalition against Sexual Assault, Pittsburgh, Pa., p. 2.
12. Interview with Ruth Koenick, coordinator of Rutgers University Sexual Assault Services, June 1994.
13. Interview with Ellie DiLapi, director of University of Pennsylvania's Women's Center, June 1994.
14. Interview with Jennifer Beeman, director of University of California, Davis, Rape Education and Prevention Program, July 1994.
15. Beth Ribet, "Fighting Campus Sexual Violence: Notes about the Coalition of Campus Organizations Addressing Rape," unpublished paper, Irvine, Calif.
16. Karen Barrett, "Date Rape: A Campus Epidemic," *Ms.*, September 1982, p. 51.
17. Mary P. Koss, Christine A. Gidycz, and Nadine Wisniewski, "The Scope of Rape: Incidence and Prevalence of Sexual Aggression and Victimization in a National Sample of Higher Education Students," *Journal of Consulting and Clinical Psychology* 55 (1987): pp. 162–70.
18. Robin Warshaw, *I Never Called It Rape: The Ms. Report on Recognizing, Fighting, and Surviving Date and Acquaintance Rape* (New York: Harper and Row, 1988), p. 11.
19. Jodi Gold, Jessie Minier, and Susan Villari, "Creating Campuses Intolerant of Rape: Peer Education and the Institutional Response to Sexual Violence" presented at the 6th International Conference on Sexual Assault and Harassment on Campus, Long Beach, Calif., November 1996.
20. Gold, Minier, and Villari, "Creating Campuses Intolerant of Rape."

21. Interview with Willa Young, director of Women Student Services and Rape Education and Prevention Programs at Ohio State University, July 1994.

22. Interview with Julie Steiner, director of the University of Michigan Sexual Assault Awareness and Prevention Center (SAPAC), July 1994.

23. Interview with Jamie Tiedemann, director of University of Minnesota's Sexual Assault Services, August 1994.

24. *Time*, June 3, 1991, p. 55.

25. Interview with Myra Hindus, Princeton University, June 1994.

26. Warshaw, *I Never Called It Rape*, p. 24.

27. Warshaw, *I Never Called It Rape*, p. 44.

28. Julie K. Ehrhart and Bernice R. Sandler, *Campus Gang Rape: Party Games?* Project on the Status and Education of Women (Washington, D.C.: Association of American Colleges, 1985).

29. Peggy Reeves Sanday, *Fraternity Gang Rape: Sex, Brotherhood, and Privilege on Campus* (New York: New York University Press, 1990).

30. Carol Bohmer and Andrea Parrot, *Sexual Assault on Campus* (New York: Lexington Books, 1993), p. 22.

31. The North American Student Conferences on Campus Sexual Violence began at the University of Pennsylvania, Philadelphia, in 1992. Jodi and Susan coordinated this first conference and, at the time, they had no idea that this conference would continue into its eighth year. Since 1993 one to three conferences have been held each year, with 1998 seeing its first Canadian conference. SpeakOut: The North American Student Coalition on Campus Sexual Violence was founded in 1994 to help oversee and coordinate these North American student conferences.

32. Py Bateman, "Keynote Address," First Annual National Student Conference on Campus Sexual Assault, University of Pennsylvania, Philadelphia, March 1992.

33. Arthur Levine, "A New Generation of Student Protesters Arises," *Chronicle of Higher Education*, February 26, 1999, p. A52.

34. Paul Rogat Loeb, *Generation at the Crossroads: Apathy and Action on the American Campus* (New Brunswick, N.J.: Rutgers University Press, 1994), p. 61.

35. Gold, Minier, and Villari, "Creating Campuses Intolerant of Rape."

36. *Ms.*, July/August 1995, p. 95.

37. Interview with Ruth Koenick, June 1994.

38. From the CCOAR listserv, June 1996.

39. Michael Kimmel, "Clarence Williams, Iron Mike, Tailhook, Senator Packwood, Spur Posse, Magic . . . and US," in *Transforming a Rape Culture*, eds. Emile Buchwald, Pamela Fletcher, and Martha Roth (Minneapolis, Minn.: Milkweed Editions, 1993), p. 121.

40. Judy Mann, "Sexists on the Net," *Washington Post*, November 15, 1995, p. E17.

✿ 149

Manifesta: Young Women, Feminism and the Future

JENNIFER BAUMGARDNER
and AMY RICHARDS

Act 1, Scene 1: 1848. The Seneca Falls Convention, the first conference in this country held expressly to discuss women's rights, takes place. Here, on a Saturday in July, in the Wesleyan Chapel in the woods of upstate New York, two hundred women and forty men come together to approve the Declaration of Sentiments, a plan of action to grant women citizen's rights. "In entering upon the great work before us," the framers of that declaration wrote, "[W]e anticipate no small amount of misconception, misrepresentation, and ridicule; but we shall use every instrumentality within our power to effect our object. We shall employ agents, circulate tracts, petition the State and National legislatures, and endeavor to enlist the pulpit and the press in our behalf. We hope this Convention will be followed by a series of Conventions embracing every part of the country." A young mother named Elizabeth Cady Stanton, one of two main convention organizers, puts forth a plank—that women must have the right to vote— which her friend Lucretia Mott almost talks her out of, asserting that its radicalism would weaken public support for other goals. And, in fact, the right of women's suffrage is the only resolution of twelve in the Declaration of Sentiments that is not approved unanimously.

Act 1, Scene 2: 1923. Women may bob their hair, "reach for a Lucky instead of a sweet," and cast a ballot in all forty-eight states. A critical mass of women who had gotten a taste of the workplace within the past half decade are at home again, replaced by men returning from World War I. The service sector is providing new jobs—laundry workers, telephone operators, and secretaries. Alice Paul, the founder of the National Woman's Party (a radical offshoot of the National American Woman Suffrage Association), is young and full of vision. So much so that after spearheading the final successful push for the vote, she publicly states that it is only an opportunity to launch a much larger battle. On the seventy-fifth anniversary of the Seneca Falls Convention, Paul announces the fight for the Equal Rights Amendment, also known as the Lucretia Mott Amendment, which states: "Men and women shall have equal rights throughout the United States and every place subject to its jurisdiction."

Act 1, Scene 3: 1998. It's sixteen years after the titanic campaign for the ERA came to a halt, the victim of a ratification time limit. That July, at the 150th anniversary commemoration of the Seneca Falls Convention in Seneca Falls, there are many needs, as there were before the First Wave ended with its focus mainly on the vote. Equal and comparable pay, reproductive freedom, eradicating violence against women—all these and more had been hammered out in a kind of Constitutional Convention for Women, the 1977 National Women's Conference in Houston, with delegates elected by every state and territory.

At this 1998 conference, however, there isn't any central campaign, agenda, activism, or feminist goal. Ellie Smeal of the Feminist Majority Foundation uses her one-hour time slot to explain the Women's Equality Act, an omnibus bill that articulates the exact arenas in which women are getting a raw deal. Getting the act into action doesn't appear to be the higher purpose of this event; sales and tourism are. A huge Barnes & Noble tent sells books about women's history; multigenerational packs of women, including Secretary of Health and Human Services Donna Shalala (followed by Secret Service men trying to blend) and sixteen-year-old Tennessee Jane Watson walk the green lawns amid outdoor booths selling crafts by women. The convention is billed simply as Celebrate '98.

But celebrate what? The fact that the ERA didn't pass? That it took seventy-two years for women to get the vote? That the Violence Against Women Act II (the one that actually protects immigrant women) is currently stalled in Congress? Presenters from Hillary Clinton to Betsy McCoy Ross, who was then campaigning to be New York's next governor, make the point that there is still plenty to be done.

So shouldn't the sesquicentennial have been called Activate '98 or Flay the Patriarchy '98?

Act 2, Scene 1: 1999. September in New York City, two women sit down to write in a studio apartment on Avenue B. The coffeemaker is on. It's late. Wafting up from the streets are the psychosis-inducing sounds of the Mister Softee truck playing "Music Box Dancer" while making its rounds. "When in the course of thirty years of uninterrupted feminism," one woman types, while the other leafs through pages of clips, notes, and correspondence, "it becomes evident that a single generation can only go so far, it behooves the next generation to pick up the reins and articulate the plot that will move their cause forward. The first two waves of feminism had clear political goals that involved holding the government accountable to its citizens, the majority of whom were getting an unequal deal. In order to have a government that responds to the Third Wave, rather than a society by the few for the few, we need a similar declaration of our sentiments. We need a Manifesta."

THIRD WAVE MANIFESTA: A THIRTEEN-POINT AGENDA

1. To out unacknowledged feminists, specifically those who are younger, so that Generation X can become a visible movement and, further, a voting block of eighteen- to forty-year-olds.

2. To safeguard a woman's right to bear or not to bear a child, regardless of circumstances, including women who are younger than eighteen or impoverished. To preserve this right throughout her life and support the choice to be childless.

3. To make explicit that the fight for reproductive rights must include birth control; the right for poor women and lesbians to have children; partner adoption for gay couples; subsidized fertility treatments for all women who choose them; and freedom from sterilization abuse. Furthermore, to support the idea that sex can be—and usually is—for pleasure, not procreation.

4. To bring down the double standard in sex and sexual health, and foster male responsibility and assertiveness in the following areas: achieving freedom from STDs; more fairly dividing the

burden of family planning as well as responsibilities such as child care; and eliminating violence against women.

5. To tap into and raise awareness of our revolutionary history, and the fact that almost all movements began as youth movements. To have access to our intellectual feminist legacy and women's history; for the classics of radical feminism, womanism, *mujeristas*, women's liberation, and all our roots to remain in print; and to have women's history taught to men as well as women as a part of all curricula.

6. To support and increase the visibility and power of lesbians and bisexual women in the feminist movement, in high schools, colleges, and the workplace. To recognize that queer women have always been at the forefront of the feminist movement, and that there is nothing to be gained—and much to be lost—by downplaying their history, whether inadvertently or actively.

7. To practice "autokeonony" ("self in community"): to see activism not as a choice between self and community but as a link between them that creates balance.

8. To have equal access to health care, regardless of income, which includes coverage equivalent to men's and keeping in mind that women use the system more often than men do because of our reproductive capacity.

9. For women who so desire to participate in all reaches of the military, including combat, and to enjoy all the benefits (loans, health care, pensions) offered to its members for as long as we continue to have an active military. The largest expenditure of our national budget goes toward maintaining this welfare system, and feminists have a duty to make sure women have access to every echelon.

10. To liberate adolescents from slut-bashing, listless educators, sexual harassment, and bullying at school, as well as violence in all walks of life, and the silence that hangs over adolescents' heads, often keeping them isolated, lonely, and indifferent to the world.

11. To make the workplace responsive to an individual's wants, needs, and talents. This includes valuing (monetarily) stay-at-home parents, aiding employees who want to spend more time with family and continue to work, equalizing pay for jobs of comparable worth, enacting a minimum wage that would bring a full-time worker with two children over the poverty line, and providing employee benefits for freelance and part-time workers.

12. To acknowledge that, although feminists may have disparate values, we share the same goal of equality, and of supporting one another in our efforts to gain the power to make our own choices.

13. To pass the Equal Rights Amendment so that we can have a constitutional foundation of righteousness and equality upon which future women's rights conventions will stand.

STANDING ON SHOULDERS

Kim Miltimore, a twenty-eight-year-old from Kent, Washington, sat down one night in the fall of 1999 and fired off an E-mail to feminist.com. "I cannot accept that insurance companies cover Viagra but won't cover infertility drugs such as Clomid," she wrote. "I want to help change this gross inequity—do you have any links to groups fighting for equality in medical coverage?"

At the same time, Jewish Women Watching, a group of feminists in New York City, sent out hundreds of cards in celebration of Yom Kippur, the Jewish New Year, which listed various excuses that institutions give for not being sympathetic to women's issues. The cards offered snappy retorts to sexist comments. For example, "We don't offer child care. If women want families, they are going to have to make career sacrifices." To which Jewish Women Watching responded: "This year, support working parents" and "Sexism Is a Sin."

In Australia, junior champion steer rider Peta Browne, age thirteen, and her friend Ayshea Clements, age fifteen, protested the fact that girls are banned from riding in the junior steer ride within the National Rodeo Association (NRA). The girls filed a complaint with the Human Rights Commission, but the HRC responded with twenty-four reasons that they and girls like them are not covered by Australia's Sexual Discrimination Act. Both have been reaching out via the Internet for support to appeal this sexist exclusion.

What all these feminists have in common is this: they saw an injustice and used their rage to become everyday activists. One can be an activist with one's voice, money, vote, creativity, privilege, or the fearlessness that comes from having nothing left to lose. Activists may work within the system—by voting, lobbying Congress, advocating at the United Nations, or monitoring a governmental agency set up to protect human rights and civil liberties. They may also work outside the system—by creating nongovernmental organizations (NGOs) to fill in the government's gaps, contributing to existing grassroots groups and foundations, organizing boycotts or protests, or doing something individual and agit-propesque, like walking from Pasadena to Washington, D.C., to demonstrate the need for campaign-finance reform. (That last is exactly what eighty-nine-year-old Doris Haddock did in anticipation of the 2000 Presidential race.) A regular woman becomes an activist when she rights some glaring human mistake, or recognizes a positive model of equality and takes the opportunity to build on it.

Webster's defines activism as "the doctrine or policy of taking positive, direct action to achieve an end." Regardless of how you define it, activism, like feminism, can be something organic to our lives, a natural reflex in the face of injustice and inequality. Also like feminism, activism is one of the most confused concepts we know.

Even among women who relate to the goal of equality and the necessity of achieving it, activism can be an alien idea. To most people, the image of an activist is someone who is out of the ordinary—someone who hoists picket signs in front of the Pakistani Embassy, marches on the Washington Mall demanding money for cancer research, or chains him- or herself to trees. Given these images, it's easy to imagine that activists are "other" people—weird or dauntingly benevolent. If news stories highlighted the real faces and sources of activism, activists would be much more mundane and familiar.

Though activism can be grand or all-consuming, it is also as common and short-term as saying "That's not funny" to a racist joke, "No" to the boss who asks only the "girls" in the office to make coffee, or calling your senator to protest the passage of the House's version of the Unborn Victims of Violence Act, which seeks to give an embryo separate legal rights, thus criminalizing women who abort or use drugs. (Needless to say, this would give embryos rights that the same right-wingers won't give gay people.) On those oddly feisty days, activism can also be organizing boycotts against Nestle for pushing its expensive baby formula in developing countries where poor women lack the clean drinking water to mix it with and should be encouraged to breast-feed in the first place. In other words, activism is everyday acts of defiance. And these acts, taken together, make up a vital feminist movement.

THE MYTHS

Knowing there is feminist work to be done, and that the second most frequently asked question at Ask Amy is "What is activism?" it seemed necessary to lay out the nuts and bolts of personal activism—from radical-feminist Yom Kippur cards to general advice, incentive, and myth-busting.

The first myth is that activism will bring an immediate and decisive victory. In reality, the journey to justice is usually damn long. So while the click of consciousness brings immediate gratification in itself, social change, even on a small scale, is slow and arduous work. . . .

For example: before Rosa Parks refused to give up her seat to a white man on December 1, 1955, the act that initiated the Montgomery Bus Boycott, she and others had spent years as activists. They had been trained at the Highlander Folk School, a progressive political training ground founded in 1932 in Tennessee. This one act, a black woman's refusal to stand up for a white man, symbolizes the civil-rights movement to modern audiences. Parks herself is often depicted as a spontaneous actor, almost an accidental activist. In actuality, her act was a conscious part of a campaign, and nearly ten more years of nonstop activism by Parks and thousands of others were necessary before the Civil Rights Act was passed in 1964. . . .

The second myth about activism is that it has to be huge—*A Million March on Washington!* Thousands of men and women marched on Washington in August 1963 to hear Martin Luther King, Jr.'s "I Have a Dream" speech. However, that glistening moment of victory and grandeur was only one event in years of unexciting, tedious, utterly essential organizing—much of it, again, women's work. Splashy events get attention, but the work behind them doesn't. Activists might not even recognize themselves as part of this process.

The third myth is the importance of the super-leader. *Gandhi organizes India! Gloria Steinem organizes American women! Martin Luther King, Jr. organizes black Americans! Cesar Chavez organizes farmworkers! Ralph Nader figures out what to boycott!* Or, in our own generation, *Rebecca Walker is the Third Wave! Katie Roiphe is the anti–Third Wave! Kathleen Hanna IS Riot Grrrl!* It is a myth that effective activism is the result of one person, or even a few. . . . For example, you know Mahatma Gandhi and Jawaharlal Nehru, but it's unlikely that you have heard about the Indian women's movement of the late nineteenth and early twentieth centuries, which pioneered nonviolent resistance and the strategy of going from community to community to organize the grass roots. Seeking independence from male colonization of their bodies and lives, they campaigned against child marriages and *sati* (widow burning). Gandhi not only borrowed their techniques but tapped into their already existing movement, which then became part of the drive toward independence from British rule. (Speaking of men creating historic events off the backs of women's organizing, the Boston Tea Party was precipitated by women who refused to buy tea that was taxed by England.)

The leader of a movement has an important but misunderstood role. Because of charisma and oratorical skills, leaders attract media and mass. They usually have a gift for inspiring hope by stating a possibility that could become real, thus raising con-

sciousness and righteous anger. But they are just the tip of the iceberg, and would have no impact without the activists who form the foundation of the movement. They are the ones who fold and mail the flyers, answer the phones, and translate the agenda to and from the grass roots—whether there is any media attention at all.

At the beginning of a new century and a new millennium, Third Wave feminists shouldn't be discouraged that we don't have the equivalent of a Betty Friedan or a Rosa Parks—an icon that the whole movement can be reduced to at our rallies. And, even when we do, nothing will be accomplished without a truly aggressive Third Wave movement to push that iceberg's tip above sea level.

Although we may not yet have a critical mass of Third Wave activists, we need to dispel the fourth and final myth: that our generation is politically, um, impotent. Our purported lack of activism is usually chalked up to vague notions of apathy. We were reared by the boob tube, and made cynical by the coldwar politics and consumerism of the Reagan-Bush era. For a while, ad executives and media pundits conjectured that Generation X was simply lazy and irresponsible—fullfilling the slacker persona of the early nineties. The apathy rap has some truth when it comes to feminism. Some people do believe that everything is fine now, and that there is no need for feminism, either because they have low expectations, or because they haven't been in the outside world long enough to experience the limitations brought on by sexism. Many younger women in general haven't yet smacked up against job discrimination by sex and race—though they have certainly, however subtly, faced it socially and culturally. But history tells us that for each big leap, for each crystal-clear moment in which people refused to give up their seats on the bus or at the lunch counter, there is a time of collecting energy and stating new visions—a time of pre-emergence. Understanding that change takes time will lead us to a redefinition of our generation politically. . . .

Most movements are undertaken or, at least, swept along by young people in response to some galvanizing moment. The Tiananmen Square uprising began as an issue of free speech at a Beijing

University newspaper. School integration, the lynching of Emmett Till, and ordering the police to turn fire hoses on peaceful marchers in Alabama by George Wallace and Bull Connor all swelled the ranks of the Student Nonviolent Coordinating Committee and the Southern Christian Leadership Conference. Many white students in the North were so outraged by these events that they went South, and soon it became a national issue, not just a community one. In turn, the chokehold that racism had on our nation was loosened. Young men's resistance to the draft for the Vietnam War sparked the antiwar and free-speech movements of the sixties. These movements, which were started on American college campuses by such organizations as Students for a Democratic Society, as well as the ongoing civil-rights struggle, spawned the radical women's movement, which then coalesced with the reformist women's movement already in progress. . . .

We have hundreds of examples of positive and innovative Third Wave activism that has not yet brought huge and sweeping change but is slowly and surely draining the power of the patriarchy. . . . There is Inga Muscio's and Eve Ensler's public reclaiming of women's private parts with the books *Cunt* and *The Vagina Monologues*, and their accompanying book tours, and the women musicians who started the Seattle-based Home Alive after the murder of the Gits' lead singer Mia Zapata, in an attempt to make the streets safe by teaching women to kick ass. There is Mary Chung, who in 1994, at the age of twenty-six, founded the National Asian Women's Health Organization because there were hardly any resources aimed at Asian women and their reproductive health. And Kory Johnson, who in 1988, at the age of nine, founded Children for a Safe Environment to mobilize the kids in her Maryvale, Arizona, neighborhood about its hazardous waste problem. Now, eleven years since that original act, Kory is a student at Arizona State University and is still organizing for the group. There is Nancy Lublin, who at twenty-four founded Dress for Success with a small inheritance of $5,000 she received from her great-grandfather. Then a student at New York University law school, Lublin noticed that women going from welfare to work often

didn't have interview suits—something that seemed trivial to legislators passing welfare reform but is actually key to landing a job. In 1996, a week after receiving her inheritance, Lublin started Dress for Success by simply asking professional women to donate their gently used suits and getting the suits to women who needed them. (She networked with the social-service agencies that were helping women move from welfare to work.) Three years after the first suiting, Dress for Success has forty-eight chapters across the United States, one apiece in London and Vancouver, and has been profiled in mainstream media ranging from *60 Minutes* to the cover of *Working Woman*.

Meanwhile, as our radical foremothers predicted, young women keep getting together for conventions. Every few years, NOW or the Feminist Majority Foundation sponsors a young women's conference, where young women prepare themselves to inherit the reins of these venerable organizations. (For instance, in April 2000, the Feminist Majority Foundation sponsored Expo 2000, which drew six thousand women from around the world, including a large contingency of young women.) In 1995, three years before Celebrate '98 promoted a crafts fair more than a campaign for fairness, fifty thousand women converged on Huairou, China, for what's known as the Beijing Women's Conference. There was a large and encouraging contingency of young women and girls from around the world, who, for an hour every day, rode on old diesel buses from downtown Beijing to the muddy, Woodstock-style fields of the conference. Women in saris, veils, blue jeans, and boubous all came together to sign the "Platform for Action," a human-rights document that included planks about issues from poverty to education and training to the rights of the "girl child." . . .

A DAY WITH FEMINISM

Regardless of where and when feminists have gathered, we are always led back to the same question, What do women want? Rather than keep you guessing, we propose imagining what a feminist future will look like.

Women and men are paid equal wages for work of comparable value, as is every race and ethnic group, co-parenting is a given, men lengthen their lives by crying and otherwise expressing emotion, and women say "I'm sorry" only when they truly should be. To the extent that we can imagine this even now, this is the equality feminists have been working for since that day in Seneca Falls in 1848. With each generation, the picture will get bigger and at the same time more finely detailed.

When Elizabeth Cady Stanton and her crew wrote the Declaration of Sentiments, they knew that this nation's Declaration of Independence would have no justice or power unless it included the female half of the country. For these women, equality was being full citizens who were able to own and inherit property, just as men were, to have the right to their own children, and the ability to vote. In 1923, Alice Paul had the vision to write the Equal Rights Amendment so that laws could not be made based on sex, any more than they could be made based on race, religion, or national origin. By the 1970s, Betty Friedan, Audre Lorde, Gloria Steinem, and Shirley Chisholm could imagine women's equality in the paid workforce, a new vision of family and sexuality, and legislative bodies that truly reflected the country. They could not have foreseen a twenty-three-year-old White House intern who owned her own libido and sexual prowess the way Monica Lewinsky did. (They certainly wouldn't have imagined that a woman with that much access to power would just want to blow it.)

Now, at the beginning of a new millennium, we have witnessed a woman running for President who has a chance of winning, a first lady who translates that unparalleled Washington experience into her own high-flying political ambitions, easily reversible male birth control, gay parenting, a women's soccer team that surpasses the popular appeal of men's, and parental leave for both parents. And we can imagine more: federally subsidized child-care centers for every child and legalized gay marriage in all fifty states. A number of leaps are still needed to bring us to a day of equality, but at least we can begin to picture what such a future might hold.

Whether children are born to a single mother, a single father, two mothers, two fathers, or a mother

and a father, a family is defined by love, commitment, and support. A child who has two parents is just as likely to have a hyphenated last name, or choose a whole new name, as she or he is to have a father's or birth mother's name. Carrying on a lineage is an individual choice, not the province of the father or the state.

Men work in child-care centers and are paid at least as well as plumbers, sanitation workers, or firefighters. When kids sit down to their breakfast Wheaties, they are as likely to confront a tennis star like Venus Williams as a golf pro like Tiger Woods. On TV, the male and female newscasters are about the same age and, whether black or white, are as likely to report foreign policy as sports. In general, people on camera come in all shapes and sizes. If you are watching drama, women are just as likely to be the rescuers as the rescued, and men are just as likely to ask for help as to give it. Women are as valued for their sense of humor as men are for their sex appeal. On Monday-night television, women's soccer or basketball is just as popular as men's basketball or football. Barbie no longer has feet too tiny to stand on or finds math hard; nor do girls. G.I. Joe, now a member of a peacekeeping force, likes to shop at the mall. In grade school, boys and girls decorate their bedrooms with posters of female athletes.

By the time girls hit junior high, they have already had the opportunity to play sports, from soccer to Little League, hockey to wrestling, and they share gymnastics and ballet classes with boys. Boys think ballet and gymnastics are cool. Kids hit puberty fully aware of how their bodies work: erections, nocturnal emissions, periods, cramps, masturbation, body hair—the works. These topics still cause giggling, curiosity, and excitement, but paralyzing shame and utter ignorance are things of the past. In fact, sweet-sixteen birthdays have given way to coming-of-age rituals for both genders, and don't assume that the birthday kid has never been kissed. Around the time that girls and boys are learning how to drive, both have mastered manual stimulation for their own sexual pleasure.

In high school, many varsity teams have coed cheerleaders, athletes all, but mostly cheering is left to the fans. Differences in girls' and boys' academic performance are as indistinguishable as differences in their athletic performance though they are very different as unique individuals. Some girls ask other girls to the prom, some boys ask boys, and that is as okay as going in as a mixed couple. Some go alone or not at all, and that's okay, too. Athletic scholarships have no more prestige or funding than arts scholarships.

Students take field trips to local museums where women are the creators of the art as often as they are its subjects. In preparation for this trip, students study art history from Artemisia Gentileschi to Mark Rothko, from Ndebele wall paintings to Yayoi Kusama. The museums themselves were designed by architects who may have been among the 11 percent of architects who were female in the 1990s. Military school is open to everyone and teaches peacekeeping as much as defense. Women's colleges no longer exist, because women no longer need a compensatory environment, and women's history, African-American history, and all those remedial areas have become people's and world history.

Women achieved parity long ago, so the idea of bean counting is irrelevant. At Harvard, 75 percent of the tenured professors are women, and at nearby Boston College, 30 percent of the tenured faculty is female. History courses cover the relevance of a movement that ended sexual violence against women. Though there is still a throwback incident now and then, men are even more outraged by it than women are. Once a year, there is a party in the quad to commemorate what was once called Take Back the Night.

Women walking through a park at night can feel just as safe as they do during the day, when kids play while white male nannies watch over them, right along with women and men of every group. In fact, it's as common to see a white man taking care of a black or a brown baby as it is to see a woman of color taking care of a white baby.

Sex is separate from procreation. Because there is now a national system of health insurance, birth control and abortions are covered right along with births, and the Hyde Amendment's ban of federal funding for abortions is regarded as a shameful moment in history, much like the time of Jim Crow laws.

A judicial decision known as *Doe v. Hyde* effectively affirmed a woman's right to bodily integrity, and went way past the right to privacy guaranteed by *Roe v. Wade*. Abortion isn't morally contested territory because citizens don't interfere with one another's life choices, and women have the right to determine when and whether to have no children, a single child, or five children.

Environmentally sound menstrual products are government-subsidized and cost the same as a month's worth of shaving supplies. After all, women's childbearing capacity is a national asset, and young, sexually active men often opt for freezing their sperm or undergoing a simple vasectomy to control their paternity. Many men choose vasectomies, given that it's the least dangerous and most foolproof form of birth control—as well as the easiest to reverse. Men are screened for chlamydia, human papilloma virus, herpes, and other sexually transmitted diseases during their annual trip to the andrologist. Doctors learn how to detect and treat all of the above, in both men and women. Although the old number of three million or so new cases of STDs each year has dropped to half that amount, STDs are still as common (and about as shameful) as the common cold—and are finally acknowledged as such.

The Equal Rights Amendment has put females in the U.S. Constitution. There are many women of all races in fields or institutions formerly considered to be the province of men, from the Virginia Military Institute and the Citadel to fire departments and airline cockpits. Women are not only free to be as exceptional as men but also as mediocre. Men are as critiqued or praised as women are. Women's salaries have jumped up 26 to 40 percent from pre-equality days to match men's. There are no economic divisions based on race, and the salary categories have been equalized. This categorization is the result of legislation that requires the private sector—even companies that employ fewer than 50 people—to report employees' wages. Many older women are averaging half a million dollars in back pay as a result of the years in which they were unjustly underpaid. Women and men in the NBA make an average of $100,000 per year. Haircuts, dry cleaning, and clothes for women cost the same as they do for men.

The media are accountable to their constituency. Magazines cover stories about congressional hearings on how to help transition men on welfare back into the workforce. Many of these men are single fathers—by choice. Welfare is viewed as a subsidy, just as corporate tax breaks used to be, and receiving government assistance to help rear one's own child is as destigmatized as it is to be paid to rear a foster child. Howard Stern, who gave up his declining radio show to become a stay-at-home granddad, has been replaced on radio by Janeane Garofalo, who no longer jokes primarily about her "back fat" and other perceived imperfections. (Primary caregiving has humanized Stern so that people no longer have to fear for his influence on his offspring.) Leading ladies and leading men are all around the same age. There is always fanfare around *Time* magazine's Person of the Year and *Sports Illustrated*'s coed swimsuit issue. *Rolling Stone* covers female pop stars and music groups in equal numbers with male stars, and women are often photographed for the cover *with* their shirts on. Classic-rock stations play Janis Joplin as often as they play Led Zeppelin.

Women who choose to have babies give birth in a birthing center with a midwife, a hospital with a doctor, or at home with a medicine woman. Paid child-care leave is for four months, and it is required of both parents (if there is more than one). Child rearing is subsidized by a trust not unlike Social Security, a concept pioneered by the welfare-rights activist Theresa Funiciello and based on Gloria Steinem's earlier mandate that every child have a minimum income. The attributed economic value of housework is figured into the gross national product (which increases the United States' GNP by almost 30 percent), and primary caregivers are paid. Whether you work in or out of the home, you are taxed only on your income; married couples and people in domestic partnerships are taxed as individuals, too. When women retire, they get as much Social Security as men do, and all people receive a base amount on which they can live.

The amount of philanthropic dollars going to programs that address or specifically include women and girls is now pushing 60 percent, to make up for all the time it was about 5 percent. More important, these female-centered programs no longer have to provide basic services, because the government does that. All school meals, vaccinations, public libraries, and museums are government-funded and thus available to everybody. Taxpayers have made their wishes clear because more than 90 percent of the electorate actually votes.

"Postmenopausal zest" is as well documented and as anticipated as puberty. Women in their fifties—free from pregnancy, menstruation, and birth control—are regarded as sexpots and envied for their wild and free libidos. "Wine and women," as the saying goes, "get better with age."

Every man and woman remembers exactly where they were the moment they heard that the Equal Rights Amendment passed. The President addressed the nation on the night of that victory and said, "Americans didn't know what we were missing before today . . . until we could truly say that all people are created equal." The first man stood at her side with a tear running down his face.

The social-justice movement, formerly known as feminism, is now just *life*.   [2000]

🌿 150

Voices of Women's Studies Graduates

Real Life: Women's Studies in Action

LORI GROSS

How has my women's studies degree affected my life? Well, it's like magically receiving the gift of an extra sense. In addition to my traditional senses: smell, taste, touch, sight and sound, having a feminist perspective is like being given a new way of experiencing and interacting with the world. It has been a profound and mind-altering experience to integrate this perspective into my life and I am grateful for every bit of it. Learning about history, art, politics, geography and literature from a feminist perspective was like being handed the most delicious and decadent dessert I have ever dreamed of. I could not get enough of it. Learning about how women's lives have shaped our world, about their achievements and the struggles they faced, has given me a new way to measure my own life, my own achievements and struggles.

It has been over ten years since I graduated with my B.A. in women's studies with a concentration in Human Services and Social Change. I have had a number of interesting jobs where my women's studies degree has clearly been a valuable asset. When I was an Activity Leader for a Nursing Home, I was eager to find out about the women's lives and about who they were in their former lives. When I learned what was important to them, it became important to me to acknowledge these things about them and incorporate these details into my interactions with them. I knew many of them had full and interesting lives before Alzheimer's disease or dementia started to take control of their brains. I knew that on some level they would appreciate being honored for the wholeness of their lives. I had a much richer experience in this job than I might have had without my feminist value system.

Another job I had was being a primary child care provider for a little girl from the time she was seven weeks old until she was about a year and a half. I was sort of in between jobs and unsure of where I was on my life's journey. And, as it turned out, this job was one of the most important and meaningful positions I have held. I felt honored to be able to help shape the life of this new being. I rejoiced at every opportunity I had to expose her to the fullest spectrum of experiences, not just activities that our sexist culture deemed gender appropriate. Before she was even a year old, I took her sailing on the Hudson River on a magnificent sailboat called *The Clearwater*, which, by the way, always seemed to have at least one female captain. I took her hiking and showed her cool things like spiders and frogs, and I allowed her to feel and express a full range of emotions. I expected her to be herself and to be respectful of herself and others, not just clean, quiet, and

"nice." In fact, I often encouraged getting messy and making a joyful noise. Before my women studies experience I might have shrugged this job off as simply a way to fill time until a more "important" opportunity arose. Now I know that this work is priceless. Unfortunately, our sexist culture devalues child care and expects women to do essential, life-affirming work for little or no wages.

I am currently a Health Educator for Planned Parenthood of the Mid-Hudson Valley, Inc. I love my job and again I am finding my women's studies degree to be incredibly valuable in my work. My position is wonderful because I have a very broad array of topics that I can teach to groups of many different ages and backgrounds. The topics range from puberty to menopause, communication skills to safer sex, homophobia to self-care. Basically, if it has anything to do with health and wellness, I can create a curriculum for it and teach it. I work in many different settings including: alcohol/substance use rehab centers, public and private schools, domestic violence shelters, hospitals, prisons, and youth centers. I also provide professional staff training for school administrators, nurses, counselors, parents, and human service workers. And, I am fortunate to be able to co-facilitate a weekly meeting for lesbian, gay, bisexual, transgender, and straight teens. I feel that my feminist perspective is essential in my work as a Health Educator and offers me a solid foundation from which to educate others on topics that are often entangled with many sexist and heterosexist value systems. It is wildly fulfilling for me to see the little glimpses of understanding in people's eyes when they are given their first taste of this new sense called feminism.

Bringing Women's Studies to a Battered Women's Shelter

COLLEEN FARRELL

I was in my mid-30s and at a point in my life where I truly felt I was ready to make a change. I returned to college as a women's studies major. That turned out to be the best decision of my life. The curriculum offered through the women's studies program enabled me to see how society's widespread notions, perceptions, and thoughts have had a major impact on my life.

All that I have learned I bring daily to my work as a Domestic Violence Advocate. My women's studies education has helped me to realize that every woman is at risk for becoming a victim of violence. I share with the women with whom I work how violence against women has been accepted and even condoned throughout history. Violence happens regardless of socioeconomic status, race, ethnicity, age, education, sexual orientation, or childhood history. In fact, being female is the only significant risk factor for being a victim of violence. Violence against women is not just a woman's problem. Violence against women is a social problem.

Many of the women who attend the Battered Women's Support Group that I facilitate talk about how they have been called lesbians by their abusers. It is at this time that I explain how society perceives a lesbian as someone who has stepped out of line and how the word lesbian has been used to hurt all women. Many women are also forced to stay in abusive and dangerous relationships because they can't support themselves and their children. My feminist perspective and women's studies background allow me to point out to the members of the support group the common elements of oppressions (sexism, racism, heterosexism, classism, etc.) and how they are linked by economic power and control.

I have also started a newsletter for my co-workers which centers on information about the history of women and women's issues such as heterosexism and sexism, titled "The Lily" (a tribute to the 19th century women's newspaper edited by Amelia Bloomer). And finally, I remind myself every day of the most important lesson I have taken with me from my time as a women's studies major at SUNY New Paltz. Never judge other women too harshly— for they too have traveled a long and difficult road. In order to end the devaluation of women and girls in our culture, we must begin to value other women as well as ourselves.

Becoming a Feminist Physician

SHARON THOMPSON

Over the last few months, I've been interviewing for residency* in obstetrics and gynecology (ob-gyn). At one of these interview sessions, one of the other applicants asked the department chair why there is only one female on the full-time faculty. He responded by explaining that the workload in the department is very demanding. While the department does not penalize its members for their priorities, it also does not make allowances for obligations outside work and requires every member to live up to the expectations and demands of the department.

Left unsaid, but clearly implied, was that women self-select out of the department for other priorities —presumably family. On the surface, this seems a reasonable approach. Everyone is held to a standard which is blind to personal differences. Unexamined are the assumptions that a work environment which precludes outside interests is reasonable and most productive, that priorities for work and family are not affected by gender, and that the added value women would bring to the department is not worth some measure of sacrifice. Uncovering the unspoken assumptions is a key lesson of women's studies.

In a few months, I will receive the Doctorate of Medicine. With it will come great responsibility for promoting and safeguarding health. It will also bring the privilege of entering private, intimate and sacred spaces. With the degree also comes power. Power to change how people feel and how they behave, to shape individual and public opinion. The services I offer, the questions I ask, the way I answer, and the issues I am willing to discuss will all contribute to normalizing certain ideas and behaviors while allowing others to remain taboo. Being realistic and intelligent about power relationships and inequities is another lesson of women's studies.

---

*During residency a new doctor acquires the knowledge and skills specific to a specialty of medicine by working full time in the field.

Being a student of women's studies did not influence my career choice, but it helped shape my values, how I view the world, and what I see as my role in it as an African-American woman. I value women as full members of society in whatever roles they choose. However, I recognize the world as gendered and unequal. I feel that I have a responsibility to change that status quo wherever possible. This has several concrete consequences for my career as an obstetrician gynecologist. I am committed to believing what women tell me, even though it means I will sometimes be wrong. In my practice, I will offer women a full range of reproductive choices including contraception, abortion and maternity care, although it may sometimes be at a risk to myself. I will expect and work to have women represented in whatever setting I may work, although it may mean added responsibility. These values are neither objective nor neutral. But the fallacy of objectivity is another lesson of women's studies.   [2002]

We hope that the many different voices in *Women: Images and Realities* have spoken to you and deepened your understanding of women's experience. While you may not have agreed with everything you read, we hope it has stimulated your thinking. We have tried to do several things in this anthology: demonstrate the commonalities and differences among women, emphasize the power of women talking and working together, stimulate thinking about the ways women of different backgrounds can work together effectively, and, finally, encourage you to participate in the process of improving women's lives. While this book is concluding, we hope your involvement with feminism continues.

Further Readings

PART I: WHAT IS WOMEN'S STUDIES

All the Women Are White, All the Blacks Are Men, But Some of Us Are Brave. Gloria T. Hull, Patricia Bell-Scott, and Barbara Smith, eds. Feminist Press, Old Westbury, NY, 1982.

The American Women's Almanac: An Inspiring and Irreverent Women's History. Louise Bernikow. In association with the National Women's History Project. Berkley Books, New York, 1997.

Changing Our Minds: Feminist Transformation of Knowledge. Susan Aiken, Karen Anderson, Myra Dinnerstein, Judy Note Lensink, and Patricia MacCorquodale, eds. SUNY Press, Albany, NY, 1988.

Feminism and Science. Oxford Readings in Feminism. Evelyn Fox Keller and Helen E. Longino, eds. Oxford University Press, New York, 1996.

Feminist Pedagogy: An Update. Frinde Maher and Nancy Schniedewind, eds. *Women's Studies Quarterly,* Fall/Winter 1993.

Feminist Thought. A Comprehensive Introduction (2nd ed.). Rosemarie Tong. Westview, Boulder, CO, 1998.

Generations: A Century of Women Speak About Their Lives. Myriam Miedziant and Alisa Malinovich, eds. Atlantic Monthly Press, New York, 1997.

The Impact of Feminist Research in the Academy. Christie Farnham, ed. Indiana University Press, Indianapolis, 1987.

Learning About Women: Gender, Politics, and Power. Jill K. Conway, Susan C. Bourque, and Joan W. Scott, eds. University of Michigan Press, Ann Arbor, 1989.

Life Notes: Personal Writings by Contemporary Black Women. Patricia Bell-Scott, ed. Norton, New York, 1994.

Myths of Gender: Biological Theories of Women and Men. Anne Fausto-Sterling. Basic Books, New York, 1992.

The New Lesbian Studies Into the Twenty-First Century. Toni A. H. McNaron, Bonnie Zimmerman. The Feminist Press, New York, 1996.

On Lies, Secrets and Silence: Selected Prose. Adrienne Rich. Norton, New York, 1979.

The Politics of Women's Studies: Testimony from 30 Founding Mothers, Florence Howe, ed. Feminist Press, New York, 2000.

Reflections on Gender and Science. Evelyn Fox Keller. Yale University Press, New Haven, CT, 1985.

Talking Back: Thinking Feminist, Thinking Black. bell hooks. South End Press, Boston, 1989.

Talking Gender: Public Images, Personal Journeys and Political Critiques. Nancy Hewitt, Jean O'Barr, and Nancy Rosebaugh, eds. University of North Carolina Press, Chapel Hill, 1996.

Thinking Feminist: Key Concepts in Women's Studies. Diane Richardson and Victoria Robinson, eds. Guilford, New York, 1993.

Transforming the Curriculum: Ethnic Studies and Women's Studies. Johnella Butler and John Walter. SUNY Press, Albany, NY, 1991.

Transforming the Disciplines: A Women's Studies Primer. Elizabeth L. MacNabb et al. Haworth Press, New York, 2001.

Questions of Gender: Perspectives and Paradoxes. Dina L. Anselmi and Anne L. Law. McGraw-Hill, New York, 1998.

Women's Studies International. Aruna Rao, ed. Feminist Press, New York, 1991.

Women's Studies in the South. Rhoda E. Barge Johnson, ed. Kendall/Hunt, Dubuque, IA, 1991.

PART II: BECOMING A WOMAN IN OUR SOCIETY

Dominant Ideas About Women

Allegra Maud Goldman. Edith Konecky. The Feminist Press, New York, 2001.

Cuentos: Stories by Latinas. Alma Gomez, Cherrie Moraga, and Mariann Roma-Carmona, eds. Kitchen Table Press, New York, 1983.

Daughters of Sorrow: Attitudes Towards Black Women 1880–1920. Beverly Guy-Sheftall. Carlsen, Brooklyn, 1990.

Disfigured Images: The Historical Assault on Afro-American Women. Patricia Morton. Greenwood, New York, 1991.

Gender Shock: Exploding the Myths of Male and Female. Phyllis Burke. Anchor, New York, 1996.

Gender: Stereotypes and Roles (3rd ed.). Susan A. Basow. Wadsworth, Belmont, CA, 1992.

Girls Speak Out: Finding Your True Self. Andrea Johnston. Scholastic Press, New York, 1997.

Our Feet Walk the Sky: Women of the South Asian Diaspora. Women of South Asian Descent Collective, ed. Aunt Lute Books, San Francisco, 1993.

Learning Gender

AAUW Report: How Schools Shortchange Girls. American Association of University Women, Washington, DC, 1993.

Body Politics: Power, Sex and Non-Verbal Communication. Nancy Henley. Prentice-Hall, Englewood Cliffs, NJ, 1977.

Cecelia Reclaimed: Feminist Perspectives on Gender and Music. Susan Cook and Judy Tsou. University of Illinois Press, Urbana, 1994.

The Chilly Classroom Climate: A Guide to Improve the Education of Women. Bernice Sandler, Lisa Silverberg, and Roberta Hall. National Association for Women in Education, Washington, DC, 1996.

Educated in Romance: Women, Achievement and College Culture. Dorothy Holland. University of Chicago Press, Chicago, 1990.

Failing at Fairness: How America's Schools Cheat Girls. Myra and David Sadker, Scribners, New York, 1994.

From Reverence to Rape: The Treatment of Women in the Movies. Molly Haskell. University of Chicago Press, Chicago, 1987.

Gender and Non-Verbal Behavior. Nancy Henley and Clara Mayo. Springer, New York, 1981.

Gender, Race and Class in the Media. Gail Dines and Jean Humez, eds. Sage, Thousand Oaks, CA, 1995.

Gendered Lives: Communication, Gender and Culture. Julia Wood. Wadsworth, Belmont, CA, 1994.

Language, Gender, and Society. Nancy Henley, Charise Kramarae, and Barrie Thorne. Newbury House, Rowley, MA, 1983.

Man Made Language. Dale Spender. Routledge, Kegan, Paul, Boston, 1985.

"Media Images, Feminist Issues." Deborah Rhode. *Signs: A Journal of Women and Culture,* vol. 20, no. 3, pp. 685–710, 1995.

Media-tions: Forays into the Culture and Gender Wars. Elayne Rapping. South End, Boston, 1994.

"Missing Voices: Women in the U.S. News Media." Special issue of *Extra,* New York, 1982.

Prime Time Feminism: Television, Media Culture and the Women's Movement Since 1970. Bonnie Dow. University of Pennsylvania Press, Philadelphia, 1996.

Putting on Appearances: Gender and Advertising. Diane Barthel. Temple University Press, Philadelphia, 1988.

"Redesigning Women." Special issue of *Media and Values*, no. 49, Winter 1989.

Representing Women: Myths of Femininity in the Popular Media. Myra McDonald. St. Martin's, New York, 1995.

Schoolgirls: Young Women, Self-Esteem, and the Confidence Gap. Peggy Orenstein. Doubleday, New York, 1994.

"Secrets in Public: Sexual Harassment in Our Schools." Nan Stein, Nancy Marshall, and Linda Tropp. Center for Research on Women, Wellesley, MA, 1993.

What's Wrong with This Picture? The Status of Women on Screen and Behind the Camera in Entertainment TV. Sally Steenland. National Commission on Working Women of Wider Opportunities for Women, Los Angeles, 1990.

You Just Don't Understand: Women and Men in Conversation. Deborah Tannen. Ballantine, New York, 1990.

PART III: GENDER AND WOMEN'S BODIES

Female Beauty

Am I Thin Enough Yet? The Cult of Thinness and the Commercialization of Identity. Sharlene Hesse-Biber. Oxford University Press, New York, 1996.

Beauty Myth: How Images of Beauty Are Used Against Women, Anchor Books, New York, 1992.

The Bluest Eye. Toni Morrison. Random House, New York, 1970.

Bodymakers: A Cultural Anthology of Women's Body Building. Leslie Heywood. Rutgers University Press, Piscataway, NJ, 1998.

Body Outlaws. Young Women Write about Body Image and Identity. Ophira Edut, ed. Seal Press, Seattle, WA, 2000.

Eating Our Hearts Out: Personal Accounts of Women's Relationship to Food. Lesléa Newman. Crossing Press, Freedom, CA, 1993.

Generations: A Memoir. Lucille Clifton. Random House, New York, 1976.

The Power of Beauty. Nancy Friday. HarperCollins, New York, 1996.

In Search of Our Mothers' Gardens. Alice Walker. Harcourt Brace Jovanovich, New York, 1983.

The Third Woman. Dexter Fisher, ed. Houghton Mifflin, Boston, 1980.

The Tribe of Dina: A Jewish Women's Anthology. Melanie Kaye Kantrowitz and Irena Klepfisz, eds. Sinister Wisdom, Montpelier, VT, 1986.

Sexuality and Relationships

"Bad Girls"/"Good Girls": Women, Sex, and Power in the Nineties. Nan Bauer Maglin and Donna Perry, eds. Rutgers University Press, New Brunswick, NJ, 1996.

Bi Lives. Bisexual Women Tell Their Stories. Kata Orndorff, ed. See Sharp Press, Tucson, AZ, 1999.

Closer to Home: Bisexuality and Feminism. Elizabeth Reba Weise, ed. Seal Press, Seattle, WA, 1992.

Embracing the Fire: Sisters Talk About Sex and Relationships. Julia Boyd. Dutton, New York, 1997.

Gorilla My Love. Toni Cade Bambara. Random House, New York, 1972.

Flirting with Danger. Young Women's Reflections on Sexuality and Domination. Lynn M. Phillips. New York University Press, New York, 2000.

Frictions II: Stories by Women. Rhea Tregebov, ed. Second Story Press, Toronto, 1993.

The Hand I Fan With. Tina McElroy Ansa. Anchor, New York, 1996.

Her Way: Young Women Remake the Sexual Revolution. Paula Kamen. New York University Press, New York, 2000.

Gendered Relationships. Julia T. Wood, ed. Mayfield, Mountain View, CA, 1996.

Invisible Lives: The Erasure of Transsexual and Transgendered People. Viviane K. Namaste. University of Chicago Press, Chicago, 2000.

Latina Realities: Essays on Healing, Migration, and Sexuality. Olivia M. Espin. Westview, Boulder, CO, 1997.

Men We Cherish: African American Women Praise the Men in Their Lives. Brooke Stephens, ed. Anchor, New York, 1997.

The Politics of Women's Bodies: Sexuality, Appearance, and Behavior. Rose Weitz, ed. Oxford University Press, New York, 1998.

Sexing the Body: Gender Politics and the Construction of Sexuality. Anne Fausto-Sterling. Basic Books, New York, 2000.

Sex Is Not a Natural Act and Other Essays. Leonore Tiefer. Westview, Boulder, CO, 1994.

Stolen Women: Reclaiming Our Sexuality, Taking Back Our Lives. Gail E. Wyatt. Wiley, New York, 1997.

Troubling the Angels: Women Living with HIV/AIDS. Patti Lather and Chris Smithies. Westview, Boulder, CO, 1997.

With the Power of Each Breath: A Disabled Woman's Anthology. Susan E. Browne, Debra Connors, and Nancy Stern, eds. Cleis, Pittsburgh, 1985.

Women on Top. Nancy Friday. Pocket Books, New York, 1991.

PART IV: INSTITUTIONS THAT SHAPE WOMEN'S LIVES

Women and Work

9to5 Guide for Combatting Sexual Harassment. Ellen Bravo, Ellen Cassidy. 9to5, Milwaukee, WI, 1999.

The Endless Day: The Political Economy of Women and Work. Bettina Berch. Harcourt Brace Jovanovich, New York, 1982.

Black Women in the Labor Force. Phyllis Wallace with Linda Datcher and Julianne Malveaux. MIT Press, Cambridge, MA, 1980.

Between Feminism and Labor: The Significance of the Comparable Worth Movement. Linda Blum. University of California Press, Berkeley, 1991.

Black Women in the Workplace: Impacts of Structural Change in the Economy. Bette Woody. Greenwood Press, New York, 1992.

The Economics of Women, Men and Work, 4th edition. Francine Blau, Marianne A. Ferber, Anne E. Winkler. Prentice Hall, Saddle River, NJ, 2000.

Fetal Rights, Women's Rights: Gender Equality in the Workplace. Suzanne Uttaro Samuels. University of Wisconsin, Madison, 1995.

For Crying Out Loud: Women's Poverty in the United States. Diane Dujon and Ann Withorn, eds. South End, Boston, 1996.

Glass Ceilings and Bottomless Pits: Women's Work, Women's Poverty. Randy Albelda and Chris Tilly. South End Press, Boston, 1997.

Keeping Jobs and Raising Families in Low-Income America: It Just Doesn't Work. Linda Dodson, Tiffany Manuel and Ellen Bravo. Radcliffe Institute for Advanced Study, Harvard University, Cambridge, MA, 2002.

Keeping Women and Children Last: America's War on the Poor. Ruth Sidel. Penguin, New York, 1996.

Making Ends Meet: How Single Mothers Survive Welfare and Low Wage Work. Kathryn Edin. Russell Sage, New York, 1997.

Mexicanas at Work in the United States. Margarita Melville. Mexican American Studies Program, University of Houston, Houston, 1988.

Never Done: A History Of American Housework. Susan Strasser. Pantheon, New York, 1982.

New Field Guide to the U.S. Economy. Nancy Folbre. New Press, New York, 1995.

Nickled and Dimed, On (Not) Getting by in America. Barbara Ehrenreich. Henry Holt, New York, 2001.

Puerto Rican Women and Work: Bridges in Transnational Labor. Altagracia Ortiz, ed. Temple, Philadelphia, 1996.

Tyranny of Kindness: Dismantling the Welfare System to End Poverty in America. Theresa Funicello. Atlantic Monthly Press, New York, 1993.

Race, Gender and Work: A Multicultural Economic History of Women in the United States. Theresa Amott and Julie Matthaei. South End, Boston, 1996.

We'll Call You If We Need You: Experiences of Women Working Construction. Susan Eisenberg. ILR Press, Ithaca, NY, 1998.

With Silk Wings: Asian American Women at Work. Elaine Kim and Janice Otani. Asian Women United of California, Oakland, 1983.

Women, the Law, and Social Policy

Alchemy of Race and Rights: Diary of a Law Professor. Patricia Williams. Harvard University Press, Cambridge, MA, 1991.

Black Women and the New World Order: Social Justice and the African American Female. Willa Mae Hemmons. Praeger, Westport, CT, 1996.

Feminist Legal Theory: Readings in Law and Gender. Katharine T. Bartlett and Rosanne Kennedy, eds. Westview, Boulder, CO, 1991.

Law, Gender, and Injustice: A Legal History of U.S. Women. Joan Hoff. New York University Press, New York, 1991.

Mothers in Law: Feminist Theory and the Legal Regulation of Motherhood. Martha Fineman and Isabel Karpin, eds. Columbia University Press, New York, 1995.

The Politics of Parenthood: Child Care, Women's Rights and the Myth of the Good Mother. Mary Frances Berry. Viking, New York, 1993.

The Price of Motherhood: Why the Most Important Job in the World Is Still the Least Valued. Ann Crittenden. Henry Holt & Co., New York, 2001.

The Rights of Women: The Basic ACLU Guide to Women's Rights. Susan Deller Ross. Southern Illinois University Press, Carbondale, IL, 1993.

Sex and Power. Susan Estrich. Riverhead Books, New York, 2000.

Women's Rights and the Law. Laura Otten. Praeger, Westport, CT, 1993.

Under Attack, Fighting Back: Women and Welfare in the United States. Mimi Abramovitz. Monthly Review Press, New York, 1996.

Welfare's End. Gwendolyn Mink. Cornell University Press, Ithaca, NY, 1998.

Women and the Family

All Our Families: New Policies for a New Century. Mary Ann Mason, Arlene Skolnick, and Stephen Sugarman, eds. University of California Press, Berkeley, 1998.

The Autobiography of My Mother. Jamaica Kincaid. Plume, New York, 1997.

Bearing Life: Women's Writings on Childlessness. Rochelle Ratner, ed. Feminist Press, New York, 2000.

Beyond the Traditional Family: Voices of Diversity. Betty Polisar Reigot and Rita Spina, eds. Springer, New York, 1996.

Black Mothers and Daughters: Their Roles and Functions in American Society. Gloria Joseph. Doubleday, New York, 1981.

Considering Parenthood: A Workbook for Lesbians. Stacey Pes. Spinsters Ink, San Francisco, 1985.

A Family Affair: The Real Lives of Black Single Mothers. Barbara Omalade. Kitchen Table Press, Latham, NY, 1986.

Families in Cultural Context: Strengths and Challenges in Diversity. Mary Kay DeGenova, ed. Mayfield, Mountain View, CA, 1997.

Farewell to Manzanar. Jeann Wakatsuki Houston. Bantam, New York, 1974.

The Impossibility of Motherhood. Feminism, Individualism and the Problem of Mothering. Patrice Diquinzio. Routledge, New York, 1999.

I've Always Wanted to Tell You: Letters to Our Mothers: An Anthology of Contemporary Women Writers. Constance Warloeed. Pocket Books, New York, 1997.

The Job-Family Challenge. Ellen Bravo. Wiley, New York, 1995.

The Joy Luck Club. Amy Tan. Putnam, New York, 1989.

Motherguilt: How Our Culture Blames Mothers for What's Wrong with Society. Diane Eyer. Random House, New York, 1996.

A Mother's Place: Taking the Debate About Motherhood Beyond Guilt and Blame. Susan Chira. HarperCollins, New York, 1998.

Of Woman Born: Motherhood as Experience and Institution. Adrienne Rich. Norton, New York, 1986.

Politics of the Heart: A Lesbian Parenting Anthology. Sandra Pollack and Jeanne Vaughn, eds. Firebrand, Ithaca, NY, 1987.

Rethinking the Family: Some Feminist Questions. Barrie Thorne with Marilyn Yalom, ed. Northeastern University Press, Boston, 1992.

The Way We Never Were: American Families and the Nostalgia Trap. Stephanie Coontz. Basic Books, Austin, TX, 2000.

Women Living Single: Thirty Women Share Their Stories of Navigating Through a Married World. Faber & Faber, Boston, 1996.

Women and Religion

Beyond God the Father: Toward a Philosophy of Women's Liberation. Mary Daly. Beacon, Boston, 1973.

The Church and the Second Sex. Mary Daly. Beacon, Boston, 1985.

Daughters of Thunder: Black Women Preachers and Their Sermons, 1850–1979. Betty Collier-Thomas. Jossey-Bass, San Francisco, CA, 1998.

Fundamentalism and the Human Rights of Women. Courtney Howland, ed. St. Martins, New York, 1999.

Gender and Judaism: The Transformation of Tradition. T. M. Rudavsky, ed. New York University Press, New York, 1995.

I Asked for Intimacy: Stories of Blessings, Betrayals and Birthings. Renita J. Weems. Lura Media, San Diego, CA, 1994.

My Soul Is a Witness: African American Spirituality. Gloria Wade-Gayles. Beacon, Boston, 1995.

Religion and Women. Arvind Sharma, ed. SUNY Press, Albany, NY, 1994.

Sexism and God-Talk: Toward a Feminist Theology. Rosemary Radford Ruether. Beacon, Boston, 1983.

Wise Women: Over 2,000 Years of Spiritual Writing by Women. Susan Cahill, ed. Norton, New York, 1996.

Women and Fundamentalism: Islam and Christianity. Shahin Gerami. Garland, New York, 1996.

Women and Goddess Traditions, in Antiquity and Today. Karen King, ed. Fortress, Minneapolis, 1997.

PART V: HEALTH AND REPRODUCTIVE FREEDOM

The Health Care System

1 in 3: Women with Cancer Confront an Epidemic. Judith Brady, ed. Cleis Press Inc., Pittsburgh, 1991.

Alive and Well: A Lesbian Health Guide. Circe Hepburn. Crossing Press, Freedom, CA, 1988.

The Black Women's Health Book: Speaking for Ourselves. Evelyn C. White, ed. Seal Press, Seattle, 1990.

Body and Soul: The Black Women's Guide to Physical Health and Emotional Well-Being. Linda Villarosa, ed. Harper Perennial, New York, 1994.

Breast Cancer: Society Shapes an Epidemic. Anne E. Kasper and Susan J. Ferguson, eds. St. Martin's Press, New York, 2000.

The Cancer Journals. Audre Lorde. Spinsters Ink, Argyles, NY, 1980.

The Gender Politics of HIV/AIDS in Women: Perspectives on the Pandemic in the United States. Nancy Goldstein and Jennifer L. Manlowe, eds. New York University Press, New York, 1997.

Living Downstream. Sandra Steingraber. Addison-Wesley Publishing Company, Inc., Reading, MA, 1997.

Living on the Margins: Women Writers on Breast Cancer. Hilda Raz, ed. R. R. Donnelly & Company, New York, 1999.

Manmade Breast Cancers. Zillah Eisenstein. Cornell University Press, Ithaca, NY, 2001.

Our Bodies, Ourselves for the New Century: A Book by and for Women. The Boston Women's Health Book Collective. Simon & Schuster, New York, 1998.

Patient No More: The Politics of Breast Cancer. Sharon Batt, Gynergy Books, Charlottetown, P. E. I., Canada, 1994.

The Politics of Breast Cancer. Maureen Hogan Casamayou. Georgetown University Press, Washington, DC, 2001.

River of Tears: The Politics of Black Women's Health Care. Delores S. Aldridge and La Frances Rodgers-Rose. Traces Publishing, Newark, NJ, 1993.

Sisters of the Yam: Black Women and Self Recovery. bell hooks. South End, Boston, 1993.

Vamps, Virgins and Victims: How Can Women Fight AIDS? Robin Gorna. Cassell, London, 1996.

What Makes Women Sick: Gender and the Political Economy of Health. Leslie Doyal, Rutgers University Press, New Brunswick, NJ, 1995.

Women and AIDS: Negotiating Safer Practices, Care and Representation. Nancy Roth and Linda Fuller, eds. Haworth, Binghamton, NY, 1998.

Women and Madness. Phyllis Chesler. Doubleday, Garden City, NY, 1972.

Reproductive Freedom

Abortion Wars: A Half Century of Struggle, 1950–2000. Rickie Solinger, ed. University of California Press, Berkeley, 1998.

Abortion Without Apology: Radical History for the 1990s. Ninia Baehr. South End Press, Boston, 1990.

Abortion and the Politics of Motherhood. Kristin Luker. University of California Press, Berkeley, 1984.

Beggars and Choosers: How the Politics of Choice Shapes Adoption, Abortion and Welfare in the United States. Rickie Solinger. Hill and Wang, New York, 2001.

Birth or Abortion? Private Struggles in a Political World. Kate Maloy and Maggie Jones Patterson. Plenum, New York, 1992.

The Choices We Made: 25 Women and Men Speak Out About Abortion. Angela Bonavoglia. Random House, New York, 1991.

Feminist Approaches to Bioethics: Theoretical Reflections and Practical Applications. Rosemarie Tong. Westview, Boulder, CO, 1996.

From Abortion to Reproductive Freedom. Marlene Gerber Fried, ed. South End, Boston, 1990.

Killing the Black Body: Race, Reproduction, and the Meaning of Liberty. Dorothy Roberts. Pantheon, New York, 1997.

Negotiating Reproductive Rights: Women's Perspectives across Countries and Cultures. Rosalind P. Petchesky and Karen Judd, eds. Zed Books, London and New York, 1998.

A Question of Choice. Sarah Weddington. Putnam, New York, 1992.

Reproductive Rights and Wrongs: The Global Politics of Population Control and Contraceptive Choice. Betsy Hartmann. Harper & Row, New York, 1987.

Roe v. Wade, cite as 93 s.ct. 705 (1973). Jane Roe, et al., appellants, v. Henry Wade, no. 70-18. Argued Dec. 13, 1971. Reargued Oct. 11, 1972. Decided Jan. 22, 1973. Supreme Court reporter.

Taking Chances: Abortion and the Decision Not to Contracept. Kristin Luker. University of California Press, Berkeley, 1975.

PART VI: THE DIFFERENCES AMONG US: DIVISIONS AND CONNECTIONS

Afrikete, An Anthology of Black Lesbian Writing. Catherine McKinley and Joyce DeLaney, eds. Doubleday, New York, 1995.

All American Women: Lines That Divide, Ties That Bind. Johnetta Cole, ed. Free Press, New York, 1986.

American Indian Women: Telling Their Lives. Gretchen M. Bataille and Kathleen Mullen Sand. University of Nebraska Press, Lincoln, NE, 1984.

Asian and Pacific American Experiences: Women's Perspectives. Nobuya Tsuchida, Linda Mealey, and Gail Thoen, eds. Asian/Pacific American Learning Resource Center and General College, University of Minnesota, Minneapolis, 1982.

Borderlands/La Frontera. Gloria Anzaldua. Spinsters/Aunt Lute, San Francisco, 1987.

Calling Home: Working Class Women's Writings: An Anthology. Janet Zandy, ed. Rutgers University Press, New Brunswick, NJ, 1990.

Daughter of Earth. Agnes Smedley. Feminist Press, Old Westbury, NY, 1973.

Farewell to Manzanar. Jeanne Wakatsuki Houston. Bantam, New York, 1994.

Food for Our Grandmothers. Joanna Kadi. South End, Boston, 1994.

The Forbidden Stitch: An Asian American Women's Anthology. Shirley Geok-Lin Lim, Mauyumi Tsutakawa, and Margarita Donnely, eds. Calyx Books, Corvalis, OR, 1989.

Homophobia: A Weapon of Sexism. Suzanne Pharr. Chardon, Little Rock, AR, 1988.

Getting Over Getting Older. Letty Cottin Pogrebin. Berkley, New York, 1996.

I Am Your Sister: Women Organizing Across Sexualities. Audre Lorde. Kitchen Table Press, Latham, NY, 1986.

Look Me in the Eye: Old Women, Aging, and Ageism. Barbara MacDonald and Cynthia Rich. Spinsters Ink, San Francisco, 1983.

Making Face, Making Soul: Creative and Critical Perspectives by Women of Color. Gloria Anzaldua, ed. Aunt Lute Books, San Francisco, 1990.

Making More Waves: An Anthology of Writings by and about Asian American Women. Elaine Kim, ed. Beacon, Boston, 1997.

Medicine Stories. Aurora Levins Morales. South End Press, Boston, 1998.

Names We Call Home: Autobiography on Racial Identity. Becky Thompson and Sangeeta Tyagi, eds. Routledge, New York, 1996.

Nice Jewish Girls: A Lesbian Anthology. Evelyn Torton Beck, ed. Beacon, Boston, 1989.

Off the Reservation: Reflections on Boundary-Busting, Border-Crossing Loose Cannons. Paula Gunn Allen. Beacon, Boston, 1998.

The Other Within Us: Feminist Explorations of Women and Aging. Marilyn Pearsall, ed. Westview, Boulder, CO, 1997.

Ourselves, Growing Older: Women Aging with Knowledge and Power. Paula Doress, Diana Laskin Siegal, Midlife and Older Women Book Project, and Boston Women's Health Book Collective. Simon & Schuster, New York, 1987.

Our Feet Walk the Sky: Women of the South Asian Diaspora. Women of South Asian Descent Collective. Aunt Lute Books, San Francisco, 1993.

A Patchwork Shawl: Chronicles of South Asian Women in America. Shamita Das Dasgupta, ed. Rutgers University Press, New Brunswick, NJ, 1998.

Race, Class, Gender, and Sexuality: The Big Questions. Naomi Zack, Laurie Schrage, and Crispin Sartwell. Blackwell Publishers, Malden, MA, 1998.

Race, Class and Gender: Common Bonds, Different Voices. Esther Ngan-ling Chow, Doris Wilkinson, and Maxine Baca Zinn. Sage, Thousand Oaks, CA, 1996.

The Sacred Hoop: Recovering the Feminine in American Indian Tradition. Paula Gunn Allen. Beacon, Boston, 1986.

Skin: Talking about Sex, Class and Literature. Dorothy Allison. Firebrand, Ithaca, NY, 1994.

Teaching for Diversity and Social Justice: A Sourcebook. Maurianne Adams, Lee Anne Bell, and Pat Griffin, eds. Routledge, New York, 1997.

That's What She Said: Contemporary Poetry and Fiction by Native American Women. Rayna Green, ed. Indiana University Press, Bloomington, 1984.

The Things That Divide Us. Faith Conlon, ed. Seal Press, Seattle, 1985.

The Tribe of Dina: A Jewish Women's Anthology. Melanie Kaye/Kantrowitz and Irena Klepfisz, eds. Beacon, Boston, 1986.

This Bridge Called My Back: Writings by Radical Women of Color. Cherrie Moraga and Gloria Anzaldua. Peresephone, Watertown, MA, 1981.

Tish Sommers, Activist, and the Founding of the Older Women's League. Patricia Huckle and Tish Sommers. University of Tennessee Press, Knoxville, TN, 1991.

Wearing Purple: Four Longtime Friends Celebrate the Joys and Challenges of Growing Older. Lydia Lewis Alexander, Marilyn Hill Harper, Otis Holloway Owens, and Mildred Lucas Peterson. Berkley, New York, 1996.

The Wedding. Dorothy West. Anchor, New York, 1995.

White Women, Race Matters: The Social Construction of Whiteness. Ruth Frankenberg, University of Minnesota Press, Minneapolis, MN, 1993.

Why Are all the Black Kids Sitting Together in the Cafeteria and Other Conversations About Race. Beverly Daniel Tatum. Basic Books, New York, 1997.

With Wings: An Anthology of Literature by and About Women with Disabilities. Marsha Saxton and Florence Howe, eds. Feminist Press, New York, 1987.

Women of Color in U.S. Society. Maxine Baca Zinn and Bonnie Thornton Dill, eds., Temple University Press, Philadelphia, 1995.

Worlds of Pain: Life in the Working Class Family. Lillian Breslow Rubin, Basic Books, New York, 1992.

PART VII: VIOLENCE AGAINST WOMEN

Violence Against Women in Intimate Relationships

Battered Wives. Del Martin. Glide, San Francisco, 1976.

Chain, Chain, Change: For Black Women Dealing with Physical and Emotional Abuse. Evelyn C. White. Seal Press, Seattle, 1985.

Compelled to Crime: The Gender Entrapment of Battered Black Women. Beth Ritchie. Routledge Press, New York, 1996.

For the Latina in an Abusive Relationship. Myrna Zambrano. Seal Press, Seattle, 1983.

Getting Away With Murder: Weapons for the War Against Domestic Violence. Raoul Felder and Barbara Victor. Simon & Schuster, New York, 1996.

Getting Free: A Handbook for Women in Abusive Relationships. Ginny NiCarthy. Seal Press, Seattle, 1986.

Heroes of Their Own Lives: The Politics and History of Family Violence, Boston, 1880–1960. Linda Gordon. Viking, New York, 1988.

No Safe Haven: Male Violence Against Women at Home, at Work, and in the Community. Mary Koss. American Psychological Association, Washington, DC, 1994.

Women and Male Violence: The Visions and Struggles of the Battered Women's Movement. Susan Schechter. South End, Boston, 1982.

Women at Risk: Domestic Violence and Women's Health. Evan Stark and Anne Flitcraft. Sage, Thousand Oaks, CA, 1996.

Sexual Violence and Rape

Acquaintance Rape: The Hidden Crime. Andrea Parrot and Laurie Bechhofer. Wiley, New York, 1991.

Against Our Will: Men, Women, and Rape. Susan Brownmiller. Simon & Schuster, New York, 1975.

Fraternity Gang Rape. Peggy Sanday. New York University Press, New York, 1990.

Incest, Work and Women: Understanding the Consequences of Incest on Women's Careers, Work and Dreams. LeslieBeth Berger. Charles C. Thomas, Springfield, IL, 1998.

I Never Called It Rape. Robin Warshaw and Mary P. Koss. Harper & Row, New York, 1988.

The Politics of Survivorship: Incest, Women's Literature, and Feminist Theory. Rosaria Champagne, New York University Press, New York, 1996.

Sexual Assault on Campus: The Problem and the Solution. Carol Bohmer and Andrea Parrot. Lexington, New York, 1993.

Surviving the Silence. Black Women's Stories of Rape. Charlotte Pierce-Baker. Norton, New York, 1998.

There Were Times I Thought I Was Crazy. A Black Woman's Story of Incest. Vanessa Alleyne, Sister Vision: Black Women and Women of Color Press, Toronto, Canada, 1997.

Transforming a Rape Culture. Emelie Buchwald, Pamela Fletcher, and Martha Roth, eds. Milkweed, Minneapolis, MN, 1993.

Warrior Marks: Female Genital Mutilation and the Sexual Blinding of Women. Alice Walker and Pratibha Parmar. Harcourt Brace, New York, 1993.

A Woman Scorned: Acquaintance Rape on Trial. Peggy Reeves Sanday, Doubleday, New York, 1996.

Incestuous Sexual Abuse

Bad Girls/Good Girls. Nan Bauer Maglin and Donna Perry, eds. Rutgers University Press, New Brunswick, NJ, 1996.

Betrayal Trauma: The Logic of Forgetting Childhood Abuse. Jennifer Freyd. Harvard University Press, Cambridge, MA, 1996.

The Courage to Heal. Ellen Bass and Laura Davis. Harper & Row, New York, 1988.

Crossing the Boundary: Black Women Survive Incest. Melba Wilson. Seal Press, Seattle, 1994.

Rocking the Cradle of Sexual Politics: What Happened When Women Said Incest. Louise Armstrong. Addison-Wesley Publishing Co., Reading, MA, 1994.

Secret Survivors: Uncovering Incest and Its Aftereffects in Women. Sue E. Blume. Wiley, New York, 1990.

The Secret Trauma: Incest in the Lives of Girls and Women. Diana E. H. Russell. Basic, New York, 1984.

Voices in the Night: Women Speaking About Incest. Toni A. H. McNaron and Yarrow Margan. Cleis, Minneapolis, MN, 1982.

PART VIII: CHANGING OUR WORLD

Feminism as a Social Movement

African American Women in the Struggle for the Vote 1850–1920. Rosalyn Terborg-Penn. University of Indiana Press, Bloomington, 1998.

Ain't I a Woman: Black Women and Feminism. bell hooks. South End, Boston, 1981.

Black Feminism and the Politics of Respectability. Frances E. White, Temple University Press, Philadelphia, 2001.

Black Feminist Thought: Knowledge, Consciousness and the Politics of Empowerment. Patricia Hill Collins. Unwin Hyman, Boston, 1990.

Century of Struggle. Eleanor Flexner. Athenaeum, New York, 1972.

The Challenge of Local Feminisms. Amrita Basu, ed. Westview, Boulder, CO, 1995.

Changing Our Lives: Lesbian Passions, Politics and Priorities. Veronica Groocock. Cassell, London, 1995.

Chicana Feminist Thought: The Basic Historical Writings. Alma Garcia, ed. Routledge, New York, 1997.

Dear Sisters: Dispatches from the Women's Liberation Movement, Rosalyn Baxandall and Linda Gordon, eds. Basic Books, New York, 2000.

Dragon Ladies: Asian American Feminists Breathe Fire. Sonia Shah, ed. South End, Cambridge, 1997.

Feminism Is for Everybody: Passionate Politics. bell hooks. South End Press, Cambridge, 2000.

Feminism in Our Time: The Essential Writings, WWII to the Present. Miriam Schneir, ed. Random House, New York, 1994.

Feminist Locations: Global and Local Theory and Practice. Marianne De Koven. Rutgers University Press. New Brunswick, NJ, 2001.

The Feminist Papers: From Adams to De Beauvoir. Alice Rossi. Northeastern University Press, Boston, 1988.

Freedom from Violence: Women's Strategies From Around the World. Margaret Schuler, ed. OEF International Unifem, New York, 1992.

A Girl's Guide to Taking over the World: Writings From the Girl Zine Revolution. Karen Green and Tristan Taormino, eds. St. Martin Griffin, New York, 1997.

Home Girls: A Black Feminist Anthology. Barbara Smith, ed. Kitchen Table Press, Latham, NY, 1983.

In Our Time: Memoir of a Revolution. Susan Brownmiller. The Dial Press, New York, 1999.

Listen Up: Voices From the Next Feminist Generation. Barbara Findlen. Seal Press, Seattle, 2001.

Living Chicana Theory. Carla Trujillo, ed. Third Woman Press, Berkeley, CA, 1998.

Ours By Right: Women's Rights as Human Rights. Joanna Kerr, ed. Zed, New York, 1993.

Sisterhood Is Global: The First Anthology of Writings from the International Women's Movement. Robin Morgan, ed. Anchor Press/Doubleday, Garden City, NY, 1984.

Tales of the Lavender Menace, A Memoir of Liberation. Karla Jay. Viking, New York, 1999.

Talking Visions: Multicultural Feminism in a Transnational Age. Ella Shohat, ed. LOGO, New York, 1999.

Third Wave Agenda: Being Feminist, Doing Feminism. Leslie Heywood and Jennifer Drake, eds. University of Minnesota Press, Minneapolis, 1997.

Third World Women and the Politics of Feminism. Chandra Mohanty, Ann Russo and Lourdes Torres. Indiana University Press, Bloomington, IN, 1991.

To Be Real: Telling the Truth and Changing the Face of Feminism. Rebecca Walker. Doubleday, New York, 1995.

Words of Fire: An Anthology of African-American Feminist Thought. Beverly Guy-Sheftall, ed. New Press, New York, 1995.

The World Split Open: How the Modern Women's Movement Changed America. Ruth Rosen. Viking, New York, 2000.

Women Organizing: Many Issues, Many Voices

Bridges of Power: Women's Multicultural Alliances. Lisa Albrecht and Rose Brewer. New Society Publishers, Philadelphia, 1990.

Community Activism and Feminist Politics: Organizing Across Race, Class and Gender. Nancy Naples, ed. Routledge, New York, 1998.

Earth Follies: Coming to Feminist Terms With the Global Environmental Crisis. Joan Seager. Routledge, New York, 1993.

Ecofeminism. Maria Mies and Vandana Shiva. Zed Books, London, 1993.

Feminist Fatale. Paula Kamin. Fine, New York, 1991.

Fighting Words: Black Women and the Search for Justice. Patricia Hill Collins, University of Minnesota Press, Minneapolis, 1998.

Frontline Feminism 1975–1995: Essays from Sojourner's First Twenty Years. Karen Cahn, ed. Aunt Lute Books, San Francisco, 1995.

National Congress of Neighborhood Women Training Sourcebook. Neighborhood Women, Brooklyn, NY, 1993.

No Middle Ground: Women and Radical Protest. Kathleen M. Blee, ed. New York University Press, New York, 1998.

Passionate Politics. Charlotte Bunch, St. Martin's Press, New York, 1987.

Peace as a Women's Issue: A History of the U.S. Movement for World Peace and Women's Rights. Harriet Alonso. Syracuse University Press, Syracuse, NY, 1993.

Rocking the Boat: Union Women's Voices, 1915–1975. Brigid O'Farrell and Joyce L. Kornbluh. Rutgers University Press, New Brunswick, NJ, 1993.

Rocking the Ship of State: Toward a Feminist Peace Politics. Adrienne Harris and Ynestra King. Westview, Boulder, CO, 1989.

Sweatshop Warriors: Immigrant Women Workers Take on the Global Factory. Miriam Ching Yoon Louie. South End Press, Boston, 2001.

A Tradition That Has No Name. Mary Field Belenky, Lynne Bond, and Jacqueline Weinstock. Basic Books, New York, 1997.

Too Heavy a Load: Black Women in Defense of Themselves, 1894–1994. Deborah Gray White. Norton, New York, 1999.

Toxic Struggles: The Theory and Practice of Environmental Justice. Richard Hofrichter. New Society, Philadelphia, 1993.

Voicing Power: Conversations with Visionary Women. Gail Hanlon, ed. Westview, Boulder, CO, 1997.

Women, AIDS, and Activism. ACT UP/NY, Women and AIDS Book Group. South End Press, Boston, 1990.

Women and Male Violence: The Visions and Struggles of the Battered Women's Movement. Susan Schechter. South End Press, Boston, 1982.

Women and the Politics of Empowerment. Ann Bookman and Sandra Morgan. Temple University Press, Philadelphia, 1988.

Women Transforming Politics: An Alternative Reader. Cathy Cohen, Kathleen Jones, and Joan Tronto. New York University Press, New York, 1997.

You Can't Kill the Spirit. Pam McAllister. New Society Publishers, Philadelphia, 1992.

Credits